6th Edition

Strategic Management

Competitiveness and Globalization

Michael A. Hitt
Texas A&M University

R. Duane Ireland
University of Richmond
and
Texas A&M University

Robert E. Hoskisson
The University of Oklahoma

THOMSON

SOUTH-WESTERN

Australia · Canada · Mexico · Singapore · Spain · United Kingdom · United States

THOMSON
SOUTH-WESTERN

Strategic Management: Competitiveness and Globalization (Concepts and Cases) 6e
Michael A. Hitt, R. Duane Ireland, and Robert E. Hoskisson

VP/Editorial Director:
Jack W. Calhoun

VP/Editor-in-Chief:
Michael P. Roche

Senior Publisher:
Melissa Acuña

Executive Editor:
John Szilagyi

Senior Developmental Editor:
Mardell Toomey

Marketing Manager:
Jacque Carrillo

Senior Production Editor:
Kara ZumBahlen

Media Developmental Editor:
Kristen Meere

Media Production Editor:
Karen Schaffer

Manufacturing Coordinator:
Rhonda Utley

Production House:
Lachina Publishing Services, Inc.

Printer:
QuebecorWorld
Versailles, KY

Internal and Cover Designer:
Anne Marie Rekow

Cover Images:
Image 100

Photography Manager:
John Hill

Photo Researcher:
Jan Siedel

ISBN: 0-324-27528-5
(Package: includes text, InfoTrac,
and student CD)
ISBN: 0-324-27529-3 (text only)

Library of Congress Control
Number:
2003115519

For permission to use material
from this text or product, submit
a request online at http://www.
thomsonrights.com.

For more information
contact South-Western,
5191 Natorp Boulevard,
Mason, Ohio 45040.
Or you can visit our Internet site at:
http://www.swlearning.com

*To Rebecca and Joe. We love you
both. For you, it is certainly true that
"two hearts are better than one."*
—*R. Duane Ireland*

*To my children, Robyn, Dale, Becky,
Angela, Joseph, and Matthew, who have
supported me throughout my career.*
—*Robert E. Hoskisson*

Brief Contents

Contents

Part 2 *Strategic Actions: Strategy Formulation*   100

Chapter 7   Acquisition and Restructuring Strategies   200

Chapter 8 International Strategy   232

| Chapter 9 | Cooperative Strategy   268

6th Edition

Strategic Management

Competitiveness and Globalization

Case Title	Industrial/ Manufacturing	Service	Consumer Goods	Food/Retail	
American International Group		X			
Apple Computer, Inc.			X		
AT&T		X			
Bloomington Hospital		X			
Brasil Telecom		X			
Breckenridge Brewery				X	
Cochlear "Bionic Ears"					
Cyberplay				X	
Daewoo Motors	X				
Diageo plc			X	X	
Collapse of Enron					
ERG					
Fashion Faux Pas			X		
Gillette Company	X		X		
Handspring, Inc., 2002			X		
HP-Compaq Merger	X				
Kerry Group				X	
McDonald's				X	
Microsoft					
MTV vs. Channel V		X			
Nestlé	X		X	X	
Nextel		X			
Pacific Cataract and Laser Institute		X			
Paper Storms: Newspaper					
Resene Paints			X	X	
Sesame Workshop					
Sonic's Drive-In				X	
Southwest Airlines		X			
Sun Life		X			
Sylvan Learning Systems		X			
Tredegar Industries	X				
United Airlines		X			
UPS vs. FedEx		X			
Vodafone AirTouch		X			
Wachovia		X			

	High Technology	Media/ Entertainment/ Communication	International Perspective	Social/ Ethical Issues	Entrepre- neurial	Industry Perspective	Chapters
			X			X	2, 8, 9
	X						4, 5
	X						2, 6
							1, 2
	X	X	X				8, 9
					X	X	12, 13
	X		X		X		5, 13
	X				X		11, 13
			X	X			7, 9, 12
			X			X	2, 4, 7
				X			1, 2, 12
	X		X				8, 9
			X				7, 10
							2, 3, 6
	X				X		12, 13
	X						7, 10
			X		X		6, 10
				X			2, 12
	X						1, 2, 9, 11
		X	X	X		X	5, 8
			X		X		3, 8, 13
	X	X				X	1, 2, 3
	X		X			X	2, 4
		X				X	2, 5
							2, 7, 11
		X	X				8, 9
						X	4, 9
						X	2, 4
			X			X	3, 7, 10
			X			X	3, 7, 11, 12
			X				6, 7
			X			X	2, 5, 9
			X				3, 5, 12
		X	X			X	2, 7, 8
						X	6, 7, 10

Preface

Our goal in writing this book was to establish a new standard in the presentation of current and up-to-date concepts in strategic management. We believe that this goal has been realized and is fully evident in this 6th edition of our market-leading book. Written in a lively and user-friendly manner, this text presents a rich and comprehensive examination of strategic management concepts and tools. Following are some of the most important features of our book and this edition.

- This text offers the most comprehensive and thorough coverage of strategic management available in the market.
- The research presented in our text is the most up-to-date in the field and most current in practice compared to all other strategic management books. Although the text is grounded in the current research, it is also strongly application oriented with more examples and applications of strategic management concepts, techniques, and tools than any other competitor on the market.
- We integrate two of the most popular and well-known theoretical concepts in the field of strategic management, industrial organization economics through the writings of such authors as Michael Porter and the resource-based view of the firm from the work of such authors as Jay Barney. No other book integrates these two theoretical perspectives to explain the process of strategic management.
- We use the ideas of prominent scholars (e.g., Michael Porter, Richard Rumelt, Kathy Eisenhardt, Gary Hamel, C. K. Prahalad, David Teece, Oliver Williamson, Don Hambrick, Dan Schendel, Richard Bettis, Sumantra Ghoshal, Kathy Harrigan, Rosabeth Kanter, and Costas Markides as well as numerous others) and prominent executives and practitioners (e.g., Carly Fiorina, John Chambers, Andy Grove, Herb Kelleher, Steven Jobs, Meg Whitman, Jeffrey Immelt, and Anne Mulcahy as well as many others) to provide an effective understanding of the theoretical base of strategic management and its application in organizations.
- We (the authors of this book) are also highly active scholars in the conduct of strategic management research and the application of the concepts derived from that research. Thus, our own research is integrated in the appropriate chapters as well.
- In this edition, we offer examples of over 100 companies' actions in the chapters' Opening Cases and Strategic Focus segments. Furthermore, the application of strategic management concepts is shown in more than 600 different companies in the book's chapters. There is no strategic management book on the market that has both the up-to-date research and the application orientation shown by this number of company examples.

Some of the highlights of our new edition include:

- **New Opening Cases and Strategic Focus Segments:** We continue our tradition of providing new Opening Cases and Strategic Focus segments and many other new examples in each chapter to describe actions companies take within the context of a chapter's topic.
- **An Exceptional Balance** between current research and applications of it in actual organizations. The content has not only the best research documentation

but also the largest amount of effective firm examples to help students understand the strategies discussed.

- **All New Cases** with an effective mix of U.S. and international organizations. Many of the cases have enhanced financial analyses as part of the Case Notes.
- **Enhanced Experiential Exercises** to support learners' efforts to understand the use of strategic management in organizations of all types.
- **Lively, Concise Writing Style** to hold readers' attention and to increase their interest in the subject matter.
- **Continuing, Updated Coverage** of vital strategic management topics such as competitive rivalry and dynamics, strategic alliances, mergers and acquisitions, international strategies, corporate governance and ethics, and strategic entrepreneurship.
- **Full Four-Color Format** to enhance readability by attracting and maintaining readers' interest.
- **New Content in Chapter 12, Strategic Leadership:** "Effectively Managing the Firm's Resource Portfolio"; "Developing Human Capital and Social Capital"; and "Emphasizing Ethical Practices." Also, expanded discussion of the **Balanced Scorecard** used by *many* corporations today.

Supplements

Instructors

IRCD (0-324-20387-X)
Key ancillaries [Instructor's Case Notes, Instructor's Resource Manual, Test Bank, ExamView™, PowerPoint®, Case Analysis Spreadsheets, and CNN Video Guide (integrates cases and videos)] are provided on CD-ROM, giving instructors the ultimate tool for customizing lectures and presentations.

INSTRUCTOR'S CASE NOTES (0-324-20381-0)
Prepared by Charles Byles, Virginia Commonwealth University; Timothy R. Mayes, Metropolitan State College of Denver; Jude Rathburn, University of Wisconsin; and Craig VanSandt, Augustana College. All-new case notes provide details about the cases found in the last part of the text following the framework supported by Hitt/Ireland/Hoskisson for preparing an effective case analysis. The case notes for the 6th edition have been written in even greater detail compared to previous editions and have been compiled by four respected case notes writers who have followed specific guidelines to ensure consistency. Questions and answers have been added throughout the case notes to facilitate their usefulness in the classroom. An additional improvement includes adding complete financial analyses for 17 of the 35 cases. Spreadsheets for those financial analyses are available for instructors on our product support website and are packaged with the text for use by students.

INSTRUCTOR'S RESOURCE MANUAL WITH VIDEO GUIDE AND TRANSPARENCY MASTERS (0-324-20382-9)
Prepared by Leslie E. Palich, Baylor University. The Instructor's Resource Manual, organized around each chapter's knowledge objectives, includes ideas about how to approach each chapter and how to reinforce essential principles with extra examples. The support product includes lecture outlines, detailed answers to end-of-chapter review questions, instructions for using each chapter's experiential exercises, guides to all available videos, and additional assignments.

TEST BANK (0-324-20383-7)

Prepared by Janelle Dozier. Thoroughly revised and enhanced, Test Bank questions are linked to each chapter's knowledge objectives and are ranked by difficulty and question type. We have increased the number of application questions throughout, and we have also retained scenario-based questions as a means of adding in-depth problem-solving questions to exams (these were new to the last edition). The Test Bank material is also available in computerized ExamView™ format for creating custom tests in both Windows and Macintosh formats.

EXAMVIEW™ (0-324-23621-2)

Computerized testing software contains all of the questions in the printed Test Bank. This program is an easy-to-use test creation software compatible with Microsoft Windows. Instructors can add or edit questions, instructions, and answers, and select questions by previewing them on the screen, selecting them randomly, or selecting them by number. Instructors can also create and administer quizzes online, whether over the Internet, a local area network (LAN), or a wide area network (WAN).

TRANSPARENCY ACETATES (0-324-20384-5)

Key figures from the main text have been re-created as colorful and attractive over-head transparencies for classroom use.

POWERPOINT® DISCUSSION SLIDES (0-324-20386-1)
POWERPOINT® LECTURE SLIDES (0-324-20385-3)

Prepared by Dennis Middlemist, Colorado State University. An all-new PowerPoint® presentation, created for this edition, provides configurations both for lecture-based teaching formats and for discussion-based teaching formats. Slides can also be used by students as an aid to note-taking

Students

STUDENT CD-ROM (0-324-22400-1)

New to This Edition! The Student CD-ROM, prepared by Timothy R. Mayes and packaged with every text, features financial case analyses to accompany 17 of the total 35 cases presented in the 6th edition. Each case analysis includes interactive spreadsheets so that students are tutored for a better understanding of the importance and creation of financial analyses.

Students and Instructors

WEBTUTOR™ TOOLBOX (0-324-23172-5—WEBCT; 0-324-23171-7—BLACKBOARD)

WebTutor™ ToolBox provides instructors with links to content from our book companion websites. WebTutor™ ToolBox also provides rich communication tools to instructors and students including a course calendar, chat, and e-mail.

WEBSITE

This edition's website offers students and instructors access to a wealth of helpful support and learning materials. Included are Instructor Resources, Student Resources, Interactive Study Center, Interactive Quizzes, links to Strategy Suite, e-Coursepacks, and Careers in Management. You will find continually updated case information, a section on how to write a case analysis along with the case analyses for this edition's applicable cases, and a new feature—interactive spreadsheets that help students understand the importance of case analyses and how to perform them. We have provided an Internet index with important strategy URLs and PowerPoint® slide presentations. We have also included additional experiential exercises, Strategic Focus applications, Ethics questions, Internet exercises, and Global Resources. Finally, for quickly finding new terms, we offer an online glossary. The *Strategic Management* website provides information about the authors and allows you to contact the authors and the publisher.

CNN VIDEO (0-324-20389-6)

"Management and Strategy" is a 45-minute video of short news clips from CNN, capitalizing on the resources of the world's first 24-hour all-news network. The 6th edition features videos that are closely linked with current case and text content for a truly integrative approach, assuring particular relevance to students of strategic management and a fresh perspective on text content. A resource guide accompanies the video, and further support is offered in the Instructor's Resource Manual.

ENTREPRENEURSHIP AND STRATEGY VIDEO (0-324-26131-4)

This is a 45-minute video based on the remarkable resources of *Small Business School*, the series on PBS stations, Worldnet, and the Web. The video features seven firms that capitalized on their beginnings and used strategic management to grow market share and create competitive advantage. A resource guide within the Instructor's Resource Manual describes each segment and provides discussion questions.

CORPORATE STRATEGY VIDEO (0-324-20390-X)

This is a 45-minute video featuring corporate strategy situations for classroom viewing. Corporate strategy and strategic planning perspectives are analyzed at an up-and-coming company, Caribou Coffee; strategy and leadership are examined at CVS; and organizational structure is studied through Student Advantage. A resource guide within the Instructor's Resource Manual describes each segment and provides discussion questions.

E-COURSEPACK

Current, interesting, and relevant articles are available to supplement each chapter of *Strategic Management* in an e-Coursepack—the result of a joint effort between the Gale Group, a world leader in e-information publishing for libraries, schools, and businesses, and South-Western. Full-length articles to complement *Strategic Management* are available 24 hours a day over the Web, from sources such as *Fortune, Across the Board, Management Today,* and the *Sloan Management Review.* Students can also access up-to-date information on key individuals, companies, and textbook cases through predefined searches of Gale databases. For more information, contact your South-Western/Thomson Learning sales representative or call Thomson Custom Publishing at 1-800-355-9983.

INFOTRAC COLLEGE EDITION

InfoTrac College Edition gives students access—anytime, anywhere—to an online database of full-text articles from hundreds of scholarly and popular periodicals, including *Newsweek* and *Fortune.* Fast and easy search tools help you find just what you're looking for from tens of thousands of articles, updated daily, all at a single site. For more information, contact your South-Western/Thomson Learning sales representative or call Thomson Custom Publishing at 1-800-355-9983.

Acknowledgments

In the words of Carly Fiorina, "We have hit our stride" in this edition. We are indebted to the following people who worked on and developed several ancillary materials to support this edition of the book:

Charles M. Byles, *Virginia Commonwealth University*
Janelle Dozier
Timothy R. Mayes, *Metropolitan State College of Denver*
R. Dennis Middlemist, *Colorado State University*
Leslie E. Palich, *Baylor University*
Jude Rathburn, *University of Wisconsin—Milwaukee*
Craig VanSandt, *Augustana College*

We also express our appreciation to the following people who reviewed chapters and offered comments to help us develop this edition:

Karen Bilda, *Cardinal Stritch University*
James Bronson, *University of Wisconsin, Whitewater*
Lowell Busenitz, *University of Oklahoma*
Charles M. Byles, *Virginia Commonwealth University*
Bruce Clemens, *James Madison University*
Refik Culpan, *Pennsylvania State University at Harrisburg*
Wade Danis, *Marquette University*
Tamela D. Ferguson, *University of Louisiana at Lafayette*
Charles Gates, *Northern Illinois University*
Ted Herbert, *Rollins College*
Mike Hergert, *San Diego State University*
Phyllis Holland, *Valdosta State University*
Carol Jacobson, *Purdue University*
Franz Kellermanns, *University of Connecticut*
David J. Ketchen, *Florida State*
Haiyang Li, *Texas A&M University*
Roman Nowacki, *Northern Illinois University*
Annette L. Ranft, *Wake Forest University*
Mark Sharfman, *University of Oklahoma*
Tony W. Tong, *Ohio State University*
Henry Van Buren, *University of Northern Iowa*
Robert Wiseman, *Michigan State University*

We also express our appreciation for the excellent support received from our editorial and production team at South-Western. We especially wish to thank John Szilagyi, our editor; Mardell Toomey, the developmental editor; and Kara ZumBahlen, the production editor. We are grateful for their dedication, commitment, and outstanding contributions to the development and publication of this book and its package of support materials.

Michael A. Hitt

R. Duane Ireland

Robert E. Hoskisson

About the Authors

Michael A. Hitt

Michael A. Hitt is a Distinguished Professor and holds the Joseph Foster Chair in Business Leadership and the C. W. and Dorothy Conn Chair in New Ventures at Texas A&M University. He received his Ph.D. from the University of Colorado. He has authored or coauthored several books and book chapters and numerous articles in such journals as the *Academy of Management Journal, Academy of Management Review, Strategic Management Journal, Journal of Applied Psychology, Organization Science, Organization Studies, Journal of Management Studies,* and *Journal of Management,* among others. His publications include several books: *Downscoping: How to Tame the Diversified Firm* (Oxford University Press, 1994); *Mergers and Acquisitions: A Guide to Creating Value for Stakeholders* (Oxford University Press, 2001); and *Competing for Advantage* (South-Western College Publishing, 2004). He is Coeditor of several recent books: *Managing Strategically in an Interconnected World* (1998); *New Managerial Mindsets: Organizational Transformation and Strategy Implementation* (1998); *Dynamic Strategic Resources: Development, Diffusion and Integration* (1999); *Winning Strategies in a Deconstructing World* (John Wiley & Sons, 2000); *Handbook of Strategic Management* (2001); *Strategic Entrepreneurship: Creating a New Integrated Mindset* (2002); *Creating Value: Winners in the New Business Environment* (Blackwell Publishers, 2002); and *Managing Knowledge for Sustained Competitive Advantage* (Jossey Bass, 2003). He has served on the editorial review boards of multiple journals including the *Academy of Management Journal, Academy of Management Executive, Journal of Applied Psychology, Journal of Management, Journal of World Business,* and *Journal of Applied Behavioral Sciences.* Furthermore, he has served as Consulting Editor (1988–90) and Editor (1991–93) of the *Academy of Management Journal.* He serves on the Board of the Strategic Management Society and is a Past President of the Academy of Management, an international organization with 13,000-plus members dedicated to the advancement of management knowledge and practice. He received the 1996 Award for Outstanding Academic Contributions to Competitiveness and the 1999 Award for Outstanding Intellectual Contributions to Competitiveness Research from the American Society for Competitiveness. He is a Fellow in the Academy of Management and a Research Fellow in the National Entrepreneurship Consortium, and received an honorary doctorate from the Universidad Carlos III de Madrid for his contributions to the field. He is a member of the *Academy of Management Journal*'s Hall of Fame. He received awards for the best article published in the *Academy of Management Executive* (1999) and *Academy of Management Journal* (2000). In 2001, he received the Irwin Outstanding Educator Award and the Distinguished Service Award from the Academy of Management.

R. Duane Ireland

R. Duane Ireland holds the W. David Robbins Chair in Strategic Management in the Robins School of Business, University of Richmond. Beginning in July 2004, he will hold the Foreman R. and Ruby S. Bennett Chair in Business Administration in the Mays Business School, Texas A&M University. He is currently serving a three-year term as a Representative-at-Large on the Board of Governors of the Academy of Management. He teaches courses at all levels (undergraduate, masters, doctoral, and executive). His research, which focuses on diversification, innovation, corporate entrepreneurship, and strategic entrepreneurship, has been published in a number of journals including *Academy of Management Journal, Academy of Management Review, Academy of Management Executive, Administrative Science Quarterly, Strategic Management Journal, Journal of Management, Human Relations,* and *Journal of Management Studies,* among others. His published books include *Competing for Advantage* (South-Western College Publishing, 2004) and *Mergers and Acquisitions: A Guide to Creating Value for Stakeholders* (Oxford University Press, 2001). He is Coeditor of *The Blackwell Entrepreneurship Encyclopedia* (Blackwell Publishers, 2004) and *Strategic Entrepreneurship: Creating a New Mindset* (Blackwell Publishers, 2001). He is serving or has served as a member of the editorial review boards for a number of journals such as *Academy of Management Journal, Academy of Management Review, Academy of Management Executive, Journal of Management, Journal of Business Venturing, Entrepreneurship Theory and Practice, Journal of Business Strategy,* and *European Management Journal,* among others. He has coedited special issues of *Academy of Management Review, Academy of Management Executive, Journal of Business Venturing, Strategic Management Journal,* and *Journal of High Technology and Engineering Management.* He received awards for the best article published in *Academy of Management Executive* (1999) and *Academy of Management Journal* (2000). In 2001, his coauthored article published in *Academy of Management Executive* won the Best Journal Article in Corporate Entrepreneurship Award from the U.S. Association for Small Business & Entrepreneurship (USASBE). He is a Research Fellow in the National Entrepreneurship Consortium. He received the 1999 Award for Outstanding Intellectual Contributions to Competitiveness Research from the American Society for Competitiveness and the USASBE Scholar in Corporate Entrepreneurship Award (2004) from USASBE.

Robert E. Hoskisson

Robert E. Hoskisson received his Ph.D. from the University of California–Irvine. Professor Hoskisson's research topics focus on international diversification, privatization and cooperative strategy, product diversification, corporate governance, and acquisitions and divestitures. He teaches courses in corporate and international strategic management, cooperative strategy, and strategy consulting, among others. Professor Hoskisson has served on several editorial boards for such publications as the *Academy of Management Journal* (including Consulting Editor and Guest Editor of a special issue), *Strategic Management Journal, Journal of Management* (including Associate Editor), and *Organization Science.* He has coauthored several books including *Strategic Management: Competitiveness and Globalization,* 5th Edition (South-Western/Thomson Learning); *Competing for Advantage* (South-Western/Thomson Learning); and *Downscoping: How to Tame the Diversified Firm* (Oxford University Press). Professor Hoskisson's research has appeared in over 85 publications including the *Academy of Management Journal, Academy of Management Review, Strategic Management Journal, Organization Science, Journal of Management, Academy of Management Executive,* and *California Management Review.* He is a Fellow of the Academy of Management and a charter member of the Academy of Management Journal's Hall of Fame. He also served for three years as a Representative-at-Large on the Board of Governors of the Academy of Management. He is also a member of the Academy of International Business and the Strategic Management Society.

6th Edition

Strategic Management

Competitiveness and Globalization

Part One

Strategic Management Inputs

Strategic Management and Strategic Competitiveness

Knowledge Objectives

Studying this chapter should provide you with the strategic management knowledge needed to:

1. Define strategic competitiveness, competitive advantage, and above-average returns.

2. Describe the 21st-century competitive landscape and explain how globalization and technological changes shape it.

3. Use the industrial organization (I/O) model to explain how firms can earn above-average returns.

4. Use the resource-based model to explain how firms can earn above-average returns.

5. Describe strategic intent and strategic mission and discuss their value.

6. Define stakeholders and describe their ability to influence organizations.

7. Describe the work of strategic leaders.

8. Explain the strategic management process.

Corel Corporation

Research and development is critical to the success of innovative companies such as Samsung, Sony, and Verizon. Continuous development of new products— although costly and sometimes difficult to achieve— is an important aspect of strategic competitiveness.

Conventional wisdom says to get back to the basics. Conventional wisdom says to cut costs. Conventional wisdom is doomed. The winners are the innovators who are making bold thinking an everyday part of doing business.

—Gary Hamel, 2002

Innovation has become an absolute necessity to survive and perform well in almost every industry. The current competitive landscape demands innovation. Gary Hamel, a well-known writer and management consultant, argues that firms cannot rely on past successes to perform well today. Furthermore, he suggests that current success will not carry firms into the future. Managers must have the foresight and courage to continuously innovate. Thus, a firm's strategy must include continuous innovation.

DuPont, once known as a highly innovative company, lost its way. As one author noted, the company has mostly "shot blanks" in the last decade. Analysts suggest that too many resources have been diverted from developing innovative products to focus on increasing the productivity of its current businesses. Furthermore, the firm's managers have been criticized for failing to evaluate the market effectively and thereby missing primary opportunities, such as in the agricultural biotechnology field. It had to sell off its pharmaceutical business because it could no longer compete against the larger and more innovative companies in the industry. Top executives are also considering divesting some of DuPont's other businesses, accounting for a major portion of its sales, because of poor market performance. Its R&D must be shifted from improving existing products to emphasizing the development of new products. DuPont executives are now in the process of changing the mix of R&D dollars spent from about one-third on creating new products and two-thirds on improving existing ones to two-thirds invested in developing innovative new market entries.

Interestingly, the large conglomerate Samsung has continued its success, largely through innovation. The conventional wisdom was that large, highly diversified firms could not be innovative and most are not. But Samsung has been very innovative and is among the leaders in many markets in which it competes. For example, it is the market leader in big-screen TVs, microwave ovens, LCD displays, and DRAM chips. It is number two in the flash memory market and number three in cell phones, MP3 players, and DVD players. Unlike many other large conglomerates, it places a high priority on investments in R&D. To remain a leader in the markets listed above requires a steady stream of innovative products.

Innovation is important in many industries, as noted above. For example, Clear Channel Communications, the largest owner of radio stations, recently announced that it would market a CD of live recordings from concerts within five minutes of the conclusion of a show. Verizon recently introduced phone booths where people can gain access to the Internet. The firm's intent is to become the market leader in providing broadband services. Sony, the current market leader in video games, is not resting on its current product line. In 2003 it announced a powerful handheld player designed to beat one of its primary competitors, Nintendo. These firms are using innovation to obtain or maintain market leadership. Without it, they would risk even survival.

While innovation is important, it is difficult and costly to achieve. For example, large pharmaceutical competitors are now considering cooperating to develop certain types of drugs because of the costs and risks involved. In fact, an industry task force has recommended establishing a research consortium of pharmaceutical companies similar to Sematech in the semiconductor industry. Sematech allowed U.S. semiconductor companies to regain competitiveness in that industry. Such a research consortium could encourage cooperation in the development of cancer fighting drugs. The costs and risks involved in R&D make some firms take a conservative approach and focus on improving current products. Such research usually has short-term payoffs but is costly in the longer term when there is a deficit of new products to market. Internal dissension exists at Hewlett-Packard (HP) because of the pressure to reduce costs in R&D, which HP scientists argue is hurting the company's level of innovation. The tight market for computer hardware and the high costs of the Compaq acquisition have caused reductions in HP's R&D budgets. Over time, HP will learn if these pressures will harm its competitiveness.

SOURCES: C. Edwards, M. Ihlwan, & P. Engardio, 2003, The Samsung way, *Business Week*, June 16, 56–64; B. J. Feder, 2003, Verizon sets up phone booths to give access to the Internet, *New York Times*, May 14, http://www.nytimes.com; Sony takes on Nintendo with new player, 2003, *New York Times*, May 14, http://www.nytimes.com; A. Pollack, 2003, Companies may cooperate on cancer drugs, *New York Times*, May 14, http://www.nytimes.com; J. Markoff, 2003, Innovation at Hewlett tries to evade the ax, *New York Times*, May 5, http://www.nytimes.com; M. Mirapaul, 2003, Concert CDs sold on the spot by a radio giant, *New York Times*, May 5, http://www.nytimes.com; G. Hamel, 2002, Innovation now! *Fast Company*, December, http://www.fastcompany.com.

Samsung and DuPont's performances are in sharp contrast. DuPont, a once highly innovative company, lost its competitive edge. Clearly, DuPont changed its strategy to emphasize productivity and improve its current product line rather than introduce innovative new products. Such actions probably improved the firm's profits in the short term. But in the long term, it had to sell off divisions that were no longer competitive and is experiencing major problems because of the lack of innovation. In contrast, Samsung is investing in innovation to remain among the leaders in multiple product markets. Again, these are outcomes of its strategy. Samsung's strategy formulation and implementation actions helped it gain an advantage over many of its competitors. Other firms operating in diverse industries are using innovation as a competitive weapon. Examples include Verizon's new telephone booths for access to the Internet, the concert CDs offered by Clear Channel Communications, and Sony's new handheld player.

The actions taken by these firms are intended to achieve strategic competitiveness and earn above-average returns. **Strategic competitiveness** is achieved when a firm

Strategic competitiveness is achieved when a firm successfully formulates and implements a value-creating strategy.

successfully formulates and implements a value-creating strategy. When a firm implements such a strategy and other companies are unable to duplicate it or find it too costly to imitate,[1] this firm has a **sustained (or sustainable) competitive advantage** (hereafter called simply *competitive advantage*). An organization is assured of a competitive advantage only after others' efforts to duplicate its strategy have ceased or failed. In addition, when a firm achieves a competitive advantage, it normally can sustain it only for a certain period.[2] The speed with which competitors are able to acquire the skills needed to duplicate the benefits of a firm's value-creating strategy determines how long the competitive advantage will last.[3]

Understanding how to exploit a competitive advantage is important for firms to earn above-average returns.[4] **Above-average returns** are returns in excess of what an investor expects to earn from other investments with a similar amount of risk. **Risk** is an investor's uncertainty about the economic gains or losses that will result from a particular investment.[5] Returns are often measured in terms of accounting figures, such as return on assets, return on equity, or return on sales. Alternatively, returns can be measured on the basis of stock market returns, such as monthly returns (the end-of-the-period stock price minus the beginning stock price, divided by the beginning stock price, yielding a percentage return). In smaller new venture firms, performance is sometimes measured in terms of the amount and speed of the growth (e.g., in annual sales) because they may not have returns early or the asset base is too small to evaluate the returns received.[6]

Firms without a competitive advantage or that are not competing in an attractive industry earn, at best, average returns. **Average returns** are returns equal to those an investor expects to earn from other investments with a similar amount of risk. In the long run, an inability to earn at least average returns results in failure. Failure occurs because investors withdraw their investments from those firms earning less-than-average returns.

Dynamic in nature, the **strategic management process** (see Figure 1.1) is the full set of commitments, decisions, and actions required for a firm to achieve strategic competitiveness and earn above-average returns.[7] Relevant strategic inputs derived from analyses of the internal and external environments are necessary for effective strategy formulation and implementation. In turn, effective strategic actions are a prerequisite to achieving the desired outcomes of strategic competitiveness and above-average returns. Thus, the strategic management process is used to match the conditions of an ever-changing market and competitive structure with a firm's continuously evolving resources, capabilities, and core competencies (the sources of strategic inputs). Effective strategic actions that take place in the context of carefully integrated strategy formulation and implementation actions result in desired strategic outcomes.[8] (See Figure 1.1.)

In the remaining chapters of this book, we use the strategic management process to explain what firms should do to achieve strategic competitiveness and earn above-average returns. These explanations demonstrate why some firms consistently achieve competitive success while others fail to do so.[9] As you will see, the reality of global competition is a critical part of the strategic management process.[10]

Several topics are discussed in this chapter. First, we examine the challenge of strategic management. This brief discussion highlights the fact that strategic actions taken to achieve and then maintain strategic competitiveness demand the best efforts of managers, employees, and their organizations on a continuous basis.[11] Second, we describe the 21st-century competitive landscape, created primarily by the emergence of a global economy and rapid technological changes. This landscape provides the context of opportunities and threats within which firms strive to meet today's competitive challenges.

We next examine two models that suggest the strategic inputs needed to select strategic actions necessary to achieve strategic competitiveness. The first model (industrial

A **sustained** *or* **sustainable competitive advantage** *occurs when a firm implements a value-creating strategy and other companies are unable to duplicate it or find it too costly to imitate.*

Above-average returns *are returns in excess of what an investor expects to earn from other investments with a similar amount of risk.*

Risk *is an investor's uncertainty about the economic gains or losses that will result from a particular investment.*

Average returns *are returns equal to those an investor expects to earn from other investments with a similar amount of risk.*

The **strategic management process** *is the full set of commitments, decisions, and actions required for a firm to achieve strategic competitiveness and earn above-average returns.*

Figure 1.1 — The Strategic Management Process

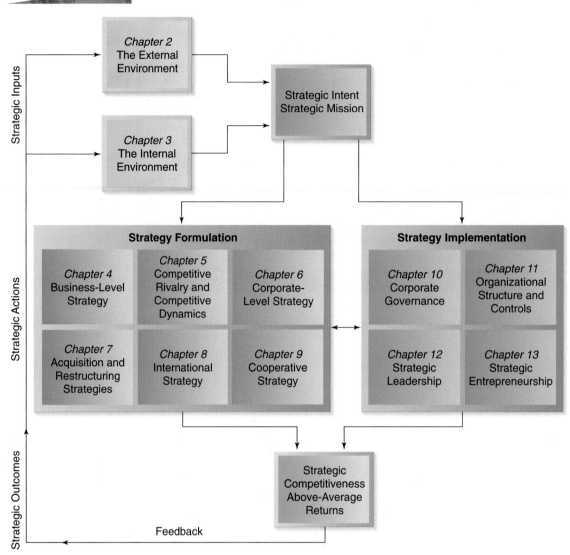

organization) suggests that the external environment is the primary determinant of a firm's strategic actions. The key to this model is identifying and competing successfully in an attractive (i.e., profitable) industry.[12] The second model (resource based) suggests that a firm's unique resources and capabilities are the critical link to strategic competitiveness.[13] Comprehensive explanations in this chapter and the next two chapters show that through the combined use of these models, firms obtain the strategic inputs needed to formulate and implement strategies successfully. Analyses of its external and internal environments provide a firm with the information required to develop its strategic intent and strategic mission (defined later in this chapter). As shown in Figure 1.1, strategic intent and strategic mission influence strategy formulation and implementation actions. The chapter's discussion then turns to the stakeholders that organizations serve. The degree to which stakeholders' needs can be met increases directly with enhancements in a firm's strategic competitiveness and its ability to earn above-average returns. Closing the chapter are introductions to strategic leaders and the elements of the strategic management process.

The goals of achieving strategic competitiveness and earning above-average returns are challenging—not only for large firms such as IBM, but also for those as small as a local computer retail outlet or dry cleaner. As suggested in the Opening Case, the performances of some companies, such as Samsung, have more than met strategic management's challenges to date.

For other firms, the challenges are substantial in the dynamic competitive landscape. Evidence the rapid changes experienced by Cisco Systems. During the 1990s, Cisco's overall performance was among the best—it was among the top ten firms whose stock price increased over 10,000 percent in that decade. However, in 2001, the firm experienced significant reductions in its stock price. One writer referred to Cisco as a fractured fairy tale.[14] Cisco's top management argued that their new strategic actions would, over time, regain the high performance once enjoyed by the firm.[15] In Spring 2003, Cisco announced that it had recovered from the substantial loss suffered in 2001. In fact, Cisco reported a profit of almost $1.9 billion for 2002, and its stock price was beginning to increase.[16]

Business failure is rather common. In 2002, for example, 38,540 U.S. businesses filed for bankruptcy, down approximately 4 percent from the number filed in 2001. But the total value of the assets reached a record in 2002. The bankruptcies filed represented $375.2 billion in assets compared to $258.5 billion in 2001.[17] These statistics suggest that competitive success is transient.[18] Thomas J. Watson, Jr., formerly IBM's chairman, once cautioned people to remember that "corporations are expendable and that success—at best—is an impermanent achievement which can always slip out of hand."[19]

As described in a Strategic Focus later in this chapter, both US Airways and United Airlines filed for bankruptcy, and American Airlines narrowly averted bankruptcy by gaining major wage concessions from its employee unions. In the Opening Case, several companies were noted to be introducing innovative new products while others' capabilities to produce innovation were questioned by knowledgable industry analysts. Without innovations, firms in most industries will not be able to survive over time. And, the innovation must be a part of an effective strategy developed to navigate in the competitive landscape of the 21st century. It is interesting to note that a survey showed CEOs did not place "strong and consistent profits" as their top priority; in fact, it was ranked fifth. A "strong and well-thought-out strategy" was regarded as the most important factor to make a firm the most respected in the future. Maximizing customer satisfaction and loyalty, business leadership and quality products and services, and concern for consistent profits followed this factor.[20] These rankings are consistent with the view that no matter how good a product or service is, the firm must select the "right" strategy and then implement it effectively. In a 2003 survey of the top 100 growth companies, *Business Week* noted that these firms thrive in a tough economy because of their risk taking (e.g., innovation) and use of smart strategies.[21]

Suggesting strategic management's challenge, Andrew Grove, Intel's former CEO, observed that only paranoid companies survive and succeed. Firms must continuously evaluate their environments and decide on the appropriate strategy. **Strategy** is an integrated and coordinated set of commitments and actions designed to exploit core competencies and gain a competitive advantage. By choosing a strategy, a firm decides to pursue one course of action over others. The firm's executives are thus setting priorities for the firm's competitive actions. Strategies are organic in that they must be adapted over time as the external environment and the firm's resource portfolio change.[22]

Firms can select effective or ineffective strategies. For example, the choice by Xerox to pursue a strategy other than the development and marketing of the personal

Strategy *is an integrated and coordinated set of commitments and actions designed to exploit core competencies and gain a competitive advantage.*

computer and laser printers was likely an ineffective one. The purpose of this book is to explain how firms develop and implement effective strategies. Partly because of Grove's approach described above, Intel continuously strives to improve in order to remain competitive. For Intel and others that compete in the 21st century's competitive landscape, Grove believes that a key challenge is to try to do the impossible—namely, to anticipate the unexpected.[23]

The Current Competitive Landscape[24]

The fundamental nature of competition in many of the world's industries is changing.[25] The pace of this change is relentless and is increasing. Even determining the boundaries of an industry has become challenging. Consider, for example, how advances in interactive computer networks and telecommunications have blurred the definition of the television industry. The near future may find companies such as ABC, CBS, NBC, and HBO competing not only among themselves, but also with AT&T, Microsoft, Sony, and others.

Other characteristics of the 21st-century competitive landscape are noteworthy as well. Conventional sources of competitive advantage, such as economies of scale and huge advertising budgets, are not as effective as they once were. Moreover, the traditional managerial mind-set is unlikely to lead a firm to strategic competitiveness. Managers must adopt a new mind-set that values flexibility, speed, innovation, integration, and the challenges that evolve from constantly changing conditions. The conditions of the competitive landscape result in a perilous business world, one where the investments required to compete on a global scale are enormous and the consequences of failure are severe.[26] Developing and implementing strategy remains an important element of success in this environment. It allows for strategic actions to be planned and to emerge when the environmental conditions are appropriate. It also helps to coordinate the strategies developed by business units in which the responsibility to compete in specific markets is decentralized.[27]

Hypercompetition is a term often used to capture the realities of the 21st-century competitive landscape. Hypercompetition results from the dynamics of strategic maneuvering among global and innovative combatants. It is a condition of rapidly escalating competition based on price-quality positioning, competition to create new know-how and establish first-mover advantage, and competition to protect or invade established product or geographic markets.[28] In a hypercompetitive market, firms often aggressively challenge their competitors in the hopes of improving their competitive position and ultimately their performance.[29]

Several factors create hypercompetitive environments and the 21st-century competitive landscape. The two primary drivers are the emergence of a global economy and technology, specifically rapid technological change.

As explained in the Strategic Focus, the global automobile market is highly competitive. The U.S. auto market is the largest and perhaps the most important, but most auto manufacturers compete in markets around the world. Both GM and Ford are headquartered in the United States, but sell their products globally. Likewise, BMW is headquartered in Germany, but considers the United States a critically important market. In fact, many of the new BMW autos were designed specifically for the U.S. market. BMW is performing well, and GM's overall performance is improving. But Ford is in trouble and may encounter challenges to turn around the firm's fortunes. Interestingly, in the mid-1990s, Ford was considered the best U.S. auto manufacturer. But poor strategic decisions and a lack of focus on creating innovative new designs have reversed its fortunes. The change in Ford exemplifies the impermanence of success, especially with global markets and competition.

Gliding above the Water, Treading Water, and Drowning

The global automobile market is highly competitive. The autos compete in market segments but performance, design, and quality are important competitive factors in all market segments. In an annual quality survey conducted by J.D. Power and Associates, some autos fared well and others performed badly. For example, the bottom five performers in quality were Hummer, Land Rover, Kia, MINI, and Saab, whereas the top five performers were Lexus, Cadillac, Infiniti, Acura, and Buick. Performance on such surveys can greatly affect sales, so it is quite important. BMW performed well above average with a score that ranked eighth, whereas two Ford products (Ford and Lincoln) and several GM products (Oldsmobile, Pontiac, GMC, and Saturn) had below-average quality scores. These outcomes are the result of differing strategies followed by these firms in past years.

BMW has developed and implemented a strategy for growth that entails designing and manufacturing a number of different autos targeted for multiple different market segments. BMW is especially targeting the large U.S. auto market, and its goal is to increase BMW's sales in the United States by 40 percent by 2008. This would be total sales of 300,000 cars annually, the largest number of luxury autos sold in one market globally, and would overtake Lexus, the current leader. This is a bold strategic move at a time when many of BMW's competitors are cutting R&D and production. However, the time may be correct for just such a move. When the economy rebounds, BMW will be in a strong position to take advantage of the enhanced market. BMW's actions have already been winning customers and converts from its primary competitor, Lexus.

In contrast, GM is "treading water" and Ford may be "drowning." For a number of years, GM's market share was declining because of multiple past strategic mistakes. The current CEO is providing reasons to believe that GM may turn around its fortunes. Rick Wagoner, CEO, is changing the culture, placing renewed emphasis on new product development and introducing competitive tactics such as zero percent financing to regain a competitive advantage. GM has also reduced both the time and cost of building its automobiles. For example, the number of labor hours required to produce a Malibu has been reduced by 25 percent, and the engineering costs on several of its autos have been reduced by one-third.

Ford, on the other hand, is in deep trouble and faces major challenges to turn around its fortunes. It lost a total of $6.4 billion in 2001–2002 and the outcomes for 2003 were not bright. The year 2003 marked Ford's 100th anniversary, but it was one of the firm's most challenging times since the early years of its existence. Ford's competitors have been relentless in developing advantages that Ford is challenged to overcome. Ford's autos were ranked last in reliability by *Consumer Reports* in 2003. Ford and GM both have substantial pension funding requirements, but much of Ford's obligations have been funded by debt. As a result, Ford's debt rating is only slightly above "junk status." Rumors suggest that there are conflicts among the top management team with turnover likely by some team members. One informed observer stated that "if it didn't have the name Ford, it would be in bankruptcy." Ford's competitors have been building and marketing vehicles that better meet customers' needs and desires. Ford managers somehow lost touch with the market over time

A 2004 BMW on display at a U.S. auto show. BMW has maintained a global sustained competitive advantage through its reputation in automobile engineering as well as its innovations in design. Its long-term strategic plan entails a 40 percent increase in U.S. sales by 2008 and greater attention to market segments especially intended for the U.S.

©Gary Conner/PhotoEdit

and did not invest in new product development while its competitors were designing new models. Currently, it is just trying to catch up to GM's lower costs and speedier production (but still using existing designs).

SOURCES: G. Edmondson, C. Palmeri, B. Grow, & C. Tierney, 2003, BMW: Will Panke's high-speed approach hurt the brand? *Business Week*, June 9, 57–60; N. Shirouzu, 2003, Ford's new development plan: Stop reinventing its wheels, *Wall Street Journal*, April 16, A1, A4; K. Kerwin, 2003, Can Ford pull out of its skid? *Business Week*, March 31, 70–71; D. Hakim, 2003, Long road ahead for Ford, *New York Times*, March 14, http://www.nytimes.com; D. Welch & K. Kerwin, 2003, Rick Wagoner's game plan, *Business Week*, February 10, 52–60; G. L. White, 2003, GM's deep-discounting strategy helps auto maker regain ground, *Wall Street Journal*, January 17, A1, A4; B. Breen, 2002, BMW: Driven by design, *Fast Company*, September, 121–134; D. Welch, 2002, A hit parade for BMW? *Business Week*, September 23, 64–65.

The Global Economy

A global economy is one in which goods, services, people, skills, and ideas move freely across geographic borders.

A **global economy** is one in which goods, services, people, skills, and ideas move freely across geographic borders. Relatively unfettered by artificial constraints, such as tariffs, the global economy significantly expands and complicates a firm's competitive environment.[30] Interesting opportunities and challenges are associated with the emergence of the global economy. For example, Europe, instead of the United States, is now the world's largest single market with 700 million potential customers. The European Union and the other Western European countries also have a gross domestic product that is over 35 percent higher than the GDP of the United States.[31] In addition, by 2015, China's total GDP will be greater than Japan's, although its per capita output will likely be lower.[32] In recent years, as the competitiveness rankings in Table 1.1 indicate, the Japanese economy has lagged behind that of the United States and a number of other countries. In fact, Japanese managers once heralded for their approach have been forced to change their style of operation in order to compete in global markets.[33] A few Asian countries, in particular Malaysia and Taiwan, have maintained their rankings, which is commendable considering the Asian financial crisis of the latter part of the 1990s.[34] Australia and Canada have also ranked highly in recent years.

Achieving improved competitiveness allows a country's citizens to have a higher standard of living. Some believe that entrepreneurial activity will continue to influence living standards during the 21st century. The role of entrepreneurship is discussed further in Chapter 13. A country's competitiveness is achieved through the accumulation of individual firms' strategic competitiveness in the global economy. To be competitive, a firm must view the world as its marketplace. For example, Procter & Gamble believes that it still has tremendous potential to grow internationally because the global market for household products is not as mature as it is in the United States. Recently, U.S. midsize and small firms are demonstrating a strong commitment to competing in the global economy as well as their larger counterparts. For example, 60 percent of U.S. firms now exporting goods are defined as small businesses.

Ikea (discussed further in Chapter 4) has benefited from competing in the global economy. It has annual sales exceeding $11 billion and employs 70,000 workers. It first moved outside its home market in Sweden in 1963 and entered the U.S. market in the mid-1980s. Currently, Ikea has over 150 stores in more than 20 countries. Much of the firm's growth and success have come from sales in international markets.[35]

The March of Globalization

Globalization is the increasing economic interdependence among countries as reflected in the flow of goods and services, financial capital, and knowledge across country bor-

Country Competitiveness Rankings (Population over 20 Million)			Table 1.1

Country	2003	2002
United States	1	1
Australia	2	3
Canada	3	2
Malaysia	4	6
Germany	5	4
Taiwan	6	7
United Kingdom	7	5
France	8	9
Spain	9	8
Thailand	10	13
Japan	11	11
China (mainland)	12	12
Brazil (Sao Paolo)	13	—
China (Zeijiang)	14	—
Korea	15	10
Colombia	16	20
Italy	17	14
South Africa	18	16
India (Maharashtra)	19	—
India	20	17
Brazil	21	15
Philippines	22	18
Romania	23	—
Mexico	24	19
Turkey	25	23
Russia	26	21
Poland	27	22
Indonesia	28	25
Argentina	29	26
Venezuela	30	24

SOURCE: From *World Competitiveness Yearbook 2003*, IMD, Switzerland. http://www.imd.ch.wcy.esummary, April. Reprinted by permission.

ders.[36] In globalized markets and industries, financial capital might be obtained in one national market and used to buy raw materials in another one. Manufacturing equipment bought from a third national market can then be used to produce products that are sold in yet a fourth market. Thus, globalization increases the range of opportunities for companies competing in the 21st-century competitive landscape.

Wal-Mart, for instance, is trying to achieve boundaryless retailing with global pricing, sourcing, and logistics. Most of Wal-Mart's original international investments were in Canada and Mexico, in proximity to the United States. However, the company

Although other discount department stores have failed to thrive, Wal-Mart currently enjoys success as the largest retailer in the world through global pricing, sourcing, and logistics. Here a shopper loads his trunk with items purchased at the largest Wal-Mart store in the world in Mexico City, Mexico.

has now moved into Europe, South America, and Asia. Wal-Mart is the largest retailer in the world and changes the structure of business in many countries it enters. In 2003, Wal-Mart had 1,295 stores in international locations representing about 27 percent of its total stores.[37]

The internationalization of markets and industries makes it increasingly difficult to think of some firms as domestic companies. For example, Daimler-Benz, the parent company of Mercedes-Benz, merged with Chrysler Corporation to create DaimlerChrysler. DaimlerChrysler has focused on integrating the formerly independent companies' operations around the world. In a similar move, Ford acquired Volvo's car division. Ford now has six global brands: Ford, Lincoln, Mercury, Jaguar, Mazda, and Aston Martin. It uses these brands to build economies of scale in the purchase and sourcing of components that make up 60 percent of the value of a car.[38]

Neither of these companies has been performing well since the turn of the 21st century. Problems with the integration of Chrysler into the Daimler organization have been blamed for the performance problems of DaimlerChrysler. The problems experienced by Ford were enumerated in the Strategic Focus. The U.S. auto market continues to change, as suggested in the Strategic Focus. In fact, it is predicted that foreign brands will control about 50 percent of this market by 2007.[39] However, auto manufacturers should no longer be thought of as European, Japanese, or American. Instead, they can be more accurately classified as global companies striving to achieve strategic competitiveness in the 21st-century competitive landscape. Some believe that because of the enormous economic benefits it can generate, globalization will not be stopped. It has been predicted that genuine free trade in manufactured goods among the United States, Europe, and Japan would add 5 to 10 percent to the three regions' annual economic output, and free trade in their service sectors would boost aggregate output by another 15 to 20 percent. Realizing these potential gains in economic output requires a commitment from the industrialized nations to cooperatively stimulate the higher levels of trade necessary for global growth. In 2001, global trade in goods and services accounted for approximately 25 percent of the world's GDP and has remained relatively constant since that time.[40]

Global competition has increased performance standards in many dimensions, including quality, cost, productivity, product introduction time, and operational efficiency. Moreover, these standards are not static; they are exacting, requiring continuous improvement from a firm and its employees. As they accept the challenges posed by these increasing standards, companies improve their capabilities and individual workers sharpen their skills. Thus, in the 21st-century competitive landscape, only firms capable of meeting, if not exceeding, global standards typically earn strategic competitiveness.[41]

The development of emerging and transitional economies also is changing the global competitive landscape and significantly increasing competition in global markets.[42] The economic development of Asian countries—outside Japan—is increasing the significance of Asian markets. Firms in the emerging economies of Asia, such as South Korea, however, are becoming major competitors in global industries. Companies such as Cemex are moving more boldly into international markets and are making important investments in Asia. Cemex, a cement producer headquartered in Mexico, also has significant investments in North America and Latin America. Thus, international investments come from many directions and are targeted for multiple regions of the world. However, firms' ability to compete is affected by the resources and institutional environments (e.g., government regulations, access to financial capital, culture) in their country. Firms from emerging market countries often are resource poor and must access resources (often through alliances with resource rich firms) to compete in global markets.[43] Thus, the different institutional frameworks in countries cause firms to follow different strategies. As a result, there are different strategies across countries, and firms entering markets will vary their strategies according to the institutional environments in those countries.[44]

There are risks with these investments (a number of them are discussed in Chapter 8). Some people refer to these risks as the "liability of foreignness."[45] Research suggests that firms are challenged in their early ventures into international markets and can encounter difficulties by entering too many different or challenging international markets. First, performance may suffer in early efforts to globalize until a firm develops the skills required to manage international operations.[46] Additionally, the firm's performance may suffer with substantial amounts of globalization. In this instance, firms may overdiversify internationally beyond their ability to manage these diversified operations.[47] The outcome can sometimes be quite painful to these firms.[48] Thus, entry into international markets, even for firms with substantial experience in them, first requires careful planning and selection of the appropriate markets to enter followed by developing the most effective strategies to successfully operate in those markets.

Global markets are attractive strategic options for some companies, but they are not the only source of strategic competitiveness. In fact, for most companies, even for those capable of competing successfully in global markets, it is critical to remain committed to and strategically competitive in the domestic market.[49] In the 21st-century competitive landscape, firms are challenged to develop the optimal level of globalization that results in appropriate concentrations on a company's domestic and global operations.

In many instances, strategically competitive companies are those that have learned how to apply competitive insights gained locally (or domestically) on a global scale.[50] These companies do not impose homogeneous solutions in a pluralistic world. Instead, they nourish local insights so that they can modify and apply them appropriately in different regions of the world.[51] Moreover, they are sensitive to globalization's potential effects. Firms with strong commitments to global success evaluate these possible outcomes in making their strategic choices.

Technology and Technological Changes

There are three categories of trends and conditions through which technology is significantly altering the nature of competition.

INCREASING RATE OF TECHNOLOGICAL CHANGE AND DIFFUSION

Both the rate of change of technology and the speed at which new technologies become available and are used have increased substantially over the last 15 to 20 years. Consider the following rates of technology diffusion:

> *It took the telephone 35 years to get into 25 percent of all homes in the United States. It took TV 26 years. It took radio 22 years. It took PCs 16 years. It took the Internet 7 years.*[52]

Perpetual innovation is a term used to describe how rapidly and consistently new, information-intensive technologies replace older ones. The shorter product life cycles resulting from these rapid diffusions of new technologies place a competitive premium on being able to quickly introduce new goods and services into the marketplace. In fact, when products become somewhat indistinguishable because of the widespread and rapid diffusion of technologies, speed to market may be the primary source of competitive advantage (see Chapter 5).[53] While some people became disenchanted with information technology because of the "bubble years" when the Internet was overvalued, the information technology industry comprises 10 percent of the U.S. economy and 60 percent of its capital spending. Thus, the waves of innovation it produces will continue to be highly important.[54]

There are other indicators of rapid technology diffusion. Some evidence suggests that it takes only 12 to 18 months for firms to gather information about their competitors' research and development and product decisions.[55] In the global economy, competitors can sometimes imitate a firm's successful competitive actions within a few days. Once a source of competitive advantage, the protection firms possessed previously through their patents has been stifled by the current rate of technological diffusion. Today, patents are thought by many to be an effective way of protecting proprietary technology only for the pharmaceutical and chemical industries. Indeed, many firms competing in the electronics industry often do not apply for patents to prevent competitors from gaining access to the technological knowledge included in the patent application.

The other factor in technological change is the development of disruptive technologies that destroy the value of existing technology and create new markets.[56] Some have referred to this concept as Schumpeterian innovation, from the work by the famous economist Joseph A. Schumpeter. Others refer to this outcome as radical or breakthrough innovation.[57] While disruptive or radical technologies generally harm industry incumbents, some are able to adapt based on their superior resources, past experience, and ability to gain access to the new technology through multiple sources (e.g., alliances, acquisitions, and ongoing internal basic research).[58]

THE INFORMATION AGE

Dramatic changes in information technology have occurred in recent years. Personal computers, cellular phones, artificial intelligence, virtual reality, and massive databases (e.g., Lexis/Nexis) are a few examples of how information is used differently as a result of technological developments. An important outcome of these changes is that the ability to effectively and efficiently access and use information has become an important source of competitive advantage in virtually all industries.

Companies are building electronic networks that link them to customers, employees, vendors, and suppliers. These networks, designed to conduct business over the Internet, are referred to as e-business,[59] and e-business is big business. Internet trade has exceeded expectations with business-to-business trade reaching $2.4 trillion and business-to-consumer trade reaching $95 billion in 2003. Productivity gains from business use of the Internet are also expected to reach $450 billion by 2005.[60]

Both the pace of change in information technology and its diffusion will continue to increase. For instance, the number of personal computers in use is expected to reach 278 million by 2010. The declining costs of information technologies and the increased accessibility to them are also evident in the 21st-century competitive landscape. The global proliferation of relatively inexpensive computing power and its linkage on a global scale via computer networks combine to increase the speed and diffusion of information technologies. Thus, the competitive potential of information technologies is now available to companies of all sizes throughout the world, not only to large firms in Europe, Japan, and North America.

The Internet provides an infrastructure that allows the delivery of information to computers in any location. Access to significant quantities of relatively inexpensive information yields strategic opportunities for a range of industries and companies. Retailers, for example, use the Internet to provide abundant shopping privileges to customers in multiple locations. The pervasive influence of electronic commerce or e-business is creating a new culture, referred to as e-culture, that affects the way managers lead, organize, think, and develop and implement strategies.[61]

INCREASING KNOWLEDGE INTENSITY

Knowledge (information, intelligence, and expertise) is the basis of technology and its application. In the 21st-century competitive landscape, knowledge is a critical organizational resource and is increasingly a valuable source of competitive advantage.[62] As a result, many companies now strive to translate the accumulated knowledge of individual employees into a corporate asset. Some argue that the value of intangible assets, including knowledge, is growing as a proportion of total shareholder value.[63] The probability of achieving strategic competitiveness in the 21st-century competitive landscape is enhanced for the firm that realizes that its survival depends on the ability to capture intelligence, transform it into usable knowledge, and diffuse it rapidly throughout the company.[64] Therefore, firms must develop (e.g., through training programs) and acquire (e.g., by hiring educated and experienced employees) knowledge, integrate it into the organization to create capabilities, and then apply it to gain a competitive advantage.[65] Thus, firms must develop a program whereby they learn and then integrate this learning into firm operations. And, they must build routines that facilitate the diffusion of local knowledge throughout the organization for use everywhere it has value.[66] To earn above-average returns, firms must be able to adapt quickly to changes in their competitive landscape. Such adaptation requires that the firm develop strategic flexibility. **Strategic flexibility** is a set of capabilities used to respond to various demands and opportunities existing in a dynamic and uncertain competitive environment. Thus, it involves coping with uncertainty and the accompanying risks.[67]

Firms should develop strategic flexibility in all areas of their operations. To achieve strategic flexibility, many firms have to develop organizational slack—slack resources that allow the firm some flexibility to respond to environmental changes.[68] When larger changes are required, firms may have to undergo strategic reorientations to change their competitive strategy. Strategic reorientations often result from a firm's poor performance. For example, when a firm earns negative returns, its stakeholders (discussed later in this chapter) are likely to pressure top executives to make major changes.[69]

To be strategically flexible on a continuing basis, a firm has to develop the capacity to learn. Continuous learning provides the firm with new and up-to-date sets of skills, which allow the firm to adapt to its environment as it encounters changes.[70] As illustrated in the Strategic Focus, most of the airlines, especially US Airways and United Airlines, have been unable to adapt to a turbulent and negative economic environment. They followed flawed strategies too long and failed. As these firms realized, being flexible, learning, and making the necessary changes are difficult, but they are necessary for continued survival.

Next, we describe two models used by firms to generate the strategic inputs needed to successfully formulate and implement strategies and to maintain strategic flexibility in the process of doing so.

Strategic flexibility is a set of capabilities used to respond to various demands and opportunities existing in a dynamic and uncertain competitive environment.

The I/O Model of Above-Average Returns

From the 1960s through the 1980s, the external environment was thought to be the primary determinant of strategies that firms selected to be successful.[71] The industrial organization (I/O) model of above-average returns explains the dominant influence of the external environment on a firm's strategic actions. The model specifies that the industry in which a firm chooses to compete has a stronger influence on the firm's performance than do the choices managers make inside their organizations.[72] The firm's performance is believed to be determined primarily by a range of industry properties, including economies of scale, barriers to market entry, diversification, product differentiation, and the degree of concentration of firms in the industry.[73] These industry characteristics are examined in Chapter 2.

Grounded in economics, the I/O model has four underlying assumptions. First, the external environment is assumed to impose pressures and constraints that determine the strategies that would result in above-average returns. Second, most firms competing within a particular industry or within a certain segment of it are assumed to control similar strategically relevant resources and to pursue similar strategies in light of those resources. The I/O model's third assumption is that resources used to implement strategies are highly mobile across firms. Because of resource mobility, any resource differences that might develop between firms will be short-lived. Fourth, organizational decision makers are assumed to be rational and committed to acting in the firm's best interests, as shown by their profit-maximizing behaviors.[74] The I/O model challenges firms to locate the most attractive industry in which to compete. Because most firms are assumed to have similar valuable resources that are mobile across companies, their performance generally can be increased only when they operate in the industry with the highest profit potential and learn how to use their resources to implement the strategy required by the industry's structural characteristics.

The five forces model of competition is an analytical tool used to help firms with this task. The model (explained in Chapter 2) encompasses several variables and tries to capture the complexity of competition. The five forces model suggests that an industry's profitability (i.e., its rate of return on invested capital relative to its cost of capital) is a function of interactions among five forces: suppliers, buyers, competitive rivalry among firms currently in the industry, product substitutes, and potential entrants to the industry.[75] Firms can use this tool to understand an industry's profit potential and the strategy necessary to establish a defensible competitive position, given the industry's structural characteristics. Typically, the model suggests that firms can earn above-average returns by manufacturing standardized products or producing standardized services at costs below those of competitors (a cost leadership strategy) or by manufacturing differentiated products for which customers are willing to pay a price premium (a differentiation strategy, described in depth in Chapter 4).

As shown in Figure 1.2, the I/O model suggests that above-average returns are earned when firms implement the strategy dictated by the characteristics of the general, industry, and competitor environments. Companies that develop or acquire the internal skills needed to implement strategies required by the external environment are likely to succeed, while those that do not are likely to fail. Hence, this model suggests that external characteristics, rather than the firm's unique internal resources and capabilities, primarily determine returns.

Research findings support the I/O model. They show that approximately 20 percent of a firm's profitability can be explained by the industry. In other words, 20 percent of a firm's profitability is determined by the industry or industries in which it chooses to operate. This research also shows, however, that 36 percent of the variance in profitability could be attributed to the firm's characteristics and actions.[76] The results of the research suggest that both the environment and the firm's characteristics play a role in determining the firm's specific level of profitability. Thus, there is likely a reciprocal relationship between the environment and the firm's strategy, thereby affecting the firm's performance.[77]

A firm is viewed as a bundle of market activities and a bundle of resources. Market activities are understood through the application of the I/O model. The develop-

1. Study the external environment, especially the industry environment.

The External Environment
- The general environment
- The industry environment
- The competitor environment

2. Locate an industry with high potential for above-average returns.

An Attractive Industry
- An industry whose structural characteristics suggest above-average returns

3. Identify the strategy called for by the attractive industry to earn above-average returns.

Strategy Formulation
- Selection of a strategy linked with above-average returns in a particular industry

4. Develop or acquire assets and skills needed to implement the strategy.

Assets and Skills
- Assets and skills required to implement a chosen strategy

5. Use the firm's strengths (its developed or acquired assets and skills) to implement the strategy.

Strategy Implementation
- Selection of strategic actions linked with effective implementation of the chosen strategy

Superior Returns
- Earning of above-average returns

ment and effective use of a firm's resources, capabilities, and core competencies are understood through the application of the resource-based model. As a result, executives must integrate the two models to develop the most effective strategy.

Profitability in the airline industry has been exceptionally low since we moved into the 21st century. In fact, it is an unattractive industry except for Southwest Airlines and a few other innovative carriers, such as JetBlue in the United States and Virgin Atlantic in the United Kingdom. The industry might become more efficient over time if opened to international competition, but this would undoubtedly lead to consolidation and fewer airlines globally. As shown in the Strategic Focus, however, the key to success is building a portfolio of valuable resources. Southwest Airlines has done so and performed much better than the other large airlines in the industry. Resources are Wal-Mart's key to success as well. Therefore, we must attempt to integrate the I/O model discussed above with the resource-based model explained next.

How Do Firms Succeed in a Highly Challenging Economic Environment with Strong Competition? It Is Resources, Stupid!

Airlines exist in one of the most challenging economic environments since the depression of the 1930s in the United States. This industry is reeling from the poor economic environment in the United States and beyond, the terrorist attack on September 11, 2001, the SARS outbreak in Asia, and war in the Middle East. Because of decreased demand and overcapacity in the industry, most airlines have had substantial net losses since the turn of the century. In fact, two major airlines, US Airways and United Airlines, had to file for bankruptcy, and others, such as American Airlines, have narrowly averted it. These major airlines are searching for new strategies and business models. As in the past, several large airlines have stated publicly that they were going to start a low-cost airline (e.g., United, Delta), while others have proclaimed that they will become a low-cost airline. Of course, these decisions are designed to emulate Southwest Airlines. (These actions are described further in Chapter 5's Opening Case.) Several airlines have tried to imitate Southwest in the past and have failed. The primary problem is that the major airlines have had cost structures substantially higher than Southwest's (from 60 percent higher to more than 100 percent higher). One industry analyst called for a relaxation of the regulations to allow foreign competition. The analyst suggested that this would lead to a more efficient industry. While correct, there are significant forces against this proposal.

Southwest Airlines has been the nemesis of the major airlines for many years. It has made a profit every year of its existence, the only airline to do so. Certainly, strategic decisions made early in its history (such as the use of only one type of aircraft) have helped it maintain a low cost structure. But many now believe that the primary reason for the phenomenal success of Southwest Airlines is its resources. Southwest has two important resources not possessed by other major airlines—substantial human capital and a positive corporate culture. Because of its positive work environment and caring culture, Southwest is able to hire outstanding employees who are loyal and productive. An example of the reason for this ability is that Southwest refused to lay off employees with the major downturn in demand after September 11. It was able to do so because it had amassed a major cache of cash in a contingency fund for use in emergencies. All other airlines had substantial employee layoffs. In *Fortune's* 2003 annual survey of the most admired companies, Southwest Airlines was ranked number two out of all possible companies. Southwest Airlines has been ranked among the top ten companies on this survey since 1999, and it ranked number two in both 2002 and 2003. We further discuss Southwest's uses of its resources in a Strategic Focus in Chapter 4.

The number one ranked firm in *Fortune's* 2003 survey was Wal-Mart, the largest company in the world. Warren Buffett provided the following description of the firm: "Wal-Mart . . . hasn't lost a bit of its dynamism that it had back when Sam Walton started it . . . I think that's enormously impressive." To be ranked number one, it had to fare well in evaluations of its financial soundness, quality of management, quality of products and services, employee talent, use of corporate assets, and innovation, among other criteria. Thus, many evaluators believe that Wal-Mart has more than economic

An airline "graveyard" shown in the Arizona desert. With few successes, and many bankruptcies or near-bankruptcies, the airline industry has experienced substantial losses for decades. Turning the industry around may depend on increasing international competition.

Airphoto—Jim Wark

power due to its size; it must have substantial resources in its human capital, ability to be innovative, etc. Resources are the key to maintaining strategic flexibility and, thus, the ability to respond to major changes in the environment. They also allow firms to develop and implement the strategies needed to gain and sustain a competitive advantage. Southwest and Wal-Mart have performed so well over time because of the resources they have and the way in which they have managed those resources.

SOURCES: M. Maynard, 2003, United shifts focus on low-cost airline, *New York Times*, http://www.nytimes.com, May 30; W. Zellner & M. Arndt, 2003, Can anything fix the airlines? *Business Week*, April 7, 52–53; K. L. Alexander, 2003, US Airways CEO talks shop, *Washington Post*, http://www.washingtonpost.com, April 4; N. Stein, 2003, America's most admired companies, *Fortune*, March 3, 81–94; W. Zellner & M. Arndt, 2003, Holding steady: As rivals sputter, can Southwest stay on top? *Business Week*, February 3, 66–68; S. McCartney, 2003, U.S. airlines would benefit from foreign competition, *Wall Street Journal*, http://www.wsj.com, January 22.

The Resource-Based Model of Above-Average Returns

The resource-based model assumes that each organization is a collection of unique resources and capabilities that provides the basis for its strategy and that is the primary source of its returns. This model suggests that capabilities evolve and must be managed dynamically in pursuit of above-average returns.[78] According to the model, differences in firms' performances across time are due primarily to their unique resources and capabilities rather than the industry's structural characteristics. This model also assumes that firms acquire different resources and develop unique capabilities. Therefore, not all firms competing within a particular industry possess the same resources and capabilities. Additionally, the model assumes that resources may not be highly mobile across firms and that the differences in resources are the basis of competitive advantage.

Resources are inputs into a firm's production process, such as capital equipment, the skills of individual employees, patents, finances, and talented managers. In general, a firm's resources can be classified into three categories: physical, human, and organizational capital. Described fully in Chapter 3, resources are either tangible or intangible in nature.

Individual resources alone may not yield a competitive advantage.[79] In general, competitive advantages are formed through the combination and integration of sets of resources. A **capability** is the capacity for a set of resources to perform a task or an activity in an integrative manner. Through the firm's continued use, capabilities become stronger and more difficult for competitors to understand and imitate. As a source of competitive advantage, a capability "should be neither so simple that it is highly imitable, nor so complex that it defies internal steering and control."[80]

The resource-based model of superior returns is shown in Figure 1.3. Instead of focusing on the accumulation of resources necessary to implement the strategy dictated by conditions and constraints in the external environment (I/O model), the resource-based view suggests that a firm's unique resources and capabilities provide the basis for a strategy. The strategy chosen should allow the firm to best exploit its core competencies relative to opportunities in the external environment.

Not all of a firm's resources and capabilities have the potential to be the basis for competitive advantage. This potential is realized when resources and capabilities are valuable, rare, costly to imitate, and nonsubstitutable.[81] Resources are *valuable* when they allow a firm to take advantage of opportunities or neutralize threats in its external environment. They are *rare* when possessed by few, if any, current and potential competitors. Resources are *costly to imitate* when other firms either cannot obtain them or are at a cost disadvantage in obtaining them compared with the firm that

Resources *are inputs into a firm's production process, such as capital equipment, the skills of individual employees, patents, finances, and talented managers.*

A **capability** *is the capacity for a set of resources to perform a task or an activity in an integrative manner.*

Figure 1.3 — The Resource-Based Model of Above-Average Returns

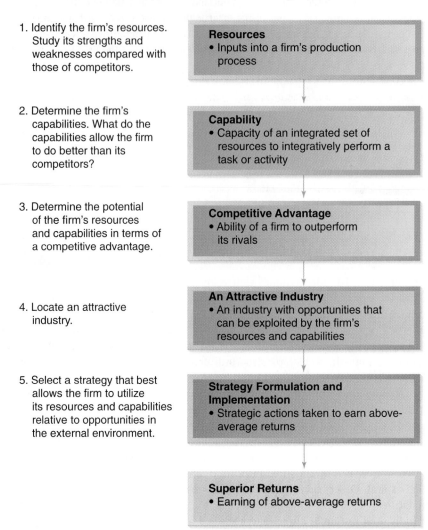

1. Identify the firm's resources. Study its strengths and weaknesses compared with those of competitors.

Resources
• Inputs into a firm's production process

2. Determine the firm's capabilities. What do the capabilities allow the firm to do better than its competitors?

Capability
• Capacity of an integrated set of resources to integratively perform a task or activity

3. Determine the potential of the firm's resources and capabilities in terms of a competitive advantage.

Competitive Advantage
• Ability of a firm to outperform its rivals

4. Locate an attractive industry.

An Attractive Industry
• An industry with opportunities that can be exploited by the firm's resources and capabilities

5. Select a strategy that best allows the firm to utilize its resources and capabilities relative to opportunities in the external environment.

Strategy Formulation and Implementation
• Strategic actions taken to earn above-average returns

Superior Returns
• Earning of above-average returns

already possesses them. And, they are *nonsubstitutable* when they have no structural equivalents. Many resources can either be imitated or substituted over time. Therefore, it is difficult to achieve and sustain a competitive advantage based on resources.[82] When these four criteria are met, however, resources and capabilities become core competencies. **Core competencies** are resources and capabilities that serve as a source of competitive advantage for a firm over its rivals. Often related to a firm's functional skills (e.g., the marketing function is a core competence of Philip Morris, a division of the Altria Group, Inc.), core competencies, when developed, nurtured, and applied throughout a firm, may result in strategic competitiveness.

Managerial competencies are important in most firms. For example, managers often have valuable human (education and experience) and social capital (ties to important customers or critical external organizations such as suppliers).[83] Such competencies may include the capability to effectively organize and govern complex and diverse operations and the capability to create and communicate a strategic vision.[84] Managerial capabilities are important in a firm's ability to take advantage of its resources. Firms must also continuously develop their competencies to keep them up

Core competencies *are resources and capabilities that serve as a source of competitive advantage for a firm over its rivals.*

to date. This development requires a systematic program for updating old skills and introducing new ones. Dynamic core competencies are especially important in rapidly changing environments, such as those that exist in high-technology industries. Thus, the resource-based model suggests that core competencies are the basis for a firm's competitive advantage, its strategic competitiveness, and its ability to earn above-average returns.

Recent research shows that both the industry environment and a firm's internal assets affect that firm's performance over time.[85] Thus, both are important in the development and implementation of firm strategy.[86] As a result, we integrate analysis of the external environment (Chapter 2) with the evaluation of the firm's internal resources and capabilities (Chapter 3) in the development of the most effective strategy for the firm.

Strategic Intent and Strategic Mission

Resulting from analyses of a firm's internal and external environments is the information required to form a strategic intent and develop a strategic mission (see Figure 1.1). Both intent and mission are linked with strategic competitiveness.

Strategic Intent

Strategic intent is the leveraging of a firm's resources, capabilities, and core competencies to accomplish the firm's goals in the competitive environment.[87] Strategic intent exists when all employees and levels of a firm are committed to the pursuit of a specific (and significant) performance criterion. Some argue that strategic intent provides employees with the only goal worthy of personal effort and commitment: to unseat the best or remain the best, worldwide.[88] Strategic intent has been effectively formed when employees believe strongly in their company's product and when they are focused on their firm's ability to outperform its competitors.

It appears as if Apple Computer is changing its strategic intent. While Steven Jobs has been able to steady a rapidly deteriorating firm after becoming CEO again in the late 1990s, Apple's market share in the computer market has decreased to 2.3 percent, down from 9.3 percent in 1993. Thus, Jobs has turned the company toward development of digital entertainment with a new online music service. His contacts in the entertainment industry have helped him obtain the agreements to offer the music of popular performers such as the Eagles through Apple's new service. The competition will be stiff; however, the change in strategic intent may be a matter of survival for Apple.[89]

It is not enough for a firm to know its own strategic intent. Performing well demands that the firm also identify its competitors' strategic intent. Only when these intentions are understood can a firm become aware of the resolve, stamina, and inventiveness (traits linked with effective strategic intents) of those competitors.[90] For example, Apple must now identify and understand not only Dell Inc.'s strategic intent but also that of Vivendi's Universal Music Group. A company's success may also be grounded in a keen and deep understanding of the strategic intent of its customers, suppliers, partners, and competitors.[91]

Apple is currently attempting to increase its market share through digital entertainment. Its success will depend on how well this change in strategic intent will carry them in an already highly competitive industry.

©Bill Aron/PhotoEdit

Strategic Mission

As the preceding discussion shows, strategic intent is internally focused. It is concerned with identifying the resources, capabilities, and core competencies on which a firm can base its strategic actions. Strategic intent reflects what a firm is capable of doing with its core competencies and the unique ways they can be used to exploit a competitive advantage.

Strategic mission is a statement of a firm's unique purpose and the scope of its operations in product and market terms.

Strategic mission flows from strategic intent. Externally focused, **strategic mission** is a statement of a firm's unique purpose and the scope of its operations in product and market terms.[92] A strategic mission provides general descriptions of the products a firm intends to produce and the markets it will serve using its core competencies. An effective strategic mission establishes a firm's individuality and is inspiring and relevant to all stakeholders.[93] Together, strategic intent and strategic mission yield the insights required to formulate and implement strategies.

The strategic mission of Johnson & Johnson focuses on customers, stating that the organization's primary responsibility is to "the doctors, nurses, and patients, mothers and fathers and all others who use our products and services."[94] An effective strategic mission is formed when the firm has a strong sense of what it wants to do and of the ethical standards that will guide behaviors in the pursuit of its goals.[95] Because Johnson & Johnson specifies the products it will offer in particular markets and presents a framework within which the firm operates, its strategic mission is an application of strategic intent.[96]

Research has shown that having an effective intent and mission and properly implementing them have a positive effect on performance as measured by growth in sales, profits, employment, and net worth.[97] When a firm is strategically competitive and earning above-average returns, it has the capacity to satisfy stakeholders' interests.

Stakeholders

Stakeholders are the individuals and groups who can affect, and are affected by, the strategic outcomes achieved and who have enforceable claims on a firm's performance.

Every organization involves a system of primary stakeholder groups with whom it establishes and manages relationships.[98] **Stakeholders** are the individuals and groups who can affect, and are affected by, the strategic outcomes achieved and who have enforceable claims on a firm's performance.[99] Claims on a firm's performance are enforced through the stakeholders' ability to withhold participation essential to the organization's survival, competitiveness, and profitability.[100] Stakeholders continue to support an organization when its performance meets or exceeds their expectations. Also, recent research suggests that firms effectively managing stakeholder relationships outperform those that do not. Stakeholder relationships can therefore be managed to be a source of competitive advantage.[101]

Although organizations have dependency relationships with their stakeholders, they are not equally dependent on all stakeholders at all times; as a consequence, not every stakeholder has the same level of influence. The more critical and valued a stakeholder's participation is, the greater is a firm's dependency on it. Greater dependence, in turn, gives the stakeholder more potential influence over a firm's commitments, decisions, and actions. Managers must find ways to either accommodate or insulate the organization from the demands of stakeholders controlling critical resources.[102]

Cisco changed from being a star to most of its stakeholders to displeasing many of them. In particular, its substantial reduction in stock price concerned shareholders. Its employee layoffs created concern and displeasure among Cisco's workforce, particularly because the need to cut costs was caused by poor strategic decisions that produced large inventories. However, as noted in the Strategic Focus, Cisco has survived the dot-com crash and its performance is improving. While Cisco's stock price is still much lower than in the heady times of the late 1990s, its future looks bright with a

Is Cisco a Survivor?

Strategic Focus

In the decade of the 1990s, Cisco Systems created more wealth for its shareholders than any other firm. Its stock price increased by 124,825 percent—a $100 investment in Cisco stock in 1990 was worth $1,248,250 by the end of the decade. Cisco was able to satisfy many of its stakeholders during the decade, but with the downturn in the U.S. economy and the poor performance of Internet-based and telecommunications firms (Cisco's major customers), its fortunes turned sour. Its stock price declined by almost 78 percent, from a high of over $71 in 2000 to below $16 in 2001, and Cisco had to lay off employees.

During the earlier strong economy, Cisco experienced delays in obtaining supplies and was unable to meet customers' orders for its systems. As a result, it signed long-term contracts with suppliers to ensure supply. When sales declined significantly, Cisco was faced with large inventories. One analyst suggested that Cisco managers did not know what to do when the economy slowed. Neither shareholders nor employees were pleased with the results.

During this slowdown, CEO John Chambers remained optimistic and vowed to stay the course. But, he compared the Internet slump to a 100-year flood that had not been anticipated by his team. Such a flood causes considerable destruction, so his analogy was appropriate. Chambers suggested that the firm's focus had changed from revenue growth to profitability, earnings contribution, and growth through internal development rather than acquisitions. While Cisco experienced a net loss of $1.0 billion in 2001, down from a $2.7 billion profit in 2000, Chambers' optimism seems well founded. Cisco reported a net profit in 2002 of almost $1.9 billion, representing a significant turnaround. Additionally, its cash reserves were higher in 2002 than they were in 2000, the previous high, and profits continued to increase in 2003. Thus, Cisco appears to be in good financial condition.

Chambers predicted that brand would become especially important and promised to protect the good brand of Cisco. Recent actions show that Chambers was serious. Cisco filed suit against Huawei Technologies, a Chinese company, for infringement of its patents. In June 2003, a U.S. federal judge issued an injunction against Huawei preventing it from selling, importing, exporting, or using the software questioned by Cisco. Huawei withdrew the products in question from the U.S. market.

SOURCES: 2003, Judge issues injunction against Chinese company in suit by Cisco, *New York Times,* http://www.nytimes.com, June 9; 2003, Cisco Annual Report 2002, http://www.cisco.com, March; B. Elgin, 2001, A do-it-yourself plan at Cisco, *Business Week,* September 10, 52; G. Anders, 2001, John Chambers after the deluge, *Fast Company,* July, 100–111; S. N. Mehta, 2001, Cisco fractures its own tale, *Fortune,* May 14, 105–112; P. Abrahams, 2001, Cisco chief must sink or swim, *Financial Times,* http://www.ft.com, April 19.

good net profit in 2002 (especially in poor economic times) and a strong cash position. Cisco is a survivor, and its stakeholders should be relieved, if not highly pleased to see the performance turnaround.

Classification of Stakeholders

The parties involved with a firm's operations can be separated into at least three groups.[103] As shown in Figure 1.4, these groups are the capital market stakeholders (shareholders and the major suppliers of a firm's capital), the product market stakeholders (the firm's primary customers, suppliers, host communities, and unions representing the workforce), and the organizational stakeholders (all of a firm's employees, including both nonmanagerial and managerial personnel).

Figure 1.4 — The Three Stakeholder Groups

Each stakeholder group expects those making strategic decisions in a firm to provide the leadership through which its valued objectives will be accomplished.[104] The objectives of the various stakeholder groups often differ from one another, sometimes placing managers in situations where trade-offs have to be made. The most obvious stakeholders, at least in U.S. organizations, are shareholders—those who have invested capital in a firm in the expectation of earning a positive return on their investments. These stakeholders' rights are grounded in laws governing private property and private enterprise.

Shareholders want the return on their investment (and, hence, their wealth) to be maximized. Maximization of returns sometimes is accomplished at the expense of investing in a firm's future. Gains achieved by reducing investment in research and development, for example, could be returned to shareholders, thereby increasing the short-term return on their investments. However, this short-term enhancement of shareholders' wealth can negatively affect the firm's future competitive ability, and sophisticated shareholders with diversified portfolios may sell their interests if a firm fails to invest in its future. Those making strategic decisions are responsible for a firm's survival in both the short and the long term. Accordingly, it is not in the interests of any stakeholders for investments in the company to be unduly minimized.

In contrast to shareholders, another group of stakeholders—the firm's customers—prefers that investors receive a minimum return on their investments. Customers could have their interests maximized when the quality and reliability of a firm's products are improved, but without a price increase. High returns to customers might come at the expense of lower returns negotiated with capital market shareholders.

Because of potential conflicts, each firm is challenged to manage its stakeholders. First, a firm must carefully identify all important stakeholders. Second, it must prioritize them, in case it cannot satisfy all of them. Power is the most critical criterion in prioritizing stakeholders. Other criteria might include the urgency of satisfying each particular stakeholder group and the degree of importance of each to the firm.[105]

When the firm earns above-average returns, the challenge of effectively managing stakeholder relationships is lessened substantially. With the capability and flexibility provided by above-average returns, a firm can more easily satisfy multiple stakeholders simultaneously. When the firm is earning only average returns, it is unable to maximize the interests of all stakeholders. The objective then becomes one of at least minimally satisfying each stakeholder. Trade-off decisions are made in light of how important the support of each stakeholder group is to the firm. For example, environmental groups may be very important to firms in the energy industry but less important to professional service firms.[106] A firm earning below-average returns does not have the capacity to minimally satisfy all stakeholders. The managerial challenge in this case is to make trade-offs that minimize the amount of support lost from stakeholders. Societal values also influence the general weightings allocated among the three stakeholder groups shown in Figure 1.4. Although all three groups are served by firms in the major industrialized nations, the priorities in their service vary because of cultural differences.

CAPITAL MARKET STAKEHOLDERS

Shareholders and lenders both expect a firm to preserve and enhance the wealth they have entrusted to it. The returns they expect are commensurate with the degree of risk accepted with those investments (that is, lower returns are expected with low-risk investments, and higher returns are expected with high-risk investments). Dissatisfied lenders may impose stricter covenants on subsequent borrowing of capital. Dissatisfied shareholders may reflect their concerns through several means, including selling their stock.

When a firm is aware of potential or actual dissatisfactions among capital market stakeholders, it may respond to their concerns. The firm's response to dissatisfied stakeholders is affected by the nature of its dependency relationship with them (which, as noted earlier, is also influenced by a society's values). The greater and more significant the dependency relationship is, the more direct and significant the firm's response becomes.

As discussed in a previous Strategic Focus, United Airlines and US Airways have both filed for bankruptcy and their stock has very little value. The capital market stakeholders in this case (i.e., stockholders and lenders) lost a large amount of money on their investments or loans. There is little that they can do to recoup their monies. In another Strategic Focus, it was noted that Cisco's stock price remains low, but the future of the firm is looking brighter. Thus, this firm's stockholders likely will want to hold on to their shares of stock in the hopes that the firm's profits will drive up the stock price. Lenders may also be feeling relief after news of Cisco's recent profits and positive future projections.

PRODUCT MARKET STAKEHOLDERS

Some might think that there is little commonality among the interests of customers, suppliers, host communities, and unions (product market stakeholders). However, all four groups can benefit as firms engage in competitive battles. For example, depending on product and industry characteristics, marketplace competition may result in lower product prices being charged to a firm's customers and higher prices being paid to its suppliers (the firm might be willing to pay higher supplier prices to ensure delivery of the types of goods and services that are linked with its competitive success).

As is noted in Chapter 4, customers, as stakeholders, demand reliable products at the lowest possible prices. Suppliers seek loyal customers who are willing to pay the highest sustainable prices for the goods and services they receive. Host communities want companies willing to be long-term employers and providers of tax revenues without placing excessive demands on public support services. Union officials are interested in secure jobs, under highly desirable working conditions, for employees they represent. Thus, product market stakeholders are generally satisfied when a firm's profit margin reflects at least a balance between the returns to capital market stakeholders (i.e., the returns lenders and shareholders will accept and still retain their interests in the firm) and the returns in which they share.

All product market stakeholders are important in a competitive business environment, but many firms emphasize the importance of the customer. As the preceding Strategic Focus suggests, Cisco experienced problems with consumer demand even before the poor economic conditions at the end of the decade. Some of Cisco's shareholders and employees (organizational stakeholders) were displeased with the firm's establishment of long-term contracts with suppliers that produced large investments in inventories when the economy slowed. These extra costs required Cisco to cut costs in other areas (e.g., by laying off employees) and contributed to a lower stock price. Cisco seems to have weathered the storm and is returning to profitability, as shown by its 2002 results and its continuing positive performance in 2003.

ORGANIZATIONAL STAKEHOLDERS

Employees—the firm's organizational stakeholders—expect the firm to provide a dynamic, stimulating, and rewarding work environment. They are usually satisfied working for a company that is growing and actively developing their skills, especially those skills required to be effective team members and to meet or exceed global work standards. Workers who learn how to use new knowledge productively are critical to organizational success. In a collective sense, the education and skills of a firm's workforce are competitive weapons affecting strategy implementation and firm performance.[107]

Strategic Leaders

Strategic leaders are the people responsible for the design and execution of strategic management processes. These individuals may also be called top-level managers, executives, the top management team, and general managers. Throughout this book, these names are used interchangeably. As discussed in Chapter 12, top-level managers can be a source of competitive advantage as a result of the value created by their strategic decisions.

Small organizations may have a single strategic leader; in many cases, this person owns the firm and is deeply involved with its daily operations. At the other extreme, large, diversified firms often have multiple top-level managers. In addition to the CEO and other top-level officials (e.g., the chief operating officer and chief financial officer), other managers of these companies are responsible for the performance of individual business units.

Top-level managers play critical roles in a firm's efforts to achieve desired strategic outcomes. In fact, some believe that every organizational failure is actually a failure of those who hold the final responsibility for the quality and effectiveness of a firm's decisions and actions. Failure can stem from changing strategic assumptions, which can cause the strategic mission to become a strategic blunder. This appears to have been a problem at United Airlines and US Airways described earlier in a Strategic Focus. While they all exist in a highly changing environment, several other airlines are not in danger of bankruptcy, and a few, especially Southwest, are profitable. This suggests that the decisions made by strategic leaders at United Airlines and US Airways were not as effective as those made by the strategic leaders at other airlines. Recent research suggests that many smart executives make major mistakes and fail. For example, these otherwise intelligent executives remove all people on the staff who disagree with them. As a result, no dissenting opinions are offered and major mistakes are inevitable.[108]

Decisions that strategic leaders make include how resources will be developed or acquired, at what price they will be obtained, and how they will be used. Managerial decisions also influence how information flows in a company, the strategies a firm chooses to implement, and the scope of its operations. In making these decisions, managers must assess the risk involved in taking the actions being considered. The level of risk is then factored into the decision.[109] The firm's strategic intent and managers' strategic orientations both affect their decisions. The decisions made by a firm's strategic leaders affect its ability to develop a competitive advantage.

Critical to strategic leadership practices and the implementation of strategies, **organizational culture** refers to the complex set of ideologies, symbols, and core values that are shared throughout the firm and that influence how the firm conducts business. Thus, culture is the social energy that drives—or fails to drive—the organization. For example, Southwest Airlines, one of the successful firms discussed in an earlier Strategic Focus, is known for having a unique and valuable culture. Its culture encourages employees to work hard but also to have fun while doing so. Moreover, its culture entails respect for others—employees and customers alike. The firm also places a premium on service, as suggested by its commitment to provide POS (Positively Outrageous Service) to each customer. These core values at Southwest Airlines provide a particular type of social energy that drives the firm's efforts. Organizational culture thus becomes a potential source of competitive advantage.

Organizational culture refers to the complex set of ideologies, symbols, and core values that are shared throughout the firm and that influence how the firm conducts business.

Given the importance of strategic leaders to a firm's success, the selection of those to fill these positions is critical. Planning for the succession of key leaders is important. Most planned successions of CEOs, for example, have been found to have positive effects on a firm's stock price regardless of whether the successor comes from the inside or outside.[110] When strategic change is needed, however, an outside successor is often selected for a key strategic leadership position. This is done because he or she can bring new ideas to the firm and is not tied to past decisions or to internal political processes. But, outside successors are disadvantaged early because of their lack of firm-specific knowledge. Thus, early performance after such a change may not be positive. Outside successors, however, are likely to make changes that have long-term positive consequences for the firm.[111] Careful decisions regarding leadership succession are important because of the potential for mistakes made by executives, as noted above. When executives are powerful, they are more likely to display hubris and make mistakes. When "heirs apparent" are selected from inside the firm relatively early, they are more likely to have greater power when they move into the strategic leadership position.[112] After the new strategic leader is chosen, his or her focus is on making effective strategic decisions.

CEOs play a critical role in creating and implementing a company's strategy. CEO Meg Whitman has successfully led eBay through global expansion and continuous reinvention of itself as a way of staying ahead of its competition.

The Work of Effective Strategic Leaders

Perhaps not surprisingly, hard work, thorough analyses, a willingness to be brutally honest, a penchant for wanting the firm and its people to accomplish more, and common sense are prerequisites to an individual's success as a strategic leader.[113] In addition to possessing these characteristics, effective

AP Photo/Paul Sakuma

strategic leaders must be able to think clearly and ask many questions. In particular, top-level managers are challenged to "think seriously and deeply . . . about the purposes of the organizations they head or functions they perform, about the strategies, tactics, technologies, systems, and people necessary to attain these purposes and about the important questions that always need to be asked."[114]

As the Internet has changed the nature of competition, it is also changing strategic decision making. Speed has become a much more prominent competitive factor, and it makes strategic thinking even more critical. Most high-tech firms operate in hypercompetitive industry environments. As a result of the intense competition in these industries, some product life cycles have decreased from a period of one to two years to a period of six to nine months, leaving less time for a company's products to generate revenue. Speed and flexibility have become key sources of competitive advantage for companies competing in these industries. Thinking strategically, in concert with others, increases the probability of identifying bold, innovative ideas.[115] When these ideas lead to the development of core competencies, they become the foundation for taking advantage of environmental opportunities.

Our discussion highlights the nature of a strategic leader's work. Strategic leaders often work long hours, and the work is filled with ambiguous decision situations for which effective solutions are not easily determined.[116] However, the opportunities afforded by this work are appealing and offer exciting chances to dream and to act. The following words, given as advice to the late Time Warner chairman and co-CEO Steven J. Ross by his father, describe the opportunities in a strategic leader's work:

> There are three categories of people—the person who goes into the office, puts his feet up on his desk, and dreams for 12 hours; the person who arrives at 5 A.M. and works for 16 hours, never once stopping to dream; and the person who puts his feet up, dreams for one hour, then does something about those dreams.[117]

The organizational term used for a dream that challenges and energizes a company is strategic intent (discussed earlier in this chapter). Strategic leaders have opportunities to dream and to act, and the most effective ones provide a vision (the strategic intent) to effectively elicit the help of others in creating a firm's competitive advantage.

Predicting Outcomes of Strategic Decisions: Profit Pools

Strategic leaders attempt to predict the outcomes of strategic decisions they make before they are implemented. In most cases, outcomes are determined only after the decisions have been implemented. For example, executives at Montana Power decided to change the firm from a utility company to a high-tech company focusing on broadband services. The firm announced in March 2000 that it would invest $1.6 billion to build a coast-to-coast fiber optic network. Unfortunately for Montana Power, the utility industry began to grow and the broadband industry declined substantially in 2001. As a result, the firm's stock price declined from $65 per share in 2000 to less than $1 per share in 2001. In fact, the new firm in which the assets were invested, Touch America, was on the verge of bankruptcy in 2003. While it may have been difficult for Montana Power to predict the rapid decline in the high-tech businesses, it should have been much easier to predict the growth in the utility business.[118] One means of helping managers understand the potential outcomes of their strategic decisions is to map their industry's profit pools. There are four steps to doing this: (1) define the pool's boundaries, (2) estimate the pool's overall size, (3) estimate the size of the value-chain activity in the pool, and (4) reconcile the calculations.[119]

A **profit pool** entails the total profits earned in an industry at all points along the value chain.[120] Analyzing the profit pool in the industry may help a firm see something others are unable to see by helping it understand the primary sources of profits in an industry. After these sources have been identified, managers must link the profit poten-

A **profit pool** *entails the total profits earned in an industry at all points along the value chain.*

tial identified to specific strategies. In a sense, they map the profit potential of their departmental units by linking to the firm's overall profits. They can then better link the strategic actions considered to potential profits.[121]

Mapping profit pools and linking potential profits to strategic actions before they are implemented should be a regular part of the strategic management process. General Motors' strategic leaders would have done well to take these actions when they decided to continue investing resources in the Oldsmobile brand instead of investing them in their Saturn brand. The firm's investments in Oldsmobile in essence starved Saturn for resources, even though Oldsmobile was no longer a successful product in the market. Finally, after making a decision to stop marketing Oldsmobile, GM decided to invest $1.5 billion in developing a full line of Saturn products.[122]

The Strategic Management Process

As suggested by Figure 1.1, the strategic management process is intended to be a rational approach to help a firm effectively respond to the challenges of the 21st-century competitive landscape. Figure 1.1 also outlines the topics examined in this book to study the strategic management process. Part 1 of this book shows how this process requires a firm to study its external environment (Chapter 2) and internal environment (Chapter 3) to identify marketplace opportunities and threats and determine how to use its resources, capabilities, and core competencies to pursue desired strategic outcomes. With this knowledge, the firm forms its strategic intent to leverage its resources, capabilities, and core competencies and to win competitive battles. Flowing from its strategic intent, the firm's strategic mission specifies, in writing, the products the firm intends to produce and the markets it will serve when leveraging those resources, capabilities, and core competencies.

The firm's strategic inputs provide the foundation for its strategic actions to formulate and implement strategies. Both formulating and implementing strategies are critical to achieving strategic competitiveness and earning above-average returns. As suggested in Figure 1.1 by the horizontal arrow linking the two types of strategic actions, formulation and implementation must be simultaneously integrated. In formulating strategies, thought should be given to implementing them. During implementation, effective strategic leaders also seek feedback to improve selected strategies. Only when these two sets of actions are carefully integrated can the firm achieve its desired strategic outcomes.

In Part 2 of this book, the formulation of strategies is explained. First, we examine the formulation of strategies at the business-unit level (Chapter 4). A diversified firm competing in multiple product markets and businesses has a business-level strategy for each distinct product market area. A company competing in a single product market has but one business-level strategy. In all instances, a business-level strategy describes a firm's actions designed to exploit its competitive advantage over rivals. On the other hand, business-level strategies are not formulated and implemented in isolation (Chapter 5). Competitors respond to and try to anticipate each other's actions. Thus, the dynamics of competition are an important input when selecting and implementing strategies.

For the diversified firm, corporate-level strategy (Chapter 6) is concerned with determining the businesses in which the company intends to compete as well as how resources are to be allocated among those businesses. Other topics vital to strategy formulation, particularly in the diversified firm, include the acquisition of other companies and, as appropriate, the restructuring of the firm's portfolio of businesses (Chapter 7) and the selection of an international strategy (Chapter 8). Increasingly important in a global economy, cooperative strategies are used by a firm to gain competitive advantage by forming advantageous relationships with other firms (Chapter 9).

To examine actions taken to implement strategies, we consider several topics in Part 3 of the book. First, the different mechanisms used to govern firms are explained (Chapter 10). With demands for improved corporate governance voiced by various stakeholders, organizations are challenged to satisfy stakeholders' interests and the attainment of desired strategic outcomes. Finally, the organizational structure and actions needed to control a firm's operations (Chapter 11), the patterns of strategic leadership appropriate for today's firms and competitive environments (Chapter 12), and strategic entrepreneurship (Chapter 13) are addressed.

As noted earlier, competition requires firms to make choices to survive and succeed. Some of these choices are strategic in nature, including those of selecting a strategic intent and strategic mission, determining which strategies to implement, choosing an appropriate level of corporate scope, designing governance and organization structures to properly coordinate a firm's work, and, through strategic leadership, encouraging and nurturing organizational innovation.[123] The goal is to achieve and maintain a competitive advantage over rivals.

Primarily because they are related to how a firm interacts with its stakeholders, almost all strategic decisions have ethical dimensions.[124] Organizational ethics are revealed by an organization's culture; that is to say, a firm's strategic decisions are a product of the core values that are shared by most or all of a company's managers and employees. Especially in the turbulent and often ambiguous 21st-century competitive landscape, those making strategic decisions are challenged to recognize that their decisions affect capital market, product market, and organizational stakeholders differently and to evaluate the ethical implications of their decisions.

As you will discover, the strategic management process examined in this book calls for disciplined approaches to the development of competitive advantage. These approaches provide the pathway through which firms will be able to achieve strategic competitiveness and earn above-average returns in the 21st century. Mastery of this strategic management process will effectively serve readers and the organizations for which they choose to work.

Summary

- Through their actions, firms seek strategic competitiveness and above-average returns. Strategic competitiveness is achieved when a firm has developed and learned how to implement a value-creating strategy. Above-average returns (in excess of what investors expect to earn from other investments with similar levels of risk) allow a firm to simultaneously satisfy all of its stakeholders.

- In the 21st-century competitive landscape, the fundamental nature of competition has changed. As a result, those making strategic decisions must adopt a new mind-set that is global in nature. Firms must learn how to compete in highly turbulent and chaotic environments that produce disorder and a great deal of uncertainty. The globalization of industries and their markets and rapid and significant technological changes are the two primary factors contributing to the 21st-century competitive landscape.

- There are two major models of what a firm should do to earn above-average returns. The I/O model suggests that the external environment is the primary determinant of the firm's strategies. Above-average returns are earned when the firm locates an attractive industry and successfully implements the strategy dictated by that industry's characteristics.

- The resource-based model assumes that each firm is a collection of unique resources and capabilities that determine its strategy. Above-average returns are earned when the firm uses its valuable, rare, costly-to-imitate, and nonsubstitutable resources and capabilities (i.e., core competencies) as the source of its competitive advantage(s).

- Strategic intent and strategic mission are formed in light of the information and insights gained from studying a firm's internal and external environments. Strategic intent suggests how resources, capabilities, and core competencies will be leveraged to achieve desired outcomes. The strategic mission is an application of strategic intent. The mission is used to specify the product markets and customers a firm intends to serve through the leveraging of its resources, capabilities, and core competencies.

- Stakeholders are those who can affect, and are affected by, a firm's strategic outcomes. Because a firm is dependent on the continuing support of stakeholders (shareholders, customers, suppliers, employees, host communities, etc.), they have enforceable claims on the company's performance. When earning above-average returns, a firm can adequately satisfy all stakeholders' interests. However, when earning only average returns, a firm's strategic leaders must carefully manage all stakeholder groups in order to retain their support. A firm earning below-average returns must minimize the amount of support it loses from dissatisfied stakeholders.

- Strategic leaders are responsible for the design and execution of an effective strategic management process.

Today, the most effective of these processes are grounded in ethical intentions and conduct. Strategic leaders can be a source of competitive advantage. The strategic leader's work demands decision trade-offs, often among attractive alternatives. Successful top-level managers work hard, conduct thorough analyses of situations, are brutally and consistently honest, and ask the right questions of the right people at the right time.

- Managers must predict the potential outcomes of their strategic decisions. To do so, they must first calculate profit pools in their industry that are linked to the value chain activities. In so doing, they are less likely to formulate and implement an ineffective strategy.

Review Questions

Review Questions Review Questions

1. What are strategic competitiveness, competitive advantage, and above-average returns?

2. What are the characteristics of the 21st-century landscape? What two factors are the primary drivers of this landscape?

3. According to the I/O model, what should a firm do to earn above-average returns?

4. What does the resource-based model suggest a firm should do to earn above-average returns?

5. What are strategic intent and strategic mission? What is their value for the strategic management process?

6. What are stakeholders? How do the three primary stakeholder groups influence organizations?

7. How would you describe the work of strategic leaders?

8. What are the elements of the strategic management process? How are they interrelated?

Experiential Exercises

Experiential Exercise

For the experiential exercises in Part 1, choose a company or an industry in which you would like to work. You can gain valuable insight about your future employment while learning about the strategic management process. You will find it helpful to peruse the business press (e.g., *Wall Street Journal, Business Week, Fortune,* and so forth) for information about the firm or industry of interest to you.

Effective Stakeholder Management

Effective stakeholder management is an important part of successful strategic management processes. Stakeholders are the individuals or groups with objectives or interests that can be affected by the firm's strategic outcomes. Each stakeholder group also has the ability to affect the outcomes achieved by the firm.

Prepare a report for the top management team at the firm of interest to you. The purpose of your report is to provide advice about how to effectively manage the firm's stakeholders. Your report should include the following:

a. Identify all important stakeholders for your company (or industry).

b. Determine the primary objectives of each stakeholder group.

c. Assess the power of each group to affect the firm's strategic outcomes and the ways in which this power may be exercised.

d. Explain how the firm may satisfy the interests or objectives of each group.

e. Recommend trade-offs that managers may make in satisfying stakeholder groups that will improve firm performance.

Strategic Mission Statements

A strategic mission describes a firm's unique purpose and the scope of its operations in terms of the products it intends to produce and the markets it will serve using its core competencies. An effective strategic mission establishes a firm's individuality and is inspiring and relevant to all stakeholders.

On the basis of this description of a strategic mission, evaluate the following mission statements of several competitors in the pharmaceutical industry. Each statement was clearly identified on the company's website as the company's mission. Examine the similarities and differences. In your opinion, which firm has the most effective mission statement? Why? Discuss ways in which the statements could be changed to provide a more effective basis for strategy formulation or implementation.

GlaxoSmithKline: GSK's mission is to improve the quality of human life by enabling people to do more, feel better and live longer.

AstraZeneca: The people of AstraZeneca are dedicated to discovering, developing and delivering innovative pharmaceutical solutions; enriching the lives of patients, families, communities and other stakeholders; and creating a challenging and rewarding work environment for everyone.

Bristol-Myers Squibb: At Bristol-Myers Squibb, our mission is to extend and enhance human life by providing the highest-quality pharmaceuticals and health care products. Our medicines are making a difference in the lives of millions of customers across the globe. And by living our mission and growing our company for well over a century, we are making a difference in the lives of our shareholders, employees and neighbors as well.

Merck & Co., Inc.: The mission of Merck is to provide society with superior products and services by developing innovations and solutions that improve the quality of life and satisfy customer needs, and to provide employees with meaningful work and advancement opportunities, and investors with a superior rate of return.

Novartis: We want to discover, develop, and successfully market innovative products to cure diseases, to ease suffering and to enhance the quality of life. We also want to provide a shareholder return that reflects outstanding performance and to adequately reward those who invest ideas and work in our company.

Pfizer: We will become the world's most valued company to patients, customers, colleagues, investors, business partners, and the communities where we work and live.

Notes

1. D. G. Sirmon & M. A. Hitt, 2003, Managing resources: Linking unique resources, management and wealth creation in family firms, *Entrepreneurship Theory and Practice*, 27(4): 339–358; D. G. Sirmon, M. A. Hitt, & R. D. Ireland, 2003, Managing the firm's resources in order to achieve and maintain a competitive advantage, presented at the Academy of Management, Seattle; C. E. Helfat, 2000, The evolution of firm capabilities, *Strategic Management Journal*, 21(Special Issue): 955–959; J. B. Barney, 1999, How firms' capabilities affect boundary decisions, *Sloan Management Review*, 40(3): 137–145.

2. T. J. Douglas & J. A. Ryman, 2003, Understanding competitive advantage in the general hospital industry: Evaluating strategic competencies, *Strategic Management Journal*, 24: 333–347; W. Mitchell, 2000, Path-dependent and path-breaking change: Reconfiguring business resources following acquisitions in the U.S. medical sector, 1978–1995, *Strategic Management Journal*, 21(Special Issue): 1061–1081.

3. E. Bonabeau & C. Meyer, 2001, Swarm intelligence, *Harvard Business Review*, 79(5): 107–114; D. J. Teece, G. Pisano, & A. Shuen, 1997, Dynamic capabilities and strategic management, *Strategic Management Journal*, 18: 509–533.

4. A. M. McGahan & M. E. Porter, 2003, The emergence and sustainability of abnormal profits, *Strategic Organization*, 1: 79–108; T. C. Powell, 2001, Competitive advantage: Logical and philosophical considerations, *Strategic Management Journal*, 22: 875–888.

5. P. Shrivastava, 1995, Ecocentric management for a risk society, *Academy of Management Review*, 20: 119.

6. F. Delmar, P. Davidsson, & W. B. Gartner, 2003, Arriving at a high-growth firm, *Journal of Business Venturing*, 18: 189–216.

7. R. P. Rumelt, D. E. Schendel, & D. J. Teece (eds.), 1994, *Fundamental Issues in Strategy*, Boston: Harvard Business School Press, 527–530.

8. M. J. Epstein & R. A. Westbrook, 2001, Linking actions to profits in strategic decision making, *Sloan Management Review*, 42(3): 39–49.

9. S. Dutta, M. J. Zbaracki, & M. Bergen, 2003, Pricing process as a capability: A resource-based perspective, *Strategic Management Journal*, 24: 615–630; Rumelt, Schendel, & Teece, *Fundamental Issues in Strategy*, 543–547.

10. S. Tallman & K. Fladmoe-Lindquist, 2002, Internationalization, globalization, and capability-based strategy, *California Management Review*, 45(1): 116–135; M. A. Hitt, R. D. Ireland, S. M. Camp, & D. L. Sexton, 2001, Strategic entrepreneurship: Entrepreneurial strategies for wealth creation, *Strategic Management Journal* 22(Special Issue): 479–491; S. A. Zahra, R. D. Ireland, & M. A. Hitt, 2000, International expansion by new venture firms: International diversity, mode of market entry, technological learning and performance, *Academy of Management Journal*, 43: 925–950.

11. P. Davidsson & B. Honig, 2003, The role of social and human capital among nascent entrepreneurs, *Journal of Business Venturing*, 18: 301–333; M. A. Hitt, L. Bierman, K. Shimizu, & R. Kochhar, 2001, Direct and moderating effects of human capital on strategy and performance in professional service firms, *Academy of Management Journal*, 44: 13–28.

12. A. Nair & S. Kotha, 2001, Does group membership matter? Evidence from the Japanese steel industry, *Strategic Management Journal*, 22: 221–235; A. M. McGahan & M. E. Porter, 1997, How much does industry matter, really? *Strategic Management Journal*, 18 (Special Issue): 15–30.

13. Sirmon & Hitt, Managing resources; J. B. Barney, 2001, Is the resource-based "view" a useful perspective for strategic management research? Yes, *Academy of Management Review*, 26: 41–56.

14. S. N. Mehta, 2001, Cisco fractures its own fairy tale, *Fortune*, 105–112.

15. S. Day, 2001, Shares surge after Cisco says its business has stabilized, *New York Times*, http://www.nytimes.com, August 25.

16. 2003, Cisco Systems 2002 Annual Report, http://www.cisco.com; K. Talley, 2003, Cisco, Apple and Dell advance, riding gains of tech shares, *Wall Street Journal Online*, http://www.wsj.com, May 6.

17. 2003, Bankruptcies, 2003, *Timesizing*, http://www.timesizing.com, February 15; M. Krantz, 2002, U.S. bankruptcies set record in 2002, *Honolulu Advertiser*, http://www.honoluluadvertiser.com, December 22.

18. Rumelt, Schendel, & Teece, *Fundamental Issues in Strategy*, 530.

19. C. J. Loomis, 1993, Dinosaurs, *Fortune*, May 3, 36–46.

20. V. Marsh, 1998, Attributes: Strong strategy tops the list, *Financial Times*, http://www.ft.com, November 30.

21. A. Barrett & D. Foust, 2003, Hot growth companies, *Business Week*, June 9, 74–77.

22. M. Farjoun, 2002, Towards an organic perspective on strategy, *Strategic Management Journal*, 23: 561–594.

23. A. Reinhardt, 1997, Paranoia, aggression, and other strengths, *Business Week*, October 13, 14; A. S. Grove, 1995, A high-tech CEO updates his views on managing and careers, *Fortune*, September 18, 229–230.

24. M. A. Hitt, B. W. Keats, & S. M. DeMarie, 1998, Navigating in the new competitive landscape: Building competitive advantage and strategic flexibility in the 21st century, *Academy of Management Executive*, 12(4): 22–42; R. A. Bettis & M. A. Hitt, 1995, The new competitive landscape, *Strategic Management Journal*, 16 (Special Issue): 7–19.

25. M. H. Zack, 2003, Rethinking the knowledge-based organization, *MIT Sloan Management Review*, 44(4): 67–71.

26. M. A. Hitt & V. Pisano, 2003, The cross-border merger and acquisition strategy, *Management Research*, 1: 133–144.

27. R. M. Grant, 2003, Strategic planning in a turbulent environment: Evidence from the oil majors, *Strategic Management Journal*, 24: 491–517.

28. R. A. D'Aveni, 1995, Coping with hypercompetition: Utilizing the new 7S's framework, *Academy of Management Executive*, 9(3): 46.

29. W. J. Ferrier, 2001, Navigating the competitive landscape: The drivers and consequences of competitive aggressiveness, *Academy of Management Journal*, 44: 858–877.

30. D. G. McKendrick, 2001, Global strategy and population level learning: The case of hard disk drives, *Strategic Management Journal*, 22: 307–334; T. P. Murtha, S. A. Lenway, & R. Bagozzi, 1998, Global mind-sets and cognitive shifts in a complex multinational corporation, *Strategic Management Journal*, 19: 97–114.

31. 2003, Economic Research Service, U.S. Department of Agriculture Long-term Macroeconomic Data, http://www.ers.usda.gov/data/macroeconomic/historicalrealGDPvalue.xls; S. Koudsi & L. A. Costa, 1998, America vs. the new Europe: By the numbers, *Fortune*, December 21, 149–156.

32. T. A. Stewart, 1993, The new face of American power, *Fortune*, July 26, 70–86.

33. S. Clegg & T. Kono, 2002, Trends in Japanese management: An overview of embedded continuities and disembedded discontinuities, *Asia Pacific Journal of Management*, 19: 269–285.

34. S. Garelli, 2001, Executive summary, *The World Competitiveness Yearbook*, http://www.imd.ch.wcy.esummary.

35. K. Kling & I. Goteman, 2003, IKEA CEO Anders Dahlvig on international growth and IKEA's unique corporate culture and brand identity, *Academy of Management Executive*, 17(1): 31–37.

36. Tallman & Fladmoe-Lindquist, Internationalization, globalization, and capability-based strategy; V. Govindarajan & A. K. Gupta, 2001, *The Quest for Global Dominance*, San Francisco: Jossey-Bass.

37. 2003, Wal-Mart website, http://www.walmartstores.com, May; D. Luhnow, 2001, Lower tariffs, retail muscle translate into big sales for Wal-Mart in Mexico, *Wall Street Journal Online*, http://www.wsj.com/articles, September 1.

38. 1999, Business: Ford swallows Volvo, *The Economist*, January 30, 58.

39. J. Porretto, 2002, Automakers face uncertain economy, growing foreign competition, union contract talks in 2003, *Dallas Morning News*, http://www.dallasnews.com, December.

40. Govindarajan & Gupta, *The Quest for Global Dominance*; R. Ruggiero, 1997, The high stakes of world trade, *Wall Street Journal*, April 28, A18.

41. M. Subramaniam & N. Venkataraman, 2001, Determinants of transnational new product development capability: Testing the influence of transferring and deploying tacit overseas knowledge, *Strategic Management Journal*, 22: 359–378; S. A. Zahra, 1999, The changing rules of global competitiveness in the 21st century, *Academy of Management Executive*, 13(1): 36–42; R. M. Kanter, 1995, Thriving locally in the global economy, *Harvard Business Review*, 73(5): 151–160.

42. D. E. Thomas, L. Eden, & M. A. Hitt, 2002, Who goes abroad? The role of knowledge and relation-based resources in emerging market firms' entry into developed markets, Paper presented at the Academy of Management, August; S. A. Zahra, R. D. Ireland, I. Gutierrez, & M. A. Hitt, 2000, Privatization and entrepreneurial transformation: Emerging issues and a future research agenda, *Academy of Management Review*, 25: 509–524.

43. L. Nachum, 2003, Does nationality of ownership make any difference and if so, under what circumstances? Professional service MNEs in global competition, *Journal of International Management*, 9: 1–32.

44. M. A. Hitt, D. Ahlstrom, M. T. Dacin, E. Levitas, & L. Svobodina, 2004, The institutional effects on strategic alliance partner selection in transition economies: China versus Russia, *Organization Science* (in press); M. W. Peng, 2002, Towards an institution-based view of business strategy, *Asia Pacific Journal of Management*, 19: 251–267.

45. S. Zaheer & E. Mosakowski, 1997, The dynamics of the liability of foreignness: A global study of survival in financial services, *Strategic Management Journal*, 18: 439–464.

46. D. Arnold, 2000, Seven rules of international distribution, *Harvard Business Review*, 78(6): 131–137; J. S. Black & H. B. Gregersen, 1999, The right way to manage expats, *Harvard Business Review*, 77(2): 52–63.

47. M. A. Hitt, R. E. Hoskisson, & H. Kim, 1997, International diversification: Effects on innovation and firm performance in product-diversified firms, *Academy of Management Journal*, 40: 767–798.

48. D'Aveni, Coping with hypercompetition, 46.

49. G. Hamel, 2001, Revolution vs. evolution: You need both, *Harvard Business Review*, 79(5): 150–156; T. Nakahara, 1997, Innovation in a borderless world economy, *Research-Technology Management*, May/June, 7–9.

50. G. Apfelthaler, H. J. Muller, & R. R. Rehder, 2002, Corporate global culture as competitive advantage: Learning from Germany and Japan in Alabama and Austria, *Journal of World Business*, 37: 108–118; J. Birkinshaw & N. Hood, 2001, Unleash innovation in foreign subsidiaries, *Harvard Business Review*, 79(3): 131–137.

51. J.-R. Lee & J-S. Chen, 2003, Internationalization, local adaptation and subsidiary's entrepreneurship: An exploratory study on Taiwanese manufacturing firms in Indonesia and Malaysia, *Asia Pacific Journal of Management*, 20: 51–72.

52. K. H. Hammonds, 2001, What is the state of the new economy? *Fast Company*, September, 101–104.

53. K. H. Hammonds, 2001, How do fast companies work now? *Fast Company*, September, 134–142; K. M. Eisenhardt, 1999, Strategy as strategic decision making, *Sloan Management Review*, 40(3): 65–72.

54. S. Lohr, 2003, Technology hits a midlife bump, *New York Times*, http://www.nytimes.com, May 4.

55. C. W. L. Hill, 1997, Establishing a standard: Competitive strategy and technological standards in winner-take-all industries, *Academy of Management Executive*, 11(2): 7–25.

56. C. Gilbert, 2003, The disruptive opportunity, *MIT Sloan Management Review*, 44(4): 27–32; C. M. Christiansen, 1997, *The Innovator's Dilemma*, Boston: Harvard Business School Press.

57. R. Adner, 2002, When are technologies disruptive? A demand-based view of the emergence of competition, *Strategic Management Journal*, 23: 667–688; G. Ahuja & C. M. Lampert, 2001, Entrepreneurship in the large corporation: A longitudinal study of how established firms create breakthrough inventions, *Strategic Management Journal*, 22(Special Issue): 521–543.

58. C. L. Nichols-Nixon & C. Y. Woo, 2003, Technology sourcing and output of established firms in a regime of encompassing technological change, *Strategic Management Journal*, 24: 651–666; C. W. L. Hill & F. T. Rothaermel, 2003, The performance of incumbent firms in the face of radical technological innovation, *Academy of Management Review*, 28: 257–274.

59. R. Amit & C. Zott, 2001, Value creation in e-business, *Strategic Management Journal*, 22(Special Issue): 493–520.

60. T. J. Mullaney, H. Green, M. Arndt, R. D. Hof, & L. Himmelstein, 2003, The e-biz surprise, *Business Week*, May 12, 60–68.

61. R. M. Kanter, 2001, *e-volve: Succeeding in the Digital Culture of Tomorrow*, Boston: Harvard Business School Press.

62. A. S. DeNisi, M. A. Hitt, & S. E. Jackson, 2003, The knowledge-based approach to sustainable competitive advantage, in S. E. Jackson, M. A. Hitt, & A. S. DeNisi (eds.), *Managing Knowledge for Sustained Competitive Advantage*, San Franciso: Jossey-Bass, 3–33.

63. S. K. McEvily & B. Chakravarthy, 2002, The persistence of knowledge-based advantage: An empirical test for product performance and technological knowledge, *Strategic Management Journal*, 23: 285–305; F. Warner, 2001, The drills for knowledge, *Fast Company*, September, 186–191; B. L. Simonin, 1999, Ambiguity and the process of knowledge transfer in strategic alliances, *Strategic Management Journal*, 20: 595–624.

64. A. W. King & C. P. Zeithaml, 2003, Measuring organizational knowledge: A conceptual and methodological framework, *Strategic Management Journal*, 24: 763–772; L. Rosenkopf & A. Nerkar, 2001, Beyond local search: Boundary-spanning, exploration, and impact on the optical disk industry, *Strategic Management Journal*, 22: 287–306.

65. Sirmon, Hitt, & Ireland, Managing the firm's resources.

66. K. Asakawa & M. Lehrer, 2003, Managing local knowledge assets globally: The role of regional innovation relays, *Journal of World Business*, 38: 31–42.

67. N. Worren, K. Moore, & P. Cardona, 2002, Modularity, strategic flexibility and firm performance: A study of the home appliance industry, *Strategic Management Journal*, 23: 1123–1140; K. R. Harrigan, 2001, Strategic flexibility in old and new economies, in M. A. Hitt, R. E. Freeman, & J. S. Harrison (eds.), *Handbook of Strategic Management*, Oxford, UK: Blackwell Publishers, 97–123.

68. H. Lee, M. A. Hitt, & E. Jeong, 2003, The impact of CEO and TMT characteristics on strategic flexibility and firm performance, Working paper, University of Connecticut; J. L. C. Cheng & I. F. Kesner, 1997, Organizational slack and response to environmental shifts: The impact of resource allocation patterns, *Journal of Management*, 23: 1–18.

69. M. A. Hitt, R. D. Ireland, & J. S. Harrison, 2001, Mergers and acquisitions: A value creating or value destroying strategy? in M. A. Hitt, R. E. Freeman, & J. S. Harrison (eds.), *Handbook of Strategic Management*, Oxford, UK: Blackwell Publishers, 384–408; W. Boeker, 1997, Strategic change: The influence of managerial characteristics and organizational growth, *Academy of Management Journal*, 40: 152–170.

70. K. Uhlenbruck, K. E. Meyer, & M. A. Hitt, 2003, Organizational transformation in transition economies: Resource-based and organizational learning perspectives, *Journal of Management Studies*, 40: 257–282; R. T. Pascale, 1999, Surviving the edge of chaos, *Sloan Management Review*, 40(3): 83–94.

71. R. E. Hoskisson, M. A. Hitt, W. P. Wan, & D. Yiu, 1999, Swings of a pendulum: Theory and research in strategic management, *Journal of Management*, 25: 417–456.

72. E. H. Bowman & C. E. Helfat, 2001, Does corporate strategy matter? *Strategic Management Journal*, 22: 1–23.

73. J. Shamsie, 2003, The context of dominance: An industry-driven framework for exploiting reputation, *Strategic Management Journal*, 24: 199–215; A. Seth & H. Thomas, 1994, Theories of the firm: Implications for strategy research, *Journal of Management Studies*, 31: 165–191.

74. Seth & Thomas, 169–173.

75. M. E. Porter, 1985, *Competitive Advantage*, New York: Free Press; M. E. Porter, 1980, *Competitive Strategy*, New York: Free Press.

76. A. M. McGahan, 1999, Competition, strategy and business performance, *California Management Review*, 41(3): 74–101; McGahan & Porter, How much does industry matter, really?

77. R. Henderson & W. Mitchell, 1997, The interactions of organizational and competitive influences on strategy and performance, *Strategic Management Journal* 18(Special Issue), 5–14; C. Oliver, 1997, Sustainable competitive advantage: Combining institutional and resource-based views, *Strategic Management Journal*, 18: 697–713; J. L. Stimpert & I. M. Duhaime, 1997, Seeing the big picture: The influence of industry, diversification, and business strategy on performance, *Academy of Management Journal*, 40: 560–583.

78. M. Blyler & R. W. Coff, 2003, Dynamic capabilities, social capital, and rent appropriation: Ties that split pies, *Strategic Management Journal*, 24: 677–686; C. Lee, K. Lee, & J. M. Pennings, 2001, Internal capabilities, external networks, and performance: A study on technology-based ventures, *Strategic Management Journal*, 22 (Special Issue): 615–640.

79. B.-S. Teng & J. L. Cummings, 2002, Trade-offs in managing resources and capabilities, *Academy of Management Executive*, 16(2): 81–91; R. L. Priem & J. E. Butler, 2001, Is the resource-based "view" a useful perspective for strategic management research? *Academy of Management Review*, 26: 22–40.

80. P. J. H. Schoemaker & R. Amit, 1994, Investment in strategic assets: Industry and firm-level perspectives, in P. Shrivastava, A. Huff, & J. Dutton (eds.), *Advances in Strategic Management*, Greenwich, CT: JAI Press, 9.

81. D. M. DeCarolis, 2003, Competencies and imitability in the pharmaceutical industry: An analysis of their relationship with firm performance, *Journal of Management*, 29: 27–50; Barney, Is the resource-based "view" a useful perspective for strategic management research? Yes; J. B. Barney, 1995, Looking inside for competitive advantage, *Academy of Management Executive*, 9(4): 56.

82. C. Zott, 2003, Dynamic capabilities and the emergence of intraindustry differential firm performance: Insights from a simulation study, *Strategic Management Journal*, 24: 97–125.

83. Davidsson & Honig, The role of social and human capital among nascent entrepreneurs.

84. R. D. Ireland, J. G. Covin, & D. F. Kuratko, 2003, Antecedents, elements, and consequences of corporate entrepreneurship as strategy, Working paper, University of Richmond.

85. G. Hawawini, V. Subramanian, & P. Verdin, 2003, Is performance driven by industry- or firm-specific factors? A new look at the evidence, *Strategic Management Journal*, 24: 1–16.

86. M. Makhija, 2003, Comparing the resource-based and market-based views of the firm: Empirical evidence from Czech privatization, *Strategic Management Journal*, 24: 433–451; T. J. Douglas & J. A. Ryman, 2003, Understanding competitive advantage in the general hospital industry: Evaluating strategic competencies, *Strategic Management Journal*, 24: 333–347.

87. G. Hamel & C. K. Prahalad, 1989, Strategic intent, *Harvard Business Review*, 67(3): 63–76.

88. Hamel & Prahalad, Strategic intent, 66.

89. P.-W. Tam, B. Orwall, & A. W. Mathews, 2003, As Apple stalls, Steve Jobs looks to digital entertainment, *Wall Steet Journal*, April 25, A1, A5.

90. Hamel & Prahalad, Strategic intent, 64.

91. M. A. Hitt, D. Park, C. Hardee, & B. B. Tyler, 1995, Understanding strategic intent in the global marketplace, *Academy of Management Executive*, 9(2): 12–19.

92. R. D. Ireland & M. A. Hitt, 1992, Mission statements: Importance, challenge, and recommendations for development, *Business Horizons*, 35(3): 34–42.

93. W. J. Duncan, 1999, *Management: Ideas and Actions*, New York: Oxford University Press, 122–125.

94. R. M. Fulmer, 2001, Johnson & Johnson: Frameworks for leadership, *Organizational Dynamics*, 29(3): 211–220.

95. P. Martin, 1999, Lessons in humility, *Financial Times*, June 22, 18.

96. I. M. Levin, 2000, Vision revisited, *Journal of Applied Behavioral Science*, 36: 91–107.

97. I. R. Baum, E. A. Locke, & S. A. Kirkpatrick, 1998, A longitudinal study of the relation of vision and vision communication to venture growth in entrepreneurial firms, *Journal of Applied Psychology*, 83: 43–54.

98. J. Frooman, 1999, Stakeholder influence strategies, *Academy of Management Review*, 24: 191–205.

99. T. M. Jones & A. C. Wicks, 1999, Convergent stakeholder theory, *Academy of Management Review*, 24: 206–221; R. E. Freeman, 1984, *Strategic Management: A Stakeholder Approach*, Boston: Pitman, 53–54.

100. G. Donaldson & J. W. Lorsch, 1983, *Decision Making at the Top: The Shaping of Strategic Direction*, New York: Basic Books, 37–40.

101. A. J. Hillman & G. D. Keim, 2001, Shareholder value, stakeholder management, and social issues: What's the bottom line? *Strategic Management Journal*, 22: 125–139.

102. R. E. Freeman & J. McVea, 2001, A stakeholder approach to strategic management, in M. A. Hitt, R. E. Freeman, & J. S. Harrison (eds.), *Handbook of Strategic Management*, Oxford, UK: Blackwell Publishers, 189–207.

103. Ibid.

104. P. Brandes, R. Dharwadkar, & G. V. Lemesis, 2003, Effective employee stock option design: Reconciling stakeholder, strategic and motivational factors, *Academy of Management Executive*, 17(1): 77–93; A. McWilliams & D. Siegel, 2001, Corporate social responsibility: A theory of the firm perspective, *Academy of Management Review*, 26: 117–127.

105. Freeman & McVea, A stakeholder approach to strategic management; R. K. Mitchell, B. R. Agle, & D. J. Wood, 1997, Toward a theory of stakeholder identification and salience: Defining the principle of who and what really count, *Academy of Management Review*, 22: 853–886.

106. A. L. Hart & M. B. Milstein, 2003, Creating sustainable value, *Academy of Management Executive*, 17(2): 56–67.

107. Hitt, Bierman, Shimizu, & Kochhar, Direct and moderating effects of human capital.

108. S. Finkelstein, 2003, *Why Smart Executives Fail: And What You Can Learn from Their Mistakes*, New York: Portfolio-Penguin Putnam Publishers.

109. P. Bromiley, K. D. Miller, & D. Rau, 2001, Risk in strategic management research, in M. A. Hitt, R. E. Freeman, & J. S. Harrison (eds.), *Handbook of Strategic Management*, Oxford, UK: Blackwell Publishers, 259–288.

110. W. Shen & A. A. Cannella, 2003, Will succession planning increase shareholder wealth? Evidence from investor reactions to relay CEO successions, *Strategic Management Journal*, 24: 191–198.

111. W. Shen & A. A. Cannella, 2002, Revisiting the performance consequences of CEO succession: The impacts of successor type, postsuccession senior executive turnover and departing CEO tenure, *Academy of Management Journal*, 45: 717–733.

112. G. A. Bigley & M. F. Wiersema, 2002, New CEOs and corporate strategic focusing: How experience as heir apparent influences the use of power, *Administrative Science Quarterly*, 47: 707–727.

113. W. C. Taylor, 1999, Whatever happened to globalization? *Fast Company*, September, 288–294.

114. T. Leavitt, 1991, *Thinking about Management*, New York: Free Press, 9.

115. K. Lovelace, D. L. Shapiro, & L. R. Weingart, 2001, Maximizing cross-functional new product teams' innovativeness and constraint adherence: A conflict communications perspective, *Academy of Management Journal*, 44: 779–793.

116. J. Brett & L. K. Stroh, 2003, Working 61 plus hours a week: Why do managers do it? *Journal of Applied Psychology*, 88: 67–78.

117. M. Loeb, 1993, Steven J. Ross, 1927–1992, *Fortune*, January 25, 4.

118. 2003, Who killed Montana Power? *CBSNews*, http://www.cbsnews.com, February 10; B. Richards, 2001, For Montana Power, a broadband dream may turn out to be more of a nightmare, *Wall Street Journal Online*, http://www.wsj.com/articles, August 22.

119. O. Gadiesh & J. L. Gilbert, 1998, How to map your industry's profit pool, *Harvard Business Review*, 76(3): 149–162.

120. O. Gadiesh & J. L. Gilbert, 1998, Profit pools: A fresh look at strategy, *Harvard Business Review*, 76(3): 139–147.

121. M. J. Epstein & R. A. Westbrook, 2001, Linking actions to profits in strategic decision making, *Sloan Management Review*, 42(3): 39–49.

122. 2001, Trading places, *Forbes*, http://www.forbes.com, June 14.

123. R. D. Ireland, M. A. Hitt, S. M. Camp, & D. L. Sexton, 2001, Integrating entrepreneurship and strategic management actions to create firm wealth, *Academy of Management Executive*, 15(1): 49–63; Rumelt, Schendel, & Teece, *Fundamental Issues in Strategy*, 9–10.

124. L. K. Trevino & G. R. Weaver, 2003, *Managing Ethics in Business Organizations*, Stanford, CA: Stanford University Press; D. R. Gilbert, 2001, Corporate strategy and ethics as corporate strategy comes of age, in M. A. Hitt, R. E. Freeman, & J. S. Harrison (eds.), *Handbook of Strategic Management*, Oxford, UK: Blackwell Publishers, 564–582.

The External Environment: Opportunities, Threats, Industry Competition, and Competitor Analysis

Chapter Two

Knowledge Objectives

Studying this chapter should provide you with the strategic management knowledge needed to:

1. Explain the importance of analyzing and understanding the firm's external environment.

2. Define and describe the general environment and the industry environment.

3. Discuss the four activities of the external environmental analysis process.

4. Name and describe the general environment's six segments.

5. Identify the five competitive forces and explain how they determine an industry's profit potential.

6. Define strategic groups and describe their influence on the firm.

7. Describe what firms need to know about their competitors and different methods used to collect intelligence about them.

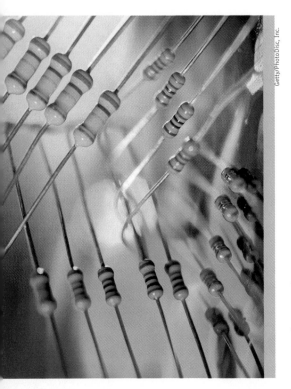

High-technology products and services have languished in the recent poor economic climate. One example of a company that has struggled to regain its former profitability is Sun Microsystems. As we saw in Chapter 1, one of the keys to turning around this company—and the industry in general—is continuous innovation.

The Economic Aftermath in High Technology: Will We Ever See the Sun Set?

The economic malaise experienced in the early part of the 21st century hit the high-technology firms especially hard. Analysts argue that it is more than a reaction to the "bubble years" in the 1990s. They suggest that the industry (actually several overlapping industries such as hardware, software, and Internet commerce) has entered a post-technology era. Many hardware products are almost becoming commodities where costs, along with quality and service, are important competitive characteristics. Additionally, the power has shifted from the supplier to the customer. Yet, many expect that the industry will continue to deliver innovation, and it has become a highly important economic engine in the United States. The high-technology industry accounts for approximately 10 percent of the U.S. economy and 60 percent of the capital spending by U.S. businesses.

There are many facets of the high-technology industry, but one of its former stars is struggling, perhaps for its very survival. Sun Microsystems once enjoyed $64 a share for its stock, but the share price fell to below $3. Scott McNealy, the founder and CEO, remains in firm control and is convinced that he has the company headed toward success. While critics believe that Sun needs to control its costs more effectively, McNealy is spending heavily on R&D to enhance innovation that will serve as a catalyst for revenue growth. His goal is to introduce sophisticated new computer hardware and cutting-edge software. In fact, in 2003, Sun introduced several new hardware and software products to increase its competitiveness in the market. These new products are directly competitive with IBM and Hewlett-Packard (HP) and target product areas in which both firms currently have products, especially network technology.

Sun faces a weak economic climate and especially strong competition from several quarters. None of its competitors is remaining static. For example, IBM's new CEO is developing a strategy of offering computing power on demand (similar to water or electricity). In this way, customers do not have to invest substantial capital in equipment and software or in knowledgeable human resources and worry about underutilizing the assets. Rather, they pay only for what they need, and they always receive high-quality service. Additionally, Sun cannot overlook Dell Inc. Dell is expanding its product lines and services and has dropped the word "computer" from its name to better represent the product lines it is planning. And, Dell was recently ranked among the top ten best-managed companies and was ranked as the second best technology firm. Sun was not ranked among the top 100. Most of Sun's competitors were among the top 100 technology companies, however.

Sun has survived and overcome major obstacles in the past. Additionally, it is investing in innovation, noted in Chapter 1 to be critical to success in most industries. There is little doubt as to the importance of innovation in the high-technology industry. Sun must even watch out for a non-firm, Linux, the open source operating system, pushed by a group of technology specialists to compete with Microsoft. Linux is backed by Intel, HP, IBM, and Dell Inc. and is being used in a number of technology-based products. Thus, Sun exists in a critical industry where innovation is required for survival. It is also an industry populated by a formidable group of competitors. Sun faces a difficult economic climate and a world of uncertainties, all of which heightens the uncertainty of its future.

SOURCES: S. Hamm, S. Rosenbush, & C. Edwards, 2003, Tech comes out swinging, *Business Week*, June 23, 62–66; S. Lohr, 2003, Technology hits a midlife bump, *New York Times*, http://www.nytimes.com, May 4; G. McWilliams, 2003, Dell pushes PC strategy into corporate products, *Wall Street Journal Online*, http://www.wsj.com, April 3; 2003, The ranking, *Business Week*, Spring (Special Annual Issue), 44–56; G. McWilliams, 2003, Pay as you go, *Wall Street Journal*, March 31, R8; 2003, Dell enters printer market, stepping up rivalry with H-P, *Wall Street Journal Online*, http://www.wsj.com, March 26; S. E. Ante, 2003, The new blue, *Business Week*, March 17, 80–88; J. Greens, 2003, The Linux uprising, *Business Week*, March 3, 78–86; S. Lohr, 2003, Sun rolls out its new effort to gain edge over 2 rivals, *New York Times*, http://www.nytimes.com, February 10; 2003, The best and worst managers of the year, *Business Week*, January 13, 58–92; J. Kerstetter & J. Greens, 2002, Will Sun rise again? *Business Week*, November 25, 120–130.

Companies' experiences and research suggest that the external environment affects firm growth and profitability.[1] Major political events such as the war in Iraq, the strength of separate nations' economies at different times, and the emergence of new technologies are a few examples of conditions in the external environment that affect firms in the United States and throughout the world. External environmental conditions such as these create threats to and opportunities for firms that, in turn, have major effects on their strategic actions.[2]

The economic problems in the early 21st century affected all industries, most negatively, but one of the industries hurt the most was high technology. Many firms in the industry were hurt, and some ceased to exist. Some firms, such as IBM, are beginning to turn around their performance, and others, such as Dell Inc., seem to continue to do well. However, one formerly successful firm, Sun Microsystems, continues to perform poorly. Its founder and CEO, Scott McNealy, claims that because of its innovation in hardware and software products, Sun will again thrive in the industry. Based on what we learned in Chapter 1, innovation is a key to success, particularly in the high-technology industry. Thus, it appears that Sun is taking the correct actions, despite analysts' criticisms. However, Sun also faces significant competition, continuing economic conditions that are challenging, and a highly uncertain environment. Regardless of the industry, the external environment is critical to a firm's survival and success. This chapter focuses on what firms do to analyze and understand the external environment. As the discussion of the high-technology industry shows, the external environment influences the firm's strategic options as well as the decisions made in light of them. The firm's understanding of the external environment is matched with knowledge about its internal environment (discussed in the next chapter) to form its strategic intent, to develop its strategic mission, and to take actions that result in strategic competitiveness and above-average returns (see Figure 1.1).

As noted in Chapter 1, the environmental conditions in the current global economy differ from those previously faced by firms. Technological changes and the continuing growth of information gathering and processing capabilities demand more timely and effective competitive actions and responses.[3] The rapid sociological changes occurring in many countries affect labor practices and the nature of products demanded by increasingly diverse consumers. Governmental policies and laws also affect where and how firms may choose to compete.[4] Deregulation and local government changes, such as those in the global electric utilities industry, affect not only the general competitive environment, but also the strategic decisions made by companies competing globally. To achieve strategic competitiveness, firms must be aware of and understand the different dimensions of the external environment.

Firms understand the external environment by acquiring information about competitors, customers, and other stakeholders to build their own base of knowledge and capabilities.[5] Firms may use this base to imitate the capabilities of their able competitors (and even may imitate successful firms in other industries), and they may use it to build new knowledge and capabilities to achieve a competitive advantage. On the basis of the new information, knowledge, and capabilities, firms may take actions to buffer themselves against environmental effects or to build relationships with stakeholders in their environment.[6] To strengthen their knowledge and capabilities and to take actions that buffer or build bridges to external stakeholders, organizations must effectively analyze the external environment.

The General, Industry, and Competitor Environments

An integrated understanding of the external and internal environments is essential for firms to understand the present and predict the future.[7] As shown in Figure 2.1, a firm's external environment is divided into three major areas: the general, industry, and competitor environments.

The **general environment** is composed of dimensions in the broader society that influence an industry and the firms within it.[8] We group these dimensions into six

The general environment is composed of dimensions in the broader society that influence an industry and the firms within it.

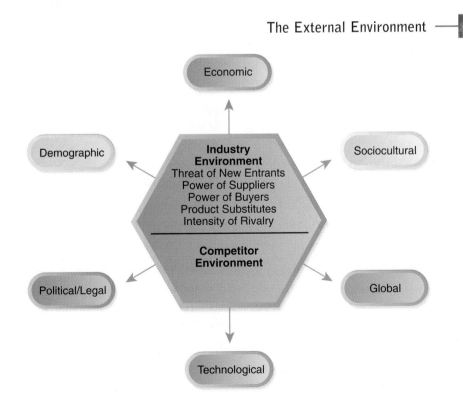

The External Environment — Figure 2.1

environmental *segments:* demographic, economic, political/legal, sociocultural, technological, and global. Examples of *elements* analyzed in each of these segments are shown in Table 2.1.

Firms cannot directly control the general environment's segments and elements. Accordingly, successful companies gather the information required to understand each segment and its implications for the selection and implementation of the appropriate strategies. For example, most firms have little individual effect on the U.S. economy, although that economy has a major effect on their ability to operate and even survive. Thus, companies around the globe were challenged to understand the effects of this economy's decline on their current and future strategies. Certainly, this is the case for Sun Microsystems as explained in the Opening Case. And there are legitimate differences of opinion regarding the particular strategies that should be followed in reaction to the economic changes. Analysts argue that Sun should be controlling costs while Sun's CEO believes that he must invest heavily in R&D if Sun is to succeed over time. We soon may learn whose evaluation of the environment and strategies was the most appropriate in Sun's case.

The **industry environment** is the set of factors that directly influences a firm and its competitive actions and competitive responses: the threat of new entrants, the power of suppliers, the power of buyers, the threat of product substitutes, and the intensity of rivalry among competitors. In total, the interactions among these five factors determine an industry's profit potential. The challenge is to locate a position within an industry where a firm can favorably influence those factors or where it can successfully defend against their influence. In fact, positioning is a major issue for Sun Microsystems, discussed in the Opening Case. It faces substantial competitive rivalry. The greater a firm's capacity to favorably influence its industry environment, the greater is the likelihood that the firm will earn above-average returns.

The industry environment *is the set of factors that directly influences a firm and its competitive actions and competitive responses: the threat of new entrants, the power of suppliers, the power of buyers, the threat of product substitutes, and the intensity of rivalry among competitors.*

Table 2.1	The General Environment: Segments and Elements	
Demographic Segment	• Population size • Age structure • Geographic distribution	• Ethnic mix • Income distribution
Economic Segment	• Inflation rates • Interest rates • Trade deficits or surpluses • Budget deficits or surpluses	• Personal savings rate • Business savings rates • Gross domestic product
Political/Legal Segment	• Antitrust laws • Taxation laws • Deregulation philosophies	• Labor training laws • Educational philosophies and policies
Sociocultural Segment	• Women in the workforce • Workforce diversity • Attitudes about the quality of work life	• Concerns about the environment • Shifts in work and career preferences • Shifts in preferences regarding product and service characteristics
Technological Segment	• Product innovations • Applications of knowledge	• Focus of private and government-supported R&D expenditures • New communication technologies
Global Segment	• Important political events • Critical global markets	• Newly industrialized countries • Different cultural and institutional attributes

How companies gather and interpret information about their competitors is called *competitor analysis*. Understanding the firm's competitor environment complements the insights provided by studying the general and industry environments. Understanding its competitor environment may be critical to Sun Microsystems' survival.

Analysis of the general environment is focused on the future; analysis of the industry environment is focused on the factors and conditions influencing a firm's profitability within its industry; and analysis of competitors is focused on predicting the dynamics of competitors' actions, responses, and intentions. In combination, the results of the three analyses the firm uses to understand its external environment influence its strategic intent, strategic mission, and strategic actions. Although we discuss each analysis separately, performance improves when the firm integrates the insights provided by analyses of the general environment, the industry environment, and the competitor environment.

External Environmental Analysis

Most firms face external environments that are highly turbulent, complex, and global—conditions that make interpreting them increasingly difficult.[9] To cope with what are often ambiguous and incomplete environmental data and to increase their understanding of the general environment, firms engage in a process called external environmental analysis. The continuous process includes four activities: scanning, monitoring, forecasting, and assessing (see Table 2.2). Those analyzing the external environment should understand that completing this analysis is a difficult, yet significant, activity.[10]

An important objective of studying the general environment is identifying opportunities and threats. An **opportunity** is a condition in the general environment that, if exploited, helps a company achieve strategic competitiveness. For example, the fact that 1 billion of the world's total population of 6.1 billion has cheap access to a telephone is a huge opportunity for global telecommunications companies.[11] And, global telephone use is growing at a rate of more than 300 billion minutes annually.[12] A **threat** is a condition in the general environment that may hinder a company's efforts to achieve strategic competitiveness.[13] The once revered firm Polaroid can attest to the seriousness of external threats. Polaroid was a leader in its industry and considered one of the top 50 firms in the United States, but it filed for bankruptcy in 2001. When its competitors developed photographic equipment using digital technology, Polaroid was unprepared and never responded effectively. Mired in substantial debt, Polaroid was unable to reduce its costs to acceptable levels (and unable to repay its debt) and eventually had to declare bankruptcy. In 2002, the former Polaroid Corp. was sold to Bank One's OEP Imaging unit, which promptly changed its name to Polaroid Corp. The old

*An **opportunity** is a condition in the general environment that, if exploited, helps a company achieve strategic competitiveness.*

*A **threat** is a condition in the general environment that may hinder a company's efforts to achieve strategic competitiveness.*

Components of the External Environmental Analysis		Table 2.2
Scanning	• Identifying early signals of environmental changes and trends	
Monitoring	• Detecting meaning through ongoing observations of environmental changes and trends	
Forecasting	• Developing projections of anticipated outcomes based on monitored changes and trends	
Assessing	• Determining the timing and importance of environmental changes and trends for firms' strategies and their management	

An old Polaroid camera now looks like an artifact that represents an earlier stage of technological development in photography. Since the time when Polaroid was a leader in the industry, other companies have long surpassed its success through the innovation of digital photography. The bankruptcy of Polaroid bears testimony to the importance of responding effectively to external threats.

Polaroid was renamed Primary PDC, Inc., but is barely in existence.[14] As these examples indicate, opportunities suggest competitive *possibilities,* while threats are potential *constraints.*

Several sources can be used to analyze the general environment, including a wide variety of printed materials (such as trade publications, newspapers, business publications, and the results of academic research and public polls), trade shows and suppliers, customers, and employees of public-sector organizations.[15] External network contacts can be particularly rich sources of information on the environment.[16] People in "boundary-spanning" positions can obtain much information. Salespersons, purchasing managers, public relations directors, and customer service representatives, each of whom interacts with external constituents, are examples of individuals in boundary-spanning positions.[17]

Scanning

Scanning entails the study of all segments in the general environment. Through scanning, firms identify early signals of potential changes in the general environment and detect changes that are already under way.[18] When scanning, the firm often deals with ambiguous, incomplete, or unconnected data and information. Environmental scanning is critically important for firms competing in highly volatile environments.[19] In addition, scanning activities must be aligned with the organizational context; a scanning system designed for a volatile environment is inappropriate for a firm in a stable environment.[20]

Some analysts expect the pressure brought to bear by the early retirement trend on countries such as the United States, France, Germany, and Japan to be quite significant and challenging. Governments in these countries appear to be offering state-funded pensions to their future elderly populations—but the costs of those pensions cannot be met with the present taxes and social security contribution rates.[21] Firms selling financial planning services and options should analyze this trend to determine if it represents an opportunity for them to help governments find ways to meet their responsibilities.

The Internet provides multiple opportunities for scanning. For example, Amazon.com, similar to many Internet companies, records significant information about individuals visiting its website, particularly if a purchase is made. Amazon then welcomes these customers by name when they visit the website again. The firm even sends messages to them about specials and new products similar to those purchased in previous visits. Additionally, many websites and advertisers on the Internet obtain information from those who visit their sites using files called "cookies." These files are saved to the visitors' hard drives, allowing customers to connect more quickly to a firm's website, but also allowing the firm to solicit a variety of information about them. Because cookies are often placed without customers' knowledge, their use can be a questionable practice. Recently, a privacy standard, Platform for Privacy Preferences, was developed that provides more control over these "digital messengers" and allows users to block the cookies from their hard drives.[22]

©Royalty-Free/CORBIS

Monitoring

When *monitoring,* analysts observe environmental changes to see if an important trend is emerging from among those spotted by scanning.[23] Critical to successful monitoring is the firm's ability to detect meaning in different environmental events and trends. For example, the size of the middle class of African Americans continues to grow in the United States. With increasing wealth, this group of citizens is beginning to more aggressively pursue investment options.[24] Companies in the financial planning sector could monitor this change in the economic segment to determine the degree to which a competitively important trend and a business opportunity are emerging. By monitoring trends, firms can be prepared to introduce new goods and services at the appropriate time to take advantage of the opportunities these trends provide.[25]

Effective monitoring requires the firm to identify important stakeholders. Because the importance of different stakeholders can vary over a firm's life cycle, careful attention must be given to the firm's needs and its stakeholder groups across time.[26] Scanning and monitoring are particularly important when a firm competes in an industry with high technological uncertainty.[27] Scanning and monitoring not only can provide the firm with information, they also serve as a means of importing new knowledge about markets and how to successfully commercialize new technologies that the firm has developed.[28]

Forecasting

Scanning and monitoring are concerned with events and trends in the general environment at a point in time. When *forecasting,* analysts develop feasible projections of what might happen, and how quickly, as a result of the changes and trends detected through scanning and monitoring.[29] For example, analysts might forecast the time that will be required for a new technology to reach the marketplace, the length of time before different corporate training procedures are required to deal with anticipated changes in the composition of the workforce, or how much time will elapse before changes in governmental taxation policies affect consumers' purchasing patterns.

Forecasting events and outcomes accurately is challenging. For example, in 2001, few would have forecasted that the U.S. Federal Reserve Board would lower the federal funds rate, which affects the short-term interest that banks charge customers, to 1 percent. Others might not have forecasted a war in Iraq in 2003. Thus, uncertainty makes forecasting a difficult task.

Assessing

The objective of *assessing* is to determine the timing and significance of the effects of environmental changes and trends on the strategic management of the firm.[30] Through scanning, monitoring, and forecasting, analysts are able to understand the general environment. Going a step farther, the intent of assessment is to specify the implications of that understanding for the organization. Without assessment, the firm is left with data that may be interesting but are of unknown competitive relevance.

Cosi, Inc., a relatively small fast-food chain with 90 stores, announced it lost $114 million in 2002. Cosi provides a good product. The food is tasty, and the stores have a lively décor. It also has some unique but flavorful sandwiches. However, while it has many positive qualities, Cosi expanded without adequate assessment of its external environment. Its all-day service throws it into competition not only with McDonald's, but also Starbucks, especially in the mornings. Recently, the firm announced that it would eliminate its all company-owned stores strategy and move to franchises. Analysts worry, however, that the firm's management has not fully assessed the challenges and requirements of successful franchising. Thus, there is much more to success than providing a good product to customers.[31]

The general environment is composed of segments (and their individual elements) that are external to the firm (see Table 2.1). Although the degree of impact varies, these environmental segments affect each industry and its firms. The challenge to the firm is to scan, monitor, forecast, and assess those elements in each segment that are of the greatest importance. Resulting from these efforts should be recognition of environmental changes, trends, opportunities, and threats. Opportunities are then matched with a firm's core competencies (the matching process is discussed further in Chapter 3).

The Demographic Segment

The **demographic segment** is concerned with a population's size, age structure, geographic distribution, ethnic mix, and income distribution.[32] Demographic segments are analyzed on a global basis because of their potential effects across countries' borders and because many firms compete in global markets.

POPULATION SIZE

Before the end of 2005, the world's population is expected to be slightly less than 6.5 billion, up from 6.1 billion in 2000. Combined, China and India accounted for one-third of the 6.1 billion. Experts speculate that the population might stabilize at 10 billion after 2200 if the deceleration in the rate of increase in the world's head count continues. By 2050, India (with over 1.5 billion people projected) and China (with just under 1.5 billion people projected) are expected to be the most populous countries.[33]

Observing demographic changes in populations highlights the importance of this environmental segment. For example, some advanced nations have a negative population growth, after discounting the effects of immigration. In 2002, Bulgaria had the lowest birthrate, with slightly over 8 births per 1,000 citizens, while Niger had the highest birthrate, with almost 50 per 1,000 citizens. The birthrate in the United States is slightly above 14 for every 1,000 people.[34] However, some believe that a baby boom will occur in the United States during the first 12 years of the 21st century and that by 2012, the annual number of births could exceed 4.3 million. Such a birthrate in the United States would equal the all-time high that was set in 1957.[35] These projections suggest major 21st-century challenges and business opportunities.

AGE STRUCTURE

In some countries, the population's average age is increasing. For example, worldwide, the number of people aged 65 and older is projected to grow by 88 percent, or almost one million people per month, by 2025.[36] Contributing to this growth are increasing life expectancies. This trend may suggest numerous opportunities for firms to develop goods and services to meet the needs of an increasingly older population. For example, GlaxoSmithKline has created a program for low-income elderly people without prescription drug coverage. The program provides drugs to these individuals at a 25 percent reduction in price. The firm's intent is to increase its sales and provide an important service to a population who might not be able to afford the drugs otherwise.[37]

It has been projected that up to one-half of the females and one-third of the males born at the end of the 1990s in

AP Photo/str

developed countries could live to be 100 years old, with some of them possibly living to be 200 or more.[38] Also, the odds that a U.S. baby boomer (a person born between the years 1946 and 1964) will reach age 90 are now one in nine.[39] If these life spans become a reality, a host of interesting business opportunities and societal issues will emerge. For example, the effect on individuals' pension plans will be significant and will create potential opportunities for financial institutions, as well as possible threats to government-sponsored retirement and health plans.[40]

GEOGRAPHIC DISTRIBUTION

For decades, the U.S. population has been shifting from the north and east to the west and south. Similarly, the trend of relocating from metropolitan to non-metropolitan areas continues and may well accelerate with the terrorist attacks in New York City and Washington, D.C. These trends are changing local and state governments' tax bases. In turn, business firms' decisions regarding location are influenced by the degree of support different taxing agencies offer as well as the rates at which these agencies tax businesses.

The geographic distribution of populations throughout the world is also affected by the capabilities resulting from advances in communications technology. Through computer technologies, for example, people can remain in their homes, communicating with others in remote locations to complete their work.

ETHNIC MIX

The ethnic mix of countries' populations continues to change. Within the United States, the ethnicity of states and their cities varies significantly. For firms, the challenge is to be sensitive to these changes. Through careful study, companies can develop and market products that satisfy the unique needs of different ethnic groups.

Changes in the ethnic mix also affect a workforce's composition. In the United States, for example, the population and labor force will continue to diversify, as immigration accounts for a sizable part of growth. Projections are that the Latino and Asian population shares will increase to 34 percent of the total U.S. population by 2050. By 2006, it is expected that (1) 72.7 percent of the U.S. labor force will be white non-Latino (down from 75.3 percent in 1996), (2) 11.7 percent will be Latino (compared with 9.5 percent in 1996), (3) 11.6 percent will be African American (up from 11.3 percent in 1996), and (4) 5.4 percent will be Asian (up from 4.3 percent in 1996). By 2020, white non-Latino workers will make up only 68 percent of the workforce.[41]

As with the U.S. labor force, other countries also are witnessing a trend toward an older workforce. By 2030, the proportion of the total labor force of 45- to 59-year-olds of countries in the Organisation for Economic Co-operation and Development (industrialized countries) is projected to increase from 25.6 to 31.8 percent; the share of workers aged 60 and over is expected to increase from 4.7 to 7.8 percent. Because a labor force can be critical to competitive success, firms across the globe, including those competing in OECD countries, must learn to work effectively with labor forces that are becoming more diverse and older.[42]

Workforce diversity is also a sociocultural issue. Effective management of a culturally diverse workforce can produce a competitive advantage. For example, heterogeneous work teams have been shown to produce more effective strategic analyses, more creativity and innovation, and higher-quality decisions than homogeneous work teams.[43] However, evidence also suggests that diverse work teams are difficult to manage to achieve these outcomes.[44]

INCOME DISTRIBUTION

Understanding how income is distributed within and across populations informs firms of different groups' purchasing power and discretionary income. Studies of income distributions suggest that although living standards have improved over time, variations exist within and between nations.[45] Of interest to firms are the average incomes of households and individuals. For instance, the increase in dual-career couples has had a notable effect on average incomes. Although real income has been declining in general, the income of dual-career couples has increased. These figures yield strategically relevant information for firms.

The Economic Segment

The health of a nation's economy affects individual firms and industries. Because of this, companies study the economic environment to identify changes, trends, and their strategic implications.

The economic environment refers to the nature and direction of the economy in which a firm competes or may compete.

The **economic environment** refers to the nature and direction of the economy in which a firm competes or may compete.[46] Because nations are interconnected as a result of the global economy, firms must scan, monitor, forecast, and assess the health of economies outside their host nation. For example, many nations throughout the world are affected by the U.S. economy.

The U.S. economy declined into a recession in 2001 that extended into 2002. However, the economy remained weak in 2003 despite efforts to revive it by the U.S. government. Interest rates in the United States reached almost record lows in 2003, equaling the rates in 1958.[47] Additionally, global trade grew in the last two decades of the 20th century. For example, equity market capitalization grew by 1,300 percent during this period to $36 trillion. The U.S. capital markets grew by 3,500 percent to $2.6 trillion.[48] Globalization and opening of new markets such as China contributed to this phenomenal growth. While bilateral trade can enrich the economies of the countries involved, it also makes each country more vulnerable to negative events. For example, the September 11, 2001, terrorist attacks in the United States have had more than a $100 billion negative effect on the U.S. economy. As a result, the European Union (E.U.) also suffered negative economic effects because of the reduction in bilateral trade between the United States and the E.U.[49]

As our discussion of the economic segment suggests, economic issues are intertwined closely with the realities of the external environment's political/legal segment.

The Political/Legal Segment

The political/legal segment is the arena in which organizations and interest groups compete for attention, resources, and a voice in overseeing the body of laws and regulations guiding the interactions among nations.

The **political/legal segment** is the arena in which organizations and interest groups compete for attention, resources, and a voice in overseeing the body of laws and regulations guiding the interactions among nations.[50] Essentially, this segment represents how organizations try to influence government and how governments influence them. Constantly changing, the segment influences the nature of competition (see Table 2.1). For example, there has been a significant global trend toward privatization of government-owned or -regulated firms. The transformation from state-owned to private firms has substantial implications for the competitive landscapes in countries and industries.[51]

Firms must carefully analyze a new political administration's business-related policies and philosophies. Antitrust laws, taxation laws, industries chosen for deregulation, labor training laws, and the degree of commitment to educational institutions are areas in which an administration's policies can affect the operations and profitability of industries and individual firms. Often, firms develop a political strategy to influence governmental policies and actions that might affect them. The effects of global governmental policies on a firm's competitive position increase the importance of forming an effective political strategy.[52]

Business firms across the globe today confront an interesting array of political/legal questions and issues. For example, the debate continues over trade policies. Some believe that a nation should erect trade barriers to protect products produced by its companies. Others argue that free trade across nations serves the best interests of individual countries and their citizens. The International Monetary Fund (IMF) classifies trade barriers as restrictive when tariffs total at least 25 percent of a product's price. At the other extreme, the IMF stipulates that a nation has open trade when its tariffs are below 9 percent. To foster trade, New Zealand initially cut its tariffs from 16 to 8.5 percent and then to 3 percent in 2000. Colombia reduced its tariffs to less than 12 percent. The IMF classifies this percentage as "relatively open."[53] Additionally, extensive trade networks are developing among the United States, Europe, Latin America, and Asia. For example, European firms acquired over 800 U.S. companies in 2000 alone.[54]

The regulations related to pharmaceuticals and telecommunications, along with the approval or disapproval of major acquisitions, shows the power of government entities. This power also suggests how important it is for firms to have a political strategy. Alternatively, the Food and Drug Administration (FDA) was criticized in 2003 for being too slow to act. A letter to TAP Pharmaceutical Products to stop misleading advertising for its drug Prevacid was held up 78 days for review by the office of the FDA's chief council. External critics with knowledge of agency operations expressed concerns that the FDA was limiting enforcement actions to avoid potential litigation. Thus, the regulations are too few for some and too many for others. Regardless, regulations tend to vary with different presidential administrations, and firms must cope with these variances.[55]

The Sociocultural Segment

The **sociocultural segment** is concerned with a society's attitudes and cultural values. Because attitudes and values form the cornerstone of a society, they often drive demographic, economic, political/legal, and technological conditions and changes.

Sociocultural segments differ across countries. For example, in the United States, 13.1 percent of the nation's GDP is spent on health care. This is the highest percentage of any country in the world. Germany allocates 10.4 percent of GDP to health care, while in Switzerland the percentage is 10.2. Interestingly, the U.S. rate of citizens' access to health care is below that of these and other countries.[56] Countries' citizens have different attitudes about retirement savings as well. In Italy, just 9 percent of citizens say that they are saving primarily for retirement, while the percentages are 18 in Germany and 48 in the United States.[57] Attitudes regarding saving for retirement affect a nation's economic and political/legal segments.

In the United States, boundaries between work and home are becoming blurred, as employees' workweeks continue to be stretched, perhaps because a strong Protestant work ethic is a part of the U.S. culture. Describing a culture's effect on a society, columnist George Will suggested that it is vital for people to understand that a nation's culture has a primary effect on its social character and health.[58] Thus, companies must understand the implications of a society's attitudes and its cultural values to offer products that meet consumers' needs.

A significant trend in many countries is increased workforce diversity. As noted earlier, the composition of the U.S. workforce is changing such that Caucasians will be in the minority

The sociocultural segment is concerned with a society's attitudes and cultural values.

As the U.S. population becomes more diverse and the number of businesses owned by women continues to increase, we can expect more service businesses like this one to appear. Currently over half of the businesses owned by women are in services such as restaurants. Whereas this restaurant would currently be considered a minority-run business, that will soon no longer be the case as Caucasians become the next minority.

©Ariel Skelley/CORBIS

in a few years. Thus, firms are trying to diversify their employee bases, but also must contend with a complex set of laws and regulations. For example, in a recent ruling, the U.S. Supreme Court declared the use of race in college and university admissions decisions to be legal if it was for the purposes of creating useful diversity among the student population and providing access to economic success for all regardless of race.[59]

As diversity increases, so does the size of the labor force in the United States. In 1993, the total workforce was slightly below 130 million, but in 2003, it was slightly over 146 million.[60] An increasing number of women are also starting and managing their own businesses. For example, the U.S. Census Bureau reports that women own approximately 5.4 million businesses that generate $819 billion in annual sales. The Center for Women's Business Research suggests that these figures substantially understate the number of women-owned businesses. The center claims that women started over 9 million businesses in 2000. Approximately 55 percent of women-owned businesses are in services, with the second largest group (about 18 percent) in some form of retailing. The number of new businesses started by women continues to increase, and thus women own a larger percentage of the total number of businesses.[61]

The growing gender, ethnic, and cultural diversity in the workforce creates challenges and opportunities,[62] including those related to combining the best of both men's and women's traditional leadership styles for a firm's benefit and identifying ways to facilitate all employees' contributions to forming and using their firm's strategies. Some companies provide training to nurture women's and ethnic minorities' leadership potential. Changes in organizational structure and management practices often are required to eliminate subtle barriers that may exist. Learning to manage diversity in the domestic workforce can increase a firm's effectiveness in managing a globally diverse workforce, as the firm acquires more international operations.

Another manifestation of changing attitudes toward work is the continuing growth of contingency workers (part-time, temporary, and contract employees) throughout the global economy. This trend is significant in several parts of the world, including Canada, Japan, Latin America, Western Europe, and the United States. The fastest growing group of contingency workers is in the technical and professional area. Contributing to this growth are corporate restructurings and downsizings in poor economic conditions along with a breakdown of lifetime employment practices (e.g., in Japan).

The continued growth of suburban communities in the United States and abroad is another major sociocultural trend. The increasing number of people living in the suburbs has a number of effects. For example, because of the resulting often-longer commute times to urban businesses, there is pressure for better transportation systems and superhighway systems (e.g., outer beltways to serve the suburban communities). On the other hand, some businesses are locating in the suburbs closer to their employees. Suburban growth also has an effect on the number of electronic telecommuters, which is expected to increase rapidly in the 21st century. This work-style option is feasible because of changes in the technological segment, including the Internet's rapid growth and evolution.[63]

The Technological Segment

Pervasive and diversified in scope, technological changes affect many parts of societies. These effects occur primarily through new products, processes, and materials. The **technological segment** includes the institutions and activities involved with creating new knowledge and translating that knowledge into new outputs, products, processes, and materials.

Given the rapid pace of technological change, it is vital for firms to thoroughly study the technological segment. The importance of these efforts is suggested by the finding that early adopters of new technology often achieve higher market shares and

The technological segment includes the institutions and activities involved with creating new knowledge and translating that knowledge into new outputs, products, processes, and materials.

earn higher returns. Thus, executives must verify that their firm is continuously scanning the external environment to identify potential substitutes for technologies that are in current use, as well as to spot newly emerging technologies from which their firm could derive competitive advantage.[64]

The importance of technology in business and our daily lives has never been greater. A fully automated plant that operates 24 hours a day exemplifies this fact. In fact, when employees arrive in the morning, they find boxes filled with gears made overnight while they slept. The employees prepare the boxes for delivery but do not participate in the manufacturing process (except in maintaining the machinery).[65]

Internet technology is playing an increasingly important role in global commerce. For example, Internet pharmacies have facilitated senior U.S. citizens' access to cheaper drugs in Canada. U.S. citizens can save as much as 80 percent on drug costs through the Internet pharmacies in Canada. Legislation was passed in the United States in 2003 to ensure that U.S. citizens could continue to access drugs from Canada. As a result, the number of Canadian Internet pharmacies grew sharply in 2003.[66]

Among its other valuable uses, the Internet is an excellent source of data and information for a firm to use to understand its external environment. Access to experts on topics from chemical engineering to semiconductor manufacturing, to the Library of Congress, and even to satellite photographs is available through the Internet. Other information available through this technology includes Securities and Exchange Commission (SEC) filings, Department of Commerce data, information from the Census Bureau, new patent filings, and stock market updates.

While the Internet was a significant technological advance providing substantial power to companies utilizing its potential, wireless communication technology is predicted to be the next critical technological opportunity. By 2003, handheld devices and other wireless communications equipment were being used to access a variety of network-based services. The use of handheld computers with wireless network connectivity, web-enabled mobile phone handsets, and other emerging platforms (i.e., consumer Internet access devices) is expected to increase substantially, soon becoming the dominant form of communication and commerce.[67]

Clearly, the Internet and wireless forms of communications are important technological developments for many reasons. One reason for their importance, however, is that they facilitate the diffusion of other technology and knowledge critical for achieving and maintaining a competitive advantage.[68] Technologies evolve over time, and new technologies are developed. Disruptive technologies, such as the Internet, are developed and implemented and, in turn, often make current technologies obsolete.[69] Companies must stay current with technologies as they evolve, but also must be prepared to act quickly to embrace important new disruptive technologies shortly after they are introduced.[70] Certainly on a global scale, the technological opportunities and threats in the general environment have an effect on whether firms obtain new technology from external sources (such as by licensing and acquisition) or develop it internally.

The Global Segment

The **global segment** includes relevant new global markets, existing markets that are changing, important international political events, and critical cultural and institutional characteristics of global markets.[71] Globalization of business markets creates both opportunities and challenges for firms.[72] For example, firms can identify and enter valuable new global markets.[73] Many global markets (such as those in some South American nations and in South Korea and Taiwan) are becoming borderless and integrated.[74] In addition to contemplating opportunities, firms should recognize potential competitive threats in these markets. China presents many opportunities and some threats for international firms.[75] Creating additional opportunities is China's

The global segment includes relevant new global markets, existing markets that are changing, important international political events, and critical cultural and institutional characteristics of global markets.

recent admission to the World Trade Organization (WTO). A Geneva-based organization, the WTO establishes rules for global trade. China's membership in this organization suggests the possibility of increasing and less-restricted participation by the country in the global economy.[76] In return for gaining entry to the WTO, China agreed to reduce trade barriers in multiple industries, including telecommunications, banking, automobiles, movies, and professional services (for example, the services of lawyers, physicians, and accountants).

Exemplifying the globalization trend is the increasing amount of global outsourcing. For example, Bank of America began major reductions of its back office operations staff (approximately 3,700), outsourcing many of the jobs to Indian businesses. In particular, Wipro Spectramind has been a major beneficiary of technology outsourcing by U.S. firms. It provides IT services, chip design, call centers, and back office functions for a number of firms. Accenture outsourced the jobs of 5,000 accounting, software, and back office employees to the Philippines. Conseco outsourced insurance claim processing to India involving 1,700 jobs, and more such actions are planned. Fluor outsourced to the Philippines 700 jobs that involved preparing architectural blueprints. And, General Electric has outsourced 20,000 jobs to companies in India for a variety of technical tasks. Over 8,000 foreign companies have outsourced IT work to the Philippines.[77]

Moving into international markets extends a firm's reach and potential. Toyota receives almost 50 percent of its total sales revenue from outside Japan, its home country. Over 60 percent of McDonald's sales revenues and almost 98 percent of Nokia's sales revenues are from outside their home countries.[78] Because the opportunity is coupled with uncertainty, some view entering new international markets to be entrepreneurial.[79] Firms can increase the opportunity to sell innovations by entering international markets. The larger total market increases the probability that the firm will earn a return on its innovations. Certainly, firms entering new markets can diffuse new knowledge they have created and learn from the new markets as well.[80]

Firms should recognize the different sociocultural and institutional attributes of global markets. Companies competing in South Korea, for example, must understand the value placed on hierarchical order, formality, and self-control, as well as on duty rather than rights. Furthermore, Korean ideology emphasizes communitarianism, a characteristic of many Asian countries. Korea's approach differs from those of Japan and China, however, in that it focuses on *Inhwa,* or harmony. Inhwa is based on a respect of hierarchical relationships and obedience to authority. Alternatively, the approach in China stresses *Guanxi*—personal relationships or good connections—while in Japan, the focus is on *Wa,* or group harmony and social cohesion.[81] The institutional context of China suggests a major emphasis on centralized planning by the government. The Chinese government provides incentives to firms to develop alliances with foreign firms having sophisticated technology in hopes of building knowledge and introducing new technologies to the Chinese markets over time.[82]

Firms based in other countries that compete in these markets can learn from them. For example, the cultural characteristics above suggest the value of relationships. In particular, Guanxi emphasizes social capital's importance when doing business in China.[83] But, social capital is important for success in most markets around the world.[84]

Global markets offer firms more opportunities to obtain the resources needed for success. For example, the Kuwait Investment Authority is the second largest shareholder of DaimlerChrysler. Additionally, Global Crossing sought financial assistance from potential investors in Europe and Asia. But, it was to no avail as Global Crossing, citing overcapacity in the telecommunications network market as the primary cause of its problems, filed for bankruptcy in 2001. Global Crossing filed a reorganization plan in 2002 and continued the struggle to turn its fortunes around in 2003.[85] Alternatively, globalization can be threatening. In particular, companies in emerging

War, Rivalry, and General Pestilence: The Airline Industry Is Experiencing Trauma

No industry has probably experienced more traumas in recent years than the airline industry. Like most industries, it suffered reduced demand because of the economic downturn in the early part of the 21st century. However, the industry was crippled by the terrorist attacks on September 11, 2001. Then foreign travel was curtailed due to the SARS crisis that occurred in 2003. The SARS epidemic in Asia was expected to reduce travel revenues by 5 percent in 2003. Two of the major firms, United Airlines and US Airways, filed for bankruptcy, as we learned in Chapter 1. And, American Airlines narrowly avoided bankruptcy because of a last minute agreement with its unions. As evidenced by these problems, the general environment in which the airline companies must operate, especially the economic, political/legal, and sociocultural dimensions, has significantly affected them.

The airlines are also greatly affected by their industry environment. In fact, the major negative effects of dimensions of the general environment have made the airlines' industry environment more salient. For example, the rivalry in the industry is severe as airlines compete for fewer air travelers. In turn, airlines have delayed or cancelled orders for new aircraft, negatively affecting major aircraft manufacturers, especially Boeing. Interestingly, even though most analysts evaluate the airline industry as being highly unattractive, it continues to have new entrants. Probably the most important of the new entrants in recent years is JetBlue, an airline that has largely imitated Southwest Airlines' strategy. In Chapter 5, we learn more about how JetBlue and Song, mentioned below, are competing in the airline industry.

Due to the success of Southwest Airlines and others such as JetBlue, and because of the general environment described earlier, the airline industry is in the process of restructuring. First, the major airlines are trying desperately to reduce their cost structures. To do this requires the approval of their unions. Unions at United Airlines and US Airways made major concessions to allow these firms to continue operations. American Airlines' CEO had to resign to achieve the wage concessions from the unions that allowed the firm to avoid bankruptcy. But, the reduction of costs is only the first step in the restructuring likely to occur.

Delta Airlines, for example, has announced the development of a low-cost airline, named Song, to compete in the low-price market niche. Other major airlines are likely to follow. British Airways has announced major changes that include a reduction of 13,000 employees, cuts in the variety of aircraft used, reductions in the number of suppliers, limitations on the amount of ticket pricing options, and an increase in the number of short-haul flights. These changes are expected to decrease the firm's costs by approximately $1.8 billion annually (almost 13 percent of total costs) and to increase its flexibility and competitiveness. Some analysts also predict consolidation in the industry as airlines are likely to merge. The

John Selvaggio, president of Song airlines, plays his trumpet on the tarmac in front of one of the company's planes at an event to inaugurate its service to Boston. Song is a low-cost carrier that represents Delta's effort to increase profit in a troubled industry environment.

AP Photo/Michael Dwyer

only thing that may prevent consolidation could be government regulations disallowing anticompetitive moves. Certainly, the future of the airline industry will be interesting to observe.

SOURCES: R. Neidl, 2003, Winners and losers as airlines restructure, *Barron's Online*, http://www.wsj.com/barrons, May 29; D. Michaels, 2003, As airlines suffer, British Air tries takeoff strategy, *Wall Street Journal*, May 22, A1, A5; S. Carey, 2003, Encountering turbulence, *Wall Street Journal*, May 1, B1, B4; M. Chung & D. Shellock, 2003, Transatlantic markets: Risky times for airlines, *Financial Times*, http://www.ft.com, May 9; N. Harris, 2003, Can Delta's song attract "discount divas"? *Wall Street Journal*, April 11, B1, B6; 2003, Death, war and pestilence. What next for corporate travel? *The Economist*, http://www.economist.com, April 3.

market countries may be vulnerable to larger, more resource-rich, and more effective competitors from developed markets.

Additionally, there are risks in global markets. A few years ago, Argentina's market was full of promise, but in 2001, Argentina experienced a financial crisis that placed it on the brink of bankruptcy. Fortunately, Argentina's economy survived, but the country continues to struggle economically.[86] Thus, the global segment of the general environment is quite important for most firms. As a result, it is necessary to have a top management team with the experience, knowledge, and sensitivity required to effectively analyze this segment of the environment.[87]

A key objective of analyzing the general environment is identifying anticipated changes and trends among external elements. With a focus on the future, the analysis of the general environment allows firms to identify opportunities and threats. As noted in the Strategic Focus, there have been and continue to be a number of threats to airlines from the general environment. Perhaps the biggest threat comes from the economy; the industry badly needs an economic recovery to increase the demand for air travel. Also critical to a firm's future operations is an understanding of its industry environment and its competitors; these issues are considered next.

Industry Environment Analysis

An industry is a group of firms producing products that are close substitutes.

An **industry** is a group of firms producing products that are close substitutes. In the course of competition, these firms influence one another. Typically, industries include a rich mix of competitive strategies that companies use in pursuing strategic competitiveness and above-average returns. In part, these strategies are chosen because of the influence of an industry's characteristics.[88] The economic malaise suffered in the early part of the 21st century showed the vulnerability of the information technology industry, as discussed in this chapter's Opening Case. Because of these problems, the industry has undergone a number of changes in recent years, including major changes in the competitive landscape (loss of firms) and major changes in the strategies employed, exemplified by IBM's new strategy of computing on demand.

Compared to the general environment, the industry environment often has a more direct effect on the firm's strategic competitiveness and above-average returns.[89] The intensity of industry competition and an industry's profit potential (as measured by the long-run return on invested capital) are functions of five forces of competition: the threats posed by new entrants, the power of suppliers, the power of buyers, product substitutes, and the intensity of rivalry among competitors (see Figure 2.2).

The five forces model of competition expands the arena for competitive analysis. Historically, when studying the competitive environment, firms concentrated on companies with which they competed directly. However, firms must search more broadly to

identify current and potential competitors by identifying potential customers as well as the firms serving them. Competing for the same customers and thus being influenced by how customers value location and firm capabilities in their decisions is referred to as the market microstructure.[90] Understanding this area is particularly important, because in recent years industry boundaries have become blurred. For example, in the electrical utilities industry, cogenerators (firms that also produce power) are competing with regional utility companies. Moreover, telecommunications companies now compete with broadcasters, software manufacturers provide personal financial services, airlines sell mutual funds, and automakers sell insurance and provide financing.[91] In addition to focusing on customers rather than on specific industry boundaries to define markets, geographic boundaries are also relevant. Research suggests that different geographic markets for the same product can have considerably different competitive conditions.[92]

The five forces model recognizes that suppliers can become a firm's competitors (by integrating forward), as can buyers (by integrating backward). Several firms have integrated forward in the pharmaceutical industry by acquiring distributors or wholesalers. In addition, firms choosing to enter a new market and those producing products that are adequate substitutes for existing products can become a company's competitors.

Threat of New Entrants

Evidence suggests that companies often find it difficult to identify new competitors.[93] Identifying new entrants is important because they can threaten the market share of existing competitors. One reason new entrants pose such a threat is that they bring additional production capacity. Unless the demand for a good or service is increasing, additional capacity holds consumers' costs down, resulting in less revenue and lower returns for competing firms. Often, new entrants have a keen interest in gaining a large market share. As a result, new competitors may force existing firms to be more effective and efficient and to learn how to compete on new dimensions (for example, using an Internet-based distribution channel).

The likelihood that firms will enter an industry is a function of two factors: barriers to entry and the retaliation expected from current industry participants. Entry barriers make it difficult for new firms to enter an industry and often place them at a competitive disadvantage even when they are able to enter. As such, high entry barriers increase the returns for existing firms in the industry and may allow some firms to dominate the industry.[94] Interestingly, there are high entry barriers in the airline industry (e.g., substantial capital costs), but new firms have entered in recent years, among them AirTran Airways and JetBlue. Both entrants are creating competitive challenges for the major airlines, especially with the economic problems in the early 21st century. Both firms compete in the low-cost segments, and the demand for low-cost air travel has increased, making the major high-cost airlines less competitive and vulnerable to these newer airlines' competitive actions.

BARRIERS TO ENTRY

Existing competitors try to develop barriers to entry. In contrast, potential entrants seek markets in which the entry barriers are relatively insignificant. The absence of entry barriers increases the probability that a new entrant can operate profitably. There are several kinds of potentially significant entry barriers.

Economies of Scale. *Economies of scale* are "the marginal improvements in efficiency that a firm experiences as it incrementally increases its size."[95] Therefore, as the quantity of a product produced during a given period increases, the cost of manufacturing each unit declines. Economies of scale can be developed in most business functions, such as marketing, manufacturing, research and development, and purchasing. Increasing economies of scale enhances a firm's flexibility. For example, a firm may choose to reduce its price and capture a greater share of the market. Alternatively, it may keep its price constant to increase profits. In so doing, it likely will increase its free cash flow, which is helpful in times of recession.

New entrants face a dilemma when confronting current competitors' scale economies. Small-scale entry places them at a cost disadvantage. Alternatively, large-scale entry, in which the new entrant manufactures large volumes of a product to gain economies of scale, risks strong competitive retaliation.

Also important for the firm to understand are competitive conditions that reduce the ability of economies of scale to create an entry barrier. Many companies now customize their products for large numbers of small customer groups. Customized products are not manufactured in the volumes necessary to achieve economies of scale. Customization is made possible by new flexible manufacturing systems (this point is discussed further in Chapter 4). In fact, the new manufacturing technology facilitated by advanced information systems has allowed the development of mass customization in an increasing number of industries. While customization is not appropriate for all products, mass customization is becoming increasingly common in manufacturing products. In fact, online ordering has enhanced the ability of customers to obtain customized products. They are often referred to as "markets of one."[96] Companies manufacturing customized products learn how to respond quickly to customers' desires rather than develop scale economies.

Product Differentiation. Over time, customers may come to believe that a firm's product is unique. This belief can result from the firm's service to the customer, effective advertising campaigns, or being the first to market a good or service. Companies such as Coca-Cola, PepsiCo, and the world's automobile manufacturers spend a great deal of money on advertising to convince potential customers of their products' distinctiveness. Customers valuing a product's uniqueness tend to become loyal to both the product and the company producing it. Typically, new entrants must allocate many resources over time to overcome existing customer loyalties. To combat the perception of uniqueness, new entrants frequently offer products at lower prices. This decision, however, may result in lower profits or even losses.

Capital Requirements. Competing in a new industry requires a firm to have resources to invest. In addition to physical facilities, capital is needed for inventories, marketing activities, and other critical business functions. Even when competing in a new industry is attractive, the capital required for successful market entry may not be available to pursue an apparent market opportunity. For example, entering the steel and defense industries would be very difficult because of the substantial resource investments required to be competitive. One way a firm could enter the steel industry, however, is with a highly efficient mini-mill. Alternatively, because of the high knowledge requirements, a firm might enter the defense industry through the acquisition of an existing firm.

Switching Costs. Switching costs are the one-time costs customers incur when they buy from a different supplier. The costs of buying new ancillary equipment and of retraining employees, and even the psychic costs of ending a relationship, may be incurred in switching to a new supplier. In some cases, switching costs are low, such as when the consumer switches to a different soft drink. Switching costs can vary as a function of time. For example, in terms of credit hours toward graduation, the cost to a student to transfer from one university to another as a freshman is much lower than it is when the student is entering the senior year. Occasionally, a decision made by manufacturers to produce a new, innovative product creates high switching costs for the final consumer. Customer loyalty programs, such as airlines' frequent flier miles, are intended to increase the customer's switching costs.

If switching costs are high, a new entrant must offer either a substantially lower price or a much better product to attract buyers. Usually, the more established the relationship between parties, the greater is the cost incurred to switch to an alternative offering.

Access to Distribution Channels. Over time, industry participants typically develop effective means of distributing products. Once a relationship with its distributors has been developed, a firm will nurture it to create switching costs for the distributors.

Access to distribution channels can be a strong entry barrier for new entrants, particularly in consumer nondurable goods industries (for example, in grocery stores where shelf space is limited) and in international markets. Thus, new entrants have to persuade distributors to carry their products, either in addition to or in place of those currently distributed. Price breaks and cooperative advertising allowances may be used for this purpose; however, those practices reduce the new entrant's profit potential.

Cost Disadvantages Independent of Scale. Sometimes, established competitors have cost advantages that new entrants cannot duplicate. Proprietary product technology, favorable access to raw materials, desirable locations, and government subsidies are examples. Successful competition requires new entrants to reduce the strategic relevance of these factors. Delivering purchases directly to the buyer can counter the advantage of a desirable location; new food establishments in an undesirable location often follow this practice. Similarly, automobile dealerships located in unattractive areas (perhaps in a city's downtown area) can provide superior service (such as picking up the car to be serviced and then delivering it to the customer) to overcome a competitor's location advantage.

Government Policy. Through licensing and permit requirements, governments can also control entry into an industry. Liquor retailing, banking, and trucking are examples of industries in which government decisions and actions affect entry possibilities. Also, governments often restrict entry into some industries because of the need to provide quality service or the need to protect jobs. Alternatively, deregulation of industries, exemplified by the airline industry (see earlier Strategic Focus) and utilities in the United States, allows more firms to enter.[97] Some of the most publicized government actions are those involving antitrust. For example, the U.S. government dropped its antitrust case against IBM in 1982 after 13 years of highly publicized litigation. More recently, the U.S. government pursued an antitrust case against Microsoft. The final settlement involved a relatively small penalty for the company.[98] In recent years, the government has reduced many regulations, such as those involving ownership of radio stations. The loosening of these restrictions allowed Clear Channel Communications to increase its market share considerably; it now owns over 1,200 radio stations as described in the Strategic Focus later in this chapter.

EXPECTED RETALIATION

Firms seeking to enter an industry also anticipate the reactions of firms in the industry. An expectation of swift and vigorous competitive responses reduces the likelihood of entry. Vigorous retaliation can be expected when the existing firm has a major stake in the industry (for example, it has fixed assets with few, if any, alternative uses), when it has substantial resources, and when industry growth is slow or constrained. For example, any firm attempting to enter the steel or IT industries at the current time can expect significant retaliation from existing competitors.

Locating market niches not being served by incumbents allows the new entrant to avoid entry barriers. Small entrepreneurial firms are generally best suited for identifying and serving neglected market segments. When Honda first entered the U.S. market, it concentrated on small-engine motorcycles, a market that firms such as Harley-Davidson ignored. By targeting this neglected niche, Honda avoided competition. After consolidating its position, Honda used its strength to attack rivals by introducing larger motorcycles and competing in the broader market. Competitive actions and competitive responses between firms such as Honda and Harley-Davidson are discussed fully in Chapter 5.

Bargaining Power of Suppliers

Increasing prices and reducing the quality of their products are potential means used by suppliers to exert power over firms competing within an industry. If a firm is unable to recover cost increases by its suppliers through its pricing structure, its profitability is reduced by its suppliers' actions. A supplier group is powerful when

- It is dominated by a few large companies and is more concentrated than the industry to which it sells.
- Satisfactory substitute products are not available to industry firms.
- Industry firms are not a significant customer for the supplier group.
- Suppliers' goods are critical to buyers' marketplace success.
- The effectiveness of suppliers' products has created high switching costs for industry firms.
- It poses a credible threat to integrate forward into the buyers' industry. Credibility is enhanced when suppliers have substantial resources and provide a highly differentiated product.

The airline industry is an example of an industry in which suppliers' bargaining power is relatively low. While the number of suppliers is low, the demand for the major aircraft is also relatively low. Boeing and Airbus compete strongly for most orders of major aircraft.[99] Also, the shift in airline strategy to short-haul flights and low costs has enhanced the fortunes of other aircraft manufacturers who make smaller and more efficient aircraft.

Bargaining Power of Buyers

Firms seek to maximize the return on their invested capital. Alternatively, buyers (customers of an industry or a firm) want to buy products at the lowest possible price—the point at which the industry earns the lowest acceptable rate of return on its invested capital. To reduce their costs, buyers bargain for higher quality, greater levels of service, and lower prices. These outcomes are achieved by encouraging competitive battles among the industry's firms. Customers (buyer groups) are powerful when

- They purchase a large portion of an industry's total output.
- The sales of the product being purchased account for a significant portion of the seller's annual revenues.
- They could switch to another product at little, if any, cost.
- The industry's products are undifferentiated or standardized, and the buyers pose a credible threat if they were to integrate backward into the sellers' industry.

Armed with greater amounts of information about the manufacturer's costs and the power of the Internet as a shopping and distribution alternative, consumers appear to be increasing their bargaining power in many industries. One reason for this shift is that individual buyers incur virtually zero switching costs when they decide to purchase from one manufacturer rather than another or from one dealer as opposed to a second or third one. These realities are also forcing airlines to change their strategies. There is very little differentiation in air travel, and the switching costs are very low.

Threat of Substitute Products

Substitute products are goods or services from outside a given industry that perform similar or the same functions as a product that the industry produces. For example, as a sugar substitute, NutraSweet places an upper limit on sugar manufacturers' prices—NutraSweet and sugar perform the same function, but with different characteristics. Other product substitutes include fax machines instead of overnight deliveries, plastic containers rather than glass jars, and tea instead of coffee. Recently, firms have introduced to the market several low-alcohol, fruit-flavored drinks that many customers substitute for beer. For example, Smirnoff's Ice was introduced with substantial advertising of the type often used for beer. Other firms have introduced lemonade with 5 percent alcohol (e.g., "Doc's" Hard Lemon) and tea and lemon combinations with alcohol (e.g., Boston Beer Company's Twisted Tea). These products are increasingly popular, especially among younger people, and as product substitutes, they have the potential to reduce overall sales of beer.[100]

In general, product substitutes present a strong threat to a firm when customers face few, if any, switching costs and when the substitute product's price is lower or its quality and performance capabilities are equal to or greater than those of the competing product. Differentiating a product along dimensions that customers value (such as price, quality, service after the sale, and location) reduces a substitute's attractiveness.

Intensity of Rivalry among Competitors

Because an industry's firms are mutually dependent, actions taken by one company usually invite competitive responses. Thus, in many industries, firms actively compete against one another. Competitive rivalry intensifies when a firm is challenged by a competitor's actions or when a company recognizes an opportunity to improve its market position.

Firms within industries are rarely homogeneous; they differ in resources and capabilities and seek to differentiate themselves from competitors.[101] Typically, firms seek to differentiate their products from competitors' offerings in ways that customers value and in which the firms have a competitive advantage. Visible dimensions on which rivalry is based include price, quality, and innovation.

As explained in the Strategic Focus, the rivalry between competitors, such as United, US Airways, American, and other major airlines, is intense. The competitive rivalry is also intense in the computer hardware and software markets, as described in the Opening Case. In fact, the rivalry is so intense, a formerly highly successful firm, Sun Microsystems, may have trouble surviving over the next several years.

As suggested by the Opening Case and Strategic Focus, various factors influence the intensity of rivalry between or among competitors. Next, we discuss the most prominent factors that experience shows to affect the intensity of firms' rivalries.

NUMEROUS OR EQUALLY BALANCED COMPETITORS

Intense rivalries are common in industries with many companies. With multiple competitors, it is common for a few firms to believe that they can act without eliciting a response. However, evidence suggests that other firms generally are aware of competitors' actions, often choosing to respond to them. At the other extreme, industries with only a few firms of equivalent size and power also tend to have strong rivalries. The large and often similar-sized resource bases of these firms permit vigorous actions and responses. The Airbus and Boeing competitive battles exemplify intense rivalry between relatively equivalent competitors.[102]

SLOW INDUSTRY GROWTH

When a market is growing, firms try to effectively use resources to serve an expanding customer base. Growing markets reduce the pressure to take customers from competitors. However, rivalry in no-growth or slow-growth markets becomes more intense as firms battle to increase their market shares by attracting competitors' customers.

Typically, battles to protect market shares are fierce. Certainly, this has been the case in the airline industry. The instability in the market that results from these competitive engagements reduces profitability for all airlines throughout the industry. Reduced profitability is one of the reasons that two major U.S.-based airlines have declared bankruptcy and others on a global basis have experienced major net losses since 2000.

HIGH FIXED COSTS OR HIGH STORAGE COSTS

When fixed costs account for a large part of total costs, companies try to maximize the use of their productive capacity. Doing so allows the firm to spread costs across a larger volume of output. However, when many firms attempt to maximize their productive capacity, excess capacity is created on an industry-wide basis. To then reduce inventories, individual companies typically cut the price of their product and offer rebates and other special discounts to customers. However, these practices, common in the automobile manufacturing industry, often intensify competition. The pattern of excess capacity at the industry level followed by intense rivalry at the firm level is observed frequently in industries with high storage costs. Perishable products, for example, lose their value rapidly with the passage of time. As their inventories grow, producers of perishable goods often use pricing strategies to sell products quickly.

LACK OF DIFFERENTIATION OR LOW SWITCHING COSTS

When buyers find a differentiated product that satisfies their needs, they frequently purchase the product loyally over time. Industries with many companies that have successfully differentiated their products have less rivalry, resulting in lower competition for individual firms. Firms that develop and sustain a differentiated product that cannot be easily imitated by competitors often earn higher returns.[103] However, when buyers view products as commodities (as products with few differentiated features or capabilities), rivalry intensifies. In these instances, buyers' purchasing decisions are based primarily on price and, to a lesser degree, service. Personal computers are becoming a commodity. Thus, the competition among Dell, HP, and other computer manufacturers is expected to be strong.

The effect of switching costs is identical to that described for differentiated products. The lower the buyers' switching costs, the easier it is for competitors to attract buyers through pricing and service offerings. High switching costs, however, at least partially insulate the firm from rivals' efforts to attract customers. Interestingly, the switching costs—such as pilot and mechanic training—are high in aircraft purchases, yet the rivalry between Boeing and Airbus remains intense because the stakes for both are extremely high.

HIGH STRATEGIC STAKES

Competitive rivalry is likely to be high when it is important for several of the competitors to perform well in the market. For example, although it is diversified and is a market leader in other businesses, Samsung has targeted market leadership in the consumer electronics market and is doing quite well. This market is quite important to Sony and other major competitors, such as Hitachi, Matsushita, NEC, and Mitsubishi. Thus, there is substantial rivalry in this market, and it is likely to continue over the next few years.

High strategic stakes can also exist in terms of geographic locations. For example, Japanese automobile manufacturers are committed to a significant presence in the U.S. marketplace. A key reason for this is that the United States is the world's largest single market for auto manufacturers' products. Because of the stakes involved in this country for Japanese and U.S. manufacturers, rivalry among firms in the U.S. and the global automobile industry is highly intense. It should be noted that while proximity tends to promote greater rivalry, physically proximate competition has potentially positive benefits as well. For example, when competitors are located near each other, it is easier for suppliers to serve them, and they can develop economies of scale that lead to lower production costs. Additionally, communications with key industry stakeholders such as suppliers are facilitated and more efficient when they are close to the firm.[104]

HIGH EXIT BARRIERS

Sometimes companies continue competing in an industry even though the returns on their invested capital are low or negative. Firms making this choice likely face high exit barriers, which include economic, strategic, and emotional factors causing companies to remain in an industry when the profitability of doing so is questionable. Exit barriers are especially high in the airline industry. Common exit barriers are

- Specialized assets (assets with values linked to a particular business or location).
- Fixed costs of exit (such as labor agreements).
- Strategic interrelationships (relationships of mutual dependence, such as those between one business and other parts of a company's operations, including shared facilities and access to financial markets).
- Emotional barriers (aversion to economically justified business decisions because of fear for one's own career, loyalty to employees, and so forth).
- Government and social restrictions (more common outside the United States, these restrictions often are based on government concerns for job losses and regional economic effects).

Will the Real Media Industry Please Stand Up?

Only a few years ago it seemed that everyone wanted to get into the media industry and to expand it farther. Although there were differences of opinion, many analysts expressed positive evaluations of such firms as AOL Time Warner, Vivendi, Bertelsmann, Sony Entertainment, and related companies (e.g., in the cable business). Yet, since the AOL Time Warner merger in 2000, the situations have soured for many of these companies. AOL Time Warner CEO Gerald Levine retired, and Steve Case stepped down as chairman. Jean-Marie Messier, CEO of Vivendi, was asked to resign, and Bertelsmann CEO Thomas Middlehof was forced to resign. All of these firms were formed into large conglomerates with the purpose of obtaining synergies and becoming the leaders across several industries.

AOL Time Warner was formed to provide content to AOL and to provide new outlets for the content beyond magazines and movies. AOL Time Warner provides Internet access (the major business of AOL), cable services, filmed entertainment, networks (e.g., CNN for news), music, and publishing. As a result, the company competes in several markets and against different firms in each one. For example, it competes against Disney in filmed entertainment and, to some degree, in networks. It competes against Comcast in cable and Sony and Apple in music. The number of and diversity among its competitors create challenges for managing this large, monolithic firm. And, unfortunately, the AOL business has been a drain on the company almost since the time of the merger. The major problem was the bursting of the Internet bubble. Beyond that, actions to create synergy by using content in AOL have not yet produced dividends. For example, the music service offered by AOL has been usurped by Apple's recent entry into providing entertainment services, especially music.

AOL has also been crippled by competition in its basic Internet access business. It has been hit from two sides—cut-rate Internet services and the new broadband services from cable providers. As a result of the two-sided competitive attack, AOL's subscriber base has declined from its high in 2002. And, although AOL has offered a new broadband service, it has largely managed only to change some of its dial-up service customers to the broadband service. It has not yet attracted much appeal beyond its current customers. Comcast, which acquired AT&T's broadband service in late 2002, has become a formidable competitor.

Essentially, AOL Time Warner must decide which problems to solve. It has so many competitors in different markets, and its inability to find synergies has caused significant problems for the firm. Some analysts have argued that the firm should spin off AOL so it does not drain the basic media business. However, Jonathon Miller, CEO of AOL, a division of AOL Time Warner, is developing a plan to revive the firm to sell subscriptions to online customers for high-demand entertainment such as *The Sopranos*. Thus, he continues to search for the elusive synergy across the businesses in the company.

SOURCES: D. D. Kirkpatrick, 2003, In HBO, AOL sees a sibling and, crucially, a role model, *New York Times*, http://www.nytimes.com, May 5; J. Angwin, 2003, America Online faces new threat from cut-rate Internet services, *Wall Street Journal*, February 3, A1, A11; J. Angwin, 2003, America Online's fate grows more uncertain, *Wall Street Journal*, January 14, B1, B4; B. Orwall & M. Peers, 2003, Facing crisis, media giants scrounge for fresh strategies, *Wall Street Journal*, January 14, A1, A6; G. Anders, 2002, AOL's true believers, *Fast Company*, July, 96–104; T. Lowry, A. Barrett, & R. Grover, 2002, A new cable giant, *Business Week*, November 18, 108–118.

Interpreting Industry Analyses

Effective industry analyses are products of careful study and interpretation of data and information from multiple sources. A wealth of industry-specific data is available to be analyzed. Because of globalization, international markets and rivalries must be included in the firm's analyses. In fact, research shows that in some industries, international variables are more important than domestic ones as determinants of strategic competitiveness. Furthermore, because of the development of global markets, a country's borders no longer restrict industry structures. In fact, movement into international markets enhances the chances of success for new ventures as well as more established firms.[105]

Following study of the five forces of competition, the firm can develop the insights required to determine an industry's attractiveness in terms of the firm's potential to earn adequate or superior returns on its invested capital. In general, the stronger competitive forces are, the lower is the profit potential for an industry's firms. An unattractive industry has low entry barriers, suppliers and buyers with strong bargaining positions, strong competitive threats from product substitutes, and intense rivalry among competitors. These industry characteristics make it very difficult for firms to achieve strategic competitiveness and earn above-average returns. Alternatively, an attractive industry has high entry barriers, suppliers and buyers with little bargaining power, few competitive threats from product substitutes, and relatively moderate rivalry.[106]

As noted in the Strategic Focus, AOL Time Warner operates in multiple industries. As such, it must analyze several industries to better know the opportunities and threats that each poses. In fact, a thorough industry analysis might have prevented Time Warner's merger with AOL, as it should have identified a number of threats faced in that industry. Interestingly, each of the media conglomerates developed in the late 1990s has suffered substantial problems since the birth of the 21st century. Next, we turn to strategic groups operating within industries.

Strategic Groups

A set of firms emphasizing similar strategic dimensions to use a similar strategy is called a **strategic group.**[107] The competition between firms within a strategic group is greater than the competition between a member of a strategic group and companies outside that strategic group. Another way of saying this is that intra-strategic group competition is more intense than is inter-strategic group competition. In fact, there is more heterogeneity in the performance of firms within strategic groups than across the groups. The performance leaders within groups are able to follow strategies similar to those of other firms in the group and yet maintain strategic distinctiveness to gain and sustain a competitive advantage.[108]

The extent of technological leadership, product quality, pricing policies, distribution channels, and customer service are examples of strategic dimensions that firms in a strategic group may treat similarly. Patterns of competition within strategic groups may be described this way: "Organizations in a strategic group occupy similar positions in the market, offer similar goods to similar customers, and may also make similar choices about production technology and other organizational features."[109] Thus, membership in a particular strategic group defines the essential characteristics of the firm's strategy.[110]

The notion of strategic groups can be useful for analyzing an industry's competitive structure. Such analyses can be helpful in diagnosing competition, positioning, and the profitability of firms within an industry.[111] High mobility barriers, high rivalry, and low resources among the firms within an industry will limit the formation of strategic groups.[112] However, research suggests that after strategic groups are formed, their membership remains relatively stable over time, making analysis easier and more useful.[113]

*A **strategic group** is a set of firms emphasizing similar strategic dimensions to use a similar strategy.*

There are approximately 30 different formats in the radio industry. These formats represent different preferences in music, scheduling, and announcer style as well as nonmusic broadcasting (news, talk radio). Resulting listening formats are specifically suited for various audiences to gain competitive advantage for each market.

©Spencer Grant/PhotoEdit

It's a Competitive World: Some Succeed and Some Fail

Home Depot is the number one home improvement company, and only a few years ago, it seemed to be unbeatable. However, its stock price reached a five-year low in 2003. Its new CEO, Bob Nardelli, has cut costs and centralized operations in the face of a bad economy. He forced the hiring of more part-time workers and increased discipline by cutting inventories. While these actions reduced costs, some customers complained that the firm reduced service. Also, the centralization allows fewer creative approaches to be used by the store managers, one of the factors often credited for Home Depot's success. As a result, Lowe's Companies, which is number two in the market, has been increasing its market share relative to Home Depot's share. Lowe's has been successful in attracting women customers, not the target for Home Depot.

Radio for many years was a highly fragmented industry. However, after the industry was deregulated through legislation, consolidation began, especially by Clear Channel Communications. In 1995, Clear Channel controlled approximately 1.3 percent of the market. By 2001, however, it had a 20.2 percent market share. It grew largely by acquisitions and now owns over 1,200 radio stations. But, Clear Channel's success comes from the synergies it has created with other businesses such as billboards. It owns more than 770,000 billboards and advertising displays. As such, it can offer advertisers "more bang for their bucks" by advertising on the radio and on billboards that people will see as they drive by listening to their radio. Clear Channel has also become the largest concert promoter (through acquisitions) and promotes those concerts on the radio. It has been accused of "strong-arm tactics" and has the economic power to do so. But, while Clear Channel is large and has built several competitive advantages through the synergies among its businesses, it still controls only about 10 percent of the radio stations in the United States.

GlaxoSmithKline is the second largest pharmaceutical firm in the world. But, it has a problem. Its pipeline of new products makes analysts and investors wary about its future. The firm has experienced strong earnings but has grown largely through acquisitions in recent years. By doing so, it has bought new products rather than developed them internally. Competition in this industry is based on the new "blockbuster" drugs developed and brought to the market. Glaxo may start paying the price for not emphasizing R&D by losing its competitive advantage as other pharmaceutical firms introduce new products and take Glaxo's market away. This concern was exacerbated when the firm failed to schedule an expected meeting with analysts to discuss its research and development program.

Paradoxically, one firm has gotten into trouble by investing heavily in R&D. Volkswagen invested billions of dollars to develop and introduce several new luxury automobiles, only to find that they were not in demand in the marketplace. One of these new cars, the Phaeton, is priced at $70,000. Sales of the Phaeton reached only 25 percent of the expected number in 2002, its year of introduction. The competition is fierce in the premium auto market. The wasted R&D investments and a lack of attention to Volkswagen's primary mid-priced auto market have allowed competitors to gain market share there as well. Thus, Volkswagen's financial results have suffered, and unless it regains a competitive advantage, its performance will continue to suffer.

SOURCES: N. E. Boudette, 2003, Volkswagen stalls on several fronts after luxury drive, *Wall Street Journal*, May 8, A1, A17; R. Abelson, 2003, For Glaxo, the answers are in the pipeline, *New York Times*, http://www.nytimes.com, May 4; C. Y. Chen, 2003, The bad boys of radio, *Fortune*, March 3, 119–122; D. Morse, 2003, A hardware chain struggles to adjust to a new blueprint, *Wall Street Journal*, January 17, A1, A6; 2003, A do-it-yourself disaster, *The Economist*, January 11, 54–55.

Using strategic groups to understand an industry's competitive structure requires the firm to plot companies' competitive actions and competitive responses along strategic dimensions such as pricing decisions, product quality, distribution channels, and so forth. Doing this shows the firm how certain companies are competing similarly in terms of how they use similar strategic dimensions. For example, there are unique radio markets because consumers prefer different music formats and programming (news radio, talk radio, and so forth). Typically, a radio format is created through choices made regarding music or nonmusic style, scheduling, and announcer style.[114] It is estimated that approximately 30 different radio formats exist, suggesting that there are many strategic groups in this industry. The strategies within each of the 30 groups are similar, while the strategies across the total set of strategic groups are dissimilar. As a result, Clear Channel Communications (described in the Strategic Focus) often owns several stations in a large city, but each uses a different format. Therefore, Clear Channel likely has stations operating in most or all of the 30 strategic groups in this industry. Thus, firms could increase their understanding of competition in the commercial radio industry by plotting companies' actions and responses in terms of important strategic dimensions, such as those we have mentioned.

Strategic groups have several implications. First, because firms within a group offer similar products to the same customers, the competitive rivalry among them can be intense. The more intense the rivalry, the greater is the threat to each firm's profitability. Second, the strengths of the five industry forces (the threats posed by new entrants, the power of suppliers, the power of buyers, product substitutes, and the intensity of rivalry among competitors) differ across strategic groups. Third, the closer the strategic groups are in terms of their strategies, the greater is the likelihood of rivalry between the groups.

Having a thorough understanding of primary competitors helps a firm formulate and implement an appropriate strategy. Clearly Home Depot and Lowe's are in a strategic group and compete directly against each other. Lowe's has been successful in selling products to women. Observing this, Home Depot has recently added new product lines to attract women to its stores. Volkswagen tried to break out of its strategic group selling mid-priced autos. But, it was unsuccessful in entering the strategic group of firms using similar strategies selling premium autos (e.g., Mercedes-Benz, BMW). Additionally, because of these efforts, VW is losing market share in its primary markets. Glaxo has used a strategy different from that of several of its primary competitors and now is in danger of losing an advantage over them. It can no longer sustain new product lines by acquisition. Research has shown that this outcome is to be expected when a firm continuously emphasizes obtaining new products through acquisitions rather than internal development.[115]

Competitor Analysis

The competitor environment is the final part of the external environment requiring study. Competitor analysis focuses on each company against which a firm directly competes. For example, Home Depot and Lowe's and GlaxoSmithKline and Merck should be keenly interested in understanding each other's objectives, strategies, assumptions, and capabilities. Furthermore, intense rivalry creates a strong need to understand competitors. In a competitor analysis, the firm seeks to understand

- What drives the competitor, as shown by its *future objectives.*
- What the competitor is doing and can do, as revealed by its *current strategy.*
- What the competitor believes about the industry, as shown by its *assumptions.*
- What the competitor's capabilities are, as shown by its *strengths* and *weaknesses.*[116]

Information about these four dimensions helps the firm prepare an anticipated response profile for each competitor (see Figure 2.3). Thus, the results of an effective competitor analysis help a firm understand, interpret, and predict its competitors' actions and responses. Understanding the actions of competitors clearly contributes to the firm's ability to compete successfully within the industry.[117]

Critical to an effective competitor analysis is gathering data and information that can help the firm understand its competitors' intentions and the strategic implications resulting from them.[118] Useful data and information combine to form **competitor intelligence:** the set of data and information the firm gathers to better understand and better anticipate competitors' objectives, strategies, assumptions, and capabilities. In competitor analysis, the firm should gather intelligence not only about its competitors, but also regarding public policies in countries across the world. Intelligence about public policies "provides an early warning of threats and opportunities emerging from the global public policy environment, and analyzes how they will affect the achievement of the company's strategy."[119]

Through effective competitive and public policy intelligence, the firm gains the insights needed to create a competitive advantage and to increase the quality of the strategic decisions it makes when deciding how to compete against its rivals. Factiva, a news and information service, has used competitor intelligence to improve its competitive position and to build an excellent service. The firm was named among the top 100 Companies in Knowledge Management by KMWorld magazine and received the 2003 Codie Award for the Best Online Business News or Information Service and the Best Online Professional Financial Information Service. Additionally, the CEO, Clare Hart,

Competitor intelligence is the set of data and information the firm gathers to better understand and better anticipate competitors' objectives, strategies, assumptions, and capabilities.

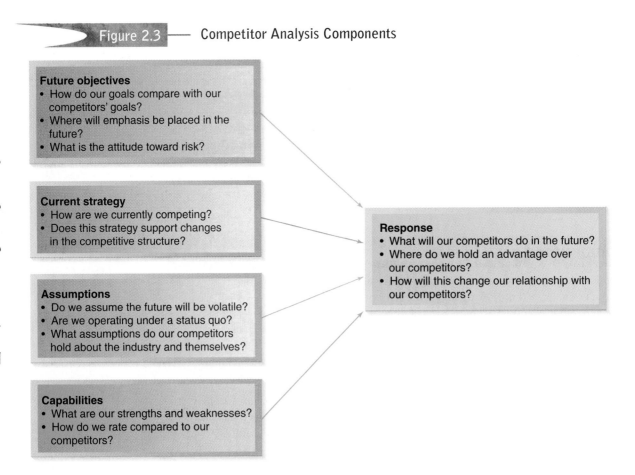

Figure 2.3 — Competitor Analysis Components

Future objectives
- How do our goals compare with our competitors' goals?
- Where will emphasis be placed in the future?
- What is the attitude toward risk?

Current strategy
- How are we currently competing?
- Does this strategy support changes in the competitive structure?

Assumptions
- Do we assume the future will be volatile?
- Are we operating under a status quo?
- What assumptions do our competitors hold about the industry and themselves?

Capabilities
- What are our strengths and weaknesses?
- How do we rate compared to our competitors?

Response
- What will our competitors do in the future?
- Where do we hold an advantage over our competitors?
- How will this change our relationship with our competitors?

states that competitor intelligence will play an important role in her firm's efforts to reach its objective of becoming the top firm in the industry.[120]

Firms should follow generally accepted ethical practices in gathering competitor intelligence. Industry associations often develop lists of these practices that firms can adopt. Practices considered both legal and ethical include (1) obtaining publicly available information (such as court records, competitors' help-wanted advertisements, annual reports, financial reports of publicly held corporations, and Uniform Commercial Code filings), and (2) attending trade fairs and shows to obtain competitors' brochures, view their exhibits, and listen to discussions about their products.

In contrast, certain practices (including blackmail; trespassing; eavesdropping; and stealing drawings, samples, or documents) are widely viewed as unethical and often are illegal. To protect themselves from digital fraud or theft by competitors that break into their employees' PCs, some companies buy insurance to protect against PC hacking.[121]

Some competitor intelligence practices may be legal, but a firm must decide whether they are also ethical, given the image it desires as a corporate citizen. Especially with electronic transmissions, the line between legal and ethical practices can be difficult to determine. For example, a firm may develop website addresses that are very similar to those of its competitors and thus occasionally receive e-mail transmissions that were intended for those competitors. According to legal experts, the legality of this "e-mail snagging" remains unclear.[122] Nonetheless, the practice is an example of the challenges companies face when deciding how to gather intelligence about competitors while simultaneously determining what to do to prevent competitors from learning too much about them.

In 2001, Procter & Gamble (P&G) notified Unilever that its own rules regarding gathering intelligence on competitors were violated when obtaining information on Unilever practices. P&G returned over 80 documents that were taken from Unilever's trash bins. The two firms then negotiated a potential settlement. Unilever wanted P&G to delay several of its planned new product launches, but P&G resisted. Moreover, both firms had to take special care in the negotiations not to violate antitrust laws, thereby spurring regulators to take action. Therefore, for several reasons, competitive intelligence must be handled with sensitivity.[123]

Open discussions of intelligence-gathering techniques can help a firm to ensure that people understand its convictions to follow ethical practices for gathering competitor intelligence. An appropriate guideline for competitor intelligence practices is to respect the principles of common morality and the right of competitors not to reveal certain information about their products, operations, and strategic intentions.[124]

Despite the importance of studying competitors, evidence suggests that only a relatively small percentage of firms use formal processes to collect and disseminate competitive intelligence. Beyond this, some firms forget to analyze competitors' future objectives as they try to understand their current strategies, assumptions, and capabilities, which will yield incomplete insights about those competitors.[125]

Summary

- The firm's external environment is challenging and complex. Because of the external environment's effect on performance, the firm must develop the skills required to identify opportunities and threats existing in that environment.

- The external environment has three major parts: (1) the general environment (elements in the broader society that affect industries and their firms), (2) the industry environment (factors that influence a firm, its competitive actions and responses, and the industry's profit potential), and (3) the competitor environment (in which the firm analyzes each major competitor's future objectives, current strategies, assumptions, and capabilities).

- The external environmental analysis process has four steps: scanning, monitoring, forecasting, and assessing. Through environmental analyses, the firm identifies opportunities and threats.

- The general environment has six segments: demographic, economic, political/legal, sociocultural, technological, and global. For each segment, the firm wants to determine the strategic relevance of environmental changes and trends.

- Compared to the general environment, the industry environment has a more direct effect on the firm's strategic actions. The five forces model of competition includes the threat of entry, the power of suppliers, the power of buyers, product substitutes, and the intensity of rivalry among competitors. By studying these forces, the firm finds a position in an industry where it can influence the forces in its favor or where it can buffer itself from the

power of the forces in order to increase its ability to earn above-average returns.

- Industries are populated with different strategic groups. A strategic group is a collection of firms that follow similar strategies along similar dimensions. Competitive rivalry is greater within a strategic group than it is between strategic groups.

- Competitor analysis informs the firm about the future objectives, current strategies, assumptions, and capabilities of the companies with whom it competes directly.

- Different techniques are used to create competitor intelligence: the set of data, information, and knowledge that allows the firm to better understand its competitors and thereby predict their likely strategic and tactical actions. Firms should use only legal and ethical practices to gather intelligence. The Internet enhances firms' capabilities to gather insights about competitors and their strategic intentions.

Review Questions

1. Why is it important for a firm to study and understand the external environment?

2. What are the differences between the general environment and the industry environment? Why are these differences important?

3. What is the external environmental analysis process? What does the firm want to learn when using this process?

4. What are the six segments of the general environment? Explain the differences among them.

5. How do the five forces of competition in an industry affect its profit potential? Explain.

6. What is a strategic group? Of what value is knowledge of the firm's strategic group in formulating that firm's strategy?

7. What is the importance of collecting and interpreting data and information about competitors? What practices should a firm use to gather competitor intelligence and why?

Experiential Exercises

Scanning the External Environment

For the company or industry of primary interest to you, scan the key segments of the external environment and identify two key trends in each segment that may present challenges to your firm in the future. Indicate whether each trend is an opportunity or a threat for your company, and briefly explain your reasoning. Which of the segments do you anticipate will have the most significant effect on your company of interest over the next five years, and why?

Five Forces Model

In order to develop your understanding of the structure of your industry of interest, conduct a brief analysis of the five forces of competition.

Rivalry of competing firms: Identify the key competitors in the industry and assess the intensity of rivalry. Briefly explain the basis of competition in the industry.

Threat of new entrants: Assess the threat of new entrants to the industry. Briefly explain the barriers to entry.

Bargaining power of suppliers: Identify key supplier groups and assess the strength of their relative bargaining power. Briefly explain the characteristics determining their power.

Bargaining power of buyers: Identify key buyer groups (from the channel of distribution to the end user) and assess the strength of their relative bargaining power. Briefly explain the characteristics determining their power.

Threat of substitute products: Identify goods or services that may serve as close substitutes for the output of the industry. Briefly explain the relative value (cost of inputs and product performance) a substitute may deliver to a buyer.

Notes

1. J. Song, 2002, Firm capabilities and technology ladders: Sequential foreign direct investments of Japanese electronics firms in East Asia, *Strategic Management Journal,* 23: 191–210; D. J. Ketchen, Jr., & T. B. Palmer, 1999, Strategic responses to poor organizational performance: A test of competing perspectives, *Journal of Management,* 25: 683–706; V. P. Rindova & C. J. Fombrun, 1999, Constructing competitive advantage: The role of firm-constituent interactions, *Strategic Management Journal,* 20: 691–710.

2. J. T. Eckhardt & S. A. Shane, 2003, Opportunities and entrepreneurship, *Journal of Management,* 29: 333–349; A. Ardichvili, R. Cardozo, & S. Ray, 2003, A theory of entrepreneurial opportunity identification and development, *Journal of Business Venturing,* 18: 105–123; P. Chattopadhyay, W. H. Glick, & G. P. Huber, 2001, Organizational actions in response to threats and opportunities, *Academy of Management Journal,* 44: 937–955.

3. J. R. Hough & M. A. White, 2003, Environmental dynamism and strategic decision-making rationality: An examination at the decision level, *Strategic Management Journal,* 24: 481–489; R. J. Herbold, 2002, Inside Microsoft: Balancing creativity and discipline, *Harvard Business Review,* 80(1): 73–79; C. M. Grimm & K. G. Smith, 1997, *Strategy as Action: Industry Rivalry and Coordination,* Cincinnati: South-Western; C. J. Fombrun, 1992, *Turning Point: Creating Strategic Change in Organizations,* New York: McGraw-Hill, 13.

4. J. M. Mezias, 2002, Identifying liabilities of foreignness and strategies to minimize their effects: The case of labor lawsuit judgments in the United States, *Strategic Management Journal,* 23: 229–244.

5. R. M. Kanter, 2002, Strategy as improvisational theater, *Sloan Management Review,* 43(2): 76–81; S. A. Zahra, A. P. Nielsen, & W. C. Bogner, 1999, Corporate entrepreneurship, knowledge, and competence development, *Entrepreneurship: Theory and Practice,* 23(3): 169–189.

6. R. M. Grant, 2003, Strategic planning in a turbulent environment: Evidence from the oil majors, *Strategic Management Journal,* 24: 491–517; M. A. Hitt, J. E. Ricart, I. Costa, & R. D. Nixon, 1998, The new frontier, in M. A. Hitt, J. E. Ricart, I. Costa, & R. D. Nixon (eds.), *Managing Strategically in an Interconnected World,* Chichester: John Wiley & Sons, 1.

7. S. A. Zahra & G. George, 2002, International entrepreneurship: The current status of the field and future research agenda, in M. A. Hitt, R. D. Ireland, S. M. Camp, & D. L. Sexton (eds.), *Strategic Entrepreneurship: Creating a New Mindset,* Oxford, UK: Blackwell Publishers, 255–288; W. C. Bogner & P. Bansal, 1998, Controlling unique knowledge development as the basis of sustained high performance, in M. A. Hitt, J. E. Ricart, I. Costa, & R. D. Nixon (eds.), *Managing Strategically in an Interconnected World,* Chichester: John Wiley & Sons, 167–184.

8. L. Fahey, 1999, *Competitors,* New York: John Wiley & Sons; B. A. Walters & R. L. Priem, 1999, Business strategy and CEO intelligence acquisition, *Competitive Intelligence Review,* 10(2): 15–22.

9. R. D. Ireland & M. A. Hitt, 1999, Achieving and maintaining strategic competitiveness in the 21st century: The role of strategic leadership, *Academy of Management Executive,* 13(1): 43–57; M. A. Hitt, B. W. Keats, & S. M. DeMarie, 1998, Navigating in the new competitive landscape: Building strategic flexibility and competitive advantage in the 21st century, *Academy of Management Executive,* 12(4): 22–42.

10. Q. Nguyen & H. Mintzberg, 2003, The rhythm of change, *MIT Sloan Management Review,* 44(4): 79–84; J. K. Sebenius, 2002, The hidden challenge of cross-border negotiations, *Harvard Business Review,* 80(3): 76–85.

11. R. Karlgaard, 1999, Digital rules: Technology and the new economy, *Forbes,* May 17, 43.

12. P. Uppaluru, 2001, The rebirth of telecommunications, *Web Voice Today,* http://www.telera.com, Winter.

13. V. Prior, 1999, The language of competitive intelligence: Part four, *Competitive Intelligence Review,* 10(1): 84–87.

14. T. Becker, 2003, Former Polaroid gets two-month extension of exclusivity, *Wall Street Journal Online,* http://www.wsj.com, March 5.

15. G. Young, 1999, "Strategic value analysis" for competitive advantage, *Competitive Intelligence Review,* 10(2): 52–64.

16. M. A. Hitt, R. D. Ireland, S. M. Camp, & D. L. Sexton, 2001, Strategic entrepreneurship: Entrepreneurial strategies for wealth creation, *Strategic Management Journal,* 22(Special Issue): 479–491.

17. L. Rosenkopf & A. Nerkar, 2001, Beyond local search: Boundary-spanning exploration, and impact in the optical disk industry, *Strategic Management Journal,* 22: 287–306.

18. D. F. Kuratko, R. D. Ireland, & J. S. Hornsby, 2001, Improving firm performance through entrepreneurial actions: Acordia's corporate entrepreneurship strategy, *Academy of Management Executive,* 15(4): 60–71; D. S. Elenkov, 1997, Strategic uncertainty and environmental scanning: The case for institutional influences on scanning behavior, *Strategic Management Journal,* 18: 287–302.

19. K. M. Eisenhardt, 2002, Has strategy changed? *Sloan Management Review,* 43(2): 88–91; I. Goll & A. M. A. Rasheed, 1997, Rational decision-making and firm performance: The moderating role of environment, *Strategic Management Journal,* 18: 583–591.

20. V. K. Garg, B. A. Walters, & R. L. Priem, 2003, Chief executive scanning emphases, environmental dynamism, and manufacturing firm performance, *Strategic Management Journal,* 24: 725–744; R. Aggarwal, 1999, Technology and globalization as mutual reinforcers in business: Reorienting strategic thinking for the new millennium, *Management International Review,* 39(2): 83–104.

21. R. Donkin, 1999, Too young to retire, *Financial Times,* July 2, 9.

22. B. Richards, 2001, Following the crumbs, *Wall Street Journal Online,* http://www.wsj.com, October 29.

23. Fahey, *Competitors,* 71–73.

24. P. Yip, 1999, The road to wealth, *Dallas Morning News,* August 2, D1, D3.

25. F. Dahlsten, 2003, Avoiding the customer satisfaction rut, *MIT Sloan Management Review,* 44(4): 73–77; Y. Luo & S. H. Park, 2001, Strategic alignment and performance of market-seeking MNCs in China, *Strategic Management Journal,* 22: 141–155.

26. K. Buysse & A. Verbke, 2003, Proactive strategies: A stakeholder management perspective, *Strategic Management Journal,* 24: 453–470; I. M. Jawahar & G. L. McLaughlin, 2001, Toward a prescriptive stakeholder theory: An organizational life cycle approach, *Academy of Management Review,* 26: 397–414.

27. M. Song & M. M. Montoya-Weiss, 2001, The effect of perceived technological uncertainty on Japanese new product development, *Academy of Management Journal,* 44: 61–80.

28. M. H. Zack, 2003, Rethinking the knowledge-based organization, *MIT Sloan Management Review,* 44(4): 67–71; H. Yli-Renko, E. Autio, & H. J. Sapienza, 2001, Social capital, knowledge acquisition, and knowledge exploitation in young technologically based firms, *Strategic Management Journal,* 22 (Special Issue): 587–613.

29. Fahey, *Competitors*.

30. Fahey, *Competitors*, 75–77.

31. J. Baily, 2003, In fast food, being bigger doesn't ensure your success, *Wall Street Journal Online*, http://www.wsj.com, March 18.

32. L. Fahey & V. K. Narayanan, 1986, *Macroenvironmental Analysis for Strategic Management*, St. Paul, MN: West Publishing Company, 58.

33. 2003, United Nations Populations Division, World Population Prospects, http://www.esa.un.org; D. Fishburn, 1999, *The World in 1999*, *The Economist* Publications, 9; 1999, Six billion . . . and counting, *Time*, October 4, 16.

34. 2002, *The World Factbook*, http://www.bartleby.com.

35. R. Poe & C. L. Courter, 1999, The next baby boom, *Across the Board*, May, 1; 1999, Trends and forecasts for the next 25 years, Bethesda, Maryland: World Future Society, 3.

36. 2001, Millennium in motion: Global trends shaping the health sciences industry, Ernst & Young, http://www.ey.com/industry/health, June.

37. M. Peterson & M. Freudenheim, 2001, Drug giant to introduce discount drug plan for the elderly, *New York Times*, http://www.nytimes.com, October 3.

38. D. Stipp, 1999, Hell no, we won't go! *Fortune*, July 19, 102–108; G. Colvin, 1997, How to beat the boomer rush, *Fortune*, August 18, 59–63.

39. J. MacIntyre, 1999, Figuratively speaking, *Across the Board*, November/December, 15.

40. Colvin, How to beat the boomer rush, 60.

41. 2001, Millennium in motion; 1999, U.S. Department of Labor, Demographic change and the future workforce, *Futurework*, http://www.dol.gov, November 8.

42. P. R. Drucker, 2002, They're not employees, they're people, *Harvard Business Review*, 80(2): 70–77.

43. D. M. Schweiger, T. Atamer, & R. Calori, 2003, Transnational project teams and networks: Making the multinational organization more effective, *Journal of World Business*, 38: 127–140; G. Dessler, 1999, How to earn your employees' commitment, *Academy of Management Executive*, 13(2): 58–67; S. Finkelstein & D. C. Hambrick, 1996, *Strategic Leadership: Top Executives and Their Effect on Organizations*, Minneapolis, MN: West Publishing Company.

44. L. H. Pelled, K. M. Eisenhardt, & K. R. Xin, 1999, Exploring the black box: An analysis of work group diversity, conflict, and performance, *Administrative Science Quarterly*, 44: 1–28.

45. 2001, Millennium in motion; E. S. Rubenstein, 1999, Inequality, *Forbes*, November 1, 158–160.

46. Fahey & Narayanan, *Macroenvironmental Analysis*, 105.

47. G. Ip, 2003, Federal Reserve maintains interest-rate target at 1%, *Wall Street Journal Online*, http://www.wsj.com, August 13.

48. 2001, Millennium in motion.

49. J. L. Hilsenrath, 2001, Shock waves keep spreading, changing the outlook for cars, hotels—even for cola, *Wall Street Journal Online*, http://www.wsj.com, October 9.

50. G. Keim, 2001, Business and public policy: Competing in the political marketplace, in M. A. Hitt, R. E. Freeman, and J. S. Harrison (eds.), *Handbook of Strategic Management*, Oxford, UK: Blackwell Publishers, 583–601.

51. J. O. De Castro & K. Uhlenbruck, 2003, The transformation into entrepreneurial firms, *Management Research*, 1: 171–184.

52. M. D. Lord, 2003, Constituency building as the foundation for corporate political strategy, *Academy of Management Executive*, 17(1): 112–124; D. A. Schuler, K. Rehbein, & R. D. Cramer, 2003, Pursuing strategic advantage through political means: A multivariate approach, *Academy of Management Journal*, 45: 659–672; A. J. Hillman & M. A. Hitt, 1999, Corporate political strategy formulation: A model of approach, participation, and strategy decisions, *Academy of Management Review*, 24: 825–842.

53. M. Carson, 1998, *Global Competitiveness Quarterly*, March 9, 1.

54. 2001, Millennium in motion.

55. M. Peterson, 2003, Who's minding the drugstore? *New York Times*, http://www.nytimes.com, June 29.

56. 2003, U.S. spends the most on healthcare but dollars do not equal health, MEDICA Portal, http://www4.medica.de; J. MacIntyre, 1999, Figuratively speaking, *Across the Board*, May 11.

57. A. R. Varey & G. Lynn, 1999, Americans save for retirement, *USA Today*, November 16, B1.

58. G. F. Will, 1999, The primacy of culture, *Newsweek*, January 18, 64.

59. J. Kronholz, R. Tomsho, D. Golden, & R. S. Greenberger, 2003, Court upholds affirmative action, *Wall Street Journal Online*, http://www.wsj.com, June 24.

60. 2003, U.S. Department of Labor, Bureau of Labor Statistics data, http://www.bls.gov, June.

61. J. Raymond, 2001, Defining women: Does the Census Bureau undercount female entrepreneurs? *Business Week Small Biz*, May 21, 12.

62. C. A. Bartlett & S. Ghoshal, 2002, Building competitive advantage through people, *MIT Sloan Management Review*, 43(2): 33–41.

63. T. Fleming, 2003, Benefits of taking the superhighway to work, *Canadian HR Reporter*, 16(11): G7.

64. C. W. L. Hill & F. T. Rothaermel, 2003, The performance of incumbent firms in the face of radical technological innovation, *Academy of Management Review*, 28: 257–274; A. Afuah, 2002, Mapping technological capabilities into product markets and competitive advantage: The case of cholesterol drugs, *Strategic Management Journal*, 23: 171–179.

65. T. Aeppel, 2002, In lights-out factories machines still make things even when no one is there, *Wall Street Journal Online*, http://www.wsj.com, November 19.

66. J. Baglole, 2003, Canada's southern drug drain, *Wall Street Journal Online*, http://www.wsj.com, March 31.

67. N. Wingfield, 2003, Anytime, anywhere: The number of Wi-Fi spots is set to explode, bringing the wireless technology to the rest of us, *Wall Street Journal*, March 31, R6, R12.

68. A. Andal-Ancion, P. A. Cartwright, & G. S. Yip, 2003, The digital transformation of traditional businesses, *MIT Sloan Management Review* 44(4): 34–41; M. A. Hitt, R. D. Ireland, & H. Lee, 2000, Technological learning, knowledge management, firm growth and performance, *Journal of Technology and Engineering Management*, 17: 231–246.

69. R. Adner, 2002, When are technologies disruptive? A demand-based view of the emergence of competition, *Strategic Management Journal*, 23: 667–688; R. Adner & D. A. Levinthal, 2002, The emergence of emerging technologies, *California Management Review*, 45(1): 50–66.

70. C. Nichols-Nixon & C. Y. Woo, 2003, Technology sourcing and output of established firms in a regime of encompassing technological change, *Strategic Management Journal*, 24: 651–666.

71. W. P. Wan & R. E. Hoskisson, 2003, Home country environments, corporate diversification strategies and firm performance, *Academy of Management Journal*, 46: 27–45; S. Zahra, R. D. Ireland, I. Gutierrez, & M. A. Hitt, 2000, Privatization and entrepreneurial transformation: Emerging issues and a future research agenda, *Academy of Management Review*, 25: 509–524.

72. F. Vermeulen & H. Barkema, 2002, Pace, rhythm, and scope: Process dependence in building a multinational corporation, *Strategic Management Journal*, 23: 637–653.

73. L. Tihanyi, R. A. Johnson, R. E. Hoskisson, & M. A. Hitt, 2003, Institutional ownership differences, and international diversification: The effects of boards of directors and technological opportunity, *Academy of Management Journal*, 46: 195–211.

74. S. M. Lee, 2003, South Korea: From the land of morning calm to ICT hotbed, *Academy of Management Executive*, 17(2): 7–18; A. K. Gupta, V. Govindarajan, & A. Malhotra, 1999, Feedback-seeking behavior within multinational corporations, *Strategic Management Journal*, 20: 205–222.

75. G. D. Bruton & D. Ahlstrom, 2002, An institutional view of China's venture capital industry: Explaining the differences between China and the West, *Journal of Business Venturing*, 18: 233–259.

76. 2003, Sales of office and commercial buildings soaring in Shenzhen, *SinoCast China Business Daily News*, August 7, D1.

77. P. Engardio, A. Bernstein, & M. Kripalani, 2003, Is your job next? *Business Week*, February 3, 50–60.

78. R. D. Ireland, M. A. Hitt, S. M. Camp, & D. L. Sexton, 2001, Integrating entrepreneurship and strategic management actions to create firm wealth, *Academy of Management Executive*, 15(1): 49–63.

79. J. W. Lu & P. W. Beamish, 2001, The internationalization and performance of SMEs, *Strategic Management Journal*, 22(Special Issue): 565–586.

80. M. Subramaniam & N. Venkataraman, 2001, Determinants of transnational new product development capability: Testing the influence of transferring and deploying tacit overseas knowledge, *Strategic Management Journal*, 22: 359–378; P. J. Lane, J. E. Salk, & M. A. Lyles, 2001, Absorptive capacity, learning and performance in international joint ventures, *Strategic Management Journal*, 22: 1139–1161.

81. G. D. Bruton, D. Ahlstrom, & J. C. Wan, 2003, Turnaround in East Asian firms: Evidence from ethnic overseas Chinese communities, *Strategic Management Journal*, 24: 519–540; S. H. Park & Y. Luo, 2001, Guanxi and organizational

dynamics: Organizational networking in Chinese firms, *Strategic Management Journal*, 22: 455–477; M. A. Hitt M. T. Dacin, B. B. Tyler, & D. Park, 1997, Understanding the differences in Korean and U.S. executives' strategic orientations, *Strategic Management Journal*, 18: 159–167.

82. M. A. Hitt, D. Ahlstrom, M. T. Dacin, E. Levitas, and L. Svobodina, 2004, The institutional effects on strategic alliance partner selection: China versus Russia, *Organization Science*, in press.

83. Park & Luo, Guanxi and organizational dynamics.

84. M. A. Hitt, H. Lee, & E. Yucel, 2002, The importance of social capital to the management of multinational enterprises: Relational capital among Asian and Western firms, *Asia Pacific Journal of Management*, 19: 353–372.

85. 2003, Global Crossing's restructuring process, http://www.globalcrossing .com, June; 2002, Global Crossing denies resemblance to Enron, *Richmond Times Dispatch*, March 22, B15; S. Romero, 2001, Global Crossing looks overseas for financing, *New York Times*, http://www.nytimes.com, December 20; T. Burt, 2001, DaimlerChrysler in talks with Kuwaiti investors, *Financial Times*, http://www.ft.com, February 11.

86. 2002, Devaluation's downbeat start, *The Economist*, http://www.economist. com, January 10; J. Fuerbringer & R. W. Stevenson, 2001, No bailout is planned for Argentina, *New York Times*, http://www.nytimes.com, July 14; K. L. Newman, 2000, Organizational transformation during institutional upheaval, *Academy of Management Review*, 25: 602–619.

87. C. A. Bartlett & S. Ghoshal, 2003, What is a global manager? *Harvard Business Review*, 81(8): 101–108; M. A. Carpenter & J. W. Fredrickson, 2001, Top management teams, global strategic posture and the moderating role of uncertainty, *Academy of Management Journal*, 44: 533–545.

88. N. Argyres & A. M. McGahan, 2002, An interview with Michael Porter, *Academy of Management Executive*, 16(2): 43–52; Y. E. Spanos & S. Lioukas, 2001, An examination into the causal logic of rent generation: Contrasting Porter's competitive strategy framework and the resource-based perspective, *Strategic Management Journal*, 22: 907–934.

89. G. Hawawini, V. Subramanian, & P. Verdin, 2003, Is performance driven by industry or firm-specific factors? A new look at the evidence, *Strategic Management Journal*, 24: 1–16.

90. S. Zaheer & A. Zaheer, 2001, Market microstructure in a global b2b network, *Strategic Management Journal*, 22: 859–873.

91. Hitt, Ricart, Costa, & Nixon, The new frontier.

92. C. Garcia-Pont & N. Nohria, 2002, Local versus global mimetism: The dynamics of alliance formation in the automobile industry, *Strategic Management Journal*, 23: 307–321; Y. Pan & P. S. K. Chi, 1999, Financial performance and survival of multinational corporations in China, *Strategic Management Journal*, 20: 359–374.

93. P. A. Geroski, 1999, Early warning of new rivals, *Sloan Management Review*, 40(3): 107–116.

94. J. Shamsie, 2003, The context of dominance: An industry-driven framework for exploiting reputation, *Strategic Management Journal*, 24: 199–215; K. C. Robinson & P. P. McDougall, 2001, Entry barriers and new venture performance: A comparison of universal and contingency approaches, *Strategic Management Journal*, 22(Special Issue): 659–685.

95. R. Makadok, 1999, Interfirm differences in scale economies and the evolution of market shares, *Strategic Management Journal*, 20: 935–952.

96. F. Keenan, S. Holmes, J. Greene, & R. O. Crockett, 2002, A mass market of one, *Business Week*, December 2, 68–72; R. Wise & P. Baumgartner, 1999, Go downstream: The new profit imperative in manufacturing, *Harvard Business Review*, 77(5): 133–141.

97. G. Walker, T. L. Madsen, & G. Carini, 2002, How does institutional change affect heterogeneity among firms? *Strategic Management Journal*, 23: 89–104.

98. 2002, The long shadow of big blue, *The Economist*, November 9, 63–64.

99. D. Michaels & J. L. Lunsford, 2003, Airbus clings to output gains, *Wall Street Journal*, January 14, B4.

100. G. Khermouch, 2001, Grown-up drinks for tender taste buds, *Business Week*, March 5, 96.

101. A. M. Knott, 2003, Persistent heterogeneity and sustainable innovation, *Strategic Management Journal*, 24: 687–705; T. Noda & D. J. Collies, 2001, The evolution of intraindustry firm heterogeneity: Insights from a process study, *Academy of Management Journal*, 44: 897–925.

102. C. Matlack & S. Holmes, 2002, Look out, Boeing: Airbus is grabbing market share, but can it make money this way? *Business Week*, October 28, 50–51.

103. D. M. De Carolis, 2003, Competencies and imitability in the pharmaceutical industry: An analysis of their relationship with firm performance, *Journal of Management*, 29: 27–50; D. L. Deephouse, 1999, To be different, or to be the same? It's a question (and theory) of strategic balance, *Strategic Management Journal*, 20: 147–166.

104. W. Chung & A. Kalnins, 2001, Agglomeration effects and performance: Test of the Texas lodging industry, *Strategic Management Journal*, 22: 969–988.

105. W. Kuemmerle, 2001, Home base and knowledge management in international ventures, *Journal of Business Venturing*, 17: 99–122; G. Lorenzoni & A. Lipparini, 1999, The leveraging of interfirm relationships as a distinctive organizational capability: A longitudinal study, *Strategic Management Journal*, 20: 317–338.

106. M. E. Porter, 1980, *Competitive Strategy*, New York: Free Press.

107. M. S. Hunt, 1972, Competition in the major home appliance industry, 1960–1970 (doctoral dissertation, Harvard University); Porter, *Competitive Strategy*, 129.

108. G. McNamara, D. L. Deephouse, & R. A. Luce, 2003, Competitive positioning within and across a strategic group structure: The performance of core, secondary, and solitary firms, *Strategic Management Journal*, 24: 161–181.

109. H. R. Greve, 1999, Managerial cognition and the mimetic adoption of market positions: What you see is what you do, *Strategic Management Journal*, 19: 967–988.

110. R. K. Reger & A. S. Huff, 1993, Strategic groups: A cognitive perspective, *Strategic Management Journal*, 14: 103–123.

111. M. Peteraf & M. Shanley, 1997, Getting to know you: A theory of strategic group identity, *Strategic Management Journal*, 18 (Special Issue): 165–186.

112. J. Lee, K. Lee, & S. Rho, 2002, An evolutionary perspective on strategic group emergence: A genetic algorithm-based model, *Strategic Management Journal*, 23: 727–746.

113. J. D. Osborne, C. I. Stubbart, & A. Ramaprasad, 2001, Strategic groups and competitive enactment: A study of dynamic relationships between mental models and performance, *Strategic Management Journal*, 22: 435–454.

114. Greve, Managerial cognition, 972–973.

115. M. A. Hitt, R. E. Hoskisson, R. A. Johnson, & D. D. Moesel, 1996, The market for corporate control and firm innovation, *Academy of Management Journal*, 39: 1084–1119.

116. Porter, *Competitive Strategy*, 49.

117. G. McNamara, R. A. Luce, & G. H. Tompson, 2002, Examining the effect of complexity in strategic group knowledge structures on firm performance, *Strategic Management Journal*, 23: 153–170.

118. P. M. Norman, R. D. Ireland, K. W. Artz, & M. A. Hitt, 2000, Acquiring and using competitive intelligence in entrepreneurial teams. Paper presented at the Academy of Management, Toronto, Canada.

119. C. S. Fleisher, 1999, Public policy competitive intelligence, *Competitive Intelligence Review*, 10(2): 24.

120. 2003, Factiva: Strategic steps to web content and solutions, http://www. factiva.com, June 20; 2001, Fuld & Co., CEO interview: Clare Hart, president and CEO, Factiva, http://www.dowjones.com, April 4.

121. V. Drucker, 1999, Is your computer a sitting duck during a deal? *Mergers & Acquisitions*, July/August, 25–28.

122. M. Moss, 1999, Inside the game of e-mail hijacking, *Wall Street Journal*, November 9, B1, B4.

123. A. Jones, 2001, P&G to seek new resolution of spy dispute, *Financial Times*, http://www.ft.com, September 4.

124. J. H. Hallaq & K. Steinhorst, 1994, Business intelligence methods: How ethical? *Journal of Business Ethics*, 13: 787–794.

125. L. Fahey, 1999, Competitor scenarios: Projecting a rival's marketplace strategy, *Competitive Intelligence Review*, 10(2): 65–85.

The Internal Environment: Resources, Capabilities, and Core Competencies

Knowledge Objectives

Studying this chapter should provide you with the strategic management knowledge needed to:

1. Explain the need for firms to study and understand their internal environment.

2. Define value and discuss its importance.

3. Describe the differences between tangible and intangible resources.

4. Define capabilities and discuss how they are developed.

5. Describe four criteria used to determine whether resources and capabilities are core competencies.

6. Explain how value chain analysis is used to identify and evaluate resources and capabilities.

7. Define outsourcing and discuss the reasons for its use.

8. Discuss the importance of preventing core competencies from becoming core rigidities.

©Tom Wagner/CORBIS SABA

Caterpillar carefully assesses its internal environment and supports its strengths by continuously investing in its resources. The company spends $4 million per day to maintain its competitive advantage through technology. It is also quick to help its worldwide dealers with whatever they need to run their businesses efficiently. Finally, Caterpillar is service oriented, utilizing 6 Sigma to change its distribution as new customer needs emerge.

Technology and Dealer Service: Caterpillar's Sources of Competitive Advantage

A *Fortune* 500 company, Caterpillar (Cat) is a manufacturer of construction and mining equipment, diesel and natural gas engines, and industrial gas turbines, and is a provider of an array of financial products. It is a technology leader in most of its manufacturing areas. The firm wants to increase its total revenue to $30 billion by 2010 while increasing its return to shareholders. A substantial commitment to participating in the development of emerging economies such as China is expected to contribute to achievement of these goals. In recent times, Cat was recognized by *Fortune* as the most admired company in the industrial and farm equipment industry, while *Forbes* named the firm to its Platinum 400 list of the best big U.S. companies.

Cat's strategic intent is to be the global leader in creating customer value. More diversified than it was ten years ago, Cat is no longer just a "tractor" company. Deriving approximately 49 percent of its sales revenue from outside the United States, Cat's distinctive yellow machines are in service in almost every country in the world. The firm's products and services are grouped into three primary business units—machinery (59 percent of revenues), engines (33 percent of revenues), and financial products (8 percent of revenues). The engines business unit derives 90 percent of its revenue from third-party customers such as Paccar Inc., manufacturer of the well-known Kenworth and Peterbilt brand tractors and trailers. As a primary area of growth, Cat expects the engines unit to account for as much as 45 percent of total revenue by 2007. According to company documents, Cat's machines are used to build the world's infrastructure, its reciprocating engines and engine systems provide power to the world, and its financial products make it possible for Cat customers around the world to buy new and used Cat machines and engines and related equipment.

Technology is one of Cat's primary competitive advantages. Cat invests approximately $4 million daily in technology. These investments are part of the firm's total allocation of over $700 million annually to research and development. Several achievements, including the fact that its employees earned over 2,800 patents in a recent six-year period, indicate that technology is a competitive advantage for Cat. Approval from the U.S. Environmental Protection Agency for its heavy-duty truck diesel engine using the firm's advanced combustion emission reduction technology, or Acert, also denotes Cat's technology competitive advantage. Cat officials indicate that Acert, developed in 2003, is a stepping-stone for the firm to meet particulate-matter standards that go into effect in 2007. In concert with a partner, Cat also recently developed a new type of stainless steel. To be used in diesel engines, this raw material permits greater engine efficiencies and fewer emissions.

A global network of independent dealers is Cat's second primary competitive advantage. In speaking to its service competence, Cat claims that its "global dealer network provides a key competitive edge—customers deal with people they know and trust." A large number of Cat's dealers have been associated with the company for decades, and many of them have relationships with their customers that span at least two generations. Regardless of customers' locations across the globe, Cat dealers support them with the machines, parts, and expertise that are required to effectively and efficiently operate their businesses.

Because service is a competitive advantage, Cat is committed to continuous improvements in order to meet the ever-changing needs of its customers. The firm is using 6 Sigma (a fact-based, data-driven discipline that focuses on maximizing customer value) to reengineer its distribution channels. This is being accomplished by focusing on processes that are common between the firm and its dealers, including e-business capabilities, customer relationship management, market segment focus, and parts and products sales opportunities.

SOURCES: 2003, Caterpillar Home Page, http://www.cat.com, July 6; 2003, Caterpillar Inc., *Standard & Poor's Stock Reports*, http://www.standardandpoors.com, July 3; J. B. Arndorfer, 2003, Cat is set to dig deeper in China, *Crain's Chicago Business*, 26(26): 4–5; J. Eig, 2003, Caterpillar's net nearly doubles amid signs of rebound in sales, *Wall Street Journal Online*, http://www.wsj.com, July 18; D. Jones, 2003, Oak Ridge, Caterpillar fashion new type of stainless steel for advanced engines, *Inside Energy*, July 7, 14–16; J. Wislocki, 2003, Caterpillar wins EPA approval for Acert heavy-duty engines, *Transport Topics*, June 16, 5.

As discussed in the first two chapters, several factors in the global economy, including the rapid development of the Internet's capabilities,[1] have made it increasingly difficult for firms to develop a competitive advantage that can be sustained for any period of time.[2] In these instances, firms try to create advantages that can be sustained longer than can others. The probability of developing a sustainable competitive advantage increases when firms use their own unique resources, capabilities, and core competencies to implement their strategies.[3] As described in the Opening Case, Caterpillar has been able to establish sustainable competitive advantages in terms of technology and dealer service. Because of their importance, Cat devotes substantial resources to support, nurture, and continuously develop these advantages.

The fact that competitive advantages and the differences in performances among firms they create continue to provide the central agenda in strategy research highlights the importance of studying competitive advantage and firm performance.[4] Research about competitive advantage is critical because "resources are the foundation for strategy and unique bundles of resources generate competitive advantages leading to wealth creation."[5] To identify and successfully use their competitive advantages over time, firms think constantly about their strategic management process and how to increase the value it creates.[6] As this chapter's discussion indicates, firms achieve strategic competitiveness and earn above-average returns when their unique core competencies are effectively acquired, bundled, and leveraged to take advantage of opportunities in the external environment.[7]

Increasingly, people are a key source of competitive advantage as organizations compete in the global economy.[8] This is true at Enterprise Rent-A-Car. Established in 1957, the firm has over 50,000 employees with 5,000-plus offices in the United States, Germany, the United Kingdom, Canada, and Ireland. When asked about his firm's ability to continue expanding, CEO Andy Taylor said that if he "had to choose one critical success factor in [the firm's] move into new markets, [he] would point to motivated, pioneering employees who have been excited about taking on a new challenge and making the business work." Taylor believes his firm succeeds because of the intellectual capital and efforts of individuals who thrive on being in charge and dream of becoming effective entrepreneurs.[9]

CEO Andy Taylor attributes Enterprise Rent-A-Car's success to employees' efforts and the intellectual capital they represent.

Over time, the benefits of any firm's value-creating strategy can be duplicated by its competitors. In other words, all competitive advantages have a limited life.[10] The question of duplication is not *if* it will happen, but *when*. In general, the sustainability of a competitive advantage is a function of three factors: (1) the rate of core competence obsolescence because of environmental changes, (2) the availability of substitutes for the core competence, and (3) the imitability of the core competence.[11]

The challenge in all firms is to effectively manage current core competencies while simultaneously developing new ones.[12] In the words of Michael Dell, CEO of Dell Inc., "No [competitive] advantage and no success is ever permanent. The winners are those who keep moving. The only constant in our business is that everything is changing. We have to be ahead of the game."[13] Only when firms develop a continuous stream of competitive advantages do they achieve strategic competitiveness, earn above-average returns, and remain ahead of competitors (see Chapter 5).

In Chapter 2, we examined general, industry, and competitor environments. Armed with this knowledge about the realities and conditions of their environments, firms have a better understanding of marketplace opportunities and the characteristics of the competitive environment in which they exist. In this chapter, we focus on the firm itself. By analyzing its internal environment, a firm determines what it *can do*— that is, the actions permitted by its unique resources, capabilities, and core competencies. As discussed in Chapter 1, core competencies are a firm's source of competitive advantage. The magnitude of that competitive advantage is a function primarily of the uniqueness of the firm's core competencies compared to those of its competitors.[14] Matching what a firm *can do* with what it *might do* (a function of opportunities and threats in the external environment) allows the firm to develop strategic intent, pursue its strategic mission, and select and implement its strategies. Outcomes resulting from internal and external environmental analyses are shown in Figure 3.1.

We begin this chapter with a discussion of the nature of an analysis of the firm's internal environment. We then discuss the roles of resources and capabilities in developing core competencies, which are the firm's competitive advantages. Included in this discussion are the techniques firms can use to identify and evaluate resources and capabilities and the criteria for selecting core competencies from among them. Resources and capabilities are not inherently valuable, but they create value when the firm can use them to perform certain activities that result in a competitive advantage. Accordingly, we also discuss in this chapter the value chain concept and examine four criteria to evaluate core competencies that establish competitive advantage.[15] The chapter closes with cautionary comments about the need for firms to prevent their core competencies from becoming core rigidities. The existence of core rigidities indicates that the firm is too anchored to its past, which prevents it from continuously developing new competitive advantages.

Figure 3.1 —— Outcomes from External and Internal Environmental Analyses

By studying the external environment, firms determine	By studying the internal environment, firms determine
• what they *might* choose to *do*	• what they *can do*

The Nature of Internal Environmental Analysis

The Context of Internal Analysis

In the global economy, traditional factors—such as labor costs, access to financial resources and raw materials, and protected or regulated markets—continue to be sources of competitive advantage, but to a lesser degree.[16] One important reason for this decline is that the advantages created by these more traditional sources can be overcome through an international strategy (discussed in Chapter 8) and by the relatively free flow of resources throughout the global economy. The need to identify additional and perhaps new sources of competitive advantage highlights the importance of looking inside the firm to carefully study its resources and capabilities.

Few firms can consistently make effective strategic decisions about how to use their resources and capabilities unless they can change. A key challenge to developing the ability to change is fostering an organizational setting in which experimentation and learning are expected and promoted in order to determine what the firm *can do* (see Figure 3.1).[17] For example, Levi Strauss previously refused to sell its jeans through Wal-Mart, believing that doing so would tarnish the value of its brand. However, "desperate" to reverse declines in the sales of its jeans, the firm began selling a new line (Levi Strauss Signature) through Wal-Mart's stores in mid-2003. The 43 percent decline in sales revenue Levi Strauss experienced between 1996 and 2002 influenced the firm's willingness to reevaluate how it was using its resources and capabilities to compete in what had become a vastly changed competitive environment for the firm.[18]

In addition to an ability to change how a firm competes, exemplified by the decision made by Levi Strauss to sell jeans through Wal-Mart, a different managerial mind-set is required for firms to effectively analyze their internal environment. Increasingly, those analyzing their firm's internal environment should use a global mind-set. A global mind-set is the ability to study an internal environment in ways that are not dependent on the assumptions of a single country, culture, or context.[19] Those with a global mind-set recognize that their firms must possess resources and capabilities that allow them to understand and appropriately respond to competitive situations that are influenced by country-specific factors as well as by unique societal cultures.

Finally, analysis of the firm's internal environment finds evaluators thinking of their firm as a *bundle* of heterogeneous resources and capabilities that can be used to create

Levi Strauss created a new product line, Levi Strauss' Signature Jeans, that is sold through a new distribution channel, Wal-Mart stores.

©David Young-Wolff/PhotoEdit

an exclusive market position.[20] This perspective suggests that individual firms possess at least some resources and capabilities that other companies do not—at least not in the same combination. Resources are the source of capabilities, some of which lead to the development of a firm's core competencies or its competitive advantages.[21] Understanding how to *leverage* the firm's unique bundle of resources and capabilities is a key outcome decision makers seek when analyzing the internal environment. Figure 3.2 illustrates the relationships among resources, capabilities, and core competencies and shows how firms use them to create strategic competitiveness. Before examining these topics in depth, we describe value and how firms use their resources, capabilities, and core competencies to create it.

Creating Value

By exploiting their core competencies or competitive advantages to at least meet if not exceed the demanding standards of global competition, firms create value for customers.[22] **Value** is measured by a product's performance characteristics and by its attributes for which customers are willing to pay.[23] Evidence suggests that increasingly, customers perceive higher value in global rather than domestic-only brands.[24] Firms create value by innovatively bundling and leveraging their resources and capabilities.[25] Firms unable to creatively bundle and leverage their resources and capabilities in ways that create value for customers suffer performance declines. In the Strategic Focus, we examine venerable Sears, Roebuck and Co. For some years now, the giant retailer has struggled in its efforts to use its resources and capabilities to create customer value. As we explain, Sears is taking multiple actions to correct this situation and to offer more value to a larger number of customers.

Value is measured by a product's performance characteristics and by its attributes for which customers are willing to pay.

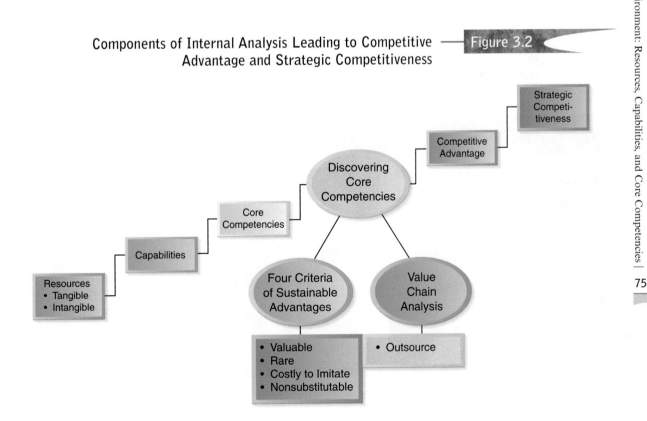

Components of Internal Analysis Leading to Competitive Advantage and Strategic Competitiveness

Figure 3.2

Sears, Roebuck and Co.: Still Where America Shops?

Sears, Roebuck and Co. is a leading retailer of appliances and home and automotive products as well as related services, such as product repairs through maintenance contracts and the installation and repair of all major brands of home products. But for some time, the firm hasn't been consistent in how it seeks to create value for customers. Over the last two decades, Sears has vacillated from soft goods to hard goods while entering and exiting a number of different businesses. Even today, some believe that "Sears is still trying to figure out what it wants to be." Others believe that "the long-term outlook for Sears as a merchandising company is very difficult" and that Sears is "still trying to figure out what its customers . . . want." Given these conditions, what is Sears trying to do to create value for customers, and how is it positioning itself to improve its ability to compete against firms such as Wal-Mart and Target?

Critical to Sears' efforts to create more customer value is the decision to refocus its operations. In mid-2003, Sears sold its credit card operation to Citigroup for approximately $3 billion. This was the last major divestiture of Sears' assets that were unrelated to its core retailing and service operations. As Sears' CEO said, selling its credit card operations was a "logical progression in [the firm's] ongoing strategy of focusing on growing [its] core retail and related-services businesses."

Appliances are a core retail and service area for Sears. To increase customer value in this product category, the firm is offering a larger number of items in the lowest-price-level categories. Sears is doing this to match competitors' (such as Lowe's and Home Depot) prices for lower-priced appliances. Sears is also increasing the size of its appliance departments and is emphasizing that it sells the top five appliance brands in addition to its own Kenmore line. To assist in improving its clothing merchandise, Sears acquired specialty-retailer Lands' End. It also jettisoned underperforming clothing lines, launching its own private labels such as Covington and introducing women's clothing by Lucy Pereda, who has been dubbed "the Hispanic Martha Stewart." Pereda hosts a popular show on Galavisión as well as a radio program on Radio Unica that concentrates on decorating and cooking. According to company officials, the relationship with Pereda was established because "Hispanics are a very fast-growing segment of the population and a very strong asset with Sears." To offer more convenience to customers, Sears is establishing stand-alone concept stores called Sears Grand. Located outside large regional malls, long the traditional location for Sears' stores, these new units are intended to help the firm sell a wider selection of merchandise and allow customers to quickly enter the store, buy merchandise, and be on their way in less time than is required to shop in Sears' mall locations.

Sears is attempting to increase its profitability by creating value for its customers. One means of doing this is marketing to the growing Hispanic community through products such as Lucy Pereda's women's clothing.

©Myrleen Ferguson Cate/PhotoEdit

SOURCES: D. Alexander, 2003, Online retailers discover value in reaching Hispanic audience, *Knight Ridder Tribune Business News,* http://www.knightridder.com, June 18; J. Bailey, 2003, For a big score, think small towns, *Wall Street Journal Online,* http://www.wsj.com, July 15; R. Crain, 2003, Recalling 25 years of "CCB" turns up reminder for Sears, *Advertising Age,* 74(24): 16; T. Kern, 2003, Sears under siege, *Home Channel News,* 29(12): 1, 56–57; M. Pacelle, R. Sidel, & A. Merrick, 2003, Citigroup agrees to buy Sears's credit-card unit, *Wall Street Journal Online,* http://www.wsj.com, July 16; L. Yue, 2003, Sears reshapes apparel division, makes stronger play for minority shoppers, *Knight Ridder Tribune Business News,* http://www.knightridder.com, June 19.

Ultimately, value creating is the source of a firm's potential to earn above-average returns. What the firm intends regarding value creation affects its choice of business-level strategy (see Chapter 4) and its organizational structure (see Chapter 11).[26] In Chapter 4's discussion of business-level strategies, we note that value is created by a product's low cost, by its highly differentiated features, or by a combination of low cost and high differentiation, compared to competitors' offerings. A business-level strategy is effective only when its use is grounded in exploiting the firm's current core competencies while actions are being taken to develop the core competencies that will be needed to effectively use "tomorrow's" business-level strategy. Thus, successful firms continuously examine the effectiveness of current and future core competencies.[27]

During the last several decades, the strategic management process was concerned largely with understanding the characteristics of the industry in which the firm competed and, in light of those characteristics, determining how the firm should position itself relative to competitors. This emphasis on industry characteristics and competitive strategy may have underestimated the role of the firm's resources and capabilities in developing competitive advantage. In fact, core competencies, in combination with product-market positions, are the firm's most important sources of competitive advantage.[28] The core competencies of a firm, in addition to its analysis of its general, industry, and competitor environments, should drive its selection of strategies. As Clayton Christensen noted, "Successful strategists need to cultivate a deep understanding of the processes of competition and progress and of the factors that undergird each advantage. Only thus will they be able to see when old advantages are poised to disappear and how new advantages can be built in their stead."[29] By emphasizing core competencies when formulating strategies, companies learn to compete primarily on the basis of firm-specific differences, but they must be very aware of how things are changing in the external environment as well.

The Challenge of Internal Analysis

The strategic decisions managers make in terms of the firm's resources, capabilities, and core competencies are nonroutine,[30] have ethical implications,[31] and significantly influence the firm's ability to earn above-average returns.[32] Making these decisions—identifying, developing, deploying, and protecting resources, capabilities, and core competencies—may appear to be relatively easy. In fact, however, this task is as challenging and difficult as any other with which managers are involved; moreover, it is increasingly internationalized.[33] Some believe that the pressure on managers to pursue only those decisions that help the firm meet the quarterly earning numbers expected by market analysts makes it harder to carefully analyze the firm's internal resources, the most valuable of which are developed across time and events.[34] Recognizing the firm's core competencies is essential before the firm can make important strategic decisions, including those related to entering or exiting markets, investing in new technologies, building new or additional manufacturing capacity, or forming strategic partnerships.[35] Patterns of interactions between individuals and groups that occur as strategic decisions affect decision quality as well as how effectively and quickly these decisions are implemented.[36]

The challenge and difficulty of making effective decisions are implied by preliminary evidence suggesting that one-half of organizational decisions fail.[37] Sometimes, mistakes are made as the firm analyzes its internal environment. Managers might, for example, select resources and capabilities as the firm's core competencies that do not create a competitive advantage. When a mistake occurs, decision makers must have the confidence to admit it and take corrective actions.[38] A firm can still grow through well-intended errors—the learning generated by making and correcting mistakes can be important to the creation of new competitive advantages.[39] Moreover, firms can learn from the failure resulting from a mistake—that is, what *not* to do when seeking competitive advantage.[40]

To facilitate developing and using core competencies, managers must have courage, self-confidence, integrity, the capacity to deal with uncertainty and complexity, and a willingness to hold people accountable for their work and to be held accountable themselves. Thus, difficult managerial decisions concerning resources, capabilities, and core competencies are characterized by three conditions: uncertainty, complexity, and intraorganizational conflicts (see Figure 3.3).[41]

Managers face *uncertainty* in terms of new proprietary technologies, rapidly changing economic and political trends, transformations in societal values, and shifts in customer demands.[42] Environmental uncertainty increases the *complexity* and range of issues to examine when studying the internal environment.[43] Biases about how to cope with uncertainty affect decisions about the resources and capabilities that will become the foundation of the firm's competitive advantage. Finally, *intraorganizational conflict* surfaces when decisions are made about the core competencies to nurture as well as how to nurture them.

In making decisions affected by these three conditions, judgment should be used. *Judgment* is the capability of making successful decisions when no obviously correct model or rule is available or when relevant data are unreliable or incomplete. In this type of situation, decision makers must be aware of possible cognitive biases. Overconfidence, for example, can often lower value when a correct decision is not obvious, such as making a judgment as to whether an internal resource is a strength or a weakness.[44]

When exercising judgment, decision makers demonstrate a willingness to take intelligent risks in a timely manner. In the current competitive landscape, executive judgment can be a particularly important source of competitive advantage. One reason for this is that, over time, effective judgment allows a firm to build a strong reputation and retain the loyalty of stakeholders whose support is linked to above-average returns.[45]

Significant changes in the value-creating potential of a firm's resources and capabilities can occur in a rapidly changing global economy. Because these changes affect a company's power and social structure, inertia or resistance to change may surface. Even though these reactions may happen, decision makers should not deny the changes needed to assure the firm's strategic competitiveness. By denying the need for change, difficult experiences can be avoided in the short run.[46] However, in the long

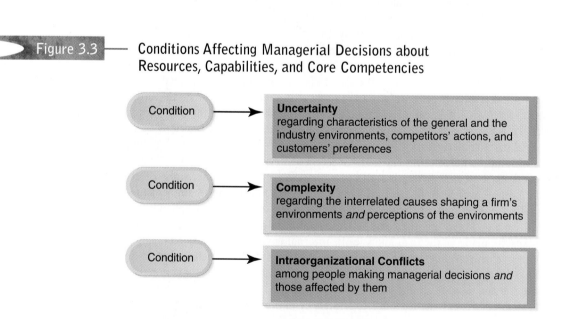

Figure 3.3 — Conditions Affecting Managerial Decisions about Resources, Capabilities, and Core Competencies

Condition → **Uncertainty** regarding characteristics of the general and the industry environments, competitors' actions, and customers' preferences

Condition → **Complexity** regarding the interrelated causes shaping a firm's environments *and* perceptions of the environments

Condition → **Intraorganizational Conflicts** among people making managerial decisions *and* those affected by them

SOURCE: Adapted from R. Amit & P. J. H. Schoemaker, 1993, Strategic assets and organizational rent, *Strategic Management Journal*, 14: 33.

run, the failure to change when needed leads to performance declines and, in the worst-case scenario, to failure. Thus, Levi Strauss' decision to begin selling its jeans in Wal-Mart stores may prevent further reductions in the firm's sales volume.

Resources, Capabilities, and Core Competencies

Resources, capabilities, and core competencies are the characteristics that make up the foundation of competitive advantage. Resources are the source of a firm's capabilities. Capabilities in turn are the source of a firm's core competencies, which are the basis of competitive advantages.[47] As shown in Figure 3.2, combinations of resources and capabilities are managed to create core competencies. In this section, we define and provide examples of these building blocks of competitive advantage.

Resources

Broad in scope, resources cover a spectrum of individual, social, and organizational phenomena.[48] Typically, resources alone do not yield a competitive advantage.[49] In fact, a competitive advantage is created through the *unique bundling of several resources.*[50] For example, Amazon.com has combined service and distribution resources to develop its competitive advantages. The firm started as an online bookseller, directly shipping orders to customers. It quickly grew large and established a distribution network through which it could ship "millions of different items to millions of different customers." Compared to Amazon's use of combined resources, traditional bricks-and-mortar companies, such as Toys 'R' Us and Borders, found it hard to establish an effective online presence. These difficulties led them to develop partnerships with Amazon. Through these arrangements, Amazon now handles the online presence and the shipping of goods for several firms, including Toys 'R' Us and Borders—which now can focus on sales in their stores. Arrangements such as these are useful to the bricks-and-mortar companies because they are not accustomed to shipping so much diverse merchandise directly to individuals.[51]

Some of a firm's resources (defined in Chapter 1 as inputs to the firm's production process) are tangible while others are intangible. **Tangible resources** are assets that can be seen and quantified. Production equipment, manufacturing plants, and formal reporting structures are examples of tangible resources. **Intangible resources** include assets that typically are rooted deeply in the firm's history and have accumulated over time. Because they are embedded in unique patterns of routines, intangible resources are relatively difficult for competitors to analyze and imitate. Knowledge, trust between managers and employees, ideas, the capacity for innovation, managerial capabilities, organizational routines (the unique ways people work together), scientific capabilities, and the firm's reputation for its goods or services and how it interacts with people (such as employees, customers, and suppliers) are all examples of intangible resources.[52]

The four types of tangible resources are financial, organizational, physical, and technological (see Table 3.1). The three types of intangible resources are human, innovation, and reputational (see Table 3.2).

TANGIBLE RESOURCES

As tangible resources, a firm's borrowing capacity and the status of its plant and equipment are visible. The value of many tangible resources can be established through financial statements, but these statements do not account for the value of all of a firm's assets, because they disregard some intangible resources.[53] As such, each of the firm's sources of competitive advantage typically is not fully reflected on corporate financial statements. The value of tangible resources is also constrained because they are difficult to leverage—it is hard to derive additional business or value from a tangible resource.

Tangible resources are assets that can be seen and quantified.

Intangible resources include assets that typically are rooted deeply in the firm's history and have accumulated over time.

Table 3.1

Tangible Resources

Financial Resources	• The firm's borrowing capacity
	• The firm's ability to generate internal funds
Organizational Resources	• The firm's formal reporting structure and its formal planning, controlling, and coordinating systems
Physical Resources	• Sophistication and location of a firm's plant and equipment
	• Access to raw materials
Technological Resources	• Stock of technology, such as patents, trademarks, copyrights, and trade secrets

SOURCES: Adapted from J. B. Barney, 1991, Firm resources and sustained competitive advantage, *Journal of Management*, 17: 101; R. M. Grant, 1991, *Contemporary Strategy Analysis*, Cambridge, U.K.: Blackwell Business, 100–102.

For example, an airplane is a tangible resource or asset, but: "You can't use the same airplane on five different routes at the same time. You can't put the same crew on five different routes at the same time. And the same goes for the financial investment you've made in the airplane."[54]

Although production assets are tangible, many of the processes to use these assets are intangible. Thus, the learning and potential proprietary processes associated with a tangible resource, such as manufacturing equipment, can have unique intangible attributes, such as quality, just-in-time management practices, and unique manufacturing processes that develop over time and create competitive advantage.[55]

Table 3.2

Intangible Resources

Human Resources	• Knowledge
	• Trust
	• Managerial capabilities
	• Organizational routines
Innovation Resources	• Ideas
	• Scientific capabilities
	• Capacity to innovate
Reputational Resources	• Reputation with customers
	• Brand name
	• Perceptions of product quality, durability, and reliability
	• Reputation with suppliers
	• For efficient, effective, supportive, and mutually beneficial interactions and relationships

SOURCES: Adapted from R. Hall, 1992, The strategic analysis of intangible resources, *Strategic Management Journal*, 13: 136–139; R. M. Grant, 1991, *Contemporary Strategy Analysis*, Cambridge, U.K.: Blackwell Business, 101–104.

INTANGIBLE RESOURCES

As suggested above, compared to tangible resources, intangible resources are a superior and more potent source of core competencies.[56] In fact, in the global economy, "the success of a corporation lies more in its intellectual and systems capabilities than in its physical assets. [Moreover], the capacity to manage human intellect—and to convert it into useful products and services—is fast becoming the critical executive skill of the age."[57]

Even though it is hard to measure the value of intangible assets such as knowledge,[58] there is some evidence that the value of intangible assets is growing relative to that of tangible assets.[59] John Kendrick, a well-known economist studying the main drivers of economic growth, found a general increase in the contribution of intangible assets to U.S. economic growth since the early 1900s: "In 1929, the ratio of intangible business capital to tangible business capital was 30 percent to 70 percent. In 1990, that ratio was 63 percent to 37 percent."[60]

Because intangible resources are less visible and more difficult for competitors to understand, purchase, imitate, or substitute for, firms prefer to rely on them rather than on tangible resources as the foundation for their capabilities and core competencies. In fact, the more unobservable (that is, intangible) a resource is, the more sustainable will be the competitive advantage that is based on it.[61] Another benefit of intangible resources is that, unlike most tangible resources, their use can be leveraged. With intangible resources, the larger the network of users, the greater is the benefit to each party.[62] For instance, sharing knowledge among employees does not diminish its value for any one person. To the contrary, two people sharing their individualized knowledge sets often can be leveraged to create additional knowledge that, although new to each of them, contributes to performance improvements for the firm.[63]

As shown in Table 3.2, the intangible resource of reputation is an important source of competitive advantage. Earned through the firm's actions as well as its words, a value-creating reputation is a product of years of superior marketplace competence as perceived by stakeholders.[64] A reputation indicates the level of awareness a firm has been able to develop among stakeholders[65] and the degree to which they hold the firm in high esteem.[66] A well-known and highly valued brand name is an application of reputation as a source of competitive advantage.[67] A continuing commitment to innovation and aggressive advertising facilitates firms' efforts to take advantage of the reputation associated with their brands.[68] Because of the desirability of its reputation, the Harley-Davidson brand name, for example, has such status that it adorns a limited edition Barbie doll, a popular restaurant in New York City, and a line of L'Oréal cologne. Moreover, Harley-Davidson MotorClothes annually generates well in excess of $100 million in revenue for the firm and offers a broad range of clothing items, from black leather jackets to fashions for tots.[69]

The Harley-Davidson name has such status that it reaches even "unlicensed" motorcycle aficionados.

©Lon C. Diehl/PhotoEdit

Capabilities

Capabilities are the firm's capacity to deploy resources that have been purposely integrated to achieve a desired end state.[70] The glue binding an organization together, capabilities emerge over time through complex interactions among tangible and intangible resources. Critical to the forming of competitive advantages, capabilities are often based on developing, carrying, and exchanging information and knowledge through the firm's human capital.[71] Because a knowledge base is grounded in organizational actions that may not be explicitly understood by all employees, repetition and practice increase the value of a firm's capabilities.[72]

The foundation of many capabilities lies in the unique skills and knowledge of a firm's employees[73] and, often, their functional expertise. Hence, the value of human capital in developing and using capabilities and, ultimately, core competencies cannot be overstated. Firms committed to continuously developing their people's capabilities seem to accept the adage that "the person who knows how will always have a job. The person who knows why will always be his boss."[74]

Global business leaders increasingly support the view that the knowledge possessed by human capital is among the most significant of an organization's capabilities and may ultimately be at the root of all competitive advantages.[75] But firms must also be able to utilize the knowledge that they have and transfer it among their operating businesses.[76] For example, researchers have suggested that "in the information age, things are ancillary, knowledge is central. A company's value derives not from things, but from knowledge, know-how, intellectual assets, competencies—all of it embedded in people."[77] Given this reality, the firm's challenge is to create an environment that allows people to fit their individual pieces of knowledge together so that, collectively, employees possess as much organizational knowledge as possible.[78]

To help them develop an environment in which knowledge is widely spread across all employees, some organizations have created the new upper-level managerial position of chief learning officer (CLO). Establishing a CLO position highlights a firm's belief that "future success will depend on competencies that traditionally have not been actively managed or measured—including creativity and the speed with which new ideas are learned and shared."[79] In general, the firm should manage knowledge in ways that will support its efforts to create value for customers.[80]

As illustrated in Table 3.3, capabilities are often developed in specific functional areas (such as manufacturing, R&D, and marketing) or in a part of a functional area (for example, advertising). Research indicates a relationship between capabilities developed in particular functional areas and the firm's financial performance at both the corporate and business-unit levels,[81] suggesting the need to develop capabilities at both levels. Table 3.3 shows a grouping of organizational functions and the capabilities that some companies are thought to possess in terms of all or parts of those functions.

Core Competencies

Defined in Chapter 1, *core competencies* are resources and capabilities that serve as a source of a firm's competitive advantage over rivals. Core competencies distinguish a company competitively and reflect its personality. Core competencies emerge over time through an organizational process of accumulating and learning how to deploy different resources and capabilities.[82] As the capacity to take action, core competencies are "crown jewels of a company," the activities the company performs especially well compared to competitors and through which the firm adds unique value to its goods or services over a long period of time.[83]

Not all of a firm's resources and capabilities are *strategic assets*—that is, assets that have competitive value and the potential to serve as a source of competitive advantage.[84] Some resources and capabilities may result in incompetence, because they represent competitive areas in which the firm is weak compared to competitors. Thus, some resources or capabilities may stifle or prevent the development of a core competence. Firms with the tangible resource of financial capital, such as Microsoft, which has a large amount of cash on hand, may be able to purchase facilities or hire the skilled workers required to manufacture products that yield customer value. However, firms without financial capital would have a weakness in regard to being able to buy

Functional Areas	Capabilities	Examples of Firms
Distribution	Effective use of logistics management techniques	Wal-Mart
Human resources	Motivating, empowering, and retaining employees	Microsoft Corp.
Management information systems	Effective and efficient control of inventories through point-of-purchase data collection methods	Wal-Mart
Marketing	Effective promotion of brand-name products	Gillette Co.
		Polo Ralph Lauren Corp.
		McKinsey & Co.
	Effective customer service	Nordstrom Inc.
		Solectron Corporation
		Norrell Corporation
	Innovative merchandising	Crate & Barrel
Management	Ability to envision the future of clothing	Gap Inc.
	Effective organizational structure	PepsiCo
Manufacturing	Design and production skills yielding reliable products	Komatsu
	Product and design quality	Gap Inc.
	Miniaturization of components and products	Sony
Research & development	Innovative technology	Caterpillar
	Development of sophisticated elevator control solutions	Otis Elevator Co.
	Rapid transformation of technology into new products and processes	Chaparral Steel
	Digital technology	Thomson Consumer Electronics

or build new capabilities. To be successful, firms must locate external environmental opportunities that can be exploited through their capabilities, while avoiding competition in areas of weakness.[85]

An important question is, "How many core competencies are required for the firm to have a sustained competitive advantage?" Responses to this question vary. McKinsey & Co. recommends that its clients identify three or four competencies around which their strategic actions can be framed.[86] Supporting and nurturing more than four core competencies may prevent a firm from developing the focus it needs to fully exploit its competencies in the marketplace.

Firms should take actions that are based on their core competencies. Recent actions by Starbucks demonstrate this point. Growing rapidly, Starbucks decided that it could use the Internet as a distribution channel to bring about additional growth. The firm quickly realized that it lacks the capabilities required to successfully distribute its products through this channel and that its unique coffee, not the delivery of that product, is its competitive advantage. In part, this recognition caused Starbucks to renew its emphasis on existing capabilities to create more value through its supply chain. Trimming the number of its milk suppliers from 65 to fewer than 25 and negotiating long-term contracts with coffee-bean growers are actions Starbucks has taken to do this. The firm also decided to place automated espresso machines in its busy units. These machines reduce Starbucks' cost while providing improved service to its customers, who can now move through the line much faster. Using its supply chain and service capabilities in these manners allows Starbucks to strengthen its competitive advantages of coffee and the unique venue in which on-site customers experience it. These efforts contributed to what analysts called Starbucks' "outstanding" performance in mid-2003.[87]

Of course, not all resources and capabilities are core competencies. The next section discusses two approaches for identifying core competencies.

Building Core Competencies

Two tools help the firm identify and build its core competencies.[88] The first consists of four specific criteria of sustainable competitive advantage that firms can use to determine those resources and capabilities that are core competencies. Because the capabilities shown in Table 3.3 have satisfied these four criteria, they are core competencies. The second tool is the value chain analysis. Firms use this tool to select the value-creating competencies that should be maintained, upgraded, or developed and those that should be outsourced.

Four Criteria of Sustainable Competitive Advantage

As shown in Table 3.4, capabilities that are valuable, rare, costly to imitate, and nonsubstitutable are core competencies. In turn, core competencies are sources of competitive advantage for the firm over its rivals. Capabilities failing to satisfy the four criteria of sustainable competitive advantage are not core competencies, meaning that although every core competence is a capability, not every capability is a core competence. In slightly different words, for a capability to be a core competence, it must be "valuable and nonsubstitutable, from a customer's point of view, and unique and inimitable, from a competitor's point of view."[89]

A sustained competitive advantage is achieved only when competitors have failed in efforts to duplicate the benefits of a firm's strategy or when they lack the confidence to attempt imitation. For some period of time, the firm may earn a competitive advantage by using capabilities that are, for example, valuable and rare, but that are imitable.[90] In this instance, the length of time a firm can expect to retain its competitive advantage is a function of how quickly competitors can successfully imitate a good, service, or process. Sustainable competitive advantage results only when all four criteria are satisfied.

VALUABLE

Valuable capabilities allow the firm to exploit opportunities or neutralize threats in its external environment. By effectively using capabilities to exploit opportunities, a firm creates value for customers.

Bricks-and-mortar grocers such as Safeway Inc. and Albertson's Inc. are using their existing capabilities to create value for online grocery shoppers. Unlike failed Internet ventures Webvan, HomeRuns.com, Streamline.com, and others of the same ilk, these established companies "stick to what they know best" to serve the needs of those wanting to buy groceries online. Rather than using expensive marketing ploys, for example, these new players advertise to those filling the online grocery market niche (no chain expects online rev-

---

Valuable capabilities *allow the firm to exploit opportunities or neutralize threats in its external environment.*

Starbucks' analysis of its core competencies has led it to deemphasize Internet distribution and place greater emphasis on its supply chain and service capabilities. Examples include its renegotiated contracts with milk and coffee bean suppliers and its installation of automated espresso machines in busy stores.

©Michael Newman/PhotoEdit

Valuable Capabilities	• Help a firm neutralize threats or exploit opportunities
Rare Capabilities	• Are not possessed by many others
Costly-to-Imitate Capabilities	• Historical: A unique and a valuable organizational culture or brand name
	• Ambiguous cause: The causes and uses of a competence are unclear
	• Social complexity: Interpersonal relationships, trust, and friendship among managers, suppliers, and customers
Nonsubstitutable Capabilities	• No strategic equivalent

enue to account for more than 5 percent of total sales volume) with the same weekly flyers and local TV ads used to promote their storefront operations. Commonly serving their affluent customers, established grocers are finding that online orders exceed average in-store ticket prices. "At Safeway, the average online order size is $120, twice that of the average in-store ticket."[91]

RARE

Rare capabilities are capabilities that few, if any, competitors possess. A key question to be answered when evaluating this criterion is, "How many rival firms possess these valuable capabilities?" Capabilities possessed by many rivals are unlikely to be sources of competitive advantage for any one of them. Instead, valuable but common (i.e., not rare) resources and capabilities are sources of competitive parity.[92] Competitive advantage results only when firms develop and exploit capabilities that differ from those shared with competitors.

Rare capabilities are capabilities that few, if any, competitors possess.

COSTLY TO IMITATE

Costly-to-imitate capabilities are capabilities that other firms cannot easily develop. Capabilities that are costly to imitate are created because of one reason or a combination of three reasons (see Table 3.4). First, a firm sometimes is able to develop capabilities because of *unique historical conditions.* "As firms evolve, they pick up skills, abilities and resources that are unique to them, reflecting their particular path through history."[93] Another way of saying this is that firms sometimes are able to develop capabilities because they were in the right place at the right time.[94]

Costly-to-imitate capabilities are capabilities that other firms cannot easily develop.

A firm with a unique and valuable *organizational culture* that emerged in the early stages of the company's history "may have an imperfectly imitable advantage over firms founded in another historical period"[95]—one in which less valuable or less competitively useful values and beliefs strongly influenced the development of the firm's culture. This may be the case for the consulting firm McKinsey & Co. "It is that culture, unique to McKinsey and eccentric, which sets the firm apart from virtually any other business organization and which often mystifies even those who engage [its] services."[96] Briefly discussed in Chapter 1, organizational culture is "something that people connect with, feel inspired by, think of as a normal way of operating. It's in their hearts and minds, and its core is voluntary behavior."[97] An organizational culture is a source of advantage when employees are held together tightly by their belief in it.[98]

UPS has been the prototype in many areas of the parcel delivery business because of its excellence in products, systems, marketing, and other operational business capabilities. "Its fundamental competitive strength, however, derives from the

Competitive Parity in the Airline Industry: The Best That Can Be Done?

Airline service has become a commodity-like good, meaning that the price variable is a primary source of competition among industry participants. Through various marketing campaigns, consumers are well aware of "discount" and "low-cost" fares that airline firms offer to induce ticket purchases. As we discuss in Chapter 5, pricing decisions are tactical rather than strategic actions. In essence, this means that although pricing decisions are easy to implement and reverse, competitors can easily imitate them, allowing the possibility of only a temporary competitive advantage at best. As discussed in Chapter 2, competing principally on the basis of price has the potential to substantially reduce firms' ability to operate profitably within an industry and virtually precludes the possibility of generating customer loyalty. However, Southwest Airlines and JetBlue Airways (discussed further in Chapters 4 and 5, respectively) operate with cost structures that allow their prices to consumers to be a competitive advantage. Even in these instances, though, the firms have other sources of differentiation that are competitive advantages. "Despite its low costs, Southwest delivers consistently high levels of service," while JetBlue "differentiates itself by flying new aircraft and offering leather seats and free direct satellite TV at every seat."

Companies prefer to be as different from competitors on as many competitive dimensions as possible. Because of this, the history of the airline industry since it was deregulated is filled with companies' efforts to distinguish themselves from competitors in ways that create value for customers. Stated more directly, each airline wants to use its resources and capabilities to establish a sustainable competitive advantage over its rivals. American Airlines, for example, launched the frequent flyer program to offer consumers a reason to frequently, if not exclusively, use its services. Although this innovation created value for customers and was rare when started, it is easily imitated. Today, virtually all carriers offer consumers a frequent flyer program, meaning that American's innovation is no longer rare nor is it a source of competitive advantage.

The third largest U.S. airline, and committed to achieving its strategic intent of providing distinctive customer service and hospitality from the heart, Delta is using its technological resources and capabilities to create what the firm believes will be a sustainable competitive advantage. At the core of this effort is a three-year commitment of $200 million to bring about a technology makeover in the firm. With a goal that no e-ticketed, self-service customer should wait more than two minutes to check in at an airport, even during peak times, Delta is rapidly installing kiosks in its airport locations. New employee roles, such as Lobby Assist Agents and Service Excellence Coordinators, and the availability of Delta Direct phones, which provide customers having complex ticket transactions with quick access to dedicated reservations agents, are other aspects of what Delta champions as a "comprehensive, hassle-free customer service system." Company officials believe that Delta is "pioneering significant changes in the way passengers will move through airports" and that how Delta customers will move through airports creates value (in the form of convenience and saved time) and is rare and imperfectly imitable. But is this the case? Delta purchases its kiosks from Kinetics Inc., a Florida-based firm that has already sold more than 3,000 of its automated check-in kiosks. Thus, any competitor with capital can purchase the same kiosk that Delta is using. Moreover, competitors can study how Delta's employees are interacting differently with technology (e.g., agents assisting customers in their use of an automated kiosk) and may be able to imitate those practices. Indeed, most other U.S. airlines are already using kiosks in manners that are similar to Delta's practices. Thus, although Delta's integrated use of technology to create customer value in the form of convenience and saved time is valuable, it may also be imitable. Once capabilities have been imitated, the competitive advantage gained by using resources and capabilities in a certain combination still creates value, but is no longer rare because competitors also possess the capabilities. Time will tell, of course. However, it seems that Delta's technological innovations may result in a temporary rather than a sustainable competitive advantage. If this proves to be the case, virtually all airline companies will develop technological deliverables similar to those available from Delta, creating a situation of competitive parity between Delta and its rivals in terms of certain technological innovations.

SOURCES: 2003, AMR Corp., *Standard & Poor's Stock Reports*, http://www.standardandpoors.com, July 16; 2003, Delta Airlines, *Standard & Poor's Stock Reports*, http://www.standardandpoors.com, July 12; 2003, Delta Airlines Home Page, Corporate information, http://www.deltaairlines.com, July 25; 2003, Southwest Airlines, *Standard & Poor's Stock Reports*, http://www.standardandpoors.com, July 19; K. Fieweger, 2003, JetBlue posts profit, like other low-cost carriers, *Reuters*, http://www.reuters.com, July 24; C. Haddad, 2003, Delta's flight to self-service, *Wall Street Journal Online*, http://www.wsj.com, July 7.

organization's unique culture, which has spanned almost a century, growing deeper all along. This culture provides solid, consistent roots for everything the company does, from skills training to technological innovation."[99]

A second condition of being costly to imitate occurs when the link between the firm's capabilities and its competitive advantage is *causally ambiguous*.[100] In these instances, competitors can't clearly understand how a firm uses its capabilities as the foundation for competitive advantage. As a result, firms are uncertain about the capabilities they should develop to duplicate the benefits of a competitor's value-creating strategy. Chaparral Steel, for example, allows competitors to tour its facilities. In the CEO's words, competitors can be shown almost "everything and we will be giving away nothing because they can't take it home with them."[101] Contributing to Chaparral Steel's causally ambiguous operations is the fact that workers use the concept of *mentefacturing,* by which they manufacture steel by using their minds instead of their hands: "In mentefacturing, workers use computers to monitor operations and don't need to be on the shop floor during production."[102]

Social complexity is the third reason that capabilities can be costly to imitate. Social complexity means that at least some, and frequently many, of the firm's capabilities are the product of complex social phenomena. Interpersonal relationships, trust, friendships among managers and between managers and employees, and a firm's reputation with suppliers and customers are examples of socially complex capabilities. Nucor Steel has been able to create "a hunger for new knowledge through a high-powered incentive system for every employee." This socially complex process has allowed Nucor "to push the boundaries of manufacturing process know-how."[103]

NONSUBSTITUTABLE

Nonsubstitutable capabilities are capabilities that do not have strategic equivalents. This final criterion for a capability to be a source of competitive advantage "is that there must be no strategically equivalent valuable resources that are themselves either not rare or imitable. Two valuable firm resources (or two bundles of firm resources) are strategically equivalent when they each can be separately exploited to implement the same strategies."[104] In general, the strategic value of capabilities increases as they become more difficult to substitute.[105] The more invisible capabilities are, the more difficult it is for firms to find substitutes and the greater the challenge is to competitors trying to imitate a firm's value-creating strategy. Firm-specific knowledge and trust-based working relationships between managers and nonmanagerial personnel are examples of capabilities that are difficult to identify and for which finding a substitute is challenging. However, causal ambiguity may make it difficult for the firm to learn as

Nonsubstitutable capabilities are capabilities that do not have strategic equivalents.

well and may stifle progress, because the firm may not know how to improve processes that are not easily codified and thus are ambiguous.[106]

For example, competitors are deeply familiar with Dell Inc.'s successful direct sales model. However, to date, no competitor has been able to imitate Dell's capabilities, as suggested by the following comment: "There's no better way to make, sell, and deliver PCs than the way Dell does it, and nobody executes that model better than Dell."[107] Moreover, no competitor has been able to develop and use substitute capabilities that can duplicate the value Dell creates by using its capabilities. Thus, experience suggests that Dell's direct sales model capabilities are nonsubstitutable.

In summary, only using valuable, rare, costly-to-imitate, and nonsubstitutable capabilities creates sustainable competitive advantage. Table 3.5 shows the competitive consequences and performance implications resulting from combinations of the four criteria of sustainability. The analysis suggested by the table helps managers determine the strategic value of a firm's capabilities. The firm should not emphasize resources and capabilities falling into the first row in the table (that is, resources and capabilities that are neither valuable nor rare and that are imitable and for which strategic substitutes exist). Capabilities yielding competitive parity and either temporary or sustainable competitive advantage, however, will be supported. Some competitors such as Coca-Cola and PepsiCo may have capabilities that result in competitive parity. In such cases, the firms will nurture these capabilities while simultaneously trying to develop capabilities that can yield either a temporary or sustainable competitive advantage.

As discussed in the Strategic Focus, it is hard for airline companies to develop sustainable competitive advantages. As mentioned earlier in the chapter, an airplane is a tangible resource. As noted in Table 3.5, competitive parity results when a resource is valuable and may or may not be substitutable, but isn't rare or costly to imitate. At best, airplanes are a source of competitive parity. Because airplanes aren't a source of competitive advantage, airline companies rely on some of their other resources and capabilities to try to create competitive advantages. While reading the Strategic Focus, try to determine if Delta Airlines' use of its technological resources and capabilities can create the competitive advantage hoped for by the company.

Table 3.5 — Outcomes from Combinations of the Criteria for Sustainable Competitive Advantage

Is the Resource or Capability Valuable?	Is the Resource or Capability Rare?	Is the Resource or Capability Costly to Imitate?	Is the Resource or Capability Nonsubstitutable?	Competitive Consequences	Performance Implications
No	No	No	No	Competitive disadvantage	Below-average returns
Yes	No	No	Yes/no	Competitive parity	Average returns
Yes	Yes	No	Yes/no	Temporary competitive advantage	Average returns to above-average returns
Yes	Yes	Yes	Yes	Sustainable competitive advantage	Above-average returns

Value Chain Analysis

Value chain analysis allows the firm to understand the parts of its operations that create value and those that do not. Understanding these issues is important because the firm earns above-average returns only when the value it creates is greater than the costs incurred to create that value.[108]

The value chain is a template that firms use to understand their cost position and to identify the multiple means that might be used to facilitate implementation of a chosen business-level strategy.[109] As shown in Figure 3.4, a firm's value chain is segmented into primary and support activities. **Primary activities** are involved with a product's physical creation, its sale and distribution to buyers, and its service after the sale. **Support activities** provide the assistance necessary for the primary activities to take place.

The value chain shows how a product moves from the raw-material stage to the final customer. For individual firms, the essential idea of the value chain is to create additional value without incurring significant costs while doing so and to capture the value that has been created. In a globally competitive economy, the most valuable links on the chain tend to belong to people who have knowledge about customers.[110] This locus of value-creating possibilities applies just as strongly to retail and service firms as to manufacturers. Moreover, for organizations in all sectors, the effects of e-commerce make it increasingly necessary for companies to develop value-adding knowledge processes to compensate for the value and margin that the Internet strips from physical processes.[111]

Primary activities are involved with a product's physical creation, its sale and distribution to buyers, and its service after the sale.

Support activities provide the assistance necessary for the primary activities to take place.

The Basic Value Chain — Figure 3.4

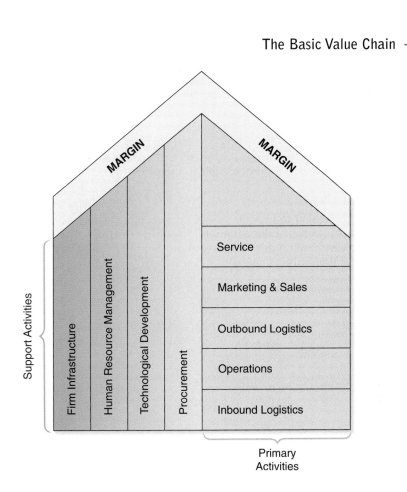

Table 3.6 lists the items to be studied to assess the value-creating potential of primary activities. In Table 3.7, the items to consider when studying support activities are shown. As with the analysis of primary activities, the intent in examining these items is to determine areas where the firm has the potential to create and capture value. All items in both tables should be evaluated relative to competitors' capabilities. To be a source of competitive advantage, a resource or capability must allow the firm (1) to perform an activity in a manner that is superior to the way competitors perform it, or (2) to perform a value-creating activity that competitors cannot complete. Only under these conditions does a firm create value for customers and have opportunities to capture that value.

Sometimes start-up firms create value by uniquely reconfiguring or recombining parts of the value chain. Federal Express (FedEx) changed the nature of the delivery business by reconfiguring outbound logistics (a primary activity) and human resource management (a support activity) to provide overnight deliveries, creating value in the process. As shown in Figure 3.5, the Internet is changing many aspects of the value chain for a broad range of firms. A key reason for this is that the Internet affects how people communicate, locate information, and buy goods and services. For example, some believe that travel products are quite suitable for selling online. Indeed, the signif-

Table 3.6 — **Examining the Value-Creating Potential of Primary Activities**

Inbound Logistics

Activities, such as materials handling, warehousing, and inventory control, used to receive, store, and disseminate inputs to a product.

Operations

Activities necessary to convert the inputs provided by inbound logistics into final product form. Machining, packaging, assembly, and equipment maintenance are examples of operations activities.

Outbound Logistics

Activities involved with collecting, storing, and physically distributing the final product to customers. Examples of these activities include finished-goods warehousing, materials handling, and order processing.

Marketing and Sales

Activities completed to provide means through which customers can purchase products and to induce them to do so. To effectively market and sell products, firms develop advertising and promotional campaigns, select appropriate distribution channels, and select, develop, and support their sales force.

Service

Activities designed to enhance or maintain a product's value. Firms engage in a range of service-related activities, including installation, repair, training, and adjustment.

Each activity should be examined relative to competitors' abilities. Accordingly, firms rate each activity as *superior, equivalent,* or *inferior.*

SOURCE: Adapted with the permission of The Free Press, an imprint of Simon & Schuster Adult Publishing Group, from *Competitive Advantage: Creating and Sustaining Superior Performance,* by Michael E. Porter, pp. 39–40, Copyright © 1985, 1998 by Michael E. Porter.

Procurement

Activities completed to purchase the inputs needed to produce a firm's products. Purchased inputs include items fully consumed during the manufacture of products (e.g., raw materials and supplies, as well as fixed assets—machinery, laboratory equipment, office equipment, and buildings).

Technological Development

Activities completed to improve a firm's product and the processes used to manufacture it. Technological development takes many forms, such as process equipment, basic research and product design, and servicing procedures.

Human Resource Management

Activities involved with recruiting, hiring, training, developing, and compensating all personnel.

Firm Infrastructure

Firm infrastructure includes activities such as general management, planning, finance, accounting, legal support, and governmental relations that are required to support the work of the entire value chain. Through its infrastructure, the firm strives to effectively and consistently identify external opportunities and threats, identify resources and capabilities, and support core competencies.

Each activity should be examined relative to competitors' abilities. Accordingly, firms rate each activity as *superior, equivalent,* or *inferior.*

SOURCE: Adapted with the permission of The Free Press, an imprint of Simon & Schuster Adult Publishing Group, from *Competitive Advantage: Creating and Sustaining Superior Performance*, by Michael E. Porter, pp. 40–43, Copyright © 1985, 1998 by Michael E. Porter.

icance of Internet-based hotel distribution routes has greatly increased over the last few years. According to industry trade data, direct hotel reservations fell from roughly 39 percent of business in 1995 to 33 percent in 1999. The shift in sales between these years went almost exclusively to electronic channels.[112] This change obviously affects the marketing and sales support activity, especially in terms of pricing, for hotels and motels.

Rating a firm's capability to execute its primary and support activities is challenging. Earlier in the chapter, we noted that identifying and assessing the value of a firm's resources and capabilities requires judgment. Judgment is equally necessary when using value chain analysis. The reason is that there is no obviously correct model or rule available to help in the process.

What should a firm do about primary and support activities in which its resources and capabilities are not a source of core competence and, hence, of competitive advantage? Outsourcing is one solution to consider.

Outsourcing

Concerned with how components, finished goods, or services will be obtained, **outsourcing** is the purchase of a value-creating activity from an external supplier.[113] Not-for-profit agencies as well as for-profit organizations are actively engaging in outsourcing.[114] During the 1990s, outsourcing became a prominent strategic action among many

Outsourcing *is the purchase of a value-creating activity from an external supplier.*

Figure 3.5 — Prominent Applications of the Internet in the Value Chain

Firm Infrastructure
- Web-based, distributed financial and ERP systems
- Online investor relations (e.g., information dissemination, broadcast conference calls)

Human Resource Management
- Self-service personnel and benefits administration
- Web-based training
- Internet-based sharing and dissemination of company information
- Electronic time and expense reporting

Technology Development
- Collaborative product design across locations and among multiple value-system participants
- Knowledge directories accessible from all parts of the organization
- Real-time access by R&D to online sales and service information

Procurement
- Internet-enabled demand planning; real-time available-to-promise/capable-to-promise and fulfillment
- Other linkage of purchase, inventory, and forecasting systems with suppliers
- Automated "requisition to pay"
- Direct and indirect procurement via marketplaces, exchanges, auctions, and buyer-seller matching

Inbound Logistics
- Real-time integrated scheduling, shipping, warehouse management, demand management, and planning, and advanced planning and scheduling across the company and its suppliers
- Dissemination throughout the company of real-time inbound and in-progress inventory data

Operations
- Integrated information exchange, scheduling and decision making in in-house plants, contract assemblers, and components suppliers
- Real-time available-to-promise and capable-to-promise information available to the sales force and channels

Outbound Logistics
- Real-time transaction of orders whether initiated by an end consumer, a salesperson, or a channel partner
- Automated customer-specific agreements and contract terms
- Customer and channel access to product development and delivery status
- Collaborative integration with customer forecasting systems
- Integrated channel management including information exchange, warranty claims, and contract management (process control)

Marketing and Sales
- Online sales channels including websites and marketplaces
- Real-time inside and outside access to customer information, product catalogs, dynamic pricing, inventory availability, online submission of quotes, and order entry
- Online product configurators
- Customer-tailored marketing via customer profiling
- Push advertising
- Tailored online access
- Real-time customer feedback through Web surveys, opt-in/opt-out marketing, and promotion response tracking

After-Sales Service
- Online support of customer service representatives through e-mail response management, billing integration, co-browse, chat, "call me now," voice-over-IP, and other uses of video streaming
- Customer self-service via websites and intelligent service request processing including updates to billing and shipping profiles
- Real-time field service access to customer account review, schematic review, parts availability and ordering, work-order update, and service parts management

← • Web-distributed supply chain management →

SOURCE: Reprinted by permission of *Harvard Business Review* from "Strategy and the Internet" by Michael E. Porter, March 2001, p. 75.

types of companies.[115] Firms engaging in effective outsourcing increase their flexibility, mitigate risks, and reduce their capital investments.[116] In multiple global industries, the trend toward outsourcing continues at a rapid pace.[117] Moreover, in some industries virtually all firms seek the value that can be captured through effective outsourcing. The auto manufacturing industry and, more recently, the electronics industry are examples of this situation.[118] As with other strategic management process decisions, careful study is required before the firm decides to engage in outsourcing.[119]

Outsourcing can be effective because few, if any, organizations possess the resources and capabilities required to achieve competitive superiority in all primary and support activities. With respect to technologies, for example, research suggests that few

The Use of Outsourcing: Nothing but Positive Outcomes?

Firms engage in outsourcing, now a global phenomenon, to complete activities in which they do not possess a competitive advantage or in which they prefer not to develop an advantage. Information technology (IT) and research and development (R&D) are two organizational functions that are commonly outsourced. In IT, offshore outsourcing is the world's fastest growing segment of the industry. A set of "global players," including companies in India, is emerging to satisfy the growing demand for IT services to be performed by outside vendors. In R&D, General Motors, IBM, Motorola, Monsanto, Siemens, Microsoft, and Nokia are just a few of the companies that have established centers in India. These corporate giants aren't alone in their decision to outsource some of their R&D activities to other nations. In fact, between 2001 and 2003, 77 global firms established R&D centers in India alone. On a more comprehensive basis, Forester Research Inc. estimates that by 2020, roughly 3.3 million U.S. services jobs and $136 billion in wages will move offshore to countries such as India, China, Russia, and the Philippines. Other analysts believe that as much as 10 percent of the existing stock of U.S. jobs could be lost due to outsourcing by the end of 2004. The results of Forester's analysis showing that outsourcing can reduce firms' costs by as much as one-half may influence the growing use of this particular strategic action.

The fact that some nations, such as the Philippines, are gearing parts of their economy toward developing competitive advantages in certain areas stimulates the use of outsourcing. In response to aggressive advertising of such advantages and to more efficiently complete certain tasks, a growing number of U.S. companies is more actively considering either using companies in the Philippines or establishing units there using local labor. JPMorgan, for example, is evaluating the possibility of forming a unit in the Philippines to handle its backroom and customer services.

The benefits of outsourcing, such as lower costs and the ability to more readily allocate resources to core competencies that create competitive advantages, are understandable. However, issues about outsourcing's consequences have been sounded. In the United States, for example, concerns have been raised about the contraction of domestic innovation. The fact that the "rate of increase for new patent applications in the IT area is down by nearly 90 percent" is one example of this concern. Workers at Boeing believe that it will be increasingly difficult for the firm to maintain its technological expertise if jobs continue to be outsourced.

Increasingly formal responses to the growing use of outsourcing are surfacing. Members of at least one of the unions representing Boeing's workers are seeking to track "where Boeing jobs are going and why." Some displaced U.S. workers are forming support groups to mount a collective challenge to the use of outsourcing. A displaced Microsoft employee, for instance, has established a website (http://www.goodetech.com) to provide a forum and to post materials about the movement of U.S. jobs to offshore locations.

SOURCES: 2003, Outsourcing ventures, *BusinessWorld*, July 15, 1; S. Aggarwal, 2003, Tech outsourcing: Two scenarios, *Business Week*, July 14, 8; C. Ansberry, 2003, The economy—the outlook: Outsourcing abroad draws debate at home, *Wall Street Journal Online*, http://www.wsj.com, July 14; A. Goldstein, 2003, Outsourcing breeds backlash at home, *Dallas Morning News*, July 9, D1, D4; M. McMillin, 2003, Union for Boeing launches effort to keep track of outsourcing, *Knight Ridder Tribune Business News*, July 10, 23; P. Fox, 2002, Avoid the decline of IT innovation, *Computerworld*, October 14, 20–21.

companies can afford to develop internally all the technologies that might lead to competitive advantage.[120] By nurturing a smaller number of capabilities, a firm increases the probability of developing a competitive advantage because it does not become overextended. In addition, by outsourcing activities in which it lacks competence, the firm can fully concentrate on those areas in which it can create value.[121]

Other research suggests that outsourcing does not work effectively without extensive internal capabilities to coordinate external sourcing as well as core competencies.[122] Dell Inc., for example, outsources most of its manufacturing and customer service activities, allowing the firm to concentrate on creating value through its service and online distribution capabilities. In addition, the value generated by outsourcing must be sufficient to cover a firm's costs. For example, research indicates that for European banks outsourcing various information technology activities, "a provider must beat a bank's internal costs by about 40 percent."[123]

To verify that the appropriate primary and support activities are outsourced, four skills are essential for managers involved in outsourcing programs: strategic thinking, deal making, partnership governance, and change management.[124] Managers should understand whether and how outsourcing creates competitive advantage within their company—they need to be able to think strategically.[125] To complete effective outsourcing transactions, these managers must also be deal makers to be able to secure rights from external providers that can be fully used by internal managers. They must be able to oversee and govern appropriately the relationship with the company to which the services were outsourced. Because outsourcing can significantly change how an organization operates, managers administering these programs must also be able to manage that change, including resolving employee resistance that accompanies any significant change effort.[126]

As explained in the Strategic Focus, some have concerns about the consequences of outsourcing. For the most part, these concerns revolve around the potential loss in firms' innovative ability and the loss of jobs within companies that decide to outsource some of their work activities to others. Companies should be aware of these issues and be prepared to fully consider the concerns about outsourcing when different stakeholders (e.g., employees) express them.

Core Competencies: Cautions and Reminders

Tools such as outsourcing help the firm focus on its core competencies as the source of its competitive advantages. However, evidence shows that the value-creating ability of core competencies should never be taken for granted. Moreover, the ability of a core competence to be a permanent competitive advantage can't be assumed. The reason for these cautions is that all core competencies have the potential to become *core rigidities*. As Leslie Wexner, CEO of Limited Brands, says: "Success doesn't beget success. Success begets failure because the more that you know a thing works, the less likely you are to think that it won't work. When you've had a long string of victories, it's harder to foresee your own vulnerabilities."[127] Thus, each core competence is a strength and a weakness—a strength because it is the source of competitive advantage and, hence, strategic competitiveness, and a weakness because, if emphasized when it is no longer competitively relevant, it can be a seed of organizational inertia.[128]

Events occurring in the firm's external environment create conditions through which core competencies can become core rigidities, generate inertia, and stifle innovation. "Often the flip side, the dark side, of core capabilities is revealed due to external events when new competitors figure out a better way to serve the firm's customers, when new technologies emerge, or when political or social events shift the ground underneath."[129] However, in the final analysis, changes in the external environment do not cause core competencies to become core rigidities; rather, strategic myopia and inflexibility on the part of managers are the cause.[130] Determining what the firm *can do* through continuous and effective analyses of its internal environment increases the likelihood of long-term competitive success.

- In the global landscape, traditional factors (e.g., labor costs and superior access to financial resources and raw materials) can still create a competitive advantage. However, this happens in a declining number of instances. In the new landscape, the resources, capabilities, and core competencies in the firm's internal environment may have a relatively stronger influence on its performance than do conditions in the external environment. The most effective firms recognize that strategic competitiveness and above-average returns result only when core competencies (identified through the study of the firm's internal environment) are matched with opportunities (determined through the study of the firm's external environment).

- No competitive advantage lasts forever. Over time, rivals use their own unique resources, capabilities, and core competencies to form different value-creating propositions that duplicate the value-creating ability of the firm's competitive advantages. In general, the Internet's capabilities are reducing the sustainability of many competitive advantages. Thus, because competitive advantages are not sustainable on a permanent basis, firms must exploit their current advantages while simultaneously using their resources and capabilities to form new advantages that can lead to competitive success in the future.

- Effective management of core competencies requires careful analysis of the firm's resources (inputs to the production process) and capabilities (capacities for teams of resources to perform a task or activity in an integrative manner). To successfully manage core competencies, decision makers must be self-confident, courageous, and willing both to hold others accountable for their work and to be held accountable for the outcomes of their own efforts.

- Individual resources are usually not a source of competitive advantage. Capabilities, which are groupings of tangible and intangible resources, are a more likely source of competitive advantages, especially relatively sustainable ones. A key reason for this is that the firm's nurturing and support of core competencies that are based on capabilities is less visible to rivals and, as such, is harder to understand and imitate.

- Increasingly, employees' knowledge is viewed as perhaps the most relevant source of competitive advantage. To gain maximum benefit from knowledge, efforts are taken to find ways for individuals' unique knowledge sets to be shared throughout the firm. The Internet's capabilities affect both the development and the sharing of knowledge.

- Only when a capability is valuable, rare, costly to imitate, and nonsubstitutable is it a core competence and a source of competitive advantage. Over time, core competencies must be supported, but they cannot be allowed to become core rigidities. Core competencies are a source of competitive advantage only when they allow the firm to create value by exploiting opportunities in the external environment. When this is no longer the case, attention shifts to selecting or forming other capabilities that do satisfy the four criteria of sustainable competitive advantage.

- Value chain analysis is used to identify and evaluate the competitive potential of resources and capabilities. By studying their skills relative to those associated with primary and support activities, firms can understand their cost structure and identify the activities through which they can create value.

- When the firm cannot create value in either a primary or support activity, outsourcing is considered. Used commonly in the global economy, outsourcing is the purchase of a value-creating activity from an external supplier. The firm must outsource only to companies possessing a competitive advantage in terms of the particular primary or support activity under consideration. In addition, the firm must continuously verify that it is not outsourcing activities from which it could create value.

Review Questions

1. Why is it important for a firm to study and understand its internal environment?

2. What is value? Why is it critical for the firm to create value? How does it do so?

3. What are the differences between tangible and intangible resources? Why is it important for decision makers to understand these differences? Are tangible resources linked more closely to the creation of competitive advantages than are intangible resources, or is the reverse true? Why?

4. What are capabilities? What must firms do to create capabilities?

5. What are the four criteria used to determine which of a firm's capabilities are core competencies? Why is it important for these criteria to be used?

6. What is value chain analysis? What does the firm gain when it successfully uses this tool?

7. What is outsourcing? Why do firms outsource? Will outsourcing's importance grow in the 21st century? If so, why?

8. What are core rigidities? Why is it vital that firms prevent core competencies from becoming core rigidities?

Scanning the Internal Environment

The resources, capabilities, and core competencies in a firm's internal environment play a critical role in determining strategic performance. A firm must have core competencies that provide the basis for responding to environmental opportunities in order to earn above-average returns.

For a company that is of interest to you, identify the four or five strongest capabilities. You may find it helpful to think in terms of functional areas or value activities to identify the strongest capabilities.

a. Evaluate each capability using the four criteria established in the chapter (see Table 3.4).

b. Which capabilities appear to provide a basis for competitive parity? Temporary competitive advantage? Sustainable competitive advantage?

c. Generate some ideas about developments in the external environment (i.e., the general, industry, and competitor environments) that may dilute or destroy the value of the existing core competencies and, thereby, erode the basis of competitive advantage.

d. Discuss the implications of these trends for the firm's strategic performance

Organizational Resources

The organizations listed in the table below have different capabilities and core competencies.

Part One. In small groups, consider each firm and use logic and consensus to complete the table. Alternatively, complete the table on an individual basis.

Organization	Capabilities	Core Competencies
Wal-Mart		
Starbucks		
U.S. Post Office		
Southwest Airlines		

Part Two. Based on your responses to the table, now compare each type of firm in terms of its resources and suggest some reasons for the differences.

	Is the Resource or Capability				Competitive consequences: • Competitive disadvantage • Competitive parity • Temporary competitive advantage • Sustainable competitive advantage	Performance implications: • Below-average returns • Average returns • Above-average returns
	Valuable?	Rare?	Costly to Imitate?	Nonsubstitutable?		
Wal-Mart						
Starbucks						
U.S. Post Office						
Southwest Airlines						

Part Three. In order to protect their competitive advantage, firms must continuously watch for developments that might dilute or destroy the value of their core competencies. For each firm, generate ideas about developments that may erode the basis of their competitive advantage.

Notes

1. A. Andal-Ancion, P. A. Cartwright, & G. S. Yip, 2003, The digital transformation of traditional businesses, *MIT Sloan Management Review*, 44(4): 34–41.

2. R. R. Wiggins & T. W. Ruefli, 2002, Sustained competitive advantage: Temporal dynamics and the incidence of persistence of superior economic performance, *Organization Science*, 13: 82–105.

3. M. Iansiti, F. W. McFarlan, & G. Westerman, 2003, Leveraging the incumbent's advantage, *MIT Sloan Management Review*, 44(4): 58–64; P. W. Roberts & G. R. Dowling, 2002, Corporate reputation and sustained superior financial performance, *Strategic Management Journal*, 23: 1077–1093.

4. S. Dutta, M. J. Zbaracki, & M. Bergen, 2003, Pricing process as a capability: A resource-based perspective, *Strategic Management Journal*, 24: 615–630; A. M. Knott, 2003, Persistent heterogeneity and sustainable innovation, *Strategic Management Journal*, 24: 687–705.

5. C. G. Brush, P. G. Greene, & M. M. Hart, 2001, From initial idea to unique advantage: The entrepreneurial challenge of constructing a resource base, *Academy of Management Executive*, 15(1): 64–78.

6. T. J. Douglas & J. A. Ryman, 2003, Understanding competitive advantage in the general hospital industry: Evaluating strategic competencies, *Strategic Management Journal*, 24: 333–347; R. Makadok, 2001, Toward a synthesis of the resource-based and dynamic-capability views of rent creation, *Strategic Management Journal*, 22: 387–401; K. M. Eisenhardt & J. A. Martin, 2000, Dynamic capabilities: What are they? *Strategic Management Journal*, 21: 1105–1121.

7. D. G. Sirmon, M. A. Hitt, & R. D. Ireland, 2003, Dynamically managing firm resources for competitive advantage: Creating value for stakeholders, Paper presented at Academy of Management, Seattle.

8. G. Hamel & L. Valikangas, 2003, The quest for resilience, *Harvard Business Review*, 81(9): 52–63; S. A. Way, 2002, High-performance work systems and intermediate indicators of firm performance within the U.S. small-business sector, *Journal of Management*, 28: 765–785; M. A. Hitt, L. Bierman, K. Shimizu, & R. Kochhar, 2001, Direct and moderating effects of human capital on strategy and performance in professional service firms: A resource-based perspective, *Academy of Management Journal*, 44: 13–28.

9. J. Schlereth, 2003, Putting people first, *BizEd*, July/August, 16–20.

10. J. Shamsie, 2003, The context of dominance: An industry-driven framework for exploiting reputation, *Strategic Management Journal*, 24: 199–215; E. Autio, H. J. Sapienza, & J. G. Almeida, 2000, Effects of age at entry, knowledge intensity, and imitability on international growth, *Academy of Management Journal*, 43: 909–924.

11. M. Makhija, 2003, Comparing the resource-based and market-based view of the firm: Empirical evidence from Czech privatization, *Strategic Management Journal*, 24: 433–451; P. L. Yeoh & K. Roth, 1999, An empirical analysis of sustained advantage in the U.S. pharmaceutical industry: Impact of firm resources and capabilities, *Strategic Management Journal*, 20: 637–653.

12. D. F. Abell, 1999, Competing today while preparing for tomorrow, *Sloan Management Review*, 40(3): 73–81; D. Leonard-Barton, 1995, *Wellsprings of Knowledge: Building and Sustaining the Sources of Innovation*, Boston: Harvard Business School Press; R. A. McGrath, J. C. MacMillan, & S. Venkataraman, 1995, Defining and developing competence: A strategic process paradigm, *Strategic Management Journal*, 16: 251–275.

13. K. M. Eisenhardt, 1999, Strategy as strategic decision making, *Sloan Management Review*, 40(3): 65–72.

14. H. K. Steensma & K. G. Corley, 2000, On the performance of technology-sourcing partnerships: The interaction between partner interdependence and technology attributes, *Academy of Management Journal*, 43: 1045–1067.

15. J. B. Barney, 2001, Is the resource-based "view" a useful perspective for strategic management research? Yes, *Academy of Management Review*, 26: 41–56.

16. M. Subramani & N. Venkataraman, 2003, Safeguarding investments in asymmetric interorganizational relationships: Theory and evidence, *Academy of Management Journal*, 46: 46–62; J. K. Sebenius, 2002, The hidden challenge of cross-border negotiations, *Harvard Business Review*, 80(3): 76–85.

17. R. Cross, W. Baker, & A. Parker, 2003, What creates energy in organizations? *MIT Sloan Management Review*, 44(4): 51–56; P. F. Drucker, 2002, They're not employees, they're people, *Harvard Business Review*, 80(2):

18. B. Grow & R. Berner, 2003, More rough-and-tumble for Lee and Wrangler, *Business Week*, June 2, 84.

19. T. M. Begley & D. P. Boyd, 2003, The need for a corporate global mind-set, *MIT Sloan Management Review*, 44(2): 25–32.

20. M. C. Bolino, W. H. Turnley, & J. M. Bloodgood, 2002, Citizenship behavior and the creation of social capital in organizations, *Academy of Management Review*, 27: 505–522; V. P. Rindova & C. J. Fombrun, 1999, Constructing competitive advantage: The role of firm-constituent interactions, *Strategic Management Journal*, 20: 691–710; M. A. Peteraf, 1993, The cornerstones of competitive strategy: A resource-based view, *Strategic Management Journal*, 14: 179–191.

21. Barney, Is the resource-based "view" a useful perspective for strategic management research? Yes; T. H. Brush & K. W. Artz, 1999, Toward a contingent resource-based theory: The impact of information asymmetry on the value of capabilities in veterinary medicine, *Strategic Management Journal*, 20: 223–250.

22. S. K. McEvily & B. Chakravarthy, 2002, The persistence of knowledge-based advantage: An empirical test for product performance and technological knowledge, *Strategic Management Journal*, 23: 285–305.

23. 1998, Pocket Strategy, *Value*, The Economist Books, 165.

24. J. Benedict, E. M. Steenkamp, R. Batra, & D. L. Alden, 2003, How perceived brand globalness creates brand value, *Journal of International Business Studies*, 34: 53–65.

25. S. Nambisan, 2002, Designing virtual customer environments for new product development: Toward a theory, *Academy of Management Review*, 27: 392–413.

26. J. Wolf & W. G. Egelhoff, 2002, A reexamination and extension of international strategy-structure theory, *Strategic Management Journal*, 23: 181–189; R. Ramirez, 1999, Value co-production: Intellectual origins and implications for practice and research, *Strategic Management Journal*, 20: 49–65.

27. V. Shankar & B. L. Bayus, 2003, Network effects and competition: An empirical analysis of the home video game industry, *Strategic Management Journal*, 24: 375–384; S. W. Floyd & B. Wooldridge, 1999, Knowledge creation and social networks in corporate entrepreneurship: The renewal of organizational capability, *Entrepreneurship: Theory and Practice*, 23(3): 123–143.

28. G. Hawawini, V. Subramanian, & P. Verdin, 2003, Is performance driven by industry- or firm-specific factors? A new look at the evidence, *Strategic Management Journal*, 24: 1–16; M. A. Hitt, R. D. Nixon, P. G. Clifford, & K. P. Coyne, 1999, The development and use of strategic resources, in M. A. Hitt, P. G. Clifford, R. D. Nixon, & K. P. Coyne (eds.), *Dynamic Strategic Resources*, Chichester: John Wiley & Sons, 1–14.

29. C. M. Christensen, 2001, The past and future of competitive advantage, *Sloan Management Review*, 42(2): 105–109.

30. J. R. Hough & M. A. White, 2003, Environmental dynamism and strategic decision-making rationality: An examination at the decision level, *Strategic Management Journal*, 24: 481–489.

31. C. J. Robertson & W. F. Crittenden, 2003, Mapping moral philosophies: Strategic implications for multinational firms, *Strategic Management Journal*, 24: 385–392.

32. C. M. Christensen & M. E. Raynor, 2003, Why hard-nosed executives should care about management theory, *Harvard Business Review*, 81(9): 66–74; T. H. Davenport, 2001, Data to knowledge to results: Building an analytic capability, *California Management Review*, 43(2): 117–138.

33. N. Checa, J. Maguire, & J. Barney, 2003, The new world disorder, *Harvard Business Review*, 81(8): 70–79; P. Westhead, M. Wright, & D. Ucbasaran, 2001, The internationalization of new and small firms: A resource-based view, *Journal of Business Venturing* 16(4): 333–358; A. McWilliams, D. D. Van Fleet, & P. M. Wright, 2001, Strategic management of human resources for global competitive advantage, *Journal of Business Strategies* 18(1): 1–24.

34. H. J. Smith, 2003, The shareholders vs. stakeholders debate, *MIT Sloan Management Review*, 44(4): 85–90; H. Collingwood, 2001, The earnings game: Everyone plays, nobody wins, *Harvard Business Review*, 79(6): 65–74.

35. Eisenhardt, Strategy as strategic decision making.

70–77; G. Verona, 1999, A resource-based view of product development, *Academy of Management Review*, 24: 132–142.

36. R. S. Dooley & G. E. Fryxell, 1999, Attaining decision quality and commitment from dissent: The moderating effects of loyalty and competence in strategic decision-making teams, *Academy of Management Journal*, 42: 389–402.

37. P. C. Nutt, 1999, Surprising but true: Half the decisions in organizations fail, *Academy of Management Executive*, 13(4): 75–90.

38. J. M. Mezias & W. H. Starbuck, 2003, What do managers know, anyway? *Harvard Business Review*, 81(5): 16–17; M. Keil, 2000, Cutting your losses: Extricating your organization when a big project goes awry, *Sloan Management Review*, 41(3): 55–68.

39. P. G. Audia, E. Locke, & K. G. Smith, 2000, The paradox of success: An archival and a laboratory study of strategic persistence following radical environmental change, *Academy of Management Journal*, 43: 837–853; R. G. McGrath, 1999, Falling forward: Real options reasoning and entrepreneurial failure, *Academy of Management Review*, 24: 13–30.

40. G. P. West III & J. DeCastro, 2001, The Achilles heel of firm strategy: Resource weaknesses and distinctive inadequacies, *Journal of Management Studies*, 38: 417–442; G. Gavetti & D. Levinthal, 2000, Looking forward and looking backward: Cognitive and experimental search, *Administrative Science Quarterly*, 45: 113–137.

41. R. Amit & P. J. H. Schoemaker, 1993, Strategic assets and organizational rent, *Strategic Management Journal*, 14: 33–46.

42. R. E. Hoskisson & L. W. Busenitz, 2001, Market uncertainty and learning distance in corporate entrepreneurship entry mode choice, in M. A. Hitt, R. D. Ireland, S. M. Camp, & D. L. Sexton (eds.), *Strategic Entrepreneurship: Creating a New Integrated Mindset*, Oxford, UK: Blackwell Publishers, 151–172.

43. C. M. Fiol & E. J. O'Connor, 2003, Waking up! Mindfulness in the face of bandwagons, *Academy of Management Review*, 28: 54–70.

44. C. Roxburgh, 2003, Hidden flaws in strategy, *The McKinsey Quarterly*, Number 2, 26–39; A. L. Zacharakis & D. L. Shepherd, 2001, The nature of information and overconfidence on venture capitalists' decision making, *Journal of Business Venturing*, 16: 311–332.

45. P. Burrows & A. Park, 2002, What price victory at Hewlett-Packard? *Business Week*, April 1, 36–37.

46. J. M. Mezias, P. Grinyer, & W. D. Guth, 2001, Changing collective cognition: A process model for strategic change, *Long Range Planning*, 34(1): 71–95.

47. D. M. De Carolis, 2003, Competencies and imitability in the pharmaceutical industry: An analysis of their relationship with firm performance, *Journal of Management*, 29: 27–50.

48. Eisenhardt & Martin, Dynamic capabilities: What are they?; M. D. Michalisin, D. M. Kline, & R. D. Smith, 2000, Intangible strategic assets and firm performance: A multi-industry study of the resource-based view, *Journal of Business Strategies*, 17(2): 91–117.

49. D. L. Deeds, D. De Carolis, & J. Coombs, 2000, Dynamic capabilities and new product development in high-technology ventures: An empirical analysis of new biotechnology firms, *Journal of Business Venturing*, 15: 211–229; T. Chi, 1994, Trading in strategic resources: Necessary conditions, transaction cost problems, and choice of exchange structure, *Strategic Management Journal*, 15: 271–290.

50. Sirmon, Hitt, & Ireland, Dynamically managing firm resources; S. Berman, J. Down, & C. Hill, 2002, Tacit knowledge as a source of competitive advantage in the National Basketball Association, *Academy of Management Journal*, 45: 13–31.

51. 2003, About Borders Group, http://www.borders.com, July 18; S. Shepard, 2001, Interview: "The company is not in the stock," *Business Week*, April 30, 94–96.

52. M. S. Feldman, 2000, Organizational routines as a source of continuous change, *Organization Science*, 11: 611–629; A. M. Knott & B. McKelvey, 1999, Nirvana efficiency: A comparative test of residual claims and routines, *Journal of Economic Behavior & Organization*, 38: 365–383.

53. Subramani & Venkataraman, Safeguarding investments; R. Lubit, 2001, Tacit knowledge and knowledge management: The keys to sustainable competitive advantage, *Organizational Dynamics*, 29(3): 164–178.

54. A. M. Webber, 2000, New math for a new economy, *Fast Company*, January/February, 214–224.

55. R. G. Schroeder, K. A. Bates, & M. A. Junttila, 2002, A resource-based view of manufacturing strategy and the relationship to manufacturing performance, *Strategic Management Journal*, 23: 105–117.

56. M. A. Hitt & R. D. Ireland, 2002, The essence of strategic leadership: Managing human and social capital, *Journal of Leadership and Organization Studies*, 9(1): 3–14.

57. J. B. Quinn, P. Anderson, & S. Finkelstein, 1996, Making the most of the best, *Harvard Business Review*, 74(2): 71–80.

58. A. W. King & C. P. Zeithaml, 2003, Measuring organizational knowledge: A conceptual and methodological framework, *Strategic Management Journal*, 24: 763–772.

59. 2003, Intellectual property, Special Advertising Section, *Business Week*, July 28.

60. Webber, New math, 217.

61. K. Funk, 2003, Sustainability and performance, *MIT Sloan Management Review*, 44(2): 65–70.

62. Bolino, Turnley, & Bloodgood, Citizenship behavior.

63. R. D. Ireland, M. A. Hitt, & D. Vaidyanath, 2002, Managing strategic alliances to achieve a competitive advantage, *Journal of Management*, 28: 416–446.

64. D. L. Deephouse, 2000, Media reputation as a strategic resource: An integration of mass communication and resource-based theories, *Journal of Management*, 26: 1091–1112.

65. Shamsie, The context of dominance.

66. Roberts & Dowling, Corporate reputation, 1078.

67. P. Berthon, M. B. Holbrook, & J. M. Hulbert, 2003, Understanding and managing the brand space, *MIT Sloan Management Review*, 44(2): 49–54; D. B. Holt, 2003, What becomes an icon most? *Harvard Business Review*, 81(3): 43–49.

68. J. Blasberg & V. Vishwanath, 2003, Making cool brands hot, *Harvard Business Review*, 81(6): 20–22.

69. 2003, Harley-Davidson MotorClothes Merchandise, http://www.harley davidson.com, July 20; M. Kleinman, 2001, Harley pushes brand prestige, *Marketing*, May 17, 16.

70. M. Blyler & R. W. Coff, 2003, Dynamic capabilities, social capital, and rent appropriation: Ties that split pies, *Strategic Management Journal*, 24: 677–686; C. E. Helfat & R. S. Raubitschek, 2000, Product sequencing: Co-evolution of knowledge, capabilities and products, *Strategic Management Journal*, 21: 961–979; Eisenhardt & Martin, Dynamic capabilities.

71. Hitt, Bierman, Shimizu, & Kochhar, Direct and moderating effects of human capital on strategy and performance in professional service firms: A resource-based perspective; M. A. Hitt, R. D. Ireland, & H. Lee, 2000, Technological learning, knowledge management, firm growth and performance: An introductory essay, *Journal of Engineering and Technology Management*, 17: 231–246; D. G. Hoopes & S. Postrel, 1999, Shared knowledge: "Glitches," and product development performance, *Strategic Management Journal*, 20: 837–865.

72. M. Burket, 2003, Funny business, *Forbes*, June 9, 173.

73. R. W. Coff & P. M. Lee, 2003, Insider trading as a vehicle to appropriate rent from R&D, *Strategic Management Journal*, 24: 183–190.

74. 1999, Thoughts on the business of life, *Forbes*, May 17, 352.

75. D. L. Deeds, 2003, Alternative strategies for acquiring knowledge, in S. E. Jackson, M. A. Hitt, & A. S. DeNisi (eds.), *Managing Knowledge for Sustained Competitive Advantage*, San Francisco: Jossey-Bass, 37–63.

76. R. A. Noe, J. A. Colquitt, M. J. Simmering, & S. A. Alvarez, 2003, Knowledge management: Developing intellectual and social capital, in S. E. Jackson, M. A. Hitt, & A. S. DeNisi (eds.), *Managing Knowledge for Sustained Competitive Advantage*, San Francisco: Jossey-Bass, 209–242; L. Argote & P. Ingram, 2000, Knowledge transfer: A basis for competitive advantage in firms, *Organizational Behavior and Human Decision Processes*, 82: 150–169.

77. G. G. Dess & J. C. Picken, 1999, *Beyond Productivity*, New York: AMACOM.

78. M. J. Tippins & R. S. Sohi, 2003, IT competency and firm performance: Is organizational learning a missing link? *Strategic Management Journal*, 24: 745–761.

79. T. T. Baldwin & C. C. Danielson, 2000, Building a learning strategy at the top: Interviews with ten of America's CLOs, *Business Horizons*, 43(6): 5–14.

80. D. F. Kuratko, R. D. Ireland, & J. S. Hornsby, 2001, Improving firm performance through entrepreneurial actions: Acordia's corporate entrepreneurship strategy, *Academy of Management Executive*, 15(4): 60–71; M. T. Hansen, N. Nhoria, & T. Tierney, 1999, What's your strategy for managing knowledge? *Harvard Business Review*, 77(2): 106–116.

81. M. A. Hitt & R. D. Ireland, 1986, Relationships among corporate level distinctive competencies, diversification strategy, corporate structure, and

performance, *Journal of Management Studies*, 23: 401–416; M. A. Hitt & R. D. Ireland, 1985, Corporate distinctive competence, strategy, industry, and performance, *Strategic Management Journal*, 6: 273–293; M. A. Hitt, R. D. Ireland, & K. A. Palia, 1982, Industrial firms' grand strategy and functional importance, *Academy of Management Journal*, 25: 265–298; M. A. Hitt, R. D. Ireland, & G. Stadter, 1982, Functional importance and company performance: Moderating effects of grand strategy and industry type, *Strategic Management Journal*, 3: 315–330; C. C. Snow & E. G. Hrebiniak, 1980, Strategy, distinctive competence, and organizational performance, *Administrative Science Quarterly*, 25: 317–336.

82. C. Zott, 2003, Dynamic capabilities and the emergence of intraindustry differential firm performance: Insights from a simulation study, *Strategic Management Journal*, 24: 97–125.

83. K. Hafeez, Y. B. Zhang, & N. Malak, 2002, Core competence for sustainable competitive advantage: A structured methodology for identifying core competence, *IEEE Transactions on Engineering Management*, 49(1): 28–35; C. K. Prahalad & G. Hamel, 1990, The core competence of the corporation, *Harvard Business Review*, 68(3): 79–93.

84. C. Bowman & V. Ambrosini, 2000, Value creation versus value capture: Towards a coherent definition of value in strategy, *British Journal of Management*, 11: 1–15; T. Chi, 1994, Trading in strategic resources: Necessary conditions, transaction cost problems, and choice of exchange structure, *Strategic Management Journal*, 15: 271–290.

85. C. Bowman, 2001, "Value" in the resource-based view of the firm: A contribution to the debate, *Academy of Management Review*, 26: 501–502.

86. C. Ames, 1995, Sales soft? Profits flat? It's time to rethink your business, *Fortune*, June 25, 142–146.

87. S. Lee, 2003, Starbucks reports outstanding August revenues, *Wall Street Journal Online*, http://www.wsj.com, August 28; N. D. Schwartz, 2001, Remedies for an economic hangover, *Fortune*, June 25, 130–138.

88. J. B. Barney, 1999, How a firm's capabilities affect boundary decisions, *Sloan Management Review*, 40(3): 137–145; J. B. Barney, 1995, Looking inside for competitive advantage, *Academy of Management Executive*, 9(4): 59–60; J. B. Barney, 1991, Firm resources and sustained competitive advantage, *Journal of Management*, 17: 99–120.

89. C. H. St. John & J. S. Harrison, 1999, Manufacturing-based relatedness, synergy, and coordination, *Strategic Management Journal*, 20: 129–145.

90. Barney, Looking inside for competitive advantage.

91. L. Lee, 2003, Online grocers: Finally delivering the lettuce, *Business Week Online*, http://www.businessweek.com, April 28.

92. Barney, Looking inside for competitive advantage, 52.

93. Ibid., 53.

94. Barney, How a firm's capabilities, 141.

95. Barney, Firm resources, 108.

96. J. Huey, 1993, How McKinsey does it, *Fortune*, November 1, 56–81.

97. J. Kurtzman, 1997, An interview with Rosabeth Moss Kanter, *Strategy & Business*, 16: 85–94.

98. L. E. Tetrick & N. Da Silva, 2003, Assessing the culture and climate for organizational learning, in S. E. Jackson, M. A. Hitt, & A. S. DeNisi (eds.), *Managing Knowledge for Sustained Competitive Advantage*, San Francisco: Jossey-Bass, 333–359; R. Burt, 1999, When is corporate culture a competitive asset? "Mastering Strategy" (Part Six), *Financial Times*, November 1, 14–15.

99. L. Soupata, 2001, Managing culture for competitive advantage at United Parcel Service, *Journal of Organizational Excellence*, 20(3): 19–26.

100. A. W. King & C. P. Zeithaml, 2001, Competencies and firm performance: Examining the causal ambiguity paradox, *Strategic Management Journal*, 22: 75–99; R. Reed & R. DeFillippi, 1990, Causal ambiguity, barriers to imitation, and sustainable competitive advantage, *Academy of Management Review*, 15: 88–102.

101. Leonard-Barton, *Wellsprings of Knowledge*, 7.

102. A. Ritt, 2000, Reaching for maximum flexibility, *Iron Age New Steel*, January, 20–26.

103. A. K. Gupta & V. Govindarajan, 2000, Knowledge management's social dimension: Lessons from Nucor Steel, *Sloan Management Review*, 42(1): 71–80.

104. Barney, Firm resources, 111.

105. Amit & Schoemaker, Strategic assets, 39.

106. M. J. Benner & M. L. Tushman, 2003, Exploitation, exploration, and process management: The productivity dilemma revisited, *Academy of Management Review*, 28: 238–256; S. K. McEvily, S. Das, & K. McCabe, 2000, Avoiding competence substitution through knowledge sharing, *Academy of Management Review*, 25: 294–311.

107. A. Serwer, 2002, Dell does domination, *Fortune*, January 21, 70–75.

108. M. E. Porter, 1985, *Competitive Advantage*, New York: Free Press, 33–61.

109. G. G. Dess, A. Gupta, J.-F. Hennart, & C. W. L. Hill, 1995, Conducting and integrating strategy research at the international corporate and business levels: Issues and directions, *Journal of Management*, 21: 376.

110. J. W. Boudreau, 2003, Strategic knowledge measurement and management, in S. E. Jackson, M. A. Hitt, & A. S. DeNisi (eds.), *Managing Knowledge for Sustained Competitive Advantage*, San Francisco: Jossey-Bass: 330–359; J. Webb & C. Gile, 2001, Reversing the value chain, *Journal of Business Strategy*, 22(2): 13–17.

111. R. Amit & C. Zott, 2001, Value creation in e-business, *Strategic Management Journal*, 22(Special Issue): 493–520; M. E. Porter, 2001, Strategy and the Internet, *Harvard Business Review*, 79(3): 62–78.

112. P. O'Connor, 2003, On-line pricing: An analysis of hotel-company practices, *Cornell Hotel and Restaurant Administration Quarterly*, 44: 88–96.

113. T. W. Gainey & B. S. Klaas, 2003, The outsourcing of training and development: Factors impacting client satisfaction, *Journal of Management*, 29: 207–229; J. Y. Murray & M. Kotabe, 1999, Sourcing strategies of U.S. service companies: A modified transaction-cost analysis, *Strategic Management Journal*, 20: 791–809.

114. M. Rola, 2002, Secrets to successful outsourcing management, *Computing Canada*, 28(23): 11.

115. C. Ansberry, 2003, The economy—the outlook: Outsourcing abroad draws debate at home, *Wall Street Journal Online*, http://www.wsj.com, July 14.

116. P. Bendor-Samuel, 2003, Outsourcing: Transforming the corporation, *Forbes*, Special Advertising Section, May 26.

117. K. Madigan & M. J. Mandel, 2003, Commentary: Outsourcing jobs: Is it bad? *Business Week Online*, http://www.businessweek.com, August 25.

118. J. Palmer, 2003, Auto supplier stands out by focusing on the inside, *Wall Street Journal Online*, http://www.wsj.com, August 17; A. Takeishi, 2001, Bridging inter- and intra-firm boundaries: Management of supplier involvement in automobile product development, *Strategic Management Journal*, 22: 403–433; H. Y. Park, C. S. Reddy, & S. Sarkar, 2000, Make or buy strategy of firms in the U.S., *Multinational Business Review*, 8(2): 89–97.

119. M. J. Leiblein, J. J. Reuer, & F. Dalsace, 2002, Do make or buy decisions matter? The influence of organizational governance on technological performance, *Strategic Management Journal*, 23: 817–833.

120. J. C. Linder, S. Jarvenpaa, & T. H. Davenport, 2003, Toward an innovation sourcing strategy, *MIT Sloan Management Review*, 44(4): 43–49.

121. Hafeez, Zhang, & Malak, Core competence for sustainable competitive advantage; B. H. Jevnaker & M. Bruce, 1999, Design as a strategic alliance: Expanding the creative capability of the firm, in M. A. Hitt, P. G. Clifford, R. D. Nixon, & K. P. Coyne (eds.), *Dynamic Strategic Resources*, Chichester: John Wiley & Sons, 266–298.

122. Takeishi, Bridging inter- and intra-firm boundaries.

123. R. Lancellotti, O. Schein, & V. Stadler, 2003, When outsourcing pays off, *The McKinsey Quarterly*, Number 1, 10.

124. M. Useem & J. Harder, 2000, Leading laterally in company outsourcing, *Sloan Management Review*, 41(2): 25–36.

125. R. C. Insinga & M. J. Werle, 2000, Linking outsourcing to business strategy, *Academy of Management Executive*, 14(4): 58–70.

126. M. Katz, 2001, Planning ahead for manufacturing facility changes: A case study in outsourcing, *Pharmaceutical Technology*, March: 160–164.

127. G. G. Dess & J. C. Picken, 1999, Creating competitive (dis)advantage: Learning from Food Lion's freefall, *Academy of Management Executive*, 13(3): 97–111.

128. De Carolis, Competencies and imitability, 28; M. Hannan & J. Freeman, 1977, The population ecology of organizations, *American Journal of Sociology*, 82: 929–964.

129. Leonard-Barton, *Wellsprings of Knowledge*, 30–31.

130. West & DeCastro, The Achilles heel of firm strategy; Keil, Cutting your losses.

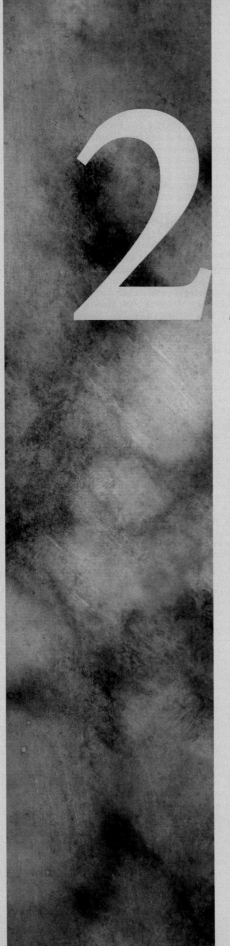

Part Two

Strategic Actions: Strategy Formulation

Business-Level Strategy

Chapter Four

4

Knowledge Objectives

Studying this chapter should provide you with the strategic management knowledge needed to:

1. Define business-level strategy.

2. Discuss the relationship between customers and business-level strategies in terms of *who, what,* and *how.*

3. Explain the differences among business-level strategies.

4. Use the five forces of competition model to explain how above-average returns can be earned through each business-level strategy.

5. Describe the risks of using each of the business-level strategies.

Corel Corporation

Krispy Kreme doughnuts utilizes a *differentiation business-level strategy* in that its products' perceived uniqueness is critical to the company's success. The uniqueness of Krispy Kreme and its products derives in part from making customers feel connected with the doughnut-making process. As one example, customers delight in anticipating the taste of the doughnuts by watching them bake in the "Doughnut Theatre."

Krispy Kreme is a leading specialty retailer of premium-quality doughnuts. The firm makes close to 3 billion doughnuts annually in approximately 280 stores in the United States and Canada. Krispy Kreme is expanding internationally into markets such as Australia, Spain, New Zealand, and the United Kingdom. As with its recently completed transaction with Grupo AXO in Mexico, much of the international expansion is taking place by forming joint venture agreements with local companies. The fact that there is a Krispy Kreme exhibit at the Smithsonian Institution's National Museum of American History is evidence that the firm is a cultural icon in the United States.

The differences in opinion about Krispy Kreme doughnuts are dramatic. Some believe that the high quality of the firm's offerings indicate that it is indeed the Michelangelo of doughnut makers and that there is "an art to making the doughnut." Others comment that Krispy Kreme doughnuts are "heavenly inspired." At the other extreme, passersby sometimes shout, "They're just doughnuts!" at loyalists waiting in line to be the first to purchase some of the products from a new Krispy Kreme store. Traffic jams and waits of two hours or more are common on the first day of a new unit. To be the first to buy doughnuts at a new location, some people begin camping out as much as 24 hours in advance of the store opening.

Krispy Kreme is implementing a differentiation business-level strategy. Discussed further in this chapter, the differentiation strategy is one in which the firm produces a good or service that customers perceive as being unique in ways that are important to them. The perception of uniqueness is critical in that it is what causes customers to buy a product that is more expensive than are offerings from competitors. The importance of uniqueness applies to Krispy Kreme as well, as suggested by an analyst who proposed, "It isn't what's inside a Krispy Kreme doughnut that creates the demand. It's what's inside the customer's head that makes a Krispy Kreme Krispy Kreme." The Doughnut Theatre—in which customers watch doughnuts being made in the store, wait for the "Hot Now" sign to illuminate, and look forward to trying the "doughnut of the month" to taste a new entry—and the firm's efforts to make customers feel that they are a part of the company and what it does are widely perceived as unique attributes of the Krispy Kreme experience and, as such, are competitive advantages for the firm. As part of the marketing effort, customers are encouraged to use the company's website to become a "Friend of Krispy Kreme." As a friend, customers receive information about product updates, warm requests for honest feedback about the firm's doughnuts and the experience surrounding their purchase and consumption, and news about Krispy Kreme's future plans. Through its marketing campaigns, Krispy Kreme attempts to find ways to create excitement that builds customer pride. Purchasing collectibles (e.g., shirts, sweatshirts, boxer shorts, mugs, hats, and toys) is thought to make customers feel as though they are a part of the company. Krispy Kreme uses its information technology capabilities (the firm's information technology department has won multiple industry awards) and its vertically integrated manufacturing process capability (the firm develops proprietary mixes which are made into doughnuts by its proprietary manufacturing equipment) to develop and support the Doughnut Theatre and marketing campaigns as competitive advantages.

Krispy Kreme also sells its doughnuts in other outlets such as grocery stores. This worries analysts who fear that the difference in quality between buying a hot doughnut in a Krispy Kreme store and buying one as a prepackaged item will dilute the value of the brand name and the bond between the firm and its on-site customers. A second major concern is the high fat content in Krispy Kreme's products. As discussed in a Strategic Focus in this chapter, McDonald's was alleged in a class-action lawsuit to be responsible for obesity in children. Might Krispy Kreme face such allegations in the future? Krispy Kreme must find ways to overcome potential problems while determining additional sources of differentiation that its customers will perceive as important to them.

SOURCES: 2003, Food brief—Krispy Kreme Doughnuts Inc.: Four inside directors resign, *Wall Street Journal Online*, http://www.wsj.com, April 10; T. Derpinghaus, 2003, Krispy Kreme restructures board, *Wall Street Journal Online*, http://www.wsj.com, April 9; C. Dyrness, 2003, Krispy Kreme adds new technologies to its arsenal, *News & Observer*, April 23; J. R. Graham, 2003, It's a Krispy Kreme world, *American Salesman*, April, 8–10; J. Harrison, 2003, Krispy Kreme chooses a bread maker as a platform for its café concept, *Mergers and Acquisitions*, 38(3): 12–13; J. Peters, 2003, Niche players seek to perk up sales with variety, *Nation's Restaurant News*, February 10, 1, 77; C. Skipp, 2003, Hot bytes, by the dozen, *Newsweek*, April 28, 42.

Increasingly important to firm success,[1] strategy is concerned with making choices among two or more alternatives. When choosing a strategy, the firm decides to pursue one course of action instead of others. Indeed, the main point of strategy is to help decision makers choose among competing priorities and alternatives.[2] Sound strategic decisions are the foundation on which successful strategies are built.[3] Business-level strategy, this chapter's focus, is the choice a firm makes when deciding how to compete in individual product markets. The choices are important, as there is an established link between a firm's strategies and its long-term performance.[4] Given the complexity of successfully competing in the global economy, these choices are difficult, often even gutwrenching.[5] Thus, Krispy Kreme's choices about how to make and distribute its products as well as how to interact with its customers will affect the firm's ability to earn above-average returns across time.

Determining the businesses in which the firm will compete is a question of corporate-level strategy and is discussed in Chapter 6. Competition in individual product markets is a question of business-level strategy. For all types of strategies, companies acquire the information and knowledge needed to make choices as they study external environmental opportunities and threats as well as identify and evaluate their internal resources, capabilities, and core competencies.

In Chapter 1, we defined a *strategy* as an integrated and coordinated set of commitments and actions designed to exploit core competencies and gain a competitive advantage. The different strategies that firms use to gain competitive advantages are shown in Figure 1.1 in Chapter 1. As described in the individual chapters outlined in the figure, the firm tries to establish and exploit a competitive advantage when using each type of strategy.[6] As explained in the Opening Case, Krispy Kreme is using a differentiation strategy to develop competitive advantages and exploit them for marketplace success.

Every firm needs a business-level strategy.[7] However, every firm may not use all the strategies—corporate-level, acquisition and restructuring, international, and cooperative—that are examined in Chapters 6 through 9. For example, the firm competing in a single-product market area in a single geographic location does not need a corporate-level strategy to deal with product diversity or an international strategy to deal with geographic diversity. Think of a local dry cleaner with only one location offering a single service (the cleaning and laundering of clothes) in a single storefront. In contrast, a diversified firm will use one of the corporate-level strategies as well as choose a separate business-level strategy for each product market area in which the company competes (the relationship between corporate-level and business-level strategies is further examined in Chapter 6). Thus, every firm—from the local dry cleaner to the multinational corporation—chooses at least one business-level strategy. Business-level strategy can be thought of as the firm's *core* strategy—the strategy that must be formed to describe how the firm will compete.[8]

Each strategy the firm uses specifies desired outcomes and how they are to be achieved.[9] Integrating external and internal foci, strategies reflect the firm's theory about how it intends to compete.[10] The fundamental objective of using each strategy is to create value for stakeholders. Strategies are purposeful, precede the taking of actions to which they apply, and demonstrate a shared understanding of the firm's strategic intent and strategic mission.[11] An effectively formulated strategy marshals, integrates, and allocates the firm's resources, capabilities, and competencies so that it will be properly aligned with its external environment.[12] A properly developed strategy also rationalizes the firm's strategic intent and strategic mission along with the actions taken to achieve them.[13] Information about a host of variables, including markets, customers, technology, worldwide finance, and the changing world economy, must be collected and analyzed to properly form and use strategies.[14] Increasingly, Internet technology affects how organizations gather and study data and information that are related to decisions about the choice and use of strategy.[15]

Business-level strategy, this chapter's focus, is an integrated and coordinated set of commitments and actions the firm uses to gain a competitive advantage by exploiting core competencies in specific product markets.[16] Only firms that continuously upgrade their competitive advantages over time are able to achieve long-term success with their business-level strategy.[17] Key issues the firm must address when choosing a business-level strategy are what good or service to offer customers, how to manufacture or create it, and how to distribute it to the marketplace. Once formed, the business-level strategy reflects where and how the firm has an advantage over its rivals.[18] The essence of a firm's business-level strategy is "choosing to perform activities differently or to perform different activities than rivals."[19]

A business-level strategy is an integrated and coordinated set of commitments and actions the firm uses to gain a competitive advantage by exploiting core competencies in specific product markets.

Customers are the foundation of successful business-level strategies and should never be taken for granted.[20] In fact, some believe that an effective business-level strategy demonstrates the firm's ability to "build and maintain relationships to the best people for maximum value creation, both 'internally' (to firm members) and 'externally' (to customers)."[21] Thus, successful organizations think of their employees as internal customers who produce value-creating products for which customers are willing to pay; such organizations also understand that the quality of their interactions with customers has a direct effect on firm performance.[22]

Because of their strategic importance, customers are the focus of discussion at the beginning of this chapter. Three issues are considered in this analysis. In selecting a business-level strategy, the firm determines (1) *who* will be served, (2) *what* needs those target customers have that it will satisfy, and (3) *how* those needs will be satisfied. Selecting customers and deciding which of their needs the firm will try to satisfy, as well as how it will do so, are challenging choices for today's organizations. Global competition, which has created many attractive options for customers, is one reason for this. In the current competitive environment, effective global competitors have become adept at identifying the needs of customers in different cultures and geographic regions as well as learning how to quickly and successfully adapt the functionality of the firms' good or service to meet those needs.

Descriptions of five business-level strategies follow the discussion of customers. These five strategies are sometimes called *generic* because they can be used in any business and in any industry.[23] Our analysis of these strategies describes how effective use of each strategy allows the firm to favorably position itself relative to the five competitive forces in the industry (see Chapter 2). In addition, we use the value chain (see Chapter 3) to show examples of the primary and support activities that are necessary to implement each business-level strategy. We also describe the different risks the firm may encounter when using one of these strategies.

Organizational structures and controls that are linked with successful use of each business-level strategy are explained in Chapter 11.

Customers: Who, What, and How

One of the key issues that firms must address in their business-level strategy is how to distribute their products to the marketplace. Amazon.com manages its relationships with its customers well by anticipating their needs. In this case, distribution of its products plays a key role as staff at online bookseller Amazon.com U.K. prepare to ship out 65,000 copies of the latest *Harry Potter* book.

Strategic competitiveness results only when the firm is able to satisfy a group of customers by using its competitive advantages as the basis for competing in individual product markets. A key reason firms must satisfy customers with their business-level strategy is that returns earned from relationships with customers are the lifeblood of all organizations.[24] Executives at Motley Fool capture this reality crisply by noting that "the customer is the person who pays us."[25]

The most successful companies such as Dell Inc. constantly seek to chart new competitive space in order to serve new customers as they simultaneously find ways to better serve existing customers. The former Dell Computer Corp. recently dropped the word *computer* from its name and became Dell Inc. This action was partly taken to signal to the market that while continuing to find ways to better serve its PC users, the company is also entering new markets and serving new customers with its network switches, handheld devices, projectors, printers, and server computers for large corporations.[26]

©Reuters NewMedia Inc./CORBIS

The Importance of Effectively Managing Relationships with Customers

The firm's relationships with its customers are strengthened when it delivers superior value to them. Superior value at Harrah's Entertainment is largely defined as providing outstanding service to customers.[27] Importantly, delivering superior value often results in increased loyalty from customers to the firm providing it. In turn, customer loyalty has a positive relationship with profitability. Ford Motor Company, for example, estimates that each percentage-point increase in customer loyalty—defined as how many Ford owners purchase a Ford product the next time—creates at least $100 million in additional profits annually. MBNA, a credit card issuer, determined that reducing customer defection rates by 5 percent increases the lifetime profitability of the average customer by 125 percent.[28] However, increased choice and easily accessible information about the functionality of firms' products are creating increasingly sophisticated and knowledgeable customers, making it difficult to earn their loyalty.[29]

A number of companies have become skilled at the art of *managing* all aspects of their relationship with their customers.[30] For example, Amazon.com is an Internet-based venture widely recognized for the quality of information it maintains about its customers, the services it renders, and its ability to anticipate customers' needs.[31] Based in Mexico, Cemex SA is the world's third largest cement maker. Cemex uses the Internet to link its customers, cement plants, and main control room, allowing the firm to automate orders and optimize truck deliveries in highly congested Mexico City. Analysts believe that Cemex's integration of Web technology with its cost leadership strategy is helping to differentiate it from competitors.[32] GE is using Internet technology to save money and to enhance relationships with its customers by reaching them faster with products of ever-increasing quality.[33]

As we discuss next, there are three dimensions of firms' relationships with customers. Companies such as Amazon.com, Cemex, and GE understand these dimensions and manage their relationships with customers in light of them.

Reach, Richness, and Affiliation

The *reach* dimension of relationships with customers is concerned with the firm's access and connection to customers. For instance, the largest physical retailer in bookstores, Barnes & Noble, carries approximately 200,000 titles in over 900 stores. By contrast, Amazon.com offers more than 4.5 million titles and is located on tens of millions of computer screens with additional customer connections being established. Thus, Amazon.com's reach is significantly magnified relative to that associated with Barnes & Noble's physical bookstores.[34] In general, firms seek to extend their reach, adding customers in the process of doing so.

Richness, the second dimension, is concerned with the depth and detail of the two-way flow of information between the firm and the customer. The potential of the richness dimension to help the firm establish a competitive advantage in its relationship with customers led traditional financial services brokers, such as Merrill Lynch, Lehman Brothers, and others, to offer online services in order to better manage information exchanges with their customers. Broader and deeper information-based exchanges allow firms to better understand their customers and their needs. Such exchanges also enable customers to become more knowledgeable about how the firm can satisfy them. Internet technology and e-commerce transactions have substantially reduced the costs of meaningful information exchanges with current and possible future customers.

Affiliation, the third dimension, is concerned with facilitating useful interactions with customers. Internet navigators such as Microsoft CarPoint help online clients find and sort information. CarPoint provides data and software to prospective car buyers that enable them to compare car models along multiple objective specifications. The program can supply this information because Internet technology allows a great deal of information to be collected from a variety of sources at a low cost. A prospective buyer who has selected a specific car based on comparisons of different models can then be linked to dealers that meet the customer's needs and purchasing requirements. An auto manufacturing company represents its own products, creating a situation in which its financial interests differ substantially from those of consumers. Because its revenues come from sources other than the final customer or end user (such as advertisements on its website, hyperlinks, and associated products and services), CarPoint represents the customer's interests, a service that fosters affiliation.[35] Viewing the world through the customer's eyes and constantly seeking ways to create more value for the customer have positive effects in terms of affiliation.

As we discuss next, effective management of customer relationships helps the firm answer questions related to the issues of *who, what,* and *how.*

Who: Determining the Customers to Serve

A crucial business-level strategy decision is the one made about the target customers for the firm's goods or services (*who*).[36] To make this decision, companies divide customers into groups based on differences in the customers' needs (needs are defined and further discussed in the next section). Called **market segmentation,** this process clusters people with similar needs into individual and identifiable groups.[37] In the animal health business, for example, the needs for food products of owners of companion pets (e.g., dogs and cats) differ from the needs for food products of those owning production animals (e.g., livestock).[38] As part of its business-level strategy, the firm develops a marketing program to effectively sell products to its particular target customer group.

Almost any identifiable human or organizational characteristic can be used to subdivide a market into segments that differ from one another on a given characteristic. Common characteristics on which customers' needs vary are illustrated in Table 4.1. Based on their internal core competencies and opportunities in the external environment, companies choose a business-level strategy to deliver value to target customers and satisfy their specific needs.

Customer characteristics are often combined to segment a large market into specific groups that have unique needs. For example, McDonald's dominates the fast-food market. However, for college students interested in healthy eating, surveys suggest that Subway is the dominant fast-food choice.[39] This more specific breakdown of the fast-food market for college students is a product of jointly studying demographic, psychological, and consumption-pattern characteristics (see Table 4.1). This knowledge suggests that on a relative basis, Subway's business-level strategy should target college students with a desire for healthier foods more aggressively than should McDonald's.

Demographic characteristics (see the discussion in Chapter 2 and Table 4.1) can also be used to segment markets into generations with unique interests and needs. Evidence suggests, for example, that direct mail is an effective communication medium for the World War II generation (those born before 1932). The Swing generation (those born between 1933 and 1945) values taking cruises and purchasing second homes. Once financially conservative but now willing to spend money, members of this generation seek product information from knowledgeable sources. The Baby Boom generation (born between 1946 and 1964) desires products that reduce the stress generated by juggling career demands and the needs of older parents with those of their own children. Ellen Tracy

Consumer Markets

1. Demographic factors (age, income, sex, etc.)
2. Socioeconomic factors (social class, stage in the family life cycle)
3. Geographic factors (cultural, regional, and national differences)
4. Psychological factors (lifestyle, personality traits)
5. Consumption patterns (heavy, moderate, and light users)
6. Perceptual factors (benefit segmentation, perceptual mapping)

Industrial Markets

1. End-use segments (identified by SIC code)
2. Product segments (based on technological differences or production economics)
3. Geographic segments (defined by boundaries between countries or by regional differences within them)
4. Common buying factor segments (cut across product market and geographic segments)
5. Customer size segments

SOURCE: Adapted from S. C. Jain, 2000, *Marketing Planning and Strategy,* Cincinnati: South-Western College Publishing, 120.

clothes, known for their consistency of fit and color, are targeted to Baby Boomer women. More conscious of hype, the 60-million-plus people in Generation X (born between 1965 and 1976) want products that deliver as promised. The Xers use the Internet as a primary shopping tool and expect visually compelling marketing. Members of this group are the fastest growing segment of mutual-fund shareholders, with their holdings overwhelmingly invested in stock funds. As employees, the top priorities of Xers are to work in a creative learning environment, to receive constant feedback from managers, and to be rewarded for using their technical skills.[40] Different marketing campaigns and distribution channels (e.g., the Internet for Generation X customers as compared to direct mail for the World War II generation) affect the implementation of strategies for those companies interested in serving the needs of different generations.

As this discussion suggests, markets are being segmented into increasingly specialized niches of customers with unique needs and interests. Generation Y (born between 1977 and 1984) is yet another market segment with specific characteristics that affect how firms use business-level strategies to serve customers' needs. Analysis of purchasing patterns shows that this segment prefers to buy in stores rather than online, but that these customers may use the Internet to study products online prior to visiting a store to make a purchase. This preference suggests that companies targeting this segment might want to combine their storefront operations with a robust and active website.[41] Other examples of targeting specific market segments include New Balance's marketing of its shoes to members of the Baby Boom generation (see the Strategic Focus in this chapter), Christopher & Banks' focusing on working women over the age of 40, and Abercrombie & Fitch's targeting of the subgroup of teenagers who demand fashion-oriented casual apparel.[42]

What: Determining Which Customer Needs to Satisfy

After the firm decides *who* it will serve, it must identify the targeted customer group's needs that its goods or services can satisfy. *Needs (what)* are related to a product's benefits and features.[43] Having close and frequent interactions with both current and potential customers helps the firm identify those individuals' and groups' current and future needs.[44] From a strategic perspective, a basic need of all customers is to buy products that create value for them. The generalized forms of value goods or services provide are either low cost with acceptable features or highly differentiated features with acceptable cost. The most effective firms continuously strive to anticipate changes in customers' needs. Failure to do this results in the loss of customers to competitors who are offering greater value in terms of product features and functionalities.[45]

In any given industry, there is great variety among consumers in terms of their needs.[46] The need some consumers have for high-quality, fresh sandwiches is what Pret A Manger seeks to satisfy with its menu items. In contrast, many large fast-food companies satisfy customer needs for lower-cost food items with acceptable quality that are delivered quickly.[47] Diversified food and soft-drink producer PepsiCo believes that "any one consumer has different needs at different times of the day." Through its soft drinks (Pepsi products), snacks (Frito-Lay), juices (Tropicana), and cereals (Quaker), PepsiCo is working on developing new products from breakfast bars to healthier potato chips "to make certain sure that it covers all those needs."[48] In the information technology area, a growing number of customers seem to want firms to help them learn how to use currently owned technologies to improve productivity.[49] Thus, instead of trying to sell increasingly sophisticated technology products, some technology companies are focusing on helping such customers improve their ability to fully use the products they've already bought. In contrast, some information technology consumers are more interested in "being on the cutting edge of the technological age," as shown by their desire to continuously buy products with the most sophisticated technological capabilities. In general, and across multiple product groups (e.g., automobiles, clothing, food), evidence suggests that middle-market consumers in the United States want to trade up to higher levels of quality and taste. These customers "are willing to pay premiums of 20% to 200% for the kinds of well-designed, well-engineered, and well-crafted goods—often possessing the artisanal touches of traditional luxury goods—not before found in the mass middle market."[50] These needs represent opportunities for some firms to pursue through their business-level strategies.

To ensure success, a firm must be able to fully understand the needs of the customers in the target group it has selected to serve. In this sense, customer needs are neither right nor wrong, good nor bad. Instead, customer needs simply represent the desires in terms of features and performance capabilities of those customers the firm has targeted to serve with its goods or services. The most effective firms are filled with people committed to understanding the customers' current as well as future needs.

How: Determining Core Competencies Necessary to Satisfy Customer Needs

As explained in Chapters 1 and 3, *core competencies* are resources and capabilities that serve as a source of competitive advantage for the firm over its rivals. Firms use core competencies (*how*) to implement value-creating strategies and thereby satisfy customers' needs. Only those firms with the capacity to continuously improve, innovate, and upgrade their competencies can expect to meet and hopefully exceed customers' expectations across time.[51]

Companies draw from a wide range of core competencies to produce goods or services that can satisfy customers' needs. IBM, for example, emphasizes its core competence in technology to rapidly develop new service-related products. Beginning in

1993, then newly appointed CEO Lou Gerstner changed IBM by leveraging its "strength in network integration and consulting to transform [the firm] from a moribund maker of mainframe computers to a sexy services company that can basically design, build, and manage a corporation's entire data system."[52] SAS Institute is the world's largest privately owned software company and is the leader in business intelligence and analytics. Customers use SAS' programs for data warehousing, data mining, and decision support purposes. Allocating over 30 percent of revenues to research and development (R&D), SAS relies on its core competence in R&D to satisfy the data-related needs of such customers as the U.S. Census Bureau and a host of consumer goods firms (e.g., hotels, banks, and catalog companies).[53] Vans Inc. relies on its core competencies in innovation and marketing to design and sell such products as skateboards. The firm also pioneered thick-soled, slip-on sneakers that can absorb the shock of 5-foot leaps on wheels. Vans uses what is recognized as an offbeat marketing mix to capitalize on its pioneering products. In lieu of mass media ads, the firm sponsors skateboarding events, supported the making of a documentary film that celebrates the "outlaw nature" of the skateboarding culture, and is building skateboard parks at malls around the country.[54]

All organizations, including IBM, SAS, and Vans Inc., must be able to use their core competencies (the *how*) to satisfy the needs (the *what*) of the target group of customers (the *who*) the firm has chosen to serve by using its business-level strategy.

Next, we discuss the business-level strategies firms use when pursuing strategic competitiveness and above-average returns.

Types of Business-Level Strategy

Business-level strategies are intended to create differences between the firm's position and those of its rivals.[55] To position itself, the firm must decide whether it intends to *perform activities differently* or to *perform different activities* as compared to its rivals.[56] Thus, the firm's business-level strategy is a deliberate choice about how it will perform the value chain's primary and support activities in ways that create unique value.

Successful use of a chosen strategy results only when the firm integrates its primary and support activities to provide the unique value it intends to deliver. Value is delivered to customers when the firm is able to use competitive advantages resulting from the integration of activities. Superior fit among primary and support activities forms an activity system. In turn, an effective activity system helps the firm establish and exploit its strategic position. We describe Southwest Airlines' activity system in the Strategic Focus. The firm's integrated cost leadership/differentiation strategy has created great wealth for shareholders in that an initial $1,000 investment in 1972 grew to $102 million by the end of 2002.[57]

The importance of fit between primary and support activities isn't unique to Southwest, in that fit among activities is a key to the sustainability of competitive advantage for all firms. As Michael Porter comments, "Strategic fit among many activities is fundamental not only to competitive advantage but also to the sustainability of that advantage. It is harder for a rival to match an array of interlocked activities than it is merely to imitate a particular sales-force approach, match a process technology, or replicate a set of product features. Positions built on systems of activities are far more sustainable than those built on individual activities."[58]

Favorably positioned firms such as Southwest Airlines have a competitive advantage over their industry rivals and are better able to cope with the five forces of competition (see Chapter 2). Favorable positioning is important in that the universal objective of all companies is to develop and sustain competitive advantages.[59] Improperly positioned firms encounter competitive difficulties and likely will fail to sustain competitive advantages. For example, its ineffective responses to competitors such as Wal-Mart left

Southwest Airlines' Activity System: Is It Imitable?

Launched in 1971 with service among three Texas cities—Dallas, Houston, and San Antonio—Southwest Airlines offers short-haul, low-cost, point-to-point service between midsized cities and secondary airports in large cities. It performs its activities in ways that drive the firm's costs lower and lower. According to company officials, Southwest is "always looking for an opportunity to make the lowest even lower" as it simultaneously provides customers with some unique, value-creating sources of differentiation (such as an "entertaining experience" while in the air).

Relying on customer service and organizational culture as its two major competitive advantages, the firm is successfully using its integrated cost leadership/differentiation strategy. As of the end of the second quarter of 2003, for example, Southwest was the only major airline to post a profit in every quarter since the September 11, 2001, terrorist attacks on the United States. Moreover, the firm hadn't canceled any flights or furloughed any employees during that time period. The posting of a 14 percent profit gain on a 7 percent rise in sales in 2003's second quarter is strong evidence of Southwest's ability to continuously drive its costs lower.

Because Southwest's fares are as much as 20 percent below those charged by mainstream carriers, the firm's effect on pricing in the markets it serves can be dramatic. Average fares in Raleigh-Durham, N.C., for example, are roughly half those in Charlotte, N.C. Southwest serves the Raleigh-Durham airport, but not the Charlotte airport. Dallas, Texas' Love Field has the lowest average fares in the country. This is important because only Southwest serves Love Field. As former CEO and cofounder Herb Kelleher said, "If you're going to be a low-fare airline, you have to charge low fares even when you don't have competition."

An activity system can be mapped to show how individual activities are integrated to achieve fit, as the map for Southwest's activities on the next page shows. Higher-order strategic themes are critical to successful use of the firm's strategy. For Southwest Airlines, these strategic themes are limited passenger service; frequent, reliable departures; lean, highly productive ground and gate crews; high aircraft utilization; very low ticket prices; and short-haul, point-to-point routes between midsized cities and secondary airports. Individual clusters of tightly linked activities make it possible for the outcome of a strategic theme to be achieved. For example, no meals, no seat assignments, and no baggage transfers form a cluster of individual activities that support the strategic theme of limited passenger service.

Southwest's tightly integrated primary and support activities make it difficult for competitors to imitate the firm's strategy. The firm's culture influences these activities and their integration and contributes to the firm's ability to continuously identify additional ways to differentiate Southwest's service from its competitors' as well as to lower its costs. In fact, the firm's unique culture and customer service, both of which are sources of differentiated customer features, are competitive advantages rivals have not been able to imitate, although some have tried. US Airways' MetroJet subsidiary, United Airlines' United Shuttle, and Continental Airlines' Continental Lite all failed in attempts to imitate Southwest's strategy. Hindsight shows that these competitors offered low prices to customers, but weren't able to operate at costs close to those of Southwest or to provide customers with any notable sources of differentiation, such as a unique experience while in the air.

(continued on next page)

SOURCES: 2003, Southwest Airlines, *Standard & Poor's Stock Reports*, http://www.standardandpoors.com, May 3; E. Torbenson, 2003, Southwest cheers its growth at annual meeting, *Dallas Morning News*, May 15, D1, D3; A. Tsao, 2003, Getting the carriers back in the air, *BusinessWeek Online*, http://www.businessweek.com, April 2; M. Arndt, 2001, A simple and elegant flight pattern, *Business Week*, June 11, 118; J. H. Gittell, 2001, Investing in relationships, *Harvard Business Review*, 79(6): 28–30; M. E. Porter, 1996, What is strategy? *Harvard Business Review*, 74(6): 61–78.

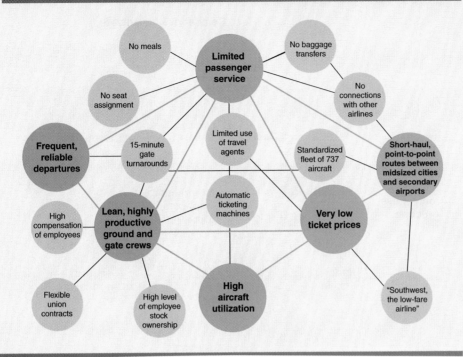

Sears, Roebuck and Co. in a weak competitive position for years. These ineffective responses resulted from the inability of Sears to properly implement strategies that were appropriate in light of its external opportunities and threats and its internal competencies. Two researchers describe this situation: "Once a towering force in retailing, Sears spent 10 years vacillating between an emphasis on hard goods and soft goods, venturing in and out of ill-chosen arenas, failing to differentiate itself in any of them, and never building a compelling economic logic."[60] As we described in Chapter 3, Sears is now taking actions to effectively position itself and to develop and effectively exploit competitive advantages.

Firms choose from among five business-level strategies to establish and defend their desired strategic position against rivals: *cost leadership, differentiation, focused cost leadership, focused differentiation,* and *integrated cost leadership/differentiation* (see Figure 4.1). Each business-level strategy helps the firm to establish and exploit a competitive advantage within a particular competitive scope. Once chosen, a firm's business-level strategy and its use demonstrate how the firm differs from competitors.[61]

When selecting a business-level strategy, firms evaluate two types of potential competitive advantage: "lower cost than rivals, or the ability to differentiate and command a premium price that exceeds the extra cost of doing so."[62] Having lower cost derives from the firm's ability to perform activities differently than rivals; being able to differentiate indicates the firm's capacity to perform different (and valuable) activities.[63] Competitive advantage is thus achieved within some scope and is the cause of superior firm performance.[64]

Scope has several dimensions, including the group of product and customer segments served and the array of geographic markets in which the firm competes. Competitive advantage is sought by competing in many customer segments when implementing either the cost leadership or the differentiation strategy. In contrast, when using focus strategies, firms seek a cost competitive advantage or a differentiation competitive

Figure 4.1 ———— Five Business-Level Strategies

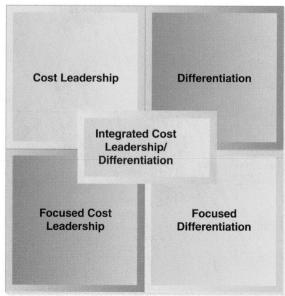

SOURCE: Adapted with the permission of The Free Press, an imprint of Simon & Schuster Adult Publishing Group, from *Competitive Advantage: Creating and Sustaining Superior Performance*, by Michael E. Porter, 12. Copyright © 1985, 1998 by Michael E. Porter.

advantage in a *narrow competitive scope, segment,* or *niche.* With focus strategies, the firm "selects a segment or group of segments in the industry and tailors its strategy to serving them to the exclusion of others."[65]

None of the five business-level strategies is inherently or universally superior to the others.[66] The effectiveness of each strategy is contingent both on the opportunities and threats in a firm's external environment and on the possibilities provided by the firm's unique resources, capabilities, and core competencies. It is critical, therefore, for the firm to select a strategy that is based on a match between the opportunities and threats in its external environment and the strengths of its internal environment as shown by its core competencies.

Cost Leadership Strategy

The cost leadership strategy is an integrated set of actions taken to produce goods or services with features that are acceptable to customers at the lowest cost, relative to that of competitors.

The **cost leadership strategy** is an integrated set of actions taken to produce goods or services with features that are acceptable to customers at the lowest cost, relative to that of competitors.[67] Cost leaders' goods and services must have competitive levels of differentiation in terms of features that create value for customers. Indeed, emphasizing cost reductions while ignoring competitive levels of differentiation is ineffective. At the extreme, concentrating only on reducing costs could find the firm very efficiently producing products that no customer wants to purchase. When the firm designs, produces, and markets a comparable product more efficiently than its rivals, there is evidence that it is successfully using the cost leadership strategy.[68] Firms using the cost leadership strategy sell no-frills, standardized goods or services (but with competitive levels of differentiation) to the industry's most typical customers. Cost leaders concentrate on finding ways to lower their costs relative to those of their competitors by constantly rethinking how to complete their primary and support activities (see Chapter 2) to reduce costs still further while maintaining competitive levels of differentiation.[69]

As primary activities, inbound logistics (e.g., materials handling, warehousing, and inventory control) and outbound logistics (e.g., collecting, storing, and distributing products to customers) often account for significant portions of the total cost to produce some goods and services. Research suggests that having a competitive advantage in terms of logistics creates more value when using the cost leadership strategy than when using the differentiation strategy.[70] Thus, cost leaders seeking competitively valuable ways to reduce costs may want to concentrate on the primary activities of inbound logistics and outbound logistics.

Cost leaders also carefully examine all support activities to find additional sources of potential cost reductions. Developing new systems for finding the optimal combination of low cost and acceptable quality in the raw materials required to produce the firm's goods or services is an example of how the procurement support activity can facilitate successful use of the cost leadership strategy.

Big Lots uses the cost leadership strategy. Committed to the strategic intent of being "The World's Best Bargain Place," Big Lots is the largest broadline closeout discount chain in the United States. Operating under the format names of Big Lots, Big Lots Furniture, Wisconsin Toy, Consolidated International, and Big Lots Wholesale, the firm strives constantly to drive its costs lower relative to its competitors' by relying on what some analysts see as a highly disciplined merchandise cost and inventory management system.[71] The firm's stores sell name-brand products at prices that are 15 to 35 percent below those of discount retailers and roughly 80 percent below those of traditional retailers.[72] Big Lots' buyers travel the country looking through manufacturer overruns and discontinued styles, finding goods priced at well below wholesale prices. In addition, the firm buys from overseas suppliers. Big Lots thinks of itself as the undertaker of the retailing business, purchasing merchandise that others can't sell or don't want. The target customer is one seeking what Big Lots calls the "closeout moment," which is the feeling customers have after they recognize their significant savings from buying a brand name item at a steeply discounted price.[73] The customer need Big Lots satisfies is to access the differentiated features and capabilities of brand-name products, but at a fraction of their initial cost. The tight integration of purchasing and inventory management activities across its full set of stores is the main core competence Big Lots uses to satisfy its customers' needs.

As described in Chapter 3, firms use value-chain analysis to determine the parts of the company's operations that create value and those that do not. Figure 4.2 demonstrates the primary and support activities that allow a firm to create value through the cost leadership strategy. Companies unable to link the activities shown in this figure typically lack the core competencies needed to successfully use the cost leadership strategy.

Effective use of the cost leadership strategy allows a firm to earn above-average returns in spite of the presence of strong competitive forces (see Chapter 2). The next sections (one for each of the five forces) explain how firms are able to do this.

RIVALRY WITH EXISTING COMPETITORS

Having the low-cost position is a valuable defense against rivals. Because of the cost leader's advantageous position, rivals hesitate to compete on the basis of price, especially before evaluating the potential outcomes of such competition.[74] Wal-Mart is known for its ability to both control and reduce costs, making it difficult for firms to compete against it on the basis of costs. The discount retailer achieves strict cost control in several ways: "Wal-Mart's 660,000-square-foot main headquarters, with its drab gray interiors and frayed carpets, looks more like a government building than the home of one of the world's largest corporations. Business often is done in the no-frills cafeteria, and suppliers meet with managers in stark, cramped rooms. Employees have to throw out their own garbage at the end of the day and double up in hotel rooms on business

Figure 4.2 — Examples of Value-Creating Activities Associated with the Cost Leadership Strategy

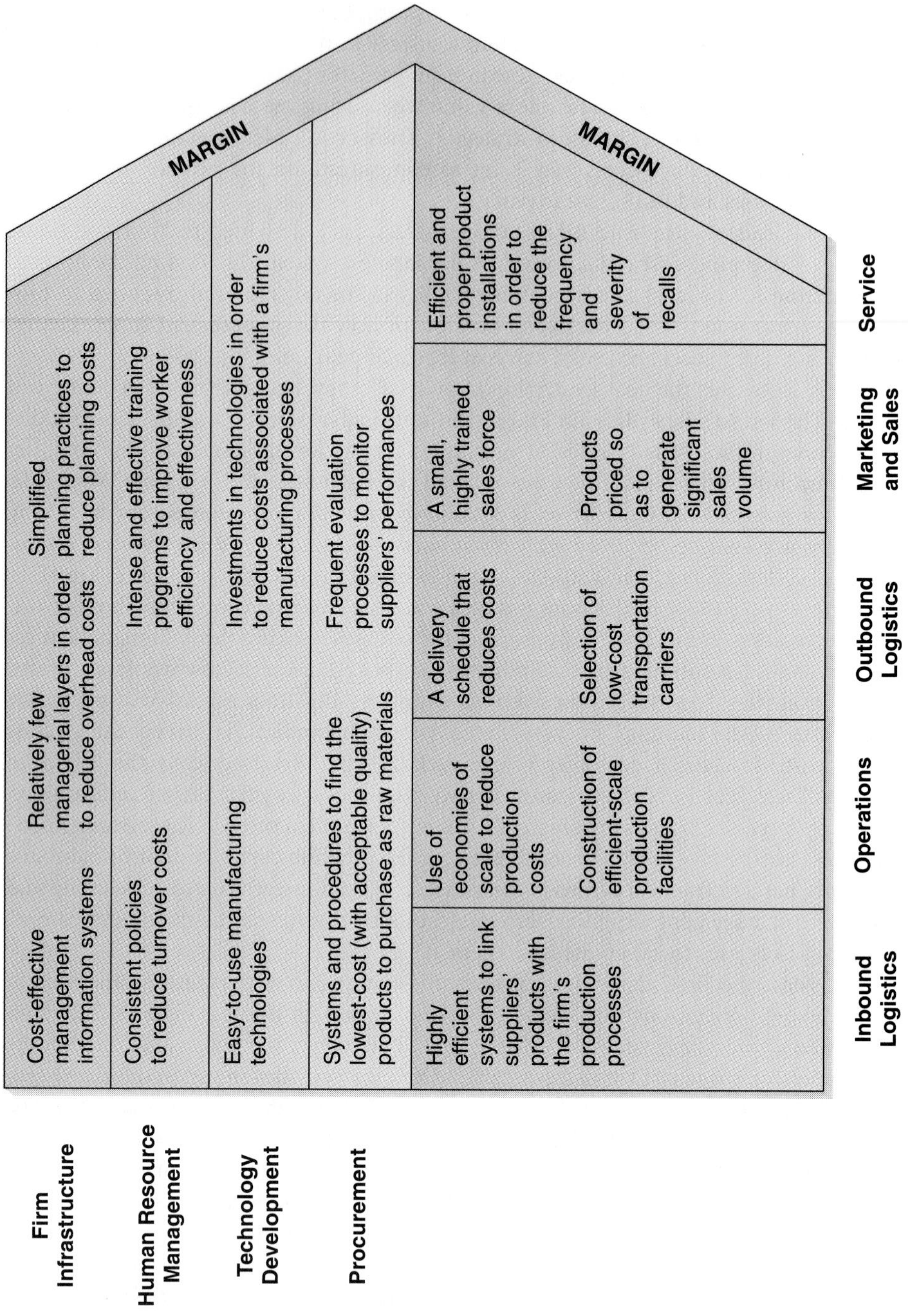

	Inbound Logistics	Operations	Outbound Logistics	Marketing and Sales	Service
Firm Infrastructure	Cost-effective management information systems — Relatively few managerial layers in order to reduce overhead costs — Simplified planning practices to reduce planning costs				
Human Resource Management	Consistent policies to reduce turnover costs — Intense and effective training programs to improve worker efficiency and effectiveness				
Technology Development	Easy-to-use manufacturing technologies — Investments in technologies in order to reduce costs associated with a firm's manufacturing processes				
Procurement	Systems and procedures to find the lowest-cost (with acceptable quality) products to purchase as raw materials — Frequent evaluation processes to monitor suppliers' performances				
	Highly efficient systems to link suppliers' products with the firm's production processes	Use of economies of scale to reduce production costs	A delivery schedule that reduces costs	A small, highly trained sales force	Efficient and proper product installations in order to reduce the frequency and severity of recalls
		Construction of efficient-scale production facilities	Selection of low-cost transportation carriers	Products priced so as to generate significant sales volume	

MARGIN

SOURCE: Adapted with the permission of The Free Press, an imprint of Simon & Schuster Adult Publishing Group, from *Competitive Advantage: Creating and Sustaining Superior Performance*, by Michael E. Porter, 47. Copyright © 1985, 1998 by Michael E. Porter.

trips."[75] Kmart's decision to compete against Wal-Mart on the basis of cost contributed to the firm's failure and subsequent bankruptcy filing. Its competitively inferior distribution system—an inefficient and high-cost system compared to Wal-Mart's—is one of the factors that prevented Kmart from having a competitive cost structure relative to Wal-Mart.

As noted earlier, research suggests that having a competitive advantage in terms of logistics significantly contributes to the cost leader's ability to earn above-average returns.[76] Because Wal-Mart developed a logistics competitive advantage that has become the world standard, the probability that Kmart could successfully engage in price competition with the retailing giant was very low. Also contending with strong pricing pressure from Wal-Mart,[77] Target Corp. relies on means other than specific price competition, including its Target credit card. With almost $6 billion in credit card receivables at the end of fiscal year 2002, Target earned $150 million in that year's fourth quarter alone from its credit card operations. Target continues to try to find ways to increase the value its customers can derive by using the Target credit card, hoping that being able to do so will create a competitive advantage for the firm.[78]

BARGAINING POWER OF BUYERS (CUSTOMERS)

Powerful customers can force a cost leader to reduce its prices, but not below the level at which the cost leader's next-most-efficient industry competitor can earn average returns. Although powerful customers might be able to force the cost leader to reduce prices even below this level, they probably would not choose to do so. Prices that are low enough to prevent the next-most-efficient competitor from earning average returns would force that firm to exit the market, leaving the cost leader with less competition and in an even stronger position. Customers would thus lose their power and pay higher prices if they were forced to purchase from a single firm operating in an industry without rivals.

BARGAINING POWER OF SUPPLIERS

The cost leader operates with margins greater than those of competitors. Among other benefits, higher margins relative to those of competitors make it possible for the cost leader to absorb its suppliers' price increases. When an industry faces substantial increases in the cost of its supplies, only the cost leader may be able to pay the higher prices and continue to earn either average or above-average returns. Alternatively, a powerful cost leader may be able to force its suppliers to hold down their prices, which would reduce the suppliers' margins in the process. Wal-Mart uses its power with suppliers (gained because it buys such large quantities from many suppliers) to extract lower prices from them. These savings are then passed on to customers in the form of lower prices, which further strengthens Wal-Mart's position relative to competitors lacking the power to extract lower prices from suppliers.[79]

POTENTIAL ENTRANTS

Through continuous efforts to reduce costs to levels that are lower than competitors', a cost leader becomes highly efficient. Because ever-improving levels of efficiency enhance profit margins, they serve as a significant entry barrier to potential competitors. New entrants must be willing and able to accept no-better-than-average returns until they gain the experience required to approach the cost leader's efficiency. To earn even average returns, new entrants must have the competencies required to match the cost levels of competitors other than the cost leader. The low profit margins (relative to margins earned by firms implementing the differentiation strategy) make it necessary for the cost leader to sell large volumes of its product to earn above-average returns. However, firms striving to be the cost leader must avoid pricing their products so low that their ability to operate profitably is reduced, even though volume increases.

PRODUCT SUBSTITUTES

Compared to its industry rivals, the cost leader also holds an attractive position in terms of product substitutes. A product substitute becomes an issue for the cost leader when its features and characteristics, in terms of cost and differentiated features, are potentially attractive to the firm's customers. When faced with possible substitutes, the cost leader has more flexibility than its competitors. To retain customers, it can reduce the price of its good or service. With still lower prices and competitive levels of differentiation, the cost leader increases the probability that customers will prefer its product rather than a substitute.

COMPETITIVE RISKS OF THE COST LEADERSHIP STRATEGY

The cost leadership strategy is not risk free. One risk is that the processes used by the cost leader to produce and distribute its good or service could become obsolete because of competitors' innovations. These innovations may allow rivals to produce at costs lower than those of the original cost leader, or to provide additional differentiated features without increasing the product's price to customers.

A second risk is that too much focus by the cost leader on cost reductions may occur at the expense of trying to understand customers' perceptions of "competitive levels of differentiation." As noted earlier, Wal-Mart is well known for constantly and aggressively reducing its costs. At the same time, however, the firm must understand when a cost-reducing decision to eliminate differentiated features (e.g., extended shopping hours, a large number of checkout counters to reduce waits) would create a loss of value for customers.

A final risk of the cost leadership strategy concerns imitation. Using their own core competencies, competitors sometimes learn how to successfully imitate the cost leader's strategy. When this occurs, the cost leader must increase the value that its good or service provides to customers. Commonly, value is increased by selling the current product at an even lower price or by adding differentiated features that customers value while maintaining price.

Differentiation Strategy

The **differentiation strategy** is an integrated set of actions taken to produce goods or services (at an acceptable cost) that customers perceive as being different in ways that are important to them.[80] While cost leaders serve an industry's typical customer, differentiators target customers who perceive that value is added by the manner in which the firm's products differ from those produced and marketed by competitors.

Firms must be able to produce differentiated products at competitive costs to reduce upward pressure on the price customers pay for them. When a product's differentiated features are produced with noncompetitive costs, the price for the product can exceed what the firm's target customers are willing to pay. When the firm has a thorough understanding of what its target customers value, the relative importance they attach to the satisfaction of different needs, and for what they are willing to pay a premium, the differentiation strategy can be successfully used.[81]

Through the differentiation strategy, the firm produces nonstandardized products for customers who value differentiated features more than they value low cost. For example, superior product reliability and durability and high-performance sound systems are among the differentiated features of Toyota Motor Corporation's Lexus products. The often-used Lexus promotional statement—"The Passionate Pursuit of Perfection"—suggests a strong commitment to overall product quality as a source of differentiation. However, Lexus offers its vehicles to customers at a competitive purchase

©TRAMONTINA GARY/CORBIS SYGMA

price. As with Lexus products, a good's or service's unique attributes, rather than its purchase price, provide the value for which customers are willing to pay. As described in the Opening Case, Krispy Kreme uses what the firm believes is a truly unique recipe to make its doughnuts. The Doughnut Theatre and interactions with its customers are other sources of differentiation for this firm.

Continuous success with the differentiation strategy results when the firm consistently upgrades differentiated features that customers value, without significant cost increases. Because a differentiated product satisfies customers' unique needs, firms following the differentiation strategy are able to charge premium prices. For customers to be willing to pay a premium price, a "firm must truly be unique at something or be perceived as unique."[82] The ability to sell a good or service at a price that substantially exceeds the cost of creating its differentiated features allows the firm to outperform rivals and earn above-average returns. For example, shirt and neckwear manufacturer Robert Talbott follows stringent standards of craftsmanship and pays meticulous attention to every detail of production. The firm imports exclusive fabrics from the world's finest mills to make men's dress shirts and neckwear. Single-needle tailoring is used, and precise collar cuts are made to produce shirts. According to the company, customers purchasing one of its products can be assured that they are being provided with the finest quality available.[83] Thus, Robert Talbott's success rests on the firm's ability to produce and sell its differentiated products at a price significantly higher than the costs of imported fabrics and its unique manufacturing processes.

Rather than costs, a firm using the differentiation strategy always concentrates on investing in and developing features that differentiate a good or service in ways that customers value. Robert Talbott, for example, uses the finest silks from Europe and Asia to produce its "Best of Class" collection of ties. Overall, a firm using the differentiation strategy seeks to be different from its competitors on as many dimensions as possible. The less similarity between a firm's goods or services and those of competitors, the more buffered it is from rivals' actions. Commonly recognized differentiated goods include Toyota's Lexus, Ralph Lauren's clothing lines, and Caterpillar's heavy-duty earth-moving equipment. Thought by some to be the world's most expensive and prestigious consulting firm, McKinsey & Co. is a well-known example of a firm that offers differentiated services.

A product can be differentiated in many ways. Unusual features, responsive customer service, rapid product innovations and technological leadership, perceived prestige and status, different tastes, and engineering design and performance are examples of approaches to differentiation. There may be a limited number of ways to reduce costs (as demanded by successful use of the cost leadership strategy). In contrast, virtually anything a firm can do to create real or perceived value is a basis for differentiation. For example, trying to differentiate its luxury products from those of global competitors, Detroit's automakers are turning to design and styling to create what the industry is calling "gotta have" products. Hard to precisely define, "gotta have" cars and trucks look different, look good, and make customers turn their heads.[84] For Detroit automakers as well as all firms using the differentiation strategy for one or more of their product lines, the challenge is to identify features that create value for the customers the firm has chosen to serve.

Firms sometimes introduce a new source of differentiation to test consumer reaction before extending it. H. J. Heinz, for example, recently added color as a source of differentiation for its highly successful ketchup. Called Blastin' Green, the first color Heinz introduced proved very popular with customers, causing the firm to experiment further by introducing Funky Purple and Wicked Orange colors as well (with additional colors being considered). Positive reactions to these product introductions suggest that color does create perceived value for at least some of Heinz's target customers.[85]

A firm's value chain can be analyzed to determine whether the firm is able to link the activities required to create value by using the differentiation strategy. Examples of primary and support activities that are commonly used to differentiate a good or service are shown in Figure 4.3. Companies without the skills needed to link these activities cannot expect to successfully use the differentiation strategy. Next, we explain how firms using the differentiation strategy can successfully position themselves in terms of the five forces of competition (see Chapter 2) to earn above-average returns.

Figure 4.3 — Examples of Value-Creating Activities Associated with the Differentiation Strategy

Support Activities:

- **Firm Infrastructure:** Highly developed information systems to better understand customers' purchasing preferences · A company-wide emphasis on the importance of producing high-quality products
- **Human Resource Management:** Compensation programs intended to encourage worker creativity and productivity · Somewhat extensive use of subjective rather than objective performance measures · Superior personnel training
- **Technology Development:** Strong capability in basic research · Investments in technologies that will allow the firm to produce highly differentiated products
- **Procurement:** Systems and procedures used to find the highest-quality raw materials · Purchase of highest-quality replacement parts

Primary Activities (MARGIN):

- **Inbound Logistics:** Superior handling of incoming raw materials so as to minimize damage and to improve the quality of the final product
- **Operations:** Consistent manufacturing of attractive products · Rapid responses to customers' unique manufacturing specifications
- **Outbound Logistics:** Accurate and responsive order-processing procedures · Rapid and timely product deliveries to customers
- **Marketing and Sales:** Extensive granting of credit buying arrangements for customers · Extensive personal relationships with buyers and suppliers
- **Service:** Extensive buyer training to assure high-quality product installations · Complete field stocking of replacement parts

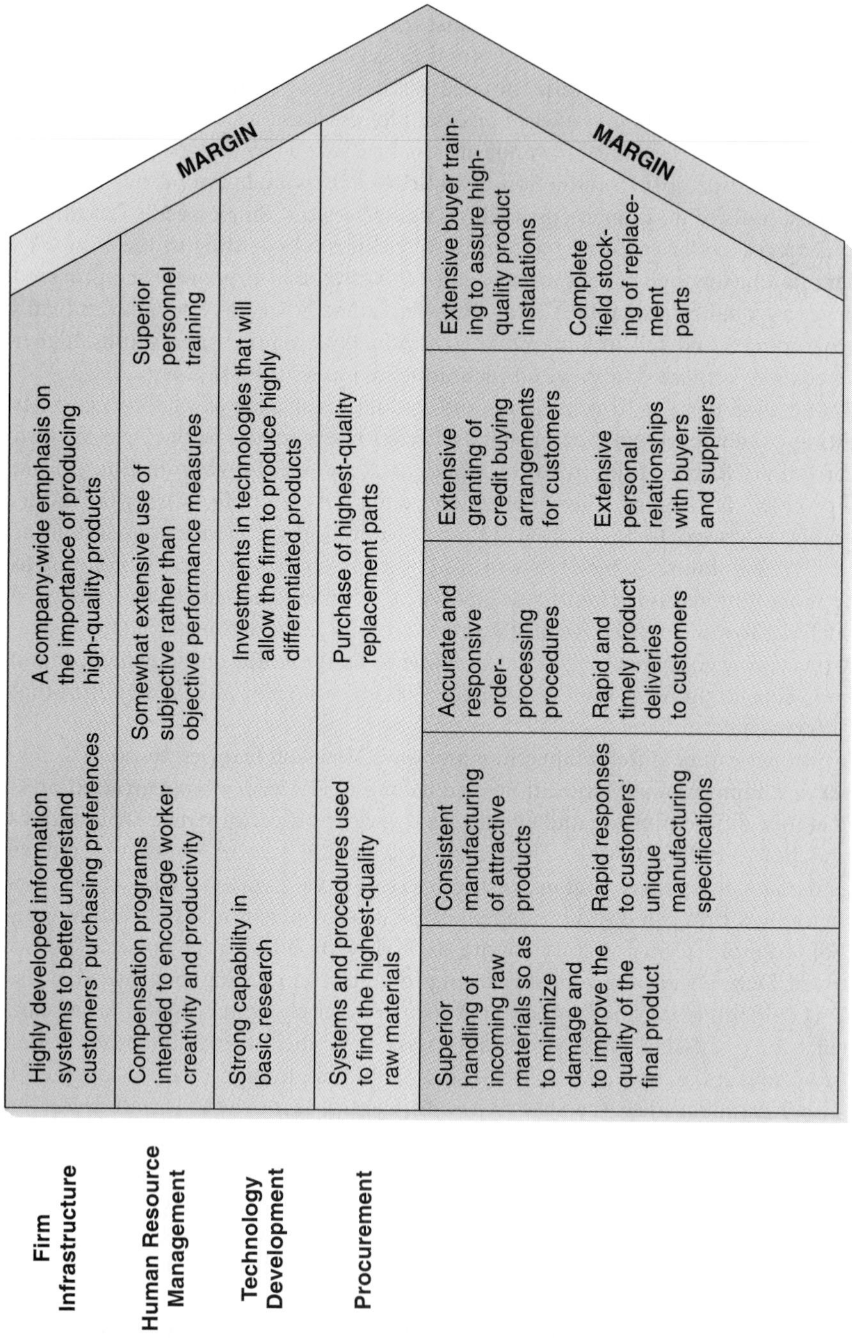

SOURCE: Adapted with the permission of The Free Press, an imprint of Simon & Schuster Adult Publishing Group, from *Competitive Advantage: Creating and Sustaining Superior Performance*, by Michael E. Porter, 47. Copyright © 1985, 1998 by Michael E. Porter.

RIVALRY WITH EXISTING COMPETITORS

Customers tend to be loyal purchasers of products that are differentiated in ways that are meaningful to them. As their loyalty to a brand increases, customers' sensitivity to price increases is reduced. The relationship between brand loyalty and price sensitivity insulates a firm from competitive rivalry. Thus, McKinsey & Co. is insulated from its competitors, even on the basis of price, as long as it continues to satisfy the differentiated needs of its customer group. Likewise, Bose is insulated from intense rivalry as long as customers continue to perceive that its stereo equipment offers superior sound quality at a competitive cost.

BARGAINING POWER OF BUYERS (CUSTOMERS)

The uniqueness of differentiated goods or services reduces customers' sensitivity to price increases. On the basis of a combination of unique materials and brand image, "L'Oréal has developed a winning formula: a growing portfolio of international brands that has transformed the French company into the United Nations of beauty. Blink an eye, and L'Oréal has just sold 85 products around the world, from Maybelline eye makeup, Redken hair care, and Ralph Lauren perfumes to Helena Rubinstein cosmetics and Vichy skin care." L'Oréal is finding success in markets stretching from China to Mexico as some other consumer product companies falter. L'Oréal's differentiation strategy seeks to convey the allure of different cultures through its many products: "Whether it's selling Italian elegance, New York street smarts, or French beauty through its brands, L'Oréal is reaching out to more people across a bigger range of incomes and cultures than just about any other beauty-products company in the world."[86]

L'Oréal seeks to satisfy customers' unique needs better than its competitors can. Some buyers are willing to pay a premium price for the firm's cosmetic items because, for these buyers, other products do not offer a comparable combination of features and cost. The lack of perceived acceptable alternatives increases the firm's power relative to that of its customers.

BARGAINING POWER OF SUPPLIERS

Because the firm using the differentiation strategy charges a premium price for its products, suppliers must provide high-quality components, driving up the firm's costs. However, the high margins the firm earns in these cases partially insulate it from the influence of suppliers in that higher supplier costs can be paid through these margins. Alternatively, because of buyers' relative insensitivity to price increases, the differentiated firm might choose to pass the additional cost of supplies on to the customer by increasing the price of its unique product.

POTENTIAL ENTRANTS

Customer loyalty and the need to overcome the uniqueness of a differentiated product present substantial entry barriers to potential entrants. Entering an industry under these conditions typically demands significant investments of resources and patience while seeking customers' loyalty.

PRODUCT SUBSTITUTES

Firms selling brand-name goods and services to loyal customers are positioned effectively against product substitutes. In contrast, companies without brand loyalty face a higher probability of their customers switching either to products that offer differentiated features that serve the same function (particularly if the substitute has a lower price) or to products that offer more features and perform more attractive functions.

COMPETITIVE RISKS OF THE DIFFERENTIATION STRATEGY

As with the other business-level strategies, the differentiation strategy is not risk free. One risk is that customers might decide that the price differential between the differentiator's product and the cost leader's product is too large. In this instance, a firm may be offering differentiated features that exceed target customers' needs. The firm then becomes vulnerable to competitors that are able to offer customers a combination of features and price that is more consistent with their needs.

Another risk of the differentiation strategy is that a firm's means of differentiation may cease to provide value for which customers are willing to pay. A differentiated product becomes less valuable if imitation by rivals causes customers to perceive that competitors offer essentially the same good or service, but at a lower price. For example, Walt Disney Company operates different theme parks, including The Magic Kingdom, Epcot Center, and the newly developed Animal Kingdom. Each park offers entertainment and educational opportunities. However, Disney's competitors, such as Six Flags Corporation, also offer entertainment and educational experiences similar to those available at Disney's locations. To ensure that its facilities create value for which customers will be willing to pay, Disney continuously reinvests in its operations to more crisply differentiate them from those of its rivals.[87]

A third risk of the differentiation strategy is that experience can narrow customers' perceptions of the value of a product's differentiated features. For example, the value of the IBM name provided a differentiated feature for the firm's personal computers for which some users were willing to pay a premium price in the early life cycle of the product. However, as customers familiarized themselves with the product's standard features, and as a host of other firms' personal computers entered the market, IBM brand loyalty ceased to create value for which some customers were willing to pay. The substitutes offered features similar to those found in the IBM product at a substantially lower price, reducing the attractiveness of IBM's product.

Counterfeiting is the differentiation strategy's fourth risk. Makers of counterfeit goods—products that attempt to convey a firm's differentiated features to customers at significantly reduced prices—are a concern for many firms using the differentiation strategy. For example, Callaway Golf Company's success at producing differentiated products that create value, coupled with golf's increasing global popularity, has created great demand for counterfeited Callaway equipment. Through the U.S. Customs Service's "Project Teed Off" program, agents seized over 110 shipments with a total of more than 100,000 counterfeit Callaway golf club components over a three-year period.[88] Altria Group's domestic tobacco division, Philip Morris USA, files lawsuits against retailers selling counterfeit versions of its cigarettes, such as Marlboro. Judgments Philip Morris has won in these suits include immediate discontinuance of selling the counterfeit products as well as significant financial penalties for any future violations.[89]

Focus Strategies

Firms choose a focus strategy when they intend to use their core competencies to serve the needs of a particular industry segment or niche to the exclusion of others. Examples of specific market segments that can be targeted by a focus strategy include (1) a particular buyer group (e.g., youths or senior citizens), (2) a different segment of a product line (e.g., products for professional painters or those for "do-it-yourselfers"), or (3) a different geographic market (e.g., the East or the West in the United States).[90] Thus, the **focus strategy** is an integrated set of actions taken to produce goods or services that serve the needs of a particular competitive segment.

Although the breadth of a target is clearly a matter of degree, the essence of the focus strategy "is the exploitation of a narrow target's differences from the balance of the industry."[91] Firms using the focus strategy intend to serve a particular segment of an industry more effectively than can industry-wide competitors. They succeed when they effectively serve a segment whose unique needs are so specialized that broad-based competitors choose not to serve that segment or when they satisfy the needs of a segment being served poorly by industry-wide competitors.[92]

To satisfy the needs of a certain size of company competing in a particular geographic market, Los Angeles–based investment banking firm Greif & Company posi-

The focus strategy is an integrated set of actions taken to produce goods or services that serve the needs of a particular competitive segment.

PART 2 / Strategic Actions: Strategy Formulation

tions itself as "The Entrepreneur's Investment Bank." Greif & Company is a "leading purveyor of merger and acquisition advisory services to medium-sized businesses based in the Western United States."[93] Partly because of costs and liability, governments are outsourcing health care to private companies. Nicknamed the "HMO behind bars," American Services Group Inc. (ASG) specializes in providing contract health care for prisons and jails such as New York's Rikers Island facility.[94] Through successful use of the focus strategy, firms such as Greif & Company and ASG gain a competitive advantage in specific market niches or segments, even though they do not possess an industry-wide competitive advantage.[95]

Firms can create value for customers in specific and unique market segments by using the focused cost leadership strategy or the focused differentiation strategy.

FOCUSED COST LEADERSHIP STRATEGY

Based in Sweden, Ikea, a global furniture retailer with locations in over 30 countries, follows the focused cost leadership strategy.[96] Young buyers desiring style at a low cost are Ikea's market segment.[97] For these customers, the firm offers home furnishings that combine good design, function, and acceptable quality with low prices. According to the firm, "low cost is always in focus. This applies to every phase of our activities."[98] The firm continues its global expansion, recently opening stores in Russia and China.[99]

Ikea emphasizes several activities to keep its costs low. For example, instead of relying primarily on third-party manufacturers, the firm's engineers design low-cost, modular furniture ready for assembly by customers. Ikea also positions its products in roomlike settings. Typically, competitors' furniture stores display multiple varieties of a single item in separate rooms, and their customers examine living room sofas in one room, tables in another room, chairs in yet another location, and accessories in still another area. In contrast, Ikea's customers can view different living combinations (complete with sofas, chairs, tables, and so forth) in a single setting, which eliminates the need for sales associates or decorators to help the customer imagine how a batch of furniture will look when placed in the customer's home. This approach requires fewer sales personnel, allowing Ikea to keep its costs low. A third practice that helps keep Ikea's costs low is expecting customers to transport their own purchases rather than providing delivery service.

Although a cost leader, Ikea also offers some differentiated features that appeal to its target customers, including in-store playrooms for children, wheelchairs for customer use, and extended hours. Stores outside those in the home country have "Sweden Shops" that sell Swedish specialties, such as herring, crisp bread, Swedish caviar, and gingerbread biscuits. Ikea believes that these services and products "are uniquely aligned with the needs of [its] customers, who are young, are not wealthy, are likely to have children (but no nanny), and, because they work for a living, have a need to shop at odd hours."[100] Thus, Ikea's focused cost leadership strategy finds the firm offering some differentiated features with its low-cost products.

Ikea is an example of a company successfully using the focused cost leadership strategy. Stores display their furniture in what look like completely furnished rooms to increase the appeal of their products as well as reduce costs by employing fewer sales personnel.

FOCUSED DIFFERENTIATION STRATEGY

Other firms implement the focused differentiation strategy. As noted earlier, firms can differentiate their products in many ways. The Internet furniture venture Casketfurniture.com, for example, targets Generation X people

©Spencer Grant/PhotoEdit

Satisfying Unique Needs: Of Shoes and Cars

Privately held New Balance Athletic Shoe Inc. concentrates on the athletic shoe needs of the Baby Boom generation (born between 1946 and 1964). Indicating the firm's focus on a particular customer segment is the perspective that "we don't want New Balance to be all things to all people." The high-quality "fit" that its shoes provide is the primary source of differentiation, for which the firm's target customer group is willing to pay a premium price.

Early research by New Balance suggested that active Baby Boomers want shoes that fit extremely well rather than shoes that are recognized for their style. A key indicator of the company's commitment to fit is that it is the only shoe manufacturer producing a complete line in a variety of widths—from AA to EEEE. New Balance's philosophy about fit is straightforward: "The better your shoes fit, the more comfortable you will be, the better you will enjoy yourself."

To support the design and manufacture of products with the "best possible fit," New Balance invests significantly in technological research and development (R&D) activities. Several patented technologies resulting from the firm's R&D efforts have been instrumental in developing suspension systems for the firm's shoes. Well-trained workers use highly sophisticated manufacturing equipment to produce the firm's differentiated products. The successful differentiation of New Balance's shoes in terms of fit is suggested by the fact that several models have received special recognition by the American Podiatric Medical Association. To further support these efforts, the firm recently installed a product-life-cycle management (PLM) software system. Linking all people involved with product development, distribution, and service after the sale, this new system facilitates New Balance's commitment to appropriately modify its products to satisfy consumer preferences in different regions of the world while continuously improving product quality.

Committed to innovation and serving an array of product niches by using its focused differentiation strategy, New Balance launched a new brand in spring 2004. Called Aravon, this line seeks to satisfy physicians' needs to prescribe running shoes for patients with unique foot characteristics.

Fiat Group, the Italian manufacturer of mass-market cars, owns 90 percent of Ferrari SpA, the famous sports car company with the well-recognized Prancing Horse emblem on its products. In the late 1990s, Ferrari bought Maserati. After a ten-year absence from the U.S. market, a Maserati product was reintroduced in early 2002 after being successfully relaunched earlier in France, Italy, Switzerland, and Germany. Demonstrating precise segmentation of the market for expensive sports cars, Ferrari determined that the Maserati would appeal to wealthy sports car enthusiasts lacking either the resources or the desire to purchase a Ferrari. The target customer is the person with "good taste who is looking for a unique emotion from driving." With a base price of approximately $80,000, the two-seater Maserati Spider (the product offered in the United States) competes against the Porsche 911 and the Jaguar XKR. Like its rivals, the Spider travels from zero to 60 miles per hour in roughly 5.3 seconds.

Early evidence suggests that the focused differentiation strategy is allowing Ferrari to use the Maserati to expand into different segments without diluting Ferrari's own brand. In late 2003, Maserati unveiled a new four-door luxury sedan as its entry into that particular segment. The firm hoped this sedan would account for half of all Maserati sales by 2006. Along with Porsche and BMW, Maserati also established an outlet in Beijing to satisfy the growing demand in China for luxury automobiles.

SOURCES: M. Davis, 2003, Frank Stephenson talks about his new life at Ferrari-Maserati, *Autoweek*, 53(4): 20–21; S. Hill, Jr., 2003, A new vision, *MSI*, 21(2): 30–32; J. Lerner, 2003, New Balance takes strides to comfort-casual market, *Boston Business Journal*, February 14, D6; C. Reidy, 2003, New Balance hopes casual-footwear line attracts younger customers, *Boston Globe*, March 14, C1; D. Roberts, 2003, Bentley Beijing: Chariots on fire, *Business Week*, March 24, 66–67; A. Bernstein, 2001, Low-skilled jobs: Do they have to move? *Business Week*, February 26, 94–95; A. Kirkman, 2001, Zoom! Zoom! *Forbes*, May 14, 208.

who are interested in using the Internet as a shopping vehicle and who want to buy items with multiple purposes. The firm offers a collection of products, including display cabinets, coffee tables, and entertainment centers, that can be easily converted into coffins if desired. The $1,975 display cabinet is the company's best-selling item. With 16 units on the East Coast, hair salon Cartoon Cuts serves children between the ages of 8 and 14. This age group is a profitable and growing niche in the $50 billion U.S. hair salon industry. Upscale bed and breakfast facilities, such as Harbor Light Inn in Boston, Mass., provide an extensive array of services for business travelers desiring the finest in amenities.[101]

In the Strategic Focus, we discuss individual sources of differentiation that two firms—New Balance and Maserati (part of Fiat Group)—have created to use the focused differentiation strategy. Technology, R&D capability, managerial creativity, and an empowered and talented workforce are the competitive advantages New Balance uses to offer customers a shoe with an ideal "fit." Relying on its advantages of reputation, design skills, and manufacturing expertise, Maserati has produced the Maserati Spider to appeal to the *emotions* of its target customer group. In both instances, perceived value is created for a narrow segment of broader markets (for athletic shoes and automobiles, respectively).

Firms must be able to complete various primary and support activities in a competitively superior manner to develop and sustain a competitive advantage and earn above-average returns with a focus strategy. The activities required to use the focused cost leadership strategy are virtually identical to the activities shown in Figure 4.2, and activities required to use the focused differentiation strategy are virtually identical to those shown in Figure 4.3. Similarly, the manner in which each of the two focus strategies allows a firm to deal successfully with the five competitive forces parallels those described with respect to the cost leadership strategy and the differentiation strategy. The only difference is that the competitive scope changes from an industry-wide market to a narrow industry segment. Thus, a review of Figures 4.2 and 4.3 and the text regarding the five competitive forces yields a description of the relationship between each of the two focus strategies and competitive advantage.

COMPETITIVE RISKS OF FOCUS STRATEGIES

With either focus strategy, the firm faces the same general risks as does the company using the cost leadership or the differentiation strategy, respectively, on an industry-wide basis. However, focus strategies have three additional risks.

First, a competitor may be able to focus on a more narrowly defined competitive segment and "outfocus" the focuser. For example, Big Dog Motorcycles is trying to outfocus Harley-Davidson, which is pursuing a broader-focus differentiation strategy. While Harley focuses solely on producing heavyweight motorcycles, Big Dog Motor-cycles builds motorcycles that target only the very high end of the heavyweight market—the high-end premium cruiser market—with such names as Pitbull, Wolf, Mastiff, and Bulldog. Big Dog Motorcycles

Big Dog Motorcycles offers several models, including Pitbull, Wolf, Mastiff, and Bulldog. Big Dog Motorcycles has arguably outfocused its major competitor, Harley-Davidson, by producing high-end heavyweight motorcycles.

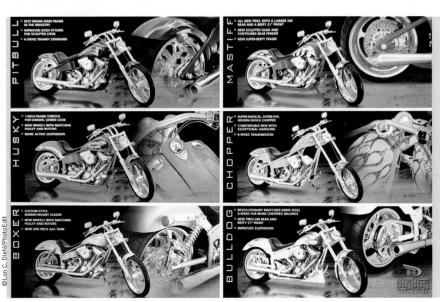

©Lon C. Diehl/PhotoEdit

is careful to differentiate its products from those of Harley-Davidson, citing its larger motors, fat rear tires, unique state-of-the-art electronics, and four-piston caliper brakes as examples of value-creating features. The estimate that eight out of ten of its customers either own or have owned a Harley-Davidson product suggests the apparent success of Big Dog Motorcycles' efforts to outfocus its major competitor.[102]

Second, a company competing on an industry-wide basis may decide that the market segment served by the focus strategy firm is attractive and worthy of competitive pursuit. For example, Building Materials Holding Company (BMHC) is a profitable regional retailer of building materials and construction services with operations in 12 western and southern states. Targeting professional contractors, BMHC provides customers with "a number of specialized services not offered by home center retailers" such as Home Depot and Lowe's.[103] Continuing growth in the size of the professional contractor market as well as the population of western and southern states might induce more concentrated efforts by Home Depot and Lowe's to learn how to serve the specialized needs of BMHC's core customer.

The third risk involved with a focus strategy is that the needs of customers within a narrow competitive segment may become more similar to those of industry-wide customers as a whole. As a result, the advantages of a focus strategy are either reduced or eliminated. At some point, for example, the needs of Ikea's customers for stylish furniture may dissipate, although their desire to buy relatively inexpensive furnishings may not. If this change in needs were to happen, Ikea's customers might buy from large chain stores that sell somewhat standardized furniture at low costs.

Integrated Cost Leadership/Differentiation Strategy

Particularly in global markets, the firm's ability to integrate the means of competition necessary to implement the cost leadership and differentiation strategies may be critical to developing competitive advantages. Compared to firms implementing one dominant business-level strategy, the company that successfully uses an integrated cost leadership/differentiation strategy should be in a better position to (1) adapt quickly to environmental changes, (2) learn new skills and technologies more quickly, and (3) effectively leverage its core competencies while competing against its rivals.

Concentrating on the needs of its core customer group (higher-income, fashion-conscious discount shoppers), Target Stores uses an integrated strategy. One reason for the use of this strategy is that, as we discussed earlier, trying to imitate major competitor Wal-Mart's cost leadership strategy is virtually impossible (because of how successfully Wal-Mart is positioned relative to the five forces of competition). Thus, Target has chosen to use its core competencies to serve the needs of a target customer group that differs from Wal-Mart's. Target relies on its relationships with Michael Graves in home, garden, and electronics products, Sonia Kashuk in cosmetics, Mossimo in apparel, and Eddie Bauer in camping and outdoor gear, among others, to offer differentiated products at discounted prices to its core customers. Committed to presenting a consistent upscale image, the firm carefully studies trends to find new branded items that it believes can satisfy its customers' needs.[104]

Evidence suggests a relationship between successful use of the integrated strategy and above-average returns.[105] Thus, firms able to produce relatively differentiated products at relatively low costs can expect to perform well.[106] Indeed, a researcher found that the most successful firms competing in low-profit-potential industries were integrating the attributes of the cost leadership and differentiation strategies.[107] Other researchers have discovered that "businesses which combined multiple forms of competitive advantage outperformed businesses that only were identified with a single form."[108] The results of another study showed that the highest-performing companies in the Korean electronics industry combined the value-creating aspects of the cost leadership and differentiation strategies.[109] This finding suggests the usefulness of the integrated strategy in settings outside the United States.

McDonald's is a corporation with a strong global brand, offering products at a relatively low cost but with some differentiated features. Historically, its global scale, relationships with franchisees, and rigorous standardization of processes have allowed McDonald's to lower its costs, while its brand recognition and product consistency have been sources of differentiation allowing the restaurant chain to charge slightly higher prices.[110] Thus, the firm uses the integrated cost leadership/differentiation strategy.[111]

The future success of McDonald's is being questioned, however. One analyst, for example, suggests, "Already in the U.S., competition is eroding its dominance; its great days are probably over. It must now manage a decline which will be bumpy, even violent."[112] Does this comment accurately describe McDonald's future as it uses the integrated strategy? Are the firm's glory days "over" as the analyst foresees? We consider these matters in the Strategic Focus.

Will McDonald's efforts to reduce costs through a more simplified menu while offering some additional differentiated features in new storefront formats be sufficient to assure success in the years to come? Only time will tell. However, information in the Strategic Focus suggests that the firm needs either to more effectively implement the integrated cost leadership/differentiation strategy or to change its strategy to one that is a better match between opportunities and threats in the firm's external environment and the core competencies of its internal environment.

Unlike McDonald's, which uses the integrated cost leadership/differentiation strategy on an industry-wide basis, air-conditioning and heating-systems maker Aaon concentrates on a particular competitive scope. Thus, Aaon is implementing a focused integrated strategy. Aaon manufactures semicustomized rooftop air conditioning systems for large retailers, including Wal-Mart, Target, and Home Depot. Aaon positions its rooftop systems between low-priced commodity equipment and high-end customized systems. The firm's innovative manufacturing capabilities allow it to tailor a production line for units with special heat-recovery options unavailable on low-end systems. Combining custom features with assembly-line production methods results in significant cost savings. Aaon's prices are approximately 5 percent higher than low-end products but are only one-third the price of comparable customized systems.[113] Thus, the firm's narrowly defined target customers receive some differentiated features (e.g., special heat-recovery options) at a low, but not the lowest, cost.

A commitment to strategic flexibility (see Chapter 1) is necessary for firms to effectively use the integrated cost leadership/differentiation strategy. Strategic flexibility results from developing systems, procedures, and methods that enable a firm to quickly and effectively respond to opportunities that reduce costs or increase differentiation. Flexible manufacturing systems, information networks, and total quality management systems are three sources of strategic flexibility that facilitate use of the integrated strategy and make firms more globally competitive as a result.[114] Valuable to the successful use of each business-level strategy, the strategic flexibility provided by these three tools is especially important to firms trying to balance the objectives of continuous cost reductions and continuous enhancements to sources of differentiation.

FLEXIBLE MANUFACTURING SYSTEMS

Flexible manufacturing systems (FMS) increase the "flexibilities of human, physical, and information resources"[115] that the firm integrates to create relatively differentiated products at relatively low costs. A *flexible manufacturing system* is a computer-controlled process used to produce a variety of products in moderate, flexible quantities with a minimum of manual intervention.[116] Particularly in situations where parts are too heavy for people to handle or when other methods are less effective in creating manufacturing and assembly flexibility, robots are integral to use of an FMS.[117] In spite of their promise, only one in five *Fortune* 1000 companies are using the productive capabilities of an FMS.[118]

Global Burgers: Are McDonald's Glory Days a Thing of the Past?

McDonald's is the world's leading global food service retailer. The firm serves approximately 46 million people daily in its 31,000 units that are located in 120 countries. System-wide sales were $41.5 billion in fiscal year 2002. However, all is not well in Ronald McDonald land. Sales grew only 2 percent in 2002 with same-store sales down in all regions except Europe and Latin America. McDonald's faces fierce competition from traditional competitors as well as from the rapidly growing fast-casual format (a segment where customers "get a meal that tastes home-cooked in a short amount of time, then sit down and eat it at their leisure"). Although the case was dismissed, McDonald's has been sued on the allegation that its fatty foods made the company responsible for the rise in childhood obesity. Even more discouraging for McDonald's stakeholders, especially shareholders, was the posting of the firm's first quarterly loss in its history during the October–December 2002 quarter.

What are the root causes of McDonald's problems? Historically, McDonald's has used value pricing (the source of relatively low costs to customers) while offering menu and storefront variety and relying on the power of its brand name (sources of differentiation). Globally, the company has tried to provide its combination of relatively low costs and some levels of differentiation in a culturally sensitive manner. In India, for example, the Maharaja Mac, which is made from lamb, substitutes for the beef-based Big Mac. Popular corn soup is offered on the chain's menu in its Japanese units while the locally oriented McNifica is popular in Argentina.

McDonald's is taking actions to improve the implementation of its integrated cost leadership/product differentiation strategy. In 1999, the firm launched its "Made for You" system. Replacing the firm's historic practice of producing food and storing it in a large tray until purchased, the new system was designed to increase product quality, variety, and delivery speed (sources of differentiation). To do this, new computer equipment and cooking and food preparation machinery were installed in each unit. Crew members and managers received extensive training to learn how to maximize efficiency by using the new system. However, after two years and a $1 billion investment, McDonald's moved from "Made for You" to a more simplified system. A primary reason for this change was that the cost of using the "Made for You" system to increase sources of differentiation exceeded acceptable levels for successful use of the integrated cost leadership/differentiation strategy.

More recently, McDonald's has tried to control costs through simplification. A decision made in this respect was to trim the standard 36-item core menu, jettisoning such items as the McFlurry. Menu simplification is appealing to a large segment of McDonald's franchisees, one of whom observed, "You can't be everything to everybody. If you do, you fracture your clientele and your business. Then you're nothing to everyone. You have to hang onto your niche and try to do that well." Other decisions have been made to improve the firm's performance, including "fixing operating inadequacies in existing restaurants; taking a more integrated and focused approach to growth, with an emphasis on increasing sales, margins and returns in existing restaurants; and ensuring the correct operating structure and resources, aligned behind focusing priorities that create benefits for its customers and restaurants." In addition, McDonald's is evaluating several sources of differentiation, such as coin changers, self-order kiosks, and cashless drive-throughs, for possible introduction by mid-2005.

SOURCES: 2003, McDonald's Corp., *Standard & Poor's Stock Reports*, http://www.standardandpoors.com, May 17; 2003, McDonald's Japan to keep low-price burgers, *Jiji Press English News Service*, May 12; B. Herzog, 2003, *Oregonian*, May 1; J. R. McPherson, A. V. Mitchell, & M. R. Mitten, 2003, Fast-food fight, *The McKinsey Quarterly*, no. 2, 11–14; R. Sims, 2003, Tallahassee, Fla., hosts McDonald's new version of its Boston Market chain, *Tallahassee Democrat*, May 7; R. Dzinkowski, 2001, McDonald's Europe, *Strategic Finance*, May, 24–27; K. MacArthur, 2001, McDonald's sees 100%, *Advertising Age*, May/June, 12–14.

The goal of an FMS is to eliminate the "low-cost-versus-product-variety" trade-off that is inherent in traditional manufacturing technologies. Firms use an FMS to change quickly and easily from making one product to making another.[119] Used properly, an FMS allows the firm to respond more effectively to changes in its customers' needs, while retaining low-cost advantages and consistent product quality.[120] Because an FMS also enables the firm to reduce the lot size needed to manufacture a product efficiently, the firm increases its capacity to serve the unique needs of a narrow competitive scope.

Thus, FMS technology is a significant technological advance that allows firms to produce a large variety of products at relatively low costs. The effective use of an FMS is linked with a firm's ability to understand the constraints these systems may create (in terms of materials handling and the flow of supporting resources in scheduling, for example) and to design an effective mix of machines, computer systems, and people.[121] In industries of all types, effective mixes of the firm's tangible assets (e.g., machines) and intangible assets (e.g., people's skills) facilitate implementation of complex competitive strategies, especially the integrated cost leadership/differentiation strategy.[122]

An FMS is a complex engineering project. UNOVA Inc. uses a differentiation strategy to develop and implement flexible manufacturing systems for end users. An industrial technologies company, UNOVA provides global customers in the automotive, aerospace, and heavy equipment industries with flexible manufacturing solutions to the need to improve their efficiency and productivity. In markets throughout the world, the firm provides customers with the most technologically advanced, high-quality systems. To increase the functionality of its FMS systems to satisfy unique customer needs, especially the need to produce a wide variety of unique products at a relatively low cost for each item, the firm forms strategic alliances with companies located in many different countries (e.g., Korea, China, and Japan). To enhance the flexibility its systems provide to end users, UNOVA continuously evaluates its own manufacturing processes to find ways to enhance the sources of value its differentiated product features create for customers.[123]

INFORMATION NETWORKS

By linking companies with their suppliers, distributors, and customers, information networks provide another source of strategic flexibility. Among other outcomes, these networks, when used effectively,[124] facilitate the firm's efforts to satisfy customer expectations in terms of product quality and delivery speed.[125] In addition, effective information networks improve the flow of work among employees in the focal firm as well as between those employees and their counterparts, such as suppliers and distributors, with whom they interact.[126]

Customer relationship management (CRM) is one form of an information-based network process that firms use to better understand customers and their needs.[127] An effective CRM system provides a 360-degree view of the company's relationship with customers, encompassing all contact points, involving all business processes, and incorporating all communication media and sales channels.[128] The firm can then use this information to determine the trade-offs its customers are willing to make between differentiated features and low cost, which is vital for companies using the integrated cost leadership/differentiation strategy.

Information networks are also critical to the establishment and successful use of an enterprise resource planning (ERP) system. ERP is an information system used to identify and plan the resources required across the firm to receive, record, produce, and ship customer orders.[129] For example, salespeople for aircraft parts distributor Aviall use handheld equipment to scan bar-code labels on bins in customers' facilities to determine when parts need to be restocked. Data gathered through this procedure are uploaded via the Web to the Aviall back-end replenishment and ERP system, allowing the order fulfillment process to begin within minutes of scanning.[130] Growth in ERP applications such as the one used at Aviall has been significant.[131] Full installations of an ERP system are expensive, running into the tens of millions of dollars for large-scale applications.

Improving efficiency on a company-wide basis is a primary objective of using an ERP system. Efficiency improvements result from the use of systems through which financial and operational data are moved rapidly from one department to another. The transfer of sales data from Aviall salespeople to the order entry point at the firm's manufacturing facility demonstrates the rapid movement of information from one function to another. Integrating data across parties that are involved with detailing product specifications and then manufacturing those products and distributing them in ways that are consistent with customers' unique needs enable the firm to respond with flexibility to customer preferences relative to cost and differentiation.

TOTAL QUALITY MANAGEMENT SYSTEMS

Total quality management is a managerial innovation that emphasizes an organization's total commitment to the customer and to continuous improvement of every process through the use of data-driven, problem solving approaches based on empowerment of employee groups and teams.

Total quality management (TQM) is a "managerial innovation that emphasizes an organization's total commitment to the customer and to continuous improvement of every process through the use of data-driven, problem-solving approaches based on empowerment of employee groups and teams."[132] Firms develop and use TQM systems in order to (1) increase customer satisfaction, (2) cut costs, and (3) reduce the amount of time required to introduce innovative products to the marketplace.[133] Ford Motor Company is relying on TQM to help "root out" its quality flaws,[134] while General Motors is "scrambling to narrow the quality gap that its executives say is the main reason consumers shy away from GM."[135] The focus by these firms on TQM to improve product and service quality is appropriate,[136] in that while U.S. auto manufacturers have made progress, "the Big Three still lag behind some foreign competitors, primarily the Japanese, by most quality measures."[137]

Firms able to simultaneously cut costs while enhancing their ability to develop innovative products increase their strategic flexibility. The increased flexibility associated with the ability to jointly reduce costs and become more innovative is particularly helpful to firms implementing the integrated cost leadership/differentiation strategy. At least meeting (and perhaps exceeding) customers' expectations regarding quality is a differentiating feature, and eliminating process inefficiencies to cut costs allows the firm to offer that quality to customers at a relatively low price. Thus, an effective TQM system helps the firm develop the flexibility needed to spot opportunities to simultaneously increase differentiation and reduce costs.

COMPETITIVE RISKS OF THE INTEGRATED COST LEADERSHIP/DIFFERENTIATION STRATEGY

The potential to earn above-average returns by successfully using the integrated cost leadership/differentiation strategy is appealing. However, experience shows that substantial risk accompanies this potential. As noted at the beginning of the chapter, selecting a business-level strategy requires the firm to make choices about how it intends to compete. Achieving the low-cost position in an industry or a segment of an industry by using a cost leadership strategy or a focused cost leadership strategy demands that the firm consistently reduce its costs relative to competitors' costs. The use of the differentiation strategy, with either an industry-wide or a focused competitive scope (see Figure 4.1), requires the firm to provide its customers with differentiated goods or services they value and for which they are willing to pay a premium price.

The firm that uses the integrated strategy yet fails to establish a leadership position risks becoming "stuck in the middle."[138] Being in this position prevents the firm from dealing successfully with the competitive forces in its industry and from having a distinguishable competitive advantage. Not only will the firm not be able to earn above-average returns, but earning even average returns will be possible only when the structure of the industry in which it competes is highly favorable or if its competitors are also in the same position.[139] Without these conditions, the firm will earn below-average returns. Thus, companies implementing the integrated cost leadership/differentiation strategy must be certain that their competitive actions allow them both to offer some differentiated features that their customers value and to provide those products at a relatively low cost. The discussion of McDonald's in the Strategic Focus suggests that the firm may be "stuck in the middle" as a result of ineffective use of the integrated cost leadership/product differentiation strategy. In contrast, the earlier description of Southwest Airlines' performance over its 30-plus years of life indicates that it continues to be extremely successful as it uses the integrated cost leadership/differentiation strategy.

In spite of McDonald's performance problems, there is very little if any research evidence showing that the attributes of the cost leadership and differentiation strategies *cannot* be effectively integrated.[140] The integrated strategy, therefore, is an appropriate strategic choice for firms with the core competencies required to produce somewhat differentiated products at relatively low costs.

Summary

- A business-level strategy is an integrated and coordinated set of commitments and actions the firm uses to gain a competitive advantage by exploiting core competencies in specific product markets. Five business-level strategies (cost leadership, differentiation, focused cost leadership, focused differentiation, and integrated cost leadership/differentiation) are examined in the chapter.

- Customers are the foundation of successful business-level strategies. When considering customers, a firm simultaneously examines three issues: *who, what,* and *how.* These issues, respectively, refer to the customer groups to be served, the needs those customers have that the firm seeks to satisfy, and the core competencies the firm will use to satisfy customers' needs. Increasing segmentation of markets throughout the global economy creates opportunities for firms to identify increasingly unique customer needs.

- Firms seeking competitive advantage through the cost leadership strategy produce no-frills, standardized products for an industry's typical customer. However, these low-cost products must be offered with competitive levels of differentiation. Above-average returns are earned when firms continuously drive their costs lower than those of their competitors, while providing customers with products that have low prices and acceptable levels of differentiated features.

- Competitive risks associated with the cost leadership strategy include (1) a loss of competitive advantage to newer technologies, (2) a failure to detect changes in customers' needs, and (3) the ability of competitors to imitate the cost leader's competitive advantage through their own unique strategic actions.

- Through the differentiation strategy, firms provide customers with products that have different (and valued) features. Differentiated products must be sold at a cost that customers believe is competitive given the product's features as compared to the cost/feature combination available through competitors' offerings. Because of their uniqueness, differentiated goods or services are sold at a premium price. Products can be differentiated along any dimension that some customer group values. Firms using this strategy seek to differentiate their products from competitors' goods or services along as many dimensions as possible. The less similarity with competitors' products, the more buffered a firm is from competition with its rivals.

- Risks associated with the differentiation strategy include (1) a customer group's decision that the differences between the differentiated product and the cost leader's good or service are no longer worth a premium price, (2) the inability of a differentiated product to create the type of value for which customers are willing to pay a premium price, (3) the ability of competitors to provide customers with products that have features similar to those associated with the differentiated product, but at a lower cost, and (4) the threat of counterfeiting, whereby firms produce a cheap "knock-off" of a differentiated good or service.

- Through the cost leadership and the differentiated focus strategies, firms serve the needs of a narrow competitive segment (e.g., a buyer group, product segment, or geographic area). This strategy is successful when firms have the core competencies required to provide value to a narrow competitive segment that exceeds the value available from firms serving customers on an industry-wide basis.

- The competitive risks of focus strategies include (1) a competitor's ability to use its core competencies to "out-focus" the focuser by serving an even more narrowly defined competitive segment, (2) decisions by industry-wide competitors to serve a customer group's specialized needs that the focuser has been serving, and (3) a reduction in differences of the needs between customers in a narrow competitive segment and the industry-wide market.

- Firms using the integrated cost leadership/differentiation strategy strive to provide customers with relatively low-cost products that have some valued differentiated features. The primary risk of this strategy is that a firm might produce products that do not offer sufficient value in terms of either low cost or differentiation. When this occurs, the company is "stuck in the middle." Firms stuck in the middle compete at a disadvantage and are unable to earn more than average returns.

Review Questions

1. What is a business-level strategy?

2. What is the relationship between a firm's customers and its business-level strategy in terms of *who*, *what*, and *how*? Why is this relationship important?

3. What are the differences among the cost leadership, differentiation, focused cost leadership, focused differentiation, and integrated cost leadership/differentiation business-level strategies?

4. How can each one of the business-level strategies be used to position the firm relative to the five forces of competition in a way that permits the earning of above-average returns?

5. What are the specific risks associated with using each business-level strategy?

Experiential Exercises

Warehouse Clubs' Strategies

Although warehouse clubs have traditionally offered low-priced merchandise to small-business owners, they are increasingly servicing the end-use consumer in this $70 billion industry. Two giants in the field are Sam's Club and Costco. Costco has surpassed Sam's in sales, nearly doubling Sam's sales on a per-store basis by some estimates. Sam's tends to offer average-quality goods in bulk at low margins. Costco increasingly offers special selections of high-quality, even designer, goods, attracting customers whose incomes are approximately twice the national average. Although each competitor regularly stocks certain products, other offerings may be one time only with limited stock. Costco uses this scenario to entice customers into the store to see what is there today, perhaps gone tomorrow. This type of shopping experience has reportedly grown into a cultural fad for some Costco shoppers, who often look for a value on high-end goods and compare bargain finds with their friends. Sam's Clubs are often located near major interstates to capitalize on their quick, efficient distribution system. Costcos are increasingly located in affluent suburbs, near their customer bases.

Use the Internet to research the home pages and annual statements of both Sam's Club and Costco. Using your knowledge of these businesses and any relevant researched information, label each strategy. (See Figure 4.1.) Based on each of their identified business strategies, how are each of these firms positioned relative to the five forces of competition? To better understand each of their competitive positions, compare total sales and sales per store; number of memberships and sales per membership; and operating income and sales growth for 2001 to 2003. Finally, how does each of these two firms appear to be positioned relative to the *who*, *what*, and *how* of customer elements of strategic competitiveness? (See Table 4.1.)

Business-Level Strategy

Natural and organic foods are the fastest growing segment of food retailing, and almost every supermarket in America has begun offering at least a limited selection of these products. According to chairman and CEO John Mackey, "Whole Foods is the 'category killer' for natural and organic products, offering the largest selection at competitive prices and the most informed customer service."

The first Whole Foods Markets opened in 1980, in Austin, Texas, and realized $4 million in sales. By 2001, the firm had become the world's largest retailer of natural and organic foods, with 126 stores across the country and the District of Columbia. A strong performer for several years with consistently high same-store sales, cash flow, gross margins, and controlled expansion, the firm's sales grew to $2.27 billion and earnings per share to $1.03 for fiscal 2001. Shares were up more than 50 percent over the previous year, and analysts expected the performance to continue, anticipating 18 percent earnings growth in fiscal 2002 and 20 percent growth in 2003.

Whole Foods purchases its products both locally and from all over the world, supporting organic farming on a global level, and prides itself on providing its customers with the highest-quality, least-processed, most flavorful and naturally preserved foods. Although the firm concedes that organic foods generally cost more than conventional foods, it notes that organic farming is not government subsidized and that organic products must meet stricter regulations governing growing, harvesting, transportation, and storage. All of these steps make the process more labor and management intensive.

Whole Foods staff members are encouraged to make their own decisions and play a critical role in helping build the store into a profitable and beneficial part of its community.

Answer the following questions and be prepared to make a short presentation or to discuss your findings with the rest of the class.

1. What type of business-level strategy does Whole Foods appear to follow, based on the above information?

2. What are some of the risks Whole Foods faces with this strategy?

3. Use the following table and show how Whole Foods might apply each strategy to its business activities, based on the information given above (also see Figures 4.2 and 4.3).

Activities	Cost Leadership Strategy	Differentiation Strategy
Inbound Logistics		
Operations		
Outbound Logistics		
Marketing and Sales		
Service		

SOURCES: L. DiCarlo, 2001, The overachievers, Forbes.com, http://www.forbes.com, December 5; 2000, Whole Foods Annual Report, Chairman's Letter, http://www.wholefoods.com/investor/ar00_letter.html.

Notes

1. L. L. Bryan, 2003, Strategic minds at work, The McKinsey Quarterly, Number 2, 6–7.

2. C. Roxburgh, 2003, Hidden flaws in strategy, The McKinsey Quarterly, Number 2, 27–39; J. Stopford, 2001, Should strategy makers become dream weavers? Harvard Business Review, 79(1): 165–169.

3. S. Kaplan & E. D. Beinhocker, 2003, The real value of strategic planning, MIT Sloan Management Review, 44(2): 71–76.

4. T. J. Douglas & J. A. Ryman, 2003, Understanding competitive advantage in the general hospital industry: Evaluating strategic competencies, Strategic Management Journal, 24: 333–347.

5. B. Pittman, 2003, Leading for value, Harvard Business Review, 81(4): 41–46.

6. D. A. Schuler, K. Rehbein, & R. D. Cramer, 2002, Pursuing strategic advantage through political means: A multivariate approach, Academy of Management Journal, 45: 659–672.

7. H. Bowman & C. E. Helfat, 2001, Does corporate strategy matter? Strategic Management Journal, 22: 1–23.

8. C. B. Dobni & G. Luffman, 2003, Determining the scope and impact of market orientation profiles on strategy implementation and performance, Strategic Management Journal, 24: 577–585; G. Hamel, 2000, Leading the Revolution, Boston: Harvard Business School Press, 71.

9. L. G. Love, R. L. Priem, & G. T. Lumpkin, 2002, Explicitly articulated strategy and firm performance under alternative levels of centralization, Journal of Management, 28: 611–627; R. S. Kaplan & D. P. Norton, 2001, The Strategy-Focused Organization, Boston: Harvard Business School Press, 90.

10. J. B. Barney, 2002, Gaining and Sustaining Competitive Advantage, 2nd ed., Upper Saddle River, NJ: Prentice-Hall, 6; D. C. Hambrick & J. W. Fredrickson, 2001, Are you sure you have a strategy? Academy of Management Executive, 15(4): 48–59.

11. R. D. Ireland, M. A. Hitt, S. M. Camp, & D. L. Sexton, 2001, Integrating entrepreneurship and strategic management actions to create firm wealth, Academy of Management Executive, 15(1): 49–63.

12. I. C. MacMillan, A. B. van Putten, & R. M. McGrath, 2003, Global gamesmanship, Harvard Business Review, 81(5): 62–71; M. A. Geletkanycez & S. S. Black, 2001, Bound by the past? Experience-based effects on commitment to the strategic status quo, Journal of Management, 27: 3–21.

13. D. F. Kuratko, R. D. Ireland, & J. S. Hornsby, 2001, The power of entrepreneurial actions: Insights from Acordia, Inc., Academy of Management Executive, 15(4): 60–71; T. J. Dean, R. L. Brown, & C. E. Bamford, 1998, Differences in large and small firm responses to environmental context: Strategic implications from a comparative analysis of business formations, Strategic Management Journal, 19: 709–728.

14. D. Farrell, T. Terwilliger, & A. P. Webb, 2002, Getting IT spending right this time, The McKinsey Quarterly, Number 2, 118–129; L. Tihanyi, A. E. Ellstrand, C. M. Daily, & D. R. Dalton, 2000, Composition of top management team and firm international diversification, Journal of Management, 26: 1157–1177.

15. A. M. Appel, A. Dhadwal, & W. E. Pietraszek, 2003, More bang for the IT buck, The McKinsey Quarterly, Number 2, 130–141; S. Nambisan, 2002, Designing virtual customer environments for new product development: Toward a theory, Academy of Management Review, 27: 392–413.

16. P. Rindova & C. J. Fombrun, 1999, Constructing competitive advantage: The role of firm-constituent interactions, Strategic Management Journal, 20: 691–710; G. G. Dess, A. Gupta, J. F. Hennart, & C. W. L. Hill, 1995, Conducting and integrating strategy research at the international, corporate, and business levels: Issues and directions, Journal of Management, 21: 357–393.

17. R. D. Ireland, M. A. Hitt, & D. G. Sirmon, 2003, A model of strategic entrepreneurship: The construct and its dimensions, Journal of Management, in press.

18. T. L. Pett & J. A. Wolff, 2003, Firm characteristics and managerial perceptions of NAFTA: An assessment of export implications for U.S. SMEs, Journal of Small Business Management, 41(2): 117–132; S. F. Slater & E. M. Olsen, 2000, Strategy type and performance: The influence of sales force management, Strategic Management Journal, 21: 813–829; M. E. Porter, 1998, On Competition, Boston: Harvard Business School Press.

19. M. E. Porter, 1996, What is strategy? Harvard Business Review, 74(6): 61–78.

20. T. A. Stewart, 2003, Dear shareholders, Harvard Business Review, 81(5): 10.

21. B. Lowendahl & O. Revang, 1998, Challenges to existing strategy theory in a postindustrial society, Strategic Management Journal, 19: 755–773.

22. D. M. De Carolis, 2003, Competencies and imitability in the pharmaceutical industry: An analysis of their relationship with firm performance, *Journal of Management*, 29: 27–50.

23. M. E. Porter, 1980, *Competitive Strategy*, New York: Free Press.

24. G. S. Day, 2003, Creating a superior customer-relating capability, *The McKinsey Quarterly*, 44(3): 77–82; L. L. Berry, 2001, The old pillars of new retailing, *Harvard Business Review*, 79(4): 131–137; A. Afuah, 1999, Technology approaches for the information age, in "Mastering Strategy" (Part One), *Financial Times*, September 27, 8.

25. N. Irwin, 2001, Motley Fool branches out, *Washington Post*, May 22, B5.

26. C. Harrison, 2003, Hoping a new name still computes, *Dallas Morning News*, May 6, D1.

27. D. O. Becker, 2003, Gambling on customers, *The McKinsey Quarterly*, Number 2, 46–59.

28. T. A. Stewart, 1999, *Intellectual Capital*, New York: Currency Doubleday, 144.

29. B. Magura, 2003, What hooks M-commerce customers? *The McKinsey Quarterly*, 44(3): 9; S. Winer, 2001, A framework for customer relationship management, *California Management Review*, 43(4): 89–105.

30. R. Dhar & R. Glazer, 2003, Hedging customers, *Harvard Business Review*, 81(5): 86–92.

31. L. K. Geller, 2002, CRM: What does it mean? *Target Marketing*, 25(8): 23–24.

32. 2003, Fitch Mexico assigns AA qualifications to certificates of Cemex, *Emerging Markets Economy*, April 8, 3; L. Walker, 2001, Plugged in for maximum efficiency, *Washington Post*, June 20, G1, G4.

33. P. Panepento, 2003, Erie, Pa., plant leads GE profits, *Erie Times-News*, April 12, B4; 2001, While Welch waited, *The Economist*, May 19, 75–76.

34. 2003, Amazon.com, *Standard & Poor's Stock Reports*, http://www.standardandpoors.com, May 3; 2003, Barnes & Noble, *Standard & Poor's Stock Reports*, http://www.standardandpoors.com, May 3.

35. 2003, http://www.carpoint.com, May 17; P. Evans & T. S. Wurster, 1999, Getting real about virtual commerce, *Harvard Business Review*, 77(6): 84–94; S. F. Slater & J. C. Narver, 1999, Market-oriented is more than being customer-led, *Strategic Management Journal*, 20: 1165–1168.

36. D. Rosenblum, D. Tomlinson, & L. Scott, 2003, Bottom-feeding for blockbuster businesses, *Harvard Business Review*, 81(3): 52–59.

37. W. D. Neal & J. Wurst, 2001, Advances in market segmentation, *Marketing Research*, 13(1): 14–18.

38. A. Baur, S. P. Hehner, & G. Nederegger, 2003, Pharma for Fido, *The McKinsey Quarterly*, Number 2, 7–10.

39. B. J. Knutson, 2000, College students and fast food—how students perceive restaurant brands, *Cornell Hotel and Restaurant Administration Quarterly*, 41(3): 68–74.

40. 2003, Unions and Gen-X: What does the future hold? *HR Focus*, March, 3; F. Marshall, 2003, Storehouse wakes up to Gen-X employees, *Furniture Today*, February 10, 2–3; J. Pereira, 2003, Best on the street, *Wall Street Journal*, May 12, R7; C. Burritt, 2001, Aging boomers reshape resort segment, *Lodging Hospitality*, 57(3): 31–32; J. D. Zbar, 2001, On a segmented dial, digital cuts wire finer, *Advertising Age*, 72(16): S12.

41. F. Warner, 2003, Learning how to speak to Gen Y, *Fast Company*, July, 36–37; T. Elkin, 2003, Study: GenY is key to convergence, *Advertising Age*, 74(17): 61; 2001, Is Gen Y shopping online? *Business Week*, June 11, 16.

42. 2003, Abercrombie & Fitch, *Standard & Poor's Stock Reports*, http://www.standardandpoors.com, May 3; D. Little, 2001, Hot growth companies, *Business Week*, June 11, 107–110.

43. D. A. Aaker, 1998, *Strategic Marketing Management*, 5th ed., New York: John Wiley & Sons, 20.

44. E. Danneels, 2003, Tight-loose coupling with customers: The enactment of customer orientation, *Strategic Management Journal*, 24: 559–576.

45. 2003, Giving people what they want, *The Economist*, May 10, 58.

46. J. P. O'Brien, 2003, The capital structure implications of pursuing a strategy of innovation, *Strategic Management Journal*, 24: 415–431.

47. L. Mazur, 2003, Forget risk-free rules to tap into customer needs, *Marketing*, April 10, 16.

48. D. Foust, F. F. Jespersen, F. Katzenberg, A. Barrett, & R. O. Crockett, 2003, The best performers, *BusinessWeek Online*, http://www.businessweek.com, March 24.

49. 2003, Less is Moore, *The Economist*, May 10, 10.

50. M. J. Silverstein & N. Fiske, 2003, Luxury for the masses, *Harvard Business Review*, 81(4): 48–57.

51. C. W. L. Hill & F. T. Rothaermel, 2003, The performance of incumbent firms in the face of radical technological innovation, *Academy of Management Review*, 28: 257–274; A. W. King, S. W. Fowler, & C. P. Zeithaml, 2001, Managing organizational competencies for competitive advantage: The middle-management edge, *Academy of Management Executive*, 15(2): 95–106.

52. S. N. Mehta, 2001, What Lucent can learn from IBM, *Fortune*, June 25, 40–44.

53. 2003, http://www.sas.com, May 15; C. A. O'Reilly III & J. Pfeffer, 2000, *Hidden Value: How Great Companies Achieve Extraordinary Results with Ordinary People*, Boston: Harvard Business School Press, 102.

54. 2003, http://www.vans.com; A. Weintraub & G. Khermouch, 2001, Chairman of the board, *Business Week*, May 28, 94.

55. M. E. Porter, 1985, *Competitive Advantage*, New York: Free Press, 26.

56. Porter, What is strategy?

57. 2003, What makes Southwest Airlines fly? *Knowledge at Wharton*, http://knowledge.wharton.upenn.edu, April 24.

58. Porter, What is strategy?

59. G. Hawawini, V. Subramanian, & P. Verdin, 2003, Is performance driven by industry- or firm-specific factors? A new look at the evidence, *Strategic Management Journal*, 24: 1–16; B. McEvily & A. Zaheer, 1999, Bridging ties: A source of firm heterogeneity in competitive capabilities, *Strategic Management Journal*, 20: 133–156.

60. Hambrick & Fredrickson, Are you sure you have a strategy?

61. C. Zott, 2003, Dynamic capabilities and the emergence of intraindustry differential firm performance: Insights from a simulation study, *Strategic Management Journal*, 24: 97–125.

62. M. E. Porter, 1994, Toward a dynamic theory of strategy, in R. P. Rumelt, D. E. Schendel, & D. J. Teece (eds.), *Fundamental Issues in Strategy*, Boston: Harvard Business School Press, 423–461.

63. Porter, What is strategy?, 62.

64. R. J. Arend, 2003, Revisiting the logical and research considerations of competitive advantage, *Strategic Management Journal*, 24: 279–284.

65. Porter, *Competitive Advantage*, 15.

66. G. G. Dess, G. T. Lumpkin, & J. E. McGee, 1999, Linking corporate entrepreneurship to strategy, structure, and process: Suggested research directions, *Entrepreneurship: Theory & Practice*, 23(3): 85–102; P. M. Wright, D. L. Smart, & G. C. McMahan, 1995, Matches between human resources and strategy among NCAA basketball teams, *Academy of Management Journal*, 38: 1052–1074.

67. Porter, *Competitive Strategy*, 35–40.

68. S. D. Dobrev & G. R. Carroll, 2003, Size (and competition) among organizations: Modeling scale-based selection among automobile producers in four major countries, 1885–1981, *Strategic Management Journal*, 24: 541–558; J. A. Parnell, 2000, Reframing the combination strategy debate: Defining forms of combination, *Journal of Management Studies*, 9(1): 33–54.

69. D. F. Spulber, 2004, *Management Strategy*, New York: McGrawHill/Irwin, 175.

70. D. F. Lynch, S. B. Keller, & J. Ozment, 2000, The effects of logistics capabilities and strategy on firm performance, *Journal of Business Logistics*, 21(2): 47–68.

71. 2003, Big Lots, *Standard & Poor's Stock Reports*, http://www.standardandpoors.com, May 3.

72. F. Green, 2003, Bargain retailers get pick of top-notch holiday goods, *San Diego Union-Tribune*, January 25, D4.

73. D. Howell, 2003, "National" Big Lots aims to expand, *DSN Retailing*, 42(8): 2.

74. L. K. Johnson, 2003, Dueling pricing strategies, *The McKinsey Quarterly*, 44(3): 10–11.

75. A. D'Innocenzio, 2001, We are paranoid, *Richmond Times-Dispatch*, June 10, E1, E2.

76. Lynch, Keller, & Ozment, The effects of logistics capabilities.

77. 2003, Target Corp., *Standard & Poor's Stock Reports*, http://www.standardandpoors.com, May 3.

78. S. Carlson, 2003, Target sees 4.4 percent earnings rise in fourth quarter, *Saint Paul Pioneer News*, February 21, B2.

79. J. Collins, 2003, Bigger, better, faster, *Fast Company*, June, 74–78.

80. Porter, *Competitive Strategy*, 35–40.

81. Ibid., 65.

82. Porter, *Competitive Advantage*, 14.

83. 2003, http://www.roberttalbott.com.

84. J. Flint, 2003, Gotta have, *Forbes*, May 26, 97.

PART 2 / Strategic Actions: Strategy Formulation

85. M. Carmichael, 2002, It's wicked—Heinz ketchup now goes an orange colour, *Grocer*, February 16, 54; 2001, Business in Brief, *Washington Post*, June 20, E2.

86. G. Edmondson, E. Neuborne, A. L. Kazmin, E. Thornton, & K. N. Anhalt, 1999, L'Oréal: The beauty of global branding, *Business Week e-biz*, June 28.

87. Barney, *Gaining and Sustaining Competitive Advantage*, 268.

88. 2003, Callaway Golf Company, *Standard & Poor's Stock Reports*, http://www.standardandpoors.com, May 3; H. R. Goldstein, A. E. Roth, T. Young, & J. D. Lawrence, 2001, US manufacturers take a swing at counterfeit golf clubs, *Intellectual Property & Technology Law Journal*, May, 23.

89. 2003, Philip Morris files to stop counterfeit cigarette sales, *Wall Street Journal Online*, http://www.wsj.com, March 3.

90. Porter, *Competitive Strategy*, 98.

91. Porter, *Competitive Advantage*, 15.

92. Ibid., 15–16.

93. D. Kasler, 2003, Sacramento, Calif., family look for buyer for records retailer, *Sacramento Bee*, May 12, B3; 1999, Lloyd Greif Center for Entrepreneurial Studies, Discussion of the Greif Center's founder, http://www.marshall.usc.edu.

94. D. Raiford, 2002, Prison health ends contract with Philly, *Nashville Business Journal*, July 12; D. Foust & B. Grow, 2001, This company likes it in jail, *Business Week*, June 11, 112.

95. Porter, *Competitive Advantage*, 15.

96. Porter, What is strategy?, 67.

97. K. Kling & I. Goteman, 2003, Ikea CEO Andres Dahlvig on international growth and Ikea's unique corporate culture and brand identity, *Academy of Management Executive*, 17(1): 31–37.

98. 2003, http://www.ikea.com.

99. W. Stewart, 2003, Ikea's flat-pack revolution changing rooms in Russia, *Knight Ridder Tribune Business News*, http://www.knightridder.com, April 24; 2003, Ikea's RMB 500-million outlet opens in Shanghai, *SinoCast China Business Daily News*, April 18.

100. G. Evans, 2003, Why some stores strike me as special, *Furniture Today*, 27(24): 91; Porter, What is strategy?, 65.

101. 2003, http://casketfurniture.com, May 20; F. Keenan, 2003, Execs cozy up to B&Bs, *Business Week*, May 19, 132; S. Jones, 2001, Cutting a swath in hair care, *Washington Post*, May 5, E1, E8.

102. D. Voorhis, 2003, Wichita, Kan., motorcycle manufacturer kicks into high gear, *Wichita Eagle*, May 9, A1; 2003, http://www.bigdogmotorcycles.com, May 20.

103. 2003, Building Materials Holding Company, *Standard & Poor's Stock Reports*, http://www.standardandpoors.com, May 3.

104. 2001, The engine that drives differentiation, *DSN Retailing Today*, April 2, 52.

105. Dess, Lumpkin, & McGee, Linking corporate entrepreneurship to strategy, 89.

106. P. Ghemawat, 2001, *Strategy and the Business Landscape*, Upper Saddle River, NJ: Prentice-Hall, 56.

107. W. K. Hall, 1980, Survival strategies in a hostile environment, *Harvard Business Review* 58(5): 75–87.

108. Dess, Gupta, Hennart, & Hill, Conducting and integrating strategy research, 377.

109. L. Kim & Y. Lim, 1988, Environment, generic strategies, and performance in a rapidly developing country: A taxonomic approach, *Academy of Management Journal*, 31: 802–827.

110. Ghemawat, *Strategy and the Business Landscape*, 56.

111. Ibid.

112. M. Naim, 2001, McAtlas shrugged, *Foreign Policy*, May/June, 26–37.

113. S. A. Forest, 2001, When cool heads prevail, *Business Week*, June 11, 114.

114. A. Aston & M. Arndt, 2003, The flexible factory: Leaning heavily on technology, some U.S. plants stay competitive with offshore rivals, *Business Week*, May 5, 90–91; J. Markoff, 2003, Computing's big shift: Flexibility in the chips, *New York Times*, http://www.nytimes.com, June 16.

115. R. Sanchez, 1995, Strategic flexibility in product competition, *Strategic Management Journal*, 16(Special Issue): 140.

116. Ibid., 105.

117. J. Portelli, 2003, Agile assembly with robots, *Manufacturing Engineering*, 130(3): 83–87; R. Olexa, 2001, Flexible parts feeding boosts productivity, *Manufacturing Engineering*, 126(4): 106–114.

118. I. Mount & B. Caulfield, 2001, The missing link, *Ecompany* Now, May, 82–88.

119. J. Baljko, 2003, Built for speed—When putting the reams of supply chain data they've amassed to use, companies are discovering that agility counts, *EBN*, 1352: 25–28.

120. 2001, ABB: Integrated drives and process control, *Textile World*, April, 60–61.

121. R. S. Russell & B. W. Taylor III, 2000, *Operations Management*, 3rd ed., Upper Saddle River, NJ: Prentice-Hall, 262–264.

122. J. B. Dilworth, 2000, *Operations Management: Providing Value in Goods and Services*, 3rd ed., Fort Worth, TX: The Dryden Press, 286–289; D. Lei, M. A. Hitt, & J. D. Goldhar, 1996, Advanced manufacturing technology, organization design and strategic flexibility, *Organization Studies*, 17: 501–523.

123. 2003, UNOVA Industrial Automotive Systems—Using strategic business alliances to tap global markets, http://activequote.fidelity.com, April 29; 2003, Fix machine tools with less fuss, *American Machinist*, 147(1): 30; R. E. Chalmers, 2001, Assembly systems maximize efficiency, *Manufacturing Engineering*, May, 130–138.

124. A. McAfee, 2003, When too much IT knowledge is a dangerous thing, *The McKinsey Quarterly*, 44(2): 83–89.

125. F. Mattern, S. Schonwalder, & W. Stein, 2003, Fighting complexity in IT, *The McKinsey Quarterly*, Number 1, 57–65.

126. K. H. Doerr, T. R. Mitchell, C. A. Schriesheim, T. Freed, & X. Zhou, 2002, Heterogeneity and variability in the context of work flows, *Academy of Management Review*, 27: 594–607.

127. S. W. Brown, 2003, The employee experience, *Marketing Management*, 12(2): 12–13.

128. S. Isaac & R. N. Tooker, 2001, The many faces of CRM, *LIMRA's Market-Facts Quarterly*, 20(1): 84–89.

129. P. J. Rondeau & L. A. Litteral, 2001, The evolution of manufacturing planning and control systems: From reorder point to enterprise resource planning, *Production and Inventory Management*, 42(2): 1–7.

130. A. L. Velocci, Jr., 2003, Near-term market offers little growth, *Aviation Week & Space Technology*, 158(1): 41–42; M. L. Songini, 2001, Companies test their wireless supply chain wings, *Computerworld*, May 21, 35.

131. V. A. Mabert, A. Soni, & M. A. Venkataramanan, 2003, Enterprise resource planning: Managing the implementation process, *European Journal of Operational Research*, 146(2): 302–314.

132. J. D. Westphal, R. Gulati, & S. M. Shortell, 1997, Customization or conformity: An institutional and network perspective on the content and consequences of TQM adoption, *Administrative Science Quarterly*, 42: 366–394.

133. V. W. S. Yeung & R. W. Armstrong, 2003, A key to TQM benefits: Manager involvement in customer processes, *International Journal of Services Technology and Management*, 4(1): 14–29; S. Sanghera, 1999, Making continuous improvement better, *Financial Times*, April 21, 28.

134. J. Muller, 2001, Ford: Why it's worse than you think, *Business Week*, June 25, 80–89.

135. J. White, G. L. White, & N. Shirouzu, 2001, Soon, the big three won't be, as foreigners make inroads, *Wall Street Journal*, August 13, A1, A12.

136. D. Welch, K. Kerwin, & C. Tierney, 2003, Way to go, Detroit—Now go a lot farther, *Business Week*, May 26, 44.

137. N. Ganguli, T. V. Kumaresh, & A. Satpathy, 2003, Detroit's new quality gap, *The McKinsey Quarterly*, Number 1, 148–151.

138. Porter, *Competitive Advantage*, 16.

139. Ibid., 17.

140. Parnell, Reframing the combination strategy debate, 33.

Competitive Rivalry and Competitive Dynamics

Knowledge Objectives

Studying this chapter should provide you with the strategic management knowledge needed to:

1. Define competitors, competitive rivalry, competitive behavior, and competitive dynamics.

2. Describe market commonality and resource similarity as the building blocks of a competitor analysis.

3. Explain awareness, motivation, and ability as drivers of competitive behavior.

4. Discuss factors affecting the likelihood a competitor will take competitive actions.

5. Discuss factors affecting the likelihood a competitor will respond to actions taken against it.

6. Explain competitive dynamics in slow-cycle, fast-cycle, and standard-cycle markets.

BrandX Pictures

JetBlue and Song are direct competitors on the east coast. Song represents Delta's strategic response to the founding of JetBlue, which could be considered JetBlue's first strategic action.

JetBlue and Song: Competitive Rivalry between Low-Cost Carriers

JetBlue was launched on February 11, 2000, with a maiden flight between John F. Kennedy (JFK) International Airport and Fort Lauderdale, Florida. Using its fleet of new Airbus A320 planes, this start-up venture serves over 20 cities with plans to serve many more over the next few years. Founder and CEO David Neeleman has extensive experience in the airline industry having started and sold Salt-Lake City Air and Morris Air as well as establishing and selling Open Skies, an e-ticketing system he developed at Morris Air. Neeleman believed that his formula of low cost and great service could be successfully used out of New York City, which is the world's largest aviation market. With much fanfare, his JetBlue Airways was founded as a new airline that "would bring humanity back to air travel." Price-conscious leisure travelers were JetBlue's target customer—a group whose needs Neeleman felt weren't being well served by existing competitors. Thus, JetBlue is the product of an entrepreneur's identification of an entrepreneurial opportunity (entrepreneurs and entrepreneurial opportunities are further discussed in Chapter 13). The decision to launch JetBlue demonstrates what is called a strategic action, a term that is defined and discussed in this chapter.

Song, a wholly owned subsidiary of Delta Air Lines, launched its maiden voyage from JFK to West Palm Beach on April 15, 2003. The primary routes initially served by Song with its fleet of Boeing 757 aircraft were between the Northeast and Florida. Company officials noted that Song was a "new airline service developed to revolutionize customer expectations for high-quality, low-fare air travel." In more specific terms, Song was established to "make flying the way it used to be—fun, exciting, interesting or simply relaxing—what the customer is looking for that day." Delta's decision to establish Song as a replacement for Delta Express, its previously established but unsuccessful low-fare venture, demonstrates a strategic response (another term defined and discussed in this chapter).

Song is competing directly with JetBlue for the leisure travel market on the east coast. As competitors, Song and JetBlue have a high degree of market commonality, another term that is discussed and defined in this chapter. Some analysts claim that one reason for the direct competition between these two companies is that Delta had to do something to "recapture customers taken by highly profitable low-fare carrier JetBlue Airways." Thus, Song represents Delta's strategic response to the founding of JetBlue, which was a strategic action. For several reasons, Delta decided to establish a new venture to compete against JetBlue instead of continuing to use low-fare carrier Delta Express or to rely on its own Delta Air Line flights to do so. The problem with Delta Express (which Song replaced) is that while the carrier matched and sometimes beat the discount airlines' (such as JetBlue and

Southwest Airlines) fares, inefficient spending increased costs to the point where it couldn't earn a profit. Full-size operators such as Delta Air Lines aren't profitable (Delta, United, and American lost a combined $9 billion in 2002) and, according to industry analysts, simply can't compete against low-cost carriers in terms of CASM (cost per available seat mile) and RASM (revenue per available seat mile).

As competitors engaged in competitive rivalry, JetBlue and Song are trying to "outcompete" each other in terms of providing value-creating services along with the lowest fare to the same customer. JetBlue, for example, is the only carrier offering passengers live satellite television with up to 24 channels of DirecTV programming free of charge at each seat. As a competitive response, Song partnered with several firms to offer customers personal video monitors at each seat with touchscreen technology and credit card "swipe" capability. In addition, Song passengers have all-digital satellite television programming from DISH Network available to them. Each JetBlue seat is leather while Song emphasizes the 33 inches of legroom between rows on its 757 jets. As competitors, JetBlue and Song can be expected to closely monitor each other's competitive actions and competitive responses as each firm seeks to outcompete the other one.

SOURCES: 2003, Delta Airlines 2002 Annual Report, http://www.delta.com, May 25; 2003, Delta Airlines Home Page, Introducing the world's most innovative low-fare airline service, http://www.delta.com, May 25; 2003, Delta's Song to offer satellite TV, *Satellite News*, 26(17): B2; 2003, JetBlue Home Page, Welcome from our CEO, http://www.jetblue.com, May 25; S. Kirsner, 2003, Song's flight plan, *Fast Company*, June, 98–107; J. Naudi, 2003, Airlines aim to recapture business with low-fare tickets, *Indianapolis Star*, February 23, D3; R. Thomaselli, 2003, Delta takes low-key approach to low-cost carrier, *Advertising Age*, 74(18): 4, 36.

Firms operating in the same market, offering similar products, and targeting similar cutomers are competitors.

Competitive rivalry is the ongoing set of competitive actions and competitive responses occurring between competitors as they compete against each other for an advantageous market position.

Competitive behavior is the set of competitive actions and competitive responses the firm takes to build or defend its competitive advantages and to improve its market position.

Firms operating in the same market, offering similar products, and targeting similar customers are **competitors**.[1] JetBlue and Song are competitors as are Teradyne and Applied Materials and PepsiCo and Coca-Cola Company. Firms interact with their competitors that are part of the broad context within which they operate while attempting to earn above-average returns.[2] The decisions firms make about who their competitors will be and especially about how they will compete against their rivals have an important effect on their ability to earn above-average returns.[3]

Competitive rivalry is the ongoing set of competitive actions and competitive responses occurring between competitors as they compete against each other for an advantageous market position. Especially in highly competitive industries, firms constantly jockey for advantage as they launch strategic actions and respond or react to rivals' moves.[4] It is important for those leading organizations to understand competitive rivalry, in that "the central, brute empirical fact in strategy is that some firms outperform others,"[5] meaning that competitive rivalry influences an individual firm's ability to gain and sustain competitive advantages.[6]

A sequence of firm-level moves, rivalry results from firms initiating their own competitive actions and then responding to actions taken by competitors.[7] **Competitive behavior** is the set of competitive actions and competitive responses the firm takes to build or defend its competitive advantages and to improve its market position.[8] Through competitive behavior, the firm tries to successfully position itself relative to the five forces of competition (see Chapter 2) and to defend and use current competitive advantages while building advantages for the future (see Chapter 3). Increasingly, competitors engage in competitive actions and responses in more than one market.[9] Firms competing against each other in several product or geographic markets are engaged in **multimarket competition.**[10] All competitive behavior—that is, the total set of actions and responses taken by all firms competing within a market—is called **competitive dynamics.** The relationships among these key concepts are shown in Figure 5.1.

This chapter focuses on competitive rivalry and competitive dynamics. The essence of these important topics is that a firm's strategies are dynamic in nature. Actions taken by one firm elicit responses from competitors that, in turn, typically result in responses from the firm that took the initial action.[11] This chain of events is illustrated in the Opening Case that describes the competitive actions and competitive responses occurring between JetBlue and Song.

Another way of highlighting competitive rivalry's effect on the firm's strategies is to say that a strategy's success is determined not only by the firm's initial competitive actions but also by how well it anticipates competitors' responses to them *and* by how well the firm anticipates and responds to its competitors' initial actions (also called attacks).[12] Although competitive rivalry affects all types of strategies (for example, corporate-level, acquisition, and international), its most dominant influence is on the firm's business-level strategy or strategies. Indeed, firms' actions and responses to those of their rivals are the basic building block of business-level strategies.[13] Recall from Chapter 4 that business-level strategy is concerned with what the firm does to successfully use its competitive advantages in specific product markets. In the global economy, competitive rivalry is intensifying,[14] meaning that the significance of its effect on firms' business-level strategies is increasing. However, firms that develop and use effective business-level strategies tend to outperform competitors in individual product markets, even when experiencing intense competitive rivalry.[15]

An expanding geographic scope contributes to the increasing intensity in the competitive rivalry between firms. Some believe, for example, that an aptitude for cross-border management practices and a facility with cultural diversity find European

Firms competing against each other in several product or geographic markets are engaged in multimarket competition.

All competitive behavior—that is, the total set of actions and responses taken by all firms competing within a market—is called competitive dynamics.

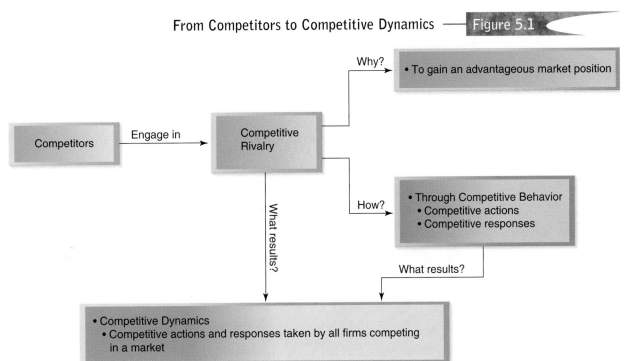

From Competitors to Competitive Dynamics — Figure 5.1

- Competitors — Engage in → Competitive Rivalry
  - Why? → • To gain an advantageous market position
  - How? → • Through Competitive Behavior
    - • Competitive actions
    - • Competitive responses
  - What results? ↓
- What results? →
- • Competitive Dynamics
  - • Competitive actions and responses taken by all firms competing in a market

SOURCE: Adapted from M.-J. Chen, 1996, Competitor analysis and interfirm rivalry: Toward a theoretical integration, *Academy of Management Review*, 21: 100–134.

Union firms emerging as formidable global competitors.[16] In the global brewing industry, for example, Belgian brewer Interbrew bought 70 percent of K.K. Brewery, the leading beer maker in Zhejiang Province, in the Yangtze delta in China. Interbrew is bringing its brewing skills to this facility to establish a strong competitive position in a highly fragmented, rapidly growing market that it believes is very attractive.[17] Similarly, Diageo PLC, the giant U.K.-based spirits and beer group, is expanding aggressively on a global scale.[18] Viewing the expansion's outcomes favorably, some analysts think that "Diageo could easily mop up 10 points of market share over the next five years in the U.S."[19] Diageo's bold entry into U.S. markets could engender strong competitive responses from Anheuser Busch and SABMiller.

A Model of Competitive Rivalry

Over time, firms take many competitive actions and responses.[20] As noted earlier, competitive rivalry evolves from this pattern of actions and responses as one firm's competitive actions have noticeable effects on competitors, eliciting competitive responses from them.[21] This pattern shows that firms are mutually interdependent, that they feel each other's actions and responses, and that marketplace success is a function of both individual strategies and the consequences of their use.[22] Increasingly, too, executives recognize that competitive rivalry can have a major and direct effect on the firm's financial performance.[23] Research findings showing that intensified rivalry within an industry results in decreased average profitability for firms competing in it support the importance of understanding these effects.[24]

We offer a model (see Figure 5.2) to show what is involved with competitive rivalry at the firm level.[25] We study rivalry at the firm level because the competitive actions and responses the firm takes are the foundation for successfully building and using its competitive advantages to gain an advantageous market position.[26] Thus, we use the model in Figure 5.2 to help us explain competition between a particular firm and each of its competitors. Successful use of the model finds companies able to predict competitors' behavior (actions and responses) and reduce the unpredictable variation or the uncertainty associated with competitors' actions.[27] Being able to predict competitors' competitive actions and responses has a positive effect on the firm's market position and its subsequent financial performance.[28] The sum of all the individual rivalries modeled in Figure 5.2 that are occurring in a particular market reflects the competitive dynamics in that market.

Figure 5.2 —— A Model of Competitive Rivalry

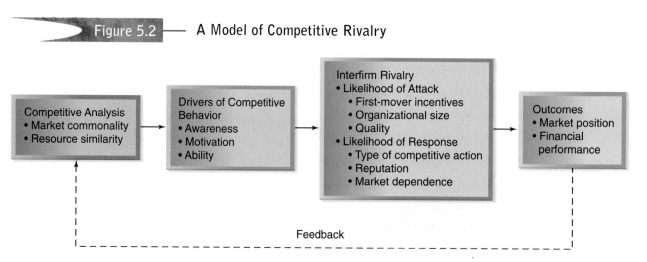

The remainder of the chapter discusses the model shown in Figure 5.2. We first describe market commonality and resource similarity as the building blocks of a competitor analysis. Next, we discuss the effects of three organizational characteristics—awareness, motivation, and ability—on the firm's competitive behavior. We then examine competitive rivalry between firms, or interfirm rivalry, in detail by describing the factors that affect the likelihood a firm will take a competitive action and the factors that affect the likelihood a firm will respond to a competitor's action. In the chapter's final section, we turn our attention to competitive dynamics to describe how market characteristics affect competitive rivalry in slow-cycle, fast-cycle, and standard-cycle markets.

Competitor Analysis

As previously noted, a competitor analysis is the first step the firm takes to be able to predict the extent and nature of its rivalry with each competitor. Recall that a competitor is a firm operating in the same market, offering similar products, and targeting similar customers. The number of markets in which firms compete against each other (called market commonality, defined below) and the similarity in their resources (called resource similarity, also defined below) determine the extent to which the firms are competitors. Firms with high market commonality and highly similar resources are "clearly direct and mutually acknowledged competitors."[29] However, being direct competitors does not necessarily mean that the rivalry between the firms will be intense. The drivers of competitive behavior—as well as factors influencing the likelihood that a competitor will initiate competitive actions and will respond to its competitor's competitive actions—influence the intensity of rivalry, even for direct competitors.[30]

In Chapter 2, we discussed competitor analysis as a technique firms use to understand their competitive environment. Together, the general, industry, and competitive environments comprise the firm's external environment. In the earlier chapter we described how competitor analysis is used to help the firm *understand* its competitors. This understanding results from studying competitors' future objectives, current strategies, assumptions, and capabilities (see Figure 2.3). In this chapter, the discussion of competitor analysis is extended to describe what firms study to be able to *predict* competitors' behavior in the form of their competitive actions and responses. The discussions of competitor analysis in Chapter 2 and Chapter 5 are complementary in that firms must first *understand* competitors (Chapter 2) before their competitive actions and competitive responses can be *predicted* (Chapter 5).

Market Commonality

Each industry is composed of various markets. The financial services industry has markets for insurance, brokerage services, banks, and so forth. Denoting an interest to concentrate on the needs of different, unique customer groups, markets can be further subdivided. The insurance market, for example, could be broken into market segments (such as commercial and consumer), product segments (such as health insurance and life insurance), and geographic markets (such as Western Europe and Southeast Asia). In general, the Internet's capabilities are shaping the nature of industry markets as well as competition within them.[31] For example, widely available electronic news sources affect how traditional print news distributors such as newspapers conduct their business.

In general, competitors agree about the different characteristics of individual markets that form an industry.[32] For example, in the transportation industry, there is an understanding that the commercial air travel market differs from the ground transportation market that is served by such firms as Yellow Freight System and J.B. Hunt Transport Services Inc. Although differences exist, most industries' markets are somewhat related in terms of technologies used or core competencies needed to develop a competitive advantage.[33] For example, different types of transportation companies need to provide reliable and timely service. Commercial air carriers such as Song and JetBlue (see the Opening Case) must therefore develop service competencies to satisfy their passengers, while Yellow Freight System and J.B. Hunt Transport Services Inc. must develop such competencies to serve the needs of those using their fleets to ship goods.

Firms competing in several or even many markets, some of which may be in different industries, are likely to come into contact with a particular competitor several times,[34] a situation that involves the concept of market commonality. **Market commonality** is concerned with the number of markets with which the firm and a competitor are jointly involved and the degree of importance of the individual markets to each.[35] Firms competing against one another in several or many markets engage in multimarket competition.[36] As noted in the Opening Case, JetBlue and Song were initially competing against each other to serve customers traveling between a number of northeast locations and Florida. McDonald's and Burger King compete against each other in multiple geographic markets across the world,[37] while Prudential and Cigna compete against each other in several market segments (institutional and retail) as well as product markets (such as life insurance and health insurance).[38] Airlines, chemicals, pharmaceuticals, and consumer foods are other industries in which firms often simultaneously engage each other in competition in multiple markets.

Firms competing in several markets have the potential to respond to a competitor's actions not only within the market in which the actions are taken, but also in other markets where they compete with the rival. This potential creates a complicated competitive mosaic in which "the moves an organization makes in one market are designed to achieve goals in another market in ways that aren't immediately apparent to its rivals."[39] This potential complicates the rivalry between competitors. In fact, research suggests that "a firm with greater multimarket contact is less likely to initiate an attack, but more likely to move (respond) aggressively when attacked."[40] Thus, in general, multimarket competition reduces competitive rivalry.[41] However, other research suggests that market commonality and multimarket competition sometimes occur almost by chance.[42] But, once it begins, the rivalry between the unexpected competitors becomes intentional and often intense.

Resource Similarity

Resource similarity is the extent to which the firm's tangible and intangible resources are comparable to a competitor's in terms of both type and amount.[43] Firms with similar types and amounts of resources are likely to have similar strengths and weaknesses and use similar strategies.[44] The competition between competitors CVS Corp. and Walgreens to be the largest drugstore chain in the United States demonstrates these expectations. These firms are using the integrated cost leadership/differentiation strategy to offer relatively low-cost goods with some differentiated features, such as services.

When performing a competitor analysis, firms analyze each of their competitors in terms of market commonality and resource similarity. With respect to market commonality, CVS and Walgreens, for example, are quite aware of the total number of markets in which they compete against each other as well as the number of storefronts each operates.[45] Recent statistics show that there are over 4,000 CVS stores in 32 states and the District of Columbia while Walgreens has over 4,000 stores in 43 states and Puerto Rico. CVS is the largest U.S. retail drugstore chain in terms of store count while Walgreens is the largest U.S. retail drug chain in terms of revenues. Thus, these firms compete against each other in many markets, indicating that there is a high degree of market commonality between them.[46]

In contrast to market commonality, assessing resource similarity can be difficult, particularly when critical resources are intangible (such as brand name, knowledge, trust, and the capacity to innovate) rather than tangible (for example, access to raw

Market commonality is concerned with the number of markets with which the firm and a competitor are jointly involved and the degree of importance of the individual markets to each.

Resource similarity is the extent to which the firm's tangible and intangible resources are comparable to a competitor's in terms of both type and amount.

materials and a competitor's ability to borrow capital). As discussed in Chapter 3, a competitor's intangible resources are difficult to identify and understand, making an assessment of their value challenging. CVS and Walgreens know the amount of each other's annual net income (a tangible resource). However, it is difficult for CVS and Walgreens to determine if any intangible resources (such as knowledge and trust among employees) its competitor possesses can lead to a competitive advantage.

©Tom Prettyman/PhotoEdit

The results of the firm's competitor analyses can be mapped for visual comparisons. In Figure 5.3, we show different hypothetical intersections between the firm and individual competitors in terms of market commonality and resource similarity. These intersections indicate the extent to which the firm and those to which it has compared itself are competitors.[47] For example, the firm and its competitor displayed in quadrant I of Figure 5.3 have similar types and amounts of resources and use them to compete against each other in many markets that are important to each. These conditions lead to the conclusion that the firms modeled in quadrant I are direct and mutually acknowledged competitors. In contrast, the firm and its competitor shown in quadrant III share few markets and have little similarity in

their resources, indicating that they aren't direct and mutually acknowledged competitors. The firm's mapping of its competitive relationship with rivals is fluid as firms enter and exit markets and as companies' resources change in type and amount. Thus, the companies with which the firm is a direct competitor change across time.

CVS and Walgreens are direct competitors with a high degree of market commonality. Their sales volume, total number of stores, and strategies are all similar.

Toyota Motor Corp. and Volkswagen AG have high market commonality as they compete in many of the same global markets. In years past, the companies also had similar types and quantities of resources. This is changing, though, in that the companies' resources are becoming dissimilar, especially in terms of profitability and sales revenue. In fact, the companies are moving in opposite directions—Toyota's sales and profits are increasing while Volkswagen's sales and profits are decreasing. Thus, quadrant II in Figure 5.3 captures the degree to which Toyota and Volkswagen are direct competitors. In the Strategic Focus, we discuss the possibility that some of Toyota's recent competitive actions may create a situation in which Volkswagen will encounter more competition from Toyota.

How will Volkswagen respond to the possibility of increased competition from Toyota in Europe and China? The challenge is daunting, in that it is difficult if not impossible to "out-Toyota Toyota."[48] Volkswagen's CEO believes that his firm is on the right course, however. Among other actions, the CEO is concentrating on reducing the

Figure 5.3 ——— A Framework of Competitor Analysis

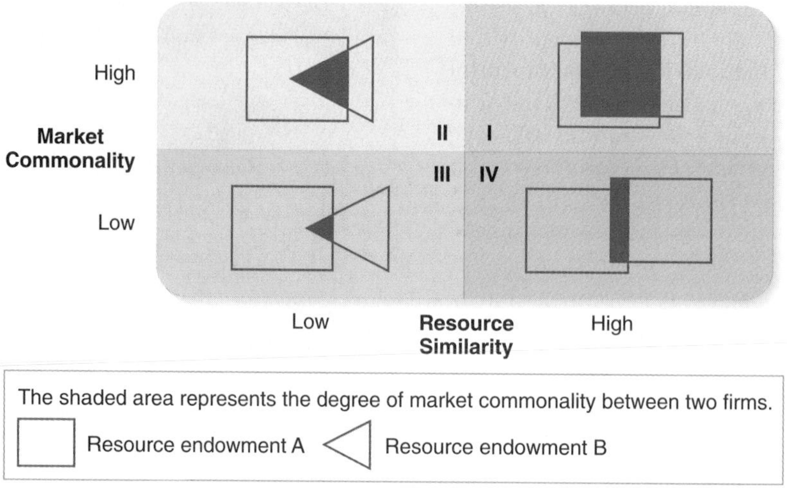

High

**Market
Commonality**

II | I

III | IV

Low

Low   **Resource
Similarity**   High

The shaded area represents the degree of market commonality between two firms.

☐ Resource endowment A   ◁ Resource endowment B

SOURCE: Adapted from M.-J. Chen, 1996, Competitor analysis and interfirm rivalry: Toward a theoretical integration, *Academy of Management Review*, 21: 100–134.

firm's costs and changing the culture to facilitate productive interactions among those designing, manufacturing, and selling the products. Reduced costs and a changed culture will help Volkswagen produce innovative vehicles to fill in gaps in its product line (such as sport-utility vehicles and minivans), the CEO believes.[49]

Drivers of Competitive Actions and Responses

As shown in Figure 5.2, market commonality and resource similarity influence the drivers (awareness, motivation, and ability) of competitive behavior. In turn, the drivers influence the firm's competitive behavior, as shown by the actions and responses it takes while engaged in competitive rivalry.[50]

Awareness, which is a prerequisite to any competitive action or response being taken by the firm or its competitor, refers to the extent to which competitors recognize the degree of their mutual interdependence that results from market commonality and resource similarity.[51] Awareness tends to be greatest when firms have highly similar resources (in terms of types and amounts) to use while competing against each other in multiple markets. CVS and Walgreens are fully aware of each other, as are JetBlue and Song and Wal-Mart and France's Carrefour, the two largest supermarket groups in the world. The last two firms' joint awareness has increased as they use similar resources to compete against each other for dominant positions in multiple European and South American markets.[52] Awareness affects the extent to which the firm understands the consequences of its competitive actions and responses. A lack of awareness can lead to excessive competition, resulting in a negative effect on all competitors' performance.[53]

Motivation, which concerns the firm's incentive to take action or to respond to a competitor's attack, relates to perceived gains and losses. Thus, a firm may be aware of competitors but may not be motivated to engage in rivalry with them if it perceives that its position will not improve as a result of doing so or that its market position won't be damaged if it doesn't respond.[54]

Market commonality affects the firm's perceptions and resulting motivation. For example, all else being equal, the firm is more likely to attack the rival with whom it

Toyota and Volkswagen: Direct Competitors or Not?

The world's third largest auto manufacturer (behind General Motors and Ford Motor Company), Toyota Motor Corporation manufactures and sells cars, trucks, recreational vehicles, minivans, trucks, buses, and related parts on a global basis under the Toyota, Lexus, and Daihatsu brand names. The firm's intention is to "build cars that people want to buy" and to participate in every market segment "wherever there's money to be made and market share to be gained." Toyota's market share is increasing in both the United States and Europe.

Evidence suggests that Toyota has competitive advantages in terms of efficiency and quality. In a recent year, for example, Toyota's profit margin per vehicle was 9.3 percent—more than a threefold increase over General Motors' at 3 percent. This efficiency advantage allows Toyota to increase product quality and/or add value-creating features with its new vehicles while simultaneously reducing the price to customers. Toyota's minivan, the Sienna, is a case in point. Compared to previous models, the all-new 2004 Sienna minivan had greater power and fuel efficiency as well as new seat configurations creating more passenger room, among other new features. However, the base price was 6 percent lower than the previous year's version of the Sienna. The 2003 results from J.D. Power's initial quality survey found Lexus again at the top of the list with only 76 problems per 100 vehicles. Products under the Toyota nameplate had 121 problems per 100 vehicles. With 143 problems per 100 vehicles, Volkswagen fell below the industry average. (The Hummer was at the other end of the initial quality scale with 225 problems per 100 vehicles.)

Volkswagen AG (VW) makes and sells cars and other vehicles on a global basis under the brand names of Volkswagen, Audi, Seat, Skoda, Lamborghini, Bugatti, Rolls Royce, and Bentley. Thus, compared to Toyota, Volkswagen's product lines are more diverse, especially at the upper end with entries from Lamborghini, Bugatti, Rolls Royce, and Bentley.

Volkswagen's current fortunes differ from those of Toyota: "Once Europe's dominant car seller by a wide margin, VW this year (2003) is only slightly ahead of No. 2 PSA Peugeot Citroen." Moreover, VW's share of the all-important U.S. market continues to decline as well.

What has caused these problems for Volkswagen? Some believe that the firm is simply "trying to compete on too many battlefields," including the luxury car market. "But, the drive for luxury diverted VW from its bread-and-butter business—making fun cars for average folks." Another problem was the decision to use the same platform for products in the different lines. This caused confusion among consumers, some of whom felt, for example, that they shouldn't pay an Audi price for a vehicle with the same platform as a VW. Compounding these problems, the firm lost its focus on quality while trying to develop new products for all of its brands.

As it looks to its future, Volkswagen faces the prospect of increasing competition from Toyota, a firm with advantages in terms of manufacturing efficiency, product quality, and available resources. Toyota is concentrating more on European markets, challenging Volkswagen as a result of doing so. Of equal concern to Volkswagen should be Toyota's decision to invest heavily in its Chinese operations. China is Volkswagen's second largest market, indicating that the firm must defend its share against the likes of Toyota as well as other competitors.

SOURCES: N. E. Boudette, 2003, Drivers wanted: Volkswagen stalls on several fronts after luxury drive, *Wall Street Journal,* Eastern edition, May 8, A1; G. Edmondson, 2003, Volkswagen needs a jump, *Business Week,* May 12, 48–49; D. Kiley, 2003, Toyota, Volkswagen take different journeys, *USA Today,* May 9, B5; D. Murphy, 2003, Volkswagen races to keep up in China, *Wall Street Journal,* Eastern edition, March 5, B.11E; L. Ulrich, 2003, Outside the box, *Money,* 32(6): 137–138; G. C. Williams III, 2003, Toyota strategy includes San Antonio expansion, *San Antonio Express-News,* February 7, C3; C. Condon, 2002, Companies head to Eastern Europe to partake in land of low costs, *Sunday Business,* November 17, D1; T. Zaun, 2002, The economy—A global journal report, *Wall Street Journal,* Eastern edition, October 31, A2.

has low market commonality than the one with whom it competes in multiple markets. The primary reason is that there are high stakes involved in trying to gain a more advantageous position over a rival with whom the firm shares many markets. As we mentioned earlier, multimarket competition can find a competitor responding to the firm's action in a market different from the one in which the initial action was taken. Actions and responses of this type can cause both firms to lose focus on core markets and to battle each other with resources that had been allocated for other purposes. Because of the high stakes of competition under the condition of market commonality, there is a high probability that the attacked firm will respond to its competitor's action in an effort to protect its position in one or more markets.[55]

In some instances, the firm may be aware of the large number of markets it shares with a competitor and may be motivated to respond to an attack by that competitor, but it lacks the ability to do so. *Ability* relates to each firm's resources and the flexibility they provide. Without available resources (such as financial capital and people), the firm lacks the ability to attack a competitor or respond to its actions. However, similar resources suggest similar abilities to attack and respond. When a firm faces a competitor with similar resources, careful study of a possible attack before initiating it is essential because the similarly resourced competitor is likely to respond to that action.

Resource *dissimilarity* also influences competitive actions and responses between firms, in that "the greater is the resource imbalance between the acting firm and competitors or potential responders, the greater will be the delay in response"[56] by the firm with a resource disadvantage. For example, Wal-Mart initially used a focused cost leadership strategy to compete only in small communities (those with a population of 25,000 or less). Using sophisticated logistics systems and extremely efficient purchasing practices as advantages, among others, Wal-Mart created what was at that time a new type of value (primarily in the form of wide selections of products at the lowest competitive prices) for customers in small retail markets. Local stores, facing resource deficiencies relative to Wal-Mart, lacked the ability to marshal resources at the pace required to respond quickly and effectively. However, even when facing competitors with greater resources (greater ability) or more attractive market positions, firms should eventually respond, no matter how daunting doing so seems.[57] Choosing not to respond can ultimately result in failure, as happened with at least some local retailers who didn't respond to Wal-Mart's competitive actions.

Competitive Rivalry

As defined earlier in the chapter, *competitive rivalry* is the ongoing set of competitive actions and competitive responses occurring between competing firms for an advantageous market position. Because the ongoing competitive action/response sequence between a firm and a competitor affects the performance of both firms,[58] it is important for companies to carefully study competitive rivalry to successfully use their strategies. Understanding a competitor's awareness, motivation, and ability helps the firm to predict the likelihood of an attack by that competitor and how likely it is that a competitor will respond to the actions taken against it.

As we described earlier, the predictions drawn from study of competitors in terms of awareness, motivation, and ability are grounded in market commonality and resource similarity. These predictions are fairly general. The value of the final set of predictions the firm develops about each of its competitors' competitive actions and responses is enhanced by studying the "Likelihood of Attack" factors (such as first-mover incentives and organizational size) and the "Likelihood of Response" factors (such as the actor's reputation) that are shown in Figure 5.2. Studying these factors allows the firm to develop a deeper understanding in order to refine the predictions it makes about its competitors' actions and responses.

Strategic and Tactical Actions

Firms use both strategic and tactical actions when forming their competitive actions and competitive responses in the course of engaging in competitive rivalry.[59] A **competitive action** is a strategic or tactical action the firm takes to build or defend its competitive advantages or improve its market position. A **competitive response** is a strategic or tactical action the firm takes to counter the effects of a competitor's competitive action. A **strategic action or a strategic response** is a market-based move that involves a significant commitment of organizational resources and is difficult to implement and reverse. A **tactical action or a tactical response** is a market-based move that is taken to fine-tune a strategy; it involves fewer resources and is relatively easy to implement and reverse. Hyundai Motor Co.'s expenditures on research and development and plant expansion to support the firm's desire to be one of the world's largest carmakers by 2010 and to sell at least one million units annually in the United States by 2010[60] are strategic actions. Likewise, Boeing Corp.'s decision to commit the resources required to build the super-efficient 7E7 midsized jetliner for delivery in 2008[61] demonstrates a strategic action. Changes in airfares are somewhat frequently announced by airlines. As tactical actions that are easily reversed, pricing decisions are often taken by these firms to increase demand in certain markets during certain periods.

As explained in the Strategic Focus, Coca-Cola Company, PepsiCo Inc., and Nestlé SA are aware of one another as they compete in the bottled water market. Moreover, this awareness influences the competitive actions and responses these firms initiate as they engage in competitive rivalry.

Of course, bottled water isn't the only product category (outside of soft drinks) in which multimarket competitors Coca-Cola and PepsiCo compete against each other. Consider the emerging competition between these firms in the milk-based products area as a case in point. Partly because of the potential damage of the price wars in the bottled water market that we describe in the Strategic Focus and in order to expand beyond soda into healthier beverages, Coca-Cola introduced Swerve in July 2003. Containing 52 percent milk and initially offered in three flavors (chocolate, blueberry, and vanilla/banana), Swerve was sold in 12-ounce cans labeled with a grinning cow in dark glasses.[62] The target market for such products was parents seeking a substitute for sugary or caffeinated drinks for their children.[63] At the time of Swerve's introduction, PepsiCo was already offering a chocolate dairy drink called Love Bus Brew, which is made with milk, vitamins, ginseng, and Dutch chocolate.[64] Swerve and Love Bus Brew were two entries in the small but growing beverage category of milk-based drinks. Because of the degree of their market commonality and resource similarity and the fact that they engage in multimarket competition, Coca-Cola and PepsiCo will continue to carefully monitor each other's competitive actions and responses in multiple product areas as part of their competitive rivalry.

A competitive action is a strategic or tactical action the firm takes to build or defend its competitive advantages or improve its market position.

A competitive response is a strategic or tactical action the firm takes to counter the effects of a competitor's competitive action.

A strategic action or a strategic response is a market-based move that involves a significant commitment of organizational resources and is difficult to implement and reverse.

A tactical action or a tactical response is a market-based move that is taken to fine-tune a strategy; it involves fewer resources and is relatively easy to implement and reverse.

Vice-president Robert Pollack presents the new 7E7 CDream Liner at an air show. Committing the resources to build this type of aircraft represents a strategic action on Boeing's part.

Water, Water Everywhere: Which to Drink?

There are simple facts about bottled water that explain why some of the world's largest companies are interested in expanding their share of the market for this product. First, bottled water in the United States alone is almost an $8 billion market on an annual basis. Moreover, demand for water is growing roughly 10 percent per year, which is faster than the growth rate for other drinks. American consumers drink an average of 21.2 gallons of bottled water per year, making it the second most popular drink (behind soft drinks at a huge 54 gallons per person, per year). Speaking to these issues, an analyst observed that competition among beverage companies in the bottled water segment is "becoming more intense as growth in the [soft drink] industry slows and consumers show a willingness to purchase less expensive private-label brands." Also making bottled water sales attractive is the 22 percent-plus margin they generate when sold in multi-packs in such outlets as discount club chains, grocery stores, and discount stores, such as Wal-Mart.

Because of market-based realities such as these, as well as the high degree of market commonality experienced by the three companies (Coca-Cola Company, Nestlé SA, and PepsiCo) dominating the U.S. bottled water market, these firms are clearly aware of one another's competitive actions and responses as they engage in intense rivalry to expand their shares of the bottled water market. Currently, the U.S. bottled water market is significantly influenced by these firms' competitive actions, largely because their combined share is close to 70 percent, with Nestlé having the largest share among the three firms. Also increasing the rivalry among these firms to sell their bottled waters is that while the brands vary by price, pedigree, and process—purified versus spring water, for example—many of them are essentially the same thing. Indeed, according to the editor of the *Beverage Digest,* all of these waters "hydrate equally well." In the United States, Nestlé offers nine domestic brands (e.g., Arrowhead and Deer Park) and five imports, including Perrier. PepsiCo makes Aquafina, which is the leading brand of water, while Coca-Cola produces Dasani, the second largest single brand, and distributes Group Danone's Evian and Dannon waters through a joint venture.

To gain market share, Coca-Cola lowered the prices of Dannon waters by 25 percent in grocery stores and mass retailers such as Wal-Mart late in the spring of 2003. Dannon waters are lower-tier bottled waters that tend to sell well in mass retail outlets. A tactical rather than a strategic action, the price reductions resulted in increased market share for Coca-Cola in these outlets. The double-digit growth of the lower-priced waters in mass retailers may have influenced Coca-Cola's decision to lower the prices on its offerings in this category in order to gain greater share in a fast-growth segment of the bottled water market. Certainly aware of Coca-Cola's tactical action, Nestlé and PepsiCo didn't respond immediately with price cuts, but vowed to defend their market positions as necessary. According to industry analysts, the initial price cut could stimulate a price war that would reduce the substantial profit margins the three competitors earn from these products in the mass retailer distribution channel. Indeed, there was concern in the industry that if one were to last for an extended period of time, a price war would result in material harm to the profitability of all three companies. As is common when companies engage in intense rivalry and are aware of each other while doing so, Nestlé and PepsiCo immediately started studying the effects of Coca-Cola's price reductions before choosing their competitive responses to Coca-Cola's competitive action.

SOURCES: 2003, Bottled water to be no. 2 U.S. drink, *Chicago Tribune*, April 6, C8; S. Day, 2003, Summer may bring a bottled water price war, *New York Times*, http://www.nytimes.com, May 10; R. Frank & B. McKay, 2002, Leading the news: Danone nears pact for purchase of Canada's Sparkling Spring, *Wall Street Journal*, Eastern edition, November 12, A3.

In addition to market commonality, resource similarity, and the drivers of awareness, motivation, and ability, other factors affect the likelihood a competitor will use strategic actions and tactical actions to attack its competitors. Three of these factors—first-mover incentives, organizational size, and quality—are discussed next.

First-Mover Incentives

A **first mover** is a firm that takes an initial competitive action in order to build or defend its competitive advantages or to improve its market position. The first-mover concept has been influenced by the work of the famous economist Joseph Schumpeter, who argued that firms achieve competitive advantage by taking innovative actions[65] (innovation is defined and described in detail in Chapter 13). In general, first movers "allocate funds for product innovation and development, aggressive advertising, and advanced research and development."[66]

A first mover is a firm that takes an initial competitive action in order to build or defend its competitive advantages or to improve its market position.

The benefits of being a successful first mover can be substantial. Especially in fast-cycle markets (discussed later in the chapter) where changes occur rapidly and where it is virtually impossible to sustain a competitive advantage for any length of time, "a first mover may experience five to ten times the valuation and revenue of a second mover."[67] This evidence suggests that although first-mover benefits are never absolute, they are often critical to firm success in industries experiencing rapid technological developments and relatively short product life cycles.[68] In addition to earning above-average returns until its competitors respond to its successful competitive action, the first mover can gain (1) the loyalty of customers who may become committed to the goods or services of the firm that first made them available and (2) market share that can be difficult for competitors to take during future competitive rivalry.[69] The general evidence that first movers have greater survival rates compared to later market entrants[70] is perhaps the culmination of first-mover benefits.

The firm trying to predict its competitors' competitive actions might rightly conclude that the benefits of being a first mover are incentives for many of them to act as first movers. However, while a firm's competitors might be motivated to be first movers, they may lack the ability to do so. First movers tend to be aggressive and willing to experiment with innovation and take higher, yet reasonable levels of risk.[71] To be a first mover, the firm must have readily available the amount of resources that is required to significantly invest in R&D as well as to rapidly and successfully produce and market a stream of innovative products.

Organizational slack makes it possible for firms to have the ability (as measured by available resources) to be first movers. *Slack* is the buffer or cushion provided by actual or obtainable resources that aren't currently in use[72] and as such, are in excess of the minimum resources needed to produce a given level of organizational output.[73] In 2003, Cisco Systems Inc. had substantial financial slack as suggested by the firm's more than $21 billion in cash and liquid investments.[74]

As a liquid resource, slack can quickly be allocated to support the competitive actions, such as R&D investments and aggressive marketing campaigns, that lead to first-mover benefits. This relationship between slack and the ability to be a first mover allows the firm to predict that a competitor who is a first mover likely has available slack and will probably take aggressive competitive actions to continuously introduce innovative products. Furthermore, the firm can predict that as a first mover, a competitor will try to rapidly gain market share and customer loyalty in order to earn above-average returns until its competitors are able to effectively respond to its first move.

Firms studying competitors should realize that being a first mover carries risk. For example, it is difficult to accurately estimate the returns that will be earned from introducing product innovations to the marketplace.[75] Additionally, the first mover's cost to develop a product innovation can be substantial, reducing the slack available to it to support further innovation. Thus, the firm should carefully study the results a competitor achieves as a first mover. Continuous success by the competitor suggests additional product innovations, while lack of product acceptance over the course of the competitor's innovations may indicate less willingness in the future to accept the risks of being a first mover.

A **second mover** is a firm that responds to the first mover's competitive action, typically through imitation. More cautious than the first mover, the second mover studies customers' reactions to product innovations. In the course of doing so, the second mover also tries to find any mistakes the first mover made so that it can avoid them and the problems they created. Often, successful imitation of the first mover's innovations allows the second mover "to avoid both the mistakes and the huge spending of the pioneers [first movers]."[76]

Second movers also have the time to develop processes and technologies that are more efficient than those used by the first mover.[77] Greater efficiencies could result in lower costs for the second mover. American Home Mortgage Holdings Inc. (AHMH) is a second mover with its Internet-based offering, MortgageSelect.com. In the words of the firm's CEO, being the second mover allowed it "to see where other firms had failed." Based on its observations of earlier Internet mortgage market entrants, AHMH doesn't brand its own services (instead providing mortgages for other companies) and has fine-tuned the offering of a "high-touch" call center to support its website.[78] Overall, the outcomes of the first mover's competitive actions may provide an effective blueprint for second and even late movers as they determine the nature and timing of their competitive responses.[79]

Determining that a competitor thinks of itself as an effective second mover allows the firm to predict that that competitor will tend to respond quickly to first movers' successful, innovation-based market entries. If the firm itself is a first mover, then it can expect a successful second mover competitor to study its market entries and to respond to them quickly. As a second mover, the competitor will try to respond with a product that creates customer value exceeding the value provided by the product initially introduced by the first mover. The most successful second movers are able to rapidly and meaningfully interpret market feedback to respond quickly, yet successfully, to the first mover's successful innovations.[80]

A **late mover** is a firm that responds to a competitive action, but only after considerable time has elapsed after the first mover's action and the second mover's response. Typically, a late response is better than no response at all, although any success achieved from the late competitive response tends to be slow in coming and considerably less than that achieved by first and second movers. Thus, the firm competing against a late mover can predict that that competitor will likely enter a particular market only after both the first and second movers have achieved success by doing so. Moreover, on a relative basis, the firm can predict that the late mover's competitive action will allow it to earn even average returns only when enough time has elapsed for it to understand how to create value that is more attractive to customers than is the value offered by the first and second movers' products. Although exceptions do exist, the firm can predict that as a competitor, the late mover's competitive actions will be relatively ineffective, certainly as compared to those initiated by first movers and second movers.

Organizational Size

An organization's size affects the likelihood that it will take competitive actions as well as the types of actions it will take and their timing.[81] In general, compared to large companies, small firms are more likely to launch competitive actions and tend to be quicker in doing so. Smaller firms are thus perceived as nimble and flexible competitors who rely on speed and surprise to defend their competitive advantages or develop new ones while engaged in competitive rivalry, especially with large companies, to gain an advantageous market position.[82] Small firms' flexibility and nimbleness allow them to develop greater variety in their competitive actions as compared to large firms, which tend to limit the types of competitive actions used when competing with rivals.[83]

Compared to small firms, large ones are likely to initiate more competitive actions as well as strategic actions during a given period.[84] Thus, when studying its competitors in terms of organizational size, the firm should use a measurement such as total sales revenue or total number of employees to compare itself with each competitor. The competitive actions the firm likely will encounter from competitors larger than it is will be different than the competitive actions it will encounter from competitors that are smaller.

The organizational size factor has an additional layer of complexity associated with it. When engaging in competitive rivalry, the firm usually wants to take a large number of competitive actions against its competitors. As we have described, large organizations commonly have the slack resources required to launch a larger number of total competitive actions. On the other hand, smaller firms have the flexibility needed to launch a greater variety of competitive actions. Ideally, the firm would like to have the ability to launch a large number of unique competitive actions. Herb Kelleher, cofounder and former CEO of Southwest Airlines, addressed this matter, "Think and act big and we'll get smaller. Think and act small and we'll get bigger."[85]

In the context of competitive rivalry, Kelleher's statement can be interpreted to mean that relying on a limited number or types of competitive actions (which is the large firm's tendency) can lead to reduced competitive success across time, partly because competitors learn how to effectively respond to what is a limited set of competitive actions taken by a given firm. In contrast, remaining flexible and nimble (which is the small firm's tendency) in order to develop and use a wide variety of competitive actions contributes to success against rivals.

Wal-Mart appears to be an example of a large firm that has the flexibility required to take many types of competitive actions. With $254 billion in sales expected in 2004 and market capitalization over $252 billion,[86] Wal-Mart is one of the world's two largest companies in terms of sales revenue (the other is ExxonMobil). In less than a decade, Wal-Mart has become one of the largest grocery retailers in the United States. This accomplishment demonstrates Wal-Mart's ability to successfully compete against its various rivals, even long-established grocers.

In spite of its size, the firm remains highly flexible as it takes both strategic actions (such as rapid global expansion) and tactical actions. A recent strategic action is the opening of more Neighborhood Markets. The company is careful to note that its freestanding grocery units won't compete against its other concepts. In the words of a company spokesperson, "Neighborhood Markets are close to residential areas in more convenient locations. They're big enough to fulfill all of shoppers' grocery needs, but small enough that you can stop in for last-minute items as well."[87] Wal-Mart is opening these stores to take more market share from its competitors in the grocery market.

Analysts believe that Wal-Mart's tactical actions are as critical to its success as are its strategic actions and that its tactical actions demonstrate a great deal of flexibility. For example, "every humble store worker has the power to lower the price on any Wal-Mart product if he spots it cheaper elsewhere."[88] Decision-making responsibility and authority have been delegated to the level of the individual worker to make certain that the firm's cost leadership business-level strategy always results in the lowest prices for customers. Managers and employees both spend a good deal of time thinking about additional strategic and tactical actions, respectively, that might enhance the firm's performance. Thus, it is possible that Wal-Mart has met the expectation suggested by

Kelleher's statement, in that it is a large firm that "remains stuck to its small-town roots" in order to think and act like the small firm capable of using a wide variety of competitive actions.[89] Wal-Mart's competitors might feel confident in predicting that the firm's competitive actions will be a combination of the tendencies shown by small and large companies.

Quality

Quality *exists when the firm's goods or services meet or exceed customers' expectations.*

Quality has many definitions, including well-established ones relating it to the production of goods or services with zero defects[90] and seeing it as a never-ending cycle of continuous improvement.[91] From a strategic perspective, we consider quality to be an outcome of how the firm completes primary and support activities (see Chapter 3). Thus, **quality** exists when the firm's goods or services meet or exceed customers' expectations. Some evidence suggests that quality may be the most critical component in satisfying the firm's customers.[92]

Customers may be interested in measuring the quality of a firm's products against a broad range of dimensions. Sample quality dimensions for goods and services in which customers commonly express an interest are shown in Table 5.1. Thus, in the eyes of customers, quality is about doing the right things relative to performance measures that are important to them.[93] Quality is possible only when top-level managers support it and when its importance is institutionalized throughout the entire organization.[94] When quality is institutionalized and valued by all, employees and managers alike become vigilant about continuously finding ways to improve quality.[95]

Quality is a universal theme in the global economy and is a necessary but not sufficient condition for competitive success. In other words, "Quality used to be a compet-

Table 5.1

Quality Dimensions of Goods and Services

Product Quality Dimensions
1. *Performance*—Operating characteristics
2. *Features*—Important special characteristics
3. *Flexibility*—Meeting operating specifications over some period of time
4. *Durability*—Amount of use before performance deteriorates
5. *Conformance*—Match with preestablished standards
6. *Serviceability*—Ease and speed of repair
7. *Aesthetics*—How a product looks and feels
8. *Perceived quality*—Subjective assessment of characteristics (product image)

Service Quality Dimensions
1. *Timeliness*—Performed in the promised period of time
2. *Courtesy*—Performed cheerfully
3. *Consistency*—Giving all customers similar experiences each time
4. *Convenience*—Accessibility to customers
5. *Completeness*—Fully serviced, as required
6. *Accuracy*—Performed correctly each time

SOURCES: Adapted from J. W. Dean, Jr., & J. R. Evans, 1994, *Total Quality: Management, Organization and Society,* St. Paul, MN: West Publishing Company; H. V. Roberts & B. F. Sergesketter, 1993, *Quality Is Personal,* New York: The Free Press; D. Garvin, 1988, *Managed Quality: The Strategic and Competitive Edge,* New York: The Free Press.

itive issue out there, but now it's just the basic denominator to being in the market."[96] Without quality, a firm's products lack credibility, meaning that customers don't think of them as viable options. Indeed, customers won't consider buying a product until they believe that it can satisfy at least their base-level expectations in terms of quality dimensions that are important to them. For years, quality was an issue for Jaguar automobiles as the carmaker endured frequent complaints from drivers about poor quality. As a result of recent actions addressing this issue, quality has improved to the point where customers now view the cars as credible products.[97]

Hyundai cars await shipment from Korea. An emphasis on quality at Hyundai Motors has turned the company around from a low point in 1999. Hyundai is now competing successfully with Honda and Toyota.

Quality affects competitive rivalry. The firm studying a competitor whose products suffer from poor quality can predict that the competitor's costs are high and that its sales revenue will likely decline until the quality issues are resolved. In addition, the firm can predict that the competitor likely won't be aggressive in terms of taking competitive actions, given that its quality problems must be corrected in order to gain credibility with customers. However, after the problems are corrected, that competitor is likely to take competitive actions emphasizing additional dimensions of competition. Hyundai Motor Co.'s experiences illustrate these expectations.

Immediately upon becoming CEO of Hyundai Motor Co. in March 1999, Mong Koo Chung started touring the firm's manufacturing facilities. Appalled at what he saw, he told workers and managers alike, "The only way we can survive is to raise our quality to Toyota's level."[98] To dramatically improve quality, a quality-control unit was established, and significant resources (over $1 billion annually) were allocated to research and development (R&D) in order to build cars that could compete on price and deliver on quality. Today, quality is still viewed as the firm's number one priority.[99]

Outcomes from Hyundai's focus on quality improvements are impressive. The 2002 *Consumer Reports* survey observed that Hyundai's ratings were among the worst of the products the magazine tested a decade ago. However, the firm's 2002 model-year vehicles were tied with those of Honda for second place in reliability.[100] In 2003, the director of automotive quality research at J.D. Power observed, "Since 1998, Hyundai is the most improved car in the initial quality survey. They have dropped their number of quality problems by 50 percent."[101] Signaling a strong belief in its products' quality, Hyundai offers a ten-year drive-train warranty in the United States, which the firm has selected as a key market.

While concentrating on quality improvements, Hyundai didn't launch aggressive competitive actions, as competitors could predict would likely be the case. However, as could also be predicted by firms studying Hyundai as a competitor, improvements to the quality of Hyundai's products helped the firm to become a more aggressive competitor.

The introduction of the Santa Fe in 2000 is one indication of Hyundai's more aggressive orientation to competition. A well-conceived sport-utility vehicle (SUV), the Santa Fe was designed and built to outperform Toyota's RAV4 and Honda's CR-V. Considered a successful market entry, partly because of its quality, the second-generation Santa Fe is to be built in Hyundai's plant in Alabama beginning in March 2005. With its quality issues perhaps behind it, Hyundai is challenging competitors on other competitive dimensions, including design and styling.[102]

The success of a firm's competitive action is affected by the likelihood that a competitor will respond to it as well as by the type (strategic or tactical) and effectiveness of that response. As noted earlier, a competitive response is a strategic or tactical action the firm takes to counter the effects of a competitor's competitive action. In general, a firm is likely to respond to a competitor's action when (1) the consequences of that action are better use of the competitor's competitive advantages or improvement in its market position, (2) the action damages the firm's ability to use its advantages, or (3) the firm's market position becomes less defensible.[103]

In addition to market commonality and resource similarity and awareness, motivation, and ability, firms study three other factors—type of competitive action, reputation, and market dependence—to predict how a competitor is likely to respond to competitive actions (see Figure 5.2).

Type of Competitive Action

Competitive responses to strategic actions differ from responses to tactical actions. These differences allow the firm to predict a competitor's likely response to a competitive action that has been launched against it. Of course, a general prediction is that strategic actions receive strategic responses while tactical responses are taken to counter the effects of tactical actions.

In general, strategic actions elicit fewer total competitive responses because strategic responses, such as market-based moves, involve a significant commitment of resources and are difficult to implement and reverse.[104] Moreover, the time needed for a strategic action to be implemented and its effectiveness assessed delays the competitor's response to that action.[105] In contrast, a competitor likely will respond quickly to a tactical action, such as when an airline company almost immediately matches a competitor's tactical action of reducing prices in certain markets. And, either strategic actions or tactical actions that target a large number of a rival's customers are likely to be targeted with strong responses.[106]

Actor's Reputation

In the context of competitive rivalry, an *actor* is the firm taking an action or a response while *reputation* is "the positive or negative attribute ascribed by one rival to another based on past competitive behavior."[107] A positive reputation may be a source of above-average returns, especially for consumer goods producers.[108] Thus, a positive corporate reputation is of strategic value[109] and affects competitive rivalry. To predict the likelihood of a competitor's response to a current or planned action, the firm studies the responses that the competitor has taken previously when attacked—past behavior is assumed to be a reasonable predictor of future behavior.

Competitors are more likely to respond to either strategic or tactical actions that are taken by a market leader.[110] For example, Home Depot is the world's largest home improvement

Home Depot is the innovator in home improvement retailing. Its EXPO Design Center, a new store format, has led to Lowe's transformation into "home improvement warehouses."

©Michael Newman/PhotoEdit

retailer and the second largest U.S. retailer (behind Wal-Mart). Known for being an innovator in its core home improvement market as well as for having an ability to develop successful new store formats (such as its EXPO Design Centers and Villager's Hardware Stores), Home Depot can predict that its competitors carefully study its actions, especially the strategic ones, and that they are likely to respond to them. Lowe's Companies, the second largest U.S. home improvement retailer and Home Depot's major competitor, is aware of Home Depot's actions. Lowe's also has both the motivation and ability to respond to actions by Home Depot. For example, partly in response to Home Depot's consistent focus on updating the retail concept of its core home improvement stores, Lowe's continues to transform "its store base from a chain of small stores into a chain of destination home improvement warehouses,"[111] increasing the similarity of its store design to Home Depot's.

Other evidence suggests that commonly successful actions, especially strategic actions, will be quickly imitated, almost regardless of the actor's reputation. For example, although a second mover, IBM committed significant resources to enter the PC market. When IBM was immediately successful in this endeavor, competitors such as Dell, Compaq, and Gateway responded with strategic actions to enter the market. IBM's reputation as well as its successful strategic action strongly influenced entry by these competitors. Thus, in terms of competitive rivalry, IBM could predict that responses would follow its entry to the PC market if that entry proved successful. In addition, IBM could predict that those competitors would try to create value in slightly different ways, such as Dell's legendary decision to sell directly to consumers rather than to use storefronts as a distribution channel.

In contrast to a firm with a strong reputation, such as IBM, competitors are less likely to take responses against companies with reputations for competitive behavior that is risky, complex, and unpredictable. The firm with a reputation as a price predator (an actor that frequently reduces prices to gain or maintain market share) generates few responses to its pricing tactical actions because price predators, which typically increase prices once their market share objective is reached, lack credibility with their competitors.[112] The opposite of a price predator in terms of reputation, Wal-Mart is widely recognized for its pricing integrity, giving the firm a great deal of credibility when it launches a tactical action or response around the prices of its goods.

Dependence on the Market

Market dependence denotes the extent to which a firm's revenues or profits are derived from a particular market.[113] In general, firms can predict that competitors with high market dependence are likely to respond strongly to attacks threatening their market position.[114] Interestingly, the threatened firm in these instances tends not to respond quickly, suggesting the importance of an effective response to an attack on the firm's position in a critical market.

A firm such as Wm. Wrigley Company would be expected to respond aggressively, but not necessarily quickly, to an attack. With such well-known brands as Spearmint, Doublemint, Juicy Fruit, Big Red, Extra, and Hubba Bubba bubble gum, Wrigley is the world's largest producer of chewing gum, accounting for roughly 50 percent of total chewing gum sales volume worldwide and over 90 percent of the U.K. market.[115] Through its Amurol Confections subsidiary (which produces several products such as liquid gel candy, suckers, and hard roll candies) and Healthcare Division (which develops and markets products using chewing gum to deliver active ingredients that provide health benefits), Wrigley has a minor amount of diversification. However, chewing gum accounts for more than 90 percent of the firm's total revenue as well as earnings.[116] Wrigley's dominant market position provides the flexibility needed to respond aggressively but carefully to actions that a competitor such as Adams might take. But, if Adams were to attack Wrigley's sugarless Extra gum through actions related to Adams' Trident, for example, it should understand that Wrigley's dependence on the chewing gum market will induce it to respond aggressively to protect its position in the sugarless gum market.

Competitive Dynamics

Whereas competitive rivalry concerns the ongoing actions and responses between a firm and its competitors for an advantageous market position, competitive dynamics concerns the ongoing actions and responses taking place among *all* firms competing within a market for advantageous positions.

To explain competitive rivalry, we described (1) factors that determine the degree to which firms are competitors (market commonality and resource similarity), (2) the drivers of competitive behavior for individual firms (awareness, motivation, and ability) and (3) factors affecting the likelihood a competitor will act or attack (first-mover incentives, organizational size, and quality) and respond (type of competitive action, reputation, and market dependence). Building and sustaining competitive advantages are at the core of competitive rivalry, in that advantages are the link to an advantageous market position.[117]

To explain competitive dynamics, we discuss the effects of varying rates of competitive speed in different markets (called slow-cycle, fast-cycle, and standard-cycle markets, defined below) on the behavior (actions and responses) of all competitors within a given market. Competitive behaviors as well as the reasons or logic for taking them are similar within each market type, but differ across market type.[118] Thus, competitive dynamics differ in slow-cycle, fast-cycle, and standard-cycle markets. The sustainability of the firm's competitive advantages is an important difference among the three market types.

As noted in Chapter 1, firms want to sustain their competitive advantages for as long as possible, although no advantage is permanently sustainable. The degree of sustainability is affected by how quickly competitive advantages can be imitated and how costly it is to do so.

Slow-Cycle Markets

Slow-cycle markets are markets in which the firm's competitive advantages are shielded from imitation for what are commonly long periods of time and where imitation is costly.[119] Competitive advantages are sustainable in slow-cycle markets.

Building a one-of-a-kind competitive advantage that is proprietary leads to competitive success in a slow-cycle market. This type of advantage is difficult for competitors to understand. As discussed in Chapter 3, a difficult-to-understand and costly-to-imitate advantage results from unique historical conditions, causal ambiguity, and/or social complexity. Copyrights, geography, patents, and ownership of an information resource are examples of what leads to one-of-a-kind advantages.[120] Once a proprietary advantage is developed, the firm's competitive behavior in a slow-cycle market is oriented to protecting, maintaining, and extending that advantage. Thus, the competitive dynamics in slow-cycle markets involve all firms concentrating on competitive actions and responses that enable them to protect, maintain, and extend their proprietary competitive advantage.

Walt Disney Co. continues to extend its proprietary characters, such as Mickey Mouse, Minnie Mouse, and Goofy. These characters have a unique historical development as a result of Walt and Roy Disney's creativity and vision for entertaining people. Products based on the characters seen in Disney's animated films are sold through Disney's theme park shops as well as freestanding retail outlets called Disney Stores. The list of character-based products is extensive, including everything from the characters to clothing with the characters' images. Because patents shield it, the proprietary nature of Disney's advantage in terms of animated characters protects the firm from imitation by competitors.

Consistent with another attribute of competition in a slow-cycle market, Disney remains committed to protecting its exclusive rights to its characters and their use as shown by the fact that "the company once sued a day-care center, forcing it to remove the likeness of Mickey Mouse from a wall of the facility."[121] As with all firms competing in slow-cycle markets, Disney's competitive actions (such as building theme parks in France and Japan and other potential locations such as China) and responses (such as lawsuits to protect its right to fully control use of its animated characters) maintain and extend its proprietary competitive advantage while protecting it. Disney has been able to establish through actions and defend through responses an advantageous market position as a result of its competitive behavior.

Patent laws and regulatory requirements such as those in the United States requiring FDA (Food and Drug Administration) approval to launch new products shield pharmaceutical companies' positions. Competitors in this market try to extend patents on their drugs to maintain advantageous positions that they (patents) provide. However, once a patent expires, the firm is no longer shielded from competition, a situation that has financial implications.

As is true with Walt Disney Co., pharmaceutical companies aggressively pursue legal courses of action to protect their patents. This is demonstrated by recent actions taken by Pfizer Inc., the maker and seller of Lipitor, the world's most prescribed cholesterol-lowering drug. In 2003, Ranbaxy applied to the U.S. Food and Drug Administration to begin immediately marketing its generic version of Lipitor. Pfizer filed a suit asking a judge to prohibit Ranbaxy from making and marketing Lipitor before its 1987 U.S. patent expires in 2010. The stakes were high, in that Pfizer generated over $8 billion in revenue from sales of Lipitor in 2002.[122] As with its competitors, Pfizer is also vigilant in working with the FDA's Criminal Investigations office to control counterfeiting. Fake versions of Lipitor are common as are counterfeit Viagra pills (Viagra is Pfizer's treatment for impotence in men). In addition to damage to its sales, Pfizer is concerned about possible serious health risks for customers who consume counterfeit versions of its products.[123]

The competitive dynamics generated by firms competing in slow-cycle markets are shown in Figure 5.4. In slow-cycle markets, firms launch a product (e.g., a new drug) that has been developed through a proprietary advantage (e.g., R&D) and then exploit it for as long as possible while the product is shielded from competition. Eventually, competitors respond to the action with a counterattack. In markets for drugs, this counterattack commonly occurs as patents expire or are broken through legal means, creating the need for another product launch by the firm seeking a shielded market position.

Fast-Cycle Markets

Fast-cycle markets are markets in which the firm's competitive advantages aren't shielded from imitation and where imitation happens quickly and perhaps somewhat inexpensively. Competitive advantages aren't sustainable in fast-cycle markets. Thus, firms competing in fast-cycle markets recognize the importance of speed, meaning that these companies appreciate that "time is as precious a business resource as money or head count—and that the costs of hesitation and delay are just as steep as going over budget or missing a financial forecast."[124]

Reverse engineering and the rate of technology diffusion in fast-cycle markets facilitate rapid imitation. A competitor uses reverse engineering to quickly gain the knowledge required to imitate or improve the firm's products, usually in only a few months. Technology is diffused rapidly in fast-cycle markets, making it available to competitors in a short period. The technology often used by fast-cycle competitors

Fast-cycle markets *are markets in which the firm's competitive advantages aren't shielded from imitation and where imitation happens quickly and perhaps somewhat inexpensively.*

Figure 5.4 —— Gradual Erosion of a Sustained Competitive Advantage

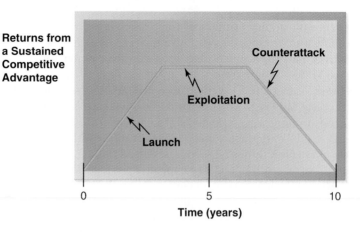

SOURCE: Adapted from I. C. MacMillan, 1988, Controlling competitive dynamics by taking strategic initiative, *Academy of Management Executive*, II(2): 111–118.

isn't proprietary, nor is it protected by patents as is the technology used by firms competing in slow-cycle markets. For example, only a few hundred parts, which are readily available on the open market, are required to build a PC. Patents protect only a few of these parts, such as microprocessor chips.[125]

Fast-cycle markets are more volatile than slow-cycle and standard-cycle markets. Indeed, the pace of competition in fast-cycle markets is almost frenzied, as companies rely on ideas and the innovations resulting from them as the engines of their growth. Because prices fall quickly in these markets, companies need to profit quickly from their product innovations. For example, rapid declines in the prices of microprocessor chips produced by Intel and Advanced Micro Devices, among others, make it possible for personal computer manufacturers to continuously reduce their prices to end users. Imitation of many fast-cycle products is relatively easy, as demonstrated by such firms as Dell Inc. and Hewlett-Packard, along with a host of local PC vendors. All of these firms have partly or largely imitated IBM's PC design to create their products. Continuous declines in the costs of parts, as well as the fact that the information required to assemble a PC isn't especially complicated and is readily available, make it possible for additional competitors to enter this market without significant difficulty.[126]

The fast-cycle market characteristics described above make it virtually impossible for companies in this type of market to develop sustainable competitive advantages. Recognizing this, firms avoid "loyalty" to any of their products, preferring to cannibalize their own before competitors learn how to do so through successful imitation. This emphasis creates competitive dynamics that differ substantially from those found in slow-cycle markets. Instead of concentrating on protecting, maintaining, and extending competitive advantages, as is the case for firms in slow-cycle markets, companies competing in fast-cycle markets focus on learning how to rapidly and continuously develop new competitive advantages that are superior to those they replace. In fast-cycle markets, firms don't concentrate on trying to protect a given competitive advantage because they understand that the advantage won't exist long enough to extend it.

The competitive behavior of firms competing in fast-cycle markets is shown in Figure 5.5. As suggested by the figure, competitive dynamics in this market type find firms taking actions and responses in the course of competitive rivalry that are oriented to rapid and continuous product introductions and the use of a stream of ever-changing competitive advantages. The firm launches a product as a competitive action and then exploits the advantage associated with it for as long as possible. However, the firm also tries to move to another temporary competitive advantage before competitors can respond to the first one (see Figure 5.5). Thus, competitive dynamics in fast-cycle markets, in which all firms seek to achieve new competitive advantages before competitors learn how to effectively respond to current ones, often result in rapid product upgrades as well as quick product innovations.[127]

As our discussion suggests, innovation has a dominant effect on competitive dynamics in fast-cycle markets. For individual firms, this means that innovation is a key source of competitive advantage. Through innovation, the firm can cannibalize its own products before competitors successfully imitate them.

In the Strategic Focus, we describe the experiences of Teradyne Inc., a company competing in a fast-cycle market. Teradyne allocates over 13 percent of sales revenue to R&D, suggesting the importance of innovation to this firm.

As noted earlier, it is difficult for firms competing in fast-cycle markets to maintain a competitive advantage in terms of their products. Partly because of this, Teradyne has chosen to emphasize its ability to design and manufacture assembly equipment and the skills it uses to serve customers as possible sources of competitive advantage. It may be difficult for competitors to fully understand and imitate these core competencies, meaning that they may be sustainable competitive advantages for a firm competing in fast-cycle markets.

Standard-Cycle Markets

Standard-cycle markets are markets in which the firm's competitive advantages are moderately shielded from imitation and where imitation is moderately costly. Competitive advantages are partially sustainable in standard-cycle markets, but only when the firm is able to continuously upgrade the quality of its competitive advantages. The competitive actions and responses that form a standard-cycle market's competitive dynamics find firms seeking large market shares, trying to gain customer loyalty through brand names, and carefully controlling their operations to consistently provide the same usage experience for customers without surprises.[128]

Standard-cycle markets are markets in which the firm's competitive advantages are moderately shielded from imitation and where imitation is moderately costly.

Developing Temporary Advantages to Create Sustained Advantage Figure 5.5

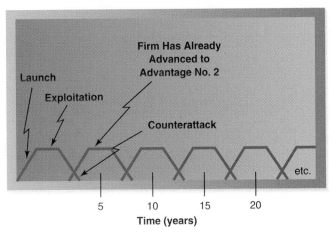

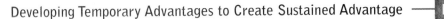

SOURCE: Adapted from I. C. MacMillan, 1988, Controlling competitive dynamics by taking strategic initiative, *Academy of Management Executive*, II(2): 111–118.

Teradyne Inc.: Life in the Fast Lane

The CEO's opening words in his letter to shareholders from Teradyne Inc.'s 2002 Annual Report capture the rollercoaster experience firms competing in fast-cycle markets may encounter: "Two years ago in this space, I was telling you about the best year in Teradyne's history. Now I am here to report our worst."

Teradyne designs and manufactures automatic test equipment and interconnection systems that are sold primarily to semiconductor, electronics, network systems, and automotive companies. Teradyne's products are used to test the performance and functionality of semiconductors, circuit boards and modules, automotive electronics, and voice and broadband networks. Teradyne products are intended to help customers more quickly introduce innovative goods to the marketplace with greater reliability and at a lower cost.

Teradyne's business is directly tied to the semiconductor industry. Beginning in 2000 and running through mid-2003, chip demand declined from the highs of the 1990s. Lower consumer demand for personal computers, cellular telephones, and other technology-related products made with semiconductors accounted for the decline in the demand for chips. Derivatively, lower demand for chips results in lower demand for equipment to test their performance and functionality, a reality that affects Teradyne's sales. In fast-cycle markets, firms must react quickly to market demand. Because of market growth in the mid- to late 1990s, Teradyne expanded to ship what it expected would be $3 billion worth of product sales in 2000. However, sales revenue of less than half of the expectation in 2002 caused Teradyne to restructure. In the company's words: "A lot of good employees had to be released and a lot of plants had to be closed. We dropped marginal product lines, and we borrowed and mortgaged to prepare for the worst. We squeezed costs wherever we could, while protecting the engineering programs vital to our future and making sure that our customers were well supported."

Teradyne is organized into four strategic business units—interconnection systems, circuit board test and inspection, automotive test and diagnosis, and broadband test. As is true for its competitors—firms such as Applied Materials Inc., KLA-Tencor Corp., and Lam Research Corp.—Teradyne's products typically have relatively short shelf lives. While engaged in competitive rivalry, these companies strive diligently to develop and introduce products that are superior to their own before competitors do so.

Proprietary assembly equipment (equipment that is designed and made in-house) and customer service are core competencies Teradyne believes are competitive advantages for the firm. One of the "latest of these innovative machines," according to the company, "is BRIM (for Backplane Rotary Insertion Machine), which automatically inserts tiny gold-plated pins into backplane modules." Allocating 13 percent or more of sales revenue to R&D, some of which supports analysis of how to develop ever more sophisticated, value-creating assembly equipment, demonstrates Teradyne's effort to sustain proprietary assembly equipment as a competitive advantage. Moreover, even when experiencing negative growth, Teradyne remains committed to providing the high level of support it believes customers expect from it. Continuous training and reliance on a total quality management system facilitate the firm's efforts to provide superior service to customers. When describing why it chose a Teradyne product to test its experimental Smart Card, users at Samsung Electronics noted that excellent local support was a key factor in their decision.

SOURCES: 2003, Teradyne and Boeing offer new avionics testing system, *Aviation Daily*, 352(68): 6; 2003, Teradyne posts narrower loss, *Wall Street Journal Online*, http://www.wsj.com, April 15; 2003, NetVendor acquires Teradyne's manufacturing group, *Wall Street Journal Online*, http://www.wsj.com, February 26; 2003, Teradyne Inc. Home Page, http://www.teradyne.com, May 28; 2002, Teradyne Inc. Annual Report, Because technology never stops, 1–9; T. Witkowsi, 2002, Weathering the storm: Teradyne Inc., *Boston Business Journal*, December 27, 22(47): 11.

Standard-cycle companies serve many customers in competitive markets. Because the capabilities and core competencies on which their competitive advantages are based are less specialized, imitation is faster and less costly for standard-cycle firms than for those competing in slow-cycle markets. However, imitation is slower and more expensive in these markets than in fast-cycle markets. Thus, competitive dynamics in standard-cycle markets rest midway between the characteristics of dynamics in slow-cycle and fast-cycle markets. The quickness of imitation is reduced and becomes more expensive for standard-cycle competitors when a firm is able to develop economies of scale by combining coordinated and integrated design and manufacturing processes with a large sales volume for its products.

A Crest spokesperson (right) explains to a customer how to apply the new Crest Whitestrips to her teeth during a nationwide unveiling in Santa Monica, California. This has been a very successful product for P&G in a standard-cycle market.

Because of large volumes, the size of mass markets, and the need to develop scale economies, the competition for market share is intense in standard-cycle markets. Procter & Gamble (P&G) and Unilever compete in standard-cycle markets. A competitor analysis reveals that P&G and Unilever are direct competitors in that they share multiple markets as they engage each other in competition in over 140 countries, and they have similar types and amounts of resources and follow similar strategies. One of the product lines in which these two firms aggressively compete for market share is laundry detergents. The market for these products is large, with an annual sales volume of over $6 billion in the United States alone. The sheer size of this market highlights the importance of market share, as a mere percentage point gain in share translates into at least a $60 million increase in revenues. As analysts have noted, in a standard-cycle market, "It's a death struggle to incrementally gain share." For P&G and Unilever, this means that the firms must "slog it out for every fraction of every share in every category in every market where they compete."[129]

Innovation can also drive competitive actions and responses in standard-cycle markets, especially when rivalry is intense. Some innovations in standard-cycle markets are incremental rather than radical in nature (incremental and radical innovations are discussed in Chapter 13). Recently, Procter & Gamble introduced high-margin incremental variations of some of its mainstay brands, such as Tide, Pampers, and Crest. Almost overnight, the introductions of Crest Whitestrips and the Crest SpinBrush, both of which are product extensions of the Crest brand, made Crest P&G's 12th brand to exceed $1 billion in annual sales revenue.[130] Because Unilever and P&G battle for every share of each market in which they compete, P&G can expect a competitive reaction from Unilever in the form of possible changes to its toothpaste products, such as Close-Up.

In the final analysis, innovation has a substantial influence on competitive dynamics as it affects the actions and responses of all companies competing within a slow-cycle, fast-cycle, or standard-cycle market. We have emphasized the importance of innovation to the firm's strategic competitiveness in earlier chapters and will do so again in Chapter 13. Our discussion of innovation in terms of competitive dynamics extends the earlier discussions by showing its importance in all types of markets in which firms compete.

- Competitors are firms competing in the same market, offering similar products, and targeting similar customers. Competitive rivalry is the ongoing set of competitive actions and competitive responses occurring between competitors as they compete against each other for an advantageous market position. The outcomes of competitive rivalry influence the firm's ability to sustain its competitive advantages as well as the level (average, below-average, or above-average) of its financial returns.

- For the individual firm, the set of competitive actions and responses it takes while engaged in competitive rivalry is called competitive behavior. Competitive dynamics is the set of actions and responses taken by all firms that are competitors within a particular market.

- Firms study competitive rivalry in order to be able to predict the competitive actions and responses that each of their competitors likely will take. Competitive actions are either strategic or tactical in nature. The firm takes competitive actions to defend or build its competitive advantages or to improve its market position. Competitive responses are taken to counter the effects of a competitor's competitive action. A strategic action or a strategic response requires a significant commitment of organizational resources, is difficult to successfully implement, and is difficult to reverse. In contrast, a tactical action or a tactical response requires fewer organizational resources and is easier to implement and reverse. For an airline company, for example, entering major new markets is an example of a strategic action or a strategic response while changing its prices in a particular market is an example of a tactical action or a tactical response.

- A competitor analysis is the first step the firm takes to be able to predict its competitors' actions and responses. In Chapter 2, we discussed what firms do to *understand* competitors. This discussion is extended in this chapter as we described what the firm does to *predict* competitors' market-based actions. Thus, understanding precedes prediction. Market commonality (the number of markets with which competitors are jointly involved and their importance to each) and resource similarity (how comparable competitors' resources are in terms of type and amount) are studied to complete a competitor analysis. In general, the greater are market commonality and resource similarity, the more firms acknowledge that they are direct competitors.

- Market commonality and resource similarity shape the firm's awareness (the degree to which it and its competitor understand their mutual interdependence), motivation (the firm's incentive to attack or respond), and ability (the quality of the resources available to the firm to attack and respond). Having knowledge of a competitor in terms of these characteristics increases the quality of the firm's predictions about that competitor's actions and responses.

- In addition to market commonality and resource similarity and awareness, motivation and ability, three more specific factors affect the likelihood a competitor will take competitive actions. The first of these concerns first-mover incentives. First movers, those taking an initial competitive action, often earn above-average returns until competitors can successfully respond to their action and gain loyal customers. Not all firms can be first movers in that they may lack the awareness, motivation, or ability required to engage in this type of competitive behavior. Moreover, some firms prefer to be a second mover (the firm responding to the first mover's action). One reason for this is that second movers, especially those acting quickly, can successfully compete against the first mover. By studying the first mover's product, customers' reactions to it, and the responses of other competitors to the first mover, the second mover can avoid the early entrant's mistakes and find ways to improve upon the value created for customers by the first mover's good or service. Late movers (those that respond a long time after the original action was taken) commonly are lower performers and are much less competitive.

  Organizational size, the second factor, tends to reduce the number of different types of competitive actions that large firms launch while it increases the variety of actions undertaken by smaller competitors. Ideally, the firm would like to initiate a large number of diverse actions when engaged in competitive rivalry.

  The third factor, quality, dampens firms' abilities to take competitive actions, in that product quality is a base denominator to successful competition in the global economy.

- The type of action (strategic or tactical) the firm took, the competitor's reputation for the nature of its competitor behavior, and that competitor's dependence on the market in which the action was taken are studied to predict a competitor's response to the firm's action. In general, the number of tactical responses taken exceeds the number of strategic responses. Competitors respond more frequently to the actions taken by the firm with a reputation for predictable and understandable competitive behavior, especially if that firm is a market leader. In general, the firm can predict that when its competitor is highly dependent for its revenue and profitability in the market in which the firm took a competitive action, that competitor is likely to launch a strong response. However, firms that are more diversified across markets are less likely to respond to a particular action that affects only one of the markets in which they compete.

- Competitive dynamics concerns the ongoing competitive behavior occurring among all firms competing in a market for advantageous positions. Market characteristics affect the set of actions and responses firms take while competing in a given market as well as the sustainability of firms' competitive advantages. In slow-cycle markets, where competitive advantages can be maintained, competitive dynamics finds firms taking actions and responses that are intended to protect, maintain, and extend their proprietary advantages. In fast-cycle markets, competition is almost frenzied as firms concentrate on developing a series of temporary competitive advantages. This emphasis is necessary because firms' advantages in fast-cycle markets aren't proprietary and, as such, are subject to rapid and relatively inexpensive imitation. Standard-cycle markets are between slow-cycle and fast-cycle markets, in that firms are moderately shielded from competition in these markets as they use competitive advantages that are moderately sustainable. Competitors in standard-cycle markets serve mass markets and try to develop economies of scale to enhance their profitability. Innovation is vital to competitive success in each of the three types of markets. Companies should recognize that the set of competitive actions and responses taken by all firms differs by type of market.

Review Questions

1. Who are competitors? How are competitive rivalry, competitive behavior, and competitive dynamics defined in the chapter?

2. What is market commonality? What is resource similarity? What does it mean to say that these concepts are the building blocks for a competitor analysis?

3. How do awareness, motivation, and ability affect the firm's competitive behavior?

4. What factors affect the likelihood a firm will take a competitive action?

5. What factors affect the likelihood a firm will initiate a competitive response to the action taken by a competitor?

6. How are competitive dynamics in slow-cycle markets described in the chapter? In fast-cycle markets? In standard-cycle markets?

Experiential Exercises

Competitive Rivalry

Part One. Define first mover and second mover, and provide examples of firms for each category.

First mover:

Second mover:

Part Two. In the following table, list the advantages and disadvantages of being the first mover and of being the second mover for the firms you identified.

First Mover		Second Mover	
Advantages	**Disadvantages**	**Advantages**	**Disadvantages**

Part Three. Based on the above information, what are the most important issues that you feel first and second movers must consider before initiating a competitive move?

Intra-Industry Competitive Rivalry

Choose an industry for which you would like to more fully understand the competitive environment, or base your work on an industry assigned by your professor. Both the popular business press and the Internet are potential information sources for this exercise, as is the InfoTrac College Edition online database that can be accessed using information on your subscription card. (See http://www.infotrac-college.com.) Additionally, efforts should be made to find industry-level information through trade councils and trade publications.

1. Analyze the general state of competitive dynamics within the industry of study. What evidence or indicators do you have that the industry operates in a slow-, fast-, or standard-cycle market? How might this influence the overall competitive environment in the industry?

2. Analyze the position of several major competitors within the industry. That is, pick a firm active in the industry, along with two or three principal competitors, and, at a minimum, analyze:

   a. Market commonality (e.g., products and customers) and resource similarities across competitors.

   b. Three major competitive actions that occurred in the industry within the past two years. Identify whether these were strategic or tactical actions, who took the actions, as well as whether and how competitors responded. How do these actions and reactions fit into the Model of Competitive Rivalry presented in Figure 5.2?

   c. Competitors in terms of market position. Will the competitive positioning and importance of major industry competitors significantly change in the next five years? Why or why not? Overall, what are the drivers of change within the industry?

Notes

1. D. F. Spulber, 2004, *Management Strategy*, Boston: McGraw-Hill/Irwin, 87–88; M.-J. Chen, 1996, Competitor analysis and interfirm rivalry: Toward a theoretical integration, *Academy of Management Review*, 21: 100–134.
2. T. Galvin, 2002, Examining institutional change: Evidence from the founding dynamics of U.S. health care interest associations, *Academy of Management Journal*, 45: 673–696.
3. B. Pittman, 2003, Leading for value, *Harvard Business Review*, 81(4): 41–46.
4. A. Nair & L. Filer, 2003, Cointegration of firm strategies within groups: A long-run analysis of firm behavior in the Japanese steel industry, *Strategic Management Journal*, 24: 145–159.
5. T. C. Powell, 2003, Varieties of competitive parity, *Strategic Management Journal*, 24: 61–86.
6. S. Jayachandran, J. Gimeno, & P. R. Varadarajan, 1999, Theory of multimarket competition: A synthesis and implications for marketing strategy, *Journal of Marketing*, 63(3): 49–66.
7. R. E. Caves, 1984, Economic analysis and the quest for competitive advantage, in *Papers and Proceedings of the 96th Annual Meeting of the American Economic Association*, 127–132.
8. G. Young, K. G. Smith, C. M. Grimm, & D. Simon, 2000, Multimarket contact and resource dissimilarity: A competitive dynamics perspective, *Journal of Management*, 26: 1217–1236; C. M. Grimm & K. G. Smith, 1997, *Strategy as Action: Industry Rivalry and Coordination*, Cincinnati: South-Western College Publishing, 53–74.
9. H. A. Haveman & L. Nonnemaker, 2000, Competition in multiple geographic markets: The impact on growth and market entry, *Administrative Science Quarterly*, 45: 232–267.
10. K. G. Smith, W. J. Ferrier, & H. Ndofor, 2001, Competitive dynamics research: Critique and future directions, in M. A. Hitt, R. E. Freeman, & J. S. Harrison (eds.), *Handbook of Strategic Management*, Oxford, UK: Blackwell Publishers, 326.
11. G. Young, K. G. Smith, & C. M. Grimm, 1996, "Austrian" and industrial organization perspectives on firm-level competitive activity and performance, *Organization Science*, 73: 243–254.
12. H. D. Hopkins, 2003, The response strategies of dominant U.S. firms to Japanese challengers, *Journal of Management*, 29: 5–25; G. S. Day & D. J. Reibstein, 1997, The dynamic challenges for theory and practice, in G. S. Day & D. J. Reibstein (eds.), *Wharton on Competitive Strategy*, New York: John Wiley & Sons, 2.
13. M.-J. Chen & D. C. Hambrick, 1995, Speed, stealth, and selective attack: How small firms differ from large firms in competitive behavior, *Academy of Management Journal*, 38: 453–482.
14. D. Foust, F. F. Jespersen, & F. Katzenberg, 2003, The best performers, *BusinessWeek Online*, http://www.businessweek.com, March 24; D. L. Deeds, D. De Carolis, & J. Coombs, 2000, Dynamic capabilities and new product development in high technology ventures: An empirical analysis of new biotechnology firms, *Journal of Business Venturing*, 15: 211–299.
15. T. J. Douglas & J. A. Ryman, 2003, Understanding competitive advantage in the general hospital industry: Evaluating strategic competencies, *Strategic Management Journal*, 24: 333–347; W. P. Putsis, Jr., 1999, Empirical analysis of competitive interaction in food product categories, *Agribusiness*, 15(3): 295–311.
16. S. Crainer, 2001, And the new economy winner is . . . Europe, *Strategy & Business*, Second Quarter, 40–47.
17. 2003, Masks off, down the hatch, *The Economist*, May 17, 57.
18. G. Khermouch & K. Capell, 2003, Spiking the booze business, *Business Week*, May 19, 77–78.
19. C. Lawton & D. Ball, 2003, Diageo mixes it up—liquor giant targets system dating to end of prohibition, *Wall Street Journal Online*, http://www.wsj.com, May 8.
20. S. J. Marsh, 1998, Creating barriers for foreign competitors: A study of the impact of anti-dumping actions on the performance of U.S. firms, *Strategic Management Journal*, 19: 25–37; K. G. Smith, C. M. Grimm, G. Young, & S. Wally, 1997, Strategic groups and rivalrous firm behavior: Toward a reconciliation, *Strategic Management Journal*, 18: 149–157.
21. W. J. Ferrier, 2001, Navigating the competitive landscape: The drivers and consequences of competitive aggressiveness, *Academy of Management Journal*, 44: 858–877; M. E. Porter, 1980, *Competitive Strategy*, New York: Free Press.
22. Smith, Ferrier, & Ndofor, Competitive dynamics research, 319.
23. J. Shamsie, 2003, The context of dominance: An industry-driven framework for exploiting reputation, *Strategic Management Journal*, 24: 199–215;

PART 2 / Strategic Actions: Strategy Formulation

K. Ramaswamy, 2001, Organizational ownership, competitive intensity, and firm performance: An empirical study of the Indian manufacturing sector, *Strategic Management Journal*, 22: 989–998.

24. K. Cool, L. H. Roller, & B. Leleux, 1999, The relative impact of actual and potential rivalry on firm profitability in the pharmaceutical industry, *Strategic Management Journal*, 20: 1–14.

25. D. R. Gnyawali & R. Madhavan, 2001, Cooperative networks and competitive dynamics: A structural embeddedness perspective, *Academy of Management Review*, 26: 431–445.

26. Young, Smith, Grimm, & Simon, Multimarket contact and resource dissimilarity, 1217; M. E. Porter, 1991, Towards a dynamic theory of strategy, *Strategic Management Journal*, 12: 95–117.

27. R. L. Priem, L. G. Love, & M. A. Shaffer, 2002, Executives' perceptions of uncertainty scores: A numerical taxonomy and underlying dimensions, *Journal of Management*, 28: 725–746.

28. I. C. MacMillan, A. B. van Putten, & R. S. McGrath, 2003, Global gamesmanship, *Harvard Business Review*, 81(5): 62–71; S. Godin, 2002, Survival is not enough, *Fast Company*, January, 90–94.

29. Chen, Competitor analysis, 108.

30. Ibid., 109.

31. A. Afuah, 2003, Redefining firm boundaries in the face of the Internet: Are firms really shrinking? *Academy of Management Review*, 28: 34–53.

32. G. K. Deans, F. Kroeger, & S. Zeisel, 2002, The consolidation curve, *Harvard Business Review*, 80(12): 20–21; E. Abrahamson & C. J. Fombrun, 1994, Macrocultures: Determinants and consequences, *Academy of Management Review*, 19: 728–755.

33. C. Salter, 2002, On the road again, *Fast Company*, January, 50–58.

34. Young, Smith, Grimm, & Simon, Multimarket contact, 1219.

35. Chen, Competitor analysis, 106.

36. J. Gimeno & C. Y. Woo, 1999, Multimarket contact, economies of scope, and firm performance, *Academy of Management Journal*, 42: 239–259.

37. K. MacArthur, 2001, McDonald's flips business strategy, *Advertising Age*, April 2, 1, 36.

38. 2003, Prudential Financial Inc., *Standard & Poor's Stock Reports*, http://www.standardandpoors.com, May 17.

39. MacMillan, van Putten, & McGrath, Global gamesmanship, 63.

40. Young, Smith, Grimm, & Simon, Multimarket contact, 1230.

41. J. Gimeno, 1999, Reciprocal threats in multimarket rivalry: Staking out "spheres of influence" in the U.S. airline industry, *Strategic Management Journal*, 20: 101–128; N. Fernandez & P. L. Marin, 1998, Market power and multimarket contact: Some evidence from the Spanish hotel industry, *Journal of Industrial Economics*, 46: 301–315.

42. H. J. Korn & J. A. C. Baum, 1999, Chance, imitative, and strategic antecedents to multimarket contact, *Academy of Management Journal*, 42: 171–193.

43. Jayachandran, Gimeno, & Varadarajan, Theory of multimarket competition, 59; Chen, Competitor analysis, 107.

44. J. Gimeno & C. Y. Woo, 1996, Hypercompetition in a multimarket environment: The role of strategic similarity and multimarket contact on competitive de-escalation, *Organization Science*, 7: 322–341.

45. M. Halkias, 2003, Three drugstores stake claims on same intersection in Collin County, Texas, *Dallas Morning News*, May 8, D1, D3.

46. 2003, CVS Corp., *Standard & Poor's Stock Reports*, http://www.standardandpoors.com, May 17; 2003, Walgreen Co., *Standard & Poor's Stock Reports*, http://www.standardandpoors.com, May 17.

47. Chen, Competitor analysis, 107–108.

48. L. Ulrich, 2003, Outside the box, *Money*, 32(6): 137–138.

49. N. E. Boudette, 2003, Drivers wanted: Volkswagen stalls on several fronts after luxury drive, *Wall Street Journal*, Eastern edition, May 8, A1.

50. Chen, Competitor analysis, 110.

51. Ibid.; W. Ocasio, 1997, Towards an attention-based view of the firm, *Strategic Management Journal*, 18 (Special Issue): 187–206; Smith, Ferrier, & Ndofor, Competitive dynamics research, 320.

52. M. Selva, 2003, Wal-Mart, France's Carrefour set sights on Ahold businesses, *Sunday Business*, April 6, B3; 2001, Wal around the world, *The Economist*, December 8, 55–56.

53. G. P. Hodgkinson & G. Johnson, 1994, Exploring the mental models of competitive strategists: The case for a processual approach, *Journal of Management Studies*, 31: 525–551; J. F. Porac & H. Thomas, 1994, Cognitive categorization and subjective rivalry among retailers in a small city, *Journal of Applied Psychology*, 79: 54–66.

54. Smith, Ferrier, & Ndofor, Competitive dynamics research, 320.

55. Chen, Competitor analysis, 113.

56. Grimm & Smith, *Strategy as Action*, 125.

57. 2002, Blue light blues, *The Economist*, January 29, 54; D. B. Yoffie & M. Kwak, 2001, Mastering strategic movement at Palm, *MIT Sloan Management Review*, 43(1): 55–63.

58. K. G. Smith, W. J. Ferrier, & C. M. Grimm, 2001, King of the hill: Dethroning the industry leader, *Academy of Management Executive*, 15(2): 59–70.

59. W. J. Ferrier & H. Lee, 2003, Strategic aggressiveness, variation, and surprise: How the sequential pattern of competitive rivalry influences stock market returns, *Journal of Managerial Issues*, 14: 162–180; G. S. Day, 1997, Assessing competitive arenas: Who are your competitors? in G. S. Day & D. J. Reibstein (eds.), *Wharton on Competitive Strategy*, New York: John Wiley & Sons, 25–26.

60. R. Truett, 2003, A chance to shape design destiny, *Automotive News*, April 7, D2; M. Ihlwan, L. Armstrong, & K. Kerwin, 2001, Hyundai gets hot, *Business Week*, December 17, 84–86.

61. 2003, Boeing says to build new 7E7 in United States, *Reuters*, http://www.reuters.com, May 16.

62. B. McKay, 2003, Coke plans to launch milk-based beverage, *Wall Street Journal Online*, http://www.wsj.com, May 23.

63. S. Day, 2003, Summer may bring a bottled water price war, *New York Times*, http://www.nytimes.com, May 12.

64. 2003, Coke aims milk-based drink at kids, teens, *Richmond Times-Dispatch*, May 27, B5.

65. J. Schumpeter, 1934, *The Theory of Economic Development*, Cambridge, MA: Harvard University Press.

66. J. L. C. Cheng & I. F. Kesner, 1997, Organizational slack and response to environmental shifts: The impact of resource allocation patterns, *Journal of Management*, 23: 1–18.

67. F. Wang, 2000, Too appealing to overlook, *America's Network*, December, 10–12.

68. G. Hamel, 2000, *Leading the Revolution*, Boston: Harvard Business School Press, 103.

69. W. T. Robinson & S. Min, 2002, Is the first to market the first to fail? Empirical evidence for industrial goods businesses, *Journal of Marketing Research*, 39: 120–128.

70. R. Agarwal, M. B. Sarkar, & R. Echambadi, 2002, The conditioning effect of time on firm survival: An industry life cycle approach, *Academy of Management Journal*, 45: 971–994.

71. Smith, Ferrier, & Ndofor, Competitive dynamics research, 331.

72. L. J. Bourgeois, 1981, On the measurement of organizational slack, *Academy of Management Review*, 6: 29–39.

73. S. W. Geiger & L. H. Cashen, 2002, A multidimensional examination of slack and its impact on innovation, *Journal of Managerial Issues*, 14: 68–84.

74. S. Thurm, 2003, Leading the news: Cisco net income rises 50% despite decline in revenue, *Wall Street Journal*, February 3, A3.

75. M. B. Lieberman & D. B. Montgomery, 1988, First-mover advantages, *Strategic Management Journal*, 9: 41–58.

76. 2001, Older, wiser, webbier, *The Economist*, June 30, 10.

77. M. Shank, 2002, Executive strategy report, IBM business strategy consulting, http://www.ibm.com, March 14; W. Boulding & M. Christen, 2001, First-mover disadvantage, *Harvard Business Review*, 79(9): 20–21.

78. B. Finkelstein, 2003, AHMH took two-pronged approach to building volume, *Origination News*, 11(4): 19.

79. K. G. Smith, C. M. Grimm, & M. J. Gannon, 1992, *Dynamics of Competitive Strategy*, Newberry Park, CA.: Sage Publications.

80. H. R. Greve, 1998, Managerial cognition and the mimetic adoption of market positions: What you see is what you do, *Strategic Management Journal*, 19: 967–988.

81. S. D. Dobrev & G. R. Carroll, 2003, Size (and competition) among organizations: Modeling scale-based selection among automobile producers in four major countries, 1885–1981, *Strategic Management Journal*, 24: 541–558; Smith, Ferrier, & Ndofor, Competitive dynamics research, 327.

82. F. K. Pil & M. Hoiweg, 2003, Exploring scale: The advantage of thinking small, *The McKinsey Quarterly*, 44(2): 33–39; Chen & Hambrick, Speed, stealth, and selective attack.

83. D. Miller & M.-J. Chen, 1996, The simplicity of competitive repertoires: An empirical analysis, *Strategic Management Journal*, 17: 419–440.

84. Young, Smith, & Grimm, "Austrian" and industrial organization perspectives.

85. B. A. Melcher, 1993, How Goliaths can act like Davids, *Business Week*, Special Issue, 193.

86. 2003, Wal-Mart Stores, *Standard & Poor's Stock Reports*, http://www.standardandpoors.com, May 17.

87. J. DeMoss, 2003, Wal-Mart grocery store concept to debut in Utah at South Ogden site, *Standard-Examiner*, March 25, B6.

88. 2001, Wal around the world, 55.

89. Ibid.

90. P. B. Crosby, 1980, *Quality Is Free*, New York: Penguin.

91. W. E. Deming, 1986, *Out of the Crisis*, Cambridge, MA: MIT Press.

92. L. B. Crosby, R. DeVito, & J. M. Pearson, 2003, Manage your customers' perception of quality, *Review of Business*, 24(1): 18–24.

93. R. S. Kaplan & D. P. Norton, 2001, *The Strategy-Focused Organization*, Boston: Harvard Business School Press.

94. R. Cullen, S. Nicholls, & A. Halligan, 2001, Measurement to demonstrate success, *British Journal of Clinical Governance*, 6(4): 273–278.

95. K. E. Weick & K. M. Sutcliffe, 2001, *Managing the Unexpected*, San Francisco: Jossey-Bass, 81–82.

96. J. Aley, 1994, Manufacturers grade themselves, *Fortune*, March 21, 26.

97. J. Green & D. Welch, 2001, Jaguar may find it's a jungle out there, *Business Week*, March 26, 62.

98. Ihlwan, Armstrong, & Kerwin, Hyundai gets hot, 84.

99. J. C. Armstrong, 2003, Hyundai Motor begins sourcing 2006 Santa Fe, *Automotive News*, April 28, 21.

100. K. Lundegaard, 2003, GM, Hyundai excel in consumer reports survey—Ford, Mercedes do poorly, *Wall Street Journal*, March 11, D3.

101. T. Box, 2003, Accelerating quality, *Dallas Morning News*, May 17, D1, D3.

102. R. Truett, 2003, A chance to shape design destiny, *Automotive News*, April 7, 2D.

103. J. Schumpeter, 1950, *Capitalism, Socialism and Democracy*, New York: Harper; Smith, Ferrier, & Ndofor, Competitive dynamics research, 323.

104. M.-J. Chen & I. C. MacMillan, 1992, Nonresponse and delayed response to competitive moves, *Academy of Management Journal*, 35: 539–570; Smith, Ferrier, & Ndofor, Competitive dynamics research, 335.

105. M.-J. Chen, K. G. Smith, & C. M. Grimm, 1992, Action characteristics as predictors of competitive responses, *Management Science*, 38: 439–455.

106. M.-J. Chen & D. Miller, 1994, Competitive attack, retaliation and performance: An expectancy-valence framework, *Strategic Management Journal*, 15: 85–102.

107. Smith, Ferrier, & Ndofor, Competitive dynamics research, 333.

108. J. Shamsie, 2003, The context of dominance: An industry-driven framework for exploiting reputation, *Strategic Management Journal*, 24: 199–215.

109. P. W. Roberts & G. R. Dowling, 2003, Corporate reputation and sustained superior financial performance, *Strategic Management Journal*, 24: 1077–1093.

110. W. J. Ferrier, K. G. Smith, & C. M. Grimm, 1999, The role of competitive actions in market share erosion and industry dethronement: A study of industry leaders and challengers, *Academy of Management Journal*, 42: 372–388.

111. 2001, Lowe's Companies, *Standard & Poor's Stock Reports*, http://www.standardandpoors.com, December 26.

112. Smith, Grimm, & Gannon, *Dynamics of Competitive Strategy*.

113. A. Karnani & B. Wernerfelt, 1985, Research note and communication: Multiple point competition, *Strategic Management Journal*, 6: 87–97.

114. Smith, Ferrier, & Ndofor, Competitive dynamics research, 330.

115. M. J. McCarthy, 2002, Wrigley must chew on its next move, *Wall Street Journal*, September 19, B1.

116. 2003, Wm. Wrigley Company, About Us, *http://www.wrigley.com*, May 26.

117. G. McNamara, P. M. Vaaler, & C. Devers, 2003, Same as it ever was: The search for evidence of increasing hypercompetition, *Strategic Management Journal*, 24: 261–278.

118. J. R. Williams, 1999, *Renewable Advantage: Crafting Strategy through Economic Time*, New York: Free Press.

119. J. R. Williams, 1992, How sustainable is your competitive advantage? *California Management Review* 34(3): 29–51.

120. Ibid., 6.

121. Ibid., 57.

122. 2003, Pfizer suit is for a blockbuster drug, *Businessline*, February 26, 13.

123. 2003, U.S. FDA says counterfeit Lipitor recalled by distributor, *Reuters*, http://www.reuters.com, May 23.

124. 2003, How fast is your company? *Fast Company*, June, 18.

125. Williams, *Renewable Advantage*, 8.

126. Ibid.

127. R. Sanchez, 1995, Strategic flexibility in production competition, *Strategic Management Journal*, 16 (Special Issue): 9–26.

128. Williams, *Renewable Advantage*, 7.

129. K. Brooker, 2001, A game of inches, *Fortune*, February 5, 98–100.

130. D. Foust, F. F. Jespersen, & F. Katzenberg, 2003, The best performers, *BusinessWeek Online*, http://www.businessweek.com, March 24.

Corporate-Level Strategy

Chapter Six

Knowledge Objectives

Studying this chapter should provide you with the strategic management knowledge needed to:

1. Define corporate-level strategy and discuss its importance to the diversified firm.

2. Describe the advantages and disadvantages of single- and dominant-business strategies.

3. Explain three primary reasons why firms move from single- and dominant-business strategies to more diversified strategies.

4. Describe how related diversified firms create value by sharing or transferring core competencies.

5. Explain the two ways value can be created with an unrelated diversification strategy.

6. Discuss the incentives and resources that encourage diversification.

7. Describe motives that can encourage managers to overdiversify a firm.

Getty/PhotoDisc, Inc.

Sony has been successful in adding technology to content in a way that has been innovative and profitable.

Sony's Chairman Idei Seeks to Foster Related Diversification

The development of technology is revolutionizing the media industry. Media content producers have sought, so far unsuccessfully, to merge their companies with content distribution firms, hoping to maximize returns by controlling outlets for their content. Bertelsmann AG, Vivendi Universal, and AOL Time Warner, for example, have multiple media and content outlet business units in publishing, movies, cable TV, and Internet websites. Despite the failure of executives Thomas Middelhoff at Bertelsmann, Jean-Marie Messier at Vivendi Universal, and Gerald M. Levin at AOL Time Warner to achieve similar goals, Nobuyuki Idei, the chairman of Sony, is undauntedly pursuing convergence in music, movies, games, and communications in all forms.

Mr. Idei argued that Sony's unique advantage over other media behemoths was that it makes the actual electronic devices (TVs, personal computers, game consoles, and mobile phones) that deliver the content Sony controls. Across its personal device divisions, Sony has achieved operational relatedness (defined later in the chapter) in its consumer electronics businesses. Now, Sony is seeking corporate relatedness (defined later in the chapter) across its electronic devices, software, and content divisions. As Sony's chairman, Idei has made significant strides in building a company where content meshes with the electronics. Many Walkmans are no longer stand-alone tape players, but can also download music from the Internet; Clié personal digital assistants (PDAs) come with cameras; CoCoonhome video recorders can be programmed from a mobile phone. "In terms of building networked products," said Lee Kun Soo, an analyst at West LB Securities in Tokyo, "no company has come so far."

But inside Sony, there remains the major challenge of balancing the divergent aims of the content divisions, which are fighting to protect their song and movie copyrights, and the gadget makers in the consumer electronics divisions, who are creating products that will allow consumers to swap content. Sony's acquisition of Columbia Pictures in the late 1980s brought the struggle between hardware and software in-house, and new technological advances are likely to make that struggle even more intense in coming years.

Chairman Idei maintains that by 2005 the telecommunications infrastructure (broadband) meshed with content products (music, video, and games software) will be in place, allowing the company to reap the benefits of the convergence of media and technology. The number of high-speed Internet and mobile phone connections is exploding. Sony's Memory Stick is now embedded in most of its new products, making it possible for users to easily swap data between cameras, computers, and PDAs. One-third, or nearly 1,200, of Sony's movies through Columbia Pictures have been digitized, which will allow them to be used on many hardware devices.

In this era of increasingly indistinguishable electronics, preserving Sony's corporate brand is paramount. "People don't just buy for economic reasons," Mr. Idei says. "When you touch a product, you should feel something." However, to accomplish this diversification strategy, the integration necessary between divisions has led to some changes in leadership. "The necessity for such bridge building led to the recent ouster of Sony Music's longtime leader, Tommy Mottola, whose unwillingness to confer with the rest of Sony on a new business model forced the change to an outsider, NBC television executive Andrew Lack." Thus, implementing the related diversification strategy and vision of Mr. Idei has not been without difficulties. Furthermore, any diversification strategy has to create value over and above the value created by the businesses involved. To this point, although the operational relatedness strategy has been fairly successful, the strategy to foster both operational and corporate relatedness has yet to achieve the desired success.

SOURCES: K. Belson, 2003, 65 and just itching for a little convergence, *New York Times*, http://www.nytimes.com, April 3; 2003, Special Report: The complete home entertainer? Sony, *The Economist*, March 1, 62–64; R. A. Guth, 2003, Sony's board will divide up responsibilities, *Wall Street Journal*, January 29, B6; S. Levy, 2003, Sony's new day, *Newsweek*, January 27, 50–53; J. Ordonez & J. Lippman, 2003, Sony taps NBC's Lack in hope success will rub off—high costs, piracy, other woes plague its sickly music unit, *Wall Street Journal*, January 13, B1.

Our discussions of business-level strategies (Chapter 4) and the competitive rivalry and competitive dynamics associated with them (Chapter 5) concentrate on firms competing in a single industry or product market.[1] When a firm chooses to diversify beyond a single industry and to operate businesses in several industries, it uses a corporate-level strategy of diversification. As explained in the Opening Case, Sony is best known for its consumer electronics business where it seeks to create synergy between businesses (operational relatedness). Now it seeks to have integration across its electronic and media businesses through corporate relatedness. A corporate-level strategy of diversification such as Sony's allows the firm to use its core competencies to pursue opportunities in the external environment.[2] In particular, the convergence among these industries is creating an opportunity that requires a diversification strategy such as Sony's. As the Opening Case illustrates, diversification strategies play a major role in the behavior of large firms.[3] Strategic choices regarding diversification are, however, fraught with uncertainty, as in the Sony illustration.[4]

A diversified company has two levels of strategy: business (or competitive) and corporate (or company-wide).[5] Each business unit in the diversified firm chooses a business-level strategy as its means of competing in individual product markets. The firm's corporate-level strategy is concerned with two key questions: what businesses the firm should be in and how the corporate office should manage the group of businesses.[6] Defined formally, **corporate-level strategy** specifies actions the firm takes to gain a competitive advantage by selecting and managing a group of different businesses competing in several industries and product markets. In the current global environment, top executives should view their firm's businesses as a portfolio of core competencies when they select new businesses and decide how to manage them.

A corporate-level strategy is expected to help the firm earn above-average returns by creating value, just as with the diversified firm's business-level strategies.[7] Some suggest that few corporate-level strategies actually create value.[8] A corporate-level strat-

PART 2 / Strategic Actions: Strategy Formulation

Corporate-level strategy *specifies actions the firm takes to gain a competitive advantage by selecting and managing a group of different businesses competing in several industries and product markets.*

egy's value is ultimately determined by the degree to which "the businesses in the portfolio are worth more under the management of the company than they would be under any other ownership."[9] Thus, the effective corporate-level strategy creates, across all business units, aggregate returns that exceed what those returns would be without the strategy[10] and contributes to the firm's strategic competitiveness and its ability to earn above-average returns.[11]

Product diversification, a primary corporate-level strategy, concerns the scope of the industries and markets in which the firm competes as well as "how managers buy, create and sell different businesses to match skills and strengths with opportunities presented to the firm."[12] Successful diversification is expected to reduce variability in the firm's profitability in that earnings are generated from several different business units.[13] Because firms incur development and monitoring costs when diversifying, the ideal business portfolio balances diversification's costs and benefits.[14] Increasingly, for example, a number of "traditional economy" firms are diversifying into Internet and e-commerce businesses in attempts to develop a properly balanced portfolio.[15]

Diversification requires the crafting of a multibusiness or corporate-level strategy. Multibusiness strategies often involve the firm with many different industry environments and product markets and, as explained in Chapter 11, require unique organizational structures. In the Opening Case, we describe Sony's use of a multibusiness diversification strategy to compete in the consumer electronics, media content, and games businesses. The prevailing logic of diversification suggests that the firm should diversify into additional markets when it has excess resources, capabilities, and core competencies with multiple value-creating uses.[16] The probability of success increases when top-level managers verify that the firm has excess, value-creating resources, capabilities, and core competencies before choosing and trying to implement a corporate-level strategy.[17]

We begin the chapter by examining different levels (from low to high) of diversification. Value-creating reasons for firms to use a corporate-level strategy are explored next. When diversification results in companies simultaneously competing against one another in multiple markets, they are engaging in multipoint competition.[18] The chapter also describes the use of the vertical integration strategy as a means to gain power over competitors. Two types of diversification strategies denoting moderate to very high levels of diversification—related and unrelated—are then examined. The chapter also explores value-neutral incentives to diversify as well as managerial motives for diversification, which can be value destructive.

Levels of Diversification

Diversified firms vary according to their level of diversification and the connections between and among their businesses. Figure 6.1 lists and defines five categories of businesses according to increasing levels of diversification. In addition to the single- and dominant-business categories, which denote relatively low levels of diversification, more fully diversified firms are classified into related and unrelated categories. A firm is related through its diversification when there are several links between its business units; for example, units may share products or services, technologies, or distribution channels. The more links among businesses, the more "constrained" is the relatedness of diversification. Unrelatedness refers to the absence of direct links between businesses.

Low Levels of Diversification

A firm pursing a *low level of diversification* uses either a single or a dominant corporate-level diversification strategy. A single-business diversification strategy is a corporate-level strategy wherein the firm generates 95 percent or more of its sales revenue from

Figure 6.1 —— Levels and Types of Diversification

Low Levels of Diversification

    Single business: More than 95% of revenue comes from a single business.

    Dominant business: Between 70% and 95% of revenue comes from a single business.

Moderate to High Levels of Diversification

    Related constrained: Less than 70% of revenue comes from the dominant business, and all businesses share product, technological, and distribution linkages.

    Related linked (mixed related and unrelated):   Less than 70% of revenue comes from the dominant business, and there are only limited links between businesses.

Very High Levels of Diversification

    Unrelated: Less than 70% of revenue comes from the dominant business, and there are no common links between businesses.

SOURCE: Adapted from R. P. Rumelt, 1974, *Strategy, Structure and Economic Performance*, Boston: Harvard Business School.

its core business area.[19] For example, focusing on the chewing-gum market, Wm. Wrigley Jr. Company historically used a single-business strategy while operating in relatively few product markets.[20] Wrigley's trademark chewing-gum brands include Spearmint, Doublemint, and Juicy Fruit. Sugarfree gums Hubba Bubba, Orbit, and Ice White were added in the 1990s. Its collaboration with Procter & Gamble (P&G) to produce a dental chewing gum caused Wrigley to become more diversified than it had been, moving it toward the dominant business strategy. The dental chewing gum is being marketed under P&G's Crest brand.[21] Furthermore, William Wrigley, Jr., the current chairman, has suggested that he would like "to double the size of the company over a number of years."[22] In fact, he sought but failed to buy out chocolate maker Hershey Foods to partially accomplish this goal.

    With the dominant-business corporate-level diversification strategy, the firm generates between 70 and 95 percent of its total revenue within a single business area. Smithfield Foods uses the dominant-business diversification strategy in that the majority of its sales are generated from raising and butchering hogs. Recently, however, Smithfield diversified into beef packing by acquiring Moyer Packing Co., a smaller beef processor. Smithfield also attempted to acquire IBP, the largest beef packer, but was outbid by Tyson Foods.[23] Also, it lost a bid to the bankruptcy court for Farmland, a large beef processing cooperative.[24] Smithfield often seeks to buy troubled companies such as Farmland and then restructure the business operations to make them more profitable. Although it is still using the dominant-business diversification strategy, the firm's addition of beef packing operations suggests that its portfolio of businesses is becoming more diversified. If Smithfield were to become even more diversified, its corporate-level strategy could be more accurately described as moderately diversified.

Moderate and High Levels of Diversification

A firm generating more than 30 percent of its sales revenue outside a dominant business and whose businesses are related to each other in some manner uses a *related diversification corporate-level strategy.* When the links between the diversified firm's businesses are rather direct, a *related constrained diversification strategy* is being used. Campbell Soup, Procter & Gamble, Kodak, and Merck & Company all use a related constrained strategy. A related constrained firm shares a number of resources and activities between its businesses.

The diversified company with a portfolio of businesses with only a few links between them is called a mixed related and unrelated firm and is using the *related linked diversification corporate-level strategy* (see Figure 6.1). Johnson & Johnson, General Electric, and Cendant follow this corporate-level diversification strategy. Compared to related constrained firms, related linked firms share fewer resources and assets between their businesses, concentrating on transferring knowledge and competencies between the businesses instead.

A highly diversified firm, which has no relationships between its businesses, follows an *unrelated diversification corporate-level strategy.* United Technologies, Textron, and Samsung are examples of firms using this type of corporate-level strategy.[25] Although many U.S. firms using the unrelated diversification strategy have refocused to become less diversified, a number continue to have high levels of diversification. In Latin America and other emerging economies such as China, Korea, and India, conglomerates (firms following the unrelated diversification strategy) continue to dominate the private sector.[26] For instance, in Taiwan, "the largest 100 groups produced one third of the GNP in the past 20 years."[27] Typically family controlled, these corporations account for the greatest percentage of private firms in India.[28] Similarly, the largest business groups in Brazil, Mexico, Argentina, and Colombia are family-owned, diversified enterprises.[29] Questions are being raised as to the viability of these large diversified business groups,[30] especially in developed economies such as Japan.[31] However, evidence suggests that where capital markets and the legal system are underdeveloped, diversification produces better performance.[32]

Reasons for Diversification

There are many reasons firms use a corporate-level diversification strategy (see Table 6.1). Typically, a diversification strategy is used to increase the firm's value by improving its overall performance. Value is created either through related diversification or through unrelated diversification when the strategy allows a company's business units to increase revenues or reduce costs while implementing their business-level strategies. Another reason for diversification is to gain market power relative to competitors. Often, this is achieved through vertical integration (see the discussion later in the chapter).

Other reasons for using a diversification strategy may not increase the firm's value; in fact, diversification could have neutral effects, increase costs, or reduce a firm's revenues and its value. These reasons include diversification to match and thereby neutralize a competitor's market power (such as to neutralize another firm's advantage by acquiring a similar distribution outlet) and diversification to expand a firm's portfolio of businesses to reduce managerial employment risk (if one of the businesses in a diversified firm fails, the top executive of the firm remains employed). Because diversification can increase a firm's size and thus managerial compensation, managers have motives to diversify a firm to a level that reduces its value.[33] Diversification rationales that may have a neutral or negative effect on the firm's value are discussed in a later section.

To provide an overview of value-creating diversification strategies, Figure 6.2 illustrates operational relatedness and corporate relatedness. Study of these independent

Table 6.1 ———— Motives, Incentives, and Resources for Diversification

Motives to Enhance Strategic Competitiveness
- Economies of scope (related diversification)
  - Sharing activities
  - Transferring core competencies
- Market power (related diversification)
  - Blocking competitors through multipoint competition
  - Vertical integration
- Financial economies (unrelated diversification)
  - Efficient internal capital allocation
  - Business restructuring

Incentives and Resources with Neutral Effects on Strategic Competitiveness
- Antitrust regulation
- Tax laws
- Low performance
- Uncertain future cash flows
- Risk reduction for firm
- Tangible resources
- Intangible resources

Managerial Motives (Value Reduction)
- Diversifying managerial employment risk
- Increasing managerial compensation

relatedness dimensions shows the importance of resources and key competencies.[34] The figure's vertical dimension points to opportunities for sharing operational activities between businesses (operational relatedness) while its horizontal dimension depicts corporate capabilities for transferring knowledge (corporate relatedness). The firm with a strong capability in managing operational synergy, especially in sharing assets between its businesses, falls in the upper left quadrant, which also represents vertical sharing of assets through vertical integration. The lower right quadrant represents a highly developed corporate capability for transferring a skill across businesses. This capability is located primarily in the corporate office. The use of either operational or corporate relatedness is based on a knowledge asset that the firm can either share or transfer.[35] Unrelated diversification is also illustrated in Figure 6.2 in the lower left quadrant. As shown, the unrelated diversification strategy creates value through financial economies rather than through either operational or corporate relatedness among business units.

Related Diversification

Economies of scope are cost savings that the firm creates by successfully transferring some of its capabilities and competencies that were developed in one of its businesses to another of its businesses.

With the related diversification corporate-level strategy, the firm builds upon or extends its resources, capabilities, and core competencies to create value.[36] The company using the related diversification strategy wants to develop and exploit economies of scope between its business units. Available to companies operating in multiple industries or product markets,[37] **economies of scope** are cost savings that the firm creates by successfully transferring some of its capabilities and competencies that were developed in one of its businesses to another of its businesses.

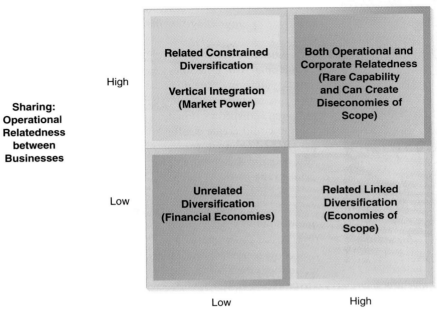

Sharing: Operational Relatedness between Businesses

High

Low

Related Constrained Diversification

Vertical Integration (Market Power)

Both Operational and Corporate Relatedness (Rare Capability and Can Create Diseconomies of Scope)

Unrelated Diversification (Financial Economies)

Related Linked Diversification (Economies of Scope)

Low

High

Corporate Relatedness: Transferring Skills into Businesses through Corporate Headquarters

As illustrated in Figure 6.2, firms seek to create value from economies of scope through two basic kinds of operational economies: sharing activities (operational relatedness) and transferring skills or corporate core competencies (corporate relatedness). The difference between sharing activities and transferring competencies is based on how separate resources are jointly used to create economies of scope. Tangible resources, such as plant and equipment or other business-unit physical assets, often must be shared to create economies of scope. Less tangible resources, such as manufacturing know-how, also can be shared.[38] However, when know-how is transferred between separate activities and there is no physical or tangible resource involved, a corporate core competence has been transferred as opposed to operational sharing of activities having taken place.

Operational Relatedness: Sharing Activities

Firms can create operational relatedness by sharing either a primary activity (such as inventory delivery systems) or a support activity (for example, purchasing practices)—see Chapter 3's discussion of the value chain. Sharing activities is quite common, especially among related constrained firms. Procter & Gamble's paper towel business and baby diaper business both use paper products as a primary input to the manufacturing process. The firm's paper production plant produces inputs for both divisions and is an example of a shared activity. In addition, these two businesses are likely to share distribution channels and sales networks, because they both produce consumer products.

Firms expect activity sharing among units to result in increased strategic competitiveness and improved financial returns.[39] For example, Hewlett-Packard's (HP) acquisition of Compaq is significantly improving the cost structure of the merged firm. One analyst observed that the team in charge of "untangling 163 overlapping product

Hewlett-Packard's acquisition of Compaq is an example of activity sharing across companies that can be complex and difficult to manage. Because of CEO Carly Fiorina's strength in the facilitation of the acquisition, the firm has experienced more positive than negative outcomes.

lines—from Intel-based home computers to Unix workstations to handhelds—[has met] the $2.5 billion in cost reductions that Carly Fiorina [CEO of HP] was promising investors."[40] In mid-2003, the team was on track to save another $500 million that year by improving the sharing of resources between the merged firms.

Other issues affect the degree to which activity sharing creates positive outcomes. For example, activity sharing requires sharing strategic control over business units. Moreover, one business unit manager may feel that another unit is receiving a disproportionate share of the gains. Such a perception could create conflicts between division managers. In the HP and Compaq transaction, 15,000 employees lost their jobs because the sharing of resources between the two firms reduced the need for these employees.[41]

Activity sharing also is risky because business-unit ties create links between outcomes. For instance, if demand for one business's product is reduced, there may not be sufficient revenues to cover the fixed costs required to operate the facilities being shared. Organizational difficulties such as these can reduce activity sharing success.[42]

Although activity sharing across business units isn't risk free, research shows that it can create value. For example, studies that examined acquisitions of firms in the same industry (called horizontal acquisitions), such as the banking industry, have found that sharing resources and activities and thereby creating economies of scope contributed to postacquisition increases in performance and higher returns to shareholders.[43] Additionally, firms that sold off related units in which resource sharing was a possible source of economies of scope have been found to produce lower returns than those that sold off businesses unrelated to the firm's core business.[44] Still other research discovered that firms with more related units had lower risk.[45] These results suggest that gaining economies of scope by sharing activities across a firm's businesses may be important in reducing risk and in creating value. Further, more attractive results are obtained through activity sharing when a strong corporate office facilitates it.[46]

Corporate Relatedness: Transferring of Core Competencies

Over time, the firm's intangible resources, such as its know-how, become the foundation of core competencies. As suggested by Figure 6.2, corporate core competencies are complex sets of resources and capabilities that link different businesses, primarily through managerial and technological knowledge, experience, and expertise.[47] One corporate capability that has been suggested by research is the ability to appropriately price new products, no matter the business line of origin.[48]

Related linked firms often transfer competencies across businesses, thereby creating value in at least two ways.[49] First, the expense of developing a competence has been incurred in one unit. Transferring it to a second business unit eliminates the need for the second unit to allocate resources to develop the competence. Resource intangibility is a second source of value creation through corporate relatedness. Intangible resources are difficult for competitors to understand and imitate. Because of this difficulty, the unit receiving a transferred competence often gains an immediate competitive advantage over its rivals.[50]

As an example of corporate relatedness, Pininfarina is famous for cars it has designed in the past, namely the Ferrari Testarossa and the Alfa Romeo Spider. But its CEO, Andrea Pininfarina, is seeking to move it into higher-margin service businesses, such as engineering new models and testing prototypes. In the CEO's words, "The

Cendant: A Diversified Service Conglomerate

Cendant Corporation was created in December 1997 by a merger between HFS, Inc., and CUC International. The merger combined a marketing company (CUC) with HFS, a diversified firm with franchising operations in several industries, including real estate, hospitality, and vehicle services. Henry Silverman, CEO of the former HFS, was appointed chairman of the merged company. Massive accounting irregularities in CUC's businesses caused Cendant's shares to lose nearly half their market value four months after the merger and resulted in criminal charges against some of CUC's former executives.

Cendant Corporation owns a diversified set of service businesses, including its fee-for-service businesses—hotels, real estate, tax preparation, rental cars, fleet and fuel cards, mortgage origination, employee relocation, and vacation exchange and rental services. Cendant grows through acquisitions as well as through internal means, such as development of new product lines, to implement its related linked corporate-level diversification strategy. Discussed in detail in the chapter, this strategy mixes related and unrelated diversification. Cendant also uses joint ventures and franchising (types of cooperative strategies that we discuss further in Chapter 9) to reach its growth objectives.

The focus of Cendant's corporate-level strategy is rapid growth through buying strong brands that are effectively positioned in the fee-for-service business area. Its businesses usually have low to moderate capital requirements but generate high margins and provide growing returns on capital and strong cash flows. Furthermore, Cendant seeks productivity improvements to lower costs by employing newer technologies.

Cendant's real estate franchises include Century 21, Coldwell Banker Commercial, and ERA—some of the most well-known franchises in the commercial and residential real estate brokerage market. Furthermore, it is one of the largest real estate retail mortgage originators in the United States. It also has a relocation service called Cendant Mobility. Real estate services generate approximately 40 percent of revenues for this diversified company.

In travel services, Cendant has a vast array of lodging franchises, including Days Inn, Howard Johnson, Ramada, Super 8, and Travelodge, among others. In fact, one in four customers in the budget segment stay in a Cendant franchised property. Because its customer base is budget conscious, the September 11, 2001, strikes on the United States had less effect on Cendant's revenues than on those of highly differentiated and more expensive lodging facilities. Cendant also owns Fairfield Resorts, Inc., through which vacation ownership interests are sold. To complement its travel business, Cendant acquired Galileo International, a distributor of electronic global reservation services for the travel industry. Customers in 115 countries use Galileo's services to access schedule and fare information, make reservations, and obtain tickets. Another recent Cendant acquisition, CheapTickets, provides additional opportunity in the online travel reservation segment. With the capability formed through its acquisitions, Cendant feels that it can effectively compete with such online travel companies as Travelocity and Priceline.com. Travel services generate approximately 28 percent of Cendant's revenues.

Cendant has a vehicle service division and is the leader in providing fleet and fuel management service cards. Avis Rent A Car System and Budget Car and Truck Rental, as well as PHH Arval and Wright Express form the core of this division. In total, this group of businesses accounts for roughly 17 percent of Cendant's sales revenue.

In regard to financial services, Cendant owns Jackson Hewitt Tax Service, the second largest U.S. tax preparation company, as well as Benefit Consultants, FISI-Madison Financial, and Long Term Preferred Care in the insurance and loyalty marketing area. On a combined basis, Cendant's financial services business unit contributes approximately 15 percent to the firm's total revenues.

Part of Cendant's related linked diversification strategy is to acquire companies that complement its prestigious branded businesses. For instance, Galileo International, originally United Airlines' Apollo reservation system, has the second largest share of the electronic travel reservation business. Sabre Holdings Corporation, a competitor that operates the Sabre computer reservation system and also controls Travelocity, holds the largest share of this market. The Galileo network connects 43,000 travel agency sites to 550 airlines, 37 car rental companies, 47,000 hotel properties, 368 tour operators, and three major cruise lines. Thus, this acquisition creates a stronger link among Cendant's travel businesses.

A key objective of Cendant's acquisition strategy is to add companies that augment growth, strengthening the various businesses or segments where the firm has competitive advantages. Its best success with cross market knowledge sharing has been in its array of real estate franchises. Although Cendant's businesses within each service type demonstrate some degree of relatedness and knowledge sharing across service businesses, it has yet to realize the potential synergy between service categories. As is the case for all diversified businesses, Cendant must provide clear and transparent reports of its operational successes so investors and other stakeholders can fairly judge the value being created by exploiting interrelationships among the firm's business units.

SOURCES: G. G. Marcial, 2003, Cendant comes back, *Business Week,* May 12, 110; A. Tsao, 2003, Just the ticket for travel stocks, *BusinessWeek Online,* http://www.businessweek.com, March 19; A. Barrett, 2002, Keep it simple, Cendant, Wall Street is slamming the company for complex financials, *Business Week,* October 14, 54; A. Serwer, 2002, Dirty rotten numbers, *Fortune,* February 18, 74–84; A. Barrett & D. Brady, 2001, Just when it seems on the mend, *Business Week,* October 15, 75–76; D. Colarusso, 2001, Wall Street is pondering Cendant's fresh start, *New York Times,* http://www.nytimes.com, April 22; M. Rich, 2001, Cendant agrees to buy CheapTickets, *Wall Street Journal,* August 14, B6; C. Rosen, 2001, Cendant ventures into travel, *Information Week,* June 25, 24; R. Sorkin & B. J. Feder, 2001, Owner of Avis and Day's Inn seen buying travel service, *New York Times,* http://www.nytimes.com, June 18; A. Barrett, S. A. Forest, & T. Lowry, 2000, Henry Silverman's long road back, *Business Week,* February 28, 126–136.

unique asset of Pininfarina is creativity." Ford has transferred the responsibility for the design, engineering, and assembly of its newest European convertible to the Italian automotive design firm. By calling on Pininfarina's talent to create and engineer the new convertible, Ford is availing itself of Pininfarina's core competence, namely, managing the creative process beyond mere design.[51]

The Strategic Focus on Cendant illustrates how this diversified services firm shares knowledge between its groups of businesses. For instance, in April 2002, Cendant unveiled the website CheapTickets.com, which allows the user to plan an entire trip, including plane tickets, hotel rooms, and car rentals. Although not devoted exclusively to Cendant brands, this website could help correlate the company's holdings in these markets. The September 11, 2001, terrorist attacks and the wars in Afghanistan and Iraq have had negative effects on the global travel market. However, the expectation of an improved travel market in the future bodes well for Cendant's businesses. The knowledge gained through the new website might also help Cendant's other businesses because online travel booking is one of the few areas of growth among Internet businesses.[52]

A number of firms have successfully transferred some of their resources and capabilities across businesses. Virgin Industries transferred its marketing skills across travel, cosmetics, music, drinks, mobile phones, and a number of other businesses. Thermo Electron uses its entrepreneurial skills to start new ventures and maintain a new-venture network. Coopers Industries manages a number of manufacturing-related businesses. Honda has developed and transferred its expertise in small and now larger engines for different types of vehicles, from motorcycles and lawnmowers to its range of automotive products.[53]

As the Strategic Focus suggests, the decision to merge CUC International with HFS seemed to have potential for improving the marketing capabilities of the merged firm, Cendant. However, because of accounting irregularities in some CUC businesses, the merger created significant difficulties, resulting in an initial precipitous decline in Cendant's market value. Also, because of the complexities in its financial statements, Cendant's market value declined subsequent to the Enron debacle.[54] Thus, there are significant risks to this strategy. Sony's chairman, Nobuyuki Idei, is finding how difficult pursuing corporate relatedness can be, as illustrated in this chapter's Opening Case.

One way managers facilitate the transfer of competencies is to move key people into new management positions.[55] However, a business-unit manager of an older division may be reluctant to transfer key people who have accumulated knowledge and experience critical to the business unit's success. Thus, managers with the ability to facilitate the transfer of a core competence may come at a premium, or the key people involved may not want to transfer. Additionally, the top-level managers from the transferring division may not want the competencies transferred to a new division to fulfill the firm's diversification objectives. As the Opening Case illustrates, because the former music businesss manager was unwilling to integrate the music content with other divisions, Idei, Sony's chairman, replaced him with Andrew Lack. However, research suggests that transferring expertise in manufacturing-based businesses often does not result in improved performance.[56] Businesses in which performance does improve often demonstrate a corporate passion for pursuing skill transfer and appropriate coordination mechanisms for realizing economies of scope.

Market Power

Related diversification can also be used to gain market power. Market power exists when a firm is able to sell its products above the existing competitive level or to reduce the costs of its primary and support activities below the competitive level, or both.[57]

One approach to gaining market power through diversification is *multipoint competition.* Multipoint competition exists when two or more diversified firms simultaneously compete in the same product areas or geographic markets.[58] The actions taken by United Parcel Service (UPS) and FedEx in two markets, overnight delivery and ground shipping, illustrate the concept of multipoint competition. UPS has moved into the stronghold of FedEx, overnight delivery, and FedEx has been buying trucking and ground shipping assets to move into the stronghold of UPS. Additionally, there is geographic competition for markets as DHL, the strongest shipping company in Europe, tries to move into the U.S. market.[59] Additionally, all three competitors are seeking to move into large foreign markets to establish market shares. For instance, because China was allowed into the World Trade Organization (WTO) and government officials have declared the market more open to foreign competition, the battle for global market share among these three top shippers is raging in China and other countries throughout the world.[60]

Some firms choose to create value by using vertical integration to gain market power (see Figure 6.2). **Vertical integration** exists when a company produces its own inputs (backward integration) or owns its own source of output distribution (forward integration). In some instances, firms

Vertical integration *exists when a company produces its own inputs (backward integration) or owns its own source of distribution of outputs (forward integration).*

DHL, UPS, and FedEx are vying for market share in large foreign markets. Here, a Chinese airport official stands near the Panda Express, a FedEx plane painted with a giant panda's face that carries live giant pandas in Beijing, China.

AP Photo/Ng Han Guan

partially integrate their operations, producing and selling their products by using company units as well as outside sources.

Vertical integration is commonly used in the firm's core business to gain market power over rivals. Market power is gained as the firm develops the ability to save on its operations, avoid market costs, improve product quality, and, possibly, protect its technology from imitation by rivals.[61] Market power also is created when firms have strong ties between their assets for which no market prices exist. Establishing a market price would result in high search and transaction costs, so firms seek to vertically integrate rather than remain separate businesses.[62]

Apple has recently forward integrated into the music business. Steven Jobs, Apple's CEO, saw people copying songs off CDs to use on their computers. Accordingly, Apple created iTunes jukebox computer software, which allows users to create their own list of songs or have the computer select songs randomly. Then, Apple developed the iPod, which is a portable device with a very large hard drive and which works seamlessly with iTunes so that music put on a personal computer becomes portable. Recently, Jobs has gone a step farther by vertically integrating forward into music purchases on the Internet, allowing iTune and iPod users as well as others to buy music directly from the Apple Store, an online store already selling more than $1 billion in hardware and software. Customers can now buy a specific song or a set of songs rather than pay a monthly subscription fee to such firms as Time Warner's music division, Pressplay, or MusicNet. One observer noted, "It's a lot easier to get people to migrate from physical CDs to buying individual songs online than it is to jump-start a subscription service."[63]

There are limits to vertical integration. For example, an outside supplier may produce the product at a lower cost. As a result, internal transactions from vertical integration may be expensive and reduce profitability relative to competitors. Also, bureaucratic costs may occur with vertical integration. And, because vertical integration can require substantial investments in specific technologies, it may reduce the firm's flexibility, especially when technology changes quickly. Finally, changes in demand create capacity balance and coordination problems. If one division is building a part for another internal division, but achieving economies of scale requires the first division to manufacture quantities that are beyond the capacity of the internal buyer to absorb, it would be necessary to sell the parts outside the firm as well as to the internal division. Thus, although vertical integration can create value, especially through market power over competitors, it is not without risks and costs.

For example, Merck, the pharmaceutical company, previously owned a pharmacy-benefits management company called Medco Health. Medco acts as a middleman between patients, insurers, and drugmakers, which led to conflicts of interest with its parent company. By revenue, Medco was 50 percent larger than Merck, but had a much smaller profit margin. Because of the legal headaches caused by the conflicts of interest, as well as the small profit margin and a desire to focus more attention on its own underlying profitability, Merck spun off Medco in mid-2003. This decision indicates that the benefits Merck expected from vertical integration did not fully materialize.[64]

Many manufacturing firms no longer pursue vertical integration.[65] In fact, deintegration is the focus of most manufacturing firms, such as Intel and Dell, and even some large auto companies, such as Ford and General Motors, as they develop independent supplier networks.[66] Solectron Corp., a contract manufacturer, represents a new breed of large contract manufacturers that is helping to foster this revolution in supply-chain management.[67] Such firms often manage their customers' entire product lines and offer services ranging from inventory management to delivery and after-sales service. Conducting business through e-commerce also allows vertical integration to be changed into "virtual integration."[68] Thus, closer relationships are possible with suppliers and customers through virtual integration or electronic means of integration, allowing firms to reduce the costs of processing transactions while improving their supply-chain management skills and tightening the control of their inventories.

Johnson & Johnson Seeks to Combine Diagnostic Devices and Drugs

Johnson & Johnson (J&J) is a 117-year-old company with 204 different and complex enterprises. It is organized into three major strategic groups: drugs, medical devices and diagnostics, and consumer products. Significantly, 61 percent of its operating profits came from the drugs group in 2002. With $36 billion in revenue, J&J is one of the largest health-care companies in the United States. In consumer products, it has prestigious brands, such as Band-Aid® and its famous Johnson & Johnson baby powder. It has a strong research and development capability as well as an effective program to acquire new products. Once it has a new product revenue stream, developed internally or acquired, the firm seeks to sell it aggressively around the world. Because of the company's size, it can offer favorable prices, for instance, to hospitals, which are likely to buy a "whole package" from J&J because of this competitiveness.

Over the last decade, Johnson & Johnson has spent $30 billion to acquire 52 businesses. However, because of the company's size, making a contribution to income through an acquisition program is very difficult, and, thus, the sustainability of an acquisition strategy is questionable. Primarily because of the acquisition strategy, as well as internal development and diversification, J&J's set of businesses is quite decentralized. The near total autonomy and independence that have been maintained in the corporation have fostered an entrepreneurial attitude that has kept J&J quite competitive in world markets.

However, William C. Weldon, J&J's current CEO, sees an opportunity for top-line growth in the scientific convergence of drugs, devices, and diagnostics. The convergence in science has allowed contributions from one discipline to another, leading to significantly greater sophistication in disease treatments. "Sutures are coated with drugs to prevent infections; tests based on genomic research could determine who would respond to a certain cancer drug; defibrillators may be linked to computers that alert doctors when patients have abnormal heart rhythms." J&J will soon release a drug-emitting stent. A stent is a tubelike device that holds arteries open in heart patients. The drug-emitting stent will release a drug that helps keep the artery from narrowing again. These stents are expected to be enormously popular with doctors and heart patients, resulting in a significant commercial success for J&J. Weldon suggests that this convergence will allow J&J to do many things it has not done before. However, convergence also requires operating relatedness between the company's various business units in a specific product area as well as corporate relatedness, which enables transfer of knowledge between different businesses.

To achieve this opportunity, however, the systems necessary to manage J&J's diversified set of businesses must change. J&J's famed autonomy (which accompanies its highly decentralized operations) must evolve to a new system that fosters better communication and much more frequent collaboration among the company's decentralized operations and between the head office and formerly independent businesses. The challenge will be to foster cooperation and collaboration among businesses without undermining the entrepreneurial

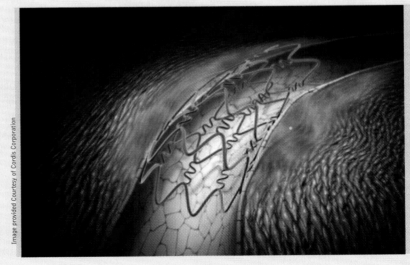

Image provided Courtesy of Cordis Corporation

Johnson & Johnson is improving its top-line growth through the convergence of drugs, devices, and diagnostics. This image shows its CYPHER™ Sirolimus-eluting Coronary Stent (a drug-emitting stent) inside an artery.

spirit that has created J&J's success. This collaboration will require more centralization than heretofore has been the norm at J&J.

In summary, capitalizing on product convergence will require that J&J move toward both operational and corporate relatedness simultaneously. This seems risky for a company that has been totally decentralized. However, Weldon is very competitive and will seek to accomplish this desirable outcome as he has in the past, by pursuing "near impossible goals for his people and holding them to it." It will be interesting to see whether J&J can effectively pursue operational and corporate relatedness simultaneously.

SOURCES: A. Barrett, 2003, Staying on top: Can he keep up the growth? *Business Week*, May 5, 60–68; J. Carey & M. Arndt, 2003, Combo medicine: The union of drugs and devices offers major breakthroughs in health care—but can regulators keep up? *Business Week*, March 25, 156–158; M. E. Egan, 2003, Patchwork, *Forbes*, http://www.forbes.com, June 9; M. Herper, 2003, For drug deals, think small, *Forbes*, http://www.forbes.com, February 10; M. Herper, 2003, J&J earnings soar, but competition looms, *Forbes*, http://www.forbes.com, January 21.

Simultaneous Operational Relatedness and Corporate Relatedness

As Figure 6.2 suggests, some firms simultaneously seek operational and corporate forms of economies of scope.[69] Because simultaneously managing two sources of knowledge is very difficult, such efforts often fail, creating diseconomies of scope.[70] Although this strategy is difficult to implement, if the firm is successful, it could create value that is hard for competitors to imitate.

Johnson & Johnson is trying to achieve both operational relatedness and corporate relatedness in a decentralized set of businesses. Johnson & Johnson's strategy, as illustrated in the Strategic Focus, may be difficult to achieve because of a corporate culture focused on decentralization.

Although it may be difficult for J&J to pursue both operational and corporate synergy, Disney's strategy has been effective compared to others when measured by revenues generated from successful movies. By using operational relatedness and corporate relatedness, Disney made $3 billion on the 150 products that were marketed with its movie *The Lion King.* Sony's *Men in Black* was a super hit at the box office and earned $600 million, but box-office and video revenues were practically the entire story. Disney was able to accomplish its great success by sharing activities around the *Lion King* theme within its movie, theme park, music, and retail products divisions, while at the same time transferring knowledge into these same divisions, creating a music CD, *Rhythm of the Pride Lands,* and producing a video, *Simba's Pride.* In addition, there were *Lion King* themes at Disney resorts and Animal Kingdom parks.[71] However, it is difficult for analysts from outside the firm to fully assess the value-creating potential of pursuing both operational relatedness and corporate relatedness. Disney's assets as well as those of other media firms such as AOL Time Warner have been discounted somewhat because "the biggest lingering question is whether multiple revenue streams will outpace multiple-platform overhead."[72]

Unrelated Diversification

Firms do not seek either operational relatedness or corporate relatedness when using the unrelated diversification corporate-level strategy. An unrelated diversification strategy (see Figure 6.2) can create value through two types of financial economies.

Financial economies are cost savings realized through improved allocations of financial resources based on investments inside or outside the firm.[73]

The first type of financial economy results from efficient internal capital allocations. This approach seeks to reduce risk among the firm's business units—for example, through the development of a portfolio of businesses with different risk profiles. The approach thereby reduces business risk for the total corporation. The second type of financial economy is concerned with purchasing other corporations and restructuring their assets. This approach finds the diversified firm buying another company, restructuring that company's assets in ways that allow it to operate more profitably, and then selling the company for a profit in the external market.[74]

Efficient Internal Capital Market Allocation

In a market economy, capital markets are thought to efficiently allocate capital. Efficiency results from investors' purchasing of firm equity shares (ownership) that have high future cash-flow values. Capital is also allocated through debt as shareholders and debtholders try to improve the value of their investments by taking stakes in businesses with high growth prospects.

In large diversified firms, the corporate office distributes capital to business divisions to create value for the overall company. Such an approach may provide gains from internal capital market allocation relative to the external capital market.[75] This happens because while managing the firm's portfolio of businesses, the corporate office may gain access to detailed and accurate information regarding those businesses' actual and prospective performance.

The corporate office needs to convey its ability to create value in this manner to the market. One way firms can do this is through tracking stocks, as General Motors (GM) has done for its Hughes Electronics division.[76] GM created a new stock listing for Hughes that conveyed better information to the market about this additional asset. This approach allows more scrutiny by the market and thus more transparency of increasingly complex and diversified internal operations. It also increases the ability to move the assets to another company through a sell-off if this becomes necessary. In fact, in 2003, News Corp. made a $6 billion offer for the Hughes assets that operate DirecTV, a satellite TV system.[77]

Compared with corporate office personnel, investors have relatively limited access to internal information and can only estimate divisional performance and future business prospects. Although businesses seeking capital must provide information to potential suppliers (such as banks or insurance companies), firms with internal capital markets may have at least two informational advantages. First, information provided to capital markets through annual reports and other sources may not include negative information, instead emphasizing positive prospects and outcomes. External sources of capital have limited ability to understand the operational dynamics of large organizations. Even external shareholders who have access to information have no guarantee of full and complete disclosure.[78] Second, although a firm must disseminate information, that information also becomes simultaneously available to the firm's current and potential competitors. With insights gained by studying such information, competitors might attempt to duplicate a firm's competitive advantage. Thus, an ability to efficiently allocate capital through an internal market may help the firm protect its competitive advantages.

If intervention from outside the firm is required to make corrections to capital allocations, only significant changes are possible, such as forcing the firm into bankruptcy or changing the top management team. Alternatively, in an internal capital market, the corporate office can fine-tune its corrections, such as choosing to adjust managerial incentives or suggesting strategic changes in a division. Thus, capital can be allocated according to more specific criteria than is possible with external market allocations. Because it has less accurate information, the external capital market may fail to allocate resources adequately to high-potential investments compared with corporate office investments. The corporate office of a diversified company can more effectively perform such tasks as disciplining underperforming management teams through resource allocations.[79]

Research suggests, however, that in efficient capital markets, the unrelated diversification strategy may be discounted.[80] "For years, stock markets have applied a 'conglomerate discount': they value diversified manufacturing conglomerates at 20 percent less, on average, than the value of the sum of their parts. The discount still applies, in good economic times and bad. Extraordinary manufacturers (like GE) can defy it for a while, but more ordinary ones (like Philips and Siemens) cannot."[81]

Some firms still use the unrelated diversification strategy.[82] These large, diversified business groups are found in many European countries (for example, Spain's Grupo Ferrovial, an industrial, engineering, and financial conglomerate) and throughout emerging economies (for example, Hong Kong's Shanghai Industrial Holdings Ltd. and Malaysia's Sime Darby Berhad). Research indicates that the conglomerate or unrelated diversification strategy has not disappeared in Europe, where the number of firms using it has actually increased.[83] Although many conglomerates, such as ITT and Hansen Trust, have refocused, other unrelated diversified firms have replaced them.

The Achilles' heel of the unrelated diversification strategy is that conglomerates in developed economies have a fairly short life cycle because financial economies are more easily duplicated than are the gains derived from operational relatedness and corporate relatedness. This is less of a problem in emerging economies, where the absence of a "soft infrastructure" (including effective financial intermediaries, sound regulations, and contract laws) supports and encourages use of the unrelated diversification strategy.[84] In fact, in emerging economies such as those in India and Chile, diversification increases performance of firms affiliated with large diversified business groups.[85]

Restructuring

Financial economies can also be created when firms learn how to create value by buying and selling other companies' assets in the external market.[86] As in the real estate business, buying assets at low prices, restructuring them, and selling them at a price exceeding their cost generates a positive return on the firm's invested capital.[87]

Sara Lee Corporation is a prime example of a diversified company that seeks to acquire and then restructure the operations acquired. It owns over 200 brands, including Jimmy Dean sausages, its namesake baked goods, Hanes underwear, and Earthgrains bread. Managing so many different brands has proven a challenge: growth has been flat for the past several years. Thus, the company has not excelled at restructuring the businesses that it has acquired. Unlike Procter & Gamble, Sara Lee hasn't discovered how to focus on key brands to drive growth. L'eggs pantyhose has had years of double-digit volume declines. Folgers has outperformed Chock full o'Nuts coffee. The current CEO, Steven McMillan, is busy sorting out which businesses and brands to keep and which to sell in an attempt to reduce the firm's diversification. One proposal suggests that the best option would be to split the firm into its three main businesses—food (52 percent of sales), apparel (37 percent), and household goods (11 percent).[88]

Under former CEO Dennis L. Kozlowski, Tyco International, Ltd., excelled at financial economies through restructuring. Tyco focused on two types of acquisitions: platform, which represent new bases for future acquisitions, and add-on, in markets in which Tyco currently has a major presence. As with many unrelated diversified firms, Tyco acquires mature product lines. However, completing large numbers of complex transactions has resulted in accounting practices that aren't as transparent as stakeholders now demand. In fact, many of Tyco's top executives, including Kozlowski, were arrested for fraud, and the new CEO, Edward Breen, has been restructuring the firm's businesses to overcome "the flagrant accounting, ethical, and governance abuses of his predecessor." Actions being taken in firms such as Tyco suggest that firms creating value through financial economies are responding to the demand for greater transparency in their practices, thus providing the information the market requires to more accurately estimate the value the diversified firm is creating when using the unrelated diversification strategy.[89]

Creating financial economies by acquiring and restructuring other companies' assets requires an understanding of significant trade-offs. Success usually calls for a focus on mature, low-technology businesses because of the uncertainty of demand for high-technology products. Otherwise, resource allocation decisions become too complex, creating information-processing overload on the small corporate staffs of unrelated diversified firms. High-technology businesses are often human resource dependent; these people can leave or demand higher pay and thus appropriate or deplete the value of an acquired firm.[90] Service businesses with a client orientation are also difficult to buy and sell because of their client-based sales orientation. Sales staffs of service businesses are more mobile than those of manufacturing-oriented businesses and may seek jobs with a competitor, taking clients with them.[91] David Bell, CEO of Interpublic Group (IPG), has found it very difficult to manage the advertising agency conglomerate. IPG bought more than 300 advertising agencies and consulting firms in five years. Saddled with significant debt because it paid high prices for some of its acquisitions, IPG has not been able to gain economies of scope between the units; very few large firms have sought to take advantage of its global scale. The separate IPG agencies seem to be fiercely independent, and clients are mainly relationship based, because advertising is sold more through personal flare than firm reputation.[92] Thus, restructuring a service business can be a difficult strategy to effectively implement.

Diversification: Incentives and Resources

The economic reasons given in the preceding section summarize conditions under which diversification strategies can increase a firm's value. Diversification, however, is also often undertaken with the expectation that it will prevent reductions in firm value. Thus, there are reasons to diversify that are value neutral. In fact, some research suggests that all diversification leads to trade-offs and some suboptimization.[93] Nonetheless, as we explain next, several incentives may lead a firm to pursue further diversification.

Incentives to Diversify

Incentives to diversify come from both the external environment and a firm's internal environment. The term *incentive* implies that managers have choices. External incentives include antitrust regulations and tax laws. Internal incentives include low performance, uncertain future cash flows, and pursuit of synergy and reduction of risk for the firm. Several of these incentives are illustrated in the Strategic Focus on Yahoo!.

ANTITRUST REGULATION AND TAX LAWS

Government antitrust policies and tax laws provided incentives for U.S. firms to diversify in the 1960s and 1970s.[94] Antitrust laws prohibiting mergers that created increased market power (via either vertical or horizontal integration) were stringently enforced during that period.[95] As a result, many of the mergers during the 1960s and 1970s were "conglomerate" in character, involving companies pursuing different lines of business. Merger activity that produced conglomerate diversification was encouraged primarily by the Celler-Kefauver Antimerger Act (1950), which discouraged horizontal and vertical mergers. For example, between 1973 and 1977, 79.1 percent of all mergers were conglomerate.[96]

Yahoo!'s Low Performance and Uncertain Future Have Led to Strategic Diversification

After a brush with bankruptcy when the Internet bubble burst in 1999, Yahoo! has managed to improve performance under the management of new CEO Terry Semel. By changing the culture at Yahoo! from that of the quintessential "go-go" Internet start-up to a more conservative and principled style, Semel has made significant progress. Yahoo! realized poor performance along with many other Internet companies when its sky-high market capitalization evaporated in 1999. In addition, Yahoo! experienced continued uncertainty due to competition. Low performance and uncertainty created an incentive to change the firm's speculative approach. Accordingly, Semel guided Yahoo! in pursuing a diversification strategy that included acquiring HotJobs.com (a job search website) and Inktomi (focused on search engine technology), and forming partnerships with Overture Services, Inc. (a web advertising specialist) and SBC Communications (to extend Yahoo!'s services on SBC's broadband network). As a result of these diversification moves, revenues have grown significantly, and Yahoo! is profitable again. However, the market is competitive, and Yahoo! must continue to make appropriate investments to diversify its offerings.

Because Yahoo! began as a free service, its biggest obstacle has been finding a way to turn all of its viewers into paying customers. Looking to the future, Semel envisions Yahoo! as a "digital theme park" where customers can access a set of appealing offerings: digital music, online games, job listings, and premium e-mail. However, other firms, including media giant AOL Time Warner and software powerhouse Microsoft, have the same strategy, each with competitive advantages. AOL, for example, has access to a huge library of popular content from Time Warner while MSN benefits from Microsoft's software muscle and significant cash reserves as well as its broadband partnerships (like Yahoo!'s partnership with SBC Communications) that get it into 27 percent more homes than Yahoo!. Thus, although Yahoo!'s diversification strategy has helped it survive, the winner of this battle for domination is unknown. In addition to competing with AOL and MSN, Yahoo! competes in its original arena—search engines. The popular search engine Google is Yahoo!'s main rival in this arena, especially since Google won 4 percent more viewers in the last quarter of 2002 than did Yahoo!. Web surfers favor Google's uncluttered searches over Internet portals such as Yahoo! and MSN. This is important because advertisers are starting to shift advertising dollars from portals like Yahoo! to search engines like Google. This trend is occurring because "people are tuned out on banner ads and tuned in to search results." Banner ads are generally ignored, but when advertised products appear when a user instigates a search through a search engine, more exposure and sales success result. Yahoo! currently uses Google's search technology, but recently purchased Inktomi, another search technology firm, and may seek to move away from Google in order to gain additional revenue from advertisers.

Yahoo! competes in two different markets—web portals and search engines—with different competitors in each market. The firm has diversified the paid product offerings on its portal, including job opportunities through HotJobs.com, and is looking into deals

Terry Semel, chairman and CEO of Yahoo!, talks with Jean-Marie Messier (left), former chairman and CEO of Vivendi Universal, before a session of the World Economic Forum in New York.

AP Photo/Henny Abrams, Pool

to add online travel and classified ads for cars. Yahoo! is now more profitable, but the competition is stiff as the Internet moves to broadband offerings. Yahoo!'s continued profitability and survival depend on the quality of its diversification strategy.

SOURCES: 2003, A dotcom revival? *The Economist*, http//:www.economist.com, May 7; B. Elgin, 2003, Yahoo! Act two, *Business Week*, June 2, 70–76; B. Elgin, 2003, Can Yahoo! make the bounce last? Maybe, if new broadband and Net search efforts succeed, *Business Week*, February 17, 41; M. Mangalindan, 2003, Leading the news: Yahoo tops profit forecasts on 47% revenue jump, *Wall Street Journal*, April 10, A3.

During the 1980s, antitrust enforcement lessened, resulting in more and larger horizontal mergers (acquisitions of target firms in the same line of business, such as a merger between two oil companies).[97] In addition, investment bankers became more open to the kinds of mergers facilitated by the change in the regulation; as a consequence, takeovers increased to unprecedented numbers.[98] The conglomerates, or highly diversified firms, of the 1960s and 1970s became more "focused" in the 1980s and early 1990s as merger constraints were relaxed and restructuring was implemented.[99]

In the late 1990s and early 2000s, antitrust concerns emerged again with the large volume of mergers and acquisitions (see Chapter 7).[100] Thus, mergers are now receiving more scrutiny than they did in the 1980s and through the early 1990s.[101]

The tax effects of diversification stem not only from individual tax rates, but also from corporate tax changes. Some companies (especially mature ones) generate more cash from their operations than they can reinvest profitably. Some argue that *free cash flows* (liquid financial assets for which investments in current businesses are no longer economically viable) should be redistributed to shareholders as dividends.[102] However, in the 1960s and 1970s, dividends were taxed more heavily than ordinary personal income. As a result, before 1980, shareholders preferred that firms use free cash flows to buy and build companies in high-performance industries. If the firm's stock value appreciated over the long term, shareholders might receive a better return on those funds than if the funds had been redistributed as dividends, because returns from stock sales would be taxed more lightly under capital gains rules than would dividends.

Under the 1986 Tax Reform Act, however, the top individual ordinary income tax rate was reduced from 50 to 28 percent, and the special capital gains tax was also changed, treating capital gains as ordinary income. These changes created an incentive for shareholders to stop encouraging firms to retain funds for purposes of diversification. These tax law changes also influenced an increase in divestitures of unrelated business units after 1984. Thus, while individual tax rates for capital gains and dividends created a shareholder incentive to increase diversification before 1986, they encouraged less diversification after 1986, unless it was funded by tax-deductible debt. The elimination of personal interest deductions, as well as the lower attractiveness of retained earnings to shareholders, might prompt the use of more leverage by firms, for which interest expense is tax deductible.

Corporate tax laws also affect diversification. Acquisitions typically increase a firm's depreciable asset allowances. Increased depreciation (a non-cash-flow expense) produces lower taxable income, thereby providing an additional incentive for acquisitions. Before 1986, acquisitions may have been the most attractive means for securing tax benefits,[103] but the 1986 Tax Reform Act diminished some of the corporate tax advantages of diversification.[104] The recent changes recommended by the Financial Accounting Standards Board (FASB) regarding the elimination of the "pooling of interests" method for accounting for the acquired firm's assets and the elimination of the write-off for research and development in process reduce some of the incentives to make acquisitions, especially related acquisitions in high-technology industries (these changes are discussed further in Chapter 7).[105]

Although there was a loosening of federal regulations in the 1980s and a retightening in the late 1990s, a number of industries have experienced increased merger activity due to industry-specific deregulation activity, including banking, telecommunications, oil and gas, and electric utilities. Regulations changes have also affected convergence between media and telecommunications industries, which has allowed a number of mergers, such as the successive Time Warner and AOL Time Warner mergers. The Federal Communications Commission (FCC) has made a highly contested ruling "allowing broadcasters to own TV stations that reach 45 percent of U.S. households, up from 35 percent, own three stations in the largest markets (up from two) and own a TV station and newspaper in the same town."[106] Critics argued that the change in regulations would allow "an orgy of mergers and acquisitions" and that "it is a victory for free enterprise, but it is not a victory for free speech."[107] Because of the impending regulatory change, a number of firms have been eyeing potential acquisitions. For example, the FCC has allowed cable companies to get into local phone service. In Orange County, California, cable TV companies now provide 25 percent of local phone service. Phone companies have also been moving into selling TV service, although technology has been hindered until recently because high frequencies, which TV signals use, fade out on thin copper wires. At one point, to overcome this problem, SBC, a large local telephone operator, considered acquiring DirecTV, a satellite TV market leader.[108] Thus, regulatory changes create incentives for diversification.

Low Performance

Sears hopes that diversification through Lands' End apparel will increase the reputation of its own apparel and help push it out of the near-bankruptcy conditions it has experienced in the last few years.

Some research shows that low returns are related to greater levels of diversification.[109] If "high performance eliminates the need for greater diversification,"[110] then low performance may provide an incentive for diversification. As the Strategic Focus on Yahoo! illustrates, firms plagued by poor performance often take higher risks.[111] Poor performance may lead to increased diversification, as it did with Sears, Roebuck and Co., especially if resources exist to do so.[112] Sears has struggled on the edge of bankruptcy the past few years. Its high-margin appliance business is under attack from Home Depot and Lowe's. Sears has strong internal reasons to diversify, and it did so by purchasing clothes maker Lands' End in 2002. Sears expects that the company's high-quality image will improve its own apparel's reputation, although some question whether this will be at the cost of Lands' End's own reputation.[113] Continued poor returns following additional diversification, however, may slow the pace of diversification and even lead to divestitures.

This has happened to Sears previously. In 1981, Sears diversified into financial services by acquiring Coldwell Banker and Dean Witter Reynolds, Inc. The anticipated synergies in financial services did not materialize, and Sears' retail performance deteriorated. In 1992, Sears announced the divestiture of financial services and a refocusing on retail operations.[114] At least, the Lands' End acquisition is closely related to Sears' core business of retail sales.

A firm can overdiversify as Sears did earlier in its history. Thus, an overall curvilinear relationship, as illustrated in Figure 6.3, may exist between diversification and performance.[115] The German media company Bertelsmann was led by its former CEO Thomas Middelhoff into a variety of new ventures, especially Internet ones, that have proved to be a drag on the company's resources and have provided very little

© Susan Van Etten/PhotoEdit

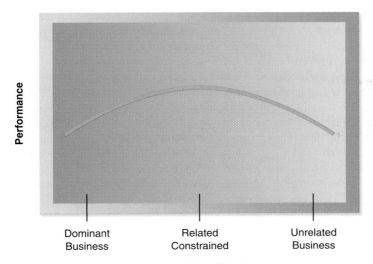

return on investment. The new CEO, Gunter Thielen, is emphasizing a return to basics by getting rid of non-core businesses, such as the Internet ventures. "The course has been pretty clear since Middelhoff left," says a German consultant: "Focus on the businesses that they understand and dominate." These businesses include producing books, magazines, music, and TV shows. Under Thielen's leadership, Bertelsmann has regrouped and refocused on what it does best.[116]

UNCERTAIN FUTURE CASH FLOWS

As a firm's product line matures or is threatened, diversification may be taken as an important defensive strategy.[117] Small firms and companies in mature or maturing industries sometimes find it necessary to diversify for long-term survival.[118] Yahoo!'s strategy has been built on diversification in order to survive competition from other portals such as AOL and MSN and search engine Google (see the Strategic Focus). Certainly, uncertainty was one of the dominant reasons for diversification among railroad firms during the 1960s and 1970s. Railroads diversified primarily because the trucking industry was perceived to have significant negative effects for rail transportation and thus created demand uncertainty. Uncertainty, however, can be derived from supply and distribution sources as well as from demand sources.

Intel is turning its core competence of technical development toward developing chips for cell phones. As the functions of PCs and phones continue to merge, Intel must learn to master wireless technology or begin to lose its core microprocessor market. With a goal to provide the "brains" of cellular phones, Intel is moving from just providing memory chips to providing the microprocessors for high-end cell phones. In the next iteration of its Manitoba chip, it will combine memory, processor, and voice transmission ability on a single chip. As Intel learns to bring its technological and financial resources (the company has $11 billion in cash) to bear on the market, it could change the handset market to a commodities market, threatening the profits and business models of handset makers.[119] But the move to diversify is driven by the uncertainty in the memory chip area for cell phones.

Diversified firms pursuing economies of scope often have investments that are too inflexible to realize synergy between business units. As a result, a number of problems may arise. **Synergy** exists when the value created by business units working together exceeds the value those same units create working independently. But, as a firm increases its relatedness between business units, it also increases its risk of corporate failure, because synergy produces joint interdependence between business units and the firm's flexibility to respond is constrained. This threat may force two basic decisions.

First, the firm may reduce its level of technological change by operating in more certain environments. This behavior may make the firm risk averse and thus uninterested in pursuing new product lines that have potential, but are not proven. Alternatively, the firm may constrain its level of activity sharing and forgo synergy's benefits. Either or both decisions may lead to further diversification. The former would lead to related diversification into industries in which more certainty exists. The latter may produce additional, but unrelated, diversification.[120] Research suggests that a firm using a related diversification strategy is more careful in bidding for new businesses, whereas a firm pursuing an unrelated diversification strategy may be more likely to overprice its bid, because an unrelated bidder may not have full information about the acquired firm.[121]

For example, Volkswagen's U.S. sales slipped almost 11 percent in the first quarter of 2003, and in Europe its Golf model was dethroned by Peugeot as the best-selling car. Net profit dropped 11.2 percent from the previous year. While there is tough competition in the auto industry, VW's conservative relatedness strategy is also partly to blame for the firm's foundering. All of its cars (from Audis to VWs to Skodas) are built on just a few platforms, which blurs brand image and cannibalizes sales within the group. Volkswagen has pursued related diversification in an effort to make operations more efficient, but in doing so, it has been too conservative in design and seems to have dimmed the distinctions between its auto brands.[122] The Crossfire, branded as a Chrysler product, is a bolder move because it is the first "synergistic" model offered to the market by Chrysler and Mercedes-Benz. Nearly 40 percent of the upscale car is based on Mercedes' content, "including its 3.2 liter engine, transmission and axles." However, the risk is that consumers will perceive it as a "Mercedes that is somewhat cheaper" and devalue the Mercedes brand.[123] Thus, although synergy is a strong incentive to diversify, it may compromise the pursuit of appropriate levels of diversification and risk.

Resources and Diversification

Although a firm may have incentives to diversify, it must also possess the resources required to create value through diversification.[124] As mentioned earlier, tangible, intangible, and financial resources all facilitate diversification. Resources vary in their utility for value creation, however, because of differences in rarity and mobility—that is, some resources are easier for competitors to duplicate because they are not rare, valuable, costly to imitate, and nonsubstitutable (see Chapter 3). For instance, free cash flows are a financial resource that may be used to diversify the firm. Because financial resources are more flexible and common, they are less likely to create value compared with other types of resources and less likely to be a source of competitive advantage.[125]

However, as a financial resource, cash can be used to invest in other resources that can lead to more valuable and less imitable advantages. For example, "Microsoft's net cash stash of $43 billion would, by itself, make it the 35th-largest company in the S&P 500 and exceeds the combined market values of Ford and General Motors."[126] With this much cash in reserve (more, by far, than any other company), Microsoft is

---

Synergy exists when the value created by business units working together exceeds the value those same units create working independently.

able to invest heavily in R&D, to gradually build a market presence with products such as Xbox, Microsoft's video game machine, and to make diversifying acquisitions of other companies and new business ventures. "Microsoft is able to spend more than $4.3 billion a year on R&D."[127] This level of cash creates significant flexibility, allowing Microsoft to invest in new product ideas and provide the support required for an idea to evolve into a possible competitive advantage. Hence, as this example suggests, excess cash can be the conduit the firm needs to create more sustainable advantages.[128]

Tangible resources usually include the plant and equipment necessary to produce a product and tend to be less-flexible assets. Any excess capacity often can be used only for closely related products, especially those requiring highly similar manufacturing technologies. Excess capacity of other tangible resources, such as a sales force, can be used to diversify more easily. Again, excess capacity in a sales force is more effective with related diversification, because it may be utilized to sell similar products. The sales force would be more knowledgeable about related-product characteristics, customers, and distribution channels.[129] Tangible resources may create resource interrelationships in production, marketing, procurement, and technology, defined earlier as activity sharing. Intangible resources are more flexible than tangible physical assets in facilitating diversification. Although the sharing of tangible resources may induce diversification, intangible resources such as tacit knowledge could encourage even more diversification.[130]

Sometimes, however, the perceived resources advantages to diversification do not work out as expected. Media companies that invested in sports teams are realizing that they don't have the resources for this type of diversification and that their resources might be better spent elsewhere. News Corp., AOL Time Warner, and Disney are trying to sell the L.A. Dodgers, the Atlanta Braves, and the Anaheim Angels, respectively. Both Disney and News Corp. overvalued the teams they purchased as programming assets and undervalued their liabilities. Additionally, the traditional use of sports teams' losses as a tax write-off is less acceptable in the current rigorous corporate governance environment. Finally, cable TV economies have changed, and companies are unable to recoup astronomical player salaries through increased charges to cable operators. Unwilling to take additional losses, the media companies are seeking to sell the teams and divert their resources elsewhere.[131]

Managerial Motives to Diversify

Managerial motives for diversification may exist independently of incentives and resources and include managerial risk reduction and a desire for increased compensation.[132] For instance, diversification may reduce top-level managers' employment risk (the risk of job loss or income reduction). That is, corporate executives may diversify a firm in order to diversify their own employment risk, as long as profitability does not suffer excessively.[133]

Diversification provides an additional benefit to managers that shareholders do not enjoy. Diversification and firm size are highly correlated, and as size increases, so does executive compensation.[134] Large firms are more complex and difficult to manage; thus, managers of larger firms usually receive more compensation.[135] Higher compensation may serve as a motive for managers to engage in greater diversification. Governance mechanisms, such as the board of directors, monitoring by owners, executive compensation ceilings, and the market for corporate control, may limit managerial tendencies to overdiversify. These mechanisms are discussed in more detail in Chapter 10.

On the other hand, governance mechanisms may not be strong, and, in some instances, managers may diversify the firm to the point that it fails to earn even average returns.[136] The loss of adequate internal governance may result in poor relative performance, thereby triggering a threat of takeover. Although takeovers may improve efficiency by replacing ineffective managerial teams, managers may avoid takeovers through defensive tactics, such as "poison pills," or may reduce their own exposure with "golden parachute" agreements.[137] Therefore, an external governance threat, although restraining managers, does not flawlessly control managerial motives for diversification.[138]

Most large publicly held firms are profitable because managers are positive stewards of firm resources, and many of their strategic actions (e.g., diversification strategies) contribute to the firm's success.[139] As mentioned, governance devices should be designed to deal with exceptions to the norms of achieving strategic competitiveness and increasing shareholder wealth through the firm's earning of above-average returns. Thus, it is overly pessimistic to assume that managers usually act in their own self-interest as opposed to their firm's interest.[140]

Managers may also be held in check by concerns for their reputation. If a positive reputation facilitates power, a poor reputation may reduce it. Likewise, a strong external market for managerial talent may deter managers from pursuing inappropriate diversification.[141] In addition, a diversified firm may police other firms by acquiring those that are poorly managed in order to restructure its own asset base. Knowing that their firms could be acquired if they are not managed successfully encourages managers to use value-creating strategies.

Even when governance mechanisms cause managers to correct a problem of poorly implemented diversification or overdiversification, these moves are not without trade-offs. For instance, firms that are spun off may not realize productivity gains, even though spinning them off is in the best interest of the divesting firm.[142] Accordingly, the assumption that managers need disciplining may not be entirely correct, and sometimes governance may create consequences that are worse than those resulting from overdiversification. Governance that is excessive may cause a firm's managers to be overly cautious and risk averse.[143]

As shown in Figure 6.4, the level of diversification that can be expected to have the greatest positive effect on performance is based partly on how the interaction of resources, managerial motives, and incentives affects the adoption of particular diversification strategies. As indicated earlier, the greater the incentives and the more flexible the resources, the higher is the level of expected diversification. Financial resources (the most flexible) should have a stronger relationship to the extent of diversification than either tangible or intangible resources. Tangible resources (the most inflexible) are useful primarily for related diversification.

As discussed in this chapter, firms can create more value by effectively using diversification strategies. However, diversification must be kept in check by corporate governance (see Chapter 10). Appropriate strategy implementation tools, such as organizational structures, are also important (see Chapter 11).

We have described corporate-level strategies in this chapter. In the next one, we discuss mergers and acquisitions as prominent means for firms to diversify. These trends toward more diversification through acquisitions, which have been partially reversed due to restructuring (see Chapter 7), indicate that learning has taken place regarding corporate-level diversification strategies.[144] Accordingly, firms that diversify should do so cautiously, choosing to focus on relatively few, rather than many, businesses.[145] In fact, research suggests that although unrelated diversification has decreased, related diversification has increased, possibly due to the restructuring that continued into the 1990s and early 21st century.[146] This sequence of diversification followed by restructuring is now taking place in Europe and other places such as Korea, mirroring actions of firms in the United States and the United Kingdom.[147] Firms can improve their strategic competitiveness when they pursue a level of diversification that is appropriate for their resources (especially financial resources) and core competencies and the opportunities and threats in their country's institutional and competitive environments.[148]

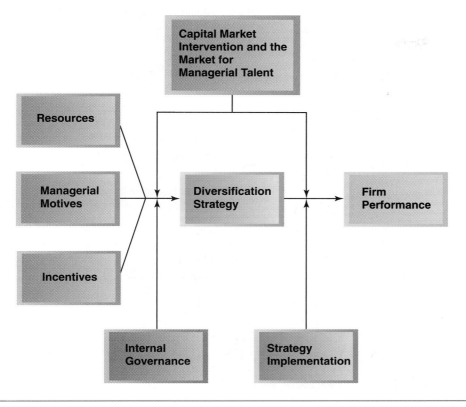

Summary Model of the Relationship between Firm Performance and Diversification

Figure 6.4

SOURCE: R. E. Hoskisson & M. A. Hitt, 1990, Antecedents and performance outcomes of diversification: A review and critique of theoretical perspectives, *Journal of Management*, 16: 498.

Summary

- Using a single- or dominant-business corporate-level strategy may be preferable to seeking a more diversified strategy, unless a corporation can develop economies of scope or financial economies between businesses, or unless it can obtain market power through additional levels of diversification. These economies and market power are the main sources of value creation when the firm diversifies.

- Related diversification creates value through the sharing of activities or the transfer of core competencies.

- Sharing activities usually involves sharing tangible resources between businesses. Transferring core competencies involves transferring core competencies developed in one business to another one. It also may involve transferring competencies between the corporate office and a business unit.

- Sharing activities is usually associated with the related constrained diversification corporate-level strategy. Activity sharing is costly to implement and coordinate, may create unequal benefits for the divisions involved in the sharing, and may lead to fewer managerial risk-taking behaviors.

- Transferring core competencies is often associated with related linked (or mixed related and unrelated) diversification, although firms pursuing both sharing activities and transferring core competencies can use it.

- Efficiently allocating resources or restructuring a target firm's assets and placing them under rigorous financial controls are two ways to accomplish successful unrelated diversification. These methods focus on obtaining financial economies.

- The primary reason a firm diversifies is to create more value. However, diversification is sometimes pursued because of incentives from tax and antitrust government policies, performance disappointments, or uncertainties about future cash flow, or to reduce risk.

- Managerial motives to diversify (including to increase compensation) can lead to overdiversification and a reduction in the firm's value-creating ability. On the other hand, managers can also be good stewards of the firm's assets.

- Managers need to pay attention to their firm's internal environment and its external environment when making decisions about the optimum level of diversification for their company. Of course, internal resources are important determinants of the direction that diversification should take. However, conditions in the firm's external environment may facilitate additional levels of diversification as might unexpected threats from competitors.

Review Questions

1. What is corporate-level strategy? Why is it important to the diversified firm?

2. What are the advantages and disadvantages of single- and dominant-business strategies, compared with those of firms with higher levels of diversification?

3. What are three reasons that firms choose to become more diversified by moving away from either a single- or a dominant-business corporate-level strategy?

4. How do firms share activities or transfer core competencies to obtain economies of scope when using a related diversification strategy?

5. What are the two ways to obtain financial economies when using an unrelated diversification strategy?

6. What incentives and resources encourage diversification?

7. What motives might encourage managers to diversify the firm beyond an appropriate level?

Experiential Exercises

Diversification: The Good and the Not So Good

As a member of the strategic management team for a very successful sporting goods firm that specializes in the manufacturing and marketing of soccer equipment, you have been asked to provide your thoughts as to whether the firm should diversify and to what extent.

Part One. List the advantages and disadvantages of diversification in the following table.

Part Two. Provide examples of related and unrelated diversification areas that you feel might be appropriate for the firm, including some specific advantages and disadvantages that the firm might find for each.

Advantages	Disadvantages

Diversification at Citibank

Organizations often anticipate that following a diversification strategy can create value on many fronts, including economies of scale and scope, along with increased market power. However, not all diversification efforts prove to be as successful as originally planned. Firms sometimes must reconsider their initial diversification strategy and frequently reverse or drastically alter their strategic decisions, often within a very short time frame. For instance, Citibank and Travelers Insurance Group merged in the late 1990s to form Citigroup, a huge financial supermarket of sorts that offered a plethora of products, including investment banking, credit cards, mortgages, insurance, and more. By 2002, Travelers Property Casualty Corporation had been spun out of Citigroup. Explore the circumstances and expected outcome of the original Travelers–Citibank merger. What went wrong? Could such problems have been avoided?

Notes

1. M. E. Porter, 1980, *Competitive Strategy*, New York: The Free Press, xvi.
2. W. P. Wan & R. E. Hoskisson, 2003, Home country environments, corporate diversification strategies and firm performance, *Academy of Management Journal*, 46: 27–45; D. D. Bergh, 2001, Diversification strategy research at a crossroads: Established, emerging and anticipated paths, in M. A. Hitt, R. E. Freeman, & J. S. Harrison (eds.), *Handbook of Strategic Management*, Oxford, UK: Blackwell Publishers, 363–383; E. Hoskisson, R. A. Johnson, D. Yiu, & W. P. Wan, 2001, Restructuring strategies of diversified business groups: Differences associated with country institutional environments, in M. A. Hitt, R. E. Freeman, & J. S. Harrison (eds.), *Handbook of Strategic Management*, Oxford, UK: Blackwell Publishers, 433–463.
3. E. H. Bowman & C. E. Helfat, 2001, Does corporate strategy matter? *Strategic Management Journal*, 22: 1–23; M. A. Hitt, R. E. Hoskisson, & H. Kim, 1997, International diversification: Effects on innovation and firm performance in product-diversified firms, *Academy of Management Journal*, 40: 767–798.
4. M. Mayer & R. Whittington, 2003, Diversification in context: A cross-national and cross-temporal extension, *Strategic Management Journal*, 24: 773–781; R. L. Simerly & M. Li, 2000, Environmental dynamism, capital structure and performance: A theoretical integration and an empirical test, *Strategic Management Journal*, 21: 31–49; D. D. Bergh & M. W. Lawless, 1998, Portfolio restructuring and limits to hierarchical governance: The effects of environmental uncertainty and diversification strategy, *Organization Science*, 9: 87–102.
5. M. E. Porter, 1987, From competitive advantage to corporate strategy, *Harvard Business Review*, 65(3): 43–59.
6. Porter, From competitive advantage to corporate strategy; C. A. Montgomery, 1994, Corporate diversification, *Journal of Economic Perspectives*, 8: 163–178.
7. M. Kwak, 2002, Maximizing value through diversification, *MIT Sloan Management Review*, 43(2): 10; R. A. Burgelman & Y. L. Doz, 2001, The power of strategic integration, *MIT Sloan Management Review*, 42(3): 28–38; C. C. Markides, 1997, To diversify or not to diversify, *Harvard Business Review*, 75(6): 93–99.
8. S. A. Mansi & D. M. Reeb, 2002, Corporate diversification: What gets discounted? *Journal of Finance*, 57: 2167–2183; P. Wright, M. Kroll, A. Lado, & B. Van Ness, 2002, The structure of ownership and corporate acquisition strategies, *Strategic Management Journal*, 23: 41–53; C. C. Markides & P. J. Williamson, 1996, Corporate diversification and organizational structure: A resource-based view, *Academy of Management Journal*, 39: 340–367.
9. A. Campbell, M. Goold, & M. Alexander, 1995, Corporate strategy: The question for parenting advantage, *Harvard Business Review*, 73(2): 120–132.
10. M. Goold & A. Campbell, 2002, Parenting in complex structures, *Long Range Planning*, 35(3): 219–243; T. H. Brush, P. Bromiley, & M. Hendrickx, 1999, The relative influence of industry and corporation on business segment performance: An alternative estimate, *Strategic Management Journal*, 20: 519–547; T. H. Brush & P. Bromiley, 1997, What does a small corporate effect mean? A variance components simulation of corporate and business effects, *Strategic Management Journal*, 18: 825–835.
11. J. B. Barney, 2002, *Gaining and Sustaining Competitive Advantage*, 2nd ed., Upper Saddle River, NJ: Prentice-Hall.
12. Bergh, Diversification strategy research at a crossroads, 363.
13. C. Kim, S. Kim, & C. Pantzalis, 2001, Firm diversification and earnings volatility: An empirical analysis of U.S.-based MNCs, *American Business Review*, 19(1): 26–38; W. Lewellen, 1971, A pure financial rationale for the conglomerate merger, *Journal of Finance*, 26: 521–537.
14. D. E. M. Sappington, 2003, Regulating horizontal diversification, *International Journal of Industrial Organization*, 21: 291–315.
15. H. von Kranenburg, M. Cloodt, & J. Hagedoorn, 2001, An exploratory story of recent trends in the diversification of Dutch publishing companies in the multimedia and information industries, *International Studies of Management & Organization*, 31(10): 64–86.
16. T. J. Douglas & J. A. Ryman, 2003, Understanding competitive advantage in the general hospital industry: Evaluating strategic competencies, *Strategic Management Journal*, 24: 333–347; B. S. Silverman, 1999, Technological resources and the direction of corporate diversification: Toward an integration of the resource-based view and transaction cost economics, *Management Science*, 45: 1109–1124; D. Collis & C. A. Montgomery, 1995, Competing on resources: Strategy in the 1990s, *Harvard Business Review*, 73(4): 118–128; M. A. Peteraf, 1993, The cornerstones of competitive advantage: A resource-based view, *Strategic Management Journal*, 14: 179–191.
17. T. J. Waite, 2002, Stick to the core—or go for more? *Harvard Business Review*, 80(2): 31–41.
18. Bergh, Diversification strategy research at a crossroads, 369.
19. R. P. Rumelt, *Strategy, Structure, and Economic Performance*, Boston: Harvard Business School, 1974; L. Wrigley, 1970, *Divisional Autonomy and Diversification* (Ph.D. dissertation), Harvard Business School.
20. J. Boorstin, 2003, Why is Wrigley so wrapper up? *Fortune*, March 3, 133–134.
21. T. Mason, 2001, Can gum and dental care mix? *Marketing*, August 23, 21.
22. Boorstin, Why is Wrigley so wrapper up?
23. S. Killman, 2001, Smithfield Foods CEO welcomes backlash over its hog farms, *Wall Street Journal*, August 21, B4; J. Forster, 2001, Who's afraid of a little mud? *Business Week*, May 21, 112–113.
24. S. Kilman, 2002, Farmland rebuffs Smithfield offer—Farm cooperative files for Chapter 11 protection, leaves door open to talks, *Wall Street Journal*, June 3, A6.
25. H. W. Choi, 2003, Korean leader poses challenge to conglomerates, *Wall Street Journal*, February 24, A13.
26. L. Fauver, J. Houston, & A. Naranjo, 2003, Capital market development, international integration, legal systems, and the value of corporate diversification: A cross-country analysis, *Journal of Financial and Quantitative Analysis*, 38: 135–157; Wan & Hoskisson, Home country environments, corporate diversification strategies and firm performance; T. Khanna & J. W. Rivkin, 2001, Estimating the performance effects of business groups in emerging markets, *Strategic Management Journal*, 22: 45–74; L. A. Keister, 2000, *Chinese Business Groups: The Structure and Impact of Inter-Firm Relations During Economic Development*, New York: Oxford University Press; T. Khanna & K. Palepu, 1997, Why focused strategies may be wrong for emerging markets, *Harvard Business Review*, 75(4): 41–50.
27. C. Chung, 2001, Markets, culture and institutions: The emergence of large business groups in Taiwan, 1950s–1970s, *Journal of Management Studies*, 38: 719–745.
28. S. Manikutty, 2000, Family business groups in India: A resource-based view of the emerging trends, *Family Business Review*, 13: 279–292.
29. 1997, Inside story, *The Economist*, December 6, 7–9.
30. S. P. Ferris, K. A. Kim, & P. Kitsabunnarat, 2003, The costs (and benefits?) of diversified business groups: The case of Korean chaebols, *Journal of Banking & Finance*, 27: 251–273; S. J. Chang & J. Hong, 2002, How much does the business group matter in Korea? *Strategic Management Journal*, 23: 265–274; K. V. Lins & H. Servaes, 2002, Is corporate diversification beneficial in emerging markets? *Financial Management*, 31(2): 5–31.
31. K. Dewenter, W. Novaes, & R. H. Pettway, 2001, Visibility versus complexity in business groups: Evidence from Japanese keiretsu, *Journal of Business*, 74: 79–100.
32. Fauver, Houston, & Naranjo, Capital market development, international integration, legal systems, and the value of corporate diversification; Wan & Hoskisson, Home country environments, corporate diversification strategies and firm performance.
33. R. K. Aggarwal & A. A. Samwick, 2003, Why do managers diversify their firms? Agency reconsidered, *Journal of Finance*, 58: 71–118; P. Wright, M. Kroll, & D. Elenkov, 2002, Acquisition returns, increase in firm size, and chief executive officer compensation: The moderating role of monitoring, *Academy of Management Journal*, 45: 599–608.
34. J. Song, 2002, Firm capabilities and technology ladders, *Strategic Management Journal*, 23: 191–210; J. Lampel & J. Shamsie, 2000, Probing the unobtrusive link: Dominant logic and the design of joint ventures at General Electric, *Strategic Management Journal*, 21: 593–602; M. Farjoun, 1998, The independent and joint effects of the skill and physical bases of relatedness in diversification, *Strategic Management Journal*, 19: 611–630.
35. R. E. Hoskisson & L. W. Busenitz, 2002, Market uncertainty and learning distance in corporate entrepreneurship entry mode choice, in M. A. Hitt, R. D. Ireland, S. M. Camp, & D. L. Sexton (eds.), *Strategic Entrepreneurship: Creating a New Mindset*, Oxford, UK: Blackwell Publishers, 150–172;

A. Seth, K. P. Song, & R. R. Pettit, 2002, Value creation and destruction in cross-border acquisitions: An empirical analysis of foreign acquisitions of U.S. firms, *Strategic Management Journal*, 23: 921–940.

36. J. A. Doukas & L. H. P. Lang, 2003, Foreign direct investment, diversification and firm performance, *Journal of International Business Studies*, 34: 153–172; L. Capron, 1999, The long term performance of horizontal acquisitions, *Strategic Management Journal*, 20: 987–1018.

37. M. E. Porter, 1985, *Competitive Advantage*, New York: The Free Press, 328.

38. R. G. Schroeder, K. A. Bates, & M.A. Junttila, 2002, A resource-based view of manufacturing strategy and the relationship to manufacturing performance, *Strategic Management Journal*, 23: 105–117.

39. D. Gupta & Y. Gerchak, 2002, Quantifying operational synergies in a merger/acquisition, *Management Science*, 48: 517–533.

40. B. Caulfield, 2003, Saving $3 billion the HP way, *Business 2.0*, May, 52–54.

41. Ibid.

42. M. L. Marks & P. H. Mirvis, 2000, Managing mergers, acquisitions, and alliances: Creating an effective transition structure, *Organizational Dynamics*, 28(3): 35–47.

43. C. Park, 2003, Prior performance characteristics of related and unrelated acquirers, *Strategic Management Journal*, 24: 471–480; G. Delong, 2001, Stockholder gains from focusing versus diversifying bank mergers, *Journal of Financial Economics*, 2: 221–252; T. H. Brush, 1996, Predicted change in operational synergy and post-acquisition performance of acquired businesses, *Strategic Management Journal*, 17: 1–24; H. Zhang, 1995, Wealth effects of U.S. bank takeovers, *Applied Financial Economics*, 5: 329–336.

44. D. D. Bergh, 1995, Size and relatedness of units sold: An agency theory and resource-based perspective, *Strategic Management Journal*, 16: 221–239.

45. M. Lubatkin & S. Chatterjee, 1994, Extending modern portfolio theory into the domain of corporate diversification: Does it apply? *Academy of Management Journal*, 37: 109–136.

46. A. Van Oijen, 2001, Product diversification, corporate management instruments, resource sharing, and performance, *Academy of Management Best Paper Proceedings* (on CD-ROM, Business Policy and Strategy Division); T. Kono, 1999, A strong head office makes a strong company, *Long Range Planning*, 32(2): 225.

47. M. Kotabe, X. Martin, & H. Domoto, 2003, Gaining from vertical partnerships: Knowledge transfer, relationship duration, and supplier performance improvement in the U.S. and Japanese automotive industries, *Strategic Management Journal*, 24: 293–316; M. Y. Brannen, J. K. Liker, & W. M. Fruin, 1999, Recontextualization and factory-to-factory knowledge transfer from Japan to the U.S.: The case of NSK, in J. K. Liker, W. M. Fruin, & P. Adler (eds.), *Remade in America: Transplanting and Transforming Japanese Systems*, New York: Oxford University Press, 117–153; L. Capron, P. Dussauge, & W. Mitchell, 1998, Resource redeployment following horizontal acquisitions in Europe and the United States, 1988–1992, *Strategic Management Journal*, 19: 631–661; A. Mehra, 1996, Resource and market based determinants of performance in the U.S. banking industry, *Strategic Management Journal*, 17: 307–322; S. Chatterjee & B. Wernerfelt, 1991, The link between resources and type of diversification: Theory and evidence, *Strategic Management Journal*, 12: 33–48.

48. S. Dutta, M. J. Zbaracki, & M. Bergen, 2003, Pricing process as a capability: A resource-based perspective, *Strategic Management Journal*, 24: 615–630.

49. L. Capron & N. Pistre, 2002, When do acquirers earn abnormal returns? *Strategic Management Journal*, 23: 781–794.

50. J. W. Spencer, 2003, Firms' knowledge-sharing strategies in the global innovation system: Empirical evidence from the flat panel display industry, *Strategic Management Journal*, 24: 217–233.

51. G. Edmondson, 2003, Pininfarina's snazzy new design—for itself, *Business Week*, March 3, 56.

52. G. Marcial, 2003, Cendant comes back, *BusinessWeek Online*, http://www.businessweek.com, May 12; A. Tsao, 2003, Just the ticket for travel stocks, *BusinessWeek Online*, http://www.businessweek.com, March 19.

53. B. Einhorn, F. Balfour, & K. Capell, 2002, More Virgin territory, *Business Week*, April 8, 25; R. Whittington, 1999, In praise of the evergreen conglomerate, "Mastering Strategy" (Part 6), *Financial Times*, November 1, 4–6; W. Ruigrok, A. Pettigrew, S. Peck, & R. Whittington, 1999, Corporate restructuring and new forms of organizing: Evidence from Europe, *Management International Review*, 39 (Special Issue): 41–64.

54. A. Barrett, 2002, Keep it simple, Cendant, Wall Street is slamming the company for complex financials, *Business Week*, October 14, 54.

55. C. Zellner & D. Fornahl, 2002, Scientific knowledge and implications for its diffusion, *Journal of Knowledge Management*, 6(2): 190–198.

56. C. St. John & J. S. Harrison, 1999, Manufacturing-based relatedness, synergy, and coordination, *Strategic Management Journal*, 20: 129–145.

57. S. Chatterjee & J. Singh, 1999, Are tradeoffs inherent in diversification moves? A simultaneous model for type of diversification and mode of expansion decisions, *Management Science*, 45: 25–41.

58. G. Symeonidis, 2002, Cartel stability with multiproduct firms, *International Journal of Industrial Organization*, 20: 339–352; J. Gimeno & C. Y. Woo, 1999, Multimarket contact, economies of scope, and firm performance, *Academy of Management Journal*, 42: 239–259.

59. R. Brooks, 2003, DHL Airways' CEO-led buyout moves forward, *Wall Street Journal* (Eastern Edition), May 22, B4.

60. L. Wozniak, 2003, DHL and FedEx race to integrate China, *Far Eastern Economic Review*, February 27, 42–44.

61. A. Darr & I. Talmud, 2003, The structure of knowledge and seller-buyer networks in markets for emergent technologies, *Organization Studies*, 24: 443–461.

62. O. E. Williamson, 1996, Economics and organization: A primer, *California Management Review*, 38(2): 131–146.

63. D. Leonard, 2003, Songs in the key of Steve, *Fortune*, May 12, 52–62.

64. R. Barker, 2003, How high will Medco fly on its own? *Business Week*, May 26, 118.

65. L. R. Kopczak & M. E. Johnson, 2003, The supply-chain management effect, *MIT Sloan Management Review*, 3: 27–34; K. R. Harrigan, 2001, Strategic flexibility in the old and new economies, in M. A. Hitt, R. E. Freeman, & J. S. Harrison (eds.), *Handbook of Strategic Management*, Oxford, UK: Blackwell Publishers, 97–123.

66. M. R. Subramani & N. Venkatraman, 2003, Safeguarding investments in asymmetric interorganizational relationships: Theory and evidence, *Academy of Management Journal*, 46: 46–62; R. E. Kranton & D. F. Minehart, 2001, Networks versus vertical integration, *Rand Journal of Economics*, 3: 570–601.

67. C. Serant, 2003, Mexico spins a new orbit—The country's venerable contract manufacturing complex is assuming a dramatic new form as China asserts its position as the EMS industry's cost leader, *EBN*, January 20, 27.

68. P. Kothandaraman & D. T. Wilson, 2001, The future of competition: Value-creating networks, *Industrial Marketing Management*, 30: 379–389.

69. K. M. Eisenhardt & D. C. Galunic, 2000, Coevolving: At last, a way to make synergies work, *Harvard Business Review*, 78(1): 91–111.

70. R. Schoenberg, 2001, Knowledge transfer and resource sharing as value creation mechanisms in inbound continental European acquisitions, *Journal of Euro-Marketing*, 10: 99–114.

71. Eisenhardt & Galunic, Coevolving, 94.

72. M. Freeman, 2002, Forging a model for profitability, *Electronic Media*, January 28, 1, 13.

73. D. D. Bergh, 1997, Predicting divestiture of unrelated acquisitions: An integrative model of ex ante conditions, *Strategic Management Journal*, 18: 715–731; C. W. L. Hill, 1994, Diversification and economic performance: Bringing structure and corporate management back into the picture, in R. P. Rumelt, D. E. Schendel, & D. J. Teece (eds.), *Fundamental Issues in Strategy*, Boston: Harvard Business School Press, 297–321.

74. Porter, *Competitive Advantage*.

75. O. E. Williamson, 1975, *Markets and Hierarchies: Analysis and Antitrust Implications*, New York: Macmillan Free Press.

76. J. T. Harper & J. Madura, 2002, Sources of hidden value and risk within tracking stock, *Financial Management*, 31(3): 91–109; M. T. Billet & D. Mauer, 2001, Diversification and the value of internal capital markets: The case of tracking stock, *Journal of Banking & Finance*, 9: 1457–1490.

77. A. Pasztor, 2003, Hughes Electronics has sharply narrower loss, *Wall Street Journal*, April 15, B3.

78. J. McTague, 2002, Security in numbers, *Barron's*, December 30, 26; C. Botosan & M. Harris, 2000, Motivations for changes in disclosure frequency and its consequences: An examination of voluntary quarterly segment disclosure, *Journal of Accounting Research*, 38: 329–353; R. Kochhar & M. A. Hitt, 1998, Linking corporate strategy to capital structure: Diversification strategy, type, and source of financing, *Strategic Management Journal*, 19: 601–610.

79. D. Miller, R. Eisenstat, & N. Foote, 2002, Strategy from the inside out: Building capability-creating organizations, *California Management Review*, 44(3): 37–54; M. E. Raynor & J. L. Bower, 2001, Lead from the center:

How to manage divisions dynamically, *Harvard Business Review*, 79(5): 92–100; P. Taylor & J. Lowe, 1995, A note on corporate strategy and capital structure, *Strategic Management Journal*, 16: 411–414.

80. J. M. Campa & S. Kedia, 2002, Explaining the diversification discount, *Journal of Finance*, 57: 1731–1762; M. Kwak, 2001, Spinoffs lead to better financing decisions, *MIT Sloan Management Review*, 42(4): 10; O. A. Lamont & C. Polk, 2001, The diversification discount: Cash flows versus returns, *Journal of Finance*, 56: 1693–1721; R. Rajan, H. Servaes, & L. Zingales, 2001, The cost of diversity: The diversification discount and inefficient investment, *Journal of Finance*, 55: 35–79.

81. 2001, Spoilt for choice, *The Economist*, http://www.economist.com, July 5.

82. D. J. Denis, D. K. Denis, & A. Sarin, 1999, Agency theory and the reference of equity ownership structure on corporate diversification strategies, *Strategic Management Journal*, 20: 1071–1076; R. Amit & J. Livnat, 1988, A concept of conglomerate diversification, *Journal of Management*, 14: 593–604.

83. Whittington, In praise of the evergreen conglomerate, 4.

84. Khanna & Rivkin, Estimating the performance effects of business groups in emerging markets.

85. T. Khanna & K. Palepu, 2000, Is group affiliation profitable in emerging markets? An analysis of diversified Indian business groups, *Journal of Finance*, 55: 867–892; T. Khanna & K. Palepu, 2000, The future of business groups in emerging markets: Long-run evidence from Chile, *Academy of Management Journal*, 43: 268–285.

86. R. E. Hoskisson, R. A. Johnson, D. Yiu, & W. P. Wan, 2001. Restructuring strategies and diversified business groups: Differences associated with country institutional environments, in M. A. Hitt, R. E. Freeman, & J. S. Harrison (eds.), *Handbook of Strategic Management*, Oxford, UK: Blackwell Publishers, 433–463; S. J. Chang & H. Singh, 1999, The impact of entry and resource fit on modes of exit by multibusiness firms, *Strategic Management Journal*, 20: 1019–1035.

87. W. Ng & C. de Cock, 2002, Battle in the boardroom: A discursive perspective, *Journal of Management Studies*, 39: 23–49.

88. P. Gogoi, 2003, Sara Lee: No piece of cake, *Business Week*, May 26, 66–68.

89. M. Warner, 2003, Exorcism at Tyco: CEO Ed Breen & Co. aim to run a big, solid, and, yes, boring company, *Fortune*, April 28, 106.

90. R. Coff, 2003, Bidding wars over R&D-intensive firms: Knowledge, opportunism, and the market for corporate control, *Academy of Management Journal*, 46: 74–85.

91. S. Nambisan, 2001, Why service businesses are not product businesses, *MIT Sloan Management Review*, 42(4): 72–80.

92. G. Khermouch, 2003, Interpublic Group: Synergy—or sinkhole? *Business Week*, April 21, 76–77.

93. E. Stickel, 2001, Uncertainty reduction in a competitive environment, *Journal of Business Research*, 51: 169–177; Chatterjee & Singh, Are tradeoffs inherent in diversification moves?

94. M. Lubatkin, H. Merchant, & M. Srinivasan, 1997, Merger strategies and shareholder value during times of relaxed antitrust enforcement: The case of large mergers during the 1980s, *Journal of Management*, 23: 61–81.

95. D. P. Champlin & J. T. Knoedler, 1999, Restructuring by design? Government's complicity in corporate restructuring, *Journal of Economic Issues*, 33(1): 41–57.

96. R. M. Scherer & D. Ross, 1990, *Industrial Market Structure and Economic Performance*, Boston: Houghton Mifflin.

97. A. Shleifer & R. W. Vishny, 1994, Takeovers in the 1960s and 1980s: Evidence and implications, in R. P. Rumelt, D. E. Schendel, & D. J. Teece (eds.), *Fundamental Issues in Strategy*, Boston: Harvard Business School Press, 403–422.

98. S. Chatterjee, J. S. Harrison, & D. D. Bergh, 2003, Failed takeover attempts, corporate governance and refocusing, *Strategic Management Journal*, 24: 87–96; Lubatkin, Merchant, & Srinivasan, Merger strategies and shareholder value; D. J. Ravenscraft & R. M. Scherer, 1987, *Mergers, Sell-Offs and Economic Efficiency*, Washington, DC: Brookings Institution, 22.

99. D. A. Zalewski, 2001, Corporate takeovers, fairness, and public policy, *Journal of Economic Issues*, 35: 431–437; P. L. Zweig, J. P. Kline, S. A. Forest, & K. Gudridge, 1995, The case against mergers, *Business Week*, October 30, 122–130; J. R. Williams, B. L. Paez, & L. Sanders, 1988, Conglomerates revisited, *Strategic Management Journal*, 9: 403–414.

100. E. J. Lopez, 2001, New anti-merger theories: A critique, *Cato Journal*, 20: 359–378; 1998, The trustbusters' new tools, *The Economist*, May 2, 62–64.

101. R. Croyle & P. Kager, 2002, Giving mergers a head start, *Harvard Business Review*, 80(10): 20–21.

102. M. C. Jensen, 1986, Agency costs of free cash flow, corporate finance, and takeovers, *American Economic Review*, 76: 323–329.

103. R. Gilson, M. Scholes, & M. Wolfson, 1988, Taxation and the dynamics of corporate control: The uncertain case for tax motivated acquisitions, in J. C. Coffee, L. Lowenstein, & S. Rose-Ackerman (eds.), *Knights, Raiders, and Targets: The Impact of the Hostile Takeover*, New York: Oxford University Press, 271–299.

104. C. Steindel, 1986, Tax reform and the merger and acquisition market: The repeal of the general utilities, *Federal Reserve Bank of New York Quarterly Review*, 11(3): 31–35.

105. M. A. Hitt, J. S. Harrison, & R. D. Ireland, 2001, *Mergers and Acquisitions: A Guide to Creating Value for Stakeholders*, New York: Oxford University Press.

106. D. B. Wilkerson & Russ Britt, 2003, It's showtime for media deals: Radio lessons fuel debate over control of TV, newspapers, CBS MarketWatch, http://cbs.marketwatch.com, May 30.

107. S. Labaton, 2003, Senators move to restore F.C.C. limits on the media, *New York Times*, http//:www.nytimes.com, June 5.

108. S. Wooley, 2003, Telco TV (take 2), *Forbes*, May 12, 68.

109. C. Park, 2002, The effects of prior performance on the choice between related and unrelated acquisitions: Implications for the performance consequences of diversification strategy, *Journal of Management Studies*, 39: 1003–1019.

110. Rumelt, *Strategy, Structure and Economic Performance*, 125.

111. M. N. Nickel & M. C. Rodriguez, 2002, A review of research on the negative accounting relationship between risk and return: Bowman's paradox, *Omega*, 30(1): 1–18; R. M. Wiseman & L. R. Gomez-Mejia, 1998, A behavioral agency model of managerial risk taking, *Academy of Management Review*, 23: 133–153; E. H. Bowman, 1982, Risk seeking by troubled firms, *Sloan Management Review*, 23: 33–42.

112. J. G. Matsusaka, 2001, Corporate diversification, value maximization, and organizational capabilities, *Journal of Business*, 74: 409–432.

113. R. Berner, 2003, Dark days in white goods for Sears, *Business Week*, March 10, 78–79.

114. S. L. Gillan, J. W. Kensinger, & J. D. Martin, 2000, Value creation and corporate diversification: The case of Sears, Roebuck & Co., *Journal of Financial Economics*, 55: 103–137.

115. L. E. Palich, L. B. Cardinal, & C. C. Miller, 2000, Curvilinearity in the diversification-performance linkage: An examination of over three decades of research, *Strategic Management Journal*, 21: 155–174.

116. J. Ewing, 2003, Back to basics, *Business Week*, March 10, 46–47.

117. A. E. Bernardo & B. Chowdhry, 2002, Resources, real options, and corporate strategy, *Journal of Financial Economics*, 63: 211–234; Simerly & Li, Environmental dynamism, capital structure and performance; Bergh & Lawless, Portfolio restructuring and limits to hierarchical governance.

118. N. W. C. Harper & S. P. Viguerie, 2002, Are you too focused? *The McKinsey Quarterly*, Mid-Summer, 29–38; J. C. Sandvig & L. Coakley, 1998, Best practices in small firm diversification, *Business Horizons*, 41(3): 33–40; C. G. Smith & A. C. Cooper, 1988, Established companies diversifying into young industries: A comparison of firms with different levels of performance, *Strategic Management Journal*, 9: 111–121.

119. C. Edwards, A. Reinhardt, & R. O. Crockett, 2003, The hulk haunting cell phones, *Business Week*, March 3, 44.

120. N. M. Kay & A. Diamantopoulos, 1987, Uncertainty and synergy: Towards a formal model of corporate strategy, *Managerial and Decision Economics*, 8: 121–130.

121. M. E. Raynor, 2002, Diversification as real options and the implications of firm-specific risk and performance, *Engineering Economist*, 47(4): 371–389; R. W. Coff, 1999, How buyers cope with uncertainty when acquiring firms in knowledge-intensive industries: Caveat emptor, *Organization Science*, 10: 144–161.

122. G. Edmondson, 2003, Volkswagen needs a jump, *Business Week*, May 12, 48–49.

123. J. Muller, 2003, Crossbreed: Is it a Chrysler or a Mercedes? Only your engineer knows for sure, *Forbes*, March 17, 54.

124. Chatterjee & Singh, Are tradeoffs inherent in diversification moves?; S. J. Chatterjee & B. Wernerfelt, 1991, The link between resources and type of diversification: Theory and evidence, *Strategic Management Journal*, 12: 33–48.

125. W. Keuslein, 2003, The Ebitda folly, *Forbes*, March 17, 165–167; Kochhar & Hitt, Linking corporate strategy to capital structure.

126. 2003, Microsoft's cash stash, *Kiplinger's Personal Finance*, May, 37; J. Greene, 2001, Microsoft: How it became stronger than ever, *Business Week*, June 4, 75–85.

127. M. Sivy, 2003, The big payoff from R&D, *Money*, June, 63–64.

128. K. Haanes & O. Fjeldstad, 2000, Linking intangible resources and competition, *European Management Journal*, 18(1): 52–62.

129. L. Capron & J. Hulland, 1999, Redeployment of brands, sales forces, and general marketing management expertise following horizontal acquisitions: A resource-based view, *Journal of Marketing*, 63(2): 41–54.

130. A. M. Knott, D. J. Bryce, & H. E. Pose, 2003, On the strategic accumulation of intangible assets, *Organization Science*, 14: 192–207; J. Castillo, 2002, A note on the concept of tacit knowledge, *Journal of Management Inquiry*, 11(1): 46–57; R. D. Smith, 2000, Intangible strategic assets and firm performance: A multi-industry study of the resource-based view, *Journal of Business Strategies*, 17(2): 91–117.

131. J. Helyar, 2003, Media strike out, *Fortune*, March 17, 42.

132. J. G. Combs & M. S. Skill, 2003, Managerialist and human capital explanation for key executive pay premiums: A contingency perspective, *Academy of Management Journal*, 46: 63–73; M. A. Geletkanycz, B. K. Boyd, & S. Finkelstein, 2001, The strategic value of CEO external directorate networks: Implications for CEO compensation, *Strategic Management Journal*, 9: 889–898; W. Grossman & R. E. Hoskisson, 1998, CEO pay at the crossroads of Wall Street and Main: Toward the strategic design of executive compensation, *Academy of Management Executive*, 12(1): 43–57; S. Finkelstein & D. C. Hambrick, 1996, *Strategic Leadership: Top Executives and Their Effects on Organizations*, St. Paul, MN: West Publishing Company.

133. Aggarwal & Samwick, Why do managers diversify their firms?; W. Shen & A. A. Cannella, Jr., 2002, Power dynamics within top management and their impacts on CEO dismissal followed by inside succession, *Academy of Management Journal*, 45: 1195–1206; W. Shen & A. A. Cannella, Jr., 2002, Revisiting the performance consequences of CEO succession: The impacts of successor type, postsuccession senior executive turnover, and departing CEO tenure, *Academy of Management Journal*, 45: 717–733; P. J. Lane, A. A. Cannella, Jr., & M. H. Lubatkin, 1998, Agency problems as antecedents to unrelated mergers and diversification: Amihud and Lev reconsidered, *Strategic Management Journal*, 19: 555–578; D. L. May, 1995, Do managerial motives influence firm risk reduction strategies? *Journal of Finance*, 50: 1291–1308; Y. Amihud and B. Lev, 1981, Risk reduction as a managerial motive for conglomerate mergers, *Bell Journal of Economics*, 12: 605–617.

134. J. J. Cordeiro & R. Veliyath, 2003, Beyond pay for performance: A panel study of the determinants of CEO compensation, *American Business Review*, 21(1): 56–66; Wright, Kroll, & Elenkov, Acquisition returns, increase in firm size, and chief executive officer compensation; S. R. Gray & A. A. Cannella, Jr., 1997, The role of risk in executive compensation, *Journal of Management*, 23: 517–540.

135. Combs & Skill, Managerialist and human capital explanation for key executive pay premiums; R. Bliss & R. Rosen, 2001, CEO compensation and bank mergers, *Journal of Financial Economics*, 1:107–138; W. G. Sanders & M. A. Carpenter, 1998, Internationalization and firm governance: The roles of CEO compensation, top team composition, and board structure, *Academy of Management Journal*, 41: 158–178.

136. J. J. Janney, 2002, Eat or get eaten? How equity ownership and diversification shape CEO risk-taking, *Academy of Management Executive*, 14(4): 157–158; J. W. Lorsch, A. S. Zelleke, & K. Pick, 2001, Unbalanced boards, *Harvard Business Review*, 79(2): 28–30; R. E. Hoskisson & T. Turk, 1990, Corporate restructuring: Governance and control limits of the internal market, *Academy of Management Review*, 15: 459–477.

137. M. Kahan & E. B. Rock, 2002, How I learned to stop worrying and love the pill: Adaptive responses to takeover law, *University of Chicago Law Review*, 69(3): 871–915.

138. R. C. Anderson, T. W. Bates, J. M. Bizjak, & M. L. Lemmon, 2000, Corporate governance and firm diversification, *Financial Management*, 29(1): 5–22; J. D. Westphal, 1998, Board games: How CEOs adapt to increases in structural board independence from management, *Administrative Science Quarterly*, 43: 511–537; J. K. Seward & J. P. Walsh, 1996, The governance and control of voluntary corporate spin offs, *Strategic Management Journal*, 17: 25–39; J. P. Walsh & J. K. Seward, 1990, On the efficiency of internal and external corporate control mechanisms, *Academy of Management Review*, 15: 421–458.

139. M. Wiersema, 2002, Holes at the top: Why CEO firings backfire, *Harvard Business Review*, 80(12): 70–77.

140. V. Kisfalvi & P. Pitcher, 2003, Doing what feels right: The influence of CEO character and emotions on top management team dynamics, *Journal of Management Inquiry*, 12(10): 42–66; R. Larsson, K. R. Brousseau, M. J. Driver, & M. Homqvist, 2003, International growth through cooperation: Brand-driven strategies, leadership, and career development in Sweden, *Academy of Management Executive*, 17(1): 7–21; W. G. Bennis & R. J. Thomas, 2002, Crucibles of leadership, *Harvard Business Review*, 80(9): 39–45; W. G. Rowe, 2001, Creating wealth in organizations: The role of strategic leadership, *Academy of Management Executive*, 15(1): 81–94.

141. E. F. Fama, 1980, Agency problems and the theory of the firm, *Journal of Political Economy*, 88: 288–307.

142. H. Chesbrough, 2003, The governance and performance of Xerox's technology spin-off companies, *Research Policy*, 32(3): 403–421; R. A. Johnson, 1996, Antecedents and outcomes of corporate refocusing, *Journal of Management*, 22: 439–483; C. Y. Woo, G. E. Willard, & U. S. Dallenbach, 1992, Spin-off performance: A case of overstated expectations, *Strategic Management Journal*, 13: 433–448.

143. M. Wright, R. E. Hoskisson, & L. W. Busenitz, 2001, Firm rebirth: Buyouts as facilitators of strategic growth and entrepreneurship, *Academy of Management Executive*, 15(1): 111–125; H. Kim & R. E. Hoskisson, 1996, Japanese governance systems: A critical review, in S. B. Prasad (ed.), *Advances in International Comparative Management*, Greenwich, CT: JAI Press, 165–189.

144. M. L. A. Hayward, 2002, When do firms learn from their acquisition experience? Evidence from 1990–1995, *Strategic Management Journal*, 23: 21–39; L. Capron, W. Mitchell, & A. Swaminathan, 2001, Asset divestiture following horizontal acquisitions: A dynamic view, *Strategic Management Journal*, 22: 817–844.

145. Bergh, Diversification strategy research at a crossroads, 370–371; W. M. Bulkeley, 1994, Conglomerates make a surprising come-back—with a '90s twist, *Wall Street Journal*, March 1, A1, A6.

146. J. P. H. Fan & L. H. P. Lang, 2000, The measurement of relatedness: An application to corporate diversification, *Journal of Business*, 73: 629–660.

147. Khanna & Palepu, The future of business groups in emerging markets; P. Ghemawat & T. Khanna, 1998, The nature of diversified business groups: A research design and two case studies, *Journal of Industrial Economics*, 46: 35–61.

148. Wan & Hoskisson, Home country environments, corporate diversification strategies, and firm performance.

Acquisition and Restructuring Strategies

Chapter Seven 7

Knowledge Objectives

Studying this chapter should provide you with the strategic management knowledge needed to:

1. Explain the popularity of acquisition strategies in firms competing in the global economy.

2. Discuss reasons firms use an acquisition strategy to achieve strategic competitiveness.

3. Describe seven problems that work against developing a competitive advantage using an acquisition strategy.

4. Name and describe attributes of effective acquisitions.

5. Define the restructuring strategy and distinguish among its common forms.

6. Explain the short- and long-term outcomes of the different types of restructuring strategies.

Getty/PhotoDisc, Inc.

News Corporation has an opportunity for complementarity through the vertical acquisition of a satellite television producer, DirecTV, to distribute the content it already produces.

Comparing the Acquisition Strategies of News Corp. and AOL Time Warner

Beginning with an Australian newspaper inherited from his father, Rupert Murdoch built News Corporation and continues to manage it today. He has a large ownership position in the company and includes family members in its management structure. He began acquiring British newspapers in the 1970s, and then began an acquisition program in the United States in 1976 when he acquired the *New York Post.* Books (Harper-Collins), magazines (*TV Guide*), television networks (Fox), and movies (Twentieth Century Fox) have been added to make News Corp. the most profitable media company in the world in 2002. Murdoch recently acquired a controlling interest in DirecTV by offering $6.6 billion to buy General Motors' 20 percent stake in Hughes Electronics. The deal for DirecTV, a satellite television producer, is a vertical acquisition (defined later in the chapter), which gives Murdoch's firm another media distribution outlet for the content that it produces. Through both vertical and horizontal acquisitions (defined later in the chapter) as well as starting businesses internally, Murdoch has made his company influential and powerful in the media industry.

Rupert Murdoch is sworn in during a hearing before the House Committee on the Judiciary, Capitol Hill, Washington, D.C., May 8, 2003. The hearing examined the state of competition in direct broadcast satellite service in the multichannel video programming distribution market, particularly in light of the recent News Corporation/ DirecTV merger announcement. Murdoch manages one of the most profitable media companies in the world.

Another media company, AOL Time Warner, is the product of an unsuccessful merger between an Internet portal and a broadscale media company. Time Warner was created by a merger of Time Inc. and Warner Communications in 1989 while the combination of Time Warner and America Online occurred in 2001. In the two years following the merger, the company's market capitalization declined in value by $223 billion. To AOL, Time Warner's content was a vertical acquisition to fill AOL's growing Internet pipeline, but to Time Warner, AOL was just another new distribution outlet to accelerate the growth of established media content businesses. The two worldviews were incompatible culturally, and the supposed complementarity from either

Getty Images

point of view never fully materialized. There is pressure on CEO Richard Parsons to spin off AOL and return Time Warner to its premerger state. While the Time Warner part of the company is still profitable and growing, AOL is struggling, and the combined company is seeking ways to pay down the debt incurred as a result of the merger.

A well-managed acquisition strategy can add much value to a company. However, when it is ill-considered and poorly implemented, it can be the downfall of a previously successful company. News Corporation and AOL Time Warner are two such polar examples. While News Corp. continues to grow and expand though its track record is far from perfect, AOL Time Warner is managing for damage control in order to establish a firmer foundation from which its strategies can be successfully implemented. News Corp. has also made poor acquisitions; its acquisition of Gemstar—TV Guide, for example, has created a significant drag on earnings and lost market capitalization. However, examining the acquisitions strategies of these two firms can be instructive. Murdoch has been careful to stay away from music and Internet acquisitions. This decision has benefited his firm compared to the other media conglomerates Bertelsmann, Vivendi, and, especially, AOL Time Warner. Like Viacom, which owns CBS and MTV, News Corp. has focused primarily on producing good content; as a result, these firms have fared better than the more diversified media firms. Choosing appropriate acquisition targets and remaining focused on their own expertise has contributed to both Viacom and News Corp.'s success.

SOURCES: 2003, News Corporation home page, http://www.newscorp.com, June 6; J. Friedman, 2003, An aging News Corp. contrasts with paralyzed AOL, http://CBS.marketwatch.com, June 2; A. Bianco & T. Lowry, 2003, Can Dick Parsons rescue AOL Time Warner? *Business Week*, May 19, 87–96; M. Gunther & D. Leonard, 2003, Murdoch's prime time, *Fortune*, February 17, 52–62; 2002, Business: Still rocking; Viacom and News Corporation, *The Economist*, November 23, 55–56.

In Chapter 6, we studied corporate-level strategies, focusing on types and levels of product diversification strategies that can build core competencies and create competitive advantage. As noted in that chapter, diversification allows a firm to create value by productively using excess resources.[1] In this chapter, we explore mergers and acquisitions, often combined with a diversification strategy, as a prominent strategy employed by firms throughout the world. The acquisition of DirecTV by News Corporation is a vertical acquisition, as DirecTV is a satellite TV company through which News Corp. can distribute more of its media content: news, movies, and television shows. As such, combining the two firms creates an opportunity for complementarity as described in the Opening Case.

In the latter half of the 20th century, acquisition became a prominent strategy used by major corporations. Even smaller and more focused firms began employing acquisition strategies to grow and to enter new markets. However, acquisition strategies are not without problems; a number of acquisitions fail. Thus, we focus on how acquisitions can be used to produce value for the firm's stakeholders.[2] Before describing attributes associated with effective acquisitions, we examine the most prominent problems companies experience with an acquisition strategy. For example, when acquisitions contribute to poor performance, a firm may deem it necessary to restructure its operations. Closing the chapter are descriptions of three restructuring strategies, as well as the short- and long-term outcomes resulting from their use. Setting the stage for these topics is an examination of the popularity of mergers and acquisitions and a discussion of the differences among mergers, acquisitions, and takeovers.

The Popularity of Merger and Acquisition Strategies

The acquisition strategy has been a popular strategy among U.S. firms for many years. Some believe that this strategy played a central role in an effective restructuring of U.S. businesses during the 1980s and 1990s and into the 21st century.[3] Increasingly, acquisition strategies are becoming more popular with firms in other nations and economic regions, including Europe. In fact, about 40 to 45 percent of the acquisitions in recent years have been made across country borders (i.e., a firm headquartered in one country acquiring a firm headquartered in another country).[4]

Five waves of mergers and acquisitions took place in the 20th century with the last two occurring in the 1980s and 1990s.[5] There were 55,000 acquisitions valued at $1.3 trillion in the 1980s, but acquisitions in the 1990s exceeded $11 trillion in value.[6] World economies, particularly the U.S. economy, slowed in the new millennium, reducing the number of mergers and acquisitions completed.[7] The annual value of mergers and acquisitions peaked in 2000 at about $3.4 trillion and fell to about $1.75 trillion in 2001.[8] Slightly more than 15,000 acquisitions were announced in 2001 compared to over 33,000 in 2000.[9] In 2002, the total value for U.S. deals was $447.8 billion, the lowest level since 1994.[10] However, the number of firms anticipating making acquisitions increased significantly from 2002 to 2003.[11]

Although acquisitions have slowed, their number remains high. In fact, an acquisition strategy is sometimes used because of the uncertainty in the competitive landscape. A firm may make an acquisition to increase its market power because of a competitive threat, to enter a new market because of the opportunity available in that market, or to spread the risk due to the uncertain environment.[12] In addition, a firm may acquire other companies as options that allow the firm to shift its core business into different markets as volatility brings undesirable changes to its primary markets.[13] Such options may arise because of industry or regulatory changes. For instance, Clear Channel Communications built its business by buying radio stations in many geographic markets when the Telecommunications Act of 1996 changed the regulations regarding such acquisitions.[14]

The strategic management process (see Figure 1.1) calls for an acquisition strategy to increase a firm's strategic competitiveness as well as its returns to shareholders. Thus, an acquisition strategy should be used only when the acquiring firm will be able to increase its economic value through ownership and the use of an acquired firm's assets.[15]

Evidence suggests, however, that at least for acquiring firms, acquisition strategies may not always result in these desirable outcomes.[16] Studies by academic researchers have found that shareholders of acquired firms often earn above-average returns from an acquisition, while shareholders of acquiring firms are less likely to do so, typically earning returns from the transaction that are close to zero.[17] In approximately two-thirds of all acquisitions, the acquiring firm's stock price falls immediately after the intended transaction is announced. This negative response is an indication of investors' skepticism about the likelihood that the acquirer will be able to achieve the synergies required to justify the premium.[18] For example, as the Opening Case illustrates, the value of AOL Time Warner, now the world's largest media company, has continued to decline since the merger.

A **merger** is a strategy through which two firms agree to integrate their operations on a relatively coequal basis. There are few true mergers, because one party is usually dominant. DaimlerChrysler AG was termed a "merger of equals" and, although Daimler-Benz was the dominant party in the automakers' transaction, Chrysler managers would not allow the business deal to be consummated unless it was termed a merger.[19]

An **acquisition** is a strategy through which one firm buys a controlling, or 100 percent, interest in another firm with the intent of making the acquired firm a subsidiary business within its portfolio. In this case, the management of the acquired firm reports to the management of the acquiring firm. While most mergers are friendly transactions, acquisitions include unfriendly takeovers.

A **takeover** is a special type of an acquisition strategy wherein the target firm does not solicit the acquiring firm's bid. For example, the Strategic Focus on Oracle's unsolicited bid for PeopleSoft illustrates a takeover attempt. Often, takeover bids spawn bidding wars. Safeway, a U.K. grocery (unrelated to its U.S. namesake), received six bids when there was a signal that its assets were for sale. Following an agreed-upon offer from Morrison J. Sainsbury PLC, Wal-Mart Stores, Inc.'s U.K. arm Asda, Tesco PLC, and Arcadia showed interest. Also, Kohlberg Kravis Roberts & Co. (KKR), a buyout specialist, considered making a leveraged buyout offer (defined later in the chapter).[20] The number of unsolicited takeover bids increased in the economic downturn of 2001–2002, a common occurrence in economic recessions, because the poorly managed firms that are undervalued relative to their assets are more easily identified.[21]

Many takeover attempts are not desired by the target firm's managers and are referred to as hostile. In a few cases, unsolicited offers may come from parties familiar to the target firm. For example, financier Kirk Kerkorian, who specializes in takeovers, has acquired Metro-Goldwyn-Mayer (MGM) five separate times. The value of his investment in MGM has grown considerably, outperforming the Standard and Poor's 500. Still, MGM has struggled against fierce competition in recent years, and Kerkorian is trying to sell it (again).[22]

On a comparative basis, acquisitions are more common than mergers and takeovers. Accordingly, this chapter focuses on acquisitions.

Reasons for Acquisitions

In this section, we discuss reasons that support the use of an acquisition strategy. Although each reason can provide a legitimate rationale for an acquisition, the acquisition may not necessarily lead to a competitive advantage.

Increased Market Power

A primary reason for acquisitions is to achieve greater market power.[23] Defined in Chapter 6, *market power* exists when a firm is able to sell its goods or services above competitive levels or when the costs of its primary or support activities are below those of its competitors. Market power usually is derived from the size of the firm and its resources and capabilities to compete in the marketplace.[24] It is also affected by the firm's share of the market. Therefore, most acquisitions designed to achieve greater market power entail buying a competitor, a supplier, a distributor, or a business in a highly related industry to allow exercise of a core competence and to gain competitive advantage in the acquiring firm's primary market. One goal in achieving market power is to become a market leader.[25] For example, two Russian oil companies, Yukos and Sibneft, recently merged to become the fourth largest oil producer in the world. The merger increases the companies' market power to the extent that the merged firm can now compete with ExxonMobil, BP, Shell, and the other "supermajors."[26] Also, as

A merger is a strategy through which two firms agree to integrate their operations on a relatively coequal basis.

An acquisition is a strategy through which one firm buys a controlling, or 100 percent, interest in another firm with the intent of making the acquired firm a subsidiary business within its portfolio.

A takeover is a special type of an acquisition strategy wherein the target firm does not solicit the acquiring firm's bid.

Oracle Tries to Build Market Power through Acquisition of PeopleSoft

Oracle, a corporate database software company, made a $5.1 billion initial hostile takeover bid for PeopleSoft, an applications company, in June 2003. These companies produce software used by corporations to manage such business functions as "human resources, inventory management, and customer relations." Hostile takeovers are rare in the software business, but Larry Ellison, Oracle's CEO, initiated it as part of a strategy to increase Oracle's market power. Having seen how Microsoft became a more potent player when it released applications bundled with its operating system, Ellison is seeking applications to bundle with Oracle's database software, which is perceived as an operating system equivalent for corporate computing comparable to Microsoft Windows XP on a PC. Ellison has said that he is most interested in PeopleSoft's customers and in switching them over to Oracle applications.

In its own effort to build more market power in a consolidating industry, People-Soft had attempted to purchase J.D. Edwards. PeopleSoft objected to Oracle's bid on the grounds that it would not pass Department of Justice antitrust scrutiny. It countered Oracle's effort by revising its all-stock offer for J.D. Edwards to one that included a large amount of cash, making it more difficult for Oracle to appeal to shareholders. "Making the deal half cash and issuing half as much stock means they are below the NASDAQ threshold and don't have to go to the PeopleSoft shareholders" to complete the transaction. Oracle also made itself less attractive as a takeover target by reducing its cash on hand. In addition, PeopleSoft mounted an ad campaign that promised refunds to PeopleSoft subscribers if Oracle won the takeover battle. Oracle executives said that this move was like "a poison pill" that would make PeopleSoft more costly to acquire.

Many analysts agreed that the software business was ripe for consolidation, especially at that time, when the economy was down and managers, trying to cut costs, were cutting software spending. Ellison's announcement would put the number two, three, and four enterprise computing companies together into one (PeopleSoft is number three and J.D. Edwards is number four). However, even with the addition of PeopleSoft, Oracle would still come in a distant second to SAP, the major enterprise computing company, potentially holding 23 percent of the market while SAP had 35 percent.

SAP could benefit from Oracle's takeover bid, whether or not it were to be completed. At that moment of turmoil, SAP looked like a reliable provider that would be around for years supporting its software, an image that appealed to corporate customers. Additionally, if the takeover were to be completed, SAP would have an even chance to convince PeopleSoft customers to switch to SAP instead of to Oracle. The company launched an ad campaign to woo discontented PeopleSoft customers and authorized financial incentives to lure them over to SAP.

On the other hand, even if the takeover bid were to fail, Oracle could gain. The chances of a successful bid were viewed as remote because of antitrust objections. However, the bid caused enough uncertainty that PeopleSoft's sales declined, and the company was expected to report lower-than-expected earnings during the second quarter of 2003 as a direct result. Whether Oracle or SAP would gain the most is undetermined. Either way, Oracle managed to paralyze its rival and gain an opportunity for growing its market share.

SOURCES: L. J. Flynn & A. R. Sorkin, 2003, PeopleSoft revises a bid in its battle with Oracle, *New York Times,* http://www.nytimes.com, June 17; S. Hamm, 2003, Why SAP is sitting pretty, *BusinessWeek Online,* http://www.businessweek.com, June 12; S. Lohr, 2003, PeopleSoft bid mirrors lofty goals of Oracle chief executive, *New York Times,* http://www.nytimes.com, June 11; M. Prince, 2003, PeopleSoft board rejects revised offer from Oracle, *Wall Street Journal Online,* http://www.wsj.com, June 20; A. R. Sorkin, 2003, Has Oracle's chief disarmed a rival? *New York Times,* http://www.nytimes.com, June 16; F. Vogel-stein, 2003, Oracle's Ellison turns hostile, *Fortune,* June 23, 28.

illustrated in the Strategic Focus, Oracle's hostile bid to acquire PeopleSoft in the corporate database software business (which facilitates management of functions such as human resources, inventory management, and customer relations) may create more market power for Oracle. The PeopleSoft acquisition would allow Oracle to remain the number two software leader in its segment behind SAP. To increase their market power, firms often use horizontal, vertical, and related acquisitions.

HORIZONTAL ACQUISITIONS

The acquisition of a company competing in the same industry in which the acquiring firm competes is referred to as a *horizontal acquisition*. Horizontal acquisitions increase a firm's market power by exploiting cost-based and revenue-based synergies.[27] Research suggests that horizontal acquisitions of firms with similar characteristics result in higher performance than when firms with dissimilar characteristics combine their operations. Examples of important similar characteristics include strategy, managerial styles, and resource allocation patterns. Similarities in these characteristics make the integration of the two firms proceed more smoothly.[28] Horizontal acquisitions are often most effective when the acquiring firm integrates the acquired firm's assets with its assets, but only after evaluating and divesting excess capacity and assets that do not complement the newly combined firm's core competencies.[29]

After a strategy dispute with Palm's chairman, Palm founders Jeff Hawkins and Donna Dubinsky split off and founded another company, Handspring, modeled on Palm. Handspring has done well, and Palm recently announced that it is acquiring Handspring, bringing the founders' talent and technology back into Palm. It hopes that Handspring's Treo device, a combination phone-PDA, will help Palm's performance, as PDA sales have declined in favor of combined devices. Palm's horizontal acquisition of Handspring will likely save about $25 million a year by eliminating overlapping programs and taking advantage of more volume in the combined firm's manufacturing operations.[30]

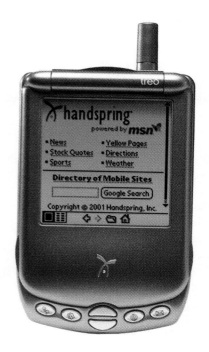

Handspring's Treo, a combination phone/PDA, is a product that occasioned a horizontal acquisition of Handspring by Palm.

Getty Images

VERTICAL ACQUISITIONS

A *vertical acquisition* refers to a firm acquiring a supplier or distributor of one or more of its goods or services.[31] A firm becomes vertically integrated through this type of acquisition, in that it controls additional parts of the value chain (see Chapters 3 and 6). Sony's acquisition of Columbia Pictures in the late 1980s was a vertical acquisition in which movie content could be used by Sony's hardware devices. Sony's additional acquisition of CBS Records, a music producer, and development of the PlayStation hardware have formed the bases for more vertical integration. The spread of broadband and the technological shift from analog to digital hardware require media firms to find new ways to sell their content to consumers. Sony's CEO, Nobuyuki Idei, believes that this shift has created a new opportunity to sell hardware that integrates this change by selling "televisions, personal computers, game consoles and handheld devices through which all of that wonderful content will one day be streaming."[32]

RELATED ACQUISITIONS

The acquisition of a firm in a highly related industry is referred to as a *related acquisition*. Tyson Foods, which has almost a quarter of the market for chicken, acquired IBP, the leader in beef and number two in pork. Most of Tyson's sales come from value-added products, such as breaded, marinated, or ready-to-microwave items, and it is hoping to apply this same recipe to its new beef and pork business, achieving economies of scope.[33] However, because of the difficulty in achieving synergy, related acquisitions are often difficult to value.[34]

Acquisitions intended to increase market power are subject to regulatory review as well as to analysis by financial markets.[35] For example, as noted in the Strategic Focus, the takeover attempt of PeopleSoft by Oracle received a significant amount of government scrutiny as well as close examination by financial analysts. European regulators did not approve the GE acquisition of Honeywell, dooming this strategic action and leaving Honeywell as a possible takeover target.[36] Thus, firms seeking growth and market power through acquisitions must understand the political/legal segment of the general environment (see Chapter 2) in order to successfully use an acquisition strategy.

Overcoming Entry Barriers

Barriers to entry (introduced in Chapter 2) are factors associated with the market or with the firms currently operating in it that increase the expense and difficulty faced by new ventures trying to enter that particular market. For example, well-established competitors may have substantial economies of scale in the manufacture or service of their products. In addition, enduring relationships with customers often create product loyalties that are difficult for new entrants to overcome. When facing differentiated products, new entrants typically must spend considerable resources to advertise their goods or services and may find it necessary to sell at prices below competitors' to entice customers.

Facing the entry barriers created by economies of scale and differentiated products, a new entrant may find the acquisition of an established company to be more effective than entering the market as a competitor offering a good or service that is unfamiliar to current buyers. In fact, the higher the barriers to market entry, the greater the probability that a firm will acquire an existing firm to overcome them. Although an acquisition can be expensive, it does provide the new entrant with immediate market access.

As it struggles to compete with UPS and FedEx in the air cargo industry, DHL Airways is finding many barriers to entry it must overcome, including a court case and a hearing before the U.S. Department of Transportation. UPS and FedEx have dominated this market for years in the United States. However, these arch rivals have banded together in an effort to exclude DHL Airways, alleging that the carrier is controlled by Deutsche Post World Net, a German firm, whose ownership may be illegal under American law. DHL Airways was formed by a takeover of Seattle-based Airborne Inc. DHL was surprised by how high the barriers to entry have become. "We had anticipated that there would be a tremendous effort to keep us from getting a toehold," said one DHL executive. "The surprise has been that it has taken on a life of its own."[37]

As in the DHL example above, firms trying to enter international markets often face quite steep entry barriers.[38] However, acquisitions are commonly used to overcome those barriers.[39] At least for large multinational corporations, another indicator of the importance of entering and then competing successfully in international markets is the fact that five emerging markets (China, India, Brazil, Mexico, and Indonesia) are among the 12 largest economies in the world, with a combined purchasing power that is already one-half that of the Group of Seven industrial nations (United States, Japan, Britain, France, Germany, Canada, and Italy).[40]

CROSS-BORDER ACQUISITIONS

Acquisitions made between companies with headquarters in different countries are called *cross-border acquisitions*. These acquisitions are often made to overcome entry barriers. In Chapter 9, we examine cross-border alliances and the reason for their use.

Compared to a cross-border alliance, a cross-border acquisition gives a firm more control over its international operations.[41]

Historically, U.S. firms have been the most active acquirers of companies outside their domestic market.[42] However, in the global economy, companies throughout the world are choosing this strategic option with increasing frequency. In recent years, cross-border acquisitions have represented as much as 45 percent of the total number of annual acquisitions.[43] The Daimler-Benz acquisition of Chrysler Corporation provides an example of this activity. Because of relaxed regulations, the amount of cross-border activity among nations within the European community also continues to increase. Accounting for this growth in the range of cross-border acquisitions, some analysts believe, is the fact that many large European corporations have approached the limits of growth within their domestic markets and thus seek growth in other markets. Research has indicated that many European and U.S. firms participated in cross-border acquisitions across Asian countries that experienced a financial crisis due to significant currency devaluations in 1997. These acquisitions, it is argued, facilitated the survival and restructuring of many large Asian companies such that these economies recovered more quickly than they would have without the cross-border acquisitions.[44]

Firms in all types of industries are completing cross-border acquisitions. For example, in 2002, the largest cross-border deal in the United States was the acquisition of Beneficial and Household Finance brands ("the largest independent consumer finance company in the United States and the country's second-largest third-party issuer of private label credit cards") by London-headquartered HSBC, now the largest foreign-owned bank in the United States.[45] In the second largest transaction, Miller Brewing was purchased from Philip Morris (now Altria Group Inc.) by South African Breweries (SAB). Although South African Breweries' acquisition (now SABMiller) "doubled its global market share and gave it a foothold in the lucrative U.S. market, . . . the beer brand's sales have fallen nearly 5 percent in the U.S."[46] As the South African Breweries experience indicates, such cross-border acquisitions can be difficult to negotiate and operate because of the differences in foreign cultures.[47]

Cost of New Product Development and Increased Speed to Market

Developing new products internally and successfully introducing them into the marketplace often require significant investments of a firm's resources, including time, making it difficult to quickly earn a profitable return.[48] Also of concern to firms' managers is achieving adequate returns from the capital invested to develop and commercialize new products—an estimated 88 percent of innovations fail to achieve adequate returns. Perhaps contributing to these less-than-desirable rates of return is the successful imitation of approximately 60 percent of innovations within four years after the patents are obtained. Because of outcomes such as these, managers often perceive internal product development as a high-risk activity.[49]

Acquisitions are another means a firm can use to gain access to new products and to current products that are new to the firm. Compared to internal product development processes, acquisitions provide more predictable returns as well as faster market entry. Returns are more predictable because the performance of the acquired firm's products can be assessed prior to completing the acquisition.[50] For these reasons, extensive bidding wars and acquisitions are more frequent in high-technology industries.[51]

Acquisition activity is also extensive throughout the pharmaceutical industry, where firms frequently use acquisitions to enter markets quickly, to overcome the high costs of developing products internally, and to increase the predictability of returns on their investments. Interestingly, although the value of the deals decreased 22 percent to $26.4 billion, the number of deals increased significantly, from 21 in 2001 to 45 in 2003. The increase in the number of smaller deals is probably "driven by the trend among pharma firms to buy biotechnology companies to bolster late-stage R&D pipelines." Although one large deal, the $60 billion acquisition of Pharmacia by Pfizer, was completed in April 2003, most firms are targeting small acquisitions to supplement market power and reinvigorate or create innovative drug pipelines.[52]

As indicated previously, compared to internal product development, acquisitions result in more rapid market entries.[53] Acquisitions often represent the fastest means to enter international markets and help firms overcome the liabilities associated with such strategic moves.[54] Acquisitions provide rapid access both to new markets and to new capabilities. Using new capabilities to pioneer new products and to enter markets quickly can create advantageous market positions.[55] Pharmaceutical firms, for example, access new products through acquisitions of other drug manufacturers. They also acquire biotechnology firms both for new products and for new technological capabilities. Pharmaceutical firms often provide the manufacturing and marketing capabilities to take the new products developed by biotechnology firms to the market.[56] Novartis, for example, has a significant ownership position in Roche, another Swiss-headquartered pharmaceutical firm, which has helped to develop the biotech powerhouse, Genentech. Through this relationship and other acquisitions over the years, Novartis' "pipeline is full." However, it would like to purchase the remaining shares of Roche to improve its position even more.[57]

Lower Risk Compared to Developing New Products

Because an acquisition's outcomes can be estimated more easily and accurately compared to the outcomes of an internal product development process, managers may view acquisitions as lowering risk.[58] The difference in risk between an internal product development process and an acquisition can be seen in the results of Novartis' strategy and that of its competitors described above.

As with other strategic actions discussed in this book, the firm must exercise caution when using a strategy of acquiring new products rather than developing them internally. While research suggests that acquisitions have become a common means of avoiding risky internal ventures (and therefore risky R&D investments), they may also become a substitute for innovation.[59] Thus, acquisitions are not a risk-free alternative to entering new markets through internally developed products.

Increased Diversification

Acquisitions are also used to diversify firms. Based on experience and the insights resulting from it, firms typically find it easier to develop and introduce new products in markets currently served by the firm. In contrast, it is difficult for companies to develop products that differ from their current lines for markets in which they lack experience.[60] Thus, it is uncommon for a firm to develop new products internally to diversify its product lines.[61] Using acquisitions to diversify a firm is the quickest and, typically, the easiest way to change its portfolio of businesses.[62] For example, Goodrich Corp. has evolved from a tire maker to a top-tier aerospace supplier through over 40 acquisitions that began in the mid-1980s. The firm has indicated that it will reduce the number of acquisitions over the next several years as it seeks to integrate its sizable acquisition of the former TRW Aeronautical Systems.[63]

Both related diversification and unrelated diversification strategies can be implemented through acquisitions.[64] For example, United Technologies has used acquisitions to

Acquisitions are a quick way for a firm to diversify. Using acquisitions, Goodrich Corp., for example, has evolved from being a tire maker to a top-tier aerospace supplier.

©Russ Schleipman

build a conglomerate—a highly unrelated diversified firm.[65] It has been building a portfolio of stable and noncyclical businesses, including Otis Elevator Co. and Carrier Corporation (air conditioners), since the mid-1970s in order to reduce its dependence on the volatile aerospace industry. Its main businesses have been Pratt & Whitney (jet engines), Sikorsky (helicopters), and Hamilton Sundstrand (aerospace parts). It has also acquired a hydrogen-fuel-cell business. However, perceiving an opportunity in security caused by problems at airports and because security has become a top concern both for governments and for corporations, United Technologies has agreed to acquire Chubb PLC, a British electronic-security company, for $1 billion. This is the largest deal United Technologies has attempted since its 2001 bid for Honeywell Inc., which failed due to an offer from General Electric (GE). However, as mentioned earlier, the GE offer did not materialize because it was not approved by European regulators.[66]

Research has shown that the more related the acquired firm is to the acquiring firm, the greater is the probability the acquisition will be successful.[67] Thus, horizontal acquisitions (through which a firm acquires a competitor) and related acquisitions tend to contribute more to the firm's strategic competitiveness than acquiring a company that operates in product markets quite different from those in which the firm competes.[68]

Reshaping the Firm's Competitive Scope

As discussed in Chapter 2, the intensity of competitive rivalry is an industry characteristic that affects the firm's profitability.[69] To reduce the negative effect of an intense rivalry on their financial performance, firms may use acquisitions to lessen their dependence on one or more products or markets. Reducing a company's dependence on specific markets alters the firm's competitive scope.

One of the arguments used in the Strategic Focus on Oracle's acquisition of PeopleSoft is that the acquisition would strengthen Oracle's competitive scope relative to its competitors. In an effort to copy Microsoft's successful strategy of bundling applications with an operating system, Oracle made a bid for PeopleSoft, a maker of human resource management software. Oracle's database in corporate computing is comparable to Microsoft's operating system on desktops, and Oracle was attempting to reduce its reliance on its database software by adding more applications to its bundle.[70] Similarly, GE reduced its emphasis in the electronics market many years ago by making acquisitions in the financial services industry. Today, GE is considered a service firm because a majority of its revenue now comes from services instead of industrial products.[71]

Learning and Developing New Capabilities

Some acquisitions are made to gain capabilities that the firm does not possess. For example, acquisitions may be used to acquire a special technological capability. Research has shown that firms can broaden their knowledge base and reduce inertia through acquisitions.[72] Therefore, acquiring firms with skills and capabilities that differ from its own helps the acquiring firm to learn new knowledge and remain agile.[73] Of course, firms are better able to learn these capabilities if they share some similar properties with the firm's current capabilities. Thus, firms should seek to acquire companies with different but related and complementary capabilities in order to build their own knowledge base.[74]

One of Cisco Systems' primary goals in its early acquisitions was to gain access to capabilities that it needed to compete in the fast-changing networking equipment industry that connects the Internet. Cisco developed an intricate process to quickly integrate the acquired firms and their capabilities (knowledge). Cisco's processes accounted for its phenomenal success in the latter half of the 1990s. However, "Cisco today is evolving from a loose federation of start-ups that rewarded 'speed at the expense of teamwork' and last-minute scrambling to grab opportunities." The goal is now more internal cooperation to "avoid the diving catch." Although Cisco continues to pursue acquisitions that build new capabilities, it completed only 10 acquisitions from January 2001 through July 2003, including four companies that Cisco cultivated, versus 23 acquisitions in 2000 alone.[75]

Problems in Achieving Acquisition Success

Acquisition strategies based on legitimate reasons described in this chapter can increase strategic competitiveness and help firms earn above-average returns. However, acquisition strategies are not risk-free. Reasons for the use of acquisition strategies and potential problems with such strategies are shown in Figure 7.1.

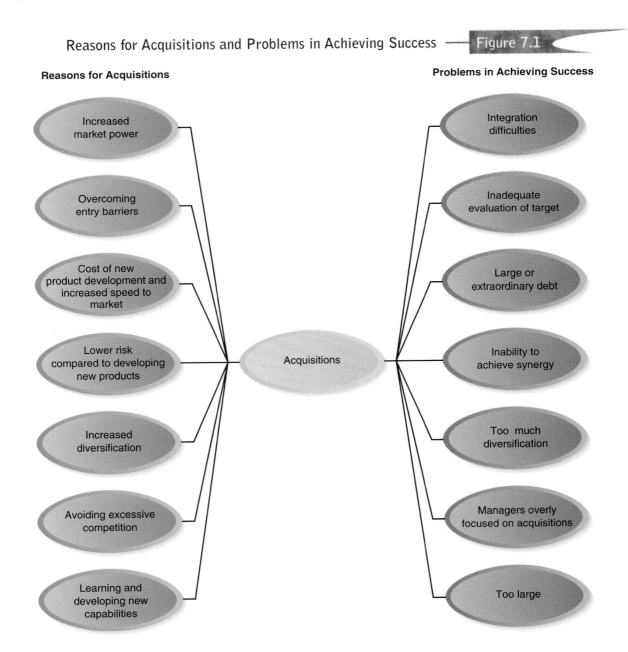

Reasons for Acquisitions and Problems in Achieving Success —— Figure 7.1

Reasons for Acquisitions

- Increased market power
- Overcoming entry barriers
- Cost of new product development and increased speed to market
- Lower risk compared to developing new products
- Increased diversification
- Avoiding excessive competition
- Learning and developing new capabilities

Acquisitions

Problems in Achieving Success

- Integration difficulties
- Inadequate evaluation of target
- Large or extraordinary debt
- Inability to achieve synergy
- Too much diversification
- Managers overly focused on acquisitions
- Too large

Research suggests that perhaps 20 percent of all mergers and acquisitions are successful, approximately 60 percent produce disappointing results, and the last 20 percent are clear failures.[76] Successful acquisitions generally involve a well-conceived strategy in selecting the target, avoiding paying too high a premium, and employing an effective integration process.[77] As shown in Figure 7.1, several problems may prevent successful acquisitions.

Integration Difficulties

Integrating two companies following an acquisition can be quite difficult. Integration challenges include melding two disparate corporate cultures, linking different financial and control systems, building effective working relationships (particularly when management styles differ), and resolving problems regarding the status of the newly acquired firm's executives.[78]

The importance of a successful integration should not be underestimated.[79] Without it, an acquisition is unlikely to produce positive returns. Thus, as suggested by a researcher studying the process, "managerial practice and academic writings show that the post-acquisition integration phase is probably the single most important determinant of shareholder value creation (and equally of value destruction) in mergers and acquisitions."[80]

Integration is complex and involves a large number of activities, which if overlooked can lead to significant difficulties. For instance, HealthSouth Corporation developed into a major power in the hospital and health-care industries through an aggressive acquisition strategy. However, the strategy's success was based primarily on generous government Medicare reimbursements. When Congress slashed the budget for such reimbursements, HealthSouth was not in a position to take advantage of its scale because the managers had not sought possible improved cost savings through integration. In fact, the CEO was accused of fraudulent reporting to make up for the significant losses, which went unreported. "Acquisitions covered a lot of sins. It allowed the company to layer on a lot of growth without necessarily digesting any of its purchases."[81]

It is important to maintain the human capital of the target firm after the acquisition. Much of an organization's knowledge is contained in its human capital.[82] Turnover of key personnel from the acquired firm can have a negative effect on the performance of the merged firm.[83] The loss of key personnel, such as critical managers, weakens the acquired firm's capabilities and reduces its value. If implemented effectively, the integration process can have a positive effect on target firm managers and reduce the probability that they will leave.[84]

Inadequate Evaluation of Target

Due diligence is a process through which a potential acquirer evaluates a target firm for acquisition. In an effective due-diligence process hundreds of items are examined in areas as diverse as the financing for the intended transaction, differences in cultures between the acquiring and target firm, tax consequences of the transaction, and actions that would be necessary to successfully meld the two workforces. Due diligence is commonly performed by investment bankers, accountants, lawyers, and management consultants specializing in that activity, although firms actively pursuing acquisitions may form their own internal due-diligence team.[85]

The failure to complete an effective due-diligence process may easily result in the acquiring firm paying an excessive premium for the target company. In fact, research shows that without due diligence, "the purchase price is driven by the pricing of other 'comparable' acquisitions rather than by a rigorous assessment of where, when, and how management can drive real performance gains. [In these cases], the price paid may have little to do with achievable value."[86]

Because many firms previously used investment banks to perform their due diligence, in the post-Enron era many firms are bringing their due diligence in-house. While investment bankers such as Credit Suisse First Boston and Citibank still play a large role in due diligence for big mergers and acquisitions, their role in smaller mergers and acquisitions seems to be decreasing. Deals completed through May 21, 2003, without any investment banking assistance for either buyer or seller, comprised 83 percent of the total number of deals, up from 73 percent during the same period ending in 2002. A growing number of companies are building their own internal operations to advise and finance mergers. First, companies are less inclined toward the sort of complex megadeals that took place regularly in the 1990s, and they don't feel that they need the investment banks' expensive counsel for small purchases. Second, some companies feel that no one should be more aware of their industry than they are; in other words, individual firms are just as capable, if not more capable, of finding appropriate partnerships for mergers or acquisitions. Third, it's much cheaper for companies to do without the expensive advice of investment bankers. However, although they are playing a lesser role, there will always be the need for an outside opinion for a company's board of directors—to reassure them about a planned merger and reduce their liability.[87]

As the Strategic Focus indicates, larger brewers have been paying too much for their latest acquisitions. Thus, better due diligence may be appropriate, even if the acquired firms increase the acquiring firm's market share.

Large or Extraordinary Debt

To finance a number of acquisitions completed during the 1980s and 1990s, some companies significantly increased their levels of debt. A financial innovation called junk bonds helped make this increase possible. *Junk bonds* are a financing option through which risky acquisitions are financed with money (debt) that provides a large potential return to lenders (bondholders). Because junk bonds are unsecured obligations that are not tied to specific assets for collateral, interest rates for these high-risk debt instruments sometimes reached between 18 and 20 percent during the 1980s.[88] Some prominent financial economists viewed debt as a means to discipline managers, causing them to act in shareholders' best interests.[89]

Junk bonds are now used less frequently to finance acquisitions, and the conviction that debt disciplines managers is less strong. Nonetheless, some firms still take on significant debt to acquire companies. For example, AOL Time Warner increased its total debt to $26 billion after its acquisition of AOL. Now it is straining to pay the debt and may need to break up the firm and sell off some of its myriad businesses (including its Internet assets [AOL], cable TV, filmed entertainment, network TV, music, and publishing) to do so.[90]

High debt can have several negative effects on the firm. For example, because high debt increases the likelihood of bankruptcy, it can lead to a downgrade in the firm's credit rating by agencies such as Moody's and Standard and Poor's.[91] In addition, high debt may preclude needed investment in activities that contribute to the firm's long-term success, such as R&D, human resource training, and marketing.[92] Still, use of leverage can be a positive force in a firm's development, allowing it to take advantage of attractive expansion opportunities. However, too much leverage (such as extraordinary debt) can lead to negative outcomes, including postponing or eliminating investments, such as R&D expenditures, that are necessary to maintain strategic competitiveness over the long term.

Inability to Achieve Synergy

Derived from *synergos,* a Greek word that means "working together," *synergy* exists when the value created by units working together exceeds the value those units could create working independently (see Chapter 6). That is, synergy exists when assets are

Consolidation in the Global Beer Industry and Firms Overpaying for Acquisitions

Large global brewers are faced with prospects for slow volume growth in their traditional developed markets. Although the world's ten largest brewers have grown more than four times relative to the total industry since the mid-1990s, combined volume of all brewers actually decreased during the same period. Consequently, this lack of growth has fueled the consolidation and acquisition process. Accordingly, this has led brewers either to make acquisitions of other brewers in already developed markets or to seek to develop strategic alliances or pursue acquisitions in developing markets. For instance, as noted earlier in the chapter, Miller Brewing was purchased by South African Breweries (SAB) from Philip Morris (now Altria Group Inc.) and the combined firm was named SAB-Miller. At the same time, this consolidation process has led to the rapid disappearance of many local brewers.

Anheuser-Busch has been very active as exemplified by its acquiring 27 percent (over time) of Tsingtao Brewery, the top brewer in China by volume sold. Coors has also joined the process by purchasing Carling Brewery in the United Kingdom, and each of Europe's leading brewers—Heineken, Interbrew, Carlsberg, and Scottish & Newcastle—has made significant acquisitions in the recent past.

AmBev, a Brazilian brewer, has made acquisitions in Latin America and aims to become a pan-American brewer, while Canada's Molson bought Kaiser, Brazil's largest competitor to AmBev. Although there is still no sign of a top global brewer, there are dominant players in each region. For instance, Heineken is big in Western Europe and the United States, but not large elsewhere.

In a recent acquisition, Heineken won the bidding for Austrian brewer BBAG, while SABMiller won the bidding for privately held Peroni, Italy's second largest brewer. However, analysts are arguing that the big five in Europe (Carlsberg, Heineken, Interbrew, SABMiller, and Scottish & Newcastle) have destroyed shareholder value and economic profit since 2001 through their acquisitions. These analysts were dumping shares of Heineken, for instance, because the acquisition of BBAG looked overpriced and would dilute Heineken's shareholder value. Heineken paid Euro 124 per share for BBAG, which was 30 percent higher than the price at which BBAG's shares had been trading.

It has been a year since SABMiller has released results, and analysts have downgraded the stock because the Miller acquisition further devalued it. The consensus was that Miller had not realized the synergies or benefits from the combination and, although Miller's performance could still turn around, the stock price has remained lower since the acquisition.

In the long run, the large brewers making these acquisitions may win out through market share dominance. In the short run, however, it might behoove some of the less nimble players to prepare for being purchased, because target firm shareholders are receiving more value from the acquisition process. Thus, for those firms willing to sell, value can be collected from selling to a bidder willing to overpay.

SOURCES: 2003, Food brief—Heineken NV: Dutch brewer set to acquire BBAG in $2.13 million deal, *Wall Street Journal*, May 5, A12; D. Bilefsky, 2003, Miller Beer aims to be icon in Europe, *Wall Street Journal*, June 13, B7; A. Caplan, 2003, Global beer: Tapping into growth, *Beverage World*, February 15, 24–29; J. Cioletti, 2003, Top 10 beers scoring 100, *Beverage World*, April 15, 29–31; B. Truscott, 2003, European trader: Is the beer stein half-full or half-empty? *Barron's*, June 2, MW6–MW7.

worth more when used in conjunction with each other than when they are used separately.[93] For shareholders, synergy generates gains in their wealth that they could not duplicate or exceed through their own portfolio diversification decisions.[94] Synergy is created by the efficiencies derived from economies of scale and economies of scope and by sharing resources (e.g., human capital and knowledge) across the businesses in the merged firm.[95]

A firm develops a competitive advantage through an acquisition strategy only when a transaction generates private synergy. *Private synergy* is created when the combination and integration of the acquiring and acquired firms' assets yield capabilities and core competencies that could not be developed by combining and integrating either firm's assets with another company. Private synergy is possible when firms' assets are complementary in unique ways; that is, the unique type of asset complementarity is not possible by combining either company's assets with another firm's assets.[96] Because of its uniqueness, private synergy is difficult for competitors to understand and imitate. However, private synergy is difficult to create.

A firm's ability to account for costs that are necessary to create anticipated revenue- and cost-based synergies affects the acquisition's success. Firms experience several expenses when trying to create private synergy through acquisitions. Called transaction costs, these expenses are incurred when firms use acquisition strategies to create synergy.[97] Transaction costs may be direct or indirect. Direct costs include legal fees and charges from investment bankers who complete due diligence for the acquiring firm. Indirect costs include managerial time to evaluate target firms and then to complete negotiations, as well as the loss of key managers and employees following an acquisition.[98] Firms tend to underestimate the sum of indirect costs when the value of the synergy that may be created by combining and integrating the acquired firm's assets with the acquiring firm's assets is calculated.

Interpublic Group is an example of a company that has failed to achieve synergy with its acquisitions. Interpublic Group (IPG) is an ad agency holding company that has bought more than 300 companies in the past five years. IPG is loaded with debt, and the promised synergies between advertising and marketing properties have failed to appear. Non-advertising businesses were supposed to hedge the notorious cycles of the ad business, but that also has not been the case in the recent downturn. CEO David Bell envisioned "one-stop shopping" for advertising, packaging, and promotions, but the subsidiary companies fought the idea. The cultural differences between advertisers and non-advertisers were wide, and clients themselves overwhelmingly believed that they should choose the best talent in each discipline, regardless of which company owned it. While CEO Bell hasn't given up yet on making the one-stop shopping concept work, many customers and investors have.[99] Similarly, as the Strategic Focus on the global brewing industry indicates, the synergies expected from many of the acquisitions between beer producers have not materialized as expected.

Too Much Diversification

As explained in Chapter 6, diversification strategies can lead to strategic competitiveness and above-average returns. In general, firms using related diversification strategies outperform those employing unrelated diversification strategies. However, conglomerates, formed by using an unrelated diversification strategy, also can be successful. For example, Virgin Group, the U.K. firm with interests ranging from cosmetics to trains, is successful.[100]

At some point, firms can become overdiversified. The level at which overdiversification occurs varies across companies because each firm has different capabilities to manage diversification. Recall from Chapter 6 that related diversification requires more information processing than does unrelated diversification. The need for related diversified firms to process more information of greater diversity is such that they become overdiversified with a smaller number of business units, compared to firms using an unrelated diversification strategy.[101] Regardless of the type of diversification strategy implemented, however, declines in performance result from overdiversification, after which business units are often divested.[102] The pattern of excessive diversification followed by divestments of underperforming business units acquired earlier is currently taking place in the media industry, as the Opening Case illustrates. Many firms in the media industry have been seeking to divest businesses bought in the boom era of the late 1990s through 2001 when the Internet economy collapsed.[103] These cycles were also frequently observed among U.S. firms during the 1960s through the 1980s.[104]

Even when a firm is not overdiversified, a high level of diversification can have a negative effect on the firm's long-term performance. For example, the scope created by additional amounts of diversification often causes managers to rely on financial rather than strategic controls to evaluate business units' performances (financial and strategic controls are defined and explained in Chapters 11 and 12). Top-level executives often rely on financial controls to assess the performance of business units when they do not have a rich understanding of business units' objectives and strategies. Use of financial controls, such as return on investment (ROI), causes individual business-unit managers to focus on short-term outcomes at the expense of long-term investments. When long-term investments are reduced to increase short-term profits, a firm's overall strategic competitiveness may be harmed.[105]

Another problem resulting from too much diversification is the tendency for acquisitions to become substitutes for innovation. Typically, managers do not intend acquisitions to be used in that way. However, a reinforcing cycle evolves. Costs associated with acquisitions may result in fewer allocations to activities, such as R&D, that are linked to innovation. Without adequate support, a firm's innovation skills begin to atrophy. Without internal innovation skills, the only option available to a firm is to complete still additional acquisitions to gain access to innovation. Evidence suggests that a firm using acquisitions as a substitute for internal innovations eventually encounters performance problems.[106]

Managers Overly Focused on Acquisitions

Typically, a fairly substantial amount of managerial time and energy is required for acquisition strategies to contribute to the firm's strategic competitiveness. Activities with which managers become involved include (1) searching for viable acquisition candidates, (2) completing effective due-diligence processes, (3) preparing for negotiations, and (4) managing the integration process after the acquisition is completed.

Top-level managers do not personally gather all data and information required to make acquisitions. However, these executives do make critical decisions on the firms to be targeted, the nature of the negotiations, and so forth. Company experiences show that participating in and overseeing the activities required for making acquisitions can divert managerial attention from other matters that are necessary for long-term competitive success, such as identifying and taking advantage of other opportunities and interacting with important external stakeholders.[107]

Both theory and research suggest that managers can get overly involved in the process of making acquisitions.[108] "The urge to merge is still like an addiction in many companies: Doing deals is much more fun and interesting than fixing fundamental problems. So, as in dealing with any other addiction or temptation maybe it is best to just say no."[109] The overinvolvement can be surmounted by learning from mistakes and by not having too much agreement in the board room. Encouraging dissent is helpful to make sure that all sides of a question are considered (see Chapter 10).[110] When failure does occur, leaders may be tempted to blame the failure on others and on unforeseen circumstances rather than on their excessive involvement in the acquisition process.[111]

Corus was created in 1999 when British and Dutch steel firms combined to become the world's third largest steel company through $6 billion of market capitalization. However, in 2003, it was worth $200 million and was threatened with bankruptcy or possible breakup. Although the merger looked good and steel prices have recently risen, problems arose because of differing management practices of the British and Dutch systems and because the managers involved became focused on protecting their countries' interests.[112] Acquisitions can consume significant amounts of managerial time and energy in both the acquiring and target firms. In particular, managers in target firms may operate in a state of virtual suspended animation during an acquisition.[113] Although the target firm's day-to-day operations continue, most of the company's executives are hesitant to make decisions with long-term consequences until negotiations have been completed. Evidence suggests that the acquisition process can create a short-term perspective and a greater aversion to risk among top-level executives in a target firm.[114]

Too Large

Most acquisitions create a larger firm that should help increase its economies of scale. These economies can then lead to more efficient operations—for example, the two sales organizations can be integrated using fewer sales reps because a sales rep can sell the products of both firms (particularly if the products of the acquiring and target firms are highly related).

Many firms seek increases in size because of the potential economies of scale and enhanced market power (discussed earlier). For example, funeral home operators Service Corporation International (SCI), Stewart Enterprises, and Loewen Group each made numerous acquisitions of funeral home operations and sought to consolidate them to increase size and achieve better economies of scale. However, all three ultimately lost significant market share because they grew too fast and in a downturn lost most of their market capitalization. Through excessive debt and a slowdown in takeovers, for example, SCI and Stewart "fell more than 90 percent to lows of less than 2 dollars," although they have improved more recently. Loewen Group ultimately filed for bankruptcy and reorganized into the Alderwoods Group.[115]

At some level, the additional costs required to manage the larger firm will exceed the benefits of the economies of scale and additional market power, as in the funeral home operators example above. Additionally, there is an incentive to grow larger because size serves as a takeover defense.[116] Research in the United Kingdom indicates that firms that acquire other firms and grow larger are less likely to be taken over.[117] However, the complexities generated by the larger size often lead managers to implement more bureaucratic controls to manage the combined firm's operations. Bureaucratic controls are formalized supervisory and behavioral rules and policies designed to ensure consistency of decisions and actions across different units of a firm. However, through time, formalized controls often lead to relatively rigid and standardized managerial behavior. Certainly, in the long run, the diminished flexibility that accompanies rigid and standardized managerial behavior may produce less innovation. Because of innovation's importance to competitive success, the bureaucratic controls resulting from a large organization (that is, built by acquisitions) can have a detrimental effect on performance.[118]

Effective Acquisitions

Earlier in the chapter, we noted that acquisition strategies do not consistently produce above-average returns for the acquiring firm's shareholders.[119] Nonetheless, some companies are able to create value when using an acquisition strategy.[120] For example, few companies have grown so successfully by acquisition as Computer Associates (CA). Charles Wang, the founder, watched and waited for software companies to show signs of weakness and then purchased them. By staying ultra-lean, CA kept many programs running and supported that otherwise would have been untenable. Although customers with existing software complained about increased fees and shoddy service after CA moved in, new customers delighted in the innovative pricing. Through its expansion, CA could serve a valuable function, especially for mainframe owners, as an alternative to IBM with its more rigid pricing and contracts, thus keeping IBM more nimble.[121]

Results from a research study shed light on the differences between unsuccessful and successful acquisition strategies and suggest that there is a pattern of actions that can improve the probability of acquisition success.[122] The study shows that when the target firm's assets are complementary to the acquired firm's assets, an acquisition is more successful. With complementary assets, integrating two firms' operations has a higher probability of creating synergy. In fact, integrating two firms with complementary assets frequently produces unique capabilities and core competencies.[123] With complementary assets, the acquiring firm can maintain its focus on core businesses and leverage the complementary assets and capabilities from the acquired firm. Often, targets were selected and "groomed" by establishing a working relationship prior to the acquisition.[124] As discussed in Chapter 9, strategic alliances are sometimes used to test the feasibility of a future merger or acquisition between the involved firms.[125]

The study's results also show that friendly acquisitions facilitate integration of the firms involved in an acquisition. Through friendly acquisitions, firms work together to find ways to integrate their operations to create synergy.[126] The acquisition of Ocean Energy Inc. by Devon Energy Corp. represents a friendly acquisition. The $5.3 billion deal created the country's largest independent oil company and gives Oklahoma City–based Devon Energy the near-term production growth it needed. Also, the premium paid was lower because the deal was friendly.[127] In hostile takeovers, animosity often results between the two top-management teams, a condition that in turn affects working relationships in the newly created firm. As a result, more key personnel in the acquired firm may be lost, and those who remain may resist the changes necessary to integrate the two firms.[128] With effort, cultural clashes can be overcome, and fewer key managers and employees will become discouraged and leave.[129]

Additionally, effective due-diligence processes involving the deliberate and careful selection of target firms and an evaluation of the relative health of those firms (financial health, cultural fit, and the value of human resources) contribute to successful acquisitions.[130] Financial slack in the form of debt equity or cash, in both the acquiring and acquired firms, also has frequently contributed to success in acquisitions. While financial slack provides access to financing for the acquisition, it is still important to maintain a low or moderate level of debt after the acquisition to keep debt costs low. When substantial debt was used to finance the acquisition, companies with successful acquisitions reduced the debt quickly, partly by selling off assets from the acquired firm, especially noncomplementary or poorly performing assets. For these firms, debt costs do not prevent long-term investments such as R&D, and managerial discretion in the use of cash flow is relatively flexible.

Another attribute of successful acquisition strategies is an emphasis on innovation, as demonstrated by continuing investments in R&D activities. Significant R&D investments show a strong managerial commitment to innovation, a characteristic that is increasingly important to overall competitiveness, as well as acquisition success.

Berkshire Hathaway is a conglomerate holding company owned by Warren Buffett, one of the world's richest men. Here Mr. Buffett talks to members of the media at a Berkshire Hathaway shareholders meeting. Looking at Table 7.1, you will see that he owes his wealth, in part, to observance of these seven attributes of successful acquisitions.

Getty Images

Flexibility and adaptability are the final two attributes of successful acquisitions. When executives of both the acquiring and the target firms have experience in managing change and learning from acquisitions, they will be more skilled at adapting their capabilities to new environments.[131] As a result, they will be more adept at integrating the two organizations, which is particularly important when firms have different organizational cultures.

Efficient and effective integration may quickly produce the desired synergy in the newly created firm. Effective integration allows the acquiring firm to keep valuable human resources in the acquired firm from leaving.[132]

The attributes and results of successful acquisitions are summarized in Table 7.1. Managers seeking acquisition success should emphasize the seven attributes that are listed. Berkshire Hathaway is a conglomerate holding company for Warren Buffett, one of the world's richest men. The company operates widely in the insurance industry and also has stakes in gems, candy, apparel, pilot training, and shoes. The company owns an interest in such well-known firms as Wal-Mart, American Express, Coca-Cola, Gillette, The Washington Post Company, and Wells Fargo, among others. Recently, Buffett has bought an interest in a Chinese energy firm, PetroChina.[133] His acquisition strategy in insurance has been particularly successful because he has followed many of the suggestions in Table 7.1.

As we have learned, some acquisitions enhance strategic competitiveness. However, the majority of acquisitions that took place from the 1970s through the 1990s did not enhance firms' strategic competitiveness. In fact, "history shows that anywhere between one-third [and] more than half of all acquisitions are ultimately divested or

Attributes of Successful Acquisitions — Table 7.1

Attributes	Results
1. Acquired firm has assets or resources that are complementary to the acquiring firm's core business	1. High probability of synergy and competitive advantage by maintaining strengths
2. Acquisition is friendly	2. Faster and more effective integration and possibly lower premiums
3. Acquiring firm conducts effective due diligence to select target firms and evaluate the target firm's health (financial, cultural, and human resources)	3. Firms with strongest complementarities are acquired and overpayment is avoided
4. Acquiring firm has financial slack (cash or a favorable debt position)	4. Financing (debt or equity) is easier and less costly to obtain
5. Merged firm maintains low to moderate debt position	5. Lower financing cost, lower risk (e.g., of bankruptcy), and avoidance of trade-offs that are associated with high debt
6. Acquiring firm has sustained and consistent emphasis on R&D and innovation	6. Maintain long-term competitive advantage in markets
7. Acquiring firm manages change well and is flexible and adaptable	7. Faster and more effective integration facilitates achievement of synergy

spun-off."[134] Thus, firms often use restructuring strategies to correct for the failure of a merger or an acquisition.

Restructuring

Defined formally, **restructuring** is a strategy through which a firm changes its set of businesses or financial structure.[135] From the 1970s into the 2000s, divesting businesses from company portfolios and downsizing accounted for a large percentage of firms' restructuring strategies. Restructuring is a global phenomenon.[136]

The failure of an acquisition strategy often precedes a restructuring strategy. Softbank, a Japanese telecommunications and Internet holding company built through acquisitions and partnering, has about 40 percent of the consumer broadband market in Japan, and sees itself within striking distance of the 3 million customers needed to break even on its digital subscriber line (DSL) service. However, the effect of the high cost of acquiring new customers (approximately $250 per customer) was obvious in the company's balance sheet, when it posted an $833 million loss in 2002. To keep the company liquid and to pay down its debt, Softbank is restructuring its holdings by selling its stakes in several companies, namely E*Trade, Yahoo!, and UTStarcom, as well as its stake in Aozora Bank, a national bank in Japan.[137]

In other instances, however, firms use a restructuring strategy because of changes in their external and internal environments. For example, opportunities sometimes surface in the external environment that are particularly attractive to the diversified firm in light of its core competencies. In such cases, restructuring may be appropriate to position the firm to create more value for stakeholders, given the environmental changes.[138]

As discussed next, there are three restructuring strategies that firms use: downsizing, downscoping, and leveraged buyouts.

Downsizing

Once thought to be an indicator of organizational decline, downsizing is now recognized as a legitimate restructuring strategy. *Downsizing* is a reduction in the number of a firm's employees and, sometimes, in the number of its operating units, but it may or may not change the composition of businesses in the company's portfolio. Thus, downsizing is an intentional proactive management strategy, whereas "decline is an environmental or organizational phenomenon that occurs involuntarily and results in erosion of an organization's resource base."[139]

In the late 1980s, early 1990s, and early 2000s, thousands of jobs were lost in private and public organizations in the United States. One study estimates that 85 percent of *Fortune* 1000 firms have used downsizing as a restructuring strategy.[140] Moreover, *Fortune* 500 firms laid off more than one million employees, or 4 percent of their collective workforce, in 2001 and into the first few weeks of 2002.[141] This trend continued in many industries in 2003. In particular, the airlines downsized in response to decreases in traffic caused by the SARS epidemic and the war in Iraq. For instance, Continental laid off 1,200 people in an effort to cut costs.[142] Firms use downsizing as a restructuring strategy for different reasons. The most frequently cited reason is that the firm expects improved profitability from cost reductions and more efficient operations, as exemplified by the Continental Airlines layoffs.

Downscoping

Compared to downsizing, downscoping has a more positive effect on firm performance.[143] *Downscoping* refers to divestiture, spin-off, or some other means of eliminating businesses that are unrelated to a firm's core businesses. Commonly, downscoping is described as a set of actions that causes a firm to strategically refocus on its core businesses.[144]

A firm that downscopes often also downsizes simultaneously. However, it does not eliminate key employees from its primary businesses in the process, because such action could lead to a loss of one or more core competencies. Instead, a firm that is simultaneously downscoping and downsizing becomes smaller by reducing the diversity of businesses in its portfolio.[145]

By refocusing on its core businesses, the firm can be managed more effectively by the top management team. Managerial effectiveness increases because the firm has become less diversified, allowing the top management team to better understand and manage the remaining businesses.[146]

In general, U.S. firms use downscoping as a restructuring strategy more frequently than do European companies, while the trend in Europe, Latin America, and Asia has been to build conglomerates. In Latin America, these conglomerates are called *grupos*. Many Asian and Latin American conglomerates have begun to adopt Western corporate strategies in recent years and have been refocusing on their core businesses. This downscoping has occurred simultaneously with increasing globalization and with more open markets that have greatly enhanced the competition. By downscoping, these firms have been able to focus on their core businesses and improve their competitiveness.[147]

Downscoping has been practiced recently by many Korean chaebol, large diversified business groups. Samsung has been very successful using this strategy. Lucky Goldstar (LG) Group is Korea's second largest chaebol with $92 billion in revenue in 2002. LG Group has been controlled by two families, the Koos and the Huhs, since its initiation in 1947. Since 1998, the two families have engaged in a major restructuring program. They have eliminated most of the cross-holding (an arrangement in which major subsidiaries held ownership in each other), which has been typical of Korean chaebol. In place of the cross-holding arrangement, they have created a holding company with more separation between subsidiaries. Although this has been a boon to investors, a shareholder lawsuit has been threatened, which suggests that the families have been shorting shareholders in many of the deals the holding company has completed. One of the major problems is that many of the diversified businesses are being sold to Koos and Huh family members as stand-alone companies. This has allowed the families, through the holding company structure, to continue in firm control of the group. Thus, although shareholders have gained from the restructuring, there is still a concern about too much family control and possible self-dealing.[148]

Leveraged Buyouts

Leveraged buyouts are commonly used as a restructuring strategy to correct for managerial mistakes or because the firm's managers are making decisions that primarily serve their own interests rather than those of shareholders.[149] A *leveraged buyout* (LBO) is a restructuring strategy whereby a party buys all of a firm's assets in order to take the firm private. Once the transaction is completed, the company's stock is no longer traded publicly. As the Strategic Focus on an LBO revival indicates, these deals have many purposes.

Usually, significant amounts of debt are incurred to finance a buyout; hence the term "leveraged" buyout. To support debt payments and to downscope the company to concentrate on the firm's core businesses, the new owners may

The Korean firm Lucky Goldstar (LG) Group has been heavily restructured through downscoping, as have other Korean chaebol that have previously been highly diversified. Shareholders are still expressing concern, however, about too much family control and self-interest. Pictured here is one of its products, a new iris scanning device (shown at Boston's Logan airport) manufactured by LG Electronics' Iris Technology Division.

Leveraged Buyouts and Private Equity Restructuring Deals Experience a Revival

Leveraged buyout associations receive funds from investors to invest in firms interested in being privately owned; as such, they are often labeled private equity funds. As the name implies, this is often done through the "leverage" of debt investment devices. Because of the Enron debacle and firms being under financial distress, assets sales through leveraged buyouts had increased. The *Wall Street Journal* indicated: "U.S. LBO volume doubled to $23 billion in 2002 from $11 billion the previous year, although it still remains below 2000 levels of $39 billion. The number of transactions held steady at 181. Worldwide LBOs increased to $81 billion, up 36% from 2001, with the number of deals falling 19.8% to 814." In commenting on the prospects of private equity funds, one analyst predicted: "With LBO shops having sufficient cash on hand, and there being a large number of distressed companies due to an adverse economic climate, there is ample reason to believe that 2003 will be a big year for LBOs."

Both investment and commercial banks often participate in these funds through syndicated arrangements to reduce risk. For example, Bain Capital, Texas Pacific Group, and Goldman Sachs helped to finance the $1.5 billion purchase of Burger King from Diageo PLC through syndicated loans among these banks.

Many firms are considering going private through leveraged buyouts through the help of private equity funds because of the increased safeguards for shareholders against corporate malfeasance. Some feel that the Sarbanes-Oxley Act of 2002 is too strict and does not allow enough flexibility for many firms, especially fast-moving technology firms and many small firms considering being listed on the NASDAQ stock exchange. Many of these firms, instead of going through an IPO, are choosing to receive funding from a private equity firm. For example, Quintiles, a pharmaceutical-testing company, pursued a private equity deal because it allowed the firm more flexibility to pursue its long-term growth, which requires expensive investments now. Dennis Gillings, the company founder, felt that market analysts of public companies were too focused on quarterly earnings and would fail to grasp his long-term strategy. Accordingly, he received $1.7 billion from Bank One's private equity arm to move forward with his strategy.

Wilbur Ross runs a private equity fund that has had significant success by buying distressed firms in mature businesses, such as textiles, carpet making, optical networking, and, lately, integrated steel mills. Ross has been steadfast in his pursuit of bankrupt and distressed companies, whether in boom or bust economic times. Carl Icahn says of Ross, "He has the abilities to see opportunities other investment bankers miss." In the past several years, Ross has bought 70 distressed properties, the largest of which are Burlington Industries in carpet making, 360 Networks in optical networking, and, most recently, Bethlehem Steel. He will seek to integrate Bethlehem Steel with previous acquisitions of LTV and Acme, which he brought together into the International Steel Group (ISG). Subsequent to the Bethlehem purchase, these steel operations will be responsible for more than 20 percent of U.S. production.

In searching for possible deals, Ross examines industries with a large concentration of high-yield financing, which he considers a red flag. Once these are identified, he tries to pick the survivors that will be able to overcome their difficulties and be successfully restructured. Regarding his steel investments, he believed that steel was "too vital to the economy and national security" to allow domestic production to disappear. Shortly after his investments, the Bush administration imposed a 30 percent tariff on foreign steel. Although ISG faces competitors from Japan, Russia, Mexico, and the European Union that are contesting the legality of U.S. tariffs at the World Trade Organization, Ross is confident that his integrated steel operations will be able to compete, given the restructuring that has been and will continue to be undertaken through the auspices of ISG managers. He is now continuing his search in real estate, energy, and other sectors for distressed firms that can be taken private through his large private equity fund.

SOURCES: J. Kahn, 2003, The burden of being public, *Fortune*, May 26, 35–36; K. Scannell, 2003, Year-end review of markets & finance 2002—LBO shops profit from scandals—buyouts accounted for 5% of 2002's M&A volume, *Wall Street Journal*, January 2, R8; N. Stein, 2003, Wilbur Ross is a man of steel, *Fortune*, May 26, 121–122; M. Sikora, 2003, Syndicated bank loans may fuel upturn in LBO deals expected in 2003, *Mergers and Acquisitions*, March, 18.

immediately sell a number of assets.[150] It is not uncommon for those buying a firm through an LBO to restructure the firm to the point that it can be sold at a profit within a five- to eight-year period.

Management buyouts (MBOs), employee buyouts (EBOs), and whole-firm buyouts, in which one company or partnership purchases an entire company instead of a part of it, are the three types of LBOs. In part because of managerial incentives, MBOs, more so than EBOs and whole-firm buyouts, have been found to lead to downscoping, an increased strategic focus, and improved performance.[151] Research has shown that management buyouts can also lead to greater entrepreneurial activity and growth.[152]

While there may be different reasons for a buyout, one is to protect against a capricious financial market, allowing the owners to focus on developing innovations and bringing them to the market.[153] As such, buyouts can represent a form of firm rebirth to facilitate entrepreneurial efforts and stimulate strategic growth.[154]

Restructuring Outcomes

The short-term and long-term outcomes resulting from the three restructuring strategies are shown in Figure 7.2. As indicated, downsizing does not commonly lead to a

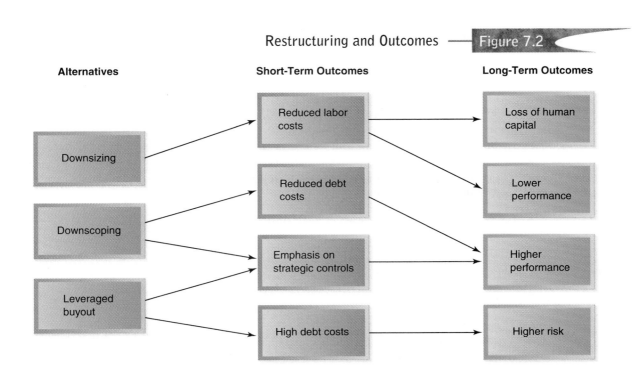

Restructuring and Outcomes — Figure 7.2

higher firm performance.[155] Still, in free-market-based societies at large, downsizing has generated an incentive for individuals who have been laid off to start their own businesses.

Research has shown that downsizing contributed to lower returns for both U.S. and Japanese firms. The stock markets in the firms' respective nations evaluated downsizing negatively. Investors concluded that downsizing would have a negative effect on companies' ability to achieve strategic competitiveness in the long term. Investors also seem to assume that downsizing occurs as a consequence of other problems in a company.[156] This is clear in the Continental Airlines layoffs mentioned above.

An unintentional outcome of downsizing, however, is that often, laid-off employees start new businesses in order to live through the disruption in their lives. Accordingly, downsizing has generated a host of entrepreneurial new ventures. For example, Richard Sheridan, a former vice-president of software development at Interface Systems, founded a software consulting business with a few other colleagues after being laid off in January 2001. His company, Menlo Innovations, broke even in 2001 and was profitable in 2002.[157]

As shown in Figure 7.2, downsizing tends to result in a loss of human capital in the long term. Losing employees with many years of experience with the firm represents a major loss of knowledge. As noted in Chapter 3, knowledge is vital to competitive success in the global economy.[158] Thus, in general, research evidence and corporate experience suggest that downsizing may be of more tactical (or short-term) value than strategic (or long-term) value.

Downscoping generally leads to more positive outcomes in both the short and the long term than does downsizing or engaging in a leveraged buyout (see Figure 7.2). Downscoping's desirable long-term outcome of higher performance is a product of reduced debt costs and the emphasis on strategic controls derived from concentrating on the firm's core businesses. In so doing, the refocused firm should be able to increase its ability to compete.

While whole-firm LBOs have been hailed as a significant innovation in the financial restructuring of firms, there can be negative trade-offs. First, the resulting large debt increases the financial risk of the firm, as is evidenced by the number of companies that filed for bankruptcy in the 1990s after executing a whole-firm LBO. Sometimes, the intent of the owners to increase the efficiency of the bought-out firm and then sell it within five to eight years creates a short-term and risk-averse managerial focus.[159] As a result, these firms may fail to invest adequately in R&D or take other major actions designed to maintain or improve the company's core competence.[160] Research also suggests that in firms with an entrepreneurial mind-set, buyouts can lead to greater innovation, especially if the debt load is not too great.[161] However, because buyouts more often result in significant debt, most LBOs have taken place in mature industries where stable cash flows are possible. This enables the buyout firm to meet the recurring debt payments as exemplified by Wilbur Ross' buyouts in the steel industry described in the Strategic Focus.

Summary

- Acquisition strategies are increasingly popular. Because of globalization, deregulation of multiple industries in many different economies, and favorable legislation, the number and size of domestic and cross-border acquisitions continues to increase.

- Firms use acquisition strategies to (1) increase market power, (2) overcome entry barriers to new markets or regions, (3) avoid the costs of developing new products and increase the speed of new market entries, (4) reduce the risk of entering a new business, (5) become more diversified, (6) reshape their competitive scope by developing a different portfolio of businesses, and (7) enhance their learning, thereby adding to their knowledge base.

- Among the problems associated with the use of an acquisition strategy are (1) the difficulty of effectively integrating the firms involved, (2) incorrectly evaluating the target firm's value, (3) creating debt loads that preclude adequate long-term investments (e.g., R&D), (4) overestimating the potential for synergy, (5) creating a firm that is too diversified, (6) creating an internal environment in which managers devote increasing amounts of their time and energy to analyzing and completing the acquisition, and (7) developing a combined firm that is too large, necessitating extensive use of bureaucratic, rather than strategic, controls.

- Effective acquisitions have the following characteristics: (1) the acquiring and target firms have complementary resources that can be the basis of core competencies in the newly created firm, (2) the acquisition is friendly thereby facilitating integration of the two firms' resources, (3) the target firm is selected and purchased based on thorough due diligence, (4) the acquiring and target firms have considerable slack in the form of cash or debt capacity, (5) the merged firm maintains a low or moderate level of debt by selling off portions of the acquired firm or some of the acquiring firm's poorly performing units, (6) the acquiring and acquired firms have experience in terms of adapting to change, and (7) R&D and innovation are emphasized in the new firm.

- Restructuring is used to improve a firm's performance by correcting for problems created by ineffective management. Restructuring by downsizing involves reducing the number of employees and hierarchical levels in the firm. Although it can lead to short-term cost reductions, they may be realized at the expense of long-term success, because of the loss of valuable human resources (and knowledge).

- The goal of restructuring through downscoping is to reduce the firm's level of diversification. Often, the firm divests unrelated businesses to achieve this goal. Eliminating unrelated businesses makes it easier for the firm and its top-level managers to refocus on the core businesses.

- Leveraged buyouts (LBOs) represent an additional restructuring strategy. Through an LBO, a firm is purchased so that it can become a private entity. LBOs usually are financed largely through debt. There are three types of LBOs: management buyouts (MBOs), employee buyouts (EBOs), and whole-firm LBOs. Because they provide clear managerial incentives, MBOs have been the most successful of the three. Often, the intent of a buyout is to improve efficiency and performance to the point where the firm can be sold successfully within five to eight years.

- Commonly, restructuring's primary goal is gaining or reestablishing effective strategic control of the firm. Of the three restructuring strategies, downscoping is aligned the most closely with establishing and using strategic controls.

Review Questions

1. Why are acquisition strategies popular in many firms competing in the global economy?

2. What reasons account for firms' decisions to use acquisition strategies as one means of achieving strategic competitiveness?

3. What are the seven primary problems that affect a firm's efforts to successfully use an acquisition strategy?

4. What are the attributes associated with a successful acquisition strategy?

5. What is the restructuring strategy and what are its common forms?

6. What are the short- and long-term outcomes associated with the different restructuring strategies?

Determining the Best Path to Firm Growth

You are on the executive board of an information technology firm that provides trafficking software to the trucking industry. One of the firm's managers feels the company should grow and has suggested expanding by creating trafficking software for rail shipments or by offering trucking trafficking services online. You know your firm is in a position to expand but are not sure about the best way to do so.

Part One. Should the firm consider a merger with or an acquisition of a firm that offers the suggested services, or should it develop them internally? List the advantages and disadvantages of each strategic option.

Part Two. Based on your findings and other information, assume that your firm decides to obtain trafficking software for rail shipments through an acquisition of an existing firm. Predict some general problems your firm might encounter in an acquisition and how they might be resolved.

Mergers and Acquisitions

Merger and acquisition activity is increasingly common, both domestically and internationally. However, such activity does not always result in the intended outcomes. In general, shareholders of acquired firms often enjoy above-average returns, while shareholders of acquiring firms are less likely to do so.

Identify a recent major merger or acquisition, such as one that made the front page of the *Wall Street Journal* or was a feature story in a business periodical such as *Fortune*, *Business Week*, or *The Economist*. Then find two or three other comprehensive articles about this merger or acquisition from more than one source, especially over a period of several weeks as the merger/acquisition events unfolded. This process of triangulation will provide a better understanding of any business activity and its results, as well as help substantiate the facts of the case.

1. What are the primary reasons for the merger or acquisition of study? Is this a horizontal, vertical, or related integration? How do you know? How is the firm's market power affected?

2. Was the merger or acquisition a success? To what extent do analysts anticipate problems in achieving success with this merger or acquisition? What issues appear to be of concern?

3. What happened to the stock prices of the involved firms before, during, and after the merger/acquisition? What actions could have been taken to make the integration more efficient and effective in achieving the acquiring firm's goals?

1. L. Capron & N. Pistre, 2002, When do acquirers earn abnormal returns? *Strategic Management Journal*, 23: 781–794.

2. K. Fuller, J. Netter, & M. Stegemoller, 2002, What do returns to acquiring firms tell us? Evidence from firms that make many acquisitions, *Journal of Finance*, 57: 1763–1793; M. A. Hitt, J. S. Harrison, & R. D. Ireland, 2001, *Mergers and Acquisitions: A Guide to Creating Value for Stakeholders*, New York: Oxford University Press.

3. G. K. Deans, F. Kroeger, & S. Zeisel, 2002, The consolidation curve, *Harvard Business Review*, 80(12): 20–21; 2000, How M&As will navigate the turn into a new century, *Mergers and Acquisitions*, January, 29–35.

4. J. A. Schmidt, 2002, Business perspective on mergers and acquisitions, in J. A. Schmidt (ed.), *Making Mergers Work*, Alexandria, VA: Society for Human Resource Management, 23–46.

5. E. R. Auster & M. L. Sirower, 2002, The dynamics of merger and acquisition waves: A three-stage conceptual framework with implications for practice, *Journal of Applied Behavioral Science*, 38: 216–244.

6. M. A. Hitt, R. D. Ireland, & J. S. Harrison, 2001, Mergers and acquisitions: A value creating or a value destroying strategy? in M. A. Hitt, R. E. Freeman, & J. S. Harrison, *Handbook of Strategic Management*, Oxford, UK: Blackwell Publishers, 385–408.

7. L. Saigol, 2002, Thin pickings in dismal year for dealmaking, *Financial Times*, http://www.ft.com, January 2; 2001, Waiting for growth, *The Economist*, http://www.economist.com, April 27.

8. 2002, Mergers snapshot: 2001 deal volume, *Wall Street Journal*, January 4, C12; 2001, The great merger wave breaks, *The Economist*, January 27, 59–60.

9. R. Sidel, 2002, Volatile U.S. markets and global slowdown cool corporate desire to merge, *Wall Street Journal*, January 2, R10.

10. J. Keough, 2003, M&A activity to rise in 2003, *Industrial Distribution*, February, 19–20.

11. L. Himelstein, L. Lee, J. Kerstetter, & P. Burrows, 2003, Let's make a deal: After a long M&A drought, corporate America is shopping around again, *Business Week*, April 21, 82–83.

12. R. Coff, 2003, Bidding wars over R&D-intensive firms: Knowledge, opportunism, and the market for corporate control, *Academy of Management Journal*, 46: 74–85; P. Chattopadhyay, W. H. Glick, & G. P. Huber, 2001, Organizational actions in response to threats and opportunities, *Academy of Management Journal*, 44: 937–955.

13. A. E. Bernardo & B. Chowdhry, 2002, Resources, real options, and corporate strategy, *Journal of Financial Economics*, 63: 211–234; M. A. Schilling & H. K. Steensma, 2002, Disentangling the theories of firm boundaries: A path model and empirical test, *Organization Science*, 13: 387–401; H. T. J. Smit, 2001, Acquisition strategies as option games, *Journal of Applied Corporate Finance*, 14(2): 79–89.

14. A. Bednarski, 2003, From diversity to duplication: Mega-mergers and the failure of the marketplace model under the Telecommunications Act of 1996, *Federal Communications Law Journal*, 55(2): 273–295.

15. L. Selden & G. Colvin, 2003, M&A needn't be a losers game, *Harvard Business Review*, 81(6): 70–73; J. P. Hughes, W. W. Lang, L. J. Mester, C.-G. Moon, & M. S. Pagano, 2003, Do bankers sacrifice value to build empires? Managerial incentives, industry consolidation, and financial performance, *Journal of Banking & Finance*, 27: 417–447.

16. K. Gugler, D. C. Mueller, R. B. Yurtoglu, & C. Zulehner, 2003, The effects of mergers: An international comparison, *International Journal of Industrial Organization*, 21: 625–653.

17. M. M. Cornett, G. Hovakimian, D. Palia, & H. Tehranian, 2003, The impact of the manager-shareholder conflict on acquiring bank returns, *Journal of Banking & Finance*, 27: 103–131; M. C. Jensen, 1988, Takeovers: Their causes and consequences, *Journal of Economic Perspectives*, 1(2): 21–48.

18. T. Wright, M. Kroll, A. Lado, & B. Van Ness, 2002, The structure of ownership and corporate acquisition strategies, *Strategic Management Journal*, 23: 41–53; Selden & Colvin, M&A needn't be a losers game; A. Rappaport & M.

19. L. Sirower, 1999, Stock or cash? *Harvard Business Review*, 77(6): 147–158.

19. A. Keeton, 2003, Class-action is approved against DaimlerChrysler, *Wall Street Journal*, June 13, B2.

20. J. Hall, 2003, Deals & deal makers: Kohlberg Kravis drops Safeway from shopping list, cites risk, *Wall Street Journal*, February 25, C5.

21. E. Thornton, F. Keesnan, C. Palmeri, & L. Himelstein, 2002, It sure is getting hostile, *Business Week*, January 14, 28–30.

22. R. Grover, 2003, Getting MGM off the back lot: Can Yemenidjian transform the studio into a media giant? *Business Week*, March 3, 101–102; J. Harding & C. Grimes, 2002, MGM owner sounds out possible suitors, *Financial Times*, http://www.ft.com, January 16; B. Pulley, 2001, The wizard of MGM, *Forbes*, May 28, 122–128.

23. P. Haspeslagh, 1999, Managing the mating dance in equal mergers, "Mastering Strategy" (Part Five), *Financial Times*, October 25, 14–15.

24. P. Wright, M. Kroll, & D. Elenkov, 2002, Acquisition returns, increase in firm size and chief executive officer compensation: The moderating role of monitoring, *Academy of Management Journal*, 45: 599–608.

25. G. Anders, 2002, Lessons from WaMu's M&A playbook, *Fast Company*, January, 100–107.

26. P. Starobin, 2003, A Russian oilman's global ambitions, *BusinessWeek Online*, http://www.businessweek.com, May 21.

27. Capron & Pistre, When do acquirers earn abnormal returns?; L. Capron, 1999, Horizontal acquisitions: The benefits and risks to long-term performance, *Strategic Management Journal*, 20: 987–1018.

28. M. Lubatkin, W. S. Schulze, A. Mainkar, & R. W. Cotterill, 2001, Ecological investigation of firm effects in horizontal mergers, *Strategic Management Journal*, 22: 335–357; K. Ramaswamy, 1997, The performance impact of strategic similarity in horizontal mergers: Evidence from the U.S. banking industry, *Academy of Management Journal*, 40: 697–715.

29. L. Capron, W. Mitchell, & A. Swaminathan, 2001, Asset divestiture following horizontal acquisitions: A dynamic view, *Strategic Management Journal*, 22: 817–844.

30. J. Markoff, 2003, Deal reunites early makers of handhelds, *New York Times*, http://www.nytimes.com, June 5.

31. M. R. Subramani & N. Venkatraman, 2003, Safeguarding investments in asymmetric interorganizational relationships: Theory and evidence, *Academy of Management Journal*, 46: 46–62; T. S. Gabrielsen, 2003, Conglomerate mergers: Vertical mergers in disguise? *International Journal of the Economics of Business*, 10(1): 1–16.

32. 2003, Special Report: The complete home entertainer? Sony, *The Economist*, March 1, 62–64.

33. W. Zellner, 2003, Tyson: Is there life outside the chicken coop? *Business Week*, March 10, 77.

34. D. Gupta & Y. Gerchak, 2002, Quantifying operational synergies in a merger/acquisition, *Management Science*, 48: 517–533.

35. D. E. M. Sappington, 2003, Regulating horizontal diversification, *International Journal of Industrial Organization*, 21: 291–315.

36. A. Barrett, 2003, "In the credibility penalty box": Can Honeywell CEO Cote restore investors' confidence? *Business Week*, April 28, 80–81.

37. A. R. Sorkin, 2003, Three's a crowd to air cargo giants, *New York Times*, http://www.nytimes.com, June 1.

38. M. Lerner, 2001, Israeli Antitrust Authority's general director David Tadmor on corporate mergers, *Academy of Management Executive*, 15(1): 8–11.

39. S. J. Chang & P. M. Rosenzweig, 2001, The choice of entry mode in sequential foreign direct investment, *Strategic Management Journal*, 22: 747–776.

40. N. Dawar & A. Chattopadhyay, 2002, Rethinking marketing programs for emerging markets, *Long Range Planning*, 35(5): 457–474; J. A. Gingrich, 1999, Five rules for winning emerging market consumers, *Strategy & Business*, 15: 19–33.

41. J. A. Doukas & L. H. P. Lang, 2003, Foreign direct investment, diversification and firm performance, *Journal of International Business Studies*, 34: 153–172; Hitt, Harrison, & Ireland, *Mergers and Acquisitions*, Chapter 10; D. Angwin &

B. Savill, 1997, Strategic perspectives on European cross–border acquisitions: A view from the top European executives, *European Management Review*, 15: 423–435.

42. A. Seth, K. P. Song, & R. R. Pettit, 2002, Value creation and destruction in cross-border acquisitions: An empirical analysis of foreign acquisitions of U.S. firms, *Strategic Management Journal*, 23: 921–940.

43. Schmidt, Business perspective on mergers and acquisitions.

44. A. M. Agami, 2002, The role that foreign acquisitions of Asian companies played in the recovery of the Asian financial crisis, *Multinational Business Review*, 10(1): 11–20.

45. 2002, Cleary Gottlieb acts in largest US cross-border deal of the year, *International Financial Law Review*, 21(12): 13.

46. D. Bilefsky, 2003, Miller Beer aims to be icon in Europe, *Wall Street Journal*, June 13, B7.

47. J. K. Sebenius, 2002, The hidden challenge of cross-border negotiations, *Harvard Business Review*, 80(3): 76–85.

48. W. Vanhaverbeke, G. Duysters, & N. Noorderhaven, 2002, External technology sourcing through alliances or acquisitions: An analysis of the application-specific integrated circuits industry, *Organization Science*, 6: 714–733; J. K. Shank & V. Govindarajan, 1992, Strategic cost analysis of technological investments, *Sloan Management Review*, 34(3): 39–51.

49. H. Gatignon, M. L. Tushman, W. Smith, & P. Anderson, 2002, A structural approach to assessing innovation: Construct development of innovation locus, type, and characteristics, *Management Science*, 48: 1103–1122; Hitt, Harrison, & Ireland, *Mergers and Acquisitions*.

50. M. A. Hitt, R. E. Hoskisson, R. A. Johnson, & D. D. Moesel, 1996, The market for corporate control and firm innovation, *Academy of Management Journal*, 39: 1084–1119.

51. Coff, Bidding wars over R&D-intensive firms: Knowledge, opportunism, and the market for corporate control.

52. 2003, Pharma and biotech M&A deal activity up in 2002, *Chemical Week*, April 2, 43.

53. T. Yoshikawa, 2003, Technology development and acquisition strategy, *International Journal of Technology Management*, 25(6,7): 666–674; K. F. McCardle & S. Viswanathan, 1994, The direct entry versus takeover decision and stock price performance around takeovers, *Journal of Business*, 67: 1–43.

54. Y. Luo, O. Shenkar, & M.-K. Nyaw, 2002, Mitigating liabilities of foreignness: Defensive versus offensive approaches, *Journal of International Management*, 8: 283–300; J. W. Lu & P. W. Beamish, 2001, The internationalization and performance of SMEs, *Strategic Management Journal*, 22(Special Issue): 565–586.

55. C. W. L. Hill & F. T. Rothaermel, 2003, The performance of incumbent firms in the face of radical technological innovation, *Academy of Management Review*, 28: 257–274; G. Ahuja & C. Lampert, 2001, Entrepreneurship in the large corporation: A longitudinal study of how established firms create breakthrough inventions, *Strategic Management Journal*, 22 (Special Issue): 521–543.

56. F. Rothaermel, 2001, Incumbent's advantage through exploiting complementary assets via interfirm cooperation, *Strategic Management Journal*, 22(Special Issue): 687–699.

57. K. Capell, 2003, Novartis CEO Daniel Vasella has a hot cancer drug and billions in the bank. What's his next big move? *Business Week*, May 26, 54.

58. G. Ahuja & R. Katila, 2001, Technological acquisitions and the innovation performance of acquiring firms: A longitudinal study, *Strategic Management Journal*, 22: 197–220; M. A. Hitt, R. E. Hoskisson, & R. D. Ireland, 1990, Mergers and acquisitions and managerial commitment to innovation in M-form firms, *Strategic Management Journal*, 11(Special Issue): 29–47.

59. Hitt, Hoskisson, Johnson, & Moesel, The market for corporate control.

60. Hill & Rothaermel, The performance of incumbent firms in the face of radical technological innovation.

61. M. A. Hitt, R. E. Hoskisson, R. D. Ireland, & J. S. Harrison, 1991, Effects of acquisitions on R&D inputs and outputs, *Academy of Management Journal*, 34: 693–706.

62. Capron, Mitchell, & Swaminathan, Asset divestiture following horizontal acquisitions; D. D. Bergh, 1997, Predicting divestiture of unrelated acquisitions: An integrative model of ex ante conditions, *Strategic Management Journal*, 18: 715–731.

63. A. L. Velocci, Jr., 2003, Goodrich curbs appetite, focuses on TRW integration, *Aviation Week & Space Technology*, February 24, 33–34.

64. C. Park, 2003, Prior performance characteristics of related and unrelated acquirers, *Strategic Management Journal*, 24: 471–480; C. Park, 2002, The effects of prior performance on the choice between related and unrelated acquisitions: Implications for the performance consequences of diversification strategy, *Journal of Management Studies*, 39: 1003–1019.

65. P. L. Moore, 2001, The most aggressive CEO, *Business Week*, May 28, 67–77.

66. A. Raghavan & R. Sidel, 2003, Deals & deal makers: United Technologies seals deal, *Wall Street Journal*, June 12, C5.

67. Hitt, Harrison, & Ireland, *Mergers and Acquisitions*.

68. J. Anand & H. Singh, 1997, Asset redeployment, acquisitions and corporate strategy in declining industries, *Strategic Management Journal*, 18(Special Issue): 99–118.

69. W. J. Ferrier, 2001, Navigating the competitive landscape: The drivers and consequences of competitive aggressiveness, *Academy of Management Journal*, 44: 858–877.

70. S. Lohr, 2003, PeopleSoft bid mirrors lofty goals of Oracle chief executive, *New York Times*, http://www.nytimes.com, June 11.

71. M. Warner, 2002, Can GE light up the market again? *Fortune*, November 11, 108–117; R. E. Hoskisson & M. A. Hitt, 1994, *Downscoping: How to Tame the Diversified Firm*, New York: Oxford University Press.

72. J. Anand & A. Delios, 2002, Absolute and relative resources as determinants of international acquisitions, *Strategic Management Journal*, 23(2): 119–134; F. Vermeulen & H. Barkema, 2001, Learning through acquisitions, *Academy of Management Journal*, 44: 457–476.

73. M. L. A. Hayward, 2002, When do firms learn from their acquisition experience? Evidence from 1990–1995, *Strategic Management Journal*, 23: 21–39.

74. J. S. Harrison, M. A. Hitt, R. E. Hoskisson, & R. D. Ireland, 2001, Resource complementarity in business combinations: Extending the logic to organizational alliances, *Journal of Management*, 27: 679–690.

75. S. Thurm, 2003, After the boom: A go-go giant of Internet age, Cisco is learning to go slow, *Wall Street Journal*, May 7, A1.

76. Schmidt, Business perspective on mergers and acquisitions.

77. Hitt, Harrison, & Ireland, *Mergers and Acquisitions*.

78. R. A. Weber & C. F. Camerer, 2003, Cultural conflict and merger failure: An experimental approach, *Management Science*, 49: 400–415; J. Vester, 2002, Lessons learned about integrating acquisitions, *Research Technology Management*, 45(3): 33–41; D. K. Datta, 1991, Organizational fit and acquisition performance: Effects of post-acquisition integration, *Strategic Management Journal*, 12: 281–297.

79. Y. Weber & E. Menipaz, 2003, Measuring cultural fit in mergers and acquisitions, *International Journal of Business Performance Management*, 5(1): 54–72.

80. M. Zollo, 1999, M&A—The challenge of learning to integrate, "Mastering Strategy" (Part Eleven), *Financial Times*, December 6, 14–15.

81. C. Haddad, A. Weintraub, & B. Grow, 2003, Too good to be true, *Business Week*, April 14, 70–72.

82. M. A. Hitt, L. Bierman, K. Shimizu, & R. Kochhar, 2001, Direct and moderating effects of human capital on strategy and performance in professional service firms, *Academy of Management Journal*, 44: 13–28.

83. J. A. Krug, 2003, Why do they keep leaving? *Harvard Business Review*, 81(2): 14–15; H. A. Krishnan & D. Park, 2002, The impact of workforce reduction on subsequent performance in major mergers and acquisitions: An exploratory study, *Journal of Business Research*, 55(4): 285–292; G. G. Dess & J. D. Shaw, 2001, Voluntary turnover, social capital and organizational performance, *Academy of Management Review*, 26: 446–456.

84. R. G. Baptiste, 2002, The merger of ACE and CARE: Two Caribbean banks, *Journal of Applied Behavioral Science*, 38: 466–480; J. A. Krug & H. Hegarty,

85. L. B. Nygaard, 2002, Mergers and acquisitions: Beyond due diligence, *Internal Auditor*, 59(2): 36–43.

86. Rappaport & Sirower, Stock or cash? 149.

87. E. Thornton, 2003, Bypassing the street, *Business Week*, June 2, 79.

88. G. Yago, 1991, *Junk Bonds: How High Yield Securities Restructured Corporate America*, New York: Oxford University Press, 146–148.

89. M. C. Jensen, 1986, Agency costs of free cash flow, corporate finance, and takeovers, *American Economic Review*, 76: 323–329.

90. A. Fass, 2003, AOL Time over? *Forbes*, June 23, 49.

91. M. A. Hitt & D. L. Smart, 1994, Debt: A disciplining force for managers or a debilitating force for organizations? *Journal of Management Inquiry*, 3: 144–152.

92. Hitt, Harrison, & Ireland, *Mergers and Acquisitions*.

93. T. N. Hubbard, 1999, Integration strategies and the scope of the company, "Mastering Strategy" (Part Eleven), *Financial Times*, December 6, 8–10.

94. Hitt, Harrison, & Ireland, *Mergers and Acquisitions*.

95. Ibid.

96. Harrison, Hitt, Hoskisson, & Ireland, Resource complementarity in business combinations; J. B. Barney, 1988, Returns to bidding firms in mergers and acquisitions: Reconsidering the relatedness hypothesis, *Strategic Management Journal*, 9(Special Issue): 71–78.

97. O. E. Williamson, 1999, Strategy research: Governance and competence perspectives, *Strategic Management Journal*, 20: 1087–1108.

98. Hitt, Hoskisson, Johnson, & Moesel, The market for corporate control.

99. G. Khermouch, 2003, Interpublic Group: Synergy—or sinkhole? *Business Week*, April 21, 76–77.

100. B. Einhorn, F. Balfour, & K. Capell, 2002, More Virgin territory, *Business Week*, April 8, 25.

101. C. W. L. Hill & R. E. Hoskisson, 1987, Strategy and structure in the multiproduct firm, *Academy of Management Review*, 12: 331–341.

102. R. A. Johnson, R. E. Hoskisson, & M. A. Hitt, 1993, Board of director involvement in restructuring: The effects of board versus managerial controls and characteristics, *Strategic Management Journal*, 14(Special Issue): 33–50; C. C. Markides, 1992, Consequences of corporate refocusing: Ex ante evidence, *Academy of Management Journal*, 35: 398–412.

103. G. Garai, 2002, Take our outfit—Please! How do you start a small business? Maybe by relieving a corporation of a rashly acquired division, as our expert explains, *BusinessWeek Online*, http://www.businessweek.com, December 18.

104. D. Palmer & B. N. Barber, 2001, Challengers, elites and families: A social class theory of corporate acquisitions, *Administrative Science Quarterly*, 46: 87–120.

105. Hitt, Harrison, & Ireland, *Mergers and Acquisitions*.

106. Ibid.

107. Hughes, Lang, Mester, Moon, & Pagano, Do bankers sacrifice value to build empires? Managerial incentives, industry consolidation, and financial performance; Hitt, Hoskisson, Johnson, & Moesel, The market for corporate control.

108. M. L. A. Hayward & D. C. Hambrick, 1997. Explaining the premiums paid for large acquisitions: Evidence of CEO hubris, *Administrative Science Quarterly* 42: 103–127; R. Roll, 1986, The hubris hypothesis of corporate takeovers, *Journal of Business*, 59: 197–216.

109. J. Pfeffer, 2003, The human factor: Curbing the urge to merge, *Business 2.0*, July, 58.

110. Hayward, When do firms learn from their acquisition experience?

111. Weber & Camerer, Cultural conflict and merger failure: An experimental approach.

112. 2003, Business: Corus of disapproval; steel, *The Economist*, March 15, 61–62.

113. Hitt, Harrison, & Ireland, *Mergers and Acquisitions*; Hitt, Hoskisson, Ireland, & Harrison, Effects of acquisitions on R&D inputs and outputs.

114. R. E. Hoskisson, M. A. Hitt, & R. D. Ireland, 1994, The effects of acquisitions and restructuring (strategic refocusing) strategies on innovation, in G. von Krogh, A. Sinatra, and H. Singh (eds.), *Managing Corporate Acquisitions*, London: Macmillan Press, 144–169.

115. H. Greenberg, 2002, The buy-'em-up boondoggle, *Fortune*, July 22, 210.

116. R. M. Cyert, S.-H. Kang, and P. Kumar, 2002, Corporate governance, takeovers, and top-management compensation: Theory and evidence, *Management Science*, 48:453–469.

117. A. P. Dickerson, H. D. Gibson, & E. Tsakalotos, 2003, Is attack the best form of defence? A competing risks analysis of acquisition activity in the UK, *Cambridge Journal of Economics*, 27: 337–357.

118. Hitt, Harrison, & Ireland, *Mergers and Acquisitions*.

119. A. P. Dickerson, H. D. Gibson, and E. Tsakalotos, 2002, Takeover risk and the market for corporate control: The experience of British firms in the 1970s and 1980s, *International Journal of Industrial Organization*, 20: 1167–1195.

120. R. M. Di Gregorio, 2003, Making mergers and acquisitions work: What we know and don't know—Part II, *Journal of Change Management*, 3(3): 259–274; R. M. Di Gregorio, 2002, Making mergers and acquisitions work: What we know and don't know—Part I, *Journal of Change Management*, 3(2): 134–148.

121. B. Musler, 2002, Requiem for a predator, *Computerworld*, December 2, 25.

122. M. A. Hitt, R. D. Ireland, J. S. Harrison, & A. Best, 1998, Attributes of successful and unsuccessful acquisitions of U.S. firms, *British Journal of Management*, 9: 91–114.

123. Harrison, Hitt, Hoskisson, & Ireland, Resource complementarity in business combinations.

124. J. Hagedoorn & G. Dysters, 2002, External sources of innovative capabilities: The preference for strategic alliances or mergers and acquisitions, *Journal of Management Studies*, 39: 167–188.

125. J. Reuer, 2001, From hybrids to hierarchies: Shareholder wealth effects of joint venture partner buyouts, *Strategic Management Journal*, 22: 27–44.

126. R. J. Aiello & M. D. Watkins, 2000, The fine art of friendly acquisition, *Harvard Business Review*, 78(6): 100–107.

127. J. Wetuski, 2003, Devon-Ocean combination to be stronger than parts, *Oil & Gas Investor*, 23(4): 119–120.

128. D. D. Bergh, 2001, Executive retention and acquisition outcomes: A test of opposing views on the influence of organizational tenure, *Journal of Management*, 27: 603–622; J. P. Walsh, 1989, Doing a deal: Merger and acquisition negotiations and their impact upon target company top management turnover, *Strategic Management Journal*, 10: 307–322.

129. M. L. Marks & P. H. Mirvis, 2001, Making mergers and acquisitions work: Strategic and psychological preparation, *Academy of Management Executive*, 15(2): 80–92.

130. S. Rovit & C. Lemire, 2003, Your best M&A strategy, *Harvard Business Review*, 81(3): 16–17.

131. Hitt, Harrison, & Ireland, *Mergers and Acquisitions*; Q. N. Huy, 2001, Time, temporal capability and planned change, *Academy of Management Review*, 26: 601–623; L. Markoczy, 2001, Consensus formation during strategic change, *Strategic Management Journal*, 22: 1013–1031.

132. R. W. Coff, 2002, Human capital, shared expertise, and the likelihood of impasse in corporate acquisitions, *Journal of Management*, 28: 107–128.

133. S. McBride, 2003, China offers challenge for Buffett, *Wall Street Journal*, May 2, C11.

134. J. Anand, 1999, How many matches are made in heaven, Mastering Strategy (Part Five), *Financial Times*, October 25, 6–7.

135. R. A. Johnson, 1996, Antecedents and outcomes of corporate refocusing, *Journal of Management*, 22: 437–481; J. E. Bethel & J. Liebeskind, 1993, The effects of ownership structure on corporate restructuring, *Strategic Management Journal*, 14(Special Issue): 15–31.

136. R. E. Hoskisson, R. A. Johnson, D. Yiu, & W. P. Wan, 2001, Restructuring strategies of diversified groups: Differences associated with country institutional environments, in M. A. Hitt, R. E. Freeman, & J. S. Harrison (eds.), *Handbook of Strategic Management*, Oxford, UK: Blackwell Publishers, 433–463; S. R. Fisher & M. A. White, 2000, Downsizing in a learning

organization: Are there hidden costs? *Academy of Management Review*, 25: 244–251; E. Bowman & H. Singh, 1990, Overview of corporate restructuring: Trends and consequences, in L. Rock & R. H. Rock (eds.), *Corporate Restructuring*, New York: McGraw-Hill.

137. 2003, Business: Hard times; Softbank's woes, *The Economist*, May 17: 78.

138. T. A. Kruse, 2002, Asset liquidity and the determinants of asset sales by poorly performing firms, *Financial Management*, 31(4): 107–129.

139. G. J. Castrogiovanni & G. D. Bruton, 2000, Business turnaround processes following acquisitions: Reconsidering the role of retrenchment, *Journal of Business Research*, 48: 25–34; W. McKinley, J. Zhao, & K. G. Rust, 2000, A sociocognitive interpretation of organizational downsizing, *Academy of Management Review*, 25: 227–243.

140. W. McKinley, C. M. Sanchez, & A. G. Schick, 1995, Organizational downsizing: Constraining, cloning, learning, *Academy of Management Executive*, 9(3): 32–44.

141. P. Patsuris, 2002, Forbes.com layoff tracker surpasses 1M mark, *Forbes*, http://www.forbes.com, January 16.

142. A. G. Keane, 2003, Up is down, *Traffic World*, May 12, 26–27.

143. Hoskisson & Hitt, *Downscoping*.

144. L. Dranikoff, T. Koller, & A. Schneider, 2002, Divestiture: Strategy's missing link, *Harvard Business Review*, 80(5): 74–83.

145. M. Rajand & M. Forsyth, 2002, Hostile bidders, long-term performance, and restructuring methods: Evidence from the UK, *American Business Review*, 20(1): 71–81.

146. Johnson, Hoskisson, & Hitt, Board of director involvement; R. E. Hoskisson & M. A. Hitt, 1990, Antecedents and performance outcomes of diversification: A review and critique of theoretical perspectives, *Journal of Management*, 16: 461–509.

147. Hoskisson, Johnson, Yiu, & Wan, Restructuring strategies.

148. J. Doebele, 2003, Ends and means: Is the restructuring of LG aimed at benefiting investors—or its family members? *Forbes*, February 17, 68–70.

149. D. D. Bergh & G. F. Holbein, 1997, Assessment and redirection of longitudinal analysis: Demonstration with a study of the diversification and divestiture relationship, *Strategic Management Journal*, 18: 557–571; C. C. Markides & H. Singh, 1997, Corporate restructuring: A symptom of poor governance or a solution to past managerial mistakes? *European Management Journal*, 15: 213–219.

150. M. F. Wiersema & J. P. Liebeskind, 1995, The effects of leveraged buyouts on corporate growth and diversification in large firms, *Strategic Management Journal*, 16: 447–460.

151. S. C. Bae & H. Jo, 2002, Consolidating corporate control: Divisional versus whole-company leveraged buyouts, *Journal of Financial Research*, 25(2): 247–262; A. Seth & J. Easterwood, 1995, Strategic redirection in large management buyouts: The evidence from post-buyout restructuring activity, *Strategic Management Journal*, 14: 251–274; P. H. Phan & C. W. L. Hill, 1995, Organizational restructuring and economic performance in leveraged buyouts: An ex-post study, *Academy of Management Journal*, 38: 704–739.

152. C. M. Daily, P. P. McDougall, J. G. Covin, & D. R. Dalton, 2002, Governance and strategic leadership in entrepreneurial firms, *Journal of Management*, 3: 387–412.

153. M. Wright, R. E. Hoskisson, L. W. Busenitz, & J. Dial, 2000, Entrepreneurial growth through privatization: The upside of management buyouts, *Academy of Management Review*, 25: 591–601.

154. M. Wright, R. E. Hoskisson, & L. W. Busenitz, 2001, Firm rebirth: Buyouts as facilitators of strategic growth and entrepreneurship, *Academy of Management Executive*, 15(1): 111–125.

155. Bergh, Executive retention and acquisition outcomes: A test of opposing views on the influence of organizational tenure.

156. H. A. Krishnan & D. Park, 2002, The impact of work force reduction on subsequent performance in major mergers and acquisitions: An exploratory study, *Journal of Business Research*, 55(4): 285–292; P. M. Lee, 1997, A comparative analysis of layoff announcements and stock price reactions in the United States and Japan, *Strategic Management Journal*, 18: 879–894.

157. L. Kroll and E. Lambert, 2003, The accidental entrepreneur, *Forbes*, May 12, 90–96.

158. Fisher & White, Downsizing in a learning organization.

159. P. Desbrieres & A. Schatt, 2002, The impacts of LBOs on the performance of acquired firms: The French case, *Journal of Business Finance & Accounting*, 29(5,6): 695–729.

160. G. D. Bruton, J. K. Keels, & E. L. Scifres, 2002, Corporate restructuring and performance: An agency perspective on the complete buyout cycle, *Journal of Business Research*, 55: 709–724; W. F. Long & D. J. Ravenscraft, 1993, LBOs, debt, and R&D intensity, *Strategic Management Journal*, 14(Special Issue): 119–135.

161. Wright, Hoskisson, Busenitz, & Dial, Entrepreneurial growth through privatization; S. A Zahra, 1995, Corporate entrepreneurship and financial performance: The case of management leveraged buyouts, *Journal of Business Venturing*, 10: 225–248.

International Strategy

Chapter Eight

8

Knowledge Objectives

Studying this chapter should provide you with the strategic management knowledge needed to:

1. Explain traditional and emerging motives for firms to pursue international diversification.

2. Explore the four factors that lead to a basis for international business-level strategies.

3. Define the three international corporate-level strategies: multidomestic, global, and transnational.

4. Discuss the environmental trends affecting international strategy, especially liability of foreignness and regionalization.

5. Name and describe the five alternative modes for entering international markets.

6. Explain the effects of international diversification on firm returns and innovation.

7. Name and describe two major risks of international diversification.

8. Explain why the positive outcomes from international expansion are limited.

South-Western Publishing

Since joining the World Trade Organization, China has attracted a large amount of foreign direct investment, especially from manufacturing firms. Volkswagen, for example, has a bigger operation in China than it does in Germany, and it is still growing!

China: Manufacturer for the World

China, since the signing of the World Trade Organization (WTO) agreement, has accumulated a significant amount of foreign direct investment (FDI). Most of this foreign direct investment has come from manufacturing firms looking for low wages, and thereby lower costs, especially in labor-intensive industries. For example, China now manufactures 60 percent of the world's bicycles; 86 percent of those are sold in the United States. Rival manufacturers in Latin America and Africa are thus struggling to survive. One analyst suggests that the bicycle industry is the symbol of what most of the world fears about China: "Its phenomenally fast growth can be sustained only at the expense of other economies, both developed and developing." Another analyst suggested that China's exports could exceed those of Japan by 2005. Furthermore, it was suggested that part of the deflation threat in other countries might be because of China's industrialization: "China's industrialization devalues manufacturing assets outside of China." In fact, in 2002, China displaced Japan as the third largest trading partner with the United States, behind Canada and Mexico.

As export quotas in the textile industry expire in 2004, it is expected that China's share of the world's garment exports will increase from 20 percent to about 50 percent by the end of the decade. Other labor-intensive industries, such as shoes, semiconductors, and televisions, are likely to follow. This is due to the very low wages and seemingly endless supply of labor of China. This supply is also increased because, as large, state-owned enterprises restructure, they lay off people who then have the opportunity to be hired in newly developing, foreign capitalized manufacturing plants. For instance, average wages in the garment industry in China are forty cents an hour, less than a third of that of Mexico.

On the other hand, one explanation for the success of bicycle exporting is that China's bicycle manufacturers have lost half their domestic market; 20 percent fewer bicycles are being sold in China whereas more cars are being sold. In 2002, one million cars were sold for the first time, and that number was expected to rise by 20 percent in 2003. The point is that these cars are being produced in China by firms such as Volkswagen and General Motors. For example, "Volkswagen is already bigger in China than it is in Germany, and it is looking to add more capacity." Also, Ford expects China to become a bigger market for its vehicles than both Germany and Japan within five years. As such, as China grows, it becomes a bigger market for other people's goods. Thus, besides representing a threat, it also represents an opportunity for sales growth.

Due to the increased trade, China's economy is already very significant. In terms of GDP, it is the sixth largest economy in the world, just somewhat smaller than France. In 2002, China had a growth rate approaching 8 percent, by far the most dynamic large economy in the world. In fact, in 2002, China surpassed the United States as the world's largest recipient of FDI, with $53 billion. (This had to do more with collapse of investment in the United States, however; in 1999 and 2000, FDI in the United States was $283 billion and $301 billion, respectively. Nonetheless, FDI has been growing over the last three years in China.)

Not only is labor-intensive manufacturing being moved to China, but also high-value manufacturing has increasingly been locating in China. This is evidenced by the battle between DHL, FedEx, and UPS, all seeking to have operations in China. These companies do a lot of business for high-value (high-technology) manufacturing that is relocating to mainland China.

In summary, the WTO agreement has led to the acceleration of firms locating to China, first to reduce expenses, but also to take advantage of a larger market, such as the auto companies and the express delivery companies mentioned. It is a significant draw for FDI for the expected future growth given the possible size of its market as its people become more able to buy high-valued goods. China will also be a significant economic player as one of the top-producing economies in the world within this decade, barring unforeseen problems that may derail its growth prospects.

SOURCES: 2003, Special Report: Is the wakening giant a monster? China's economy, *The Economist*, February 15, 63–65; J. T. Areddy, 2003, China is allowing companies more flexibility over the yuan, *Wall Street Journal Online*, http//:www.wsj.com, June 22; J. Flint, 2003, China: How big, how fast, how dangerous? *Forbes*, http://www.forbes.com, July 1; F. Hansen, 2003, China in the WTO, *Business Credit*, May, 59–62; F. Hu, 2003, The Zhu Rongji's decade, *Wall Street Journal Online*, http//:www.wsj.com, March 10; G. Ip, 2003, The economy: Trade gap widens to record level—monthly deficit combines with other data to point to trouble for recovery, *Wall Street Journal*, February 21, A2; P. M. Norton & K. Almstedt, 2003, China joins the trade wars, *China Business Review*, January/February, 22–29; L. Weymouth, 2003, What's right, not popular, *Newsweek*, June 2, 32; L. Wozniak, 2003, DHL and FedEx race to integrate China, *Far Eastern Economic Review*, February 27, 42–44.

As the Opening Case indicates, China's entry into the World Trade Organization (WTO) has brought change not only to China and its trading partners, but also to firms in other countries such as Mexico that have depended on labor-intensive industry foreign direct investment to employ its people. Many of the potential investments in Mexican firms are losing out to Chinese firms.[1] While many firms have entered and will enter China in the coming years, foreign firms who have done so have found it difficult to manage the risk and establish legitimacy.[2]

China and its entrance into the WTO clearly illustrate how entering international markets features both opportunities and threats for firms that choose to compete in global markets. This chapter examines opportunities facing firms as they seek to develop and exploit core competencies by diversifying into global markets. In addition, we discuss different problems, complexities, and threats that might accompany use of the firm's international strategies.[3] Although national boundaries, cultural differences, and geographical distances all pose barriers to entry into many markets, significant opportunities draw businesses into the international arena. A business that plans to operate globally must formulate a successful strategy to take advantage of these global opportunities.[4] Furthermore, to mold their firms into truly global companies, managers must develop global mind-sets.[5] Especially in regard to managing human resources, traditional means of operating with little cultural diversity and without global sourcing are no longer effective.[6]

As firms move into international markets, they develop relationships with suppliers, customers, and partners, and then learn from these relationships. Such activity is evident in the pharmaceuticals industry as firms compete against each other in global markets and invest in all areas of the world in order to learn about new markets and new potential drugs.[7]

In this chapter, as illustrated in Figure 1.1, we discuss the importance of international strategy as a source of strategic competitiveness and above-average returns. The chapter focuses on the incentives to internationalize. Once a firm decides to compete internationally, it must select its strategy and choose a mode of entry into international markets. It may enter international markets by exporting from domestic-based operations, licensing some of its products or services, forming joint ventures with international partners, acquiring a foreign-based firm, or establishing a new subsidiary. Such international diversification can extend product life cycles, provide incentives for more innovation, and produce above-average returns. These benefits are tempered by political and economic risks and the problems of managing a complex international firm with operations in multiple countries.

Figure 8.1 provides an overview of the various choices and outcomes. The relationships among international opportunities, and the exploration of resources and capabilities that result in strategies and modes of entry that are based on core competencies as well as strategic competitiveness outcomes, are explored in this chapter.

©Reuters NewMedia Inc.

Signing an agreement for China's entry into the World Trade Organization.

Opportunities and Outcomes of International Strategy — Figure 8.1

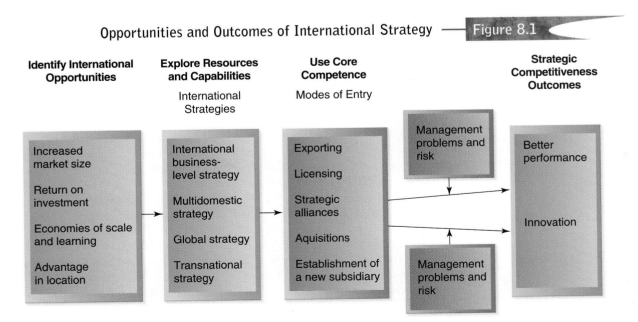

Identify International Opportunities	Explore Resources and Capabilities	Use Core Competence		Strategic Competitiveness Outcomes
	International Strategies	Modes of Entry		
Increased market size	International business-level strategy	Exporting	Management problems and risk	Better performance
Return on investment	Multidomestic strategy	Licensing		
Economies of scale and learning	Global strategy	Strategic alliances		Innovation
Advantage in location	Transnational strategy	Aquisitions		
		Establishment of a new subsidiary	Management problems and risk	

An international strategy is a strategy through which the firm sells its goods or services outside its domestic market.

An **international strategy** is a strategy through which the firm sells its goods or services outside its domestic market.[8] One of the primary reasons for implementing an international strategy (as opposed to a strategy focused on the domestic market) is that international markets yield potential new opportunities.[9]

Raymond Vernon captured the classic rationale for international diversification.[10] He suggested that, typically, a firm discovers an innovation in its home-country market, especially in an advanced economy such as that of the United States. Some demand for the product may then develop in other countries, and exports are provided by domestic operations. Increased demand in foreign countries justifies direct foreign investment in production capacity abroad, especially because foreign competitors also organize to meet increasing demand. As the product becomes standardized, the firm may rationalize its operations by moving production to a region with low manufacturing costs.[11] Vernon, therefore, suggests that firms pursue international diversification to extend a product's life cycle.

Another traditional motive for firms to become multinational is to secure needed resources. Key supplies of raw material—especially minerals and energy—are important in some industries. For instance, aluminum producers need a supply of bauxite, tire firms need rubber, and oil companies scour the world to find new petroleum reserves. Other industries, such as clothing, electronics, watch making, and many others, seek low-cost factors of production, and have moved portions of their operations to foreign locations in pursuit of lower costs as illustrated in the Opening Case on China.

Although these traditional motives persist, other emerging motivations also drive international expansion (see Chapter 1). For instance, pressure has increased for a global integration of operations, mostly driven by more universal product demand. As nations industrialize, the demand for some products and commodities appears to become more similar. This "nation-less," or borderless, demand for globally branded products may be due to similarities in lifestyle in developed nations. Increases in global communication media also facilitate the ability of people in different countries to visualize and model lifestyles in different cultures.[12] Benetton, an Italian casual-wear apparel company, although it has been forced to restructure given the global economic downturn, has used its global brand and well-established retail presence to more effectively manage its worldwide supply and manufacturing networks with improved communications technology.[13]

In some industries, technology drives globalization because the economies of scale necessary to reduce costs to the lowest level often require an investment greater than that needed to meet domestic market demand. The major Korean car manufacturers Daewoo, Hyundai, and Kia certainly found this to be true; accordingly, they have sought to enhance their operations in the United States and elsewhere.[14] There is also pressure for cost reductions, achieved by purchasing from the lowest-cost global suppliers. For instance, research and development expertise for an emerging business start-up may not exist in the domestic market.[15]

New large-scale, emerging markets, such as China and India, provide a strong internationalization incentive because of the potential demand in them.[16] Because of currency fluctuations, firms may also choose to distribute their operations across many countries, including emerging ones, in order to reduce the risk of devaluation in one country.[17] However, the uniqueness of emerging markets presents both opportunities and challenges.[18] While India, for example, differs from Western countries in many respects, including culture, politics, and the precepts of its economic system,[19] it also offers a huge potential market. Many international firms perceive Chinese markets as almost untouched markets, without exposure to many modern and sophisticated products. Once China is exposed to these products, these firms believe that demand will develop. However, the differences between China and Western countries pose serious challenges to Western competitive paradigms that emphasize the skills needed to manage financial, economic, and political risks.[20]

A large majority of U.S.-based companies' international business is in European markets, where 60 percent of U.S. firms' assets that are located outside the domestic market are invested.[21] Companies seeking to internationalize their operations in Europe, as elsewhere, need to understand the pressure on them to respond to local, national, or regional customs, especially where goods or services require customization because of cultural differences or effective marketing to entice customers to try a different product.[22]

Of course, all firms encounter challenges when using an international strategy. For example, Unilever is a large European-centered global food and consumer products firm that adapts its products to local tastes as it moves into new national markets.[23] Its investors expect Unilever executives to create global mega-brands, which have the most growth potential and margins, even though most of Unilever's growth has come through acquisition and the selling of the acquired, unique local brands. Establishing mega-brands while also dealing with the forces for localization is difficult.[24]

Local repair and service capabilities are another factor influencing an increased desire for local country responsiveness.[25] This localization may even affect industries that are seen as needing more global economies of scale, for example, white goods (home appliances, such as refrigerators). Alternatively, suppliers often follow their customers, particularly large ones, into international markets, which eliminates the firm's need to find local suppliers.[26] The transportation costs of large products and their parts, such as heavy earthmoving equipment, are significant, which may preclude a firm's suppliers from following the firm to an international market.

Employment contracts and labor forces differ significantly in international markets. For example, it is more difficult to lay off employees in Europe than in the United States because of employment contract differences. In many cases, host governments demand joint ownership, which allows the foreign firm to avoid tariffs. Also, host governments frequently require a high percentage of procurements, manufacturing, and R&D to use local sources. These issues increase the need for local investment and responsiveness compared to seeking global economies of scale.[27]

We've discussed incentives influencing firms to use international strategies. When successful, firms can derive four basic benefits from using international strategies: (1) increased market size; (2) greater returns on major capital investments or on investments in new products and processes; (3) greater economies of scale, scope, or learning; and (4) a competitive advantage through location (for example, access to low-cost labor, critical resources, or customers). We examine these benefits in terms of both their costs (such as higher coordination expenses and limited access to knowledge about host country political influences[28]) and their managerial challenges.

Increased Market Size

Firms can expand the size of their potential market—sometimes dramatically—by moving into international markets. Qualcomm, a chip maker for cell phones, views the large-scale, emerging markets in Asia as an incentive for its international strategy. Qualcomm holds a 90 percent market share for its chip technology, CDMA, and has aggressively and profitably pursued expansion into Asia. The company has been especially successful in China, where the telephone infrastructure has become mostly digital. Qualcomm has also devoted much research money to the next generation of CDMA, called WCDMA, which is becoming popular in Europe. The enormous market potential around the world has led to Qualcomm's pursuit of its international strategy.[29]

Although changing consumer tastes and practices linked to cultural values or traditions is not simple, following an international strategy is a particularly attractive option to firms competing in domestic markets that have limited growth opportunities. For example, firms in the beer industry lack significant growth opportunities in their domestic markets. Accordingly, as discussed in Chapter 7, most large global brewers have pursued a strategy of acquiring other brewers, both in developed markets and in emerging economies. For instance, Miller Brewing was purchased by South African Breweries (SAB) to form SABMiller, and Anheuser-Busch acquired a controlling interest in China's Tsingtao Brewery, a top volume brewer in China.[30]

The size of an international market also affects a firm's willingness to invest in R&D to build competitive advantages in that market.[31] Larger markets usually offer higher potential returns and thus pose less risk for a firm's investments. The strength of the science base in the country in question also can affect a firm's foreign R&D investments. Most firms prefer to invest more heavily in those countries with the scientific knowledge and talent to produce value-creating products and processes from their R&D activities.[32]

Return on Investment

Large markets may be crucial for earning a return on significant investments, such as plant and capital equipment or R&D. Therefore, most R&D-intensive industries such as electronics are international. This can be exampled by firms in the electronics-manufacturing services industry such as Flextronics. Before the electronics industry experienced a recent downturn, Flextronics flourished by buying "underused factories around the world from the likes of Hewlett-Packard, Siemens, and IBM."[33] Flextronics survived the downturn better than some of its competitors "by cutting the workforce in high-cost locations and adding in low-cost places."[34] However, because the firm moved a significant amount of capacity to China, its productivity was threatened by the SARS epidemic.[35] In addition to the need for a large market to recoup heavy investment in R&D, the development pace for new technology is increasing. As a result, new products become obsolete more rapidly. Therefore, investments need to be recouped more quickly. Moreover, firms' abilities to develop new technologies are expanding, and because of different patent laws across country borders, imitation by competitors is more likely. Through reverse engineering, competitors are able to take apart a product, learn the new technology, and develop a similar product that imitates the new technology. Because their competitors can imitate the new technology relatively quickly, firms need to recoup new product development costs even more rapidly. Consequently, the larger markets provided by international expansion are particularly attractive in many industries such as computer hardware, because they expand the opportunity for the firm to recoup significant capital investments and large-scale R&D expenditures.[36]

Regardless of other issues, however, the primary reason for investing in international markets is to generate above-average returns on investments. Still, firms from different countries have different expectations and use different criteria to decide whether to invest in international markets.[37] Turkey, for example, has experienced significant growth due to foreign direct investment over the last several decades because it has a fairly large market, but concerns about too much bureaucracy and instability have recently lowered levels of investment, especially due to the Iraq conflict.[38]

Economies of Scale and Learning

By expanding their markets, firms may be able to enjoy economies of scale, particularly in their manufacturing operations. To the extent that a firm can standardize its products across country borders and use the same or similar production facilities, thereby coordinating critical resource functions, it is more likely to achieve optimal economies of scale.[39]

Economies of scale are critical in the global auto industry. China's decision to join the World Trade Organization will allow carmakers from other countries to enter the country and lower tariffs to be charged (in the past, Chinese carmakers have had an advantage over foreign carmakers due to tariffs). Ford, Honda, General Motors, and Volkswagen are each producing an economy car to compete with the existing cars in China. Because of global economies of scale, all of these companies are likely to obtain market share in China.[40] As the Opening Case indicates, Ford expects to sell more cars in China than in both Germany and Japan within five years. Volkswagen already sells more cars in China than in Germany.[41] As a result, Chinese carmakers will have to change the way they do business to effectively compete against foreign carmakers.

Firms may also be able to exploit core competencies in international markets through resource and knowledge sharing between units across country borders.[42] This sharing generates synergy, which helps the firm produce higher-quality goods or services at lower cost. In addition, working across international markets provides the firm with new learning opportunities.[43] Multinational firms have substantial occasions to learn from the different practices they encounter in separate international markets. Even firms based in developed markets can learn from operations in emerging markets.[44]

Location Advantages

Firms may locate facilities in other countries to lower the basic costs of the goods or services they provide. These facilities may provide easier access to lower-cost labor, energy, and other natural resources. Other location advantages include access to critical supplies and to customers.[45] Once positioned favorably with an attractive location, firms must manage their facilities effectively to gain the full benefit of a location advantage.[46]

China's Internet portals have found their location to be a great advantage in reaching customers. All three of the major Chinese portals are profitable because they have focused less on computer Internet users and more on cell phone Internet users by building their business around text message updates sent to cell phones and sold on subscription. Even the SARS epidemic has been helpful—subscriptions to news updates increased 25 percent between March and June 2003.[47]

International Strategies

Firms choose to use one or both of two basic types of international strategies: business-level international strategy and corporate-level international strategy. At the business level, firms follow generic strategies: cost leadership, differentiation, focused cost leadership, focused differentiation, or integrated cost leadership/differentiation. There are three corporate-level international strategies: multidomestic, global, or transnational (a combination of multidomestic and global). To create competitive advantage, each strategy must realize a core competence based on difficult-to-duplicate resources and capabilities.[48] As discussed in Chapters 4 and 6, firms expect to create value through the implementation of a business-level strategy and a corporate-level strategy.[49]

International Business-Level Strategy

Each business must develop a competitive strategy focused on its own domestic market. We discuss business-level generic strategies in Chapter 4 and competitive rivalry and competitive dynamics in Chapter 5. International business-level strategies have some unique features. In an international business-level strategy, the home country of operation is often the most important source of competitive advantage.[50] The resources

Italy has become the leader in the shoe industry because of related and supporting industries such as leather processing, distribution through tourism in Italy, leather working, and design.

and capabilities established in the home country frequently allow the firm to pursue the strategy into markets located in other countries. However, as a firm continues its growth into multiple international locations, research indicates that the country of origin diminishes in importance as the dominant factor.[51]

Ikea, a furniture manufacturer and retailer, initiated its business-level strategy in its home market in Sweden in 1963. Later, Ikea entered the U.S. market in the mid-1980s. Currently, Ikea has 70,000 employees globally with 150 stores in over 30 countries; its sales total over $11 billion. Ikea's international success could not have been achieved in its domestic market alone, although it developed a strong culture and brand identity in its domestic market.[52]

Michael Porter's model, illustrated in Figure 8.2, describes the factors contributing to the advantage of firms in a dominant global industry and associated with a specific country or regional environment.[53] The first dimension in Porter's model is *factors of production*. This dimension refers to the inputs necessary to compete in any industry—labor, land, natural resources, capital, and infrastructure (such as transportation, postal, and communication systems). There are basic (for example, natural and labor resources) and advanced (such as digital communication systems and a highly educated workforce) factors. Other production factors are generalized (highway systems and the supply of debt capital) and specialized (skilled personnel in a specific industry, such as the workers in a port that specialize in handling bulk chemicals). If a country has both advanced

Figure 8.2 — Determinants of National Advantage

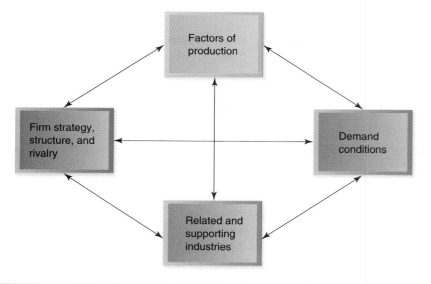

SOURCE: Adapted with the permission of The Free Press, an imprint of Simon & Schuster Adult Publishing Group, from *Competitive Advantage of Nations*, by Michael E. Porter, p. 72. Copyright ©1990, 1998 by Michael E. Porter.

and specialized production factors, it is likely to serve an industry well by spawning strong home-country competitors that also can be successful global competitors.

Ironically, countries often develop advanced and specialized factors because they lack critical basic resources. For example, some Asian countries, such as South Korea, lack abundant natural resources but offer a strong work ethic, a large number of engineers, and systems of large firms to create an expertise in manufacturing. Similarly, Germany developed a strong chemical industry, partially because Hoechst and BASF spent years creating a synthetic indigo dye to reduce their dependence on imports, unlike Britain, whose colonies provided large supplies of natural indigo.[54]

The second dimension in Porter's model, *demand conditions,* is characterized by the nature and size of buyers' needs in the home market for the industry's goods or services. The sheer size of a market segment can produce the demand necessary to create scale-efficient facilities.

Chinese manufacturing companies have spent years focused on building their businesses in China, and only recently are beginning to look at markets beyond their borders. Companies such as Legend (personal computers) and Haier (small appliances) have begun the difficult process of building their brand equity in other countries, beginning in the Far East and seeking to make subsequent moves into the West. These companies have been helped by China's entry to the World Trade Organization and are looking to overseas markets to increase market share and profits.[55] The efficiency built in a large-scale market could help lead to ultimate domination of the industry in other countries, although this could be difficult for firms coming from an emerging economy.

Specialized demand may also create opportunities beyond national boundaries. For example, Swiss firms have long led the world in tunneling equipment because of the need to tunnel through mountains for rail and highway passage in Switzerland. Japanese firms have created a niche market for compact, quiet air conditioners, which are important in Japan because homes are often small and close together.[56]

Related and supporting industries are the third dimension in Porter's model. Italy has become the leader in the shoe industry because of related and supporting industries; a well-established leather-processing industry provides the leather needed to construct shoes and related products. Also, many people travel to Italy to purchase leather goods, providing support in distribution. Supporting industries in leather-working machinery and design services also contribute to the success of the shoe industry. In fact, the design services industry supports its own related industries, such as ski boots, fashion apparel, and furniture. In Japan, cameras and copiers are related industries. Similarly, it is argued that the "creative resources nurtured by [the] popular cartoons and animation sector, combined with technological knowledge accumulated in the consumer electronics industry, facilitated the emergence of a successful video game industry in Japan."[57]

Firm strategy, structure, and rivalry make up the final country dimension and also foster the growth of certain industries. The dimension of strategy, structure, and rivalry among firms varies greatly from nation to nation. Because of the excellent technical training system in Germany, there is a strong emphasis on methodical product and process improvements. In Japan, unusual cooperative and competitive systems have facilitated the cross-functional management of complex assembly operations. In Italy, the national pride of the country's designers has spawned strong industries in sports cars, fashion apparel, and furniture. In the United States, competition among computer manufacturers and software producers has favored the development of these industries.

The four basic dimensions of the "diamond" model in Figure 8.2 emphasize the environmental or structural attributes of a national economy that contribute to national advantage. Government policy also clearly contributes to the success and failure of many firms and industries. DHL Worldwide Express seeks to enter the U.S.

domestic shipping market through the acquisition of Airborne, a Seattle-based air cargo firm, which would cause it to be in competition with UPS and FedEx. The combined company is hoping to take market share from UPS' and FedEx's small and mid-sized business accounts, which tend to have higher margins than large corporate accounts that are typically heavily discounted. UPS and FedEx are afraid that Deutsche Post (the German post office monopoly that controls DHL) will subsidize DHL-Airborne, allowing it to offer discount prices and thus gain market share. As such, UPS and FedEx have banded together to lobby the U.S. government to prohibit DHL's Airborne acquisition.[58]

Although each firm must create its own success, not all firms will survive to become global competitors—not even those operating with the same country factors that spawned the successful firms. The actual strategic choices managers make may be the most compelling reason for success or failure. Accordingly, the factors illustrated in Figure 8.2 are likely to produce competitive advantages only when the firm develops and implements an appropriate strategy that takes advantage of distinct country factors. Thus, these distinct country factors are necessary to consider when analyzing the business-level strategies (i.e., cost leadership, differentiation, focused cost leadership, focused differentiation, and integrated cost leadership/differentiation discussed in Chapter 4) in an international context.

International Corporate-Level Strategy

The international business-level strategies are based at least partially on the type of international corporate-level strategy the firm has chosen. Some corporate strategies give individual country units the authority to develop their own business-level strategies; other corporate strategies dictate the business-level strategies in order to standardize the firm's products and sharing of resources across countries.[59]

International corporate-level strategy focuses on the scope of a firm's operations through both product and geographic diversification.[60] International corporate-level strategy is required when the firm operates in multiple industries and multiple countries or regions.[61] The headquarters unit guides the strategy, although business or country-level managers can have substantial strategic input, given the type of international corporate level strategy followed. The three international corporate-level strategies are multidomestic, global, and transnational, as shown in Figure 8.3.

MULTIDOMESTIC STRATEGY

A **multidomestic strategy** is an international strategy in which strategic and operating decisions are decentralized to the strategic business unit in each country so as to allow that unit to tailor products to the local market.[62] A multidomestic strategy focuses on competition within each country. It assumes that the markets differ and therefore are segmented by country boundaries. In other words, consumer needs and desires, industry conditions (e.g., the number and type of competitors), political and legal structures, and social norms vary by country. With multidomestic strategies, the firm can customize its products to meet the specific needs and preferences of local customers. Therefore, these strategies should maximize a firm's competitive response to the idiosyncratic requirements of each market.[63]

The use of multidomestic strategies usually expands the firm's local market share because the firm can pay attention to the needs of the local clientele.[64] However, the use of these strategies results in more uncertainty for the corporation as a whole, because of the differences across markets and thus the different strategies employed by local country units.[65] Moreover, multidomestic strategies do not allow for the achievement of economies of scale and can be more costly. As a result, firms employing a multidomestic strategy decentralize their strategic and operating decisions to the business

A multidomestic strategy is an international strategy in which strategic and operating decisions are decentralized to the strategic business unit in each country so as to allow that unit to tailor products to the local market.

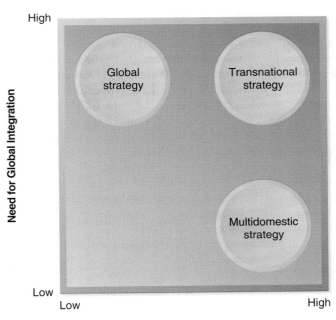

units operating in each country. Historically, Unilever has had a very decentralized approach to managing its international operations.[66] Although firms have expected the Internet to facilitate global integration across borders, research suggests that firms need to pay attention to local aspects of its use,[67] as the example about Chinese Internet portals noted above illustrates. The multidomestic strategy has been more commonly used by European multinational firms because of the variety of cultures and markets found in Europe.[68]

In the brewing industry, many firms have been following a multidomestic strategy by making acquisitions in regions of interest. Belgian brewer Interbrew, for example, bought 70 percent of K.K. Brewery, the leading beer maker in Zhejiang Province, in the Yangtze Delta in China. Interbrew is bringing its brewing skills to this facility to establish a strong competitive position in a highly fragmented, rapidly growing market that it believes is very attractive.[69] Similarly, Diageo PLC, the giant U.K.-based spirits and beer group (it owns the Guinness brand), is expanding aggressively in many countries and regions.[70] Viewing its expansion's outcomes favorably, some analysts think that "Diageo could easily mop up 10 points of market share over the next five years in the U.S."[71] Diageo's bold entry into U.S. markets could, however, engender strong competitive responses from Anheuser Busch and SABMiller.

GLOBAL STRATEGY

In contrast to a multidomestic strategy, a global strategy assumes more standardization of products across country markets.[72] As a result, a global strategy is centralized and controlled by the home office. The strategic business units operating in each country are assumed to be interdependent, and the home office attempts to achieve integration across these businesses.[73] A **global strategy** is an international strategy through which the firm offers standardized products across country markets, with competitive strategy being dictated by the home office. Thus, a global strategy emphasizes economies

*A **global strategy** is an international strategy through which the firm offers standardized products across country markets, with competitive strategy being dictated by the home office.*

of scale and offers greater opportunities to utilize innovations developed at the corporate level or in one country in other markets. This strategy is being facilitated through improved global accounting and financial reporting standards.[74]

While a global strategy produces lower risk, the firm may forgo growth opportunities in local markets, either because those markets are less likely to be identified as opportunities or because opportunities require that products be adapted to the local market.[75] The global strategy is not as responsive to local markets and is difficult to manage because of the need to coordinate strategies and operating decisions across country borders. Consequently, achieving efficient operations with a global strategy requires sharing of resources and coordination and cooperation across country boundaries, which in turn require centralization and headquarters control. Many Japanese firms have successfully used the global strategy.[76]

Cemex, a Monterrey, Mexico-based cement maker, is the world's third largest cement manufacturer, behind France's Lafarge and Switzerland's Holcim. Cemex's aggressive acquisition strategy was noticed more prominently by the media in the United States when it acquired Southdown, the U.S. cement company, for $3 billion at the end of 2001 and began to consolidate this operation with its other U.S. assets. Cemex has the leading market position in Spain with around 72 percent of the production capacity in the Spanish cement industry. Besides its significant assets in North and South America and southern Europe, the firm is also making inroads in Asia through acquisitions. Notwithstanding its presence in developed markets, "its real specialty lies in supplying cement in places that lack easy-to-navigate roads, solid telephone networks and highly skilled workers."[77] Accordingly, Cemex specializes "in supplying cement in countries such as Bangladesh, Thailand and Venezuela."[78] In these places, cement "can be sold at higher margins in bags for small-scale building, rather than in mixed ready-made quantities."[79]

To integrate its businesses globally, Cemex uses the Internet as one way of increasing revenue and lowering its cost structure. By using the Internet to improve logistics and manage an extensive supply network, Cemex can significantly reduce costs. "The advent of technology meant that every truck had a computer and a global-positioning system receiver. By combining the trucks' positions with the output at the plants and the order from customers, Cemex has been able to produce a system that not only calculates which truck should go where, but also lets dispatchers redirect trucks en route. Delivery time is now down to 20 minutes."[80] Thus, Cemex is using a global strategy to integrate many aspects of its worldwide operations.[81]

TRANSNATIONAL STRATEGY

A **transnational strategy** is an international strategy through which the firm seeks to achieve both global efficiency and local responsiveness. Realizing these goals is difficult: one requires close global coordination while the other requires local flexibility. "Flexible coordination"—building a shared vision and individual commitment through an integrated network—is required to implement the transnational strategy.[82] In reality, it is difficult to successfully use the transnational strategy because of the conflicting

A transnational strategy is an international strategy through which the firm seeks to achieve both global efficiency and local responsiveness.

New York Stock Exchange President William Johnson (third from left) joined executives from Cemex, S.A. de C.V. of Mexico, the third largest cement company in the world, as they rang the opening bell at the NYSE in New York. Chairman Lorenzo Zambrano (fourth from left) is the architect of the company's global strategy.

©Reuters NewMedia Inc./CORBIS

Large U.S. Auto Manufacturers and the Transnational Strategy

The Big Three auto manufacturers—General Motors, Ford, and Chrysler (now part of DaimlerChrysler)—found their sales, market share, and revenues were hurt so much by the globalization of competition that their dominance in the crucial North American market was significantly diminished. For 60 years these three companies controlled the American car market. As recently as the late 1990s, these companies earned record profits. However, the market shares of foreign car manufacturers have grown from their original, anemic level, and these firms are now serious competitors to domestic U.S. dominance. As Ford considered its centennial celebration, it learned that Toyota had overtaken Ford as the number two global market share leader. "Toyota is well on its way to achieving its audacious goal of grabbing 15 percent of the world's auto market by early in the next decade," up from 10 percent in 2001 and 11.7 percent in the first quarter of 2003. Although Ford's sales rose to 1.58 million, Toyota's increased more—to 1.66 million.

General Motors has long fought an image that it does not build quality vehicles. Despite its ranking in a recent survey as being the most reliable domestic U.S. carmaker after sales, GM still placed behind Toyota, Honda, and Nissan overall. "Japanese automakers continue to lead in durability, with 228 problems per 100 cars for the average Japanese brand, 282 for the average Big Three [U.S.] brand, 331 for European brands and 406 for Korean brands." For many consumers, quality is one of the major factors affecting their car purchase.

Manufacturing efficiency is also a problem. Toyota's "not-so-secret weapons are its plants, at home and, increasingly, abroad, which consistently rank among the world's most efficient."

Although domestic U.S. companies are improving, some foreign carmakers already have a good reputation and a known reliability rating. At the low end of the market, companies such as Hyundai and Kia are capturing market share. As price competition increases, domestic automakers have seen their market share shrink proportionally.

In response to this situation, U.S. firms and other large automakers are using international corporate-level strategies. For example, General Motors has invested billions of dollars in foreign car companies, moving toward a more transnational strategy for its automobiles. The company owns Saab and Opel and also has stakes in Daewoo, Fiat, Subaru, and Suzuki Motor. In the past, GM used a multidomestic strategy by which its foreign business units were managed in a decentralized way and each unit could decide what cars to design and build. This laissez-faire management approach produced poor financial results.

GM CEO G. Richard Wagoner Jr. decided to overcome this problem by implementing a transnational strategy. The senior managers from its partners' headquarters and product development centers now report directly to a top-ranking GM executive in the relevant region of the world. Thus, GM's top management team has more control over events in each of its foreign car companies but can continue to be responsive to regional or country needs. In particular, GM has focused on the Asia Pacific region because it expects the global market for cars to increase 12 million units by 2012 with half of that coming from the region (particularly from China, India, South Korea, and Thailand). However, the firm realizes it is important to maintain a country focus as well. Thus, GM has sought to balance efficiency and responsiveness through the transnational strategy.

SOURCES: J. Flint, 2003, China: How big, how fast, how dangerous? *Forbes*, http//:www.forbes.com, July 1; K. Greenberg, 2003, Imports look for big gains in minivan market, *Brandweek*, March 3; D. Hakim, 2003, American cars show gains in a survey of dependability, *New York Times*, http//:nytimes.com, July 9, 12; J. Palmer, 2003, Taking on the world, *Barron's*, May 5, 15–16; A. Taylor III, 2003, And it's Toyota by a nose! *Fortune*, June 9, 34; F. Warner, 2003, Learning how to speak to Gen Y, *Fast Company*, July, 36–37; S. A. Webster, 2003, GM alters strategy in Asia Pacific; Its global leadership position is at stake as it focuses more on China, less on Japan, *Detroit News*, June 12, 1.

goals (see Chapter 11 for more on implementation of this and other corporate-level international strategies). On the positive side, effective implementation of a transnational strategy often produces higher performance than does implementation of either the multidomestic or global international corporate-level strategies.[83]

The Strategic Focus on the global auto industry suggests that many large auto manufacturers choose the transnational strategy to deal with global trends. Renault has used this strategy to reinvigorate Nissan, in which Renault bought a controlling interest in 1999. Since then, Carlos Ghosn, CEO of Nissan, has brought Nissan back from being a very poor performer to achieving a "10.8 percent operating margin, the highest of any major carmaker, and a 19.5 percent return on invested capital."[84] The business units of Renault cooperate to achieve efficiencies and adapt to local market conditions. "For example, diesel engines have zero penetration in the Japanese market, but they power more than a third of the cars sold in Europe. So Nissan equips diesel cars it sells in Europe with Renault engines."[85]

Environmental Trends

Although the transnational strategy is difficult to implement, emphasis on global efficiency is increasing as more industries begin to experience global competition. To add to the problem, there is also an increased emphasis on local requirements: global goods and services often require some customization to meet government regulations within particular countries or to fit customer tastes and preferences. In addition, most multinational firms desire coordination and sharing of resources across country markets to hold down costs, as illustrated by the Cemex example above.[86] Furthermore, some products and industries may be more suited than others for standardization across country borders.

As a result, most large multinational firms with diverse products employ a multidomestic strategy with certain product lines and a global strategy with others. Many multinational firms may require this type of flexibility if they are to be strategically competitive, in part due to trends that change over time. Two important trends are the liability of foreignness, which has increased after the terrorist attacks and the war in Iraq, and regionalization.

Liability of Foreignness

The dramatic success of Japanese firms such as Toyota and Sony in the United States and other international markets in the 1980s was a powerful jolt to U.S. managers and awakened them to the importance of international competition in what were rapidly becoming global markets. In the 1990s, Eastern Europe and China represented potential major international market opportunities for firms from many countries, including the United States, Japan, Korea, and European nations.[87] However, as described in the Strategic Focus, there are legitimate concerns about the relative attractiveness of global strategies. Research shows that global strategies are not as prevalent as once thought and are very difficult to implement, even when using Internet-based strategies.[88] The September 11, 2001, attacks and the war in Iraq in 2003 are two explanations for these concerns.[89]

In the 21st century, firms may focus less on truly global markets and more on regional adaptation. Although parallel developments in the Internet and mobile telecommunication facilitate communications across the globe, as noted earlier, the implementation of Web-based strategies also requires local adaptation.

The globalization of businesses with local strategies is demonstrated by the online operation of Lands' End, Inc., using local Internet portals to offer its products for sale. Lands' End, formerly a direct-mail catalog business and now a part of Sears,

Uncertainty, Liability of Foreignness, and Regionalization

The U.S. economy is the biggest in the world, twice the size of the second largest. When certainty regarding the initiation of conflict in Iraq began to escalate in the United States, the uncertainty of the outcome negatively affected consumer spending, and large-scale capital investment and other potential creators of economic wealth in the global economy were affected. Easing concerns about the hostilities in Iraq provided "some lift to business and consumer confidence," but "the effect has not been dramatic." Until the U.S. economy improves, it is unlikely that the global economy will pick up as well. Political maneuvering and conflicts have also affected trade relations between the United States and Europe. American executives visiting France were scolded by their French counterparts for the aggressive Bush administration policy toward Iraq. European firms were reluctant to invest in the United States for fear of American retaliation.

Other countries will probably bear the economic effects of the war in Iraq differently. Japan's economy continues to shrink, only mildly exacerbated by the war, and China's continues to grow, also relatively unaffected by the war and higher oil prices. South Korea, besides its neighbor North Korea's nuclear threat, is also threatened by its dependence on imported oil. However, it has built formidable financial reserves, and its large companies have reduced their debt loads. Already suffering from enormous debt and increased oil prices, Turkey probably faces the worst repercussions. Tourism, a major source of revenue, is expected to drop off, and Turkey's unwilling support of U.S. armed forces lessens its chances of receiving an aid package from the American government.

Similarly, the September 11, 2001, terrorist attacks as well as the war in Afghanistan created uncertainty about the progress of globalization. Although these shocks put a short-term damper on increased globalization, research also suggests that globalization is not as pervasive as once believed. In only a few sectors, such as consumer electronics, is a global strategy as defined above economically viable. For most manufacturing (such as automobiles), national responsiveness and implementation of the transnational strategy are increasingly important.

In fact, even in a service sector such as banking and retailing, the more successful multinationals design their strategies on a regional basis, while the less successful multinationals pursue global strategies. Also, research suggests that geography still matters in regard to competition and rivalry of firms who use the Internet. Although events such as war and terrorist attacks that create shocks of uncertainty are likely to slow the process of globalization, they are not likely to reverse it. Furthermore, even though innovations such as the Internet may foster globalization, they are not likely to do away with the need for local responsiveness or regionalization. For example, although Internet commerce has reduced the need for local sales outlets, firms with local physical outlets still have an advantage.

SOURCES: B. Davis, 2003, For global economy, much rides on how the U.S. war plays out, *Wall Street Journal*, March 20, A1; G. Ip, 2003, Fed find few signs economy picked up after end of Iraq war, *Wall Street Journal*, June 12, A2; P. Magnusson, 2003, Ire over Iraq starts tripping up trade with Europe, *Business Week*, March 17, 51; R. L. Mecham III, 2003, Success for the new global manager: What you need to know to work across distances, countries, and cultures, *Leadership Quarterly*, 14: 347–352; A. Rugman & S. Girod, 2003, Retail multinationals and globalization: The evidence is regional, *European Management Journal*, 21(1): 24–37; A. M. Rugman & A. Verbeke, 2003, Extending the theory of the multinational enterprise: Internalization and strategic management perspectives, *Journal of International Business Studies*, 34: 125–137; J. Stell, 2003, War uncertainties delay construction projects, *Oil & Gas Journal*, April 14, 66–73; E. Scardino, 2003, Does a fast war mean a fast economic recovery? Not so fast, *DSN Retailing Today*, April 21, 30–34; L. Walczak, S. Crock, & P. Dwyer, 2003, America and the world, *BusinessWeek Online*, http://www.businessweek.com, April 21; D. Xu & O. Shenkar, 2002, Institutional distance and the multinational enterprise, *Academy of Management Review*, 27: 608–618.

Roebuck and Co., launched its web-based business in 1995. The firm established websites in the United Kingdom and Germany in 1999, and in France, Italy, and Ireland in 2000 prior to initiating a catalog business in those countries. With limited online advertising and word-of-mouth, a website business can be built in a foreign country without a lot of initial marketing expenses. Once the online business is large enough, a catalog business can be launched with mailing targeted to customers who have used the business online. Thus, even smaller companies can sell their goods and services globally when facilitated by electronic infrastructure without having significant (brick-and-mortar) facilities outside of their home location. But significant local adaptation is still needed in each country or region.[90]

Regionalization

Regionalization is a second trend that has become more common in global markets. Because a firm's location can affect its strategic competitiveness,[91] it must decide whether to compete in all or many global markets, or to focus on a particular region or regions. Competing in all markets provides economies that can be achieved because of the combined market size. Research suggests that firms that compete in risky emerging markets can also have higher performance.[92]

However, a firm that competes in industries where the international markets differ greatly (in which it must employ a multidomestic strategy) may wish to narrow its focus to a particular region of the world. In so doing, it can better understand the cultures, legal and social norms, and other factors that are important for effective competition in those markets. For example, a firm may focus on Far East markets only rather than competing simultaneously in the Middle East, Europe, and the Far East. Or, the firm may choose a region of the world where the markets are more similar and some coordination and sharing of resources would be possible. In this way, the firm may be able not only to better understand the markets in which it competes, but also to achieve some economies, even though it may have to employ a multidomestic strategy. For instance, research suggests that most large retailers are better at focusing on a particular region rather than being truly global.[93]

Countries that develop trade agreements to increase the economic power of their regions may promote regional strategies. The European Union (EU) and South America's Organization of American States (OAS) are country associations that developed trade agreements to promote the flow of trade across country boundaries within their respective regions.[94] However, the European Union is moving closer to unity, with a draft constitution on the table and plans for a more powerful president and foreign minister. If the EU's planned enlargement in 2004 succeeds, it will contain 25 countries and about 450 million people, and have about the same amount of wealth as the United States.[95] Many European firms acquire and integrate their businesses in Europe to better coordinate pan-European brands as the EU creates more unity in European markets. With a more united Europe, this process is likely to continue as new countries are added to the agreement.

The North American Free Trade Agreement (NAFTA), signed by the United States, Canada, and Mexico, facilitates free trade across country borders in North America and may be expanded to include other countries in South America, such as Argentina, Brazil, and Chile.[96] NAFTA loosens restrictions on international strategies within a region and provides greater opportunity for international strategies. NAFTA does not exist for the sole purpose of U.S. businesses moving across its borders. In fact, Mexico is the number two trading partner of the United States, and NAFTA greatly increased Mexico's exports to this country. Research suggests that managers of small and medium-sized firms are influenced by the strategy they implement (those with a differentiation strategy are more positively disposed to the agreement than are those pursuing a cost leadership strategy) and by their experience and rivalry with exporting firms.[97] Although Vicente Fox's election as president of Mexico and Mexico's new spirit of democracy have created opportunity for change, the poor U.S. economy and the September 11, 2001, attacks have lowered the economic outlook for Mexico. However, the Iraq War was a boon for Mexico as the price of oil was driven higher and trade became more regionally focused during the conflict. However, as the Opening Case indicates, China threatens to displace Mexico as the second largest U.S. trading partner. China displaced Japan as the third largest trading partner in 2002.[98]

Most firms enter regional markets sequentially, beginning in markets with which they are more familiar. They also introduce their largest and strongest lines of business into these markets first, followed by their other lines of business once the first lines are successful.[99]

After the firm selects its international strategies and decides whether to employ them in regional or world markets, it must choose a market entry mode.[100]

Choice of International Entry Mode

International expansion is accomplished by exporting products, participating in licensing arrangements, forming strategic alliances, making acquisitions, and establishing new wholly owned subsidiaries. These means of entering international markets and their characteristics are shown in Table 8.1. Each means of market entry has its advantages and disadvantages. Thus, choosing the appropriate mode or path to enter international markets affects the firm's performance in those markets.[101]

Exporting

Many industrial firms begin their international expansion by exporting goods or services to other countries.[102] Exporting does not require the expense of establishing operations in the host countries, but exporters must establish some means of marketing and distributing their products. Usually, exporting firms develop contractual arrangements with host-country firms.

The disadvantages of exporting include the often high costs of transportation and possible tariffs placed on incoming goods. Furthermore, the exporter has less control over the marketing and distribution of its products in the host country and must either pay the distributor or allow the distributor to add to the price to recoup its costs and earn a profit.[103] As a result, it may be difficult to market a competitive product

Global Market Entry: Choice of Entry Mode — Table 8.1

Type of Entry	Characteristics
Exporting	High cost, low control
Licensing	Low cost, low risk, little control, low returns
Strategic alliances	Shared costs, shared resources, shared risks, problems of integration (e.g., two corporate cultures)
Acquisition	Quick access to new market, high cost, complex negotiations, problems of merging with domestic operations
New wholly owned subsidiary	Complex, often costly, time consuming, high risk, maximum control, potential above-average returns

through exporting or to provide a product that is customized to each international market.[104] However, evidence suggests that cost leadership strategies enhance the performance of exports in developed countries, whereas differentiation strategies are more successful in emerging economies.[105]

Firms export mostly to countries that are closest to their facilities because of the lower transportation costs and the usually greater similarity between geographic neighbors. For example, U.S. NAFTA partners Mexico and Canada account for more than half of the goods exported from Texas. The Internet has also made exporting easier as illustrated by the Lands' End system described earlier.[106] Even small firms can access critical information about foreign markets, examine a target market, research the competition, and find lists of potential customers. Governments also use the Internet to facilitate applications for export and import licenses. Although the terrorist threat is likely to slow its progress, high-speed technology is still the wave of the future.[107]

Small businesses are most likely to use the exporting mode of international entry.[108] Currency exchange rates are one of the most significant problems small businesses face. The Bush administration has supported a dollar weak against the euro, which makes imports more expensive and U.S. goods less costly to foreign buyers, thus providing some economic relief for U.S. exporters.[109]

Licensing

Licensing is one of the forms of organizational networks that are becoming common, particularly among smaller firms.[110] A licensing arrangement allows a foreign firm to purchase the right to manufacture and sell the firm's products within a host country or set of countries.[111] The licenser is normally paid a royalty on each unit produced and sold. The licensee takes the risks and makes the monetary investments in facilities for manufacturing, marketing, and distributing the goods or services. As a result, licensing is possibly the least costly form of international expansion.

Licensing is also a way to expand returns based on previous innovations. Even if product life cycles are short, licensing may be a useful tool. For instance, because the toy industry faces relentless change and an unpredictable buying public, licensing is used and contracts are often completed in foreign markets where labor may be less expensive.[112]

Licensing also has disadvantages. For example, it gives the firm very little control over the manufacture and marketing of its products in other countries. Thus, license deals must be structured properly.[113] In addition, licensing provides the least potential returns, because returns must be shared between the licenser and the licensee. Worse, the international firm may learn the technology and produce and sell a similar competitive product after the license expires. Komatsu, for example, first licensed much of its technology from International Harvester, Bucyrus-Erie, and Cummins Engine to compete against Caterpillar in the earthmoving equipment business. Komatsu then dropped these licenses and developed its own products using the technology it had gained from the U.S. companies.[114]

In addition, if a firm wants to move to a different ownership arrangement, licensing may create some inflexibility. Thus, it is important that a firm think ahead and consider sequential forms of entry in international markets.[115]

Strategic Alliances

In recent years, strategic alliances have become a popular means of international expansion.[116] Strategic alliances allow firms to share the risks and the resources required to enter international markets.[117] Moreover, strategic alliances can facilitate the development of new core competencies that contribute to the firm's future strategic competitiveness.[118]

Most strategic alliances are formed with a host-country firm that knows and understands the competitive conditions, legal and social norms, and cultural idiosyncrasies of the country, which should help the expanding firm manufacture and market a competitive product. In return, the host-country firm may find its new access to the expanding firm's technology and innovative products attractive. Each partner in an alliance brings knowledge or resources to the partnership.[119] Indeed, partners often enter an alliance with the purpose of learning new capabilities. Common among those desired capabilities are technological skills.[120]

China is home to several large energy companies that are finally forming a global strategy. China's increasing petroleum needs and dependence on the Middle East are spurring the companies to seek out foreign oil sources and joint ventures with other companies. Recently, the oil companies have acquired stakes in the Caspian Sea region, Indonesia, and Australia, and are working to develop a joint venture with Russian companies to build a pipeline that would bring Russian crude oil to the northeast corner of China. The Caspian Sea deal in particular illustrates China's rising presence. "This gives us a firm foothold in probably the most prolific oil and gas basin outside the Middle East," says Mark Qiu, CFO of China National Offshore Oil Corporation (CNOOC).[121]

Not all alliances are successful; in fact, many fail.[122] The primary reasons for failure include incompatible partners and conflict between the partners.[123] International strategic alliances are especially difficult to manage.[124] Several factors may cause a relationship to sour. Trust between the partners is critical and is affected by at least four fundamental issues: the initial condition of the relationship, the negotiation process to arrive at an agreement, partner interactions, and external events.[125] Trust is also influenced by the country cultures involved in the alliance or joint venture.[126]

Research has shown that equity-based alliances, over which a firm has more control, tend to produce more positive returns[127] (strategic alliances are discussed in greater depth in Chapter 9). However, if conflict in a strategic alliance or joint venture will not be manageable, an acquisition may be a better option.[128] Research suggests that alliances are more favorable in the face of high uncertainty and where cooperation is needed to share knowledge between partners and where strategic flexibility is important, such as with small and medium-sized firms.[129] Acquisitions are better in situations with less need for strategic flexibility and when the transaction is used to maintain economies of scale or scope.[130]

Acquisitions

As free trade has continued to expand in global markets, cross-border acquisitions have also been increasing significantly. In recent years, cross-border acquisitions have comprised more than 45 percent of all acquisitions completed worldwide.[131] As explained in Chapter 7, acquisitions can provide quick access to a new market. In fact, acquisitions may provide the fastest, and often the largest, initial international expansion of any of the alternatives.[132]

Although acquisitions have become a popular mode of entering international markets, they are not without costs. International acquisitions carry some of the disadvantages of domestic acquisitions (see Chapter 7). In addition, they can be expensive and often require debt financing, which also carries an extra cost. International negotiations for acquisitions can be exceedingly complex and are generally more complicated than for domestic acquisitions. For example, it is estimated that only 20 percent of the cross-border bids made lead to a completed acquisition, compared to 40 percent for domestic acquisitions.[133] Dealing with the legal and regulatory requirements in the target firm's country and obtaining appropriate information to negotiate an agreement frequently present significant problems.[134] Finally, the problems of merging the new firm into the acquiring firm often are more complex than in domestic acquisitions. The acquiring firm must deal not only with different corporate cultures, but also with potentially different social cultures and practices. Therefore, while international acquisitions have been popular because of the rapid access to new markets they provide, they also carry with them important costs and multiple risks.

An ice cream rivalry is taking shape in the United States, but not between two U.S. firms. Through international acquisitions, Swiss-headquartered Nestlé and Anglo-Dutch giant Unilever have sought a strong presence in the U.S. ice cream market. Unilever holds 17 percent of the U.S. market through its Good Humor, Ben & Jerry's, and Breyers brands, while Nestlé's acquisition of Dreyer will allow it to own a similar market share by adding this brand to its Häagen-Dazs and Drumstick brands. Because this market requires freezer technology and a lot of ice cream is sold at scoop shops, "distribution headaches long made ice cream the province of small local dairies."[135] However, these two firms have exploited a strategy in Europe where branded ice cream freezers are visible everywhere. They expect to do the same in the United States by "exploiting on-the-go outlets, such as convenience stores, gas stations, video shops and vending machines."[136] "Unilever already sells ice cream in hundreds of Toys 'R' Us, True Value, Blockbuster and Family Dollar stores out of branded freezers."[137] Each firm will also exploit its well-known candy brands by mixing these candies with ice cream to create new flavors, such as "Nestlé's Butterfinger ice cream or Unilever's Klondike Caramel & Peanut bars with Planters peanuts."[138] The firms also expect to create licensing opportunities, such as Dreyer's deal with Walt Disney Co. for a *Finding Nemo* ice cream product that can be promoted with the movie. Acquisitions have allowed both firms to increase their presence quickly while obtaining distribution assets. Distribution to "on-the-go outlets" can be added to distribution runs to supermarkets.[139] Because the ice cream market is quite mature, an acquisition strategy worked well, although there are always integration difficulties as described in Chapter 7, and these only increase with cross-border deals.

New Wholly Owned Subsidiary

The establishment of a new wholly owned subsidiary is referred to as a **greenfield venture.** This process is often complex and potentially costly, but it affords maximum control to the firm and has the most potential to provide above-average returns. This potential is especially true of firms with strong intangible capabilities that might be leveraged through a greenfield venture.[140]

The risks are also high, however, because of the costs of establishing a new business operation in a new country. The firm may have to acquire the knowledge and expertise of the existing market by hiring either host-country nationals, possibly from competitors, or consultants, which can be costly. Still, the firm maintains control over the technology, marketing, and distribution of its products.[141] Alternatively, the company must build new manufacturing facilities, establish distribution networks, and learn and implement appropriate marketing strategies to compete in the new market.[142]

As the consumer electronics industry began to globalize, this trend had implications for electronic component distribution companies such as Avnet and Arrow, which sell parts to

The establishment of a new wholly owned subsidiary is referred to as a greenfield venture.

Unilever, a European-centered global food and consumer products firm, offers ice cream brands in the United States such as Good Humor, Ben & Jerry's, and Breyers. Its strongest rival in the United States is not a U.S. firm but, rather, the Swiss-headquartered European Nestlé.

AP Photo

OEMs as well as to retail distributors. At first they expanded to Europe, mainly by making acquisitions, and then sought to integrate them by creating a centralized information system. This was difficult and often done in stages. However, a pure acquisition strategy has been more difficult to accomplish in Asia as component distributors have expanded into this region because there was more fragmentation among the existing distributors relative to Europe. As such, they have been doing more greenfield investment. Also, both TTI and Future, small distributors relative to Avnet and Arrow, have mostly used a greenfield approach because "they have a unique business model they want to preserve as they expand and staying on a single IT platform has its advantages."[143] Such an approach allows more centralized control, but takes longer to implement and longer to build local relationships than through acquiring a local distributor as in the ice cream example above.

Dynamics of Mode of Entry

A firm's choice of mode of entry into international markets is affected by a number of factors.[144] Initially, market entry will often be achieved through export, which requires no foreign manufacturing expertise and investment only in distribution. Licensing can facilitate the product improvements necessary to enter foreign markets, as in the Komatsu example. Strategic alliances have been popular because they allow a firm to connect with an experienced partner already in the targeted market. Strategic alliances also reduce risk through the sharing of costs. All three modes therefore are best for early market development tactics. Also, the strategic alliance is often used in more uncertain situations, such as an emerging economy.[145] However, if intellectual property rights in the emerging economy are not well protected, the number of firms in the industry is growing fast, and the need for global integration is high, the wholly owned entry mode is preferred.[146]

To secure a stronger presence in international markets, acquisitions or greenfield ventures may be required. Large aerospace firms Airbus and Boeing have used joint ventures, while military equipment firms such as Lockheed Martin have used acquisitions to build a global presence.[147] Many Japanese auto manufacturers, such as Honda, Nissan, and Toyota, have gained a presence in the United States through both greenfield ventures and joint ventures.[148] Toyota has particularly strong intangible production capabilities that it has been able to transfer through greenfield ventures.[149] Both acquisitions and greenfield ventures are likely to come at later stages in the development of an international strategy. In addition, both strategies tend to be more successful when the firm making the investment possesses valuable core competencies.[150] Large diversified business groups, often found in emerging economies, not only gain resources through diversification, but also have specialized abilities in managing differences in inward and outward flows of foreign direct investment. In particular, Korean *chaebol* have been adept at making acquisitions in emerging economies.[151]

Thus, to enter a global market, a firm selects the entry mode that is best suited to the situation at hand. In some instances, the various options will be followed sequentially, beginning with exporting and ending with greenfield ventures.[152] In other cases, the firm may use several, but not all, of the different entry modes, each in different markets. The decision regarding which entry mode to use is primarily a result of the industry's competitive conditions, the country's situation and government policies, and the firm's unique set of resources, capabilities, and core competencies.

Strategic Competitiveness Outcomes

Once its international strategy and mode of entry have been selected, the firm turns its attention to implementation issues (see Chapter 11). It is important to do this, because as explained next, international expansion is risky and may not result in a competitive advantage (see Figure 8.1). The probability the firm will achieve success by using an international strategy increases when that strategy is effectively implemented.

International Diversification and Returns

As noted earlier, firms have numerous reasons to diversify internationally. **International diversification** is a strategy through which a firm expands the sales of its goods or services across the borders of global regions and countries into different geographic locations or markets. Because of its potential advantages, international diversification should be related positively to firms' returns. Research has shown that, as international diversification increases, firms' returns increase.[153] In fact, the stock market is particularly sensitive to investments in international markets. Firms that are broadly diversified into multiple international markets usually achieve the most positive stock returns, especially when they diversify geographically into core business areas.[154] There are also many reasons for the positive effects of international diversification, such as potential economies of scale and experience, location advantages, increased market size, and the opportunity to stabilize returns. The stabilization of returns helps reduce a firm's overall risk.[155] All of these outcomes can be achieved by smaller and newer ventures, as well as by larger and established firms. New ventures can also enjoy higher returns when they learn new technologies from their international diversification.[156]

Firms in the Japanese auto industry, especially Toyota (as indicated in the Strategic Focus on the global auto industry), have found that international diversification may allow them to better exploit their core competencies, because sharing knowledge resources between operations can produce synergy. Also, a firm's returns may affect its decision to diversify internationally. For example, poor returns in a domestic market may encourage a firm to expand internationally in order to enhance its profit potential. In addition, internationally diversified firms may have access to more flexible labor markets, as the Japanese do in the United States, and may thereby benefit from global scanning for competition and market opportunities. Also, through global networks with assets in many countries, firms can develop more flexible structures to adjust to changes that might occur.[157] Petronas has developed such a strong global network and, even though it is a state-owned oil company in Malaysia, its operations are profitable, which is counter to most state-owned monopolies. Because Malaysia's oil reserves have dwindled and because few domestic opportunities exist to drill for new reserves, Petronas expanded its operations abroad to fill the potentially growing reserve challenge. It has done so successfully; it "established itself as the developing world's most aggressive foreign investor, with operations in 32 countries."[158] It has gone to Iraq and the Sudan, among other places, where more technologically developed "Western rivals have feared to tread."[159] In the process, Petronas has become a truly global company. However, it must still deal with Malaysian politics because of its state-owned status, which can cause problems during political transitions.[160] Multinational firms, such as Petronas, with efficient and competitive operations are more likely to produce above-average returns for their investors and better products for their customers than are solely domestic firms. However, as explained later, international diversification can be carried too far.

International Diversification and Innovation

In Chapter 1, we indicated that the development of new technology is at the heart of strategic competitiveness. As noted in Porter's model (see Figure 8.2), a nation's competitiveness depends, in part, on the capacity of its industry to innovate. Eventually and inevitably, competitors outperform firms that fail to innovate and improve their operations and products. Therefore, the only way to sustain a competitive advantage is to upgrade it continually.[161]

International diversification provides the potential for firms to achieve greater returns on their innovations (through larger or more numerous markets) and lowers the often substantial risks of R&D investments. Therefore, international diversification provides incentives for firms to innovate.[162]

In addition, international diversification may be necessary to generate the resources required to sustain a large-scale R&D operation. An environment of rapid technological obsolescence makes it difficult to invest in new technology and the capital-intensive operations required to take advantage of such investment. Firms operating solely in domestic markets may find such investments problematic because of the length of time required to recoup the original investment. If the time is extended, it may not even be possible to recover the investment before the technology becomes obsolete.[163] As a result, international diversification improves a firm's ability to appropriate additional and necessary returns from innovation before competitors can overcome the initial competitive advantage created by the innovation. In addition, firms moving into international markets are exposed to new products and processes. If they learn about those products and processes and integrate this knowledge into their operations, further innovation can be developed.[164]

The relationship among international diversification, innovation, and returns is complex. Some level of performance is necessary to provide the resources to generate international diversification, which in turn provides incentives and resources to invest in research and development. The latter, if done appropriately, should enhance the returns of the firm, which then provides more resources for continued international diversification and investment in R&D.[165]

Because of the potential positive effects of international diversification on performance and innovation, such diversification may even enhance returns in product-diversified firms. International diversification would increase market potential in each of these firms' product lines, but the complexity of managing a firm that is both product diversified and internationally diversified is significant. Research suggests that firms in less developed countries gain from being product diversified when partnering with multinational firms from a more developed country that are looking to enter a less developed country in pursuit of increased international diversification.[166]

Asea Brown Boveri (ABB) demonstrates these relationships. This firm's operations involve high levels of both product and international diversification, yet ABB's performance was strong until the recent downturn. Weaknesses have appeared, however. Some believe that the firm's inability to effectively implement the transnational strategy was ultimately due to overdiversification in both product and geographic markets. ABB assembled culturally diverse corporate and divisional management teams that facilitated the simultaneous achievement of global integration and local responsiveness, but too much diversification, especially in emerging markets such as Korea, forced a reorganization. ABB also bought companies that created "huge liabilities from asbestos litigation."[167] Although the firm's strategy failed, many local companies benefited, especially those that were already product diversified, such as those in Korea.

Evidence suggests that more culturally diverse top-management teams often have a greater knowledge of international markets and their idiosyncrasies[168] (top-management teams are discussed further in Chapter 12). Moreover, an in-depth understanding of diverse markets among top-level managers facilitates intrafirm coordination and the use of long-term, strategically relevant criteria to evaluate the performance of managers and their units.[169] In turn, this approach facilitates improved innovation and performance.[170]

Complexity of Managing Multinational Firms

Although firms can realize many benefits by implementing an international strategy, doing so is complex and can produce greater uncertainty.[171] For example, multiple risks are involved when a firm operates in several different countries. Firms can grow only so large and diverse before becoming unmanageable, or before the costs of managing them exceed their benefits.[172] Other complexities include the highly competitive nature of global markets, multiple cultural environments, potentially rapid shifts in the value of different currencies, and the possible instability of some national governments.

Risks in an International Environment

International diversification carries multiple risks.[173] Because of these risks, international expansion is difficult to implement and manage. The chief risks are political and economic. Taking these risks into account, highly internationally diversified firms are accustomed to market conditions yielding competitive situations that differ from what was predicted. Sometimes, these situations contribute to the firm's strategic competitiveness; on other occasions, they have a negative effect on the firm's efforts.[174] Specific examples of political and economic risks are shown in Figure 8.4.

Political Risks

Political risks are risks related to instability in national governments and to war, both civil and international. Instability in a national government creates numerous problems, including economic risks and uncertainty created by government regulation; the existence of many, possibly conflicting, legal authorities or corruption; and the potential nationalization of private assets.[175] Foreign firms that invest in another country may have concerns about the stability of the national government and what might happen to their investments or assets because of unrest and government instability.[176]

Economic Risks

As illustrated in the Strategic Focus on intellectual property rights, economic risks are interdependent with political risks. If firms cannot protect their intellectual property, foreign direct investment decreases. Countries therefore need to create and sustain strong intellectual property rights and their enforcement, or they risk losing their reputation in the eyes of potential investing firms and might also risk sanctions from international political bodies such as the WTO.

As noted earlier, foremost among the economic risks of international diversification are the differences and fluctuations in the value of different currencies.[177] The value of the dollar relative to other currencies determines the value of the international assets and earnings of U.S. firms; for example, an increase in the value of the U.S. dollar can reduce the value of U.S. multinational firms' international assets and earnings in other countries. Furthermore, the value of different currencies can also, at times, dramatically affect a firm's competitiveness in global markets because of its effect on the prices of goods manufactured in different countries.[178]

An increase in the value of the dollar can harm U.S. firms' exports to international markets because of the price differential of the products. Currently the dollar is weak, meaning that overseas profits for American companies do not look as good as they might in other years. A weak dollar could also contribute eventually to a slide into deeper recession for the American economy, another major risk for companies that invest in America.[179]

Limits to International Expansion: Management Problems

Firms tend to earn positive returns on early international diversification, but the returns often level off and become negative as the diversification increases past some point.[180] There are several reasons for the limits to the positive effects of international diversification. First, greater geographic dispersion across country borders increases the costs

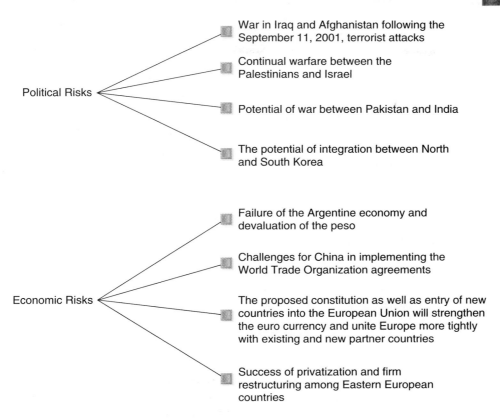

Political Risks
- War in Iraq and Afghanistan following the September 11, 2001, terrorist attacks
- Continual warfare between the Palestinians and Israel
- Potential of war between Pakistan and India
- The potential of integration between North and South Korea

Economic Risks
- Failure of the Argentine economy and devaluation of the peso
- Challenges for China in implementing the World Trade Organization agreements
- The proposed constitution as well as entry of new countries into the European Union will strengthen the euro currency and unite Europe more tightly with existing and new partner countries
- Success of privatization and firm restructuring among Eastern European countries

SOURCES: 2003, Finance and economics: The perils of convergence; Economics focus, *The Economist*, April 5, 71; K. D. Brouthers, 2003, Institutional, cultural and transaction cost influences on entry mode choice and performance, *Journal of International Business Studies*, 33: 203–221; F. Bruni, 2003, With a constitution to ponder, Europeans gather in Greece, *New York Times*, http://www.nytimes.com, June 20; B. Davis, R. Buckman, & C. Rhoads, 2003, A global journal report: For global economy, much rides on how the U.S. war plays out, *Wall Street Journal*, March 20, A1; J. Flint, 2003, China: How big, how fast, how dangerous? *Forbes*, http://www.forbes.com, July 1; G. A. Fowler, 2003, Copies `R' Us—Pirates in China move fast to pilfer toy makers' ideas, *Wall Street Journal*, January 31, B1; W. Rugg, 2003, A down dollar's lure—and peril, *Business-Week Online*, http://www.businessweek.com, May 22; J. H. Zhao, S. H. Kim, & J. Du, 2003, The impact of corruption and transparency on foreign direct investment: An empirical analysis, *Management International Review*, 43(1): 41–62; M. Kripalani, N. Mangi, F. Balfour, P. Magnusson, & R. Brady, 2002, Now, will India and Pakistan get serious about peace? *Business Week*, January 14, 51; M. Wallin, 2002, Argentina grapples with postdevaluation, *Wall Street Journal*, January 10, A8; P. Engardio, R. Miller, G. Smith, D. Brady, M. Kripalani, A. Borrus, & D. Foust, 2001, What's at stake: How terrorism threatens the global economy, *Business Week*, October 22, 33–34; D. Eisenberg, 2001, Arafat's dance of death, *Time*, December 24, 64–65; B. Fulford, 2001, Another enemy, *Forbes*, October 29, 117; K. E. Myer, 2001, Institutions, transaction costs, and entry model choice in Eastern Europe, *Journal of International Business Studies*, 32: 357–367.

of coordination between units and the distribution of products. Second, trade barriers, logistical costs, cultural diversity, and other differences by country (e.g., access to raw materials and different employee skill levels) greatly complicate the implementation of an international diversification strategy.[181]

Institutional and cultural factors can present strong barriers to the transfer of a firm's competitive advantages from one country to another. Marketing programs often have to be redesigned and new distribution networks established when firms expand into new countries. In addition, firms may encounter different labor costs and capital charges. In general, it is difficult to effectively implement, manage, and control a firm's international operations.[182]

Intellectual Property Rights in China and Southeast Asia

The lack of protection for intellectual property in China and Southeast Asia has made it very difficult for Western firms to be successful there, and it includes all sorts of industries, from movies and music to software and textiles.

General Motors has a Chinese joint venture partner named SAIC. Together, they built Buicks and other models in China. GM developed a new car called the Matiz, which was to be released in China. Rumors surfaced that SAIC had produced a very similar subcompact car called the QQ. Government officials commented on the cars' similarity. When GM approached its partner with its concerns, SAIC denied imitating the design from GM's plans. GM has not decided yet what it is going to do to resolve its concern. Despite the growth in the auto industry in China (sales increased 50 percent from 2002 to 2003), GM is not alone in its piracy concerns. Toyota has filed suit against Geely Auto Group, a private Chinese auto company, for trademark infringement.

Toy makers have also encountered problems in China. The toy industry has evolved such that the molds used for casting can be copied within a few hours, and toy makers at conventions to showcase new toys find themselves face-to-face with copies at these conventions. China produces 70 percent of the world's toys, and as a manufacturing hub, it is very open to design theft. The big toy companies, Mattel and Hasbro, don't attend toy fairs to showcase new toys; instead, they hold their own invitation-only fairs once a year. Small toy companies can't afford to do that. They also can't afford to legally register their toys, although the law does not provide much relief from imposters. For example, the penalty for piracy doesn't include jail time. One owner reports having chased away would-be copiers with cameras, sketch pads, and Palm Pilots from her booth. Another retailer keeps its toys locked in hotel rooms, where only invited guests may see them.

Software is undeniably one of the most commonly pirated items in China. It is estimated that 92 percent of all software in China was counterfeit in 2001. This includes not only disks sold to end consumers, but also preinstalled software that comes with computers. As a result, companies such as Microsoft struggle to be profitable in China. Microsoft, attracted by a growing number of computer owners and the opening market in China, moved in through Taiwan and Hong Kong starting in 1989. The dream is that computers and software will follow the same trajectory as the mobile phone in China: 24 million cell phones in 1998 increased to 200 million cell phones in 2003.

Unfortunately, Microsoft began with an overconfident attitude unappealing to the Chinese. It followed that with an aggressive attack of lawsuits against pirates, which made it look like a foreign bully thrashing small Chinese companies. Microsoft has invested millions of dollars already in China and has yet to earn a profit, nor does it look likely that the firm will achieve profitability any time soon. Having evaluated its approach, Microsoft is now trying to rebuild its reputation by investing heavily in China, spending approximately $750 million. This includes sponsoring research at universities and forming joint ventures with Chinese companies as well as training Chinese software engineers and building research labs.

Cisco Systems filed suit in February 2003 against the Chinese company Huawei, alleging that Huawei had stolen its designs and software code for

Steamroller crushes approximately two million illegal CDs, DVDs, and videocassettes of local and foreign films during a ceremony highlighting the Philippine government's fight against piracy in suburban Quezon City. The pirated CDs, including music and pornographic movies, were seized in three days of raids by police of sidewalk stalls and shops in the city.

routers. For years, customers had wondered at the similarities, right down to the layout of the user handbook and the keyboard programming commands. 3Com, a Cisco rival that recently formed a joint venture with Huawei, was unalarmed at the suit, and said that Huawei had done its best to appease its own and Cisco's concerns with the venture, including a clause in the agreement that guarantees there is no pirated software in what will be produced.

China has begun taking steps to protect intellectual property rights, especially because of requirements for entry into the World Trade Organization. As China seeks to become a global player in the software industry, like India, it wants to overcome its reputation for piracy. It continues to stiffen its laws, making it easier for companies to sue and applying hefty fines to violators. Progress has been made in Hong Kong especially since 1999, when the city's Intellectual Property Investigation Bureau established a special antipiracy unit. China has amended its laws so that even offers to sell pirated products, not just actual sales, are illegal. And in February 2003, a Chinese court handed down a remarkable decision in favor of Lego, the Danish toy company, which clearly protected Lego's intellectual property rights.

Despite legal steps, enforcement remains scanty. Local governments might own the factory producing pirated products and choose Chinese jobs over the potential of foreign lawsuits. Progress will mostly come as the Chinese begin to see themselves as the creators of intellectual property and seek intellectual property rights in their own interest.

SOURCES: S. M. Andrews, 2003, Design thieves menace survival, *Home Textiles Today*, January 27, 10; G. A. Fowler, 2003, Copies `R' Us— Pirates in China move fast to pilfer toy makers' ideas, *Wall Street Journal*, January 31, B1; B. Einhorn, 2003, Cisco: Making a federal case out of it, *Business Week*, February 10, 36; B. Einhorn, 2003, China learns to say, "Stop, thief!" *BusinessWeek Online*, http//:www.businessweek.com, February 10; D. Ackman, 2003, Building blocks of Chinese IP law, *Forbes*, http//:www.forbes.com, February 11; R. Meredith, 2003, Microsoft's long march, *Forbes*, February 17, 78–86; P. D. Henig, 2003, Cross border IP hits the spotlight: With more tech startups operating in India and China, protecting IP has become ever more critical, *Venture Capital Journal*, March 1, 1; S. Thurm, 2003, China's Huawei, 3Com to form venture to compete with Cisco, *Wall Street Journal*, March 20, B5; P. Burrows, 2003, Cisco: In hot pursuit of a Chinese rival, *Business-Week Online*, http//:www.businessweek.com, May 19; K. Leggett, 2003, U.S. auto makers find promise—and peril—in China, *Wall Street Journal*, June 19, B1.

Wal-Mart made significant mistakes in markets around the world as it internationalized. For example, its first Mexican stores carried ice skates, riding lawn mowers, fishing tackle—even clay pigeons for skeet shooting. To get rid of the clay pigeons, they would be radically discounted, "only to have automated inventory systems linked to Wal-Mart's corporate headquarters in Bentonville, Arkansas, order a fresh batch."[183] As Wal-Mart began to get the right mix of products, the Mexican currency was devalued in 1994. However, over time, Wal-Mart has become very successful in Latin America, especially in Mexico, and elsewhere in the world. It has been able to increase its market share by taking advantage of local sourcing, and especially by taking advantage of the lower wages, for instance, in Mexico through NAFTA. It has made acquisitions in Europe and will have increased the number of stores in 2003 from 25 to 40 in China alone.[184]

The amount of international diversification that can be managed varies from firm to firm and according to the abilities of each firm's managers. The problems of central coordination and integration are mitigated if the firm diversifies into more friendly countries that are geographically close and have cultures similar to its own country's culture. In that case, there are likely to be fewer trade barriers, the laws and customs are better understood, and the product is easier to adapt to local markets.[185] For example, U.S. firms may find it less difficult to expand their operations into Mexico, Canada, and Western European countries than into Asian countries.

Management must also be concerned with the relationship between the host government and the multinational corporation.[186] Although government policy and regulations are often barriers, many firms, such as Toyota and General Motors, have turned to strategic alliances to overcome those barriers. By forming interorganizational networks, such as strategic alliances, firms can share resources and risks but also build flexibility.[187]

Summary

- The use of international strategies is increasing not only because of traditional motivations, but also for emerging reasons. Traditional motives include extending the product life cycle, securing key resources, and having access to low-cost labor. Emerging motivations focus on the combination of the Internet and mobile telecommunications, which facilitates global transactions. Also, there is increased pressure for global integration as the demand for commodities becomes borderless, and yet pressure is also increasing for local country responsiveness.

- An international strategy usually attempts to capitalize on four benefits: increased market size; the opportunity to earn a return on large investments; economies of scale and learning; and advantages of location.

- International business-level strategies are usually grounded in one or more home-country advantages, as Porter's diamond model suggests. The diamond model emphasizes four determinants: factors of production; demand conditions; related and supporting industries; and patterns of firm strategy, structure, and rivalry.

- There are three types of international corporate-level strategies. A multidomestic strategy focuses on competition within each country in which the firm competes. Firms using a multidomestic strategy decentralize strategic and operating decisions to the business units operating in each country, so that each unit can tailor its goods and services to the local market. A global strategy assumes more standardization of products across country boundaries; therefore, competitive strategy is centralized and controlled by the home office. A transnational strategy seeks to combine aspects of both multidomestic and global strategies in order to emphasize both local responsiveness and global integration and coordination. This strategy is difficult to implement, requiring an integrated network and a culture of individual commitment.

- Although the transnational strategy's implementation is a challenge, environmental trends are causing many multinational firms to consider the need for both global efficiency and local responsiveness. Many large multinational firms—particularly those with many diverse products—use a multidomestic strategy with some product lines and a global strategy with others.

- The threat of wars and terrorist attacks increases the risks and costs of international strategies. Furthermore, research suggests that the liability of foreignness is more difficult to overcome than once thought.

- Some firms decide to compete only in certain regions of the world, as opposed to viewing all markets in the world as potential opportunities. Competing in regional markets allows firms and managers to focus their learning on specific markets, cultures, locations, resources, etc.

- Firms may enter international markets in one of several ways, including exporting, licensing, forming strategic alliances, making acquisitions, and establishing new wholly owned subsidiaries, often referred to as greenfield ventures. Most firms begin with exporting or licensing, because of their lower costs and risks, but later may expand to strategic alliances and acquisitions. The most expensive and risky means of entering a new international market is through the establishment of a new wholly owned subsidiary. On the other hand, such subsidiaries provide the advantages of maximum control by the firm and, if they are successful, the greatest returns.

- International diversification facilitates innovation in a firm, because it provides a larger market to gain more and faster returns from investments in innovation. In addition, international diversification may generate the resources necessary to sustain a large-scale R&D program.

- In general, international diversification is related to above-average returns, but this assumes that the diversification is effectively implemented and that the firm's international operations are well managed. International diversification provides greater economies of scope and learning, which, along with greater innovation, help produce above-average returns.

- Several risks are involved with managing multinational operations. Among these are political risks (e.g., instability of national governments) and economic risks (e.g., fluctuations in the value of a country's currency).

- There are also limits to the ability to manage international expansion effectively. International diversification increases coordination and distribution costs, and management problems are exacerbated by trade barriers, logistical costs, and cultural diversity, among other factors.

1. What are the traditional and emerging motives that cause firms to expand internationally?

2. What four factors provide a basis for international business-level strategies?

3. What are the three international corporate-level strategies? How do they differ from each other? What factors lead to their development?

4. What environmental trends are affecting international strategy?

5. What five modes of international expansion are available, and what is the normal sequence of their use?

6. What is the relationship between international diversification and innovation? How does international diversification affect innovation? What is the effect of international diversification on a firm's returns?

7. What are the risks of international diversification? What are the challenges of managing multinational firms?

8. What factors limit the positive outcomes of international expansion?

Experiential Exercises

Modes of Entry into China

As pointed out in the Opening Case, China's 2001 entry into the World Trade Organization (WTO) is potentially one of the most significant international trade events in recent times. Substantial business discussion has focused on China's relative competitive advantage with regard to labor, which allows the production and exportation of vast quantities of goods at very low costs. Conversely, Chinese markets provide a substantial potential opportunity for non-Chinese firms to export into them. The huge market size (1.2 billion plus in population) is a key factor, as are virtually untapped consumer markets for many goods and services for increasingly sophisticated Chinese needs and tastes, which are often modest by Western standards. However, conflicting business and social goals in the macro Chinese environment have underscored the liability of foreignness. That is, being a foreign firm often increases the difficulty of management and the likelihood of failure. This is primarily due to unfamiliarity with cultural, political, economic, and other environmental differences and their potential effect on business operations, as well as to the need for coordination across geographic distance, among other factors. Organizational and strategic influences on firm survival in foreign banking and financial services markets have been linked to levels of technology adaptations, mode of internal control, and intensity of competition, as well as general levels of competitiveness of both the home and the host country. Furthermore, variance in the degree to which former state-owned businesses have been encouraged, or even allowed, to approach free-market status has caused further difficulties. For instance, before September 2003, certification for import/export business activity was tightly controlled by the Ministry of Commerce at the national level and generally limited to large, well-connected firms that could satisfy relatively high capitalization and operational requirements. These requirements were relaxed in response to WTO commitments, while primary responsibility for examination and

registration of firms was delegated to the local government level. This should permit more (smaller) firms across industries to engage in import/export business activity but also is likely to create potential discrepancies in the certification process for import/export status.

Chinese and U.S. businesses have an inverse relationship concerning import and export patterns for goods and services. China is a net exporter of goods to the United States, while the United States is a net exporter of services to China. Based on this and chapter information, your own knowledge of Chinese and Western business practices, as well as Internet resources, explore the differences between Western and Chinese business practices. Using this information, evaluate the most appropriate mode of entry (see Table 8.1) into China by:

1. A U.S. financial services firm, such as a bank; and

2. A U.S. manufacturer of heavy goods, such as an auto company.

Developing and Implementing International Mode of Entry Strategies

In the late 1990s, Motorola Inc., a leading U.S. telecom supplier, viewed the telecommunication market in Turkey as promising. The rapidly growing Turkish economy presented substantial growth potential to U.S. firms seeking entry into this market, where subscribers grew from two to nine million during 1999–2001 alone, in a country of sixty-five million. Likewise, opportunity abounded for those awarded lucrative Turkish wireless telecom licenses, such as Telsim, a local (domestic) firm. Telsim was and is controlled by the powerful Turkish Uzan family. This family has substantial affiliations across construction, banking, media, and politics. In general, Telsim reportedly needed a strong partner to take advantage of market opportunities, and Motorola sought to enter the potentially lucrative telecommunication market in Turkey.

In February 2000, Motorola and Telsim announced an agreement for Motorola to expand wireless telephone service in Turkey by providing infrastructure, handsets, and associated services to supplement Telsim's global satellite network. As part of the agreement, Telsim named Motorola as its exclusive regional supplier of most equipment over the next three years. Motorola estimated that revenues from this supplier agreement would be at least $1.5 billion USD. In October 2000, Motorola and Telsim signed another agreement for the supply and deployment of a third generation (3G) mobile network capable of providing advanced multimedia services. Motorola estimated the potential value of the contract to be in excess of $2 billion USD. During the course of these interactions, Motorola loaned nearly $2 billion USD to Telsim (mostly in the form of cash and some equipment).

By the middle of 2001, the initially excellent business relations between Motorola and Telsim became troubled and were viewed by many as less than successful. This came during a general downturn in the global telecom market, making the industry as a whole less attractive. On January 28, 2002, Motorola filed a lawsuit against Telsim in the U.S. District Court for the Southern District of New York alleging criminal actions, including diversion of funds and fraud, on the part of Telsim. This lawsuit was filed under the Racketeer Influenced and Corrupt Organizations (RICO) Act. Motorola sought more than $2 billion USD in compensatory damages as well as unspecified punitive damages.

1. Briefly discuss various choices of market entry modes originally available to Motorola in this case. Table 8.1 provides a summary of market entry modes.

2. Working in small groups, students should update this case by developing and defending an approach to deal with this situation. What should Motorola do next? Pull out of the Turkish market? Find another licensing company? Wait until the lawsuits are completely settled in the courts? Change the mode of entry?

3. Can such disputes influence other firms interested in developing business relationships in Turkey? How? Class discussion will follow.

Understanding International Strategies

Divide the class into small groups. For each company in the table, indicate the international strategy being implemented. You may support your determination by using the content of Chapter 8, as it gives some clues regarding possible strategies used. Groups will discuss the selection with the class.

Company	Strategy	Supporting the Choice of Strategy
Unilever		1. 2. 3.
Coca-Cola		1. 2. 3.
Tricon Global Restaurants		1. 2. 3.
Flextronics		1. 2. 3.
Cemex		1. 2. 3.
DaimlerChrysler		1. 2. 3.
Lands' End		1. 2. 3.
General Motors		1. 2. 3.
Wal-Mart		1. 2. 3.

Company	Strategy	Supporting the Choice of Strategy
British American Tobacco (BAT)		1. 2. 3.
Asea Brown Boveri (ABB)		1. 2. 3.

Notes

1. G. Smith, 2003, Wasting away: Despite SARS, Mexico is still losing export ground to China, *Business Week*, June 2, 42–44.

2. H. Chen, M. Y. Hu, & P. S. Hu, 2002, Ownership strategy of multinationals from ASEAN: The case of their investment in Sino-foreign joint ventures, *Management International Review*, 42(3): 309–326; D. Ahlstrom & G. D. Bruton, 2001, Learning from successful local private firms in China: Establishing legitimacy, *Academy of Management Executive*, 15(4): 72–83.

3. S. Werner, 2002, Recent developments in international management research: A review of 20 top management journals, *Journal of Management*, 28: 277–305.

4. R. A. Kapp, 2003, Internationalizing China: Domestic interests and global linkages, *China Business Review*, 30(2): 80; A. K. Gupta & V. Govindarajan, 2001, Converting global presence into global competitive advantage, *Academy of Management Executive*, 15(2): 45–57.

5. T. M. Begley & D. P. Boyd, 2003, The need for a corporate global mind-set, *MIT Sloan Management Review*, 44(2): 25–32.

6. R. L. Mecham III, 2003, Success for the new global manager: What you need to know to work across distances, countries, and cultures, *Leadership Quarterly*, 14: 347–352; R. J. Trent & R. M. Monczka, 2002, Pursuing competitive advantage through integrated global sourcing, *Academy of Management Executive*, 16(2): 66–80; A. McWilliams, D. D. Van Fleet, & P. M. Wright, 2001, Strategic management of human resources for global competitive advantage, *Journal of Business Strategies*, 18(1): 1–24; B. L. Kedia & A. Mukherji, 1999, Global managers: Developing a mindset for global competitiveness, *Journal of World Business*, 34(3): 230–251.

7. D. M. De Carolis, 2003, Competencies and imitability in the pharmaceutical industry: An analysis of their relationship with firm performance, *Journal of Management*, 29: 27–50; J. S. Childers, Jr., R. L. Somerly, & K. E. Bass, 2002, Competitive environments and sustained economic rents: A theoretical examination of country-specific differences within the pharmaceutical industry, *International Journal of Management*, 19(1): 89–98; G. Bottazzi, G. Dosi, M. Lippi, F. Pammolli, & M. Riccaboni, 2001, Innovation and corporate growth in the evolution of the drug industry, *International Journal of Industrial Organization*, 19: 1161–1187.

8. S. Tallman & K. Fladmoe-Lindquist, 2002, Internationalization, globalization, and capability-based strategy, *California Management Review*, 45(1): 116–135; S. Tallman, 2001, Global strategic management, in M. A. Hitt, R. E. Freeman, & J. S. Harrison (eds.), *Handbook of Strategic Management*, Oxford, UK: Blackwell Publishers, 462–490; C. W. L. Hill, 2000, *International Business: Competing in the Global Marketplace*, 3d ed., Boston: Irwin/McGraw Hill, 378–380.

9. W. Hejazi & P. Pauly, 2003, Motivations for FDI and domestic capital formation, *Journal of International Business Studies*, 34: 282–289.

10. R. Vernon, 1996, International investment and international trade in the product cycle, *Quarterly Journal of Economics*, 80: 190–207.

11. H. F. Lau, C. C. Y. Kwok, & C. F. Chan, 2000, Filling the gap: Extending international product life cycle to emerging economies, *Journal of Global Marketing*, 13(4): 29–51.

12. L. Yu, 2003, The global-brand advantage, *MIT Sloan Management Review*, 44(3): 13.

13. G. Edmondson & C. Passariello, 2003, Has Benetton stopped unraveling? Its new boss plans sweeping changes, and investors are happy, *Business Week*, June 23, 22.

14. J. Flint, 2003, Too much globalism, *Forbes*, February 17, 96; Y. S. Pak, J. Lee, & J. M. An, 2002, Lessons learned from Daewoo Motors' experience in emerging markets, *Multinational Business Review*, 10(2): 122–128; B. Kim & Y. Lee, 2001, Global capacity expansion strategies: Lessons learned from two Korean carmakers, *Long Range Planning*, 34(3): 309–333.

15. D. Rigby & C. Zook, 2003, Open-market innovation, *Harvard Business Review*, 89(10): 80–89; J.-R. Lee & J.-S. Chen, 2003, Internationalization, local adaptation and subsidiary's entrepreneurship: An exploratory study on Taiwanese manufacturing firms in Indonesia and Malaysia, *Asia Pacific Journal of Management*, 20: 51–72; K. Macharzina, 2001, The end of pure global strategies? *Management International Review*, 41(2): 105.

16. Y. Luo, 2003, Market-seeking MNEs in an emerging market: How parent-subsidiary links shape overseas success, *Journal of International Business Studies*, 34: 290–309; 2003, Special Report: Two systems, one grand rivalry—India and China, *The Economist*, June 21, 66–68; Y. Luo, 2000, Entering China today: What choices do we have? *Journal of Global Marketing*, 14(2): 57–82.

17. C. C. Y. Kwok & D. M. Reeb, 2000, Internationalization and firm risk: An upstream-downstream hypothesis, *Journal of International Business Studies*, 31: 611–629; J. J. Choi & M. Rajan, 1997, A joint test of market segmentation and exchange risk factor in international capital markets, *Journal of International Business Studies*, 28: 29–49.

18. R. E. Hoskisson, L. Eden, C. M. Lau, & M. Wright, 2000, Strategy in emerging economies, *Academy of Management Journal*, 43: 249–267; D. J. Arnold & J. A. Quelch, 1998, New strategies in emerging markets, *Sloan Management Review*, 40: 7–20.

19. P. Engardio, A. Bernstein, & M. Kripalani, 2003, Is your job next? *Business Week*, February 3, 50–60; M. Wright, A. Lockett, & S. Pruthi, 2002, Internationalization of Western venture capitalists into emerging markets: Risk assessment and information in India, *Small Business Economics*, 19(1): 13–29.

20. M. Peng, 2003, Institutional transitions and strategic choices, *Academy of Management Review*, 28: 275–296.

21. T. Aeppel, 2003, Manufacturers spent much less abroad last year—U.S. firms cut investing overseas by estimated 37 percent; the "high-wage paradox," *Wall Street Journal*, May 9, A8.

22. W. Kuemmerle, 2001, Go global—or not? *Harvard Business Review*, 79(6): 37–49; Y. Luo & M. W. Peng, 1999, Learning to compete in a transition economy: Experience, environment and performance, *Journal of International Business Studies*, 30: 269–295.

23. G. Jones, 2002, Control, performance, and knowledge transfers in large multinationals: Unilever in the United States, 1945–1980, *Business History Review*, 76(3): 435–478.

24. A. P. Raman, 2003, HBR case study: The global brand face-off, *Harvard Business Review*, 81(6): 35–46.

25. Lee & Chen, Internationalization, local adaptation and subsidiary's entrepreneurship.

26. D. Skarmeas, C. S. Katsikeas, & B. B. Schlegelmilch, 2002, Drivers of commitment and its impact on performance in cross-cultural buyer-seller relationships: The importer's perspective, *Journal of International Business Studies*, 33: 757–783; X. Martin, A. Swaminathan, & W. Mitchell, 1999, Organizational evolution in the interorganizational environment: Incentives and constraints on international expansion strategy, *Administrative Science Quarterly*, 43: 566–601.

27. P. Ghemawat, 2001, Distance still matters: The hard reality of global expansion, *Harvard Business Review*, 79(8): 137–147.

28. S. R. Miller & A. Parkhe, 2002, Is there a liability of foreignness in global banking? An empirical test of banks' x-efficiency, *Strategic Management Journal*, 23: 55–75; T. Kostova & S. Zaheer, 1999, Organizational legitimacy under conditions of complexity: The case of the multinational enterprise, *Academy of Management Review*, 24: 64–81; S. Zaheer & E. Mosakowski, 1997, The dynamics of the liability of foreignness: A global study of survival in financial services, *Strategic Management Journal*, 18: 439–464.

29. O. Kharif, 2003, Qualcomm's mixed signals, *BusinessWeek Online*, http://www.businessweek.com, May 8.

30. A. Caplan, 2003, Global beer: Tapping into growth, *Beverage World*, February 15, 24–29.

31. K. Asakawa & M. Lehrer, 2003, Managing local knowledge assets globally: The role of regional innovation relays, *Journal of World Business*, 38: 31–42.

32. W. Chung & J. Alcacer, 2002, Knowledge seeking and location choice of foreign direct investment in the United States, *Management Science*, 48(12): 1534–1554.

33. 2003, Weathering the tech storm: How Michael Marks boosted efficiency at contract manufacturer Flextronics, *Business Week*, May 5, B24.

34. Ibid.

35. M. L. Clifford & P. Engardio, 2003, Standing guard: How a big factory is keeping SARS out, *Business Week*, May 5, 46–48.

36. C. R. Gowen III & W. J. Tallon, 2002, Turnaround strategies of American and Japanese electronics corporations—How do they differ in formulating plans and achieving results? *Journal of High Technology Management Research*, 13(2): 225–248; W. Shan & J. Song, 1997, Foreign direct investment and the sourcing of technological advantage: Evidence from the biotechnology industry, *Journal of International Business Studies*, 28: 267–284.

37. W. Chung, 2001, Identifying technology transfer in foreign direct investment: Influence of industry conditions and investing firm motives, *Journal of International Business Studies*, 32: 211–229.

38. B. Davis, R. Buckman, & C. Rhoads, 2003, A global journal report: For global economy, much rides on how the U.S. war plays out, *Wall Street Journal*, March 20, A1; F. Erdal & E. Tatoglu, 2002, Locational determinants of foreign direct investment in an emerging market economy: Evidence from Turkey, *Multinational Business Review*, 10(1): 21–28.

39. A. J. Mauri & A. V. Phatak, 2001, Global integration as inter-area product flows: The internalization of ownership and location factors influencing product flows across MNC units, *Management International Review*, 41(3): 233–249.

40. 2003, Business: The great leap forward; cars in China, *The Economist*, February 1, 53–56.

41. J. Flint, 2003, China: How big, how fast, how dangerous? *Forbes*, http://www.forbes.com, July 1.

42. W. Kuemmerle, 2002, Home base and knowledge management in international ventures, *Journal of Business Venturing*, 2: 99–122; H. Bresman, J. Birkinshaw & R. Nobel, 1999, Knowledge transfer in international acquisitions, *Journal of International Business Studies*, 30: 439–462; J. Birkinshaw, 1997, Entrepreneurship in multinational corporations: The characteristics of subsidiary initiatives, *Strategic Management Journal*, 18: 207–229.

43. S. Makino, C. M. Lau, & R. S. Yeh, 2002, Asset-exploitation versus asset-seeking: Implications for location choice of foreign direct investment from newly industrialized economies, *Journal of International Business Studies*, 33(3): 403–421.

44. K. Uhlenbruck, K. E. Meyer, & M. A. Hitt, 2003, Organizational transformation in transition economies: Resource-based and organizational learning perspectives, *Journal of Management Studies*, 40: 257–282; Ahlstrom & Bruton, Learning from successful local private firms in China; S. A. Zahra, R. D. Ireland, & M. A. Hitt, 2000, International expansion by new venture firms: International diversity, mode of market entry, technological learning, and performance, *Academy of Management Journal*, 43: 925–950.

45. K. Ito & E. L. Rose, 2002, Foreign direct investment location strategies in the tire industry, *Journal of International Business Studies*, 33(3): 593–602.

46. J. Bernstein & D. Weinstein, 2002, Do endowments predict the location of production? Evidence from national and international data, *Journal of International Economics*, 56(1): 55–76.

47. B. Einhorn, 2003, China's homegrown stars, *BusinessWeek Online*, http://www.businessweek.com, May 12.

48. Tallman & Fladmoe-Lindquist, Internationalization, globalization, and capability-based strategy; D. A. Griffith & M. G. Harvey, 2001, A resource perspective of global dynamic capabilities, *Journal of International Business Studies*, 32: 597–606; D. J. Teece, G. Pisano, & A. Shuen, 1997, Dynamic capabilities and strategic management, *Strategic Management Journal*, 18: 509–533.

49. Y. Luo, 2000, Dynamic capabilities in international expansion, *Journal of World Business*, 35(4): 355–378.

50. H. W.-C. Zhao, 2002, Entrepreneurship in international business: An institutional perspective, *Asia Pacific Journal of Management*, 19: 29–61.

51. L. Nachum, 2001, The impact of home countries on the competitiveness of advertising TNCs, *Management International Review*, 41(1): 77–98.

52. K. Kling & I. Goteman, 2003, IKEA CEO Anders Dahlvig on international growth and IKEA's unique corporate culture and brand identity, *Academy of Management Executive*, 17(1): 31–37.

53. M. E. Porter, 1990, *The Competitive Advantage of Nations*, New York: The Free Press.

54. Porter, *The Competitive Advantage of Nations*, 84.

55. G. Khermouch, B. Einhorn, & D. Roberts, 2003, Breaking into the name game, *Business Week*, April 7, 54.

56. Porter, *The Competitive Advantage of Nations*, 89.

57. Y. Aoyama & H. Izushi, 2003, Hardware gimmick or cultural innovation? Technological, cultural, and social foundations of the Japanese video game industry, *Research Policy*, 32: 423–443.

58. Khermouch, Einhorn, & Roberts, Breaking into the name game.

59. J. Birkinshaw, 2001, Strategies for managing internal competition, *California Management Review*, 44(1): 21–38.

60. W. P. Wan & R. E. Hoskisson, 2003, Home country environments, corporate diversification strategies and firm performance, *Academy of Management Journal*, 46: 27–45; J. M. Geringer, S. Tallman, & D. M. Olsen, 2000, Product and international diversification among Japanese multinational firms, *Strategic Management Journal*, 21: 51–80.

61. Wan and Hoskisson, Home country environments, corporate diversification strategies and firm performance; M. A. Hitt, R. E. Hoskisson, & R. D. Ireland, 1994, A mid-range theory of the interactive effects of international and product diversification on innovation and performance, *Journal of Management*, 20: 297–326.

62. J. Pla-Barber, 2002, From Stopford and Wells's model to Bartlett and Ghoshal's typology: New empirical evidence, *Management International Review*, 42(2): 141–156; J. Sheth, 2001, From international to integrated marketing, *Journal of Business Research*, 9: 5–9; A.-W. Harzing, 2000, An empirical analysis and extension of the Bartlett and Ghoshal typology of multinational companies, *Journal of International Business Studies*, 32: 101–120; S. Ghoshal, 1987, Global strategy: An organizing framework, *Strategic Management Journal*, 8: 425–440.

63. L. Nachum, 2003, Does nationality of ownership make any difference and if so, under what circumstances? Professional service MNEs in global competition, *Journal of International Management*, 9: 1–32; Sheth, From international to integrated marketing; J. Taggart & N. Hood, 1999, Determinants of autonomy in multinational corporation subsidiaries, *European Management Journal*, 17: 226–236.

64. Y. Luo, 2001, Determinants of local responsiveness: Perspectives from foreign subsidiaries in an emerging market, *Journal of Management*, 27: 451–477.

65. M. Geppert, K. Williams, & D. Matten, 2003, The social construction of contextual rationalities in MNCs: An Anglo-German comparison of subsidiary choice, *Journal of Management Studies*, 40: 617–641; M. Carpenter & J. Fredrickson, 2001, Top management teams, global strategic posture, and the moderating role of uncertainty, *Academy of Management Journal*, 44: 533–545; T. T. Herbert, 1999, Multinational strategic planning: Matching central expectations to local realities, *Long Range Planning*, 32: 81–87.

66. Jones, Control, performance, and knowledge transfers in large multinationals: Unilever in the United States, 1945–1980.

67. A. Afuah, 2003, Redefining firm boundaries in the face of the Internet: Are firms really shrinking? *Academy of Management Review*, 28: 34–53; M. F. Guillen, 2002, What is the best global strategy for the Internet? *Business Horizons*, 45(3): 39–46.

68. A.-W. Harzing & A. Sorge, 2003, The relative impact of country of origin and universal contingencies in internationalization strategies and corporate control in multinational enterprises: Worldwide and European perspectives, *Organization Studies*, 24: 187–214.

69. 2003, Masks off, down the hatch, *The Economist*, May 17, 57.

70. G. Khermouch & K. Capell, 2003, Spiking the booze business, *Business Week*, May 19, 77–78.

PART 2 / Strategic Actions: Strategy Formulation

71. C. Lawton & D. Ball, 2003, Diageo mixes it up—liquor giant targets system dating to end of prohibition, *Wall Street Journal Online*, http://www.wsj.com, May 8.

72. Harzing, An empirical analysis and extension of the Bartlett and Ghoshal typology.

73. I. C. MacMillan, A. B. van Putten, & R. G. McGrath, 2003, Global gamesmanship, *Harvard Business Review*, 81(5): 62–71.

74. R. G. Barker, 2003, Trend: Global accounting is coming, *Harvard Business Review*, 81(4): 24–25.

75. A. Yaprak, 2002, Globalization: Strategies to build a great global firm in the new economy, *Thunderbird International Business Review*, 44(2): 297–302; D. G. McKendrick, 2001, Global strategy and population level learning: The case of hard disk drives, *Strategic Management Journal*, 22: 307–334.

76. H. D. Hopkins, 2003, The response strategies of dominant US firms to Japanese challengers, *Journal of Management*, 29: 5–25; S. Massini, A. Y. Lewin, T. Numagami, & A. Pettigrew, 2002, The evolution of organizational routines among large Western and Japanese firms, *Research Policy*, 31(8,9): 1333–1348; M. W. Peng, S. H. Lee, & J. J. Tan, 2001, The keiretsu in Asia: Implications for multilevel theories of competitive advantage, *Journal of International Management*, 7: 253–276; A. Bhappu, 2000, The Japanese family: An institutional logic for Japanese corporate networks and Japanese management, *Academy of Management Review*, 25: 409–415; J. K. Johansson & G. S. Yip, 1994, Exploiting globalization potential: U.S. and Japanese strategies, *Strategic Management Journal*, 15: 579–601.

77. S. Roy, 2003, Cementing global success, *Strategic Direct Investor*, March, 12–13.

78. Ibid.

79. Ibid.

80. Ibid.

81. J. Barham, 2002, From local manufacturer to global player, *LatinFinance*, April, 25–26.

82. Y. Doz, J. Santos, & P. Williamson, 2001, *From Global to Metanational: How Companies Win in the Knowledge Economy*, Boston: Harvard Business School Press; C. A. Bartlett & S. Ghoshal, 1989, *Managing across Borders: The Transnational Solution*, Boston: Harvard Business School Press.

83. J. Child & Y. Yan, 2001, National and transnational effects in international business: Indications from Sino-foreign joint ventures, *Management International Review*, 41(1): 53–75.

84. B. James, 2003, Ghosn's local vision plays on a world stage, *International Herald Tribune*, May 3, 9.

85. Ibid.

86. A. M. Rugman & A. Verbeke, 2003, Extending the theory of the multinational enterprise: Internalization and strategic management perspectives, *Journal of International Business Studies*, 34: 125–137.

87. T. Isobe, S. Makino, & D. B. Montgomery, 2000, Resource commitment, entry timing and market performance of foreign direct investments in emerging economies: The case of Japanese international joint ventures in China, *Academy of Management Journal*, 43: 468–484.

88. S. Zaheer & A. Zaheer, 2001, Market microstructure in a global B2B network, *Strategic Management Journal*, 22: 859–873.

89. J. A. Trachtenberg & B. Steinberg, 2003, Plan B for Marketers—in a time of global conflict, companies consider changing how they push products, *Wall Street Journal*, March 20, B7.

90. S. Reda, 2003, Retailers take multi-faceted approaches to multi-channel success, *Stores*, June, 22–26.

91. F. X. Molina-Morales, 2001, European industrial districts: Influence of geographic concentration on performance of the firm, *Journal of International Management*, 7: 277–294; M. E. Porter & S. Stern, 2001, Innovation: Location matters, *Sloan Management Review*, 42(4): 28–36.

92. C. Pantzalis, 2001, Does location matter? An empirical analysis of geographic scope and MNC market valuation, *Journal of International Business Studies*, 32: 133–155.

93. A. Rugman & S. Girod, 2003, Retail multinationals and globalization: The evidence is regional, *European Management Journal*, 21(1): 24–37.

94. R. D. Ludema, 2002, Increasing returns, multinationals and geography of preferential trade agreements, *Journal of International Economics*, 56: 329–358; L. Allen & C. Pantzalis, 1996, Valuation of the operating flexibility of multinational corporations, *Journal of International Business Studies*, 27: 633–653.

95. F. Bruni, 2003, With a constitution to ponder, Europeans gather in Greece, *New York Times*, http://www.nytimes.com, June 20.

96. J. I. Martinez, J. A. Quelch, & J. Ganitsky, 1992, Don't forget Latin America, *Sloan Management Review*, 33(Winter): 78–92.

97. T. L. Pett & J. A. Wolff, 2003, Firm characteristic and managerial perceptions of NAFTA: An assessment of export implications for U.S. SMEs, *Journal of Small Business Management*, 41(2): 117–132.

98. G. Ip, 2003, The economy: Trade gap widens to record level–monthly deficit combines with other data to point to trouble for recovery, *Wall Street Journal*, February 21, A2.

99. D. Xu & O. Shenkar, 2002, Institutional distance and the multinational enterprise, *Academy of Management Review*, 27(4): 608–618; J. Chang & P. M. Rosenzweig, 1998, Industry and regional patterns in sequential foreign market entry, *Journal of Management Studies*, 35: 797–822.

100. K. D. Brouthers, L. E. Brouthers, & S. Werner, 2003, Industrial sector, perceived environmental uncertainty and entry mode strategy, *Journal of Business Research*, 55: 495–507; S. Zahra, J. Hayton, J. Marcel, & H. O'Neill, 2001, Fostering entrepreneurship during international expansion: Managing key challenges, *European Management Journal*, 19: 359–369.

101. K. D. Brouthers, 2003, Institutional, cultural and transaction cost influences on entry mode choice and performance, *Journal of International Business Studies*, 33: 203–221; R. Konopaske, S. Werner, & K. E. Neupert, 2002, Entry mode strategy and performance: The role of FDI staffing, *Journal of Business Research*, 55: 759–770; Zahra, Ireland, & Hitt, International expansion by new venture firms.

102. R. Isaak, 2002, Using trading firms to export: What can the French experience teach us? *Academy of Management Executive*, 16(4): 155–156; M. W. Peng, C. W. L. Hill, & D. Y. L. Wang, 2000, Schumpeterian dynamics versus Williamsonian considerations: A test of export intermediary performance, *Journal of Management Studies*, 37: 167–184.

103. Y. Chui, 2002, The structure of the multinational firm: The role of ownership characteristics and technology transfer, *International Journal of Management*, 19(3): 472–477.

104. Luo, Determinants of local responsiveness.

105. L. E. Brouthers & K. Xu, 2002, Product stereotypes, strategy and performance satisfaction: The case of Chinese exporters, *Journal of International Business Studies*, 33: 657–677; M. A. Raymond, J. Kim, & A. T. Shao, 2001, Export strategy and performance: A comparison of exporters in a developed market and an emerging market, *Journal of Global Marketing*, 15(2): 5–29; P. S. Aulakh, M. Kotabe, & H. Teegen, 2000, Export strategies and performance of firms from emerging economies: Evidence from Brazil, Chile and Mexico, *Academy of Management Journal*, 43: 342–361.

106. W. Dou, U. Nielsen, & C. M. Tan, 2003, Using corporate Websites for export marketing, *Journal of Advertising Research*, 42(5): 105–115.

107. B. Walker & D. Luft, 2001, Exporting tech from Texas, *Texas Business Review*, August, 1–5.

108. P. Westhead, M. Wright, & D. Ucbasaran, 2001, The internationalization of new and small firms: A resource-based view, *Journal of Business Venturing*, 16: 333–358.

109. W. Rugg, 2003, A down dollar's lure—and peril, *BusinessWeek Online*, http://www.businessweek.com, May 22.

110. D. Kline, 2003, Sharing the corporate crown jewels, *MIT Sloan Management Review*, 44(3): 83–88; M. A. Hitt & R. D. Ireland, 2000, The intersection of entrepreneurship and strategic management research, in D. L. Sexton & H. Landstrom (eds.), *Handbook of Entrepreneurship*, Oxford, UK: Blackwell Publishers, 45–63.

111. A. Arora & A. Fosfuri, 2000, Wholly owned subsidiary versus technology licensing in the worldwide chemical industry, *Journal of International Business Studies*, 31: 555–572.

112. M. Johnson, 2001, Learning from toys: Lessons in managing supply chain risk from the toy industry, *California Management Review*, 43(3): 106–124.

113. Rigby & Zook, Open-market innovation.

114. C. A. Bartlett & S. Rangan, 1992, Komatsu limited, in C. A. Bartlett & S. Ghoshal (eds.), *Transnational Management: Text, Cases and Readings in Cross-Border Management*, Homewood, IL: Irwin, 311–326.

115. Chang & Rosenzweig, The choice of entry mode in sequential foreign direct investment; B. Petersen, D. E. Welch, & L. S. Welch, 2000, Creating meaningful switching options in international operations, *Long Range Planning*, 33(5): 688–705.

116. R. Larsson, K. R. Brousseau, M. J. Driver, & M. Homqvist, 2003, International growth through cooperation: Brand-driven strategies, leadership, and career development in Sweden, *Academy of Management Executive*, 17(1): 7–21; J. W. Lu & P. W. Beamish, 2001, The internationalization and performance of SMEs, *Strategic Management Journal*, 22 (Special Issue): 565–586; M. Koza & A. Lewin, 2000, Managing partnerships and strategic alliances: Raising the odds of success, *European Management Journal*, 18(2): 146–151.

117. J. S. Harrison, M. A. Hitt, R. E. Hoskisson, & R. D. Ireland, 2001, Resource complementarity in business combinations: Extending the logic to organization alliances, *Journal of Management*, 27: 679–690; T. Das & B. Teng, 2000, A resource-based theory of strategic alliances, *Journal of Management*, 26: 31–61.

118. M. A. Hitt, D. Ahlstrom, M. T. Dacin, E. Levitas, & L. Svobodina, 2004, The institutional effects on strategic alliance partner selection in transition economies: China versus Russia, *Organization Science*, in press; M. Peng, 2001, The resource-based view and international business, *Journal of Management*, 27: 803–829.

119. H. Chen & T. Chen, 2003, Governance structures in strategic alliances: Transaction cost versus resource-based perspective, *Journal of World Business*, 38(1): 1–14; E. W. K. Tsang, 2002, Acquiring knowledge by foreign partners for international joint ventures in a transition economy: Learning-by-doing and learning myopia, *Strategic Management Journal*, 23(9): 835–854; P. J. Lane, J. E. Salk, & M. A. Lyles, 2002, Absorptive capacity, learning, and performance in international joint ventures, *Strategic Management Journal*, 22: 1139–1161; B. L. Simonin, 1999, Transfer of marketing know-how in international strategic alliances: An empirical investigation of the role and antecedents of knowledge ambiguity, *Journal of International Business Studies*, 30: 463–490; M. A. Lyles & J. E. Salk, 1996, Knowledge acquisition from foreign parents in international joint ventures: An empirical examination in the Hungarian context, *Journal of International Business Studies*, 27 (Special Issue): 877–903.

120. P. Almeida, J. Song, & R. M. Grant, 2002, Are firms superior to alliances and markets? An empirical test of cross-border knowledge building, *Organization Science*, 13(2): 147–161; Shrader, Collaboration and performance in foreign markets; M. A. Hitt, M. T. Dacin, E. Levitas, J. L. Arregle, & A. Borza, 2000, Partner selection in emerging and developed market contexts: Resource based and organizational learning perspectives, *Academy of Management Journal*, 43: 449–467.

121. P. Engardio & D. Roberts, 2003, Growing up fast, *Business Week*, March 31, 52–53.

122. M. W. Peng & O. Shenkar, 2002, Joint venture dissolution as corporate divorce, *Academy of Management Executive*, 16(2): 92–105; O. Shenkar & A. Yan, 2002, Failure as a consequence of partner politics: Learning from the life and death of an international cooperative venture, *Human Relations*, 55: 565–601.

123. J. A. Robins, S. Tallman, & K. Fladmoe-Lindquist, 2002, Autonomy and dependence of international cooperative ventures: An exploration of the strategic performance of U.S. ventures in Mexico, *Strategic Management Journal*, 23(10): 881–901; Y. Gong, O. Shenkar, Y. Luo, & M-K. Nyaw, 2001, Role conflict and ambiguity of CEOs in international joint ventures: A transaction cost perspective, *Journal of Applied Psychology*, 86: 764–773.

124. D. C. Hambrick, J. Li, K. Xin, & A. S. Tsui, 2001, Compositional gaps and downward spirals in international joint venture management groups, *Strategic Management Journal*, 22: 1033–1053; M. T. Dacin, M. A. Hitt, & E. Levitas, 1997, Selecting partners for successful international alliances: Examination of U.S. and Korean Firms, *Journal of World Business*, 32: 3–16.

125. J. Child & Y. Yan, 2003, Predicting the performance of international joint ventures: An investigation in China, *Journal of Management Studies*, 40(2): 283–320; J. P. Johnson, M. A. Korsgaard, & H. J. Sapienza, 2002, Perceived fairness, decision control, and commitment in international joint venture management teams, *Strategic Management Journal*, 23(12): 1141–1160; A. Arino, J. de la Torre, & P. S. Ring, 2001, Relational quality: Managing trust in corporate alliances, *California Management Review*, 44(1): 109–131.

126. L. Huff & L. Kelley, 2003, Levels of organizational trust in individualist versus collectivist societies: A seven-nation study, *Organization Science*, 14(1): 81–90.

127. Y. Pan & D. K. Tse, 2000, The hierarchical model of market entry modes, *Journal of International Business Studies*, 31: 535–554; Y. Pan, S. Li, & D. K. Tse, 1999, The impact of order and mode of market entry on profitability and market share, *Journal of International Business Studies*, 30: 81–104.

128. J. J. Reuer, 2002, Incremental corporate reconfiguration through international joint venture buyouts and selloffs, *Management International Review*, 42: 237–260.

129. G. A. Knight & P. W. Liesch, 2002, Information internalisation in internationalising the firm, *Journal of Business Research*, 55(12): 981–995; M. Supphellen, S. A. Haugland, & T. Korneliussen, 2002, SMBs in search of international strategic alliances: Perceived importance of personal information sources, *Journal of Business Research*, 55(9): 785–795.

130. W. H. Hoffmann & W. Schaper-Rinkel, 2001, Acquire or ally? A strategy framework for deciding between acquisition and cooperation, *Management International Review*, 41(2): 131–159.

131. M. A. Hitt, J. S. Harrison, & R. D. Ireland, 2001, *Creating Value through Mergers and Acquisitions*, New York: Oxford University Press.

132. M. A. Hitt & V. Pisano, 2003, The cross-border merger and acquisition strategy, *Management Research*, 1: 133–144.

133. 1999, French dressing, *The Economist*, July 10, 53–54.

134. Xu & Shenkar, Institutional distance and the multinational enterprise.

135. D. Ball, 2003, Ice cream rivals prepare to wage a new cold war, *Wall Street Journal*, June 26, B1.

136. Ibid.

137. Ibid.

138. Ibid.

139. Ibid.

140. A.-W. Harzing, 2002, Acquisitions versus greenfield investments: International strategy and management of entry modes, *Strategic Management Journal*, 23: 211–227; K. D. Brouthers & L. E. Brouthers, 2000, Acquisition or greenfield start-up? Institutional, cultural and transaction cost influences, *Strategic Management Journal*, 21: 89–97.

141. P. Deng, 2003, Determinants of full-control mode in China: An integrative approach, *American Business Review*, 21(1): 113–123.

142. R. Belderbos, 2003, Entry mode, organizational learning, and R&D in foreign affiliates: Evidence from Japanese firms, *Strategic Management Journal*, 34: 235–259.

143. B. Jorgensen, 2003, Act global, think local, *Electronic Business*, April 15, 42–50.

144. V. Gaba, Y. Pan, & G. R. Ungson, 2002, Timing of entry in international market: An empirical study of U.S. Fortune 500 firms in China, *Journal of International Business Studies*, 33(1): 39–55; S.-J. Chang & P. Rosenzweig, 2001, The choice of entry mode in sequential foreign direct investment, *Strategic Management Journal*, 22: 747–776.

145. K. E. Myer, 2001, Institutions, transaction costs, and entry mode choice in Eastern Europe, *Journal of International Business Studies*, 32: 357–367.

146. Deng, Determinants of full-control mode in China; Y. Luo, 2001, Determinants of entry in an emerging economy: A multilevel approach, *Journal of Management Studies*, 38: 443–472.

147. A. Antoine, C. B. Frank, H. Murata, & E. Roberts, 2003, Acquisitions and alliances in the aerospace industry: An unusual triad, *International Journal of Technology Management*, 25(8): 779–790.

148. L. J. Howell & J. C. Hsu, 2002, Globalization within the auto industry, *Research Technology Management*, 45(4): 43–49; A. Takeishi, 2001, Bridging inter- and intra-firm boundaries: Management of supplier involvement in automobile product development, *Strategic Management Journal*, 22: 403–433.

149. D. K Sobek II, A. C. Ward, & J. K. Liker, 1999, Toyota's principles of set-based concurrent engineering, *Sloan Management Review*, 40(2): 53–83.

150. J. Hagedoorn & G. Dysters, 2002, External sources of innovative capabilities: The preference for strategic alliances or mergers and acquisitions, *Journal of Management Studies*, 39: 167–188; H. Chen, 1999, International performance of multinationals: A hybrid model, *Journal of World Business*, 34: 157–170.

151. H. S. Tu, S. Y. Kim, & S. E. Sullivan, 2002, Global strategy lessons from Japanese and Korean business groups, *Business Horizons*, 45(2): 39–46; S.-J. Chang & J. Hong, 2002, How much does the business group matter in Korea? *Strategic Management Journal*, 23: 265–274.

152. J. Song, 2002, Firm capabilities and technology ladders: Sequential foreign direct investments of Japanese electronics firms in East Asia, *Strategic Management Journal*, 23: 191–210.

153. Wan & Hoskisson, Home country environments, corporate diversification strategies and firm performance; M. Ramirez-Aleson & M. A. Espitia-Escuer, 2001, The effect of international diversification strategy on the performance of Spanish-based firms during the period 1991–1995, *Management International Review*, 41(3): 291–315; A. Delios & P. W. Beamish, 1999, Geographic scope, product diversification, and the corporate performance of Japanese firms, *Strategic Management Journal*, 20: 711–727.

154. J. A. Doukas & L. H. P. Lang, 2003, Foreign direct investment, diversification and firm performance, *Journal of International Business Studies*, 34: 153–172; Pantzalis, Does location matter?; C. Y. Tang & S. Tikoo, 1999,

Operational flexibility and market valuation of earnings, *Strategic Management Journal*, 20: 749–761.

155. Kwok & Reeb, 2000, Internationalization and firm risk; J. M. Geringer, P. W. Beamish, & R. C. daCosta, 1989, Diversification strategy and internationalization: Implications for MNE performance, *Strategic Management Journal*, 10: 109–119; R. E. Caves, 1982, *Multinational Enterprise and Economic Analysis*, Cambridge, MA: Cambridge University Press.

156. Zahra, Ireland, & Hitt, International expansion by new venture firms.

157. T. W. Malnight, 2002, Emerging structural patterns within multinational corporations: Toward process-based structures, *Academy of Management Journal*, 44: 1187–1210.

158. L. Lopez, 2003, A well-oiled money machine, *Far Eastern Economic Review*, March 13, 40–43.

159. Ibid.

160. Ibid.

161. Hagedoorn & Dysters, External sources of innovative capabilities; G. Hamel, 2000, *Leading the Revolution*, Boston: Harvard Business School Press.

162. L. Tihanyi, R. A. Johnson, R. E. Hoskisson, & M. A. Hitt, 2003, Institutional ownership differences and international diversification: The effects of board of directors and technological opportunity, *Academy of Management Journal*, 46: 195–211.

163. F. Bradley & M. Gannon, 2000, Does the firm's technology and marketing profile affect foreign market entry? *Journal of International Marketing*, 8(4): 12–36; M. Kotabe, 1990, The relationship between off-shore sourcing and innovativeness of U.S. multinational firms: An empirical investigation, *Journal of International Business Studies*, 21: 623–638.

164. Asakawa & Lehrer, Managing local knowledge assets globally: The role of regional innovation relays; I. Zander & O. Solvell, 2000, Cross border innovation in the multinational corporation: A research agenda, *International Studies of Management and Organization*, 30(2): 44–67; Y. Luo, 1999, Time-based experience and international expansion: The case of an emerging economy, *Journal of Management Studies*, 36: 505–533.

165. O. E. M. Janne, 2002, The emergence of corporate integrated innovation systems across regions: The case of the chemical and pharmaceutical industry in Germany, the UK and Belgium, *Journal of International Management*, 8: 97–119; N. J. Foss & T. Pedersen, 2002, Transferring knowledge in MNCs: The role of sources of subsidiary knowledge and organizational context, *Journal of International Management*, 8: 49–67; Z. Liao, 2001, International R&D project evaluation by multinational corporations in the electronics and IT industry of Singapore, *R&D Management*, 31: 299–307.

166. Wan & Hoskisson, Home country environments, corporate diversification strategies and firm performance.

167. S. Reed & M. Arndt, 2003, Working his magic: Can Dormann bring ABB back? *Business Week*, February 10, 26; D. Bilefsky & A. Raghavan, 2003, Blown fuse: How "Europe's GE" and its star CEO tumbled to earth—Percy Barnevik's leadership made ABB a global name, but also may have hurt it—lingering asbestos woes, *Wall Street Journal*, January 23, A1.

168. P. Herrmann, 2002, The influence of CEO characteristics on the international diversification of manufacturing firms: An empirical study in the United States, *International Journal of Management*, 19(2): 279–289; M. Carpenter & J. Fredrickson, 2001, Top management teams, global strategic posture, and the moderating role of uncertainty, *Academy of Management Journal*, 44: 533–545; S. Finkelstein & D. C. Hambrick, 1996, *Strategic Leadership: Top Executives and Their Effects on Organizations*, St. Paul, MN: West Publishing Company.

169. H. A. Krishnan & D. Park, 2003, Power in acquired top management teams and post-acquisition performance: A conceptual framework, *International Journal of Management*, 20: 75–80; A. McWilliams, D. D. Van Fleet, & P. M. Wright, 2001, Strategic management of human resources for global competitive advantage, *Journal of Business Strategies*, 18(1): 1–24.

170. M. A. Hitt, R. E. Hoskisson, & H. Kim, 1997, International diversification: Effects on innovation and firm performance in product-diversified firms, *Academy of Management Journal*, 40: 767–798.

171. J. Child, L. Chung, & H. Davies, 2003, The performance of cross-border units in China: A test of natural selection, strategic choice and contingency theories, *Journal of International Business Studies*, 34: 242–254; D. Rondinelli,

B. Rosen, & I. Drori, 2001, The struggle for strategic alignment in multinational corporations: Managing readjustment during global expansion, *European Management Journal*, 19: 404–405; Carpenter & Fredrickson, Top management teams, global strategic posture, and the moderating role of uncertainty.

172. Y.-H. Chiu, 2003, The impact of conglomerate firm diversification on corporate performance: An empirical study in Taiwan, *International Journal of Management*, 19: 231–237; Luo, Market-seeking MNEs in an emerging market: How parent-subsidiary links shape overseas success.

173. A. Delios & W. J. Henisz, 2003, Policy uncertainty and the sequence of entry by Japanese firms, 1980–1998, *Journal of International Business Studies*, 34: 227–241; D. M. Reeb, C. C. Y. Kwok, & H. Y. Baek, 1998, Systematic risk of the multinational corporation, *Journal of International Business Studies*, 29: 263–279.

174. C. Pompitakpan, 1999, The effects of cultural adaptation on business relationships: Americans selling to Japanese and Thais, *Journal of International Business Studies*, 30: 317–338.

175. J. H. Zhao, S. H. Kim, & J. Du, 2003, The impact of corruption and transparency on foreign direct investment: An empirical analysis, *Management International Review*, 43(1): 41–62.

176. S. Globerman & D. Shapiro, 2003, Governance infrastructure and US foreign direct investment, *Journal of International Business Studies*, 34(1): 19–39.

177. L. L. Jacque & P. M. Vaaler, 2001, The international control conundrum with exchange risk: An EVA framework, *Journal of International Business Studies*, 32: 813–832.

178. S. Mudd, R. Grosse, & J. Mathis, 2002, Dealing with financial crises in emerging markets, *Thunderbird International Business Review*, 44(3): 399–430.

179. Rugg, A down dollar's lure—and peril.

180. Wan & Hoskisson, Home country environments, corporate diversification strategies and firm performance; Hitt, Hoskisson, & Kim, International diversification; S. Tallman & J. Li, 1996, Effects of international diversity and product diversity on the performance of multinational firms, *Academy of Management Journal*, 39: 179–196; Hitt, Hoskisson, & Ireland, A mid-range theory of interactive effects; Geringer, Beamish, & daCosta, Diversification strategy.

181. A. K. Rose & E. van Wincoop, 2001, National money as a barrier to international trade: The real case for currency union, *American Economic Review*, 91: 386–390.

182. I. M. Manev & W. B. Stevenson, 2001, Nationality, cultural distance, and expatriate status: Effects on the managerial network in a multinational enterprise, *Journal of International Business Studies*, 32: 285–303.

183. D. Luhnow, 2001, How NAFTA helped Wal-Mart transform the Mexican market. *Wall Street Journal*, August 31, A1, A2.

184. B. Saporito, 2003, Can Wal-Mart get any bigger? (Yes, a lot bigger . . . here's how), *Time*, January 13, 38–43.

185. V. Miroshnik, 2002, Culture and international management: A review, *Journal of Management Development*, 21(7,8): 521–544; P. Ghemawat, 2001, Distance still matters, *Harvard Business Review*, 79(8): 137–147; D. E. Thomas & R. Grosse, 2001, Country-of-origin determinants of foreign direct investment in an emerging market: The case of Mexico, *Journal of International Management*, 7: 59–79.

186. T. P. Blumentritt & D. Nigh, 2002, The integration of subsidiary political activities in multinational corporations, *Journal of International Business Studies*, 33: 57–77; J. Feeney & A. Hillman, 2001, Privatization and the political economy of strategic trade policy, *International Economic Review*, 42: 535–556; R. Vernon, 2001, Big business and national governments: Reshaping the compact in a globalizing economy, *Journal of International Business Studies*, 32: 509–518; B. Shaffer & A. J. Hillman, 2000, The development of business-government strategies by diversified firms, *Strategic Management Journal*, 21: 175–190.

187. U. Andersson, M. Forsgren, & U. Holm, 2002, The strategic impact of external networks: Subsidiary performance and competence development in the multinational corporation, *Strategic Management Journal*, 23: 979–996; B. Barringer & J. Harrison, 2000, Walking the tightrope: Creating value through interorganizational relationships, *Journal of Management*, 26: 367–404.

Cooperative Strategy

Chapter Nine

Chapter Nine

Knowledge Objectives

Studying this chapter should provide you with the strategic management knowledge needed to:

1. Define cooperative strategies and explain why firms use them.

2. Define and discuss three types of strategic alliances.

3. Name the business-level cooperative strategies and describe their use.

4. Discuss the use of corporate-level cooperative strategies in diversified firms.

5. Understand the importance of cross-border strategic alliances as an international cooperative strategy.

6. Describe cooperative strategies' risks.

7. Describe two approaches used to manage cooperative strategies.

©Getty Images

Phone companies and satellite TV providers have formed both business- and corporate-level alliances, allowing them to respond effectively to cable company offerings in phone services. The alliance between EchoStar and SBC, for example, will allow customers to sign up for as many as five services (local, long distance, and cellular phone plus satellite TV and broadband). The newly formed SBC DISH Network should please customers, who will receive one bill for several diverse services.

Alliances in Response to Rivalry: Telecommunication versus Cable Firms

Demand for broadband Internet connections has surged in the United States, and telephone companies have scrambled to maintain pace with the cable companies as they respond to the demand. The phone companies are relative latecomers to broadband. Cable operators, which invested heavily in the 1990s in expanding and modernizing their networks, dominate the market. Comcast, the biggest provider, had 4.1 million subscribers at the end of March 2003, far ahead of the leading phone companies—SBC Communications with 2.5 million, Verizon with 1.8 million, and BellSouth with 1.1 million.

Offering broadband also allowed the cable companies to offer phone service (once regulatory agencies allowed it) through cable, something they have aggressively pursued. In 2003, cable operators had registered over three million phone customers, often offering discounts if a customer subscribed to more than one service (cable television, phone, broadband). In response to the competition, phone companies formed alliances to better contend with the cable companies' aggressive moves into phone service.

SBC Communications has agreed to an alliance with EchoStar Communications Corp. EchoStar offers satellite TV services (DISH Network). Under the SBC plan, starting early in 2004 the phone company's customers were able to sign up for EchoStar TV services by calling SBC sales representatives. Customers could receive as many as five services—local phone, long distance, cellular phone, satellite TV, and broadband—consolidated on one SBC bill. SBC and EchoStar intended to brand their service "SBC DISH Network." In return, SBC will invest $500 million in EchoStar's convertible debt. Qwest is building a similar alliance with DirecTV, another satellite TV provider.

The SBC-EchoStar alliance builds on "bundling," the practice of selling diverse kinds of services under a single bill, which one analyst declares is the future of telecommunications. Bundling services is more profitable for the telecommunication companies than giving a customer a single service, because it creates switching costs for the customer. As another analyst noted: "When customers use multiple services, it becomes increasingly difficult to compare and contrast to competitive offerings so they tend to stay put." As phone companies seek to defend themselves, "you'll see more and more bundled deals," adds Michael Bowen, a telecommunication analyst at SoundView Technology Group.

SBC has made other alliances to diversify the services it offers. For example, a deal announced with Yahoo! Inc. made the popular site part of SBC's broadband package. SBC subscribers who sign up for the service automatically reach the Web through a Yahoo! portal. Users can check their e-mail through Yahoo! Mail and customize their home screen with special Yahoo!

content. Under the terms of the deal, SBC will pay Yahoo! an estimated $5 a month for each subscriber; Yahoo!, in return, will give SBC an undisclosed percentage of any premium services subscribers purchase beyond the basic package, like real-time stock quotes or expanded e-mail storage.

The competition response alliances (defined later in this chapter) between phone companies and satellite TV providers have not only allowed them to respond to cable companies' strategic moves into phone services, but have also allowed phone companies to diversify their service offerings. Thus, these examples represent both business- as well as corporate-level alliances, which are discussed in this chapter.

SOURCES: A. Latour & P. Grant, 2003, SBC, Qwest strike partnerships with providers of satellite TV, *Wall Street Journal Online*, http://www.wsj.com, July 22; L. J. Flynn, 2003, EchoStar deal lets SBC offer satellite TV in phone bill, *New York Times*, http://www.nytimes.com, July 22; 2003, SBC, Qwest in satellite TV partnerships, *New York Times*, http://www.nytimes.com, July 21; B. Simon, 2003, Some bet the future of broadband belongs to regional Bells, not cable, *New York Times*, http://www.nytimes.com, July 21; A. Latour, 2003, BellSouth unveils DSL Lite service as Bells step up subscriber battle, *Wall Street Journal Online*, www.http://www.wsj.com, July 8; D. Roth, 2002, Terry Semel thinks Yahoo should grow up already, *Fortune*, September 30, 107–110; B. Elgin, 2002, Can Yahoo make them pay? *BusinessWeek Online*, http://www.businessweek.com, September 9.

Pursuing internal opportunities (doing better than competitors through strategic execution or innovation) and merging with or acquiring other companies are the two primary means by which firms grow that we have discussed to this point in the book. In this chapter, we examine cooperative strategies, which are the third major alternative firms use to grow, develop value-creating competitive advantages, and create differences between themselves and competitors.[1] Defined formally, a **cooperative strategy** is a strategy in which firms work together to achieve a shared objective.[2] Thus, cooperating with other firms is another strategy that is used to create value for a customer that exceeds the cost of constructing that value in other ways[3] and to establish a favorable position relative to competition (see Chapters 2, 4, 5, and 8).[4] The Opening Case provides an example of SBC Communications and EchoStar Communications forming an alliance. This partnership will provide SBC, a phone service company, with a stronger position against cable companies' thrust into phone services by giving SBC a satellite TV service offering. The increasing importance of cooperative strategies as a growth engine shouldn't be underestimated. Increasingly, cooperative strategies are formed by firms competing against one another,[5] as illustrated by the number of alliances between rivals in the auto industry.[6] This means that effective competition in the 21st-century landscape results when the firm learns how to cooperate with as well as compete against competitors.[7]

Because they are the primary type of cooperative strategy that firms use, strategic alliances (defined in the next section) are this chapter's focus. Although not frequently used, collusive strategies are another type of cooperative strategy discussed in this chapter. In a *collusive strategy*, two or more firms cooperate to raise prices above the fully competitive level.[8]

We examine several topics in this chapter. First, we define and offer examples of different strategic alliances as primary types of cooperative strategies. Next, we discuss the extensive use of cooperative strategies in the global economy and reasons for this use. In succession, we then describe business-level (including collusive strategies), corporate-level, international, and network cooperative strategies—most in the form of strategic alliances. The chapter closes with discussions of the risks of using cooperative strategies as well as how effective management of them can reduce those risks.

A cooperative strategy is a strategy in which firms work together to achieve a shared objective.

Strategic Alliances as a Primary Type of Cooperative Strategy

Strategic alliances are increasingly popular.[9] Two researchers describe this popularity by noting that an "unprecedented number of strategic alliances between firms are being formed each year. [These] strategic alliances are a logical and timely response to intense and rapid changes in economic activity, technology, and globalization, all of which have cast many corporations into two competitive races: one for the world and the other for the future."[10]

A **strategic alliance** is a cooperative strategy in which firms combine some of their resources and capabilities to create a competitive advantage.[11] Thus, as linkages between them, strategic alliances involve firms with some degree of exchange and sharing of resources and capabilities to co-develop or distribute goods or services.[12] Strategic alliances let firms leverage their existing resources and capabilities while working with partners to develop additional resources and capabilities as the foundation for new competitive advantages.[13]

Many firms, especially large global competitors, establish multiple strategic alliances. General Motors' alliances, for example, include collaboration with Honda on internal combustion engines, with Toyota on advanced propulsion, with Renault on medium- and heavy-duty vans for Europe and, in the United States, with AM General on the brand and distribution rights for the Hummer.[14] Focusing on developing advanced technologies, Lockheed Martin has formed over 250 alliances with firms in more than 30 countries as it concentrates on its primary business of defense modernization.[15] In general, strategic alliance success requires cooperative behavior from all partners. Actively solving problems, being trustworthy, and consistently pursuing ways to combine partners' resources and capabilities to create value are examples of cooperative behavior known to contribute to alliance success.[16]

A competitive advantage developed through a cooperative strategy often is called a collaborative or relational advantage.[17] As previously discussed, particularly in Chapter 4, competitive advantages significantly influence the firm's marketplace success.[18] Rapid technological changes and the global economy are examples of factors challenging firms to constantly upgrade current competitive advantages while they develop new ones to maintain strategic competitiveness.[19]

A strategic alliance is a cooperative strategy in which firms combine some of their resources and capabilities to create a competitive advantage.

Three Types of Strategic Alliances

There are three major types of strategic alliances—joint venture, equity strategic alliance, and nonequity strategic alliance.

A **joint venture** is a strategic alliance in which two or more firms create a legally independent company to share some of their resources and capabilities to develop a competitive advantage. Joint ventures are effective in establishing long-term relationships and in transferring tacit knowledge. Because it can't be codified, tacit knowledge is learned through experiences[20] such as those taking place when people from partner firms work together in a joint venture. As discussed in Chapter 3, tacit knowledge is an important source of competitive advantage for many firms.[21]

Typically, partners in a joint venture own equal percentages and contribute equally to its operations. In China, Shui On Construction and entrepreneur Paul S. P. Tung created a 50-50 joint venture called TH Group to invest in cement factories. Cement is big business in China as the government seeks to develop the infrastructure (ports, highways, etc.) of the western provinces. Mr. Tung contributed money, and Shui On the expertise, necessary to develop a large, well-run cement company.[22] Overall, evidence suggests that a joint venture may be the optimal alliance when firms need to combine their resources and capabilities to create a competitive advantage that is substantially different from any they possess individually and when the partners intend to enter highly uncertain markets.[23]

A joint venture is a strategic alliance in which two or more firms create a legally independent company to share some of their resources and capabilities to develop a competitive advantage.

An **equity strategic alliance** is an alliance in which two or more firms own differ-ent percentages of the company they have formed by combining some of their resources and capabilities to create a competitive advantage. Many foreign direct investments, such as those made by Japanese and U.S. companies in China, are completed through equity strategic alliances.[24]

For example, Citigroup Inc. is forming a strategic alliance with Shanghai Pudong Development Bank Co. It is doing so through an initial equity investment totaling 5 per-cent. However, it was allowed to raise that stake to almost 25 percent and will be the first foreign bank to own more than 20 percent of a bank in the PRC (People's Republic of China). Shanghai Pudong Development Bank is China's ninth largest bank, and Citi-group's investment will make it a significant shareholder. This equity strategic alliance "will serve as a launchpad for Citigroup to enter the Chinese credit-card business."[25]

A **nonequity strategic alliance** is an alliance in which two or more firms develop a contractual relationship to share some of their unique resources and capabilities to create a competitive advantage. In this type of strategic alliance, firms do not establish a separate independent company and therefore don't take equity positions. Because of this, nonequity strategic alliances are less formal and demand fewer partner commit-ments than do joint ventures and equity strategic alliances.[26] The relative informality and lower commitment levels characterizing nonequity strategic alliances make them unsuitable for complex projects where success requires effective transfers of tacit knowledge between partners.[27]

However, firms today increasingly use this type of alliance in many different forms, such as licensing agreements, distribution agreements, and supply contracts.[28] For example, Sears, Roebuck and Co. recently announced an agreement to outsource its credit card business to Citigroup Inc. for $3 billion. Sears was one of the few com-panies that still held total control over its private-label credit cards, as most depart-ment stores favored co-branding nonequity alliances with financial institutions. The terms of the deal allow Sears to outsource its financing business by forming an alliance with Citigroup to manage its credit card operations. Under a ten-year marketing-and-servicing agreement, Citigroup will absorb costs associated with Sears' 0 percent financing program, which Sears said will save it more than $200 million a year. Sears also said that it expects to receive approximately $200 million in annual performance payments from Citigroup under the agreement. This strategic alliance will give Sears a chance to refocus on its struggling retail business.[29] A key reason for the growth in types of cooperative strategies is the complexity and uncertainty that characterize most global industries such as the global agrochemical industry, making it difficult for firms to be successful without partnerships.[30]

Typically, outsourcing commitments take the form of a nonequity strategic alliance.[31] Discussed in Chapter 3, *outsourcing* is the purchase of a value-creating pri-mary or support activity from another firm. Johnson Controls, Inc. (JCI) has become a leading manufacturer of automotive interior systems, automotive batteries, and auto-mated building control systems. A wide range of cooperative strategies has served as the engine of its growth. JCI has used a cooperative strategy with many of its suppliers. For example, it worked out an agreement with IKON Office Solutions to provide networked copiers for its offices and plants nationwide. Instead of paying a flat fee, however, it pays per use, and this arrangement has cut printing and copying costs by 35 percent.[32]

Reasons Firms Develop Strategic Alliances

As previously noted, the use of cooperative strategies as a path to strategic competi-tiveness is on the rise[33] in for-profit firms of all sizes as well as in public organiza-tions.[34] Thus, cooperative strategies are becoming more important to companies. For example, recently surveyed executives of technology companies stated that strategic alliances are central to their firms' success.[35] Speaking directly to the issue of technology acquisition and development for these firms, a manager noted that "you have to partner today or you will miss the next wave. You cannot possibly acquire the technology fast enough, so partnering is essential."[36]

Some even suggest that strategic alliances "may be the most powerful trend that has swept American business in a century."[37] Among other benefits, strategic alliances allow partners to create value that they couldn't develop by acting independently[38] and to enter markets more quickly.[39] Moreover, most (if not all) firms lack the full set of resources and capabilities needed to reach their objectives, which indicates that partnering with others will increase the probability of reaching them.[40]

For example, Ann Taylor and its owner, United Retail Group, have partnered with a private-label credit service to build and strengthen their existing credit card programs. The firms worked with Alliance Data's proprietary credit network to provide credit processing at each store, which allowed Ann Taylor to link all of its stores and receive critical market testing data, thereby providing "a new way to communicate and market messages to its customers."[41]

The effects of the greater use of cooperative strategies—particularly in the form of strategic alliances—are noticeable. In large firms, for example, alliances now account for more than 20 percent of revenue.[42] Booz Allen Hamilton, Inc. predicted that by 2003, alliances would account for as much as 35 percent of revenue for the 1,000 largest U.S. companies.[43] Supporting this expectation is the belief of many senior-level executives that alliances are a prime vehicle for firm growth.[44]

In some industries, alliance versus alliance is becoming more prominent than firm against firm as a point of competition. In the global airline industry, for example, competition is increasingly between large alliances rather than between airlines.[45] This increased use of cooperative strategies and its results are not surprising in that the mid-1990s and early 21st century saw predictions that cooperative strategies were the wave of the future.[46]

The individually unique competitive conditions of slow-cycle, fast-cycle, and standard-cycle markets[47] find firms using cooperative strategies to achieve slightly different objectives (see Table 9.1). We discuss these three market types in Chapter 5, where we study competitive rivalry and competitive dynamics. *Slow-cycle markets* are markets where the firm's competitive advantages are shielded from imitation for relatively long periods of time and where imitation is costly. These markets are close to monopolistic conditions. Railroads and, historically, telecommunications, utilities, and financial services are examples of industries characterized as slow-cycle markets. In *fast-cycle markets,* the firm's competitive advantages aren't shielded from imitation, preventing their long-term sustainability. Competitive advantages are moderately shielded from imitation in *standard-cycle markets,* typically allowing them to be sustained for a longer period of time compared to fast-cycle market situations, but for a shorter period of time than in slow-cycle markets.

Strategic alliances through outsourcing allow partners to create value they couldn't otherwise develop on their own. Ann Taylor, for example, has improved its marketing through testing data it receives from its partner, a proprietary credit network.

Table 9.1

Reasons for Strategic Alliances by Market Type

Market	Reason
Slow-Cycle	• Gain access to a restricted market
	• Establish a franchise in a new market
	• Maintain market stability (e.g., establishing standards)
Fast-Cycle	• Speed up development of new goods or services
	• Speed up new market entry
	• Maintain market leadership
	• Form an industry technology standard
	• Share risky R&D expenses
	• Overcome uncertainty
Standard-Cycle	• Gain market power (reduce industry overcapacity)
	• Gain access to complementary resources
	• Establish better economies of scale
	• Overcome trade barriers
	• Meet competitive challenges from other competitors
	• Pool resources for very large capital projects
	• Learn new business techniques

SLOW-CYCLE MARKETS

Firms in slow-cycle markets often use strategic alliances to enter restricted markets or to establish franchises in new markets. For example, due to consolidating acquisitions, the American steel industry has three major players: U.S. Steel, ISG, and Nucor. In an effort to compete in a global steel market, these companies are looking overseas. They have made strategic alliances in Europe and Asia and are investing in ventures in South America and Australia. U.S. Steel, for example, bought a Slovakian steel producer, VSZ, in 2000. ISG is bidding for a Korean steel producer, Kia Steel Co., and Nucor is investing in joint ventures in Brazil and Australia. While the global consolidation continues, these companies are increasing their competitiveness through their strategic alliances overseas.[48]

In another example, the opening of India's previously restricted insurance market prompted a number of international insurers to enter this large potential market. "Most are joint ventures between Indian companies and international insurers like AIG, MetLife, and Prudential, all eager to get in at the ground floor of what they believe will be a huge opportunity."[49] For example, American International Group (AIG) formed a joint venture—Tata AIG—with Mumbai-based Tata Group, one of the country's largest conglomerates.[50] Prior to the privatization process in India, state-operated insurers had played a monopolistic role for decades.

Slow-cycle markets are becoming rare in the 21st-century competitive landscape for several reasons, including the privatization of industries and economies, the rapid expansion of the Internet's capabilities in terms of the quick dissemination of information, and the speed with which advancing technologies make quickly imitating even complex products possible.[51] Firms competing in slow-cycle markets should recognize the future likelihood that they'll encounter situations in which their competitive advantages become partially sustainable (in the instance of a standard-cycle market) or unsustainable (in the case of a fast-cycle market). Cooperative strategies can be helpful to firms making the transition from relatively sheltered markets to more competitive ones.[52]

FAST-CYCLE MARKETS

Fast-cycle markets tend to be unstable, unpredictable, and complex.[53] Combined, these conditions virtually preclude the establishment of long-lasting competitive advantages, forcing firms to constantly seek sources of new competitive advantages while creating value by using current ones. Alliances between firms with current excess resources and capabilities and those with promising capabilities help companies competing in fast-cycle markets to make an effective transition from the present to the future and also to gain rapid entry to new markets.

Getty Images

The information technology (IT) industry is a fast-cycle market. The IT landscape will continue to change rapidly as businesses are becoming more focused on selecting a handful of strategic partners to help drive down costs, integrate technologies that provide significant business advantage or productivity gains, and aggressively look for applications that can be shifted to more flexible and cost-effective platforms. For example, Dell Inc. is striving to maintain its market leadership through responsiveness to customers. As a result of customers' requests, it is making servers and storage more modular and more customizable. It also sees wireless as the next technology that will be demanded by corporations, and thus is making it a standard feature on all corporate laptops by 2004. Strategic partners who help Dell remain on top of new innovations accomplish much of this work.[54]

Sometimes, companies establish venture capital programs to facilitate changes that occur rapidly in an industry.[55] Even after significant write-offs after the technology "bubble" burst in 2000, Intel continues to make venture capital partnership investments through its Intel Capital operation. In the first six months of 2003, Intel's venture unit made ten deals, including five in the United States and five abroad. "In addition to its interest in wireless, Intel says its new deals will fall into three other major categories: the digital home, network infrastructure and the enterprise market."[56]

Henry Liu, who works for MTV Online, does some work using free wireless high-speed Internet access on his laptop in Bryant Park in New York City. The Bryant Park Wireless Network provides free high-speed Wi-Fi (short for wireless fidelity) Internet access to users anywhere in the park at up to 11 megabits per second, faster than DSL or cable modem lines. Wireless communication on laptops is becoming standard, and Dell Inc. is taking advantage of this through alliances.

STANDARD-CYCLE MARKETS

In standard-cycle markets, which are often large and oriented toward economies of scale (e.g., commercial aerospace), alliances are more likely to be made by partners with complementary resources and capabilities. While airline alliances were originally set up to increase revenue, airlines have recently realized that they could also be used to reduce costs. SkyTeam (chaired by Delta and Air France) has set up an internal website to speed joint-buying and let member carriers swap tips on pricing. Managers at Oneworld (American Airlines and British Airways) believe the alliance's members have already saved up to $200 million through joint purchasing, and Star (United and Lufthansa) estimates that its member airlines save up to 25 percent on joint orders. Some airlines have taken this new buying power up to their biggest-ticket item: airplanes. Four airlines (Air Canada, Lufthansa, Austrian Airlines, and Scandinavian Airlines System) are seeking to buy together as many as 100 planes. Alitalia and Air France are attempting to purchase regional jets together. Airplane makers are intrigued and pleased by the new arrangements. "Group buys are something that we have envisioned for years," says Kent Fisher, vice-president for future customers and markets at Boeing. The trick will be getting the airlines to agree on things that previously were points of differentiation:

cabin décor, galley layout, cockpit arrangement. If the airlines succeed in agreeing upon a common plan, they will possibly realize even greater savings than just the cost of the plane. If, for example, members in the same alliance used exactly the same plane, there would be international economies of scale in equipment and training previously unrealized. Thus, this example illustrates that alliances of companies in this standard-cycle market are often geared toward obtaining potential economies of scale.[57]

Companies also may cooperate in standard-cycle markets to gain market power. As discussed in Chapter 6, market power allows the firm to sell its product above the existing competitive level or to reduce its costs below the competitive level, or both. Vivendi Universal, in a bid to avoid insolvency, signaled that it was selling many of its entertainment assets and has attracted many bidders. NBC, a television network owned by General Electric, instead of seeking an outright purchase of the assets, wanted to form an alliance with Vivendi. In 2003, NBC did complete a transaction to combine its broadcast and cable television operations with Vivendi Universal's entertainment assets in an arrangement that would give NBC majority control, but also much more market share, increasing its market power.[58] The alliance may avoid significant government scrutiny relative to an acquisition and would allow NBC to reduce excess capacity without an outright purchase.

Business-Level Cooperative Strategy

A business-level cooper-
ative strategy *is used to
help the firm improve its
performance in individual
product markets.*

A **business-level cooperative strategy** is used to help the firm improve its performance in individual product markets. As discussed in Chapter 4, business-level strategy details what the firm intends to do to gain a competitive advantage in specific product markets. Thus, the firm forms a business-level cooperative strategy when it believes that combining its resources and capabilities with those of one or more partners will create competitive advantages that it can't create by itself and that will lead to success in a specific product market. There are four business-level cooperative strategies (see Figure 9.1).

Complementary Strategic Alliances

Complementary strategic
alliances *are business-level
alliances in which firms
share some of their resources
and capabilities in complementary ways to develop
competitive advantages.*

Complementary strategic alliances are business-level alliances in which firms share some of their resources and capabilities in complementary ways to develop competitive advantages.[59] There are two types of complementary strategic alliances—vertical and horizontal (see Figure 9.1).

VERTICAL COMPLEMENTARY STRATEGIC ALLIANCE
In a *vertical complementary strategic alliance,* firms share their resources and capabilities from different stages of the value chain to create a competitive advantage (see

Figure 9.1 —— Business-Level Cooperative Strategies

- Complementary strategic alliances
  - Vertical
  - Horizontal
- Competition response strategy
- Uncertainty reducing strategy
- Competition reducing strategy

Figure 9.2).[60] Universal Music Group (UMG), a division of Vivendi Universal, has put together a vertical strategic alliance by forming a venture to create a new label in the music business, recruiting executives who have relationships with music artists. The "all-star" team includes executives from Interscope, Island Def Jam, Universal Motown, and Bad Boy Entertainment. Tommy Mottola, formerly of Sony Music, has agreed to serve as CEO of the new venture. UMG will fund the new label, called Casablanca, with about $15 million over the next five years. By putting together talent from several labels, UMG hopes to develop hits and improve its bottom line. In the

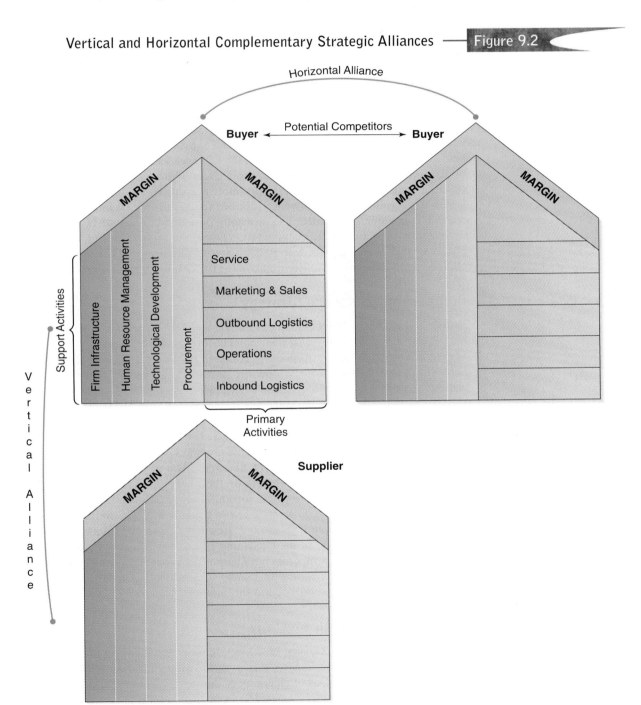

Vertical and Horizontal Complementary Strategic Alliances — Figure 9.2

words of UMG CEO Doug Morris, "It's so similar to a sports team, it's unbelievable. If you have no one on your team who can get hits, you're out of business."[61] This is a vertical alliance because of the executives' relationships to suppliers of music.

HORIZONTAL COMPLEMENTARY ALLIANCE

A *horizontal complementary strategic alliance* is an alliance in which firms share some of their resources and capabilities from the same stage of the value chain to create a competitive advantage (see Figure 9.2). Commonly, firms use this type of alliance to focus on long-term product development and distribution opportunities.[62] Bell Canada and Microsoft Canada have entered into an alliance to provide Internet services in Canada through a new portal. Although they will share the day-to-day operations of the portal, Bell Canada will be responsible for content development and for customer support, billing, and marketing. Microsoft will provide access to its portal infrastructure and to online services such as Hotmail and MSN Messenger.[63]

Hyundai Motor Company has seen its sales increase across the globe, and has set an ambitious goal to move from being the world's number nine automaker to being number five. Horizontal complementary strategic alliances and joint ventures are a key part of its strategy. In February 2003, Hyundai and DaimlerChrysler were scheduled to launch a joint venture in Korea to build 90,000 trucks annually. Hyundai has also set up strategic relationships to allow it to reach China's huge emerging market. In 2002, it set up a joint venture with Beijing Automotive Industry Holding Co., China's sixth largest auto company, through which it hoped to sell 50,000 cars in 2003, increasing to 500,000 cars annually by 2010. Kia, a wholly owned subsidiary of Hyundai, also has agreements with Chinese car manufacturers Dongfeng Motor Co. and Yueda Automobile Co., and was poised to sell 50,000 cars in China in 2003. Hyundai's strategic alliances have done much to help improve the firm's growth potential.[64]

Competition Response Strategy

As discussed in Chapter 5, competitors initiate competitive actions to attack rivals and launch competitive responses to their competitors' actions. Strategic alliances can be used at the business level to respond to competitors' attacks. Because they can be difficult to reverse and expensive to operate, strategic alliances are primarily formed to respond to strategic rather than tactical actions.

As the Opening Case indicates, because cable services continue to lead the telephone companies as broadband Internet providers, BellSouth has entered into an alliance with Movielink (see the Strategic Focus). BellSouth has been offering its service at a cheaper rate to compete with cable providers. "By becoming more aggressive in the broadband arena, the Bells hope to achieve two goals: to compete better with cable operators and to make customers of their core phone services more loyal."[65] Accordingly, the alliance is a response to similar services offered by cable companies but will not require BellSouth "to own or run content itself."[66] Similarly, as noted in the Opening Case, SBC and Qwest are striking partnerships with EchoStar and DirecTV, respectively, who run the DISH and DirecTV satellite TV networks, to offer billing services. The cable companies have been moving aggressively into phone service. This will allow SBC, for instance, to bundle local phone, long distance, cell phone, satellite TV, and high-speed broadband Internet service.[67]

Uncertainty Reducing Strategy

Particularly in fast-cycle markets, business-level strategic alliances are used to hedge against risk and uncertainty.[68] Also, they are used where uncertainty exists, such as in entering new product markets or emerging economies. For example, Dutch bank ABN

Competition Response Alliances in the Media Content, Internet, Software, and Cell Phone Equipment Industries

In highly competitive markets, companies often form alliances in response to competitors' actions. Telecommunication companies such as SBC Communications and Verizon Communications are battling with cable companies like Comcast to be chosen as Internet broadband providers for households and businesses. In addition to cutting prices and offering special services, the telecommunication companies are reaching out to form alliances in response to the competition with cable companies, which have traditionally offered more services.

For example, BellSouth has entered into an alliance with Movielink. Movielink LLC, headquartered in Santa Monica, California, is an Internet-based movie-rental service formed as a joint venture that is owned by Metro-Goldwyn-Mayer Studios, Paramount Pictures, Sony Pictures Entertainment, Universal, and Warner Bros. Movielink, because of its affiliation with its owners, can offer recently released movies as well as films owned by members of the closely held joint venture. Movielink offers a downloadable service that allows appropriately formatted films to be played on television sets. The aim of the Movielink alliance with BellSouth is to store movies closer to the customer on BellSouth's network, thus shortening the download time for the customer and making BellSouth's Internet service more appealing.

In another example, in response to competition from Microsoft, RealNetworks recently announced an alliance agreement with Vodafone, the mobile-phone operator, to use its software. RealNetworks makes audio and video software in competition with Microsoft. It hopes that by pushing into the mobile-phone market, it will persuade content owners to make audio and video available in its format, rather than in Microsoft's, or in other popular formats such as MPEG. RealNetworks pioneered the delivery of audio and video over the Internet and is seeking to strengthen its weakening position. Vodafone controls operations in 16 countries, and it says it plans to use RealNetworks' server software to deliver video and audio clips of its Vodafone Live! suite of multimedia services. It will also ask handset suppliers to include RealNetworks' phone software on their products. An analyst with International Data Corporation says that mobile-phone users are less likely than PC owners to download additional video players, and therefore suppliers of video software are "scrambling to sign up as many partners and devices as possible."

Nokia Corporation, the world's largest cell phone maker, is mounting a comeback in the U.S. market that is largely connected to its alliance relationship with Sprint PCS, one of the United States' largest mobile-phone operators. Motorola overtook Nokia in 2002 in North America and had a 32 percent U.S. market share by unit sales in the first quarter of 2003, compared with 29 percent for Nokia. Pekka Vartiainen, general manager of Nokia Mobile Phones–Americas, says that Nokia's 3585i handset is the top-selling low-end phone in the Sprint PCS portfolio of handsets, and an analyst attributes Nokia's market-share gains in the second quarter of 2003 to "a strong showing at Sprint." This is important for Nokia, because Sprint hadn't sold Nokia phones for three years prior to the launch of the 3585i in February 2003. These examples illustrate that to maintain competitiveness, alliances are often used to respond to rivals' competitive moves.

SOURCES: 2003, The generation game, *The Economist*, http://www.economist.com, May 30; D. Pringle, 2003, RealNetworks beats Microsoft in Vodafone clip-delivery deal, *Wall Street Journal Online*, http://www.wsj.com, June 30; A. Latour, 2003, BellSouth unveils DSL Lite service as Bells step up subscriber battle, *Wall Street Journal Online*, http://www.wsj.com, July 8; D. Pringle, 2003, Nokia spurs comeback in U.S. with new handsets, promotions, *Wall Street Journal Online*, http://www.wsj.com, July 10; S. Alsop, 2002, Hollywood's latest flop, *Fortune*, December 9, 56.

AMRO signed on to a venture called ShoreCap International. This commercial company is a multisector partnership of organizations, including private businesses, financial institutions, development funds, and foundations. ShoreCap will invest capital in and advise local financial institutions that do small and microbusiness lending in developing economies, targeting Asia, Africa, and Central and Eastern Europe. The venture's leading sponsor, ShoreBank Corporation, is a for-profit community development and environmental bank. It has a history of collaboration with financial institutions and other partners, including the World Bank. Through this cooperative strategy with other financial institutions, ShoreBank hopes to be able to reduce the risk of providing credit to smaller borrowers in disadvantaged regions. It also hopes to reduce poverty in the regions where it invests.[69]

In other instances, firms form business-level strategic alliances to reduce the uncertainty associated with developing new products or establishing a technology standard. Wind Infostrada SpA, Italy's third largest telecom company, recently signed an agreement with Japan's NTT DoCoMo Inc. to become the sole provider of DoCoMo's i-mode technology. I-mode technology, which allows users to access the Internet on their mobile-phone handsets, has been a noteworthy success in Japan. DoCoMo sees this relationship as an opportunity to establish a foothold for its standard in cell phone technology, and Wind is going to share the risk with DoCoMo, as they test to see if i-mode will also be a successful standard in Europe.[70] Thus, the uncertainty and risk of the 21st-century landscape finds firms, such as those competing in the cell phone and telecommunication industries, forming multiple strategic alliances to increase their strategic competitiveness.

Competition Reducing Strategy

Used to reduce competition, collusive strategies differ from strategic alliances in that collusive strategies are often an illegal type of cooperative strategy. There are two types of collusive strategies—explicit collusion and tacit collusion.

Explicit collusion "exists when firms directly negotiate production output and pricing agreements in order to reduce competition."[71] Explicit collusion strategies are illegal in the United States and most developed economies (except in regulated industries).

Firms that use explicit collusion strategies may face litigation and may be found guilty of noncompetitive actions. For instance, in 2003, cosmetics firms, including Estée Lauder, and a group of retail firms settled a price-fixing lawsuit out of court for a $175-million cosmetic products giveaway program. In regard to the suit, one of the winning attorneys stated: "Virtually every woman who buys cosmetics knows that department-store cosmetics are never discounted, never go on sale and are priced identically in any department store in any city. This kind of conduct does not happen in a competitive environment without collusion."[72]

Tacit collusion exists when several firms in an industry indirectly coordinate their production and pricing decisions by observing each other's competitive actions and responses.[73] Tacit collusion results in below fully competitive production output and prices that are above fully competitive levels. Unlike explicit collusion, firms engaging in tacit collusion do not directly negotiate output and pricing decisions.

Discussed in Chapter 6, *mutual forbearance* is a form of tacit collusion "in which firms avoid competitive attacks against those rivals they meet in multiple markets."[74] Rivals learn a great deal about each other when engaging in multimarket competition, including how to deter the effects of their rival's competitive attacks and responses. Given what they know about each other as a competitor, firms choose not to engage in what could be destructive competitions in multiple product markets.[75]

AOL dominates the instant-messaging (IM) business, with almost 60 million users. Yahoo! and MSN also operate IM services, but unlike e-mail, instant messages cannot cross over programs, which irritates many users. AOL and Microsoft quietly announced in 2003 that they would make their IM services work together. MSN has the next largest group of IM users (23.6 million) and through this strategic agreement with AOL will be able to reduce the level of competition.[76]

Tacit collusion tends to be used as a business-level competition reducing strategy in highly concentrated industries, such as breakfast cereals. Firms in these industries recognize that they are interdependent and that their competitive actions and responses significantly affect competitors' behavior toward them. Understanding this interdependence and carefully observing competitors because of it tend to lead to tacit collusion.

Four firms (Kellogg, General Mills, Post, and Quaker) have accounted for as much as 80 percent of sales volume in the ready-to-eat segment of the U.S. cereal market.[77] Some believe that this high degree of concentration results in "prices for branded cereals that are well above [the] costs of production."[78] Prices above the competitive level in this industry suggest the possibility that the dominant firms use a tacit collusion cooperative strategy.

At a broad level in free-market economies, governments need to determine how rivals can collaborate to increase their competitiveness without violating established regulations.[79] Reaching this determination is challenging when evaluating collusive strategies, particularly tacit ones. For example, regulation of pharmaceutical and biotech firms who must collaborate to meet global competition might lead to too much price fixing and, therefore, regulation is required to make sure that the balance is right, although sometimes the regulation gets in the way of good market functioning.[80] For individual companies, the issue is to understand the effect of a competition reducing strategy on their performance and competitiveness.

Assessment of Business-Level Cooperative Strategies

Firms use business-level strategies to develop competitive advantages that can contribute to successful positioning and performance in individual product markets. For a competitive advantage to be developed by using an alliance, the particular set of resources and capabilities that is combined and shared in a particular manner through the alliance must be valuable, rare, imperfectly imitable, and nonsubstitutable (see Chapter 3).

Evidence suggests that complementary business-level strategic alliances, especially vertical ones, have the greatest probability of creating a sustainable competitive advantage.[81] Horizontal complementary alliances are sometimes difficult to maintain because they are often between rivalrous competitors. The international airline industry, in an effort to skirt laws blocking international mergers, as noted earlier, has been forming global partnerships for a number of years. The largest is Star, built around United Airlines, Lufthansa, and All Nippon Airways. The fact that United entered Chapter 11 bankruptcy proceedings in 2003 and threatened Chapter 7 bankruptcy (liquidation) has destabilized these partnerships. KLM, based in the Netherlands, has been mainly on the outside of the big partnerships, its only joint venture being with Northwest Airlines on transatlantic routes. However, Northwest recently won approval to work with Delta and Continental on joint domestic flights, which would make it logical for KLM and Northwest to join SkyTeam, the partnership anchored by Delta and Air France. KLM is also considering joining Oneworld, partnering with British Airways and American Airlines. If United does go into Chapter 7 bankruptcy, which would dissolve its assets, the Star alliance will probably strive to lure either Delta or American into the fold to replace United. This would in turn destabilize the alliance to which they formerly belonged. Because of the high rivalry among partners in the airline industry, the horizontal alliances formed are often unstable.[82]

Although strategic alliances designed to respond to competition and to reduce uncertainty can also create competitive advantages, these advantages tend to be more temporary than those developed through complementary (both vertical and horizontal) strategic alliances. The primary reason is that complementary alliances have a stronger focus on the creation of value compared to competition reducing and uncertainty reducing alliances, which tend to be formed to respond to competitors' actions or reduce uncertainty rather than to attack competitors.

Of the four business-level cooperative strategies, the competition reducing strategy has the lowest probability of creating a sustainable competitive advantage. Research suggests that firms following a foreign direct investment strategy using alliances can be due to a follow-the-leader imitation approach without regard to strong strategic or learning goals. Thus, such investment may be attributable to tacit collusion, or interdependence, among the participating firms rather than for obtaining significant strategic or competitive advantage.[83] This suggests that companies using such competition reducing business-level strategic alliances should carefully monitor them as to the degree to which they are facilitating the firm's efforts to develop and successfully create competitive advantages.

Corporate-Level Cooperative Strategy

A corporate-level cooperative strategy *is used by the firm to help it diversify in terms of products offered or markets served, or both.*

A firm uses a **corporate-level cooperative strategy** to help it diversify in terms of products offered or markets served, or both. Diversifying alliances, synergistic alliances, and franchising are the most commonly used corporate-level cooperative strategies (see Figure 9.3).

Firms use diversifying alliances and synergistic alliances to grow and diversify their operations through a means other than a merger or an acquisition.[84] When a firm seeks to diversify into markets in which the host nation's government prevents mergers and acquisitions, alliances become an especially appropriate option. Corporate-level strategic alliances are also attractive compared to mergers and particularly acquisitions, because they require fewer resource commitments[85] and permit greater flexibility in terms of efforts to diversify partners' operations.[86] An alliance can be used as a way to determine if the partners might benefit from a future merger or acquisition between them. This "testing" process often characterizes alliances completed to combine firms' unique technological resources and capabilities.[87]

Diversifying Strategic Alliance

A diversifying strategic alliance *is a corporate-level cooperative strategy in which firms share some of their resources and capabilities to diversify into new product or market areas.*

A **diversifying strategic alliance** is a corporate-level cooperative strategy in which firms share some of their resources and capabilities to diversify into new product or market areas. Shell Petrochemicals and China National Offshore Oil Corporation (CNOOC) have announced a joint venture focused on the construction of a $4.3 billion petrochemicals complex in southern China. The emphasis will be to produce products for

Figure 9.3 —— Corporate-Level Cooperative Strategies

- Diversifying alliances
- Synergistic alliances
- Franchising

"Guangdong and high-consumption areas along the country's coastal economic zones."[88] CNOOC's business has been mainly upstream, especially in offshore oil production. "For CNOOC, the development is part of its continuing diversification from its core upstream business."[89]

©Philip Gould/CORBIS

Besides creating more diversification, cooperative ventures are also used to reduce diversification in firms that have overdiversified. Japanese chipmakers Fujitsu, Mitsubishi Electric, Hitachi, NEC, and Toshiba have been using joint ventures to consolidate and then spin off diversified businesses that were a drag on earnings. Hitachi and Mitsubishi Electric created a joint venture called Renesas that focuses on producing large-scale integrated circuits. Hitachi further entered a joint venture with NEC called Elpida, which is considered the last Japanese DRAM maker. Toshiba and Fujitsu announced an alliance last year. Fujitsu, realizing that memory chips were becoming a financial burden, dumped its flash-memory business into a joint venture company controlled by Advanced Micro Devices. These alliances resulted in the involved firms being able to refocus on their core businesses, reduce excessive diversification, and add value to their firm.[90]

Synergistic Strategic Alliance

A **synergistic strategic alliance** is a corporate-level cooperative strategy in which firms share some of their resources and capabilities to create economies of scope. Similar to the business-level horizontal complementary strategic alliance, synergistic strategic alliances create synergy across multiple functions or multiple businesses between partner firms.

Grupo Televisa SA, a Mexican entertainment company, is seeking an alliance with Univision Communications Inc., the largest U.S. Spanish-language television network. Univision captures four-fifths of the U.S. Spanish-language cable audience, and it already licenses Televisa's shows. Such a large and relatively wealthy market is very appealing to Emilio Azcarraga Jean, head of Televisa. Since Univision has not shown interest in allying with Televisa, another way for Televisa to increase its U.S. market exposure would be through purchasing an equity stake in Entravision Communications Corp., which owns a large group of Univision affiliates as well as Spanish-language radio stations, billboards, and a newspaper. An alliance with either company would create economies of scope for Grupo Televisa and hence is an example of a potential synergistic alliance.[91] The Opening Case also illustrated how SBC Communications and EchoStar Communications were synergistically diversified by the arrangement to offer satellite TV billing services through SBC's system. Thus, a synergistic strategic alliance is different from a complementary business-level alliance in that it diversifies both firms into a new business, but in a synergistic way.

Franchising

Franchising is a corporate-level cooperative strategy in which a firm (the franchisor) uses a franchise as a contractual relationship to describe and control the sharing of its resources and capabilities with partners (the franchisees).[92] A *franchise* is a "contractual

Shell Petrochemicals and China National Offshore Oil Corporation (CNOOC) have announced a joint venture focused on the construction of a petrochemicals complex in south China. This venture helps diversify both firms: CNOOC experiences increased product diversification, while Shell Petrochemicals experiences increased international diversification.

A **synergistic strategic alliance** *is a corporate-level cooperative strategy in which firms share some of their resources and capabilities to create economies of scope.*

Franchising *is a corporate-level cooperative strategy in which a firm (the franchisor) uses a franchise as a contractual relationship to describe and control the sharing of its resources and capabilities with partners (the franchisees).*

agreement between two legally independent companies whereby the franchisor grants the right to the franchisee to sell the franchisor's product or do business under its trademarks in a given location for a specified period of time."[93]

Franchising is a popular strategy: companies using it account for $1 trillion in annual U.S. retail sales and compete in more than 75 industries. As the Cendant strategy outlined in a Strategic Focus in Chapter 6 indicates, franchising can be used successfully across a number of businesses. Cendant has used franchising in real estate, for example, through its Century 21 and ERA brands. Already frequently used in developed nations, franchising is expected to account for significant portions of growth in emerging economies in the 21st century's first two decades.[94] As with diversifying and synergistic strategic alliances, franchising is an alternative to pursuing growth through mergers and acquisitions.

McDonald's, Hilton International, and Krispy Kreme are well-known examples of firms that use the franchising corporate-level cooperative strategy. 7-Eleven, Inc., the convenience store company, has successfully used franchising in its expansion, both domestically and internationally. The chain now has over 25,000 outlets worldwide and sales of $3 billion. 7-Eleven is especially popular in Asia, where convenience stores are more like pantries for city dwellers short on space. There are 77 stores per million people in Japan and 148 per million in Taiwan, far more than the 20 per million in the United States.[95]

In the most successful franchising strategy, the partners (the franchisor and the franchisees) closely work together.[96] A primary responsibility of the franchisor is to develop programs to transfer to the franchisees the knowledge and skills that are needed to successfully compete at the local level.[97] In return, franchisees should provide feedback to the franchisor regarding how their units could become more effective and efficient.[98] Working cooperatively, the franchisor and its franchisees find ways to strengthen the core company's brand name, which is often the most important competitive advantage for franchisees operating in their local markets.[99]

Franchising is a particularly attractive strategy to use in fragmented industries, such as retailing and commercial printing. In fragmented industries, a large number of small and medium-sized firms compete as rivals; however, no firm or small set of firms has a dominant share, making it possible for a company to gain a large market share by consolidating independent companies through contractual relationships.[100] La Quinta Inns decided to use franchising as a corporate-level cooperative strategy in order to increase its market share. Even though the lodging industry isn't as fragmented as it once was, La Quinta's decision to franchise has been viewed favorably. It is seeking to have 1,000 La Quinta Inn and La Quinta Inn & Suites properties by 2010, which would represent significant growth from its 353 branded properties in 2003. Alan Talis, executive vice-president at La Quinta, speaking of the relationship to its franchisees, said, "There is absolutely no difference between our company-owned properties and our franchised properties. They are not our customers. They are our operating partners."[101]

Assessment of Corporate-Level Cooperative Strategies

Costs are incurred with each type of cooperative strategy.[102] Compared to those at the business-level, corporate-level cooperative strategies commonly are broader in scope and more complex, making them relatively more costly. Those forming and using cooperative strategies, especially corporate-level ones, should be aware of alliance costs and carefully monitor them.

In spite of these costs, firms can create competitive advantages and value when they effectively form and use corporate-level cooperative strategies.[103] The likelihood of this being the case increases when successful alliance experiences are internalized.

In other words, those involved with forming and using corporate-level cooperative strategies can also use them to develop useful knowledge about how to succeed in the future. To gain maximum value from this knowledge, firms should organize it and verify that it is always properly distributed to those involved with the formation and use of alliances.[104]

We explain in Chapter 6 that firms answer two questions to form a corporate-level strategy—in which businesses will the diversified firm compete, and how will those businesses be managed? These questions are also answered as firms form corporate-level cooperative strategies. Thus, firms able to develop corporate-level cooperative strategies and manage them in ways that are valuable, rare, imperfectly imitable, and nonsubstitutable (see Chapter 3) develop a competitive advantage that is in addition to advantages gained through the activities of individual cooperative strategies. Later in the chapter, we further describe alliance management as a source of competitive advantage.

International Cooperative Strategy

A **cross-border strategic alliance** is an international cooperative strategy in which firms with headquarters in different nations combine some of their resources and capabilities to create a competitive advantage. For example, British Petroleum (BP) agreed to invest over $6 billion in a joint venture with Russian oil company Tyumen Oil. The venture will combine BP's Russian assets, a stake in Russian oil company Sidanco, with Tyumen. The new company will be the tenth largest oil producer in the world, increasing its competitive advantage against other, smaller oil companies.[105] Taking place in virtually all industries, the number of cross-border alliances being completed continues to increase,[106] in some cases at the expense of mergers and acquisitions.[107] However, as the Strategic Focus on cross-border aerospace industry alliances illustrates, although cross-border alliances can be complex, they may be necessary to improve technology as well as win government support for new orders in the aerospace industry.

There are several reasons for the increasing use of cross-border strategic alliances. In general, multinational corporations outperform firms operating on only a domestic basis,[108] so a firm may form cross-border strategic alliances to leverage core competencies that are the foundation of its domestic success to expand into international markets.[109] Nike has used its core competence with celebrity marketing as it expands overseas, especially because its U.S. business growth has slowed. It has sought to duplicate its marketing strategy in international markets, signing big-name athletes to sell shoes and apparel. In the United States, Nike's focus has been on basketball, while in other nations, soccer is more popular, and Nike has alliance agreements with Brazilian soccer star Ronaldo and the world's most popular soccer team, Manchester United. As a result of these alliances, Nike's global soccer business generated $720 million in sales in 2003, up from $500 million in fiscal year 2002.[110]

A cross-border strategic alliance is an international cooperative strategy in which firms with headquarters in different nations combine some of their resources and capabilities to create a competitive advantage.

In the United States, Nike has focused on marketing its shoes through celebrity basketball players who use and endorse its products. That celebrity marketing strategy is adapted abroad. In Europe and Central and South America, soccer is more popular than in the United States, and Nike has sought alliance agreements with soccer players such as Brazilian star Ronaldo (center) and Manchester United, the world's most popular soccer team.

AP Photo/Laurent Rebours

Strategic Focus

Cross-Border Alliances Battle to Win the President's Entourage: S-92 versus EH101 Helicopters

An analyst speaking about firms in the aerospace industry said, "If an aerospace company is not good at alliances, it's not in business." Commonly, these alliances are formed across borders. Aerospace is one of the industries in which highly diversified United Technologies competes. The firm is involved with over 100 worldwide cooperative strategies, including cross-border alliances and joint ventures. One of United Technologies' cooperative strategies was the cross-border alliance formed by the firm's Sikorsky business unit to produce the S-92 helicopter. Five firms from four continents joined Sikorsky to form this alliance.

This alliance's partners (called "Team S-92") and their responsibilities were: (1) Japan's Mitsubishi Heavy Industries (main cabin section), (2) Jingdezhen Helicopter Group/CATIC of the People's Republic of China (vertical tail fin and stabilizer), (3) Spain's Gamesa Aeronautica (main rotor pylon, engine nacelles, aft tail transition section, and cabin interior), (4) Aerospace Industrial Development Corporation of Taiwan (the electrical harnesses, flight controls, hydraulic lines, and environmental controls forming the cockpit), and (5) Embraer of Brazil (main landing gear and fuel system). As the sixth member of the alliance, Sikorsky was responsible for the main and tail rotor head components and the S-92's transmissions, along with final assembly and launch-ready certification.

The FAA certified the S-92 in December 2002. The Air Force is seeking to revitalize its search-and-rescue operations, and as part of that wants to replace aging helicopters. It has chosen the S-92 as the "front-runner," according to Maj. General Randall M. Schmidt. The Navy has decided to replace the fleet of 1970s helicopters that transport the American president. Although the contract is small in scope (11 helicopters in all), the prestige is enormous, and could translate into marketing gains for the winner.

However, the S-92 faces stiff competition from other helicopter manufacturers for the Navy contract, including AgustaWestland. AgustaWestland is a joint venture by a British company, GKN, and an Italian company, Finmeccanica. The venture was created in 2001 to strengthen the product range and increase the global reach of both companies. In July 2002, AgustaWestland signed an agreement with American company Lockheed Martin to jointly market the EH101 helicopter for American government applications. In May 2003, it also chose an American partner, Bell Helicopter, a division of Textron, a large diversified conglomerate, to build the machine should it win the contracts.

In the contest for the president's entourage of helicopters, some say that the American president should not fly in a foreign helicopter. Stephen C. Moss, president of AgustaWestland's U.S. subsidiary, noted that the foreign pedigree of the EH101 won't matter, largely because much of the Sikorsky helicopter was built by foreign partners.

Both Sikorsky and AgustaWestland are using cross-border alliances to facilitate doing business. Sikorsky's Team S-92 alliance smoothed the development of a new helicopter. AgustaWestland itself is a product of a cross-border alliance, and it is building strategic alliance relationships with American companies in order to win contracts from the American government.

SOURCES: R. Wall, 2003, Coming to America: AgustaWestland expands U.S. ties in pursuit of Pentagon programs, facing Sikorsky in heated competition for new presidential helo, *Aviation Week & Space Technology*, May 19, 32; J. L. Lunsford, 2003, Should U.S. president use a foreign copter? *Wall Street Journal*, May 12, B1; 2003, AgustaWestland Company History, http://www.agustawestland.com, July 19; M. A. Taverna, 2002, AgustaWestland teams with Lockheed Martin, Thales, *Aviation Week & Space Technology*, July 29, 39; R. Wall, 2002, USAF to bolster pilot rescue ability, *Aviation Week & Space Technology*, August 12, 30–32; 2002, Sikorsky S-92 awarded FAA type certification, United Technologies, http://www.utc.com, December 19.

Limited domestic growth opportunities are another reason firms use cross-border alliances. Hewlett-Packard has formed an alliance with NEC, a large computer manufacturer, to help NEC manage information-technology systems of Japanese companies. The alliance also has plans to target other customers in Asia. "Joe Hogan, H-P's vice president of marketing for managed services, said the pact is likely to generate more than $1 billion in revenues over the next few years." The alliance will likely increase the growth rates for both companies.[111]

Another reason for forming cross-border alliances is government economic policies. As discussed in Chapter 8, local ownership is an important national policy objective in some nations. In India and China, for example, governmental policies reflect a strong preference to license local companies. Morgan Stanley has created a joint venture with China Construction Bank to dispose of mainland China's nonperforming loans, the first foreign bank to do so. China Construction Bank sees the deal as an opportunity to use Western banking expertise to clean up its bad loan problem, while Morgan Stanley views this as an opportunity to move further into China's opening market. "But the communist bureaucracy isn't known for its quickness in instituting ground-breaking reforms. For instance, Morgan Stanley's new bad loan deal has yet to be cleared by the bureaucrats at the People's Bank of China, the China Banking Regulatory Commission, or the Ministry of Finance."[112] Thus, in spite of Morgan Stanley's efforts, it may not be able to follow up fully on this joint venture,[113] indicating that in some countries, the full range of entry mode choices that we describe in Chapter 8 may not be available to firms wishing to internationally diversify. Indeed, investment by foreign firms in these instances may be allowed only through a partnership with a local firm, such as in a cross-border alliance. A cross-border strategic alliance can also be helpful to foreign partners from an operational perspective, because the local partner has significantly more information about factors contributing to competitive success such as local markets, sources of capital, legal procedures, and politics.[114]

Firms also use cross-border alliances to help transform themselves or to better use their advantages to benefit from opportunities surfacing in the rapidly changing global economy. Starbucks, the Seattle-based purveyor of gourmet coffee, has been expanding quickly into China and Japan. In China, the firm hopes to benefit from improved income of the emerging middle class. Although China is a nation of tea drinkers who generally don't care for coffee, Starbucks is counting on its image of relaxed affluence to attract the Chinese. In Japan, Starbucks has opened 470 stores in seven years, and is reaching the saturation point in several cities. Japanese consumers eagerly embrace new ideas, and as a result Starbucks views Japan as an ideal test market. It now offers alcohol at one store and assorted new coffee drinks at other stores. In 2003, the chain began serving food in some Japanese stores. Products that are popular in Japan can often be exported to the United States, like Starbucks' green tea Frappucino, which was devised in Japan and Taiwan and may soon be sold in the United States. Thus, the firm expects to learn a great deal from its ventures in Asia, which may be costly initially but ultimately may help improve performance in the United States and in other markets around the world.[115]

In general, cross-border alliances are more complex and risky than domestic strategic alliances. However, the fact that firms competing internationally tend to outperform domestic-only competitors suggests the importance of learning how to diversify into international markets. Compared to mergers and acquisitions, cross-border alliances may be a better way to learn this process, especially in the early stages of the firms' geographic diversification efforts. As mentioned earlier, when Starbucks was looking to expand overseas, it wanted to do so quickly in order to keep its first-mover advantage. Thus, it agreed to a complex series of joint ventures in many countries in the interest of speed. Lately, its overseas stores have been unprofitable, and it seems that the complexity of the joint ventures is partly to blame. While the company gets a slice of revenues and profits as well as licensing fees for supplying its coffee, controlling costs abroad is more difficult than in the United States.[116] However, as noted above, the firm hopes to learn a great deal from serving multiple markets. Careful and thorough study of a proposed cross-border alliance contributes to success[117] as do precise specifications of each partner's alliance role.[118] These points are explored later in our discussion of how to best manage alliances.

Network Cooperative Strategy

Increasingly, firms are involved with more than one cooperative strategy. In addition to forming their own alliances with individual companies, a growing number of firms are joining forces in multiple cooperative strategies. A **network cooperative strategy** is a cooperative strategy wherein several firms agree to form multiple partnerships to achieve shared objectives.

A network cooperative strategy is particularly effective when it is formed by geographically clustered firms,[119] as in California's Silicon Valley and Singapore's Silicon Island.[120] Effective social relationships and interactions among partners while sharing their resources and capabilities make it more likely that a network cooperative strategy will be successful,[121] as does having a productive *strategic center firm* (discussed further in Chapter 11). In Europe, there has recently been an increased emphasis on joint venture film production. As the European Union prepared for its expansion to 25 countries in 2004, production houses across Europe were learning to use film festivals such as Cannes to strike alliances and pool their resources. With these joint ventures, firms from countries with minimal film budgets, such as Portugal, can get off the ground. For example, in May 2003, RAI Cinema and Europa Corp., from Italy and France, respectively, signed a coproduction and distribution agreement through 2005. The geographic closeness of the members of the European Union facilitates effective use of this strategy.[122]

The early research evidence suggests the positive financial effects of network cooperative strategies will make these strategies important contributors to the 21st-century success of both supplier and buyer partners involved.[123]

Alliance Network Types

An important advantage of a network cooperative strategy is that firms gain access "to their partners' partners."[124] Having access to multiple collaborations increases the likelihood that additional competitive advantages will be formed as the set of resources and capabilities being shared expands.[125] In turn, increases in competitive advantages further stimulate the development of product innovations that are so critical to strategic competitiveness in the global economy.[126]

The set of partnerships, such as strategic alliances, that result from the use of a network cooperative strategy is commonly called an *alliance network*. The alliance networks that companies develop vary by industry conditions. A *stable alliance network* is formed in mature industries where demand is relatively constant and predictable. Through a stable alliance network, firms try to extend their competitive advantages to other settings while con-

Joint venture film production benefits countries with smaller film budgets, as production houses pool their resources. Film festivals, such as the one pictured here in Cannes, foster these alliances.

Getty Images

tinuing to profit from operations in their core, relatively mature industry. Thus, stable networks are built for *exploitation* of the economies (scale and/or scope) available between firms.[127] *Dynamic alliance networks* are used in industries characterized by frequent product innovations and short product life cycles.[128] For instance, the pace of innovation in the information technology (IT) industry is too fast for any one company to maintain success over time. Therefore, the ability to develop and nurture strategic partnerships can make the difference between success and failure. As such, independent software vendors earn more than 40 percent of their revenue through successful partnering. After IBM's "near-death experience" in the early 1990s, the power of its alliances with more than 90,000 business partners helped shape its turnaround. By partnering, companies play on "teams," fielding the best players at every position and thus providing stamina and flexibility for customers. Through partnerships, a company can offer a broader range of IT solutions and improve the probability of market success.[129]

Thus, dynamic alliance networks are primarily used to stimulate rapid, value-creating product innovations and subsequent successful market entries, demonstrating that their purpose is often *exploration* of new ideas.[130] Often, large firms in such industries as software and pharmaceuticals create networks of smaller entrepreneurial start-up firms to accomplish this goal.[131] Small firms also build credibility faster by being engaged in such joint network relationships.[132]

Competitive Risks with Cooperative Strategies

Stated simply, many cooperative strategies fail.[133] In fact, evidence shows that two-thirds of cooperative strategies have serious problems in their first two years and that as many as 70 percent of them fail.[134] This failure rate suggests that even when the partnership has potential complementarities and synergies, alliance success is elusive.[135] We describe two failed alliances, MusicNet and Pressplay, in the Strategic Focus.

Although failure is undesirable, it can be a valuable learning experience. Certainly, it appears that MusicNet and Pressplay have learned from the more positive results and customer demand experienced by Apple's iTunes venture, as the Strategic Focus indicates. Companies willing to carefully study a cooperative strategy's failure may gain insights that can be used to successfully develop and use future cooperative strategies.[136] Thus, companies should work equally hard to avoid cooperative strategy failure and to learn from failure if it occurs. In the construction industry, cooperation on a project between the main contractor and subcontractors is very important. Without managing areas of mistrust, including suspected incompetence and potential dishonesty, success can be elusive, and failure of the alliance can be very costly.[137] Prominent cooperative strategy risks are shown in Figure 9.4.

Managing Competitive Risks in Cooperative Strategies —— Figure 9.4

Rivalry and Mistrust: Failure and Success of Music Industry Alliances

The music industry is in the middle of a significant change. Increasingly, music is being pirated online and industry executives are having a hard time finding a viable way to curtail the losses associated with the illegal behavior. Napster, the biggest online music swap service, was shut down by a lawsuit filed by the music companies. The music companies promised to launch paid services with the same ease of access. Accordingly, Warner Music, BMG, EMI, and RealNetworks started an alliance called MusicNet, while Sony and Vivendi Universal formed a joint venture called Pressplay. Instead of making digital music easier to obtain legally, however, these two joint ventures apparently increased the difficulty.

The record companies were afraid of cannibalizing CD sales and decided to "rent" music to customers through the Internet. Customers were expected to pay a monthly subscription fee for songs from MusicNet and Pressplay. However, MusicNet tunes could be downloaded only onto a computer, but not burned onto CDs, and they disappeared off the computer (through the downloading software) if the customer's bill was not paid. To make matters worse for the consumer, the two joint ventures fought over who would dominate instead of trying to work together on a standard to attract customers. Pressplay wouldn't share its songs with MusicNet, and MusicNet withheld its tunes from Pressplay. As a result, neither service had enough songs to attract paying customers. All of these factors contributed to the ventures' lack of success. Although their executives insist otherwise, both could be considered initial failures.

Apple, on the other hand, opened an online music store called iTunes as a venture with most major record companies and artists. It is not a subscription service like MusicNet and Pressplay. Instead, an iTunes customer pays 99 cents per song and from then on owns the music, although sharing with others is still illegal. Also, the purchased tune can be downloaded to portable MP3 players, burned on a CD, or arranged in a play list for the PC, and it never goes away. In its first week, iTunes sold over one million songs, in contrast to the subscribership of MusicNet and Pressplay, estimated at 225,000 altogether since their initiation. Another sign of iTunes' success is that both the MusicNet and Pressplay joint ventures have scrambled to add a service like Apple's to their offerings.

SOURCES: J. Ellis, 2003, Digital squared: Living in an iTunes world, *Fast Company*, August, 59; C. Haddad, 2003, How Apple spells future: i-P-O-D, *BusinessWeek Online*, http://www.businessweek.com, July 2; D. Leonard, 2003, Songs in the key of Steve, *Fortune*, http://www.fortune.com, April 28; D. Leonard, 2003, Leader of the digital music pack? *Fortune*, http://www.fortune.com, April 28; D. Leonard, 2003, Apple takes a big bite, *Fortune*, http://www.fortune.com, May 13; N. Wingfield & A. W. Matthews, 2003, Behind the missing music, *Wall Street Journal*, July 2, D1.

One cooperative strategy risk is that a partner may act opportunistically. Opportunistic behaviors surface either when formal contracts fail to prevent them or when an alliance is based on a false perception of partner trustworthiness. Not infrequently, the opportunistic firm wants to acquire as much of its partner's tacit knowledge as it can.[138] Full awareness of what a partner wants in a cooperative strategy reduces the likelihood that a firm will suffer from another's opportunistic actions.[139]

TVS Motor, an Indian motorcycle company, was created as a joint venture with Suzuki Motor Co., but when Suzuki refused to provide financial guarantees for TVS after a devastating strike, TVS initiated a strategy to become independent. Having learned much from Suzuki, including the implementation of Japanese-style quality programs, Venu Srinivasan, CEO of TVS, improved the company's situation through upgrading plants, nurturing in-house design, and investing in new technology. When sales of its new Victor motorcycle took off in 2001, TVS decided to go its own way and ended its relationship with Suzuki.[140]

Some cooperative strategies fail when it is discovered that a firm has misrepresented the competencies it can bring to the partnership. 3Com Corporation recently agreed to a joint venture with Huawei Technologies, China's equivalent to Cisco Systems for developing network infrastructure that supports the Internet. On paper, the combination of Huawei and 3Com appears very promising. It provides Huawei with 3Com's global distribution system, along with a strong base in the United States, and it lets 3Com fill gaps in its product line and exploit Huawei's low-cost operations in China. Unfortunately, Cisco, 3Com's major rival, has accused Huawei of stealing its intellectual property and has filed suit against the company. For years, others have noticed how similar Huawei's products were to Cisco's, down to the model number and manual. Now Cisco says that it has found some of its own bugs in Huawei's software, which would be an extremely unlikely coincidence. 3Com CEO Bruce Claflin says the company agreed to the joint venture only after a detailed investigation of Huawei's source code. Terms of the venture include warranties by Huawei that its products do not infringe intellectual rights. Even if certain Huawei products turn out to have Cisco code, Claflin believes it was not done with management's blessing and has confidence in the company's future offerings. The furor already endangers the joint venture, however: Cisco has threatened to sue 3Com as well as Huawei.[141] The risk of competence misrepresentation is more common when the partner's contribution is grounded in some of its intangible assets. Superior knowledge of local conditions is an example of an intangible asset that partners often fail to deliver. Asking the partner to provide evidence that it does possess the resources and capabilities (even when they are largely intangible) it is to share in the cooperative strategy may be an effective way to deal with this risk.

Another risk is that a firm won't actually make available to its partners the resources and capabilities (such as its most sophisticated technologies) that it committed to the cooperative strategy. This risk surfaces most commonly when firms form an international cooperative strategy.[142] In these instances, different cultures can result in different interpretations of contractual terms or trust-based expectations.

A final risk is that the firm may make investments that are specific to the alliance while its partner does not. For example, the firm might commit resources and capabilities to develop manufacturing equipment that can be used only to produce items coming from the alliance. If the partner isn't also making alliance-specific investments, the firm is at a relative disadvantage in terms of returns earned from the alliance compared to investments made to earn the returns.

For example, Pixar and Disney have partnered to release several computer graphics animated features, including *Toy Story, Monsters Inc.*, and *A Bug's Life*, all of which have been box-office hits. Disney is seeing the risks in its partnership as the firm's managers consider the possible expiration of the agreement with Pixar. Pixar may have more bargaining power to strike another deal—with Disney or with someone else. All of Pixar's films have done better at the box office than have Disney's recent animated features, and Pixar contributed 35 percent of Disney's studio operating profits in 2002. Pixar's chairman Steve Jobs has been meeting with executives from other studios, which puts pressure on Disney to sweeten its offer for continued partnership, perhaps by allowing Pixar to keep more of its profits.[143] If Disney had more of a commitment in the form of equity ownership in Pixar, it would have more control due to such investment.

As our discussion has shown, cooperative strategies are an important option for firms competing in the global economy.[144] However, our study of cooperative strategies also shows that they are complex.[145]

Firms gain the most benefit from cooperative strategies when they are effectively managed. Being able to flexibly adapt partnerships is a crucial aspect of managing cooperative strategies.[146] The firm that learns how to manage cooperative strategies better than its competitors do may develop a competitive advantage in terms of this activity.[147] Because the ability to effectively manage cooperative strategies is unevenly distributed across organizations in general, assigning managerial responsibility for a firm's cooperative strategies to a high-level executive or to a team improves the likelihood that the strategies will be well managed.

Those responsible for managing the firm's set of cooperative strategies coordinate activities, categorize knowledge learned from previous experiences, and make certain that what the firm knows about how to effectively form and use cooperative strategies is in the hands of the right people at the right time. Firms use one of two primary approaches to manage cooperative strategies—cost minimization and opportunity maximization[148] (see Figure 9.4). This is the case whether the firm has formed a separate cooperative strategy management function or not.

In the *cost minimization* management approach, the firm develops formal contracts with its partners. These contracts specify how the cooperative strategy is to be monitored and how partner behavior is to be controlled. The goal of this approach is to minimize the cooperative strategy's cost and to prevent opportunistic behavior by a partner. The focus of the second managerial approach—*opportunity maximization*—is on maximizing a partnership's value-creation opportunities. In this case, partners are prepared to take advantage of unexpected opportunities to learn from each other and to explore additional marketplace possibilities. Less formal contracts, with fewer constraints on partners' behaviors, make it possible for partners to explore how their resources and capabilities can be shared in multiple value-creating ways.

Firms can successfully use either approach to manage cooperative strategies. However, the costs to monitor the cooperative strategy are greater with cost minimization, in that writing detailed contracts and using extensive monitoring mechanisms is expensive, even though the approach is intended to reduce alliance costs. Although monitoring systems may prevent partners from acting in their own best interests, they also preclude positive responses to those situations where opportunities to use the alliance's competitive advantages surface unexpectedly. Thus, formal contracts and extensive monitoring systems tend to stifle partners' efforts to gain maximum value from their participation in a cooperative strategy and require significant resources to put into place and use.[149]

For example, Sony Ericsson Mobile Communications was a joint venture formed by Sony and Ericsson to become the top seller of multimedia mobile-phone handsets. Although it was growing at three times the overall market rate in its core areas, the venture posted a loss for the second quarter of 2003. Notably, the loss was attributed to costs from job cuts and closing units, such as research parks in Munich, Germany, and North Carolina. Such cost-cutting activities may create difficulties for strategic alliances built to explore opportunities. "The question is whether they can continue such an exceptional performance given that they are cutting costs rather than growing."[150]

The relative lack of detail and formality that is a part of the contract developed by firms using the second management approach of opportunity maximization means that firms need to trust each other to act in the partnership's best interests. A psychological state, *trust* is a willingness to be vulnerable because of the expectations of positive behavior from the firm's alliance partner.[151] When partners trust each other, there is less need to write detailed formal contracts to specify each firm's alliance behaviors,[152] and the cooperative relationship tends to be more stable.[153] On a relative basis, trust tends to be more difficult to establish in international cooperative strategies compared to domestic ones. Differences in trade policies, cultures, laws, and politics that are part of cross-border alliances account for the increased difficulty.[154] When trust exists, partners' monitoring costs are reduced and opportunities to create value are maximized.[155]

Research showing that trust between partners increases the likelihood of alliance success[156] seems to highlight the benefits of the opportunity maximization approach to managing cooperative strategies. Trust may also be the most efficient way to influence and control alliance partners' behaviors.[157] Research indicates that trust can be a capability that is valuable, rare, imperfectly imitable, and often nonsubstitutable.[158] Thus, firms known to be trustworthy can have a competitive advantage in terms of how they develop and use cooperative strategies both internally and externally.[159] One reason is that it is impossible to specify all operational details of a cooperative strategy in a formal contract. Confidence that its partner can be trusted reduces the firm's concern about the inability to contractually control all alliance details.

Summary

- A cooperative strategy is one in which firms work together to achieve a shared objective. Strategic alliances, cooperative strategies in which firms combine some of their resources and capabilities to create a competitive advantage, are the primary form of cooperative strategies. Joint ventures (where firms create and own equal shares of a new venture that is intended to develop competitive advantages), equity strategic alliances (where firms own different shares of a newly created venture), and non-equity strategic alliances (where firms cooperate through a contractual relationship) are the three basic types of strategic alliances. Outsourcing, discussed in Chapter 3, commonly occurs as firms form nonequity strategic alliances.

- Collusive strategies are the second type of cooperative strategies (with strategic alliances being the other). In many economies and certainly developed ones, explicit collusive strategies are illegal unless sanctioned by government policies. With increasing globalization, fewer government-sanctioned situations of explicit collusion exist. Tacit collusion, also called mutual forbearance, is a cooperative strategy through which firms tacitly cooperate to reduce industry output below the potential competitive output level, thereby raising prices above the competitive level.

- Reasons firms use cooperative strategies vary by slow-cycle, fast-cycle, and standard-cycle market conditions. To enter restricted markets (slow-cycle), to move quickly from one competitive advantage to another (fast-cycle), and to gain market power (standard-cycle) demonstrate the differences among reasons by market type for use of cooperative strategies.

- There are four business-level cooperative strategies (a business-level cooperative strategy is used to help the firm improve its performance in individual product markets). Through vertical and horizontal complementary alliances, companies combine their resources and capabilities to create value in different parts (vertical) or the same parts (horizontal) of the value chain. Competition responding strategies are formed to respond to competitors' actions, especially strategic ones. Competition reducing strategies are used to avoid excessive competition while the firm marshals its resources and capabilities to improve its competitiveness. Uncertainty reducing strategies are used to hedge against the risks created by the conditions of uncertain competitive environments (such as new product markets). Complementary alliances have the highest probability of yielding a sustainable competitive advantage; competition reducing alliances have the lowest probability of doing so.

- Corporate-level cooperative strategies are used when the firm wants to pursue product and/or geographic diversification. Through diversifying strategic alliances, firms agree to share some of their resources and capabilities to enter new markets or produce new products. Synergistic alliances are ones where firms share resources and capabilities to develop economies of scope. This alliance is similar to the business-level horizontal complementary alliance in which firms try to develop operational synergy whereas synergistic alliances are used to develop synergy at the corporate level. Franchising is a corporate-level cooperative strategy where the franchisor uses a franchise as a contractual relationship to describe the sharing of its resources and capabilities with franchisees.

- As an international cooperative strategy, a cross-border alliance is used for several reasons, including the performance superiority of firms competing in markets outside their domestic market and governmental restrictions on growth through mergers and acquisitions. Cross-border alliances tend to be riskier than their domestic counterparts, particularly when partners aren't fully aware of each other's purpose for participating in the partnership.

- A network cooperative strategy is one wherein several firms agree to form multiple partnerships to achieve shared objectives. One of the primary benefits of a network cooperative strategy is the firm's opportunity to gain access "to its partner's other partnerships." When this happens, the probability greatly increases that partners will find unique ways to uniquely share their resources and capabilities to form competitive advantages. Network cooperative strategies are used to form either a stable alliance network or a dynamic alliance network. Used in mature industries, partners use stable networks to extend competitive advantages into new areas. In rapidly changing environments where frequent product innovations occur, dynamic networks are primarily used as a tool of innovation.

- Cooperative strategies aren't risk free. If a contract is not developed appropriately, or if a partner misrepresents its competencies or fails to make them available, failure is likely. Furthermore, a firm may be held hostage through asset-specific investments made in conjunction with a partner, which may be exploited.

- Trust is an increasingly important aspect of successful cooperative strategies. Firms recognize the value of partnering with companies known for their trustworthiness. When trust exists, a cooperative strategy is managed to maximize the pursuit of opportunities between partners. Without trust, formal contracts and extensive monitoring systems are used to manage cooperative strategies. In this case, the interest is to minimize costs rather than to maximize opportunities by participating in a cooperative strategy.

Review Questions

1. What is the definition of cooperative strategy and why is this strategy important to firms competing in the 21st-century competitive landscape?

2. What is a strategic alliance? What are the three types of strategic alliances firms use to develop a competitive advantage?

3. What are the four business-level cooperative strategies and what are the differences among them?

4. What are the three corporate-level cooperative strategies? How do firms use each one to create a competitive advantage?

5. Why do firms use cross-border strategic alliances?

6. What risks are firms likely to experience as they use cooperative strategies?

7. What are the differences between the cost-minimization approach and the opportunity-maximization approach to managing cooperative strategies?

Alliance Strategy

Assume that you are the CEO of Century Pharmaceuticals, Inc., seeking a strategic alliance with Excel Research, an independent, full-service research organization. Excel Research specializes in working with pharmaceutical companies to efficiently and effectively navigate the regulatory approval process and bring new drug therapies to market. Century will be consulting with Excel about submissions to the Food and Drug Administration (FDA) for new and current products as well as general development projects. As CEO, you believe that Century Pharmaceuticals and Excel Research can successfully work together to create novel therapies to fill unmet needs in dermatology and other therapeutic arenas.

You expect that the strategic alliance between Century Pharmaceuticals and Excel Research will provide enhanced benefits for both companies. Century, under your leadership, is committed to continuing to grow by implementing its differentiation strategy, which specifies the objectives of acquiring new products, extending the product life cycle of existing products, and introducing new uses for therapies in specific markets. Excel Research has an established and proven track record of success in supporting and providing the evaluation required to bring new therapies and new uses for existing therapies to market.

Based on this information, determine answers to the following questions and make a brief presentation to the class as the Board of Directors:

1. Is the above case a complementary strategic alliance? If so, what kind of complementary strategic alliance?

2. Is it a competition response strategy? If so, who are the competitors and what are they doing?

3. Is it an uncertainty reducing strategy? If so, how can uncertainty be reduced?

4. Is it a competition reducing strategy? If so, explain how it works.

Cooperative Strategy Risk

Your firm manufactures fasteners for industrial applications. As the senior vice president of sales, you have developed several long-term relationships with your customers. Your main competitor has recently approached you about establishing a strategic alliance with your firm.

1. Because you are not sure if this alliance would be beneficial to your firm, you decide to bring the proposal to your firm's executive committee for a preliminary discussion. You anticipate that the committee will ask several basic questions. What information should you be able to provide?

2. After several weeks of investigating the value of an alliance, your firm decides that it would be financially beneficial, but the executive committee now wants you to present the risks that an alliance might entail and how you would suggest minimizing them. What risks do you foresee? How can they be prevented?

3. Before a contract between your firm and your competitor can be signed, you begin negotiations with one of your competitor's largest customers to provide new products based on a new technology your firm has developed. In your opinion, does the alliance raise legal or ethical issues that your firm should consider before proceeding with your negotiations?

1. J. Hagedoorn & G. Dysters, 2002, External sources of innovative capabilities: The preference for strategic alliances or mergers and acquisitions, *Journal of Management Studies*, 39: 167–188; K. M. Eisenhardt, 2002, Has strategy changed? *MIT Sloan Management Review*, 43(2): 88–91; T. B. Lawrence, C. Hardy, & N. Phillips, 2002, Institutional effects of interorganizational collaborations: The emergence of proto-institutions, *Academy of Management Journal*, 45: 281–290; E. B. Roberts & W. K. Liu, 2002, Ally or acquire? *MIT Sloan Management Review*, 43(1): 26–34.

2. T. A. Hemphill, 2003, Cooperative strategy, technology innovation and competition policy in the United States and the European Union, *Technology Analysis & Strategic Management*, 15(1): 93–101; J. B. Barney, 2002, *Gaining and Sustaining Competitive Advantage*, 2nd ed., Upper Saddle River, NJ: Prentice-Hall, 339.

3. M. Takayama, C. Watanabe, & C. Griffy-Brown, 2002, Alliance strategy as a competitive strategy for successively creative new product development: The proof of the co-evolution of creativity and efficiency in the Japanese pharmaceutical industry, *Technovation*, 22(10): 607–614; W. S. Desarbo, K. Jedidi, & I. Sinha, 2001, Customer value in a heterogeneous market, *Strategic Management Journal*, 22: 845–857.

4. C. Young-Ybarra & M. Wiersema, 1999, Strategic flexibility in information technology alliances: The influence of transaction cost economics and social exchange theory, *Organization Science*, 10: 439–459; M. E. Porter & M. B. Fuller, 1986, Coalitions and global strategy, in M. E. Porter (ed.), *Competition in Global Industries*, Boston: Harvard Business School Press, 315–344.

5. M. A. Hitt, R. D. Ireland, S. M. Camp, & D. L. Sexton, 2002, Strategic entrepreneurship: Integrating entrepreneurial and strategic management perspectives, in M. A. Hitt, R. D. Ireland, S. M. Camp, & D. L. Sexton (eds.), *Strategic Entrepreneurship: Creating a New Mindset*, Oxford, UK: Blackwell Publishers, 8.

6. C. Garcia-Pont & N. Nohria, 2002, Local versus global mimetism: The dynamics of alliance formation in the automobile industry, *Strategic Management Journal*, 23: 307–321; S. Royer, 2002, Successful horizontal alliances between competitors: Evidence from the automobile industry, *International Journal of Human Resources Development and Management*, 2(3,4): 445–462.

7. J. Bowser, 2001, Strategic co-opetition: The value of relationships in the networked economy, *IBM Business Strategy Consulting*, http://www.ibm.com, March 12.

8. Barney, *Gaining and Sustaining Competitive Advantage*, 339.

9. D. Rigby & C. Zook, 2003, Open-market innovation, *Harvard Business Review*, 89(10): 80–89.

10. Y. L. Doz & G. Hamel, 1998, *Alliance Advantage: The Art of Creating Value through Partnering*, Boston: Harvard Business School Press, xiii.

11. R. D. Ireland, M. A. Hitt, & D. Vaidyanath, 2002, Alliance management as a source of competitive advantage, *Journal of Management*, 28: 413–446; J. G. Coombs & D. J. Ketchen, 1999, Exploring interfirm cooperation and performance: Toward a reconciliation of predictions from the resource-based view and organizational economics, *Strategic Management Journal*, 20: 867–888.

12. M. R. Subramani & N. Venkatraman, 2003, Safeguarding investments in asymmetric interorganizational relationships: Theory and evidence, *Academy of Management Journal*, 46(1): 46–62; P. Kale, H. Singh, & H. Perlmutter, 2000, Learning and protection of proprietary assets in strategic alliances: Building relational capital, *Strategic Management Journal*, 21: 217–237.

13. P. Kale, J. H. Dyer, & H. Singh, 2002, Alliance capability, stock market response, and long-term alliance success: The role of the alliance function, *Strategic Management Journal*, 23: 747–767; D. F. Kuratko, R. D. Ireland, & J. S. Hornsby, 2001, Improving firm performance through entrepreneurial actions: Acordia's corporate entrepreneurship strategy, *Academy of Management Executive*, 15(4): 60–71.

14. 2002, Borrego blurs traditional lines, *Dallas Morning News*, February 24, M4.

15. A. Antoine, C. B. Frank, H. Murata, & E. Roberts, 2003, Acquisitions and alliances in the aerospace industry: An unusual triad, *International Journal of Technology Management*, 25(8): 779–790; 2002, Lockheed Martin, Responsive global partnerships, http://www.lockheedmartin.com, March 17.

16. Ireland, Hitt, & Vaidyanath, Alliance management as a source of competitive advantage; J. H. Tiessen & J. D. Linton, 2000, The JV dilemma: Cooperating and competing in joint ventures, *Revue Canadienne des Sciences de l'Administration*, 17(3): 203–216.

17. M. Harvey, M. B. Myers, & M. M. Novicevic, 2003, The managerial issues associated with global account management: A relational contract perspective, *Journal of Management Development*, 22(1,2): 103–129; T. K. Das & B.-S. Teng, 2001, A risk perception model of alliance structuring, *Journal of International Management*, 7: 1–29; J. H. Dyer & H. Singh, 1998, The relational view: Cooperative strategy and sources of interorganizational competitive advantage, *Academy of Management Review*, 23: 660–679.

18. A. Afuah, 2002, Mapping technological capabilities into product markets and competitive advantage: The case of cholesterol drugs, *Strategic Management Journal*, 23: 171–179; A. Arino, 2001, To do or not to do? Non-cooperative behavior by commission and omission in interfirm ventures, *Group & Organization Management*, 26(1): 4–23; C. Holliday, 2001, Sustainable growth, the DuPont way, *Harvard Business Review*, 79(8): 129–134.

19. Y. Kim & K. Lee, 2003, Technological collaboration in the Korean electronic parts industry: Patterns and key success factors, *R&D Management*, 33(1): 59–77; M. A. Geletkanycz & S. S. Black, 2001, Bound by the past? Experience-based effects on commitment to the strategic status quo, *Journal of Management*, 27: 3–21.

20. S. L. Berman, J. Down, & C. W. L. Hill, 2002, Tacit knowledge as a source of competitive advantage in the National Basketball Association, *Academy of Management Journal*, 45: 13–31.

21. Tiessen & Linton, The JV dilemma, 206; P. E. Bierly III & E. H. Kessler, 1999, The timing of strategic alliances, in M. A. Hitt, P. G. Clifford, R. D. Nixon, & K. P. Coyne (eds.), *Dynamic Strategic Resources: Development, Diffusion and Integration*, Chichester: John Wiley & Sons, 299–345.

22. M. Clifford, 2003, Concrete lessons in reform, *BusinessWeek Online*, http://www.businessweek.com, June 16.

23. R. E. Hoskisson & L. W. Busenitz, 2002, Market uncertainty and learning distance in corporate entrepreneurship entry mode choice, in M. A. Hitt, R. D. Ireland, S. M. Camp, & D. L. Sexton (eds.), *Strategic Entrepreneurship: Creating a New Mindset*, Oxford, UK: Blackwell Publishers, 151–172.

24. A.-W. Harzing, 2002, Acquisitions versus greenfield investments: International strategy and management of entry modes, *Strategic Management Journal*, 23: 211–227; S.-J. Chang & P. M. Rosenzweig, 2001, The choice of entry mode in sequential foreign direct investment, *Strategic Management Journal*, 22: 747–776; Y. Pan, 1997, The formation of Japanese and U.S. equity joint ventures in China, *Strategic Management Journal*, 18: 247–254.

25. J. T. Areddy, 2003, Citigroup may bolster 5% stake in Pudong Development Bank, *Wall Street Journal*, January 6, C7; 2003, Citibank can boost China stake, *Wall Street Journal*, April 28, C11.

26. S. Das, P. K. Sen, & S. Sengupta, 1998, Impact of strategic alliances on firm valuation, *Academy of Management Journal*, 41: 27–41.

27. Bierly & Kessler, The timing of strategic alliances, 303.

28. T. B. Folta & K. D. Miller, 2002, Real options in equity partnerships, *Strategic Management Journal*, 23: 77–88; Barney, *Gaining and Sustaining Competi-*

tive Advantage, 339; S. D. Hunt, C. J. Lambe, & C. M. Wittmann, 2002, A theory and model of business alliance success, *Journal of Relationship Marketing*, 1(1): 17–35.

29. M. Pacelle, R. Sidel, & A. Merrick, 2003, Citigroup agrees to buy Sears's credit-card unit, *Wall Street Journal Online*, http://www.wsj.com, July 15.

30. A. Hinterhuber, 2002, Value chain orchestration in action and the case of the global agrochemical industry, *Long Range Planning*, 35(6): 615–635; A. C. Inkpen, 2001, Strategic alliances, in M. A. Hitt, R. E. Freeman, & J. S. Harrison (eds.), *Handbook of Strategic Management*, Oxford, UK: Blackwell Publishers, 409–432.

31. M. Delio, 1999, Strategic outsourcing, *Knowledge Management*, 2(7): 62–68.

32. E. Chabrow, 2003, Creative pressure, *InformationWeek*, June 16, 38–44.

33. J. J. Reuer, M. Zollo, & H. Singh, 2002, Post-formation dynamics in strategic alliances, *Strategic Management Journal*, 23: 135–151.

34. D. Campbell, 2001, High-end strategic alliances as fundraising opportunities, *Nonprofit World*, 19(5): 8–12; M. D. Hutt, E. R. Stafford, B. A. Walker, & P. H. Reingen, 2000, Case study: Defining the social network of a strategic alliance, *Sloan Management Review*, 41(2): 51–62.

35. M. J. Kelly, J.-L. Schaan, & H. Jonacas, 2002, Managing alliance relationships: Key challenges in the early stages of collaboration, *R&D Management*, 32(1): 11–22.

36. A. C. Inkpen & J. Ross, 2001, Why do some strategic alliances persist beyond their useful life? *California Management Review*, 44(1): 132–148.

37. M. Schifrin, 2001, Partner or perish, *Forbes*, May 21, 28.

38. C. Hardy, N. Phillips, & T. B. Lawrence, 2003, Resources, knowledge and influence: The organizational effects of interorganizational collaboration, *Journal of Management Studies*, 40(2): 321–347; Inkpen, Strategic alliances, 411.

39. L. Fuentelsaz, J. Gomez, & Y. Polo, 2002, Followers' entry timing: Evidence from the Spanish banking sector after deregulation, *Strategic Management Journal*, 23: 245–264.

40. K. R. Harrigan, 2001, Strategic flexibility in the old and new economies, in M. A. Hitt, R. E. Freeman, & J. S. Harrison (eds.), *Handbook of Strategic Management*, Oxford, UK: Blackwell Publishers, 97–123.

41. D. M. Amato-McCoy, 2003, Outsourced private label credit card program brings flexibility in-house, *Stores*, 85(2): 38–40.

42. G. W. Dent, Jr., 2001, Gap fillers and fiduciary duties in strategic alliances, *Business Lawyer*, 57(1): 55–104.

43. S. Ulfelder, 2001, Partners in profit, *Computerworld*, July/August, 24–28.

44. M. Gonzalez, 2001, Strategic alliances, *Ivey Business Journal*, 66(1): 47–51.

45. M.-J. Oesterle & K. Macharzina, 2002, Editorial: De-regulation, liberalization, and concentration in the airline industry, *Management International Review*, 42(2): 115–119; M. Johnson, 2001, Airlines rush for comfort alliances, *Global Finance*, 15(11): 119–120.

46. J. Child & D. Faulkner, 1998, *Strategies of Co-operation: Managing Alliances, Networks, and Joint Ventures*, New York: Oxford University Press.

47. J. R. Williams, 1998, *Renewable Advantage: Crafting Strategy through Economic Time*, New York: The Free Press.

48. M. Arndt, 2003, Up from the scrap heap, *BusinessWeek Online*, http://www.businessweek.com, July 21.

49. J. Slater, 2002, India seeds a new market, *Far Eastern Economic Review*, October 31, 50–51.

50. Ibid.; V. Kumari, 2001, Joint ventures bolster credibility of new players in India, *National Underwriter*, 105(14): 46.

51. S. A. Zahra, R. D. Ireland, I. Gutierrez, & M. A. Hitt, 2000, Privatization and entrepreneurial transformation: Emerging issues and a future research agenda, *Academy of Management Review*, 25: 509–524.

52. I. Filatotchev, M. Wright, K. Uhlenbruck, L. Tihanyi, & R. E. Hoskisson, 2003, Governance, organizational capabilities, and restructuring in transition economies, *Journal of World Business*, in press.

53. Eisenhardt, Has strategy changed? 88.

54. M. Dell, 2003, Collaboration equals innovation, *InformationWeek*, January 27, 24–26; H. D'Antoni, 2003, Behind the numbers: Business alliances merit closer examination, *InformationWeek*, January 27, 88.

55. H. W. Chesbrough, 2002, Making sense of corporate venture capital, *Harvard Business Review*, 80(3): 90–99.

56. C. Braunschweig, 2003, Big write-downs won't slow Intel Capital, *Venture Capital Journal*, March 1, 1.

57. D. Michaels & J. L. Lunsford, 2003, Airlines move toward buying planes jointly, *Wall Street Journal*, May 20, A3.

58. E. Nelson & M. Peros, 2003, Vivendi, GE sign pact, shift focus to acquiring Diller stakes, *Wall Street Journal*, October 9, B6.

59. D. R. King, J. G. Covin, & H. Hegarty, 2003, Complementary resources and the exploitation of technological innovations, *Journal of Management*, 29: 589–606; J. S. Harrison, M. A. Hitt, R. E. Hoskisson, & R. D. Ireland, 2001, Resource complementarity in business combinations: Extending the logic to organizational alliances, *Journal of Management*, 27: 679–699; S. H. Park & G. R. Ungson, 1997, The effect of national culture, organizational complementarity, and economic motivation on joint venture dissolution, *Academy of Management Journal*, 40: 297–307.

60. Subramani & Venkatraman, Safeguarding investments in asymmetric interorganizational relationships.

61. 2003, Mottola joins Universal all-stars, *New York Times*, http://www.nytimes.com, July 13.

62. M. Kotabe & K. S. Swan, 1995, The role of strategic alliances in high technology new product development, *Strategic Management Journal*, 16: 621–636.

63. J. Li, 2003, Bell Canada, Microsoft in Internet service alliance, *Wall Street Journal Online*, http://www.wsj.com, June 16.

64. M. Ihlwan, L. Armstrong, & G. Edmondson, 2003, Hyundai's hurdles, *BusinessWeek Online*, http://www.businessweek.com, July 21.

65. A. Latour, 2003, BellSouth unveils DSL Lite service as Bells step up subscriber battle, *Wall Street Journal Online*, http://www.wsj.com, July 8.

66. Ibid.

67. A. Latour & P. Grant, 2003, SBC, Qwest strikes partnership with providers of satellite TV; alliances with EchoStar, DirecTV aim to fend off rivalry from cable firms, *Wall Street Journal*, July 22, B11.

68. S. Chatterjee, R. M. Wiseman, A. Fiegenbaum, & C. E. Devers, 2003, Integrating behavioural and economic concepts of risk into strategic management: The twain shall meet, *Long Range Planning*, 36(1), 61–80; Hitt, Ireland, Camp, & Sexton, *Strategic Entrepreneurship*, 9; R. G. McGrath, 1999, Falling forward: Real options reasoning and entrepreneurial failure, *Academy of Management Journal*, 22: 13–30.

69. Dow Jones, 2003, ABN, ShoreBank set up co to invest in developing economies, *Wall Street Journal Online*, http://www.wsj.com, July 10.

70. V. Alessio & L. Di Leo, 2003, Wind, NTT DoCoMo set up strategic alliance, *Wall Street Journal Online*, http://www.wsj.com, June 25.

71. Barney, *Gaining and Sustaining Competitive Advantage*, 339.

72. 2003, Cosmetics makers agree to give-aways, *Wall Street Journal*, July 21, B2.

73. D. Leahy & S. Pavelin, 2003, Follow-my-leader and tacit collusion, *International Journal of Industrial Organization*, 21(3): 439–454.

74. S. Jayachandran, J. Gimeno, & P. Rajan, 1999, Theory of multimarket competition: A synthesis and implications for marketing strategy, *Journal of Marketing*, 63(3): 49–66.

75. B. R. Golden & H. Ma, 2003, Mutual forbearance: The role of intrafirm integration and rewards, *Academy of Management Review*, 28: 479–493.

76. 2003, AOL, Microsoft vow messaging cooperation, *New York Times*, http://www.nytimes.com, June 4.

77. G. K. Price & J. M. Connor, 2003, Modeling coupon values for ready-to-eat breakfast cereals, *Agribusiness*, 19(2): 223–244.

78. G. K. Price, 2000, Cereal sales soggy despite price cuts and reduced couponing, *Food Review*, 23(2): 21–28.

79. S. B. Garland & A. Reinhardt, 1999, Making antitrust fit high tech, *Business Week*, March 22, 34–36.

80. E. G. Rogoff & H. S. Guirguis, 2002, Legalized price-fixing, *Forbes*, December 9, 48.

81. G. Gari, 1999, Leveraging the rewards of strategic alliances, *Journal of Business Strategy*, 20(2): 40–43.

82. 2003, Who gains if United should die? *The Economist*, May 10, 56.

83. Leahy & Pavelin, Follow-my-leader and tacit collusion.

84. Harrison, Hitt, Hoskisson, & Ireland, Resource complementarity, 684–685; S. Chaudhuri & B. Tabrizi, 1999, Capturing the real value in high-tech acquisitions, *Harvard Business Review*, 77(5): 123–130; J.-F. Hennart & S. Reddy, 1997, The choice between mergers/acquisitions and joint ventures in the United States, *Strategic Management Journal*, 18: 1–12.

85. A. E. Bernardo & B. Chowdhry, 2002, Resources, real options, and corporate strategy, *Journal of Financial Economics*, 63: 211–234; Inkpen, Strategic alliances, 413.

86. J. L. Johnson, R. P.-W. Lee, A. Saini, & B. Grohmann, 2003, Market-focused strategic flexibility: Conceptual advances and an integrative model, *Academy of Marketing Science Journal*, 31: 74–90; Young-Ybarra & Wiersema, Strategic flexibility, 439.

87. Folta & Miller, Real options in equity partnerships, 77.

88. 2002, CNOOC adds petrochemicals to downstream strategy, *Petroleum Economist*, December, 39.

89. Ibid.

90. J. Yang, 2003, One step forward for Japan's chipmakers, *BusinessWeek Online*, http://www.businessweek.com, July 7.

91. M. Allen & E. Porter, 2003, Grupo Televisa chief considers U.S. citizenship to pursue bid, *Wall Street Journal Online*, http://www.wsj.com, July 1.

92. J. G. Combs & D. J. Ketchen, Jr., 2003, Why do firms use franchising as an entrepreneurial strategy? A meta-analysis, *Journal of Management*, 29: 427–443; S. A. Shane, 1996, Hybrid organizational arrangements and their implications for firm growth and survival: A study of new franchisers, *Academy of Management Journal*, 39: 216–234.

93. F. Lafontaine, 1999, Myths and strengths of franchising, "Mastering Strategy" (Part Nine), *Financial Times*, November 22, 8–10.

94. G. G. Marcial, 2003, Cendant comes back, *Business Week*, May 12, 110; L. Fenwick, 2001, Emerging markets: Defining global opportunities, *Franchising World*, 33(4): 54–55.

95. J. Wilgoren, 2003, In the urban 7-Eleven, the Slurpee looks sleeker, *New York Times*, http://www.nytimes.com, July 13.

96. S. C. Michael, 2002, Can a franchise chain coordinate? *Journal of Business Venturing*, 17: 325–342; R. P. Dant & P. J. Kaufmann, 1999, Franchising and the domain of entrepreneurship research, *Journal of Business Venturing*, 14: 5–16.

97. M. Gerstenhaber, 2000, Franchises can teach us about customer care, *Marketing*, March 16, 18.

98. P. J. Kaufmann & S. Eroglu, 1999, Standardization and adaptation in business format franchising, *Journal of Business Venturing*, 14: 69–85.

99. S. C. Michael, 2002, First mover advantage through franchising, *Journal of Business Venturing*, 18: 61–81; L. Wu, 1999, The pricing of a brand name product: Franchising in the motel services industry, *Journal of Business Venturing*, 14: 87–102.

100. Barney, *Gaining and Sustaining Competitive Advantage*, 110–111.

101. D. Blank, 2003, La Quinta moves ahead with long-term plans, *Hotel and Motel Management*, 218(8): 28; J. Higley, 2000, La Quinta jumps into franchising, *Hotel and Motel Management*, 215(13): 1, 54.

102. M. Zollo, J. J. Reuer, & H. Singh, 2002, Interorganizational routines and performance in strategic alliances, *Organization Science*, 13: 701–714; P. J. Buckley & M. Casson, 1996, An economic model of international joint venture strategy, *Journal of International Business Studies*, 27: 849–876; M. J. Dowling & W. L. Megginson, 1995, Cooperative strategy and new venture performance: The role of business strategy and management experience, *Strategic Management Journal*, 16: 565–580.

103. Ireland, Hitt, & Vaidyanath, Alliance management.

104. P. Almeida, G. Dokko, & L. Rosenkopf, 2003, Startup size and the mechanisms of external learning: Increasing opportunity and decreasing ability? *Research Policy*, 32(2): 301–316; B. L. Simonin, 1997, The importance of collaborative know-how: An empirical test of the learning organization, *Academy of Management Journal*, 40: 1150–1174.

105. H. Timmons, 2003, BP signs deal with Russian firm for venture in oil and gas, *New York Times*, June 27, W1.

106. M. A. Hitt, M. T. Dacin, E. Levitas, J.-L. Arregle, & A. Borza, 2000, Partner selection in emerging and developed market contexts: Resource-based and organizational learning perspectives, *Academy of Management Journal*, 43: 449–467; M. D. Lord & A. L. Ranft, 2000, Organizational learning about new international markets: Exploring the internal transfer of local market knowledge, *Journal of International Business Studies*, 31: 73–589.

107. D. Kovaleski, 2003, More firms shaking hands on strategic partnership agreements, *Pensions & Investments*, February 3, 20; A. L. Velocci, Jr., 2001, U.S.-Euro strategic alliances will outpace company mergers, *Aviation Week & Space Technology*, 155(23): 56.

108. I. M. Manev, 2003, The managerial network in a multinational enterprise and the resource profiles of subsidiaries, *Journal of International Management*, 9: 133–152; M. A. Hitt, R. E. Hoskisson, & H. Kim, 1997, International diversification: Effects on innovation and firm performance in product diversified firms, *Academy of Management Journal*, 40: 767–798; R. N. Osborn & J. Hagedoorn, 1997, The institutionalization and evolutionary dynamics of interorganizational alliances and networks, *Academy of Management Journal*, 40: 261–278.

109. L. Nachum & D. Keeble, 2003, MNE linkages and localized clusters: Foreign and indigenous firms in the media cluster of Central London, *Journal of International Management*, 9: 171–192; J. Hagedoorn, 1995, A note on international market leaders and networks of strategic technology partnering, *Strategic Management Journal*, 16: 241–250.

110. S. Holmes, 2003, The real Nike news is happening abroad, *BusinessWeek Online*, http://www.businessweek.com, July 21.

111. 2002, H-P says it has alliance with NEC in Asia, *Wall Street Journal*, December 12, B2; A. Rogers, 2002, NEC, HP to form outsourcing services alliance, *CRN*, December 23–30, 70.

112. D. Roberts & M. L. Clifford, 2003, Morgan Stanley: What great wall? *BusinessWeek Online*, http://www.businessweek.com, July 28.

113. Ibid.

114. S. R. Miller & A. Parkhe, 2002, Is there a liability of foreignness in global banking? An empirical test of banks' x-efficiency, *Strategic Management Journal*, 23: 55–75; Y. Luo, 2001, Determinants of local responsiveness: Perspectives from foreign subsidiaries in an emerging market, *Journal of Management*, 27: 451–477.

115. G. A. Fowler, 2003, Starbucks' road to China, *Wall Street Journal Online*, http://www.wsj.com, July 14; J. Singer & M. Fackler, 2003, In Japan, adding beer, wine to the latte list, *Wall Street Journal Online*, http://www.wsj.com, July 14.

116. S. Holmes, 2003, For Starbucks, there's no place like home, *BusinessWeek Online*, http://www.businessweek.com, June 9.

117. H. J. Teegen & J. P. Doh, 2002, US-Mexican alliance negotiations: Impact of culture on authority, trust, performance, *Thunderbird International Business Review*, 44(6): 749–775; P. Ghemawat, 2001, Distance matters: The hard reality of global expansion, *Harvard Business Review*, 79(8): 137–147.

118. J. K. Sebenius, 2002, The hidden challenge of cross-border negotiations, *Harvard Business Review*, 80(3): 76–85.

119. C. B. Copp & R. L. Ivy, 2001, Networking trends of small tourism businesses in post-socialist Slovakia, *Journal of Small Business Management*, 39: 345–353.

120. M. Ferrary, 2003, Managing the disruptive technologies life cycle by externalising the research: Social network and corporate venturing in the Silicon Valley, *International Journal of Technology Management*, 25(1,2): 165–180; S. S. Cohen & G. Fields, 1999, Social capital and capital gains in Silicon Valley, *California Management Review*, 41(2): 108–130; J. A. Matthews, 1999, A silicon island of the east: Creating a semiconductor

industry in Singapore, *California Management Review*, 41(2): 55–78; M. E. Porter, 1998, Clusters and the new economics of competition, *Harvard Business Review*, 78(6): 77–90; R. Pouder & C. H. St. John, 1996, Hot spots and blind spots: Geographical clusters of firms and innovation, *Academy of Management Review*, 21: 1192–1225.

121. A. C. Cooper, 2001, Networks, alliances, and entrepreneurship, in M. A. Hitt, R. D. Ireland, S. M. Camp, & D. L. Sexton (eds.), *Strategic Entrepreneurship: Creating a New Mindset*, Oxford, UK: Blackwell Publishers, 203–222.

122. C. Passariello, 2003, Doing the continental at Cannes, *BusinessWeek Online*, http://www.businessweek.com, May 23.

123. S. Chung & G. M. Kim, 2003, Performance effects of partnership between manufacturers and suppliers for new product development: The supplier's standpoint, *Research Policy*, 32: 587–604.

124. R. S. Cline, 2001, Partnering for strategic alliances, *Lodging Hospitality*, 57(9): 42.

125. M. Rudberg & J. Olhager, 2003, Manufacturing networks and supply chains: An operations strategy perspective, *Omega*, 31(1): 29–39.

126. G. J. Young, M. P. Charns, & S. M. Shortell, 2001, Top manager and network effects on the adoption of innovative management practices: A study of TQM in a public hospital system, *Strategic Management Journal*, 22: 935–951.

127. E. Garcia-Canal, C. L. Duarte, J. R. Criado, & A. V. Llaneza, 2002, Accelerating international expansion through global alliances: A typology of cooperative strategies, *Journal of World Business*, 37(2): 91–107; F. T. Rothaermel, 2001, Complementary assets, strategic alliances, and the incumbent's advantage: An empirical study of industry and firm effects in the biopharmaceutical industry, *Research Policy*, 30: 1235–1251.

128. V. Shankar & B. L. Bayus, 2003, Network effects and competition: An empirical analysis of the home video game industry, *Strategic Management Journal*, 24: 375–384.

129. B. Duncan, 2003, Five steps to successful strategic partnering, *InformationWeek*, http://www.informationweek.com, July 21.

130. Z. Simsek, M. H. Lubatkin, & D. Kandemir, 2003, Inter-firm networks and entrepreneurial behavior: A structural embeddedness perspective, *Journal of Management*, 29: 401–426; H. W. Volberda, C. Baden-Fuller, & F. A. J. van den Bosch, 2001, Mastering strategic renewal: Mobilising renewal journeys in multi-unit firms, *Long Range Planning*, 34(2): 159–178.

131. King, Covin, & Hegarty, Complementary resources and the exploitation of technological innovations.

132. A. I. Goldberg, G. Cohen, & A. Fiegenbaum, 2003, Reputation building: Small business strategies for successful venture development, *Journal of Small Business Management*, 41(2): 168–186; S. Das, P. K. Sen, & S. Sengupta, 2003, Strategic alliances: A valuable way to manage intellectual capital? *Journal of Intellectual Capital*, 4(1): 10–19.

133. D. C. Hambrick, J. Li, K. Xin, & A. S. Tsui, 2001, Compositional gaps and downward spirals in international joint venture management groups, *Strategic Management Journal*, 22: 1033–1053; T. K. Das & B.-S. Teng, 2000, Instabilities of strategic alliances: An internal tensions perspective, *Organization Science*, 11: 77–101.

134. M. P. Koza & A. Y. Lewin, 1999, Putting the S-word back in alliances, "Mastering Strategy" (Part Six), *Financial Times*, November 1, 12–13; S. H. Park & M. Russo, 1996, When cooperation eclipses competition: An event history analysis of joint venture failures, *Management Science*, 42: 875–890.

135. A. Madhok & S. B. Tallman, 1998, Resources, transactions and rents: Managing value through interfirm collaborative relationships, *Organization Science*, 9: 326–339.

136. D. De Cremer & D. van Knippenberg, 2002, How do leaders promote cooperation? The effects of charisma and procedural fairness, *Journal of Applied Psychology*, 87: 858–867.

137. S.-O. Cheung, T. S. T. Ng, S.-P. Wong, & H. C. H. Suen, 2003, Behavioral aspects in construction partnering, *International Journal of Project Management*, 21: 333–344.

138. P. M. Norman, 2002, Protecting knowledge in strategic alliances—Resource and relational characteristics, *Journal of High Technology Management Research*, 13(2): 177–202; P. M. Norman, 2001, Are your secrets safe? Knowledge protection in strategic alliances, *Business Horizons*, November/December, 51–60.

139. M. A. Hitt, M. T. Dacin, B. B. Tyler, & D. Park, 1997, Understanding the differences in Korean and U.S. executives strategic orientations, *Strategic Management Journal*, 18: 159–168.

140. 2003, Venu Srinivasan, *BusinessWeek Online*, http://www.businessweek.com, June 9.

141. P. Burrows, 2003, Cisco: In hot pursuit of a Chinese rival, *BusinessWeek Online*, http://www.businessweek.com, May 19.

142. R. Abratt & P. Motlana, 2002, Managing co-branding strategies: Global brands into local markets, *Business Horizons*, 45(5): 43–50; P. Lane, J. E. Salk, & M. A. Lyles, 2001, Absorptive capacity, learning, and performance in international joint ventures, *Strategic Management Journal*, 22: 1139–1161.

143. R. Grover, 2003, Is Steve about to move his cheese? *Business Week*, February 10, 72.

144. R. Larsson, K. R. Brousseau, M. J. Driver, & M. Homqvist, 2003, International growth through cooperation: Brand-driven strategies, leadership, and career development in Sweden, *Academy of Management Executive*, 17(1): 7–21; R. Larsson, L. Bengtsson, K. Henriksson, & J. Sparks, 1998, The interorganizational learning dilemma: Collective knowledge development in strategic alliances, *Organization Science*, 9: 285–305.

145. Ireland, Hitt, & Vaidyanath, Alliance management.

146. Reuer, Zollo, & Singh, Post-formation dynamics, 148.

147. J. H. Dyer, P. Kale, & H. Singh, 2001, How to make strategic alliances work, *MIT Sloan Management Review*, 42(4): 37–43.

148. J. H. Dyer, 1997, Effective interfirm collaboration: How firms minimize transaction costs and maximize transaction value, *Strategic Management Journal*, 18: 535–556.

149. J. H. Dyer & C. Wujin, 2003, The role of trustworthiness in reducing transaction costs and improving performance: Empirical evidence from the United States, Japan, and Korea, *Organization Science*, 14: 57–69.

150. 2003, Sony Ericsson venture to close sites and cut 500 jobs, *New York Times*, http://www.nytimes.com, June 25; J. L. Schenker, 2003, Sony Ericsson posts loss despite sales gain, *New York Times*, http://www.nytimes.com, July 16.

151. Hutt, Stafford, Walker, & Reingen, Case study: Defining the social network, 53.

152. D. L. Ferrin & K. T. Dirks, 2003, The use of rewards to increase and decrease trust: Mediating processes and differential effects, *Organization Science*, 14(1): 18–31; D. F. Jennings, K. Artz, L. M. Gillin, & C. Christodouloy, 2000, Determinants of trust in global strategic alliances: Amrad and the Australian biomedical industry, *Competitiveness Review*, 10(1): 25–44.

153. V. Perrone, A. Zaheer, & B. McEvily, 2003, Free to be trusted? Boundary constraints on trust in boundary spanners, *Organization Science*, 14: 422–439; H. K. Steensma, L. Marino, & K. M. Weaver, 2000, Attitudes toward cooperative strategies: A cross-cultural analysis of entrepreneurs, *Journal of International Business Studies*, 31: 591–609.

154. J. Child & Y. Yan, 2003, Predicting the performance of international joint ventures: An investigation in China, *Journal of Management Studies*, 40(2): 283–320.

155. L. Huff & L. Kelley, 2003, Levels of organizational trust in individualist versus collectivist societies: A seven-nation study, *Organization Science*, 14(1): 81–90.

156. S. J. Carson, A. Madhok, R. Varman, & G. John, 2003, Information processing moderators of the effectiveness of trust-based governance in interfirm R&D collaboration, *Organization Science*, 14(1): 45–56; A. Arino & J. de la Torre, 1998, Learning from failure: Towards an evolutionary model of collaborative ventures, *Organization Science*, 9: 306–325; J. B. Barney & M. H. Hansen, 1994, Trustworthiness: Can it be a source of competitive advantage? *Strategic Management Journal*, 15(Special Issue): 175–203.

157. Dyer & Wujin, The role of trustworthiness in reducing transaction costs and improving performance; R. Gulati & H. Singh, 1998, The architecture of cooperation: Managing coordination costs and appropriation concerns in strategic alliances, *Administrative Science Quarterly*, 43: 781–814; R. Gulati, 1996, Social structure and alliance formation patterns: A longitudinal analysis, *Administrative Science Quarterly*, 40: 619–652.

158. J. H. Davis, F. D. Schoorman, R. C. Mayer, & H. H. Tan, 2000, The trusted general manager and business unit performance: Empirical evidence of a competitive advantage, *Strategic Management Journal*, 21: 563–576; R. C. Mayer, J. H. Davis, & F. D. Schoorman, 1995, An integrative model of organizational trust, *Academy of Management Review*, 20: 709–734.

159. B. Hillebrand & W. G. Biemans, 2003, The relationship between internal and external cooperation: literature review and propositions, *Journal of Business Research*, 56: 735–744.

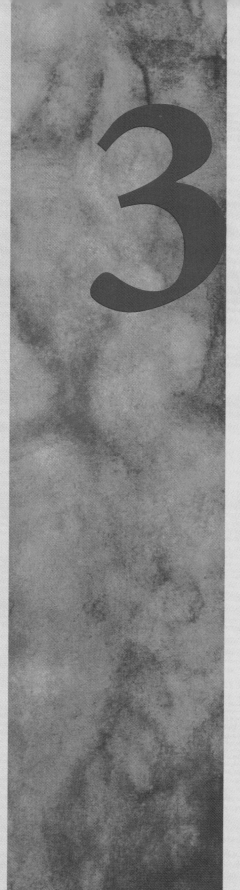

Part Three

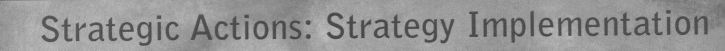

Strategic Actions: Strategy Implementation

Corporate Governance

Knowledge Objectives

Studying this chapter should provide you with the strategic management knowledge needed to:

1. Define corporate governance and explain why it is used to monitor and control managers' strategic decisions.

2. Explain why ownership has been largely separated from managerial control in the modern corporation.

3. Define an agency relationship and managerial opportunism and describe their strategic implications.

4. Explain how three internal governance mechanisms—ownership concentration, the board of directors, and executive compensation—are used to monitor and control managerial decisions.

5. Discuss the types of compensation executives receive and their effects on strategic decisions.

6. Describe how the external corporate governance mechanism—the market for corporate control—acts as a restraint on top-level managers' strategic decisions.

7. Discuss the use of corporate governance in international settings, in particular in Germany and Japan.

8. Describe how corporate governance fosters ethical strategic decisions and the importance of such behaviors on the part of top-level executives.

Digital Vision

Boards of directors are now under pressure to better control CEO pay and compensation. Given the amount of money involved, these decisions are integral to the strategic management process.

In light of the corporate scandals among large U.S. firms, the poor economy and bad performance of many companies, and the substantial layoffs and high unemployment engendered by the economy and poor corporate performance, high executive pay, especially for CEOs, has been controversial in the last few years. Given the substantial media publicity about CEO pay, scandals, and layoffs, many (e.g., union leaders, major investors, congressional representatives, and compensation experts) have questioned what they believe to be excessive pay received by CEOs. The question is, has this controversy and the heavy publicity changed pay practices in major corporations? The answer is twofold. In selected companies, changes have been made in pay practices, but in the aggregate, overall pay for CEOs remains largely unchanged.

Executive pay is difficult to compare because of the multiple components and comparison group. CEO pay, for example, is often composed of salary, bonuses, stock issued, and stock options. And, should total compensation include stock options valued at the time issued or the value when exercised? Also, average pay depends on the firms and the executives included in the group. For example, the *Wall Street Journal* reported that the top CEO pay in 2002 was $116.4 million given to Jeffrey Barbakow, CEO of Tenet Healthcare. The *Journal* focused on direct pay, however, including only the value of stock options exercised. Alternatively, *USA Today* reported the top CEO income for 2002 to be $188.8 million, given to Jeffrey Barbakow; but that figure included the value of options issued but not exercised. The *New York Times* reported that total CEO compensation declined by 20 percent in 2002 to an average $10.83 million, yet salaries, amount of stock received (not options), and other perquisites increased such that the median direct compensation grew by almost 17 percent. Therefore, the value of options decreased because of declines in the stock market, but boards of directors tried to "compensate" for this decline by increasing CEOs' direct compensation. These actions suggest that there have been few material changes in the CEO compensation practices in large U.S. firms.

Overall, CEO pay has remained high; the changes are relatively small. And, some CEOs are cashing out their stock holdings (or exercising options and then selling). In fact, if cashing out were included in the pay, Lee Raymond, CEO of ExxonMobil, would have been among those receiving the most compensation in 2002. And, Bill Gates sold $2.6 billion of Microsoft stock in 2002. But, some believe that potentially major changes are on the horizon. For example, some boards of directors are barring executives from making large sales of stock at one time. James Rogers, executive with Cinergy Corp., acquired 239,894 shares of stock by exercising options, but he is barred by policy from selling until 90 days after he leaves the company. Boards are now under strong pressure to better control CEO compensation and thus are more likely to take action than at any time in the past.

SOURCES: G. Strauss & B. Hansen, 2003, Bubble hasn't burst yet on CEO salaries despite the times, *USA Today*, http://www.usatoday.com, July 3; 2003, How CEO salary and bonus packages compare, *USA Today*, http://www.usatoday.com, July 3; 2003, How CEO compensation packages compare, *USA Today*, http://www.usatoday.com, July 3; 2003, Who made the biggest bucks, *Wall Street Journal Online*, http://www.wsj.com, April 14; J. Lublin, 2003, Why the get-rich-quick days for executives may be over, *Wall Street Journal Online*, http://www.wsj.com, April 14; J. Lublin, 2003, Under the radar, *Wall Street Journal Online*, http://www.wsj.com, April 14; L. Browning, 2003, The perks still flow (but with less fizz), *New York Times*, http://www.nytimes.com, April 6; D. Leonhardt, 2003, Is that your CEO cashing out? *New York Times*, http://www.nytimes.com, April 6; P. McGeehan, 2003, Again, money follows the pinstripes, *New York Times*, http://www.nytimes.com, April 6; S. Craig, 2003, Wall Street's CEOs still get fat paychecks despite woes, *Wall Street Journal Online*, http://www.wsj.com, March 4.

As the Opening Case illustrates, corporate governance is an increasingly important part of the strategic management process.[1] If the board makes the wrong decision in compensating the firm's strategic leader, the CEO, the shareholders, and the firm suffer. Compensation is used to motivate CEOs to act in the best interests of the firm—in particular, the shareholders. When they do, the firm's value should increase.

What are a CEO's actions worth? The Opening Case suggests that they are worth a significant amount in the United States. While some critics argue that U.S. CEOs are paid too much, the hefty increases in their compensation in recent years ostensibly have come from linking their pay to their firms' performance, and U.S. firms have performed better than many companies in other countries. However, research suggests that firms with a smaller pay gap between the CEO and other top executives perform better, especially when collaboration among top management team members is more important.[2] The performance improvement is attributed to better cooperation among the top management team members. Other research suggests that CEOs receive excessive compensation when corporate governance is the weakest.[3] Also, as noted in the Opening Case, there has been little change in the compensation practices used for top executives over the last several years despite increasing criticism. However, it appears that some changes in policy are beginning to occur, such as the restriction barring the selling of stock gained from options until after the executive's employment with the company ends.

Corporate governance represents the relationship among stakeholders that is used to determine and control the strategic direction and performance of organizations.[4] At its core, corporate governance is concerned with identifying ways to ensure that strategic decisions are made effectively.[5] Governance can also be thought of as a means corporations use to establish order between parties (the firm's owners and its top-level managers) whose interests may conflict. Thus, corporate governance reflects and enforces the company's values.[6] In modern corporations—especially those in the United States and the United Kingdom—a primary objective of corporate governance is to ensure that the interests of top-level managers are aligned with the interests of the shareholders. Corporate governance involves oversight in areas where owners, managers, and members of boards of directors may have conflicts of interest. These areas include the election of directors, the general supervision of CEO pay and more focused supervision of director pay, and the corporation's overall structure and strategic direction.[7]

Corporate governance has been emphasized in recent years because, as the Opening Case illustrates, corporate governance mechanisms occasionally fail to adequately monitor and control top-level managers' decisions. This situation has resulted in changes in governance mechanisms in corporations throughout the world, especially with respect to efforts intended to improve the performance of boards of directors. A second and more positive reason for this interest is that evidence suggests that a well-

Corporate governance represents the relationship among stakeholders that is used to determine and control the strategic direction and performance of organizations.

functioning corporate governance and control system can create a competitive advantage for an individual firm.[8] For example, one governance mechanism—the board of directors—has been suggested to be rapidly evolving into a major strategic force in U.S. business firms.[9] Thus, in this chapter, we describe actions designed to implement strategies that focus on monitoring and controlling mechanisms, which can help to ensure that top-level managerial actions contribute to the firm's strategic competitiveness and its ability to earn above-average returns.

Effective corporate governance is also of interest to nations.[10] As stated by one scholar, "Every country wants the firms that operate within its borders to flourish and grow in such ways as to provide employment, wealth, and satisfaction, not only to improve standards of living materially but also to enhance social cohesion. These aspirations cannot be met unless those firms are competitive internationally in a sustained way, and it is this medium- and long-term perspective that makes good corporate governance so vital."[11]

Corporate governance, then, reflects company standards, which in turn collectively reflect societal standards.[12] In many individual corporations, shareholders hold top-level managers accountable for their decisions and the results they generate. As with these individual firms and their boards, nations that effectively govern their corporations may gain a competitive advantage over rival countries. In a range of countries, but especially in the United States and the United Kingdom, the fundamental goal of business organizations is to maximize shareholder value.[13] Traditionally, shareholders are treated as the firm's key stakeholders, because they are the company's legal owners. The firm's owners expect top-level managers and others influencing the corporation's actions (for example, the board of directors) to make decisions that will result in the maximization of the company's value and, hence, of the owners' wealth.[14]

In the first section of this chapter, we describe the relationship providing the foundation on which the modern corporation is built: the relationship between owners and managers. The majority of this chapter is used to explain various mechanisms owners use to govern managers and to ensure that they comply with their responsibility to maximize shareholder value.

Three internal governance mechanisms and a single external one are used in the modern corporation (see Table 10.1). The three internal governance mechanisms we describe in this chapter are (1) ownership concentration, as represented by types of shareholders and their different incentives to monitor managers, (2) the board of directors, and (3) executive compensation. We then consider the market for corporate control, an external corporate governance mechanism. Essentially, this market is a set of potential owners seeking to acquire undervalued firms and earn above-average returns on their investments by replacing ineffective top-level management teams.[15] The chapter's focus then shifts to the issue of international corporate governance. We briefly describe governance approaches used in German and Japanese firms whose traditional governance structures are being affected by the realities of global competition. In part, this discussion suggests the possibility that the structures used to govern global companies in many different countries, including Germany, Japan, the United Kingdom, and the United States, are becoming more, rather than less, similar. Closing our analysis of corporate governance is a consideration of the need for these control mechanisms to encourage and support ethical behavior in organizations.

Importantly, the mechanisms discussed in this chapter can positively influence the governance of the modern corporation, which has placed significant responsibility and authority in the hands of top-level managers. The most effective managers understand their accountability for the firm's performance and respond positively to corporate governance mechanisms.[16] In addition, the firm's owners should not expect any single mechanism to remain effective over time. Rather, the use of several mechanisms allows owners to govern the corporation in ways that maximize strategic competitiveness and

Table 10.1 ——— Corporate Governance Mechanisms

Internal Governance Mechanisms

Ownership Concentration
- Relative amounts of stock owned by individual shareholders and institutional investors

Board of Directors
- Individuals responsible for representing the firm's owners by monitoring top-level managers' strategic decisions

Executive Compensation
- Use of salary, bonuses, and long-term incentives to align managers' interests with shareholders' interests

External Governance Mechanism

Market for Corporate Control
- The purchase of a company that is underperforming relative to industry rivals in order to improve the firm's strategic competitiveness

increase the financial value of their firm. With multiple governance mechanisms operating simultaneously, however, it is also possible for some of the governance mechanisms to be in conflict.[17] Later, we review how these conflicts can occur.

Separation of Ownership and Managerial Control

Historically, the founder-owners and their descendants managed U.S. firms. In these cases, corporate ownership and control resided in the same persons. As firms grew larger, "the managerial revolution led to a separation of ownership and control in most large corporations, where control of the firm shifted from entrepreneurs to professional managers while ownership became dispersed among thousands of unorganized stockholders who were removed from the day-to-day management of the firm."[18] These changes created the modern public corporation, which is based on the efficient separation of ownership and managerial control. Supporting the separation is a basic legal premise suggesting that the primary objective of a firm's activities is to increase the corporation's profit and, thereby, the financial gains of the owners (the shareholders).[19]

The separation of ownership and managerial control allows shareholders to purchase stock, which entitles them to income (residual returns) from the firm's operations after paying expenses. This right, however, requires that they also take a risk that the firm's expenses may exceed its revenues. To manage this investment risk, shareholders maintain a diversified portfolio by investing in several companies to reduce their overall risk.[20] As shareholders diversify their investments over a number of corporations, their risk declines. The poor performance or failure of any one firm in which they invest has less overall effect. Thus, shareholders specialize in managing their investment risk.

In small firms, managers often are high percentage owners, so there is less separation between ownership and managerial control. In fact, there are a large number of family-owned firms in which ownership and managerial control are not separated. In the United States, families have a substantial ownership of at least one-third of the S&P top 500 firms. Furthermore, families own about 18 percent of the outstanding equity. And, family-owned firms perform better when a member of the family is CEO than when the CEO is an outsider.[21] In many countries outside the United States, such as in Latin America, Asia, and some European countries, family-owned firms represent the dominant form.[22] The primary purpose of most of these firms is to increase the family's wealth, which explains why a family CEO often is better than an outside CEO.[23] There are at least two critical issues for family-controlled firms. First, as they grow, they may not have access to all of the skills needed to effectively manage the firm and maximize its returns for the family. Thus, they may need outsiders. Also, as they grow, they may need to seek outside capital and thus give up some of the ownership. In these cases, protection of the minority owners' rights becomes important.[24] To avoid these potential problems, when these firms grow and become more complex, their owner-managers may contract with managerial specialists. These managers make major decisions in the owner's firm and are compensated on the basis of their decision-making skills. As decision-making specialists, managers are agents of the firm's owners and are expected to use their decision-making skills to operate the owners' firm in ways that will maximize the return on their investment.[25]

Without owner (shareholder) specialization in risk bearing and management specialization in decision making, a firm may be limited by the abilities of its owners to manage and make effective strategic decisions. Thus, the separation and specialization of ownership (risk bearing) and managerial control (decision making) should produce the highest returns for the firm's owners.

Shareholder value is reflected by the price of the firm's stock. As stated earlier, corporate governance mechanisms, such as the board of directors or compensation based on the performance of a firm, is the reason that CEOs show general concern about the firm's stock price. For example, Cisco earned the dubious honor in 2001 of losing the most in shareholder value: $156 billion for the year. Furthermore, it lost $456 billion between March 2000 and December 2001. On a more positive note, it is fair to report that over its lifetime, Cisco has created significant wealth for its investors and managers; it ranks 11th overall in regard to wealth creation.[26] And, while Cisco experienced a net loss of slightly over $1 billion in fiscal 2001, it had a net profit of more than $1.8 billion in fiscal 2002. And, its stock price in July 2003 (the end of its fiscal year) was approximately 8.5 percent higher than the highest price achieved in its fourth quarter of fiscal 2002.[27] As a result, Cisco's future is looking much brighter, and it is beginning to rebuild shareholder value.

An agency relationship exists when one or more persons (the principal or principals) hire another person or persons (the agent or agents) as decision-making specialists to perform a service.

CEO John Chambers is helping to rebuild Cisco's lost shareholder value.

©Reuters NewMedia Inc./CORBIS

Agency Relationships

The separation between owners and managers creates an agency relationship. An **agency relationship** exists when one or more persons (the principal or principals) hire another person or persons (the agent or agents) as decision-making specialists to perform a service.[28] Thus, an agency relationship exists when one party delegates decision-making responsibility to a second party for compensation (see Figure 10.1).[29] In addition to shareholders and top executives, other examples of agency relationships are consultants and clients and insured and insurer. Moreover, within organizations, an agency relationship exists between managers and their employees, as well as between top executives and the firm's owners.[30] In the modern corporation, managers must understand the links between these relationships and the firm's effectiveness.[31] Although the agency relationship between managers and their employees is important, in this chapter we focus on the agency relationship between the firm's owners (the principals) and top-level managers (the principals' agents), because this relationship is related directly to how the firm's strategies are implemented.

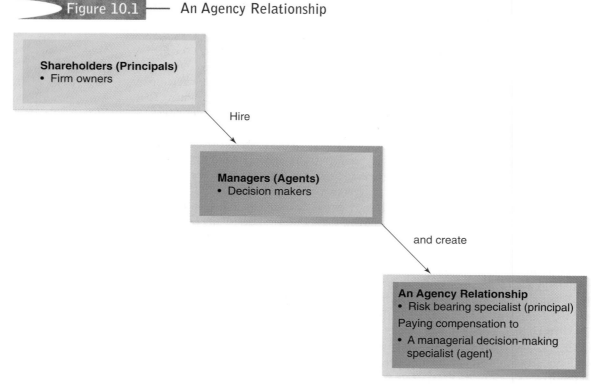

Figure 10.1 — An Agency Relationship

Shareholders (Principals)
• Firm owners

Hire

Managers (Agents)
• Decision makers

and create

An Agency Relationship
• Risk bearing specialist (principal)

Paying compensation to

• A managerial decision-making
  specialist (agent)

The separation between ownership and managerial control can be problematic. Research evidence documents a variety of agency problems in the modern corporation.[32] Problems can surface because the principal and the agent have different interests and goals, or because shareholders lack direct control of large publicly traded corporations. Problems also arise when an agent makes decisions that result in the pursuit of goals that conflict with those of the principals. Thus, the separation of ownership and control potentially allows divergent interests (between principals and agents) to surface, which can lead to managerial opportunism.

Managerial opportunism is the seeking of self-interest with guile (i.e., cunning or deceit).[33] Opportunism is both an attitude (e.g., an inclination) and a set of behaviors (i.e., specific acts of self-interest).[34] It is not possible for principals to know beforehand which agents will or will not act opportunistically. The reputations of top executives are an imperfect predictor, and opportunistic behavior cannot be observed until it has occurred. Thus, principals establish governance and control mechanisms to prevent agents from acting opportunistically, even though only a few are likely to do so.[35] Any time that principals delegate decision-making responsibilities to agents, the opportunity for conflicts of interest exists. Top executives, for example, may make strategic decisions that maximize their personal welfare and minimize their personal risk.[36] Decisions such as these prevent the maximization of shareholder wealth. Decisions regarding product diversification demonstrate these possibilities.

Managerial opportunism is the seeking of self-interest with guile (i.e., cunning or deceit).

Product Diversification as an Example of an Agency Problem

As explained in Chapter 6, a corporate-level strategy to diversify the firm's product lines can enhance a firm's strategic competitiveness and increase its returns, both of which serve the interests of shareholders and the top executives. However, product diversification can result in two benefits to managers that shareholders do not enjoy, so top executives may prefer more product diversification than do shareholders.[37]

First, diversification usually increases the size of a firm, and size is positively related to executive compensation. Also, diversification increases the complexity of managing a firm and its network of businesses and may thus require more pay because of this complexity.[38] Thus, increased product diversification provides an opportunity for top executives to increase their compensation.[39]

Second, product diversification and the resulting diversification of the firm's portfolio of businesses can reduce top executives' employment risk. Managerial employment risk is the risk of job loss, loss of compensation, and loss of managerial reputation.[40] These risks are reduced with increased diversification, because a firm and its upper-level managers are less vulnerable to the reduction in demand associated with a single or limited number of product lines or businesses. For example, Gemplus International named Antonio Perez as its CEO in 2000. With his 25-year career at Hewlett-Packard, Perez had a good reputation in the business world and his Hewlett-Packard experience seemed to be perfect preparation for his new position. Gemplus, headquartered at the time in France, is the world's top producer of smart cards (microchips used in telephones and credit cards), and is highly focused on a narrow product market. Perez' appointment was met with outrage by the French media over the $97 million worth of stock and options he received when he was hired. This focus has positive attributes, but the substantial downturn in telecommunications, the major market for smart cards, and the economic slump led to a major reduction in Gemplus' revenues and large net losses. Perez gave back the options trying to appease shareholders. However, the poor performance and a battle with the company founder led to Perez' resignation, forced by the firm's major shareholders. Perez' employment risk was higher because the firm lacked significant product diversification, which is probably why he received significant compensation in the form of stock and options when he began his tenure with Gemplus.[41] In fact, Gemplus has had two CEOs in the short time since Perez left, and has engaged in significant restructuring, showing the risks of low diversification.[42]

Another concern that may represent an agency problem is a firm's free cash flows over which top executives have control. Free cash flows are resources remaining after the firm has invested in all projects that have positive net present values within its current businesses.[43] In anticipation of positive returns, managers may decide to invest these funds in products that are not associated with the firm's current lines of business to increase the firm's level of diversification. The managerial decision to use free cash flows to overdiversify the firm is an example of self-serving and opportunistic managerial behavior. In contrast to managers, shareholders may prefer that free cash flows be distributed to them as dividends, so they can control how the cash is invested.[44]

Curve S in Figure 10.2 depicts the shareholders' optimal level of diversification. Owners seek the level of diversification that reduces the risk of the firm's total failure while simultaneously increasing the company's value through the development of economies of scale and scope (see Chapter 6). Of the four corporate-level diversification strategies shown in Figure 10.2, shareholders likely prefer the diversified position noted by point A on curve S—a position that is located between the dominant business and related-constrained diversification strategies. Of course, the optimum level of diversification owners seek varies from firm to firm.[45] Factors that affect shareholders' preferences include the firm's primary industry, the intensity of rivalry among competitors in that industry, and the top management team's experience with implementing diversification strategies.

As do principals, upper-level executives—as agents—also seek an optimal level of diversification. Declining performance resulting from too much product diversification increases the probability that corporate control of the firm will be acquired in the market. After a firm is acquired, the employment risk for the firm's top executives

Figure 10.2 — Manager and Shareholder Risk and Diversification

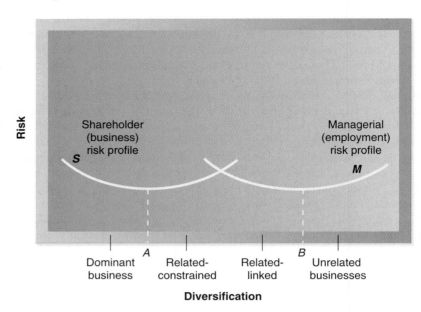

Figure 10.2 — Manager and Shareholder Risk and Diversification

increases substantially. Furthermore, a manager's employment opportunities in the external managerial labor market (discussed in Chapter 12) are affected negatively by a firm's poor performance. Therefore, top executives prefer diversification, but not to a point that it increases their employment risk and reduces their employment opportunities.[46] Curve *M* in Figure 10.2 shows that executives prefer higher levels of product diversification than do shareholders. Top executives might prefer the level of diversification shown by point *B* on curve *M*.

In general, shareholders prefer riskier strategies and more focused diversification. They reduce their risk through holding a diversified portfolio of equity investments. Alternatively, managers obviously cannot balance their employment risk by working for a diverse portfolio of firms. Therefore, top executives may prefer a level of diversification that maximizes firm size and their compensation and that reduces their employment risk. Product diversification, therefore, is a potential agency problem that could result in principals incurring costs to control their agents' behaviors.

Agency Costs and Governance Mechanisms

The potential conflict illustrated by Figure 10.2, coupled with the fact that principals do not know which managers might act opportunistically, demonstrates why principals establish governance mechanisms. However, the firm incurs costs when it uses one or more governance mechanisms. **Agency costs** are the sum of incentive costs, monitoring costs, enforcement costs, and individual financial losses incurred by principals, because governance mechanisms cannot guarantee total compliance by the agent. If a firm is diversified, governance costs increase because it is more difficult to monitor what is going on inside the firm.[47]

In general, managerial interests may prevail when governance mechanisms are weak, as is exemplified by allowing managers a significant amount of autonomy to make strategic decisions. If, however, the board of directors controls managerial autonomy, or if other strong governance mechanisms are used, the firm's strategies should better reflect the interests of the shareholders.

Agency costs are the sum of incentive costs, monitoring costs, enforcement costs, and individual financial losses incurred by principals, because governance mechanisms cannot guarantee total compliance by the agent.

Research suggests that even using more governance mechanisms may produce major changes in strategies. Firms acquired unrelated businesses at approximately the same rate in the 1980s as they did in the 1960s, even though more governance mechanisms were employed in the 1980s. Thus, governance mechanisms are an imperfect means of controlling managerial opportunism.[48] Alternatively, other evidence suggests that active shareholders, especially institutional investors, are more willing to try to remove the CEO leading a firm that is performing poorly. The actions taken at Gemplus International, as explained above, demonstrate this willingness.[49]

Next, we explain the effects of different governance mechanisms on the decisions managers make about the choice and the use of the firm's strategies.

Ownership Concentration

Both the number of large-block shareholders and the total percentage of shares they own define **ownership concentration. Large-block shareholders** typically own at least 5 percent of a corporation's issued shares. Ownership concentration as a governance mechanism has received considerable interest because large-block shareholders are increasingly active in their demands that corporations adopt effective governance mechanisms to control managerial decisions.[50]

In general, diffuse ownership (a large number of shareholders with small holdings and few, if any, large-block shareholders) produces weak monitoring of managers' decisions. Among other problems, diffuse ownership makes it difficult for owners to effectively coordinate their actions. Diversification of the firm's product lines beyond the shareholders' optimum level can result from ineffective monitoring of managers' decisions. Higher levels of monitoring could encourage managers to avoid strategic decisions that harm shareholder value. In fact, research evidence shows that ownership concentration is associated with lower levels of firm product diversification.[51] Thus, with high degrees of ownership concentration, the probability is greater that managers' strategic decisions will be intended to maximize shareholder value. Much of this concentration has come from increasing equity ownership by institutional investors.

The Growing Influence of Institutional Owners

A classic work published in the 1930s argued that the "modern" corporation had become characterized by a separation of ownership and control.[52] This change occurred primarily because growth prevented founders-owners from maintaining their dual positions in their increasingly complex companies. More recently, another shift has occurred: ownership of many modern corporations is now concentrated in the hands of institutional investors rather than individual shareholders.[53]

Institutional owners are financial institutions such as stock mutual funds and pension funds that control large-block shareholder positions. Because of their prominent ownership positions, institutional owners, as large-block shareholders, are a powerful governance mechanism. Institutions of these types now own more than 50 percent of the stock in large U.S. corporations, and of the top 1,000 corporations, they own, on average, 56 percent of the stock. Pension funds alone control at least one-half of corporate equity.[54]

These ownership percentages suggest that as investors, institutional owners have both the size and the incentive to discipline ineffective top-level managers and can significantly influence a firm's choice of strategies and overall strategic decisions.[55] Research evidence indicates that institutional and other large-block shareholders are becoming more active in their efforts to influence a corporation's strategic decisions. Initially, these shareholder activists and institutional investors concentrated on the performance and accountability of CEOs and contributed to the ouster of a number of them. They are now targeting what they believe are ineffective boards of directors.[56]

Ownership concentration *is defined by both the number of large-block shareholders and the total percentage of shares they own.*

Large-block shareholders *typically own at least 5 percent of a corporation's issued shares.*

Institutional owners *are financial institutions such as stock mutual funds and pension funds that control large-block shareholder positions.*

For example, CalPERS provides retirement and health coverage to over 1.3 million current and retired public employees.[57] As the largest public employee pension fund in the United States, CalPERS is generally thought to act aggressively to promote decisions and actions that it believes will enhance shareholder value in companies in which it invests. As noted in the Strategic Focus, CalPERS is currently focusing on problems with executive compensation as exemplified by the addition of executive pay to its corporate governance principles. However, CalPERS has also become a target because of concerns about its own governance. As a result, it announced in 2003 that it would begin releasing information on the performance of fund-of-fund investments (e.g., on Grove Street Advisors, which manages about $2 billion of CalPERS monies).[58] The largest institutional investor, TIAA-CREF, has taken actions similar to those of CalPERS, but with a less publicly aggressive stance. To date, research suggests that these institutions' activism may not have a direct effect on firm performance, but that its influence may be indirect through its effects on important strategic decisions, such as those concerned with international diversification and innovation.[59]

The Strategic Focus suggests that institutional investors are not the only ones who have become active. Small investors, such as in the case of John Hancock Financial Services, and large investors, such as KKR, a buyout firm that forced out a CEO with which it disagreed on strategy, are becoming more active on governance issues. Thus, shareholder activism has become an important issue related to corporate governance.

Shareholder Activism: How Much Is Possible?

The U.S. Securities and Exchange Commission (SEC) has issued several rulings that support shareholder involvement and control of managerial decisions. For example, the SEC eased its rule regarding communications among shareholders. Historically, shareholders could communicate among themselves only through a cumbersome and expensive filing process. Now, with a simple notification to the SEC of an upcoming meeting, shareholders can convene to discuss a corporation's strategic direction. If a consensus on an issue exists, shareholders can vote as a block. As a result of the new policies, proxy fights are becoming more common.[60]

Some argue that greater latitude should be extended to those managing the funds of large institutional investor groups, believing that allowing these individuals to hold positions on boards of firms in which their organizations have significant investments might enable fund managers to better represent the interests of those they serve.[61] However, the actions of traditionally activist institutional investor CalPERS were potentially compromised by investments it had in Enron. Institutional activism should create a premium for companies with good corporate governance. However, trustees for these funds sometimes have other relationships that compromise their effectiveness, as apparently was the case for CalPERS. It is more often the case that large *private* pension funds, which have other business relationships with companies in their fund's portfolio, reduce effective monitoring.[62] Alternatively, mutual funds such as the Vanguard Group also have increasing influence because of their substantial equity holdings.

Also, the degree to which institutional investors can effectively monitor the decisions being made in all of the companies in which they have investments is questionable. Historically, CalPERS targeted 12 companies at a time for improvement. The New York State Teachers' Retirement System, another activist institutional investor, focuses on 25 of the 1,300-plus companies in its investment portfolio. Given limited resources, even large-block shareholders tend to concentrate on corporations in which they have significant investments. Thus, although shareholder activism has increased, institutional investors face barriers to the amount of active governance they can realistically employ.[63] Furthermore, at times, activist institutional shareholders may have conflicting goals.[64] Other means of corporate governance are needed.

In addition to institutional owners, other owners are able to influence the decisions managers make as agents. Although other investors have significant influence, battles are

The Growing Activism of Shareholders

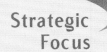

Institutional Shareholder Services Inc. (ISS) has developed a service that evaluates companies and ranks them based on the quality of their governance. ISS provides advice and information to institutional investors on proxy issues. It is a powerful organization that has over $40 million in revenue. An ISS rating results in a numerical score, but the criteria used provide guidelines for improving a firm's governance. Some of the criteria used for the evaluation include the percentage of outside board members, the independence of key board committees, the existence of poison pill defenses against takeovers, and the type and amount of executive compensation. Others provide these services, and some criteria in the ISS evaluation scheme have been criticized for lack of a basis in research. The ISS tool, called the Corporate Governance Quotient, has become influential, and many companies are buying access to it to improve their governance and ratings.

CalPERS (California Public Employees Retirement System) is a large institutional investor known for its activism. For example, in June 2003, it announced actions to ensure that firms carefully consider shareholders' interests when they develop executive compensation plans. These actions are designed to focus on abusive executive compensation. The leadership at CalPERS is especially concerned about practices that provide incentives, purposeful or otherwise, for short-term oriented or self-interested behavior on the part of executives. As an example, CalPERS actively opposed the planned $35 million "golden farewell" for the CEO of GlaxoSmithKline, Jean-Pierre Garnier, at the firm's annual shareholders' meeting held in 2003. While the vote was purely advisory to the board, it forced the board to publicly defend its actions.

Other shareholders are following CalPERS lead and taking up the gauntlet. For example, Halliburton shareholders expressed dissatisfaction that the board had developed severance agreements that shareholders considered excessive. Although a vote to require all future agreements to have shareholder approval failed, 36.5 percent voted for the measure, putting the board on notice. A lawsuit was filed against John Hancock Financial Services regarding excessive pay to its CEO and other senior executives. Highfields Capital Management, the largest shareholder in the Janus Capital Group, opposed a $15 million bonus for five executives because of the lack of disclosure in the 2002 proxy statement regarding significant compensation paid to top executives. Other top executives have been pressured by major shareholders to take specific actions. For example, shareholders pressured the CEO of Hollinger International, Lord Black, to restructure the shareholder voting procedures and to accept less compensation. More extreme, KKR, as a major shareholder, pressured the CEO of Primedia, Thomas Rogers, to resign.

Other institutional investors have become active in a different way. Jack Brennan is CEO of Vanguard Group, the second largest mutual fund with approximately $557 billion in assets in 2003. Brennan wrote a letter to 450 companies in which it owns at least 3 percent of the stock to express the emphasis that Vanguard now places on effective governance and honest accounting processes (and outcomes). Brennan believes that incentive pay for executives should be linked to long-term performance of the firm. His advice is being sought by such firms as General Electric on ways to make boards of directors more independent.

SOURCES: J. B. Treaster, 2003, Shareholder sues John Hancock over executive pay levels, *New York Times*, http://www.nytimes.com, May 29; S. Kirchgaessner & A. Beard, 2003, Hollinger chief bows to investor pressure, *Financial Times*, http://www.ft.com, May 23; 2003, Revolting shareholders, *The Economist*, http://www.economist.com, May 22; S. McNulty, 2003, Halliburton investors kick against pay, *Financial Times*, http://www.ft.com, May 21; G. Dyer, 2003, CalPERS to take stance on executive pay at GSK, *Financial Times*, http://www.ft.com, May 9; J. Earle, 2003, Investors oppose Janus bosses' $15m bonuses, *Financial Times*, http://www.ft.com, May 8; M. Rose, 2003, Pressured by KKR, Primedia CEO resigns, *Wall Street Journal*, April 18, B1, B3; J. Sonnenfeld, 2003, Some research is missing in governance quotients, *Wall Street Journal Online*, http://www.wsj.com, April 1; A. Lucchetti, 2003, Vanguard CEO Jack Brennan makes his demands heard, *Wall Street Journal Online*, http://www.wsj.com, February 6; M. Langley, 2003, Want to lift your firm's rating on governance? Buy the test, *Wall Street Journal*, June 6, A1, A6.

not likely to be won or lost unless institutional investors are involved because they currently are such significant shareholders. Texas billionaire Sam Wyly sold his company, Sterling Software, to Computer Associates in 2000. Wyly fought to elect a new Computer Associates board that would in turn elect him to be Computer Associates' chairman. He argued that Computer Associates, the fourth largest software company in the world, had not performed well since 1996 and had alienated customers and employees.[65] Wyly was unsuccessful in his attempt to take over the leadership of Computer Associates, but his revised plan won the support of CalPERS and other investors. Even though Wyly lost his attempt at leadership, Computer Associates made significant improvements in its corporate governance procedures. It made a commitment to financial transparency and to using "state-of-the-art" corporate governance principles. For example, it developed a policy of having 75 percent of the board members be independent outsiders and established a lead director position.[66]

Corporate governance may also by affected by the recent phenomenon of increased managerial ownership of the firm's stock. There are many positive reasons for managerial ownership. However, an unexpected outcome of managerial ownership has been reduced support for shareholder-sponsored proposals to repeal anti-takeover provisions. Institutional owners generally support the repeal of these provisions because shareholder wealth is typically increased if a takeover is offered, while managerial owners, whose jobs are at risk if a takeover is executed, generally oppose their repeal. Thus, managerial ownership provides managers with power to protect their own interests.[67]

Board of Directors

Typically, shareholders monitor the managerial decisions and actions of a firm through the board of directors. Shareholders elect members to their firm's board. Those who are elected are expected to oversee managers and to ensure that the corporation is operated in ways that will maximize its shareholders' wealth. Even with large institutional investors having major equity ownership in U.S. firms, diffuse ownership continues to exist in most firms, which means that monitoring and control of managers by individual shareholders is limited in large corporations. Furthermore, large financial institutions, such as banks, are prevented from directly owning stock in firms and from having representatives on companies' boards of directors, although this is not the case in Europe and elsewhere.[68] These conditions highlight the importance of the board of directors for corporate governance. Unfortunately, over time, boards of directors have not been highly effective in monitoring and controlling top management's actions.[69] As noted in the Strategic Focus, boards are experiencing increasing pressure from shareholders, lawmakers, and regulators to become more forceful in their oversight role and thereby forestall inappropriate actions by top executives. While boards of directors are imperfect, they have the potential to positively influence both managers and the companies they serve.[70] If changes are instituted as recommended by the panel described in the Strategic Focus, boards will have even more power to influence the actions of managers and the directions of their companies. Furthermore, boards not only serve a monitoring role, but they also provide resources to firms. These resources include their personal knowledge and expertise as well as their access to resources of other firms through their external contacts and relationships.[71]

The **board of directors** is a group of elected individuals whose primary responsibility is to act in the owners' interests by formally monitoring and controlling the corporation's top-level executives.[72] Boards have power to direct the affairs of the organization, punish and reward managers, and protect shareholders' rights and interests.[73] Thus, an appropriately structured and effective board of directors protects owners from managerial opportunism. Board members are seen as stewards of their company's resources, and the way they carry out these responsibilities affects the society in which their firm operates.[74]

The **board of directors** is a group of elected individuals whose primary responsibility is to act in the owners' interests by formally monitoring and controlling the corporation's top-level executives.

Generally, board members (often called directors) are classified into one of three groups (see Table 10.2). *Insiders* are active top-level managers in the corporation who are elected to the board because they are a source of information about the firm's day-to-day operations.[75] *Related outsiders* have some relationship with the firm, contractual or otherwise, that may create questions about their independence, but these individuals are not involved with the corporation's day-to-day activities. *Outsiders* provide independent counsel to the firm and may hold top-level managerial positions in other companies or may have been elected to the board prior to the beginning of the current CEO's tenure.[76]

Recently, a number of critics have argued that many boards are not fulfilling their primary fiduciary duty to protect shareholders. Among other possibilities, it may be that boards represent a managerial tool: they do not question managers' actions, and they readily approve managers' self-serving initiatives.[77] In general, those critical of boards as a governance mechanism believe that inside managers dominate boards and exploit their personal ties with them. A widely accepted view is that a board with a significant percentage of its membership from the firm's top executives tends to provide relatively weak monitoring and control of managerial decisions.[78]

Critics advocate reforms to ensure that independent outside directors represent a significant majority of the total membership of a board.[79] Critics have become highly vocal as indicated in the Strategic Focus. As suggested in the Strategic Focus, changes are likely to be made that strengthen the boards and weaken the power of CEOs, in particular. For example, Cendant Corporation has instituted major changes, including the requirement that two-thirds of the directors be independent outsiders. Recent research suggests that firms with more independent outside directors tend to make higher-quality strategic decisions.[80] Alternatively, others argue that having outside directors is not enough to resolve the problems; it depends on the power of the CEO. In some cases, the CEO's power reduces the effectiveness of outside board members.[81]

One criticism of boards has been that some have not been vigilant enough in hiring and then monitoring the behavior of CEOs. For example, Albert Dunlap, the former CEO at Sunbeam, agreed to settle a shareholder lawsuit brought against him (and other former executives) for $15 million out of his own pocket. A number of questionable acquisitions had been made by the Dunlap team, ultimately spreading the company too thin and causing Sunbeam to file for Chapter 11 bankruptcy.[82] The Sunbeam board must share the blame in the failure for two reasons. First, it selected the CEO. Second, the board should have been actively involved in the development of the firm's strategy—if the strategy fails, the board has failed.[83] Sunbeam emerged from bankruptcy in late 2002 and changed its name to American Household. The firm is not in good financial shape (its stock sold at less than four cents when it came out of bankruptcy). The former CEO and the board of Sunbeam obviously failed the shareholders.[84]

Classifications of Boards of Directors' Members	Table 10.2

Insiders
- The firm's CEO and other top-level managers

Related outsiders
- Individuals not involved with the firm's day-to-day operations, but who have a relationship with the company

Outsiders
- Individuals who are independent of the firm in terms of day-to-day operations and other relationships

Other issues, in addition to criticisms of their work, affect today's corporate boards. For example, there is some disagreement about the most appropriate role of outside directors in a firm's strategic decision-making process.[85] In 1984, the New York Stock Exchange started requiring that listed firms have board audit committees composed solely of outside directors.[86] As a result of external pressures, boards of large corporations have more outside members. Therefore, there are potential strategic implications associated with the movement toward having corporate boards dominated by outsiders. But, with the recent scandals, the Sarbanes-Oxley corporate governance bill was passed and signed into law. It requires CEOs and chief financial officers (CFOs) to sign their accounting reports, certifying the reports' accuracy. They are threatened with criminal prosecution if they knowingly certify false documents. Thus, top executives have pressure to hire audit help to ensure the accuracy of their reports. Furthermore, their desire for a strong audit committee on the board of directors is increased.[87]

Alternatively, a large number of outside board members can also create some problems. Outsiders do not have contact with the firm's day-to-day operations and typically do not have easy access to the level of information about managers and their skills that is required to effectively evaluate managerial decisions and initiatives. Outsiders can, however, obtain valuable information through frequent interactions with inside board members, during board meetings and otherwise. Insiders possess such information by virtue of their organizational positions. Thus, boards with a critical mass of insiders typically are better informed about intended strategic initiatives, the reasons for the initiatives, and the outcomes expected from them.[88] Without this type of information, outsider-dominated boards may emphasize the use of financial, as opposed to strategic, controls to gather performance information to evaluate managers' and business units' performances. A virtually exclusive reliance on financial evaluations shifts risk to top-level managers, who, in turn, may make decisions to maximize their interests and reduce their employment risk. Reductions in R&D investments, additional diversification of the firm, and the pursuit of greater levels of compensation are some of the results of managers' actions to achieve financial goals set by outsider-dominated boards.[89]

Enhancing the Effectiveness of the Board of Directors

Because of the importance of boards of directors in corporate governance and as a result of increased scrutiny from shareholders—in particular, large institutional investors—the performances of individual board members and of entire boards are being evaluated more formally and with greater intensity.[90] Given the demand for greater accountability and improved performance, many boards have initiated voluntary changes. Among these changes are (1) increases in the diversity of the backgrounds of board members (for example, a greater number of directors from public service, academic, and scientific settings; a greater percentage of boards with ethnic minorities and women; and members from different countries on boards of U.S. firms), (2) the strengthening of internal management and accounting control systems, and (3) the establishment and consistent use of formal processes to evaluate the board's performance.[91] Additional changes suggested in the

Renault board of directors during a typical business meeting. Increased pressure is being applied to all boards of directors for greater accountability and improved performance. One of the many cited areas in need of improvement is increased diversity, because many boards are still composed primarily of Caucasian males.

©PITCHAL FREDERIC/CORBIS SYGMA

Controversy in the Boardroom

According to a special report on corporate governance published in the *Wall Street Journal*, "Boards of directors have been put on notice." Because of the major scandals in U.S. corporations, shareholders, congressional representatives, and regulators are placing strong pressure on boards of directors to make a number of changes that, in effect, shift the power from CEOs to directors. This pressure includes expectations that directors will be more conscientious in the discharge of their responsibilities.

Institutional investors are placing pressures on firms and boards to separate the roles of chairman of the board and CEO. CEOs who hold both positions have substantial power. They can largely control the agenda of the board and, many times, its membership as well. And, in almost two-thirds of the major U.S. companies, the CEO also is chairman of the board. A blue-ribbon panel, the Commission on Public Trust and Private Enterprise, created by the Conference Board, recommended separating these two roles. The panel also recommended creating the position of "lead director," an action that would weaken the CEO's power over the board. The lead director would set the board agenda, oversee executive sessions of nonmanagement directors, and have the authority to call board meetings. In addition, there are calls for more outside and independent directors, and for more diversity on boards that are overwhelmingly male and Caucasian. Data suggest that the few women and minorities on boards are outside directors and are independent: approximately 86 percent of women directors and 82 percent of minority directors are independent.

What is needed is a board that is not afraid to confront senior management if needed. To do so, the board must be strong and independent, and have a good working relationship among the directors. Trying to create such a board, Cendant Corporation announced major changes to its board of directors. One of the new policies requires that two-thirds of the board members be independent. Additionally, stock options have been eliminated as compensation for directors, and directors on major governance committees can have no other relationship with the company for which they are compensated. Cendant has also appointed a "lead director" to manage executive sessions of nonmanagement directors. The lead director idea is being adopted at other major U.S. companies, such as GE and Walt Disney.

The fervor for change has even extended to the New York Stock Exchange (NYSE), which has pushed for governance change itself. External parties have expressed criticism of the composition of the NYSE board, the compensation of its top executives, and potential inappropriate practices on the trading floor. Therefore, the NYSE board announced a major review of its governance process to be completed by the end of 2003. Governance experts argue that the NYSE governance processes require more transparency. The primary catalyst for this review was the controversy that occurred over the nomination for the NYSE board of Sanford Weill, CEO and chairman of Citigroup Inc. Weill became a subject of controversy because of questionable actions in his job. After substantial criticism, the nomination was withdrawn. The pressure for change has reached beyond U.S. companies. For example, Toyota Motor Corporation announced that its board would be reduced in size by 50 percent, and foreign managers would be added. The firm hopes these moves will speed the decision process and enrich its globalization efforts.

SOURCES: C. Hymowitz, 2003, In the U.S., what will it take to create diverse boardrooms? *Wall Street Journal*, July 8, B1; V. Boland, 2003, NYSE probe will focus on the boardroom, *Financial Times*, http://www.ft.com, May 25; 2003, Have fat cats had their day? *The Economist*, http://www.economist.com, May 22; M. O'Neal, 2003, Expectations (and pay) climb for directors, *New York Times*, http://www.nytimes.com, April 6; C. Hymowitz, 2003, Changing the rules, *Wall Street Journal Online*, http://www.wsj.com, February 24; M. Rich, 2003, Cendant makes major changes to corporate governance rules, *Wall Street Journal Online*, http://www.wsj.com, February 7; J. S. Lublin, 2003, Separating top posts trims CEO's power, some believe, *Wall Street Journal Online*, http://www.wsj.com, January 10; C. Hymowitz, 2002, Building a board that's independent, strong and effective, *Wall Street Journal*, November 19, B1.

Strategic Focus include (4) the creation of a "lead director" role that has strong powers with regard to the board agenda and oversight of nonmanagement board member activities, and (5) changes in the compensation of directors, especially reducing or eliminating stock options as a part of the package.

Boards have become more involved in the strategic decision-making process, so they must work collaboratively. Research shows that boards working collaboratively make higher-quality strategic decisions, and they make them faster.[92] In fact, some argue that improving the processes used by boards to make decisions and monitor managers and firm outcomes is the key to increasing board effectiveness.[93] Moreover, because of the increased pressure from owners and the potential conflict among board members, procedures are necessary to help boards function effectively in facilitating the strategic decision-making process.[94] In addition to being increasingly involved in important strategic decisions, boards also are becoming more active in expressing their view about CEO succession, as opposed to readily supporting the incumbent's choice. In general, however, boards have relied on precedence (past decisions) for guidance in the selection process. Also, they are most likely to consider inside candidates before looking for outside candidates.[95] Outside directors have the power to facilitate the firm's transition to a new CEO. When an internal heir apparent CEO candidate is associated with a high-performing firm, outside directors are likely to help the heir apparent make the transition. However, if firm performance is problematic, outside directors are less likely to support the chosen successor and are often skeptical of someone chosen to follow in the footsteps of the former CEO.[96]

Increasingly, outside directors are being required to own significant equity stakes as a prerequisite to holding a board seat. In fact, some research suggests that firms perform better if outside directors have such a stake.[97] Director compensation has increased partly because of their need to perform more work. The average director annual pay is slightly over $152,000.[98] Additionally, while critics have argued that directors serving on several boards cannot be effective, research suggests that directors have the opportunity to serve on more boards when they are on the board of firms that perform well. Research also shows that directors on boards where poor strategic decisions are made (i.e., not in the best interests of the shareholders) are less likely to serve on multiple boards.[99] Other research suggests that diverse boards help firms make more effective strategic decisions and perform better over time.[100] One activist concludes that boards need three foundational characteristics to be effective: director stock ownership, executive meetings to discuss important strategic issues, and a serious nominating committee that truly controls the nomination process to strongly influence the selection of new board members.[101]

Executive Compensation

As the Opening Case illustrates, the compensation of top-level managers, and especially of CEOs, generates a great deal of interest and strongly held opinions. One reason for this widespread interest can be traced to a natural curiosity about extremes and excesses. Another stems from a more substantive view, that CEO pay is tied in an indirect but tangible way to the fundamental governance processes in large corporations: Who has power? What are the bases of power? How and when do owners and managers exert their relative preferences? How vigilant are boards? Who is taking advantage of whom?[102]

Executive compensation is a governance mechanism that seeks to align the interests of managers and owners through salaries, bonuses, and long-term incentive compensation, such as stock awards and options.[103] Long-term incentive plans are becoming a critical part of compensation packages in U.S. firms. The use of longer-term pay helps firms cope with or avoid potential agency problems.[104] Because of this, the stock

| PART 3 / Strategic Actions: Strategy Implementation

Executive compensation *is a governance mechanism that seeks to align the interests of managers and owners through salaries, bonuses, and long-term incentive compensation, such as stock options.*

market generally reacts positively to the introduction of a long-range incentive plan for top executives.[105]

Sometimes the use of a long-term incentive plan prevents major stockholders (e.g., institutional investors) from pressing for changes in the composition of the board of directors, because they assume that the long-term incentives will ensure that top executives will act in shareholders' best interests. Alternatively, stockholders largely assume that top-executive pay and the performance of a firm are more closely aligned when firms have boards that are dominated by outside members.[106]

Effectively using executive compensation as a governance mechanism is particularly challenging to firms implementing international strategies. For example, the interests of owners of multinational corporations may be best served when there is less uniformity among the firm's foreign subsidiaries' compensation plans.[107] Developing an array of unique compensation plans requires additional monitoring and increases the firm's potential agency costs. Importantly, levels of pay vary by regions of the world. For example, managers receive the highest compensation in the United States, while managerial pay is much lower in Asia. Compensation is lower in India partly because many of the largest firms have strong family ownership and control.[108] As corporations acquire firms in other countries, the managerial compensation puzzle becomes more complex and may cause additional executive turnover.[109]

A Complicated Governance Mechanism

For several reasons, executive compensation—especially long-term incentive compensation—is complicated. First, the strategic decisions made by top-level managers are typically complex and nonroutine, so direct supervision of executives is inappropriate for judging the quality of their decisions. The result is a tendency to link the compensation of top-level managers to measurable outcomes, such as the firm's financial performance. Second, an executive's decision often affects a firm's financial outcomes over an extended period, making it difficult to assess the effect of current decisions on the corporation's performance. In fact, strategic decisions are more likely to have long-term, rather than short-term, effects on a company's strategic outcomes. Third, a number of other factors affect a firm's performance besides top-level managerial decisions and behavior. Unpredictable economic, social, or legal changes (see Chapter 2) make it difficult to discern the effects of strategic decisions. Thus, although performance-based compensation may provide incentives to top management teams to make decisions that best serve shareholders' interests,[110] such compensation plans alone are imperfect in their ability to monitor and control managers.[111] Still, annual bonuses as incentive compensation represent a significant portion of many executives' total pay. For example, the ten highest CEO salaries and bonuses in 2002 ranged from $5.5 million to just under $8 million.[112]

Although incentive compensation plans may increase the value of a firm in line with shareholder expectations, such plans are subject to managerial manipulation. For instance, annual bonuses may provide incentives to pursue short-run objectives at the expense of the firm's long-term interests. Supporting this conclusion, some research has found that bonuses based on annual performance were negatively related to investments in R&D when the firm was highly diversified, which may affect the firm's long-term strategic competitiveness.[113] However, research has found a positive relationship between investments in R&D and long-term compensation in non-family firms.[114]

Although long-term, performance-based incentives may reduce the temptation to underinvest in the short run, they increase executive exposure to risks associated with uncontrollable events, such as market fluctuations and industry decline. The longer the focus of incentive compensation, the greater are the long-term risks borne by top-level managers. Also, because long-term incentives tie a manager's overall wealth to the firm in a way that is inflexible, such incentives and ownership may not be valued as highly by a manager as by outside investors who have the opportunity to diversify their wealth in a number of other financial investments.[115] Thus, firms may have to overcompensate managers using long-term incentives, as the next section suggests.

The Effectiveness of Executive Compensation

The compensation recently received by some top-level managers, especially CEOs, has angered many stakeholders, including shareholders. Table 10.3 lists the compensation received by the highest-paid U.S. CEOs in 2002. The table shows those receiving the largest direct compensation (including exercised options) and those receiving the largest total compensation, including stock and stock options, for the same time period. As the table shows, Jeffrey Barbakow received the highest direct compensation as well as the highest total compensation including the value of stock and stock options awarded. However, Steven Jobs, CEO of Apple Computer, received the highest total compensation and value of stock options granted, with $381 million and $872 million, respectively, in 2000. Thus, the value of his total compensation that year was over $1 billion.[116] As Table 10.3 indicates, stock and stock options are the primary component of large compensation packages.

The primary reason for compensating executives in stock is that the practice affords them an incentive to keep the stock price high and hence aligns managers' interests with shareholders' interests. However, there may be some unintended consequences. Managers who own more than 1 percent of their firm's stock may be less

Table 10.3

Highest Paid CEOs in 2002

Executive	Company	Total Pay Received (Millions)	Total Pay with Options Granted (Millions)
J. C. Barbakow	Tenet Healthcare	$116.4	$188.8
D. M. Cote	Honeywell	3.2	145.5
R. I. Lipp	Travelers P&C	1.8	129.8
P. T. Stokes	Anheuser-Busch	17.9	125.6
M. S. Dell	Dell	82.3	119.7
E. D. Breen	Tyco	4.1	103.5
J. T. Chambers	Cisco	0.0	99.2
E. E. Whitacre	SBC Comm.	6.1	88.4
A. G. Lafley	Procter & Gamble	5.0	87.7
S. G. McNealy	Sun Microsystems	25.8	87.1

Considering only compensation received without the value of options granted (but not exercised), the following people would be in the above list:

I. M. Jacobs	Qualcomm	63.2	
C. M. Cawley	MBNA	48.3	
O. C. Smith	Starbucks	38.8	
R. S. Fuld	Lehman Brothers	28.7	
V. D. Coffman	Lockheed Martin	23.9	

SOURCES: 2003, Who made the biggest bucks?, *Wall Street Journal Online*, http://www.wsj.com, April 14; 2003, How CEO compensation packages compare, *USA Today*, http://www.usatoday.com, March 31.

likely to be forced out of their jobs, even when the firm is performing poorly.[117] Furthermore, a review of the research suggests that over time, firm size has accounted for more than 50 percent of the variance in total CEO pay, while firm performance has accounted for less than 5 percent of the variance.[118] Thus, the effectiveness of pay plans as a governance mechanism is suspect.

Another way that boards may compensate executives is through loans with favorable, or no, interest for the purpose of buying company stock. If appropriately used, this practice can be a governance tool, since it aligns executives' priorities with those of the shareholders in that the executives hold stock, instead of only options on the stock. They gain or lose money along with the shareholders. "When people exercise most stock options, they pay the regular income-tax rate—close to 40 percent for executives—on the difference between the option's exercise price and the share price at that time. But if executives buy shares with borrowed money instead of receiving options, the government considers their profit to be an investment gain, not a part of their salary, and they pay only the capital-gains tax of 20 percent or less."[119]

While some stock option–based compensation plans are well designed with option strike prices substantially higher than current stock prices, too many have been designed simply to give executives more wealth that will not immediately show up on the balance sheet.[120] Research of stock option repricing where the strike price value of the option has been lowered from its original position suggests that action is taken more frequently in high-risk situations. However, it also happens when firm performance was poor to restore the incentive effect for the option. Evidence also suggests that politics are often involved.[121] Additionally, research has found that repricing stock options does not appear to be a function of management entrenchment or ineffective governance. These firms often have had sudden and negative changes to their growth and profitability. They also frequently lose their top managers.[122] Interestingly, institutional investors prefer compensation schemes that link pay with performance, including the use of stock options.[123] Again, this evidence shows that no internal governance mechanism is perfect.

While stock options became highly popular as a means of compensating top executives and linking pay with performance, they also have become controversial of late. It seems that option awards became a means of providing large compensation packages, and the options awarded did not relate to the firm's performance, particularly when boards showed a propensity to reprice options at a lower strike price when stock prices fell precipitously.[124] Because of the large number of options granted in recent years and the increasingly common practice of repricing them, several analysts, compensation experts, and politicians have called for expensing the options by the firm at the time they are awarded. This action could be quite costly to many firms' stated profits. Thus, some firms have begun to move away from granting stock options. In fact, Microsoft announced in July 2003 that it would no longer grant stock options to its employees. The firm is replacing options with awards of restricted stock that will vest over a five-year period. Some suggest that Microsoft's action may spell the end of stock options as a means of compensation.[125]

Market for Corporate Control

The **market for corporate control** is an external governance mechanism that becomes active when a firm's internal controls fail.[126] The market for corporate control is composed of individuals and firms that buy ownership positions in or take over potentially undervalued corporations so they can form new divisions in established diversified companies or merge two previously separate firms. Because the undervalued firm's executives are assumed to be responsible for formulating and implementing the strategy that led to poor performance, they are usually replaced. Thus, when the market for

The market for corporate control *is an external governance mechanism that becomes active when a firm's internal controls fail.*

corporate control operates effectively, it ensures that managers who are ineffective or act opportunistically are disciplined.[127]

The market for corporate control governance mechanism should be triggered by a firm's poor performance relative to industry competitors. A firm's poor performance, often demonstrated by the firm's earning below-average returns, is an indicator that internal governance mechanisms have failed; that is, their use did not result in managerial decisions that maximized shareholder value. This market has been active for some time. As noted in Chapter 7, the decade of the 1990s produced the largest number and value of mergers and acquisitions. The major reduction in the stock market resulted in a significant drop in acquisition activity in the first part of the 21st century. However, the number of mergers and acquisitions began to increase in 2003, with the number expected to reach almost 25,000 by the end of the year.[128] And, the market for corporate control has become increasingly international with over 40 percent of the merger and acquisition activity involving two firms from different countries.[129]

While some acquisition attempts are intended to obtain resources important to the acquiring firm, most of the hostile takeover attempts are due to the target firm's poor performance.[130] Therefore, target firm managers and members of the boards of directors are highly sensitive about hostile takeover bids. First, it frequently means that they have not done an effective job in managing the company because of the performance level inviting the bid. If they accept the offer, they are likely to lose their jobs; the acquiring firm will insert its own management. If they reject the offer and fend off the takeover attempt, they must improve the performance of the firm or risk losing their jobs as well.[131]

In 2003, the increasing number of hostile bids provided evidence of the merger and acquisition market heating up. For example, Oracle made a hostile bid for PeopleSoft; PeopleSoft rejected the offer, but Oracle remained in the takeover battle. The takeover attempt invited considerable attention from regulatory authorities in both the United States and Europe.[132] Also in 2003, smaller rival ArvinMeritor launched a hostile takeover attempt of its larger competitor, Dana, with a cash bid of $4.4 billion. But, analysts believed that the attempt would encourage others to make bids as well, making the takeover more expensive.[133] In fact, the takeover attempt of Safeway involved six bidders, but some were disapproved because of the potential concentration that might be created by the acquisition.[134]

Jean-Marie Messier, former CEO of Vivendi Universal, won an arbitration award for his severance pay package of $23.3 million. However, in late 2003, the SEC filed a suit to stop payment.

AP Photo/Jacques Brinon

Managerial Defense Tactics

Hostile takeovers are the major activity in the market for corporate control governance mechanism. Not all hostile takeovers are prompted by poorly performing targets, and firms targeted for hostile takeovers may use multiple defense tactics to fend off the takeover attempt. Historically, the increased use of the market for corporate control has enhanced the sophistication and variety of managerial defense tactics that are used to reduce the influence of this governance mechanism. The market for corporate control tends to increase risk for managers. As a result, managerial pay is often augmented indirectly through golden parachutes (wherein a CEO can receive up to three years' salary if his or her firm is taken over). Golden parachutes, similar to most other defense tactics, are controversial. For example, Jean-Marie Messier was given a golden parachute near the end of his tenure as CEO of Vivendi Universal, presumably to encourage him to resign. The package involved a $23.3 million payment, but it was delayed by court tests after he departed. The board claimed that no vote was taken to approve the severance payment. While the American Arbitration Association ruled in favor of Messier, Vivendi appealed the ruling to the French supreme court, which suspended the payment. Thus, the payment remains in litigation.[135]

Among other outcomes, takeover defenses increase the costs of mounting a takeover, causing the incumbent management to become entrenched, while reducing the chances of introducing a new management team.[136] Some defense tactics require asset restructuring created by divesting one or more divisions in the diversified firm's portfolio. Others necessitate only changes in the financial structure of the firm, such as repurchasing shares of the firm's outstanding stock.[137] Some tactics (e.g., reincorporation of the firm in another state) require shareholder approval, but the greenmail tactic, wherein money is used to repurchase stock from a corporate raider to avoid the takeover of the firm, does not. These defense tactics are controversial, and the research on their effects is inconclusive. Alternatively, most institutional investors oppose the use of defense tactics. TIAA-CREF and CalPERS have taken actions to have several firms' poison pills eliminated.[138] Hewlett-Packard's board adopted a policy that a poison pill could not be established in the future without taking a shareholder vote for approval. The stockholders also wanted approval on future executive severance pay packages.[139] But, there can be advantages to severance packages because they may encourage executives to accept takeover bids that are attractive to shareholders. Also, as in the case of Messier, it may encourage a CEO doing a poor job to depart.[140]

A potential problem with the market for corporate control is that it may not be totally efficient. A study of several of the most active corporate raiders in the 1980s showed that approximately 50 percent of their takeover attempts targeted firms with above-average performance in their industry—corporations that were neither undervalued nor poorly managed.[141] The targeting of high-performance businesses may lead to acquisitions at premium prices and to decisions by managers of the targeted firm to establish what may prove to be costly takeover defense tactics to protect their corporate positions.[142]

Although the market for corporate control lacks the precision of internal governance mechanisms, the fear of acquisition and influence by corporate raiders is an effective constraint on the managerial-growth motive.[143] The market for corporate control has been responsible for significant changes in many firms' strategies and, when used appropriately, has served shareholders' interests.[144] But this market and other means of corporate governance vary by region of the world and by country. Accordingly, we next address the topic of international corporate governance.

International Corporate Governance

Understanding the corporate governance structure of the United Kingdom and the United States is inadequate for a multinational firm in today's global economy.[145] The Strategic Focus suggests that the governance systems in many countries have been affected by the realities of the global economy. While the stability associated with German and Japanese governance structures has historically been viewed as an asset, some believe that it may now be a burden.[146] And the governance in Germany and Japan is changing, just as it is in other parts of the world. As suggested in the Strategic Focus, the corporate governance systems are becoming more similar. These changes are partly the

Corporate Governance Is Changing across the World

The pressures to change corporate governance practices have extended well beyond the United States. For example, a new report commissioned by the British government recommends significant changes in the governance practices of British companies. The report has a number of recommendations but two are especially important. First, the report suggests that firms should designate a nonexecutive director to attend regular management meetings with major shareholders. Second, it recommends that instead of the chairperson of the board, a nonexecutive director should chair the nomination committee. British top executives have expressed serious concerns about the changes.

Similarly, there have been calls for changes in the governance of French firms. The emphasis in France has been on increasing the number of independent directors on corporate boards. The most recent recommendation is to increase the number of independent directors to 50 percent of the total number of directors on the board. However, a major problem is that most "independent" directors (nonmanagement, outside members) are not truly independent. They have connections to the top executives in the company or to other board members or both. Thus, they are selected based on these connections instead of their expertise or independence.

Changes are also occurring in Switzerland and Japan. Similar to the United States, Switzerland has experienced corporate scandals in recent years. The bankruptcy of Swiss Air and the government rescue of it have created a public furor. Additionally, the disclosure that ABB awarded $170 million in pensions and other benefits to two former CEOs produced calls for governance changes. As a result, the Swiss stock market leaders have issued new regulations requiring disclosure of board members' total stock holdings and options, the highest paid director, and the names of all boards on which directors serve (to avoid conflicts of interest).

Even in Japan, changes in governance similar to those taking place in Europe are moving Japanese firms toward the U.S. system. For example, Sony announced that it would appoint more outsiders to its board and would have a majority of outsiders on the three critical board committees—compensation, audit, and nominating. In a similar move, Toyota announced that its board would be reduced by 50 percent and that the firm would simultaneously appoint more foreign managers. Its stated reasons are different from Sony's. Sony suggested that its changes are designed to make the firm's corporate governance more similar to that of U.S. firms. Toyota says that its moves are designed to help it compete in global markets, yet the changes also make Toyota's governance slightly more similar to that in the United States.

While there have been changes in Latin American firms' governance systems, they have been minor, largely because of the severe economic problems occurring in many Latin American countries. For example, shareholders do not have to be concerned about excessive executive compensation in Argentina. Because of the severe recession coupled with a devaluation of the peso and an increasing inflation rate, executives have received an average 30 percent pay cut. The job market for top executives in Argentina is highly limited.

SOURCES: T. Smith, 2003, Shrinking salaries hit home in Argentina, *New York Times*, http://www.nytimes.com, April 6; T. Zaun, 2003, Toyota to halve board, add foreign managers, *Wall Street Journal Online*, http://www.wsj.com, March 31; 2003, Hating Higgs, *The Economist*, http://www.economist.com, March 15; 2003, Independent? Moi? *The Economist*, http://www. economist.com, March 15; G. Mijuk, 2003, Money talks a little, *Wall Street Journal Online*, http://www.wsj.com, February 24; R. A. Guth, 2003, Sony's board will divide up its responsibilities in future, *Wall Street Journal Online*, http://www.wsj.com, January 29.

result of multinational firms operating in many different countries and attempting to develop a more global governance system.[147] While the similarity is increasing, differences remain evident, and firms employing an international strategy must understand these differences in order to operate effectively in different international markets.[148]

Corporate Governance in Germany

In many private German firms, the owner and manager may still be the same individual. In these instances, there is no agency problem.[149] Even in publicly traded German corporations, there is often a dominant shareholder. Thus, the concentration of ownership is an important means of corporate governance in Germany, as it is in the United States.[150]

Historically, banks have been at the center of the German corporate governance structure, as is also the case in many other European countries, such as Italy and France. As lenders, banks become major shareholders when companies they financed earlier seek funding on the stock market or default on loans. Although the stakes are usually under 10 percent, the only legal limit on how much of a firm's stock banks can hold is that a single ownership position cannot exceed 15 percent of the bank's capital. Through their shareholdings, and by casting proxy votes for individual shareholders who retain their shares with the banks, three banks in particular—Deutsche, Dresdner, and Commerzbank—exercise significant power. Although shareholders can tell the banks how to vote their ownership position, they generally do not do so. A combination of their own holdings and their proxies results in majority positions for these three banks in many German companies. Those banks, along with others, monitor and control managers, both as lenders and as shareholders, by electing representatives to supervisory boards.

German firms with more than 2,000 employees are required to have a two-tiered board structure. Through this structure, the supervision of management is separated from other duties normally assigned to a board of directors, especially the nomination of new board members. Germany's two-tiered system places the responsibility for monitoring and controlling managerial (or supervisory) decisions and actions in the hands of a separate group.[151] While all the functions of direction and management are the responsibility of the management board (the Vorstand), appointment to the Vorstand is the responsibility of the supervisory tier (the Aufsichtsrat). Employees, union members, and shareholders appoint members to the Aufsichtsrat.

Because of the role of local government (through the board structure) and the power of banks in Germany's corporate governance structure, private shareholders rarely have major ownership positions in German firms. Large institutional investors, such as pension funds and insurance companies, are also relatively insignificant owners of corporate stock. Thus, at least historically, German executives generally have not been dedicated to the maximization of shareholder value that is occurring in many countries.

Volkswagen (VW) made an amazing turnaround in the latter half

Volkswagen's foray into manufacturing luxury cars such as the $70,000 Phaeton has not proven successful. The internal corporate governance system at the company has failed to control costly strategic errors and has put Volkswagen's survival in jeopardy. Here an employee polishes a Phaeton at its factory in Dresden, eastern Germany.

AP Photo/Matthias Rietschel

of the 1990s. The company became much more profitable than it had been, and it appeared to be headed to new heights. Despite these promising signs, many investors had uneasy feelings about VW. The company would not release financial data, including operating profits that investors wanted to examine. In 2001, VW's market capitalization was less than Bayerische Motoren Werke's (BMW's), another German carmaker, in spite of the fact that VW generated twice as much revenue as did BMW.

As we learned in Chapter 2, Volkswagen invested billions of dollars to develop and introduce several new luxury automobiles, only to find that they were not in demand in the marketplace. One of these new cars, the Phaeton, is priced at $70,000 and its sales reached only 25 percent of the expected number in 2002, its year of introduction. The competition is fierce in the premium auto market. Lack of attention to Volkswagen's primary midpriced auto market allowed competitors to gain market share. Thus, Volkswagen's financial results have suffered, and unless it regains a competitive advantage, its performance will continue to suffer. The internal corporate governance system in Volkswagen has not controlled managerial behavior, allowing serious strategic errors. As a result, Volkswagen's survival may be in question.[152]

Corporate governance in Germany is changing, at least partially, because of the increasing globalization of business. Many German firms are beginning to gravitate toward the U.S. system. Recent research suggests that the traditional system produced some agency costs because of a lack of external ownership power. Alternatively, firms with stronger external ownership power were less likely to undertake governance reforms. Firms that adopted governance reforms often divested poorly performing units and achieved higher levels of market performance.[153]

Corporate Governance in Japan

Attitudes toward corporate governance in Japan are affected by the concepts of obligation, family, and consensus.[154] In Japan, an obligation "may be to return a service for one rendered or it may derive from a more general relationship, for example, to one's family or old alumni, or one's company (or Ministry), or the country. This sense of particular obligation is common elsewhere but it feels stronger in Japan."[155] As part of a company family, individuals are members of a unit that envelops their lives; families command the attention and allegiance of parties throughout corporations. Moreover, a *keiretsu* (a group of firms tied together by cross-shareholdings) is more than an economic concept; it, too, is a family. Consensus, an important influence in Japanese corporate governance, calls for the expenditure of significant amounts of energy to win the hearts and minds of people whenever possible, as opposed to top executives issuing edicts.[156] Consensus is highly valued, even when it results in a slow and cumbersome decision-making process.

As in Germany, banks in Japan play an important role in financing and monitoring large public firms. The bank owning the largest share of stocks and the largest amount of debt—the main bank—has the closest relationship with the company's top executives. The main bank provides financial advice to the firm and also closely monitors managers. Thus, Japan has a bank-based financial and corporate governance structure, whereas the United States has a market-based financial and governance structure.[157]

Aside from lending money, a Japanese bank can hold up to 5 percent of a firm's total stock; a group of related financial institutions can hold up to 40 percent. In many cases, main-bank relationships are part of a horizontal keiretsu. A keiretsu firm usually owns less than 2 percent of any other member firm; however, each company typically has a stake of that size in every firm in the keiretsu. As a result, somewhere between 30 and 90 percent of a firm is owned by other members of the keiretsu. Thus, a keiretsu is a system of relationship investments.

As is the case in Germany, Japan's structure of corporate governance is changing. For example, because of Japanese banks' continuing development as economic organizations, their role in the monitoring and control of managerial behavior and firm outcomes is less significant than in the past.[158] The Asian economic crisis in the latter part of the 1990s made the governance problems in Japanese corporations apparent. The problems were readily evidenced in the large and once-powerful Mitsubishi keiretsu. Many of its core members lost substantial amounts of money in the late 1990s.[159]

Still another change in Japan's governance system has occurred in the market for corporate control, which was nonexistent in past years. Japan experienced three recessions in the 1990s and is dealing with another early in the 21st century. As a whole, managers are unwilling to make the changes necessary to turn their companies around. As a result, many firms in Japan are performing poorly, but could, under the right guidance, improve their performance. Still, recent research suggests that the Japanese stewardship management approach leads to greater investments in long-term R&D projects than does the more financially oriented system in the United States.[160]

Global Corporate Governance

The 21st-century competitive landscape is fostering the creation of a relatively uniform governance structure that will be used by firms throughout the world.[161] As markets become more global and customer demands more similar, shareholders are becoming the focus of managers' efforts in an increasing number of companies. Investors are becoming more and more active throughout the world as evidenced by the shareholder outrage at the severance package given to Jean-Marie Messier, former CEO of Vivendi Universal.

Changes in governance are evident in many countries and are moving the governance models closer to that of the United States, as suggested in the Strategic Focus. Firms in Europe, especially in France and the United Kingdom, are developing boards of directors with more independent members. Similar actions are occurring in Japan, where the boards are being reduced in size and foreign members added.

Even in transitional economies, such as those of China and Russia, changes in corporate governance are occurring.[162] However, changes are implemented more slowly in these economies. Chinese firms have found it helpful to use stock-based compensation plans, thereby providing an incentive for foreign companies to invest in China.[163] Because Russia has reduced controls on the economy and on business activity much faster than China has, the country needs more effective governance systems to control its managerial activities. In fact, research suggests that ownership concentration leads to lower performance in Russia, primarily because minority shareholder rights are not well protected through adequate governance controls.[164]

Governance Mechanisms and Ethical Behavior

The governance mechanisms described in this chapter are designed to ensure that the agents of the firm's owners—the corporation's top executives—make strategic decisions that best serve the interests of the entire group of stakeholders, as described in Chapter 1. In the United States, shareholders are recognized as a company's most significant stakeholder. Thus, governance mechanisms focus on the control of managerial decisions to ensure that shareholders' interests will be served, but product market stakeholders (e.g., customers, suppliers, and host communities) and organizational stakeholders (e.g., managerial and nonmanagerial employees) are important as well.[165] Therefore, at least the minimal interests or needs of all stakeholders must be satisfied through the firm's actions. Otherwise, dissatisfied stakeholders will withdraw their support from one firm and provide it to another (for example, customers will purchase products from a supplier offering an acceptable substitute).

The firm's strategic competitiveness is enhanced when its governance mechanisms take into consideration the interests of all stakeholders. Although the idea is subject to debate, some believe that ethically responsible companies design and use governance mechanisms that serve all stakeholders' interests. There is, however, a more critical relationship between ethical behavior and corporate governance mechanisms. The Enron disaster illustrates the devastating effect of poor ethical behavior not only on a firm's stakeholders, but also on other firms.

In addition to Enron, recent scandals at WorldCom, HealthSouth, and Ahold NV show that all corporate owners are vulnerable to unethical behaviors by their employees, including top-level managers—the agents who have been hired to make decisions that are in shareholders' best interests. The decisions and actions of a corporation's board of directors can be an effective deterrent to these behaviors. In fact, some believe that the most effective boards participate actively to set boundaries for their firms' business ethics and values.[166] Once formulated, the board's expectations related to ethical decisions and actions of all of the firm's stakeholders must be clearly communicated to its top-level managers. Moreover, as shareholders' agents, these managers must understand that the board will hold them fully accountable for the development and support of an organizational culture that results in ethical decisions and behaviors. As explained in Chapter 12, CEOs can be positive role models for ethical behavior.

Only when the proper corporate governance is exercised can strategies be formulated and implemented that will help the firm achieve strategic competitiveness and earn above-average returns. As the discussion in this chapter suggests, corporate governance mechanisms are a vital, yet imperfect, part of firms' efforts to select and successfully use strategies.

Summary

- Corporate governance is a relationship among stakeholders that is used to determine a firm's direction and control its performance. How firms monitor and control top-level managers' decisions and actions affects the implementation of strategies. Effective governance that aligns managers' decisions with shareholders' interests can help produce a competitive advantage.

- There are three internal governance mechanisms in the modern corporation—ownership concentration, the board of directors, and executive compensation. The market for corporate control is the single external governance mechanism influencing managers' decisions and the outcomes resulting from them.

- Ownership is separated from control in the modern corporation. Owners (principals) hire managers (agents) to make decisions that maximize the firm's value. As risk-bearing specialists, owners diversify their risk by investing in multiple corporations with different risk profiles. As decision-making specialists, owners expect their agents (the firm's top-level managers) to make decisions that will lead to maximization of the value of their firm. Thus, modern corporations are characterized by an agency relationship that is created when one party (the firm's own-

ers) hires and pays another party (top-level managers) to use its decision-making skills.

- Separation of ownership and control creates an agency problem when an agent pursues goals that conflict with principals' goals. Principals establish and use governance mechanisms to control this problem.

- Ownership concentration is based on the number of large-block shareholders and the percentage of shares they own. With significant ownership percentages, such as those held by large mutual funds and pension funds, institutional investors often are able to influence top executives' strategic decisions and actions. Thus, unlike diffuse ownership, which tends to result in relatively weak monitoring and control of managerial decisions, concentrated ownership produces more active and effective monitoring. Institutional investors are an increasingly powerful force in corporate America and actively use their positions of concentrated ownership to force managers and boards of directors to make decisions that maximize a firm's value.

- In the United States and the United Kingdom, a firm's board of directors, composed of insiders, related outsiders, and outsiders, is a governance mechanism expected to represent shareholders' collective interests. The percentage of outside directors on many boards now exceeds the percentage of inside directors. Outsiders are expected to be more independent of a firm's top-level managers compared to those selected from inside the firm.

- Executive compensation is a highly visible and often criticized governance mechanism. Salary, bonuses, and long-term incentives are used to strengthen the alignment between managers' and shareholders' interests. A firm's board of directors is responsible for determining the effectiveness of the firm's executive compensation system. An effective system elicits managerial decisions that are in shareholders' best interests.

- In general, evidence suggests that shareholders and boards of directors have become more vigilant in their control of managerial decisions. Nonetheless, these mechanisms are insufficient to govern managerial behavior in many large companies. Therefore, the market for corporate control is an important governance mechanism. Although it, too, is imperfect, the market for corporate control has been effective in causing corporations to combat inefficient diversification and to implement more effective strategic decisions.

- Corporate governance structures used in Germany and Japan differ from each other and from that used in the United States. Historically, the U.S. governance structure has focused on maximizing shareholder value. In Germany, employees, as a stakeholder group, have a more prominent role in governance. By contrast, until recently, Japanese shareholders played virtually no role in the monitoring and control of top-level managers. However, all of these systems are becoming increasingly similar, as are many governance systems both in developed countries, such as France and Spain, and in transitional economies, such as Russia and China.

- Effective governance mechanisms ensure that the interests of all stakeholders are served. Thus, long-term strategic success results when firms are governed in ways that permit at least minimal satisfaction of capital market stakeholders (e.g., shareholders), product market stakeholders (e.g., customers and suppliers), and organizational stakeholders (managerial and nonmanagerial employees; see Chapter 2). Moreover, effective governance produces ethical behavior in the formulation and implementation of strategies.

Review Questions

1. What is corporate governance? What factors account for the considerable amount of attention corporate governance receives from several parties, including shareholder activists, business press writers, and academic scholars? Why is governance necessary to control managers' decisions?

2. What does it mean to say that ownership is separated from managerial control in the modern corporation? Why does this separation exist?

3. What is an agency relationship? What is managerial opportunism? What assumptions do owners of modern corporations make about managers as agents?

4. How is each of the three internal governance mechanisms—ownership concentration, boards of directors, and

executive compensation—used to align the interests of managerial agents with those of the firm's owners?

5. What trends exist regarding executive compensation? What is the effect of the increased use of long-term incentives on executives' strategic decisions?

6. What is the market for corporate control? What conditions generally cause this external governance mechanism to become active? How does the mechanism constrain top executives' decisions and actions?

7. What is the nature of corporate governance in Germany and Japan?

8. How can corporate governance foster ethical strategic decisions and behaviors on the part of managers as agents?

Experiential Exercises

Corporate Governance and the Board of Directors

The composition and actions of the firm's board of directors have a profound effect on the firm. "The most important

thing a board can ask itself today is whether it is professionally managed in the same way that the company itself is professionally managed," says Carolyn Brancato, director of the Global Corporate Governance Research Center at The Conference Board, which creates and disseminates knowledge about management and the marketplace. "The collegial nature of boards must give way to a new emphasis on professionalism, and directors must ask management the hard questions."

Following are several questions about boards of directors and corporate governance. Break into small groups and use the content of this chapter to discuss these questions. Be prepared to defend your answers.

1. How can corporate governance keep a company viable and maintain its shareholders' confidence?

2. How should boards evaluate CEOs? How can the board learn of problems in the CEO's performance? How does a board decide when a CEO needs to be replaced? How should succession plans be put in place?

3. Who should serve on a board? What human factors affect board members' interactions with each other, and how can those factors be used to best advantage?

4. Should independent directors meet on a regular basis without management present? Does the board have a role in setting corporate strategy?

5. What should a CEO expect of directors? How can a CEO move unproductive participants off a board?

6. What processes can be put in place to help make the board more aware of problems in company operations? How can the board be assured of receiving appropriate information? How can the board fulfill its monitoring role while relying on information provided by management and external accountants?

Developing and Analyzing Executive Compensation Packages

To date, A. G. Lafley, the chairman, president, and chief executive officer (CEO) of Procter & Gamble (P&G) can be proud of the company's financial performance under his leadership. Procter & Gamble's net income rose 19 percent in the fiscal year ended June 30, 2003, while unit volume grew 8 percent and net sales rose 8 percent to $43.38 billion. In general, the shareholders were pleased with wealth creation based on these performance-related outcomes. The board of directors carefully listens to presentations by Mr. Lafley and the Compensation Committee concerning CEO

compensation for the next year. The fiduciary duty of the board requires that its members make decisions that are in the best interest of P&G shareholders.

Break the class into three groups.

Phase 1: Group Work

• Group A will represent Mr. Lafley. This group should develop a list of three to five major changes in executive compensation that will be presented to the P&G board of directors for approval. The list should contain some changes that are primarily beneficial to shareholders and other changes that are primarily beneficial to Mr. Lafley and other senior managers (it's important to have both). The list could be created using this chapter's contents or other sources. Students may refer to the P&G website at http://www.pg.com to gather useful information.

• Group B will represent the Compensation Committee. This group believes that Mr. Lafley deserves a compensation increase, largely because his incentives lagged the industry average. The group will prepare a new compensation offer for Mr. Lafley. Use this chapter's contents for ideas of executive compensation incentives.

• Group C will act as a Board of Directors. To prepare for phase 2 of the exercise, this group will discuss various aspects of managerial opportunism, various ways to compensate top managers, and the importance to all stakeholders of retaining competent CEOs.

Phase 2: Role Playing

A representative of group A presents the list of major changes that Mr. Lafley proposes. Group C listens to the proposal and approves or disapproves each item. The discussion is in front of the class. Members may differ in opinions—there is no right or wrong position. Items that do not benefit shareholders should not be approved.

A representative of group B presents a new compensation plan for Mr. Lafley. Group C discusses the plan and approves it, disapproves it, or suggests changes.

Phase 3: Analysis and Feedback

The instructor leads the entire class in an analysis of what has transpired while completing this exercise.

Notes

1. M. Carpenter & J. Westphal, 2001, Strategic context of external network ties: Examining the impact of director appointments on board involvement in strategic decision making, *Academy of Management Journal*, 44: 639–660.

2. A. Henderson & J. Fredrickson, 2001, Top management team coordination needs and the CEO pay gap: A competitive test of economic and behavioral views, *Academy of Management Journal*, 44: 96–117.

3. F. Elloumi & J.-P. Gueyie, 2001, CEO compensation, IOS and the role of corporate governance, *Corporate Governance*, 1(2): 23–33; J. E. Core, R. W. Holthausen, & D. F. Larcker, 1999, Corporate governance, chief executive officer compensation, and firm performance, *Journal of Financial Economics*, 51: 371–406.

4. M. D. Lynall, B. R. Golden, & A. J. Hillman, 2003, Board composition from adolescence to maturity: A multitheoretic view, *Academy of Management Review*, 28: 416–431; A. J. Hillman, G. D. Keim, & R. A. Luce, 2001, Board composition and stakeholder performance: Do stakeholder directors make a difference? *Business and Society*, 40: 295–314.

5. C. M. Daily, D. R. Dalton, & A. A. Cannella, 2003, Corporate governance: Decades of dialogue and data, *Academy of Management Review*, 28: 371–382; P. Stiles, 2001, The impact of the board on strategy: An empirical examination, *Journal of Management Studies*, 38: 627–650.

6. D. Finegold, E. E. Lawler III, & J. Conger, 2001, Building a better board, *Journal of Business Strategy*, 22(6): 33–37.

7. E. F. Fama & M. C. Jensen, 1983, Separation of ownership and control, *Journal of Law and Economics*, 26: 301–325.

8. J. Henderson & K. Cool, 2003, Corporate governance, investment bandwagons and overcapacity: An analysis of the worldwide petrochemical industry, 1975–95, *Strategic Management Journal*, 24: 393–413; R. Charan, 1998, *How Corporate Boards Create Competitive Advantage*, San Francisco: Jossey-Bass.

9. A. Cannella, Jr., A. Pettigrew, & D. Hambrick, 2001, Upper echelons: Donald Hambrick on executives and strategy, *Academy of Management Executive*, 15(3): 36–52; J. D. Westphal & E. J. Zajac, 1997, Defections from the inner circle: Social exchange, reciprocity and diffusion of board independence in U.S. corporations, *Administrative Science Quarterly*, 42: 161–212.

10. J. McGuire & S. Dow, 2002, The Japanese keiretsu system: An empirical analysis, *Journal of Business Research*, 55: 33–40.

11. J. Charkham, 1994, *Keeping Good Company: A Study of Corporate Governance in Five Countries*, New York: Oxford University Press, 1.

12. A. Cadbury, 1999, The future of governance: The rules of the game, *Journal of General Management*, 24: 1–14.

13. R. Aguilera & G. Jackson, 2003, The cross-national diversity of corporate governance: Dimensions and determinants, *Academy of Management Review*, 28: 447–465; Cadbury Committee, 1992, *Report of the Cadbury Committee on the Financial Aspects of Corporate Governance*, London: Gee.

14. C. K. Prahalad & J. P. Oosterveld, 1999, Transforming internal governance: The challenge for multinationals, *Sloan Management Review*, 40(3): 31–39.

15. M. A. Hitt, R. A. Harrison, & R. D. Ireland, 2001, *Mergers and Acquisitions: A Guide to Creating Value for Stakeholders*, New York: Oxford University Press; M. A. Hitt, R. E. Hoskisson, R. A. Johnson, & D. D. Moesel, 1996, The market for corporate control and firm innovation, *Academy of Management Journal*, 39: 1084–1119.

16. K. Ramaswamy, M. Li, & R. Veliyath, 2002, Variations in ownership behavior and propensity to diversify: A study of the Indian context, *Strategic Management Journal*, 23: 345–358.

17. R. E. Hoskisson, M. A. Hitt, R. A. Johnson, & W. Grossman, 2002, Conflicting voices: The effects of ownership heterogeneity and internal governance on corporate strategy, *Academy of Management Journal*, 45: 697–716.

18. G. E. Davis & T. A. Thompson, 1994, A social movement perspective on corporate control, *Administrative Science Quarterly*, 39: 141–173.

19. R. Bricker & N. Chandar, 2000, Where Berle and Means went wrong: A reassessment of capital market agency and financial reporting, *Accounting, Organizations and Society*, 25: 529–554; M. A. Eisenberg, 1989, The structure of corporation law, *Columbia Law Review*, 89(7): 1461 as cited in R. A. G. Monks & N. Minow, 1995, *Corporate Governance*, Cambridge, MA: Blackwell Business, 7.

20. R. M. Wiseman & L. R. Gomez-Mejia, 1999, A behavioral agency model of managerial risk taking, *Academy of Management Review*, 23: 133–153.

21. R. C. Anderson & D. M. Reeb, 2003, Founding-family ownership and firm performance: Evidence from the S&P 500, *Journal of Finance*, 58: in press.

22. N. Anthanassiou, W. F. Crittenden, L. M. Kelly, & P. Marquez, 2002, Founder centrality effects on the Mexican family firm's top management group: Firm culture, strategic vision and goals and firm performance, *Journal of World Business*, 37: 139–150.

23. G. Redding, 2002, The capitalist business system of China and its rationale, *Asia Pacific Journal of Management*, 19: 221–249.

24. M. Carney & E. Gedajlovic, 2003, Strategic innovation and the administrative heritage of East Asian family business groups, *Asia Pacific Journal of Management*, 20: 5–26; D. Miller & I. Le Breton-Miller, 2003, Challenge versus advantage in family business, *Strategic Organization*, 1: 127–134.

25. E. E. Fama, 1980, Agency problems and the theory of the firm, *Journal of Political Economy*, 88: 288–307.

26. D. Stires, 2001, America's best & worst wealth creators, *Fortune*, December 10, 137–142.

27. 2003, Information obtained from Cisco's financial data presented on its website, http://www.cisco.com, July.

28. D. Dalton, C. Daily, T. Certo, & R. Roengpitya, 2003, Meta-analyses of financial performance and equity: Fusion or confusion? *Academy of Management Journal*, 46: 13–26; M. Jensen & W. Meckling, 1976, Theory of the firm: Managerial behavior, agency costs, and ownership structure, *Journal of Financial Economics*, 11: 305–360.

29. L. R. Gomez-Mejia, M. Nunez-Nickel, & I. Gutierrez, 2001, The role of family ties in agency contracts, *Academy of Management Journal*, 44: 81–95.

30. M. G. Jacobides & D. C. Croson, 2001, Information policy: Shaping the value of agency relationships, *Academy of Management Review*, 26: 202–223.

31. R. Mangel & M. Useem, 2001, The strategic role of gainsharing, *Journal of Labor Research*, 2: 327–343; T. M. Welbourne & L. R. Gomez-Mejia, 1995, Gainsharing: A critical review and a future research agenda, *Journal of Management*, 21: 577.

32. A. J. Hillman & T. Dalziel, 2003, Boards of directors and firm performance: Integrating agency and resource dependence perspectives, *Academy of Management Review*, 28: 383–396; Jacobides & Croson, Information policy: Shaping the value of agency relationships.

33. Hoskisson, Hitt, Johnson, & Grossman, Conflicting voices; O. E. Williamson, 1996, *The Mechanisms of Governance*, New York: Oxford University Press, 6.

34. C. C. Chen, M. W. Peng, & P. A. Saparito, 2002, Individualism, collectivism, and opportunism: A cultural perspective on transaction cost economics, *Journal of Management*, 28: 567–583; S. Ghoshal & P. Moran, 1996, Bad for practice: A critique of the transaction cost theory, *Academy of Management Review*, 21: 13–47.

35. K. H. Wathne & J. B. Heide, 2000, Opportunism in interfirm relationships: Forms, outcomes, and solutions, *Journal of Marketing*, 64(4): 36–51.

36. L. Tihanyi, R. A. Johnson, R. E. Hoskisson, & M. A. Hitt, 2003, Institutional ownership differences and international diversification: The effects of boards of directors and technological opportunity, *Academy of Management Journal*, 46: 195–211; Y. Amihud & B. Lev, 1981, Risk reduction as a managerial motive for conglomerate mergers, *Bell Journal of Economics*, 12: 605–617.

37. R. C. Anderson, T. W. Bates, J. M. Bizjak, & M. L. Lemmon, Corporate governance and firm diversification, *Financial Management*, 29(1): 5–22; R. E. Hoskisson & T. A. Turk, 1990, Corporate restructuring: Governance and control limits of the internal market, *Academy of Management Review*, 15: 459–477.

38. M. A. Geletkanycz, B. K. Boyd, & S. Finkelstein, 2001, The strategic value of CEO external directorate networks: Implications for CEO compensation, *Strategic Management Journal*, 9: 889–898.

39. P. Wright, M. Kroll, & D. Elenkov, 2002, Acquisition returns, increase in firm size and chief executive officer compensation: The moderating role of monitoring, *Academy of Management Journal*, 45: 599–608; S. Finkelstein & D. C. Hambrick, 1989, Chief executive compensation: A study of the intersection of markets and political processes, *Strategic Management Journal*, 16: 221-239.

40. Gomez-Mejia, Nunez-Nickel, & Gutierrez, The role of family ties in agency contracts.

41. C. Matlack, 2001, Gemplus: No picnic in Provence, *BusinessWeek Online*, http://www.businessweek.com, August 6; C. Matlack, 2001, A global clash at France's Gemplus, *BusinessWeek Online*, http://www.businessweek.com, December 21.

42. 2003, Gemplus Profile and Company Information, http://www.gemplus.com, July.

43. M. S. Jensen, 1986, Agency costs of free cash flow, corporate finance, and takeovers, *American Economic Review*, 76: 323–329.

44. T. H. Brush, P. Bromiley, & M. Hendrickx, 2000, The free cash flow hypothesis for sales growth and firm performance, *Strategic Management Journal*, 21: 455–472; H. DeAngelo & L. DeAngelo, 2000, Controlling stockholders and the disciplinary role of corporate payout policy: A study of the Times Mirror Company, *Journal of Financial Economics*, 56: 153–207.

45. Ramaswamy, Li, & Veliyath, Variations in ownership behavior and propensity to diversify.

46. P. Wright, M. Kroll, A. Lado, & B. Van Ness, 2002, The structure of ownership and corporate acquisition strategies, *Strategic Management Journal*, 23: 41–53.

47. R. Rajan, H. Servaes, & L. Zingales, 2001, The cost of diversity: The diversification discount and inefficient investment, *Journal of Finance*, 55: 35–79; A. Sharma, 1997, Professional as agent: Knowledge asymmetry in agency exchange, *Academy of Management Review*, 22: 758–798.

48. P. Lane, A. A. Cannella, Jr., & M. H. Lubatkin, 1999, Agency problems as antecedents to unrelated mergers and diversification: Amihud and Lev reconsidered, *Strategic Management Journal*, 19: 555–578.

49. David Champion, 2001, Off with his head? *Harvard Business Review*, 79(9): 35–46.

50. J. Coles, N. Sen, & V. McWilliams, 2001, An examination of the relationship of governance mechanisms to performance, *Journal of Management*, 27: 23–50.

51. S.-S. Chen & K. W. Ho, 2000, Corporate diversification, ownership structure, and firm value: The Singapore evidence, *International Review of Financial Analysis*, 9: 315–326; R. E. Hoskisson, R. A. Johnson, & D. D. Moesel, 1994, Corporate divestiture intensity in restructuring firms: Effects of governance, strategy, and performance, *Academy of Management Journal*, 37: 1207–1251.

52. A. Berle & G. Means, 1932, *The Modern Corporation and Private Property*, New York: Macmillan.

53. P. A. Gompers & A. Metrick, 2001, Institutional investors and equity prices, *Quarterly Journal of Economics*, 116: 229–259; M. P. Smith, 1996, Shareholder activism by institutional investors: Evidence from CalPERS, *Journal of Finance*, 51: 227–252.

54. Hoskisson, Hitt, Johnson, & Grossman, Conflicting voices; C. M. Dailey, 1996, Governance patterns in bankruptcy reorganizations, *Strategic Management Journal*, 17: 355–375.

55. Hoskisson, Hitt, Johnson, & Grossman, Conflicting voices; R. E. Hoskisson & M. A. Hitt, 1994, *Downscoping: How to Tame the Diversified Firm*, New York: Oxford University Press.

56. K. Rebeiz, 2001, Corporate governance effectiveness in American corporations: A survey, *International Management Journal*, 18(1): 74–80.

57. 2002, CalPERS at a glance, http://www.calpers.com, April 24.

58. A. Grimes, 2003, Calpers is to widen disclosure on its private-equity returns, *Wall Street Journal Online*, http://www.wsj.com, March 18; 2003, Cronyism at Calpers, *Wall Street Journal Online*, http://www.wsj.com, January 31.

59. Tihanyi, Johnson, Hoskisson, & Hitt, Institutional ownership differences and international diversification; Hoskisson, Hitt, Johnson, & Grossman, Conflicting voices; P. David, M. A. Hitt, & J. Gimeno, 2001, The role of institutional investors in influencing R&D, *Academy of Management Journal*, 44: 144–157.

60. 2001, Shareholder activism is rising, *Investor Relations Business*, August 6, 8.

61. M. J. Roe, 1993, Mutual funds in the boardroom, *Journal of Applied Corporate Finance*, 5(4): 56–61.

62. R. A. G. Monks, 1999, What will be the impact of active shareholders? A practical recipe for constructive change, *Long Range Planning*, 32(1): 20–27.

63. B. S. Black, 1992, Agents watching agents: The promise of institutional investor's voice, *UCLA Law Review*, 39: 871–893.

64. Hoskisson, Hitt, Johnson, & Grossman, Conflicting voices; T. Woidtke, 2002, Agents watching agents: Evidence from pension fund ownership and firm value, *Journal of Financial Economics*, 63: 99–131.

65. A. Berenson, 2001, The fight for control of Computer Associates, *New York Times*, http://www.nytimes.com, June 25.

66. 2003, Computer Associates corporate governance and financial transparency initiatives 2002: Year in review, http://www.ca.com/governance/2002_review.htm, January.

67. C. Sundaramurthy & D. W. Lyon, 1998, Shareholder governance proposals and conflict of interests between inside and outside shareholders, *Journal of Managerial Issues*, 10: 30–44.

68. S. Thomsen & T. Pedersen, 2000, Ownership structure and economic performance in the largest European companies, *Strategic Management Journal*, 21: 689–705.

69. D. R. Dalton, C. M. Daily, A. E. Ellstrand, & J. L. Johnson, 1998, Meta-analytic reviews of board composition, leadership structure, and financial performance, *Strategic Management Journal*, 19: 269–290; M. Huse, 1998, Researching the dynamics of board-stakeholder relations, *Long Range Planning*, 31: 218–226.

70. A. Dehaene, V. De Vuyst, & H. Ooghe, 2001, Corporate performance and board structure in Belgian companies, *Long Range Planning*, 34(3): 383–398.

71. Hillman & Dalziel, Boards of directors and firm performance.

72. Rebeiz, Corporate governance effectiveness in American corporations; J. K. Seward & J. P Walsh, 1996, The governance and control of voluntary corporate spinoffs, *Strategic Management Journal*, 17: 25–39.

73. S. Young, 2000, The increasing use of non-executive directors: Its impact on UK board structure and governance arrangements, *Journal of Business Finance & Accounting*, 27(9/10): 1311–1342; P. Mallete & R. L. Hogler, 1995, Board composition, stock ownership, and the exemption of directors from liability, *Journal of Management*, 21: 861–878.

74. J. Chidley, 2001, Why boards matter, *Canadian Business*, October 29, 6; D. P. Forbes & F. J. Milliken, 1999, Cognition and corporate governance:

75. Understanding boards of directors as strategic decision-making groups, *Academy of Management Review*, 24: 489–505.

76. Carpenter & Westphal, Strategic context of external network ties: Examining the impact of director appointments on board involvement in strategic decision making; E. J. Zajac & J. D. Westphal, 1996, Director reputation, CEO-board power, and the dynamics of board interlocks, *Administrative Science Quarterly*, 41: 507–529.

77. A. Hillman, A. Cannella, Jr., & R. Paetzold, 2000, The resource dependence role of corporate directors: Strategic adaptation of board composition in response to environmental change, *Journal of Management Studies*, 37: 235–255; J. D. Westphal & E. J. Zajac, 1995, Who shall govern? CEO/board power, demographic similarity, and new director selection, *Administrative Science Quarterly*, 40: 60–83.

78. J. S. Lublin, 2003, More work, more pay, *Wall Street Journal Online*, http://www.wsj.com, February 24; J. Westphal & L. Milton, 2000, How experience and network ties affect the influence of demographic minorities on corporate boards, *Administrative Science Quarterly*, June, 45(2): 366–398.

79. 2003, The hot seat, *Wall Street Journal Online*, http://www.wsj.com, February 24; 2001, The fading appeal of the boardroom series, *The Economist*, February 10 (Business Special): 67–69.

80. G. Kassinis & N. Vafeas, 2002, Corporate boards and outside stakeholders as determinants of environmental litigation, *Strategic Management Journal*, 23: 399–415.

81. H. L. Tosi, W. Shen, & R. J. Gentry, 2003, Why outsiders on boards can't solve the corporate governance problem, *Organizational Dynamics*, 32: 180–192.

82. K. Greene, 2002, Dunlap agrees to settle suit over Sunbeam, *Wall Street Journal*, January 15, A3, A8.

83. P. Stiles, The impact of the board on strategy: An empirical examination, *Journal of Management Studies*, 38: 627–650; J. A. Byrne, 1999, Commentary: Boards share the blame when the boss fails, *BusinessWeek Online*, http://www.businessweek.com, December 27.

84. 2002, Sunbeam emerges from Chapter 11 bankruptcy, *Muzi News*, http://www.latelinenews.com, December 12; J. S. Lublin, 2002, Sunbeam's chief tells how he kept afloat amid crisis, *Wall Street Journal Online*, http://www.wsj.com, November 12.

85. E. Perotti & S. Gelfer, 2001, Red barons or robber barons? Governance and investment in Russian financial-industrial groups, *European Economic Review*, 45(9): 1601–1617; I. M. Millstein, 1997, Red herring over independent boards, *New York Times*, April 6, F10; W. Q. Judge, Jr., & G. H. Dobbins, 1995, Antecedents and effects of outside directors' awareness of CEO decision style, *Journal of Management*, 21: 43–64.

86. I. E. Kesner, 1988, Director characteristics in committee membership: An investigation of type, occupation, tenure and gender, *Academy of Management Journal*, 31: 66–84.

87. The hot seat.

88. J. Coles & W. Hesterly, 2000, Independence of the chairman and board composition: Firm choices and shareholder value, *Journal of Management*, 26: 195–214; S. Zahra, 1996, Governance, ownership and corporate entrepreneurship among the *Fortune* 500: The moderating impact of industry technological opportunity, *Academy of Management Journal*, 39: 1713–1735.

89. Hoskisson, Hitt, Johnson, & Grossman, Conflicting voices.

90. A. Conger, E. E. Lawler, & D. L. Finegold, 2001, *Corporate Boards: New Strategies for Adding Value at the Top*, San Francisco: Jossey-Bass; J. A. Conger, D. Finegold, & E. E. Lawler III, 1998, Appraising boardroom performance, *Harvard Business Review*, 76(1): 136–148.

91. J. Marshall, 2001, As boards shrink, responsibilities grow, *Financial Executive*, 17(4): 36–39.

92. C. A. Simmers, 2000, Executive/board politics in strategic decision making, *Journal of Business and Economic Studies*, 4: 37–56.

93. S. Finkelstein & A. C. Mooney, 2003, Not the usual suspects: How to use board process to make boards better, *Academy of Management Executive*, 17: 101–113.

94. Hoskisson, Hitt, Johnson, & Grossman, Conflicting voices.

95. W. Ocasio, 1999, Institutionalized action and corporate governance, *Administrative Science Quarterly*, 44: 384–416.

96. A. A. Cannella, Jr. & W. Shen, 2001, So close and yet so far: Promotion versus exit for CEO heirs apparent, *Academy of Management Journal*, 44: 252–270.

97. M. Gerety, C. Hoi, & A. Robin, 2001, Do shareholders benefit from the adoption of incentive pay for directors? *Financial Management*, 30: 45–61; D. C. Hambrick & E. M. Jackson, 2000, Outside directors with a stake: The linchpin in improving governance, *California Management Review*, 42(4): 108–127.

98. Lublin, More work, more pay.

99. J. L. Coles & C.-K. Hoi, 2003, New evidence on the market for directors: Board membership and Pennsylvania Bill 1310, *Journal of Finance*, 58: 197–230; S. P. Ferris, M. Jagannathan, & A. C. Pritchard, 2003, Too busy to mind the business? Monitoring by directors with multiple board appointments, *Journal of Finance*, 58: in press.

100. I. Filatotchev & S. Toms, 2003, Corporate governance, strategy and survival in a declining industry: A study of UK cotton textile companies, *Journal of Management Studies*, 40: 895–920.

101. J. Kristie, 2001, The shareholder activist: Nell Minow, *Directors and Boards*, 26(1): 16–17.

102. M. A. Carpenter & W. G. Sanders, 2002, Top management team compensation: The missing link between CEO pay and firm performance, *Strategic Management Journal*, 23: 367–375; D. C. Hambrick & S. Finkelstein, 1995, The effects of ownership structure on conditions at the top: The case of CEO pay raises, *Strategic Management Journal*, 16: 175.

103. J. S. Miller, R. M. Wiseman, & L. R. Gomez-Mejia, 2002, The fit between CEO compensation design and firm risk, *Academy of Management Journal*, 45: 745–756; L. Gomez-Mejia & R. M. Wiseman, 1997, Reframing executive compensation: An assessment and outlook, *Journal of Management*, 23: 291–374.

104. J. McGuire & E. Matta, 2003, CEO stock options: The silent dimension of ownership, *Academy of Management Journal*, 46: 255–265; W. G. Sanders & M. A. Carpenter, 1998, Internationalization and firm governance: The roles of CEO compensation, top team composition and board structure, *Academy of Management Journal*, 41: 158–178.

105. N. T. Hill & K. T. Stevens, 2001, Structuring compensation to achieve better financial results, *Strategic Finance*, 9: 48–51; J. D. Westphal & E. J. Zajac, 1999, The symbolic management of stockholders: Corporate governance reform and shareholder reactions, *Administrative Science Quarterly*, 43: 127–153.

106. L. Gomez-Mejia, M. Larraza-Kintana, & M. Makri, 2003, The determinants of executive compensation in family-controlled public corporations, *Academy of Management Journal*, 46: 226–237; Elloumi & Gueyie, CEO compensation, IOS and the role of corporate governance; M. J. Conyon & S. I. Peck, 1998, Board control, remuneration committees, and top management compensation, *Academy of Management Journal*, 41: 146–157.

107. S. O'Donnell, 2000, Managing foreign subsidiaries: Agents of headquarters, or an interdependent network? *Strategic Management Journal*, 21: 521–548; K. Roth & S. O'Donnell, 1996, Foreign subsidiary compensation: An agency theory perspective, *Academy of Management Journal*, 39: 678–703.

108. K. Ramaswamy, R. Veliyath, & L. Gomes, 2000, A study of the determinants of CEO compensation in India, *Management International Review*, 40(2): 167–191.

109. J. Krug & W. Hegarty, 2001, Predicting who stays and leaves after an acquisition: A study of top managers in multinational firms, *Strategic Management Journal*, 22: 185–196.

110. Carpenter & Sanders, Top management team compensation.

111. S. Bryan, L. Hwang, & S. Lilien, 2000, CEO stock-based compensation: An empirical analysis of incentive-intensity, relative mix, and economic determinants, *Journal of Business*, 73: 661–693.

112. 2003, How CEO salary and bonus packages compare, *USA Today*, http://www.usatoday.com, March 31.

113. R. E. Hoskisson, M. A. Hitt, & C. W. L. Hill, 1993, Managerial incentives and investment in R&D in large multiproduct firms, *Organization Science*, 4: 325–341.

114. Gomez-Mejia, Larraza-Kintana, & Makri, 2003, The determinants of executive compensation in family-controlled public corporations.

115. L. K. Meulbroek, 2001, The efficiency of equity-linked compensation: Understanding the full cost of awarding executive stock options, *Financial Management*, 30(2): 5–44.

116. G. Colvin, 2001, The great CEO pay heist, *Fortune*, June 25, 67.

117. J. Dahya, A. A. Lonie, & D. A. Power, 1998, Ownership structure, firm performance and top executive change: An analysis of UK firms, *Journal of Business Finance & Accounting*, 25: 1089–1118.

118. L. Gomez-Mejia, 2003, What should be done about CEO pay? *Academy of Management Issues Forum*, July; H. Tosi, S. Werner, J. Katz, & L. Gomez-Mejia, 2000, How much does performance matter? A meta-analysis of CEO pay studies, *Journal of Management*, 26: 301–339.

119. D. Leonhardt, 2002, It's called a "loan," but it's far sweeter, *New York Times*, http://www.nytimes.com, February 3.

120. G. Strom, Even last year, option spigot was wide open, *New York Times*, http://www.nytimes.com, February 3.

121. T. G. Pollock, H. M. Fischer, & J. B. Wade, 2002, The role of politics in repricing executive options, *Academy of Management Journal*, 45: 1172–1182; M. E. Carter and L. J. Lynch, 2001, An examination of executive stock option repricing, *Journal of Financial Economics*, 59: 207–225; D. Chance, R. Kumar, & R. Todd, 2001, The "repricing" of executive stock options, *Journal of Financial Economics*, 59: 129–154.

122. N. K. Chidambaran & N. R. Prabhala, 2003, Executive stock option repricing, internal governance mechanisms and management turnover, *Journal of Financial Economics*, 61: in press.

123. J. C. Hartzell & L. T. Starks, 2003, Institutional investors and executive compensation, *Journal of Finance*, 61: in press.

124. P. Brandes, R. Dharwadkar, & G. V. Lemesis, 2003, Effective stock option design: Reconciling stakeholder, strategic and motivational factors, *Academy of Management Executive*, 17(1): 77–93.

125. J. Greene, C. Edwards, S. Hamm, D. Henry, & L. Lavelle, 2003, Will stock options lose their sex appeal? *Business Week*, July 21, 23–24.

126. R. Coff, 2002, Bidding wars over R&D intensive firms: Knowledge, opportunism and the market for corporate control, *Academy of Management Journal*, 46: 74–85; Hitt, Hoskisson, Johnson, & Moesel, The market for corporate control and firm innovation; J. P. Walsh & R. Kosnik, 1993, Corporate raiders and their disciplinary role in the market for corporate control, *Academy of Management Journal*, 36: 671–700.

127. D. Goldstein, 2000, Hostile takeovers as corporate governance? Evidence from 1980s, *Review of Political Economy*, 12: 381–402.

128. R. Sidel & A. Raghavan, 2003, Merger activity sizzles again, *Wall Street Journal*, July 9, C1, C5.

129. M. A. Hitt & V. Pisano, 2003, The cross-border merger and acquisition strategy, *Management Research*, 1: 133–144; B. Venard, 2003, Les acquisitions transnationales en hongrie: Vers une taxonomie des attitudes face au changement, *Management International*, 7: 19–30.

130. J. Anand & A. Delios, 2002, Absolute and relative resources as determinants of international acquisitions, *Strategic Management Journal*, 23: 119–134.

131. J. Harford, 2003, Takeover bids and target directors' incentives: The impact of a bid on directors' wealth and board seats, *Journal of Financial Economics*, 61: in press; S. Chatterjee, J. S. Harrison, & D. D. Bergh, 2003, Failed takeover attempts, corporate governance and refocusing, *Strategic Management Journal*, 24: 87–96.

132. F. Guerrera & R. Waters, 2003, EU probe looms over Oracle merger plans, *Financial Times*, http://www.ft.com, July 2; M. Lander, 2003, Ringside at PeopleSoft bout, SAP hopes to share in the prize, *New York Times*, http://www.nytimes.com, June 30.

133. M. Maynard & F. Warner, 2003, Rival makes hostile bid for Dana, *New York Times*, http://www.nytimes.com, July 9; J. Grant, 2003, ArvinMeritor launches hostile bid for Dana, *Financial Times*, http://www.ft.com, July 8.

134. D. Ball, J. R. Hagerly, & R. Sidel, 2003, List of Safeway suitors keeps growing, *Wall Street Journal*, January 23, C1, C9.

135. J. Johnson, 2003, Ex-Vivendi chief in transatlantic legal battle, *Financial Times*, http://www.ft.com, July 11; A. R. Sorkin, 2003, Arbitrators say Vivendi owes Messier millions, *New York Times*, http://www.nytimes.com, July 1.

136. C. Sundaramurthy, J. M. Mahoney, & J. T. Mahoney, Board structure, antitakeover provisions, and stockholder wealth, *Strategic Management Journal*, 18: 231–246.

137. J. Westphal & E. Zajac, 2001, Decoupling policy from practice: The case of stock repurchase programs, *Administrative Science Quarterly*, 46: 202–228.

138. H. W. Jenkins, 2003, Don't sweat it, *Wall Street Journal*, http://www.wsj.com, February 24; J. A. Byrne, 1999, Poison pills: Let shareholders decide, *Business Week*, May 17, 104.

139. P.-W. Tam, 2003, H-P severance curbs get support, *Wall Street Journal*, April 3, B5.
140. A. Almanzan & J. Suarez, 2003, Entrenchment and severance pay in optimal governance structures, *Journal of Finance*, 58: 519–548.
141. Walsh & Kosnik, Corporate raiders.
142. A. Chakraborty & R. Arnott, 2001, Takeover defenses and dilution: A welfare analysis, *Journal of Financial and Quantitative Analysis*, 36: 311–334.
143. A. Portlono, 2000, The decision to adopt defensive tactics in Italy, *International Review of Law and Economics*, 20: 425–452.
144. C. Sundaramurthy, 2000, Antitakeover provisions and shareholder value implications: A review and a contingency framework, *Journal of Management*, 26: 1005–1030.
145. B. Kogut, G. Walker, & J. Anand, 2002, Agency and institutions: National divergence in diversification behavior, *Organization Science*, 13: 162–178; D. Norburn, B. K. Boyd, M. Fox, & M. Muth, 2000, International corporate governance reform, *European Business Journal*, 12(3): 116–133; M. Useem, 1998, Corporate leadership in a globalizing equity market, *Academy of Management Executive*, 12(3): 43–59.
146. Y. Yafeh, 2000, Corporate governance in Japan: Past performance and future prospects, *Oxford Review of Economic Policy*, 16(2): 74–84; H. Kim & R. E. Hoskisson, 1996, Japanese governance systems: A critical review, in B. Prasad (ed.), *Advances in International Comparative Management*, Greenwich, CT: JAI Press, 165–189.
147. L. Nanchum, 2003, Does nationality of ownership make any difference and if so, under what circumstances? Professional service MNEs in global competition, *Journal of International Management*, 9: 1–32.
148. Aguilera & Jackson, The cross-national diversity of corporate governance: Dimensions and determinants.
149. S. Klein, 2000, Family businesses in Germany: Significance and structure, *Family Business Review*, 13: 157–181.
150. J. Edwards & M. Nibler, 2000, Corporate governance in Germany: The role of banks and ownership concentration, *Economic Policy*, 31: 237–268; E. R. Gedajlovic & D. M. Shapiro, 1998, Management and ownership effects: Evidence from five countries, *Strategic Management Journal*, 19: 533–553.
151. S. Douma, 1997, The two-tier system of corporate governance, *Long Range Planning*, 30(4): 612–615.
152. N. E. Boudette, 2003, Volkswagen stalls on several fronts after luxury drive, *Wall Street Journal*, May 8, A1, A17; C. Tierney, 2001, Volkswagen, *BusinessWeek Online*, http://www.businessweek.com, July 23.
153. A. Tuschke & W. G. Sanders, 2003, Antecedents and consequences of corporate governance reform: The case of Germany, *Strategic Management Journal*, 24: 631–649.
154. T. Hoshi, A. K. Kashyap, & S. Fischer, 2001, *Corporate Financing and Governance in Japan*, Boston: MIT Press.
155. Charkham, *Keeping Good Company*, 70.
156. M. A. Hitt, H. Lee, & E. Yucel, 2002, The importance of social capital to the management of multinational enterprises: Relational networks among Asian and Western Firms, *Asia Pacific Journal of Management*, 19: 353–372.
157. P. M. Lee & H. M. O'Neill, 2003, Ownership structures and R&D investments of U.S. and Japanese firms: Agency and stewardship perspectives, *Academy of Management Journal*, 46: 212–225.
158. B. Bremner, 2001, Cleaning up the banks—finally, *Business Week*, December 17, 86; 2000, Business: Japan's corporate-governance u-turn, *The Economist*, November 18, 73.
159. B. Bremner, E. Thornton, & I. M. Kunii, 1999, Fall of a keiretsu, *Business Week*, March 15, 87–92.
160. Lee & O'Neill, Ownership structures and R&D investments of U.S. and Japanese firms.
161. J. B. White, 2000, The company we'll keep, *Wall Street Journal Online*, http://www.wsj.com, January 17.
162. K. Uhlenbruck, K. E. Meyer, & M. A. Hitt, 2003, Organizational transformation in transition economies: Resource-based and organizational learning perspectives, *Journal of Management Studies*, 40: 257–282; P. Mar & M. Young, 2001, Corporate governance in transition economies: A case study of 2 Chinese airlines, *Journal of World Business*, 36(3): 280–302.
163. L. Chang, 1999, Chinese firms find incentive to use stock-compensation plans, *Wall Street Journal*, November 1, A2; T. Clarke & Y. Du, 1998, Corporate governance in China: Explosive growth and new patterns of ownership, *Long Range Planning*, 31(2): 239–251.
164. M. A. Hitt, D. Ahlstrom, M. T. Dacin, E. Levitas, & L. Svobodina, 2004, The institutional effects on strategic alliance partner selection in transition economies: China versus Russia, *Organization Science*, in press; I. Filatotchev, R. Kapelyushnikov, N. Dyomina, & S. Aukutsionek, 2001, The effects of ownership concentration on investment and performance in privatized firms in Russia, *Managerial and Decision Economics*, 22(6): 299–313; E. Perotti & S. Gelfer, 2001, Red barons or robber barons? Governance and investment in Russian financial-industrial groups, *European Economic Review*, 45(9): 1601–1617.
165. Hillman, Keim, & Luce, Board composition and stakeholder performance; R. Oliver, 2000, The board's role: Driver's seat or rubber stamp? *Journal of Business Strategy*, 21: 7–9.
166. A. Felo, 2001, Ethics programs, board involvement, and potential conflicts of interest in corporate governance, *Journal of Business Ethics*, 32: 205–218.

Organizational Structure and Controls

Chapter Eleven

11

Knowledge Objectives

Studying this chapter should provide you with the strategic management knowledge needed to:

1. Define organizational structure and controls and discuss the difference between strategic and financial controls.

2. Describe the relationship between strategy and structure.

3. Discuss the functional structures used to implement business-level strategies.

4. Explain the use of three versions of the multidivisional (M-form) structure to implement different diversification strategies.

5. Discuss the organizational structures used to implement three international strategies.

6. Define strategic networks and strategic center firms.

©Reuters NewMedia Inc./Corbis

The success of Amaze Entertainment, creator of Sony's Playstation2, is partly a function of the match between its corporate-level strategy and organizational structure.

Amaze Entertainment: Bringing Video-Game Excitement Directly to You!

Amaze Entertainment was founded in 1996. It has become one of the world's largest and most successful independent developers of interactive video-game entertainment. The firm believes that it is quite skilled at "creating reliable, solid, interactive experiences for platforms ranging from PCs and Macs to handheld devices and gaming consoles—including next-generation systems like the Nintendo Game Cube, Microsoft X-Box and Sony Playstation2." As this array of products suggests, Microsoft, Mattel, Sony, and Electronic Arts are but a few of Amaze's clients. Designing and producing games linked to Hollywood blockbusters is an important source of the firm's profitable growth. Amaze's games based on *Harry Potter and the Sorcerer's Stone*, *The Lord of the Rings: The Two Towers*, *Finding Nemo*, and *Daredevil*, for example, have been highly successful.

Although relatively small (with approximately 220 employees in mid-2003), Amaze Entertainment is a diversified company with an organizational structure featuring five core business units (called studios) serving different markets. Each specialized studio is guided by a unique vision and has its own culture. However, all the studios rely on technical sophistication and skilled designers to produce their products. The goal of the Adrenium studio is to surprise, amuse, and captivate even the most seasoned gamer. Azurik is one of its popular games. Griptonite is Amaze's handheld entertainment studio. In addition to *Harry Potter*, Griptonite has produced handheld games based on *Star Wars*, Barbie, and Ren and Stimpy, among others. The PC entertainment studio is called KnowWonder. Oriented to family fun, KnowWonder creates digital entertainment products for use on PCs. Titles produced by KnowWonder are intended to educate as well as entertain. The Fizz Factor studio was acquired by Amaze. The "Fizz" unit seeks to be a premiere developer of original character-driven console and handheld titles for customers such as Hasbro and Nickelodeon. Black Ship studios is the newest Amaze business unit. After gaining success in its U.S. domestic market, Amaze decided to expand into what it envisions to be a lucrative Asian market, starting with Japan. The former president of Nintendo Software USA is heading Black Ship, which is focused on developing partnerships and superior products by working with the best publishers in Asia. Amaze believes that Black Ship has the potential to eventually account for as much as 33 percent of the firm's total revenues.

Amaze Entertainment is using a related constrained corporate-level strategy, with each of its five studios implementing a differentiation business-level strategy. The cooperative multidivisional organizational structure (discussed later in the chapter) is used at Amaze to support its related constrained corporate-level strategy. This structure means that while Amaze's studios work independently, all five of them share the firm's strength in innovative game technologies as well as its ability to share knowledge among its employees regarding their game development skills. The corporate office centralizes strategic planning and marketing efforts to foster cooperation among the five studios. This proper match between corporate-level strategy and structure has contributed to the firm's ability to establish a niche with Hollywood producers. Indeed, as an Amaze executive says, "There really isn't another studio in the world that can do what we do. With one contract, publishers can get a great PC game, a great Game Boy game and a great console game—nobody that I know of offers that." Family-oriented games form the other market niche analysts believe Amaze dominates.

SOURCES: 2003, Amaze Entertainment, http://www.amazeentertainment.com, July 7; 2003, One market at a time, *Business Week Online*, http://www.businessweek.com, April 15; S. Ernst, Fast-growing Amaze builds on its Hollywood ties, *Puget Sound Business Journal*, 23(41): 12; L. Hawkins, 2003, Computer-game maker puts Fizz back into Austin, Texas, industry, *Austin American-Statesman*, June 23.

As described in Chapter 4, all firms use one or more business-level strategies. In Chapters 6–9, we discuss the other strategies that might be used (corporate-level, international, and cooperative strategies). Once selected, strategies can't be implemented in a vacuum. Organizational structure and controls, this chapter's topic, provide the framework within which strategies are used in both for-profit organizations and not-for-profit agencies.[1] However, as we explain, separate structures and controls are required to successfully implement different strategies. For example, Amaze Entertainment uses a form of the multidivisional structure to support use of its related constrained corporate-level strategy, while each of its business units or studios employs a version of the functional structure to effectively implement the differentiation business-level strategy. Top-level managers have the final responsibility for ensuring that the firm has matched each of its strategies with the appropriate organizational structure and that changes to both take place when needed.[2] The match or degree of fit between strategy and structure influences the firm's attempts to earn above-average returns.[3] Thus, the ability to select an appropriate strategy and match it with the appropriate structure is an important characteristic of effective strategic leadership.[4]

This chapter opens with an introduction to organizational structure and controls. We then provide more details about the need for the firm's strategy and structure to be properly matched. Executives at Amaze Entertainment are aware of this need and are committed to maintaining a proper match between its corporate-level strategy and the structure used to implement it. Affecting firms' efforts to match strategy and structure is the fact that they influence each other.[5] As we discuss, strategy has a more important influence on structure, although once in place, structure influences strategy.[6]

The chapter then describes the relationship between growth and structural change that successful firms experience. This is followed with discussions of the different organizational structures that firms use to implement the separate business-level, corporate-level, international, and cooperative strategies. A series of figures highlights the different structures firms match with strategies. Across time and based on their experiences, organizations, especially large and complex ones, customize these general structures to meet their unique needs.[7] Typically, the firm tries to form a structure that is complex enough to facilitate use of its strategies but simple enough for all to effectively implement.[8] For example, the main priority of the organizational structure developed by DnB NOR, Norway's largest commercial bank, was "to adapt the functional organization as far as possible to our customer activities, making sure that the chosen structure will enable us to realize potential synergies."[9]

Organizational Structure and Controls

Research shows that organizational structure and the controls that are a part of it affect firm performance.[10] In particular, when the firm's strategy isn't matched with the most appropriate structure and controls, performance declines.[11] An ineffective match between strategy and structure is thought to account for Zurich Financial Services' recent performance declines.[12] Recognizing this mismatch, the firm is restructuring its business portfolio to focus on its core non-life insurance programs. Less diversification and a renewed concentration on its core business area are expected to result in a match between corporate-level strategy and structure.[13] Even though mismatches between strategy and structure do occur, such as the one at Zurich Financial Services, research evidence suggests that managers try to act rationally when forming or changing their firm's structure.[14]

Organizational Structure

Organizational structure specifies the firm's formal reporting relationships, procedures, controls, and authority and decision-making processes.[15] Developing an organizational structure that effectively supports the firm's strategy is difficult,[16] especially because of the uncertainty (or unpredictable variation[17]) about cause-effect relationships in the global economy's rapidly changing and dynamic competitive environments.[18] When a structure's elements (e.g., reporting relationships, procedures, and so forth) are properly aligned with one another, that structure facilitates effective implementation of the firm's strategies.[19] Thus, organizational structure is a critical component of effective strategy implementation processes.[20]

A firm's structure specifies the work to be done and how to do it, given the firm's strategy or strategies.[21] Thus, organizational structure influences how managers work and the decisions resulting from that work.[22] Supporting the implementation of strategies,[23] structure is concerned with processes used to complete organizational tasks.[24] Effective structures provide the stability a firm needs to successfully implement its strategies and maintain its current competitive advantages, while simultaneously providing the flexibility to develop competitive advantages that will be needed for its future strategies.[25] Thus, *structural stability* provides the capacity the firm requires to consistently and predictably manage its daily work routines,[26] while *structural flexibility* provides the opportunity to explore competitive possibilities and then allocate resources to activities that will shape the competitive advantages the firm will need to be successful in the future.[27] An effective organizational structure allows the firm to *exploit* current competitive advantages while *developing* new ones.[28]

Modifications to the firm's current strategy or selection of a new strategy call for changes to its organizational structure. However, research shows that once in place, organizational inertia often inhibits efforts to change structure, even when the firm's performance suggests that it is time to do so.[29] In his pioneering work, Alfred Chandler found that organizations change their structures only when inefficiencies force them to do so.[30] Firms seem to prefer the structural status quo and its familiar working relationships until the firm's performance declines to the point where change is absolutely necessary.[31] In addition, top-level managers hesitate to conclude that there are problems with the firm's structure (or its strategy, for that matter), in that doing so suggests that their previous choices weren't the best ones.[32] Because of these inertial tendencies, structural change is often induced instead by the actions of stakeholders

Organizational structure specifies the firm's formal reporting relationships, procedures, controls, and authority and decision-making processes.

who are no longer willing to tolerate the firm's performance. For example, continuing losses of customers who have become dissatisfied with the value created by the firm's products could force change, as could reactions from capital market stakeholders (see Chapter 2). This appears to be the case for Sears, Roebuck and Co. Because of dissatisfactions expressed by those it tried to serve, Sears recently changed its organizational structure in ways that it believes allows it to better satisfy customers' needs.[33]

In spite of the timing of structural change described above, many companies make changes prior to substantial performance declines. Appropriate timing of structural change happens when top-level managers quickly recognize that a current organizational structure no longer provides the coordination and direction needed for the firm to successfully implement its strategies.[34] As we discuss in the Strategic Focus, Eastman Chemical Company has made various changes to its organizational structure prior to significant performance declines. Indeed, in commenting about one of the changes to the firm's structure, a company official asserted, "This was not a company that reorganized in response to plummeting sales, laying off thousands of workers to stay afloat. This was restructuring from strength."[35]

As we discuss next, effective organizational controls help managers recognize when it is time to change the firm's structure. Eastman Chemical Company uses a mixture of strategic and financial controls to judge its overall performance. In addition, the controls in place at Eastman help the firm determine when to make changes to its organizational structure.

Organizational Controls

Organizational controls are an important aspect of structure.[36] **Organizational controls** guide the use of strategy, indicate how to compare actual results with expected results, and suggest corrective actions to take when the difference between actual and expected results is unacceptable. The fewer the differences between actual and expected outcomes, the more effective are the organization's controls.[37] It is hard for the company to successfully exploit its competitive advantages without effective organizational controls.[38] Properly designed organizational controls provide clear insights regarding behaviors that enhance firm performance.[39] Firms rely on strategic controls and financial controls as part of their structures to support use of their strategies.[40]

Strategic controls are largely subjective criteria intended to verify that the firm is using appropriate strategies for the conditions in the external environment and the company's competitive advantages. Thus, strategic controls are concerned with examining the fit between what the firm *might do* (as suggested by opportunities in its external environment) and what it *can do* (as indicated by its competitive advantages; see Figure 3.1). Effective strategic controls help the firm understand what it takes to be successful.[41] Strategic controls demand rich communications between managers responsible for using them to judge the firm's performance and those with primary responsibility for implementing the firm's strategies (such as middle- and first-level managers). These frequent exchanges are both formal and informal in nature.[42]

Strategic controls are also used to evaluate the degree to which the firm focuses on the requirements to implement its strategies. For a business-level strategy, for example, the strategic controls are used to study primary and support activities (see Tables 3.8 and 3.9) to verify that those critical to successful execution of the business-level strategy are being properly emphasized and executed. With related corporate-level strategies, strategic controls are used to verify the sharing of appropriate strategic factors such as knowledge, markets, and technologies across businesses. To effectively use strategic controls when evaluating related diversification strategies, executives must have a deep understanding of each unit's business-level strategy.[43]

Partly because strategic controls are difficult to use with extensive diversification,[44] financial controls are emphasized to evaluate the performance of the firm following the

Organizational controls *guide the use of strategy, indicate how to compare actual results with expected results, and suggest corrective actions to take when the difference between actual and expected results is unacceptable.*

Strategic controls *are largely subjective criteria intended to verify that the firm is using appropriate strategies for the conditions in the external environment and the company's competitive advantages.*

Effective Timing of Structural Change at Eastman Chemical Company

Founded in 1920 to supply basic photographic materials to Eastman Kodak Company, Eastman Chemical Company (ECC) was spun off and became an independently traded public company in 1994. A global firm with sales exceeding $5 billion annually and with production operations in 17 countries, ECC manufactures and markets more than 1,200 plastics, chemicals, and fibers products. Collectively, this array of products and their success has resulted in ECC becoming the world's largest supplier of polyester plastics for packaging, a leading supplier of coatings, raw materials, specialty chemicals, and plastics, and a major supplier of cellulose acetate fibers and basic chemicals.

On September 1, 1999, ECC announced that it had created two major business groups—one for its polymers business and one for its chemicals business. From 1994 until the 1999 reorganization, ECC had operated through a functional structure. However, the functional structure was no longer capable of dealing with the firm's increasing product and market complexity and diversity. Following analysis of the situation, executives concluded that organizing the firm around two core product divisions would lead to stronger relationships with customers. Increased efficiency, primarily in the form of quicker response to customers' needs, and greater accountability for performance were other benefits expected from the new structure in addition to an enhanced focus on customers. With the new structure, each business group was given direct responsibility for manufacturing, sales, and pricing and product management decisions. Thus, the polymers and chemicals businesses were each to operate with an independent set of organizational functions.

ECC's structure was changed again in 2002. In this instance, 1994's product divisions were changed to create the Eastman Division and the Voridian Division. The purpose of this structural change was to allow ECC to "strategically focus on the unique needs of individual markets." The Eastman Division consists of three product segments—coatings, adhesives, specialty polymers, and inks; specialty plastics; and performance chemicals and intermediates. Polymers and fibers, the product groups formed in 1999, became Voridian's two core segments in 2002. In general, Voridian uses the cost leadership business-level strategy while the differentiation strategy is used in the Eastman Division, primarily to continuously develop innovative products.

In 2003, Developing Businesses became the third division in ECC's multidivisional structure. Soon after its formation, this division had 20 to 30 projects in the pipeline in various stages of development. The purpose of creating this division was to provide a unique environment to "leverage Eastman's technology expertise, intellectual property and know-how into business models that extend to new customers and markets." For the most part, Developing Businesses focuses on service businesses that are less capital intensive compared to the products that are the mainstay of the Eastman and Voridian Divisions.

Eastman Chemical Company was originally a division of Eastman Kodak Company, a supplier of photographic materials. Eastman Chemical now produces a variety of consumer goods, some of which are featured here. The organizational controls that led to Eastman Chemical's independence from its parent company allow each company to better handle its own market complexities and customer needs.

Photo courtesy of the Eastman Chemical Company

SOURCES: 2003, Eastman introduces new business unit, *Chemical Market Reporter*, 263(13): 3; 2003, Eastman Chemical Company, *Standard & Poor's Stock Reports*, http://www.standardandpoors.com, June 3; 2003, The company profile, http://www.eastmanchemicals.com, July 10; 2003, Eastman facts, http://www.eastmanchemicals.com, July 9; 1999, Eastman announces management reorganization, http://www.eastmanchemicals.com, July 27.

unrelated diversification strategy. The unrelated diversification strategy's focus on financial outcomes (see Chapter 6) requires the use of standardized financial controls to compare performances between units and managers.[45] **Financial controls** are largely objective criteria used to measure the firm's performance against previously established quantitative standards. Accounting-based measures, such as return on investment and return on assets, and market-based measures, such as economic value added, are examples of financial controls.

When using financial controls, firms evaluate their current performance against previous outcomes as well as their performance compared to competitors and industry averages. In the global economy, technological advances are being used to develop highly sophisticated financial controls, making it possible for firms to more thoroughly analyze their performance results and to assure compliance with regulations. For example, Oracle Corp. developed software tools that automate processes firms can use to meet the financial reporting requirements specified by the Sarbanes-Oxley Act.[46] (This act requires a firm's principal executive and financial officers to certify corporate financial and related information in quarterly and annual reports submitted to the Securities and Exchange Commission.) Pfizer Inc.'s expectations of sophisticated financial controls are that they will: "(1) safeguard the firm's assets, (2) ensure that transactions are properly authorized, and (3) provide reasonable assurance, at reasonable cost, of the integrity, objectivity, and reliability of the financial information."[47]

Both strategic and financial controls are important aspects of each organizational structure, and any structure's effectiveness is determined by using a combination of strategic and financial controls. However, the relative use of controls varies by type of strategy. For example, companies and business units of large diversified firms using the cost leadership strategy emphasize financial controls (such as quantitative cost goals), while companies and business units using the differentiation strategy emphasize strategic controls (such as subjective measures of the effectiveness of product development teams).[48] As explained above, a corporate-wide emphasis on sharing among business units (as called for by related diversification strategies) results in an emphasis on strategic controls, while financial controls are emphasized for strategies in which activities or capabilities aren't shared (e.g., in an unrelated diversification).

Relationships between Strategy and Structure

Strategy and structure have a reciprocal relationship.[49] This relationship highlights the interconnectedness between strategy formulation (Chapter 4 and Chapters 6–9) and strategy implementation (Chapters 10–13). In general, this reciprocal relationship finds structure flowing from or following the selection of the firm's strategy. Once in place, structure can influence current strategic actions as well as choices about future strategies. The general nature of the strategy/structure relationship means that changes to the firm's strategy create the need to change how the organization completes its work. In the "structure influences strategy" direction, firms must be vigilant in their efforts to verify that how their structure calls for work to be completed remains consistent with the implementation requirements of chosen strategies. Research shows, however, that "strategy has a much more important influence on structure than the reverse."[50]

Regardless of the strength of the reciprocal relationships between strategy and structure, those choosing the firm's strategy and structure should be committed to matching each strategy with a structure that provides the stability needed to use current competitive advantages as well as the flexibility required to develop future advantages. This means, for example, that when changing strategies, the firm should simultaneously consider the structure that will be needed to support use of the new strategy. Aware of this mandate, executives at the new Hewlett-Packard continue to adjust the firm's structure in light of the strategies being used following the combining of the former Hewlett-

Packard and Compaq Computer Corp.[51] The fact that a proper strategy/structure match can be a competitive advantage[52] supports actions such as those being taken at Hewlett-Packard. When the firm's strategy/structure combination is a competitive advantage, it contributes to the earning of above-average returns.[53]

Evolutionary Patterns of Strategy and Organizational Structure

Research suggests that most firms experience a certain pattern of relationships between strategy and structure. Chandler[54] found that firms tended to grow in somewhat predictable patterns: "first by volume, then by geography, then integration (vertical, horizontal) and finally through product/business diversification"[55] (see Figure 11.1). Chandler interpreted his findings to indicate that the firm's growth patterns determine its structural form.

As shown in Figure 11.1, sales growth creates coordination and control problems that the existing organizational structure can't efficiently handle. Organizational growth

Strategy and Structure Growth Pattern —— Figure 11.1

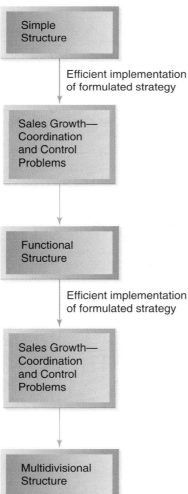

creates the opportunity for the firm to change its strategy to try to become even more successful. However, the existing structure's formal reporting relationships, procedures, controls, and authority and decision-making processes lack the sophistication required to support use of the new strategy. A new structure is needed to help decision makers gain access to the knowledge and understanding required to effectively integrate and coordinate actions to implement the new strategy.[56]

Three major types of organizational structures are used to implement strategies: simple structure, functional structure, and multidivisional structure.

Simple Structure

The simple structure is a structure in which the owner-manager makes all major decisions and monitors all activities while the staff serves as an extension of the manager's supervisory authority.

The functional structure is a structure consisting of a chief executive officer and a limited corporate staff, with functional line managers in dominant organizational areas, such as production, accounting, marketing, R&D, engineering, and human resources.

The **simple structure** is a structure in which the owner-manager makes all major decisions and monitors all activities while the staff serves as an extension of the manager's supervisory authority.[57] Typically, the owner-manager actively works in the business on a daily basis. Informal relationships, few rules, limited task specialization, and unsophisticated information systems describe the simple structure. Frequent and informal communications between the owner-manager and employees make it relatively easy to coordinate the work that is to be done. The simple structure is matched with focus strategies and business-level strategies as firms commonly compete by offering a single product line in a single geographic market. Local restaurants, repair businesses, and other specialized enterprises are examples of firms relying on the simple structure to implement their strategy.

As the small firm grows larger and becomes more complex, managerial and structural challenges emerge. For example, the amount of competitively relevant information requiring analysis substantially increases, placing significant pressure on the owner-manager. Additional growth and success may cause the firm to change its strategy. Even if the strategy remains the same, the firm's larger size dictates the need for more sophisticated workflows and integrating mechanisms. At this evolutionary point, firms tend to move from the simple structure to a functional organizational structure.[58]

Casketfurniture.com may need to change from a simple to a functional structure. MHP Enterprises Ltd. is a good example of a smaller firm that has grown more complex with its success.

Casketfurniture.com, a firm mentioned in Chapter 4 as an example of a company using the focus differentiation strategy, may soon move from the simple structure to a functional structure. Family-owned and managed, this venture is a new part of MHP Enterprises Ltd.'s operations. As a small family firm, MHP has long been managed through the simple structure. In 1997, MHP decided to expand its distribution by establishing Casketfurniture.com. Using the Internet, this venture sells what it believes are creative products throughout the world. The continuing success of Casketfurniture.com could create coordination and control problems for MHP that may be solved only by the firm changing from the simple to the functional structure.[59]

Functional Structure

The **functional structure** is a structure consisting of a chief executive officer and a limited corporate staff, with functional line managers in dominant organizational areas, such as production, accounting, marketing, R&D, engineering, and human resources.[60] This structure allows for functional specialization,[61] thereby facilitating active sharing of knowledge within each functional area. Knowledge sharing facilitates career paths as well as the professional development of functional specialists. However, a functional orientation can have a negative effect on communication and coordination among those representing different organizational functions. Because of this, the CEO must work hard to verify that the decisions and actions of individual business functions promote the entire firm rather than a single function.[62] The functional structure supports implementation of business-level strategies and some corporate-level strategies (e.g., single or dominant business) with low levels of diversification.

Multidivisional Structure

With continuing growth and success, firms often consider greater levels of diversification. However, successful diversification requires analysis of substantially greater amounts of data and information when the firm offers the same products in different markets (market or geographic diversification) or offers different products in several markets (product diversification). In addition, trying to manage high levels of diversification through functional structures creates serious coordination and control problems.[63] Thus, greater diversification leads to a new structural form.[64]

The **multidivisional (M-form) structure** consists of operating divisions, each representing a separate business or profit center in which the top corporate officer delegates responsibilities for day-to-day operations and business-unit strategy to division managers. Each division represents a distinct, self-contained business with its own functional hierarchy.[65] As initially designed, the M-form was thought to have three major benefits: "(1) it enabled corporate officers to more accurately monitor the performance of each business, which simplified the problem of control; (2) it facilitated comparisons between divisions, which improved the resource allocation process; and (3) it stimulated managers of poorly performing divisions to look for ways of improving performance."[66] Active monitoring of performance through the M-form increases the likelihood that decisions made by managers heading individual units will be in shareholders' best interests. Diversification is a dominant corporate-level strategy in the global economy, resulting in extensive use of the M-form.[67]

Used to support implementation of related and unrelated diversification strategies, the M-form helps firms successfully manage the many demands (including those related to processing vast amounts of information) of diversification.[68] Chandler viewed the M-form as an innovative response to coordination and control problems that surfaced during the 1920s in the functional structures then used by large firms such as DuPont and General Motors.[69] Research shows that the M-form is appropriate when the firm grows through diversification.[70] Partly because of its value to diversified corporations, some consider the multidivisional structure to be one of the 20th century's most significant organizational innovations.[71]

No organizational structure (simple, functional, or multidivisional) is inherently superior to the other structures.[72] In Peter Drucker's words: "There is no one right organization. . . . Rather, the task . . . is to select the organization for the particular task and mission at hand."[73] In our context, Drucker is saying that the firm must select a structure that is "right" for the particular strategy that has been selected to pursue the firm's strategic intent and strategic mission. Because no single structure is optimal in all instances, managers concentrate on developing proper matches between strategies and organizational structures rather than searching for an "optimal" structure.

We now describe the strategy/structure matches that evidence shows positively contribute to firm performance.

The **multidivisional (M-form) structure** *consists of operating divisions, each representing a separate business or profit center in which the top corporate officer delegates responsibilities for day-to-day operations and business-unit strategy to division managers.*

Matches between Business-Level Strategies and the Functional Structure

Different forms of the functional organizational structure are used to support implementation of the cost leadership, differentiation, and integrated cost leadership/differentiation strategies. The differences in these forms are accounted for primarily by different uses of three important structural characteristics or dimensions—*specialization* (concerned with the type and number of jobs required to complete work[74]), *centralization* (the degree to which decision-making authority is retained at higher managerial levels[75]), and *formalization* (the degree to which formal rules and procedures govern work[76]).

USING THE FUNCTIONAL STRUCTURE TO IMPLEMENT THE COST LEADERSHIP STRATEGY

Firms using the cost leadership strategy want to sell large quantities of standardized products to an industry's or a segment's typical customer. Simple reporting relationships, few layers in the decision-making and authority structure, a centralized corporate staff, and a strong focus on process improvements through the manufacturing function rather than the development of new products through an emphasis on product R&D characterize the cost leadership form of the functional structure[77] (see Figure 11.2). This structure contributes to the emergence of a low-cost culture—a culture in which all employees constantly try to find ways to reduce the costs incurred to complete their work.

In terms of centralization, decision-making authority is centralized in a staff function to maintain a cost-reducing emphasis within each organizational function (for example, engineering, marketing, etc.). While encouraging continuous cost reductions, the centralized staff also verifies that further cuts in costs in one function won't adversely affect the productivity levels in other functions.

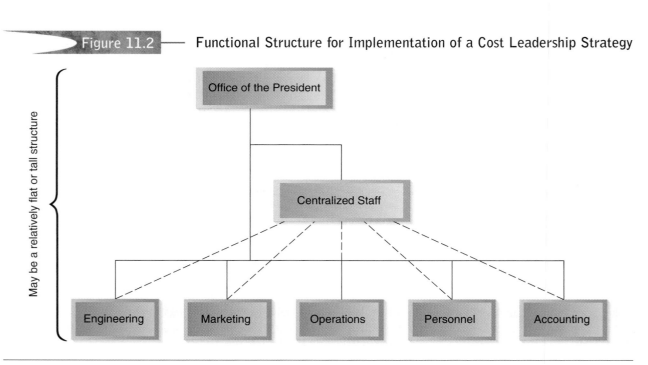

> **Figure 11.2** — Functional Structure for Implementation of a Cost Leadership Strategy

Notes:
- Operations is the main function
- Process engineering is emphasized rather than new product R&D
- Relatively large centralized staff coordinates functions
- Formalized procedures allow for emergence of a low-cost culture
- Overall structure is mechanistic; job roles are highly structured

Jobs are highly specialized in the cost leadership functional structure. Job specialization is accomplished by dividing work into homogeneous subgroups. Organizational functions are the most common subgroup, although work is sometimes batched on the basis of products produced or clients served. Specializing in their work allows employees to increase their efficiency, reducing the firm's costs as a result. Highly formalized rules and procedures, often emanating from the centralized staff, guide the work completed in the cost leadership form of the functional structure. Predictably following formal rules and procedures creates cost-reducing efficiencies. Known for its commitment to EDLP ("everyday low price"), Wal-Mart's functional organizational structures in both its retail (e.g., Wal-Mart Stores, Supercenters, Sam's Club) and specialty (e.g., Wal-Mart Vacations, Used Fixture Auctions) divisions are formed to continuously drive costs lower.[78] As discussed in Chapter 4, competitors' efforts to duplicate the success of Wal-Mart's cost leadership strategies have failed, partly because of the effective strategy/structure matches in Wal-Mart's business units.

USING THE FUNCTIONAL STRUCTURE TO IMPLEMENT THE DIFFERENTIATION STRATEGY

Firms using the differentiation strategy produce products that customers perceive as being different in ways that create value for them. With this strategy, the firm wants to sell nonstandardized products to customers with unique needs. Relatively complex and flexible reporting relationships, frequent use of cross-functional product development teams, and a strong focus on marketing and product R&D rather than manufacturing and process R&D (as with the cost leadership form of the functional structure) characterize the differentiation form of the functional structure (see Figure 11.3). This structure contributes to the emergence of a development-oriented culture—a culture in which employees try to find ways to further differentiate current products and to develop new, highly differentiated products.

Functional Structure for Implementation of a Differentiation Strategy — Figure 11.3

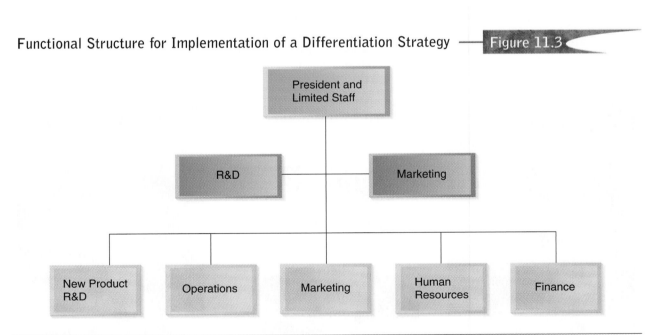

Notes: • Marketing is the main function for keeping track of new product ideas
- New product R&D is emphasized
- Most functions are decentralized, but R&D and marketing may have centralized staffs that work closely with each other
- Formalization is limited so that new product ideas can emerge easily and change is more readily accomplished
- Overall structure is organic; job roles are less structured

Thinking Globally, Acting Locally: The Foundations of Procter & Gamble's Multidivisional Structure

Consumer giant Procter & Gamble (P&G) has a bold self-perception, believing that its rightful place in corporate America is as a company that is admired, imitated, and uncommonly profitable. Historical successes suggest that this perception is reasonably consistent with reality. Across time, P&G has been quite profitable while analysts have viewed the firm's management techniques as setting "the gold standard" for others to emulate. Two of the innovations and subsequent skills for which P&G is recognized are brand management and excellence in managerial training. CEOs Jeff Immelt (GE), Meg Whitman (eBay) and W. James McNerney, Jr. (3M) are just a few of the alumni who have achieved great success following their P&G careers.

As with all successful firms, P&G is challenged to continuously reinvent itself while striving to outperform its competitors. Rivals such as Unilever are launching intense campaigns to improve their competitive positions relative to P&G. Unilever began restructuring in 1999 to deliver on the promises of its "Path to Growth" agenda. Unilever's five-year restructuring involves a major overhaul of its portfolio. The firm "has sold low-growth businesses and acquired new-growth drivers, most notably Best-foods, which it bought for $24 billion in 2000. The company also snapped up diet brand SlimFast and Ben & Jerry's ice cream."

P&G also restructured its operations in 1999. Framed around the objective of having an organizational structure that would allow the firm to "think globally and act locally," P&G formed a unique version of the cooperative multidivisional structure to support use of its related constrained diversification strategy. This structure, which P&G officials believe is a source of competitive advantage for the firm, features five global business product units (GBUs) (baby, feminine and family care, fabric and home care, food and beverage, and health and beauty care) and seven market development organizations (MDOs), each formed around a region of the world, such as Northeast Asia. Using the five global product units to create strong brand equities through ongoing innovation is how P&G thinks globally; interfacing with customers to ensure that a division's marketing plans fully capitalize on local opportunities is how P&G acts locally. Information is shared between the product-oriented and the marketing-oriented efforts to enhance the corpora-

Well-known CEOs Jeff Immelt, Meg Whitman, and W. James McNerney may owe their current success to the skills acquired during their employment at P&G, which is known for its excellence in managerial training.

tion's performance. Indeed, some corporate staff members are responsible for focusing on making certain that knowledge is meaningfully categorized and then rapidly transferred throughout P&G's businesses. Those working to achieve this objective are part of P&G's Global Business Services (GBS) group. Last, the Corporate Functions group is essentially a set of consultants ready to assist those working in the global business units and the market development organizations in their efforts to use "best practices" in terms of organizational functions, such as external relations, information technology management, and human resources practices. In summary, P&G's cooperative structure uses GBUs to define a brand's equity, MDOs to adapt a brand to local preferences, the GBS group to support operations through infrastructure services such as accounting and employee benefits and payroll, and Corporate Functions to assure that the latest and most effective methodologies are being used to conduct the firm's product- and marketing-oriented operations.

SOURCES: 2003, Procter & Gamble Home Page, http://www.procter&gamble.com, July 5; 2003, Procter & Gamble corporate structure, http://www.procter&gamble.com, July 9; D. Ball, 2003, Unilever cuts sales estimates as U.S. competition stiffens, *Wall Street Journal Online*, http://www.wsj.com, June 23; R. Berner, 2003, P&G: New and improved, *Business Week*, July 7, 52–63.

Continuous product innovation demands that people throughout the firm be able to interpret and take action based on information that is often ambiguous, incomplete, and uncertain. With a strong focus on the external environment to identify new opportunities, employees often gather this information from people outside the firm, such as customers and suppliers. Commonly, rapid responses to the possibilities indicated by the collected information are necessary, suggesting the need for decision-making responsibility and authority to be decentralized. To support creativity and the continuous pursuit of new sources of differentiation and new products, jobs in this structure are not highly specialized. This lack of specialization means that workers have a relatively large number of tasks in their job descriptions. Few formal rules and procedures are also characteristics of this structure. Low formalization, decentralization of decision-making authority and responsibility, and low specialization of work tasks combine to create a structure in which people interact frequently to exchange ideas about how to further differentiate current products while developing ideas for new products that can be differentiated to create value for customers.

USING THE FUNCTIONAL STRUCTURE TO IMPLEMENT THE INTEGRATED COST LEADERSHIP/DIFFERENTIATION STRATEGY

Firms using the integrated cost leadership/differentiation strategy want to sell products that create value because of their relatively low cost and reasonable sources of differentiation. The cost of these products is low "relative" to the cost leader's prices while their differentiation is "reasonable" compared to the clearly unique features of the differentiator's products.

The integrated cost leadership/differentiation strategy is used frequently in the global economy, although it is difficult to successfully implement. This difficulty is due largely to the fact that different primary and support activities (see Chapter 3) must be emphasized when using the cost leadership and differentiation strategies. To achieve the cost leadership position, emphasis is placed on production and process engineering, with infrequent product changes. To achieve a differentiated position, marketing and new product R&D are emphasized while production and process engineering are not. Thus, effective use of the integrated strategy results when the firm successfully combines activities intended to reduce costs with activities intended to create additional differentiation features. As a result, the integrated form of the functional structure must have decision-making patterns that are partially centralized and partially decentralized. Additionally, jobs are semispecialized, and rules and procedures call for some formal and some informal job behavior.

Matches between Corporate-Level Strategies and the Multidivisional Structure

As explained earlier, Chandler's research showed that the firm's continuing success leads to product or market diversification or both.[79] The firm's level of diversification is a function of decisions about the number and type of businesses in which it will compete as well as how it will manage the businesses (see Chapter 6). Geared to managing individual organizational functions, increasing diversification eventually creates information processing, coordination, and control problems that the functional structure can't handle. Thus, use of a diversification strategy requires the firm to change from the functional structure to the multidivisional structure to develop an appropriate strategy/structure match.

As defined in Figure 6.1 in Chapter 6, corporate-level strategies have different degrees of product and market diversification. The demands created by different levels of diversification highlight the need for each strategy to be implemented through a unique organizational structure (see Figure 11.4).

USING THE COOPERATIVE FORM OF THE MULTIDIVISIONAL STRUCTURE TO IMPLEMENT THE RELATED CONSTRAINED STRATEGY

The cooperative form is a structure in which horizontal integration is used to bring about interdivisional cooperation.

The **cooperative form** is a structure in which horizontal integration is used to bring about interdivisional cooperation. The divisions in the firm using the related constrained diversification strategy commonly are formed around products, markets, or both. We discuss related constrained firm Procter & Gamble's (P&G's) cooperative form of the multidivisional structure in the Strategic Focus. As we explain, P&G's organizational structure is intended to allow the firm to "think globally, yet act locally."

In Figure 11.5, we use product divisions as part of the representation of the cooperative form of the multidivisional structure, although as the P&G example in the Strategic Focus suggests, market divisions could be used instead of or in addition to product divisions to develop the figure. Thus, P&G has modified the core cooperative form of the multidivisional structure to satisfy its unique strategy/structure match requirements.

Figure 11.4 ——— Three Variations of the Multidivisional Structure

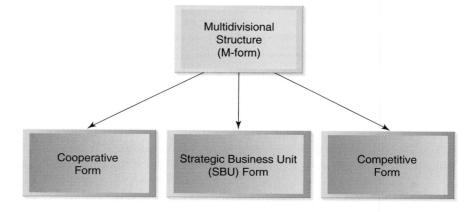

Cooperative Form of the Multidivisional Structure for Implementation of a Related Constrained Strategy

Figure 11.5

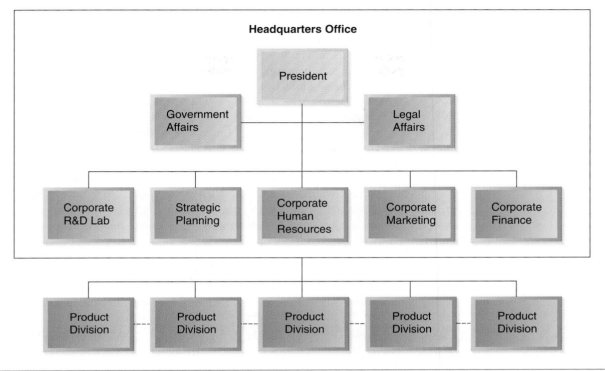

Notes:
- Structural integration devices create tight links among all divisions
- Corporate office emphasizes centralized strategic planning, human resources, and marketing to foster cooperation between divisions
- R&D is likely to be centralized
- Rewards are subjective and tend to emphasize overall corporate performance in addition to divisional performance
- Culture emphasizes cooperative sharing

All of the related constrained firm's divisions share one or more corporate strengths. Production competencies, marketing competencies, or channel dominance are examples of strengths that the firm's divisions might share.[80] Production expertise is one of the strengths shared across P&G's divisions. At Halliburton Co., the world's largest oilfield services company, the firm's competence in the development and application of sophisticated technologies is shared between its two major divisions.[81]

The sharing of divisional competencies facilitates the corporation's efforts to develop economies of scope. As explained in Chapter 6, economies of scope (cost savings resulting from the sharing of competencies developed in one division with another division) are linked with successful use of the related constrained strategy. Interdivisional sharing of competencies depends on cooperation, suggesting the use of the cooperative form of the multidivisional structure.[82] Increasingly, it is important that the links resulting from effective use of integration mechanisms support the cooperative sharing of both intangible resources (such as knowledge) as well as tangible resources (such as facilities and equipment).[83]

Different characteristics of structure are used as integrating mechanisms by the cooperative structure to facilitate interdivisional cooperation. Defined earlier in the discussion of functional organizational structures, centralization is one of these mechanisms. Centralizing some organizational functions (human resource management, R&D, marketing, and finance) at the corporate level allows the linking of activities among divisions. Work completed in these centralized functions is managed by the firm's central office with the purpose of exploiting common strengths among divisions by sharing competencies. The intent is to develop a competitive advantage in the divisions as they implement their cost leadership, differentiation, or integrated cost leadership/differentiation business-unit strategies that exceeds the value created by the advantages used by nondiversified rivals' implementation of these strategies.[84]

Frequent, direct contact between division managers, another integrating mechanism, encourages and supports cooperation and the sharing of either competencies or resources that have the possibility of being used to create new advantages. Sometimes, liaison roles are established in each division to reduce the amount of time division managers spend integrating and coordinating their unit's work with the work occurring in other divisions. Temporary teams or task forces may be formed around projects whose success depends on sharing competencies that are embedded within several divisions. Formal integration departments might be established in firms frequently using temporary teams or task forces. Ultimately, a matrix organization may evolve in firms implementing the related constrained strategy. A *matrix organization* is an organizational structure in which there is a dual structure combining both functional specialization and business product or project specialization.[85] Although complicated, an effective matrix structure can lead to improved coordination among a firm's divisions.[86]

The success of the cooperative multidivisional structure is significantly affected by how well information is processed among divisions. But because cooperation among divisions implies a loss of managerial autonomy, division managers may not readily commit themselves to the type of integrative information-processing activities that this structure demands. Moreover, coordination among divisions sometimes results in an unequal flow of positive outcomes to divisional managers. In other words, when managerial rewards are based at least in part on the performance of individual divisions, the manager of the division that is able to benefit the most by the sharing of corporate competencies might be viewed as receiving relative gains at others' expense. Strategic controls are important in these instances, as divisional managers' performance can be evaluated at least partly on the basis of how well they have facilitated interdivisional cooperative efforts. Furthermore, using reward systems that emphasize overall company performance, besides outcomes achieved by individual divisions, helps overcome problems associated with the cooperative form.

USING THE STRATEGIC BUSINESS UNIT FORM OF THE MULTIDIVISIONAL STRUCTURE TO IMPLEMENT THE RELATED LINKED STRATEGY

When the firm has fewer links or less constrained links among its divisions, the related linked diversification strategy is used. The strategic business unit form of the multidivisional structure supports implementation of this strategy. The **strategic business unit (SBU) form** is a structure consisting of three levels: corporate headquarters, strategic business units (SBUs), and SBU divisions (see Figure 11.6).

The divisions within each SBU are related in terms of shared products or markets or both, but the divisions of one SBU have little in common with the divisions of the other SBUs. Divisions within each SBU share product or market competencies to develop economies of scope and possibly economies of scale. The integration mechanisms used by the divisions in a cooperative structure can be equally well used by the divisions within the individual strategic business units that are part of the SBU form of the multidivisional structure. In the SBU structure, each SBU is a profit center that is controlled and evaluated by the headquarters office. Although both financial and strategic controls are important, on a relative basis, financial controls are vital to headquarters' evaluation of each SBU; strategic controls are critical when the heads of SBUs evaluate their divisions' performance. Strategic controls are also critical to the

The strategic business unit (SBU) form *is a structure consisting of three levels: corporate headquarters, strategic business units (SBUs), and SBU divisions.*

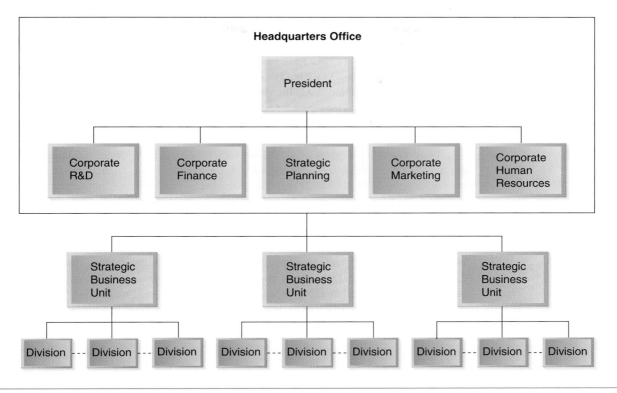

Notes: • Structural integration among divisions within SBUs, but independence across SBUs
   • Strategic planning may be the most prominent function in headquarters for managing the strategic planning approval process of SBUs for the president
   • Each SBU may have its own budget for staff to foster integration
   • Corporate headquarters staff serve as consultants to SBUs and divisions, rather than having direct input to product strategy, as in the cooperative form

headquarters' efforts to determine if the company has chosen an effective portfolio of businesses and if those businesses are being successfully managed.

Used by large firms, the SBU structure can be complex, with the complexity reflected by the organization's size and product and market diversity. Related linked firm GE, for example, has over 20 strategic business units, each with multiple divisions. GE Aircraft Engines, Appliances, Power Systems, NBC, and GE Capital are a few of the firm's SBUs. As is frequently the case with large diversified corporations, the scale of GE's business units is striking. GE Aircraft Engines, for example, is the world's leading manufacturer of jet engines for civil and military aircraft. With almost 30 divisions, GE Capital is a diversified financial services company creating comprehensive solutions to increase client productivity and efficiency. The GE Power Systems business unit has 21 divisions, including GE Energy Rentals, GE Distributed Power, and GE Water Technologies.[87]

In many of GE's SBUs, efforts are undertaken to form competencies in services and technology as a source of competitive advantage. Recently, technology was identified as an advantage for the GE Medical Systems SBU, as that unit's divisions share technological competencies to produce an array of sophisticated equipment, including computed tomography (CT) scanners, magnetic resonance imaging (MRI) systems, nuclear medicine cameras, and ultrasound systems.[88] Once a competence is developed in one of GE Medical Systems' divisions, it is quickly transferred to the other divisions in that SBU so that the competence can be leveraged to increase the unit's overall performance.[89] The sharing of competencies among units within an SBU is an important characteristic of the SBU form of the multidivisional structure (see the legend to Figure 11.6).

USING THE COMPETITIVE FORM OF THE MULTIDIVISIONAL STRUCTURE TO IMPLEMENT THE UNRELATED DIVERSIFICATION STRATEGY

Firms using the unrelated diversification strategy want to create value through efficient internal capital allocations or by restructuring, buying, and selling businesses.[90] The competitive form of the multidivisional structure supports implementation of this strategy.

The competitive form is a structure in which there is complete independence among the firm's divisions.

The **competitive form** is a structure in which there is complete independence among the firm's divisions (see Figure 11.7). Unlike the divisions included in the cooperative structure, the divisions that are part of the competitive structure do not share common corporate strengths (e.g., marketing competencies or channel dominance). Because strengths aren't shared, integrating devices aren't developed for use by the divisions included in the competitive structure.

The efficient internal capital market that is the foundation for use of the unrelated diversification strategy requires organizational arrangements that emphasize divisional competition rather than cooperation.[91] Three benefits are expected from the internal competition that the competitive form of the multidivisional structure facilitates. First, internal competition creates flexibility—corporate headquarters can have divisions working on different technologies to identify those with the greatest future

| Figure 11.7 | Competitive Form of the Multidivisional Structure for Implementation of an Unrelated Strategy |

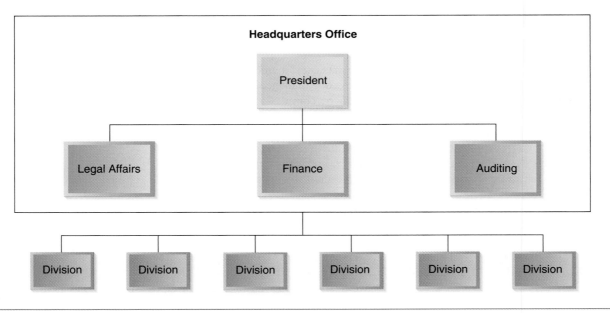

Notes: • Corporate headquarters has a small staff
- Finance and auditing are the most prominent functions in the headquarters office to manage cash flow and assure the accuracy of performance data coming from divisions
- The legal affairs function becomes important when the firm acquires or divests assets
- Divisions are independent and separate for financial evaluation purposes
- Divisions retain strategic control, but cash is managed by the corporate office
- Divisions compete for corporate resources

United Technologies Corp.: Where Strategy and Structure Are Matched

United Technologies is a diversified corporation providing high-technology products to the aerospace and building systems industries throughout the world. Operating in over 180 countries and employing more than 155,000 people worldwide and with annual sales revenue of approximately $28 billion, the firm's recent market capitalization exceeded $33 billion. United Technologies' multidivisional structure features six business units (Sikorsky, Pratt & Whitney, Hamilton Sundstrand, UTC Fuel Cells, Otis, and Carrier) as well as a corporate-level research center. Operating independently, these units compete against one another for resources that are allocated from corporate headquarters. The firm spends more than $2.5 billion annually on R&D, with the clear majority of these funds allocated to the corporate-level research center. This center's primary responsibility is to work individually with the six units to assist in developing product and process innovations that are unique to each unit's operations.

During the 1990s, United Technologies' unrelated diversification strategy was implemented very successfully as demonstrated by the fact that the firm's stock outperformed the S&P 500 index, rising at a ten-year average annual rate of 21 percent versus 15 percent for the index. However, the aftermath of the September 11, 2001 attacks has affected the firm's independent business units. As analysts noted, "Ongoing cuts in Boeing and Airbus commercial aircraft production should continue to temper near-term demand for UTX's Pratt & Whitney jet engines and Hamilton Sundstrand aircraft components." The Otis Elevator business unit has cushioned the firm's bottom line while these other two units continue to be affected by the worst slump in aviation history. Between 2002 and 2003, for example, the percentage of the firm's operating profits accounted for by Otis grew from 24.8 percent to 27.4 percent while Pratt & Whitney's percentage of total operating profits declined from 38.3 percent to 33.2 percent.

To continue reducing its dependence on the volatile airline industry, United Technologies acquired Chubb PLC for $1 billion in 2003. Based in the United Kingdom, Chubb specializes in electronic security products (e.g., hotel locks and burglar alarms) and services (e.g., security guards). A cross-border transaction, this strategic acquisition reflects United Technologies' desire to build a portfolio of businesses that are more stable and less cyclical compared to those competing in the aviation industry. In addition to being available at an attractive price, Chubb appealed to United Technologies because electronic security is one of the few sectors of the global economy that emerged stronger after the September 11, 2001 attacks. Company officials anticipate that in the current environment, Chubb will join Otis as a primary contributor to the corporation's operating profits. As part of United Technologies, Chubb will compete with all other business units for corporate resources and will operate independently from them as called for by the competitive form of the multidivisional structure.

SOURCES: J. L. Lunsford, 2003, United Technologies' formula: A powerful lift from elevators, *Wall Street Journal Online*, http://www.wsj.com, July 2; A. Raghavan, 2003, U.S. firms are shopping for European M&A deals, *Wall Street Journal Online*, http://www.wsj.com, June 30; A. Raghavan & R. Sidel, 2003, United Technologies to buy Chubb PLC for $1 billion, *Wall Street Journal Online*, http://www.wjs.com, June 12; 2003, United Tech gets U.S. clearance to buy Chubb, *Reuters*, http://www.reuters.com, July 1; 2003, United Technologies, *Standard & Poor's Stock Reports*, http://www.standardandpoors.com, July 3; 2003, UTC Fuel Cells, United Technologies Home Page, http://www.unitedtechnologies.com, July 10.

potential, for example. Resources can then be allocated to the division that is working with the most promising technology to fuel the entire firm's success. Second, internal competition challenges the status quo and inertia, because division heads know that future resource allocations are a product of excellent current performance as well as superior positioning of their division in terms of future performance. Last, internal competition motivates effort. The challenge of competing against internal peers can be as great as the challenge of competing against external marketplace competitors.[92]

Independence among divisions, as shown by a lack of sharing of corporate strengths and the absence of integrating devices, allows the firm using the unrelated diversification strategy to form specific profit performance expectations for each division to stimulate internal competition for future resources. The benefits of internal capital allocations or restructuring cannot be fully realized unless divisions are held accountable for their own independent performance. In the competitive structure, organizational controls (primarily financial controls) are used to emphasize and support internal competition among separate divisions and as the basis for allocating corporate capital based on divisions' performances. At Textron Inc., for example, return on invested capital is the primary measure used to assess the performance of the firm's unrelated business units. According to the firm, "return on invested capital serves as both a compass to guide every investment decision and a measurement of Textron's success."[93]

To emphasize competitiveness among divisions, the headquarters office maintains an arms-length relationship with them and does not intervene in divisional affairs, except to audit operations and discipline managers whose divisions perform poorly. In this situation, the headquarters office relies on strategic controls to set rate-of-return targets and financial controls to monitor divisional performance relative to those targets. The headquarters office then allocates cash flow on a competitive basis, rather than automatically returning cash to the division that produced it. Thus, the focus of the headquarters' work is on performance appraisal, resource allocation, and long-range planning to verify that the firm's portfolio of businesses will lead to financial success.[94]

As explained in the Strategic Focus, United Technologies Corp. uses the competitive form of the multidivisional structure to support use of its unrelated diversification strategy.

The three major forms of the multidivisional structure should each be paired with a particular corporate-level strategy. As explained in the Strategic Focus, United Technologies uses the competitive form of the multidivisional structure to implement the unrelated diversification strategy. Table 11.1 shows these structures' characteristics. Differences are seen in the degree of centralization, the focus of the performance appraisal, the horizontal structures (integrating mechanisms), and the incentive compensation schemes. The most centralized and most costly structural form is the cooperative structure. The least centralized, with the lowest bureaucratic costs, is the competitive structure. The SBU structure requires partial centralization and involves some of the mechanisms necessary to implement the relatedness between divisions. Also, the divisional incentive compensation awards are allocated according to both SBUs and corporate performance.

Matches between International Strategies and Worldwide Structures

As explained in Chapter 8, international strategies are becoming increasingly important for long-term competitive success.[95] Among other benefits, international strategies allow the firm to search for new markets, resources, core competencies, and technologies as part of its efforts to outperform competitors.[96]

As with business-level and corporate-level strategies, unique organizational structures are necessary to successfully implement the different international strategies.[97] Forming proper matches between international strategies and organizational structures facilitates the firm's efforts to effectively coordinate and control its global operations.[98] More importantly, recent research findings confirm the validity of the international strategy/structure matches we discuss here.[99]

Table 11.1

	Overall Structural Form		
Structural Characteristics	Cooperative M-Form (Related Constrained Strategy)[a]	SBU M-Form (Related Linked Strategy)[a]	Competitive M-Form (Unrelated Diversification Strategy)[a]
Centralization of operations	Centralized at corporate office	Partially centralized (in SBUs)	Decentralized to divisions
Use of integration mechanisms	Extensive	Moderate	Nonexistent
Divisional performance appraisals	Emphasize subjective (strategic) criteria and objective (financial) criteria	Use a mixture of subjective (strategic)	Emphasize objective (financial) criteria
Divisional incentive compensation	Linked to overall corporate performance	Mixed linkage to corporate, SBU, and divisional performance	Linked to divisional performance

Characteristics of the Structures Necessary to Implement the Related Constrained, Related Linked, and Unrelated Diversification Strategies

[a]Strategy implemented with structural form.

USING THE WORLDWIDE GEOGRAPHIC AREA STRUCTURE TO IMPLEMENT THE MULTIDOMESTIC STRATEGY

The *multidomestic strategy* decentralizes the firm's strategic and operating decisions to business units in each country so that product characteristics can be tailored to local preferences. Firms using this strategy try to isolate themselves from global competitive forces by establishing protected market positions or by competing in industry segments that are most affected by differences among local countries. The worldwide geographic area structure is used to implement this strategy. The **worldwide geographic area structure** is a structure emphasizing national interests and facilitating the firm's efforts to satisfy local or cultural differences (see Figure 11.8).

Because using the multidomestic strategy requires little coordination between different country markets, integrating mechanisms among divisions in the worldwide geographic area structure aren't needed. Hence, formalization is low, and coordination among units in a firm's worldwide geographic area structure is often informal.

The multidomestic strategy/worldwide geographic area structure match evolved as a natural outgrowth of the multicultural European marketplace. Friends and family members of the main business who were sent as expatriates into foreign countries to develop the independent country subsidiary often implemented this type of structure for the main business. The relationship to corporate headquarters by divisions took place through informal communication among "family members."[100]

Unilever, the giant Dutch consumer products firm and major competitor for Procter & Gamble, has refocused its business operations.[101] As a result, the firm grouped its worldwide operations into two global divisions—foods, and home and personal care. The firm uses the worldwide geographic area structure. For the foods division (known as Unilever Bestfoods), regional presidents are responsible for results from operations in the region to which they have been assigned. Asia, Europe, North America, Africa, the Middle East and Turkey, and Latin America are the regions of

The worldwide geographic area structure is a structure emphasizing national interests and facilitating the firm's efforts to satisfy local or cultural differences.

Figure 11.8 Worldwide Geographic Area Structure for Implementation of a Multidomestic Strategy

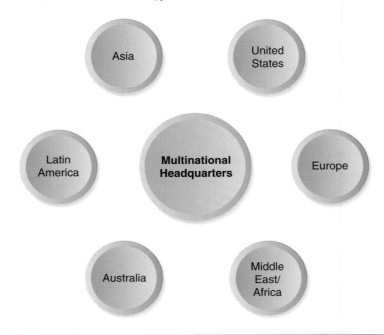

Notes:
- The perimeter circles indicate decentralization of operations
- Emphasis is on differentiation by local demand to fit an area or country culture
- Corporate headquarters coordinates financial resources among independent subsidiaries
- The organization is like a decentralized federation

Unilever's worldwide geographic structure has regionalized its food division, allowing it to be in better touch with customers in each area.

the foods division. The firm describes the match between the multidomestic strategy and Unilever's worldwide geographic structure (in terms of the firm's foods division): "Unilever Bestfoods' strength lies in our ability to tailor products to different markets as well as to anticipate consumer trends and demands. This comes from our deep understanding of the countries in which we operate and our policy of listening to our customers."[102]

A key disadvantage of the multidomestic strategy/worldwide geographic area structure match is the inability to create global efficiency. With an increasing emphasis on lower-cost products in international markets, the need to pursue worldwide economies of scale has also increased. These changes have fostered the use of the global strategy and its structural match, the worldwide product divisional structure.

USING THE WORLDWIDE PRODUCT DIVISIONAL STRUCTURE TO IMPLEMENT THE GLOBAL STRATEGY

With the corporation's home office dictating competitive strategy, the *global strategy* is one through which the firm offers standardized products across country markets. The firm's success depends on its ability to develop and take advantage of economies of scope and scale on a global level. Decisions to outsource some primary or support activities to the world's best providers are particularly helpful when the firm tries to develop economies of scale.

The worldwide product divisional structure supports use of the global strategy. In the **worldwide product divisional structure,** decision-making authority is centralized in the worldwide division headquarters to coordinate and integrate decisions and actions among divisional business units (see Figure 11.9). This structure is often used in rapidly growing firms seeking to manage their diversified product lines effectively, as in Japan's Kyowa Hakko. With businesses in pharmaceuticals, chemicals, biochemicals, and liquor and food, this company uses the worldwide product divisional structure to facilitate its decisions about how to successfully compete in what it believes are rapidly shifting global competitive environments.[103]

Integrating mechanisms are important to effective use of the worldwide product divisional structure. Direct contact between managers, liaison roles between departments, and temporary task forces as well as permanent teams are examples of these mechanisms. One researcher describes the use of these mechanisms in the worldwide structure: "There is extensive and formal use of task forces and operating committees to supplement communication and coordination of worldwide operations."[104] The evolution of a shared vision of the firm's strategy and how structure supports its implementation is one of the important outcomes resulting from these mechanisms' effective use. The disadvantages of the global strategy/worldwide structure combination are the difficulty involved with coordinating decisions and actions across country borders and the inability to quickly respond to local needs and preferences.

The worldwide product divisional structure is a structure in which decision-making authority is centralized in the worldwide division headquarters to coordinate and integrate decisions and actions among divisional business units.

Worldwide Product Divisional Structure for Implementation of a Global Strategy

Figure 11.9

Worldwide Products Division

Worldwide Products Division

Worldwide Products Division

Global Corporate Headquarters

Worldwide Products Division

Worldwide Products Division

Worldwide Products Division

Notes: • The headquarters' circle indicates centralization to coordinate information flow among worldwide products
• Corporate headquarters uses many intercoordination devices to facilitate global economies of scale and scope
• Corporate headquarters also allocates financial resources in a cooperative way
• The organization is like a centralized federation

The *transnational strategy* calls for the firm to combine the multidomestic strategy's local responsiveness with the global strategy's efficiency. Thus, firms using this strategy are trying to gain the advantages of both local responsiveness and global efficiency.[105] The combination structure is used to implement the transnational strategy. The **combination structure** is a structure drawing characteristics and mechanisms from both the worldwide geographic area structure and the worldwide product divisional structure.

The fits between the multidomestic strategy and the worldwide geographic area structure and between the global strategy and the worldwide product divisional structure are apparent. However, when a firm wants to implement both the multidomestic and the global strategies simultaneously through a combination structure, the appropriate integrating mechanisms for the two structures are less obvious. The structure used to implement the transnational strategy must be simultaneously centralized and decentralized; integrated and nonintegrated; formalized and nonformalized. These seemingly opposite characteristics must be managed by an overall structure that is capable of encouraging all employees to understand the effects of cultural diversity on a firm's operations.

This requirement highlights the need for a strong educational component to change the whole culture of the organization. If the cultural change is effective, the combination structure should allow the firm to learn how to gain competitive benefits in local economies by adapting its core competencies, which often have been developed and nurtured in less culturally diverse competitive environments. As firms globalize and move toward the transnational strategy, the idea of a corporate headquarters has become increasingly important in fostering leadership and a shared vision to create a stronger company identity.[106]

The combination structure is a structure drawing characteristics and mechanisms from both the worldwide geographic area structure and the worldwide product divisional structure.

Matches between Cooperative Strategies and Network Structures

As discussed in Chapter 9, a network strategy exists when partners form several alliances in order to improve the performance of the alliance network itself through cooperative endeavors.[107] The greater levels of environmental complexity and uncertainty companies face in today's competitive environment are causing increasing numbers of firms to use cooperative strategies such as strategic alliances and joint ventures.[108]

The breadth and scope of firms' operations in the global economy create many opportunities for firms to cooperate.[109] In fact, the firm can develop cooperative relationships with many of its stakeholders, including customers, suppliers, and competitors.[110] When the firm becomes involved with combinations of cooperative relationships, it is part of a strategic network, or what others call an alliance constellation.[111]

A *strategic network* is a group of firms that has been formed to create value by participating in multiple cooperative arrangements, such as alliances and joint ventures. An effective strategic network facilitates the discovery of opportunities beyond those identified by individual network participants.[112] A strategic network can be a source of competitive advantage for its members when its operations create value that is difficult for competitors to duplicate and that network members can't create by themselves.[113] Strategic networks are used to implement business-level, corporate-level, and international cooperative strategies.

Commonly, a strategic network is a loose federation of partners who participate in the network's operations on a flexible basis. At the core or center of the strategic network, the *strategic center firm* is the one around which the network's cooperative relationships revolve (see Figure 11.10).

Because of its central position, the strategic center firm is the foundation for the strategic network's structure. Concerned with various aspects of organizational struc-

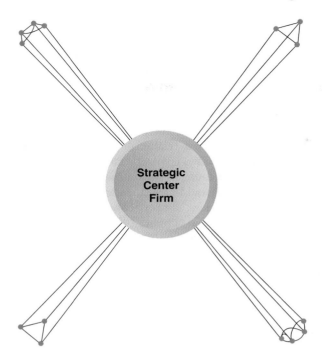

Strategic Center Firm

ture, such as formal reporting relationships and procedures, the strategic center firm manages what are often complex, cooperative interactions among network partners. The strategic center firm is engaged in four primary tasks as it manages the strategic network and controls its operations:[114]

Strategic outsourcing. The strategic center firm outsources and partners with more firms than do other network members. At the same time, the strategic center firm requires network partners to be more than contractors. Members are expected to find opportunities for the network to create value through its cooperative work.

Competencies. To increase network effectiveness, the strategic center firm seeks ways to support each member's efforts to develop core competencies that can benefit the network.

Technology. The strategic center firm is responsible for managing the development and sharing of technology-based ideas among network members. The structural requirement that members submit formal reports detailing the technology-oriented outcomes of their efforts to the strategic center firm facilitates this activity.

Race to learn. The strategic center firm emphasizes that the principal dimensions of competition are between value chains and between networks of value chains. Because of this, the strategic network is only as strong as its weakest value-chain link. With its centralized decision-making authority and responsibility, the strategic center firm guides participants in efforts to form network-specific competitive advantages. The need for each participant to have capabilities that can be the foundation for the network's competitive advantages encourages friendly rivalry among participants seeking to develop the skills needed to quickly form new capabilities that create value for the network.[115]

As noted in Chapter 9, there are two types of business-level complementary alliances: vertical and horizontal. Firms with competencies in different stages of the value chain form a vertical alliance to cooperatively integrate their different, but complementary, skills. Firms that agree to combine their competencies to create value in the same stage of the value chain form a horizontal alliance. Vertical complementary strategic alliances, such as those developed by Toyota Motor Company, are formed more frequently than horizontal alliances. Acting as the strategic center firm, Toyota fashioned its lean production system around a network of supplier firms.[116]

A strategic network of vertical relationships, such as the network in Japan between Toyota and its suppliers, often involves a number of implementation issues.[117] First, the strategic center firm encourages subcontractors to modernize their facilities and provides them with technical and financial assistance to do so, if necessary. Second, the strategic center firm reduces its transaction costs by promoting longer-term contracts with subcontractors, so that supplier-partners increase their long-term productivity. This approach is diametrically opposed to that of continually negotiating short-term contracts based on unit pricing. Third, the strategic center firm enables engineers in upstream companies (suppliers) to have better communication with those companies with whom it has contracts for services. As a result, suppliers and the strategic center firm become more interdependent and less independent.[118]

The lean production system pioneered by Toyota has been diffused throughout the Japanese and U.S. auto industries. However, no auto company has learned how to duplicate the manufacturing effectiveness and efficiency Toyota derives from the cooperative arrangements in its strategic network.[119] A key factor accounting for Toyota's manufacturing-based competitive advantage is the cost other firms would incur to imitate the structural form used to support Toyota's application. In part, then, the structure of Toyota's strategic network that it created as the strategic center firm facilitates cooperative actions among network participants that competitors can't fully understand or duplicate.

In vertical complementary strategic alliances, such as the one between Toyota and its suppliers, the strategic center firm is obvious, as is the structure that firm establishes. However, this is not always the case with horizontal complementary strategic alliances where firms try to create value in the same part of the value chain, as with airline alliances that are commonly formed to create value in the marketing and sales primary activity segment of the value chain (see Table 3.6). Because air carriers commonly participate in multiple vertical complementary alliances, it is difficult to select the strategic center firm. Moreover, participation in several alliances can cause firms to question partners' true loyalties and intentions. For these reasons, horizontal complementary alliances are used less frequently than their vertical counterpart.

Strategic networks have been important to Cisco Systems Inc. The worldwide leader in networking for the Internet, Cisco provides a broad line of solutions for transporting data, voice, and video in multiple settings[120] and has been involved with a number of strategic networks in its pursuit of competitive success. Cisco recently announced that it was changing its organizational structure. Historically, the firm's structure featured three primary business units—enterprise, service provider, and commercial. In late 2001, Cisco changed its structure to create 11 technology areas.[121] Will cooperative strategies be as critical to the firm as it completes its work through the dictates of a new organizational structure? In all likelihood, this will be the case, although the evolution of strategy and structure at Cisco will ultimately decide this issue.

Implementing Corporate-Level Cooperative Strategies

Corporate-level cooperative strategies (such as franchising) are used to facilitate product and market diversification. As a cooperative strategy, franchising allows the firm to use its competencies to extend or diversify its product or market reach, but without completing a merger or an acquisition. For example, McDonald's, the largest fast-food company in the world, has more than 50 percent of its almost 31,000 restaurants outside the United States and serves more than 46 million customers daily.[122]

The McDonald's franchising system is a strategic network. McDonald's headquarters office serves as the strategic center firm for the network's franchisees. The headquarters office uses strategic controls and financial controls to verify that the franchisees' operations create the greatest value for the entire network. One strategic control issue is the location of franchisee units. McDonald's believes that its greatest expansion opportunities are outside the United States. Density percentages seem to support this conclusion. "While in the United States there are 22,000 people per McDonald's, in the rest of the world there is only one McDonald's for every 605,000 people."[123] As a result, as the strategic center firm, McDonald's is devoting its capital expenditures (over 70 percent in the last three years) primarily to develop units in non–U.S. markets. Financial controls are framed around requirements an interested party must satisfy to become a McDonald's franchisee as well as performance standards that are to be met when operating a unit.[124]

Implementing International Cooperative Strategies

Strategic networks formed to implement international cooperative strategies result in firms competing in several countries.[125] Differences among countries' regulatory environments increase the challenge of managing international networks and verifying that at a minimum, the network's operations comply with all legal requirements.[126]

Distributed strategic networks are the organizational structure used to manage international cooperative strategies. As shown in Figure 11.11, several regional strategic

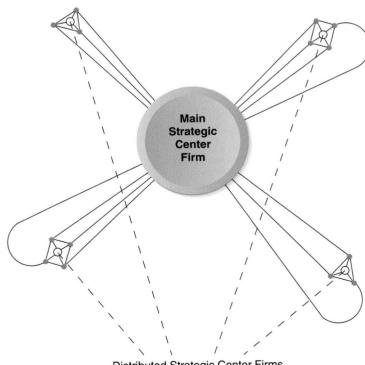

A Distributed Strategic Network — Figure 11.11

Distributed Strategic Center Firms

center firms are included in the distributed network to manage partner firms' multiple cooperative arrangements.[127] Strategic centers for Ericsson (telecommunications exchange equipment) and Electrolux (white goods, washing machines) are located in countries throughout the world, instead of only in Sweden where the firms are headquartered. Ericsson, for example, is active in more than 140 countries and employs more than 90,000 people. Using the SBU structure, Ericsson has five strategic business units and has formed cooperative agreements with companies throughout the world in each unit. As a founding member of an Ethernet alliance (Intel and Cisco are also members), Ericsson acts as the strategic center firm for this cooperative arrangement, which seeks to solve the wireline access bottleneck by promoting open industry standards.[128]

Summary

- Organizational structure specifies the firm's formal reporting relationships, procedures, controls, and authority and decision-making processes. Influencing managerial work, structure essentially details the work to be done and how that work is to be accomplished. Organizational controls guide the use of strategy, indicate how to compare actual and expected results, and suggest actions to take to improve performance when it falls below expectations. When properly matched with the strategy for which they were intended, structure and controls can be a competitive advantage.

- Strategic controls (largely subjective criteria) and financial controls (largely objective criteria) are the two types of organizational controls used to successfully implement the firm's chosen strategy. Both types of controls are critical, although their degree of emphasis varies based on individual matches between strategy and structure.

- Strategy and structure influence each other, although strategy has an overall stronger influence on structure. Research indicates that firms tend to change structure when declining performance forces them to do so. Effective managers anticipate the need for structural change, quickly modifying structure to better accommodate the firm's strategy implementation needs when evidence calls for that action.

- Business-level strategies are implemented through the functional structure. The cost leadership strategy requires a centralized functional structure—one in which manufacturing efficiency and process engineering are emphasized. The differentiation strategy's functional structure decentralizes implementation-related decisions, especially those concerned with marketing, to those involved with individual organizational functions. Focus strategies, often used in small firms, require a simple structure until such time that the firm diversifies in terms of products and/or markets.

- Unique combinations of different forms of the multidivisional structure are matched with different corporate-level diversification strategies to properly implement these strategies. The cooperative M-form, used to implement the related constrained corporate-level strategy, has a centralized corporate office and extensive integrating mechanisms. Divisional incentives are linked to overall corporate performance. The related linked SBU M-form structure establishes separate profit centers within the diversified firm. Each profit center may have divisions offering similar products, but the centers are unrelated to each other. The competitive M-form structure, used to implement the unrelated diversification strategy, is highly decentralized, lacks integrating mechanisms, and utilizes objective financial criteria to evaluate each unit's performance.

- The multidomestic strategy, implemented through the worldwide geographic area structure, emphasizes decentralization and locates all functional activities in the host country or geographic area. The worldwide product divisional structure is used to implement the global strategy. This structure is centralized in order to coordinate and integrate different functions' activities so as to gain global economies of scope and scale. Decision-making authority is centralized in the firm's worldwide division headquarters.

- The transnational strategy—a strategy through which the firm seeks the local responsiveness of the multidomestic strategy and the global efficiency of the global strategy—is implemented through the combination structure. Because it must be simultaneously centralized and decentralized, integrated and nonintegrated, and formalized and nonformalized, the combination structure is difficult to organize and manage successfully.

- Increasingly important to competitive success, cooperative strategies are implemented through organizational structures framed around strategic networks. Strategic center firms are critical to the management of strategic networks.

1. What is organizational structure and what are organizational controls? What are the differences between strategic controls and financial controls?

2. What does it mean to say that strategy and structure have a reciprocal relationship?

3. What are the characteristics of the functional structures that are used to implement the cost leadership, differentiation, integrated cost leadership/differentiation, and focused business-level strategies?

4. What are the differences among the three versions of the multidivisional (M-form) organizational structures that are used to implement the related constrained, related linked, and unrelated corporate-level diversification strategies?

5. What organizational structures are used to implement the multidomestic, global, and transnational international strategies?

6. What is a strategic network? What is a strategic center firm?

Experiential Exercises

Organizational Structure and Controls

As an executive board member for a successful 50-partner firm that provides accounting services to corporate clients, you are interested in expanding to offer management consulting services to these clients. Another possibility for your firm is offering both types of services to smaller clients.

Part One. You are concerned about how your organizational structure may need to change to support these services. Based on the material in the chapter, use the chart to rank each type of organizational structure against the activities—information processing, coordination, and control—that you anticipate will need to be strengthened.

Part Two. You are also very concerned that there may be a potential conflict of interest if your firm provides both accounting and management consulting services to the same client. In small groups, discuss whether it is possible for a firm to use organizational structure and controls to achieve its strategic objectives but also to prevent conflicts of interest among its divisions.

	Information processing	Coordination	Control
Simple structure			
Functional structure			
Multidivisional structure			

Structural Issues of Related Diversification

For years, Kodak used the cooperative form of the multidivisional structure to implement the related-constrained diversification strategy. Following this structure, primary organizational functions such as manufacturing, customer care, and strategic planning were centralized, which allowed such

expertise to be shared among Kodak's seven product divisions. The cooperative structure worked well for Kodak as it used the related-constrained strategy to compete in what for many years had been relatively stable markets. However, innovative technologies and increased competition disrupted these markets, making the sharing of the firm's technologies and related skills across product divisions less competitively valuable. Moreover, sharing key resources and their corresponding costs across many business units with increased competition in unstable markets made it difficult for Kodak to assess the profitability of its product divisions (Consumer Imaging, Digital and Applied Imaging, Kodak Professional, Health Imaging, Document Imaging, Entertainment Imaging) and operational divisions (Commercial and Government, Federal Government Contracts, and Worldwide Transportation).

Analysis of the external environment as well as of Kodak's resources, capabilities, and core competencies resulted in management concluding that the firm should reduce the number of links between its business units and their products and services. Kodak subsequently made two consecutive changes to the SBU structure. First, Kodak moved to a three SBU structure in October 2000 (see Figure 11.12). This combined the previous seven product divisions into two broad customer-oriented SBUs (Consumer and Commercial), while the third (Global Operations) handled Kodak's governmental contracts along with various supply chain and operational needs. The resulting structure was viewed as less than optimal by Kodak executives, who concluded that another form of the SBU structure might be necessary. A new version of the SBU structure was implemented by Kodak in November 2001 (see Figure 11.13).

1. How might these rapid, consecutive, and fundamental changes in the corporate structure both facilitate and hinder Kodak's ability to realistically implement its corporate-level strategy?

2. Do either of the newest Kodak organizational charts match well with the related-constrained or related-linked corporate strategies? Why or why not?

Figure 11.12

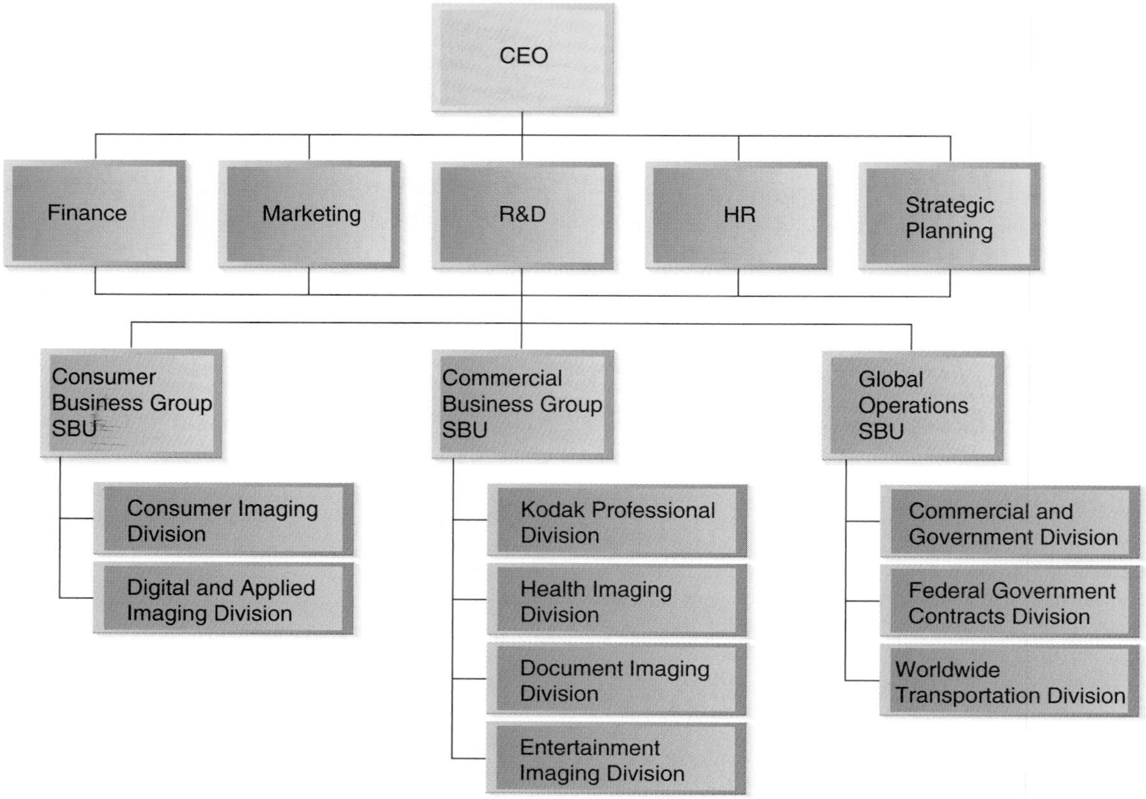

CEO

Finance | Marketing | R&D | HR | Strategic Planning

Consumer Business Group SBU

- Consumer Imaging Division
- Digital and Applied Imaging Division

Commercial Business Group SBU

- Kodak Professional Division
- Health Imaging Division
- Document Imaging Division
- Entertainment Imaging Division

Global Operations SBU

- Commercial and Government Division
- Federal Government Contracts Division
- Worldwide Transportation Division

Figure 11.13

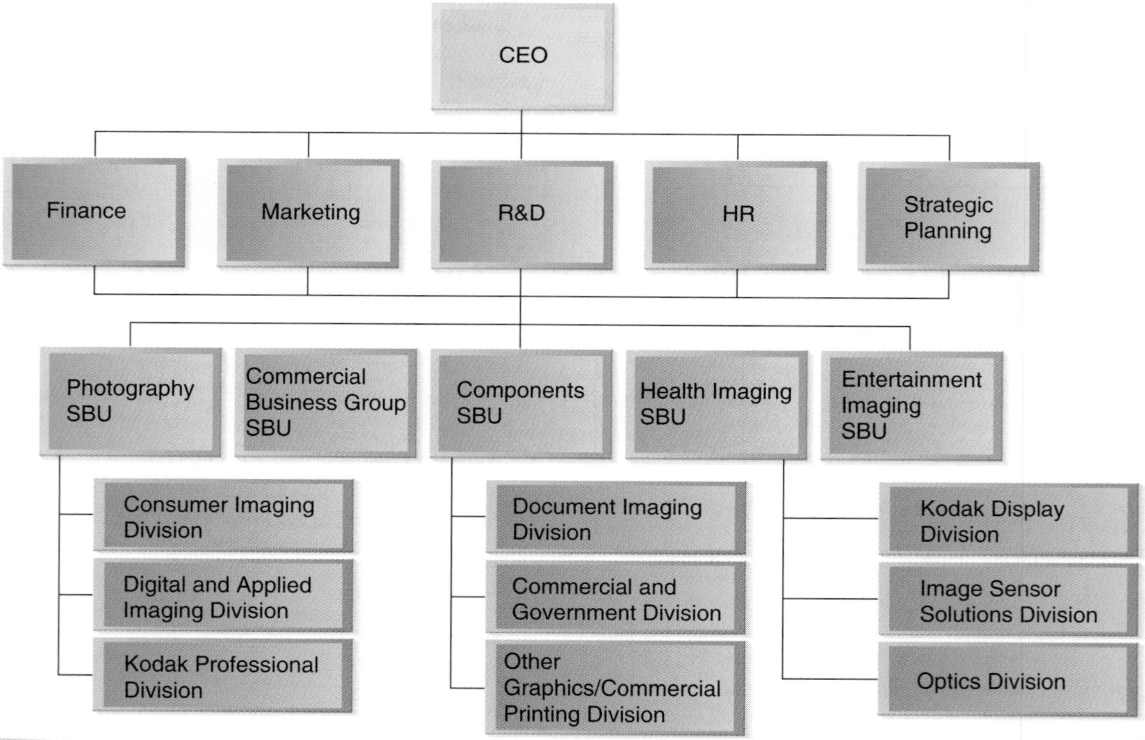

CEO

Finance | Marketing | R&D | HR | Strategic Planning

Photography SBU

- Consumer Imaging Division
- Digital and Applied Imaging Division
- Kodak Professional Division

Commercial Business Group SBU

Components SBU

- Document Imaging Division
- Commercial and Government Division
- Other Graphics/Commercial Printing Division

Health Imaging SBU

Entertainment Imaging SBU

- Kodak Display Division
- Image Sensor Solutions Division
- Optics Division

Notes

1. J. Hauser, 2003, Organizational lessons for nonprofits, *The McKinsey Quarterly*, Special Edition: 60–69.

2. R. J. Herbold, 2002, Inside Microsoft: Balancing creativity and discipline, *Harvard Business Review*, 80(1): 73–79.

3. R. E. Miles & C. C. Snow, 1978, *Organizational Strategy, Structure and Process*, New York: McGraw-Hill.

4. N. Nohria, W. Joyce, & B. Roberson, 2003, What really works, *Harvard Business Review*, 81(7): 42–52.

5. T. Amburgey & T. Dacin, 1994, As the left foot follows the right? The dynamics of strategic and structural change, *Academy of Management Journal*, 37: 1427–1452.

6. B. Keats & H. O'Neill, 2001, Organizational structure: Looking through a strategy lens, in M. A. Hitt, R. E. Freeman, & J. S. Harrison (eds.), *Handbook of Strategic Management*, Oxford, UK: Blackwell Publishers, 520–542.

7. R. E. Hoskisson, C. W. L. Hill, & H. Kim, 1993, The multidivisional structure: Organizational fossil or source of value? *Journal of Management*, 19: 269–298.

8. F. Warner, 2002, Think lean, *Fast Company*, February, 40–42.

9. 2003, DnB, Gjensidige NOR outline merged bank's structure, *Wall Street Journal Online*, http://www.wsj.com, June 11.

10. T. Burns & G. M. Stalker, 1961, *The Management of Innovation*, London: Tavistok; P. R. Lawrence & J. W. Lorsch, 1967, *Organization and Environment*, Homewood, IL: Richard D. Irwin; J. Woodward, 1965, *Industrial Organization: Theory and Practice*, London: Oxford University Press.

11. M. Bower, 2003, Organization: Helping people pull together, *The McKinsey Quarterly*, Number 2, http://www.premium.mckinseyquarterly.com; P. Jenster & D. Hussey, 2001, *Company Analysis: Determining Strategic Capability*, Chichester: John Wiley & Sons, 135–171.

12. B. Rigby & T. Johnson, 2002, Zurich scraps plan to see U.S. unit, *Reuters Business News*, http://www.fidelity.com, January 9.

13. 2003, Zurich sells U.S. life unit for $500 million, *Reuters Business News*, http://www.fidelity.com, May 30.

14. Keats & O'Neill, Organizational structure, 520–542; J. R. Galbraith, 1995, *Designing Organizations*, San Francisco: Jossey-Bass, 6.

15. Keats & O'Neill, Organizational structure, 533; Galbraith, *Designing Organizations*, 6.

16. H. J. Leavitt, 2003, Why hierarchies thrive, *Harvard Business Review*, 81(3): 96–102.

17. R. L. Priem, L. G. Love, & M. A. Shaffer, 2002, Executives' perceptions of uncertainty sources: A numerical taxonomy and underlying dimensions, *Journal of Management*, 28: 725–746.

18. J. D. Day, 2003, The value in organization, *The McKinsey Quarterly*, Number 2: 4–5; V. P. Rindova & S. Kotha, 2001, Continuous "morphing": Competing through dynamic capabilities, form, and function, *Academy of Management Journal*, 44: 1263–1280.

19. H. Barth, 2003, Fit among competitive strategy, administrative mechanisms, and performance: A comparative study of small firms in mature and new industries, *Journal of Small Business Management*, 41: 133–147; J. G. Covin, D. P. Slevin, & M. B. Heeley, 2001, Strategic decision making in an intuitive vs. technocratic mode: Structural and environmental consideration, *Journal of Business Research*, 52: 51–67.

20. H. Barkema, J. A. C. Baum, & E. A. Mannix, 2002, Management challenges in a new time, *Academy of Management Journal*, 45: 916–930.

21. Jenster & Hussey, *Company Analysis*, 169; L. Donaldson, 1997, A positivist alternative to the structure-action approach, *Organization Studies*, 18: 77–92.

22. M. A. Schilling & H. K. Steensma, 2001, The use of modular organizational forms: An industry-level analysis, *Academy of Management Journal*, 44: 1149–1168.

23. C. B. Dobni & G. Luffman, 2003, Determining the scope and impact of market orientation profiles on strategy implementation and performance, *Strategic Management Journal*, 24: 577–585; D. C. Hambrick & J. W. Fredrickson, 2001, Are you sure you have a strategy? *Academy of Management Executive*, 15(4): 48–59.

24. C. M. Fiol, 2003, Organizing for knowledge-based competitiveness: About pipelines and rivers, in S. E. Jackson, M. A. Hitt, & A. S. DeNisi (eds.), *Managing Knowledge for Sustained Competitive Advantage*, San Francisco: Jossey-Bass, 64–93; G. G. Dess & G. T. Lumpkin, 2001, Emerging issues in strategy process research, in M. A. Hitt, R. E. Freeman, & J. S. Harrison (eds.), *Handbook of Strategic Management*, Oxford, UK: Blackwell Publishers, 3–34.

25. R. D. Ireland, J. G. Covin, & D. F. Kuratko, 2003, Antecedents, elements and consequences of corporate entrepreneurship as strategy, *Proceedings of the Sixty-third Annual Meeting of the Academy of Management (CD)*, ISSN 1543-8643.

26. G. A. Bigley & K. H. Roberts, 2001, The incident command system: High-reliability organizing for complex and volatile task environments, *Academy of Management Journal*, 44: 1281–1299.

27. J. Child & R. M. McGrath, 2001, Organizations unfettered: Organizational form in an information-intensive economy, *Academy of Management Journal*, 44: 1135–1148.

28. T. W. Malnight, 2001, Emerging structural patterns within multinational corporations: Toward process-based structures, *Academy of Management Journal*, 44: 1187–1210; A. Sharma, 1999, Central dilemmas of managing innovation in firms, *California Management Review*, 41(3): 146–164; H. A. Simon, 1991, Bounded rationality and organizational learning, *Organization Science*, 2: 125–134.

29. B. W. Keats & M. A. Hitt, 1988, A causal model of linkages among environmental dimensions, macroorganizational characteristics, and performance, *Academy of Management Journal*, 31: 570–598.

30. A. Chandler, 1962, *Strategy and Structure*, Cambridge, MA: MIT Press.

31. J. D. Day, E. Lawson, & K. Leslie, 2003, When reorganization works, *The McKinsey Quarterly*, Number 2, 20–29.

32. M. Robb, P. Todd, & D. Turnbull, 2003, Untangling underperformance, *The McKinsey Quarterly*, Number 2, 52–59; Keats & O'Neill, Organizational structure, 535.

33. C. Sloan, 2003, Sears revamps home management, *Furniture Today*, 27(36): 2.

34. C. H. Noble, 1999, The eclectic roots of strategy implementation research, *Journal of Business Research*, 45: 119–134.

35. J. Lyne, 1992, Eastman Chemical CEO Earnest Deavenport: Restructuring to become a major global player, *Site Selection*, August, 1–5.

36. P. K. Mills & G. R. Ungson, 2003, Reassessing the limits of structural empowerment: Organizational constitution and trust as controls, *Academy of Management Review*, 28: 143–153.

37. S. Venkataraman & S. D. Sarasvathy, 2001, Strategy and entrepreneurship: Outlines of an untold story, in M. A. Hitt, R. E. Freeman, & J. S. Harrison (eds.), *Handbook of Strategic Management*, Oxford, UK: Blackwell Publishers, 650–668.

38. C. Sundaramurthy & M. Lewis, 2003, Control and collaboration: Paradoxes of governance, *Academy of Management Review*, 28: 397–415.

39. D. F. Kuratko, R. D. Ireland, & J. S. Hornsby, 2001, Improving firm performance through entrepreneurial actions: Acordia's corporate entrepreneurship strategy, *Academy of Management Executive*, 15(4): 60–71.

40. J. S. Harrison & C. H. St. John, 2002, *Foundations in Strategic Management*, 2nd ed., Cincinnati: South-Western College Publishing, 118–129.

41. S. D. Julian & E. Scifres, 2002, An interpretive perspective on the role of strategic control in triggering strategic change, *Journal of Business Strategies*, 19: 141–159.

42. R. E. Hoskisson, M. A. Hitt, & R. D. Ireland, 1994, The effects of acquisitions and restructuring strategies (strategic refocusing) on innovation, in G. von Krogh, A. Sinatra, & H. Singh (eds.), *Managing Corporate Acquisition*, London: MacMillan, 144–169.

43. M. A. Hitt, R. E. Hoskisson, R. A. Johnson, & D. D. Moesel, 1996, The market for corporate control and firm innovation, *Academy of Management Journal*, 39: 1084–1119.

44. R. E. Hoskisson & M. A. Hitt, 1988, Strategic control and relative R&D investment in multiproduct firms, *Strategic Management Journal*, 9: 605–621.

45. D. J. Collis, 1996, Corporate strategy in multibusiness firms, *Long Range Planning*, 29: 416–418.

46. M. L. Songini, 2003, Oracle tools designed to help monitor financial controls, *Computerworld*, 37(22): 49.

47. 2002, Pfizer Inc., Management's report, http://www.pfizer.com, January 27.

48. J. B. Barney, 2002, *Gaining and Sustaining Competitive Advantage*, 2nd ed., Upper Saddle River, NJ: Prentice-Hall.

49. M. Sengul, 2001, Divisionalization: Strategic effects of organizational structure, Paper presented during the 21st Annual Strategic Management Society Conference.

50. Keats & O'Neill, Organizational structure, 531.

51. 2003, Fitch affirms Hewlett-Packard; outlook stable, *Wall Street Journal Online*, http://www.wsj.com, June 27.

52. D. Miller & J. O. Whitney, 1999, Beyond strategy: Configuration as a pillar of competitive advantage, *Business Horizons*, 42(3): 5–17.

53. S. Tallman, 2001, Global strategic management, in M. A. Hitt, R. E. Freeman, & J. S. Harrison (eds.), *Handbook of Strategic Management*, Oxford, UK: Blackwell Publishers, 464–490.

54. Chandler, *Strategy and Structure*.

55. Keats & O'Neill, Organizational structure, 524.

56. G. M. McNamara, R. A. Luce, & G. H. Thompson, 2002, Examining the effect of complexity in strategic group knowledge structures on firm performance, *Strategic Management Journal*, 23: 153–170; J. P. Walsh, 1995, Managerial and organizational cognition: Notes from a trip down memory lane, *Organization Science*, 6: 280–321.

57. C. Levicki, 1999, *The Interactive Strategy Workout*, 2nd ed., London: Prentice-Hall.

58. J. J. Chrisman, A. Bauerschmidt, & C. W. Hofer, 1998, The determinants of new venture performance: An extended model, *Entrepreneurship Theory & Practice*, 23(3): 5–29; H. M. O'Neill, R. W. Pouder, & A. K. Buchholtz, 1998, Patterns in the diffusion of strategies across organizations: Insights from the innovation diffusion literature, *Academy of Management Review*, 23: 98–114.

59. 2003, Casketfurniture.com, About our company, http://www.casketfurniture.com, July 7.

60. Galbraith, *Designing Organizations*, 25.

61. Keats & O'Neill, Organizational structure, 539.

62. Lawrence & Lorsch, *Organization and Environment*.

63. O. E. Williamson, 1975, *Markets and Hierarchies: Analysis and Anti-trust Implications*, New York: The Free Press.

64. Chandler, *Strategy and Structure*.

65. J. Greco, 1999, Alfred P. Sloan, Jr. (1875–1966): The original organizational man, *Journal of Business Strategy*, 20(5): 30–31.

66. Hoskisson, Hill, & Kim, The multidivisional structure, 269–298.

67. W. G. Rowe & P. M. Wright, 1997, Related and unrelated diversification and their effect on human resource management controls, *Strategic Management Journal*, 18: 329–338; D. C. Galunic & K. M. Eisenhardt, 1996, The evolution of intracorporate domains: Divisional charter losses in high-technology, multidivisional corporations, *Organization Science*, 7: 255–282.

68. A. D. Chandler, 1994, The functions of the HQ unit in the multibusiness firm, in R. P. Rumelt, D. E. Schendel, & D. J. Teece (eds.), *Fundamental Issues in Strategy*, Cambridge, MA: Harvard Business School Press, 327.

69. O. E. Williamson, 1994, Strategizing, economizing, and economic organization, in R. P. Rumelt, D. E. Schendel, & D. J. Teece (eds.), *Fundamental Issues in Strategy*, Cambridge, MA: Harvard Business School Press, 361–401.

70. R. M. Burton & B. Obel, 1980, A computer simulation test of the M-form hypothesis, *Administrative Science Quarterly*, 25: 457–476.

71. O. E. Williamson, 1985, *The Economic Institutions of Capitalism: Firms, Markets, and Relational Contracting*, New York: Macmillan.

72. Keats & O'Neill, Organizational structure, 532.

73. M. F. Wolff, 1999, In the organization of the future, competitive advantage will be inspired, *Research Technology Management*, 42(4): 2–4.

74. R. H. Hall, 1996, *Organizations: Structures, Processes, and Outcomes*, 6th ed., Englewood Cliffs, NJ: Prentice-Hall, 13; S. Baiman, D. F. Larcker, & M. V. Rajan, 1995, Organizational design for business units, *Journal of Accounting Research*, 33: 205–229.

75. L. G. Love, R. L. Priem, & G. T. Lumpkin, 2002, Explicitly articulated strategy and firm performance under alternative levels of centralization, *Journal of Management*, 28: 611–627.

76. Hall, *Organizations*, 64–75.

77. Barney, *Gaining and Sustaining Competitive Advantage*, 257.

78. 2002, Wal-Mart stores pricing policy, http://www.walmart.com, February 2.

79. Chandler, *Strategy and Structure*.

80. R. Rumelt, 1974, *Strategy, Structure and Economic Performance*, Boston: Harvard University Press.

81. 2002, Halliburton Co., http://www.halliburton.com, February 1.

82. C. C. Markides & P. J. Williamson, 1996, Corporate diversification and organizational structure: A resource-based view, *Academy of Management*

Journal, 39: 340–367; C. W. L. Hill, M. A. Hitt, & R. E. Hoskisson, 1992, Cooperative versus competitive structures in related and unrelated diversified firms, *Organization Science*, 3: 501–521.

83. P. F. Drucker, 2002, They're not employees, they're people, *Harvard Business Review*, 80(2): 70–77; J. Robins & M. E. Wiersema, 1995, A resource-based approach to the multibusiness firm: Empirical analysis of portfolio interrelationships and corporate financial performance, *Strategic Management Journal*, 16: 277–299.

84. C. C. Markides, 1997, To diversify or not to diversify, *Harvard Business Review*, 75(6): 93–99.

85. J. G. March, 1994, *A Primer on Decision Making: How Decisions Happen*, New York: The Free Press, 117–118.

86. P. Walter, 2003, Executive Agenda Column, *Bangkok Post*, http://www.proquest.umi.com, May 1.

87. 2002, GE businesses, http://www.ge.com, February 4.

88. 2002, General Electric Co., Argus Research, http://argusresearch.com, February 4.

89. J. Welch with J. A. Byrne, 2001, *Jack: Straight from the Gut*, New York: Warner Business Books.

90. R. E. Hoskisson & M. A. Hitt, 1990, Antecedents and performance outcomes of diversification: A review and critique of theoretical perspectives, *Journal of Management*, 16: 461–509.

91. Hill, Hitt, & Hoskisson, Cooperative versus competitive structures, 512.

92. J. Birkinshaw, 2001, Strategies for managing internal competition, *California Management Review*, 44(1): 21–38.

93. 2002, Textron profile, http://www.textron.com, February 4.

94. T. R. Eisenmann & J. L. Bower, 2000, The entrepreneurial M-form: Strategic integration in global media firms, *Organization Science*, 11: 348–355.

95. Y. Luo, 2002, Product diversification in international joint ventures: Performance implications in an emerging market, *Strategic Management Journal*, 23: 1–20.

96. T. M. Begley & D. P. Boyd, 2003, The need for a corporate global mindset, *MIT Sloan Management Review*, 44(2): 25–32; Tallman, Global strategic management, 467.

97. T. Kostova & K. Roth, 2003, Social capital in multinational corporations and a micro-macro model of its formation, *Academy of Management Review*, 28: 297–317.

98. Malnight, Emerging structural patterns, 1188.

99. J. Wolf & W. G. Egelhoff, 2002, A reexamination and extension of international strategy-structure theory, *Strategic Management Journal*, 23: 181–189.

100. C. A. Bartlett & S. Ghoshal, 1989, *Managing across Borders: The Transnational Solution*, Boston: Harvard Business School Press.

101. I. C. MacMillan, A. B. van Putten, & R. G. McGrath, 2003, Global gamesmanship, *Harvard Business Review*, 81(5): 62–71.

102. 2002, Unilever today, http://www.unilever.com, February 5.

103. 2001, Kyowa Hakko, Semiannual report, September 30.

104. Malnight, Emerging structural patterns, 1197.

105. Barney, *Gaining and Sustaining Competitive Advantage*, 533.

106. R. J. Kramer, 1999, Organizing for global competitiveness: The corporate headquarters design, *Chief Executive Digest*, 3(2): 23–28.

107. Y. L. Doz & G. Hamel, 1998, *Alliance Advantage: The Art of Creating Value through Partnering*, Boston: Harvard Business School Press, 222.

108. S. X. Li & T. J. Rowley, 2002, Inertia and evaluation mechanisms in interorganizational partner selection: Syndicate formation among U.S. investment banks, *Academy of Management Journal*, 45: 1104–1119; A. C. Inkpen, 2001, Strategic alliances, in M. A. Hitt, R. E. Freeman, & J. S. Harrison (eds.), *Handbook of Strategic Management*, Oxford, UK: Blackwell Publishers, 409–432.

109. Luo, Product diversification in international joint ventures, 2.

110. M. Sawhney, E. Prandelli, & G. Verona, 2003, The power of innomediation, *MIT Sloan Management Review*, 44(2): 77–82; R. Gulati, N. Nohria, & A. Zaheer, 2000, Strategic networks, *Strategic Management Journal*, 21(Special Issue): 203–215; B. Gomes-Casseres, 1994, Group versus group: How alliance networks compete, *Harvard Business Review*, 72(4): 62–74.

111. T. K. Das & B.-S. Teng, 2002, Alliance constellations: A social exchange perspective, *Academy of Management Review*, 27: 445–456.

112. C. Lee, K. Lee, & J. M. Pennings, 2001, Internal capabilities, external networks, and performance: A study on technology-based ventures, *Strategic Management Journal* 22(Special Issue): 615–640.

113. M. B. Sarkar, R. Echambadi, & J. S. Harrison, 2001, Alliance entrepreneurship and firm market performance, *Strategic Management Journal*, 22(Special Issue): 701–711.

114. S. Harrison, 1998, *Japanese Technology and Innovation Management*, Northampton, MA: Edward Elgar.

115. P. Dussauge, B. Garrette, & W. Mitchell, 2000, Learning from competing partners: Outcomes and duration of scale and link alliances in Europe, North America and Asia, *Strategic Management Journal*, 21: 99–126; G. Lorenzoni & C. Baden-Fuller, 1995, Creating a strategic center to manage a web of partners, *California Management Review*, 37(3): 146–163.

116. J. H. Dyer & K. Nobeoka, 2000, Creating and managing a high-performance knowledge-sharing network: The Toyota case, *Strategic Management Journal*, 21(Special Issue): 345–367; J. H. Dyer, 1997, Effective interfirm collaboration: How firms minimize transaction costs and maximize transaction value, *Strategic Management Journal*, 18: 535–556.

117. M. Kotabe, X. Martin, & H. Domoto, 2003, Gaining from vertical partnerships: Knowledge transfer, relationship duration and supplier performance improvement in the U.S. and Japanese automotive industries, *Strategic Management Journal*, 24: 293–316.

118. T. Nishiguchi, 1994, *Strategic Industrial Sourcing: The Japanese Advantage*, New York: Oxford University Press.

119. W. M. Fruin, 1992, *The Japanese Enterprise System*, New York: Oxford University Press.

120. 2003, News @ Cisco, http://www.cisco.com, July 9.

121. 2002, Q&A with John Chambers, http://www.cisco.com, February 10.

122. 2003, McDonald's Corp., *Standard & Poor's Stock Reports*, http://www.fidelity.com, July 5.

123. Ibid.

124. 2003, McDonald's USA franchising, http://www.mcdonalds.com, July 9.

125. C. Jones, W. S. Hesterly, & S. P. Borgatti, 1997, A general theory of network governance: Exchange conditions and social mechanisms, *Academy of Management Review*, 22: 911–945.

126. J. M. Mezias, 2002, Identifying liabilities of foreignness and strategies to minimize their effects: The case of labor lawsuit judgments in the United States, *Strategic Management Journal*, 23: 229–244.

127. R. E. Miles, C. C. Snow, J. A. Mathews, G. Miles, & J. J. Coleman, Jr., 1997, Organizing in the knowledge age: Anticipating the cellular form, *Academy of Management Executive*, 11(4): 7–20.

128. 2002, Ericsson NewsCenter, http://www.ericsson.com, February 10.

Strategic Leadership

Chapter Twelve

12

Knowledge Objectives

Studying this chapter should provide you with the strategic management knowledge needed to:

1. Define strategic leadership and describe top-level managers' importance as a resource.

2. Define top management teams and explain their effects on firm performance.

3. Describe the internal and external managerial labor markets and their effects on developing and implementing strategies.

4. Discuss the value of strategic leadership in determining the firm's strategic direction.

5. Describe the importance of strategic leaders in managing the firm's resources, with emphasis on exploiting and maintaining core competencies, human capital, and social capital.

6. Define organizational culture and explain what must be done to sustain an effective culture.

7. Explain what strategic leaders can do to establish and emphasize ethical practices.

8. Discuss the importance and use of organizational controls.

AP Photo/Marty Lederhandler

Andrea Jung, CEO of Avon Products (center), in New York's Central Park. Emphasizing women's health and self-esteem, Avon Products recently launched "Avon Running—Global Women's Circuit," a series of 10K and 5K fitness walks and prerace clinics in 11 U.S. cities and 16 countries. Andrea Jung, together with Susan Kropf (COO), have strengthened Avon domestically and abroad.

"The truth is that CEOs are flawed individuals who are operating in a complex and imperfect world. . . . They are intensely driven to achieve and they operate in a marketplace that measures achievement almost wholly in the short term. They confront a world that moves faster than ever before, and really, there is little about their unwieldy organizations that they easily control." Despite the major scandals and poor performance of corporations, the current crop of CEOs is no worse overall than previous CEOs. According to Keith Hammonds, the difference is that they now play in a different "sandbox" than they did ten years ago. In 1993, the CEOs of American Express, IBM, and Westinghouse were all forced to resign in the same week. Their companies were performing poorly. Today, a number of companies are performing poorly and a good number of CEOs have resigned because of their company's performance (or because of unethical practices that have come to light).

Regardless of the challenges, some effective and successful strategic leaders do exist. For example, the team of Andrea Jung, CEO, and Susan Kropf, COO, of Avon Products deftly avoided a potential disaster for the company in the economic free fall experienced in Argentina, and have taken other actions to solidify Avon's position in domestic and international markets. While 5 percent of Avon's sales came from Argentina, Jung and Kropf have effectively expanded sales in other parts of the world. They have made Avon a major player in the $500 million market in Central and Eastern Europe and have increased sales by 30 percent in China. In 2002, Avon achieved its third consecutive year in which its earnings per share increased by more than 10 percent (an accomplishment in a very weak economy).

Another successful strategic leader is James Morgan, recently retired CEO of Applied Materials. Before his retirement, Morgan had the distinction of being the longest-serving CEO in Silicon Valley, having held the position for 25 years. Morgan was thought of as a forward thinker, but actions leading to this description caused some analysts to question his strategies. Morgan took bold actions in slow economic times, a strategy that often produced revenue and market share growth when the economic turnaround began. In the 1980s, he moved into Asian markets before most U.S. firms perceived the opportunities there. Although Morgan's action was heavily criticized, he was active in China ten years before his competitors, and his firm recently received a $200 million contract there. In fact, Morgan's goal was to have 5 percent of the firm's revenue come from China by 2005. The company's stock has appreciated in value by 5,600 percent during the previous 20 years, compared to a 500 percent increase in the Standard & Poor's Stock Index for the same time period.

A number of other successful strategic leaders exist. For example, Lindsay Owen-Jones, CEO of L'Oréal, claims part of his success comes from allowing employees to make mistakes and to learn from those mistakes. He also believes if no one makes mistakes, the firm is taking no risks and likely is overlooking opportunities. Fujio Cho, CEO of Toyota, has been highly successful in changing the firm to become a global automaker by expanding into Eastern Europe and China. Toyota's goal is to achieve a 15 percent share of the global auto market, up from 10 percent today. Cho nurtures a culture of managing costs and simultaneously achieving high quality. Michael O'Leary, CEO of Ryanair, transferred the concept of a low-cost airline from the United States (and Southwest Airlines) to Europe. Ryanair's fares on average are about 50 percent lower than those of its competitors. The firm provides low levels of service in terms of food and other amenities on flights, but has fast turnarounds on the ground (20 minutes). The firm's revenues increased by 32 percent and profits grew by 49 percent in 2002. Many of the successful executives can be described as pathfinders and pragmatists, and as having the right value set.

The list of failing strategic leaders is too long to present. Recent failures include William Smithburg, former CEO of Quaker Oats; Jean-Marie Messier, former CEO of Vivendi Universal; Dennis Kozlowski, former CEO of Tyco; Jill Barad, former CEO of Mattel; George Shaheen, former CEO of Webvan; and Samuel Waksal, former CEO of ImClone. The reasons for their failures vary, but identification of those reasons may help others avoid similar pitfalls. According to Sydney Finkelstein, these leaders and many others fail for one or more of the following reasons: they overestimate their ability to control the firm's external environment; there is no boundary between their interests and the company's; they believe that they can answer all questions; they eliminate all who disagree with them; they become obsessed with the company's image; and they underestimate obstacles and rely on what worked in the past. Many of these reasons can be summarized by the terms *arrogance* or *managerial hubris.* There is at least one other critical reason not in the preceding list: a lack of strong ethical values. While Dennis Kozlowski and Sam Waksal suffered from several of the characteristics noted above, both have been charged with crimes, and Waksal has already been convicted and sentenced.

"And so, the razor's edge. You are a CEO. You have the title, the visibility, and the responsibility. You're also isolated. You're under extraordinary pressure to deliver results. And, you're deathly afraid of failing." Being CEO is a very difficult job.

SOURCES: S. Finkelstein, 2003, 7 habits of spectacularly unsuccessful executives, *Fast Company*, July, 84–89; C. Hymowitz, 2003, CEOs value pragmatists with broad, positive views, *Wall Street Journal Online*, http://www.wsj.com, January 28; C. Hymowitz, 2003, CEOs raised in affluence confront new vulnerability, *Wall Street Journal Online*, http://www.wsj.com, January 21; 2003, The best and worst managers of the year, *Business Week*, January 13, 58–92; K. H. Hammonds & J. Collins, 2002, The secret life of the CEO, *Fast Company*, October, 81–86; N. Byrnes, J. A. Byrne, C. Edwards, & L. Lee, 2002, The good CEO, *Business Week*, September 23, 80–88.

As the Opening Case illustrates, all CEOs encounter significant risk, but they also can make a significant difference in how a firm performs. If a strategic leader can create a strategic vision for the firm using the forward thinking that was evident during James Morgan's leadership of Applied Materials, and then energize the firm's human capital, positive outcomes can be achieved. Although the challenge of strategic leadership is significant, the Opening Case provides examples of several highly successful CEOs. However, it is difficult to build and maintain success over a sustained period of time. Some of the CEOs who failed miserably, as described in the Opening Case, had been recognized for their previous success (e.g., Dennis Kozlowski of Tyco).

As this chapter makes clear, it is through effective strategic leadership that firms are able to successfully use the strategic management process. As strategic leaders, top-level managers must guide the firm in ways that result in the formation of a strategic intent and strategic mission. This guidance may lead to goals that stretch everyone in the organization to improve their performance.[1] Moreover, strategic leaders must facilitate the development of appropriate strategic actions and determine how to implement them. These actions on the part of strategic leaders culminate in strategic competitiveness and above-average returns,[2] as shown in Figure 12.1.

Strategic Leadership and the Strategic Management Process — Figure 12.1

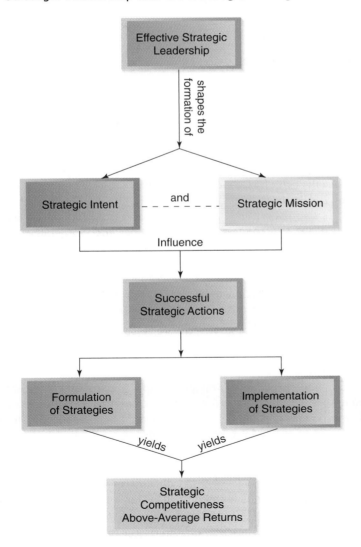

As noted in the Opening Case, there are a number of successful strategic leaders and several who have been highly unsuccessful. The Opening Case also suggests that the job of CEO is challenging and stressful, even more so than it was in previous years. Research suggests that CEO tenure on the job is likely to be three to ten years. The average tenure of a CEO in 1995 was 9.5 years. In the early 21st century, the average had decreased to 7.3 years. Additionally, the boards of directors of companies are showing an increased tendency to go outside the firm for new CEOs or to select "dark horses" from within the firm. They seem to be searching for an executive who is unafraid to make changes in the firm's traditional practices. Still, many new CEOs fail (as we learn later in this chapter).[3]

This chapter begins with a definition of strategic leadership and its importance as a potential source of competitive advantage. Next, we examine top management teams and their effects on innovation, strategic change, and firm performance. Following this discussion is an analysis of the internal and external managerial labor markets from which strategic leaders are selected. Closing the chapter are descriptions of the five key components of effective strategic leadership: determining a strategic direction, effectively managing the firm's resource portfolio, sustaining an effective organizational culture, emphasizing ethical practices, and establishing balanced organizational control systems.

Strategic Leadership

Strategic leadership *is the ability to anticipate, envision, maintain flexibility, and empower others to create strategic change as necessary.*

Strategic leadership is the ability to anticipate, envision, maintain flexibility, and empower others to create strategic change as necessary. Multifunctional in nature, strategic leadership involves managing through others, managing an entire enterprise rather than a functional subunit, and coping with change that continues to increase in the 21st-century competitive landscape, as suggested in the Opening Case. Because of this landscape's complexity and global nature, strategic leaders must learn how to effectively influence human behavior, often in uncertain environments. By word or by personal example, and through their ability to envision the future, effective strategic leaders meaningfully influence the behaviors, thoughts, and feelings of those with whom they work.[4]

The ability to manage human capital may be the most critical of the strategic leader's skills.[5] In the 21st century, intellectual capital, including the ability to manage knowledge and create and commercialize innovation, affects a strategic leader's success.[6] Competent strategic leaders also establish the context through which stakeholders (such as employees, customers, and suppliers) can perform at peak efficiency.[7] "When a public company is left with a void in leadership, for whatever reason, the ripple effects are widely felt both within and outside the organization. Internally, a company is likely to suffer a crisis of morale, confidence and productivity among employees and, similarly, stockholders may panic when a company is left rudderless and worry about the safety and future of their investment."[8] The crux of strategic leadership is the ability to manage the firm's operations effectively and sustain high performance over time.[9]

A firm's ability to achieve strategic competitiveness and earn above-average returns is compromised when strategic leaders fail to respond appropriately and quickly to changes in the complex global competitive environment. The inability to respond or to identify the need to respond is one of the reasons that some of the CEOs mentioned in the Opening Case failed. A firm's "long-term competitiveness depends on managers' willingness to challenge continually their managerial frames."[10] Strategic leaders must learn how to deal with diverse and complex competitive situations. Individual judgment is an important part of learning about and analyzing the firm's external conditions.[11] However, managers also make errors in their evaluation of the competitive conditions. These errors in perception can produce less-effective decisions. But, usually, it means that managers must make decisions under more uncertainty. Some can do this well, but some cannot. Those who cannot are likely to be ineffective and short-term managers. However, to survive, managers do not have to make optimal decisions. They only need to make better decisions than their competitors.[12] Effective strategic leaders are willing to make candid and courageous, yet pragmatic, decisions—decisions that may be difficult, but necessary—through foresight as they reflect on external conditions facing the firm. They also need to understand how such decisions will affect the internal systems currently in use in the firm. Effective strategic leaders use visioning to motivate employees. They often solicit corrective feedback from peers, superiors, and employees about the value of their difficult decisions and vision. Ultimately, they develop strong partners internally and externally to facilitate execution of their strategic vision.[13]

The primary responsibility for effective strategic leadership rests at the top, in particular, with the CEO. Other commonly recognized strategic leaders include members of the board of directors, the top management team, and divisional general managers. Regardless of their title and organizational function, strategic leaders have substantial decision-making responsibilities that cannot be delegated.[14] Strategic leadership is an extremely complex, but critical, form of leadership. Strategies cannot be formulated and implemented to achieve above-average returns without effective strategic leaders. Because strategic leadership is a requirement of strategic success, and because organizations may be poorly led and over-managed, firms competing in the 21st-century competitive landscape are challenged to develop effective strategic leaders.[15]

Managers as an Organizational Resource

As we have suggested, top-level managers are an important resource for firms seeking to formulate and implement strategies effectively.[16] The strategic decisions made by top-level managers influence how the firm is designed and whether or not goals will be achieved. Thus, a critical element of organizational success is having a top management team with superior managerial skills.[17]

Managers often use their discretion (or latitude for action) when making strategic decisions, including those concerned with the effective implementation of strategies.[18] Managerial discretion differs significantly across industries. The primary factors that determine the amount of decision-making discretion a manager (especially a top-level manager) has include (1) external environmental sources (such as the industry structure, the rate of market growth in the firm's primary industry, and the degree to which products can be differentiated), (2) characteristics of the organization (including its size, age, resources, and culture), and (3) characteristics of the manager (including commitment to the firm and its strategic outcomes, tolerance for ambiguity, skills in working with different people, and aspiration levels) (see Figure 12.2). Because strategic leaders' decisions are intended to help the firm gain a competitive advantage, how managers exercise discretion when determining appropriate strategic actions is critical to the firm's success.[19] Top executives must be action oriented; thus, the decisions that they make should spur the company to action.

A top-level executive leads a discussion at a Nike Ethnic Diversity Council meeting. Top executives can have a major effect on a firm's culture and cultural values.

©Mark Richards/PhotoEdit

Figure 12.2 —— Factors Affecting Managerial Discretion

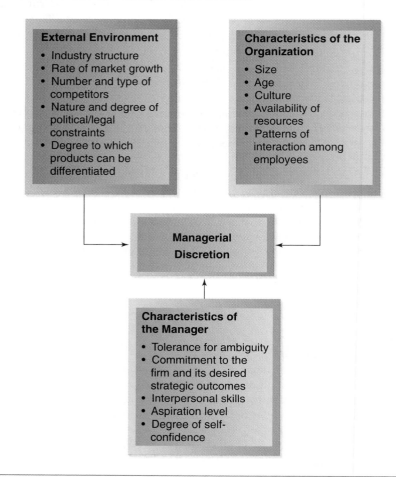

SOURCE: Adapted from S. Finkelstein & D. C. Hambrick, 1996, *Strategic Leadership: Top Executives and Their Effects on Organizations*, St. Paul, MN: West Publishing Company.

In addition to determining new strategic initiatives, top-level managers develop the appropriate organizational structure and reward systems of a firm. In Chapter 11, we described how the organizational structure and reward systems affect strategic actions taken to implement different strategies. Top executives also have a major effect on a firm's culture. Evidence suggests that managers' values are critical in shaping a firm's cultural values.[20] Accordingly, top-level managers have an important effect on organizational activities and performance.[21]

The effects of strategic leaders on the firm's performance are evident at Avon, described in the Opening Case. Avon received approximately 5 percent of its revenue from Argentina before the country experienced an economic disaster. Top executives Andrea Jung and Susan Kropf acted quickly to avoid revenue and cash problems for the firm. In short, they promoted and enhanced Avon's sales in Eastern Europe and in China to overcome the revenue losses in Argentina.

The decisions and actions of strategic leaders can make them a source of competitive advantage for the firm. In accordance with the criteria of sustainability discussed in Chapter 3, strategic leaders can be a source of competitive advantage only when their work is valuable, rare, costly to imitate, and nonsubstitutable. Effective strategic leaders become a source of competitive advantage when they focus their work on the key issues that ultimately shape the firm's ability to earn above-average returns.[22]

Top Management Teams

The complexity of the challenges faced by the firm and the need for substantial amounts of information and knowledge require teams of executives to provide the strategic leadership of most firms. The **top management team** is composed of the key managers who are responsible for selecting and implementing the firm's strategies. Typically, the top management team includes the officers of the corporation, defined by the title of vice-president and above or by service as a member of the board of directors.[23] The quality of the strategic decisions made by a top management team affects the firm's ability to innovate and engage in effective strategic change.[24]

TOP MANAGEMENT TEAM, FIRM PERFORMANCE, AND STRATEGIC CHANGE

The job of top-level executives is complex and requires a broad knowledge of the firm's operations, as well as the three key parts of the firm's external environment—the general, industry, and competitor environments, as discussed in Chapter 2. Therefore, firms try to form a top management team that has the appropriate knowledge and expertise to operate the internal organization, yet also can deal with all the firm's stakeholders as well as its competitors.[25] This normally requires a heterogeneous top management team. A **heterogeneous top management team** is composed of individuals with different functional backgrounds, experience, and education. The more heterogeneous a top management team is, with varied expertise and knowledge, the more capacity it has to provide effective strategic leadership in *formulating* strategy.[26]

Members of a heterogeneous top management team benefit from discussing the different perspectives advanced by team members. In many cases, these discussions increase the quality of the top management team's decisions, especially when a synthesis emerges from the diverse perspectives that is generally superior to any one individual perspective.[27] For example, heterogeneous top management teams in the airline industry have the propensity to take stronger competitive actions and reactions than do more homogeneous teams.[28] The net benefit of such actions by heterogeneous teams has been positive in terms of market share and above-average returns. Research shows that more heterogeneity among top management team members promotes debate, which often leads to better strategic decisions. In turn, better strategic decisions produce higher firm performance.[29]

It is also important that the top management team members function cohesively. In general, the more heterogeneous and larger the top management team is, the more difficult it is for the team to effectively implement strategies.[30] Comprehensive and long-term strategic plans can be inhibited by communication difficulties among top executives who have different backgrounds and different cognitive skills.[31] Alternatively, communication among diverse top management team members can be facilitated through electronic communications, sometimes reducing the barriers before face-to-face meetings.[32] As a result, a group of top executives with diverse backgrounds may inhibit the process of decision making if it is not effectively managed. In these cases, top management teams may fail to comprehensively examine threats and opportunities, leading to a sub-optimal strategic decision.

Having members with substantive expertise in the firm's core functions and businesses is also important to the effectiveness of a top management team. In a high-technology industry, it may be critical for a firm's top management team to have R&D expertise, particularly when growth strategies are being implemented.[33]

The characteristics of top management teams are related to innovation and strategic change.[34] For example, more heterogeneous top management teams are associated

The top management team is composed of the key managers who are responsible for selecting and implementing the firm's strategies.

A heterogeneous top management team is composed of individuals with different functional backgrounds, experience, and education.

positively with innovation and strategic change. The heterogeneity may force the team or some of the members to "think outside of the box" and thus be more creative in making decisions.[35] Therefore, firms that need to change their strategies are more likely to do so if they have top management teams with diverse backgrounds and expertise. When a new CEO is hired from outside the industry, the probability of strategic change is greater than if the new CEO is from inside the firm or inside the industry.[36] While hiring a new CEO from outside the industry adds diversity to the team, the top management team must be managed effectively to use the diversity in a positive way. Thus, to create strategic change, the CEO should exercise transformational leadership.[37] A top management team with various areas of expertise is more likely to identify environmental changes (opportunities and threats) or changes within the firm that require a different strategic direction.[38]

THE CEO AND TOP MANAGEMENT TEAM POWER

As noted in Chapter 10, the board of directors is an important governance mechanism for monitoring a firm's strategic direction and for representing stakeholders' interests, especially those of shareholders. In fact, higher performance normally is achieved when the board of directors is more directly involved in shaping a firm's strategic direction.[39]

Boards of directors, however, may find it difficult to direct the strategic actions of powerful CEOs and top management teams.[40] It is not uncommon for a powerful CEO to appoint a number of sympathetic outside board members or have inside board members who are also on the top management team and report to the CEO.[41] In either case, the CEO may have significant control over the board's actions. "A central question is whether boards are an effective management control mechanism . . . or whether they are a 'management tool,' . . . a rubber stamp for management initiatives . . . and often surrender to management their major domain of decision-making authority, which includes the right to hire, fire, and compensate top management."[42]

In the poor performance of Vivendi Universal and Tyco mentioned in the Opening Case, the board of directors can clearly be faulted. In both firms, the CEOs, Jean-Marie Messier (Vivendi Universal) and Dennis Kozlowski (Tyco) made multiple acquisitions that eventually greatly harmed the financial strength of the companies. The boards should have stopped these actions before they caused such harm. Alternatively, recent research shows that social ties between the CEO and board members may actually increase board members' involvement in strategic decisions. Thus, strong relationships between the CEO and the board of directors may have positive or negative outcomes.[43]

CEOs and top management team members can achieve power in other ways. A CEO who also holds the position of chairman of the board usually has more power than the CEO who is not simultaneously serving as chairman of the firm's board.[44] Although this practice of CEO duality (when the CEO and the chairperson of the board are the same) has become more common in U.S. businesses, it has come under heavy criticism. Duality has been blamed for poor performance and slow response to change in a number of firms.[45]

DaimlerChrysler CEO Jürgen Schrempp, who holds the dual positions of chairman of the board and CEO, has substantial power in the firm. In fact, insiders suggest that he was purging those individuals who are outspoken and who represent potential threats to his dominance. In particular, many former Chrysler executives left the firm, although research suggests that retaining key employees after an acquisition contributes to improved post-acquisition performance.[46] Thus, it has been particularly difficult to turn around the U.S. operations.[47] Dieter Zetsche, a German who is likely next in line to be CEO at DaimlerChrysler, is leading the team that is seeking to reverse Chrysler's fortunes. However, Chrysler's fortunes have not been reversed since the acquisition in 1998. In July 2003, Zetsche called on Joe Eberhardt, manager of the company's operations in the United Kingdom, to try to fix Chrysler's sales and marketing strategy problems and thereby reverse its performance. Simultaneous with Eberhardt's appointment was an announcement of a $1.2 billion loss by Chrysler in the second quarter of 2003.[48]

Although it varies across industries, duality occurs most commonly in the largest firms. Increased shareholder activism, however, has brought CEO duality under scrutiny and attack in both U.S. and European firms. Historically, an independent board leadership structure in which the same person did not hold the positions of CEO and chair was believed to enhance a board's ability to monitor top-level managers' decisions and actions, particularly in terms of the firm's financial performance.[49] And, as reported in Chapter 10, many believe these two positions should be separate in most companies today in order to make the board more independent from the CEO. Stewardship theory, on the other hand, suggests that CEO duality facilitates effective decisions and actions. In these instances, the increased effectiveness gained through CEO duality accrues from the individual who wants to perform effectively and desires to be the best possible steward of the firm's assets. Because of this person's positive orientation and actions, extra governance and the coordination costs resulting from an independent board leadership structure would be unnecessary.[50]

Top management team members and CEOs who have long tenure—on the team and in the organization—have a greater influence on board decisions.[51] And, CEOs with greater influence may take actions in their own best interests, the outcomes of which increase their compensation from the company.[52] Long tenure is known to restrict the breadth of an executive's knowledge base. With the limited perspectives associated with a restricted knowledge base, long-tenured top executives typically develop fewer alternatives to evaluate in making strategic decisions.[53] However, long-tenured managers also may be able to exercise more effective strategic control, thereby obviating the need for board members' involvement because effective strategic control generally produces higher performance.[54]

To strengthen the firm, boards of directors should develop an effective relationship with the firm's top management team. The relative degrees of power held by the board and top management team members should be examined in light of an individual firm's situation. For example, the abundance of resources in a firm's external environment and the volatility of that environment may affect the ideal balance of power between boards and top management teams.[55] Moreover, a volatile and uncertain environment may create a situation where a powerful CEO is needed to move quickly, but a diverse top management team may create less cohesion among team members and prevent or stall a necessary strategic move.[56] Through the development of effective working relationships, boards, CEOs, and other top management team members are able to serve the best interests of the firm's stakeholders.[57]

Managerial Labor Market

The choice of top executives—especially CEOs—is a critical organizational decision with important implications for the firm's performance.[58] Many companies use leadership screening systems to identify individuals with managerial and strategic leadership potential. The most effective of these systems assess people within the firm and gain valuable information about the capabilities of other companies' managers, particularly their strategic leaders.[59] Based on the results of these assessments, training and development programs are provided for current managers in an attempt to preselect and shape the skills of people who may become tomorrow's leaders. The "ten-step talent" management development program at GE, for example, is considered one of the most effective in the world.[60]

Organizations select managers and strategic leaders from two types of managerial labor markets—internal and external.[61] An **internal managerial labor market** consists of

*An **internal managerial labor market** consists of the opportunities for managerial positions within a firm.*

The Times Are Changing: Is Wonder Woman Still Required for Top Executive Positions in the 21st Century?

Total employment in the United States is expected to increase by 22.2 million jobs during the period 2000–2010. The number of women in the workforce is expected to increase by 15.1 percent to 75.5 million, while the number of men in the workforce is projected to climb by 9.3 percent to 82.2 million. As such, women should compose approximately 48 percent of the workforce in 2010. However, despite gains, only a few of the major U.S. corporations have women CEOs. Do they have to be wonder women to attain such positions? To receive consideration for a CEO position requires an exceptional record. Still, corporate America seems to be highly underutilizing a valuable asset, female human capital. But, times are changing. Ten percent of the *Fortune* 500 companies have women in 25 percent of their corporate officer teams. This represents an increase from 5 percent of the *Fortune* 500 in 1995. And, most of the women who now hold officer positions no longer refer to their gender. However, important issues remain in the gender gap. For example, a wage gap between men and women holding the same jobs is prevalent in most industries. This gap exists not only in the United States, but also in Europe. The gap is smallest in Luxembourg (11 percent) and largest in Austria (33 percent). However, the women who are members of top management teams enjoy more pay equity than women in other positions.

Anne Mulcahy, CEO of Xerox, has quietly but successfully turned around the financial performance of the firm she leads. Currently only 10 percent of *Fortune* 500 companies have women in 25 percent of their corporate officer teams—that represents an increase of only 5 percent since 1995.

There are many more examples of successful women executives in the current corporate environment than in the past. Well-known women CEOs include Carly Fiorina (Hewlett-Packard), Anne Mulcahy (Xerox), and Meg Whitman (eBay). But there are others who might be considered as "trail blazers" who should also receive recognition. For example, Catherine Elizabeth Hughes began her career in 1969 and became the first African American woman to head a firm that was publicly traded on a U.S. stock exchange. Muriel Siebert began her career in 1954 and in 1967 became the first woman to purchase a seat on the New York Stock Exchange. Judith Regan started as a secretary and then became a reporter for the *National Enquirer* in the late 1970s. She then developed a highly successful series of books for Simon and Schuster in the 1980s on celebrities such as Rush Limbaugh and Howard Stern. In 1994, she was given her own imprint at HarperCollins called ReganBooks, along with a TV show on Fox News. Today, two of the highest-profile women CEOs are Anne Mulcahy and Carly Fiorina.

Anne Mulcahy was promoted to president and COO of Xerox only a short time before it encountered significant difficulties and performance declined precipitously. Many questioned whether or not Xerox could survive. But, it has done so under Mulcahy's steady guidance. Because of her leadership, Xerox has returned to profitability, and she has become the chairman and CEO of the company. As CEO, she has several priorities for Xerox. Her first priority is to provide value to customers and growth for Xerox. Her second priority is people, those who work for the company. In fact, she argues that the success of Xerox is fully based on the Xerox human capital. Her third priority is shareholder value; many CEOs have this as their first and only priority. Her fourth priority is corporate governance. She has taken several important actions to improve the governance processes at Xerox. And, her fifth priority is to provide effective leadership. She claims that the most successful leaders are self-effacing and give credit to others. Yet, they have a strong resolve to take whatever actions

Getty Images

are necessary to see that the firm succeeds. The future of Xerox looks bright with Anne Mulcahy as the CEO.

Carly Fiorina is perhaps the highest-profile woman strategic leader as CEO of Hewlett-Packard. She has had many challenges during her relatively short tenure as CEO, the most prominent of which was the contested acquisition of Compaq. With each of these challenges, beginning with her appointment as CEO, analysts argued that she would fail. To date, although sometimes scarred in battle, she has overcome all of the major challenges. Fiorina was hired as CEO of HP in 1998 with a mandate from the board to transform the firm and breathe new life into it. To do so, she has had to take on and change long-standing practices and traditions as well as revise and revive the innovative culture that once existed. Fiorina has made shrewd strategic moves and has shown that she can "play the game" with the best of them and win. She has made HP more nimble and lean and a company that is active and on the move. Time will tell if HP and Fiorina will be truly successful, but there is little doubt that Fiorina has also been a trail blazer. Because of her leadership as CEO, few are likely to question if a woman CEO knows how to fight and win. She has shown that she can do both.

SOURCES: J. Gettings & D. Johnson, 2003, Wonder Women: Profiles of leading female CEOs and business executives, *Infoplease*, http://www.infoplease.com, July 13; 2003, Online Fact Book, Xerox at a glance, http://www.xerox.com, July 13; 2003, Facts on Working Women, U.S. Department of Labor, http://www.dol.gov/wb, May; 2003, Remarks by Anne M. Mulcahy, chairman and chief executive officer, http://www.uschamber.com, April 2; 2003, Equality through pay equity, *Trade Union World*, http://www.dol.gov/wb, March; 2003, Showdown, *Business Week*, February 17, 70–72; G. Anders, 2003, The Carly chronicle, *Fast Company*, February, 66–73; 2003, Carly Fiorina, up close, *Wall Street Journal*, January 13, B1, B6.

the opportunities for managerial positions within a firm, whereas an **external managerial labor market** is the collection of career opportunities for managers in organizations other than the one for which they work currently. Several benefits are thought to accrue to a firm when the internal labor market is used to select an insider as the new CEO. Because of their experience with the firm and the industry environment in which it competes, insiders are familiar with company products, markets, technologies, and operating procedures. Also, internal hiring produces lower turnover among existing personnel, many of whom possess valuable firm-specific knowledge. When the firm is performing well, internal succession is favored to sustain high performance. It is assumed that hiring from inside keeps the important knowledge necessary to sustain the performance.

Given the phenomenal success of GE and its highly effective management development program, an insider, Jeffrey Immelt, was chosen to succeed Jack Welch.[62] As noted in a later Strategic Focus, Immelt is making a number of changes in GE. This is surprising because new CEOs from inside the firm are less likely to make changes, and GE has performed better than many other firms over the last two decades. However, changes in the economic and competitive environments have produced needs for changes in the firm. Thus, Immelt is trying to create a new strategy and ensure continued success for the firm. One of his actions has been to create a more independent board and improve the governance system. For an inside move to the top to occur successfully, firms must develop and implement effective succession management programs. In that way, managers can be developed so that one will eventually be prepared to ascend to the top.[63] Immelt was well prepared to take over the CEO job at GE.

It is not unusual for employees to have a strong preference for the internal managerial labor market to be used to select top management team members and the CEO. In the past, companies have also had a preference for insiders to fill top-level management positions because of a desire for continuity and a continuing commitment to the firm's current strategic intent, strategic mission, and chosen strategies.[64] However,

An external managerial labor market is the collection of career opportunities for managers in organizations other than the one for which they work currently.

because of a changing competitive landscape and varying levels of performance, even at companies such as GE, an increasing number of boards of directors have been going to outsiders to succeed CEOs.[65] A firm often has valid reasons to select an outsider as its new CEO. For example, research suggests that executives who have spent their entire career with a particular firm may become "stale in the saddle."[66] Long tenure with a firm seems to reduce the number of innovative ideas top executives are able to develop to cope with conditions facing their firm. Given the importance of innovation for a firm's success in today's competitive landscape (see Chapter 13), an inability to innovate or to create conditions that stimulate innovation throughout a firm is a liability for a strategic leader. Figure 12.3 shows how the composition of the top management team and CEO succession (managerial labor market) may interact to affect strategy. For example, when the top management team is homogeneous (its members have similar functional experiences and educational backgrounds) and a new CEO is selected from inside the firm, the firm's current strategy is unlikely to change.

On the other hand, when a new CEO is selected from outside the firm and the top management team is heterogeneous, there is a high probability that strategy will change. When the new CEO is from inside the firm and a heterogeneous top management team is in place, the strategy may not change, but innovation is likely to continue. An external CEO succession with a homogeneous team creates a more ambiguous situation.

To have an adequate number of top managers, firms must take advantage of a highly qualified labor pool, including one source of managers that has often been overlooked: women. Firms are beginning to utilize women's potential managerial talents with substantial success, as described in the Strategic Focus. As noted in the Strategic Focus, women, such as Catherine Elizabeth Hughes, Muriel Siebert, and Judith Regan, have made important contributions as strategic leaders. A few firms have gained value by using the significant talents of women leaders. But many more have not done so, which represents an opportunity cost to them. Alternatively, the Strategic Focus explains that women are being recognized for their leadership skill and are being selected for prominent strategic leadership positions, such as those held by Anne Mulcahy, CEO of Xerox, and Carly Fiorina, CEO of Hewlett-Packard.

Figure 12.3 — **Effects of CEO Succession and Top Management Team Composition on Strategy**

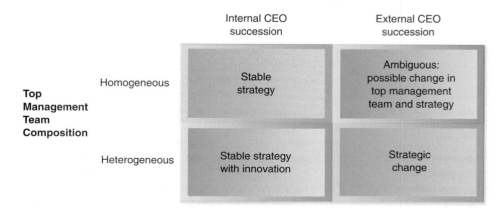

More women are now being appointed to the boards of directors for organizations in both the private and public sectors. These additional appointments suggest that women's ability to represent stakeholders' and especially shareholders' best interests in for-profit companies at the level of the board of directors is being more broadly recognized. However, in addition to appointments to the board of directors, firms competing in the complex and challenging global economy—an economy demanding the best of an organization—may be well served by adding more female executives to their top management teams. It is important for firms to create diversity in leadership positions. Organizations such as Johnson & Johnson, the World Bank, and Royal Dutch Shell are creating more diverse leadership teams in order to deal with complex, heterogeneous, and ambiguous environments.[67] To build diverse teams, firms must break down their glass ceilings to allow all people regardless of gender or ethnicity to move into key leadership positions.[68] In so doing, firms more effectively use the human capital in their workforce. They also provide more opportunities for all people in the firm to satisfy their needs, such as their need for self-actualization; therefore, employees should be more highly motivated, leading to higher productivity for the firm.[69]

Key Strategic Leadership Actions

Several identifiable actions characterize strategic leadership that positively contributes to effective use of the firm's strategies.[70] We present the most critical of these actions in Figure 12.4. Many of the actions interact with each other. For example, managing the firm's resources effectively includes developing human capital and contributes to establishing a strategic direction, fostering an effective culture, exploiting core competencies, using effective organizational control systems, and establishing ethical practices.

Determining Strategic Direction

Determining the strategic direction of a firm involves developing a long-term vision of the firm's strategic intent. A long-term vision typically looks at least five to ten years into the future. A philosophy with goals, this vision consists of the image and character the firm seeks.[71]

Determining the strategic direction of a firm involves developing a long-term vision of the firm's strategic intent.

Exercise of Effective Strategic Leadership —— Figure 12.4

Effective Strategic Leadership

Determining Strategic Direction

Establishing Balanced Organizational Controls

Effectively Managing the Firm's Resource Portfolio

Sustaining an Effective Organizational Culture

Emphasizing Ethical Practices

©Keith Dannemiller/CORBIS SABA

A former Cinemex movie theatre in Mexico City, Mexico. In 2001, the year prior to its sale to Loews Cineplex, Cinemex generated a profit of $40 million. Its success came from recognizing a need for quality movie theaters in a huge potential market.

The ideal long-term vision has two parts: a core ideology and an envisioned future. While the core ideology motivates employees through the company's heritage, the envisioned future encourages employees to stretch beyond their expectations of accomplishment and requires significant change and progress in order to be realized.[72] The envisioned future serves as a guide to many aspects of a firm's strategy implementation process, including motivation, leadership, employee empowerment, and organizational design.

Matthew D. Heyman came out of Harvard Business School in 1993 with a vision of building lavish movie theaters in Mexico City, a city with 20 million inhabitants. The Mexican theater industry was in shambles because of government price controls, and so a vacuum existed for quality movie theaters. After finding financial backing for his company, Cinemex, Heyman and his partners began constructing movie theaters. Heyman decided early on to target the largest market in Mexico City, the working poor. His theaters charged about half as much for tickets in poor areas of the city as did theaters in wealthy areas, even though they were just as extravagant. In 2001, Cinemex generated a profit of approximately $40 million.[73] In 2002, Cinemex was sold for $286 million to a Canadian partnership that owned Loews Cineplex, the fourth largest theater chain in the United States. At the time of the sale, Cinemex had 31 theaters with 349 screens.[74]

Most changes in strategic direction are difficult to design and implement, but Jeffrey Immelt has an even greater challenge at GE. As explained in the Strategic Focus, GE performed exceptionally well under Jack Welch's leadership. While there is need for a change because the competitive landscape is shifting, stakeholders accustomed to Jack Welch and high performance may not readily accept Immelt's changes, especially in strategy. Immelt is trying to effect critical changes in strategy and governance and simultaneously gain stakeholders' commitment to them. A charismatic CEO may foster stakeholders' commitment to a new vision and strategic direction. Nonetheless, it is important not to lose sight of the strengths of the organization in making changes required by a new strategic direction. Immelt must use the strengths of GE to ensure continued positive performance. The goal is to pursue the firm's short-term need to adjust to a new vision while maintaining its long-term survivability by managing its portfolio of resources effectively.

Effectively Managing the Firm's Resource Portfolio

Probably the most important task for strategic leaders is effectively managing the firm's portfolio of resources. Firms have multiple resources that can be categorized into one of the following: financial capital, human capital, social capital, and organizational capital (including organizational culture).[75] Strategic leaders manage the firm's portfolio of resources by organizing them into capabilities, structuring the firm to use the capabilities, and developing and implementing a strategy to leverage those resources to achieve a competitive advantage.[76] In particular, strategic leaders must exploit and maintain the firm's core competencies and develop and retain the firm's human and social capital.

Changing the House That Jack Built—A New GE

Jack Welch built an incredibly successful company during his tenure as CEO of GE. In 2002, the firm enjoyed revenues of $131.7 billion, 40 percent of which came from international operations. Thus, it is a truly global company. In 2002, the return on sales was 11.5 percent with earnings per share of $1.51. GE was chosen by the *Financial Times* as the world's most respected company in 1999, 2000, 2001, 2002, and 2003. However, the competitive landscape has been changing; the sands are shifting. With the economy down and political uncertainties around the world, GE is unable to grow as quickly as it has in the past. And, many argue that Welch fueled growth by reducing jobs and costs, making acquisitions, and developing a large and powerful financial services unit. Unfortunately, the same opportunities no longer exist. As a result, analysts predict that GE is likely to grow between 3 and 13 percent in the foreseeable future, with growth under 10 percent most of the time. Jeffrey Immelt, who succeeded Welch, will need to achieve growth largely by emphasizing the core industrial companies that Welch deemphasized. Thus, the job is even more challenging.

In 2002, GE's net income grew by 7.1 percent. This is clearly respectable growth in poor economic and uncertain times. But, net income grew at more than 10 percent for the ten preceding years. GE also has come under criticism for its accounting practices, suggesting some of the previous growth reported may have been the result of questionable accounting practices related to acquisitions. Therefore, Immelt faces substantial challenges and is making changes as a result. He is emphasizing the industrial and consumer goods businesses. Thus, he must refocus the firm's marketing and innovation capabilities. Immelt does have some bright areas on which he can build, one of which is the jet engine business. GE controls approximately 64 percent of the global jet engine market. It has done so by emphasizing quality, innovation, and vision. For example, while it has monopolized the engine market for large jets, executives predicted the development of the small, regional jet market. Therefore, they invested in R&D to develop an excellent engine for the small jet market. The timing was almost perfect as the number of regional jets in service grew from 85 in 1993 to 1,300 in 2003. Immelt has to strongly support this type of vision and innovation in all of GE's major businesses.

Immelt is emphasizing more transparency in accounting practices and is developing a more independent board of directors. Additionally, he expects GE managers to excel in many areas including exercising high personal integrity while simultaneously gaining high sales. It is very difficult to follow an icon, especially a highly respected and successful CEO such as Jack Welch. However, the challenge is even greater when the firm's performance is suffering and the new CEO must make major changes in the firm's strategy and managerial practices. While the environment is requiring that firms such as GE seek growth in ways different from the recent past, and GE's performance is lower than in the previous decade, GE's board seems satisfied with Immelt's performance to date. He received pay and stock options valued at $43 million for 2002. In taking this action, the GE board emphasized Immelt's integrity, his commitment to effective corporate governance (including changes in the board membership), and his determination to take actions that enhance long-term shareholder value.

SOURCES: G. Strauss & B. Hansen, 2003, Bubble hasn't burst yet on CEO salaries despite the times, *USA Today*, http://www.usatoday.com, July 3; 2003, Fact Sheet, http://www.ge.com, June 20; K. Kranhold, 2003, GE appliances don't wash with "growth," *Wall Street Journal Online*, http://www.wsj.com, April 3; A. Slywotzky & R. Wise, 2003, Double digit growth in no-growth times, *Fast Company*, April, 66–72; M. Murray, 2003, GE's Immelt starts renovations on the house that Jack built, *Wall Street Journal*, February 6, A1, A6; S. Holmes, 2003, GE: Little engines that could, *Business Week*, January 20, 62–63; C. Hymowitz, 2002, Resolving to let the new year be a year of better leadership, *Wall Street Journal Online*, http://www.wsj.com, December 31.

The Heart and Soul-Mates Support Network jointly promotes Tropicana Pure Premium and Quaker Oatmeal products, representing PepsiCo's exploitation of core competencies across organizational units.

EXPLOITING AND MAINTAINING CORE COMPETENCIES

Examined in Chapters 1 and 3, *core competencies* are resources and capabilities that serve as a source of competitive advantage for a firm over its rivals. Typically, core competencies relate to an organization's functional skills, such as manufacturing, finance, marketing, and research and development. As shown by the descriptions that follow, firms develop and exploit core competencies in many different functional areas. Strategic leaders must verify that the firm's competencies are emphasized in strategy implementation efforts. Intel, for example, has core competencies of *competitive agility* (an ability to act in a variety of competitively relevant ways) and *competitive speed* (an ability to act quickly when facing environmental and competitive pressures).[77]

In many large firms, and certainly in related diversified ones, core competencies are effectively exploited when they are developed and applied across different organizational units (see Chapter 6). For example, PepsiCo purchased Quaker Oats, which makes the sports drink Gatorade. PepsiCo uses its competence in distribution systems to exploit the Quaker assets. For example, Pepsi soft drinks (e.g., Pepsi Cola and Mountain Dew) and Gatorade share the logistics activity. Similarly, PepsiCo uses this competence to distribute Quaker Oats' healthy snacks and Frito Lay's salty snacks through the same channels. In 2003, PepsiCo launched the Heart and Soul-Mates Support Network offering nutritional tips, motivational messages, and coaching advice to jointly promote its Tropicana Pure Premium and Quaker Oatmeal products.[78]

Firms must continuously develop or even change their core competencies to stay ahead of the competition. If they have a competence that provides an advantage but do not change it, competitors will eventually imitate that competence and reduce or eliminate the firm's competitive advantage. Additionally, firms must guard against the competence becoming a liability thereby preventing change. If this occurs, competitors will eventually develop a more valuable competence, eliminating the firm's competitive advantage and taking its market share away.[79] Most core competencies require high-quality human capital.

DEVELOPING HUMAN CAPITAL AND SOCIAL CAPITAL

Human capital refers to the knowledge and skills of a firm's entire workforce.

Human capital refers to the knowledge and skills of a firm's entire workforce. From the perspective of human capital, employees are viewed as a capital resource that requires investment.[80] These investments are productive, in that much of the development of U.S. industry can be attributed to the effectiveness of its human capital. This fact suggests that "as the dynamics of competition accelerate, people are perhaps the only truly sustainable source of competitive advantage."[81] Human capital's increasing importance suggests a significant role for the firm's human resource management activities.[82] As a support activity (see Chapter 2), human resource management practices facilitate people's efforts to successfully select and especially to use the firm's strategies.[83]

Human capital is important in all types of organizations, large and small, new and established. For example, a major factor in the decision by venture capitalists to invest in an entrepreneurial venture is the quality of the human capital involved. In fact, it may be of equal or more importance to the quality of the entrepreneurial opportunity.[84] J. W. Marriott, Jr., CEO of Marriott International, argued strongly that the primary reason for the long-term success of the company has been the belief that its human capital is the most important asset of the firm. Thus, the company built and maintained a homelike and friendly environment that supports the growth and development of its employees, called "associates in Marriott." He also suggested that the firm invests significant effort in hiring caring and dependable people who are ethical and trustworthy. The firm then trains and rewards them for high-quality performance.[85]

Effective training and development programs increase the probability that a manager will be a successful strategic leader. These programs have grown progressively important to the success of firms as knowledge has become more integral to gaining and sustaining a competitive advantage.[86] Additionally, such programs build knowledge and skills, inculcate a common set of core values, and offer a systematic view of the organization, thus promoting the firm's strategic vision and organizational cohesion. The programs also contribute to the development of core competencies.[87] Furthermore, they help strategic leaders improve skills that are critical to completing other tasks associated with effective strategic leadership, such as determining the firm's strategic direction, exploiting and maintaining the firm's core competencies, and developing an organizational culture that supports ethical practices. Thus, building human capital is vital to the effective execution of strategic leadership.[88]

Strategic leaders must acquire the skills necessary to help develop human capital in their areas of responsibility. When human capital investments are successful, the result is a workforce capable of learning continuously. Continuous learning and leveraging the firm's expanding knowledge base are linked with strategic success.[89] Learning also can preclude making errors. Strategic leaders tend to learn more from their failures than their successes because they sometimes make the wrong attributions for the successes.[90] It is important to learn from both successes and failures.

Learning and building knowledge are important for creating innovation in firms.[91] And, innovation leads to competitive advantage.[92] Overall, firms that create and maintain greater knowledge usually achieve and maintain competitive advantages. However, as noted with core competencies, strategic leaders must guard against allowing high levels of knowledge in one area to lead to myopia and overlooking knowledge development opportunities in other important areas of the business.[93]

Programs that achieve outstanding results in the training of future strategic leaders become a competitive advantage for a firm. As noted earlier, GE's system of training and development of future strategic leaders is comprehensive and thought to be among the best.[94] Accordingly, it may be a source of competitive advantage for the firm.

Because of the economic downturn in 2001–2002 and the continuing economic malaise for some time thereafter, many firms laid off key people. Layoffs can result in a significant loss of the knowledge possessed by a firm's human capital. Research has shown that moderate-sized layoffs may improve firm performance, but large layoffs produce stronger performance downturns in firms because of the loss of human capital.[95] Although it is also not uncommon for restructuring firms to reduce their expenditures on, or investments in, training and development programs, restructuring may actually be an important time to increase investments in these programs. Restructuring firms have less slack and cannot absorb as many errors; moreover, the employees who remain after layoffs may find themselves in positions without all of the skills or knowledge they need to perform the required tasks effectively.[96] Improvements in information technology can facilitate better use of human resources when a downsizing event occurs.[97]

Viewing employees as a resource to be maximized rather than a cost to be minimized facilitates the successful implementation of a firm's strategies. The implementation of such strategies also is more effective when strategic leaders approach layoffs in a manner that employees believe is fair and equitable.[98] A critical issue for employees is the fairness in the layoffs and in treatment in their jobs.[99]

Social capital *involves relationships inside and outside the firm that help the firm accomplish tasks and create value for customers and shareholders.*

Social capital involves relationships inside and outside the firm that help the firm accomplish tasks and create value for customers and shareholders.[100] Social capital is a critical asset for a firm. Inside the firm, employees and units must cooperate to get the work done. In multinational organizations, units often must cooperate across country boundaries on activities such as R&D to produce outcomes needed by the firm (e.g., new products).[101]

External social capital has become critical to firm success in the last several years. Few, if any, firms have all of the resources that they need to compete in global (or domestic) markets. Thus, they establish alliances with other firms that have complementary resources in order to gain access to them. These relationships must be effectively managed to ensure that the partner trusts the firm and is willing to share the desired resources.[102] In fact, the success of many types of firms may partially depend on social capital. Large multinational firms often must establish alliances in order to enter new foreign markets. Likewise, entrepreneurial firms often must establish alliances to gain access to resources, venture capital, or other types of resources (e.g., special expertise that the entrepreneurial firm cannot afford to maintain in-house.)[103] Retaining quality human capital and maintaining strong internal social capital can be affected strongly by the firm's culture.

Sustaining an Effective Organizational Culture

An organizational cul-
ture *consists of a complex
set of ideologies, symbols,
and core values that is
shared throughout the firm
and influences the way
business is conducted.*

An **organizational culture** consists of a complex set of ideologies, symbols, and core values that is shared throughout the firm and influences the way business is conducted. Evidence suggests that a firm can develop core competencies in terms of both the capabilities it possesses and the way the capabilities are leveraged by strategies to produce desired outcomes. In other words, because the organizational culture influences how the firm conducts its business and helps regulate and control employees' behavior, it can be a source of competitive advantage.[104] Thus, shaping the context within which the firm formulates and implements its strategies—that is, shaping the organizational culture— is a central task of strategic leaders.[105] Ikea's CEO, Anders Dahlvig, attributes the success of his firm partly to its unique corporate culture.[106]

ENTREPRENEURIAL ORIENTATION

An organizational culture often encourages (or discourages) the pursuit of entrepreneurial opportunities, especially in large firms.[107] Entrepreneurial opportunities are an important source of growth and innovation.[108] In Chapter 13, we describe how large firms use strategic entrepreneurship to pursue entrepreneurial opportunities and to gain first-mover advantages. Medium- and small-sized firms also rely on strategic entrepreneurship when trying to develop innovations as the foundation for profitable growth. In firms of all sizes, strategic entrepreneurship is more likely to be successful when employees have an entrepreneurial orientation.[109] Five dimensions characterize a firm's entrepreneurial orientation: autonomy, innovativeness, risk taking, proactiveness, and competitive aggressiveness.[110] In combination, these dimensions influence the activities of a firm to be innovative and launch new ventures.

The first of an entrepreneurial orientation's five dimensions, *autonomy,* allows employees to take actions that are free of organizational constraints and permits individuals and groups to be self-directed. The second dimension, *innovativeness,* "reflects a firm's tendency to engage in and support new ideas, novelty, experimentation, and creative processes that may result in new products, services, or technological processes."[111] Cultures with a tendency toward innovativeness encourage employees to think beyond existing knowledge, technologies, and parameters in efforts to find creative ways to add value. *Risk taking* reflects a willingness by employees and their firm to accept risks when pursuing entrepreneurial opportunities. These risks can include assuming significant levels of debt and allocating large amounts of other resources (e.g., people) to projects that may not be completed. The fourth dimension of an entrepreneurial orientation, *proactiveness,* describes a firm's ability to be a market leader rather than a follower. Proactive organizational cultures constantly use processes to anticipate future market needs and to satisfy them before competitors learn how to do so. Finally, *competitive aggressiveness* is a firm's propensity to take actions that allow it to consistently and substantially outperform its rivals.[112]

CHANGING THE ORGANIZATIONAL CULTURE AND RESTRUCTURING

Changing a firm's organizational culture is more difficult than maintaining it, but effective strategic leaders recognize when change is needed. Incremental changes to the firm's culture typically are used to implement strategies.[113] More significant and, sometimes, even radical changes to organizational culture are used to support the selection of strategies that differ from those the firm has implemented historically. Regardless of the reasons for change, shaping and reinforcing a new culture require effective communication and problem solving, along with the selection of the right people (those who have the values desired for the organization), effective performance appraisals (establishing goals and measuring individual performance toward goals that fit in with the new core values), and appropriate reward systems (rewarding the desired behaviors that reflect the new core values).[114]

Evidence suggests that cultural changes succeed only when the firm's CEO, other key top management team members, and middle-level managers actively support them.[115] To effect change, middle-level managers in particular need to be highly disciplined to energize the culture and foster alignment with the strategic vision.[116]

As noted earlier, selecting new top management team members from the external managerial labor market is a catalyst for changes to organizational culture. This is illustrated by the example of Carlos Ghosn, a Brazilian-born manager working for Renault. Ghosn was charged with turning around Nissan, partially owned by Renault, which was suffering from lost market share. But, transforming an organization and its culture is challenging. Ghosn implemented several major changes. He closed plants and significantly reduced costs. In so doing, however, he gave generous bonuses of over five months' pay to the employees who were laid off. He dismantled the keiretsu investments, allowing him to revise the supply chain relationships. As a result, he returned Nissan to profitability. Renault's CEO now sees Nissan as an important asset for his firm and is integrating Renault's and Nissan's complementary resources to create global growth for the firm.[117]

Because of the actions of executives like those at Tenet HealthCare, Ahold, HealthSouth, and the major Wall Street investment firms described in the Strategic Focus, the world of corporate governance is changing, as described in Chapter 10. These changes have significant implications for the strategic leadership in individual companies. This is evidenced by the action taken by Michael Capellas, CEO of MCI, to have his top 300 executives sign an ethics pledge.

Emphasizing Ethical Practices

The effectiveness of processes used to implement the firm's strategies increases when they are based on ethical practices. Ethical companies encourage and enable people at all organizational levels to act ethically when doing what is necessary to implement the firm's strategies. In turn, ethical practices and the judgment on which they are based

As Corporate Scandals and Ethical Dilemmas Proliferate, Heads Roll

Corporate scandals have created a crisis of confidence in the practices of major corporations worldwide. In the United States, the multiple scandals of major proportion caused Congress to pass the Sarbanes-Oxley Act. The primary goal is to prevent accounting manipulations by top executives. While the names of Enron, Tyco, and WorldCom are prominent in these scandals, there are others. For example, Tenet Healthcare was investigated by the U.S. Justice Department regarding allegations that the company overbilled the U.S. government for services provided to senior citizens under the Medicare program. The CEO at the time, Jeffrey Barbakow, who received the highest compensation of any CEO in 2002, was forced to resign by the board of Tenet. Prior to these problems, Tenet's stock price was greater than $50, but fell dramatically to less than $20 per share after the allegations came to light.

Scandal was not limited to U.S. companies. Royal Ahold NV, a large international supermarket chain headquartered in the Netherlands, had major accounting problems. Specifically, Ahold's U.S. Foodservice division overstated its earnings in 2001 and 2002. Ahold also discovered potentially illegal transactions in its Argentine subsidiary. Because of these problems, the CEO and chief financial officer of Ahold were discharged. The "accounting problems" caused Ahold to reduce its operating earnings by $500 million.

Federal prosecutors investigated massive accounting fraud at HealthSouth Corporation. The prosecutors negotiated plea arrangements with five HealthSouth employees in which they would testify that they were directed by the company's chairman and CEO, Richard Scrushy, to inflate the financial results. In fact, the Securities and Exchange Commission (SEC) accused the company (and Scrushy) of inflating the profits by $1.4 billion over the period 1999–2002. The government believes that these practices may have been common in the company since its founding in 1986, so the overstatement of profits may be much greater. According to the SEC, company managers falsified accounting entries, overstated cash and other assets, and created numbers to fill in the differences between actual and desired earnings. The board of directors for HealthSouth fired the CEO, Richard Scrushy, upon learning of further allegations that he may have established offshore bank accounts to avoid taxes.

The scandals also engulfed major Wall Street firms. In fact, the top ten investment firms on Wall Street settled an inquiry by the U.S. government into irregularities, such as potential conflicts of interest whereby firms received secret payments (supposedly for research conducted) from companies for which they gave potential investors strong recommendations to buy. Other firms were accused of gaining favor with corporate clients by selling hot stock offerings to their senior executives (who could then sell the shares for almost guaranteed profits).

To avoid problems similar to those noted above and those made by its predecessor company, WorldCom, the new MCI CEO, Michael Capellas (former CEO of Compaq), required the top 300 executives in the firm to sign an ethics pledge. His intent is to restore investor confidence in the company. He stated that "we will operate at a higher standard than the rest of the world. The burden of proof is on us."

SOURCES: S. Morrison & P. T. Larsen, 2003, MCI executives sign ethics pledge, *Financial Times*, http://www.ft.com, May 8; L. R. Roth & A. Hill, 2003, Tenet chief forced to quit, *Financial Times*, http://www.ft.com, May 27; S. Labaton, 2003, 10 Wall St. firms settle with U.S. in analyst inquiry, *New York Times*, http://www.nytimes.com, April 29; C. Terhune & C. Mollenkamp, 2003, Five HealthSouth employees may plead guilty to fraud, *Wall Street Journal Online*, http://www.wsj.com, March 31; M. Freudenheim, 2003, HealthSouth inquiry looks for accounts held offshore, *New York Times*, http://www.nytimes.com, March 31; M. Freudenheim, 2003, HealthSouth fires its embattled chairman, *New York Times*, http://www.nytimes.com, March 31; M. Wallin, L. Norman, & J. Quintanilha, 2003, Ahold replaces management at Argentine unit, ends probe, *Wall Street Journal Online*, http://www.wsj.com, February 28; D. Ball, J. S. Lublin, & M. Karnitschnig, 2003, Ahold scandal raises questions about directors' responsibilities, *Wall Street Journal Online*, http://www.wsj.com, February 27; D. Ball, A. Zimmerman, & M. Veen, 2003, Supermarket giant Ahold ousts CEO in big accounting scandal, *Wall Street Journal*, February 25, A1, A10.

create "social capital" in the organization in that "goodwill available to individuals and groups" in the organization increases.[118] Alternately, when unethical practices evolve in an organization, they become like a contagious disease.[119]

To properly influence employees' judgment and behavior, ethical practices must shape the firm's decision-making process and be an integral part of an organization's culture. In fact, research has found that a value-based culture is the most effective means of ensuring that employees comply with the firm's ethical requirements.[120] As discussed in Chapter 10, in the absence of ethical requirements, managers may act opportunistically, making decisions that are in their own best interests, but not in the firm's best interests. In other words, managers acting opportunistically take advantage of their positions, making decisions that benefit themselves to the detriment of the firm's owners (shareholders).[121]

Managerial opportunism may explain the behavior and decisions of a few key executives at HealthSouth, where, as described in the Strategic Focus, substantial accounting irregularities were discovered. In fact, the investigations suggested that the company overstated its performance for many years, thereby propping up its stock price. Firms that have been reported to have poor ethical behavior, such as perpetrating fraud or having to restate financial results, see their overall corporate value in the stock market drop precipitously.[122]

While the Strategic Focus also explains the accounting irregularities completed by Ahold, Tenet Healthcare overcharged the U.S. government for Medicare payments. Interestingly, Tenet's CEO, Jeffrey Barbakow, was the highest-paid CEO in 2002. Yet Barbakow and the CEO and CFO of Ahold lost their jobs when the irregularities came to light. Thus, in addition to the firms' shareholders, they paid a high price for the indiscretions.

These incidents suggest that firms need to employ ethical strategic leaders—leaders who include ethical practices as part of their long-term vision for the firm, who desire to do the right thing, and for whom honesty, trust, and integrity are important.[123] Strategic leaders who consistently display these qualities inspire employees as they work with others to develop and support an organizational culture in which ethical practices are the expected behavioral norms.[124]

The effects of white-collar fraud are substantial.[125] Estimates in the United States suggest that white-collar fraud ranges from $200 billion to as much as $600 billion annually. Furthermore, this fraud usually equals from 1 to 6 percent of the firm's sales, and white-collar crime causes as much as 30 percent of new venture firms to fail. These amounts are incredibly high when compared to the total cost of approximately $20 billion for street crime in the United States.[126] Certainly, executives in multinational firms must understand that there are differences in ethical values across cultures globally.[127] Beyond this, however, research has shown that a positive relationship exists between ethical values (character) and an executive's health. So, ethical practices have many possible benefits to the firm and the executive.[128] Strategic leaders are challenged to take actions that increase the probability that an ethical culture will prevail in their organizations. One action that has gained favor is to institute a formal program to manage ethics. Operating much like control systems, these programs help inculcate values throughout the organization.[129] Therefore, when these efforts are successful, the practices associated with an ethical culture become institutionalized in the firm; that is, they become the set of behavioral commitments and actions accepted by most of the firm's employees and other stakeholders with whom employees interact.

Additional actions strategic leaders can take to develop an ethical organizational culture include (1) establishing and communicating specific goals to describe the firm's ethical standards (e.g., developing and disseminating a code of conduct); (2) continuously revising and updating the code of conduct, based on inputs from people throughout the firm and from other stakeholders (e.g., customers and suppliers); (3) disseminating the code of conduct to all stakeholders to inform them of the firm's ethical standards and practices; (4) developing and implementing methods and procedures to use in achieving the firm's ethical standards (e.g., using internal auditing practices that are consistent with the standards); (5) creating and using explicit reward systems that recognize acts of courage (e.g., rewarding those who use proper channels and procedures to report observed wrongdoings); and (6) creating a work environment in which all people are treated with dignity.[130] The effectiveness of these actions increases when they are taken simultaneously, thereby making them mutually supportive. When managers and employees do not engage in such actions—perhaps because an ethical culture has not been created—problems are likely to occur. As we discuss next, formal organizational controls can help prevent further problems and reinforce better ethical practices.

Establishing Balanced Organizational Controls

Organizational controls are basic to a capitalistic system and have long been viewed as an important part of strategy implementation processes.[131] Controls are necessary to help ensure that firms achieve their desired outcomes.[132] Defined as the "formal, information-based . . . procedures used by managers to maintain or alter patterns in organizational activities," controls help strategic leaders build credibility, demonstrate the value of strategies to the firm's stakeholders, and promote and support strategic change.[133] Most critically, controls provide the parameters within which strategies are to be implemented, as well as corrective actions to be taken when implementation-related adjustments are required. In this chapter, we focus on two organizational controls—strategic and financial—that were introduced in Chapter 11. Our discussion of organizational controls here emphasizes strategic and financial controls because strategic leaders are responsible for their development and effective use.

Evidence suggests that, although critical to the firm's success, organizational controls are imperfect. *Control failures* have a negative effect on the firm's reputation and divert managerial attention from actions that are necessary to effectively use the strategic management process.

As explained in Chapter 11, financial control focuses on short-term financial outcomes. In contrast, strategic control focuses on the *content* of strategic actions, rather than their *outcomes*. Some strategic actions can be correct, but poor financial outcomes may still result because of external conditions, such as a recession in the economy, unexpected domestic or foreign government actions, or natural disasters.[134] Therefore, an emphasis on financial control often produces more short-term and risk-averse managerial decisions, because financial outcomes may be caused by events beyond managers' direct control. Alternatively, strategic control encourages lower-level managers to make decisions that incorporate moderate and acceptable levels of risk because outcomes are shared between the business-level executives making strategic proposals and the corporate-level executives evaluating them.

THE BALANCED SCORECARD

The **balanced scorecard** is a framework that firms can use to verify that they have established both strategic and financial controls to assess their performance.[135] This technique is most appropriate for use when dealing with business-level strategies, but can also apply to corporate-level strategies.

The underlying premise of the balanced scorecard is that firms jeopardize their future performance possibilities when financial controls are emphasized at the expense of strategic controls,[136] in that financial controls provide feedback about outcomes achieved from past actions, but do not communicate the drivers of the firm's future performance.[137] Thus, an overemphasis on financial controls could promote organizational behavior that has a net effect of sacrificing the firm's long-term value-creating potential for short-term performance gains.[138] An appropriate balance of strategic

The balanced scorecard is a framework that firms can use to verify that they have established both strategic and financial controls to assess their performance.

controls and financial controls, rather than an overemphasis on either, allows firms to effectively monitor their performance.

Four perspectives are integrated to form the balanced scorecard framework: *financial* (concerned with growth, profitability, and risk from the shareholders' perspective), *customer* (concerned with the amount of value customers perceive was created by the firm's products), *internal business processes* (with a focus on the priorities for various business processes that create customer and shareholder satisfaction), and *learning and growth* (concerned with the firm's effort to create a climate that supports change, innovation, and growth). Thus, using the balanced scorecard framework allows the firm to understand how it looks to shareholders (financial perspective), how customers view it (customer perspective), the processes it must emphasize to successfully use its competitive advantage (internal perspective), and what it can do to improve its performance in order to grow (learning and growth perspective).[139] Generally speaking, strategic controls tend to be emphasized when the firm assesses its performance relative to the learning and growth perspective, while financial controls are emphasized when assessing performance in terms of the financial perspective. Study of the customer and internal business processes perspectives often is completed through virtually an equal emphasis on strategic controls and financial controls.

Firms use different criteria to measure their standing relative to the scorecard's four perspectives. Sample criteria are shown in Figure 12.5. The firm should select the number of criteria that will allow it to have both a strategic understanding and a financial understanding of its performance without becoming immersed in too many details.[140]

Strategic Controls and Financial Controls in a Balanced Scorecard Framework — Figure 12.5

Perspectives	Criteria
Financial	• Cash flow • Return on equity • Return on assets
Customer	• Assessment of ability to anticipate customers' needs • Effectiveness of customer service practices • Percentage of repeat business • Quality of communications with customers
Internal Business Processes	• Asset utilization improvements • Improvements in employee morale • Changes in turnover rates
Learning and Growth	• Improvements in innovation ability • Number of new products compared to competitors' • Increases in employees' skills

Strategic leaders play an important role in determining a proper balance between strategic controls and financial controls for their firm. This is true in single-business firms as well as in diversified firms. A proper balance between controls is important, in that "wealth creation for organizations where strategic leadership is exercised is possible because these leaders make appropriate investments for future viability [through strategic control], while maintaining an appropriate level of financial stability in the present [through financial control]."[141] In fact, most corporate restructuring is designed to refocus the firm on its core businesses, thereby allowing top executives to reestablish strategic control of their separate business units.[142] Thus, as emphasized in Chapter 11, both strategic controls and financial controls support effective use of the firm's corporate-level strategy.

Successful use of strategic control by top executives frequently is integrated with appropriate autonomy for the various subunits so that they can gain a competitive advantage in their respective markets.[143] Strategic control can be used to promote the sharing of both tangible and intangible resources among interdependent businesses within a firm's portfolio. In addition, the autonomy provided allows the flexibility necessary to take advantage of specific marketplace opportunities. As a result, strategic leadership promotes the simultaneous use of strategic control and autonomy.[144]

Balancing strategic and financial controls in diversified firms can be difficult. Failure to maintain an effective balance between strategic controls and financial controls in these firms often contributes to a decision to restructure the company. For example, Jean-Pierre Garnier, CEO of GlaxoSmithKline, is trying to reinvent the company by streamlining its costs (financial controls) and simultaneously enhancing its development of innovative and valuable new drugs (strategic controls). In fact, the firm must achieve a balance in these controls in order to survive in the strongly competitive pharmaceuticals industry.[145]

Samsung provides another example of the need to achieve a balance in these types of control. Following the 1997 Southeast Asian currency crisis, Samsung Electronics, a large Korean firm, was heading into a significant crisis in its Chinese operations. It was a large diversified firm with businesses throughout the world. Its Chinese operations included selling everything from washing machines to VCRs. Each product division had established Chinese factories and a nationwide sales organization by the mid-1990s. However, in China, these divisions encountered significant losses, losing $37 million in 1998.

When Jong-Yong Yun took over as Samsung's CEO in 1997, he shut down all 23 sales offices and declared that each of the seven mainland factories would have to become profitable on its own to survive. Thus, he instituted strong financial controls that were to be followed to verify that each

The recent successes of Samsung, through the leadership of its CEO, Jong-Yong Yun, represent an effective use of the balanced scorecard, which helps put strategic and financial controls in balance.

HKGCC
Hong Kong General Chamber of Commerce
香港總商會 1861

©AFP/CORBIS

division was operating profitably. Additionally, based on market survey results, Samsung executives decided that the firm would focus on ten major cities in China. Furthermore, the firm carefully selected products and supported them with intense marketing. Thus, the firm improved strategic controls using a "top-down marketing strategy." Overall, Samsung increased its revenue from $18.45 billion in 1998 to $40.51 billion in 2002. Its net income increased from $313 million in 1998 to $7.05 billion in 2002. A more effective balance between strategic and financial controls has helped Samsung to improve its performance and to make progress toward its goal of establishing marquee brands in China, comparable to Sony and Motorola.[146]

Summary

- Effective strategic leadership is a prerequisite to successfully using the strategic management process. Strategic leadership entails the ability to anticipate events, envision possibilities, maintain flexibility, and empower others to create strategic change.

- Top-level managers are an important resource for firms to develop and exploit competitive advantages. In addition, when they and their work are valuable, rare, imperfectly imitable, and nonsubstitutable, strategic leaders can themselves be a source of competitive advantage.

- The top management team is composed of key managers who play a critical role in the selection and implementation of the firm's strategies. Generally, they are officers of the corporation or members of the board of directors.

- There is a relationship among the top management team's characteristics, a firm's strategies, and its performance. For example, a top management team that has significant marketing and R&D knowledge positively contributes to the firm's use of growth strategies. Overall, most top management teams are more effective when they have diverse skills.

- When the board of directors is involved in shaping a firm's strategic direction, that firm generally improves its performance. However, the board may be less involved in decisions about strategy formulation and implementation when CEOs have more power. CEOs increase their power when they appoint people to the board and when they simultaneously serve as the CEO and board chair.

- Strategic leaders are selected from either the internal or the external managerial labor market. Because of their effect on performance, the selection of strategic leaders has implications for a firm's effectiveness. There are valid reasons to use either the internal or the external market

when choosing the firm's strategic leaders. In most instances, the internal market is used to select the firm's CEO, but the number of outsiders chosen is increasing. Outsiders often are selected to initiate changes.

- Effective strategic leadership has five major components: determining the firm's strategic direction, effectively managing the firm's resource portfolio (including exploiting and maintaining core competencies and managing human capital and social capital), sustaining an effective organizational culture, emphasizing ethical practices, and establishing balanced organizational controls.

- A firm must develop a long-term vision of its strategic intent. A long-term vision is the driver of strategic leaders' behavior in terms of the remaining four components of effective strategic leadership.

- Strategic leaders must ensure that their firm exploits its core competencies, which are used to produce and deliver products that create value for customers, through the implementation of strategies. In related diversified and large firms in particular, core competencies are exploited by sharing them across units and products.

- A critical element of strategic leadership and the effective implementation of strategy is the ability to manage the firm's resource portfolio. This includes integrating resources to create capabilities and leveraging those capabilities through strategies to build competitive advantages. Perhaps the most important resources are human capital and social capital.

- As a part of managing the firm's resources, strategic leaders must develop a firm's human capital. Effective strategic leaders and firms view human capital as a resource to be maximized, rather than as a cost to be minimized. Resulting from this perspective is the development and use of programs intended to train current and future strategic leaders to build the skills needed to nurture the rest of the firm's human capital.

- Effective strategic leaders also build and maintain internal and external social capital. Internal social capital promotes cooperation and coordination within and across units in the firm. External social capital provides access to resources that the firm needs to compete effectively.

- Shaping the firm's culture is a central task of effective strategic leadership. An appropriate organizational culture encourages the development of an entrepreneurial orientation among employees and an ability to change the culture as necessary.

- In ethical organizations, employees are encouraged to exercise ethical judgment and to behave ethically at all times. Improved ethical practices foster social capital. Setting specific goals to describe the firm's ethical standards, using a code of conduct, rewarding ethical behaviors, and creating a work environment in which all people are treated with dignity are examples of actions that facilitate and support ethical behavior within the firm.

- Developing and using balanced organizational controls is the final component of effective strategic leadership. An effective balance between strategic and financial controls allows for the flexible use of core competencies, but within the parameters indicated by the firm's financial position. The balanced scorecard is a tool used by the firm and its strategic leaders to develop an appropriate balance between its strategic and financial controls.

Review Questions

1. What is strategic leadership? In what ways are top executives considered important resources for an organization?

2. What is a top management team, and how does it affect a firm's performance and its abilities to innovate and make appropriate strategic changes?

3. What are the differences between the internal and external managerial labor markets? What are the effects of each type of labor market on the formulation and implementation of strategies?

4. How does strategic leadership affect the determination of the firm's strategic direction?

5. How do strategic leaders effectively manage their firm's resource portfolio such that its core competencies are exploited, and the human capital and social capital are leveraged to achieve a competitive advantage?

6. What is organizational culture? What must strategic leaders do to develop and sustain an effective organizational culture?

7. As a strategic leader, what actions could you take to establish and emphasize ethical practices in your firm?

8. What are organizational controls? Why are strategic controls and financial controls important parts of the strategic management process?

Using the Balanced Scorecard Framework

This experiential exercise is based on the Balanced Scorecard Framework (Figure 12.5). Form groups of three or four students each. Assume that you are strategists for a multinational sportswear manufacturing and marketing company with millions of dollars in sales worldwide. In designing your business-level strategy (see Chapter 4), you are expected to

define the objectives associated with that strategy concerning financial performance, customer service, internal processes, and learning and growth. Additionally, your task is to define measures and initiatives necessary for each category of objectives. Measures refer to the definition of specific criteria for each objective, and initiatives refer to the specific actions that should be taken to achieve a particular objective. Use the table below to record your definitions.

Financial Performance:		
Objectives	Measures	Initiatives
1.	1.	1.1 1.2
2.	2.	2.1 2.2

Customer Service:		
Objectives	Measures	Initiatives
1.	1.	1.1 1.2
2.	2.	2.1 2.2

Internal Processes:		
Objectives	Measures	Initiatives
1.	1.	1.1 1.2
2.	2.	2.1 2.2

Learning and Growth:		
Objectives	Measures	Initiatives
1.	1.	1.1 1.2
2.	2.	2.1 2.2

Strategic Leadership

The executive board for a large company is concerned that the firm's future leadership needs to be developed. Several top-level managers are expected to leave the firm in the next three to seven years. You have been put in charge of a committee to determine how the firm should prepare for these departures.

Part 1 (individual). Use the information provided within this chapter and your own perceptions to complete the following chart. Be prepared to discuss in class.

Candidates	Internal Managerial Labor Market	External Managerial Labor Market
Strengths		
Weaknesses		

Part 2 (individually or in small groups). The firm's executive board feels that the external managerial labor market is beyond its control—the managerial resources the firm will need may or may not be available when they are needed. The board has then asked your committee to consider a program that would develop the firm's internal managerial labor market. Outline the objectives that you want your program to achieve, the steps you would take to reach them, and the time frame involved. Also consider potential problems in such a program and how they could be resolved.

Notes

1. R. D. Ireland, M. A. Hitt, S. M. Camp, & D. L. Sexton, 2001, Integrating entrepreneurship and strategic management actions to create firm wealth, *Academy of Management Executive*, 15(1): 49–63; K. R. Thompson, W. A. Hochwarter, & N. J. Mathys, 1997, Stretch targets: What makes them effective? *Academy of Management Executive*, 11(3): 48–59.
2. A. Cannella, Jr., A. Pettigrew, & D. Hambrick, 2001, Upper echelons: Donald Hambrick on executives and strategy, *Academy of Management Executive*, 15(3): 36–52; R. D. Ireland & M. A. Hitt, 1999, Achieving and maintaining strategic competitiveness in the 21st century: The role of strategic leadership, *Academy of Management Executive*, 12(1): 43–57; D. Lei, M. A. Hitt, & R. Bettis, 1996, Dynamic core competencies through meta-learning and strategic context, *Journal of Management*, 22: 547–567.
3. L. Greiner, T. Cummings, & A. Bhambri, 2002, When new CEOs succeed and fail: 4-D theory of strategic transformation, *Organizational Dynamics*, 32: 1–16.
4. S. Green, F. Hassan, J. Immelt, M. Marks, & D. Meiland, 2003, In search of global leaders, *Harvard Business Review*, 81(8): 38–45; T. J. Peters, 2001, Leadership: Sad facts and silver linings, *Harvard Business Review*, 79(11): 121–128.
5. M. A. Hitt & R. D. Ireland, 2002, The essence of strategic leadership: Managing human and social capital, *Journal of Leadership and Organizational Studies*, 9: 3–14; J. Collins, 2001, Level 5 leadership: The triumph of humility and fierce resolve, *Harvard Business Review*, 79(1): 66–76.
6. A. S. DeNisi, M. A. Hitt, & S. E. Jackson, 2003, The knowledge-based approach to sustainable competitive advantage, in S. E. Jackson, M. A. Hitt, & A. S. DeNisi (eds.), *Managing Knowledge for Sustained Competitive Advantage*, San Francisco: Jossey-Bass, 3–33; D. J. Teece, 2000, *Managing Intellectual Capital: Organizational, Strategic and Policy Dimensions*, Oxford: Oxford University Press.
7. J. E. Post, L. E. Preston, & S. Sachs, 2002, Managing the extended enterprise: The new stakeholder view, *California Management Review*, 45(1): 6–28.
8. D. C. Carey & D. Ogden, 2000, *CEO Succession: A Window on How Boards Can Get It Right When Choosing a New Chief Executive*, New York: Oxford University Press.
9. M. Maccoby, 2001, Making sense of the leadership literature, *Research Technology Management*, 44(5): 58–60; T. Kono, 1999, A strong head office makes a strong company, *Long Range Planning*, 32: 225–246.
10. G. Hamel & C. K. Prahalad, 1993, Strategy as stretch and leverage, *Harvard Business Review*, 71(2): 75–84.
11. C. L. Shook, R. L. Priem, & J. E. McGee, 2003, Venture creation and the enterprising individual: A review and synthesis, *Journal of Management*, 29: 379–399.
12. J. M. Mezias & W. H. Starbuck, 2003, Studying the accuracy of managers' perceptions: A research odyssey, *British Journal of Management*, 14: 3–17.
13. M. Maccoby, 2001, Successful leaders employ strategic intelligence, *Research Technology Management*, 44(3): 58–60.
14. S. Finkelstein & D. C. Hambrick, 1996, *Strategic Leadership: Top Executives and Their Effects on Organizations*, St. Paul, MN: West Publishing Company, 2.
15. Collins, Level 5 leadership.
16. R. Castanias & C. Helfat, 2001, The managerial rents model: Theory and empirical analysis, *Journal of Management*, 27: 661–678; H. P. Gunz & R. M. Jalland, 1996, Managerial careers and business strategy, *Academy of Management Review*, 21: 718–756.
17. M. Beer & R. Eisenstat, 2000, The silent killers of strategy implementation and learning, *Sloan Management Review*, 41(4): 29–40; C. M. Christensen, 1997, Making strategy: Learning by doing, *Harvard Business Review*, 75(6): 141–156; M. A. Hitt, B. W. Keats, H. E. Harback, & R. D. Nixon, 1994, Rightsizing: Building and maintaining strategic leadership and long-term competitiveness, *Organizational Dynamics*, 23: 18–32.
18. R. Whittington, 2003, The work of strategizing and organizing: For a practice perspective, *Strategic Organization*, 1: 117–125; M. Wright, R. E. Hoskisson, L. W. Busenitz, & J. Dial, 2000, Entrepreneurial growth through

privatization: The upside of management buyouts, *Academy of Management Review*, 25: 591–601; M. J. Waller, G. P. Huber, & W. H. Glick, 1995, Functional background as a determinant of executives' selective perception, *Academy of Management Journal*, 38: 943–974; N. Rajagopalan, A. M. Rasheed, & D. K. Datta, 1993, Strategic decision processes: Critical review and future directions, *Journal of Management*, 19: 349–384.

19. W. Rowe, 2001, Creating wealth in organizations: The role of strategic leadership, *Academy of Management Executive*, 15(1): 81–94; Finkelstein & Hambrick, *Strategic Leadership*, 26–34.

20. J. A. Petrick & J. F. Quinn, 2001, The challenge of leadership accountability for integrity capacity as a strategic asset, *Journal of Business Ethics*, 34: 331–343; R. C. Mayer, J. H. Davis, & F. D. Schoorman, 1995, An integrative model of organizational trust, *Academy of Management Review*, 20: 709–734.

21. S. Gove, D. Sirmon, & M. A. Hitt, 2003, Relative resource advantages: The effect of resources and resource management on organizational performance, Paper presented at the Strategic Management Society Conference, Baltimore; J. J. Sosik, 2001, Self-other agreement on charismatic leadership: Relationships with work attitudes and managerial performance, *Group & Organization Management*, 26: 484–511.

22. J. E. Dutton, S. J. Ashford, R. M. O'Neill, & K. A. Lawrence, 2001, Moves that matter: Issue selling and organizational change, *Academy of Management Journal*, 44: 716–736.

23. I. Goll, R. Sambharya, & L. Tucci, 2001, Top management team composition, corporate ideology, and firm performance, *Management International Review*, 41(2): 109–129.

24. J. Bunderson, 2003, Team member functional background and involvement in management teams: Direct effects and the moderating role of power and centralization, *Academy of Management Journal*, 46: 458–474; L. Markoczy, 2001, Consensus formation during strategic change, *Strategic Management Journal*, 22: 1013–1031.

25. Post, Preston, & Sachs, Managing the extended enterprise; C. Pegels, Y. Song, & B. Yang, 2000, Management heterogeneity, competitive interaction groups, and firm performance, *Strategic Management Journal*, 21: 911–923.

26. H. Lee, M. A. Hitt, & E. Jeong, 2003, The impact of CEO and TMT characteristics on strategic flexibility and firm performance, Working paper, Texas A&M University.

27. Markoczy, Consensus formation during strategic change; D. Knight, C. L. Pearce, K. G. Smith, J. D. Olian, H. P. Sims, K. A. Smith, & P. Flood, 1999, Top management team diversity, group process, and strategic consensus, *Strategic Management Journal*, 20: 446–465.

28. D. C. Hambrick, T. S. Cho, & M. J. Chen, 1996, The influence of top management team heterogeneity on firms' competitive moves, *Administrative Science Quarterly*, 41: 659–684.

29. J. J. Distefano & M. L. Maznevski, 2000, Creating value with diverse teams in global management, *Organizational Dynamics*, 29(1): 45–63; T. Simons, L. H. Pelled, & K. A. Smith, 1999, Making use of difference, diversity, debate, and decision comprehensiveness in top management teams, *Academy of Management Journal*, 42: 662–673.

30. Finkelstein & Hambrick, *Strategic Leadership*, 148.

31. S. Barsade, A. Ward, J. Turner, & J. Sonnenfeld, 2000, To your heart's content: A model of affective diversity in top management teams, *Administrative Science Quarterly*, 45: 802–836; C. C. Miller, L. M. Burke, & W. H. Glick, 1998, Cognitive diversity among upper-echelon executives: Implications for strategic decision processes, *Strategic Management Journal*, 19: 39–58.

32. B. J. Avolio & S. S. Kahai, 2002, Adding the "e" to e-leadership: How it may impact your leadership, *Organizational Dynamics*, 31: 325–338.

33. U. Daellenbach, A. McCarthy, & T. Schoenecker, 1999, Commitment to innovation: The impact of top management team characteristics, *R&D Management*, 29(3): 199–208; D. K. Datta & J. P. Guthrie, 1994, Executive succession: Organizational antecedents of CEO characteristics, *Strategic Management Journal*, 15: 569–577.

34. W. B. Werther, 2003, Strategic change and leader-follower alignment, *Organizational Dynamics*, 32: 32–45; S. Wally & M. Becerra, 2001, Top manage-

ment team characteristics and strategic changes in international diversification: The case of U.S. multinationals in the European community, *Group & Organization Management*, 26: 165–188.

35. A. Tomie, 2000, Fast pack 2000, *Fast Company Online*, http://www.fastcompany.com, March 1.

36. Y. Zhang & N. Rajagopalan, 2003, Explaining the new CEO origin: Firm versus industry antecedents, *Academy of Management Journal*, 46: 327–338.

37. T. Dvir, D. Eden, B. J. Avolio, & B. Shamir, 2002, Impact of transformational leadership on follower development and performance: A field experiment, *Academy of Management Journal*, 45: 735–744.

38. Wally & Becerra, Top management team characteristics and strategic changes in international diversification; L. Tihanyi, C. Daily, D. Dalton, & A. Ellstrand, 2000, Composition of the top management team and firm international diversification, *Journal of Management*, 26: 1157–1178.

39. L. Tihanyi, R. A. Johnson, R. E. Hoskisson, & M. A. Hitt, 2003, Institutional ownership and international diversification: The effects of boards of directors and technological opportunity, *Academy of Management Journal*, 46: 195–211; B. Taylor, 2001, From corporate governance to corporate entrepreneurship, *Journal of Change Management*, 2(2): 128–147.

40. B. R. Golden & E. J. Zajac, 2001, When will boards influence strategy? Inclination times power equals strategic change, *Strategic Management Journal*, 22: 1087–1111.

41. M. Carpenter & J. Westphal, 2001, Strategic context of external network ties: Examining the impact of director appointments on board involvement in strategic decision making, *Academy of Management Journal*, 44: 639–660.

42. J. D. Westphal & E. J. Zajac, 1995, Who shall govern? CEO/board power, demographic similarity, and new director selection, *Administrative Science Quarterly*, 40: 60.

43. J. D. Westphal, 1999, Collaboration in the boardroom: Behavioral and performance consequences of CEO-board social ties, *Academy of Management Journal*, 42: 7–24.

44. J. Roberts & P. Stiles, 1999, The relationship between chairmen and chief executives: Competitive or complementary roles? *Long Range Planning*, 32(1): 36–48.

45. J. Coles, N. Sen, & V. McWilliams, 2001, An examination of the relationship of governance mechanisms to performance, *Journal of Management*, 27: 23–50; J. Coles & W. Hesterly, 2000, Independence of the chairman and board composition: Firm choices and shareholder value, *Journal of Management*, 26: 195–214; B. K. Boyd, 1995, CEO duality and firm performance: A contingency model, *Strategic Management Journal*, 16: 301.

46. D. D. Bergh, 2001, Executive retention and acquisition outcomes: A test of opposing views on the influence of organizational tenure, *Journal of Management*, 27: 603–622.

47. J. Muller, J. Green, & C. Tierney, 2001, Chrysler's rescue team, *Business Week*, January 15, 48–50.

48. J. B. White & N. E. Boudette, 2003, His mission: Shift Chrysler out of reverse, *Wall Street Journal*, July 16, B1, B4.

49. C. M. Daily & D. R. Dalton, 1995, CEO and director turnover in failing firms: An illusion of change? *Strategic Management Journal*, 16: 393–400.

50. R. Albanese, M. T. Dacin, & I. C. Harris, 1997, Agents as stewards, *Academy of Management Review*, 22: 609–611; J. H. Davis, F. D. Schoorman, & L. Donaldson, 1997, Toward a stewardship theory of management, *Academy of Management Review*, 22: 20–47.

51. M. A. Carpenter, 2002, The implications of strategy and social context for the relationship between top management team heterogeneity and firm performance, *Strategic Management Journal*, 23: 275–284.

52. J. G. Combs & M. S. Skill, 2003, Managerialist and human capital explanations for key executive pay premiums: A contingency perspective, *Academy of Management Journal*, 46: 63–73.

53. N. Rajagopalan & D. Datta, 1996, CEO characteristics: Does industry matter? *Academy of Management Journal*, 39: 197–215.

54. R. A. Johnson, R. E. Hoskisson, & M. A. Hitt, 1993, Board involvement in restructuring: The effect of board versus managerial controls and characteristics, *Strategic Management Journal*, 14(Special Issue): 33–50.

55. Boyd, CEO duality and firm performance: A contingency model.

56. Lee, Hitt, & Jeong, The impact of CEO and TMT characteristics on strategic flexibility; M. Carpenter & J. Fredrickson, 2001, Top management teams, global strategic posture, and the moderating role of uncertainty, *Academy of Management Journal*, 44: 533–545.

57. M. Schneider, 2002, A stakeholder model of organizational leadership, *Organization Science*, 13: 209–220.

58. M. Sorcher & J. Brant, 2002, Are you picking the right leaders? *Harvard Business Review*, 80(2): 78–85; D. A. Waldman, G. G. Ramirez, R. J. House, & P. Puranam, 2001, Does leadership matter? CEO leadership attributes and profitability under conditions of perceived environmental uncertainty, *Academy of Management Journal*, 44: 134–143.

59. W. Shen & A. A. Cannella, 2002, Revisiting the performance consequences of CEO succession: The impacts of successor type, postsuccession senior executive turnover, and departing CEO tenure, *Academy of Management Journal*, 45: 717–734; A. Kakabadse & N. Kakabadse, 2001, Dynamics of executive succession, *Corporate Governance*, 1(3): 9–14.

60. R. Charan, 2000, GE's ten-step talent plan, *Fortune*, April 17, 232.

61. R. E. Hoskisson, D. Yiu, & H. Kim, 2000, Capital and labor market congruence and corporate governance: Effects on corporate innovation and global competitiveness, in S. S. Cohen & G. Boyd (eds.), *Corporate Governance and Globalization*, Northampton, MA: Edward Elgar, 129–154.

62. S. B. Shepard, 2002, A talk with Jeff Immelt: Jack Welch's successor charts a course for GE in the 21st century, *Business Week*, January 28, 102–104.

63. Carey & Ogden, *CEO Succession*.

64. W. Shen & A. A. Cannella, 2003, Will succession planning increase shareholder wealth? Evidence from investor reactions to relay CEO successions, *Strategic Management Journal*, 24: 191–198; V. Kisfalvi, 2000, The threat of failure, the perils of success and CEO character: Sources of strategic persistence, *Organization Studies*, 21: 611–639.

65. Greiner, Cummings, & Bhambri, When new CEOs succeed and fail.

66. D. Miller, 1991, Stale in the saddle: CEO tenure and the match between organization and environment, *Management Science*, 37: 34–52.

67. R. M. Fulmer & M. Goldsmith, 2000, *The Leadership Investment: Promoting Diversity in Leadership*, New York: American Management Association.

68. S. Foley, D. L. Kidder, & G. N. Powell, 2002, The perceived glass ceiling and justice perceptions: An investigation of Hispanic law associates, *Journal of Management*, 28: 471–496.

69. N. M. Carter, W. B. Gartner, K. G. Shaver, & E. J. Gatewood, 2003, The career reasons of nascent entrepreneurs, *Journal of Business Venturing*, 18: 13–39.

70. B. Dyck, M. Mauws, F. Starke, & G. Mischke, 2002, Passing the baton: The importance of sequence, timing, technique and communication in executive succession, *Journal of Business Venturing*, 17: 143–162.

71. M. A. Hitt, B. W. Keats, & E. Yucel, 2003, Strategic leadership in global business organizations, in W. H. Mobley & P. W. Dorfman (eds.), *Advances in Global Leadership*, Oxford, UK: Elsevier Science, Ltd., 9–35; J. J. Rotemberg & G. Saloner, 2000, Visionaries, managers, and strategic direction, *RAND Journal of Economics*, 31: 693–716.

72. I. M. Levin, 2000, Vision revisited, *Journal of Applied Behavioral Science*, 36: 91–107; J. C. Collins & J. I. Porras, 1996, Building your company's vision, *Harvard Business Review*, 74(5): 65–77.

73. G. Gori, 2001, An American directs Mexico City's cinema revival, *New York Times*, http://www.nytimes.com, July 15.

74. 2002, Onex slides into Mexico with Cinemex purchase, http://www.latinfilm network.com, July 17.

75. J. Barney & A. M. Arikan, 2001, The resource-based view: Origins and implications, in M. A. Hitt, R. E. Freeman, & J. S. Harrison (eds.), *Handbook of Strategic Management*, Oxford, UK: Blackwell Publishers, 124–188.

76. D. G. Sirmon, M. A. Hitt, & R. D. Ireland, 2003, Managing firm resources for advantage: Creating value for stakeholders, Paper presented at the Academy of Management, Seattle, August.

77. R. A. Burgelman, 2001, *Strategy Is Destiny: How Strategy-Making Shapes a Company's Future*, New York: The Free Press.

78. 2003, History, http://www.pepsico.com, July; 2003, PepsiCo, Inc., http://www.hoovers.com, July; S. Jaffe, 2001, Do Pepsi and Gatorade mix? *BusinessWeek Online*, http://www.businessweek.com, August 14.

79. Barney & Arikan, The resource-based view.

80. C. A. Lengnick-Hall & J. A. Wolff, 1999, Similarities and contradictions in the core logic of three strategy research streams, *Strategic Management Journal*, 20: 1109–1132.

81. M. A. Hitt, L. Bierman, K. Shimizu, & R. Kochhar, 2001, Direct and moderating effects of human capital on strategy and performance in professional service firms: A resource-based perspective, *Academy of Management Journal*, 44: 13–28; S. A. Snell & M. A. Youndt, 1995, Human resource management and firm performance: Testing a contingency model of executive controls, *Journal of Management*, 21: 711–737.

82. S. E. Jackson, M. A. Hitt, & A. S. DeNisi (eds.), 2003, *Managing Knowledge for Sustained Competitive Advantage: Designing Strategies for Effective Human Resource Management*, Oxford, UK: Elsevier Science, Ltd.; P. Caligiuri & V. Di Santo, 2001, Global competence: What is it, and can it be developed through global assignments? *Human Resource Planning*, 24(3): 27–35.

83. A. McWilliams, D. D. Van Fleet, & P. M. Wright, 2001, Strategic management of human resources for global competitive advantage, *Journal of Business Strategies* 18(1): 1–24; J. Pfeffer, 1994, *Competitive Advantage through People*, Cambridge, MA: Harvard Business School Press, 4.

84. W. Watson, W. H. Stewart, & A. Barnir, 2003, The effects of human capital, organizational demography, and interpersonal processes on venture partner perceptions of firm profit and growth, *Journal of Business Venturing*, 18: 145–164.

85. H. B. Gregersen & J. S. Black, 2002, J. W. Marriott, Jr., on growing the legacy, *Academy of Management Executive*, 16(2): 33–39.

86. R. A. Noe, J. A. Colquitt, M. J. Simmering, & S. A. Alvarez, 2003, Knowledge management: Developing intellectual and social capital, in S. E. Jackson, M. A. Hitt, & A. S. DeNisi (eds.), 2003, *Managing Knowledge for Sustained Competitive Advantage: Designing Strategies for Effective Human Resource Management*, Oxford, UK: Elsevier Science, Ltd., 209–242; C. A. Bartlett & S. Ghoshal, 2002, Building competitive advantage through people, *MIT Sloan Management Review*, 43(2): 34–41.

87. G. P. Hollenbeck & M. W. McCall, Jr., 2003, Competence, not competencies: Making a global executive development work, in W. H. Mobley & P. W. Dorfman (eds.), *Advances in Global Leadership*, Oxford, UK: Elsevier Science, Ltd., 101–119; J. Sandberg, 2000, Understanding human competence at work: An interpretative approach, *Academy of Management Journal*, 43: 9–25.

88. Hitt, Keats, & Yucel, Strategic leadership in global business organizations; J. J. Distefano & M. L. Maznevski, 2003, Developing global managers integrating theory, behavior, data and performance, in W. H. Mobley & P. W. Dorfman (eds.), *Advances in Global Leadership*, Oxford, UK: Elsevier Science, Ltd., 341–371.

89. J. S. Bunderson & K. M. Sutcliffe, 2003, Management team learning orientation and business unit performance, *Journal of Applied Psychology*, 88: 552–560; C. R. James, 2003, Designing learning organizations, *Organizational Dynamics*, 32(1): 46–61; Bartlett & Ghoshal, Building competitive advantage through people.

90. J. D. Bragger, D. A. Hantula, D. Bragger, J. Kirnan, & E. Kutcher, 2003, When success breeds failure: History, Hysteresis, and delayed exit decisions, *Journal of Applied Psychology*, 88: 6–14.

91. J. W. Spencer, 2003, Firms' knowledge-sharing strategies in the global innovation system: Empirical evidence from the flat-panel display industry, *Strategic Management Journal*, 24: 217–233; M. Harvey & M. M. Novicevic, 2002, The hypercompetitive global marketplace: The importance of intuition and creativity in expatriate managers, *Journal of World Business*, 37: 127–138.

92. S. K. McEvily & B. Charavarthy, 2002, The persistence of knowledge-based advantage: An empirical test for product performance and technological knowledge, *Strategic Management Journal*, 23: 285–305.

93. K. D. Miller, 2002, Knowledge inventories and managerial myopia, *Strategic Management Journal*, 23: 689–706.

94. H. Collingwood & D. L. Coutu, 2002, Jack on Jack, *Harvard Business Review*, 80(2): 88–94.

95. R. D. Nixon, M. A. Hitt, H. Lee, & E. Jeong, 2003, Market reactions to corporate announcements of downsizing actions and implementation strategies, Unpublished working paper, University of Louisville.

96. J. Di Frances, 2002, 10 reasons why you shouldn't downsize, *Journal of Property Management*, 67(1): 72–73.

97. A. Pinsonneault & K. Kraemer, 2002, The role of information technology in organizational downsizing: A tale of two American cities, *Organization Science*, 13: 191–208.

98. Nixon, Hitt, Lee, & Jeong, Market reactions to corporate announcements of downsizing actions; M. David, 2001, Leadership during an economic slowdown, *Journal for Quality and Participation*, 24(3): 40–43.

99. T. Simons & Q. Roberson, 2003, Why managers should care about fairness: The effects of aggregate justice perceptions on organizational outcomes, *Journal of Applied Psychology*, 88: 432–443; M. L. Ambrose & R. Cropanzano, 2003, A longitudinal analysis of organizational fairness: An examination of reactions to tenure and promotion decisions, *Journal of Applied Psychology*, 88: 266–275.

100. P. S. Adler & S.-W. Kwon, 2002, Social capital: Prospects for a new concept, *Academy of Management Review*, 27: 17–40.

101. A. Mendez, 2003, The coordination of globalized R&D activities through project teams organization: An exploratory empirical study, *Journal of World Business*, 38: 96–109.

102. R. D. Ireland, M. A. Hitt, & D. Vaidyanath, 2002, Managing strategic alliances to achieve a competitive advantage, *Journal of Management*, 28: 413–446.

103. J. Florin, M. Lubatkin, & W. Schulze, 2003, *Academy of Management Journal*, 46: 374–384; P. Davidsson & B. Honig, 2003, The role of social and human capital among nascent entrepreneurs, *Journal of Business Venturing*, 18: 301–331.

104. A. K. Gupta & V. Govindarajan, 2000, Knowledge management's social dimension: Lessons from Nucor Steel, *Sloan Management Review*, 42(1): 71–80; C. M. Fiol, 1991, Managing culture as a competitive resource: An identity-based view of sustainable competitive advantage, *Journal of Management*, 17: 191–211; J. B. Barney, 1986, Organizational culture: Can it be a source of sustained competitive advantage? *Academy of Management Review*, 11: 656–665.

105. V. Govindarajan & A. K. Gupta, 2001, Building an effective global business team, *Sloan Management Review*, 42(4): 63–71; S. Ghoshal & C. A. Bartlett, 1994, Linking organizational context and managerial action: The dimensions of quality of management, *Strategic Management Journal*, 15: 91–112.

106. K. Kling & I. Goteman, 2003, IKEA CEO Anders Dahlvig on international growth and IKEA's unique corporate culture and brand identity, *Academy of Management Executive*, 17(1): 31–37.

107. D. F. Kuratko, R. D. Ireland, & J. S. Hornsby, 2001, Improving firm performance through entrepreneurial actions: Acordia's corporate entrepreneurship strategy, *Academy of Management Executive*, 15(4): 60–71.

108. A. Ardichvilli, R. Cardoza, & S. Ray, 2003, A theory of entrepreneurial opportunity identification and development, *Journal of Business Venturing*, 18: 105–123; T. E. Brown, P. Davidsson, & J. Wiklund, 2001, An operationalization of Stevenson's conceptualization of entrepreneurship as opportunity-based firm behavior, *Strategic Management Journal*, 22: 953–968.

109. R. D. Ireland, M. A. Hitt, & D. Sirmon, 2003, A model of strategic entrepreneurship: The construct and its dimensions, *Journal of Management*, in press.

110. G. T. Lumpkin & G. G. Dess, 1996, Clarifying the entrepreneurial orientation construct and linking it to performance, *Academy of Management Review*, 21: 135–172.

111. Ibid., 142.

112. Ibid., 137.

113. R. R. Sims, 2000, Changing an organization's culture under new leadership, *Journal of Business Ethics*, 25: 65–78.

114. R. A. Burgelman & Y. L. Doz, 2001, The power of strategic integration, *Sloan Management Review*, 42(3): 28–38; P. H. Fuchs, K. E. Mifflin, D. Miller, & J. O. Whitney, 2000, Strategic integration: Competing in the age of capabilities, *California Management Review*, 42(3): 118–147.

115. J. S. Hornsby, D. F. Kuratko, & S. A. Zahra, 2002, Middle managers' perception of the internal environment for corporate entrepreneurship: Assessing a measurement scale, *Journal of Business Venturing*, 17: 253–273; J. E. Dutton, S. J. Ashford, R. M. O'Neill, E. Hayes, & E. E. Wierba, 1997, Reading the wind: How middle managers assess the context for selling issues to top managers, *Strategic Management Journal*, 18: 407–425.

116. B. Axelrod, H. Handfield-Jones, & E. Michaels, 2002, A new game plan for C players, *Harvard Business Review*, 80(1): 80–88.

117. 2003, Louis Schweitzer: The interview, http://www.renault.com, July; C. Dawson, 2002, Nissan bets big on small, *BusinessWeek Online*, http://www.businessweek.com, March 4; C. Ghosn, 2002, Saving the business without losing the company, *Harvard Business Review*, 80(1): 37–45; M. S. Mayershon, 2002, Nissan's u-turn to profits, *Chief Executive*, January, 12–16; A. Raskin, 2002, Voulez-vous completely overhaul this big, slow company and start making some cars people actually want avec moi? *Business 2.0*, January, 61–67.

118. P. S. Adler & S.-W. Kwon, Social capital.

119. D. J. Brass, K. D. Butterfield, & B. C. Skaggs, 1998, Relationships and unethical behavior: A social network perspective, *Academy of Management Review*, 23: 14–31.

120. L. K. Trevino, G. R. Weaver, D. G. Toffler, & B. Ley, 1999, Managing ethics and legal compliance: What works and what hurts, *California Management Review*, 41(2): 131–151.

121. C. W. L. Hill, 1990, Cooperation, opportunism, and the invisible hand: Implications for transaction cost theory, *Academy of Management Review*, 15: 500–513.

122. W. Wallace, 2000, The value relevance of accounting: The rest of the story, *European Management Journal*, 18(6): 675–682.

123. C. J. Robertson & W. F. Crittenden, 2003, Mapping moral philosophies: Strategic implications for multinational firms, *Strategic Management Journal*, 24: 385–392; E. Soule, 2002, Managerial moral strategies—In search of a few good principles, *Academy of Management Review*, 27: 114–124.

124. L. M. Leinicke, J. A. Ostrosky, & W. M. Rexroad, 2000, Quality financial reporting: Back to the basics, *CPA Journal*, August, 69–71.

125. J. Ivancevich, T. N. Duening, J. A. Gilbert, & R. Konopaske, 2003, Deterring white-collar crime, *Academy of Management Executive*, 17(2): 114–127.

126. K. Schnatterly, 2003, Increasing firm value through detection and prevention of white-collar crime, *Strategic Management Journal*, 24: 587–614.

127. S. Watson & G. Weaver, 2003, How internationalization affects corporate ethics: Formal structures and informal management behavior, *Journal of International Management*, 9: 75–93.

128. J. H. Gavin, J. C. Quick, C. L. Cooper, & J. D. Quick, 2003, A spirit of personal integrity: The role of character in executive health, *Organizational Dynamics*, 32: 165–179.

129. J. R. Cohen, L. W. Pant, & D. J. Sharp, 2001, An examination of differences in ethical decision-making between Canadian business students and accounting professionals, *Journal of Business Ethics*, 30: 319–336; G. R. Weaver, L. K. Trevino, & P. L. Cochran, 1999, Corporate ethics programs as control systems: Influences of executive commitment and environmental factors, *Academy of Management Journal*, 42: 41–57.

130. P. E. Murphy, 1995, Corporate ethics statements: Current status and future prospects, *Journal of Business Ethics*, 14: 727–740.

131. G. Redding, 2002, The capitalistic business system of China and its rationale, *Asia Pacific Journal of Management*, 19: 221–249.

132. J. H. Gittell, 2000, Paradox of coordination and control, *California Management Review*, 42(3): 101–117; L. J. Kirsch, 1996, The management of complex tasks in organizations: Controlling the systems development process, *Organization Science*, 7: 1–21.

133. M. D. Shields, F. J. Deng, & Y. Kato, 2000, The design and effects of control systems: Tests of direct- and indirect-effects models, *Accounting, Organizations and Society*, 25: 185–202; R. Simons, 1994, How new top managers use control systems as levers of strategic renewal, *Strategic Management Journal*, 15: 170–171.

134. K. J. Laverty, 1996, Economic "short-termism": The debate, the unresolved issues, and the implications for management practice and research, *Academy of Management Review*, 21: 825–860.

135. R. S. Kaplan & D. P. Norton, 2001, The strategy-focused organization, *Strategy & Leadership*, 29(3): 41–42; R. S. Kaplan & D. P. Norton, 2000,

The Strategy-Focused Organization: How Balanced Scorecard Companies Thrive in the New Business Environment, Boston: Harvard Business School Press.

136. B. E. Becker, M. A. Huselid, & D. Ulrich, 2001, *The HR Scorecard: Linking People, Strategy, and Performance*, Boston: Harvard Business School Press, 21.

137. Kaplan & Norton, The strategy-focused organization.

138. R. S. Kaplan & D. P. Norton, 2001, Transforming the balanced scorecard from performance measurement to strategic management: Part I, *Accounting Horizons*, 15(1): 87–104.

139. R. S. Kaplan & D. P. Norton, 1992, The balanced scorecard—measures that drive performance, *Harvard Business Review*, 70(1): 71–79.

140. M. A. Mische, 2001, *Strategic Renewal: Becoming a High-Performance Organization*, Upper Saddle River, NJ: Prentice-Hall, 181.

141. Rowe, Creating wealth in organizations: The role of strategic leadership.

142. R. E. Hoskisson, R. A. Johnson, D. Yiu, & W. P. Wan, 2001, Restructuring strategies of diversified business groups: Differences associated with country institutional environments, in M. A. Hitt, R. E. Freeman, & J. S. Harrison (eds.), *Handbook of Strategic Management*, Oxford, UK: Blackwell Publishers, 433–463; R. A. Johnson, 1996, Antecedents and outcomes of corporate refocusing, *Journal of Management*, 22: 437–481; R. E. Hoskisson & M. A. Hitt, 1994, *Downscoping: How to Tame the Diversified Firm*, New York: Oxford University Press.

143. J. Birkinshaw & N. Hood, 2001, Unleash innovation in foreign subsidiaries, *Harvard Business Review*, 79(3): 131–137.

144. Ireland & Hitt, Achieving and maintaining strategic competitiveness.

145. R. C. Morais, 2003, Mind the gap, *Forbes*, http://www.forbes.com, July 21.

146. 2003, About Samsung, http://www.samsung.com, July; M. Ihlwan & D. Roberts, 2002, How Samsung plugged into China, *BusinessWeek Online*, http://www.businessweek.com, March 4.

Strategic Entrepreneurship

Chapter Thirteen

Knowledge Objectives

Studying this chapter should provide you with the strategic management knowledge needed to:

1. Define and explain strategic entrepreneurship.

2. Describe the importance of entrepreneurial opportunities, innovation, and entrepreneurial capabilities.

3. Discuss the importance of international entrepreneurship.

4. Describe autonomous and induced strategic behavior—the two forms of internal corporate venturing.

5. Discuss how cooperative strategies such as strategic alliances are used to develop innovation.

6. Explain how firms use acquisitions to increase their innovations and enrich their innovative capabilities.

7. Describe the importance of venture capital and initial public offerings to entrepreneurial activity.

8. Explain how strategic entrepreneurship creates value in all types of firms.

Getty/PhotoDisc, Inc.

Entrepreneurship involves taking unique actions to fulfill business and consumer needs as those opportunities become apparent. Anne Maxfield and Leslie Frank, for example, founded a company called Project Solvers, which acts as an agent by connecting firms and individuals involved in designing, making, and selling fashion clothing.

There is a wide variety of types of entrepreneurs, but no one formula for success. However, there are many successful entrepreneurs. For example, Marion McCaw Garrison was one of the first female accounting graduates of the University of Washington in 1939. While she was told that it was unlikely she could ever earn her CPA because she was a woman, she completed her degree in accounting anyway. At 22 years of age, she bought 40 acres of land and became a real estate developer, one of the first women to do so. After she married, she helped her husband manage their businesses, including radio and television stations and real estate. When her husband died suddenly, she took over the management of the businesses. She moved out of the radio business and entered cable television and wireless communications. The company went public in 1987, and in 1994, McCaw Cellular Communications was sold to AT&T for more than $11 billion. Garrison was successful because of her strong business knowledge and determination.

Clothing designers Anne Maxfield and Leslie Frank worked for a large fashion design company for more than a decade. Their assignments often found them assembling outside teams of illustrators, designers, and art directors to complete specific projects. Observing that "all creative people working in New York had agents except for fashion designers," Maxfield and Frank launched Project Solvers, Inc. Using their uniquely developed comprehensive database of people involved in all activities associated with designing, making, and selling fashion clothing, Project Solvers serves firms' needs to hire talented individuals/artists to complete specific projects. Their ability to envision an entrepreneurial opportunity that others hadn't seen is the foundation of the success achieved by entrepreneurs Maxfield and Frank.

Entrepreneurs sometimes establish new ventures from the base of an existing one. An entrepreneurial family business venture, International Visual Corp. (IVC) manufactures fixtures for department stores such as Nordstrom and JCPenney. By the end of the 1990s, declines in business with IVC's core department store customers had reduced the firm's profit margin from 40 percent to 20 percent. However, IVC continued to develop innovative products even as its margins declined. A thermoplastic wall panel became a valuable innovation for the firm. This innovative panel's modular design, strength, durability, and consistent color made it very attractive to department stores. But, IVC looked on with dismay as its sales, even of its valued new innovation, declined. Along with his partner, IVC's president, the founder's son, originated the idea of selling the panel to homeowners who could use the product as a base for attaching cabinets, shelves, and other components. Their idea appealed to home builders, and an innovative application of the firm's panel quickly became a success. After securing funding from a venture capital firm, the entrepreneurs established GarageTek and sold IVC to one of their former material suppliers (who retained the rights to sell the panel to retailers). Operating in an established firm, these entrepreneurs understood that proprietary technologies may have uses in multiple markets.

Each of these successful entrepreneurs took unique actions and had some special traits, but they all had a passion for the businesses they developed. According to Michael Dell, founder and CEO of Dell Inc., passion must be the driving force for starting a company. Dell also emphasizes the importance of identifying and exploiting opportunities. All of the entrepreneurs described identified opportunities and were passionate about exploiting them.

SOURCES: P. Thomas, 2003, A change of scenery boosts special project, *Wall Street Journal Online*, http://www.wsj.com, May 27; P. Thomas, 2003, When employees quit to become competitors, *Wall Street Journal Online*, http://www.wsj.com, April 29; 2001, Marion McCaw Garrison: An entrepreneurial woman, *Business*, University of Washington Business School, Fall, 40.

Several factors are important to the success of the entrepreneurs described in the Opening Case. They all have a passion for their business and a willingness to take calculated risks to pursue their entrepreneurial vision. Other factors, such as determination (Marion McCaw Garrison), an ability to see opportunities that others haven't seen (Maxfield and Frank) and a recognition that proprietary, innovative technology may have applications in several markets (IVC's leaders) also contributed to their success.

For several reasons, including the fact that entrepreneurship is the economic engine driving many nations' economies in the global competitive landscape,[1] it is important for firms' managers to understand how to act entrepreneurially. Entrepreneurship and innovation are important for young and old and for large and small firms, for service companies as well as manufacturing firms and high-technology ventures.[2] In the global competitive landscape, the long-term success of new ventures and established firms is a function of the ability to meld entrepreneurship with strategic management.[3]

This chapter focuses on strategic entrepreneurship. **Strategic entrepreneurship** is taking entrepreneurial actions using a strategic perspective. More specifically, strategic entrepreneurship involves engaging in simultaneous opportunity seeking and competitive advantage seeking behaviors to design and implement entrepreneurial strategies to create wealth.[4] These actions can be taken by individuals or by corporations and are of increasing importance in the evolving 21st-century competitive landscape.[5]

The competitive landscape that has evolved in the 21st century presents firms with substantial change, a global marketplace, and significant complexity and uncertainty.[6] Because of this uncertain environment, firms cannot easily predict the future.[7] As a result, they must develop strategic flexibility to have a range of strategic alternatives that they can implement as needed. To do so, they must acquire resources and build the capabilities that allow them to take necessary actions to adapt to a dynamic environment or to be proactive in that environment.[8] In this environment, entrepreneurs and entrepreneurial managers design and implement actions that capture more of existing markets from less aggressive and innovative competitors while creating new markets.[9] In effect, they are trying to create tomorrow's businesses.[10]

Creating tomorrow's businesses requires identifying opportunities, as argued by Michael Dell in the Opening Case, and developing innovation. In other words, firms must be entrepreneurial and innovative, yet strategic in their thinking and actions. Innovations are critical to companies' efforts to differentiate their goods or services from competitors in ways that create additional or new value for customers.[11] Thus,

Strategic entrepreneurship *is taking entrepreneurial actions using a strategic perspective.*

entrepreneurial competencies are important for firms to achieve and sustain competitive advantages.[12]

To describe how firms produce and manage innovation, we consider several topics in this chapter. First, we examine strategic entrepreneurship and innovation in a strategic context. Included as parts of this analysis are definitions of entrepreneurs and the entrepreneurial opportunities they pursue. Next, we discuss international entrepreneurship, a phenomenon reflecting the increased use of entrepreneurship in economies throughout the world. The chapter then shifts to discussions of the three ways firms innovate, with internal innovation being the first method. Most large, complex firms use all three methods to innovate. Internally, firms innovate through either autonomous or induced strategic behavior. We then describe actions firms take to implement the innovations resulting from those two types of strategic behavior. In addition to innovating through internal activities, firms can develop innovations by using cooperative strategies, such as strategic alliances, and by acquiring other companies to gain access to their innovations and innovative capabilities. The method the firm chooses to innovate can be affected by the firm's governance mechanisms. Research evidence suggests, for example, that inside board directors with equity positions favor internal innovation while outside directors with equity positions prefer acquiring innovation.[13] Descriptions of capital that is available to support entrepreneurial ventures and a final assessment of how firms use strategic entrepreneurship to create value and earn above-average returns close the chapter.

Strategic Entrepreneurship and Innovation

Joseph Schumpeter viewed entrepreneurship as a process of "creative destruction," through which existing products or methods of production are destroyed and replaced with new ones.[14] Thus, *entrepreneurship* is "concerned with the discovery and exploitation of profitable opportunities."[15] Entrepreneurial activity is an important mechanism for creating change, as well as for helping firms adapt to change created by others.[16] Firms that encourage entrepreneurship are risk takers, are committed to innovation, and act proactively in that they try to create opportunities rather than waiting to respond to opportunities created by others.[17]

Increasingly, entrepreneurship is viewed by some as a means of bringing about changes that have implications for broader societies. Called social entrepreneurship, different interpretations of the term and the actions associated with it remain.[18] In reading about social entrepreneurship in the Strategic Focus, notice that social entrepreneurs share some if not many of the traits associated with the entrepreneurs described in the Opening Case. In other words, strategic entrepreneurship is also appropriate for use by those wanting to be social entrepreneurs.

Entrepreneurial opportunities represent conditions in which new goods or services can satisfy a need in the market. The essence of entrepreneurship is to identify and exploit these opportunities.[19] Importantly, entrepreneurs or entrepreneurial managers must be able to identify opportunities not perceived by others. As explained in the Strategic Focus, social entrepreneurs find opportunities to fulfill socially oriented purposes to which others haven't committed.

Identifying opportunities in a dynamic and uncertain environment requires an entrepreneurial mind-set that entails the passionate pursuit of opportunities.[20] Discussed further later in the chapter, a mind-set can be a source of competitive advantage because of the actions resulting from its focus,[21] such as the actions taken when entrepreneurs passionately pursue opportunities. For example, three cofounders who had started other entrepreneurial ventures recently established Supply Marketing Inc. The firm sells advertising space on virtually all disposable items that are used in physicians' offices. Tongue depressors, bandages, sterile paper covering examining tables,

Entrepreneurial opportunities represent conditions in which new goods or services can satisfy a need in the market.

Social Entrepreneurship: Innovative, Proactive, Risk-oriented, and Purposeful

Coming primarily from countries or regions where entrepreneurship as a business model is well established (e.g., Asia, Latin America, and the United States), social entrepreneurs are passionate about their projects and have a single-minded focus in pursuing outcomes to which they are committed. Deliberate in their choices, social entrepreneurs work on projects throughout the world, believing that virtually all societies have groups who could benefit from their services. Those who for a variety of reasons aren't actively participating in formal economic markets, such as minorities, women, and disabled people, are social entrepreneurs' primary targets.

Social entrepreneurs practice social entrepreneurship, a process that "melds the enterprise and innovation often associated with the private sector with the grassroots accountability necessary to sustain solutions in the public sector." In slightly different words, "social entrepreneurship strives to combine the heart of business with the heart of the community through the creativity of the individual."

As we noted above, entrepreneurship is concerned with discovering and exploiting opportunities to earn profits. To do this, entrepreneurs commit to the importance of innovation, are willing to take risks, and are proactive in finding opportunities rather than waiting to respond to opportunities generated by others. In a like manner, social entrepreneurship is concerned with discovering and exploiting opportunities to achieve a social mission in the face of moral complexity. As decision makers, social entrepreneurs also commit to innovation's importance, take calculated risks, and seek opportunities to serve rather than waiting for others to act. Commonly, social entrepreneurs seek to help others establish ventures through which targeted individuals will be able to earn income. Because of growing successes, public policy makers in a variety of countries are evaluating the possibility of more actively supporting social entrepreneurship as an approach to alleviating social disadvantage.

The projects resulting from social entrepreneurship are diverse. Social entrepreneur Karen Tse, a lawyer and minister, is building networks of public defenders in China, Vietnam, and Cambodia. Located in the United Kingdom, Big Issue provides homeless individuals with an opportunity to earn income. The organization's profits are donated to a charity studying homelessness to determine how to eliminate its causes. ApproTEC creates and markets simple and inexpensive tools in Kenya and Tanzania. An irrigation pump called the MoneyMaker is the firm's most successful product. Costing only $38 for the standard size, this pump can be operated simply. The MoneyMaker "eliminates the need to haul water from a well with ropes and buckets and dramatically increases the productivity of rural gardens."

In the final analysis, social entrepreneurship "involves combining commercial aims with social objectives to reap strategic or competitive benefits." Thus, the most effective social entrepreneurs learn how to proactively use the strategic management process to create competitive advantages through which social purposes can be served. Sound strategic management practices are at the core of the social entrepreneur's success and are the foundation on which effective social entrepreneurship is built.

SOURCES: 2003, Social entrepreneurs: Playing the role of change agents in society, *Knowledge at Wharton*, http://www.knowledge.wharton.penn.edu, June 2; 2003, Globalization with a human face—and a social conscience, *Knowledge at Wharton*, http://www.knowledge.wharton.penn.edu, June 2; K. Hammonds, 2003, Investing in social change, *Fast Company*, June, 54; G. S. Mort, J. Weeawardena, & K. Carnegie, 2003, Social entrepreneurship: Toward a conceptualisation, *International Journal of Nonprofit and Voluntary Sector Marketing*, 8(1): 76–88; M. Pomerantz, 2003, The business of social entrepreneurship in a "down economy," *In Business*, 25(2): 25–28.

and rubber gloves are just a few of the products on which advertising can be placed. Financed with $250,000 in venture capital, Supply Marketing provides ad-covered products to physicians. Believing deeply in the potential of the entrepreneurial opportunity they've identified, the cofounders have contacted many companies to solicit their business. Wyeth Labs Inc., Schering-Plough Corp., Novartis AG, and Fujisawa Pharmaceutical Co., Ltd., are examples of companies that have placed orders with Supply Marketing to advertise their products on various disposable items.[22]

Supply Marketing Inc. sells advertising space on products used in doctors' offices, such as the tongue depressors shown here with the slogan "Fewer Coughs, Wetter Coughs."

After identifying opportunities, entrepreneurs must act to develop capabilities that will become the basis of their firm's core competencies and competitive advantages. The process of identifying opportunities is entrepreneurial, but this activity alone is not sufficient to create maximum wealth or even to survive over time.[23] As we learned in Chapter 3, to successfully exploit opportunities, a firm must develop capabilities that are valuable, rare, difficult to imitate, and nonsubstitutable. When capabilities satisfy these four criteria, the firm has one or more competitive advantages to exploit the identified opportunities (as described in Chapter 3). Without a competitive advantage, the firm's success will be only temporary (as explained in Chapter 1). An innovation may be valuable and rare early in its life, if a market perspective is used in its development. However, competitive actions must be taken to introduce the new product to the market and protect its position in the market against competitors to gain a competitive advantage. These actions combined represent strategic entrepreneurship.

Innovation

Peter Drucker argues that "innovation is the specific function of entrepreneurship, whether in an existing business, a public service institution, or a new venture started by a lone individual."[24] Moreover, Drucker suggests that innovation is "the means by which the entrepreneur either creates new wealth-producing resources or endows existing resources with enhanced potential for creating wealth."[25] Thus, entrepreneurship and the innovation resulting from it are important for large and small firms, as well as for start-up ventures, as they compete in the 21st-century competitive landscape.[26] Therefore, we can conclude that "entrepreneurship and innovation are central to the creative process in the economy and to promoting growth, increasing productivity and creating jobs."[27]

Innovation is a key outcome firms seek through entrepreneurship and is often the source of competitive success, especially in turbulent, highly competitive environments.[28] For example, research results show that firms competing in global industries that invest more in innovation also achieve the highest returns.[29] In fact, investors often react positively to the introduction of a new product, thereby increasing the price of a firm's stock. Innovation, then, is an essential feature of high-performance firms.[30] Furthermore, "innovation may be required to maintain or achieve competitive parity, much less a competitive advantage in many global markets."[31] The most innovative firms understand that financial slack should be available at all times to support the pursuit of entrepreneurial opportunities.[32]

Invention *is the act of creating or developing a new product or process.*

Innovation *is the process of creating a commercial product from an invention.*

Imitation *is the adoption of an innovation by similar firms.*

In his classic work, Schumpeter argued that firms engage in three types of innovative activity.[33] **Invention** is the act of creating or developing a new product or process. **Innovation** is the process of creating a commercial product from an invention. Thus, an invention brings something new into being, while an innovation brings something new into use. Accordingly, technical criteria are used to determine the success of an invention, whereas commercial criteria are used to determine the success of an innovation.[34] Finally, **imitation** is the adoption of an innovation by similar firms. Imitation usually leads to product or process standardization, and products based on imitation often are offered at lower prices, but without as many features.

In the United States in particular, innovation is the most critical of the three types of innovative activity that occur in firms. Many companies are able to create ideas that lead to inventions, but commercializing those inventions through innovation has, at times, proved difficult. Approximately 80 percent of R&D occurs in large firms, but these same firms produce fewer than 50 percent of the patents.[35] Patents are a strategic asset and the ability to regularly produce them can be an important source of competitive advantage, especially for firms competing in knowledge-intensive industries[36] (e.g., pharmaceuticals).

Corporate entrepreneurship *is a process whereby an individual or a group in an existing organization creates a new venture or develops an innovation.*

Innovations produced in large established firms are the products of **corporate entrepreneurship**, which is a process whereby an individual or a group in an existing organization creates a new venture or develops an innovation.[37] Corporate entrepreneurship practices are facilitated when the firm's human capital successfully uses the strategic management process.[38] Determining how to harness the ingenuity of a firm's employees and how to reward them for it while retaining some of the benefits of the entrepreneurial efforts for shareholders also supports corporate entrepreneurship.[39] The most successful firms remain aware of the continuing need for corporate entrepreneurship. Having formed an e-commerce powerhouse known as USA Interactive, for example, CEO Barry Diller is concentrating on creating synergies among his firm's businesses while leaving them entrepreneurial and independent as the basis for generating additional value for shareholders.[40]

Entrepreneurs and Entrepreneurial Capabilities

Entrepreneurs *are individuals, acting independently or as part of an organization, who create a new venture or develop an innovation and take risks entering it into the marketplace.*

Entrepreneurs are individuals, acting independently or as part of an organization, who create a new venture or develop an innovation and take risks entering it into the marketplace. Entrepreneurs can be independent individuals or serve in an organization at any level. Thus, top-level managers, middle- and first-level managers, staff personnel, and those producing the company's good or service can all be entrepreneurs.

Firms need employees who think entrepreneurially. Top-level managers should try to establish an entrepreneurial culture that inspires individuals and groups to engage in corporate entrepreneurship.[41] Apple Computer's Steve Jobs is committed to this effort, believing one of his key responsibilities is to help Apple become more entrepreneurial. And, as described in Chapter 6, Apple has introduced some innovative products, such as the iPod portable digital music player, thought to be the gold standard of the industry. Competitors "are feverishly working on iPod clones."[42] As a competitive response, Apple redesigned its product, making it thinner and lighter than the original version while being capable of packing in more songs.[43] Another Apple innovation is iTunes, an online music store. When launched, this website sold songs for 99 cents per download or roughly $10 per album. Users of iTunes can hear songs on an unlimited number of iPod digital-music players and burn as many as ten compact discs with the same playlists. Expecting to sell one million songs during the first month of iTunes' operation, Apple reached this initial sales target in the first week.[44]

Of course, to create and commercialize products such as the iPod and iTunes requires not only intellectual capital, but an entrepreneurial mind-set as well. An entrepreneurial mind-set finds individuals using a prevailing sense of uncertainty to develop unique products.[45] Entrepreneurial competence supports development and use of an entrepreneurial mind-set. In most cases, knowledge must be transferred to others in the organization, even in smaller ventures, to enhance the entrepreneurial competence of the firm. The transfer is likely to be more difficult in larger firms. Research has shown, however, that units within firms are more innovative if they have access to new knowledge.[46]

Transferring knowledge can be difficult, because the receiving party must have adequate absorptive capacity (or the ability) to learn the knowledge.[47] This requires that the new knowledge be linked to the existing knowledge. Thus, managers will need to develop the capabilities of their human capital to build on their current knowledge base while incrementally expanding that knowledge.[48]

Developing innovations and achieving success in the marketplace require effective human capital. In particular, firms must have strong intellectual capital in their R&D organization.[49] However, a firm must have strong human capital throughout its workforce if employees are to be innovative. For example, WinSpec West Manufacturing Inc. credits its positive market position to innovation produced by its strong employee base. In fact, the managers are very careful in hiring. Even in jobs with seemingly low challenges, they try to hire high-potential employees. For one secretarial position, the managers hired a person with an MBA in finance; that person went on to serve as the acting chief financial officer.[50]

Steve Jobs demonstrates how to download favorite tunes with Apple's iTunes.

International Entrepreneurship

Entrepreneurship is a global phenomenon.[51] In general, internationalization leads to improved firm performance,[52] a fact influencing the practice of entrepreneurship on a global scale. Nonetheless, decision makers should recognize that the decision to internationalize exposes their firms to various risks, including those of unstable foreign currencies, problems with market efficiencies, insufficient infrastuctures to support businesses, and limitations on market size, among others.[53] Thus, the decision to engage in international entrepreneurship should be a product of careful analysis.

Because of its positive benefits, entrepreneurship is at the top of public policy agendas in many of the world's countries, including Finland, Germany, Israel, Ireland, and France, among others. Placing entrepreneurship on these agendas may be appropriate in that some argue that regulation hindering innovation and entrepreneurship is the root cause of Europe's productivity problems.[54] In Northern Ireland, the minister for enterprise, trade, and investment told businesspeople that their current and future commercial success would be affected by the degree to which they decided to emphasize R&D and innovation (critical components of entrepreneurship).[55]

While entrepreneurship is a global phenomenon, the rate of entrepreneurship differs across countries. A recent study of 29 countries found that the percentage of adults involved in entrepreneurial activity ranged from a high of more than 20 percent in Mexico to a low of approximately 5 percent in Belgium. The United States had a rate of about 13 percent. Importantly, this study also found a strong positive relationship between the rate of entrepreneurial activity and economic development in the country.[56]

Culture is one of the reasons for the differences in rates of entrepreneurship among different countries. For example, the tension between individualism and collectivism is important for entrepreneurship; research shows that entrepreneurship declines as collectivism is emphasized. Simultaneously, however, research results suggest that exceptionally high levels of individualism might be dysfunctional for entrepreneurship. Viewed collectively, these results appear to call for a balance between individual initiative and a spirit of cooperation and group ownership of innovation. For firms to be entrepreneurial, they must provide appropriate autonomy and incentives for individual initiative to surface, but also promote cooperation and group ownership of an innovation if it is to be implemented successfully. Thus, international entrepreneurship often requires teams of people with unique skills and resources, especially in cultures where collectivism is a valued historical norm.[57]

The level of investment outside of the home country made by young ventures is also an important dimension of international entrepreneurship. In fact, with increasing globalization, a greater number of new ventures have been "born global."[58] Research has shown that new ventures that enter international markets increase their learning of new technological knowledge and thereby enhance their performance.[59] Because of positive outcomes such as the ones we've described, the amount of international entrepreneurship has been increasing in recent years.[60]

The probability of entering international markets increases when the firm has top executives with international experience.[61] Furthermore, the firm has a higher likelihood of successfully competing in international markets when its top executives have international experience.[62] Because of the learning and economies of scale and scope afforded by operating in international markets, both young and established internationally diversified firms often are stronger competitors in their domestic market as well. Additionally, as research has shown, internationally diversified firms are generally more innovative.[63]

International entrepreneurship has been an important factor in the economic development of Asia. In fact, private companies owned by Chinese families outside of China compose the fourth largest economic power in the world. Significant learning from their international ventures occurs in these businesses, and this learning enhances their success with future ventures.[64] The learning that occurs contributes to a firm's knowledge of operating in international markets.[65] It also contributes knowledge that can enhance a firm's new product development, on which we focus in the next section.

New Product Development and Internal Corporate Ventures

Most corporate innovation is developed through research and development (R&D). In many industries, the competitive battle for the market begins in the R&D labs. In fact, R&D may be the most critical factor in gaining and sustaining a competitive advantage in some industries, such as pharmaceuticals. Larger, established firms use R&D labs to create the competence-destroying new technology and products envisioned by Schumpeter. Such radical innovation has become an important component of competition in many industries.[66] Although critical to long-term corporate success, the outcomes of R&D investments are uncertain and often not achieved in the short term,[67] meaning that patience is required as firms examine the benefits of their allocations to R&D.

Incremental and Radical Innovation

Firms can produce and manage incremental or radical innovations. Most innovations are *incremental*—that is, they build on existing knowledge bases and provide small improvements in the current product lines. Alternatively, *radical innovations* usually provide significant technological breakthroughs and create new knowledge.[68] Improving existing processes is an important aspect of incremental innovations.[69] In contrast, developing new processes is a critical part of producing radical innovations. Both types of innovation can create value, meaning that firms should determine when it is appropriate to emphasize either incremental or radical innovation.[70]

Radical innovations are rare because of the difficulty and risk involved in developing them.[71] There is substantial uncertainty with radical innovation regarding the technology and the market opportunities.[72] Because radical innovation creates new knowledge and uses only some or little of a firm's current product or technological knowledge, creativity is required. However, creativity does not create something from nothing. Rather, creativity discovers, combines, or synthesizes current knowledge, often from diverse areas.[73] This knowledge is then used to develop new products or services that can be used in an entrepreneurial manner to move into new markets, capture new customers, and gain access to new resources.[74] Such innovations are often developed in separate business units that start internal ventures.[75]

Internal corporate venturing is the set of activities used to create inventions and innovations through internal means.[76] Spending on R&D is linked to success in internal corporate venturing. Put simply, firms are unable to invent or innovate without significant R&D investments.

As shown in Figure 13.1, there are two forms of internal corporate venturing: autonomous strategic behavior and induced strategic behavior.

Autonomous Strategic Behavior

Autonomous strategic behavior is a bottom-up process in which product champions pursue new ideas, often through a political process, by means of which they develop and coordinate the commercialization of a new good or service until it achieves success in the marketplace. A *product champion* is an organizational member with an entrepreneurial vision of a new good or service who seeks to create support for its commercialization. Product champions play critical roles in moving innovations forward.[77] The primary reason for this is that "no business idea takes root purely on its own merits; it has to be sold."[78] Autonomous strategic behavior is based on a firm's wellsprings of knowledge and resources that are the sources of the firm's innovation.

Internal corporate venturing is the set of activities used to create inventions and innovations through internal means.

Autonomous strategic behavior is a bottom-up process in which product champions pursue new ideas, often through a political process, by means of which they develop and coordinate the commercialization of a new good or service until it achieves success in the marketplace.

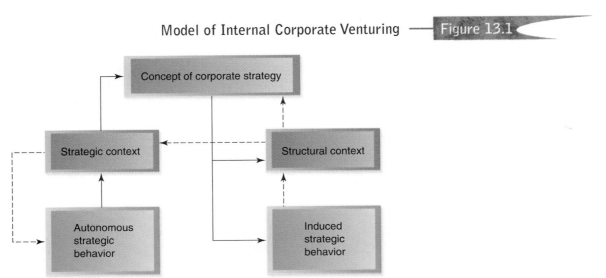

Model of Internal Corporate Venturing — Figure 13.1

SOURCE: Adapted from R. A. Burgelman, 1983, A model of the interactions of strategic behavior, corporate context, and the concept of strategy, *Academy of Management Review*, 8: 65.

Thus, a firm's technological capabilities and competencies are the basis for new products and processes.[79] GE depends on autonomous strategic behavior on a regular basis to produce innovations. Essentially, "the search for marketable services can start in any of GE's myriad businesses. [For example], an operating unit seeks out appropriate technology to better do what it already does. Having mastered the technology, it then incorporates it into a service it can sell to others."[80]

Changing the concept of corporate-level strategy through autonomous strategic behavior results when a product is championed within strategic and structural contexts (see Figure 13.1). The strategic context is the process used to arrive at strategic decisions (often requiring political processes to gain acceptance). The best firms keep changing their strategic context and strategies because of the continuous changes in the current competitive landscape. Thus, some believe that the most competitively successful firms reinvent their industry or develop a completely new one across time as they compete with current and future rivals.[81]

To be effective, an autonomous process for developing new products requires that new knowledge be continuously diffused throughout the firm. In particular, the diffusion of tacit knowledge is important for development of more effective new products.[82] Interestingly, some of the processes important for the promotion of autonomous new product development behavior vary by the environment and country in which a firm operates. For example, the Japanese culture is high on uncertainty avoidance. As such, research has found that Japanese firms are more likely to engage in autonomous behaviors under conditions of low uncertainty.[83]

Induced Strategic Behavior

Induced strategic behavior *is a top-down process whereby the firm's current strategy and structure foster product innovations that are closely associated with that strategy and structure.*

The second of the two forms of internal corporate venturing, **induced strategic behavior,** is a top-down process whereby the firm's current strategy and structure foster product innovations that are closely associated with that strategy and structure. In this form of venturing, the strategy in place is filtered through a matching structural hierarchy.

The ability to substitute aluminum for steel in some parts used to manufacture Jaguar automobiles is an innovation that resulted from induced strategic behavior. Ford Motor Company bought Jaguar in 1990. Part of Ford's differentiation business-level strategy for Jaguar called for innovation to be the source of improved competitiveness for Jaguar cars. Because aluminum parts are roughly half the weight of their steel counterparts, "Jaguar's new $60,000 XJ sedan boasts a body as light as a Mini's, accelerates quicker than a Mercedes 430 and is put together using a clever assembly method that weds aircraft-style metal bonding to mass-production-style metal shaping."[84] Thus, by using the differentiation strategy and a particular form of the functional structure (see Chapter 11), Jaguar's strategy and structure have elicited value-creating innovations.

Implementing New Product Development and Internal Ventures

To be innovative and develop internal ventures requires an entrepreneurial mind-set. In Chapter 12, we discuss an entrepreneurial orientation that includes several dimensions, such as risk propensity. Clearly, firms and individuals must be willing to take risks to commercialize new products. While they must continuously attempt to identify opportunities, they must also select and pursue the best opportunities and do so with discipline. Thus, employing an entrepreneurial mind-set entails not only developing new products and markets but also placing an emphasis on execution. Those with an entrepreneurial mind-set "engage the energies of everyone in their domain," both inside and outside the organization.[85]

Having processes and structures in place through which a firm can successfully implement the outcomes of internal corporate ventures and commercialize the innovations is critical. Indeed, the successful introduction of innovations into the marketplace reflects implementation effectiveness.[86] In the context of internal corporate ventures, processes are the "patterns of interaction, coordination, communication, and decision making employees use" to convert the innovations resulting from either autonomous or induced strategic behaviors into successful market entries.[87] As we describe in Chapter 11, organizational structures are the sets of formal relationships supporting organizational processes.

A detailer at Jaguar polishes an aluminum Jaguar XJ-R concept car in preparation for the North American International Auto Show in Detroit, 2003. The use of aluminum to partly manufacture the new Jaguar is an innovation induced by Ford that has resulted in a lighter car.

Effective integration of the various functions involved in innovation processes—from engineering to manufacturing and, ultimately, market distribution—is required to implement the innovations resulting from internal corporate ventures.[88] Increasingly, product development teams are being used to integrate the activities associated with different organizational functions. Product development teams are commonly used to produce cross-functional integration. Such integration involves coordinating and applying the knowledge and skills of different functional areas in order to maximize innovation.[89] Effective product development teams also create value when they "pull the plug" on a project.[90] Although difficult, sometimes because of emotional commitments to innovation-based projects, effective teams recognize when conditions change in ways that preclude the innovation's ability to create value as originally anticipated.

Cross-Functional Product Development Teams

Cross-functional teams facilitate efforts to integrate activities associated with different organizational functions, such as design, manufacturing, and marketing. In addition, new product development processes can be completed more quickly and the products more easily commercialized when cross-functional teams work effectively.[91] Using cross-functional teams, product development stages are grouped into parallel or overlapping processes to allow the firm to tailor its product development efforts to its unique core competencies and to the needs of the market.

Horizontal organizational structures support the use of cross-functional teams in their efforts to integrate innovation-based activities across organizational functions.[92] Therefore, instead of being built around vertical hierarchical functions or departments, the organization is built around core horizontal processes that are used to produce and manage innovations. Some of the core horizontal processes that are critical to innovation efforts are formal; they may be defined and documented as procedures and practices. More commonly, however, these processes are informal: "They are routines or ways of working that evolve over time."[93] Often invisible, informal processes are critical to successful product innovations and are supported properly through horizontal organizational structures more so than through vertical organizational structures.

Two primary barriers that may prevent the successful use of cross-functional teams as a means of integrating organizational functions are independent frames of reference of team members and organizational politics.[94]

Team members working within a distinct specialization (i.e., a particular organizational function) may have an independent frame of reference typically based on common backgrounds and experiences. They are likely to use the same decision criteria to evaluate issues such as product development efforts as they do within their functional units. Research suggests that functional departments vary along four dimensions: time orientation, interpersonal orientation, goal orientation, and formality of structure.[95] Thus, individuals from different functional departments having different orientations on these dimensions can be expected to perceive product development activities in different ways. For example, a design engineer may consider the characteristics that make a product functional and workable to be the most important of the product's characteristics. Alternatively, a person from the marketing function may hold characteristics that satisfy customer needs most important. These different orientations can create barriers to effective communication across functions.[96]

Organizational politics is the second potential barrier to effective integration in cross-functional teams. In some organizations, considerable political activity may center on allocating resources to different functions. Interunit conflict may result from aggressive competition for resources among those representing different organizational functions. This dysfunctional conflict between functions creates a barrier to their integration.[97] Methods must be found to achieve cross-functional integration without excessive political conflict and without changing the basic structural characteristics necessary for task specialization and efficiency.

Facilitating Integration and Innovation

Shared values and effective leadership are important to achieve cross-functional integration and implement innovation.[98] Highly effective shared values are framed around the firm's strategic intent and mission, and become the glue that promotes integration between functional units. Thus, the firm's culture promotes unity and internal innovation.[99]

Strategic leadership is also highly important for achieving cross-functional integration and promoting innovation. Leaders set the goals and allocate resources. The goals include integrated development and commercialization of new goods and services. Effective strategic leaders also ensure a high-quality communication system to facilitate cross-functional integration. A critical benefit of effective communication is the sharing of knowledge among team members.[100] Effective communication thus helps create synergy and gains team members' commitment to an innovation throughout the organization. Shared values and leadership practices shape the communication systems that are formed to support the development and commercialization of new products.[101]

Creating Value from Innovation

The model in Figure 13.2 shows how firms can create value from the internal processes they use to develop and commercialize new goods and services. An entrepreneurial mind-set is necessary so that managers and employees will consistently try to identify entrepreneurial opportunities that the firm can pursue by developing new goods and services and new markets. Cross-functional teams are important to promote integrated new product design ideas and commitment to their implementation thereafter. Effective leadership and shared values promote integration and vision for innovation and commitment to it. The end result for the firm is the creation of value for the customers and shareholders by developing and commercializing new products.[102]

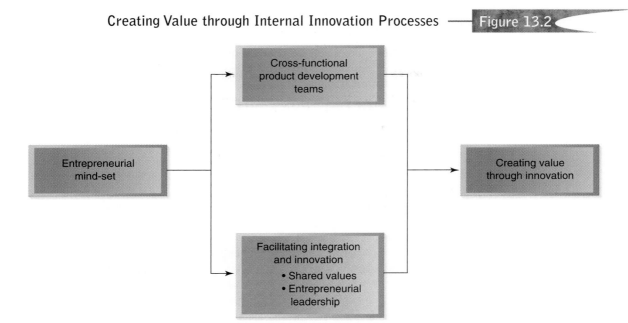

In the next two sections, we discuss the other ways firms can develop innovations—through use of cooperative strategies and acquisitions of other companies.

Cooperative Strategies for Entrepreneurship and Innovation

It is unlikely that a firm possesses all the knowledge and resources required for it to be entrepreneurial and innovative in dynamic competitive markets. Knowledge and resources are needed to develop new products and serve new markets.[103] To successfully commercialize inventions, firms may therefore choose to cooperate with other organizations and integrate their knowledge and resources.[104] Entrepreneurial new ventures, for example, may seek investment capital as well as the distribution capabilities of more established firms to implement a new product idea and introduce it to the market.[105] Alternatively, more established companies may need new technological knowledge and can gain access to it through alliances with start-up ventures.[106] Alliances between large pharmaceutical firms and biotechnology companies have increasingly been formed to integrate the knowledge and resources of both to develop new products and bring them to market.[107]

As suggested by the descriptions in the Strategic Focus, established firms also partner with one another to share their knowledge and skills in order to produce or manage innovations. Notice that the innovations described in the Strategic Focus all involve the combining of partners' unique skills. Commonly, the skills and knowledge contributed by each alliance partner are technology-based, a fact suggesting how rapidly technologies and their applications change in the 21st-century competitive landscape.

Because of the importance of alliances, particularly in the development of new technology and in commercializing innovations, firms are beginning to build networks of alliances that represent a form of social capital to them.[108] This social capital in the form of relationships with other firms helps them to obtain the knowledge and other resources necessary to develop innovations.[109] Knowledge from these alliances helps firms develop new capabilities.[110] Some firms now even allow other

Partnering to Innovate

GE Fleet Services is one of the largest fleet management companies in the world with more than 1.2 million commercial cars and trucks under lease and service management. Founded in the United Kingdom, Minorplanet Systems PLC serves close to 1,500 customers and has an installed base of 23,000 vehicles. Targeting similar customers, these firms formed a strategic alliance to develop and sell Vehicle Management Information (VMI) systems, initially in the United Kingdom and then in the United States as well. These products "provide innovative productivity solutions to help reduce fleet costs," according to officials involved with the alliance. In 2000, the firms won the "Innovation of the Year" award for productivity from *Fleet News*, the United Kingdom's leading fleet management trade publication. The award was given because one of the VMI products developed by the alliance partners was determined to radically improve the management of commercial fleets. Technologically sophisticated, this product leverages satellite and Internet technologies to help fleet operators plan routes, track vehicles on a live basis, and engage in intra-fleet text messaging, among other capabilities.

Especially early in its growth, Cisco Systems acquired innovations as it bought high-technology companies. However, Cisco also emphasizes strategic alliances to produce innovations. BearingPoint is one of the companies with which Cisco has an alliance that is designed to produce innovations. The alliance combines Cisco's expertise in network design and integrated IP-based solutions with BearingPoint's experience in assessing, designing, and implementing corporate networks. These firms combine their skills to develop what they consider to be innovative, end-to-end Internet-business solutions. Atlantic Health System (AHS) was one of the alliance's customers. To improve the reliability and performance of AHS's network, Cisco and BearingPoint developed a "state-of-the-art gigabit Ethernet infrastructure that enables digital medical-imaging and other high-bandwidth applications, increased collaboration between staff members at facilities within the group, and increased network reliability and performance."

Cisco also partners with KPMG Consulting to develop innovations. In this partnership, Cisco provides its intelligent enterprise-wide infrastructure solutions skills while KPMG offers its development and consulting expertise. Boise Cascade Office Products is a customer that the alliance served. In this instance, the alliance worked with its customer to design and implement the computer-telephony integration and Web collaboration aspects of Boise Cascade Office Products' new customer contact center. A business-to-business distributor of office products, Boise Cascade wanted to develop a differentiated, high-value-added customer contact center as a competitive advantage in what is essentially a highly competitive commodity-based business.

SOURCES: 2003, Boise Cascade thinks globally, sells locally, *Business Solutions*, http://www.business.cisco.com, June 6; 2003, Network transfusion for Atlantic Health System, *Welcome to IQ Magazine*, http://www.business.cisco.com, June 6; 2003, GE Fleet Services, UK's Minorplanet to extend strategic alliance to North America, *GE Fleet Services*, http://www.gefleet.com, June 8.

companies to participate in their internal new product development processes. It is not uncommon, for example, for firms to have supplier representatives on their cross-functional innovation teams because of the importance of the suppliers' input to ensure quality materials for any new product developed.[111]

However, alliances formed for the purpose of innovation are not without risks, including the risk that a partner will appropriate a firm's technology or knowledge and use it to enhance its own competitive abilities.[112] To prevent or at least minimize this risk, firms, particularly new ventures, need to select their partners carefully. The ideal partnership is one in which the firms have complementary skills as well as compatible strategic goals.[113] However, because firms are operating in a network of firms and thus may be participating in multiple alliances simultaneously, they encounter challenges in managing the alliances.[114] Research has shown that firms can become involved in too many alliances, which can harm rather than facilitate their innovation capabilities.[115] Thus, effectively managing the cooperative relationships to produce innovation is critical.

Acquisitions to Buy Innovation

As described in the Strategic Focus, firms sometimes acquire companies to gain access to their innovations and to their innovative capabilities. One of the reasons that firms turn to acquisitions is that the capital market values growth; acquisitions provide a means to rapidly extend the product line and increase the firm's revenues. Novartis AG likely cannot achieve its growth goal of becoming one of the world's pharmaceutical giants without acquiring other companies. Pfizer's acquisition of Pharmacia Corp. improves the likelihood that it will reach its goal of improving its percentage of converting experimental compounds into successful commercial applications that will lead to increased sales and profitability. Additional information about the relationship between acquisitions and innovation for these firms appears in the Strategic Focus.

Similar to internal corporate venturing and strategic alliances, acquisitions are not a risk-free approach to producing and managing innovations. A key risk of acquisitions is that a firm may substitute an ability to buy innovations for an ability to produce innovations internally. In support of this contention, research shows that firms engaging in acquisitions introduce fewer new products into the market.[116] This substitution may take place because firms lose strategic control and focus instead on financial control of their original and especially of their acquired business units.

We note in Chapter 7 that companies can also learn new capabilities from firms they acquire. As such, firms can gain capabilities to produce innovation from an acquired company. Additionally, firms that emphasize innovation and carefully select companies for acquisition that also emphasize innovation are likely to remain innovative.[117]

Capital for Entrepreneurial Ventures

Venture capital is a resource that is typically allocated to entrepreneurs who are involved in projects with high growth potential. The intent of venture capitalists is to achieve a high rate of return on the funds they invest.[118] In the late 1990s, the number of venture capital firms and the amount of capital invested in new ventures reached unprecedented levels with the amount of venture capital invested in new ventures reaching a high of $106 billion in 2000.[119] Venture capitalists desire to receive large returns on their investments and take major risks by investing in new ventures. Research has shown that venture capitalists may earn large returns or experience significant losses. For example, one study found that 34 percent of venture capitalists experienced a loss, while 23 percent gained a rate of return on their investments of 50 percent or greater.[120]

In addition to the benefit of financial resources, the firm receiving venture capital gains *legitimacy* (a social judgment of acceptance, appropriateness, and desirability). In turn, legitimacy increases the probability a new venture will appeal to other resources such as human capital.[121]

Venture capitalists place weight on the competence of the entrepreneur or the human capital in the firms in which they consider investing. They also weigh the expected scope of competitive rivalry the firm is likely to experience and the degree of instability in the market addressed.[122] However, the characteristics of the entrepreneur

Acquisitions as a Pathway to Innovation

Pfizer Inc. spent $14.4 billion on R&D during the three years prior to announcing in 2002 that it would acquire competitor Pharmacia. Although Pfizer spent more on R&D than any other company over that three-year period, it filed for Food and Drug Administration (FDA) approval for just three new medicines that were discovered by its own scientists. In response to this disappointing performance in its own labs, Pfizer chose to pay approximately $58 billion to acquire Pharmacia. This transaction was the third largest of all time in the pharmaceutical industry, exceeded in value only by Pfizer's previous acquisition in 2000 of Warner Lambert for $100 billion and by Glaxo Wellcome PLC's $77.26 billion purchase of SmithKline Beecham PLC. Almost ten months were required for regulatory approval to be completed in the United States and Europe. The largest hurdle to the acquisition was cleared when Pfizer agreed to sell an experimental incontinence drug to Novartis AG for $225 million. Officially, Pharmacia (formerly the world's ninth largest drugmaker) and Pfizer became a single entity in April 2003.

The newly created Pfizer intended to overhaul its R&D operations to enhance the "firm's ability to discover new medicines." Oncology research is one area in which Pharmacia excelled, resulting in a decision to lay off some Pfizer scientists working in that area. Pfizer officials believed that combining the two firms' areas of R&D expertise created a company with significant growth potential in three areas—eye care, growth disorders, and oncology. In addition to gaining access to Pharmacia's ability to develop innovative oncology drugs, Pfizer also acquired Pharmacia's eplerenone, a blood-pressure drug. In a major study, eplerenone improved "survival among heart-failure patients by 15% when tested against the best available current drug treatments." Because of a stretch of disappointing drug trials against heart disease, analysts viewed eplerenone's test results as a "home run." Thus, Pfizer's acquisition of Pharmacia allowed it to gain access to specific innovations (e.g., eplerenone) as well as to innovative capabilities, such as those concerned with oncology-related drugs.

Novartis AG also acquires innovations and innovative capabilities. Following what analysts call a "targeted acquisition" program, Novartis recently purchased a 51 percent controlling stake in Idenix Pharmaceuticals. A biotechnology company, Idenix had developed two promising hepatitis treatment drugs that interested Novartis. The acquisition of a controlling interest in Idenix gave Novartis "an instant entrée into antiviral hepatitis therapies, a market that's growing about 30% a year and in which Swiss rival Roche Holding AG is a big player." Committed to becoming one of the world's pharmaceutical giants, Novartis is trying to build a portfolio of superior drugs and is more than willing to acquire rivals to do so. In mid-2003, Schering-Plough was identified as a firm Novartis might acquire to expand its portfolio of innovative drugs as well as to enhance its innovative capabilities.

SOURCES: 2003, Novartis acquires hepatitis C franchise, *Chemical Market Reporter*, 263(13): 2; K. Capell, 2003, Novartis: CEO Daniel Vasella has a hot cancer drug and billions in the bank, *BusinessWeek Online*, http://www.businessweek.com, May 26; V. Fuhrmans, 2003, Novartis to acquire 51% of Idenix Pharmaceuticals, *Wall Street Journal Online*, http://www.wsj.com, March 27; S. Hensley, 2003, Pfizer to overhaul research following its Pharmacia deal, *Wall Street Journal Online*, http://www.wsj.com, April 30; S. Hensley, 2003, Pfizer to sell drug to Novartis to satisfy FTC, *Wall Street Journal Online*, http://www.wsj.com, March 18; R. Frank, 2002, Deals & deal makers: Pfizer's Pharmacia deal draws mixed opinions for M&A game, *Wall Street Journal Online*, http://www.wsj.com, July 16.

or firm in which venture capitalists invest as well as the rate of return expected will vary with the type of venture in which investments are made.[123]

Increasingly, venture capital is being used to support the acquisition of innovations. To provide such support, some firms establish their own venture-capital divisions. These divisions carefully evaluate other companies to identify those with innovations or innovative capabilities that might yield a competitive advantage. In other instances, a firm might decide to serve as an internal source of capital for innovative product ideas that can be spun off as independent or affiliated firms. New enterprises that are backed by venture capital provide an important source of innovation and new technology. The amount of corporate venture capital invested grew exponentially at the end of the 1990s and in 2000. For example, it grew from about $2 billion in 1998 to almost $11 billion in 1999. In 2000, the amount of corporate venture capital invested was slightly over $18 billion.[124]

Some relatively new ventures are able to obtain capital through initial public offerings (IPOs). Firms that offer new stock in this way must have high potential in order to sell their stock and obtain adequate capital to finance the growth and development of the firm. This form of capital can be substantial and is often much larger than the amounts obtained from venture capitalists. Investment bankers frequently play major roles in the development and offering of IPOs. Research has shown that founder-managed firms generally receive lower returns from IPOs than do professionally managed firms.[125] The IPO market values experienced managers more than founders who frequently do not have substantial managerial experience. JetBlue Airways created a lot of interest from investors because of its low costs, strong customer demand, and highly experienced CEO (who also happens to be the firm's founder).[126] Investors believe that the firm with an experienced CEO is more likely to succeed. Also, firms that have received venture capital backing usually receive greater returns from IPOs.[127]

Creating Value through Strategic Entrepreneurship

Newer entrepreneurial firms often are more effective than larger firms in identifying opportunities.[128] Some believe that these firms tend to be more innovative as well because of their flexibility and willingness to take risks. Alternatively, larger and well-established firms often have more resources and capabilities to exploit opportunities that are identified.[129] So, younger, entrepreneurial firms are generally opportunity seeking, and more established firms are advantage seeking. However, to compete effectively in the 21st century's competitive landscape, firms must identify and exploit opportunities, but do so while achieving and sustaining a competitive advantage.[130] Thus, newer entrepreneurial firms must learn how to gain a competitive advantage, and older, more established firms must relearn how to identify entrepreneurial opportunities.

Well-established Blockbuster Inc. recently created a new position called executive vice-president and president of emerging brands. Responsibilities attached to this position include those of finding entrepreneurial opportunities and then helping the firm decide if the innovations necessary to pursue them should be developed internally or acquired.[131] The concept of strategic entrepreneurship suggests that established and successful firms such as Blockbuster can be simultaneously entrepreneurial and strategic as can all firms, regardless of their size and age.

To be entrepreneurial, firms must develop an entrepreneurial mind-set among their managers and employees. Managers must emphasize the management of their resources, particularly human capital and social

Blockbuster Inc. is trying new innovations to expand its business. At a store in the Little Havana section of Miami, Florida, for example, it is targeting the growing Hispanic market by increasing its selection of Spanish-subtitled and dubbed movies.

Getty Images

capital.[132] The importance of knowledge to identify and exploit opportunities as well as to gain and sustain a competitive advantage suggests that firms must have strong human capital.[133] Social capital is critical for access to complementary resources from partners in order to compete effectively in domestic and international markets.[134]

Many entrepreneurial opportunities remain in international markets. Thus, firms should seek to enter and compete in international markets. Firms can learn new technologies and management practices from international markets and diffuse this knowledge throughout the firm. Furthermore, the knowledge firms gain can contribute to their innovations. Research has shown that firms operating in international markets tend to be more innovative.[135] Small and large firms are now regularly moving into international markets. Both types of firms must also be innovative to compete effectively. Thus, by developing resources (human and social capital), taking advantage of opportunities in domestic and international markets, and using the resources and knowledge gained in these markets to be innovative, firms achieve competitive advantages.[136] In so doing, they create value for their customers and shareholders.

Firms practicing strategic entrepreneurship contribute to a country's economic development. In fact, some countries such as Ireland have made dramatic economic progress by changing the institutional rules for businesses operating in the country. This could be construed as a form of institutional entrepreneurship. Likewise, firms that seek to establish their technology as a standard, also representing institutional entrepreneurship, are engaging in strategic entrepreneurship because creating a standard produces a sustainable competitive advantage for the firm.[137]

Research shows that because of its economic importance and individual motives, entrepreneurial activity is increasing across the globe. Furthermore, more women are becoming entrepreneurs because of the economic opportunity entrepreneurship provides and the individual independence it affords.[138] In future years, entrepreneurial activity may increase the wealth of less-affluent countries and continue to contribute to the economic development of the more-affluent countries. Regardless, the companies that practice strategic entrepreneurship are likely to be the winners in the 21st century.[139]

Summary

- Strategic entrepreneurship is taking entrepreneurial actions using a strategic perspective. More specifically, it involves engaging in simultaneous opportunity seeking and competitive advantage seeking behaviors to design and implement entrepreneurial strategies to create wealth.

- The concepts of entrepreneurial opportunity, innovation, and capabilities are important to firms. Entrepreneurial opportunities represent conditions in which new goods or services can satisfy a need in the market. The essence of entrepreneurship is to identify and exploit these opportunities. Innovation is the process of commercializing the products or processes that surfaced through invention. Entrepreneurial capabilities include building an entrepreneurial culture, having a passion for the business, and having a desire for measured risk.

- Increasingly, entrepreneurship is being practiced in many countries. As used by entrepreneurs, entrepreneurship and corporate entrepreneurship are strongly related to a nation's economic growth.

- Three basic approaches are used to produce and manage innovation: internal corporate venturing, cooperative strategies such as strategic alliances, and acquisitions. Autonomous strategic behavior and induced strategic behavior are the two processes of internal corporate venturing. Autonomous strategic behavior is a bottom-up process through which a product champion facilitates the commercialization of an innovative good or service. Induced strategic behavior is a top-down process in which a firm's current strategy and structure facilitate product or process innovations that are associated with them. Thus, induced strategic behavior is driven by the organization's current corporate strategy and structure.

- To create incremental and radical innovation requires effective innovation processes and practices. Increasingly, cross-functional integration is vital to a firm's efforts to develop and implement internal corporate venturing activities and to commercialize the resulting innovation. Additionally, integration and innovation can be facilitated by the development of shared values and the practice of entrepreneurial leadership.

- To gain access to the kind of specialized knowledge that often is required to innovate in the complex global economy, firms may form a cooperative relationship such as a strategic alliance with other firms, sometimes even with competitors.

- Acquisitions provide another means for firms to produce and manage innovation. Innovation can be acquired through direct acquisition, or firms can learn new capabilities from an acquisition, thereby enriching their internal innovation processes.

- Entrepreneurial activity requires capital for development. Venture capitalists are a prime source for this capital. The amount of venture capital available increased dramatically in the 1990s. While it decreased recently due to economic problems, it remains much higher than in earlier years. Initial public offerings (IPOs) also have become a common means of obtaining capital for new ventures.

- The practice of strategic entrepreneurship by all types of firms, large and small, new and more established, creates value for all stakeholders, especially for shareholders and customers. Strategic entrepreneurship also contributes to the economic development of entire nations.

Review Questions

1. What is strategic entrepreneurship? What is its importance for firms competing in the global economy?

2. What are entrepreneurial opportunities, innovation, and entrepreneurial capabilities, and what is their importance?

3. What is international entrepreneurship and why is it increasingly being used in the global economy?

4. What is autonomous strategic behavior? What is induced strategic behavior?

5. How do firms use cooperative strategies such as strategic alliances to help them produce innovation?

6. How can a firm use acquisitions to increase the number of innovations it produces and improve its capability to produce innovations?

7. What is the importance of venture capital and initial public offerings to entrepreneurial activity?

8. How does strategic entrepreneurship create value for stakeholders and contribute to economic development?

Experiential Exercises

Strategic Entrepreneurship

Assume that you are a partner in a new venture energy company called Currence. You have approached an investor group for capital to fund the first three years of your operation. Following the preliminary presentation, you find that the group is very impressed by Currence and by its six start-up partners, each of whom brings unique, yet critical skills, experience, contacts, and other knowledge to the venture. Before the investor group decides to fund your company, however, it has asked for a brief presentation about how the Currence partners will be rewarded.

Part 1 (complete individually). Indicate how Currence will determine the approximate salary, fringe benefits, and shares of stock (as a percentage) each partner will be allocated upon closing the financing of your new venture. Also indicate your rationale for these amounts.

Part 2 (in small groups). Compare your responses to Part 1 with others in your small group. Reach a consensus on the criteria your small group would use to determine how to

reward each partner. Appoint one small group member to present your consensus and how your team reached it to the class.

Part 3 (in small groups). Following the presentations in Part 2, discuss the following issues and indicate any important lessons and implications:

1. Why would an entrepreneurial venture such as Currence be asked to provide this type of information to an investor group?

2. What criteria did the groups use concerning salaries and stock? Why?

3. What patterns did you perceive in the approaches taken by each team?

4. Did the groups make salaries or stock equal for all Currence partners? Why or why not? What reasons would there be for providing different rewards for different partners?

5. How difficult was it for the small groups to reach a consensus?

Entrepreneurial Culture

One of your responsibilities as an entrepreneurial leader is to build shared values that will support entrepreneurial behavior. Describe the steps that you would follow to build an entrepreneurial culture.

Option A: Take the perspective of a manager within a large corporation who has just been given responsibility to lead a newly acquired business unit that has an innovative product. Prepare a report for the top management team that describes the steps you will take. Provide a brief rationale for your recommendations.

Option B: Take the perspective of an entrepreneur who has personally developed an innovation and is establishing a new start-up to produce and market the innovation. Prepare a report for investors about how you plan to build an entrepreneurial culture so that the investors will be willing to provide financial resources for your venture. Explain how your efforts to build an entrepreneurial culture will lead to strategic competitiveness.

Notes

1. R. G. Holcombe, 2003, The origins of entrepreneurial opportunities, *Review of Austrian Economics*, 16: 25–54; C. M. Daily, P. P. McDougall, J. G. Covin, & D. R. Dalton, 2002, Governance and strategic leadership in entrepreneurial firms, *Journal of Management*, 28: 387–412.

2. S. Thomke, 2003, R&D comes to services, *Harvard Business Review*, 81(4): 70–79.

3. R. D. Ireland, M. A. Hitt, & D. G. Sirmon, 2003, A model of strategic entrepreneurship: The construct and its dimensions, *Journal of Management*, in press.

4. M. A. Hitt, R. D. Ireland, S. M. Camp, & D. L. Sexton, 2002, Strategic entrepreneurship: Integrating entrepreneurial and strategic management perspectives, in M. A. Hitt, R. D. Ireland, S. M. Camp, & D. L. Sexton (eds.), *Strategic Entrepreneurship: Creating a New Mindset*, Oxford, UK: Blackwell Publishers, 1–16; M. A. Hitt, R. D. Ireland, S. M. Camp, & D. L. Sexton, 2001, Strategic entrepreneurship: Entrepreneurial strategies for wealth creation, *Strategic Management Journal*, 22(Special Issue): 479–491; R. D. Ireland, M. A. Hitt, S. M. Camp, & D. L. Sexton, 2001, Integrating entrepreneurship and strategic management actions to create firm wealth, *Academy of Management Executive*, 15(1): 49–63.

5. R. D. Ireland, D. F. Kuratko, & J. G. Covin, 2003, Antecedents, elements, and consequences of corporate entrepreneurship strategy, Working paper, University of Richmond.

6. B. Bowonder, J. J. Thomas, V. M. Rokkam, & A. Rokkam, 2003, The global pharmaceutical industry: Changing competitive landscape, *International Journal of Technology Management*, 25(3,4): 211–226; I. C. MacMillan, A. B. van Putten, & R. M. McGrath, 2003, Global gamesmanship, *Harvard Business Review*, 81(5): 62–71.

7. H. G. Barkema, J. A. C. Baum, & E. A. Mannix, 2002, Management challenges in a new time, *Academy of Management Journal*, 45: 916–930.

8. H. Lee, M. A. Hitt, & E. K. Jeong, 2003, The impact of CEO and TMT characteristics on strategic flexibility and firm performance, Working paper, Texas A&M University.

9. G. Hamel, 2000, *Leading the Revolution*, Boston, MA: Harvard Business School Press.

10. S. Michael, D. Storey, & H. Thomas, 2002, Discovery and coordination in strategic management and entrepreneurship, in M. A. Hitt, R. D. Ireland, S. M. Camp, & D. L. Sexton (eds.), *Strategic Entrepreneurship: Creating a New Mindset*, Oxford, UK: Blackwell Publishers, 45–65.

11. R. Katila & G. Ahuja, 2002, Something old, something new: A longitudinal study of search behavior and new product innovation, *Academy of Management Journal*, 45: 1183–1194.

12. T. W. Y. Man, T. Lau, & K. F. Chan, 2002, The competitiveness of small and medium enterprises: A conceptualization with focus on entrepreneurial competencies, *Journal of Business Venturing*, 17: 123–142.

13. R. E. Hoskisson, M. A. Hitt, R. A. Johnson, & W. Grossman, 2002, Conflicting voices: The effects of institutional ownership heterogeneity and internal governance on corporate innovation strategies, *Academy of Management Journal*, 45: 697–716.

14. J. Schumpeter, 1934, *The Theory of Economic Development*, Cambridge, MA: Harvard University Press.

15. S. Shane & S. Venkataraman, 2000, The promise of entrepreneurship as a field of research, *Academy of Management Review*, 25: 217–226.

16. E. Danneels, 2002, The dynamics of product innovation and firm competencies, *Strategic Management Journal*, 23: 1095–1121.

17. R. Katila, 2002, New product search over time: Past ideas in their prime? *Academy of Management Journal*, 45: 995–1010; B. R. Barringer & A. C. Bluedorn, 1999, The relationship between corporate entrepreneurship and strategic management, *Strategic Management Journal*, 20: 421–444.

18. J. L. Thompson, 2002, The world of the social entrepreneur, *The International Journal of Public Sector Management*, 15(4–5): 412–431.

19. G. D. Meyer, H. M. Neck, & M. D. Meeks, 2002, The entrepreneurship-strategic management interface, in M. A. Hitt, R. D. Ireland, S. M. Camp, & D. L. Sexton (eds.), *Strategic Entrepreneurship: Creating a New Mindset*, Oxford, UK: Blackwell Publishers, 19–44; I. Kirzner, 1997, Entrepreneurial discovery and the competitive market process: An Austrian approach, *Journal of Economic Literature*, 35(1): 60–85.

20. R. G. McGrath & I. MacMillan, 2000, *The Entrepreneurial Mindset*, Boston, MA: Harvard Business School Press.

21. T. M. Begley & D. P. Boyd, 2003, The need for a corporate global mind-set, *MIT Sloan Management Review*, 44(2): 25–32.

22. R. Kanaley, 2003, Advertising on bandages is just beginning for King of Prussia, Pa., firm, *The Philadelphia Inquirer*, April 28, B6.

23. C. W. L. Hill & F. T. Rothaermel, 2003, The performance of incumbent firms in the face of radical technological innovation, *Academy of Management Review*, 28: 257–274.

24. P. F. Drucker, 1998, The discipline of innovation, *Harvard Business Review*, 76(6): 149–157.

25. Ibid.

26. J. D. Wolpert, 2002, Breaking out of the innovation box, *Harvard Business Review*, 80(8): 77–83.

27. P. D. Reynolds, M. Hay, & S. M. Camp, 1999, *Global Entrepreneurship Monitor, 1999 Executive Report*, Babson Park, MA: Babson College.

28. J. E. Perry-Smith & C. E. Shalley, 2003, The social side of creativity: A static and dynamic social network perspective, *Academy of Management Review*, 28: 89–106.

29. R. Price, 1996, Technology and strategic advantage, *California Management Review*, 38(3): 38–56; L. G. Franko, 1989, Global corporate competition: Who's winning, who's losing and the R&D factor as one reason why, *Strategic Management Journal*, 10: 449–474.

30. J. W. Spencer, 2003, Firms' knowledge-sharing strategies in the global innovation system: Empirical evidence from the flat panel display industry, *Strategic Management Journal*, 24: 217–233; K. M. Kelm, V. K. Narayanan, &

G. E. Pinches, 1995, Shareholder value creation during R&D innovation and commercialization stages, *Academy of Management Journal*, 38: 770–786.

31. M. A. Hitt, R. D. Nixon, R. E. Hoskisson, & R. Kochhar, 1999, Corporate entrepreneurship and cross-functional fertilization: Activation, process and disintegration of a new product design team, *Entrepreneurship: Theory and Practice*, 23(3): 145–167.

32. J. P. O'Brien, 2003, The capital structure implications of pursuing a strategy of innovation, *Strategic Management Journal*, 24: 415–431.

33. Schumpeter, *The Theory of Economic Development.*

34. P. Sharma & J. L. Chrisman, 1999, Toward a reconciliation of the definitional issues in the field of corporate entrepreneurship, *Entrepreneurship: Theory and Practice*, 23(3): 11–27; R. A. Burgelman & L. R. Sayles, 1986, *Inside Corporate Innovation: Strategy, Structure, and Managerial Skills*, New York: Free Press.

35. R. E. Hoskisson & L. W. Busenitz, 2002, Market uncertainty and learning distance in corporate entrepreneurship entry mode choice, in M. A. Hitt, R. D. Ireland, S. M. Camp, & D. L. Sexton (eds.), *Strategic Entrepreneurship: Creating a New Mindset*, Oxford, UK: Blackwell Publishers, 151–172.

36. D. Somaya, 2003, Strategic determinants of decisions not to settle patent litigation, *Strategic Management Journal*, 24: 17–38.

37. G. G. Dess, R. D. Ireland, S. A. Zahra, S. W. Floyd, J. J. Janney, & P. J. Lane, 2003, Emerging issues in corporate entrepreneurship, *Journal of Management*, 29: 351–378.

38. J. S. Hornsby, D. F. Kuratko, & S. A. Zahra, 2002, Middle managers' perception of the internal environment for corporate entrepreneurship: Assessing a measurement scale, *Journal of Business Venturing*, 17: 253–273.

39. S. D. Sarasvathy, 2000, Seminar on research perspectives in entrepreneurship (1997), *Journal of Business Venturing*, 15: 1–57.

40. R. Grover, D. Foust, & B. Elgin, 2003, From media mogul to web warlord, *Business Week*, May 19, 46.

41. D. F. Kuratko, R. D. Ireland, & J. S. Hornsby, 2001, Improving firm performance through entrepreneurial actions: Acordia's corporate entrepreneurship strategy, *Academy of Management Executive*, 15(4): 60–71; J. Birkinshaw, 1999, The determinants and consequences of subsidiary initiative in multinational corporations, *Entrepreneurship: Theory and Practice*, 24(1): 9–36.

42. W. S. Mossberg, 2003, Apple's iPod just keeps getting better as top digital play, *Wall Street Journal*, Eastern edition, May 1, B1.

43. Ibid.

44. 2003, Apple Computer Inc.: In first week, iTunes web site sells over one million songs, *Wall Street Journal*, Eastern edition, May 6, C9.

45. S. Godin, 2003, What did you do during the 2000s? *Fast Company*, June, 70.

46. W. Tsai, 2001, Knowledge transfer in intraorganizational networks: Effects of network position and absorptive capacity on business unit innovation and performance, *Academy of Management Journal*, 44: 996–1004.

47. S. A. Zahra & G. George, 2002, Absorptive capacity: A review, reconceptualization, and extension, *Academy of Management Review*, 27: 185–203.

48. M. A. Hitt, L. Bierman, K. Shimizu, & R. Kochhar, 2001, Direct and moderating effects of human capital on strategy and performance in professional service firms: A resource-based perspective, *Academy of Management Journal*, 44: 13–28.

49. R. Belderbos, 2003, Entry mode, organizational learning, and R&D in foreign affiliates: Evidence from Japanese firms, *Strategic Management Journal*, 24: 235–259; I. Bouty, 2000, Interpersonal and interaction influences on informal resource exchanges between R&D researchers across organizational boundaries, *Academy of Management Journal*, 43: 5–65.

50. 2001, Some like it hot, *Entrepreneur.com*, October 30.

51. C. G. Brush, L. F. Edelman, & P. G. Greene, 2002, Internationalization of small firms: Personal factors revisited, *International Small Business Journal*, 20(1): 9–31; J. W. Lu & P. W. Beamish, 2001, The internationalization and performance of SMEs, *Strategic Management Journal*, 22(Special Issue): 565–585.

52. L. Tihanyi, R. A. Johnson, R. E. Hoskisson, & M. A. Hitt, 2003, Institutional ownership differences and international diversification: The effects of boards of directors and technological opportunity, *Academy of Management Journal*, 46: 195–211.

53. A. E. Ellstrand, L. Tihanyi, & J. L. Johnson, 2002, Board structure and international political risk, *Academy of Management Journal*, 45: 769–777.

54. D. Farrell, H. Fassbender, T. Kneip, S. Kriesel, & E. Labaye, 2003, Reviving French and German productivity, *The McKinsey Quarterly*, Number One, 40–53.

55. 2000, Business innovation urged, *Irish Times*, February 9, 23.

56. P. D. Reynolds, S. M. Camp, W. D. Bygrave, E. Autio, & M. Hay, 2002, *Global Entrepreneurship Monitor*, Kauffman Center for Entrepreneurial Leadership, Ewing Marion Kauffman Foundation.

57. M. H. Morris, 1998, *Entrepreneurial Intensity: Sustainable Advantages for Individuals, Organizations, and Societies*, Westport, CT: Quorum Books, 85–86.

58. S. A. Zahra & G. George, 2002, International entrepreneurship: The state of the field and future research agenda, in M. A. Hitt, R. D. Ireland, S. M. Camp, & D. L. Sexton (eds.), *Strategic Entrepreneurship: Creating a New Mindset*, Oxford, UK: Blackwell Publishers, 255–288.

59. S. A. Zahra, R. D. Ireland, & M. A. Hitt, 2000, International expansion by new venture firms: International diversity, mode of market entry, technological learning and performance, *Academy of Management Journal*, 43: 925–950.

60. P. P. McDougall & B. M. Oviatt, 2000, International entrepreneurship: The intersection of two paths, *Academy of Management Journal*, 43: 902–908.

61. A. Yan, G. Zhu, & D. T. Hall, 2002, International assignments for career building: A model of agency relationships and psychological contracts, *Academy of Management Review*, 27: 373–391.

62. H. Barkema & O. Chvyrkov, 2002, What sort of top management team is needed at the helm of internationally diversified firms? in M. A. Hitt, R. D. Ireland, S. M. Camp, & D. L. Sexton (eds.), *Strategic Entrepreneurship: Creating a New Mindset*, Oxford, UK: Blackwell Publishers, 290–305.

63. T. S. Frost, 2001, The geographic sources of foreign subsidiaries' innovations, *Strategic Management Journal*, 22: 101–122.

64. E. W. K. Tsang, 2002, Learning from overseas venturing experience: The case of Chinese family businesses, *Journal of Business Venturing*, 17: 21–40.

65. W. Kuemmerle, 2002, Home base and knowledge management in international ventures, *Journal of Business Venturing*, 17: 99–122.

66. C. D. Charitou & C. C. Markides, 2003, Responses to disruptive strategic innovation, *MIT Sloan Management Review*, 44(2): 55–63; R. Leifer, G. Colarelli, & M. Rice, 2001, Implementing radical innovation in mature firms: The role of hubs, *Academy of Management Executive*, 15(3): 102–113.

67. P. M. Lee & H. M. O'Neill, 2003, Ownership structures and R&D investments of U.S. and Japanese firms: Agency and stewardship perspectives, *Academy of Management Journal*, 46: 212–225.

68. G. Ahuja & M. Lampert, 2001, Entrepreneurship in the large corporation: A longitudinal study of how established firms create breakthrough inventions, *Strategic Management Journal*, 22(Special Issue): 521–543.

69. M. J. Benner & M. L. Tushman, 2003, Exploitation, exploration, and process management: The productivity dilemma revisited, *Academy of Management Review*, 28: 238–256.

70. J. E. Ashton, F. X. Cook, Jr., & P. Schmitz, 2003, Uncovering hidden value in a midsize manufacturing company, *Harvard Business Review*, 81(6): 111–119; L. Fleming & O. Sorenson, 2003, Navigating the technology landscape of innovation, *MIT Sloan Management Review*, 44(2): 15–23.

71. J. Goldenberg, R. Horowitz, A. Levav, & D. Mazursky, 2003, Finding your innovation sweet spot, *Harvard Business Review*, 81(3): 120–129.

72. G. C. O'Connor, R. Hendricks, & M. P. Rice, 2002, Assessing transition readiness for radical innovation, *Research Technology Management*, 45(6): 50–56.

73. R. I. Sutton, 2002, Weird ideas that spark innovation, *MIT Sloan Management Review*, 43(2): 83–87.

74. K. G. Smith & D. Di Gregorio, 2002, Bisociation, discovery, and the role of entrepreneurial action, in M. A. Hitt, R. D. Ireland, S. M. Camp, & D. L. Sexton (eds.), *Strategic Entrepreneurship: Creating a New Mindset*, Oxford, UK: Blackwell Publishers, 129–150.

75. Hoskisson & Busenitz, Market uncertainty and learning distance.

76. R. A. Burgelman, 1995, *Strategic Management of Technology and Innovation*, Boston: Irwin.

77. S. K. Markham, 2002, Moving technologies from lab to market, *Research Technology Management*, 45(6): 31–42.

78. T. H. Davenport, L. Prusak, & H. J. Wilson, 2003, Who's bringing you hot ideas and how are you responding? *Harvard Business Review*, 81(2): 58–64.

79. M. A. Hitt, R. D. Ireland, & H. Lee, 2000, Technological learning, knowledge management, firm growth and performance, *Journal of Engineering and*

Technology Management, 17: 231–246; D. Leonard-Barton, 1995, Well-springs of Knowledge: Building and Sustaining the Sources of Innovation, Cambridge, MA: Harvard Business School Press.

80. S. S. Rao, 2000, General Electric, software vendor, Forbes, January 24, 144–146.

81. H. W. Chesbrough, 2002, Making sense of corporate venture capital, Harvard Business Review, 80(3): 90–99.

82. M. Subramaniam & N. Venkatraman, 2001, Determinants of transnational new product development capability: Testing the influence of transferring and deploying tacit overseas knowledge, Strategic Management Journal, 22: 359–378.

83. M. Song & M. M. Montoya-Weiss, 2001, The effect of perceived technological uncertainty on Japanese new product development, Academy of Management Journal, 44: 61–80.

84. J. Turrettini, 2003, Beware of cat, Forbes, June 9, 164–168.

85. McGrath and MacMillan, Entrepreneurial Mindset.

86. 2002, Building scientific networks for effective innovation, MIT Sloan Management Review, 43(3): 14.

87. C. M. Christensen & M. Overdorf, 2000, Meeting the challenge of disruptive change, Harvard Business Review, 78(2): 66–77.

88. L. Yu, 2002, Marketers and engineers: Why can't we just get along? MIT Sloan Management Review, 43(1):13.

89. P. S. Adler, 1995, Interdepartmental interdependence and coordination: The case of the design/manufacturing interface, Organization Science, 6: 147–167.

90. I. Royer, 2003, Why bad projects are so hard to kill, Harvard Business Review, 81(2): 48–56.

91. B. L. Kirkman & B. Rosen, 1999, Beyond self-management: Antecedents and consequences of team empowerment, Academy of Management Journal, 42: 58–74; A. R. Jassawalla & H. C. Sashittal, 1999, Building collaborative cross-functional new product teams, Academy of Management Executive, 13(3): 50–63.

92. Hitt, Nixon, Hoskisson, & Kochhar, Corporate entrepreneurship.

93. Christensen & Overdorf, Meeting the challenge of disruptive change.

94. Hitt, Nixon, Hoskisson, & Kochhar, Corporate entrepreneurship.

95. A. C. Amason, 1996, Distinguishing the effects of functional and dysfunctional conflict on strategic decision making: Resolving a paradox for top management teams, Academy of Management Journal, 39: 123–148; P. R. Lawrence & J. W. Lorsch, 1969, Organization and Environment, Homewood, IL: Richard D. Irwin.

96. D. Dougherty, L. Borrelli, K. Muncir, & A. O'Sullivan, 2000, Systems of organizational sensemaking for sustained product innovation, Journal of Engineering and Technology Management, 17: 321–355; D. Dougherty, 1992, Interpretive barriers to successful product innovation in large firms, Organization Science, 3: 179–202.

97. Hitt, Nixon, Hoskisson, & Kochhar, Corporate entrepreneurship.

98. E. C. Wenger & W. M. Snyder, 2000, Communities of practice: The organizational frontier, Harvard Business Review, 78(1): 139–144.

99. Hamel, Leading the Revolution.

100. McGrath & MacMillan, Entrepreneurial Mindset.

101. Hamel, Leading the Revolution.

102. Hitt, Ireland, Camp, & Sexton, Strategic entrepreneurship; S. W. Fowler, A. W. King, S. J. Marsh, & B. Victor, 2000, Beyond products: New strategic imperatives for developing competencies in dynamic environments, Journal of Engineering and Technology Management, 17: 357–377.

103. R. K. Kazanjian, R. Drazin, & M. A. Glynn, 2002, Implementing strategies for corporate entrepreneurship: A knowledge-based perspective, in M. A. Hitt, R. D. Ireland, S. M. Camp, & D. L. Sexton (eds.), Strategic Entrepreneurship: Creating a New Mindset, Oxford, UK: Blackwell Publishers, 173–199.

104. R. Gulati & M. C. Higgins, 2003, Which ties matter when? The contingent effects of interorganizational partnerships on IPO success, Strategic Management Journal, 24: 127–144.

105. A. C. Cooper, 2002, Networks, alliances and entrepreneurship, in M. A. Hitt, R. D. Ireland, S. M. Camp, & D. L. Sexton (eds.), Strategic Entrepreneurship: Creating a New Mindset, Oxford, UK: Blackwell Publishers, 204–222.

106. S. A. Alvarez & J. B. Barney, 2001, How entrepreneurial firms can benefit from alliances with large partners, Academy of Management Executive, 15(1): 139–148; F. T. Rothaermel, 2001, Incumbent's advantage through exploiting complementary assets via interfirm cooperation, Strategic Management Journal, 22(Special Issue): 687–699.

107. J. Hagedoorn & N. Roijakkers, 2002, Small entrepreneurial firms and large companies in inter-firm R&D networks—the international biotechnology industry, in M. A. Hitt, R. D. Ireland, S. M. Camp, & D. L. Sexton (eds.), Strategic Entrepreneurship: Creating a New Mindset, Oxford, UK: Blackwell Publishers, 223–252.

108. D. Kline, 2003, Sharing the corporate crown jewels, MIT Sloan Management Review, 44(3): 89–93.

109. H. Yli-Renko, E. Autio, & H. J. Sapienza, 2001, Social capital, knowledge acquisition and knowledge exploitation in young technology-based firms, Strategic Management Journal, 22(Special Issue): 587–613.

110. C. Lee, K. Lee, & J. M. Pennings, 2001, Internal capabilities, external networks and performance: A study of technology-based ventures, Strategic Management Journal, 22(Special Issue): 615–640.

111. A. Takeishi, 2001, Bridging inter- and intra-firm boundaries: Management of supplier involvement in automobile product development, Strategic Management Journal, 22: 403–433.

112. R. D. Ireland, M. A. Hitt, & D. Vaidyanath, 2002, Strategic alliances as a pathway to competitive success, Journal of Management, 28: 413–446.

113. M. A. Hitt, M. T. Dacin, E. Levitas, J.-L. Arregle, & A. Borza, 2000, Partner selection in emerging and developed market contexts: Resource-based and organizational learning perspectives, Academy of Management Journal, 43: 449–467.

114. J. J. Reuer, M. Zollo, & H. Singh, 2002, Post-formation dynamics in strategic alliances, Strategic Management Journal, 23: 135–151.

115. F. Rothaermel & D. Deeds, 2002, More good things are not always necessarily better: An empirical study of strategic alliances, experience effects, and new product development in high-technology start-ups, in M. A. Hitt, R. Amit, C. Lucier, & R. Nixon (eds.), Creating Value: Winners in the New Business Environment, Oxford, UK: Blackwell Publishers, 85–103.

116. M. A. Hitt, R. E. Hoskisson, R. A. Johnson, & D. D. Moesel, 1996, The market for corporate control and firm innovation, Academy of Management Journal, 39: 1084–1119.

117. M. A. Hitt, J. S. Harrison, & R. D. Ireland, 2001, Mergers and Acquisitions: A Guide to Creating Value for Stakeholders, New York: Oxford University Press.

118. J. A. Timmons, 1999, New Venture Creation: Entrepreneurship for the 21st Century, 5th ed., New York: Irwin/McGraw-Hill.

119. L. Stern, 2003, VCs open the wallets, Newsweek, April 21, E2.

120. C. M. Mason & R. T. Harrison, 2002, Is it worth it? The rates of return from informal venture capital investments, Journal of Business Venturing, 17: 211–236.

121. M. A. Zimmerman & G. J. Zeitz, 2002, Beyond survival: Achieving new venture growth by building legitimacy, Academy of Management Review, 27: 414–431.

122. D. A. Shepherd & A. Zacharakis, 2002, Venture capitalists' expertise: A call for research into decision aids and cognitive feedback, Journal of Business Venturing, 17: 1–20.

123. S. Manigart, K. de Waele, M. Wright, K. Robbie, P. Desbrieres, H. J. Sapienza, & A. Beekman, 2002, Determinants of required return in venture capital investments: A five-country study, Journal of Business Venturing, 17: 291–312.

124. M. Maula & G. Murray, 2002, Corporate venture capital and the creation of U.S. public companies: The impact of sources of capital on the performance of portfolio companies, in M. A. Hitt, R. Amit, C. Lucier, & R. Nixon (eds.), Creating Value: Winners in the New Business Environment, Oxford, UK: Blackwell Publishers, 164–187.

125. S. T. Certo, J. G. Covin, C. M. Daily, & D. R. Dalton, 2001, Wealth and the effects of founder management among IPO-stage new ventures, Strategic Management Journal, 22(Special Issue): 641–658.

126. L. DeCarlo, 2002, JetBlue IPO will fly right for investors, Forbes, http://www.forbes.com, February, 13.

127. Maula & Murray, Corporate venture capital.

128. Ireland, Hitt, & Sirmon, A model of strategic entrepreneurship.
129. Ibid.
130. Hitt, Ireland, Camp, & Sexton, Strategic entrepreneurship.
131. M. Halkias, 2003, Blockbuster seeking new ventures, *Dallas Morning News*, May 21, D2.
132. D. G. Sirmon, M. A. Hitt, & R. D. Ireland, 2003, Dynamically managing firm resources for competitive advantage: Creating value for stakeholders. Paper presented at the Academy of Management meeting, Seattle, August.
133. Hitt, Bierman, Shimizu, & Kochhar, Direct and moderating effects of human capital.
134. M. A. Hitt, H. Lee, & E. Yucel, 2002, The importance of social capital to the management of multinational enterprises: Relational networks among Asian and Western firms, *Asia Pacific Journal of Management*, 19: 353–372.
135. M. A. Hitt, R. E. Hoskisson, & H. Kim, 1997, International diversification: Effects on innovation and firm performance in product diversified firms, *Academy of Management Journal*, 40: 767–798.
136. M. A. Hitt & R. D. Ireland, 2002, The essence of strategic leadership: Managing human and social capital, *Journal of Leadership and Organization Studies*, 9(1): 3–14.
137. R. Garud, S. Jain, & A. Kumaraswamy, 2002, Institutional entrepreneurship in the sponsorship of common technological standards: The case of Sun Microsystems and JAVA, *Academy of Management Journal*, 45: 196–214.
138. Reynolds, Camp, Bygrave, Autio, & Hay, *Global Entrepreneurship Monitor.*
139. Hitt, Ireland, Camp, & Sexton, Strategic entrepreneurship.

Case Studies

Preparing an Effective Case Analysis

introduction

In most strategic management courses, cases are used extensively as a teaching tool.[1] A key reason is that cases provide active learners with opportunities to use the strategic management process to identify and solve organizational problems. Thus, by analyzing situations that are described in cases and presenting the results, active learners (i.e., students) become skilled at effectively using the tools, techniques, and concepts that combine to form the strategic management process.

The cases that follow are concerned with actual companies. Presented within the cases are problems and situations that managers and those with whom they work must analyze and resolve. As you will see, a strategic management case can focus on an entire industry, a single organization, or a business unit of a large, diversified firm. The strategic management issues facing not-for-profit organizations also can be examined using the case analysis method.

Basically, the case analysis method calls for a careful diagnosis of an organization's current conditions (as manifested by its external and internal environments) so that appropriate strategic actions can be recommended in light of the firm's strategic intent and strategic mission. Strategic actions are taken to develop and then use a firm's core competencies to select and implement different strategies, including business-level, corporate-level, acquisition and restructuring, international, and cooperative strategies. Thus, appropriate strategic actions help the firm to survive in the long run as it creates and uses competitive advantages as the foundation for achieving strategic competitiveness and earning above-average returns. The case method that we are recommending to you has a rich heritage as a pedagogical approach to the study and understanding of managerial effectiveness.[2]

As an active learner, your preparation is critical to successful use of the case analysis method. Without careful study and analysis, active learners lack the insights required to participate fully in the discussion of a firm's situation and the strategic actions that are appropriate.

Instructors adopt different approaches in their application of the case analysis method. Some require active learners/students to use a specific analytical procedure to examine an organization; others provide less structure, expecting students to learn by developing their own unique analytical method. Still other instructors believe that a moderately structured framework should be used to analyze a firm's situation and make appropriate recommendations. Your professor will determine the specific approach you take. The approach we are presenting to you is a moderately structured framework.

We divide our discussion of a moderately structured case analysis method framework into four sections. First, we describe the importance of understanding the skills active learners can acquire through effective use of the case analysis method. In the second section, we provide you with a process-oriented framework. This framework can be of value in your efforts to analyze cases and then present the results of your work. Using this framework in a classroom setting yields valuable experiences that can, in turn, help you successfully complete assignments that you will receive from your employer. The third section is where we describe briefly what you can expect to occur during in-class case discussions. As this description shows, the relationship and interactions between instructors and active learners/students during case discussions are different than they are during lectures. In the final section, we present a moderately structured framework that we believe can help you prepare effective oral and written presentations. Written and oral communication skills also are valued highly in many organizational settings; hence, their development today can serve you well in the future.

Skills Gained Through Use of the Case Analysis Method

The case analysis method is based on a philosophy that combines knowledge acquisition with significant involvement from students as active learners. In the words of Alfred North Whitehead, this philosophy "rejects the doctrine that students had first learned passively, and then, having learned should apply knowledge."[3] In contrast to this philosophy, the case analysis method is based on principles that were elaborated upon by John Dewey:

> Only by wrestling with the conditions of this problem at hand, seeking and finding his own way out, does [the student] think. . . . If he cannot devise his own solution (not, of course, in isolation, but in correspondence with the teacher and other pupils) and find his own way out he will not learn, not even if he can recite some correct answer with a hundred percent accuracy.[4]

The case analysis method brings reality into the classroom. When developed and presented effectively, with rich and interesting detail, cases keep conceptual discussions grounded in reality. Experience shows that simple fictional accounts of situations and collections of actual organizational data and articles from public sources are not as effective for learning as fully developed cases. A comprehensive case presents you with a partial clinical study of a real-life situation that faced managers as well as other stakeholders including employees. A case presented in narrative form provides motivation for involvement with and analysis of a specific situation. By framing alternative strategic actions and by confronting the complexity and ambiguity of the practical world, case analysis provides extraordinary power for your involvement with a personal learning experience. Some of the potential consequences of using the case method are summarized in Exhibit 1.

As Exhibit 1 suggests, the case analysis method can assist active learners in the development of their analytical and judgment skills. Case analysis also helps you learn how to ask the right questions. By this we mean questions that focus on the core strategic issues that are included in a case. Active learners/students with managerial aspirations can improve their ability to identify underlying problems rather than focusing on superficial symptoms as they develop skills at asking probing yet appropriate questions.

The collection of cases your instructor chooses to assign can expose you to a wide variety of organizations and decision situations. This approach vicariously broadens your experience base and provides insights into many types of managerial situations, tasks, and responsibilities. Such indirect experience can help you make a more informed career decision about the industry and managerial situation you believe will prove to be challenging and satisfying. Finally, experience in analyzing cases definitely enhances your problem-solving skills, and research indicates that the case method for this class is better than the lecture method.[5]

Furthermore, when your instructor requires oral and written presentations, your communication skills will be honed through use of the case method. Of course, these added skills depend on your preparation as well as your instructor's facilitation of learning. However, the primary responsibility for learning is yours. The quality of case discussion is generally acknowledged to require, at a minimum, a thorough mastery of case facts and some independent analysis of them. The case method therefore first requires that you read and think carefully about each case. Additional comments about the preparation you should complete to successfully discuss a case appear in the next section.

Exhibit 1   Consequences of Student Involvement with the Case Method

1. Case analysis requires students to practice important managerial skills—diagnosing, making decisions, observing, listening, and persuading—while preparing for a case discussion.

2. Cases require students to relate analysis and action, to develop realistic and concrete actions despite the complexity and partial knowledge characterizing the situation being studied.

3. Students must confront the *intractability of reality*—complete with absence of needed information, an imbalance between needs and available resources, and conflicts among competing objectives.

4. Students develop a general managerial point of view—where responsibility is sensitive to action in a diverse environmental context.

Source: 1993, C. C. Lundberg and C. Enz, A framework for student case preparation, *Case Research Journal,* 13 (Summer): 134.

STUDENT PREPARATION FOR CASE DISCUSSION

If you are inexperienced with the case method, you may need to alter your study habits. A lecture-oriented course may not require you to do intensive preparation for *each* class period. In such a course, you have the latitude to work through assigned readings and review lecture notes according to your own schedule. However, an assigned case requires significant and conscientious *preparation before class*. Without it, you will be unable to contribute meaningfully to in-class discussion. Therefore, careful reading and thinking about case facts, as well as reasoned analyses and the development of alternative solutions to case problems, are essential. Recommended alternatives should flow logically from core problems

identified through study of the case. Exhibit 2 shows a set of steps that can help you familiarize yourself with a case, identify problems, and propose strategic actions that increase the probability that a firm will achieve strategic competitiveness and earn above-average returns.

GAINING FAMILIARITY

The first step of an effective case analysis process calls for you to become familiar with the facts featured in the case and the focal firm's situation. Initially, you should become familiar with the focal firm's general situation (e.g., who, what, how, where, and when). Thorough familiarization demands appreciation of the nuances as well as the major issues in the case.

Gaining familiarity with a situation requires you to study several situational levels, including interactions

	An Effective Case Analysis Process **EXHIBIT 2**
Step 1: *Gaining Familiarity*	a. In general—determine who, what, how, where, and when (the critical facts of the case).
	b. In detail—identify the places, persons, activities, and contexts of the situation.
	c. Recognize the degree of certainty/uncertainty of acquired information.
Step 2: *Recognizing Symptoms*	a. List all indicators (including stated "problems") that something is not as expected or as desired.
	b. Ensure that symptoms are not assumed to be the problem (symptoms should lead to identification of the problem).
Step 3: *Identifying Goals*	a. Identify critical statements by major parties (e.g., people, groups, the work unit, etc.).
	b. List all goals of the major parties that exist or can be reasonably inferred.
Step 4: *Conducting the Analysis*	a. Decide which ideas, models, and theories seem useful.
	b. Apply these conceptual tools to the situation.
	c. As new information is revealed, cycle back to substeps a and b.
Step 5: *Making the Diagnosis*	a. Identify predicaments (goal inconsistencies).
	b. Identify problems (discrepancies between goals and performance).
	c. Prioritize predicaments/problems regarding timing, importance, etc.
Step 6: *Doing the Action Planning*	a. Specify and prioritize the criteria used to choose action alternatives.
	b. Discover or invent feasible action alternatives.
	c. Examine the probable consequences of action alternatives.
	d. Select a course of action.
	e. Design an implementation plan/schedule.
	f. Create a plan for assessing the action to be implemented.

Source: 1993, C. C. Lundberg and C. Enz, A framework for student case preparation, *Case Research Journal*, 13 (Summer): 144.

between and among individuals within groups, business units, the corporate office, the local community, and the society at large. Recognizing relationships within and among levels facilitates a more thorough understanding of the specific case situation.

It is also important that you evaluate information on a continuum of certainty. Information that is verifiable by several sources and judged along similar dimensions can be classified as a *fact*. Information representing someone's perceptual judgment of a particular situation is referred to as an *inference*. Information gleaned from a situation that is not verifiable is classified as *speculation*. Finally, information that is independent of verifiable sources and arises through individual or group discussion is an *assumption*. Obviously, case analysts and organizational decision makers prefer having access to facts over inferences, speculations, and assumptions.

Personal feelings, judgments, and opinions evolve when you are analyzing a case. It is important to be aware of your own feelings about the case and to evaluate the accuracy of perceived "facts" to ensure that the objectivity of your work is maximized.

RECOGNIZING SYMPTOMS

Recognition of symptoms is the second step of an effective case analysis process. A symptom is an indication that something is not as you or someone else thinks it should be. You may be tempted to correct the symptoms instead of searching for true problems. True problems are the conditions or situations requiring solution before the performance of an organization, business unit, or individual can improve. Identifying and listing symptoms early in the case analysis process tends to reduce the temptation to label symptoms as problems. The focus of your analysis should be on the *actual causes* of a problem, rather than on its symptoms. Thus, it is important to remember that symptoms are indicators of problems; subsequent work facilitates discovery of critical causes of problems that your case recommendations must address.

IDENTIFYING GOALS

The third step of effective case analysis calls for you to identify the goals of the major organizations, business units, and/or individuals in a case. As appropriate, you should also identify each firm's strategic intent and strategic mission. Typically, these direction-setting statements (goals, strategic intents, and strategic missions) are derived from comments made by central characters in the organization, business unit, or top management team as described in the case and/or from public documents (e.g., an annual report).

Completing this step successfully sometimes can be difficult. Nonetheless, the outcomes you attain from this step are essential to an effective case analysis because identifying goals, intent, and mission helps you to clarify the major problems featured in a case and to evaluate alternative solutions to those problems. Direction-setting statements are not always stated publicly or prepared in written format. When this occurs, you must infer goals from other available factual data and information.

CONDUCTING THE ANALYSIS

The fourth step of effective case analysis is concerned with acquiring a systematic understanding of a situation. Occasionally cases are analyzed in a less-than-thorough manner. Such analyses may be a product of a busy schedule or the difficulty and complexity of the issues described in a particular case. Sometimes you will face pressures on your limited amounts of time and may believe that you can understand the situation described in a case without systematic analysis of all the facts. However, experience shows that familiarity with a case's facts is a necessary, but insufficient, step in the development of effective solutions—solutions that can enhance a firm's strategic competitiveness. In fact, a less-than-thorough analysis typically results in an emphasis on symptoms, rather than problems and their causes. To analyze a case effectively, you should be skeptical of quick or easy approaches and answers.

A systematic analysis helps you understand a situation and determine what can work and probably what will not work. Key linkages and underlying causal networks based on the history of the firm become apparent. In this way, you can separate causal networks from symptoms.

Also, because the quality of a case analysis depends on applying appropriate tools, it is important that you use the ideas, models, and theories that seem to be useful for evaluating and solving individual and unique situations. As you consider facts and symptoms, a useful theory may become apparent. Of course, having familiarity with conceptual models may be important in the effective analysis of a situation. Successful students and successful organizational strategists add to their intellectual tool kits on a continual basis.

MAKING THE DIAGNOSIS

The fifth step of effective case analysis—diagnosis—is the process of identifying and clarifying the roots of the problems by comparing goals to facts. In this step, it is useful to search for predicaments. Predicaments are situations in which goals do not fit with known facts. When you evaluate the actual performance of an organization, business unit, or individual, you may identify over- or underachievement (relative to established goals). Of course, single-problem situations are rare. Accordingly, you should recognize that the case situations you study probably will be complex in nature.

Effective diagnosis requires you to determine the problems affecting longer term performance and those requiring immediate handling. Understanding these issues will aid your efforts to prioritize problems and predicaments, given available resources and existing constraints.

DOING THE ACTION PLANNING

The final step of an effective case analysis process is called action planning. Action planning is the process of identifying appropriate alternative actions. In the action planning step you select the criteria you will use to evaluate the identified alternatives. You may derive these criteria from the analyses; typically, they are related to key strategic situations facing the focal organization. Furthermore, it is important that you prioritize these criteria to ensure a rational and effective evaluation of alternative courses of action.

Typically, managers "satisfice" when selecting courses of action; that is, they find *acceptable* courses of action that meet most of the chosen evaluation criteria. A rule of thumb that has proved valuable to strategic decision makers is to select an alternative that leaves other plausible alternatives available if the one selected fails.

Once you have selected the best alternative, you must specify an implementation plan. Developing an implementation plan serves as a reality check on the feasibility of your alternatives. Thus, it is important that you give thoughtful consideration to all issues associated with the implementation of the selected alternatives.

WHAT TO EXPECT FROM IN-CLASS CASE DISCUSSIONS

Classroom discussions of cases differ significantly from lectures. The case method calls for instructors to guide the discussion, encourage student participation, and solicit alternative views. When alternative views are not forthcoming, instructors typically adopt one view so students can be challenged to respond to it thoughtfully. Often students' work is evaluated in terms of both the quantity and the quality of their contributions to in-class case discussions. Students benefit by having their views judged against those of their peers and by responding to challenges by other class members and/or the instructor.

During case discussions, instructors listen, question, and probe to extend the analysis of case issues. In the course of these actions, peers or the instructor may challenge an individual's views and the validity of alternative perspectives that have been expressed. These challenges are offered in a constructive manner; their

intent is to help students develop their analytical and communication skills. Instructors should encourage students to be innovative and original in the development and presentation of their ideas. Over the course of an individual discussion, students can develop a more complex view of the case, benefiting from the diverse inputs of their peers and instructor. Among other benefits, experience with multiple-case discussions should help students increase their knowledge of the advantages and disadvantages of group decision-making processes.

Student peers as well as the instructor value comments that contribute to the discussion. To offer *relevant* contributions, you are encouraged to use independent thought and, through discussions with your peers outside of class, to refine your thinking. We also encourage you to avoid using "I think," "I believe," and "I feel" to discuss your inputs to a case analysis process. Instead, consider using a less emotion-laden phrase, such as "My analysis shows." This highlights the logical nature of the approach you have taken to complete the six steps of an effective case analysis process.

When preparing for an in-class case discussion, you should plan to use the case data to explain your assessment of the situation. Assume that your peers and instructor know the case facts. In addition, it is good practice to prepare notes before class discussions and use them as you explain your view. Effective notes signal to classmates and the instructor that you are prepared to engage in a thorough discussion of a case. Moreover, thorough notes eliminate the need for you to memorize the facts and figures needed to discuss a case successfully.

The case analysis process just described can help you prepare to effectively discuss a case during class meetings. Adherence to this process results in consideration of the issues required to identify a focal firm's problems and to propose strategic actions through which the firm can increase the probability that it will achieve strategic competitiveness.

In some instances, your instructor may ask you to prepare either an oral or a written analysis of a particular case. Typically, such an assignment demands even more thorough study and analysis of the case contents. At your instructor's discretion, oral and written analyses may be completed by individuals or by groups of two or more people. The information and insights gained through completing the six steps shown in Exhibit 2 often are of value in the development of an oral or written analysis. However, when preparing an oral or written presentation, you must consider the overall framework in which your information and inputs will be presented. Such a framework is the focus of the next section.

PREPARING AN ORAL/WRITTEN CASE STRATEGIC PLAN

Experience shows that two types of thinking are necessary to develop an effective oral or written presentation (see Exhibit 3). The upper part of the model in Exhibit 3 outlines the *analysis* stage of case preparation.

In the analysis stage, you should first analyze the general external environmental issues affecting the firm. Next your environmental analysis should focus on the particular industry (or industries, in the case of a diversified company) in which a firm operates. Finally, you should examine the competitive environment of the focal firm. Through study of the three levels of the external environment, you will be able to identify a firm's opportunities and threats. Following the external environmental analysis is the analysis of the firm's internal environment, which results in the identification of the firm's strengths and weaknesses.

As noted in Exhibit 3, you must then change the focus from analysis to *synthesis*. Specifically, you must *synthesize* information gained from your analysis of the firm's internal and external environments. Synthesizing information allows you to generate alternatives that can resolve the significant problems or challenges facing the focal firm. Once you identify a best alternative, from an evaluation based on predetermined criteria and goals, you must explore implementation actions.

Exhibit 4 and Exhibit 5 outline the sections that should be included in either an oral or a written strategic plan presentation: introduction (strategic intent and mission), situation analysis, statements of strengths/weaknesses and opportunities/threats, strategy formulation, and implementation plan. These sections, which can be completed only through use of the two types of thinking featured in Exhibit 3, are described in the following discussion. Familiarity with the contents of this book's 13 chapters is helpful because the general outline

| EXHIBIT 3 | Types of Thinking in Case Preparation: Analysis and Synthesis |

ANALYSIS

External environment

General environment
Industry environment
Competitor environment

Internal environment

Statements of
strengths,
weaknesses,
opportunities,
and threats

Alternatives
Evaluations of alternatives
Implementation

SYNTHESIS

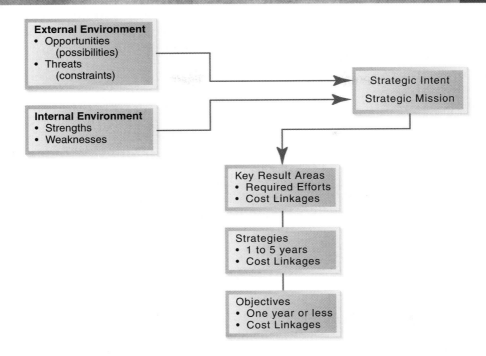

- *Strategic planning* is a *process* through which a firm determines what it seeks to accomplish and the actions required to achieve desired outcomes
  - ✓ *Strategic planning*, then, is a *process* that we use to determine *what* (outcomes to be reached) and *how* (actions to be taken to reach outcomes)
- The effective *strategic plan* for a firm would include statements and details about the following:
  - ✓ *Opportunities* (possibilities) and *threats* (constraints)
  - ✓ *Strengths* (what we do especially well) and *weaknesses* (deficiencies)
  - ✓ *Strategic intent* (an indication of a firm's ideal state)
  - ✓ *Strategic mission* (purpose and scope of a firm's operations in product and market terms)
  - ✓ *Key result areas* (KRAs) (categories of activities where efforts must take place to reach the mission and intent)
  - ✓ *Strategies* (actions for each KRA to be completed within one to five years)
  - ✓ *Objectives* (specific statements detailing actions for each strategy that are to be completed in one year or less)
  - ✓ *Cost linkages* (relationships between actions and financial resources)

for an oral or a written strategic plan shown in Exhibit 5 is based on an understanding of the strategic management process detailed in these chapters.

EXTERNAL ENVIRONMENT ANALYSIS

As shown in Exhibit 5, a general starting place for completing a situation analysis is the external environment. The *external environment* is composed of outside (external) conditions that affect a firm's performance. Your analysis of the environment should consider the effects of the *general environment* on the focal firm. Following that evaluation, you should analyze the *industry and competitor environmental* trends.

These trends or conditions in the external environment shape the firm's strategic intent and mission. The external environment analysis essentially indicates what a firm *might choose to do.* Often called an *environmental scan,* an analysis of the external environment allows a firm to identify key conditions that are beyond its direct control. The purpose of studying the external environment is to identify a firm's opportunities and threats. *Opportunities* are conditions in the external environment that appear to have the potential to contribute to a firm's success. In essence, opportunities represent *possibilities. Threats* are conditions in the external environment that appear to have the potential to prevent a firm's success. In essence, threats represent potential *constraints.*

When studying the external environment, the focus is on trying to *predict* the future (in terms of local, regional, and international trends and issues) and to *predict* the expected effects on a firm's operations. The external environment features conditions in the broader society *and* in the industry (area of competition) that influence the firm's possibilities and constraints. Areas to be considered (to identify opportunities and threats) when studying the general environment are listed in Exhibit 6. Many of these issues are explained more fully in Chapter 2.

Once you analyze the general environmental trends, you should study their effect on the focal industry. Often the same environmental trend may have a significantly different impact on separate industries. Furthermore, the same trend may affect firms within the same industry differently. For instance, with deregulation of the airline industry, older, established airlines had a significant decrease in profitability, while many smaller airlines such as Southwest Airlines, with lower cost structures and greater flexibility, were able to aggressively enter new markets.

Porter's five forces model is a useful tool for analyzing the specific industry (see Chapter 2). Careful study of how the five competitive forces (i.e., supplier power, buyer power, potential entrants, substitute products, and rivalry among competitors) affect a firm's strategy is important. These forces may create threats or opportunities relative to the specific business-level strategies (i.e., differentiation, cost leadership, focus) being implemented. Often a strategic group's analysis reveals how different environmental trends are affecting industry competitors. Strategic group analysis is useful for understanding the industry's competitive structures and firm constraints and possibilities within those structures.

Firms also need to analyze each of their primary competitors. This analysis should identify competitors' current strategies, strategic intent, strategic mission, capabilities, core competencies, and a competitive response profile. This information is useful to the focal firm in formulating an appropriate strategic intent and mission. Sources that can be used to gather information about a general environment, industry, and companies

with whom the focal firm competes are listed in Appendix I. Included in this list is a wide range of websites; publications, such as periodicals, newspapers, bibliographies, and directories of companies; industry ratios; forecasts; rankings/ratings; and other valuable statistics.

INTERNAL ENVIRONMENT ANALYSIS

The *internal environment* is composed of strengths and weaknesses internal to a firm that influence its strategic competitiveness. The purpose of completing an analysis of a firm's internal environment is to identify its strengths and weaknesses. The strengths and weaknesses in a firm's internal environment shape the strategic intent and strategic mission. The internal environment essentially indicates what a firm *can do.* Capabilities or skills that allow a firm to do something that others cannot do or that allow a firm to do something better than others do it are called strengths. *Strengths* can be categorized as something that a firm does especially well. Strengths help a firm take advantage of external opportunities or overcome external threats. Capabilities or skill deficiencies that prevent a firm from completing an important activity as well as others do it are called weaknesses. *Weaknesses* have the potential to prevent a firm from taking advantage of external opportunities or succeeding in efforts to overcome external threats. Thus, *weaknesses* can be thought of as something the firm needs to improve.

Analysis of the primary and support activities of the value chain provides opportunities to understand how external environmental trends affect the specific activities of a firm. Such analysis helps highlight strengths and weaknesses (see Chapter 3 for an explanation of the value chain). For purposes of preparing an oral or written presentation, it is important to note that strengths are internal resources and capabilities that have the potential to be core competencies. Weaknesses, on the other hand, have the potential to place a firm at a competitive disadvantage relative to its rivals.

When evaluating the internal characteristics of the firm, your analysis of the functional activities emphasized is critical. For instance, if the strategy of the firm is primarily technology-driven, it is important to evaluate the firm's R&D activities. If the strategy is market-driven, marketing functional activities are of paramount importance. If a firm has financial difficulties, critical financial ratios would require careful evaluation. In fact, because of the importance of financial health, most cases require financial analyses. Appendix II lists and operationally defines several common financial ratios. Included are exhibits describing profitability, liquidity, leverage, activity, and shareholders' return

Technology	• Information technology continues to become cheaper and have more practical applications
	• Database technology allows organization of complex data and distribution of information
	• Telecommunications technology and networks increasingly provide fast transmission of all sources of data, including voice, written communications, and video information
Demographic Trends	• Computerized design and manufacturing technologies continue to facilitate quality and flexibility
	• Regional changes in population due to migration
	• Changing ethnic composition of the population
	• Aging of the population
	• Aging of the "baby boom" generation
Economic Trends	• Interest rates
	• Inflation rates
	• Savings rates
	• Trade deficits
	• Budget deficits
	• Exchange rates
Political/Legal Environment	• Anti-trust enforcement
	• Tax policy changes
	• Environmental protection laws
	• Extent of regulation/deregulation
	• Developing countries privatizing state monopolies
	• State-owned industries
Sociocultural Environment	• Increasing number of women in the workforce
	• Awareness of health and fitness issues
	• Concern for the environment
	• Concern for customers
Global Environment	• Currency exchange rates
	• Free trade agreements
	• Trade deficits
	• New or developing markets

ratios. Other firm characteristics that should be examined to study the internal environment effectively include leadership, organizational culture, structure, and control systems.

IDENTIFICATION OF STRATEGIC INTENT AND MISSION

Strategic intent is associated with a mind-set that managers seek to imbue within the company. Essentially, a mind-set captures how we view the world and our intended role in it. Strategic intent reflects or identifies a firm's ideal state. Strategic intent flows from a firm's opportunities, threats, strengths, and weaknesses. However, the major influence on strategic intent is a firm's *strengths*. Strategic intent should reflect a firm's intended character and reflects a commitment to

"stretch" available resources and strengths in order to reach what may seem to be unattainable strategies and objectives in terms of key result areas (KRAs). When established effectively, strategic intent can cause each employee to perform in ways never imagined possible. Strategic intent has the ability to reflect what may be the most worthy goal of all: to unseat the best or to be the best on a regional, national, or even international basis. Examples of strategic intent include:

- The relentless pursuit of perfection (Lexus).
- It's our strategic intent that customers worldwide view us as their most valued pharmaceutical partner (Eli Lilly).
- To be the top performer in everything that we do (Phillips Petroleum).

- To become a high performance multinational energy company—not the biggest, but the best (Unocal Corporation).
- We are dedicated to being the world's best at bringing people together (AT&T).
- Ben & Jerry's is dedicated to the creation and demonstration of a new corporate concept—linked prosperity.
- Our intent is to be better than the best (Best Products).
- The Children's Defense Fund exists to provide a strong and effective voice for the children of America who cannot vote, lobby, or speak for themselves.
- We build homes to meet people's dreams (Kaufman & Broad).
- We will be a leader in the emerging energy services industry by challenging conventional wisdom and creating superior value in a safe and environmentally responsible manner (PSI Energy, Inc.).
- We intend to become the single source of information technology for the home (Dell Computer Corporation).
- To be a premier provider of services and products that contribute to the health and well-being of people (MDS Health Group Limited).
- We seek to set the standard for excellence, leadership and integrity in the utility industry (New York State Electric & Gas Corp.).

The strategic mission flows from a firm's strategic intent; it is a statement used to describe a firm's unique intent and the scope of its operations in product and market terms. In its most basic form, the strategic mission indicates to stakeholders what a firm seeks to accomplish. An effective strategic mission reflects a firm's individuality and reveals its leadership's predisposition(s). The useful strategic mission shows how a firm differs from others and defines boundaries within which the firm intends to operate. Examples of strategic missions include:

- To make, distribute, and sell the finest quality all-natural ice cream and related products in a wide variety of innovative flavors made from Vermont dairy products (Ben & Jerry's).
- To serve the natural and LP needs of the customers in the Clearwater and surrounding Florida Sun-Coast area in the most safe, reliable and economical manner possible while optimizing load growth, customer satisfaction, financial return to the City of Clearwater and the equity value of the Clearwater Gas System (Clearwater Gas System).
- Public Service Company of Colorado is an energy company that primarily provides gas, electricity and related services to present and potential markets.

- Our mission is to understand and satisfy customer expectations for quality and energy and energy-related products and services and profitably serve Oklahoma markets (Public Service Company of Oklahoma).
- Children's Hospital Medical Center is dedicated to serving the health-care needs of infants, children, and adolescents and to providing research and teaching programs that ensure delivery of the highest quality pediatric care to our community, the nation, and the world (Children's Hospital Medical Center).
- To provide services and products which will assist physicians, health care institutions, corporations, government agencies, and communities to improve the health and well-being of the people for whom they are responsible (MDS Health Group Limited).
- The William Penn Foundation is a private grant making organization created in 1945 by Otto Haas and his wife, Phoebe. The principal mission of the Foundation is to help improve the quality of life in the Delaware Valley (William Penn Foundation).

KEY RESULT AREAS (KRAs)

Once the strategic intent and mission have been defined, the analysis can turn to defining KRAs to help accomplish the intent and mission. *Key result areas* are categories of activities that must receive attention if the firm is to achieve its strategic intent and strategic mission. A rationale or justification and specific courses of action for each KRA should be specified. Typically, a firm should establish no more than six KRAs. KRAs should suggest (in broad terms) a firm's concerns and intended directions.

Flowing from the nature of a firm's KRAs, *strategies* are courses of action that must be taken to satisfy the requirements suggested by each KRA. Strategies typically have a one-, two-, or three-year time horizon (although it can be as long as five years). Strategies are developed to describe approaches to be used or methods to follow in order to attain the strategic intent and strategic mission (as suggested by the KRAs). Strategies reflect a group's action intentions. Flowing from individual strategies, *objectives* are specific and measurable statements describing actions that are to be completed to implement individual strategies. Objectives, which are more specific in nature than strategies, usually have a one-year or shorter time horizon.

Strategic planning should also result in cost linkages to courses of action. Once key cost assumptions are specified, these financial requirements can be tied to strategies and objectives. Once linked with strategies and objectives, cost or budgetary requirements can be related back to KRAs.

Hints for Presenting an Effective Strategic Plan

There may be a temptation to spend most of your oral or written case analysis on results from the analysis. It is important, however, that you make an equal effort to develop and evaluate KRA alternatives and to design implementation for the chosen alternatives. In your presentation, the *analysis* of a case should not be overemphasized relative to the *synthesis* of results gained from your analytical efforts (see Exhibit 3).

Strategy Formulation: Choosing Key Result Areas

Once you have formulated a strategic intent and mission, choosing among alternative KRAs is often one of the most difficult steps in preparing an oral or written presentation. Each alternative should be feasible (i.e., it should match the firm's strengths, capabilities, and especially core competencies), and feasibility should be demonstrated. In addition, you should show how each alternative takes advantage of the environmental opportunity or avoids/buffers against environmental threats. Developing carefully thought out alternatives requires synthesis of your analyses and creates greater credibility in oral and written case presentations.

Once you develop strong alternative KRAs, you must evaluate the set to choose the best ones. Your choice should be defensible and provide benefits over the other alternatives. Thus, it is important that both the alternative development and evaluation of alternatives be thorough. The choice of the best alternative should be explained and defended.

Key Result Area Implementation

After selecting the most appropriate KRAs (that is, those with the highest probability of enhancing a firm's strategic competitiveness), you must consider effective implementation. Effective synthesis is important to ensure that you have considered and evaluated all critical implementation issues. Issues you might consider include the structural changes necessary to implement the new strategies and objectives associated with each KRA. In addition, leadership changes and new controls or incentives may be necessary to implement these strategic actions. The implementation actions you recommend should be explicit and thoroughly explained. Occasionally, careful evaluation of implementation actions may show the strategy to be less favorable than you originally thought. A strategy is only as good as the firm's ability to implement it effectively. Therefore, expending the effort to determine effective implementation is important.

Process Issues

You should ensure that your presentation (either oral or written) has logical consistency throughout. For example, if your presentation identifies one purpose, but your analysis focuses on issues that differ from the stated purpose, the logical inconsistency will be apparent. Likewise, your alternatives should flow from the configuration of strengths, weaknesses, opportunities, and threats you identified through the internal and external analyses.

Thoroughness and clarity also are critical to an effective presentation. Thoroughness is represented by the comprehensiveness of the analysis and alternative generation. Furthermore, clarity in the results of the analyses, selection of the best alternative KRAs, and design of implementation actions are important. For example, your statement of the strengths and weaknesses should flow clearly and logically from the internal analyses presented.

Presentations (oral or written) that show logical consistency, thoroughness, and clarity of purpose, effective analyses, and feasible recommendations are more effective and will receive more positive evaluations. Being able to withstand tough questions from peers after your presentation will build credibility for your strategic plan presentation. Furthermore, developing the skills necessary to make such presentations will enhance your future job performance and career success.

Notes

1. 2000, M. A. Lundberg, B. B. Levin, & H. I. Harrington, *Who Learns What From Cases and How? The Research Base for Teaching and Learning with Cases* (Englewood Cliffs, New Jersey: Lawrence Erlbaum Associates).
2. 1994, L. B. Barnes, A. J. Nelson, & C. R. Christensen, *Teaching and the Case Method: Text, Cases and Readings* (Boston: Harvard Business School Press); 1993, C. C. Lundberg, Introduction to the case method, in C. M. Vance (ed.), *Mastering Management Education* (Newbury Park, Calif.: Sage); 1989, C. Christensen, *Teaching and the Case Method* (Boston: Harvard Business School Publishing Division).
3. 1993, C. C. Lundberg & E. Enz, A framework for student case preparation, *Case Research Journal*, 13 (Summer): 133.
4. 1971, J. Solitis, John Dewey, in L. E. Deighton (ed.), *Encyclopedia of Education* (New York: Macmillan and Free Press).
5. 1987, F. Bocker, Is case teaching more effective than lecture teaching in business administration? An exploratory analysis, *Interfaces*, 17(5): 64–71.

APPENDIX I: SOURCES FOR INDUSTRY AND COMPETITOR ANALYSES

Strategic Management Websites

Search Engines (may be the broadest sources of information on companies and industries)	Alta Vista— *http://www.altavista.digital.com*
	Excite— *http://www.excite.com*
	InfoSeek— *http://www.infoseek.com*
	Lycos— *http://www.lycos.com*
	WebCrawler— *http://www.webcrawler.com*
	Yahoo!— *http://www.yahoo.com*

Professional Societies

Academy of Management <*http://www.aom.pace.edu*> publishes *Academy of Management Journal, Academy of Management Review, and Academy of Management Executive,* three publications that often print articles on strategic management research, theory, and practice. The Academy of Management is the largest professional society for management research and education and has a large Business Policy and Strategy Division.

Strategic Management Society <*http://www.smsweb.org*> publishes the *Strategic Management Journal* (a top academic journal in strategic management).

Government Sources of Company Information and Data

Census Bureau <*http://www.census.gov*> provides useful links and information about social, demographic, and economic information.

Federal Trade Commission <*http://www.ftc.gov*> includes discussion on several antitrust and consumer protection laws useful to businesses looking for accurate information about business statutes.

Free EDGAR <*http://www.freeedgar.com*> provides free, unlimited access to real-time corporate data filed with the Securities and Exchange Commission (SEC).

Better Business Bureau <*http://www.bbb.org*> provides a wide variety of helpful publications, information, and other resources to both consumers and businesses to help people make informed marketplace decisions.

Publication Websites

Business Week <*http://www.businessweek.com*> allows search of *Business Week* magazine's articles by industry or topic, such as strategy.

Forbes <*http://www.forbes.com*> provides searching of *Forbes* magazine business articles and data.

Fortune <*http://www.fortune.com*> allows search of *Fortune* magazine and other articles, many of which are focused on strategy topics.

Financial Times <*http://www.ft.com*> provides access to many *Financial Times* articles, data, and surveys.

Wall Street Journal <*http://www.wsj.com*> *The Wall Street Journal Interactive* edition provides an excellent continuing stream of strategy-oriented articles and announcements.

Abstracts and Indexes

Periodicals

ABI/Inform
Business Periodicals Index
InfoTrac (CD-ROM computer multidiscipline index)
Investext (CD-ROM)
Predicasts F&S Index United States
Predicasts Overview of Markets and Technology (PROMT)
Predicasts R&S Index Europe
Predicasts R&S Index International
Public Affairs Information Service Bulletin (PAIS)
Reader's Guide to Periodical Literature

Newspapers

NewsBank
Business NewsBank
New York Times Index
Wall Street Journal Index

| Industry Ratios | Dun & Bradstreet, *Industry Norms and Key Business Ratios*
Robert Morris Associates Annual Statement Studies
Troy Almanac of Business and Industrial Financial Ratios |

| Industry Forecasts | International Trade Administration, *U.S. Industrial Outlook*
  Predicasts Forecasts |

| Rankings & Ratings | Annual Report on American Industry in *Forbes*
Business Rankings and Salaries
Business One Irwin Business and Investment Almanac
Corporate and Industry Research Reports (CIRR)
Dun's Business Rankings
Moody's Industrial Review
Rating Guide to Franchises
Standard & Poor's Industry Report Service
Value Line Investment Survey
Ward's Business Directory |

| Statistics | *American Statistics Index (ASI)* Bureau of the Census, U.S.
  Department of Commerce, *Economic Census Publications*
Bureau of the Census, U.S. Department of Commerce, *Statistical*
  Abstract of the United States
Bureau of Economic Analysis, U.S. Department of Commerce,
  Survey of Current Business
Internal Revenue Service, U.S. Treasury Department, *Statistics of*
  Income: Corporation Income Tax Returns
Statistical Reference Index (SRI) |

APPENDIX II: FINANCIAL ANALYSIS IN CASE STUDIES

EXHIBIT A-1 Profitability Ratios

Ratio	Formula	What It Shows
1. Return on total assets	$\dfrac{\text{Profits after taxes}}{\text{Total assets}}$	The net return on total investment of the firm
	or	or
	$\dfrac{\text{Profits after taxes} + \text{interest}}{\text{Total assets}}$	The return on both creditors' and shareholders' investments
2. Return on stockholders' equity (or return on net worth)	$\dfrac{\text{Profits after taxes}}{\text{Total stockholders' equity}}$	How effectively the company is utilizing shareholders' funds
3. Return on common equity	$\dfrac{\text{Profit after taxes} - \text{preferred stock dividends}}{\text{Total stockholders' equity} - \text{par value of preferred stock}}$	The net return to common stockholders
4. Operating profit margin (or return on sales)	$\dfrac{\text{Profits before taxes and before interest}}{\text{Sales}}$	The firm's profitability from regular operations
5. Net profit margin (or net return on sales)	$\dfrac{\text{Profits after taxes}}{\text{Sales}}$	The firm's net profit as a percentage of total sales

Ratio	Formula	What It Shows
1. Current ratio	$\dfrac{\text{Current assets}}{\text{Current liabilities}}$	The firm's ability to meet its current financial liabilities
2. Quick ratio (or acid-test ratio)	$\dfrac{\text{Current assets} - \text{inventory}}{\text{Current liabilities}}$	The firm's ability to pay off short-term obligations without relying on sales of inventory
3. Inventory to net working capital	$\dfrac{\text{Inventory}}{\text{Current assets} - \text{current liabilities}}$	The extent of which the firm's working capital is tied up in inventory

Ratio	Formula	What It Shows
1. Debt-to-assets	$\dfrac{\text{Total debt}}{\text{Total assets}}$	Total borrowed funds as a percentage of total assets
2. Debt-to-equity	$\dfrac{\text{Total debt}}{\text{Total shareholders' equity}}$	Borrowed funds versus the funds provided by shareholders
3. Long-term debt-to-equity	$\dfrac{\text{Long-term debt}}{\text{Total shareholders' equity}}$	Leverage used by the firm
4. Times-interest-earned (or coverage ratio)	$\dfrac{\text{Profits before interest and taxes}}{\text{Total interest charges}}$	The firm's ability to meet all interest payments
5. Fixed charge coverage	$\dfrac{\text{Profits before taxes and interest} + \text{lease obligations}}{\text{Total interest charges} + \text{lease obligations}}$	The firm's ability to meet all fixed-charge obligations including lease payments

Ratio	Formula	What It Shows
1. Inventory turnover	$\dfrac{\text{Sales}}{\text{Inventory of finished goods}}$	The effectiveness of the firm in employing inventory
2. Fixed assets turnover	$\dfrac{\text{Sales}}{\text{Fixed assets}}$	The effectiveness of the firm in utilizing plant and equipment
3. Total assets turnover	$\dfrac{\text{Sales}}{\text{Total assets}}$	The effectiveness of the firm in utilizing total assets
4. Accounts receivable turnover	$\dfrac{\text{Annual credit sales}}{\text{Accounts receivable}}$	How many times the total receivables have been collected during the accounting period
5. Average collection period	$\dfrac{\text{Accounts receivable}}{\text{Average daily sales}}$	The average length of time the firm waits to collect payments after sales

Ratio	Formula	What It Shows
1. Dividend yield on common stock	$\dfrac{\text{Annual dividends per share}}{\text{Current market price per share}}$	A measure of return to common stockholders in the form of dividends.
2. Price-earnings ratio	$\dfrac{\text{Current market price per share}}{\text{After-tax earnings per share}}$	An indication of market perception of the firm. Usually, the faster-growing or less risky firms tend to have higher PE ratios than the slower-growing or more risky firms.
3. Dividend payout ratio	$\dfrac{\text{Annual dividends per share}}{\text{After-tax earnings per share}}$	An indication of dividends paid out as a percentage of profits.
4. Cash flow per share	$\dfrac{\text{After-tax profits} + \text{depreciation}}{\text{Number of common shares outstanding}}$	A measure of total cash per share available for use by the firm.

Back to the Roots: American International Group Returns to China

C-1

case one

Guido Meyerhans
INSEAD

Qiwen Lu
INSEAD

INTRODUCTION

When Deng Xiaoping came to power in the late '70s, the concept of insurance was virtually unknown in China. The big, state-owned conglomerates were mostly "self insured"[1], and life insurance accounted for less than 1% of the total premium volume, compared to over 50% in industrialized countries.

Deng's reform in the Eighties stimulated the growth of privately-owned manufacturing and trade businesses. Their emergence, combined with increasing infrastructure projects (e.g., power plants), created the need for more and more sophisticated insurance businesses. As a result, the government started reforming the financial service sector which allowed domestic competition to enter the insurance market in 1988. To reduce the gap in international insurance companies, China opened some cities to foreign insurance companies "on an experimental basis".

In 1992, American International Group (AIG)[2] was back where it all began: Shanghai. The reopening of a wholly-owned branch was the beginning of a success story, and AIG, one of the largest life insurance companies worldwide, is nowadays considered, together with other companies such as Coca Cola, a role model of how to do business in China. Within less than two years, AIG captured a significant stake in the life insurance market in Shanghai, and basically rewrote the history of insurance in China.

This case was written by Guido Meyerhans under the supervision of Qiwen Lu, Professor at INSEAD. It is intended to be used as a basis for class discussion rather than to illustrate either effective or ineffective handling of an administrative situation.

Copyright © 2002 INSEAD-EAC, Fontainebleau, France. Reprinted by permission.

This paper will address the strategy of AIG and the license acquisition as well as the status of the Chinese life insurance industry at the beginning of the '90s. [See Exhibit 1 for more information on the history of AIG.]

STATUS AND DEVELOPMENT OF THE CHINESE INSURANCE INDUSTRY BEFORE THE ENTRY OF AIG (1992)

COMMUNIST TAKE-OVER AND CULTURAL REVOLUTION

Until 1949, the insurance industry in China was dominated by foreign, mostly British, companies. Among these companies was AIG, which was founded in 1921 by former ice-cream parlor owner, Cornelius Vander Starr. Already in the early Twenties, AIG focused on selling life insurance to the Chinese community in the Shanghai area.

After the communist take-over in 1949, all foreign insurance companies were forced to leave. The government created the People's Insurance Company of China (PICC), a subsidiary of the banking regulatory body, the People's Bank of China (PBOC). PICC was from then on the only insurance company authorized to operate in China. The development of PICC came to an end during the unrest period from 1959 to 1979. "The cultural revolution" put an end to most of the insurance business and limited PICC's activities to mainly international (Sino-foreign) marine cargo and aviation insurance. The domestic business had basically ceased to exist, and life insurance could not be developed.

By the end of 1980, the insurance industry was characterized by an annual premium volume of only RMB 640 million (US$ 170 million). On a per capita basis, insurance was virtually non-existent.

EXHIBIT 1   AIG's Expansion Steps in China

Year	Event
1921	AIG founded in Shanghai
1950	AIG forced to leave China
1975	Greenberg reactivates contacts with PR China
1980	AIG opens representative office
1980	Joint venture between AIG and PICC (China-American Insurance Company) in New York
1985	Start of construction of Shanghai Center (business/residential complex) with AIG as minority shareholder (construction completed in 1989)
1990	Greenberg appointed to chairman of foreign business leaders' advisory council to the city's government (Shanghai)
1992	AIG opens branch in Shanghai
1993	Greenberg elected chairman of the US-China business council
1994	Insurance seminars with Chinese ministries (e.g., China State Bureau of Technical Supervision: Seminar for product liability)
1995	Greenberg appointed as "senior economic advisor" to the Beijing city government
1996	AIG starts operations in Guangzhou. AIG is the only foreign insurer that offers life and P&C insurance in two provinces
1997	Greenberg becomes honorary citizen of Shanghai

THE DENG XIAOPING ERA

Economic reforms started with Deng's appointment to vice-prime minister in the fall of 1979, and the insurance industry gradually recovered. The reforms took place in two different fields:

- *Strengthening of the legal framework.* After 1980, some laws were introduced which can be seen as a basic, but preliminary, framework for insurance activities in China: Economic Contract Law (1981); Property Insurance Contract Ordinance (1983); Provisional Ordinance of Insurance Enterprise (1985) and Marine Commercial Law (1985). These first insurance laws can by no means be compared with regulations in industrialized countries, as they are merely the first signs of a reevaluation of the role of the insurance sector. Application of the laws remained unclear, and the coverage was insufficient. Good relations with local and central authorities remained the basis for doing business in China. In addition, certain insurance activities, i.e., the social security system, were explicitly excluded from the Provisional Ordinance of Insurance Enterprise. The PBOC, acting as the state insurance regulatory body, administered the Insurance Ordinance. At the same time, PICC remained a subsidiary of the People's Bank—a situation not necessarily conducive to objectivity and independence. The PBOC had complete control over the insurance industry. Its power included the licensing

of insurance companies, product and price approval, and, as it inspected and audited company accounts, it could even close down existing insurance firms.

- *Introduction of domestic competition.* "Competition" in insurance was officially introduced in China in 1988, although PICC still held a quasi-monopolistic position, given its relationship with PBOC, and the fact that some businesses had to be exclusively transacted by the former monopolist (e.g., international reinsurance). At the time AIG entered the Chinese market, there were 8 domestic life insurers operating. Half of these insurers, e.g., Beijing Insurance Company, were de facto former regional offices of PICC, which had gained independent status, although they were still linked to PICC on a contractual basis. The two life insurers, besides PICC, which gained some importance, were China Pacific Insurance Company (China Pacific) and Ping An Insurance Company (Ping An). PICC thus continued to dominate the market until the early '90s, with an estimated share of 90–95% (Exhibit 2).

MACROECONOMIC AND SOCIAL CHANGES

Apart from the changing legal situation, there were other important macroeconomic factors which helped to trigger the growth of the life insurance market from 1991 onwards.

Exhibit 2 — Market Share in Total Insurance Market (1994)

Insurance company*	Premium share (Estimates)
PICC	76%
China Pacific Insurance	15%
Ping An	7%
AIG	0.6%

*Ping An and AIG have an over proportional share in life insurance.

Source: Press reports

- *Little emperors:* China had a new mini-dynasty of so-called "little emperors", the doted-on only children of China's one child policy. This led to a behavioral change in the area of life and health insurance. The child in question needed to be preserved at all costs, and parents of average financial circumstances were turning to insurance to guarantee their ability to pay medical and school bills.[3] The second consequence of the one child policy was that parents, who, in more prolific generations may have been able to rely on at least one of their many offspring to care for them in old age, no longer had the same family support to rely on—another reason for the growth of the life/health insurance market.

- *Economic deregulation:* With economic deregulation in many sectors of Chinese industry, China's state-owned enterprises were beginning to see that they could not depend forever on the state to support their social welfare obligations, because employers and privately-held enterprises were excluded from the state pension system. Alternatives to provide pensions and casualty coverage, in addition to covering for risks inherent in their business, were provided by the newly-emerging insurance industry.

- *International relations:* In the first half of the '90s, talks about the successor to the GATT started, and China would like to have become one of the founding members of the World Trade Organization (WTO). Preconditions for China entering GATT included the opening of its financial markets to outside participants. From the US government's point of view in particular, service industries such as insurance potentially offered a useful counter to the imbalance of trade in other sectors.

- *GDP per capita growth:* One of the characteristics of life insurance is that the premium as a percentage of GDP remains constant up to a GDP per capita of approximately US$ 1,000 to US$ 1,300. After this target is reached, premiums start to grow over proportionally (Appendix A). Some of the Chinese provinces have reached this trigger, thus resulting in a high premium growth.

Status of the Industry after the Reforms

These changes in the first 10 years of Deng's legacy paved the way to a more competitive insurance market in China, and led to substantial growth in the overall insurance market (Exhibit 3). Up to 1991, the life and non-life markets had similar growth rates of 30% per year.[4] Then the life market started to grow rapidly (i.e., in 1992, with over 70%, compared to 18% in the non-life sector).

Compared with international markets, life insurance was, in 1991, of little importance in the Chinese insurance sector. The share of life insurance was, for example, 67% in India, compared with only 23% in China (1991) (Exhibit 4).

These overall growth figures hide one important factor. The People's Republic of China is so large and heterogeneous that a closer look at individual provinces

Exhibit 3 — Direct Insurance Premiums in China

Year	Total insurance (RMB billion)	Total insurance (US$ billion)	Life insurance (RMB billion)	Non-life insurance (RMB billion)
1986	5.09	1.37	1.03	4.06
1987	7.45	2.00	1.59	5.86
1988	10.06	2.70	2.23	7.83
1989	12.24	2.59	2.46	9.79
1990	14.76	2.83	3.10	11.66
1991	18.20	3.35	4.23	13.97
1992	24.00	4.21	7.50	16.50

Source: PICC annual report, Sigma (SwissRe), Asian Insurance Review

EXHIBIT 4 — International Comparison of Chinese Insurance Market, 1991

Country	Total premium (US$ million)	Share of life insurance
China	3,094	23.2%
Mexico	3,533	35.6%
India	3,966	67.9%
Taiwan	8,254	69.7%
South Korea	31,702	80.3%

Source: Sigma (SwissRe)

is required. Several of China's over 30 provinces have a higher population than that of Germany. In the early '90s, Sichuan, China's most densely populated province, with 112 million people, was about the same population size as Japan (124 million). The most important province economically, Guangdong, had a similar GDP to that of Ireland, and the GDP per capita in Shanghai reached nearly the same level as that of Eastern Europe (Exhibit 5). These local factors played a key role for foreign insurance companies in selecting the provinces with the best potential: The municipality of Shanghai, with the highest GDP per capita, and Guangdong, with its high overall GDP and its proximity to Hong Kong. In addition, both provinces had governments that were very reform-oriented.

The framework laid down by Deng was now established, but as the country had been virtually shielded from the outside world for 40 years, industry know-how was poor. The government therefore decided to open the county stepwise to foreign insurers, so that domestic companies could acquire and improve product design, underwriting and customer service skills.

AIG's POSITION AND STRATEGY IN ASIA PRIOR TO ITS ENTRY IN CHINA

Is AIG an American multinational or a domestic insurer in Asia? Legally, the company is housed in New York, but its long presence in Asia gives the American insurer a special position. People in many Southeast Asian countries do not look on AIG and its life subsidiary AIA (American International Assurance) as a foreign new entrant. The reason for this is the three-ingredient success recipe of AIG.

- *Importance of Asian business:* Today, AIG makes over half of its revenues in Asian markets (Exhibit 6).

In nearly half a dozen markets, the American insurer is either market leader or the biggest foreign company with a long tradition in Asia. Even outside the insurance industry, the profit contribution that AIG gets from Asia is impressive:

Company	Pre-tax profits in the Far East (1997, US$ billion)
AIG	1.7
Citicorp	1.2
Coca Cola	1.5*

*The far East and Middle East combined.

- *Entering during an early stage of market development:* AIG entered many Asian markets (with the exception of Hong Kong) long before other insurers started to sell policies in these countries. This strategy continued through the '90s, and currently includes the former CCCP, e.g., Kazakhstan and Uzbekistan. This early entry had the advantage that AIG often got "grandfathered", and could keep its fully-owned subsidiaries.[5]
- *Use of management:* Another big success factor was localized management. By the time other insurers entered the market, AIG had already built a strong domestic management and were more familiar with local market conditions. A strong domestic management also helped in the company's expansion in countries with similar cultural backgrounds (e.g., AIG's operations in China were run from Hong Kong and Taiwan, and sales force organization concepts were imported from South-East Asian countries).

By 1975, AIG showed its first interest in China. The company was the biggest foreign life insurer in Hong Kong, Japan, Malaysia, the Philippines, Singapore and Taiwan, and the only insurer with worldwide sales and support facilities. Its sterling reputation and hard work helped it become the second US-owned insurer[6] to enter the South Korean[7] market in 1987 (Exhibit 7).

AIG's WAY TO GET A CHINA LICENSE AND TO MAINTAIN A UNIQUE POSITION

The fact that AIG was the first insurance company to return to China was mainly the merit of one man: Maurice R. "Hank" Greenberg, CEO of AIG. Long before anyone started to talk about China, the American insurer increased its efforts in China. As Greenberg puts it "I have probably been on 40 or more trips. We

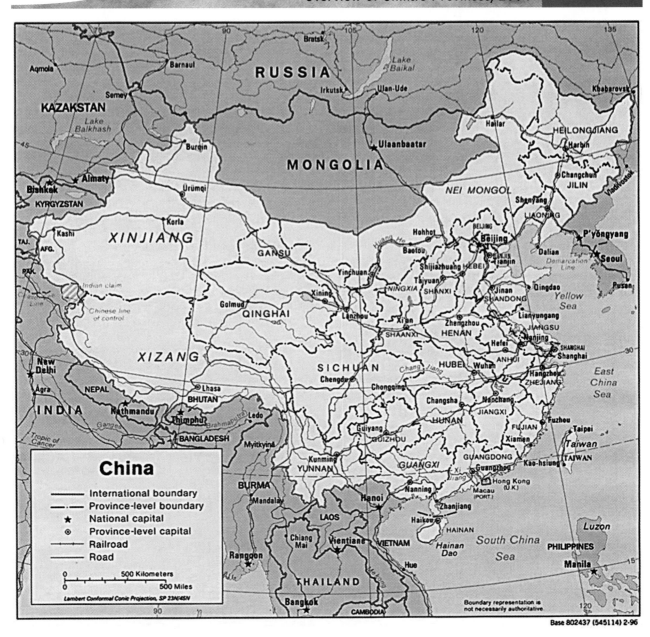

Case 1 / Back to the Roots: American International Group Returns to China   C-5

Note: Hong Kong (SAR), Macau and Taiwan are not part of this paper, and respective figures are not included under PR China.

(continued on next page)

have done many things for China. . . . We have worked hard on US-China relations. . . . [The success of AIG] has nothing to do with who we know and everything to do with what we do." The stages of the market entry are summarized in Exhibit 1.

Realizing that success in China would not come overnight, Greenberg undertook his first visit in 1975. This journey, three years after Nixon's historic visit to China, took place before Sino-American relations became normalized. In the following years, Greenberg traveled several times to the Asian country and maintained relationships even when tensions between the US and China rose (e.g., following the Tiananmen incident or renewal of most-favored-nation (MFN) trade status). Greenberg's lobbying was not limited to China; it also included the home country of the insurer. As chairman

EXHIBIT 5   Overview of China's Provinces, 1994 *(continued)*

Province, Municipality	Population (millions)	GDP 1994 (US$ billion)	GDP per Capita (US$)	Life premium* (US$ million)	Life premium in % GDP*
Beijing	11.3	12.6	1,118	54	0.42%
Tianjin	9.4	8.4	900	31	0.36%
Hebel	63.9	24.9	390	64	0.25%
Shanxi	30.5	9.9	325	24	0.24%
Inner Mongolia	22.6	7.9	350	20	0.25%
Liaoning	40.7	30.0	737	100	0.32%
Jilin	25.7	11.2	437	30	0.26%
Heilongjiang	36.7	18.8	511	53	0.28%
Shanghai	13.6	22.9	1,687	142	0.61%
Jiangsu	70.2	47.1	671	149	0.31%
Zhejiang	42.9	30.9	721	101	0.32%
Anhui	59.6	17.3	290	42	0.24%
Fujian	31.8	19.6	614	60	0.30%
Jiangxi	40.2	12.0	298	29	0.24%
Shandong	86.7	44.9	518	128	0.28%
Henan	90.3	25.5	283	61	0.23%
Hubei	57.2	21.8	381	56	0.25%
Hunan	63.6	19.7	309	48	0.24%
Guangdong	66.9	49.2	736	163	0.32%
Guangxi	44.9	14.4	321	35	0.24%
Hainan	7.1	3.8	540	11	0.28%
Sichuan	112.1	32.2	287	77	0.23%
Guizhou	34.6	6.0	175	13	0.22%
Yunnan	39.4	11.3	287	27	0.23%
Tibet	2.4	0.5	225	1	0.22%
Shaanxi	34.8	9.8	282	23	0.23%
Gansu	23.8	5.2	220	12	0.22%
Qinghai	4.7	1.6	338	4	0.24%
Ningxia	5.0	1.6	308	4	0.24%
Xinjiang	16.3	7.8	479	22	0.27%
Total	1,188.7	528.9	445	1,586	0.30%

*Life premiums estimated based on life insurance demand S-curve of Asian countries, where Chinese ethnicity dominates economy (Hong Kong, Indonesia, Malaysia, PR China, Singapore, Vietnam). Estimation was made with real GDP/capita (1994–1996) as driver.

Source: Statistical Yearbook of China; premiums estimated.

of the US-China Business Council, he was instrumental, for example, in getting the Clinton administration to drop the wrangle over China's human rights record and the renewal of China's most-favored-nation (MFN) trade status. A brief look at the names of the company's board of directors reflects AIG's political connections.

At the beginning of the China operation, the board included Martin Feldstein, Harvard University economics professor and former chairman of the President's Council of Economic Advisors; Carla A. Hills, former US trade representative and Barber B. Conable, former congressman and president of the World Bank.

Geographical Split of AIG Business Segments — EXHIBIT 6

Business segment	Pre-tax revenue share, 1997
Domestic general	32.3%
Foreign general*	18.9%
Life**	33.8%
Financial services	15.0%

*Mostly Asian business.
**Significant share of Asian business.

Source: Annual report

In addition, Henry A. Kissinger chaired the international advisory board of the company.

After the first contacts were established, AIG opened a representative office in China in 1980. In the same year, the China-American Insurance Company was founded as a joint venture between AIG and PICC. The company, registered in Delaware, Bermuda and Hong Kong, was created to focus on insurance related to Sino-American trade and to write worldwide reinsurance. While the joint venture was never a big commercial success, and remained focused on a small niche market, it was evidence of AIG's commitment to China, and could be used as a vehicle for know-how transfer for PICC.

From now on, Shanghai was the center of AIG's interest. The port city was of special significance as the early home of AIG, although, more important, was the wealth distribution and political situation in this province. AIG's investments in the city started in 1985, with a US$ 195 million participation from the Shanghai Center office-residential complex, which became a landmark in the city. The investment was seen as a firm commitment to China, and paved the way for the healthy, long-term relationship between Maurice Greenberg and Zhu Rongji, who was, at that time, mayor of Shanghai. Five years later, Greenberg was a founding member, and subsequently, chairman of the International Business Advisory Council for the Mayor of Shanghai. The council was hailed as a major step toward re-establishing the city as one of Asia's leading financial and industrial centers. A Western investment analyst in the city noted that:

> " . . . with the backing of international business behind him, Mr. Zhu can now go to the central party leaders in Beijing and outline specific proposals to attract more foreign investment, and allow Shanghai greater autonomy in the development of the economy. . . ."

For AIG, of equal importance was the establishment of the council. Zhu Rongji was more likely to get strong central backing for his reform plan of the financial sector, which had repeatedly been stalled by Beijing's central planners. Greenberg supported this argument during the council's opening session, when he mentioned:

> "Shanghai has an ambitious vision for the turn of the century, and the purpose of this council is to provide recommendations on how to achieve this vision. . . . The opening of Shanghai's financial sector to greater foreign participation would play an important role in invigorating the tertiary sector and the economy as a whole. . . . We discussed the need for a comprehensive legal and financial structure that began with earnings, progressed through savings, investments, life insurance and production, and completes the cycle back to earnings."

> Maurice R. Greenberg.
> Speech at council's opening session,
> March 25, 1990.

To strengthen the thinking process about reforms of the financial sector, the council sponsored conferences

AIG in Asia — EXHIBIT 7

Hong Kong
Market share AIG: 43%

Singapore
Market share AIG: 33%

Market share AIG bigger than 30%

AIG biggest foreign life insurer

and meetings in Shanghai. The city was the focus of Greenberg's activities, but his networking was not confined to Shanghai. In 1990, he met with several members of the Chinese government, among them:

- Jiang Zemin, General Secretary of the Chinese communist party central committee
- Rong Yiren, vice-chairman of the National People's Congress Standing Committee and chairman of the China International Trust and Investment Corporation (CITIC)
- Li Yumin, chairman and president of PICC

Two years later, in the fall of 1992, AIG obtained the first license to sell insurance in China since 1949. Other international insurers had to wait. Evidently, AIG invested a lot in China, and contact with Zhu Rongji, who was at the time vice-prime minister had some impact, but those were not the only factors that distinguished AIG from other multinational insurers. There are at least two other important differences: AIG supported local reform efforts and demonstrated a deep understanding of the Chinese culture.

PARTNERSHIP FOR REFORMS

The discussions AIG executives had with Chinese officials were not restricted to the insurance industry itself. Greenberg became a "sparring partner" for Zhu Rongji, in a series of exchanges on infrastructure, projects, trade, reform of financial sectors, etc. Insurance was an element in many conversations, but not the only common talking point, by any means.

UNDERSTANDING OF THE CHINESE CULTURE

Worldwide, no other multinational insurer has more senior executives of Chinese ethnicity than AIG, and no other company does as much insurance business in countries where Chinese people dominate the economy.[8] This presence certainly helped AIG to gain considerable insights into the Chinese way of thinking. The degree to which the company incorporated the understanding of the culture of the new market can be seen by the lengths to which they went in order to return the "Bronze Windows".

The Bronze Windows

Hand-cast in the late eighteenth century, the ten Bronze Windows disappeared from the Emperor's Summer Palace in Beijing at the turn of the century. The official line is that they were taken by foreign forces during the Boxer Revolution (1900). The windows were acquired by a French banker and shipped to Europe in 1912,

where they were hidden away for nearly 80 years until 1992, when they suddenly reappeared. Edmund Tse, executive vice-president of AIG, was informed of their reappearance by an American collector, and bought the windows through the Starr Foundation[9] for US$ 515,000. They were then donated and returned to China, thus creating an overwhelming reaction:

> ". . . The recovery of these missing relics has always been the cherished desire of generations of Chinese people . . . gold is valuable, whereas goodwill is invaluable." [Chinese saying].
>
> Zhang Dequin, Director of State Bureau of Cultural Relics.

> "No foreign corporation had ever returned missing relics to us. They only took things away from us."
>
> Chinese official, during the donation ceremony.

> "The American International Group donated the 10 Bronze Windows to China in a ceremony this afternoon in Beijing's summer palace, the first time for a foreign corporation to donate missing precious relics to China."
>
> Xinhua News Agency, December 2, 1993.

It cannot be said that there is a link between the donation and the subsequent approval granted to AIG to conduct business in Shanghai, but in a country where guanxi (relationships) is a major business driver, AIG's generosity definitely scored high marks.

AIG's INTERNATIONAL COMPETITORS IN THE CHINESE MARKET

The attractiveness of the Chinese insurance market is so great that it is no surprise that other international insurers followed in the footsteps of AIG. The first company to follow was Tokyo Marine & Fire. The Chinese government granted the license to the Japanese insurer as a rebuff to the Americans over some tensions with the US government. Other insurers followed, and, by 1998, all the top-ranked global insurers, apart from the Japanese life insurance companies,[10] had licenses in China. Exhibit 8 gives an overview of the activities of international insurers in China.

Even if competition is increasing now, early market entry clearly paid off for AIG:

- AIG remains the only foreign insurer who can offer life and non-life insurance.[11]

Company	Chinese partner	Ownership structure	License granted	Line of business
AIG	—	100% US	1992	Life, Non-life
Tokyo Marine & Fire	—	100% Japan	1992	Non-life
AIU (Guangzhou)*	—	100% US	1995	Non-life
AIA (Guangzhou)**	—	100% US	1995	Life
Manulife	Sinochem***	50% Canadian	1996	Life
Winterthur	—	100% Swiss	1996	Non-life
Allianz	Dazhong Insurance	50% German	1997	Life
AXA-UAP	China Mining Group	50% French	1997	Life
Aetna	China Pacific Insurance	50% US	1997	Life
Royal & Sun Alliance	—	100% UK	1998	Non-life
Colonial Mutual	PICC****	50% Australian	1998	Life

*Non-life subsidiary of AIG.
**Life subsidiary of AIG.
***China National Chemicals Import and Export Corp.
****PICC Shanghai Branch.

- No other non-domestic insurer has a wholly-owned life subsidiary. All other life companies have to build joint ventures with Chinese firms.

With these start advantages and business experience in Asia, "Hank" Greenberg is probably right in saying:

> *"This historic building was our home many years ago, and AIG is pleased to be the first foreign business organization to return to its early home on Shanghai's famous Bund. . . . AIG is very proud of our Chinese heritage and history, and we look forward to serving the insurance needs of Shanghai and China for many years to come."*
>
> *M. R. Greenberg, July 15, 1998.*
> *Inauguration ceremony of the Bund, the old corporate head office in Shanghai, which now serves as AIG's China head office.*

NOTES

1. The need for insurance has not been evaluated in detail, and reserves for future payments are mostly inexistent or under-funded. The old Chinese way of "self insurance" cannot be compared with modern thinking of self insurance as part of an alternative risk transfer (ART) concept.
2. AIG is the parent company of American International Assurance (AIA).
3. Education is government financed. The insurance funds (e.g., children endowment/education funds) are used either for private classes or to give the child the possibility to be educated abroad.
4. 1986–91 in local currency (20% compounded annual growth in US$ terms).
5. Examples are Malaysia, Russia and PR China.
6. Chubb was the first US insurer to enter South Korea. The culture and product focus of the two companies are fundamentally different.
7. In the South Korean market, AIG experienced similar difficulties to those of other international insurers. Cultural differences initially created poor labor relations in Korea.
8. AIG is a top-tier life insurance company in Hong Kong (#1), Singapore (#1), Thailand (#1), Malaysia (#2) and Taiwan (#3).
9. The Starr Foundation, named after the founder of AIG, is a charitable foundation closely linked to AIG and headed by M. R. Greenberg.
10. Some Japanese life insurers have opened representative offices.
11. AIG originally had a composite license, and legally separated the life and non-life part in 1995.

Premium assumptions for Chinese provinces are calculated on the base of life insurance experience in the following countries and territories: Hong Kong, Indonesia, Malaysia, China, Singapore, Thailand and Taiwan. All these areas are economically dominated by Chinese ethnicity, and have therefore been used as a proxy for the development of the Chinese life insurance industry.

The real premium levels of 1994 to 1996 have been taken as a reference to build an S-Curve of the development of life insurance as a function of GDP per capita:

$$\frac{Life\ insurance\ premium}{GDP} = \frac{1}{A + B \cdot C^{\frac{GDP}{Capita}}}$$

where A, B, and C define the S-Curve.

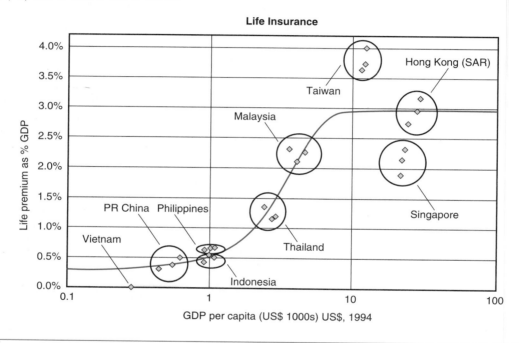

Life Insurance

Source: Wharton Econometric Forecast, Sigma.

case two

Kenneth Keith
Min Ma
Trey Olson
Santhosh Parameswaran
Hua Kun Sun

Innovation distinguishes between a leader and a follower.

—*Steve Jobs*

We started out to get a computer in the hands of everyday people, and we succeeded beyond our wildest dreams.

—*Steve Jobs*

INTRODUCTION

Apple Computer, cofounded by Steve Jobs and Steve Wozniak, has had a tumultuous journey during its 25 years in the computer industry. With a mission of providing easy-to-use computers to everyday people, Apple grew to become stronger than IBM in the personal computer segment. In 1984, with the introduction of the Macintosh, Apple revolutionized the personal computer market by providing the first widely available graphical user interface (GUI) operating system (O/S).

However, Apple now occupies a precarious position on the lower tier of financial performance in the computer industry. Microsoft offers competition in the form of operating systems and software, Dell, Hewlett Packard, and Gateway compete head-to-head for direct computer system sales, and IBM and Sun Microsystems compete in the server industry. Though Apple earned $1 billion in net income in 2001, it has recently posted net losses for the first time in the last five years.

The company continues to innovate with several new product offerings, such as the iPod, newer versions of the iMac, revisions of the iBook and PowerBook, and a new operating system based on Unix technology. However, Apple is ranked number six among the competitors listed above, with a market share of only 3.48 percent.[1] Worldwide, Apple fares worse; it is in ninth place with 2.4 percent market share.[2]

Apple Computer has recently focused on its home-consumer markets with software development including iTunes, iDVD, iPhoto, and iMovie. A report suggests that Apple's "biggest opportunity for growth is in the horizontal market, which is basically consumers. . . . The other big segment is content creation professionals and they [Apple] are pretty safe there. Those people pay a premium because they want the Mac hardware and software—the whole universe of people that do work in that segment are Mac people."[3]

To combat sliding market share, Apple is entering new sales channels. In 2001, Apple opened its first Apple Store near Washington, D.C., and has over 50 locations across the United States. Apple has also targeted Windows users to "switch," expounding the ease of moving Windows documents and files to Mac OS. These moves may prevent further declines in Apple market share by attracting new customers instead of merely retaining current customers.

COMPANY HISTORY

Think different.

Apple Computer was the creation of Steve Wozniak and Steve Jobs, friends from high school who joined to sell Wozniak's invention, which became the Apple I in 1976. By 1980, Apple Computer had grown large enough to house several thousand employees and to

This case is intended to be used as the basis for class discussion rather than to illustrate either effective or ineffective handling of an administrative or strategic situation. We appreciate the direction of Professor Robert E. Hoskisson in the development of this case. Reprinted by permission.

require a board of directors, which was assembled from the investors. After a plane crash in 1981, Steve Wozniak left the company and Steve Jobs became the chairman of Apple Computer. Jobs focused on preparing the Macintosh, the first affordable computer with a graphical user interface, which was released in 1984.

John Sculley came on board as president and CEO in April 1983. In 1985, after a confrontation about the direction the company was taking, Jobs resigned, leaving Sculley in charge. Sculley's campaign started with significant change: Apple posted its first quarterly loss and one-fifth of the employees were laid off. The emergence of Apple as an inexpensive publishing solution began with the introduction of the LaserWriter, an affordable laser printer, and PageMaker, one of the earliest desktop publishing programs.

Despite temporary successes with the Mac II in 1987 and the PowerBook in 1991, Apple lost market share quickly as PC clones flooded the marketplace and Microsoft launched its response to Mac OS, offering a similar graphical user interface. In 1993, Sculley was relieved of his position by the board of directors, and Michael Spindler stepped up from COO to CEO.

Spindler's time with Apple Computer was short. In 1994, Apple introduced the PowerMac line of computers, utilizing the PowerPC chip developed by IBM and Motorola. The PowerPC chip allowed Apple to outperform some offerings from Intel.[4] Though the company had historically decided against licensing its operating system, Spindler succeeded in licensing to select Macintosh clone vendors. However, a $68 million quarterly loss at the end of 1995 prompted the replacement of Spindler by Gil Amelio, former president of National Semiconductor.

Though Amelio made several attempts to return Apple to profitability, such as changing the corporate structure to create seven distinct profit centers, his time with Apple was also brief. In December 1996, Apple announced its plans to acquire NeXT, Steve Jobs' new software company, and its operating system technology, along with Steve Jobs. Six months later Amelio resigned as CEO and Steve Jobs accepted the title of "interim CEO."

STEVE JOBS—APPLE'S WHITE KNIGHT?

With the return of Steve Jobs, many changes happened at Apple Computer. The board of directors was restructured, and new products and an aggressive advertising campaign were unveiled, along with a surprising announcement of an alliance with historical adversary Microsoft. In return for an undisclosed settlement regarding the use of Mac technology in the development of the Windows graphical user interface, Microsoft received Apple stock and announced the development of Microsoft Office '98 for the Mac OS.[5] Microsoft was now able to expand its office suite's user base, and Apple gained compatibility with the massive PC market.

Though Spindler had believed Macintosh clone vendors were useful in spreading market penetration by the Mac OS, most clone sales were direct competition for Apple products. Jobs quickly killed the project and acquired one of the clone companies, Power Computing, utilizing its resources to allow Apple's entry into the direct sales channel. In November 1997, Apple began to sell directly to its customers over the web and by phone. The online Apple Store was a phenomenal success and quickly became the third largest e-commerce site.[6]

By January 1998, Apple returned to profitability and began to perform solidly again. To tackle the low-end consumer market, Steve Jobs introduced the iMac in 1998, an affordable computer with an innovative design, and newer versions of the PowerBook and PowerMac series. Profitability improved due to the success of the iMac, the best-selling computer in the fall of 1998.

Taking advantage of the popularity of the iMac, Apple introduced the iBook in July 1999. Serving the same low-end consumer market, the iBook brought performance and style to the consumer portable market. Jobs became the permanent CEO in the beginning of 2000, and announced a new Internet focus called iTools. iTools (now called .Mac) is a suite of Apple-exclusive Internet applications such as e-mail, website, iDisk online storage, and virus protection. Apple's stock price escalated to over $130 per share in March 2000 as Steve Jobs revived investor confidence.

As the computer industry dwindled in the post-Y2K economy, Apple performed unprofitably once again in the second half of 2000. Apple introduced the PowerMac G4 Cube in July 2000, a computer with a novel form and style for those who did not want a monitor included with the computer. However, the Cube was a complete failure, and production was halted a year later. The shortcomings of 2000 led Apple to reevaluate its position in the computer industry and address the needs of its customers.

THE COMPUTER INDUSTRY

The computer industry that we know today began in 1971 with the fourth generation of computing technology. Intel released its 4004 chip, which located all the computer components (central processing unit, memory, and input and output controls) on a tiny chip. Machines that once filled a small room could now be stored on a desktop.

During the mid-1970s, industry pioneers such as Apple began marketing personal computers to the general public. They released machines that were capable of both word-processing and spreadsheet functions. Apple became the industry leader and remained on top until 1981, when IBM introduced its first PC. The 1980s saw computers invade homes, businesses, and schools at a staggering rate. The number of personal computers in use grew from 5.5 million in 1982 to 65 million in 1992.[7]

Both IBM and Apple had installed proprietary operating systems during the 1970s. Therefore, control of the hardware sector was tantamount to control of the software sector. However, before releasing its PC in 1981, IBM approached Bill Gates, who had recently founded Microsoft with his friend Paul Allen. Gates reluctantly agreed to provide an operating system for IBM, but realized his firm would not have enough time to develop the new software. In order to meet the deadline, Microsoft purchased the rights to an operating system called QDOS from Seattle Computer Products for $75,000.[8]

IBM was satisfied with the software and agreed to a contractual provision that prohibited IBM from licensing DOS, but allowed Microsoft unfettered discretion to license the product. Incredibly, this simple clause led to the rapid decline in IBM's market power while catapulting Microsoft to a position of dominance. With unlimited rights to license DOS, Microsoft contracted with numerous companies manufacturing IBM clones. IBM's ability to distinguish itself from competitors diminished because the clone manufacturers were able to obtain and run the same operating system. Established rivals Hewlett-Packard (HP) and Compaq gained significant market share as a result.

Dell Inc. and Gateway were founded in 1984 and 1985, respectively. Michael Dell recognized that while people were satisfied with the PC as it existed, they were eager for a simpler way to obtain the product. His company responded to this desire by creating a direct sales approach. Rather than going to a brick-and-mortar store and purchasing a PC from a salesperson, consumers can order the machine they want by telephone or online at a discounted price. Gateway employs similar methods to sell its products, but has not captured the market share that Dell now commands.

THE COMPETITIVE ENVIRONMENT IN THE HARDWARE SECTOR

Today, the personal computer has reached the status of a commodity and the battle for market share is all the more intense (see Exhibits 1 and 2). Clearly, the market has reached maturity and only the strong survive. The boom of the late 1990s is over, and weathering the storm has led all the players in the industry to reevaluate the way they do business.

Today the only way to increase market share is to take customers away from the competition. Dell continues to adhere to its direct marketing approach focused on the corporate segment, with a great deal of success. Gateway uses a similar strategy, but seeks to differentiate itself by offering a PC with unique features focused on the consumer segment, including distinctive design and packaging as well as outstanding customer service. Some companies, on the other hand, are surviving through consolidation. The acquisition of Compaq by HP is an example of such a strategic move. While acquisition is typically viewed as a tool for expansion during an economic boom, these two companies have joined forces to weather the economic downturn and develop new technologies faster. Finally, IBM hopes to remain an industry leader by retaining its installed base and attracting new customers by developing the most advanced computing technologies. Each company's strategy merits a closer look.

THE DELL DIRECT MODEL

Dell's direct-to-customer business model adds value in five ways.[9] First, Dell customers avoid delays and price markups because there is no middleman. Second, Dell's model allows for customization; customers get exactly what they want. Third, the direct model allows Dell customers to receive outstanding service after the sale that is tailored to their needs. Fourth, Dell is able to implement the latest technological advances in computer hardware and software quickly because the time between assembly and delivery is so short. Fifth, Dell's efficiency creates shareholder value.

BUILDING LIFELONG RELATIONSHIPS AT GATEWAY

Gateway believes that customer service is the key to success. "From financing and consulting to training and support, we're here to help at every stage in the relationship, so you get the most from your investment."[10] While advertising and promotions are a part of Gateway's strategy, the company hopes to attract many of its customers by word of mouth, believing that no marketing technique is as effective as satisfied customers who promote Gateway to their friends and family. Gateway is most notably distinguishable from Dell in that it operates brick-and-mortar stores. Customers who wish to use a computer or talk to a sales representative in person are able to do so at these locations.

EXHIBIT 1

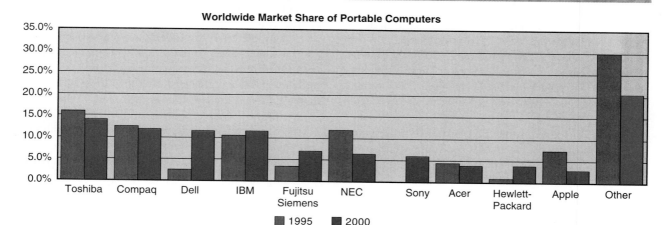

Worldwide Market Share of Portable Computers

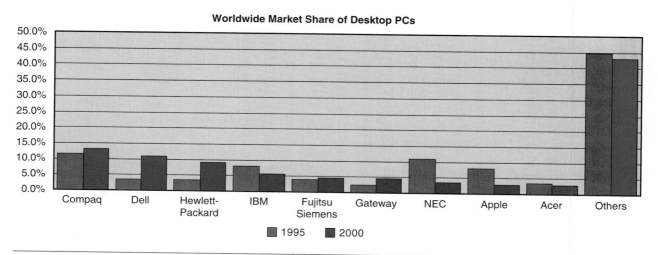

Worldwide Market Share of Desktop PCs

Source: 2002, http://www.infotechtrends.com, November 15.

INVENTION: HP AND COMPAQ

The new entity resulting from the acquisition of Compaq by HP promises to distinguish itself from the pack through innovation. Scientists at laboratories from both companies in the merged firm are eager to collaborate to expand current capabilities, particularly in the area of handheld and wireless devices. "It gives us a virtual size much larger than our real size," says Rich Zippel, director of the Cambridge Research Lab. "We feel we're part of a much bigger organization."[11] Although HP/Compaq remains a dominant force in the PC market, the company's primary focus is currently on communication technology.

IBM: LEADERSHIP THROUGH RESEARCH AND DEVELOPMENT

The goal at IBM is to facilitate the continued evolution of computing technology. "[IBM's] worldwide research

labs work in all areas of information technology, from physics and cognitive science to leading-edge application research. It invents innovative materials and structures and uses them to create exciting machine designs and architectures."[12] IBM works with the governmental and academic communities to provide customers with the most sophisticated products that technology will permit.

THE COMPETITIVE ENVIRONMENT IN THE SOFTWARE SECTOR

In the software market, the industry profile is radically different. Rather than being defined by rigorous competition, the market is dominated by Microsoft. Its Windows operating system comes standard on nearly every PC that a consumer may purchase. While Apple offers its own operating system that comes standard on

EXHIBIT 2

Financial Performance in 2002

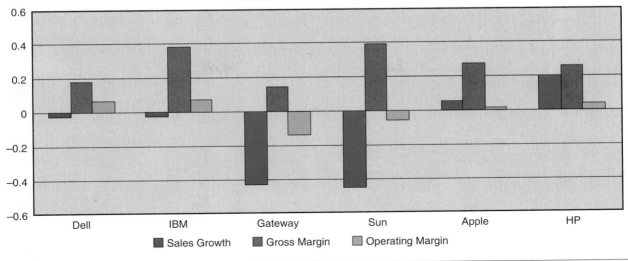

Source: Bloomberg Database, July 16, 2003.

all Apple computers, the software is not compatible with PCs. The result is that Apple software sales are limited by the amount of Apple hardware sales.

Sun Microsystems is the other player worth noting in the software market for PCs. Sun's CEO, Scott McNealy, holds documented animosity for Microsoft. For McNealy, taking market share from Microsoft is not just a necessity for surviving in the software industry; it is a personal quest. Since 1982, Sun has attempted to distinguish itself by its vision. Rather than meeting today's computing needs in homes and workplaces, Sun attempts to thrust computing into the next generation with innovative products and services.

Sun stands the test of time because the company understands that computing technology is rapidly evolving. "While others protected proprietary, standalone architectures, [Sun] focused on taking companies into the network age, providing systems and software with the scalability and reliability needed to drive the electronic marketplace."[13] Despite its unique strategy, Sun has enjoyed little success in taking customers from Microsoft.

THE BATTLE FOR MARKET SHARE

Apple's share of the worldwide desktop market in 2000 was just over 6 percent and in the portable market, just below 10 percent. HP/Compaq is the most established player in the industry. Before the acquisition, Compaq commanded over 10 percent of the portable market and

nearly 15 percent of the desktop market, while HP was also a major player. Dell and Gateway occupy the direct marketing channel. Dell alone captured over 10 percent of the market for both desktops and portable computers in 2000. The most alarming fact is that between 1995 and 2000, Apple's share of the market for both products decreased by half (see Exhibit 1).

Apple's dominance in the education market throughout the 1990s is being lost to Dell, who is leading with 35 percent of the market.[14] A number of factors may be contributing to this loss in education market share: aggressive pricing from Dell, PC price–performance ratios, and the proliferation of the PC in most sectors. While teachers may prefer Apple for their educational needs, administrators and parents often question the benefit provided by not using a PC. Apple is struggling to hold on to its 15.2 percent market share in this industry, offering its new operating system to all K–12 teachers free of charge in October 2002 (see Exhibit 3).

Finally, Apple appears to be positioning itself to attack Microsoft in the software market. The company's new Switcher campaign aims directly at converting Microsoft customers to Apple by promoting the ease of use that Apple products provide. Apple is also challenging the dominance of Microsoft Office on Mac OS by providing its AppleWorks office suite with the purchase of Apple hardware. The newest version of Mac OS X also includes applications that provide improved e-mail, calendar, and synchronization functionality previously provided by Microsoft Office.[15]

EXHIBIT 3

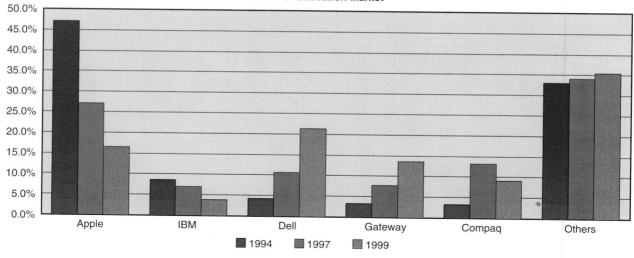

Share of Education Market

Source: 2002, http://www.infotechtrends.com, November 15.

APPLE'S CURRENT PRODUCTS AND SERVICES

The nature of competition in both the hardware and software markets has laid the groundwork for a discussion of the products and services that Apple now offers. Though the benefits of the Apple and the PC have been heavily debated, in reality there is little difference between the two when it comes to hardware. The primary differences lie in the operating system software and in applications that are unique to each system. Apple has also developed certain peripheral products that go beyond the computer and basic operating system.

APPLE HARDWARE

Apple offers its computers in two categories: for beginners and for advanced users who will pay a higher price for higher performance. In the desktop computer segment, the iMac is the least expensive, aimed at the general computer user. PowerMac is Apple's high-end desktop computer and is generally marketed within the multimedia industry. Apple has also created a specially designed computer called the eMac that fits on a school desktop and comes with applications for learning. The "e" stands for *education,* and this computer is sold to schools and other academic institutions, one of Apple's most important niche markets.

Like the desktops, Apple's portable computers are also segmented into two specific product lines. Both are designed to accompany the user wherever he or she goes, but they differ in performance and price. The iBook portables are priced for consumers on a budget, while PowerBook portable computers boast much higher performance and represent Apple's most expensive consumer product line.

Apple also markets customizable servers, keyboards, mice, and other accessories, all of which are designed to coordinate with the CPUs and monitors. Apple computers offer great color choices and are artistically designed to interest customers who are conscious of aesthetic factors. Apple offers a variety of case designs for their monitors and CPUs that give their products a unique and elegant look. See Table 1 for more information about Apple's computers.

With the objective of diversifying its products and businesses, Apple launched an ultralight, portable, pocket-size audio player called the iPod that plays MP3-formatted digital audio. The company shifted orientation significantly and offered the product to Microsoft users as well. Music is downloaded from PCs to the iPod and can be enjoyed on the go for the ten hours of battery life. Apple has equipped its computers with software that greatly decreases the time required to download the songs to the iPod. With this product, Apple has entered a new competitive arena with consumer electronics firms producing products for the entertainment industry.

APPLE SOFTWARE

Though Apple might have had an entirely different history if it had licensed its operating system for IBM-

TABLE 1

	Entry-Level Users	Educational Institutions	Professional Users
Desktop	iMac	eMac	PowerMac
Portable	iBook	–	PowerBook

compatible PCs before Microsoft's Windows took hold, Apple has instead created proprietary software that complements its hardware. Even though Windows XP and Mac OS are similar in many respects, Mac OS is more stable because it runs only on Apple machines. Alternatively, Windows offers greater flexibility and more hardware choices for its users. While Apple's operating system would be difficult to adapt to diverse hardware configurations, Windows has been built from the ground up to match the specifications followed by numerous vendors. The most recent version of Mac OS, Mac OS X Version 10.2, code-named Jaguar, is intended to be more reliable and easier to use than previous models.[16] Apple's O/S for its servers, Mac OS X, supports interoperability with competing operating systems, namely Windows, Unix, and Linux. It is also designed for optimal performance, scalable networking, and tight security standards.

Apple has developed innovative software applications that encourage digital creativity. The company's QuickTime Player is one of the leading media players. QuickTime is available for computers running Windows and offers compatibility for digital media technology used on the Internet. Apple is steering its future software releases toward video (iMovie), music, and photo design and printing (iPhoto) for home users. For corporate and advanced users, the focus is on web publishing, network management, and Internet applications.

MARKETING AND DISTRIBUTION

ADVERTISING

For years, Apple has marketed its products with creative and dazzling (and sometimes expensive) advertising campaigns. Examples include the famous 1984 commercial that introduced the Macintosh during the Super Bowl and the five-year-old "Think Different" campaign, which features archived footage about "the Crazy Ones" (Einstein, Gandhi, Picasso, etc.). Apple has won many advertising awards, including the second annual primetime Emmy Award for best commercial.[17]

During the summer of 2002, in an aggressive bid to win over Windows users, Apple started a "Switchers" advertising campaign. Eight people were chosen to share the story of why they switched from Windows. After the initial televised advertisement, potential customers flooded the Apple Switch website. The site had 1.7 million visitors in the first month following the launch, 60 percent of whom were Windows users.[18]

In the four quarters ending March 2002, Apple spent 2 percent of the company's net sales on advertising, nearly three times the percentage that Dell spent on advertising during the same period.[19] This leaves some analysts wondering whether Apple's advertising expenditures are justified.

In the mature PC market, value shoppers who are bored and unhappy with Microsoft and Intel products might turn to Apple for a new and exciting computer experience. Converting PC users has become the key to gaining share in this market. Increased market exposure would only benefit Apple. If Apple could convince even 1 percent of Windows users to switch, the company's market share would increase by 20 to 35 percent.[20]

INTEGRATED SUPPLY CHAIN AND DISTRIBUTION

In the personal computer market, product availability, customer service, and ability to respond to volatile market conditions are critical for survival and success. A well-managed supply chain is essential. Before Steve Jobs returned, Apple had long been plagued with a sluggish and bloated supply chain. Management tried to restructure the whole chain by implementing cutting-edge SAP R/3 software, but due to a lack of top-down commitment, the effort was not fruitful. In the 1997 fiscal year, Apple had $437 million tied up in inventory.[21] Apple had struggled with both insufficient supply and excess inventory because of its shaky forecasting ability.

Upon Jobs' return to Apple in 1997, a former Compaq Computer executive, Timothy D. Cook, was brought in and given full authority to clean up the supply chain. His aim was to reduce inventory stocked in channels and decrease order-to-delivery time. SAP R/3 (an enterprise resource planning [ERP] system) was finally fully adopted. Within a year, order-to-delivery time was reduced by half. Most of Apple's manufacturing and assembly work was outsourced to contract manufacturers. This outsourcing resulted in reduced costs, improved economies of scale, and faster time to market. Much of the firm's logistics and transportation planning was also outsourced.[22]

Not all solutions came as a result of outsourcing. In mid-1997, Apple began channel assembly to complement this new supply chain strategy. The company consolidated its component suppliers to stimulate faster response to market changes. Apple increased standardization of parts and worked more closely with suppliers to minimize errors in forecasting demand.

In addition to trimming the supply chain, Apple also shaped up its distribution chain. Only distributors with the highest sales volumes continued as partners. In 1998, Apple stopped its relationship with national consumer electronics retailers Best Buy and Circuit City in favor of an exclusive "store-in-store" program with CompUSA, while maintaining traditional relationships with a few regional retailers.[23] "The amount of emphasis on retail is about the same; the strategy has just changed," marketing manager Grace Kvamme said. "Now we can merchandise that area with the message we'd like communicated. We don't have to work as hard to advertise within CompUSA [now] because Apple customers are drawn into that area."[24] Results were quite satisfactory as retail sales increased over 8 percent in 1998.

Not all distribution changes were reductive. In late 1997, Apple opened its online store. Build-to-order was open to all customers. During its first 12 hours of operation, the online store received more than 4.4 million hits and booked more than a half million dollars in product orders.[25] And, after three years of supply chain restructuring, Apple opened its first company-controlled retail stores near Los Angeles and Washington, D.C., in May 2001. Expecting to double market share of 5 percent at that time, Apple opened another 25 stores across the United States by the end of 2001, most of which were located in high-traffic locations such as shopping malls and urban shopping districts. The company hopes the stores will attract those of the digital generation who are as yet unfamiliar with Apple computers.[26] In addition to selling the firm's own hardware and software products, Apple retail stores carry a variety of third-party hardware and software, as well as certain hardware support services.

While the revamped distribution chain has been good for Apple, it hasn't been good for everyone. Since the debut of the Internet direct sales model, resellers have been experiencing lower sales. The situation worsened when Apple streamlined its distributors, which cut sources for resellers to get a better price. Resellers were concerned about whether they could remain profitable.

As a result, Apple developed online configuration programs for resellers to lessen the direct competition created by the build-to-order model. While most resellers saw long-term benefits, some claimed that the programs did little to solve the problem.

Unlike its Internet direct sales model niche-player competitors, Apple is looking for a practical balance among different channels through an integrated supply chain and distribution system. Charles Smulders, senior PC analyst with Gartner, forecasted that the home PC market would improve in 2003.[27] With its existing channel management and aggressive advertising campaign, Apple could expect significant growth in market share.

Apple has been even more creative in its distribution plans for the iPod. To help generate more sales during the holidays in 2002, Best Buy began stocking iPod for both Windows and Mac on its front shelves on September 15. Retailer Target also sold iPod in stores nationwide, adding to the existing Apple retail stores and CompUSAs carrying the iPod. Even Dell, one of Apple's strong competitors in the PC market, began offering iPods for Windows through its website. Analysts estimated iPod to be a $650 million market in 2003, which is 12 percent of the company's $5.4 billion 2001 revenues.[28] Apple has hovered under 5 percent market share in the personal computer market for the past four years, and this shift to consumer electronics may be a sign of the company's aspiration to "think different."

JOBS' DILEMMA

As Thanksgiving of 2002 approached, Steve Jobs sat in his office contemplating his keynote address for the semiannual Macworld Conference and Expo, which was held in San Francisco in early January 2003. Many of Apple's recent initiatives appear to have been quite successful. Approximately 50 Apple Stores are in operation. The Apple Store increases the visibility of and excitement for Apple products. Combined with the Switcher campaign, it finally seems to be attracting new customers away from Microsoft.

Apple has also seen success in the consumer electronics market with the popularity of the iPod for both Apple and Windows users. The distribution agreements with Dell, Target, and Best Buy seem likely to generate revenue. Apple is positioning itself to become the entertainment hub of the future with the development of such software applications as iMovie, iDVD, and iTunes, which make desktop video and music creation even easier.

Despite these advancements, Steve Jobs is worried about the $45 million loss posted in the fourth quarter of

2002 (see Exhibits 4, 5, and 6). While graphics, publishing, and the education sector have traditionally been areas of strength, the company has struggled even in these areas during this period of economic uncertainty. Apple will confront three specific challenges in the coming years. First, it must find a way to successfully compete with Dell, Gateway, and the new HP in the general PC market. Second, it must realistically evaluate the possibilities for success in the education sector, a traditional area of strength. Finally, it must work at increasing market share in the software industry by taking customers from Microsoft as well as by convincing current Mac users to upgrade to the newest version of Mac OS X.

Apple has a long history of innovation and tenacity in the personal computer market in the face of stiff competition. At previous Macworld keynote addresses, Jobs introduced Mac OS X and the iMac. The 2003 address also needed to provide exciting news to reinvigorate the Apple faithful and restore investor confidence in Apple's future.

Income Statement — EXHIBIT 4

APPLE COMPUTER
Annual Income Statement
(in Millions except EPS data)
Fiscal Year End for APPLE COMPUTER (AAPL) falls in the month of September.

	9/30/2002	9/30/2001	9/30/2000	9/30/1999	9/30/1998
Sales	1,443.00	5,363.00	7,983.00	6,134.00	5,941.00
Cost of Goods	1,062.00	4,128.00	5,817.00	4,438.00	4,462.00
Gross Profit	381.00	1,235.00	2,166.00	1,696.00	1,479.00
Selling & Administrative & Depr. & Amort. Expenses	396.00	1,568.00	1,546.00	1,310.00	1,211.00
Income after Depreciation and Amortization	−15.00	−333.00	620.00	386.00	268.00
Non-Operating Income	−45.00	281.00	472.00	290.00	61.00
Interest Expense	N/A	0	0	0	0
Pretax Income	−60.00	−52.00	1,092.00	676.00	329.00
Income Taxes	−15.00	−15.00	306.00	75.00	20.00
Minority Interest	N/A	0	0	0	0
Investment Gains/Losses (`)	N/A	0	0	0	0
Other Income/Charges	N/A	0	0	0	0
Income from Cont. Operations	−45.00	−37.00	786.00	601.00	309.00
Extras and Discontinued Operations	0	12.00	0	0	0
Net Income	−45.00	−25.00	786.00	601.00	309.00
Earnings per Share Data					
Average Shares	361.79	345.61	360.32	348.33	335.83
Diluted EPS before Non-Recurring Items	0.32	10.23	2.01	1.28	0.98
Diluted Net EPS	0.18	−0.07	2.18	1.80	1.05

EXHIBIT 5   Balance Sheet

APPLE COMPUTER
Annual Balance Sheet
(in Millions except Book Value per Share)
Fiscal Year End for APPLE COMPUTER (AAPL) falls in the month of September.

	9/30/2002	9/30/2001	9/30/2000	9/30/1999	9/30/1998
Assets					
Cash and Marketable Securities	4,337.00	4,336.00	4,027.00	3,226.00	2,300.00
Receivables	565.00	466.00	953.00	681.00	955.00
Notes Receivable	N/A	0	0	0	0
Inventory	45.00	11.00	33.00	20.00	78.00
Total Current Assets	5,388.00	5,143.00	5,427.00	4,285.00	3,698.00
Net Property Plant and Equipment	621.00	564.00	313.00	318.00	348.00
Investment and Advances	N/A	128.00	786.00	0	0
Other Non-Current Assets	39.00	0	0	0	0
Deferred Charges	N/A	0	0	0	0
Intangibles	119.00	0	0	0	0
Deposits and Other Assets	131.00	186.00	277.00	558.00	243.00
Total Assets	6,298.00	6,021.00	6,803.00	5,161.00	4,289.00
Liabilities					
Notes Payable	N/A	0	0	0	0
Accounts Payable	911.00	801.00	1,157.00	812.00	719.00
Current Portion Long-Term Debt	N/A	0	0	0	0
Current Portion of Capital Leases	N/A	0	0	0	0
Accrued Expenses	747.00	717.00	776.00	737.00	801.00
Income Taxes Payable	N/A	0	0	0	0
Other Current Liabilities	N/A	0	0	0	0
Total Current Liabilities	1,658.00	1,518.00	1,933.00	1,549.00	1,520.00
Mortgages	N/A	0	0	0	0
Deferred Taxes/Income	229.00	266.00	463.00	208.00	173.00
Convertible Debt	N/A	0	0	0	0
Long-Term Debt	316.00	317.00	300.00	300.00	954.00
Non-Current Capital Leases	N/A	0	0	0	0
Other Long-Term Liabilities	N/A	0	0	0	0
Minority Interest (Liabilities)	N/A	0	0	0	0
Total Liabilities	2,203.00	2,101.00	2,696.00	2,057.00	2,647.00
Shareholders' Equity					
Preferred Stock	N/A	0	76.00	150.00	150.00
Common Stock (Net)	1,826.00	1,693.00	1,502.00	1,349.00	633.00
Capital Surplus	N/A	0	0	0	0
Retained Earnings	2,325.00	2,260.00	2,285.00	1,499.00	898.00
Other Equity Adjustments	−56.00	−33.00	244.00	106.00	−39.00
Treasury Stock (−)	N/A	0	0	0	0
Shareholders' Equity	4,095.00	3,920.00	4,107.00	3,104.00	1,642.00
Total Liabilities and Shareholders' Equity	6,298.00	6,021.00	6,803.00	5,161.00	4,289.00
Common Equity	4,095.00	3,920.00	4,031.00	2,954.00	1,492.00
Average Shares	361.79	345.61	360.32	348.33	335.83
Book Value Per Share	11.41	11.17	12.40	9.18	5.54

Fiscal Year End for APPLE COMPUTER (AAPL) falls in the month of September.

	9/30/2002	9/30/2001	9/30/2000	9/30/1999	9/30/1998
Cash Flow from Operating, Investing, and Financing Activities					
Net Income (Loss)	N/A	−25.00	786.00	601.00	309.00
Depreciation/Amortization and Depletion	N/A	102.00	84.00	85.00	111.00
Net Change from Assets/ Liabilities	N/A	211.00	157.00	377.00	387.00
Net Cash from Discontinued Operations	N/A	−12.00	0	0	0
Other Operating Activities	N/A	−91.00	−201.00	−265.00	−32.00
Net Cash from Operating Activities	N/A	185.00	826.00	798.00	775.00
Property and Equipment	N/A	−232.00	−96.00	−24.00	43.00
Acquisition/Disposition of Subsidiaries	N/A	0	0	0	−10.00
Investments	N/A	1,160.00	−796.00	−948.00	−566.00
Other Investing Activities	N/A	−36.00	−38.00	8.00	−10.00
Net Cash from Investing Activities	N/A	892.00	−930.00	−964.00	−543.00
Uses of Funds					
Issuance (Repurchase) of Capital Stock	N/A	42.00	−31.00	11.00	41.00
Issuance (Repayment) of Debt	N/A	0	0	0	3.00
Increase (Decrease) Short-Term Debt	N/A	0	0	0	−25.00
Payment of Dividends and Other Distributions	N/A	0	0	0	0
Other Financing Activities	N/A	0	0	0	0
Net Cash from Financing Activities	N/A	42.00	−31.00	11.00	19.00
Effect of Exchange Rate Changes	N/A	0	0	0	0
Net Change in Cash and Equivalents	N/A	1,119.00	−135.00	−155.00	251.00
Cash and Equivalents					
Cash at Beginning of Period	N/A	1,191.00	1,326.00	1,481.00	1,230.00
Cash at End of Period	N/A	2,310.00	1,191.00	1,326.00	1,481.00
Diluted Net EPS	0.18	−0.07	2.18	1.80	1.05

NOTES

1. 2002, Apple market share rises slightly, http://maccentral.macworld.com, November 15.
2. Ibid.
3. Ibid.
4. 2002, http://www.apple-history.com, November 15.
5. Ibid.
6. Ibid.
7. 2002, Computers: History and development, *Jones Telecommunications and Multimedia Encyclopedia*, http://www.digitalcentury.com, October 24.
8. 2002, Using the tools: A case study of the computer industry, *Industrial Organization*, Chapter 17, http://www.aw.com, November 15.
9. 2002, http://www.dell.com, October 24.
10. 2002, http://www.gateway.com/about/coinfo/index.shtml, November 15.
11. 2002, http://www.hp.com, November 15.
12. 2002, http://www.research.ibm.com, November 15.
13. 2002, www.sun.com, November 15.
14. 2002, Apple, the saddest school dropout, *BusinessWeek Online*, http://www.businessweek.com, November 15.
15. 2002, MS/Apple: Can this marriage be saved? (I doubt it), http://www.zdnet.com, November 15.
16. Ibid.
17. 2002, http://www.apple.com/pr/library/1998/aug/31emmy.html, November 15.
18. 2002, "Switch" hits from Apple's sales supremo; Steve Jobs's top marketing guy talks about converting Windows users, the price of Jaguar, and the "challenge" facing Microsoft, *BusinessWeek Online*, http://www.businessweek.com, November 15.
19. M. Boland, 2002, Core problem, *Forbes ASAP*, 170(7): 13.
20. J. Youn, 2002, MacAttack! Apple's efforts to lure new users means a business boom for Hawaii's Mac market, *Hawaii Business*, 48(5) 52–54.
21. D. Bartholomew, 1999, What's really driving Apple's recovery? *Industry Week*, 248(6): 34.
22. 2002, http://www.apple.com, November 15.
23. N. Wanchek, 1998, Apple's last resort: No Club Med, *MC Technology Marketing Intelligence*, 18(4): 12.
24. Ibid.
25. 2002, http://www.apple.com, November 15.
26. 2002, Apple's new store is sweet, as long as the economy doesn't get too sour, *DSN Retailing Today*, 41(1): 13(1).
27. Boland, Core problem.
28. Youn, MacAttack!

case three

Dominik Woessner
Thunderbird

Andrew C. Inkpen
Thunderbird

In October 2000, AT&T Corporation (AT&T) announced a sweeping restructuring plan that would break the company up into separate wireless, broadband, business long distance, and consumer long distance companies. This announcement was the culmination of twenty years of change for the company that once dominated virtually all of U.S. telecommunications. AT&T hoped that the restructuring would attract new investors and provide cash to reduce the enormous debt load that had accumulated through various acquisitions. AT&T also announced that it would sell non-strategic assets. The result of the restructuring meant that AT&T businesses, for the third time in twenty years, would be split apart and forced to establish new corporate identities.

EARLY YEARS

The company that later became AT&T started in 1875, when Alexander Graham Bell received funding from two financial backers, Gardiner Hubbard and Thomas Sanders, to complete his work on the telephone (see Exhibit 1 for a history of AT&T). The following year, Bell succeeded in his invention of the telephone and earned a patent. In 1877 the three men founded the Bell Telephone Company, and one year later the first telephone exchange opened in New Haven under license from Bell Telephone. Within the following three years, telephone exchanges with licenses from the company were set up in most major cities and towns in the United States.

In 1882 the company, now called American Bell Telephone Company, acquired a majority interest in the

Western Electric Company, which became the firm's manufacturing unit. In addition, American Bell acquired most of its licensees across the United States during those years, which resulted in the company becoming known as the Bell system, or more colloquially as Ma Bell.

The American Telephone and Telegraph Company (AT&T) was incorporated in 1885 as a wholly owned subsidiary of American Bell, with the objective of building and operating a long distance network. Fourteen years later, in 1899, AT&T became the parent company of the Bell system when it acquired the assets of American Bell.

Bell's second patent expired in 1894, which resulted in the incorporation of over six thousand new telephone companies during the following ten years. Bell Telephone and its licensees were no longer the only companies that could legally operate telephone systems in the United States. With new areas getting wired and other areas getting competition, the number of telephones increased from 285,000 to 3,317,000 during the ten years from 1894–1904. The problem, however, was that there was no interconnection, meaning that subscribers to different telephone companies could not call each other.[1]

THE BELL SYSTEM

In 1907 AT&T's president Theodore Vail formulated the principle that the telephone and its technology would operate most efficiently as a monopoly providing universal service. Initially, the United States government accepted this principle, which led to an agreement in 1913 known as the Kingsbury Commitment. AT&T agreed to connect competitors to its network and divest its controlling interest in Western Union Telegraph.

EXHIBIT 1   History of AT&T

1875	Alexander Graham Bell achieved financing of his work on the talking telegraph.
1876	Bell patents the telephone.
1877	Bell and his two financial backers found Bell Telephone Company.
1882	Establishment of telephone exchanges in major cities completed.
1885	American Telephone & Telegraph is incorporated as a wholly owned subsidiary of American Bell. AT&T begins work on the first long distance network.
1894	Dramatically increased telephone usage and competition after patent expiration.
1899	AT&T acquires the assets of its parent company, American Bell.
1913	After antitrust threats, AT&T stops acquiring companies and allows competitors to interconnect with the Bell system.
1925	Company founds Bell Labs. AT&T has achieved a virtual monopoly on local telephone service.
1926	AT&T begins trans-Atlantic telephone service via two-way radio.
1934	FCC established, setting a goal of nationwide communication service.
1947	The transistor is invented at Bell Labs; first microwave relay system comes one year later.
1949	Federal antitrust suit filed alleging company abuses.
1956	AT&T settles the antitrust suit, agreeing to restrict its activities to the regulated business of the national telephone system and government work.
1962	The company launches its first satellite.
1971	FCC opens private-line service to all competitors and opens rates investigation.
1974	Government files antitrust suit, charging monopolization and conspiracy to monopolize the supply of telecom service and equipment.
1977	AT&T installs the first fiber optic cable.
1982	Antitrust lawsuit settled; AT&T agrees to divest itself of the wholly owned Bell operating companies that provided the local exchange service.
1991	AT&T acquires computer maker NCR.
1992	AT&T acquires McCaw Cellular Communications that becomes AT&T Wireless.
1995	AT&T's restructuring into AT&T, the service company; Lucent, the products and systems company; and NCR.
1996	Telecommunications Act allows AT&T to get back into the local telephone business; the company launches AT&T WorldNet Internet service.
1998	AT&T acquires TCG, the largest local telecommunications service.
1999	AT&T acquires cable company TCI and forms AT&T Broadband; the company creates a tracking stock for AT&T Wireless.
2000	AT&T announces it will break into four separate companies with the broadband, wireless, and business services divisions all separate, publicly traded entities and the consumer business trading as a tracking stock.

Source: 26 October 2000, "From Bell to Behemoth to Breakup," *Wall Street Journal*, A12.

Several times over the next few decades, federal administrations investigated the U.S. telephone monopoly. The only notable result, however, was an antitrust lawsuit filed in 1949, alleging company abuses. This led to a settlement in 1956, whereby AT&T agreed to restrict its activities to the regulated business of the national telephone system and government work. But the restriction did not influence the rapid development of the system and its steady progress towards its goal of universal service. The penetration of telephone service into American households increased from 50% in 1945 to 90% in 1969.

The rapid development of the telecommunications industry was mainly due to the technology developed at

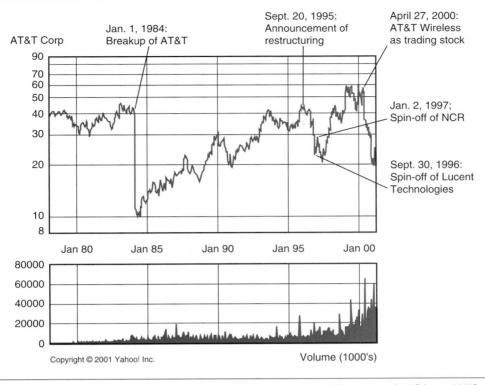

AT&T Corp

Jan. 1, 1984:
Breakup of AT&T

Sept. 20, 1995:
Announcement of
restructuring

April 27, 2000:
AT&T Wireless
as trading stock

Jan. 2, 1997;
Spin-off of NCR

Sept. 30, 1996:
Spin-off of Lucent
Technologies

Copyright © 2001 Yahoo! Inc.   Volume (1000's)

AT&T's Bell Telephone Laboratories subsidiary. One of the new technologies, microwave relay systems, provided an alternative to copper wires for long distance telephone transmission in the late 1940s. With the launch of its first communications satellite in 1962, AT&T provided an additional alternative for international communications. Furthermore, the transition to electronic components allowed more powerful and less-expensive customer and network equipment.

As AT&T grew, its culture became more and more rigid. According to one source,

AT&T's safety from competition also fostered a management culture that ultimately would play a large part in the company's undoing. AT&T's managers saw profit as a way to support and extend the monopoly, not an end in itself. Cost control was an issue less for corporate efficiency than for ensuring that outlays didn't upset the company's regulatory overseers. With customers taken for granted, sales representatives received a straight salary, no commissions, and were warned not to oversell. . . . This culture of control created managers who were averse to risk.[2]

Eventually, the Federal Communications Commission (FCC) signaled its interest in more competition and allowed competitors to use some of Bell Labs' technology and, therefore, competition became established in the general long distance service by the mid-1970s. In 1974 the U.S. government filed an antitrust lawsuit against AT&T, believing that a monopoly was still valid for the local exchanges, but no longer for long distance, manufacturing, and research and development. Competition was deemed appropriate for those segments.

The lawsuit was settled in 1982 when AT&T agreed to divest itself of the wholly owned Bell operating companies that provided local exchange service, creating the "Baby Bells" (see Exhibit 2 for AT&T's share price over the past 20 years). The government, in return, agreed to lift the constraints of the 1956 agreement.[3]

THE DIVESTITURE—AT&T AND THE REGIONAL BELL OPERATING COMPANIES

The AT&T divestiture took place on January 1, 1984. The Bell System was replaced by a new AT&T and seven operating companies, known as RBOCs (regional

Bell operating companies) or Baby Bells. The new AT&T retained $34 billion of the $149.5 billion in assets and 373,000 of its previous 1,009,000 employees. The Bell logo was given to the regional telephone companies. Most significantly, AT&T lost its ability to reach almost every consumer in the United States by its wires and bills. With the divestiture, the "last mile" would be controlled by the RBOCs.

Although the new AT&T could build on great technological and personnel strength, the transition from a regulated monopoly (the Bell System) to a competitive environment required the reinvention of the company as a competitive player and a significant change in corporate culture. In addition, the company had to keep up with emerging technologies, such as fiber optic transmission. Therefore, with the long distance telephone service becoming more competitive, it was inevitable that AT&T's long distance market share would fall. From 1984 to 1996, market share fell from over 90% in 1984 to 50% in 1996.[4]

In addition to AT&T's long distance service, its manufacturing operations faced increasing challenges during its transition from monopoly to competition.

Prior to the divestiture, AT&T purchased most of its equipment from its own manufacturing subsidiary, AT&T Network Systems. Now, AT&T's equipment arm had to compete for business with the now-independent RBOCs. Increasingly, the RBOCs saw AT&T more as a competitor than a partner.

Lastly, the Telecommunications Act of 1996 allowed the regional Bells and other competitors to compete in long distance service. This act increased the pressure on AT&T and the other long distance operators such as Sprint and MCI-WorldCom. The 1996 act also paved the way for the former regional Bells, Verizon Communications,[5] SBC Communications Inc.,[6] Qwest Communications International Inc.,[7] and BellSouth Corp., to become the strategically best-positioned telecommunications firms in the United States (Exhibit 3 shows AT&T's share price trend in comparison with the regional Bell operating companies; Exhibit 4 shows market capitalization for AT&T and the RBOCs immediately after the 1984 divestiture and in 2000). Because the regional Bells and their descendants controlled local networks, it had proved very difficult for new operators to succeed. In 2001 AT&T was lobbying state regulators

---

EXHIBIT 3   Industry Stock Price Development

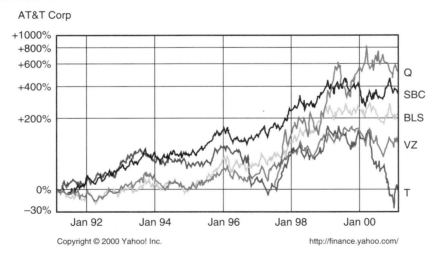

AT&T Corp

Copyright © 2000 Yahoo! Inc.   http://finance.yahoo.com/

Q: Qwest Communications (includes the former RBOC U.S. West)
SBC: SBC Communications (SBC includes the former RBOCs Ameritech, Southwestern Bell, and Pacific Bell)
BLS: BellSouth Corporation
VZ: Verizon Communications (formed by the merger of the former RBOCs Bell Atlantic and Nynex plus the acquisition of GTE)
T: AT&T

Source: "Yahoo Finance: Quotes AT&T," 17 February 2001 [Internet, http://finance.yahoo.com/ q?s=t&d=my&c=VZ%2C+SBC%2C+Q%2C+BLS, Accessed: 17 February 2001].

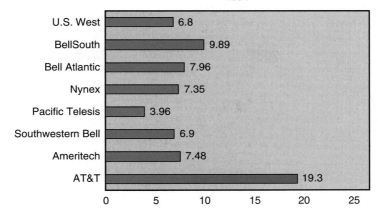

**Market capitalization (bn$) year-end
1984**

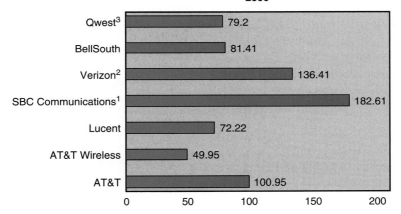

**Market capitalization (bn$) Oct. 24,
2000**

[1] SBC Communications: Southwestern Bell, Pacific Telesis and Ameritech
[2] Verizon: Nynex, Bell Atlantic, plus acquisition of GTE
[3] Qwest: Acquired U.S. West

Source: 26 October 2000, "Before . . . and after," *WSJ*, C1.

to break the regional Bells into two companies: one that would sell services such as basic dial tone and DSL, and another that would lease the network to both competitors and to the incumbent local phone company. The regional Bells countered this position by arguing that they should not have to provide access to their network at a discounted price.

AT&T's Strategy after the Divestiture

In 1984 AT&T was a firm without a local network into offices and homes. Instead of building its own network to match the regional Bells' facilities, AT&T had to negotiate agreements with the regional Bells to lease parts of their networks and resell the service to its own customers. But AT&T realized that, eventually, given the high fees for leased access, the company would have to find new ways of reaching the last mile. Options investigated included fixed wireless technology and cable television lines. Although AT&T would become the biggest cable provider, universal access to all American households, a privilege held before 1984,[8] was lost forever.

One result of the 1984 divestiture agreement was that AT&T's business activities were no longer restricted to the regulated business of the national telephone system and government work. Although AT&T

was steadily losing market share after 1984, the company continued to generate enormous positive cash flows. A decision was made to diversify away from a reliance on telecom service and equipment manufacturing. AT&T acquired several companies in the early 1990s. In 1991 AT&T acquired computer maker NCR Corp. for $7.4 billion in a hostile takeover. The rationale for the acquisition was that with the convergence of communications and computing, AT&T could link these different businesses and capture unique synergies.[9] In a 1994 acquisition, AT&T acquired the then U.S. leader in the wireless business, McCaw Cellular Communications Inc., for $11.5 billion.[10] The McCaw deal established AT&T as a leading force in the fast-growing wireless telecommunications industry and gave the company direct access to consumers for the first time in a decade.[11]

THE RESTRUCTURING—LUCENT AND NCR SPIN-OFFS

AT&T's strategy became increasingly problematic as the 1990s progressed. There were few synergies between the telecom operator and manufacturing businesses. As well, the two businesses became obstacles to each other's growth. Both businesses were becoming more complex and more global, leading to questions about the viability of AT&T as a single diversified corporation.

The result was a second divestiture involving AT&T, although this time it was voluntary and not mandated by the government. In addition to the changing telecom environment and increasing deregulation, problems at the company's NCR computer subsidiary were a catalyst for the restructuring of AT&T into three companies: a systems and equipment company (which became Lucent Technologies), a computer company (NCR), and a communications services company (which remained AT&T).[12,13]

In January 1996 AT&T announced that a post-tax charge of approximately $4 billion was necessary to cover the costs of implementing the restructuring. The expenses included the elimination of nearly 40,000 jobs over three years, with about 70% completed by the end of 1996. The charge reduced fourth quarter net income by about $2.50 a share, with earnings for the first nine months of 1995 at about $1.77 per share (see Exhibit 2).

AT&T completed its spin-off of Lucent Technologies on September 30, 1996, by providing its shareholders with 525 million shares of the new company. The spin-off included its telecom network, switching and transmission equipment business, as well as its famous Bell Labs. The new company had revenue totaling about $20 billion and 125,000 employees.[14]

As mentioned above, the spin-off was necessary because of the absence of synergies across AT&T's business and because of the emergence of new competitors. An analyst described AT&T's dilemma:

Not too many years ago, AT&T had two global competitors: MCI Communications and Sprint. Today you'd be hard pressed to find any telecom service company not competing with AT&T.

The new telecom competitors, including cable firms, RBOCs, and mobile service companies, had many options from whom to buy their equipment. By a company's placing an order with AT&T, AT&T not only would have insight into competitors' plans, AT&T could also use the profits from the equipment contracts against them. However, after the spin-off of Lucent removed these obstacles, Lucent was able to win contracts it would probably never have won when it was part of AT&T.[15]

The spin-off of NCR was more difficult to digest because the company's strategy clearly failed. AT&T's decade-long ambition to be a major force in the computer industry resulted in the $7.4 billion hostile takeover of NCR in 1991. The computer subsidiary's management was left alone to operate semi-autonomously for two years, but AT&T eventually stepped in as the subsidiary's losses mounted. This intervention, however, decreased the unit's performance even more, since the corporate culture clash resulted in confusion, complacency, and loss of direction. In addition, the commitment to becoming one of the world's top three PC makers resulted in a product line and an expense structure that was out of line with market demand. From 1993 to 1996, the computer unit lost about $5.9 billion and forced AT&T to inject about $2.8 billion into the business. The NCR spin-off was done by distributing 101.4 million NCR shares on December 31, 1996. The spin-off valued NCR at $3.96 billion, which meant that AT&T had lost about $10 billion in its NCR debacle.[16]

ARMSTRONG'S VISION

Michael Armstrong was appointed Chairman and CEO of AT&T in November 1997. Prior to joining AT&T, Armstrong was CEO of Hughes Electronics Corp. Armstrong wrote in the 1998 Annual Report:

We're transforming AT&T from a long distance company to an "any-distance" company. From a company that handles mostly voice calls to a company that connects you to information in any form that is useful to you—voice, data, and video. From a primarily domestic company to a truly global company.[17]

Following Armstrong's appointment, AT&T began to implement the vision of a global company by integrating the cable, wireless, and long distance businesses. In January 1998 the company announced a refocused strategy and cost-cutting measures to make AT&T the low-cost provider in the communications industry. The company planned to achieve a significant amount of the savings by cutting the workforce in its long distance business by 15,000 to 18,000 people over the following two years and by offering a voluntary retirement program for managers.[18]

In addition, AT&T initiated a series of joint ventures and acquisitions (see Exhibit 5 for major AT&T deals 1998–2000). One goal was to broaden the company's

July 24, 1998	Acquisition of Teleport Communications Group Inc. (TCG) for $11.5 billion.
July 26, 1998	AT&T and British Telecom announced the creation of a global venture equally owned by the two companies.
February 1, 1999	AT&T announced the formation of a joint venture with Time Warner to offer AT&T's broadband cable telephony service to residential and small business customers over Time Warner's existing cable television systems in 33 states.
March 1999	Merger with Tele-Communications Inc. (TCI) worth $37.3 billion. TCI becomes AT&T's newest business unit: AT&T Broadband & Internet Services.
May 1999	AT&T completed its acquisition of the IBM Global Network business. AT&T agreed to acquire the IBM Global Network business for $5 billion in cash in December 1998. AT&T renamed the business AT&T Global Network Services.
June 1, 1999	AT&T Canada Corp. merged with MetroNet Communications Corp.
August 1999	AT&T acquired Honolulu Cellular Telephone Company from BellSouth.
August 1999	AT&T finalized transactions with British Telecommunications to jointly acquire a 33% equity stake in Rogers Cantel Mobile Communications, Inc. for an aggregate of approximately $934 million.
February 2000	AT&T and Dobson Communications Corporation completed the acquisition of American Cellular Corporation for approx. $2.4 billion, through a newly created joint venture.
March 28, 2000	AT&T acquired GRC International, Inc. for $15.00 per share.
April 10, 2000	AT&T, through its subsidiary Liberty Media Group, acquired 100% of Four Media's issued and outstanding common stock by converting it into the right to receive 0.16129 of a share of AT&T's Class A Liberty Media Group Stock and $6.25 in cash.
June 2000	AT&T acquired Wireless One Network L.P.
June 9, 2000	AT&T's subsidiary Liberty Media Corp. acquired Ascent Entertainment Group, Inc. for $15.25 per share.
June 15, 2000	AT&T completed a merger with MediaOne in a cash and stock transaction valued at approximately $56 billion. AT&T shares had an aggregate market value of approximately $21 billion and cash payments totaled approximately $24 billion. In addition, the transaction included debt and other obligations of MediaOne totaling approximately $11 billion.
July 2000	AT&T closed its purchase of the remaining partnership interests in the Bay Area Cellular Telephone Company, a joint partnership of AT&T Wireless and Vodafone/Airtouch.
August 2000	AT&T completed its investment of $1.4 billion in Net2Phone giving AT&T a 39% voting stake and a 32% economic stake in Net2Phone for a total cash investment of approximately $1.4 billion.

Source: "Company Data Report: AT&T Corp.," 2001 [Internet, http://www.fisonline.com/mds/find.csv, Accessed: 21 March 2001].

scope to areas such as data networking services, digital voice encryption, broadband cable telephony, and video telephony. The other goal was to increase AT&T's global reach.[19]

TRANSFORMING AT&T

In 1998 AT&T acquired Teleport Communications Group (TCG) for $11.5 billion. TCG was the leading local telecommunication service provider for business customers in the United States. TCG was an attractive target for AT&T, because it provided networks that were an alternative to those of the regional Bells. The TCG acquisition was intended to provide AT&T with the ability to offer high-speed service to businesses in major U.S. urban areas. The acquisition of TCG allowed AT&T to save tens of millions of dollars in access charges previously paid to connect its customers to the Baby Bells' networks.

In support of the TCG acquisition, AT&T argued that the incentive was to acquire access to local business customers and provide these customers with a complete communications solution by integrating TCG's local services with AT&T's end-to-end telecommunications services packages for business customers. Within two years, however, almost all of TCG's former top executives had left the company, many because they missed the entrepreneurial spirit that existed at TCG prior to the acquisition.

The biggest steps made towards the vision of an integrated cable, wireless, and long distance company were undertaken in 1999 and 2000. In 1999 AT&T acquired Tele-Communications, Inc. (TCI), the second largest cable company in the United States, for $55 billion. Armstrong said at the time:

> The closing of the merger is a major step forward in the transformation of AT&T from a long distance into an "any distance" company.[20]

After the TCI deal was announced, AT&T's stock fell about 12% from the day before the announcement. AT&T next completed an acquisition of MediaOne, a Denver-based cable operator, in a cash and stock transaction valued at approximately $56 billion. The two cable acquisitions resulted in AT&T becoming the leading cable television operator in the nation. The FCC approved the deal on June 15, 2000, but insisted that AT&T would have to undergo a serious revamping within one year. The FCC gave AT&T three choices: divest MediaOne's 25% stake in Time Warner Entertainment; sell Liberty Media Group, a minority stake in Rainbow Media Holdings Inc. and MediaOne's programming networks; or sell 9.7 million cable subscribers, which was more than half of the company's current subscribers. These requirements didn't tarnish Armstrong's enthusiasm for the deal:

> The combination of AT&T and MediaOne means that far more American consumers will have a real choice and lower prices in local phone service, faster Internet access, and better cable TV. By year-end, most of our networks will be upgraded, making analog and digital video, high-speed Internet access, cable telephony and interactive television available to more of our customers.[21]

The acquisition of the cable Internet and TV services led to the creation of AT&T's newest division: AT&T Broadband and Internet Services. In addition, the deals would again give the company access to local phone services and (theoretically, since there were questions about technological viability) positioned AT&T as a one-stop shop for a wide range of communications services. AT&T was, in a sense, back in the position it was in 1984, when AT&T was broken up.[22]

Despite Armstrong's positive statements, two crucial issues had to be solved. One, AT&T had to accelerate cable system upgrades in order to introduce digital and telephony services to cable customers. Two, AT&T had to succeed in negotiations with other cable operators to achieve its goal of offering branded telephony coverage to at least 60% of U.S. homes.[23,24] In anticipation of succeeding with these tasks, AT&T forecasted cable telephony revenues of $6 billion within five years. To achieve this goal, the company would require a compounded annual growth rate of 111%.[25]

FAILED STRATEGY

In total, Armstrong's vision of transforming AT&T into a global company offering TV, local and long distance telephone services, and Internet services resulted in investments of $115 billion in cable systems. Unfortunately, the reality of creating the vision was much more difficult than Armstrong anticipated. The idea of providing an array of communications services, most of them delivered digitally by cable, proved to be harder than expected because of the expensive and time-consuming process of upgrading cable lines to make them suitable for voice phone calls. By 2001 AT&T was only able to upgrade about 65% of the cable lines within its cable network, which matched only about one fourth of AT&T's 60 million total customer base. In doing the upgrade, AT&T spent as much as $5 billion and moved aggressively to secure new customers. Had the firm waited, newer Internet technologies would have substantially lowered the upgrade cost. According to analysts, AT&T was spending about $1,200 to add a phone subscriber to the cable network. By 2001 new technologies had lowered the cost of converting cable to allow phone service to about $700 per subscriber. The majority of cable companies (with the exception of AT&T and Cox Communications) decided to wait for cable phone technologies to mature before investing significant sums on upgrades. In addition, AT&T did not succeed in striking a deal with other cable operators to lease their lines, which was necessary in order to broaden AT&T's cable telephony customer base. Although AT&T announced a joint venture with Time Warner cable business in February 1999, the two companies failed to reach an agreement.[26]

The result was that AT&T's prediction of millions of cable telephony customers by the end of 2001 had to be downgraded to no more than 650,000, the number the company should have achieved by the end of 2000.[27] Coupled with the failure to build the cable telephony business, AT&T's core long distance business was shrinking and many analysts expected the price of long distance voice service to drop to nearly zero. The long distance business, which made up about 80% of AT&T's revenues in 1997, was projected to decrease to only 35% of revenues by the end of 2002. Moreover, the company had not succeeded in entering local phone service competition with the regional Bells. In addition, the acquisitions of TCI and MediaOne left the company with $64 billion in debt, making AT&T one of the industry's most indebted companies and leaving the company's stock price far behind its competitors (see Exhibit 3).[28] The industry consensus was that AT&T overpaid for MediaOne because of concerns that rivals might acquire the company. As well, AT&T's expectations that it could easily sell some of MediaOne's stakes in other companies proved to be unfounded.

Two areas of the business that were growing were AT&T Wireless, expected to grow by about 30% in 2000, and AT&T's high-speed services, sold under the brand Excite@Home, which was gaining customers rapidly.

Finally, AT&T failed in another area. In 1997 AT&T entered the Internet service provider business with WorldNet. In a few months, the company attracted about a million customers. At the time, WorldNet was growing faster than America Online. When sales began to slow, AT&T chose not to make the marketing investments necessary to maintain growth rates. By late 2000 WorldNet had about two million customers and America Online had 21 million.

DISAPPOINTING RESULTS

AT&T's third quarter results for 2000 confirmed an overall downward trend. Earnings in the Business Services division grew less than expected and revenue in the consumer long distance business fell 11%. AT&T Broadband reported revenue growth of 10.8%, less than the 13% forecasted by analysts. As mentioned earlier, the only bright spot was AT&T Wireless, which grew 37%, compared to the same period one year before. However, AT&T's revenues, totaling $16.97 billion, increased only slightly by 3.7%. In addition, the company's third quarter earnings of 38 cents per diluted share were down 24% compared to the same period a year ago (see Exhibits 6 and 7 for 2000 financial results).

	AT&T Income Statement		EXHIBIT 6	
	12/31/2000	12/31/1999	Variance	%
Net Sales	65,981,000	62,391,000	3,590,000	5.75
Cost of Revenue	31,105,000	29,071,000	2,034,000	7.00
Gross Profit	34,876,000	33,320,000	1,556,000	4.67
Depreciation and Amortization	10,267,000	7,439,000	2,828,000	38.02
Interest Expense	3,183,000	1,651,000	1,532,000	92.79
Income Tax Expense	3,342,000	3,257,000	85,000	2.61
Income From Con't Operation	4,669,000	3,428,000	1,241,000	36.20
Net Income	4,669,000	3,428,000	1,241,000	36.20
EPS - Con't Oprs	0.890	1.770	(0.880)	−49.72
EPS - Net Income	0.890	1.770	(0.880)	−49.72
EPS From Con't Oprs Diluted	0.880	1.740	(0.860)	−49.43
EPS - Net Income - Diluted	0.880	1.740	(0.860)	−49.43

Source: "Company Data Report: AT&T Corp.," 2001 [Internet, http://www.fisonline.com/mds/find.csv, Accessed: 21 March 2001].

EXHIBIT 7   AT&T Balance Sheet

	12/31/2000	12/31/1999	Variance	%
Cash & Cash Equivalents	2,228,000	1,024,000	1,204,000	117.58
Net Receivable-Receivables, net	13,659,000	11,740,000	1,919,000	16.35
Inventories	4,074,000	3,633,000	441,000	12.14
Other Current Assets	0	0	0	0.00
Total Current Assets	17,087,000	13,884,000	3,203,000	23.07
Long Term Investments	68,551,000	57,826,000	10,725,000	18.55
Fixed Assets	51,161,000	39,618,000	11,543,000	29.14
Other Assets	122,511,000	71,962,000	50,549,000	70.24
Total Assets	242,223,000	169,406,000	72,817,000	42.98
Accounts Payable	6,455,000	6,771,000	(316,000)	−4.67
Current Long-term Debt	31,947,000	12,633,000	19,314,000	152.89
Other Current Liabilities	12,465,000	8,803,000	3,662,000	41.60
Total Current Liabilities	50,867,000	28,207,000	22,660,000	80.33
Total Long-term Debt	33,092,000	21,591,000	11,501,000	53.27
Total Liabilities	139,025,000	90,479,000	48,546,000	53.65
Preferred Stock	0	0	0	0.00
Total Common Equity	103,198,000	78,927,000	24,271,000	30.75
Total Liabilities & Equity	242,223,000	169,406,000	72,817,000	42.98

Source: "Company Data Report: AT&T Corp.," 2001 [Internet, http://www.fisonline.com/mds/find.csv, Accessed: 21 March 2001]

Michael Armstrong blamed falling long distance prices for the company's disappointing performance and subsequently lowered the company's earnings projections for the fourth quarter of 2000 as well as the whole year. Moreover, the company said that it will review its dividend policy by the end of the year and might, for the first time ever, cut its dividend of currently $3.38 billion a year, or 88 cents a share. According to the company, AT&T needed to conserve cash to pay down debt that carried an interest expense of $2.1 billion for the first three quarters ($3.2 billion for the year 2000). On top of all the negative financial news, Moody's Investor Service, the debt rating company, put AT&T's ratings on review.[29]

BREAKUP PLANS

It's hard to escape the feeling that a corporate funeral took place today. It's really the end of an icon and no matter how they try to put a positive spin on it, it's the death of a corporate giant.

Ken McGee, Analyst, Gartner Group

On October 25, 2000, AT&T announced a plan to split the company into four parts: AT&T Broadband, AT&T Wireless, AT&T Business Services, and AT&T Consumer Services (see Exhibit 8 for an overview of the planned restructuring). Under the breakup plan, the parent company would own the Business Services and Consumer Services (long distance) units. A tracking stock[30] would be introduced for the Consumer Services unit at the end of 2001. AT&T's 85% stake in AT&T Wireless, already traded as a tracking stock, would be converted into a common stock and spun off in mid-2001. Finally, the cable business was to be separated as a tracking stock, followed by an IPO in 2002.

The announced intent of the breakup was to give the individual companies more flexibility in raising money for repaying debt or for acquisitions. As well, the breakup was designed to boost the company's stock price by separating the various divisions into more easily understood stand-alone businesses (see Exhibit 9 for a comparison of AT&T's share price and three industry sector share price graphs). However, given AT&T's market capitalization of about $90 billion excluding debt and the company's stake in AT&T Wireless, which

	AT&T Broadband	AT&T Wireless	AT&T Business Services	AT&T Consumer Services
Plans	Tracking stock for summer of 2001 and independent stock in 2002	Spin-off stake in current tracking stock, forming common stock by mid 2001	Will be the parent company and legally own the AT&T brand name	AT&T tracking stock by third quarter 2001
Offerings	Video, cable telephony, pay-TV, high-speed Internet and video-on-demand; will assume AT&T's interest in Excite@Home	Mobile phones, calling plans and data services to individuals, businesses and government agencies	Long distance calling, Internet hosting, and data networking to corporate customers	Residential long distance service and dial-up and DSL-based Internet access
Strengths	Nation's largest cable-TV company	Invented "one rate" calling plan; many business customers	Still the largest phone service provider to corporations	Reputation of reliability, loyal base of long-time customers
Weaknesses	Systems need upgrading, incompatible billing systems	Rising competition in national networks, one-rate plans	Facing growing competition; sales-force problems	Revenue gains drying up as long distance price plummets
Major Competitors	Time Warner, Charter Communications, Cox, Comcast	Verizon, Sprint PCS, Cingular (BellSouth-SBC joint venture)	WorldCom, Sprint, Qwest	WorldCom, Sprint, Verizon, SBC
Headquarters	Englewood, Colo.	Redmond, Wash.	Basking Ridge, N.J.	Basking Ridge, N.J.
Current Head	Daniel E. Somers, president	John D. Zeglis, CEO	Richard R. Roscitt, president	Robert Aquilina, Howard McNally, co-presidents
Employees	37,000	18,260	38,000	18,000
Subscribers	16.1 million	12.6 million	About six million	60 million

Source: "Four for the future," 26 October 2000, *WSJ*, B1.

33

accounted for about half the value, the combined equity value of the remaining businesses was only $45 billion. Given the disappointing performance of these divisions, few analysts expected that valuations would be higher just because they were managed as separate businesses.[31]

NOTES

1. "About AT&T: Origins," 28 February 2001 [Internet: http://www.att.com/history/history1.html, Accessed: 28 February 2001].

2. Cynthia Crossen, Deborah Solomon, 26 October 2000, "AT&T takes on a humbler role," *WSJ*, p. A12.

3. "About AT&T: The Bell System," 28 February 2001 [Internet, http://www.att.com/history/history3.html, Accessed: 28 February 2001].

4. "About AT&T: Post-Divestiture AT&T," 28 February 2001 [Internet, http://www.att.com/history/ history4.html, Accessed: 28 February 2001].

5. Verizon: Nynex, Bell Atlantic, plus acquisition of GTE.

6. SBC Communications: Southwestern Bell, Pacific Telesis and Ameritech.

7. Qwest: Acquired U.S. West.

8. Crossen and Solomon, 2000.

9. Acquisition by converting 71.4 million shares of NCR common stock into approximately 203 million shares of AT&T's common stock as well as assuming and converting 2.9 million NCR stock options.

10. Acquisition of McCaw by converting 197.5 million shares of McCaw common stock into shares of AT&T common stock as well as assuming and converting 11.3 million McCaw stock options.

11. "About AT&T: Post-Divestiture AT&T," 28 February 2001 [Internet, http://www.att.com/history/ history4.html, Accessed: 28 February 2001].

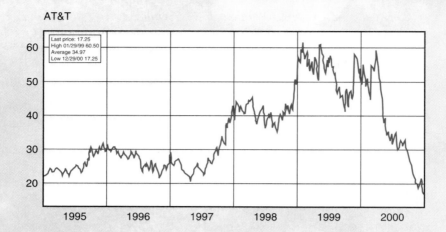

AT&T

Last price: 17.25
High 01/29/99 60.50
Average 34.97
Low 12/29/00 17.25

DJUSFC (Dow Jones US Fixed Line Communication)

Last price: 331.46
High 12/03/99 562.03
Average 311.60
Low 05/26/95 131.17

Source: Bloomberg

12. "About AT&T: Post-Divestiture AT&T," 28 February 2001 [Internet, http://www.att.com/history/ history4.html, Accessed: 28 February 2001].

13. In addition to the restructuring into three publicly traded companies, AT&T sold its 86% interest in AT&T Capital, a diversified equipment leasing and finance company providing financing support for AT&T equipment sales.

14. "Company Data Report: AT&T Corp.," 2001 [Internet, http://www.fisonline.com/mds/find.csv, Accessed: 21 March 2001].

15. Brian Deagon, 26 September 1996, "Lucent, free from AT&T, finds room to be nimble," *Investor's Business Daily,* p. A8.

16. "Spinoff sets NCR's value at $3.96 billion," 17 December 1996, *New York Times (National Edition),* p. C18.

17. "Annual Reports & SEC Filings: Annual reports," 1999 [Internet, http://www.att.com/ar-1998/ shareowners/, Accessed: 26 March 2001].

18. "Company Data Report: AT&T Corp.," 2001 [Internet, http://www.fisonline.com/mds/find.csv, Accessed: 21 March 2001].

19. In 1998 AT&T announced Concert, a Joint Venture with British Telecom, which combined the two companies' trans-border assets and operations. The Joint Venture included their existing international networks, all of their international traffic, all of their trans-border products for business customers, and AT&T and BT's multinational accounts in selected industry sectors.

20. Sylvia Dennis, 9 March 1999, "AT&T closes TCI merger/acquisition," *Newsbytes News Network.*

21. Brian Krebs, 15 June 2000, "AT&T completes MediaOne purchase," *Newsbytes News Network.*

22. Sylvia Dennis, 9 March 1999, "AT&T Closes TCI merger/acquisition," *Newsbytes News Network.*

23. Long-term agreements were sought with Time Warner Cable, Comcast Corp., Cox Communications, Cablevision Systems, and other cable operators.

24. Diane Mermigas, 15 March 1999, "The old TCI meets the new: Hindery ponders future at AT&T," *Electronic Media,* p. 1 ff.

25. Tom Kerver, Charles Paikert, 14 June 1999, "Now comes the really hard part: Execution," *CableVision* 23 (20), p. 27 f.

26. The joint venture was supposed to offer AT&T branded cable telephony service to residential and small- business customers over Time Warner's existing cable television systems in 33 states. "Company Data Report:

DJUSWC (Dow Jones US Wireless Communication)

Last price: 500.27
High 03/24/00 1220.26
Average 394.98
Low 04/25/97 134.55

BBCI (Bloomberg Broadcasting and Cable Index)

Last price: 329.87
High 01/21/00 407.55
Average 222.15
Low 01/05/95 100.23

Source: Bloomberg

AT&T Corp.," 2001 [Internet, http://www.fisonline.com/mds/find.csv, Accessed: 21 March 2001].

27. Leslie Cauley, 18 October 2000, "Armstrong's vision of AT&T cable empire unravels on the ground," *WSJ*, p. A1.

28. Richard Waters, 28 February 2001, "Ma Bell starts to empty nest in effort to cut debts," *Financial Times*, p. 20.

29. Deborah Solomon, Nikhil Deogun, 26 October 2000, "AT&T: Disconnected," *WSJ*, p. B1.

30. Tracking stocks are designed to represent the results of a unit without actually owning the underlying assets of the operation.

31. Deborah Solomon, Nikhil Deogun, 26 October 2000, "AT&T splits amid ongoing business declines," *WSJ*, p. B4.

case four

Brian K. Burton
Western Washington University

W. Harvey Hegarty
Indiana University

"It was the first time in my six-year tenure on the board that we were invited to a meeting," said Frank Vilardo, a professor at Indiana University's School of Public and Environmental Affairs and a member of the Bloomington Hospital board of directors. The board knew something was up when it got the invitation in March of 1993 to attend a meeting of the Monroe-Owen Medical Society. Rumors had been flying that the medical society had taken a vote that indicated a great lack of confidence in hospital administration, and an article appearing in the local paper, the Bloomington Herald-Times, had contained only, "The medical society does not have a comment about that statement at this time," from the society's president. The headline of the article read, "Doctors, hospital differ on serving community."[1] The hospital's president, Roland Kohr, was quoted in the article as saying that his job was on the line: "I am under tremendous pressure right now," he said. One of the major points of disagreement was the hospital's announced decision to start an open-heart surgery program.

The only hospital in Bloomington, Indiana, began exploring the possibility of a cardiovascular (CV) surgery program in 1990 as the outgrowth of an exercise in strategic planning. Three years after the beginning of this process, in March 1993, the hospital's board of directors found itself faced with a crisis in relations with key stakeholders. Decisions had to be made, not

By Brian K. Burton, Assistant Professor of Management at Western Washington University, and W. Harvey Hegarty, Professor and Chairperson, Department of Management, Kelley School of Business, Indiana University. This case is the result of field interviews supplemented with published information and is intended only as a basis for class discussion. The authors would like to thank Linda Swayne and an anonymous reviewer for their help and suggestions.

only regarding the program, but about the fates of hospital administrators.

BLOOMINGTON HOSPITAL

In the early 1990s Bloomington Hospital was a nonprofit, 269-bed hospital owned by a nonprofit corporation, Bloomington Hospital Inc. The Local Council of Women, a social organization, founded the hospital in 1905 and owned it until 1987, when the ownership structure was reorganized and title to real estate and hospital assets transferred to the corporation. The council retained veto power on major decisions, but for operating matters hospital administration answered to the hospital's board of directors. The hospital was considered a secondary-care facility. Primary care would include the patient's first contact with the health system, typically made through a physician at an office or clinic or through a smaller hospital offering only such services as emergency rooms, x-ray facilities, and rooms for patients. Secondary-care facilities like Bloomington Hospital offered more services than primary-care facilities, including such specialized services as cardiac catheterizations and neurosurgery, and were often used as referral centers for specific regions. Tertiary-care facilities, such as large metropolitan hospitals, provided more specialized services such as trauma centers, burn units, and cardiovascular units.

Monroe County, Indiana, had a population in 1995 of approximately 115,000 (see Appendix A for population data). Bloomington, the county seat and its largest city, contained approximately 60,000 people. Its largest employer was Indiana University, a large multicampus research institution whose 32,000-student main campus and administrative offices were in Bloomington. Other large employers included the Cook Group, a diversified corporation owned by William Cook, who started as a manufacturer of medical equipment; as well as manufacturing facilities owned by Thomson Consumer Electronics, General Electric, Asea Brown Bovari, and Otis Elevator. The hospital was a regional referral center for a multi-county area including Owen, Clay, Greene, Martin, Lawrence, Orange, and Crawford counties, as well as parts of Brown County, in the southwestern part of central Indiana (see Appendix B for a map of the region). Hospitals in Indianapolis, the state capital 50 miles north of Bloomington with a metropolitan area population of 1.1 million, provided tertiary care (such as CV surgery) for patients from the Bloomington area who needed care Bloomington Hospital did not provide. Those hospitals included the Indiana University Medical Center, St. Vincent's Hospital, Methodist Hospital, and St. Francis Medical Center. Columbus Regional Hospital in Columbus, a city of approximately 30,000 people 40 miles east of Bloomington, offered secondary care to the southeastern part of central Indiana. Bloomington Hospital did not specifically compete with Columbus Regional Hospital for secondary-care services, or with other, specialized hospitals in the area. However, keeping and enhancing its status as a secondary-care facility required that the hospital offer certain types of specialized medicine.

In the early 1990s, the hospital board consisted of 16 members. Seven were appointed by the Local Council of Women; seven were appointed by the commissioners of Monroe County; and two were appointed by the hospital's medical staff. The directors' terms were for three years, and a director could serve at most two consecutive terms on the board.

STRATEGIC PLANNING AND CARDIOVASCULAR SURGERY

The hospital's consideration of beginning an open-heart surgery program began as an outgrowth of both the board's vision for the hospital and the process by which the board wished to direct that vision. As the 1990s began, the hospital board and its administration, particularly president Kohr, saw Bloomington Hospital as a regional hospital, one that would attract referrals from physicians not only in Bloomington but throughout the area south and west of Monroe County. Other hospitals covered the areas to the north and east of Bloomington. Indianapolis hospitals were used by physicians north of Monroe County for referrals, while physicians in the eastern part of Brown County sent patients to Columbus Regional Hospital.

Vilardo noted that specialized services were likely to feed off one another; specialists would attract specialists,

and the hospital's general reputation among physicians would grow. It was with this understanding that the board made the strategic decision to expand its range of services, and thus expand the hospital's physical plant in 1990 (see Appendix C for a time line listing the various decisions made and faced by the board). A consultant was hired by the board to look at various new procedures the hospital could begin to offer. The first area to arise in discussions was that of CV surgery, or surgery concerned with the heart and its adjoining blood vessels. This area of surgery consisted at the time of three basic procedures. The first was coronary artery bypass grafting (CABG), in which a vein was taken from one area of the body and used to change the flow of blood around blocked arteries that connect to the heart itself. In this procedure, the heart was stopped and the patient was connected to a heart-lung machine. It typically lasted several hours. Another CV surgical procedure was percutaneous transluminal coronary angioplasty (PTCA), in which a catheter (a hollow tube) was inserted into the patient and moved to the coronary artery at the point of blockage. A balloon inside the catheter was then inflated to widen the artery and press the blocking material against the arterial wall. The third CV surgical procedure was valve replacement, in which the surgeon actually cut into the heart, removed a defective heart valve, and replaced it with either a mechanical valve or a tissue valve. As with the CABG procedure, during valve replacement the patient's heart was stopped.

MORE INVESTIGATION AND ISSUES

Other additions to the hospital's service menu, such as an obstetrics unit (including operating facilities), a pediatric and neonatal intensive care unit, an expansion of the emergency department and operating room space, and additional medical-surgical floor space, were approved. But while CV surgery, like those additions, was deemed attractive, at first appearances offering it at Bloomington Hospital did not seem feasible. "It was the cost of the procedure and somewhat the uniqueness of the procedure," Vilardo remembered. "My view was probably that we couldn't do it." Nonetheless, the board decided to investigate the possibility further. Another consultant was hired to do a feasibility study of CV surgery.

The second consultant's feasibility study came back more enthusiastic than might have been expected. "They came out pretty positively on the need and feasibility for the service," Vilardo said. Therefore, the board decided to investigate the issue in a little more detail. One priority was the quality of the service. While quality was important for all service providers, it was particularly important for Bloomington Hospital. If quality was substandard at a hospital, patients could take longer to recover or even die. In a specialty such as CV surgery, with physicians and nurses working with seriously ill patients, the quality issue became of paramount importance. "If we were going to do it, it would have to be a high-quality program," Vilardo stated.

Another issue to be resolved was the status of the surgeon. Even the most optimistic projections for the number of surgeries the hospital would perform barely reached 300, and the most realistic number seemed to be around 200. CV surgeons typically would perform about this number of surgeries annually, so the demand could only support one surgeon. However, one surgeon working alone—not affiliated with any larger group of surgeons—would have no surgeons available to relieve him or her for vacations, family emergencies, and other times when the primary surgeon was unavailable. "We didn't want a surgeon working solo," Vilardo said.

The board formed a study team in late 1990 to examine these and other questions about the service, working with the consultant. Vilardo termed the board's attitude toward CV surgery at this point as "skeptical at best." But as the study team scrutinized the data in the feasibility study, the pro forma financial statements showed that the breakeven point for the service would be reached in about three years. It was determined that the quality of the program and the surgeon issue could be addressed by contracting with one of several surgical groups in Indianapolis to provide a primary surgeon to live in Bloomington with backup surgeons available from the Indianapolis-based group. Based on these findings, the study team recommended in the fall of 1991 that CV surgery be added to the expansion plans.

"At this point the decision was pretty straightforward," Vilardo said. "Then it began to get interesting."

CONCERNS AND OBJECTIONS

Hospital administration had held forums for physicians on the strategic plan and expansion project. Vilardo recalled that typically only physicians with direct interests in the project's components attended those forums. "Obstetricians would come to talk about OB (obstetrics), emergency physicians would come for the emergency department expansion, and cardiologists would come," he said. But once the decision regarding the CV surgery program was announced, other physicians began to come forward with objections. Vilardo listed the major concerns as the program's cost and its use of resources. Some primary-care physicians, according to Vilardo, were worried that CV surgery "would be a

dominant force. 'My gall-bladder surgery will not get done because of open-heart surgery.' Too many of the hospital's resources (space, operating room staff) would be used by CV surgery. Also, they were concerned that it would use up too much of the capital budget."

This last point was echoed by some local general practitioners (GPs). They pointed out that the hospital's debt had gone from zero to more than $60 million in 15 years. Most of that increase came in the 1990s and resulted from the expansion (which was finally approved and begun in 1991). Of course, that expansion included other departments besides CV surgery, and the GPs' concerns ran beyond that department itself to the entire expansion project. "Many general practitioners are concerned about the hospital's financial liability as a result of this," said Larry Ratts, a longtime Bloomington GP who was knowledgeable about his fellow GPs' opinions. At the time of the expansion project, however, a bond rating service gave the hospital its highest possible rating.

Physicians also thought the decision process was flawed, as they claimed the addition of the CV surgery program was based on a ballpark construction estimate that kept rising until the actual bid was double the original estimate. The entire expansion cost $34 million, of which about $7 million was for CV surgery. Also, the GPs felt that the decision process did not have enough input. "At that time there was widespread concern that people hadn't been involved in the process," Ratts said.

A third objection of GPs concerned the need for CV surgery, given its cost. People who needed CV surgery, whether emergency or otherwise, were sent to an Indianapolis hospital. Some of those who needed emergency surgery would not survive the 50-mile trip. Estimates were that the program would save around 12 lives a year. The GPs were unsure of those figures or the basis for them. Ratts said, "The CV unit might save a couple lives a year, but not the 10 to 12 some people are talking about."

A fourth objection involved a financial analysis that showed the program would break even in its third year. Given the approximately $7 million they claimed that CV surgery would add to the hospital's debt, physicians questioned whether enough procedures would be performed that the program's share of the debt would be serviced by the program itself. "Most doctors are not clear in their own minds that this will be a financially viable unit for the hospital," Ratts said.

THE BOARD'S RESPONSE

Vilardo said that while the board heard these objections, its consultants were saying that the unit would actually increase resources and increase other surgeries as a result of the availability of CV surgery. Also, the availability of CV surgery as a backup would allow cardiologists to perform more cardiac catheterizations (a diagnostic procedure in which dye is carried through a catheter and injected into the coronary arteries to allow the physician to examine blood flow through the arteries) and PTCAs, as some procedures required surgical capabilities in case emergencies arose during the procedure. As for complaints about the process, particularly the involvement of physicians in it, Vilardo noted that few if any GPs attended the forums. He also commented, "They said we didn't listen to them. They did have a say, we just didn't do what they said."

Other issues relating to costs and income faced the board. Medicare payments had become increasingly important to hospitals. But at that time, Medicare was considering a program called "Centers of Excellence," under which a minimum annual number of procedures needed to be performed to ensure Medicare funding for those procedures it would ordinarily cover. The number of procedures for a CV surgery program was rumored to be around 200, just equaling the approximate number of surgeries projected to be performed at Bloomington Hospital. If the number ended up being below that, the hospital might not receive Medicare funding for those procedures. That eventuality would seriously compromise the financial viability of the program.

Another threat was bundled pricing, or a single fixed price for the surgery instead of separate billings, and the fact that the price was decreasing dramatically for such procedures. In 1992 the board's information was that the average price for a triple bypass procedure, a commonly used standard for costs, was $60,000 nationally and in the mid-$30,000 range in Indiana. But a hospital in Atlanta advertised that its price was $19,000. "At that point, you could send your employee to the Bahamas to recuperate and still come out ahead," Vilardo said.

A DECISION AND THE CONSEQEUENCES

Despite physician objections, the board approved the final version of the strategic plan, including CV surgery, in April 1991. Construction on the expansion began, and the staff for the unit, mostly nurses, began to be hired. During this same time, the board was attempting to find a group of surgeons with which to contract for the CV surgeon. In the fall of 1992, Schumacker, Isch, Jolly, Fitzgerald, Fess and Glasser, M.D.s Inc. was selected. This group was associated with St. Vincent Hospital in Indianapolis. Schumacker, Isch proposed that the surgeon selected to perform CV sur-

gery in Bloomington would reside in the city, a crucial point to the hospital. Also, the group would provide backup, vacation substitutes, and training for staff. At that point, the board made the final decision to go ahead with CV surgery.

These twin decisions began to generate a significant fallout. Some Bloomington physicians were already upset with the hospital's administration, particularly Kohr, because of other moves the hospital had made. A local eye doctor had begun an outpatient surgery center away from hospital grounds, and the hospital became a financial partner in the center. Also, the hospital had bought land adjacent to the center for an outpatient cancer treatment center. One physician criticized the hospital for what he perceived as a failure to prevent the opening of the outpatient center; others reproached the hospital for becoming a partner in the center and for buying land away from the hospital campus for the cancer treatment center. Some even were concerned that a second hospital might be in the making just a few miles from Bloomington Hospital. Jean Creek, a Bloomington internist, was quoted in the Herald-Times as saying, "It's the hospital I don't understand," referring to all the activity. "The physicians thought they didn't have a say in all this," Vilardo said. "CV was the straw that broke the camel's back."

Another straw for some in the community was that the hospital had chosen a surgical group affiliated with St. Vincent Hospital over one affiliated with the Indiana University Medical Center in Indianapolis. Although Bloomington was the location of Indiana University's main campus and administrative offices, the medical school was located in Indianapolis because the university had taken over a private medical school/hospital facility. Many Bloomington physicians received their undergraduate degrees from the Bloomington campus, were trained at Indiana's medical school, and moved back to Bloomington to practice, so ties between the medical school and Bloomington's community of physicians were close.

Some physicians were not pleased that a non-Indiana University-affiliated group was chosen, particularly because they desired closer ties with the university for teaching purposes. However, perhaps more important, Indiana University itself was not pleased with the decision. "IU was very unhappy when they found out we went with Schumacker, Isch," Vilardo recalled.

The decision to go with Schumacker, Isch was a "no-brainer," according to Vilardo, but not because of anything inherently wrong with the university. Instead, the problem was with the proposal from Cardiothoracic Surgeons Inc., the group of CV surgeons affiliated with the medical center. "Schumacker, Isch had a full proposal," Vilardo said. "IU was late—we had to call them to ask if they were interested in submitting a proposal—and sent a two-page proposal." Another factor in the decision was that Schumacker, Isch had selected an experienced, respected CV surgeon as its Bloomington-based physician. This selection, given the hospital board's concern for immediate quality in the CV surgery program, was a key to Schumacker, Isch's proposal.

The decision to go with Schumacker, Isch was not the only issue giving the university administration pause. IU officials were quoted at the time as being concerned about what the expansion would do to health-care costs in the area, particularly as the university was self-insured. Early in 1993, the hospital had announced an 11 percent rate increase, about half of which was designed to help pay for the expansion. In a Herald-Times article, Dan Rives, the university's director of benefits, was quoted as saying, "An 11 percent increase certainly has a substantial impact on health care costs at Indiana University. I'm definitely concerned." Then-university president Thomas Erlich was openly in opposition to the decision, and he was often quoted in the community regarding his views. The university, having already offered employees the option to join a health maintenance organization (HMO), threatened to open its own primary-care facility in Bloomington that would be staffed with physicians from the university's medical school. "The threat was that IU would be the preferred provider for patient care (for IU employees)," Vilardo said. "The question was, could we still break even without the IU employees? We ran the numbers and felt we could."

THE MARCH MASSACRE

As physician unrest simmered through the winter of 1992–93, with at least part of the battle being waged in newspapers, the hospital's plans continued. Staff members were trained and construction work, begun in the summer of 1991, went forward.

In early 1993 the hospital board received an invitation from the Monroe-Owen Medical Society, the local physicians' organization, to attend the society's March meeting. The hospital board requested that it meet only with the society's executive committee, but the society insisted that the hospital board meet with the full membership.

The meeting, called by Vilardo the "March Massacre," turned out to be an airing of grievances for those physicians who opposed the CV decision. Many physicians, some reading prepared remarks, criticized Roland Kohr, other hospital administrators, and the board itself. Kohr was a target in part because of the previous dis-

agreements with physicians. The physicians called for the resignation or firing of Kohr and all the hospital's vice presidents. This call was affirmed by what the hospital board was told was a strong majority vote of the executive committee, although no vote of the entire membership on the call was taken at the meeting.

The physicians cited various reasons in their criticisms. Cost was one factor. The physicians also accused the hospital of hiring consultants who would follow the hospital's lead instead of giving an independent judgment on the decision. The perceived lack of communication from the hospital was cited. Another factor that came again to the board's attention at this meeting was the alleged opposition of the Cook Group, and particularly of William Cook himself. Cook had begun his company by making catheters in the bedroom of his apartment in the late 1960s. By 1993, he had made the *Forbes* 400 and was head of more than 40 companies. His firms employed nearly 2,000 people in the Monroe and neighboring Owen counties, making the Cook Group one of the five largest employers in the area.

Vilardo said that the board really didn't know Cook's position on the CV matter at that time. As chairman of the strategic planning committee, Vilardo was the focal point of much discussion and debate. He received a letter from Cook that he described as "strange," in which Cook's main objection to CV surgery at Bloomington Hospital seemed to be the duplication of services offered 50 miles away in Indianapolis. This objection was similar to the physicians' feelings that the large expenditures on CV surgery would not be justified by the need. If Indianapolis hospitals offered high-quality CV surgery, a hospital in Bloomington would not need to offer the same service since the vast majority of patients could be sent to a hospital in Indianapolis—as was the case in 1993.

Other high-ranking Cook officials had criticized the hospital administration's vision of the hospital as a regional referral center in print, although they were not directly quoted. They believed hospitals were moving in the opposite direction, toward forming networks that would offer complementary services, not compete with each other. Under this scenario, Cook officials believed, Bloomington Hospital would not be well positioned to be a provider of CV surgery in such a network.

THE BOARD'S DILEMMA

Not only did the board not know Cook's feelings, it was not sure of the opinions of the other large employers in Bloomington and of Bloomington and Monroe County government officials. But it had found out exactly where the physicians stood. Firing the entire hospital administration was not an option. "That is ludicrous on its face," Vilardo argued. "How are you going to fire six people? It would leave chaos." However, as much of the criticism was directed at Kohr himself, asking for his resignation was a possibility. After the "March Massacre," members of the board began to wonder whether Kohr's effectiveness as a hospital administrator was eroded given the obvious conflicts between Kohr and the physicians. This question was also raised by physicians at Schumacker, Isch, who were starting to become concerned about the lack of community support for the program and about what to do with the surgeon who was to locate in Bloomington.

Firing administrators would not provide an answer to the questions regarding CV surgery, however. And between the decision to offer the service and the "March Massacre," another potential problem had arisen in the election of Bill Clinton to the U.S. presidency and his stated goal of major health-care reform. Particularly important to Bloomington Hospital and its decision on CV surgery was the idea of managed competition. Under this plan, employers would form large pools and bargain with health-care providers to gain the lowest cost for services. Competition could force attrition, with only two or three providers for any one service. Bloom-

ington Hospital would be at a competitive disadvantage compared to Indianapolis hospitals offering CV surgery under such a system, for it could not hope to gain the kinds of economies the larger hospitals had.

This imponderable, combined with the opposition from physicians and area employers, put cardiovascular surgery at Bloomington Hospital at a crossroads. The board had three possible courses of action regarding CV surgery. First, it could plow ahead and keep the program on line. Second, it could drop the idea completely. Third, it could put the program on hold and investigate the pros and cons further, making a final decision when more information was gathered. Each option had both positive and negative effects on the board's various constituencies. To make a decision, the board had to consider those effects, as well as problems and opportunities that might arise from each option, and decide which option presented the best set of trade-offs. The board had this, as well as the fate of the hospital administration, to decide quickly, for delay would only increase the pressure and the problems.

NOTE

1. Bloomington Herald-Times, February 14, 1993, p. A1.

1995 Population, Monroe County, Indiana, and Surrounding Counties, with Projections for Monroe County (state population estimates)	APPENDIX A

County	Population
Monroe	
1995 (estimate)	115,208
2000 (projected)	118,900
2005 (projected)	123,000
2010 (projected)	126,900
2020 (projected)	131,100
2030 (projected)	127,500
Bartholomew	68,065
Brown	15,098
Clay	26,306
Crawford	10,442
Greene	32,696
Lawrence	45,097
Marion (including Indianapolis)	817,604
Martin	10,545
Morgan	62,115
Orange	19,011
Owen	19,663

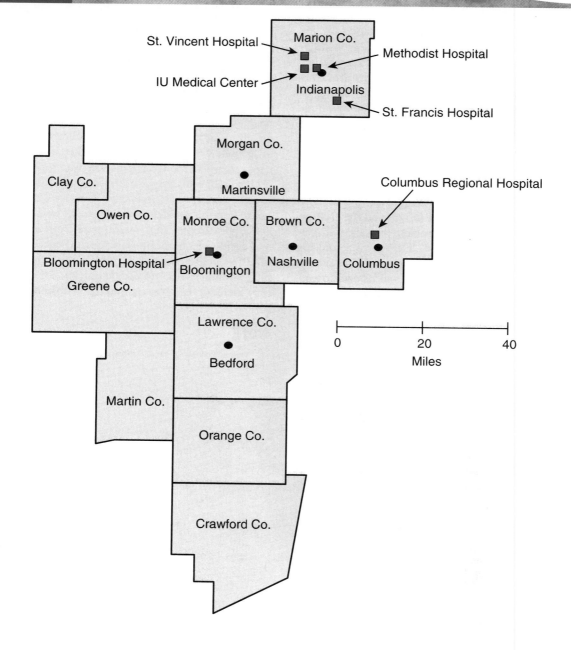

Time Line of Decisions Faced and Made by the Bloomington
Hospital Board of Directors Regarding Cardiovascular (CV) Surgery

APPENDIX C

1989: Expansion in principle approved; many services approved; the possibility of adding CV surgery studied.

1990: Board's study team recommends adding CV surgery to hospital's range of services.

1991: Final strategic plan (including CV surgery) approved; construction and hiring begun.

1993: Unrest among stakeholders reaches climax; "March Massacre" meeting; board faces decisions regarding CV surgery and hospital administration.

Brasil Telecom S.A.

case five

Michael Moffett
Kannan Ramaswamy
Thunderbird, The American Graduate
School of International Management

Ideas and leadership, however, are not enough. They need to be nurtured with money. Companies that cannot depend on steady access to the capital markets will not prosper. In some ways, the solution is simple: the only way for Latin American companies to sustain access to the international capital markets is to stop being or, at least, stop being perceived as "Latin American" companies. In many cases, this means dramatically changing corporate behavior, becoming more like the GEs, Enrons, and ABBs of the world. These companies—and hundreds of others like them—which have virtually unfettered access to the global capital markets, define best practices that attract and retain global investment capital.

What do investors want? First, of course, investors want performance: strong predictable earnings and sustainable growth. Second, they want transparency, accountability, open communications and effective corporate governance. Companies that fail to move toward international standards in each of these areas will fail to attract and retain international capital.

"The Brave New World of Corporate Governance,"
Latinfinance, *May 2001*

It was July 16, 2001. Mr. Luis Octavio de Motta Veiga, the Chairman of Brasil Telecom, leaned out of his office window as the brilliant morning sunshine flooded into his office. The sprawling city of Brasilia was coming back to life after a quiet weekend. It had proven to be a challenging morning for Mr. Veiga and Brasil Tele-

com (BT). The controlling shareholders of BT, CVC/Opportunity and Telecom Italia (TI) had decided to seek arbitration of their dispute over the future direction of the company. Unfortunately CVC/Opportunity and Telecom Italia had very different ideas of where the Brazilian telecommunications industry was going, and how they as individual entities would attempt to exploit it. Consequently, the two camps failed to see eye to eye on critical issues of capital expenditure, spending priorities, and strategy. At a time when BT needed—more than ever—a clear sense of where it was going, both for internal and external constituents, the in-fighting between owners was creating an image of a company that had lost control of its own destiny. As recently as June, BT's shares, listed on the New York Stock Exchange (American Depositary Receipts, ADRs; symbol: BRP) were down more than 120% from their peak in early 2000. BT was now facing an ownership-leadership crisis at a pivotal point in the development of the Brazilian telecom marketplace.

The impasse put at risk not only the operation of Brasil Telecom, their joint venture, but also TI's plans to expand its mobile operations in Brazil. The telecom regulatory agency Anatel had stipulated that Brasil Telecom had to meet specified network installation and quality targets before Telecom Italia Mobile (TIM), the mobile telephony subsidiary of TI, would be permitted to use two recently acquired mobile telephone licenses. Eager to meet targets early, the Italians proposed installing an additional 1.5m phone lines by January 2002 rather than by 2003. It was apparent that an early fulfillment of the targets would allow TIM to leverage its license investments and start capitalizing its first mover advantage ahead of other rivals such as Telefonica and Portugal Telecom that were not far behind. However, the majority shareholder in Brasil Telecom, the investment company Opportunity, opposed the move. Mr. Veiga had made his conclusions clear to the press recently. "There are other lines of business that are much more profitable," he had told them.

Mr. Veiga had to take stock of the deteriorating situation and recommend a course of action to the Board shortly. What opportunities would BT forego if it chose to abandon the drive to meet Anatel targets early? Would the promise of meteoric growth in the wireless segment emerge soon enough to marginalize BT given its lack of a wireless presence? Would BT be able to hold its own against other wireline operators after 2003 when true free market competition was permitted in Brazil? Of more immediate concern was developing a proposed settlement that CVC/Opportunity would like to see emerge after the arbitration in London. Needless to say, Mr. Veiga had to marshal all his resources to predict the likely path that TI would take at the arbitration proceedings. He had much preparation to do.

PRIVATIZATION OF THE BRAZILIAN TELECOM MARKET

On July 29, 1998, Telebrás, the Brazilian telecom giant, was sold by the Brazilian government in 12 pieces to the highest bidders for a total of R$22 billion (US$19 billion). Telebrás, however, was not wholly owned by the government. The Brazilian government was actually selling *its* shares, not sole ownership. The auction, which was carried live on Brazilian television, yielded nearly US$5 billion more than expected. It was the second largest telecom privatization in history, falling second only to the US$70 billion sale of Japan's NTT in 1986.

The expected outcomes of privatization were similar to those around the world: rapid injections of technology, capital, expertise, and service quality, in addition to the windfall profits accruing to governments. Telebrás, which had controlled more than 90% of the Brazilian telecommunications market, had suffered from under investment for many years. Brazil had 11.5 phones per 100 people in 1998 compared to 66 in the United States. It was estimated that over 20 million Brazilians were waiting for telephone lines, waiting on average two years, and then paying an average installation fee of US$836, a fortune in a country where the per capita income was US$4350. The backlog for telephone line installations had reached such desperate proportions that the black market for telephone lines quoted prices in newspapers like stock quotations.

The sale broke Telebrás up into 12 separate units over the three basic dimensions of telecommunications services:

1. One long-distance and international operator—Embratel[1]
2. Three fixed-line phone service companies—Telesp, Tele Norte-Nordeste-Leste, and Tele Centro-Sul;
3. Eight A-band cellular companies for mobile cellular communications.

As illustrated by Exhibit 1, the auction resulted in substantial premiums to the Brazilian government. The privatization also facilitated the entry of some of the world's largest telecom players into the Brazilian marketplace.

Although the Brazilian government was criticized for its relative tardiness in privatizing the telecommunications sector, it had devised a staged privatization program under which all areas of Brazil would be required to have at least two rival operators for both fixed-line and mobile services. And, significantly, a single firm could not provide both fixed-line and mobile services within the same region.

	Select Results of the July 1998 Privatization Auction of Telebrás (billions)			EXHIBIT 1
Telebrás Unit	**Acquiring Company**	**Asking Price**	**Actual Price**	**Premium**
Telesp wire	Telefonica of Spain	$3.0	$4.9	63%
Tele Centro-Sul	Telecom Italia	$1.6	$1.7	6%
Embratel	MCI	$1.5	$2.2	47%
Telesp cellular	Portugal Telefonica	$0.9	$3.0	233%
Telesudeste cellular	Telefonica of Spain	$0.5	$1.1	120%

Source: *Fortune*, September 7, 1998, p. 181.

The Brazilian telecommunications regulatory authority, Agência Nacional de Telecomunicações, Anatel, was charged with the intricate task of managing the staged deregulation of the newly privatized telecom sector. It was Anatel's objective to significantly improve the telecom infrastructure in Brazil through careful implementation of its universalization plan. Exhibit 2 identifies the key dimensions of the *universalization* and service quality targets specified by Anatel.

Anatel's privatization plan was a well-laid-out blueprint that would usher in complete deregulation and free market competition to the sector by December 31, 2003. In moving toward this goal, Anatel had set forth very specific network build-out and service quality targets for all wireline and wireless companies. All incumbents were restricted to operating within their allocated regions until such time as they met the targets specified. Meeting the targets early was a prerequisite for a company that sought to offer expanded services or enter other regions outside its own. The prospects were clear: the entire Brazilian telecom market would be completely opened in 2003.

BRAZILIAN WIRELINE MARKET

The Brazilian wireline market structure was organized into four well-defined *duopoly* (two monopolistic competitors) markets with artificially constructed competi-

---

EXHIBIT 2 — Anatel's Universalization and Service Quality Requirements

Universal Service Plan Build-out Requirements

1. Services to be available in all communities with a population of 600 or more inhabitants
2. Minimum of 7.5 public phones per 1,000 inhabitants
3. Minimum network digitalisation level of 95%

Quality of Service Requirements

1. Maximum billing error of 4 bills per 1,000
2. 98% of calls must have dial tone within 3 seconds
3. Maximum of three repair requests per 100 lines per month
4. Minimum of 60% of calls must be completed

---

tion. The four markets consisted of three geographically defined wireline regions and a fourth region covering the interregional and international long-distance markets. The four wireline segment concessions were awarded in the July 1998 Telebrás auction. This was followed by the auctioning of a second license in each region to create *mirror companies,* new artificial competitors for each region, in February 1999. While the incumbent player in each region was a part of the former Telebrás, the mirror companies were newly created in order to assure that there were two competitors in each region. The mirror companies were expected to gain market shares of 20% and 50% in fixed-line and long-distance services within five years. The result, as illustrated in Exhibit 3, was a wireline market of roughly three comparable fixed-line markets with a long distance overlay.

In attempting to level the playing field, the mirror companies were given unique advantages over existing concession holders. First, they were allowed to set their own tariffs without prior approval from Anatel. Second, instead of being given targets for line installation and service quality by Anatel, they set their own targets as part of their initial license bid. Third, they were exclusively licensed to adopt Wireless Local Loop (WLL) technology for two years in regions of more than 50,000 inhabitants. Under this system, a call carried by a mirror company would originate and terminate using a wireless network instead of the copper wire network that the incumbents controlled at the local level. The mirror companies were allowed to utilize the trunk line network and junction switches of the incumbent players at preset fees determined by Anatel. This was powerful, as it allowed the newly created mirror companies to be effective competitors using a large part of the existing concessionaires' infrastructure.

The experience to date, however, was mixed, as the limitations of WLL had become apparent very quickly. WLL possessed limited capacity for data transmission (thought to be the largest potential growth segment of the market), and a relatively slower Internet access speed capability. Building these networks, although still a considerably smaller task than the original baseline wireline, had also proven to be very expensive, with the resulting prices still higher than that needed for greater market penetration.

Region I: North East

Tele Norte Leste, Telemar (NYSE: TNE), held the wireline concession for Region I. It was the only wireline company in the country which did not have an international telecom operator among its controllers. It possessed the largest single regional wireline concession within Brazil, including the city of Rio de Janeiro. With

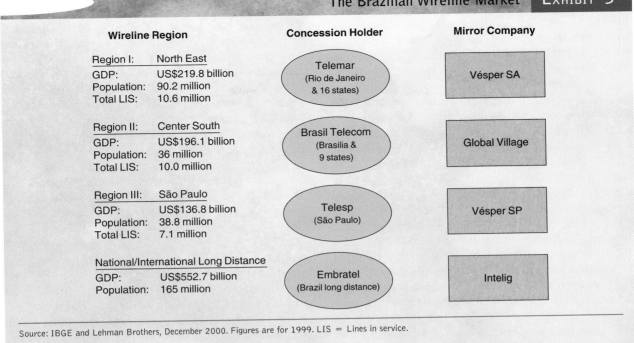

Wireline Region	Concession Holder	Mirror Company
Region I: North East GDP: US$219.8 billion Population: 90.2 million Total LIS: 10.6 million	Telemar (Rio de Janeiro & 16 states)	Vésper SA
Region II: Center South GDP: US$196.1 billion Population: 36 million Total LIS: 10.0 million	Brasil Telecom (Brasilia & 9 states)	Global Village
Region III: São Paulo GDP: US$136.8 billion Population: 38.8 million Total LIS: 7.1 million	Telesp (São Paulo)	Vésper SP
National/International Long Distance GDP: US$552.7 billion Population: 165 million	Embratel (Brazil long distance)	Intelig

Source: IBGE and Lehman Brothers, December 2000. Figures are for 1999. LIS = Lines in service.

a regional market of more than 90 million people, it had more than 11.1 million lines in service (LIS) at end of year 2000.

Telemar was moving aggressively to meet Anatel requirements before the December 31, 2003 deadline, and was known to have ambitions of expanding into personal communication services (PCS) as soon as possible. The mirror company for Region I, Vésper SA, had gained little market share as a result of technical problems (insufficient transmission speeds prevented Internet access for clients, among others). Select local cable operators actually posed a more real threat to Telemar.

Financially, Telemar enjoyed greater than 50% EBITDA margins,[2] low debt levels, and high cash levels. This financial footing would allow it to meet capital expenditure needs easily.

Region II: Center South

Brasil Telecom was the designated incumbent operator in this region. Brasil Telecom Participações SA (formerly Telepar) provides fixed-line telecommunications services in nine states of western, southern, and central Brazil (Acre, Rondônia, Mato Grosso, Mato Grosso do Sul, Tocantins, Goiás, Paraná, Santa Catarina, Rio Grande do Sul), and the federal district under license from the Brazilian federal government. The company's original service area covered roughly 30% of Brazil's

geographic territory and 18% of Brazil's population (29 million people), but this grew substantially with the acquisition of Companhia Rio Grandense de Telecomunicações (CRT) in the summer of 2000, expanding geographic territory to 34% and population coverage to 26% (39 million inhabitants). This wireline concession covered the smallest of the three regions by population, and hence had important investment implications for BT. The firm would be required to meet Anatel requirements for build-out of fixed-lines, lines-in-service, for a relatively sparsely populated region of Brazil.

BT's mirror company rival was Global Village Telecom (GVT), a subsidiary (93%) of its Dutch parent of the same name. GVT was moving ahead at a rapid pace in the installation of its required lines, completing 354 lines by end of year 2000, well ahead of the Anatel requirement of 238. GVT was expected to continue to expand LIS well ahead of requirements, including the establishment of its fiber optic backbone in the Brasilia area specifically in 2001. Although specific numbers for lines in service (LIS) were unknown, it was expected that GVT had only 100,000 LIS at end of year 2000, representing less than 1.5% of the total 7.4 million LIS market of Region II. At best, GVT was expected to achieve a 3.0% market share of LIS by end of year 2001. Other than a small change in free pulses per month (from 90 to 100), GVT had not yet had any appreciable impact on pricing.

Region III: São Paulo

Telecomunicações de São Paulo SA Telesp, owned by Telefonica of Spain, had won the wireline concession for São Paulo in the 1998 auction. Telesp operated in Brazil's wealthiest and most populous state, and was generally regarded as the premier wireline provider in Brazil in terms of potential, but not particularly for quality of service. It competed against Vésper SP, the mirror company created through the February 1999 auction for competitive rights.

Although all regions were ahead of assigned targets, Telesp in Region III was clearly moving rapidly to create the infrastructure that it believed was needed to expand its telecom services into the margins expected by its investors.

In terms of market potential for wireline services, it appeared that Regions I and III were well suited to benefit from the explosion in data and video services as well as Internet connectivity. Both regions encompassed large commercial centers, usually the premium markets for a telecom provider. The corporate segment is typically the segment of choice since this group of buyers has a wide range of needs across the spectrum of voice, data, and video, offering considerable scope for the provision of packaged value added services. The residential segment, on the other hand, is a fairly unpredictable group since it demands high levels of services but is also riddled with problems such as credit and collection. Regulatory agencies usually mandate levels of residential service making it difficult for providers to discriminate in terms of economic wealth and ability to pay. Thus, the market for value added services such as digital subscriber lines (DSL), call-waiting, three-way calling, and short messaging is typically limited to a small, wealthier market segment.

LONG-DISTANCE WIRELINE

Embratel (NYSE: EMT) was the sole domestic long-distance (DLD) and international long-distance (ILD) concession sold in the July 1998 auction of Telebrás services. It is 51.8% owned (voting shares) by MCI World-Com, with the remaining 48.2% publicly traded. Embratel brought with it the only nationwide infrastructure for Internet Service Providers (ISP), ready access to large corporate users given its existing network, and an established position in the high-margin data transmission market. Although MCI WorldCom's interest had been thought an asset given its expertise and experience, WorldCom's failed merger with Sprint led to rumors that the company was about to sell off its Latin American properties, Embratel and Avantel.

Embratel was facing stiff competition in the domestic long-distance market because the regional incumbents were permitted to offer long-distance services within their specific regions in 2001. Intelig, Embratel's mirror company, had made significant inroads and was estimated to hold 17% of the ILD market. It was placing significant pricing pressure on Embratel, offering call rates that were lower than Embratel could afford in some segments. Pricing was critical because residential service was still something of a luxury to the general Brazilian population. Market forces were expected to continue to drive ILD prices downward about 4% annually over the prospective future, but local interconnection charges were expected to fall even faster, allowing the company to complete long-distance calls for its customers much more cheaply. This would help Embratel in improving margins, as interconnection net revenues made up nearly half of all net revenues.

THE OUTLOOK FOR WIRELINE

The future for the wireline segment included one certainty: heightened competition arising from total deregulation of the telecom sector in 2003. The privatization reforms called for a complete dismantling of the regulatory regime as of December 31, 2003, allowing regional incumbents and mirror companies to cross into other regions. Given the lucrative corporate markets in Regions I and III, the intensity of competition in these regions was expected to escalate. Dominant incumbents such as Telesp, controlled by Telefonica, could breach Region II and challenge Brasil Telecom for market share. The long-distance market was also expected to face increasing competition from regional players. To exacerbate matters, telecom players who had wireless assets could also try to leverage wireline-wireless synergies across regions. Wireless penetration was expected to increase substantially to make these synergies tangible bases for launching attacks. In terms of market niches, the corporate data market was expected to grow at a steady pace of 25% per year along with increasing demand for Internet enabled services. With the onset of total deregulation, all operators would struggle to prevent their business lines from turning into telecom commodities.

BRAZILIAN WIRELESS MARKET

Unlike the wireline market that was a mosaic of organized duopolies, the wireless market was a lot more chaotic and fragmented. The original privatization of Telebrás had created eight cellular companies capable of providing mobile services. Given the mix of alternative technologies and bandwidths, and successive rounds of bandwidth auctions, there were now at least three or four players in each geographic market space.

There were two basic types of mobile network formats, *cellular communications* and *personal communications* services (PCS). *Cellular* telephone is a type of shortwave analog or digital transmission in which a subscriber has a wireless connection from a mobile telephone to a relatively nearby transmitter. The transmitter's span of coverage is called a *cell*. Generally, cellular telephone service is available in urban areas and along major highways. As the cellular telephone user moves from one cell, one area of coverage, to another, the call is passed to the local cell transmitter. *Personal Communications Services, PCS,* is a wireless phone service somewhat similar to cellular telephone service, but emphasizes personal service and extended mobility. Like cellular, PCS is for mobile users and requires a number of antennas to blanket an area of coverage. As a user moves around, the user's phone signal is picked up by the nearest antenna and then forwarded to a base station that connects to the wired network. The phone itself is slightly smaller than a cellular phone. PCS has a shorter range but was ideal for densely populated regions.

Within these two broad domains, companies had to choose among TDMA (Time Division Multiple Access), CDMA (Code Division Multiple Access), and GSM (Global System for Mobile Communication) to structure their services. These were alternative ways of managing the bandwidth spectrum that each firm had licensed. A third wireless format broadly referred to as 3G or *third generation* was already on the horizon. This technology promised much greater mobility and far higher data transmission speeds. Nokia, a leading equipment manufacturer for the 3G sector, boasted that the technology would allow callers "to hold a video conference in a taxi while driving to the airport." Anatel was likely to auction 3G spectrum in 2003.

WIRELESS CONCESSIONS

The network of wireless concessions was originally organized into ten geographic regions unlike the three that had been used in the privatization of the wireline segment. Concessions were defined by bandwidths A through E. Band A concessions had been determined in the 1998 Telebrás privatization, following Band B license auctions in 1997. Bands A and B had limited carrying capacity which, when coupled with the multiple regions, led to fragmentation.

Anatel followed up with auctions of bandwidths C, D, and E in 2001 and, in so doing, changed some of the fundamental rules of the game. These bandwidths were assigned to three regions, instead of ten, that corresponded to the original wireline markets. The bandwidths were PCS bands capable of much greater data transmission volumes giving the potential winners a

technological edge over their Band A and B counterparts. The original Band A and B firms were offered additional spectrum capacity by Anatel through a separate auctioning process to allow them to eventually migrate to PCS services.

This new round of wireless auctions was possibly the last opportunity for new entrants to stake their claims in the Brazilian wireless landscape. This was particularly crucial for wireline operators because this was the first time they were permitted to bid for PCS Bands (D and E only). The winners in these auctions were permitted to offer national and international long-distance services beginning January 1, 2002. It also offered the first real hope for wireline operators to develop a competitive range of value added services, including voice, data, DLD, ILD, and wireless along with their basic wireline offering.

THE WIRELESS LANDSCAPE

While there were 18 Band A and B providers prior to the new auctions of Bands C, D, and E, in effect there were only four major firms that seemed to have the power to realize the potential of the wireless segment. The key players were Portugal Telecom, Telefonica de España, Telecom Italia Mobile who were global operators, and Brazilian operators Telpart, controlled in part by Opportunity, the majority shareholder of BT and some pension funds and Telemar PCS, the wireless subsidiary of wireline operator Telemar in Region I.

Telefonica de España

Telefonica de España operated in the mobile segment under the aegis of its subsidiary Telefónica Móviles. It controlled three mobile communications operators in Brazil, namely TeleSudeste Celular in Río de Janeiro and Espírituo Santo, CRT Celular in Rio Grande do Sul and TeleLeste Celular in Bahía and Sergipe. Collectively these companies had over 4.6 million customers, and 66% of total mobile communications customers in the states in which they operated as of 2000. It was widely expected that Telefonica, the wireline parent would be well placed to exploit synergies across its wireline and wireless business as soon as total deregulation was implemented.

Portugal Telecom

Portugal Telecom, another European telecom entrant, was a key player in the wireless segment via its mobile company Telesp Cellular. It was the market leader in the lucrative São Paulo area (Region III) and the largest mobile operator in South America. It had a market share of 63% and 4.3 million customers in 2000. It also controlled Mobitel which provided personal calling and paging services in six metropolitan areas of

Brazil. Portugal Telecom and Telefónica Móviles had announced the creation of a single company to collectively manage the mobile assets of both partners. This would give rise to the largest mobile player in the Latin American market, with close to 9 million customers in Brazil alone.

Telecom Italia

TI's subsidiary Telecom Italia Mobile (TIM) handled TI's mobile assets in Brazil. It was a potent and aggressive player in the wireless segment. TIM had gathered enough PCS licenses through open bidding to become the only company that was capable of offering a national wireless/PCS network, an important factor that could drive valuable synergies in marketing, operations, and financing. Industry analysts believed that the overlapping wireline operations of Brasil Telecom in Region II along with TIM's GSM license in the region could offer the potential for powerful wireless-wireline synergies.

TIM's strategy was predicated on the acceptance of GSM standards in an environment where competing standards (TDMA and CDMA) existed. TIM would have to build an entire GSM network since dual mode handsets were not yet available in Brazil. However, TI's debt capacity had been fully tapped, and further increases in debt could be troublesome. These developments had prompted TI to declare that it would focus on traffic growth and international asset rationalization as opposed to recent patterns of rapid asset growth.

Telpart

Telpart, a consortium comprising investment bank Opportunity and a group of pension funds, controlled two cellular Band A operators, Telemig Cellular and Tele Norte Cellular, and one Band B operator, Americel. It was widely believed that many of these assets would come into play as part of the coming wave of consolidation. Of this portfolio, Telemig and Tele Norte were quite strong with an average market share of 70% in their respective regions.

Telemar PCS

Telemar PCS was the first wireline incumbent to have realistic opportunities to blend wireline and wireless operations. In terms of geographic area it had the PCS license covering the second largest region (Region I) and was second only to TIM in terms of its wireless footprint. Telemar had emphasized that this move was a defensive one, fundamental to its long-term strategic plan. Unlike TIM that planned on using dual mode handsets capable of switching between GSM and TDMA platforms, Telemar PCS intended to use the cheaper GSM only handsets.

PROSPECTS IN THE WIRELESS SEGMENT

Competitive bidding for bandwidth had increased the cost of entry into most regions. However, wireless penetration was still not high enough to make most operations profitable. For example, Telefonica/Portugal Telecom and TIM, the two leading wireless players, had penetration rates of only 16% and 10%, respectively. Many investors believed that the exorbitant license prices could simply not be justified under these low penetration rates.

The market has been unforgiving of telecom operators who have gone on spending sprees for footprint.

David Kabile, Dresdner Kleinwort Wasserstein, Rio de Janeiro

There were signs that the mobile landscape would gain steam and reward some of the early investors. As of early 2001, Brazil had 25 million mobile subscribers, representing a 50% increase over the previous year, with continued growth expected. However, as illustrated in Exhibit 4, the rate of penetration varied significantly across regions. For example, metropolitan São Paolo had a penetration rate of 25.8%, while the northeast states (part of the new Telemar PCS concession) had a penetration rate of only 8.8%. Analysts believed that, similar to wireline potential, wireless penetration held the most promise in the major cities of São Paolo and Rio de Janeiro where it was expected to top 50%. More than 60% of current mobile users were prepaid, and 92% of all new subscribers were prepaid customers. This assured operators of steady revenues and customer retention over the contract period, but renewal of contracts was then critical to going forward.

The prospects for value-added services such as the mobile Internet using *wireless application protocol* (WAP) was also mixed. Currently only 2% of Brazilian mobile users used WAP, although this was expected to grow to 20% by 2004. The prices were still beyond the reach of average users. As Antonio Schuh, a principal consultant at the telecom consulting company Diamond Cluster, observed, *"Prices are brutally high, especially for prepaid cell phones—a phenomenon in the country—which costs 50 cents a minute."*

BRASIL TELECOM

Brasil Telecom Participações,[3] controlled the nine Brazilian state local fixed-line telecommunications operating subsidiaries covered by the privatization award. At end of year 2000, BT had R$4.5 billion in net sales, net profits of R$315 million, R$14.2 billion in total assets, and employed more than 10,600 people. (Appendixes 1-4 provide a synopsis of the financial and

Wireless Region	State/Region	1st Qtr 2001	4th Qtr 2000	1st Qtr 2000
	São Paulo—state	20.3%	20.5%	14.8%
1	São Paulo—metro	25.8%	25.0%	19.6%
2	São Paulo—interior	16.8%	16.0%	10.1%
3	Rio de Janeiro/E. Santo	24.8%	24.1%	17.8%
4	Minas Gerais	13.9%	13.1%	8.7%
5	Paraná/Santa Catarina	12.7%	11.8%	8.2%
6	Rio Grande do Sul	21.5%	20.3%	13.6%
7	Central West states	14.5%	13.3%	8.5%
8	Amazon states	7.8%	7.1%	3.3%
9	Bahia and Sergipe	8.0%	7.3%	5.9%
10	Northeast states	8.8%	8.5%	7.1%
	Brazil	15.3%	14.5%	10.3%

Source: Morgan Stanley Dean Witter, June 8, 2001.

operative performance for Brasil Telecom in addition to comparisons with other large established global telecom companies.)

This task of combining nine separate state operators into a cohesive and effective wireline operator was a big one. To its credit, BT accomplished the task with both haste and efficiency. "Quality of service" was quickly promoted and adopted throughout the organization. While being aware of its traditional engineering mentality, the company steadfastly worked to refocus its attention on the customer rather than the technology.

As of January 2001, BT was licensed to provide all fixed-line telecommunications services in its service region. This included (a) local services, (b) intrastate long-distance services in states within Region II, (c) interstate long-distance service between states in Region II, and (d) network services, e.g., interconnection, leasing, voice-to-data networks, and fixed-to-mobile.

By December 31, 2003, it was expected that Brazil would have 33 million individual telephone lines and 981,300 public phones installed. If BT met its December 31, 2003, goals early, it could begin offering services in other regions outside its current concession area as early as January 1, 2002. The potential revenue growth from expanding out of Region II into the more established markets such as Region I and III in addition to the possibility of offering an expanded suite of value added services was strong motivation to meet targets early. Many believed that first mover advantage was crucial and those that were able to leverage the cross format (wireless-wireline) synergies, e.g., network man-

agement, brand building, would emerge victorious once total deregulation was implemented. However, even meeting Anatel targets as scheduled, much less early, would require an enormous capital expansion program by BT. (Appendix 5 shows a map of the three wireless territories in Brasil after privatization.)

CORPORATE GOVERNANCE

In the July 1998 auction, a consortium called *Solpart* purchased the Brazilian government's stake of Telebrás' Region II operations, gaining 51.8% control of the voting stock (and 19.3% of the total outstanding shares, voting and non-voting). Solpart consisted of Telecom Italia, Techold Participações (a group of pension funds) in partnership with Opportunity (a Brazilian investment bank), and Timepart Participações, a holding company controlled by Opportunity. Over half of Opportunity's invested capital in BT was from Citibank Venture Capital (CVC). The result was a company controlled by two separate and powerful groups, TI and Opportunity (see Exhibit 5).

TI possessed significant telecom operating experience and would provide the operating expertise for Solpart's ownership. The two owners divided senior management positions between them: Opportunity would hold the CEO, the CFO, and Director for Purchasing positions; TI would hold the COO position, as well as Directorships of Marketing, Networks, and Information Technology.

Problems between the two controllers arose almost immediately. TI failed to fill the position of COO for a

EXHIBIT 5   The Ownership Structure of Brasil Telecom

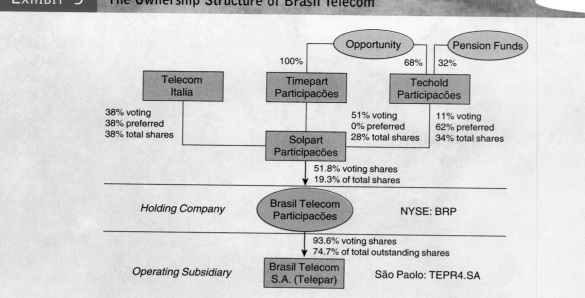

full year. Accusations arose that the appointees by TI were former Italian government workers who were ill-prepared for the complex and demanding task of bringing BT into the competitive private sector. CVC/Opportunity soon found itself the *de facto* operator.

CVC/Opportunity

Banco Opportunity was established as an investment banking firm, with offices in São Paulo and Rio de Janeiro, in 1994. Citibank Venture Capital (CVC) and Opportunity Asset Management, a subsidiary of Banco Opportunity, formed the joint venture *CVC/Opportunity Equity Partners* for private equity investments[4] in the Brazilian telecom market in the spring of 1997. Citibank provided the capital, and Opportunity provided the investment selection and management.

> *The Fund's objective is to seek long-term capital appreciation by investing primarily in Brazilian privatization and private sector investment opportunities. The Funds focus [is] on companies that the General Partner believes will likely benefit, directly or indirectly, from the substantial economic and regulatory changes that the Brazilian economy is undergoing.*[5]

In this pursuit, CVC/Opportunity, spearheaded by Manoel Brito, Director, had invested more than $6.3 billion in acquiring interests in six different telecom companies operating in Brazil (see Exhibit 6). Two of these investments were in the year prior to the privatization of Telebrás, three were positions acquired in the July 1998

privatization auctions (including its interest in BT), and the final one—Tele Norte Leste or *Telemar*—was acquired one year later in July 1999.

CVC/Opportunity's strategy was to position itself for the expected shake out in the Brazilian telecom sector by consolidating: 1) existing properties in order to increase shareholders and subscribers; 2) its position in the market through acquisitions in already existing operations or acquisition of new licenses (PCS); 3) its position as a market leader, expanding its presence in non-traditional telecom activities such as line-related services, IP backbone, etc.; and 4) synergies between wireless-wireline operators.[6]

Telecom Italia

Telecom Italia (TI), one of the leading telecom companies in post-privatized Europe, was incorporated in 1994. Widely renowned for its network management expertise and its geographically diversified portfolio of telecom assets, it had network operations in Europe (Austria, Belgium, France, Germany, Netherlands, Spain, Switzerland, and the United Kingdom), and Latin America (Argentina, Chile, Bolivia, Cuba, and Brazil), where it is one of the largest foreign operators and investors. Most of its international operations were the result of joint ventures with incumbents that emerged from several rounds of privatization.

While a large part of its pan-European strategy was built around optical fiber networks, TI had taken a different approach in Latin America. In navigating the regulatory quagmire that prohibited ownership of wireline

Company	Industry Segment	Date of Investment	Initial Outlay (mm US$)	Controlling Interest
Americel	B-band cellular	June 1997	$ 442	42%
Telet	B-band cellular	April 1997	322	41%
Amazonia	A-band cellular	July 1998	162	51%
Telemig Celular	A-band cellular	July 1998	649	51%
Brasil Telecom	Wireline	July 1998	1,778	11%
Telemar	Wireline	July 1999	2,949	na%
Total			$6,302	

na = not available.

"Interest controlled" is CVC/Opportunity in conjunction with the voting shares of a number of major Brazilian pension funds under existing voting agreements.

Source: www.opportunitysv.com.

licenses in more than one region, TI had chosen to blend wireless and wireline assets to gain network leverage in Brazil. Besides the wireline operator BT, TI is active in 16 states through Telecom Italia Mobile making it the only global operator with a national footprint in the country. TIM also held three crucial GSM licenses in the regions of Brasilia, São Paulo, and Rio de Janeiro, all part of a grand scheme of a pan-American network that the company hoped to establish linking Chile, Peru, Venezuela, Bolivia, Argentina, and Brazil.

THE CRT ACQUISITION

In August 2000 BT acquired Telefonica's stake in Companhia Rio Grandense de Telecomunicações (CRT) for US$800 million. BT, after acquiring additional shares from other sources, held 93% of the voting shares. The acquisition was a valuable one for BT because CRT's service area was wealthier on a per capita basis than any other in BT's service area. It instantly added 33% to BT's installed line base. CRT had been operating in a geographically important tri-state region that channeled traffic from the economically productive states of Parana, Santa Caterina, and Rio Grande do Sul.

The CRT negotiations revealed the increasing divergence among the interests of BT's controllers, TI and Opportunity. Two of BT's Board of Directors who were representatives of TI purportedly divulged critical details of internal meetings with BT where the acquisition price for CRT was discussed. It was reported that this breach led Telefonica to gain the upper hand in the negotiations for the sale of CRT. Ultimately, it was believed that BT ended up paying a much higher price than internally planned as a consequence. It was not readily apparent whether TI had anything to gain from

divulging pricing details to Telefonica as it was alleged to have done.

The conflict between TI and CVC/Opportunity escalated in February, when TI rejected a buyout offer. On February 6, 2001, TI made a public statement that "it was seeking control of Brasil Telecom and was not willing to sell its share." TI did note, however, that it was not making an aggressive attempt to take over the company and only sought to find more productive solutions to the differences. BT responded more aggressively. BT's Chairman, Luis Octavio de Motta Veiga, stated, "This is either going to end up in court or with Telecom Italia selling its stake."

In April, BT filed a lawsuit, charging TI with "breach of fiduciary duties and misappropriation of business opportunities that rightfully belong to Brasil Telecom." In June, BT filed similar charges against the two TI-designated directors asserting that they "repeatedly breached their fiduciary duties by putting the interests of TI ahead of the interests of Brasil Telecom." BT argued that this behavior was both unethical and illegal. The lawsuit was a direct result of the CRT acquisition.

Although it appeared that Opportunity held control, this was dependent on its ability to maintain an alliance with the pension funds holding 32% of Techold and holding significant amounts of freely floating shares. The pension funds were increasingly frustrated with Opportunity's leadership, wishing to exert more control over the interests in which the funds invested. According to Mr. Henrique Pizzolato, Director of Previ, the largest Brazilian pension fund and a contributor of over $500 million to CVC/Opportunity, the funds lost patience with CVC/Opportunity when the firm supported a BT restructuring which cost 3000 jobs, but then appointed a new CEO with an annual salary exceeding $1 million.

> *"Telecom Italia is an operator with a long-term objective in Brazil and Opportunity is an investor seeking to maximise returns," said Rodrigo Pereira, a telecom analyst with Banco Pactual in Rio de Janeiro.[7]*

TI and CVC/Opportunity obviously differed in their opinions of the most likely scenario in the telecommunications industry in the near future. TI had acquired a strong suite of wireless licenses and was already the most likely company to build a national wireless network. However, it would have to persuade CVC/Opportunity to see things its way if it wanted to start utilizing some of its wireless licenses. The topic of wireless licenses was yet another touchy one for CVC/Opportunity.

THE PCS AUCTION: A MISSED OPPORTUNITY FOR BT?

The PCS auctions for Band D and E licenses represented an important window of opportunity for BT to secure a stake in the wireless segment. For the first time, wireline incumbents were allowed to enter the auctions. BT's ownership conflicts, however, posed a major hurdle in its ability to implement its strategy. As BT attempted to solidify its strategy for the upcoming auctions, it became clear that one of its controllers, TI, was planning to bid for licenses on its own. BT, Telemar, and TI were interested in the Band D license for São Paolo. TI now had wireless interests scattered about Brazil, but needed the São Paolo license to compete head-to-head with the Telefonica/Portugal Telecom alliance. BT and Telemar, however, through their newly formed partnership *Brasmar*, were more interested in the Region I and Region II concessions (their home wireline territories).

Although TI did not explicitly block BT from bidding on the board level, the conditions that it wished to impose on any such bid made a BT bid almost impossible. Some of the restrictions TI wished to impose were limiting the cost of any funding to unrealistic levels, imposing the same ownership agreement on the PCS license subsidiary as BT itself had (giving TI veto power on all decisions) and holding management explicitly responsible for any errors or problems arising, even though TI itself still possessed veto power over management proposals in general.

Although temporarily postponed by a number of legal injunctions in late January and early February 2001, the auctions for Band C and Band D licenses were finally held in late February. The Band C license auc-

tion was a failure, with no bids reaching the Anatel minimum. The Band D license auction was dominated by TI, as it gained two of the three Regional licenses awarded, those in Region I and Region III. (Appendix 6 shows the geographic territories controlled by the major wireless companies after the Band D auctions.) TI needed only the north to southeast region—Region II—to complete a national wireless network. The Band E license auction scheduled for March would provide that opportunity. This was the auction in which BT was unable to participate. TI wound up as the only bidder for the licenses and, in fact, was able to negotiate a substantial discount from the asking price set by Anatel.

CVC/Opportunity believed it held the trump card in determining whether or not TI would ultimately benefit from the wireless licenses that its subsidiary TIM had secured. Since TI held an ownership stake in TIM, Anatel expected TI to ensure that BT met universalization targets before harnessing the value of the wireless licenses. CVC/Opportunity as the majority shareholder in BT had a major say in whether meeting targets ahead of schedule was a course that BT should follow.

GROWING DEBATE

BT had been very vocal throughout 2000 that it intended to meet Anatel targets early, probably by end of year 2001, so that it could expand services beyond its current coverage area to Regions I and III, and international long-distance early. Externally, the company planned a media campaign to promote its brand in new areas beyond 2000 coverage. Internally, it was putting together an incentive plan for employees that would effectively double annual bonuses if the company met Anatel targets by end of year 2001.

In order to achieve Anatel goals, either on-schedule or early, required BT to install lines in low population/low density areas, a high-cost low-return activity. If BT postponed these investments, it could redeploy the capital toward investments with higher expected returns. The $3 to $4 billion investment could not be postponed indefinitely, but time was money. The downside risk was that it could lose two years in its ability to expand to other areas and other telecom services.

> *While shaky shareholder control groups contribute to some of this uncertainty, we believe that the complexity of the opportunities facing all communications players make it difficult for the market and for companies themselves to define a clear strategic path, over the long-term, with real conviction.[8]*

By June, BT's management was facing an industry in rapid consolidation and owners who could not agree on any avenue of action. Speculation turned from which directions in wireline and wireless to move, to how to resolve the conflict between owners. To add kindling to the fire, new speculation arose over whether to meet Anatel universalization targets early, thereby allowing BT to make an acquisition, or to simply stay on schedule with Anatel and allow the market to continue its own consolidations and shake outs. The first path was one of choice; the second appeared to be one of default.

NOTES

1. The bidding for Embratel became so heated and active between Sprint and MCI that the process reverted from sealed written bids to open outcry bidding on the floor of the Rio de Janeiro stock exchange. Each bidder sequentially bested the competitor in $8.5 million increments until Sprint withdrew at $2.2 billion.

2. EBITDA, Earnings before interest, taxes, depreciation, and amortization, is a measure of corporate profitability (from the income statement) used to focus on the basic business line of the company before taking into account issues related to acquisitions (amortization), and capital expenditure (depreciation).

3. Brasil Telecom Participações was the holding company for the sole operating subsidiary, Brasil Telecom SA. The operating subsidiary was listed on the São Paulo Bovespa (São Paulo Stock Exchange), while the holding company itself was later listed on the New York Stock Exchange (symbol: BRP). Companies which are incorporated outside the United States, but wish to be listed on U.S. equity exchanges, are listed as *American Depositary Receipts*, ADRs. An ADR represents a receipt against the ownership of company shares held on deposit at a bank in the country of origin.

4. *Private equity* was the acquisition of privately held or previously government-owned businesses for rejuvenation and resale. The investor is typically a fund focused on specific industrial segments (telecom, medical services, etc.), with established expertise in those segments. The investor's strategy is to inject capital and managerial expertise into the enterprise to garner market share, profitability, and key strategic positions, to build enterprise value. The investor then sells the firm, privately or publicly, at the end of three to five years, to capture the profits.

5. "New TIW Company to Exclusively Offer InfoSpace's Platform to All Brazilian Cellular Operators," Press Release, May 25, 2000, Redmond, Washington and Montreal, Canada (TIW).

6. www.opportunitysv.com/who_we_are/comp_telecommunication.html, 2001.

7. "Companies & Finance, The Americas," *Financial Times*, February 7, 2001, p. 32.

8. "Brazilian Fixed-Line: Future Shock?" BBVA Securities, January 26, 2001, p. 3.

Brasil Telecom Income Statement, Actual and Forecast (millions of Brazilian reals)

	2000	2001E	2002E	2003E
Revenues				
Long distance	787	942	1,079	1,258
Local	2,851	4,081	5,141	6,061
Data transmission	441	695	1,022	1,309
Fixed-to-mobile calls	1,122	1,669	1,877	2,028
Interconnection	663	1,009	1,051	1,066
Other	182	259	314	362
Gross revenues	6,046	8,655	10,484	12,084
Deductions	(1,536)	(2,164)	(2,621)	(3,021)
Net revenues	4,510	6,491	7,863	9,063
% change	7%	44%	21%	15%
Operating Costs				
Personnel	(373)	(450)	(477)	(507)
Materials	(76)	(110)	(145)	(175)
Interconnection	(752)	(1,185)	(1,352)	(1,480)
Third party services	(752)	(1,175)	(1,559)	(1,741)
Other operating expenses	(352)	512	(642)	(656)
Total operating costs	(2,305)	(3,432)	(4,175)	(4,559)
EBITDA	2,205	3,059	3,688	4,504
EBITDA margin	48.9%	47.1%	46.9%	49.7%
Depreciation	(1,584)	(1,813)	(1,763)	(1,835)
Operating Income (EBIT)	621	1,246	1,925	2,669
% change	−6%	101%	54%	39%
% margin	14%	19%	24%	29%
Financial income	302	216	126	177
Financing expenses	(208)	(514)	(584)	(681)
Other non-operating expenses	(69)	(92)	(113)	(132)
Employee profit sharing	(330)	(40)	64	(96)
Earnings before Taxes (EBT)	616	816	2,290	1,937
Income tax and social contribution	(217)	(243)	(384)	(577)
Minority interest	(85)	146	(230)	(346)
Net Income (NI)	314	427	676	1,014
% change	−51%	36%	58%	50%
% margin	7%	7%	9%	11%
Exchange rate (R$/$)	1.87	2.30	2.08	2.13
Net Income in US$	$168	$186	$325	$476

Source: Based on data extracted from "Telecom-Wireline: Brasil," Morgan Stanley Dean Witter, July 12, 2001, p. 63.

Assets	2000	2001E	2002E	2003E
Cash and deposits	2,019	954	669	1,273
Accounts receivable	1,198	1,529	1,509	1,542
Deferred taxes	408	363	318	273
Other current assets	197	306	377	441
Current assets	3,822	3,152	2,873	3,529
Gross property, plant and equipment	19,554	21,196	22,981	22,996
Less accumulated depreciation	(10,725)	(10,798)	(10,866)	(10,870)
Net property, plant and equipment	8,829	10,398	12,025	12,126
Deferred taxes	614	547	519	441
Investments	106	153	189	220
Other fixed assets	839	800	800	800
Non-current assets	1,559	1,500	1,508	1,461
Total Assets	14,210	15,050	16,406	17,116
Liabilities				
Accounts payable	905	1,110	895	1,047
Payroll and related accruals	66	153	189	220
Income taxes payable	237	344	330	220
Short-term loans and financing	1,187	1,247	1,503	1,570
Other current liabilities	468	415	429	362
Current liabilities	2,863	3,269	3,346	3,419
Long-term loans and financing	2,354	2,544	3,411	3,646
Minority interest	2,439	2,439	2,439	2,439
Taxes payable	100	76	71	55
Other liabilities and provisions	332	348	366	384
Total Liabilities	8,088	8,676	9,633	9,943
Shareholders' equity	6,122	6,374	6,773	7,173
Total Liabilities and Shareholders' Equity	14,210	15,050	16,406	17,116

Source: Based on data extracted from "Telecom-Wireline: Brasil," Morgan Stanley Dean Witter, July 12, 2001, p. 63.

Wireline Companies 1999

Company	NYSE Symbol	Revenues	EBITDA	Earnings	Assets	EBITDA/ Revenues	Earnings/ Revenues	Earnings/ Assets
Brasil Telecom	BRT	1,737	852	105	5,332	49%	6%	2%
Telemar	THE	3,361	1,477	(28)	10,092	44%	−1%	0%
Telecom de São Paulo	TSP	3,091		374			12%	
Embratel	EMT	2,800	826	140	5,396	30%	5%	3%

Wireline Companies 2000

Company	NYSE Symbol	Revenues	EBITDA	Earnings	Assets	EBITDA/ Revenues	Earnings/ Revenues	Earnings/ Assets
Brasil Telecom	BRT	2,190	1,059	191	6,062	48%	9%	3%
Telemar	TNE	4,440	2,210	302	9,472	50%	7%	3%
Telecom de São Paulo	TSP	4,466		754			17%	
Embratel	EMT	3,746	1,035	286	6,146	28%	8%	5%

Wireless Companies 1999

Company	NYSE Symbol	Revenues	EBITDA	Earnings	Assets	EBITDA/ Revenues	Earnings/ Revenues	Earnings/ Assets
Tele Celular Sul	TSU	371	97	12	644	26%	3%	2%
Telemig Celular	TMB	284	96	15	884	34%	5%	2%
Telesp Celular	TCP	1,195	453	61	3,049	38%	5%	2%

Wireless Companies 2000

Company	NYSE Symbol	Revenues	EBITDA	Earnings	Assets	EBITDA/ Revenues	Earnings/ Revenues	Earnings/ Assets
Tele Celular Sul	TSU	396	108	18	930	27%	5%	2%
Telemig Celular	TMB	383	126	10	846	33%	3%	1%
Telesp Celular	TCP	1,528	496	94	3,559	32%	6%	3%

Firm	EBITDA 2000 mil US$	Net Debt mil US$	Net Debt/ EBITDA	Mkt Cap mil US$	Net Debt/ Mkt Cap	Subscribers millions
Verizon	26,848	54,959	2.05	137,926	39.8%	25.60
AT&T	21,236	62,811	2.96	72,850	86.2%	na
SBC	20,491	25,319	1.24	143,407	17.7%	37.25
British Telecom	13,164	39,118	2.97	51,179	76.4%	31.40
Bell South	12,425	18,971	1.53	73,719	25.7%	24.00
Deutsche Telecom	12,420	54,151	4.36	77,803	69.6%	66.70
Telecom Italia	10,698	12,615	1.18	59,625	21.2%	30.60
Telefonica	10,091	21,935	2.17	67,867	32.3%	21.50
FT	9,030	52,430	5.81	60,014	87.4%	38.10
Telemar	2,017	924	0.46	5,429	17.0%	14.50
Brasil Telecom	1,100	719	0.65	2,752	26.1%	9.38

Firm	Firm Value (EV) mil US$	EV/ EBITDA	EBITDA/ Subscriber	EV/ Subscriber
Verizon	192,885	7.18	1,049	7,535
AT&T	135,661	6.39	na	na
SBC	168,726	8.23	550	4,530
British Telecom	90,297	6.86	419	2,876
Bell South	92,690	7.46	518	3,862
Deutsche Telecom	131,954	10.62	186	1,978
Telecom Italia	72,240	6.75	350	2,361
Telefonica	89,802	8.90	469	4,177
FT	112,444	12.45	237	2,951
Telemar	6,353	3.15	139	438
Brasil Telecom	3,471	3.16	117	370

Enterprise Value (EV) = Market Capitalization + Net Debt.
Market Capitalization = Share Price × Shares Outstanding.

Source: Unibanco/Empresa, May 2001.

Wireline Regions

Region I: North East

Region II: Center South

Region III: São Paulo

APPENDIX 6   The Results of the Band D Wireless Auctions

Band D Winner By Region

Region I: Telemar

Region II: Telecom Italia

Region III: Telecom Italia

case six

Sarah Sittig
University of Denver

John W. Mullins
University of Denver

Gregory D. Leidich
University of Denver

On a crisp, sunny November afternoon in 1997, Richard Squire, Founder and President of Breckenridge Brewery, threw his skis over his shoulder and headed back to his car. Mother Nature had been generous last night, and Richard reveled in the two feet of powder that he had enjoyed all morning. He was disappointed that he had to quit early, but he had to make it back to the office by 4 p.m. That afternoon Richard was scheduled to interview a potential new hire for Breckenridge Brewery. This was not any new hire however; the person selected might eventually end up being the CEO or President of Breckenridge Brewery, and Richard's boss.

Richard had started brewing beer in the 1980's while living in Alta, Utah. He took his job as a "ski bum" very seriously, and when his brewing started to interfere with his skiing, he knew he had to make some changes. One season of skiing in Breckenridge, in the heart of Colorado's Summit County, high in the Rockies, provided Richard with an opportunity to move from being a ski bum to a brewmaster. Breckenridge Brewery came into being and grew steadily for nearly ten years. By late 1997, the combined revenues of its brewery, two microbreweries/brewpubs, and five brewpubs[1] had grown to an annualized rate of more than $15 million, and its beers were distributed in more than 30 states. While Richard's company now enjoyed a significant presence in the craft brewing industry, the company was not yet profitable (see Exhibit 1). Thus, while Breckenridge Brewery had been quite successful by

some measures, it sat somewhat precariously in a growing, but very competitive microbrewery industry and the even more competitive restaurant business.

As Richard drove down into Denver, he thought back to the days when he was licking labels and bottling two bottles of brew at a time with his original filling machine by himself. He had brought the business a long way, and dreamed of taking it farther. The afternoon interview was more than just another interview; it had the potential of changing the future of Breckenridge Brewery. If bringing in new leadership were the right thing to do (and Richard wasn't sure that it was), Richard wondered in what direction the company should go and who would be capable of taking it there.

HISTORY OF BRECKENRIDGE BREWERY

FOUNDING THE COMPANY

Richard had grown up in New York City, "survived" (as he put it) prep school in Massachusetts, and gone to work for his father's garment business after graduating. He stayed in the garment industry for 20 years. By following his intuition and launching a successful line of ladies sportswear, Richard had made enough money that he could sell his business, put his money in the bank, and follow his dream. As Richard put it, what he really wanted was "totally uninterrupted skiing." He moved to Utah, bought a house on the mountain in Alta, and retired as a veritable ski bum.

However, Richard soon found a problem that 150 days of skiing a year could not solve. There was no fresh, high quality beer in Utah! Richard's passion for life and good beer motivated him to begin brewing his own beer. By sharing a fresh home brew with his close

	Pro Forma December 28, 1997	Actual December 29, 1996
Assets		
Current Assets:		
Cash and cash equivalents	$ 467,056	$ 686,435
Short-term investments, restricted	400,000	150,000
Accounts receivable	271,681	21,509
Inventories	302,915	30,241
Receivables from affiliates	629,485	479,280
Other current assets	30,945	1,899
Total current assets	2,102,082	1,369,364
Property and equipment, net	4,149,468	628,940
Investment in joint ventures	103,968	481,686
Investment in future breweries	32,187	239,907
Goodwill and other intangible assets	4,885,033	—
Deferred charges and other assets	85,551	123,286
Total assets	$11,358,289	$ 2,843,183
Liabilities and Stockholders' Equity		
Current liabilities:		
Accounts payable and accrued liabilities	$ 1,228,405	$ 217,575
Payable to shareholders of acquired company	77,193	—
Accounts payable to affiliates	—	3,164
Long-term debt due within one year	1,481,363	17,632
Total current liabilities	2,786,961	238,371
Long-term debt	3,230,114	824,052
Stockholders' equity:		
Common stock, $.001 par value, 20,000,000 shares authorized, 2,408,762 and 1,821,177 shares issued and outstanding as of December 28, 1997 and December 29, 1996, respectively	2,409	1,821
Preferred stock, $.10 par value, 5,000,000 shares authorized, no shares issued and outstanding	—	—
Additional paid-in capital	9,488,191	4,225,059
Accumulated deficit	(4,149,386)	(2,446,120)
Total stockholders' equity	5,341,214	1,780,760
Total liabilities and stockholders' equity	$11,358,289	$ 2,843,183

	Pro Forma for 52 Weeks Ending December 28, 1997	Actual for 52 Weeks Ended December 29, 1996
Revenues:*		
Brewery	$ 498,114	$ —
Restaurants	3,337,851	766,089
Total revenues	3,835,965	766,089
Operating costs and expenses:		
Cost of sales	1,169,256	238,968
Restaurant salaries and benefits	1,480,737	405,184
Operating expenses	1,043,855	278,193
Sales, general and administrative	673,839	575,927
Depreciation and amortization	400,434	243,349
Total operating costs and expenses	4,768,121	1,741,621
Loss from operations	(932,156)	(975,532)
Other income (expense):		
Interest income	25,361	57,895
Interest expense	(231,019)	(49,741)
Equity in losses of joint ventures	(670,433)	(307,347)
Loss related to brewpub relocations	—	(1,044,741)
Other	104,981	1,536
Loss before income taxes	(1,703,266)	(2,317,930)
Income tax benefit	—	—
Net income	$ (1,703,266)	$ (2,317,930)

*Note: Financial performance for units *partially* owned by BHC (Kalamath Street Brewery, microbrewery/brewpub in Buffalo, NY, and Omaha, NE brewpub) is reported under Other Income — Equity in losses of joint ventures. These figures comprise the BHC share of net revenues less expenses for these partially owned ventures. Revenue and expense reported elsewhere on this Statement of Operations includes that generated by all *wholly owned* units (Blake Street, Denver, CO microbrewery/brewpub; and brewpubs in Breckenridge, CO; Birmingham, AL; Tucson, AZ; and Memphis, TN). Dates upon which units opened and/or became wholly owned are shown in Exhibit 9.

circle of friends, Richard thought he had solved his one problem in Alta. Unfortunately it wasn't that simple. As word of his good home brew got out, his small circle of friends got bigger, and Richard eventually found himself rushing home from skiing so that he could brew enough beer to keep his friends happy.

Because Richard brewed the kind of beer he liked, and paid little attention to national trends or consumer interests, he brewed big, strong ales and stouts,[2] in batches of five gallons at a time. In solving his original problem, though, Richard created a new one. He brewed beer that people liked, and that created growing demand. As Richard recalled, "Enough people pull on your coat and say, 'Hey, this stuff is really good; you ought to be making it for the great unfortunate out there who can't get it.'" Eventually Richard realized that, to meet the demand, he would have to amend his laid-back lifestyle.

A 1989 jaunt to Breckenridge, Colorado for the upcoming ski season provided Richard with the impetus for what would become Breckenridge Brewery. Said Richard, "I decided to buy a piece of property across from the Breckenridge ski area, build a brewery, and see if I could make the jump from homebrewer to commercial brewer." A Japanese company had just bought Breckenridge Ski Area, and Richard identified what he saw as a lucrative chance to hedge his bet on the brewery with a real estate deal. "Even if the brewery flops," recalled Richard, "I'll still make money on the real estate, as long as Japanese money keeps flowing into Breckenridge." He bought the property, an old Texaco gas station, and wrote a business plan. After asking questions like "Is there a need for quality beer? Is there a niche? Can I make money at brewing?" Richard used intuition and his knack for making good beer to open the Breckenridge Brewery and Pub in late 1989.

THE GROWTH STAGES

In each of its first two years, Breckenridge Brewery and Pub sold out of its annual maximum capacity of 3,000 barrels per year. The brewery tried to keep up with off-premises demand from other bars, restaurants, and liquor stores in Colorado's mountain resort communities through the use of kegs and 22-ounce bottles, but production and packaging capacity limited growth. By 1992, Richard sought to expand. He bought an old warehouse on Blake Street in lower downtown Denver (eventually a neighbor to the new Coors Field, the home of Major League Baseball's Colorado Rockies), installed stainless steel brewing vessels and equipment, and opened his second brewpub and brewery, Breckenridge Brewery of Denver, in November. This facility boasted a yearly brewing and packaging capacity of approximately 12,000 barrels, supplying both on-site restaurant consumption and off-premise sales. During this time, Breckenridge Brewery's signature beer, Avalanche, was becoming a well-known name in the microbrew industry. The balance of its product line, Mountain Wheat, India Pale Ale, Oatmeal Stout, and other seasonal brews, was enjoying success as well. Restaurant and bar managers requested kegs and beer distributors approached Richard asking if they could sell Breckenridge beers in bottles. By the end of 1994, the production capacity of the facility in Denver was no longer sufficient to meet demand.

To accommodate production demands, Richard opened a regional specialty brewery, Breckenridge Brewery of Colorado, on Kalamath Street, in an industrial area of Denver, in May 1996. This facility began with a production capacity of 20,000 barrels per year, grew quickly to 36,000 barrels, and had enough space to increase its production capacity to 60,000 barrels per year with additional fermentation tanks. While its predecessor, Breckenridge Brewery of Denver, was equipped to package beer in 22-ounce bottles and kegs, Breckenridge Brewery of Colorado would package exclusively in the more market-oriented 12-ounce bottles.

In addition to its growth in Colorado, Breckenridge Brewery expanded eastward during the mid 1990's. In December 1995, its first brewpub outside of Colorado opened in Buffalo, New York, with restaurant facilities and a brewing capacity of 10,000 barrels per year. In the following two years, in response to opportunities that arose from investors in several cities, but without any particular strategic plan, Breckenridge Brewery opened five additional brewpubs (all without bottling capacity) in Tucson, Arizona; Birmingham, Alabama; Memphis, Tennessee; Dallas, Texas; and Omaha, Nebraska (see Exhibit 2 for the company's current production capacity and distribution).

THE BEER INDUSTRY

The beer industry overall was stagnant during the 1990's, with total shipments from domestic brewers and importers barely growing from just under 196 million barrels in 1991 to 200 million barrels in 1996 (Exhibit 3). The top four producers (Anheuser Busch, Miller, Coors, and Stroh) accounted for more than 80% of the market, and their collective market share was increasing, at the expense of smaller regional brewers. The popularity of beer was holding its own, however, compared to other alcoholic beverages, since per capita consumption of other alcoholic beverages had actually declined.[3]

The craft portion of the industry was another story (see Exhibits 4 and 5). From 1994 to 1995, sales in the craft beer segment grew 51%, and they grew another 26% in 1996. No single firm dominated this segment. However, by 1997, the growth curve for craft beers started to flatten and growth in shipments was expected to be less than 10% for the year as a whole. Many craft breweries reported for the first time that they had capacity greater than demand. Nonetheless, industry observers expected craft brewers to continue to grow faster than the large breweries and to ultimately account for as much as 10% of the American beer market, compared to their 1996 share of 2.8%. "That still leaves room for the competitive microbreweries to at least quadruple their current market share!" noted Krisahn Gren, Breckenridge's Director of Marketing.

State	Number of Distributors	Number of Brewpubs	Brewing Capacity	Year Opened
Alabama	0	1	3,000 BBL	December 1996
Alaska	1	0		
Arkansas	1	0		
Arizona	1	1	3,000 BBL	January 1997
Colorado:				
Brewpubs:				
Breckenridge			3,000 BBL	October 1989
Blake St. Denver			12,000 BBL	November 1992
Brewery: Kalamath St.	8	2	36,000 BBL*	May 1996
Connecticut	1	0		
Florida	5	0		
Georgia	3	0		
Idaho	2	0		
Illinois	1	0		
Kansas	1	0		
Kentucky	1	0		
Louisiana	1	0		
Maryland	1	0		
Michigan	1	0		
Missouri	3	0		
Montana	4	0		
Nebraska	1	1	3,000 BBL	September 1997
New Hampshire	2	0		
New Jersey	1	0		
New Mexico	1	0		
North Carolina	1	0		
New York	5	1	10,000 BBL	December 1995
Ohio	3	0		
Oklahoma	1	0		
Rhode Island	1	0		
South Carolina	1	0		
South Dakota	2	0		
Tennessee	3	1	3,000 BBL	May 1997
Texas	3	0		
Virginia	5	0		
Wyoming	6	0		
Totals	69	7	73,000 BBL	

*Can grow to 60,000 barrels with additional equipment.

EXHIBIT 3 | Beer Industry Shipments 1991–1996 BBL (000)

Brewer	1991	1992	1993	1994	1995	1996
Anheuser Busch	86,037	86,846	87,306	88,529	87,539	91,000
Miller*	43,462	42,221	44,024	45,243	45,006	43,799
Coors	19,550	20,000	20,000	20,200	20,000	20,045
Stroh*	14,800	14,000	12,610	11,850	19,010	17,810
Heileman	9,377	9,133	8,940	8,315		
Pabst	6,675	6,900	7,000	6,630	6,550	5,610
Heineken	2,230	2,400	2,575	2,775	2,900	3,190
Labatt USA*	1,420	1,500	1,730	2,215	2,240	2,500
Genessee	2,220	2,150	2,000	1,800	1,870	1,800
Barton	750	825	945	1,070	1,340	1,680
Gambrinus	465	537	618	685	975	1,305
Boston*	174	294	475	714	961	1,213
Guinness*	870	910	1,000	1,080	950	980
Beck's	575	605	605	590	640	605
Molson	1,410	1,350	440			
McKenzie River	300	350	400	500		
Other Domestic	4,514	5,895	5,887	6,336	7,370	7,341
Other Import	1,159	1,216	1,375	1,035	1,378	1,361
Total	195,988	197,132	197,930	199,567	198,729	200,246

*Notes: Miller includes Molson from 4/93. Stroh includes Heileman and McKenzie River from 1/95. Labatt USA includes Wisdom brands from 1994, Dos Equis 1996. Guinness includes Dos Equis through 1995. Boston excludes Hudepohl-Schoenling. Moosehead included with Other Import. Pete's included with Other Domestic.

Source: Data provided by *Beer Marketer's Insights,* West Nyack, NY.

LARGE BREWERS

The production and marketing strategies of the major domestic breweries differed dramatically from those of the craft brewing industry. With annual brewing capacities of over 1,000,000 barrels, large brewers focused on mass production of beers that tended to sacrifice freshness for longer shelf lives. In spite of the rapid growth of craft brewed beers, mass production brewers still dominated the industry, though their growth had come to a virtual standstill (see Exhibit 3).

CRAFT BREWERS

Craft brewing represented a "blend of art and science" where the focus was on variety, freshness, and quality. For most craft brewers, freshness was the key. By only using the purest and finest ingredients, no adjuncts,[4] and no pasteurization,[5] these brewers felt that the quality of craft beers stood apart from the mass production of other more prominent beers. Although this process sacrificed shelf life and required constant (and costly) refrigeration, the result, in the eyes of brewers like Richard, was a uniquely crafted, flavorful microbrew.

Distinct demographic trends supported the growth of the craft brewing industry. According to *American Demographics* magazine, education and income were the two most significant factors in microbrew consumption, with relatively younger and higher income consumers leading the way. A 1996 National Restaurant Association report[6] reported that 18.9% of consumers with incomes of more than $50,000 reported ordering more microbrewed beer than two years ago. The same report indicated that Generation Xers were loyal to microbrewed beers, that 70% of those under the age of 34 purchased local or microbrewed beers, and that only 40% of those over the age of 55 exhibited the same buying patterns. This young and relatively affluent population spurred the rapid growth of the microbrew industry, and industry observers expected that these same individuals would continue to support fresh, flavorful microbrews.

Beer Industry Market Share by Market Segment — EXHIBIT 4

Market Share—Beer	1995	1996
Domestic Specialty/"Craft"	2.3%	2.8%
Imports	6.1%	6.7%
Large Brewers & Traditional Regional Breweries	91.6%	90.5%
Total	100.0%	100.0%

Source: *North American Brewers Resource Directory* 1997–98, Institute for Brewing Studies.

The craft brewing industry was divided into several categories, as outlined by the Institute for Brewing Studies in Boulder, Colorado:[7] microbreweries, brewpubs, contract brewers, and regional breweries. These definitions helped to differentiate the size and scope of craft breweries operating across the country. The traditional *microbrewery* produced less than 15,000 barrels of beer per year. These microbreweries sold to the public through restaurants and retail liquor stores. The *brewpub* was a combination restaurant-brewery that sold more than 50% of its production capacity for on-site consumption.[8] A *contract brewer* hired another company to produce its beer, while it focused on marketing, sales, and distribution. Among the best known craft brewers were contract brewers like the Boston Beer Company, well known for its Samuel Adams brand, which led the craft beer industry with a craft beer market share of 22.6% in 1996; and Pete's Brewing Company, known for its Pete's Wicked Ale, which held an 8.1% market share in the same year. Finally, a *regional specialty brewery* was a regional-scale brewery with a capacity to brew between 15,000 and 1,000,000 barrels per year, and typically focused on an all-malt (i.e., no corn or rice) specialty beer. Prominent western regional specialty breweries included the New Belgium Brewing Company in Fort Collins, Colorado; Red Hook Ale Brewing in Seattle, Washington; and Sierra Nevada Brewing Company and Anchor Brewing Company, both located in California.

In 1996 the United States had 33 regional specialty breweries, 418 microbreweries, and 799 brewpubs. In 1996, microbreweries operated with an average failure rate of one in seven, and one in eight brewpubs failed. Because microbrews relied so much on freshness, production practices revolved around small batches and hands-on processes. Some observers felt the industry would most likely remain fragmented. Others felt that the breakneck pace of growth was bound to slow and that some consolidation of the industry was inevitable. Richard expected consolidation, but felt his company was well positioned. As he saw it, "A shake-out is inevitable in this industry, but Breckenridge makes quality beer and has good market position. It will survive and be one of the few to remain on top."

LEADERSHIP AT BRECKENRIDGE BREWERY

Although Richard Squire had founded Breckenridge Brewery, the leadership of the company had evolved into a partnership between Richard and former legal counsel, now partner, Ed Cerkovnik. In November 1997, Richard and Ed each owned about 20% of the stock in Breckenridge Holding Company, with other investors holding the remaining 60%. Richard described their partnership as "the Yin and Yang of business," with Ed being "the voice of sanity and reason" while Richard remained the "visionary and father figure."

RICHARD SQUIRE

"Richard's entrepreneurial spirit drives the company," said Ed Cerkovnik. Richard felt his greatest strength centered on selling a product in which he believed

Growth in the Craft Beer Industry — EXHIBIT 5

Unit Growth: Craft Brewing Facilities	1986	1987	1988	1989	1990	1991	1992	1993	1994	1995	1996
Regional Specialty Breweries	1	1	1	3	3	5	6	9	16	27	33
Microbreweries	30	44	54	64	84	88	103	133	192	276	362
Brewpubs	16	29	69	107	124	155	186	240	333	502	691
Total number of craft brewing facilities	47	74	124	174	211	248	295	382	541	804	1086

Source: *North American Brewers Resource Directory* 1997–98, Institute for Brewing Studies.

passionately. His tenuous management skills, however, had often sent both new and seasoned employees packing. As Richard put it, "I am, without a doubt, the world's worst manager." Even those who marveled at Richard's passion and commitment to building the company tended to agree. "He can be impatient in dealing with people or ideas with which he disagrees, and he sometimes makes decisions abruptly without carefully communicating with those concerned," said Human Resource Director Dick Esser.

His limitations notwithstanding, Richard's vision and energy had propelled Breckenridge Brewery into a very competitive position within the industry. While his creative ideas didn't always work out, some of Richard's innovations had been highly successful, including the creation of a special beer honoring the visit of Pope John Paul to Denver in 1993. Breckenridge Brewery's Popus Visitus won mentions in the local press, and was the subject of a short feature broadcast nationally on network television. In addition, Richard's idea for a seasonal specialty beer program had contributed significantly to the company's sales.

Caty Hayes, now the company's Plant Coordinator, had joined Breckenridge Brewery in 1990. Initially, as she described it, Caty was Richard's "girl Friday, to keep the books and count the money when it was kept in a cigar box." Caty felt Richard had matured over the years. "He used to be going a mile a minute; now he can actually take an idea and think it through. But what Richard does best is sell. He is charismatic and charming, brazen and somewhat intimidating. He motivates people to believe in Breckenridge Brewery and to work together for a common goal."

During the company's eight short years, Richard had brewed beer, licked labels, kept the books, set up distribution channels, and hired and fired employees. One by one, Richard had hired others to fill those roles, leaving him in late 1997 in a position of leadership with few specific responsibilities. As he put it, Richard wanted to be a "road warrior" for the company, and was on the road selling about 50% of the time. However, he feared being out of touch and becoming a company figurehead "like Kentucky Fried Chicken's Colonel Sanders."

Despite this fear, Richard cautiously welcomed the idea of a new level of management and of sharing the success of the company. "I'm a social guy and feel good about getting a bunch of people together and succeeding together." He wanted to find "somebody that can wow me," someone that will come in and take care of business, and take the company to the next level.

ED CERKOVNIK
Most of the people at Breckenridge Brewery agreed that Ed was "brilliant" and "looked to for leadership."

Since his arrival at Breckenridge Brewery, Ed had provided legal counsel, credibility with various sources of financing, as well as deal structuring and negotiating skills, and had been looked to as the unofficial COO of the company. He brought ten years of business law experience to Breckenridge Brewery when he joined Richard as a 50/50 partner in 1994.

Ed had been a partner in the law firm that represented Breckenridge Brewery when he decided to make the move from law to business. Richard's pursuit of Ed had begun with an offer of 20% of the business, but Ed had different ideas and responded, "I'm not sure I want to work *for* you. If we do it, it's a 50/50 partnership." Ed had watched securities and acquisitions deals come and go over the years, and while he had earned fees for legal services, he had never built any equity. "Breckenridge Brewery provided an opportunity for me to be part of something, to build equity and value, and, if all goes well, to make a substantial amount of money."

Ed had assisted with several rounds of financing before the relationship developed from legal counsel to a personal business relationship. In each round of financing, the then-current as well as new investors bought shares in the company's growing range of facilities, from breweries to brewpubs. Once on board, Ed began laying the foundation for the Breckenridge Holding Company, to bring all the assets under common ownership. He blended a philosophy incorporating business and law, developing an ability to assess the risks and the opportunities on both sides, to structure negotiations, and to make tough deals work. While his efforts resulted in a growing family of brewpubs spread across the country, Ed acknowledged that the company had a difficult time managing the rapid growth. "I can build this thing but I don't know how to run it. I don't have the skills to run a restaurant company. We've come to a point where we need someone else, someone with a set of managerial and strategic skills that neither Richard nor I possess."

THE MANAGEMENT TEAM
The two partners agreed that their contrasting personalities had in fact worked well together in creating a work environment that was both professional and "like a family." Richard provided a great deal of vision and creativity. Ed provided discipline and strong analytical skills. Surrounding them was a team of players that made significant contributions (see Exhibit 6).

In July of 1996, Ed and Richard had added CFO Dave Runberg to their team. Dave brought extensive experience as an audit manager with Arthur Andersen & Co. and as the Chief Accounting Officer of Gillett Holdings, Inc. At Breckenridge, he had developed formal financial models to analyze costs and profitability

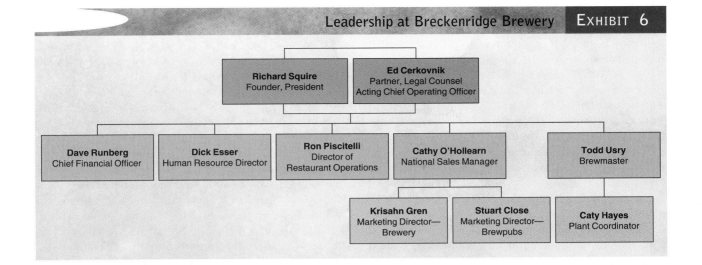

of the brewery and restaurant businesses and had implemented new accounting controls and financial reporting procedures that helped generate accurate financial information on a timely basis.

Richard and Ed felt that Dave had built a strong team within the accounting department, and that the company had benefited greatly from the controls and systems that had been implemented since his arrival. Dave noted, "As the company has grown from owning one or two units into a true multi-unit operation, we had to have controls and procedures in place that were documented, trainable, and enforceable. My staff and I have basically taken the company's accounting, budgeting, and financial analysis systems to the level necessary for an expanding, multi-unit company. Everybody now better understands the cost structure of each portion of our business."

Dave was not the only valuable addition to the management team. Richard and Ed had also hired a Director of Restaurant Operations, Ron Piscitelli, an experienced, hands-on, day-to-day supervisor for the brewpubs, with more than 25 years of restaurant industry experience; a National Sales Manager, Cathy O'Hollearn, who brought 13 years of sales and sales management experience from Anheuser Busch, the country's leading brewer; a Director of Marketing for the wholesale beer business Krisahn Gren, a recent MBA graduate whose family had been in the beer distribution business for many years; and part-time Human Resource Director, Dick Esser.

Richard and Ed also relied heavily on a committed team of long-time employees: Todd Usry, Breckenridge Brewery's Brewmaster (six years); Caty Hayes, Plant Coordinator (nine years); and Stuart Close, Director of Marketing for Brewpubs (seven years, virtually his entire career since his graduation from college). The team was clearly committed to Breckenridge beers, to growth, and to developing a strategy that would keep Breckenridge on top.

BRECKENRIDGE HOLDING COMPANY

When Ed had joined Breckenridge Brewery in 1994, he saw that his first major tasks were to consolidate ownership, raise new capital, and solidify license and development agreements within the increasingly complex structure of the company. Ed viewed these as critical steps in the formation of the company and in its ability to develop the Breckenridge Brewery concept. The business structure that had evolved to date, in Ed's words, "had become convoluted," weaving together various partners, investors, and legal entities. As a result, each Breckenridge microbrewery/brewpub was owned by a different, though partially overlapping, set of investors. Ed knew that ultimately, in order to provide a profitable exit for its investors, the company might wish to go public in an IPO or seek acquisition by another company. To do so, it would need to be an entity with common ownership, as well as a sufficient concentration of voting rights to enable a future deal to be struck.

To simplify the complex ownership structure, Richard and Ed created Breckenridge Holding Company (BHC) in 1994 as an umbrella company that would eventually own all the physical and intellectual property, trade rights, and trade dress[9] for Breckenridge Brewery and its various products. By late 1997, Breckenridge Holding Company had developed into a privately held corporation with a total of 250 shareholders and 2.2 million shares outstanding. BHC now owned 100% of some of its units, and lesser shares in others (see note to Exhibit 1).

Under the umbrella of BHC were two distinct operating concepts: the wholesale beer business and the brewpub business. Richard's vision was two tiered. It included fresh brewed beer with "the Colorado mystique," as Richard called it, as well as a growing chain of brewpubs that Richard saw as America's brewpub. Throughout the development of the company, from its start in Breckenridge to opening its most recent brewpub in Omaha, Nebraska, Ed and Richard had focused on building a business that produced quality beer, promoted the Breckenridge concept, and ran attractive brewpubs.

Unfortunately, while this mission made sense on paper, Ed and Richard struggled to unite the two sides of the business and to run the brewpubs profitably. In fact, the brewpub operation was losing large sums of money, and Ed, Richard, and Ron Piscitelli had made little progress in improving the brewpubs' profitability. Ed and Richard were struggling to balance, manage, and grow both sides of the business. A few weeks ago, the two of them had met for an afternoon to reflect on where each side of the business now stood, and the prospect of each side of the business for growth and profitability.

BRECKENRIDGE BREWERY'S WHOLESALE BEER BUSINESS

As Richard liked to say, "Brewing beer is the foundation of Breckenridge Brewery, and that is what we have always done best." With production capacity of between 15,000 and 500,000 barrels per year, a regional brewery's main function is production and distribution for off-premises sales in the form of kegs or bottles. Breckenridge Brewery of Colorado, the main brewing facility on Kalamath Street in Denver, had grown its production capacity to 36,000 barrels per year by late 1997. Its sales were expected to consume all of that capacity, with the lion's share of its output packaged in 12-ounce bottles. Breckenridge Brewery of Denver, the company's brewpub on Blake Street across the street from Coors Field, with the capability to package beer in kegs and 22-ounce bottles, had an annual production capacity of 12,000 barrels.

Todd Usry was Breckenridge Brewery's Brewmaster. He was responsible for quality control of brewing processes, hiring and training brewmasters for all of the brewpubs, plant layout and design, and a variety of other responsibilities. He took his job of brewing beer very seriously. Todd had learned the nuts-and-bolts of setting up a brewery and of brewing quality beer by working under a Canadian brewmaster at Breckenridge Brewery for nearly two years. When the Canadian left, Richard had promoted Todd to brewmaster and sent

him to the world-renowned Siebel Institute of Brewing in Chicago, Illinois for additional training. In September of 1995, Todd took charge of the design, layout, and installation of the new brewery in Denver. With that experience under his belt, he then did the same for the Buffalo facility, then for the other brewpubs. He focused on hiring quality brewmasters at each brewpub and stressed consistency and quality. He developed a template for the brewpubs and set up all supplier arrangements and contracts, as well as inventories and specs, before the new brewmaster came on board. Todd acknowledged that while "brewing beer in various locations with limited quality control resources presents a challenge, the recipes, ingredients, times, temperatures, and facility cleanliness are consistent from brewery to brewery." His ability to ensure that these components were communicated and in place before the new brewery or brewpub opened laid a foundation of success that supported Breckenridge Brewery's consistency and quality on the beer side of the business.

While Todd managed the process of beer making, Cathy O'Hollearn, Breckenridge Brewery's National Sales Manager, made sure that the beer was sold across the country. Cathy had spent 13 years in sales with Anheuser Busch Inc. and decided to join Breckenridge Brewery as she watched the rapid growth in the microbrew industry and saw the challenge offered by the young company. She was also attracted to the two-tiered concept of the brewery and brewpub, and considered that structure as a built-in marketing tool. When she was hired at Breckenridge Brewery, she walked into a production driven company that had no sales staff, no formal sales mechanism, no sales support or organization. The company was in a position in which it had to sell as much beer as it made, with or without a sales structure. Cathy viewed her charge from Richard as "Just sell as much beer as you can, wherever you can."

Working diligently and rapidly, Cathy built a sales staff of eight in as many states and a distribution network that reached 32 states. Once sales in a given state warranted personal attention, Cathy would hire a sales representative to act as the State Sales Manager, working hand-in-hand with distributors and, if applicable, brewpubs in their state. She also oversaw marketing efforts and worked closely with Director of Marketing Krisahn Gren.

Since Cathy's arrival at Breckenridge Brewery in February of 1996, annual wholesale sales had increased from 10,691 barrels to an anticipated 32,000 barrels in 1997. While this sales growth was aided by the company's strategic move to 12-ounce bottles in six-packs, as well as by the beer's exposure in its brewpubs, her efforts toward establishing a sales network had paid off. At the end of 1997, strong overall sales allowed Cathy to make the strategic decision to begin scaling down states of distribution, "so that our talent and limited resources are focused on the states with the best growth potential."

The talents of Todd and Cathy, supported by many others, spurred the success of the beer side of the business through quality, consistency, and steadily growing sales. The benchmark retail price in Colorado for Breckenridge beers was $5.99 per 12-ounce six-pack, about $1.50 more than domestic beers from mass-market brewers like Coors and Anheuser Busch. The beers were brewed in state of the art equipment in a facility that had been designed to maximize its efficiency, in spite of the higher costs of premium ingredients and the relatively smaller scale (compared to the mass-market brewers) at which Breckenridge beers were produced.

BRECKENRIDGE BREWERY'S BREWPUB BUSINESS

Though brewpubs were a part of the craft brewing industry, they were also part of the much larger restaurant industry, which had 1996 sales of $320 billion overall, of which $104 billion comprised the full-service segment (see Exhibit 7). Brewpubs were a small part of this full-service segment, and their numbers were growing rapidly (see Exhibit 5).

Even though the restaurant business was considered highly competitive, and had a large failure rate compared to other businesses, the nearly instant profitability of the first Breckenridge Brewery and Pub in Breckenridge, Colorado had convinced Richard that the brewpub side of the business could be lucrative, too. "We've got a terrific concept," said Richard, "and a great burger with great beer should sell anywhere, especially if people want to get a little of our Colorado mystique when they get back home!" The size of the restaurant industry indicated to Richard that there would be plenty of room for growth, if future brewpubs performed as well as the first one in Breckenridge had.

A typical brewpub had production capacity of approximately 3,000 barrels per year. Its main function was to produce beer for on-site consumption, though the company's Buffalo, New York brewpub and microbrewery had additional brewing capacity intended to serve the east coast wholesale beer market. In addition to its beer brewing capacity, a brewpub also focused heavily on food and food service. Between 1990 and 1997 Breckenridge Brewery had opened eight brewpubs across the country, one of which, in Dallas, Texas, had since been closed. It seems that no one had fully understood Texas laws concerning brewpubs, and operating one meant that Breckenridge was prohibited from selling beer through distributors in Texas.[10] Poor performance of the brewpub and the desire to tap the large Texas retail beer market had led Richard and Ed to close the Dallas brewpub soon after it opened.

Although Breckenridge Brewery had become a contender in the brewpub market, Dick Esser reflected that "it's been a deal oriented business, making a deal versus making a plan." The deal-driven strategy had allowed the brewpub side of the business to grow rapidly, but in the direction of facility deals instead of strong demographic trends. Stuart Close, Director of Marketing for Brewpubs, observed that "each brewpub was a new venture where there was no template and limited consistency from one brewpub to the next. The growth was deal-driven and lacked thorough planning, communication, and a detailed, company-wide strategy."

1996 Industry Sales Comparison: Beer versus Restaurant Industries		EXHIBIT 7	
	Beer Sales		**Restaurant Sales**
Craft Beer	$2.9 billion	**Full-Service Restaurants**	$104 billion
	47% *annual* compound growth since 1991; 41% growth 1995–96		
Total Beer	$50 billion	**Total Restaurant**	$320 billion
	2% *total* growth since 1991		4% *annual* compound growth since 1991; 5% projected for 1996–1997

Sources: *Restaurant Industry Operations Report*, National Restaurant Association, 1996; and *North American Brewers Resource Directory* 1997–98, Institute for Brewing Studies.

In January 1997, Richard and Ed had hired Ron Piscitelli as Director of Restaurant Operations. Ron had worked in the restaurant business continuously since he was 14. His experience ranged from an education at the US Culinary Institute and twelve years in the hotel industry to line management in the restaurant industry. Richard and Ed viewed Ron not as a strategic leader, but as a hands-on supervisor who could properly oversee the company's growing chain of brewpubs. Ron saw Breckenridge's potential, and recognized that Breckenridge Brewery was a "brewery selling food" in a restaurant market that was extremely competitive. Ron developed the idea that "food is critical" and convinced the rest of the management team that Breckenridge Brewery could not survive in the food business unless it improved its food quality to match that of its beer.

Ron's role was to "get into the stores and work with the people." He hired new people, fired others, revamped menus, and emphasized the sentiment that "we're all fighting for one company." He fought internally for getting Breckenridge Brewery's food up to the same level as its beer. Ed lamented the lost time before hiring Ron, and

admitted that he "should have acted sooner," and that "it has cost us several months from where we are today."

BRECKENRIDGE BREWERY'S OPERATING PERFORMANCE

The results of the company's expansion of its brewpub business were rapid sales growth and problems on the bottom line. For several years, cash flow for the operations as a whole had been negative, due in part to the expenses of adding both brewing capacity and staff, and also to heavy start-up and market entry expenses in new states and for new brewpubs. Accounts receivable from affiliates (the entities that owned the partially owned units) were mounting (see Exhibit 1). Several rounds of private capital had been raised to finance these investments and losses.

With the 1997 year drawing to a close, CFO Dave Runberg had prepared updated pro forma projections for the beer and brewpub sides of the business (see Exhibits 8 and 9). Collectively, they were not a pretty sight. The good news was that the beer business was now contributing to overhead and profit (see Exhibit 8),

| EXHIBIT 8 | Projected 1997 Income Statement for Breckenridge Beer Business |

Projected Consolidated Statement of Income ($000)
Breckenridge Wholesale Beer Business
For the Year Ended December 31, 1997

	Kalamath Street Brewery*	Blake Street Wholesale**	Total
Revenues	$2833.2	$498.1	$3331.3
Cost of Goods Sold	1153.8	100.2	1254.0
Gross Profit	1679.4	397.9	2077.3
Payroll	282.7	77.4	360.1
Sales/Marketing	559.1	79.9	639.0
Operating Expenses	390.4	96.0	486.4
Rent and Occupancy	153.9	41.0	194.9
Brewery General and Administrative	95.2	6.6	101.8
EBITDA	198.1	97.0	295.1
Depreciation and Amortization	141.2	62.6	203.8
Income from Operations	56.9	34.4	91.3
Interest and Other	109.4	6.7	116.1
Net Income Before Taxes (Net Loss)	($ 52.5)	$ 27.7	($ 24.8)

Projections are updated as of November 1, 1997.

*Figures represent twelve months operation. The Kalamath Street Brewery is 50% owned by BHC.
**The Blake Street Brewpub was acquired by Breckenridge Holding Company in late August 1997. Projected 1997 figures represent wholesale beer sales for approximately four months of operation. Total 1997 wholesale beer sales for Blake Street were $1.6 million.

though the Kalamath Street brewery was only 50% owned by BHC, thereby limiting BHC's benefit to half its cash flow. The bad news was that most of the brewpubs were struggling to turn a profit (see Exhibits 9 and 10), and most were deeply in the red. Pre-opening costs were significant, high initial sales sometimes turned into mediocre sales, and some units ended up over-staffed and over-spent. The brewpubs ranged widely in weekly sales, from $20,000 to $55,000. Overall, the brewpub side of the business was a huge cash drain, a significant problem, since it now accounted for more than 80% of BHC's sales (see Exhibit 1), and over 70% of the sales of the Breckenridge family of entities.

The company's adverse operating results in 1997 as compared to the much better results that had been expected early in the year were caused by two primary factors:

1. The microbrewery in Buffalo and the brewpubs in Birmingham, Memphis, Tucson, and Omaha fell short of projected revenue levels, which significantly limited their ability to cover operating expenses and generate positive cash flows.
2. The acquisition by the holding company[11] of the original brewpub in Breckenridge and the Blake Street microbrewery/brewpub in Denver were

					Brecken-	Blake		
Projected 1997 Income Statement for Breckenridge Brewpub Business								**EXHIBIT 9**

Projected Consolidated Statement of Income ($000)
Breckenridge Brewpub Business
For the Year Ended December 31, 1997

	Buffalo*	Birmingham†	Tucson‡	Memphis**	Brecken-ridge††	Blake Street‡‡	Omaha***	Total
% owned by BHC in November 1997	30%	100%	100%	100%	100%	100%	50%	
Revenues	1492.1	1647.1	1646.1	1505.4	1287.0	446.4	328.2	8352.3
Cost of Goods Sold	508.3	463.4	461.2	442.3	349.1	143.8	113.5	2481.6
Gross Profit	983.8	1183.7	1184.9	1063.1	937.9	302.6	214.7	5870.7
Payroll	579.2	777.1	728.8	631.7	503.2	195.7	193.3	3609.0
Sales/Marketing	90.4	50.2	101.9	58.7	75.5	47.9	12.3	436.9
Operating Expenses	273.1	401.7	290.2	297.5	168.8	73.5	60.4	1565.2
Rent and Occupancy	123.8	150.9	187.7	157.6	121.5	40.2	21.1	802.8
Store Level General and Admin	36.9	42.9	45.7	47.7	13.7	9.9	17.7	214.5
EBITDA	−119.6	−239.1	−169.4	−130.1	55.2	−64.6	−90.1	−757.7
Depreciation and Amortization	129.9	290.6	297.4	150.6	59.7	20.5	38.7	987.4
Income from Operations	−249.5	−529.7	−466.8	−280.7	−4.5	−85.1	−128.8	−1745.1
Interest and Other	91.3	83.5	48.7	30.6	54.5	10.8	2.6	322.0
Net Income Before Taxes (Net Loss)	($ 340.8)	($ 613.2)	($ 515.5)	($ 311.3)	($ 59.0)	($ 95.9)	($ 131.4)	($ 2067.1)

*Opened December 1995. 1997 figures represent total revenue for twelve months operation, brewpub only. Buffalo was no longer brewing for wholesale in 1997.
†Opened December 1996. 1997 figures represent total revenue for twelve months operation.
‡Opened January 1997. 1997 figures represent total revenue for twelve months operation.
**Opened May 1997. 1997 figures represent total revenue for eight months operation.
††Acquired June 1997. 1997 figures represent total revenue for seven months operation.
‡‡Acquired August 1997. 1997 figures represent total revenue for approximately four months operation. Due to baseball, Blake Street brewpub is expected to earn $50,000 on sales of $1.6 million in 1998.
***Opened September 1997. 1997 figures represent total revenue for four months operation.

EXHIBIT 10   1996 Sales and Income (000) for Brewpubs Open in 1996

	Buffalo (12 Months)*	Birmingham (1 Month)	Breckenridge (12 Months)	Blake Street (12 Months)**
Sales Revenue	$1,752.2	$177.1	$2,951,225.0	$1,736.3
Income from Operations***	($542.4)	($0.6)	$552,859.0	$279.9

*Buffalo had an additional $720,088 in brewery revenue from wholesale beer sales.
**Blake Street had an additional $2,065,899 in brewery revenue from wholesale beer sales.
***Income from operations includes margins and expenses for wholesale beer sales from Buffalo and Blake Street locations, and excludes interest and income tax.

projected to close in April 1997, but did not close until June 1997 and August 1997, respectively, which deprived BHC of the profitable operations of these two entities for several months.

All in all, 1997 had started out as a promising year, but by year's end the company had experienced some significant disappointments. Of greatest concern, restaurant revenues were below expectations, and costs were higher, leaving the company with a significant loss. A new brewpub in Dallas had performed poorly, and in February of 1997 the decision had been made to close it and take the appropriate losses. These losses and the complexity of operating a restaurant company forced Ed and Richard to carefully ponder their future needs.

THE FUTURE OF THE COMPANY

Ed and Richard agreed that, compared to the micro-brew industry, there was significantly more room for growth on the restaurant side of the business. They believed their two-tiered strategy of building both the brewery and the brewpub sides of the business still made sense and offered the opportunity for marketing synergy. As Richard pointed out, "When we opened our brewpub in Tucson last year, our beer sales in Arizona tripled."

Ed and Richard both felt that the company enjoyed extraordinary potential, but they had begun to doubt that they possessed the right mix of managerial skills to ensure that its potential would be realized. Both were extremely frustrated by their company's poor profit performance in 1997, in spite of the fact that, as Ed put it, "We've got good people." They felt that the brewery side of the business was well developed and efficient, but the brewpub side seemed more complex and lacked both consistency and quality. As Richard said, "Ron Piscitelli has made considerable progress for us, but the bottom line profitability in the brewpub business is still miserable, and it may be that our strategy has inherent

problems that Ron is not equipped to fix." The question was what they should do about this problem. "Clearly, something or someone is missing, and our deteriorating balance sheet makes it imperative that we move quickly!"

As Ed and Richard saw it, there were two questions they needed to answer. First, if new leadership could help solve the company's performance problems, what level person should they add to the team? Should they add a full-fledged partner, or even a COO or CEO to assume overall leadership of the company? Or should they bring in a heavy-hitter to run either the brewery side or the restaurant side of the business? Second, what sort of background should they be looking for? Would someone with a strong background in the beer or beverage distribution business make sense? Beer, after all, still represented the focus of the company, and ultimately, Breckenridge Brewery was a beer business at heart. Or did they need someone with a strong background in developing and managing a chain restaurant concept? Brewpubs, it was clear, were restaurants, and it was also clear that the company had not yet figured out how to run its restaurant business consistently and profitably. Further, Richard was not entirely certain that the hiring question was the right issue to be focused on. Cash was running out, and it was not clear whether more cash could be raised. Should he and Ed forget about hiring someone for now, and renew their efforts to address the company's performance problems themselves?

It was with these thoughts running through his head that Richard had spent the day on the slopes. He wasn't even sure that today's candidate, the first of several he would talk to, was a viable one, because he wasn't yet sure which way to go.

Richard arrived at the main bottling facility and Breckenridge Brewery headquarters in Denver. Before going to the conference room he walked to the back, past the straight lines of stainless steel fermentation tanks, and savored the rich smell of barley and hops.

The bottling line was running smoothly, the staff looked cheerful and busy. His brewery business had come a long way.

As Richard made his way to the conference room he thought about his vision for the company, a two-tiered concept with a top microbrewery producing fresh, quality beer and a chain of brewpubs known as America's brewpub. He had made progress on the first part of that concept, but still wondered what kind of leadership it would take to develop Breckenridge Brewery's brewery and brewpub concepts, and to successfully integrate the two sides of the company. With these thoughts weighing heavily on his mind, he walked into the interview.

Notes

1. The Breckenridge Holding Company owned some or all of each of these businesses. Richard and his partner, Ed Cerkovnik, and various private investors owned the remaining portions. See Exhibit 1 and note thereto.

2. Most ales were golden to copper colored and many had a distinctive bitterness resulting from the hops used in brewing them. Stouts were generally very dark and had a dry-roasted caramel-like flavor profile.

3. *Restaurant Industry Operations Report*, National Restaurant Association, 1996.

4. Mass production brewers typically used corn or rice, in addition to the more traditional hops and barley, in brewing their beers. These adjunct ingredients resulted in beers that were lighter in flavor and lower in cost than beers brewed only with hops and barley.

5. Pasteurization of beer lengthened its shelf life and made refrigeration unnecessary. Most, but not all, mass-produced beers were pasteurized.

6. *Restaurant Industry Operations Report*, National Restaurant Association, 1996.

7. *North American Brewers Resource Directory*, 1997–1998, Institute for Brewing Studies, Association of Brewers, Boulder, Colorado, 1997.

8. Some states required that *all* the output of a brewpub must be sold on premises.

9. Trade dress included label and package designs and the design of point of purchase and other graphic material.

10. Texas and 18 other states prohibited brewpubs from selling beer to distributors for sale at retail.

11. BHC acquired these units from their original investors, a process that took longer than anticipated.

Cochlear Hearing Devices: Maintaining Global Leadership

C-7

case seven

Professor Gary J. Stockport and Fernando R. Chaddad
The University of Western Australia

"The deaf community is not disabled. The problem lies with the hearing world, which is embarrassed by not being able to communicate."

—Martin Tucker and Anna Willoughby, parents of deaf 3-year-old Honesty and founders of *'Parents Against Childhood Experimentation'*,[1] a US-based non-profit organisation with deaf and hearing members that vigorously oppose 'cochlear' technology.

"Losing my sight and hearing has been extraordinarily difficult. My circumstances improved significantly when I received the 'cochlear' implant in my left ear, but without the benefit of sight, I still have major challenges like localizing warning signals [such as] sirens, car horns [. . .]. I hope that being implanted with the new technology in my other ear will help connect me to the world more completely."

—Rudy Vener, a 46-year-old computer programmer who gradually became blind and deaf due to a disease called *Retinitis Pigmentosa*.[2]

INTRODUCTION

Fiscal year 2001 was good for Sydney based Cochlear Limited (see Exhibit 1). The company was on-track toward the consistent delivery of 20% plus annual growth target rates. Founded in 1981, Cochlear had expanded far beyond its Australian roots and by 2001 accounted for a worldwide share of around 70% in the implantable hearing devices market. With a global distribution arm and operating companies in key markets (see Exhibits 2 and 3), it was widely known as the technology leader in this niche—

fittingly known as the 'cochlear' segment. 2000 had been a year of important changes for Cochlear. Its high-profile CEO, Catherine Livingstone, had stepped down after 6 years of service as CEO. The press had frequently cited her as 'the most powerful woman in Australian business'. She had guided the company through its highly successful IPO (initial public offering) in 1996 (see Exhibits 4 and 5) and Australian investors had been very enthusiastic, buying enough Cochlear stock to take the company's market capitalisation to around AUS$1.5bn—around US$800m.

Cochlear's incoming CEO, Jack O'Mahony, knew he would face tremendous challenges as the head of Cochlear. These included the recent technology breakthroughs of Advanced Bionics, a North American new entrant in the 'cochlear' segment. But what was probably the heaviest barrier against Cochlear's immediate growth was the bitter public debate that raged within the US and European deaf communities in the early 2000's. Parents such as Martin Tucker and Anna Willoughby, founders of a US-based non-profit initiative called *'Parents Against Childhood Experimentation'*, could be a public relations nightmare for Cochlear and were certain to heat the public debate on 'cochlear' technology even further. For O'Mahony, an executive proud of his company's values (see Exhibit 6), this debate was disappointing but it also underlined once again the importance of public awareness in the medical devices industry.

THE BEGINNING— PROFESSOR CLARK'S DREAM

In 1967, Professor Graeme Clark of the University of Melbourne in Australia began researching implantable hearing devices. Having grown up in a home with a deaf father, he set out to improve the quality of life for those

Fiscal year ended 30/06

	1996	1997	1998	1999	2000	2001
Selected P&L Data						
Net Revenues [A$m]	$ 72.3	$ 71.9	$ 91.7	$127.2	$144.2	$197.2
R&D Expenditures [A$m]	$ 11.0	$ 10.6	$ 11.6	$ 13.5	$ 20.2	NA
EBIT [A$m]	$ 13.3	$ 14.3	$ 17.5	$ 23.0	$ 34.8	NA
After-Tax Net Profit [A$m]	$ 10.8	$ 10.8	$ 13.3	$ 16.3	$ 20.2	$ 31.2
EPS [A$]	$0.217	$0.216	$0.266	$0.322	$0.396	NA
Selected Managerial Data	**1996**	**1997**	**1998**	**1999**	**2000**	**2001**
Total Assets [A$m]	NA	NA	NA	$ 82.9	$ 93.8	NA
Group Sales [units]	$2,756	$3,128	$3,507	4,128	4,941	NA
Headcount [-]	334	350	376	432	543	NA

Source: Annual Report at www.cochlear.com

Operating Company	Cochlear Ownership	Base Country
Cochlear Ltd	100%	Australia
Cochlear Europe	100%	UK
Cochlear AG	100%	Switzerland
Cochlear (UK) Ltd	100%	UK
Cochlear GmbH	100%	Germany
Cochlear Corporation	100%	USA
Cochlear (HK) Ltd	100%	Hong Kong
Nihon Cochlear Co Ltd	100%	Japan
Neopraxis Pty Ltd	100%	Australia

Source: www.cochlear.com

who could not hear. In 1978, his dream led to a significant breakthrough in audiology as a patient surgically received a 10-channel implantable device. The operation went well and the recipient could hear his wife speaking to him after the recovery period. Subsequent implants led Professor Clark to believe that his implants could be improved further.

In 1979, Nucleus, a group of companies that manufactured highly specialised medical equipment, became interested in the potential of Dr. Clark's work being made available to the wider community. With the support of both the University of Melbourne and the Australian Government, Nucleus set out to develop a commercially viable implantable device and to carry out a worldwide clinical trial. In 1981, Cochlear was established as a corporate entity in order to continue its business operations.[3] As Cochlear dedicated its efforts year after year to the further development of implantable hearing devices, this Australian company would literally become synonymous with the devices that the deaf community worldwide would know and refer to as 'cochlear implants'.

| EXHIBIT | 3 | Geographic Breakdown of Operations |

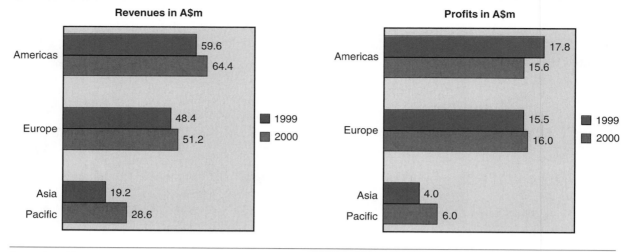

Source: Annual Report at www.cochlear.com

| EXHIBIT | 4 | Cochlear Market Cap in AUS$m and Trading Range in AUS$ |

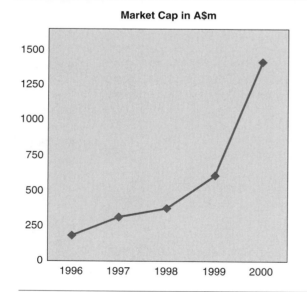

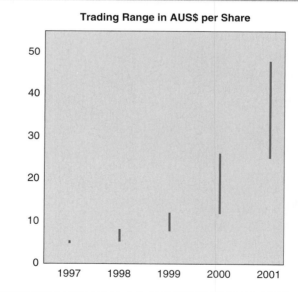

Source: 2000 Annual Report at www.cochlear.com

THE HUMAN EAR

The human ear consists of three parts (see Exhibit 7). The outer ear is the visible outer portion of the ear and ear canal. The middle ear is comprised of the eardrum and three tiny bones or ossicles. The inner ear is the fluid-filled cochlea, which contains thousands of tiny sound receptors called hair cells. For people with normal functioning hearing, sound passes through all three parts of the ear. The outer ear collects the sound and directs it to the eardrum, causing it to vibrate. This cre-

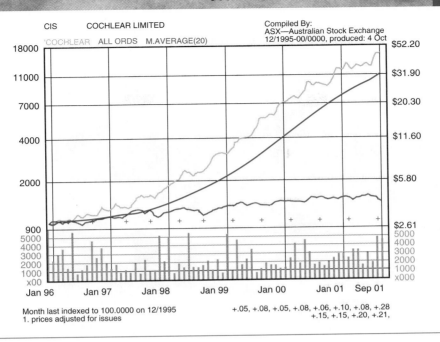

CIS COCHLEAR LIMITED

'COCHLEAR ALL ORDS M.AVERAGE(20)

Compiled By:
ASX—Australian Stock Exchange
12/1995-00/0000, produced: 4 Oct

Month last indexed to 100.0000 on 12/1995
1. prices adjusted for issues

+.05, +.08, +.05, +.08, +.06, +.10, +.08, +.28
+.15, +.15, +.20, +.21,

Source: www.asx.com.au

Our Mission

- Clinical teams and recipients embrace Cochlear as their Partner in Hearing for Life. This choice is made out of continuing preference for the benefits provided by Cochlear services and products and for the values resonated by Cochlear people.

Our Values

- Cochlear expects the highest standard of business practice from all its employees. We encourage:
  - Mutual respect
  - Performance
  - Professionalism
  - Continuous improvement

Source: www.cochlear.com

---

ates a chain reaction in the middle ear ossicles. The motion of these bones causes fluid to move throughout the inner ear, or cochlea. As the fluid moves, thousands of tiny receptors—called hair cells—that line the cochlea bend back and forth. When the hair cells move, they send electrical signals to the hearing nerve, which carries them to the brain where they are interpreted as sound.[4]

HEARING IMPAIRMENT

Hearing impairment can be characterised according to its physiological source. There are two general categories of hearing impairment: conductive and sensorineural—although sometimes a combination of the two may arise. Conductive hearing impairment results from diseases or disorders that limit the transmission of sound through the outer or middle ear. Conductive hearing impairment is often treated surgically with an implanted prosthesis to replace part or all of the ossicles. People with a conductive hearing loss represent 10% of the total hearing-impaired population. Sensorineural hearing impairment occurs in the inner ear or neural pathways and accounts for the vast majority of hearing impairment—typically 90% of a hearing impaired population. In patients with sensorineural hearing impairment, the external and middle ear function normally. The sound vibrations pass undisturbed

EXHIBIT 7   How Humans Hear

The human ear consists of three parts: the outer ear (including the visible part of the ear and the ear canal), the middle ear (air-filled space separated from the outer ear by the eardrum), and the inner ear (including the cochlea).

How Hearing Works

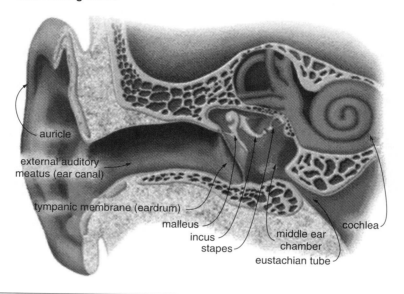

Source: www.symphonix.com

through the eardrum and ossicles, and fluid waves are created in the cochlea. However, because some or many of the delicate sensory hair cells inside the cochlea have degenerated or been damaged, the inner ear cannot detect the full intensity and quality of the sound. Sensorineural hearing impairment typically occurs as a result of aging or exposure to loud noise over a protracted period of time.[5]

ESTABLISHING ROOTS—THE AUSTRALIAN MEDICAL DEVICES MARKET

Australia was a mature market for medical equipment, representing about 1% of the global market. The size of the Australian medical equipment market in 1994–95 was estimated at about AUS$1.1bn. By 1997, the market was estimated at about AUS$1.2bn and was growing at an average long-term rate of about 8% per year. Imports accounted for about half of the Australian market. The main exporters of medical equipment to Australia were the USA (50%), Europe (25%) and Japan (10%). Many US medical companies had businesses in Australia, including 3M, Abbott, Bristol Myers, Johnson & Johnson and Pfizer. Although a relatively small market, Australia's high per capita income

meant that there was demand for a full range of sophisticated medical equipment.[6]

The Australian medical equipment industry was characterised by a large number of small companies, and a small number of large multinational firms. According to 1995 estimates, about 70 manufacturers of medical equipment operated in the country. More than 70% of these companies had less than 5 employees, and more than 90% had less than 10. Approximately 65% of the Australian equipment output was exported, mainly to ASEAN countries, New Zealand, Hong Kong, Korea and Japan. There was only a small amount of local production. Australian companies invested in R&D and many were high value-added and research-intensive companies. When they did manufacture, it tended to be for niche markets.

The health care system in Australia was pluralistic, complex and loosely organised. A distinguishing feature was the extent to which responsibilities were split between the different levels of government. The system involved Commonwealth, State and Local Governments, which were increasingly influencing the structure of health services. Private practitioners provided most medical and dental care. Australia had a universal system of health insurance—Medicare—that came into operation in 1984. Private health insurance was also purchased to cover charges in private hospitals, and for private status in public hospitals.

A number of factors influenced the demand for medical equipment in Australia. One of the major influences was government policy and activity in the provision of public health services. The public hospital system was a major end-user of hospital equipment. Quality, service and price were the main considerations when purchasing medical equipment. Known brands were preferred, so new suppliers in the high technology field needed to have a world reputation to gain a share of the Australian market. Also, safety standards had to be met. In the case of high technology equipment, hospitals demanded that service be available 24 hours per day. Hospital medical and nursing staff heavily influenced purchase decisions and sales representatives from medical firms regularly visited medical and nursing staff to promote their product ranges.

GLOBAL DEMAND FOR HEARING AIDS

The global demand for hearing aids arises from the adverse effects of hearing loss and impacts upon not only the quality of life, but also upon the psychological well-being of hearing-impaired people. Hearing-impaired individuals often withdraw from discussions and other social interactions to avoid frustration and embarrassment from not being able to fully participate in and understand conversations. Difficulty in communicating effectively can lead to negative emotions and attitudes, increased stress levels, reduced self-confidence, reduced sociability and effectiveness in the workplace.

The demographics of hearing impairment are powerful. In the US, for instance, approximately 28 million people are hearing-impaired, the equivalent of around 6.4% of the population. Hearing loss is one of the most prevalent chronic health conditions in the world, affecting people of all ages, in all segments of the population and across all socio-economic levels. In the US, hearing loss affects approximately 17 in 1,000 children under age 18. Incidence increases with age and approximately 314 in 1,000 people over age 65 have hearing loss.[7] Hearing loss can be hereditary, or it can result from disease, trauma, or long-term exposure to damaging noise or medications. Hearing loss can vary from a mild but important loss of sensitivity, to a total loss of hearing.

The global market for hearing aid devices was comprised of two segments. The traditional approaches to the treatment of mild to severe sensorineural hearing impairment involved the use of hearing aids. This was the type of hearing impairment that 85% of the typical hearing-impaired population had, and could be usually treated with individual or group devices (see Exhibit 8 for product examples). As of 2001, the global market for such devices was extremely fragmented, with intense competition in 5 continents providing all sorts of practical, often low cost solutions. See Exhibit 9 for a selected list of manufacturers of hearing aids for mild hearing loss. Technological barriers to entry were relatively low and regulation by health authorities was not terribly stringent in many countries.

Profound hearing loss, on the other hand, was more complex both in technological and regulatory terms. This type of hearing impairment usually touched only 5% of a hearing-impaired population. 'Cochlear' implants had been primarily used for this segment of the market. As 'cochlear' implants were surgically placed into patients, health authorities around the world demanded clinical trials before approving the commercial use of such products.

Hearing Aid Devices for Mild Hearing Loss EXHIBIT 8

Source: www.medel.com

- Aurilink: ready-to-wear hearing aids for people who need an extra boost
- Bionic Ear: maker of a surgically implanted assistive device
- Elkon: a range of products for assessment and rehabilitation of the hearing and speech
- Miracle-ear: advancements in hearing technology
- Oticon Inc: digital hearing aids
- Phonak: developer and manufacturer of hearing technology
- Phonic Ear: assistive listening products designed to improve signal-to-noise ratio
- Rexton: hearing aid manufacturer
- Siemens: professional products and services
- Songbird Hearing: disposable hearing aids
- Starkey Laboratories: hearing aid manufacturer
- Telex Hearing: hearing aid manufacturer
- Unitron Industries: manufacturer of hearing aids

Source: www.yahoo.com

GLOBAL PLAYERS IN PROFOUND HEARING IMPAIRMENT AIDS

By 2001, the bulk of the segment characterised as the global market for hearing devices that treat severe to profound hearing impairment was served mainly by three competitors:

- Founded in 1981, **Cochlear Ltd** was the Australian company that pioneered 'cochlear' implant technology. By 2001, the company accounted for around 75% of the estimated 45,000 'cochlear' implants that were in use worldwide. The company was known for many technological breakthroughs in audiology and was fully committed to the further advancement of 'cochlear' technology;

- **Advanced Bionics Corporation** was founded in the United States in 1993 as a result of the efforts of Dr. Robert Schindler, head of the University of California at San Francisco's 'cochlear' implant programme, who tried to seek a partner that could provide engineering talent and financial resources to commercialise his multi-channel implant system. Dr. Schindler approached Alfred Mann, a world-renowned innovator of implantable medical devices and philanthropist, and asked for support. As a consequence, Alfred Mann pledged a personal gift of US$200m to develop a biomedical research institute in one of the largest personal donations to higher education ever. Alfred Mann's experience came from founding the world's second-largest heart pacemaker manufacturer (Pacesetter Systems), the largest manufacturer of implantable external insulin pumps (MiniMed) and several other high-tech companies. With the founding of Advanced Bionics in 1993, Alfred Mann formed his third highly successful medical devices company and brought the newly re-engineered implant, called Clarion, to market. As of 2001, Advanced Bionics was working on 'bionic' technologies to treat other disabilities. As Chairman Mann affirmed, *"we seek to enable the deaf to hear, the blind to see, and the lame to walk."*[8] In 2001, Advanced Bionics accounted for roughly 10% of 'cochlear' implants in use worldwide;

- Founded in Austria in 1989, **MedEl** was headquartered in Innsbruck and accounted for roughly 5% of 'cochlear' implants in use worldwide. By early 2001, the company had 13 subsidiaries around the globe and was growing by 25% per year in sales. The US Food and Drug Administration (FDA) approval MedEl received in 2001 for its Combi 40 system to be used in both adults and children was an important breakthrough for the company. The Combi 40 system was designed as the thinnest implant package available, which made it an attractive alternative for children.

In addition to the 'cochlear' implants that Cochlear Ltd, Advanced Bionics and MedEl manufactured, technologies alternative to implants were being developed for the profoundly deaf. As an example, **Symphonix Devices** from California was developing during the early 2000's a proprietary semi-implantable and implantable technology for the management of mild to severe hearing impairment. While 'cochlear' technologies had indirectly driven the ossicles by amplifying sound to increase the vibrations of the tympanic membrane, Symphonix proposed a device that was attached directly to the ossicles and enhanced the natural movement of these vibratory structures.

Another example was ultrasound technology, which was in the early 2000's the focus of research at **Hearing Innovations Incorporated** from Arizona, USA. Ultrasound research was still in its early stages and commercial development was not expected in the short term, but the longer-term implications for audiology could be significant. Finally, it was noteworthy that several research groups worldwide were working on pure biological research, such as cell therapy that could be used to replace damaged cells in the human ear.

COCHLEAR AND PACIFIC DUNLOP

During 1988, Pacific Dunlop, the Australian conglomerate (see Exhibit 10), acquired Nucleus, the medical equipment group that had helped bring Cochlear to life in 1981. Along with Nucleus came Cochlear, which became one of the many subsidiaries of Pacific Dunlop, which had been established back in 1920 and since then had grown to annual sales of more than AUS$3bn, mainly through unrelated acquisitions. As of the late 1990's, this diversified company had interests in batteries, clothing, sporting goods, industrial goods, electronics, latex products, medical products and tires.

In the mid-1990's, Pacific Dunlop reviewed its portfolio of businesses and decided to divest Cochlear. Thus, Cochlear Limited (ticker symbol: COH) was listed in the Australian Stock Exchange in December 1995. The Australian press would later comment: *"Few company divestments rank as unfortunate as Pacific Dunlop's AUS$125m float in 1995 of ear implant maker Cochlear Limited. While Pacific Dunlop closed at AUS$1.60 on 14 February 2000, Cochlear was at AUS$23.30. [With] a market value of AUS$1.2bn, [Cochlear's market cap] is fast approaching that of its one-time parent at AUS$1.65bn."*[9]

The IPO (initial public offering) was overseen by Cochlear's CEO Catherine Livingstone, who would later attract a lot of media attention as Cochlear's stock price initiated an impressive climb. The stock debuted at AUS$3.50 in 1995 and by late 2000 it was trading at around AUS$25, valuing the company at AUS$1.6bn. In her stint as Cochlear's CEO, Catherine Livingstone doubled both revenues and profits. From the shareholder's perspective, her stint had been important as the Cochlear's share price jumped sevenfold. She was the only female Australian CEO heading one of the Top 100 Australian companies. Cochlear was then constantly in the business press headlines, which followed every earnings report with great interest.

| | Pacific Dunlop | EXHIBIT 10 |

Pacific Dunlop was founded in Victoria in 1920. Until the late 1960's, Dunlop was basically a rubber company, with interests in tires, batteries, bedding and sporting goods, but in a spending spree during 1969–1972 it acquired a wide range of companies in unrelated fields. As of 2001, it also had interests in industrial goods, electronics, latex products and medical products. It also had installations or offices in China, Japan, Hong Kong, Thailand, Malaysia, Sri Lanka, New Zealand, North America and the European Community, with 151 manufacturing facilities, 1300 retail outlets and about 40,000 employees worldwide.

Item	2000	2001
Sales Revenue [A$m]	$ 4157	$ 5726
Operating loss after tax [A$m]	$ (139)	$ (87)
Total assets [A$m]	$ 3137	$ 4008
Return on shareholders' equity [%]	(13.1)	(5.8)
Earnings per share [A$ cents]	(14.4)	(8.4)
Dividend per share [A$ cents]	5.0	10.0

Source: www.pacdunlop.com

COCHLEAR TECHNOLOGY

A 'cochlear' implant is a device that electrically stimulates the inner-ear nerve and sends the message of sound to the brain. This is a process that does not happen naturally in the deaf. The benefits of this procedure can be profound. As an example, this implant procedure can give a deaf child some access to sound and parents the opportunity of communicating with their child. The implant is only suitable for those whom standard hearing aids cannot help. The technology is not too dissimilar to the base technology used in cardiac pacemakers and it is based upon artificial electrical stimulation.[10]

This clinically proven treatment for severe to profound sensorineural hearing loss in both ears has been in use since the 1980's. In the early 2000's, the treatment consisted of externally worn and surgically implanted components (see Exhibit 11). The externally worn components captured sound in the environment and processed it into digital code. The digital code was transmitted via radio waves to the surgically implanted electronics, which delivered electrical impulses via the electrode array. The electrode array was inserted into the inner ear and delivered electrical current to hearing nerve fibres. The nerve fibres then carried the electrical signals to the brain where they are heard as sound.

PRODUCT INNOVATION

Since 1981, Cochlear had been fully committed to the further development of their implantable hearing device technology. Building on the original 10-channel research of the first implants, Cochlear developed the more advanced 22-channel implant and the WSP (wearable speech processor). The design philosophy was to make a flexible cochlear implant with sophisticated sound processing in the externally worn speech processor. This allowed the recipient to take advantage of improvements in technology without surgically replacing their implanted device. A brief summary of Cochlear's innovations includes: the first to bring 'cochlear' implants to market; the first system to gain

---

EXHIBIT 11 How a 'Cochlear' Implant Works

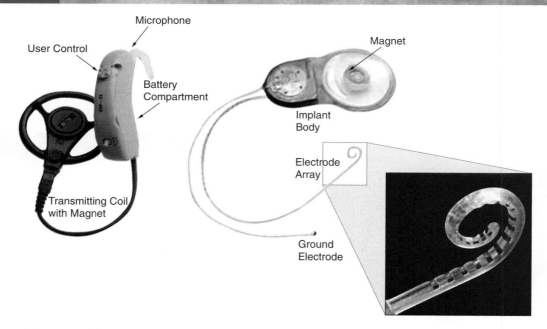

1. Sound is received by microphone at the top of the ear-level speech processor (left-most figure)
2. Sound is processed by internal chip to encode useful speech information (left-most figure)
3. The signal is sent to the transmitter then across the skin to the internal implant (central figure)
4. Internal implant converts code to electrical signals (central figure, detail in right-most figure)
5. Signals are sent to electrodes to stimulate nerve fibres, which then send hearing signals to the brain (right-most figure)

Source: www.cochlear.com

worldwide approval for use by adults and children; and the first to offer breakthrough proprietary technologies such as Neural Response Telemetry (NRT™), a method to directly record neural responses within the cochlea after stimulation. Since it did not require the 'cochlear' recipient to behaviorally respond to stimuli, it made the implant ideal for infants and young children.

By the late 1990's, Cochlear had introduced the Nucleus 24 Contour in all but the Australian and Japanese markets—which were still expecting the approval of governmental regulatory agencies. The response from surgeons to Nucleus 24 Contour's self-curling electrode array technology used in the implant had been favourable. The design also won the prestigious "Medical Design Excellence Award" in New York in May 2001. The continuous R&D investments over several years made the company the world's leader in 'cochlear' technology. By the late 1990's, the company was investing double-digit percentages of annual sales in R&D (see Exhibit 1).

GLOBAL EXPANSION

Being essentially a niche-player of highly specialised medical equipment with roots in the small Australian market, Cochlear set out to expand overseas early on. By early 2000, Cochlear had a distribution and service network that spanned over 60 countries in 5 continents. The company also had subsidiaries in the UK, Switzerland, Germany, the USA, Hong Kong and Japan, and operated R&D facilities in Australia and Belgium.

Cochlear was organised around three geographical business groups. The Americas accounted for 44% of fiscal year 2000 revenues; Europe accounted for 35% of revenues; and the Asia Pacific region was responsible for 21% of revenues. All three regions were profitable and growing (see Exhibit 3). In its 2000 annual report, Cochlear announced to its shareholders that it had maintained a world market share of 'cochlear' implants of between 60% and 65%. For Cochlear, to be the worldwide leader in 'cochlear' technology also meant a high exposure to currency risks. The company adhered to its Board policy regarding risk management issues such as hedging, and in the typical fiscal year the group revenues were influenced by currency exchange movements. In broad terms, the overall outlook for Cochlear in fiscal 2001 and beyond was positive as the company expected global demand for 'cochlear' implants to continue growing by a long-term growth rate of 20%. This rate was also the target growth rate for Cochlear.[11]

A HEATED PUBLIC DEBATE EMERGES

During April 2000, a very intense debate broke through the deaf community worldwide as director Josh Aronson's full-length documentary *"Sound and Fury"* premiered as part of the opening weekend of the Philadelphia Festival of World Cinema. The controversial documentary followed the lives of the Artinian Family, and their struggle with and debate over 'cochlear' implants.[12] The documentary also raised the question as of what was the best or right way for parents to bring up their children.

The film portrayed the Artinian Family of Long Island, USA. Part of the extended family was Peter Artinian, the deaf father of three deaf children who claimed: *"I'm happy being deaf. It's very peaceful."*[13] But the extended family also included hearing members such as Chris, Peter's brother, and his wife, Mari Artinian. After they had learnt that their baby was deaf, they fought with their deaf relatives over their decision to implant their child. Their son thus underwent surgery and heard sound for the first time in his life. But the child's uncle, Peter, was an outspoken leader of the anti-implant deaf community in Long Island, and his world was turned upside down by his daughter's request for a cochlear implant. Initially, Peter and his wife, Nita, suspended their long-standing opposition to the implant, but as they learned more about how deaf children with implants were mainstreamed into the hearing world, they became afraid that their daughter would lose her deaf identity and reject their sign language. So they decided to move away from their hearing relatives in Long Island in order to become part of a more supportive deaf community in Maryland. The on-screen controversy of the Artinian family quickly spilled into the real world upon the launch of the documentary.

OPPONENTS

Opponents of 'cochlear' technology argued that the operation was a traumatic experience: a hole was drilled in the skull and a tiny wire attached to a nerve. The whole idea of having an electromagnetic device in a child's head was worrying: sometimes it could get attached to the facial nerves and leave the child with a paralysed face. Also, for a child with a 'cochlear' implant, the spontaneity of childhood could be lost. Children going down a slide or getting out of a car had to be caught by their parents to 'ground' them, because otherwise they would get an electrical shock. The most radical opponents assailed 'cochlear' as the demise of sign language in specific and deaf culture in general, and organised around movements such as *'Parents Against Childhood Experimentation'*.

PROPONENTS

Proponents of the technology described 'cochlear' as a miraculous surgical procedure that could restore hearing in both children and sometimes adults. For many deaf patients, both adults and children, it was the only technology available for some access to sound and thus the only source of hope. Proponents admitted that the technology still had room for improvement. But proponents also observed that technological progress in the field of audiology was incremental enough to make them confident that, soon, every argument put forth by opponents would no longer be valid.

Indeed, as of early 2000, the scientific community working on 'cochlear' were still fighting with the limits of science. The latest generation of implants worked by stimulating the auditory nerve, which was still the only treatment available to the profoundly deaf. However, they restored only a rudimentary level of hearing. According to Professor Holley of the University of Sheffield, United Kingdom: *"Cochlear implants work very well in a limited way but they can't be given to long-term deaf people because their auditory nerves have degenerated too far. Replacement nerve cells could improve the electrical contact between the implant and the brain. This opens up the prospect of making implants more effective. We may be in a position to make these advances in 3–5 years."*[14]

The controversial debate triggered by the *"Sound and Fury"* documentary put Cochlear centre-stage as the world's leader in 'cochlear' implants, and reminded incoming CEO Jack O'Mahony of what could be a formidable barrier to success and growth in the medical equipment industry: public awareness.

COMPETITOR'S BREAKTHROUGH

In July 2000, an announcement made overseas reached the office of Cochlear's CEO Jack O'Mahony. California-based Advanced Bionics Corporation announced that its new Clarion HiFocus Electrode had received approval from the FDA for use in postlingually deafened adults. According to Jeff Greiner, President of Advanced Bionics: *"Scientists have attempted for many years to develop an electrode that can selectively stimulate targeted groups of hearing nerve fibres. The HiFocus Electrode is the first FDA approved technology which is designed to achieve this goal."*[15]

The new technology allowed, for the first time, focused directional coupling between a 'cochlear' implant system and a deaf patient's auditory nerve. According to Albert Maltan, Advanced Bionics VP of Product Management: *"Advanced Bionics is proud to be the first in the race to get this technology to market because patient performance results have exceeded our expectations."*[16] The HiFocus Electrode was guided into position during surgery by the use of the patented Elec-

trode Positioning System™. It was also designed to occupy the space in the human cochlea where scar (fibrous) tissue can form. This was good news for 'cochlear' implant users, especially children, who would make use of future technologies in their lifetimes. By the time of the FDA approval, the company employed over 350 scientists, engineers and professionals around the globe and was one of the fastest growing medical device manufacturers in the world. Advanced Bionics seemed to be catching up quickly with the technology gap that Cochlear had established after decades of research (see Exhibit 12).

NEW INITIATIVES IN EMERGING MARKETS

In the meantime, Cochlear continued to expand overseas, this time embarking into an initiative geared toward emerging markets. The rationale was that the first-wave of 'cochlear' implants in developed markets was well underway, and that immediate growth could be achieved in emerging markets. This push, however, would be linked to difficulties additional to the ones Cochlear was used to. Amongst those were the relative scarcity of physical resources such as hospitals and equipment, as well as the scarceness of trained personnel to handle the complex 'cochlear' implants and maintenance.

Cochlear announced in early 2001 a plan to establish more implant centres in Thailand. According to Albert Sorrell, Cochlear's general manager for the Asia Pacific region, the market in Thailand was very small for Cochlear due to a lack of awareness and funding, but the company believed that the Thai operation would be developed into a profitable market in 3 to 5 years. Cochlear would invest in hospital facilities, which would become capable of offering 'cochlear' technology to patients. The required investment included surgical and mapping equipment, as well as the training of a team of surgeons, audiologists, speech therapists and teachers of the deaf. Emerging markets such as Thailand could be a great opportunity to Cochlear, which had up to this point expanded overseas mainly into developed countries. For example, a study by the Otological Centre in Bangkok and 17 provinces showed that hearing disabilities affected 13.6% of the country's 62 million people. Whereas only about 14,900 were seen as 'cochlear' implant candidates, just 30 had received them by early 2001. But even though the average cost of treatment for 'cochlear' patients was relatively low in comparison to other treatments (see Exhibit 13), the cost was still much too high for the broader segments of emerging market populations.

According to Cochlear:

Criterion	Advanced Bionics Clarion	Cochlear Nucleus	MedEl Combi 40 +
Electrode array design	Straight	Self-Curling	Straight
Number of channels	16	22	12
Number of virtual channels	15	21	NA
Magnetic interference safety	None	1.5 Tesla	1.5 Tesla
Neural response telemetry	No	Yes	No
External casing	Ceramic	Titanium	Ceramic

According to Advanced Bionics:

Criterion*	Advanced Bionics Clarion	Cochlear Nucleus	MedEl Combi 40 +
Sound processing options	3	3	2
Information delivery available	5	1	1
Non-simultaneous delivery rate	2	1	2
Simultaneous delivery rate	3	0	0
Number of output circuits	5	1	1
Potential channels	1	3	2
Software upgrade	5	1	1

*1 is lowest, 5 is highest score

Source: www.cochlear.com, www.bionicear.com

CEO AGENDA

After 6 years at the helm of Cochlear, Catherine Livingstone announced in March 2000 that she would be leaving by year's end. The company's Board appointed Jack O'Mahony as Cochlear's new CEO in the 2000 Board meeting. The business press later announced that Catherine Livingstone would be joining the board of directors of Telstra, Australia's telecom and one of the country's largest companies.[17] O'Mahony took over in September 2000. He had spent all of his professional life in the medical equipment industry, and had been President of Howmedica, the US-based orthopaedics company associated with Pfizer.

As Livingstone departed, the Australian business press continued to praise Cochlear: "*Cochlear Limited boosted its net profit for the year to June 2000 to AUS$20.2m, up 23.5% on last year. The Australian company said on 22 August it was confident of sustaining earnings growth above 20% a year. The final dividend was AUS$0.15 a share. Earnings per share for the year rose to AUS$0.396 from AUS$0.323. Cochlear's shares rose AUS$0.30 to close at AUS$27.50.*"[18]

In his first few months as the new CEO, Jack O'Mahony thought about his new role at the company. He pondered about Cochlear's unique place in the medical devices industry as the undisputed leader of the implantable hearing devices segment, with a worldwide market share of around 70%. He also pondered about the company's strong track record and 20% plus growth targets. How could he best steer the company toward its goals? In writing the CEO Agenda, O'Mahony wanted to structure his thoughts around the most important issues he would face as the CEO of Cochlear. He thought about the following:

• **Economies of Scale:** It seemed to Jack O'Mahony that the company still had not reached the desired economies of scale in production due to the lack of public awareness of the product. This resulted in a high price to customers worldwide, especially in emerging markets. The product required highly skilled labour to assemble the device that includes a tiny electrode array. The company had about 200 people working at microscopes in a sterile room and each device required some 16 hours of handwork to

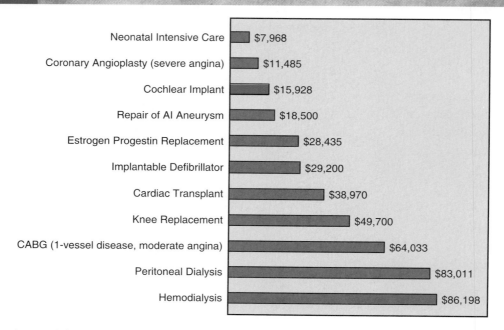

Neonatal Intensive Care	$7,968
Coronary Angioplasty (severe angina)	$11,485
Cochlear Implant	$15,928
Repair of AI Aneurysm	$18,500
Estrogen Progestin Replacement	$28,435
Implantable Defibrillator	$29,200
Cardiac Transplant	$38,970
Knee Replacement	$49,700
CABG (1-vessel disease, moderate angina)	$64,033
Peritoneal Dialysis	$83,011
Hemodialysis	$86,198

Note: figures are in 1993 US dollars and denote the cost per quality-adjusted life year (QALY). The original source is the Maryland Hospital State Rate Setting Commission database and others.

Source: 2000 Annual Report at www.cochlear.com

complete. CEO O'Mahony wondered how he could push Cochlear up the production scale experience curve. According to O'Mahony: *"The market is very much bigger than people give us credit for. It is just difficult to get into in lots of ways."*[19] See Exhibit 14 for statistics on hearing disabilities for selected countries. Specifically within the severe hearing loss segment, one estimate was that 500,000 patients in the US alone could benefit from a Cochlear implant, plus another 200,000 in Germany, whereas fewer than 10,000 implants were being installed each year;

- **Public Awareness:** Hand-in-hand with the economies of scale problem came the issue of public awareness. Initiatives such as *'Parents Against Childhood Experimentation'* were a major threat to O'Mahony. Having spent his entire career in the medical devices industry, he considered ethics as one of his most important values. It was not the first time he had heard of public debates about 'cochlear', but this time it had been very intense. CEO O'Mahony con-

sidered public awareness one of the most formidable challenges in his stint at the helm of Cochlear;

- **Competitor and Substitute Technologies:** Throughout much of its history, Cochlear was arguably alone in the 'cochlear' market, which was complex in technological and regulatory terms. In 2000, however, Advanced Bionics from California experienced a major breakthrough as the American FDA cleared its products, in essence allowing the company to enter the 'cochlear' market. O'Mahony knew Advanced Bionics had deep skills in implantable prostheses and miniaturization. After all, it was the world's second-largest manufacturer of pacemakers. CEO O'Mahony wondered whether this new entrant would be a threat to Cochlear in what was Cochlear's most important market: the Americas. He also wondered whether this new competitor could be an ally in the battle for public awareness. Furthermore, he wondered whether he was at risk of being outflanked not by its most visible competitor, Advanced Bionics, but by alterna-

Estimated Populations with All Types of Hearing Impairment for Selected Countries

EXHIBIT 14

Country	Hearing Impairment [% of Population]
Argentina	8.4%
Australia	5.5%
Brazil	6.0%
Canada	5.7%
China	7.2%
France	5.0%
Germany	5.3%
India	8.8%
Iran	6.7%
Iraq	5.2%
Japan	6.0%
Mexico	6.2%
Nigeria	6.6%
South Africa	9.0%
South Korea	5.6%
Spain	4.6%
Sweden	6.3%
Switzerland	5.7%
UK	5.0%
USA	6.4%
Zambia	5.7%

Source: http://frontpage.erie.net/dwm/default.htm

tion. What would happen if they could not continue to meet the expectations of the IR community by not continuing to produce 20% plus annual growth figures?

During the process of writing the CEO Agenda for Cochlear, however, he was absolutely sure other issues would arise throughout his administration. But he needed to set specific targets and priorities for at least the next 2–3 years.

BIBLIOGRAPHY

1. *"Body and Mind: Second Opinion..."*—The Observer, April 30, 2000
2. *"PR Newswire: Blind and Deaf Man to Receive..."*—PR Newswire, August 22, 2000
3. www.cochlear.com
4. www.symphonix.com
5. www.symphonix.com
6. *"Australia: Medical Equipment Market"*—Industry Sector Analysis, January 30, 1997
7. Symphonix annual report at www.symphonix.com
8. www.bionicear.com
9. *"Bad-move Sales"*—Sydney Morning Herald, February 15, 2000
10. *"Body and Mind: Second Opinion..."*—The Observer, April 30, 2000
11. Annual report available at *www.cochlear.com*
12. *"Philadelphia Festival of World Cinema 2000..."*—PR Newswire, April 26, 2000
13. *"Philadelphia Festival of World Cinema 2000..."*—PR Newswire, April 26, 2000
14. *"Nerve Cell Implants Offer Prospect of Hearing to the Deaf"*—The Independent, March 26, 2001
15. *"FDA Approves New Cochlear Implant..."*—PR Newswire, July 20, 2000
16. *"FDA Approves New Cochlear Implant..."*—PR Newswire, July 20, 2000
17. *"She's One in a Hundred but This CEO Is Quitting"*—Sydney Morning Herald, March 14, 2000
18. *"Cochlear Ready to Do It Again..."*—Sydney Morning Herald, August 23, 2000
19. *"Biotech—Volume Rising"*—Australian Shares May 2001, page 22–24.

tive technologies such as the semi-implantable devices that were the focus at Symphonix Devices. Finally, O'Mahony wondered whether Cochlear should get involved with the biological or ultrasound basic research, which he believed could impact the industry in the longer term;

- **Investor Relations (IR):** The Cochlear stock was doing very well despite global bearishness in equity markets. CEO O'Mahony wondered whether the company was reasonably valued in the latter part of 2001 as Cochlear's share price approached AUS$50. He also wondered about the likely impacts in his day-to-day responsibilities by a Cochlear stock with a less optimistic market valua-

William A. Andrews
Stetson University

The boutiques on the hill overlooking Lake Dora were all adorned in their Christmas regalia. Gazing out his office window toward the lake, Steve Shamrock, founder and CEO of Cyberplay faced a plethora of financing options for his four-year-old company. After three years of mostly nickel-and-dime fund raising from friends and family, he now had three substantial investors willing to contribute over $5 million in capital. This infusion would allow the company to pay off its debt of over $5 million (some at an agreed upon discount) on which it had defaulted, give the company a positive net worth, plus provide enough working capital to carry the company for a year as operating cash flows took off. Shamrock's objective was an IPO or merger in about 12 months. Despite all of the good news on the financing side, Shamrock had two concerns about operations that bore directly on the value of a potential IPO or merger, and even on the survival of the company. The cash burn rate was about $250,000 per month and the company's capabilities no longer seemed to match its strategy. Unless these issues were carefully resolved, he feared he would run through the $5 million before he achieved a positive operating cash flow, or at least before significant revenues materialized. Such a scenario would seriously jeopardize the future of the company.

COMPANY CONCEPT AND HISTORY

After a family visit to Discovery Zone, a children's recreational center with lots of juvenile diversions, Shamrock wondered whether or not an educational, computer-based center might not make an excellent business concept. Shamrock raised about $800,000 from friends and family and opened the original Cyberplay store in October 1995, in Winter Park, Florida, an Orlando suburb.

The store coupled state-of-the-art computer hardware and software with an award-winning futuristic store design. The original Cyberplay business model was based on three related revenue streams: pay-for-play services, software sales, and software training. Pay-for-play services allowed users to play the latest software games on state-of-the-art computers. Educational games for younger children were in one area, while combat and competitive games were in another. Additionally, users could use e-mail and Internet capabilities, as well as the full complement of Microsoft Office products. Time could be purchased by the hour, day, or month, and usage was debited on a magnetic-strip debit card that was issued to new customers. This revenue stream was anticipated to have been the largest of the three. Software sales occurred as customers liked programs that they had just tested on Cyberplay's network. Software training services included classes in Microsoft Office software applications.

Cyberplay soon began receiving very high profile awards for its store design including the Retail Innovation Technology Award (RITA), and the Retail Store of the Year award from *Chain Store Age*, a prominent retail trade publication. Perhaps the most prestigious award was the Smithsonian Medal, received for integrating technology into education. Among other things, the judges were impressed with the company's proprietary technology that allowed multiple users to simultaneously use a single CD.

By June 1996 Intel had become a modest investor in Cyberplay with an investment of around $300,000 and an option to invest more based on company performance. A second store was opened in Atlanta where Intel had set up its pavilion for the 1996 Summer Olympics. Later that year Cyberplay was invited by Sony to build a center at Sony's Wonder Technology Lab, its premier promotional exhibit, on Madison Avenue, New York City. Cyberplay was the only other brand name at this site, visited by 200,000 people per year.

Concurrent with the opening of the new stores, Cyberplay hired two software specialists with Ph.D.s to develop training programs for popular software applications. Recounts Shamrock, "Most corporate training modules came in six-hour blocks. From talking to training managers, we learned that few employees were willing to be out of the office for a whole day. As a result, corporate training budgets were often not spent. We developed a three-hour module that would cover the most commonly used functions, complete with a reference book and delivered by an instructor. This way, trainees could get off work at, say, 3:00 p.m., go to the training, and still be home in time for supper. We launched these courses through our Winter Park facility. One of the great strengths is our curriculum and its developers. Another is our retail store design and awards. The exposure and industry contacts that the store design brought us allowed us to make the shift to the corporate training market."

A Strategic Shift

It soon became apparent to Shamrock that the original business concept was not going to be financially successful. After tweaking the marketing "200 different ways," Shamrock concluded that other revenue streams had to be pursued. Commenting on the reasons for not being able to make the "edutainment" business work, Shamrock speculated, "Between 1995 when we first got the idea of Cyberplay, and 1997, the cost of computer hardware dropped dramatically from about $2500 for a great machine to about $1250. This resulted in many of our potential retail customers buying their own hardware."

While visiting the Atlanta facility, Shamrock received a call that a very close friend had died suddenly of a heart attack at age 36. He caught the next flight to Orlando. Noticing Shamrock's fallen countenance, the man in the seat next to him asked if something was the matter. As it turned out, the man was on the board of directors for Prudential Insurance, and had heard of Cyberplay through a recent article in *Business Week*. Their conversation converged on Prudential's corporate computer training needs, and the flight ended with the board member promising to have someone contact Shamrock.

"I didn't expect to hear from anyone again, but amazingly, several days later I did receive a call. Within a few months we had an agreement in principle to offer training at their site in Jacksonville to some 6000 employees. Nevertheless, it took one year before we received a signed training contract from them. We were, of course, slowly starving to death for lack of cash." So Cyberplay began its migration from being in the "edutainment" business at the retail level, to being in the computer-training business at the business-to-business level.

Shamrock noted, "We had similar success with AT&T in that we became an approved vendor with the highest scores ever awarded to a software training company. By June of 1998, we signed a contract to become the preferred provider for ADP, and they wanted to market our training to their enormous customer base." Later that summer, Cyber Technology Engineering (CTE), an outfit that specialized in computer simulation training for police officers, selected Cyberplay as the medium through which to deliver their training. CTE's simulations would be enhanced greatly by the absolute latest in technology, and for this reason they were particularly impressed with Cyberplay's innovative Winter Park facility. Since the police officers would be required to complete a certain amount of training annually, training usage rates were estimated at 50% of eligible officers per year.

By September, EVC, a company that supplied college-level courses from established universities over the Internet, signed with Cyberplay to use its courses for teaching software applications. In sum, in one year Cyberplay had moved from being a retail "edutainment" company to being a corporate training firm. Appendix A shows pricing and revenue assumptions that emerged from contract discussions with each of the major clients.

Recounts Shamrock, "By this time, we were in default on several million dollars of bank and corporate debt. Our legal counsel advised us to file bankruptcy and basically start over as a new business. I really grappled with this question, but decided to seek forbearance agreements with the bankers for two reasons. First, I believed that we were very close to being very successful. Second, most of the shareholders and bondholders were community people to whom I felt I had more than just a legal obligation. The banks agreed to cooperate, so we rested our future on the corporate training market." The alternative to this strategic shift was bankruptcy, and the opportunities had emerged fortuitously, so successfully concluded contracts substituted for systematic market entry analysis.

The Training Industry

In 1998, the information technology and training market was estimated to be about $12 billion worldwide and $5 billion in the U.S. These numbers were expected to grow to about $17 billion and $7.5 billion, respectively, by the year 2000.

The industry was highly fragmented, with no competitor having a significant share of the market. The industry was subdivided according to the medium of delivery: (1) classroom-based training organization

(Executrain, New Horizons, Productivity Point), (2) retail-based training organizations (Best Buy, CompUSA, Gateway Country Stores), (3) client-site training companies, and (4) Internet-based training companies (Ziff Davis). Significantly, Cyberplay had beaten all of the major training companies in landing the AT&T, ADP, and Prudential accounts. It had been particularly successful against CompUSA, which was the largest training provider in the country. Moreover, CompUSA recognized the strategic importance of the training market and was eager to expand its share. Initially, Shamrock believed that the target market, the *Fortune* 1000, did not want Internet-based training, preferring instead the personal touch of a trainer. Some companies had their own in-house training departments that provided competition for Cyberplay.

Cyberplay felt that one of its competitive advantages was its ability to secure excellent trainers. Cyberplay had used a national search firm to find qualified applicants in the various cities in which it was training. These individuals were required to have strong interpersonal and communication skills in addition to being technically competent. A. R. Robinson, VP of operations, put it this way, "We are looking for a very special person—someone who is energetic, pleasant, and knowledgeable." Although the rapid acquisition of trainers would be critical to success, Robinson believed the firm had a proven method for securing such employees.

OPERATING STRATEGY

If Cyberplay could not provide training facilities quickly, it would soon lose credibility with its customers. Building Cyberplay centers would not be feasible due to capital costs and time constraints, unless a franchising structure was utilized. Shamrock pursued the franchising route, talking with some of the most experienced consultants and franchisers in the U.S. Eventually, he decided that there was a better way to access training facilities than through franchising.

To quickly access the facilities needed to meet the demands of their clients, Cyberplay entered into a strategic alliance with Computer City (CC), the second-largest retailer of computer equipment, to train at their facilities. CC was thrilled with the alliance as it gave them a strong presence in the training market where they had lagged behind CompUSA. The agreement allowed for a 50-50 split of revenues, with Cyberplay being responsible for the curriculum, teaching, and marketing, and CC being responsible for the location, hardware, and software. Hours before this alliance was to close on July 1, 1998, CompUSA purchased CC, and the Cyberplay–CC

deal was placed on hold. Eventually, CompUSA agreed to essentially the same deal, but this delayed the start-up of Cyberplay's training contracts by about two months. Given the cash flow needs, this was precious time wasted. Furthermore, Shamrock had some reluctance about being associated with one of Cyberplay's closest competitors, fearing that CompUSA would dump them as a partner once they were able to imitate the bases for Cyberplay's competitive advantages.

By the end of 1998, the Prudential contract was up and running at the projected levels, and the ADP contract was producing about two-thirds of projected amounts. The employee at ADP charged with overseeing the training had not received an expected promotion, and had been traveling a bit, so Cyberplay found themselves in the all-too-frequent position of waiting for someone else to do something. Shamrock remarked, "We are learning the realities of dealing with office politics. We have asked ADP to give us another person to work through, and they said they would do something about it in January of 1999."

The CTE contract, while approved at the Cyberplay end, awaited final approval and adoption from various federal, state, and municipal law enforcement agencies at the CTE end. Because this training would be required of law enforcement officers, this contract was potentially huge.

The EVC contract had yet to produce material income, as EVC was also a new company. Nevertheless, Cyberplay felt that through this association, it could take its training online using EVC's proprietary interactive technology that allowed all class participants to interact with all others from multiple locations. Shamrock wondered whether the clients would prefer shifting all of Cyberplay's training to online delivery. He sensed it would result in another major strategic shift because of the implications it would have for staffing, organizational structure, and the cost to deliver.

Finally, Shamrock had to determine what to do with the original Cyberplay retail store. Cyberplay had two retail facilities that were significant drags on earnings and cash flow. These facilities had won the firm international recognition and had been the subject of articles in *Business Week* and other leading periodicals. Cyberplay's market had evolved, however, from a retail business concept to a corporate-client business, and it was not clear how these facilities would fit into the new strategy. In June 1998, the Atlanta facility was closed, and only the Winter Park facility remained. The facilities were very significant in securing the contract with CTE. Should the Winter Park facility be closed also? Appendix B provides the profit and loss statement for the Winter Park facility.

THE PERSONNEL

The executives and entire headquarters staff seemed very personable, and the work pace seemed laid-back. Most everyone lived in the rural area just north of Orlando, and all seemed sensitive to Cyberplay's role and reputation in the community. Several of the executives attended the same conservative church, and there was a sense that the "old values" of honesty, fair play, commitment, hard work, and congeniality formed the shared values of the firm.

Steve Shamrock, 38, chairman and CEO, had been involved as a managing partner in a real estate development and construction company for about 12 years prior to starting Cyberplay. He was regarded as an experienced, honest businessman in his community and had outstanding "people skills." These attributes figured prominently in his ability to raise so much money from the community without having to go the venture-capital route.

Shamrock felt the pressure of ensuring that the company succeeded since virtually everyone he knew in his community—not to mention his family members—were investors. His people skills were largely responsible for initiating the discussions that resulted in the major training contracts. By his own admission, he "barely knew how to turn a computer on," but he felt that gave him the perspective of many of his clients who would require training. He was totally dedicated to seeing the business succeed, and had over $1 million of his own money in the venture. Remarked Shamrock, "I cannot describe all of the hurdles we have had to overcome, but we have singular focus on making this venture be successful. 'Can't' is not in our vocabulary." Shamrock's annual salary was $200,000.

Bruce Lagravinese, 31, was the chief information and technology officer. He had managed national accounts with Data General Corporation, and was largely responsible for the technology that won Cyberplay the Smithsonian Medal. He had expertise in information systems design, management, and training. He was a good complement to Shamrock in that he was completely comfortable in the world of cyber-speak on both the hardware and software fronts. His current responsibilities focused around three areas. First, he maintained the proprietary information system that provided reports to Cyberplay's clients on the employee utilization and client billings. Second, he was the systems designer for new delivery networks that might be installed in a client's on-site training facility. Third, he evaluated the technological and cost features of potential contracts. Lagravinese's salary was $82,000.

Ron Young, 38, executive vice president, had built a career designing custom aircraft interiors for Page Avjet Corporation. His expertise had contributed to the award-winning design of the Cyberplay centers, and his familiarity with modular design allowed them to be installed in seven days. He also had experience in the real estate industry and was part of Cyberplay's founding management team. Ron also had excellent people skills. He was in charge of the office staff and was a longtime friend of Shamrock's. Young's salary was $62,000.

A. R. Robinson, 43, vice president of operations, had extensive experience in store rollout, having worked for 12 years with Target during that company's rapid expansion. He had been in charge of bringing new stores on line. He also had a successful stint with Blockbuster Video, where he had turned around one of the least profitable regions. He was in charge of managing the facilities rollout for Cyberplay, for ensuring the recruitment of the trainers, and for ultimate customer satisfaction. Robinson, like Shamrock, had magical people skills, and conveyed a genuine warmth, enthusiasm, and confidence. Robinson's annual salary was $70,000.

Rick Barron, 46, the vice president of finance, was responsible for assessing the financial effect of potential operating and financial decisions, for ensuring the control function, and for producing the necessary accounting statements. Barron had worked for 12 years as the finance VP of Filene's Basement, a publicly held retail company. Barron had a pleasant personality, especially for a controller, but was not quite as outgoing as Robinson or Shamrock. Barron's annual salary was $60,000.

Bob Kolter, 27, vice president of marketing, had worked for a label company selling to national accounts. His present responsibilities focused on getting smaller local companies to use Cyberplay training. These accounts offered a shorter sales cycle compared to the national accounts, and since cash flow was still a problem, such accounts were deemed a priority. Kolter's annual salary was $45,000.

Appendix C shows the organizational chart.

MARKETING

The Prudential account came to Cyberplay through Shamrock's fortuitous meeting with a Prudential board member on a plane. The ADP account was the result of a cold call while visiting the Prudential office in New Jersey. Again, Shamrock was the force behind this call, assisted by Bob Kolter. EVC was a referral to Cyberplay when a contact at ADP recommended that Cyberplay handle EVC's computer training. The CTE contract was also a result of a referral when a former employee assisted in getting the two sides together to discuss CTE's need for training sites.

Managing national accounts required that Cyberplay have someone to promote and coordinate the training within the companies. Client employees needed to be prodded to take the training, otherwise it tended to be something that would be done "tomorrow." Cyberplay billed its clients on a per-student per-course-taken basis; hence, it needed to be working with its clients to ensure that employees received the training.

Lagravinese had developed a database program that could be accessed by client companies and that allowed managers to identify each eligible employee, what the company's training standards were for that person, whether the employee had taken the training, and how he had done on the test. Shamrock remarked, "This is like having someone from our office pressing the managers to make sure their employees go to the training. In light of our recent ADP experience though, there may be more we can do." ADP was running significantly behind expectations, and getting the training back on track seemed out of Cyberplay's control.

FINANCIAL PERFORMANCE

Cyberplay had losses totaling about $6 million over its first three years of operations. As of the beginning of 1999, it had a negative net worth of about $2.5 million. In the past year alone, it had lost $3.6 million. It was in default on over $3 million of bank debt and had arranged a forbearance agreement whereby the bank would be paid off with the proceeds from the new funding at $0.50 on the dollar. It was also in default on about $2.5 million of corporate debt that would be paid in full at the refinancing.

Appendix D shows the financial statements for the past year.

Appendix A (previously referenced) shows the projections for the next three years. Clearly, if Cyberplay grew as rapidly as anticipated, it would be profitable after 1999, and would need about $1.5 million in external financing for 1999—an amount that would be provided by the financing options already being considered. However, the enormous revenue growth projections, while viewed as realistic and based on successful implementation of current contracts, carried an amount of uncertainty with them.

THE DECISION

Shamrock realized that at present, Cyberplay had been spending about $250,000 a month to support about $15,000 of monthly revenue. Clearly, this situation could not last long. No amount of expense reduction could make the company profitable from its retail operations. But even as the training revenues materialized, they would need to materialize according to schedule or else large deficits would persist. Even though the financial deal that was expected to close soon would leave them with about $1.5 million in working capital—enough to cover a years' worth of negative operating cash flow and get them to a positive cash flow position—several questions troubled Shamrock:

(1) Should he reduce corporate expenses to bare-bones levels in case contracts were slow to materialize? Would such a move jeopardize the success of these contracts?

(2) If he were to reduce expenses, what should be cut?

(3) Was Cyberplay doing everything it could to ensure the growth of the current revenue streams? What should be the relative emphasis between generating additional revenues from existing accounts and generating new accounts?

(4) Were new positions necessary? Was the present organizational structure adequate?

(5) If Cyberplay could shift its clients to online training on the Internet, how would this impact staffing requirements, expenses, and organizational structure? Would such a shift be acceptable to Cyberplay's clients? Should Cyberplay pursue such a shift?

The past four years had taken a toll on Shamrock's health, and although he found challenges invigorating, he admitted that he was tired. He was eager to get the revenues and profits up to a level that would reward the shareholders for their patience. He also recognized that failure to show strong revenue and profit progress could cause the firm to lose momentum in the capital markets for future needs. The year 1999 needed to be a good year on the income statement, not just on the balance sheet.

(000's)	1999	2000	2001
Total Fiscal Sales	$ 1,773	$26,536	$54,366
Operating Margin	328	9,551	20,381
Corporate Expense	1,441	4,492	6,589
Profit Before Tax and Interest	(1,113)	5,059	13,792

Source: Company records.

Specific Revenue Assumptions:

CTE

General Assumptions: 50% officer participation rate, 3 classes annually per officer, $60.00 per officer class.

Population Base: Orlando 10,000, Remainder of Florida 32,000, Texas 56,000, Michigan 31,000, and California 139,000.

FI 1999:
Orlando: 1 additional classroom: Begin 2/99 in Winter Park, 1 additional location by 3/99.
Florida (remaining): 5 classrooms: Begin 5/99 and complete by 9/99.
Texas: 9 classrooms: Begin 4/99 and complete by 11/99.
Michigan: 5 classrooms: Begin 4/99 and complete by 8/99.
California: 23 classrooms: Begin 6/99 and complete by 5/00.

EVC

General Assumptions: 15% employee participation rate, 2 classes annually per participating employee, $60.00 per class.

Total Employee Population Base: 1,350,000
Each Phase is assumed to be in groups of 150,000 employees

ADP National Accounts

General Assumptions: 60% participation rate, 2.0 classes annually per participating employee, $55.00 per student class.

Populations: Each location 750.
Ramped up to targeted levels over 12 months.
FI 1999:
Boston (2/99), Atlanta (2/99), Chicago (2/99), Roseland (3/99).

ADP Major Accounts

General assumptions: 25% participation rate, 2.0 classes annually per participating employee, $55.00 per student class.

Population: 7,000
Begin 3/99
Ramped up to targeted levels over 12 months.

ADP Emerging Business

General assumptions: 25% participation rate, 2.0 classes annually per participating employee, $55.00 per student class.

Population: 5,000

FI 1999:
Begin 3/99
Ramped up to targeted levels over 12 months.

Prudential

General Assumptions: 25% participation rate, 2 classes annually per participating employee, $70.00 per student class.

Populations: Atlanta (2,000), Jacksonville (6,000)

FI 1999:
Atlanta (11/98), Jacksonville (10/98).
Ramped up to targeted levels over 12 months.

EVC

1st Phase of 150,000 begins 2/99
2nd Phase begins 3/99
3rd Phase begins 6/99
4th Phase begins 7/99
5th Phase begins 8/99
6th Phase begins 9/99
7th Phase begins 12/99
8th Phase begins 7/2000
9th Phase begins 8/2000

ADP Client Access

General Assumptions: 1.5% company participation rate, 15% employee participation rate within participating companies, 400 employees per participating company, 2 classes annually per participating employee, $60.00 per student class.

Total Company Population Base: 100,000
Ramped up to targets levels over 12 months.

FI 1999:
Phases are assumed in groups of 10,000 companies
1st Phase begins 6/99
2nd Phase begins 10/99
3rd Phase begins 6/2000
4th Phase begins 2/2001
Remaining 60,000 companies to be prospected after this 3 year LRP.

ADP Proprietary

120,000 Potential companies, 7.5% company participation rate, 2 employees per company, 3 classes per participating employee, $45.00 per student class.

Begin 2/99

Ramped up to targeting levels over 12 months.

Income Statement, 1998–9
Winter Park Retail Facility

(in $)

Net Revenue	$ 347,706
Cost of Goods Sold	206,365
Gross Profit	141,341
General and Admin. Expenses	
Payroll	96,716
Rent	72,626
Advert. and Mkt.	23,840
Communications	24,033
Deprec. and Amort.	124,957
Other	58,100
Total Expenses	400,272
Operating Profit (loss)	$(259,930)

Source: Company records.

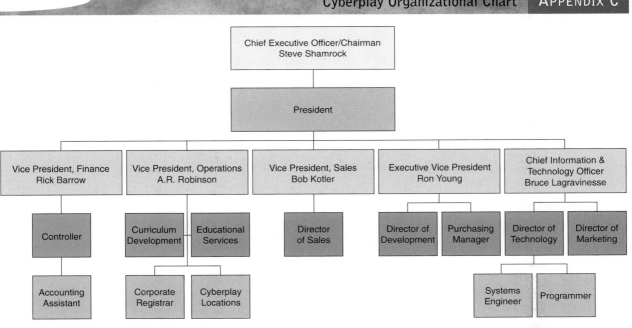

Year End June 30, 1998

Net Sales	$ 579,027.75
Cost of Goods Sold	252,524.00
Gross Profit	326,503.75
Expenses	
Payroll	1,541,709.38
Rent	255,168.94
Advertising and Marketing	78,390.85
Payroll Taxes	189,814.13
Utilities	31,024.08
Depreciation and Amortization	264,150.98
Property Tax	29,237.28
Atlanta Closing Costs	131,874.95
Other GSA Expenses	671,222.00
Total Expenses	3,163,355.40
Operating Profit	(2,836,851.65)
Other Income & Expenses	
Project Income	99,407.60
Interest Expense	465,415.56
Loss on Disposal of Assets	395,528.65
Misc. Incl. Expenses	11,647.00
Total Other Income & Expenses	749,888.50
Profit Before Taxes	(3,586,740.15)
Net Loss	($3,586,740.15)

Balance Sheet Highlights
(Unaudited; approximate)

Cash	1,000
Total Current Assets	2,500
Total Current Liabilities	350,000
Long-term Debt	5,000,000

Source: Company records.

The Fall of Daewoo Motors

case nine

D. Sirisha
Vivek Gupta
ICFAI Center for Management Research

"In a drive to go global, it (Daewoo Motors) refused to quit when it was behind."

—BusinessWeek, *August 23, 1999.*

"Kim Woo Choong has been stealing money from the company and we should not be punished for the mess he created."

—Choi Jong Hak, *Daewoo Motor Labor Union representative, in 2001.*

A COMPANY IN TROUBLE

In the late 1990s, leading South Korean car manufacturer, Daewoo Motors (Daewoo), was in deep financial trouble. For the financial year ending 1999-2000, Daewoo generated revenues of $197.8 million and a net loss after tax of $10.43 billion (13.7 trillion won). The company's revenues had dropped by 94% since 1999. The loss reported was also three times higher than that reported in 1999, and was ranked as South Korea's largest ever corporate loss. In addition, the company's domestic market share fell from 33% in 1998 to just 23% in 2000.

According to analysts, Daewoo's borrowings for its expansion programs were responsible for its losses. The company's domestic and foreign debt amounted to more than $16.06 billion in December 1999. Moreover, its expansion into risky and uncertain markets like Vietnam and its decision to sell products at very low prices to gain market share had negatively affected its financial condition. Labor unrest was also one of the

reasons cited by market observers for Daewoo's poor financial performance. The workers at many of its plants went on strike protesting against low wages, layoffs, and lack of job security. The Southeast Asian financial crisis[1] of 1997–98 further deepened the problems. The company's creditors started demanding repayments.

However, some analysts felt that the primary reason for Daewoo's problems was mismanagement and the corrupt corporate governance practices adopted by Kim Woo Choong (Kim), the founder of the Daewoo Group. An analyst commented, "The ill management and inability of Daewoo companies resulted in bankruptcy. The run-away irresponsible previous owner, Kim is now hiding somewhere in the world."[2] Analysts commented that because of his financial mismanagement, not only Daewoo but also the entire Daewoo Group was deep in debt.

In November 2000, the Korean government officially announced Daewoo's bankruptcy and its assets were put on sale. Amid controversies and almost a year of negotiations with the Korean government, GM signed a preliminary agreement in September 2001 to buy Daewoo's assets for $1.2 billion. However, this agreement ran into problems when GM reported a discrepancy in Daewoo's overseas accounts. With so many skeletons in Daewoo's closet, market observers wondered when the company would find a buyer and when its problems would be solved.

BACKGROUND NOTE

There were five major business conglomerates or Chaebols[3] in South Korea—LG, Samsung, Sunkyong, Hyundai and the Daewoo Group. In 1967, Kim established the Daewoo Group as a textiles business. The then Korean President Park Chung Hee[4] (Park) helped Kim by handing over the management of bankrupt companies, which were slated for restructuring by the

This case was written by D. Sirisha under direction of Vivek Gupta, ICFAI Center for Management Research (ICMR). It is intended to be used as a basis for class discussion rather than to illustrate either effective or ineffective handling of a management situation.

The case was compiled from published sources.

Korean government. Park also helped Kim with essential resources and official assistance. Kim also developed close contacts with politicians and managed to get huge amounts of funds from several Korean banks.

Funded by government-approved borrowings, the Daewoo Group witnessed significant growth and diversified into several businesses during the 1970s and 1980s. In the early 1990s, the Group expanded overseas and soon became the 18th largest corporation in the world. The Group had investments in more than 400 projects in about 85 countries. The Daewoo Group consisted of 24 companies, the major ones including Daewoo Motors, Daewoo Shipbuilding, Daewoo Telecom, Daewoo Engineering and Construction, Daewoo Electronics, Daewoo International, Daewoo Heavy Industries, Daewoo Securities etc. Of the 24 companies, nine were listed while the remaining were privately owned.

The Group's management believed that expansion equaled success. However, little attention was paid to the profitability of the new businesses. In the mid-1990s, the Daewoo Group was charged for corrupt corporate governance practices. Reportedly Kim, along with 34 executives and accountants of the Group, had generated $20 billion officially and $38 billion unofficially in the form of illegal foreign exchange loans. They also pooled funds from the different subsidiaries of the Group through false documents.

The Daewoo Group had also reportedly manipulated its accounts to show fictitious profits and decrease liabilities (see Exhibit 1) to present a rosy picture of its overall financial performance. The Group seemed to have hidden many of its failed ventures and also swapped assets among the Group's companies. For instance, during 1997–98, in spite of a recession in the Korean economy, the combined profit of Daewoo Heavy Industries, Daewoo Corporation, and Daewoo Electronics was reported as $272 million. The income statements of these companies showed $2.7 billion in gains resulting from sales of assets to other companies in the Group. One of the Group's companies sold an asset to another much above the stated book value and posted the capital gain as profit. Government lawyers reported that the assets were actually worth far less than the quoted price. Lee Dong Gull, former economic adviser to the Korean President Kim Dae Jung, said, "By swapping their shares and other assets at inflated prices, they generated

| EXHIBIT 1 | Assets and Liabilities of Daewoo Group's Twelve Affiliates | | | | | | |

(Unit: 1 billion won)

Company	As of End of June 1999			Due Diligence Audits by Korean Government, As of End of August 1999			(B-A)
	Assets	Liabilities	Capital(A)	Assets	Liabilities	Capital(B)	
Daewoo Corporation	29,203.0	26,590.9	2,612.1	17,458.6	31,994.4	−14,535.8	−17,147.9
Daewoo Telecom Ltd.	3,294.1	2,985.2	308.9	2,260.3	3,159.3	−899.0	−1,207.9
The Diners Club of Korea	1,399.5	1,267.6	131.9	886.0	1,271.6	−385.6	−517.5
Daewoo Electronics Company	8,230.1	7,665.3	564.8	5,046.7	7,729.0	−2,682.3	−3,247.1
Daewoo Electronics Components	395.1	276.0	119.1	365.0	292.6	72.4	−46.7
Daewoo Heavy Industries Ltd.	13,794.1	10,661.4	3,132.7	12,028.3	11,009.3	1,019.0	−2,113.7
Daewoo Motor Company	20,646.2	15,560.2	5,086.0	12,935.9	18,638.3	−5,702.4	−10,788.4
Daewoo Motor Sales Company	2,130.2	1,367.3	762.9	1,397.3	1,215.6	181.7	−581.2
Ssangyong Motor Company	3,347.6	2,976.9	370.7	2,762.2	3,097.8	−335.6	−706.3
Keangnam Enterprises Ltd.	1,087.1	851.7	235.4	626.4	696.8	−70.4	−305.8
Orion Electric Company	1,801.7	1,363.1	438.6	1,897.4	1,719.5	177.9	−260.7
Daewoo Capital Company	6,564.4	6,202.0	362.4	3,566.8	5,993.8	−2,427.0	−2,789.4
Total	91,893.1	77,767.6	14,125.5	61,230.9	86,818.0	−25,587.1	−39,712.6

The figures for Daewoo Heavy Industries Ltd. are as of end of July 1999.

Source: www.cfo.com.

all the gains without exchanging even a single cent. Once these fictitious profits were deleted, the three companies collectively lost $2.4 billion."

The economic scenario changed dramatically in the late 1990s. With the Southeast Asian financial crisis in 1997-98, bankers became more concerned about their funds and started demanding repayment. By that time, the Daewoo Group had taken huge loans. According to Korean Government estimates, by the end of December 1999, the Daewoo Group owed about $80 billion to various bankers as domestic and foreign debt, and the interest payments amounted to more than $6 billion per annum. Daewoo's foreign currency debt totaled $9.9 billion: $6.8 billion from foreign creditors and $3.1 billion from Korean creditors in foreign currency. The foreign currency debt borrowed from foreign creditors was concentrated on four leading companies of the Group (refer to Table 1 and Table 2).

THE DAEWOO MOTORS STORY

The Daewoo Group entered the automobile industry in 1978 by acquiring a 50% stake in Saehan Motor Company (Saehan). Founded in 1972, Saehan was a 50-50 joint venture between Shinjin Motors,[5] and GM.[6] In 1976, Shinjin Motors faced financial problems and sold its 50% stake in Saehan to the Korea Development Bank (KDB). In 1978, the Daewoo Group acquired the equity stake and management rights from KDB.

In 1982, Saehan owned a car assembly plant in Bupyong, a truck assembly plant in Pusan and a foundry at Inchon. In 1983, GM and the Daewoo Group agreed to rename their venture Daewoo Motor Company (Daewoo). In 1984, the partners decided to build additional assembly, stamping and engine facilities at Bupyong. The plants were dedicated to the production of a passenger car, Pontiac LeMans, based on

	Daewoo Group's Total Debt	TABLE 1
(In US $ billion)	Daewoo's Calculation of Debt (in June 1999)	Govt.'s Calculation of Debt (in December 1999)
Daewoo Corporation	23.84	30.51
Daewoo Motor	13.96	16.06
Daewoo Electronics	6.87	7.65
Daewoo Telecom	2.67	2.93
Other Companies	22.36	22.65
Total Debt of Daewoo Group	69.70	79.80

Source: BusinessWeek, September 2, 2000.

	Daewoo Group's Foreign Debt—1999	TABLE 2
Company	Amount of Foreign Currency Debt (in $ billion)	Percentage of Total
Daewoo Corporation	2.7	53%
Daewoo Motors	1.5	30%
Daewoo Electronics	0.6	12%
Daewoo Heavy Industries Ltd.	0.2	4%
Total	5.0	
Convertible Bonds	1.8	
Total	6.8	

Source: www.cfo.com.

the Opel Kadett platform. Production started in 1987 and about 50% of the cars were exported to the US and other international markets.

Pontiac LeMans was not successful in many of the international markets in which it was launched. This strained the relationship between GM and the Daewoo Group. Moreover, there were also quality problems and delayed deliveries. The partners had different opinions about capacity expansion, debt leverage, profitability objectives, marketing issues etc. Daewoo wanted to expand globally, but GM could not support the plan since it was facing financial problems in the US during the early 1990s. In 1992, GM withdrew the partnership and the Daewoo Group acquired the remaining 50% stake in the venture for $170 million. Soon after, Daewoo became the leading automaker in South Korea.

In January 1993, Daewoo established Daewoo Motor Sales and separated the sales and manufacturing operations. In the same year, the company established assembly plants in East Europe and Asia. At these plants, Daewoo manufactured successful models like Lanos, Nubira and Leganza. In late 1993, Daewoo became the first Asian carmaker to earn ISO 9001.

As other companies of the Daewoo Group were not performing well, Kim concentrated on the automobile division and invested heavily in Daewoo. The company expanded its capacity rapidly. With low price and interest free installment offers, Daewoo soon became the leader in the South Korean passenger car market, displacing Hyundai and Kia Motors. Kim wanted to make Daewoo one of the world's top ten automakers, and to do so, he took more foreign debt for the company's expansion programs.

In 1994, Daewoo acquired an automobile engineering company IAD in the UK, and established the Worthing Technical Center. It also set up the Munich Technical Center in Germany to develop power trains. Daewoo seemed to have broken the rules of the industry when it established its own direct selling operations instead of a dealer network. The company also appointed Halfords[7] to provide after-sales services in the UK.

Because of its price competitiveness and attractive servicing and warranty offers, Daewoo's cars attracted good demand in the international markets. By 1996–97, the company's totally indigenous cars, Lanos, Nubira and Leganza, had captured significant market share in the UK.

In 1998, Daewoo acquired SsangYong Motor and added new vehicles to its range, including the small car Matiz. In 1998, Daewoo Motors America was established to market Daewoo products. The company also expanded quickly to Japan and other countries.

However, the rapid expansion and the Southeast Asian financial crisis of 1997–98 left the company financially vulnerable. By the late 1990s, Daewoo had approximately $14.5 billion domestic and $1.5 billion foreign currency debt. As Daewoo's debts were huge, its creditors became concerned and started demanding repayment.

PROBLEMS AT DAEWOO MOTORS

Daewoo's problems started when Kim took huge debts to expand the automobile business. About $1.3 billion was spent on Daewoo's expansion in developing countries. It acquired an additional $1.1 billion debt to buy SsangYong Motor. It was also reported that Kim had expanded Daewoo's global manufacturing capacities recklessly. He had established factories in Ukraine, Romania, Vietnam, and Uzbekistan with low investments and by making many false promises to the governments concerned. For example, in Poland, Daewoo acquired the government owned auto manufacturer by promising to invest $1.1 billion and to provide job opportunities for 20,000 workers. The company failed to fulfill its promises.

The company was unable to fulfill its promises because it overestimated demand in these countries. In 1994, one year after Daewoo started assembling cars in Vietnam, the country's economy witnessed a recession, which led to a 30% reduction in the demand for cars. The demand fell to just 5000 vehicles per annum. Daewoo recorded sales of only 423 units. Despite poor demand, Daewoo launched the Matiz in Vietnam, expecting a 50% increase in total demand by 1997–98. However, the actual demand did not match their expectations. To make the matters worse, the entry of competitors in the late 1990s resulted in a decline in demand for Daewoo's cars.

By late 1998, Daewoo faced problems in domestic as well as global markets. In 1998, total car sales decreased by 56% (to 234,000 units) in South Korea while Daewoo doubled its capacity, thus leaving substantial production capacity underutilized. In the same year, Daewoo America aimed to sell 100,000 cars in the US. Due to poor demand for its cars, the company offered steep rebates to increase volumes, but this move resulted in huge losses. In India, Daewoo lost more than $30 million per annum due to the discounts offered. In Western Europe, during 1998–99, Daewoo's revenues increased in UK, Germany and Italy only when it offered large discounts and interest free financing options. However, analysts expected that the trend would not continue for long.

To save Daewoo from collapsing, Kim came up with a restructuring plan in April 1999. He planned to sell about $7.5 billion worth of assets of other companies of the Group and concentrate on the automobiles and finance business. Though the creditors appreciated the plan, it seemed difficult to execute. Lee Name, Director, Samsung Securities, explained, "Daewoo's problem is that nobody really wants to buy whatever they are selling—and certainly nowhere near their asking price."

Kim planned to sell Daewoo Group's shipyards to a Japanese company for $4 billion. But Japan was planning to reduce its own shipyards by 50% due to over capacity. Kim also planned to sell the group's two Hilton hotels in Seoul and Kyongju. He expected $250 million for the hotel in Seoul. However, it was reported that offers did not exceed $180 million. Some analysts felt that the Group could not command the price it wanted because it lacked a strong brand name and reputation. Hunsaker, an analyst with ING Barings commented, "Daewoo never had a brand name; they were never a leader in anything; they never invested much money in research and development. Hyundai may be as deep in debt, but it has a reputation, a brand name, and has invested in technology. You can't say that about Daewoo."

Kim also planned to exchange the Group's electronics business for the Samsung Group's car division. However, Samsung was not interested in buying the debt-ridden Daewoo Electronics. A banker in Seoul said, "The only reason Samsung might want to buy Daewoo Electronics is to shut it down." As part of the plan, in mid-1999, Daewoo laid off about 3000 workers and also slashed the wages of remaining workers by 30%.

Since Kim was not able to execute his restructuring plan successfully, in July 1999, the South Korean government declared Daewoo insolvent and put the company on sale. The government also set up a committee for restructuring Daewoo. In August 1999, the creditors of the Daewoo Group agreed to a restructuring program for the company. Thereafter, the Korean government released the Capital Structure Improvement (Special) Agreement (CSIA) for the Daewoo Group (see Exhibit 2). As the foreign creditors were not participants in the CSIA, separate negotiations were planned with them.

| | Daewoo Group—CSIA Restructuring Plan | | EXHIBIT 2 |

	Method	Time Schedule (in 1999)	Retained Business
Daewoo Corp.*	Separation of construction unit from Daewoo Group (DG) following accounting separation	4th quarter	Daewoo Corp. • trading division
Daewoo Heavy Industry*	Sell-off of its ship-building unit following separation from DG	4th quarter contract	Daewoo Heavy Industry • machinery unit
Daewoo Motors* / Ssangyong Motors	• Acquisition of Ssangyong Motors • Induction of foreign investment into automobiles unit • Sell-off of its bus/truck unit	4th quarter contract	Daewoo Motors
Daewoo Motor Sales*			Daewoo Motor Sales
Daewoo Electronics	Overseas sale following separation from DG	3rd quarter contract & 4th quarter receipt of funds	
Daewoo Telecom*	TDX unit sold. PC unit to be sold-off	TDX: 3rd quarter receipt of funds. PC: 4th quarter contract	Daewoo Telecom • auto parts unit
Keangnam Ent.*	Sell-off following separation from DG	4th quarter contract	
Daewoo Securities*	Sell-off to 3rd party following takeover by creditors	3rd quarter contract	
Daewoo Capital*			Daewoo Capital
Daewoo Leisure*	Sell-off	4th quarter contract	

*Nine affiliates which were to remain under the previous CSIA.
Note: 14 other affiliates not mentioned in the table will either be sold-off or merged.

Source: www.mofe.go.kr.

Meanwhile, Daewoo employees opposed the sale of the company to a foreign automaker. There were strikes at all of Daewoo's plants in Korea. One of South Korea's largest trade union groups, Korean Confederation of Trade Unions, also protested the sell-off. There were also protests from a group of activists comprising some high-profile members of the country. The group launched a campaign offering to buy Daewoo and make it a 'people's company.' The South Korean Finance Minister commented, "The campaigners are misguided. I think it's not the right direction. The most critical thing, if they want to revive Daewoo Motors, they should get labor and management and push them towards an agreement. That is the right direction."

In February 2000, GM, Ford and DaimlerChrysler expressed interest in acquiring Daewoo. By June 2000, Ford entered into negotiations with the committee. However, after a few months of negotiations, Ford reported that its due diligence had revealed some discrepancies in Daewoo's valuation of its assets. In September 2000, Ford announced the withdrawal of its offer, citing the discrepancies in Daewoo's accounts as the primary reason. From August 2000, Daewoo stopped paying its 19,000 employees since further loans were not sanctioned to the company.

In October 2000, GM and its partners, including Isuzu Motors, Fuji Heavy Industries and Suzuki Motors, announced their interest in acquiring a part of Daewoo's assets. GM also insisted on the completion of the restructuring plan, which involved laying off hundreds of workers at various Daewoo plants. In November 2000, Daewoo was officially declared bankrupt and was put under court-receivership.[8]

In February 2001, the Supreme Public Prosecution Office (SPPO)[9] in Korea announced the arrest of Kim and seven of his close associates on four criminal charges (refer to Exhibit 3). They were charged with organizing Asia's biggest single 'financial fraud-false accounting' between 1997–98, inflating the group's equity by $32 billion. Kim fled the country to avoid prosecution. The seven associates were tried in court and eventually jailed.

Amidst revolts and controversies, an agreement was reached between the Korean government and GM in September 2001. GM signed a memorandum of understanding with Daewoo's creditors to acquire two plants in Korea and one each in Egypt and Vietnam, along with all their outstanding debts for $1.2 billion. The agreement also included the acquisition of 22 sales units of the company across the world.

In February 2002, GM made a renewed bid for some of Daewoo's assets to its main creditor KDB. In this new bid, GM expressed interest in only 9 sales units of Daewoo as against the earlier 22. It also refused to pay the $260 million debt of these units as it had dis-

---

EXHIBIT 3   Daewoo Group—the Prosecutors' Allegations

London Slush Fund

Prosecutors charged Kim with setting up a London-based shell company called British Finance Center (BFC) for raising slush funds for lobbying at home and abroad. Daewoo Group had forged documents to show import-export transactions worth $2.6 billion that never occurred. The group also transferred an additional $1.5 billion from car-export revenues. Prosecutors did not say how the money was spent, but industry executives and analysts think that at least part of it was earmarked for Kim's personal use and for bribing government officials around the world and executives at client companies and banks.

Accounting Dodge

To book profitable results at a failed factory in Ukraine, Daewoo Motor got fully built Korean cars, tore them down, reassembled them at the Ukraine plant, and then booked the sales as if produced by the plant. Value of all Daewoo Motor manipulations: $3.6 billion.

Inflating Asset Values

Daewoo Heavy Industry artificially generated profits in 1998 by selling assets to Daewoo Motor at inflated prices, when it actually posted a loss of $670 million. Asset values inflated by $4 billion.

Deceitful Borrowing

Daewoo Electronics took loans amounting to nearly $1 billion from financial institutions in 1997 after concealing that losses had wiped out shareholders' equity. Value of inflated equity: $2.9 billion.

Source: BusinessWeek, February 19, 2001.

covered new debts in some of Daewoo's overseas operations, including Daewoo's plant in Egypt. GM announced that it would not honor the previous agreement if its new conditions were not accepted.

In April 2002, GM and Daewoo's creditors arrived at an agreement. According to this agreement, GM would create a new company (most likely to be named GM-Daewoo Motors), which would be owned jointly by Daewoo's creditors and GM. GM would own a 67%[10] stake in the new company, with an investment of $400 million. Creditors were to pay $137 million for the remaining 33% stake. The new venture also assumed $537 million in debt.

THE FUTURE

According to analysts, GM's acquisition of Daewoo seemed to be the ideal solution for the latter's problems. An analyst commented, "GM badly needs Daewoo to establish a beachhead in the Asian market. And without GM, Daewoo will simply collapse." They also opined that GM was the ideal buyer as it had owned a 50% stake in Daewoo till 1992. Moreover, most of Daewoo's vehicle designs were based on GM's. Analysts felt that in the long run, GM could use Daewoo to gain a foothold in Asia. Prior to the acquisition, GM depended solely on its European subsidiary Adam Opel to manufacture small cars for developing countries. As GM's small car was not very successful, it planned to use Daewoo's expertise in developing such cars to tap Asian markets. The company felt that China, India and Thailand, were the key markets for the next 10 years. Alan Perriton (Perriton), who was in charge of GM's business development in Asia, commented that Daewoo's acquisition, "gives us high-quality, low-cost products for the rest of Asia."

However, some analysts felt that making Daewoo's acquisition successful would be a big challenge for GM. They said that restoring Daewoo's brand image would require a lot of time and money. Commenting on the damage done, Perriton explained, "Sales have been hit badly because Koreans weren't sure Daewoo would survive. We have to let customers know that the company is back in business and stands behind its products." By 2001, Daewoo's domestic market share had fallen to less than 15%.

Moreover, GM was itself facing problems in the US. Though its sales were more than those of Daimler-Chrysler and Ford, net earnings were decreasing. Some analysts felt that GM was adding to its problems by acquiring a company like Daewoo. Scott Sprinzen, a managing director at Standard & Poor, New York, said, "GM would seem to have its hands full with other challenges: struggling overseas alliances, including ones with Italy's Fiat and Japan's Isuzu Motors."

Will GM be able to integrate Daewoo's operations successfully (see Exhibit 4)? According to analysts, if the

---

Daewoo Motors' Production Facilities Worldwide EXHIBIT 4

Pupyong Plant
Pupyong-gu
Inchon, Korea

Kunsan Plant
Kunsan, Chonbuk, Korea

Changwon Plant
Kyungnam, Korea

Pyongtaek Plant
Kyonggi, Korea

Pusan Plant
Pusan, Korea

China
Guilin-Daewoo Bus Co., Ltd.
Guilin, Guangxi, China

Czech Republic
Daewoo Avia AS
Prague, Czech Republic

Egypt
Daewoo Motor Egypt S.A.E.
Cairo, Egypt

India
Daewoo Motor India Limited
Suraipur-203 207
Distt Ghaziabad (UP)

Iran
Kerman Motor Corporation
Tehran, Iran

Philippines
Filipinas Daewoo Industries Corp.
Cavite, Philippines

Poland
Daewoo-FSO Motor Corp.
Warsaw, Poland and Daewoo Motor Poland Co., Ltd.
Lublin, Poland

Romania
Daewoo Automobile Romania S.A.
Craiova, Romania

Ukraine
CJSC, AvtoVAZ-Daewoo
Zaporozhye, Ukraine

Uzbekistan
UZ-Daewoo Auto Co.
Asaka City, Andijan Region Uzbekistan

Vietnam
Hanoi, Vietnam

Source: www.daewoomotors.com.

integration is successful, GM would be able to compete with Ford—world's No. 2 automaker—more effectively. An analyst commented, "If its game plan works out, the new Daewoo venture, for which it projects annual sales of $5 billion within a couple of years, could help GM put more distance between it and the No. 2 auto maker, Ford, which has been narrowing the gap."[11]

QUESTIONS FOR DISCUSSION

1. Comment on Daewoo Motors' international expansion strategy in several developed and developing markets. Briefly explain how the company built its presence in these markets. Do you agree with the approach adopted by the company?

2. To what extent was the promoter responsible for Daewoo's downfall? Comment on the culture, the ethical standards, and the corporate governance standards of the company.

3. Analysts seem to be divided over GM's decision to acquire Daewoo Motors. Briefly describe the synergies GM can achieve through the acquisition. What challenges will the acquisition pose for GM? Do you think acquiring Daewoo Motors was a good move on GM's part?

NOTES

1. The Southeast Asian financial crisis arose mainly due to a shortage of foreign exchange that had caused the value of currencies and equity shares in Thailand, Indonesia, South Korea and other Southeast Asian countries to fall drastically.
2. As quoted in workers.labor.net.au.
3. In South Korea, large family-owned conglomerates were called Chaebol. The system, which Japanese colonialists first started in the 1920s and 1930s, was greatly expanded by President Park Chung Hee in the 1960s and 1970s. In this system, the central government selected a few companies and granted them all kinds of preferential treatment.
4. Park was a student of Kim's father.
5. Established in 1965 in Korea, Shinjin Motors set the foundation for the Korean automobile industry. It started its business by re-building scrapped US military vehicles.
6. Established in 1908, GM was the world's largest automobile manufacturer, with operations spread over 60 countries. Its products (including cars and trucks) were sold in more than 200 countries; GM's popular brands included Chevrolet, Pontiac, Buick, Oldsmobile, Cadillac, Saturn, Hummer, Saab, Opel, Vauxhall and Holden.
7. Halfords is UK's leading retailer of car and motor bike parts and accessories.
8. A procedure that installed new management and froze all debts for an insolvent company. In the case of Daewoo, the creditor banks and the Korean government gained control over all of Daewoo's financial matters.
9. Korea's top law-enforcement agency.
10. GM holds 42.1% and its partners hold 24.9%.
11. As quoted in Business Week, October 8, 2001.

Diageo plc

case ten

Armand Gilinsky, Jr.
Sonoma State University

Richard Castaldi
San Francisco State University

Wine is a small percentage of our sales, the growth rates are very exciting, and Sterling [Vineyards] will give us a sound platform. But wine is capital intensive and we must be confident we can maximize capital investment and drive an appropriate return for our shareholders.

—*Paul Walsh, Chief Executive Officer,*
Diageo PLC

As a company, if you're looking to invest in spirits or wine, it's spirits every time. I hugely admire what companies like Southcorp are doing, but let me tell you: if they had a decent portfolio of spirits brands, they wouldn't be bothering.

—*Jack Keenan, President, United Distillers*
and Vintners, Diageo PLC

Wine is a very dynamic and attractive segment to Diageo. The premium end of the business is still growing at double-digit rates. There is a lot of demand out there for premium wine, and we expect demand for these wines will continue to be very strong.

—*Ray Chadwick, President, Diageo Chateau*
and Estate Wines

This case study was prepared by Professors Armand Gilinsky, Jr., Sonoma State University, and Richard Castaldi, San Francisco State University, with the assistance of researchers Dan Dhruva and James Cavanagh, MBA students at San Francisco State University, as a basis for class discussion, not to illustrate either effective or ineffective handling of an administrative situation. The authors gratefully acknowledge a Business and International Education (BIE) grant from the U.S. Department of Education and a matching grant from the College of Business at San Francisco State University in support of this research.

In April 2002, Diageo plc (Diageo) announced its intent to sell its Glen Ellen and MG Vallejo wine subsidiaries to the Wine Group for $83 million. The sale was to include the Glen Ellen and MG Vallejo brand names and all existing inventory but not the vineyards/facilities of the two wineries. Glen Ellen and MG Vallejo wines typically sold for about $5–$7 a bottle. These brands did not fit into Diageo's increasing emphasis on marketing premium wine brands that sold for $10–$15 a bottle and higher. Wine industry observers viewed the sale of Glen Ellen and MG Vallejo as a move towards brand rationalization, that is, allowing Diageo to concentrate its marketing efforts on a smaller number of more upscale brands.

Six months later, in October 2002, Ray Chadwick, President of Diageo Chateau & Estate Wines, reviewed his company's remaining wine portfolio. Diageo Chateau & Estate Wines was based in Napa, California. Chadwick was pondering which, if any further changes to the portfolio should be made:

> *If you were to ask me, "Will there be changes to the portfolio?" We understand and pay attention to the desires of our consumers. We're constantly evaluating our business. We own over 2,000 acres in the Napa Valley. We have long-term leases on over 300 acres in Napa. That makes us the largest grape grower in the Napa Valley. We are still open to acquiring new vineyards if we can do so at a price that makes sense. The economics have to be right. We are currently looking at several vineyard opportunities in the Napa Valley. I can tell you that we have no plans to sell any of our vineyards at this time. We have a very large vineyard operation in Monterey County, Paris Valley Ranch (approximately 1,500 acres). We have in addition to that probably another 700 acres or so of coastal vineyards in the south coast [of California].*

To justify his evaluation and recommendations, Chadwick needed to determine which, if any, synergies could be achieved between his division's premium wine holdings in California and Diageo's holdings of some of the most highly recognized spirits and beer brands in the world. Diageo also owned 34 percent of Moët Hennessy, the wine and spirits unit of French luxury goods maker LVMH Moët Hennessy Louis Vuitton.

Cost synergy appeared to have become the main driver of growth at Diageo. In 2001 Diageo had sold its Guinness World Records business to a media company, Gullane Entertainment, for $63 million. In a rebranding move to emphasize the Diageo name, the company scrapped its Guinness/UDV unit and folded those operations into a new premium drinks division. Diageo also decided to sell its Pillsbury unit to General Mills for $10.5 billion as part of the company's effort to focus on its spirits, wine, and beer businesses and to shed less

profitable operations. The Pillsbury divestiture gave Diageo a 33 percent stake in General Mills.

Diageo's stock price began to rise in response, reaching a 52-week high on the New York Stock Exchange of $55.40 on May 3, 2002. Yet, securities analysts over the summer and early fall 2002 had been progressively downgrading their recommendations on Diageo's stock from "strong buy" to "under-perform, medium risk." See Exhibit 1 for Diageo's stock price chart, 1997–2002, and analysts' forecasts.

Diageo subsequently announced that it has gone back to the drawing board in an attempt to unload its Burger King business (the number two burger chain, after McDonald's, with more than 11,300 locations). Diageo's July 2002 agreement to sell Burger King for $2.26 billion unraveled after a group composed of Texas Pacific Group, Bain Capital, and Goldman Sachs Capital Partners backed out of the deal in November

---

EXHIBIT 1 Diageo plc—Stock Price Movements, 1997–2002

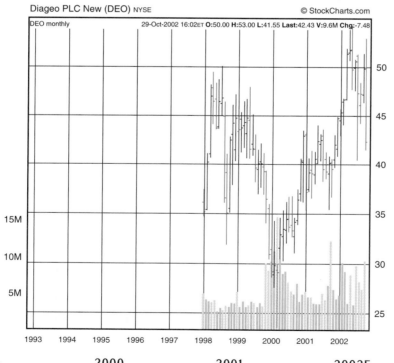

Diageo (NYSE:DEO)	2000	2001	2002E	2003E
P/E ratio	19.9x	17.3x	17.0x	14.3x
Dividend yield	2.8%	3.0%	3.2%	3.4%
ROI	19.3%	20.1%	18.4%	20.7%
Core EPS growth	8.5%	15.1%	1.6%	14.5%

Sources: www.StockCharts.com, accessed October 28, 2002; Diageo company reports, and Salomon Smith Barney estimates as of October 25, 2002.

2002. New suitors reportedly interested in Burger King included Warren Buffett's Berkshire Hathaway, owner of Dairy Queen, although Buffett publicly denied he had an interest in buying Burger King.

Almost one year earlier, Diageo had finally acquired the beverage assets of the Canada-based Joseph E. Seagram Company (Seagram's) in a hotly contested bidding war with rival Allied Domecq. Following the acquisition of Seagram's liquor and wine portfolio, Diageo became the largest spirits and wine holding company in the world. The acquisition included two major California brands, Sterling Vineyards and Beaulieu Vineyards, as well as importing rights and/or partial ownership in about 200 French wines and champagne, including many estate-bottled French Burgundies, wines from Barton & Guestier (Bordeaux, France), and F.E. Trimbach wines (Alsace, France).

Although senior executives at Diageo wanted the conglomerate to be viewed by the financial markets as a growth company, its recent growth in profits had primarily come from divestitures and cost savings. Some security analysts predicted that the underlying growth at Diageo would remain low relative to its peer group in the beverages industry, despite the promise of its new ready-to-drink brands based on malt liquor beverages. Diageo's clout in global drinks markets had been continually undermined by the group's poorer performing regional brands. Diageo appeared extremely reluctant to bite the bullet and dispose of these poor quality assets. For these reasons and others, Diageo's stock price performance had not yet met investors' and investment analysts' expectations.

Diageo and Seagram Chateau & Estate Wines (the acquired Seagram wine brands) had combined estimated wine revenues of nearly $600 million. However, its rivals in the wine industry were ahead or in close pursuit: E&J Gallo Winery held the number one position at an estimated $1.5 billion in sales. Other rivals included: Foster's Group (Beringer Blass Wine Estates) at $818 million in sales; Constellation Brands at $713 million; Robert Mondavi, at $481 million; and Kendall-Jackson Wine Estates at $366 million. See Exhibit 2 for a comparison of the world's largest winemakers, ranked by sales.

COMPANY BACKGROUND

Based in London, England, Diageo was created in 1997 through the merger of two British companies, Grand Metropolitan plc and Guinness plc. Diageo—from the Latin word for "day" and the Greek word for "world"—competed in the food, alcoholic beverages,

	World's Biggest Wine Makers, ranked by sales ($ millions)		EXHIBIT 2

Rank	Company[1]	Country	Wine Sales in CY 2000
1.	E&J Gallo Winery[2]	U.S.	$1,500
2.	Foster's Group[3]	Australia	818
3.	Seagram[4]	Canada	800
4.	Constellation Brands[5]	U.S.	712
5.	Southcorp	Australia	662
6.	Castel Frères	France	625
7.	Diageo[6]	Britain	590
8.	Henkell & Sonlein	Germany	528
9.	Robert Mondavi	U.S.	481
10.	Kendall-Jackson	U.S.	366

NOTES
[1]List excludes France's LVMH, which earned more than 75% of its $1.6 billion wine sales in champagne.
[2]Includes Gallo of Sonoma (Healdsburg, CA) with estimated sales of $190 million.
[3]Includes Beringer Blass Wine Estates (Napa, CA) with estimated sales of $440 million.
[4]Includes Seagram Chateau & Estate (Napa, CA) with estimated sales of $273 million.
[5]Includes Franciscan Estates (Rutherford, CA) with estimated sales of $200 million.
[6]Includes Guinness (Rutherford, CA) with estimated sales of $303 million.

Sources: *Business Week*, September 3, 2001, p. 57; *North Bay Business Journal* estimates, June 11, 2001.

and fast-food restaurants sectors, although it had publicly stated its intention to exit from all sectors except the beverage industry.

Prior to their 1997 merger, Scottish-based Guinness/United Distillers (Guinness) and London-based Grand Metropolitan (GrandMet) owned beer and hard liquor (spirits) brands. Guinness had well-known beer (Guinness Stout, Bass Ale, and Harp Lager) and spirit brands and experience distributing products in emerging markets such as Asia and Latin America. Guinness, through its United Distillers (UD) division, also owned whisky (Johnnie Walker, Bell's) and gin (Gordon's, Tanqueray) brands and various alcohol brands. GrandMet, through its International Distillers and Vintners (IDV) division, was a holding company with vodka (Smirnoff), liqueur (Bailey's), rum (Malibu), and tequila (through its partnership with José Cuervo) brands. GrandMet also owned Pillsbury Foods and the Burger King fast-food restaurant chain, enabling it to maintain a sizable presence in the American market.

Both holding companies had foreseen a consolidation in the spirits/beer industry and sought acquisitions of related lines of business. In April 1997, George Bull, chairman of GrandMet, and Tony Greener, chairman of Guinness, met in London and reached a tentative agreement to merge the two companies.

Publicly, both companies gave a number of reasons for the merger. The merger would create one of the largest providers of branded food and beverages in the world. The major reason for the merger, though, was the specific benefits or "synergies" to be realized from combining the premium spirits brands of Guinness and GrandMet. Both companies had extensive experience selling and distributing internationally and the combined portfolio of brands covered the entire spirits spectrum. At the time it was consummated, the merger was expected to save £175 million (roughly $263 million at an exchange rate of £1 = $1.50), although this synergy cost savings was later estimated to be £290 million (about $435 million). One of the first consequences of the merger was that the spirits divisions were combined to form a new division called United Distillers and Vintners (UDV). Under the new Diageo holding company corporate structure, Guinness Brewing became one division, UDV another, and Pillsbury and Burger King were combined into a separate food division.

From 1997 to the year 2000, the merger was not received as favorably by the investment community as Diageo had originally hoped. During this period, Diageo's stock price lagged behind the London Stock Index by 20 percent. By 2000, its food division, which had been facing intense price competition, contributed about 35 percent of total company operating profits. The Guinness and UDV divisions contributed the remaining 65 percent of group operating profits. Exhibits 3–6 present 1998–2002 financial statements and ratios. Exhibit 7 presents 2000–2001 company segment information by line of business and by geographical region.

Hired two years after the merger, Paul Walsh, Diageo's CEO, stated his intention to focus on the "drinks" business. See Exhibit 8 for a list of Diageo's portfolio of beverage brands. In 2000, Walsh merged Guinness Brewing with United Distillers and Vintners to create a more focused core of beverage businesses (now named Guinness UDV) upon which to build future earnings growth.

In 2000, Seagram Corporation was in the process of being acquired by Vivendi Corporation. Vivendi was interested in Seagram's entertainment-related assets and made public its plan to sell off Seagram's numerous liquor brands. At this juncture, Diageo already owned twelve of the top one hundred spirits brands in the world. In seeking Seagram's liquor brands, CEO Walsh was moving Diageo further along the spirits-oriented strategy.

Meanwhile, Allied Domecq, another British alcoholic beverages conglomerate, joined the chase for ownership of Seagram's valuable drinks brands. Allied Domecq, the number two distiller of alcohol in the world behind Diageo, had already entered into negotiations with Seagram to purchase the Captain Morgan rum brand. Allied Domecq was consolidating alcohol brands under one corporate umbrella and had already begun to shed some of its core non-drinks businesses, including a donut chain in Spain and its pub operations in the United Kingdom.

Diageo prevailed in the battle for Seagram's, and in December 2000, Diageo and the French company Pernod Ricard agreed to jointly purchase Seagram's alcohol assets and divide them between the two companies. Diageo paid $5 billion, while Pernod Ricard contributed $3.15 billion to the deal. Diageo stood to gain the Seagram whisky (Seven Crown brand) and Seagram wine assets. These wine assets included Sterling Vineyards (Napa Valley), Monterey Vineyard, and Mumm Cuvée Napa. It also included numerous wine brands with which Seagram had import agreements, such as Barton & Guestier (France) and San Telmo (Argentina). Industry analysts predicted that many of Seagram's remaining smaller brands would then be divested.

A large stumbling block to completing the deal was the United States Federal Trade Commission (FTC). Even though European and Canadian (Seagram's home country) regulators had approved the deal, the FTC was concerned that Diageo would have a monopoly over the United States rum market if the deal went through. On October 23, 2001, the members of the

FY June 30
All quantities converted from £ sterling to dollar amounts in millions except per share amounts.

	2002	2001	2000	1999	1998
Turnover—continuing operations	$13,881	$12,933	$18,010	$18,716	$29,229
Turnover—acquisitions	860	—	—	—	—
Turnover—discontinued operations	2,183	6,299	—	—	176
Total turnover	16,924	19,232	18,010	18,716	29,405
Operating costs	(14,444)	(16,422)	(15,307)	(16,309)	(25,803)
Operating profit	2,480	2,810	2,704	2,407	3,602
Share of profits of associates	424	305	296	286	452
Trading profit	2,903	3,115	3,000	2,693	4,054
Disposal of fixed assets	(33)	29	8	(16)	(3)
Sale of businesses—continuing operations	749	42	(255)	(165)	(869)
Merger expenses					141
Sale of businesses—discontinued operations					452
Utilization of provision					415
Total				149	688
Interest payable (net)	(599)	(525)	(551)	(514)	(807)
Profit on ordinary activities before tax	3,504	2,584	2,202	2,328	3,934
Taxation on profit on ordinary activities	(949)	(653)	(608)	(698)	(1,510)
Profit on ordinary activities after tax	$ 2,555	$ 1,930	$ 1,593	$ 1,630	$ 2,424
Minority interests—equity	(74)	(65)	(56)	(78)	(111)
Minority interests—non-equity	(57)	(55)	(56)	(57)	(90)
Profit for the year	2,426	1,810	1,481	1,495	2,223
Dividends	(1,151)	(1,126)	(1,082)		
Transferred to reserves	1,275	684	399		
Average ordinary shares outstanding—basic	4,779	5,148	5,606	6,447	
Average ordinary shares outstanding—diluted	4,784	5,156	5,633	6,598	
Year end ordinary shares outstanding	4,828	5,192	5,440	5,938	
Earnings per share—basic	$0.73	$0.54	$0.44	$0.42	$0.57
Earnings per share—diluted	$0.73	$0.54	$0.44	$0.42	$0.57

Source: Diageo *Annual Reports.*

FTC voted to seek a preliminary injunction to block the sale. Joe Simmons, the director of the FTC's bureau of competition, said at the time, "This will create a dangerous likelihood of reduced competition and higher prices for consumers of rum." The FTC's reasoning was that Diageo would own the second largest rum producer in the United States (Seagram's Captain Morgan brand) and the third largest (Diageo's Malibu brand). The FTC indicated that Diageo would probably have to sell one of its rum brands in order to finalize the Seagram purchase.

In a press release following the FTC announcement, Paul Walsh stated, "We are encouraged by the FTC's willingness to have further discussions."

EXHIBIT 4   Diageo plc, Consolidated Balance Sheets, 1998–2002

FYE June 30
All quantities converted from £ sterling to dollar amounts in millions.

	2002	2001	2000	1999	1998
Fixed Assets					
Intangible assets	$ 8,151	$ 8,028	$ 8,025	$ 8,232	$ 7,854
Tangible assets, net	3,818	4,764	4,670	5,043	4,994
Investments	4,775	2,210	2,270	2,149	2,067
Total fixed assets	16,744	15,002	14,965	15,424	14,915
Current Assets					
Inventory stocks	3,474	3,348	3,246	3,494	3,715
Debtors due within one year	3,314	2,948	2,799	3,064	3,384
Debtors due after one year	1,815	1,926	1,801	2,047	1,660
Debtors subject to fin. arrangements			59	60	30
Investments					804
Cash at bank and in hand	2,394	2,763	1,613	1,741	4,159
Total current assets	10,997	10,985	9,518	10,406	13,752
Creditors due within one year					
Borrowings	(5,577)	(5,990)	(4,652)	(6,196)	(7,849)
Other creditors	(5,468)	(5,243)	(4,969)	(5,605)	(5,855)
	(11,045)	(10,646)	(9,621)	(11,801)	(13,704)
Creditors due after one year					
Borrowings	(5,567)	(5,990)	(5,638)	(5,387)	(4,808)
Other creditors	(74)	(144)	(152)	(159)	(404)
	(5,640)	(6,134)	(5,790)	(5,546)	(5,212)
Provision for liabilities and charges	(1,221)	(1,094)	(1,053)		(1,171)
	9,834	8,594	8,019	7,288	8,580
Capital and reserves					
Called up share capital	1,395	1,481	1,502	1,574	1,892
Share premium account	1,986	1,971	1,950	2,012	1,863
Revaluation reserve	194	206	209	275	316
Capital redemption reserve	4,518	4,431	4,475	4,659	4,772
Profit and loss account		(404)	(988)	(2,131)	(1,151)
Reserves attributable to equity shareholders	7,607	6,204	5,646	4,814	5,799
Shareholders' funds before minority interest	9,002	7,685	7,148	6,388	7,691
Minority interest—equity	276	311	256	284	281
Minority interest—non-equity	557	599	615	616	608
Total minority interests	833	909	871	900	889
Total capital and reserves	9,834	8,594	8,019	7,288	8,580

Source: Diageo *Annual Reports.*

All quantities converted from £ sterling to dollar amounts in millions.

FYE Jun 30	2001	2000	1999	1998
Net Operating Cash Flow	$ 2,361.0	$ 2,108.0	$ 589.0	$ 3,201.7
Net Investing Cash Flow	(785.0)	(59.0)	191.0	1,498.4
Net Financing Cash Flow	(1,435.0)	(2,256.0)	(552.0)	(4,071.7)
Net Change in Cash	141.0	(208.0)	227.0	628.3
Depreciation and Amortization	570.0	553.0	535.0	806.7
Capital Expenditures	(813.0)	(1,059.0)	(599.0)	(953.4)
Cash Dividends Paid	(1,025.0)	(1,036.0)	(1,054.0)	(1,813.4)

Source: Diageo *Annual Reports* and *10-K.*

In late October 2001, Diageo completed the sale of its Pillsbury unit to General Mills, and plans were already under way to spin off its Burger King unit by summer 2002. Diageo received a 33 percent minority stake in the newly merged General Mills and Pillsbury as well as $4.5 billion in cash. Despite intense focus on what it now called its "global priority" brands, Diageo had not yet succeeded in mitigating its high (relative to the industry) financial and operating leverage, vestiges of the 1997 merger. However, some industry analysts remained skeptical that Diageo wasn't yet completely drinks/alcohol focused. After the Pillsbury deal was announced, Morgan Stanley Dean Witter beverage analyst Alexandra Oldroyd remarked, "People are disappointed that they [Diageo] didn't get out of the food [sector] altogether." Walsh rebutted Oldroyd's criticism by pointing out that the General Mills cash-and-stock deal was the only one available since "not many companies have $10.5 billion in cash."

On December 21, 2001, the FTC gave its final approval to Diageo to complete the Seagram deal, based upon Diageo's promise to sell its Malibu rum brand. Commenting on the FTC's decision, Paul Walsh said, "Last summer we announced Diageo's strategic realignment behind premium drinks. Our strategy is to focus on our priority brands in their most important markets." In February of 2002 Diageo sold Malibu rum to its rival, Allied Domecq, for $795 million. Diageo also sold one of Seagram's wine brands, Mumm Cuvée Napa, to Allied Domecq for $39 million. By the end of the wheeling and dealing, Diageo had strengthened its position in the rum market and had also procured significant wine assets in terms of wineries, brands, and export rights.

OVERVIEW OF THE WINE INDUSTRY

Wine, the German poet Goethe once wrote, "rejoices the heart of men, and joy is the mother of virtue." Wine has been a part of civilization for thousands of years. One legend that is believed to have arisen in 3500 B.C. described how a tasting of accidentally fermented grape juices turned King Jamshid of Sumer and thus the entire kingdom into wine lovers. Regardless of the validity of legends concerning the origins of wine, grape growing and wine making are essentially the same today as they had become by the time of the Roman Empire (220 A.D.). Selected vines were planted and cared for, grapes harvested and crushed, and grape juice transformed into wine through the process of fermentation and then blending, bottling, and labeling. Over the centuries, grape growers and wine makers developed small refinements and improvements in the procedure so as to help the natural process along.

Wine is a complex beverage. It contains so many natural substances that scientists are still discovering new facts about it (including the purported health benefits of red wine on preventing heart disease, known as "the French paradox"). Its complexity has accounted for the vast number of producers in the United States and around the world, and the great variety of wines found in the marketplace. According to the *Adams Wine Handbook*, there are more producers of wine than any other beverage product.

Unlike the production of beer or spirits beverages (e.g., whisky, vodka, rum, and gin), wine production is primarily an agricultural pursuit. A wine maker could really only further improve the quality of the wine by using better quality grapes. A bad grape crop (e.g., due

EXHIBIT 6   Diageo plc, Selected Financial Ratios, 1998–2001

	2001	2000	1999	1998
Profitability				
Return on Total Equity (%)	$25.61	$25.11	$20.55	$13.22
Return on Assets (%)	9.13	8.03	7.02	6.64
Return on Invested Capital (%)	12.15	10.92	9.45	8.90
Cash Earnings Return on Equity (%)	36.66	38.05	21.36	21.66
Cost of Goods Sold to Sales (%)	75.05	70.67	66.24	59.72
Gross Profit Margin (%)	20.29	26.12	30.34	36.53
Operating Profit Margin (%)	19.64	16.20	18.49	18.50
Pretax Margin (%)	13.88	10.61	12.88	14.05
Net Margin (%)	11.18	8.22	9.49	9.03
Activity				
Assets per Employee ($)	$344,496	$333,540	$350,909	$381,522
Assets Turnover (x)	0.64	0.78	0.64	0.57
Inventory Turnover (x)	3.72	3.97	3.00	2.56
Net Sales to Gross Fixed Assets (x)	2.18	2.61	2.07	2.12
Capital Expend Pct Sales (%)	4.00	4.61	5.38	6.42
Leverage				
Total Debt Pct Common Equity (%)	152.17	149.29	187.77	169.56
LT Debt Pct Common Equity (%)	80.29	82.10	87.74	64.76
LT Debt Pct Total Capital (%)	41.74	42.17	43.38	36.19
Equity Pct Total Capital (%)	51.98	51.37	49.44	55.89
Total Debt Pct Total Assets (%)	43.83	42.82	45.65	44.41
Total Capital Pct Total Assets (%)	55.41	55.83	49.17	46.86
Liquidity				
Quick Ratio (x)	0.50	0.43	0.39	0.56
Current Ratio (x)	0.85	0.80	0.71	0.88
Cash Ratio (x)	30.54	20.90	20.82	41.04
Receivables Pct Current Assets (%)	28.85	32.17	33.81	22.00
Inventories Pct Current Assets (%)	37.01	42.06	41.80	30.72
Inventories Days Held (days)	96.71	90.78	120.16	140.58

Source: Diageo *Annual Reports*.

to weather or pest infestation) could result in a shortage of supply and inconsistent quality in the year-to-year vintages. On the other hand, a glut of grapes due to a bountiful harvest would alleviate supply shortages but not always guarantee consistency of quality.

Spirits and beer production were mostly process-related. A better technical process in the efficiency of distilling, for example, could lead to larger quantities being produced as well as improved taste and perceived quality of the final product. Raw materials and ingredients supply and demand imbalances had little effect on quality and quantity of production, due to the longer shelf lives of both raw materials inputs (e.g., grains, yeast, and water) and production outputs (e.g., beer, whisky, gin).

The nature and circumstances of wine, spirits, and beer consumption could be varied as well. Wine

EXHIBIT 7

Diageo plc, Segment Analysis, 2001 and 2000
(millions, British £ sterling)

	FY 2001						FY 2000					
	Revenue		Oper. Profit		Total Assets		Revenue		Oper. Profit		Total Assets	
Line of Business												
Premium Drinks	£ 7,580	59%	£1,432	67%	£ 5,123	48%	£ 7,117	60%	£1,286	65%	£ 4,972	49%
Quick Service Restaurant	1,042	8%	177	8%	1,432	13%	941	8%	202	10%	1,356	13%
Packaged Food	4,199	33%	518	24%	4,077	38%	3,812	32%	492	25%	3,734	37%
TOTAL	£12,821	100%	£2,127	100%	£10,632	100%	£11,870	100%	£1,980	100%	£10,062	100%
Geographical Area												
Europe	£ 4,073	32%	£ 614	29%	£ 3,763	35%	£ 4,181	35%	£585	30%	£ 3,804	38%
North America	6,401	50%	1,001	47%	6,193	58%	5,639	48%	956	48%	5,696	57%
Asia Pacific	990	8%	206	10%	246	2%	886	7%	170	9%	183	2%
Latin America	776	6%	188	9%	216	2%	697	6%	165	8%	252	3%
Rest of World	581	5%	118	6%	214	2%	467	4%	104	5%	127	1%
TOTAL	£12,821	100%	£2,127	100%	£10,632	100%	£11,870	100%	£1,980	100%	£10,062	100%

NOTE: Percentages may not add up to 100% due to rounding

Source: Diageo *Annual Reports.*

EXHIBIT 8   Diageo's Portfolio of Drinks Businesses and Priority Brands

Global Priority Brands in 2002

Brand	Recent news
Johnnie Walker	net sales up 4%
Baileys	volume up 10%
J&B	volume up 5% in Spain
Tanqueray	re-launched with marketing spend up 11%
Smirnoff Red	volume up 7%
Smirnoff flavours	now 1 million cases; Ice up 98%
Cuervo	US market share up 1.1%
Guinness	creating a platform for future growth
Captain Morgan	growing volume and market share in US

Local Priority Brands in 2002 and 2003

Brand	Market	Brand	Market
Archers	Great Britain	Dimple/Pinch	Korea
Beaulieu Wines	United States	Goldschlager	United States
Bells	Great Britain	Gordons gin	Great Britain
Bells	South Africa	Gordons gin	United States
Buchanan's	United States	Harp	Ireland
Buchanan's	Venezuela	Old Parr	Japan
Budweiser	Ireland	Red Stripe	Jamaica
Bundaberg rum	Australia	Romana Sambuca	United States
Cardhu	Spain	Rumple Minze	United States
Carlsberg	Ireland	Smithwicks	Ireland

Added for 2003

Brand	Market	Brand	Market
Cacique	Spain	Seagram's 7	United States
Crown Royal	United States	Seagram's VO	United States
Malta	Africa	Sterling Vineyards	United States
Myers's Rum	United States	Tusker	Kenya
Pilsner	Kenya	Windsor Premier	Korea

Source: Diageo's presentation to Securities' Analysts and Investors, London, September 5, 2002.

consumption was historically part of daily life in Mediterranean countries. Wine was consumed with the cuisine of the area, and the two complemented each other. In other countries, however, wine was seldom a part of mainstream culture. The markets of Japan, East Asia, and India consumed little wine, and future consumption in those areas was confounded by the fact that traditional wine varieties were not known to be well suited to the diverse cuisines of those regions. Hard liquor (whiskies) and beer dominated alcohol consumption in the United States. In the United States in particular, a strong lobby of anti-alcohol groups, along with other publicity regarding the effects of alcohol on health and public safety, were considered by some industry observers to have had a lasting negative impact on wine, beer, and spirits sales and consumption. Anti-alcohol groups advocated stringent labeling and distribution requirements for all alcoholic beverages.

THE UNITED STATES WINE INDUSTRY

The United States wine industry was composed of approximately 1,500 wineries in all 50 states; however, it was highly concentrated, with the top ten wineries accounting for 70 percent (by volume) of United States production, according to the 1999 *Adams Wine Handbook*. California dominated the United States wine industry with over 800 wineries, which accounted for more than 90 percent of the wine produced in and exported by the United States. Washington, Oregon, and Idaho had attracted approximately 200 wineries and were developing an export presence and a reputation for quality wines.

During the 1990s several major trends emerged in the United States wine industry. These trends included: (1) consolidation of the industry's "three-tier" distribution network (winery-wholesaler/distributor-retailer); (2) market segmentation due to consumers' "trading up" from inexpensive jug wines to premium-priced "varietal" wines, such as Chardonnay, Merlot, and Cabernet Sauvignon;[1] and (3) the emergence of global markets for wines, notably the increasing share of foreign imports in the United States wine market.

DISTRIBUTION CHANNELS

Wine was sold through a three-tier distribution system. Wineries (the first tier) or importers sold wine to wholesalers (the second tier), who provided legal fulfillment of wine products to local retail businesses (the third tier) within a certain state. Wine was a controlled substance, and laws in each state differed regarding how wine could be sold. Typically, wine passed through the second tier via wholesalers and distributors, making direct shipping to retailers or selling wine through the Internet and wine-buying clubs difficult or impossible in all but 13 states. Thus, access to wholesale distribution channels was considered by wineries to be critical. Meanwhile, second-tier distribution channels were consolidating due to the advantages of scale and scope afforded to larger distributors, and due to the fact that there was similar consolidation under way in the third tier, primarily on the retail (off-premises) side.

The third tier of the distribution system consisted of retail and non-retail outlets. According to *Adams Wine Handbook,* supermarkets, convenience stores, club stores, mail order and Internet retailers, specialty stores, and wine clubs accounted for 78 percent of total sales volume. Supermarkets alone accounted for 41 percent of retail wine sales and were very influential in wine distribution. They were dominant in food and drink retailing and made one-stop shopping an appealing concept for consumers. Furthermore, supermarkets had considerable bargaining leverage with wholesalers. The role of specialty stores in wine distribution diminished due to the increasing power of supermarkets. Specialty stores' share of retail wine sales was about 23 percent in 1998. Nevertheless, specialty stores were not likely to disappear soon because they provided superior customer service. Moreover, their sales staff had extensive knowledge of wines. Specialty stores also carried specialty brands and limited production labels, attracting wine connoisseurs and enthusiasts. On-premises sales via non-retail outlets such as restaurants, hotels, and airlines accounted for the remaining 22 percent of wine volume in the United States, according to *Adams Wine Handbook.* See Exhibit 9 for an estimated breakdown of percentage sales for each distribution channel by country.

MARKET SEGMENTATION

"Table" wines were those with 7–14 percent alcohol content by volume and were traditionally consumed with food. This was in contrast to other wine products such as sparkling wines (champagnes), wine coolers, and fortified wines, which were typically consumed as stand-alone beverages. Table wines that retailed at less than $3.00 per 750 ml. bottle were generally considered to be generic or "jug" wines, while those selling for more than $3.00 per bottle were considered "premium" wines.

Premium wines generally had a vintage date on their labels. This meant that the product was made with at least 95 percent of grapes harvested, crushed, and fermented in the calendar year shown on the label and used grapes from an appellation of origin (for example, Napa Valley, Sonoma Valley, Central Coast, etc.).[2] Within the premium table wine category, a number of market segments emerged, based on retail price points. "Popular premium" wines generally fell into the $3.00–$7.00 per bottle range, while "premium wines" retailed for $7.00–$10.00 and "super premium wines" retailed for $10.00–$15.00. The "ultra premium" category sold for $15.00–$30.00 per bottle. Any retail price above $30.00 per bottle was considered "luxury premium." See Exhibit 10 for wine market segmentation by price point.

The Wine Institute estimated that 1999 United States wine market retail sales had reached $18 billion, growing from $11.7 billion in 1990. The United States wine market ranked third in the world behind France and Italy. However, the United States ranked thirtieth in the world in per capita consumption of wine in 1999. The greatest concentration of table wine consumers was in the 35-to-55 age bracket. About the same proportion of men and women consumed wine. While all income

EXHIBIT 9 Wine Distribution Channels by Country, Year 2000

	HORECA* (%)	Supermarkets	Specialists	Other**
Western Europe				
Austria	26	41	4	30
Belgium	44	39	7	10
France	28	38	19	14
Greece	30	36	20	14
Germany	20	43	7	30
Italy	14	34	8	44
Netherlands	12	62	21	5
Portugal	10	81	5	6
Spain	57	33	7	4
UK	20	59	18	2
Americas				
Argentina	15	10	2	75
Canada	24	5	65	6
Chile	45	26	14	14
US	22	41	23	14
Other				
South Africa	34	28	34	3
Australia	57	15	19	9
Japan	61	7	17	15

*HORECA = Hotels, Restaurants, and Cafes
**Other includes direct sales, mail orders, corner and food shops

Source: *Euromonitor.*

levels consumed wine, higher income was associated with greater wine consumption. In 1998, adults in families earning over $75,000 annually represented 18.7 percent of the population and 31.4 percent of the domestic table wine consumption. Still, according to the *Adams Wine Handbook,* barely more than 10 percent of the adults in the United States consumed 86 percent of all wine sold. See Exhibit 11 for wine consumption patterns in the United States by year, 1981–2000, and Exhibit 12 for a table comparing wine consumption in the top ten wine consuming nations in 2000.

GLOBAL MARKETS

By 2000, the United States had become the second largest market for exported wine and the fourth leading producer of wine in the world. In 2000, United States wine exports to 164 countries totaled $560 million, of which more than 90 percent came from California. Wine was produced commercially in over 60 countries with 23 percent (by volume) of the wine produced in the

world being exported to international markets according to *Wines & Vines.* Leading wine producers included the "Old World" wineries in France, Italy, and Spain, which were also the leading exporters. So-called "New World" producers, such as the United States, Australia, Chile, Argentina, and South Africa, had been making both production and export inroads globally over the past few decades. For example, France, Italy, and Spain all exported more than 25 percent of the wine they produced, Australia exported over 40 percent, and Chile over 80 percent of its production. Many observers attributed Australia and Chile's high rates of growth in exports to the comparatively smaller size of their home markets. See Exhibits 13, 14, and 15 for year 2000 comparisons among wine producing nations, ranked by grapes produced, volume of wine produced, and volume of wine exported.

Until the mid-1990s, the United States wine market remained largely a domestic industry, with some imports from France, Italy, and Spain competing with

United States Consumers' Wine Purchases in Food Stores, Year 2000 — EXHIBIT 10

AC Nielsen/Adams Category	Volume Share	Case Removals Change (000)	Volume % Change	Revenue % Change
Total Wine	100%	1,266	3%	10%
Up to $3	39%	−920	−4%	−4%
$3 to $7	41%	539	3%	3%
$7 up to $10	13%	1,298	22%	24%
$10 up to $14	5%	468	23%	25%
$14 and over	2%	146	18%	24%

Sources: Gomberg-Fredrikson & Associates' data, compiled from AC Nielsen/Adams.

U.S. Per Capita Wine Consumption, 1981–2000 — EXHIBIT 11

Year	Total Wine per Resident, Gallons	Total Wine, Gallons	Total Table Wine, Gallons
2000	2.01	565	505
1999	2.02	551	482
1998	1.95	526	466
1997	1.94	520	461
1996	1.89	500	439
1995	1.77	464	404
1994	1.77	459	395
1993	1.74	449	381
1992	1.87	476	405
1991	1.85	466	394
1990	2.05	509	423
1989	2.11	524	432
1988	2.24	551	457
1987	2.39	581	481
1986	2.43	587	487
1985	2.43	580	378
1984	2.34	555	401
1983	2.25	528	402
1982	2.22	514	397
1981	2.20	506	387

Source: The Wine Institute.org. Key Facts.

EXHIBIT 12 | Top 10 Wine Consuming Nations, 2000

Country	Wine Consumption (million liters)	Share of World Consumption %
France	3,290	15.0
Italy	3,080	14.0
USA	2,140	9.8
Germany	1,956	8.9
Spain	1,450	6.6
Argentina	1,276	5.8
United Kingdom	915	4.2
China (inc. Taiwan)	553	2.5
Russia	550	2.5
Romania	521	2.5

Source: G. Dutruc-Rosset, extracted from the *Report on World Vitiviniculture.* Presented at the World Congress of the OIV in Adelaide, 12 October 2001.

Country	Grape Production (million tons)	% Share of World Production
Italy	8,871	14.2
France	7,627	12.2
USA	6,792	10.9
Spain	6,641	10.6
Turkey	3,400	5.4
China (inc. Taiwan)	3,013	4.8
Iran	2,300	3.8
Argentina	2,191	3.5
Chile	1,900	3.0
Germany	1,408	2.5
Rest of world	18,266	29.1
World	62,409	100.0

Note: percentages may not add up to 100% due to rounding.

Source: G. Dutruc-Rosset, extracted from the *Report on World Vitiviniculture.* Presented at the World Congress of the OIV in Adelaide, 12 October 2001.

United States wineries. By 1999, however, imports had risen to 20 percent of the United States market, seven percentage points above 1995, according to *Wine Business Monthly.* Australian and Chilean wines began making rapid inroads into the United States market. For example, from 1995 to 1999, Australia increased the value of its exports to the United States by 243 percent and Chile by 152 percent. Since 1995, the unfavorable

balance of trade for wine in the United States had increased by 78 percent. Tariffs and trade barriers played a pivotal role in obstructing United States wineries' access to various country markets.

Wine exports from the United States nevertheless grew consistently, from a base of $137 million in 1990 to $548 million in 1999, according to the U.S. Department of Commerce. Also, the United States wine industry

World's Top 10 Wine Producing Nations, Ranked by Volume, 2000 — EXHIBIT 14

Country	Wine Production (million liters)	% Share of World Production
France	5,754	20.9
Italy	5,162	18.8
Spain	4,113	15.0
USA	2,210	8.0
Argentina	1,254	4.6
Germany	985	3.6
Australia	859	3.1
South Africa	695	2.4
Portugal	669	2.4
Chile	667	2.4
Rest of world	5,123	18.8
World	27,491	100.0

Note: percentages may not add up to 100% due to rounding.

Source: G. Dutruc-Rosset, extracted from the *Report on World Vitiviniculture*. Presented at the World Congress of the OIV in Adelaide, 12 October 2001.

Top 10 Exporters of Wine in the World, 2000 — EXHIBIT 15

Country	Wine Exports (million liters)	% Share of World Exports
Italy	1,780	27.5
France	1,508	23.3
Spain	865	13.4
USA	297	4.6
Australia	285	4.4
Chile	270	4.2
Germany	254	3.9
Portugal	210	3.2
Moldavia	152	2.3
South Africa	139	2.1
Rest of world	714	11.0
World	6,474	100.0

Note: percentages may not add up to 100% due to rounding.

Source: G. Dutruc-Rosset, extracted from the *Report on World Vitiviniculture*. Presented at the World Congress of the OIV in Adelaide, 12 October 2001.

enjoyed the highest rate of increased wine exports (19.3 percent) in 1998, among the major wine producing countries listed in the *2000 World Vineyard, Grape, and Wine Report*. At the same time, United States wineries also faced increasing threats to their domestic market share due to globalization in the wine industry. *Wines & Vines* reported in 1999 that the United States had only 4.2 percent (by volume) of the world export wine market, while producing 8 percent (by volume) of the wine produced in the world. The United States wine industry exported only 13 percent of the wine it produced, while other countries had more intensely developed their export markets. Ten United States wineries accounted for more than 89 percent of exports. Nearly 50 percent of United States wineries exported their products.

The leading United States exporter by volume was Ernest and Julio (E&J) Gallo, accounting for about half of United States exports and more than four times the volume of its nearest export competitor. E&J Gallo exported approximately 13 percent of its total production. United States wineries typically exported only a small percentage of their production. Wente Vineyards was a notable exception. Wente had made exports a cornerstone of its long-term strategy, as 60 percent of its annual case sales were in 147 different country markets.

By 2001, the super-premium and ultra-premium market segments had become highly fragmented, composed of hundreds of individual, small to large wine-producing operations, all competing to produce the most acclaimed wines each year. Although the largest among these producers held advantages in scale and capital, the smallest wineries were able to compete by consistently producing high quality wines in limited quantities (known in the industry as "on-allocation"). On-allocation wines often gained critical acclaim from wine enthusiasts, in part because of their scarcity. Smaller wine producers, however, remained at a disadvantage when trying to compete for grape sources against larger better-financed competitors, such as Foster's Group's Beringer Blass Wine Estates, Robert Mondavi Corporation, Kendall-Jackson, Sebastiani Vineyards, E&J Gallo, and Constellation Brands' Canandaigua division. Many of these rival firms owned portfolios of brands, invested in wine-making facilities and vineyards across California and abroad, and produced wines across the price spectrum of the premium, super-premium, and ultra-premium market segments. The ability of a winery to produce brands in multiple segments appealed to distributors and retailers, who were in turn hoping to sell broad product lines to consumers.

Due to the globalization of markets and the creation of the European Union, trade barriers were falling worldwide. The worldwide consolidation trend accelerated among wineries and distributors. For example, Allied Domecq (United Kingdom), BRL Hardy (Australia), Brown-Forman Corporation (United States), Constellation Brands (United States), Foster's Group (Australia), and Southcorp (Australia) had all courted larger premium wineries in Northern California, such as Buena Vista and Kendall-Jackson, for acquisitions. Wine industry analysts anticipated further consolidation in the wine industry as large wine and alcoholic beverage conglomerates continued to acquire smaller winery operations across national borders, in order to gain access to premium and ultra-premium brands, as well as access to the growing markets for those brands.

COMPETITION

Diageo Chateau & Estate Wines competed with two major types of businesses: stand-alone wineries and conglomerates. Diageo's primary stand-alone winery competitors in the United States included publicly-traded Robert Mondavi, and the privately held Kendall-Jackson, E&J Gallo, and a host of small to medium-size wineries primarily based in Northern California. Large conglomerate competitors included Allied Domecq, Brown-Forman's Wine Estates division, Constellation Brands' Canandaigua division, Fortune Brands, Foster's Group's Beringer Blass Wine Estates division, Louis Vuitton Möet Hennesey (LVMH), Southcorp, and UST (formerly known as U.S. Tobacco). Comparative historical financial data for many of Diageo's publicly-traded competitors in the alcoholic beverages industry are shown in Exhibits 16 and 17.

Since the end of Prohibition in 1933, the jug wine segment had been almost completely dominated both in the United States and global markets by E&J Gallo, a family-owned wine business. However, during the 1980s, large alcoholic beverage companies, such as Canandaigua and The Wine Group, entered and competed with E&J Gallo in the jug wine market segment. Although Modesto, California-based E&J Gallo was still the single largest wine producer in the world, comprising approximately 45 percent of California wine sales, it had failed to capitalize on changes in consumer demand toward a preference for premium wines. In recent years, E&J Gallo, like many other jug wine producers, sought to enter the premium wine market, choosing to develop and launch new E&J Gallo brands from 2,300 acres of prime vineyards in Sonoma County, acreage acquired to supply the development of new premium and ultra-premium brands.

Besides the wine companies, several large food and beverage conglomerates, such as Nestlé, Pillsbury, Suntory, PepsiCo, and Coca-Cola, entered the premium

EXHIBIT 16

Selected Financial and Operating Highlights of Global Alcohol and Beverage Conglomerates, 1999 and 2000

Company	HQ Location	Sales ($ millions)			Net Income ($ millions)			ROE (%)		ROA (%)	
		2001	2000	1999	2001	2000	1999	2001	2000	2001	2000
Allied Domecq[1]	Bristol, England	$4,318	$6,154	$ 3,948	$516	$476	$114	117.7	N/A	12.7	N/A
Brown-Forman	Louisville, KY	2,180	2,009	2,134	233	202	218	19.6	20.8	19.3	19.3
Constellation Brands, Inc.	Fairport, NY	3,154	2,340	1,497	136	97.3	77.4	14.4	15.8	3.9	3.3
Fortune Brands	Lincolnshire, IL	5,678	5,579	5,844	385	(891)	(138)	18.9	-6.2	7.5	-2.3
Foster's Group[2]	Australia	2,244	1,874	1,656	256	236	203	12.2	18.5	9.0	12.8
Louis Vuitton Moët Hennessy (LVMH) [3]	Paris, France	1,168	8,589	10,909	10	696	680	0.2	10.3	2.0	8.4
Southcorp[2]	Australia	1,375	1,441	1,554	118	168	11	15.2	N/A	N/A	N/A
UST	Greenwich, CT	1,670	1,548	1,512	492	442	469	84.6	163.3	24.4	26.8

N/A = Not Available.

[1]Converted from British £ sterling to U.S. dollars at a rate of £1 = $1.50 U.S.
[2]Converted from Australian dollars to U.S. dollars at a rate of $1 Australian = $0.55 U.S.
[3]Converted from Euros to U.S. dollars at a rate of 1€ = $0.95 U.S.

Sources: Company reports, *Value Line*, and WSRN.com, accessed October 25, 2002.

Exhibit 17

Selected Stock Price and Financial Data for Publicly-Traded U.S. Alcohol Beverage Companies, 2002

Stock	Ticker Symbol	Recent Stock Price	P/E Ratio (x)	12 mo. Trail EPS	30 Day Price Change (%)	1 Year Price Change (%)	Beta	Div. Yield (%)	Stk. Mkt. Capitaliz. ($ million)	Return on Equity (%)	Pre-tax Margin (%)	LTD to Capital (%)
Brown-Forman Corp.	BF.B	$75.00	23	$3.29	13%	23%	0.44	1.9	2,963	18.3	17.8	2.8
Chalone Wine Group	CHLN	8.65	62	0.14	8%	−10%	0.25	Nil	104	2.8	6.5	38.6
Constellation Brands	STZ	25.50	14	1.82	0%	19%	0.30	Nil	1,994	17.5	8.2	53.6
Diageo plc (ADS)	DEO	46.14	15	2.98	−8%	15%	0.39	3.1	39,346	24.8	13.4	40.5
Robert Mondavi Corp.	MOND	31.86	14	2.21	6%	−1%	0.82	Nil	305	6.1	9.3	41.0

Source: Compiled by casewriters in October 2002 from statistics prepared by Richard Joy, *Standard & Poor's Rankings*.

market by acquiring premium to ultra-premium wineries in the 1970s. However, during the 1980s, each of these food and beverage companies divested their wine holdings, choosing instead to focus on their core businesses. The beneficiaries of these divestitures were the wine and alcoholic beverage companies that continued to build their portfolios of wine brands. For example, while Diageo and Allied Domecq owned a host of other diversified businesses, Constellation/Canandaigua focused primarily on alcoholic beverages and related products such as bottled water. All three firms, however, were firmly rooted in distilled spirits, and continued to expand their wine businesses.

Diageo's Chateau & Estate division faced intense global competition in the premium and ultra-premium wine segments. Rival beverage conglomerates such as Brown-Forman, Foster's Group, and Constellation/Canandaigua continued to build their wine portfolios through acquisitions and partnership arrangements. Diageo's conglomerate competitors had historically expanded their wine portfolios through acquisitions of independent wineries as well as purchases of and majority interests in the beverage divisions of other conglomerates. In 2000 and 2001, conglomerates began divesting those satellite businesses that diverted resources from their core beverage businesses, notably Allied Domecq's sale of the majority of its food operations. Exhibit 18 presents a comparison of portfolios and recent strategic moves by several major competitors in the wine industry.

At the wine industry's annual trade conference in Sacramento, California in January 2002, several industry experts predicted that the wine industry would continue to grow despite the challenges of economic uncertainty, consolidation, and oversupply of grapes. The experts opined that the accelerating trend of worldwide consolidation in the producer and trade segments would be more than offset by several factors. These included the continuing increase in the number of small wineries, a fundamental increase in consumer demand, the increasing affluence of the wine-buying public, and the results of decade-long efforts directed toward improving quality in production, sales, and service. Vic Motto, of Motto Kryla Fisher, a wine industry consultant, remarked:

> *Globalization has created a world market with a trend towards worldwide normalization of taste and stylistic standards. Global communication networks have also created the potential for small brands to access the same consumers as large ones. However, no one has succeeded in building a global brand—yet.*

FUTURE UNCERTAINTIES

At the time of Ray Chadwick's promotion in December 2001 to President of the Chateau & Estate wine division, another Diageo executive had said publicly:

> *With Ray Chadwick's rich and long history in the wine business, he will bring a thorough understanding of what it takes to be successful in a competitive industry. Additionally, Ray has a command of the intricate financial issues, as well as the strategic vision critical to leading a portfolio that will contain some of the finest wines in the world. Key to being successful in the wine industry is how well you build and maintain relationships.*

As Chadwick considered changes in the portfolio for his Chateau & Estate wine division, many observers still questioned Diageo's wisdom of entering the wine industry at all, with its comparatively (to spirits and beer) lower profit margins and the industry's increased reliance on an uncertain grape supply and consumer demand. Exhibit 19 presents Chadwick's biography.

In a January 2002 interview with a reporter at *Wine Business Insider*, Chadwick spoke of Diageo's philosophy behind entering the wine business:

> *Wines are a very attractive consumer segment with a strong growth potential. Wine is definitely a complement to Diageo's strategy to be a total beverage alcohol company. Diageo is very focused on the consumer and we think about "consumer need" states and what types of beverage alcohol consumers tend to drink in these various need states. There's one need state which is the dinner table: wine tends to be the choice when people choose to consume beverage alcohol. When people sit at the table and they eat, they tend to use wine.*

Still, some observers argued that the wine market required a completely different set of skills from Diageo's other beverages brand businesses, and that wine was more about vintage than brand, so there would be little transfer of skills in the Seagram acquisition. An anonymous critic, quoted in *Marketing Week,* said:

> *I would question the long-term growth potential of a company that moves from being a conglomerate with lots of diverse interests to being a business focused purely on high-value drinks. The alcoholic drinks market is not a high growth industry—the only way to grow is to take market share from someone else.*

However, other observers believed that global trends favored Diageo. As beverages analyst Alan Gray of

Profiles of Diageo's Major Wine Industry Competitors: Brand Portfolios and Recent Strategic Moves

EXHIBIT 18

Company	Portfolio Brands—Wine	Other Portfolio Brands	Annual Wine Production	Recent Strategic Moves
Allied Domecq	Clos du Bois, Callaway Coastal, Atlas Peak, William Hill, Bodegas Balbi, Graffigna & Ste Sylvie, Montana, Marques de Arienzo, Harveys, Cockburn's, La Ina, Mumm and Perrier-Jouet.	*Spirits:* Ballantine's, Beefeater, Kahlua, Sauza, Stolichnaya, Tia Maria, Maker's Mark, Courvoisier, Canadian Club *Fast-food:* Dunkin' Donuts, Baskin-Robbins and Togo's	Atlas Peak: 40,000 cases; 500 acres owned Callaway: 340,000 cases; 40 acres owned, 605 leased or controlled Clos du Bois: 1.4 million cases; 640 acres owned, 160 leased or controlled	Unsuccessfully bid to acquire Seagram's drinks businesses assets in 2001.
Constellation (Canandaigua)	Almaden, Arbor Mist, Franciscan Oakville Estate, Simi, Estancia, Talus, Taylor, Vendange	*Spirits and Beer:* Paul Masson brandy, Corona Extra, Modelo Especial, St. Pauli Girl, Alice White, Black Velvet, Fleischmann's, Schenley, Ten High, Stowells of Chelsea	30 million cases; 765 acres owned, 2,600 leased or controlled.	Acquired Ravenswood Estates (Sonoma, CA) for $148 million in cash and assumed debt in July 2001.
E&J Gallo	E&J Gallo (Modesto, CA): Gallo, Thunderbird, Carol Rossi, Bartles & Jaymes Gallo of Sonoma (Healdsburg, CA): E&J Gallo Estate, Gallo of Sonoma, Anapamu, Marcelina, Rancho Zabacho, Indigo Hills	None	E&J Gallo (Modesto, CA): 90 million cases (est.) Gallo of Sonoma (Healdsburg, CA): 1 million cases (est.); 3,000 acres	Is world's largest wine producer and leading U.S. wine exporter; selling in 85 countries; wines also account for over 25% of all U.S. wine sales; exports one million bottles annually to the French market; plans to create first-mover advantage in the Indian wine market.
Kendall-Jackson	Kendall-Jackson, Pepi, La Crema, Edmeades Estate, Camelot, Tapiz, Villa Arceno, Calina	None	4 million cases; 12,000 acres	Launched new Australian line, Yangarra Park in 2001; in May 2001, rejected several takeover bids, including one by BFC; also lost five-year battle with Gallo over alleged theft of trade secrets.
Robert Mondavi	Robert Mondavi Winery, Robert Mondavi Coastal, Woodbridge, La Famiglia de Robert Mondavi, Byron, Arrowood, Vichon Mediterranean, Opus One, Caliterra, Luce	None	Unknown; 7,730 acres	Formed joint ventures with producers in France, Chile, and Italy; created a $10 million wine country attraction in 2001 at Disney's California Adventure theme park; began shift from vineyard development to production—internal grape supply expected to rise from 7% to 20% by 2004.

Sources: Dow Jones Interactive On-line, accessed October 25, 2002, and *Wines and Vines' 2001 Annual Buyers' Guide.*

Ray Chadwick
President, Diageo Chateau & Estate

Chadwick was appointed president of Diageo's wine operations in December 2001. At that time he assumed responsibility for the integrated wine operations of Guinness North America and Seagram Chateau & Estate Wines. Previously, Chadwick served as Executive Vice President and Chief Financial Officer of the Seagram Chateau & Estate Wines Company, where his responsibilities included the overall direction of the finance function, long range and strategic planning, international sales, business development, information services, and environmental affairs. Chadwick served concurrently as Managing Director of Barton & Guestier, S.A., and had functional responsibility for the finance function at the Seagram Beverage Company. Chadwick first joined Seagram in 1974 and has worked in a variety of roles, including market research, sales and finance.

He also spent time in London in an international marketing role for Brown-Forman. Chadwick served as integration leader when The Seagram Classics Wine Company and Seagram Chateau and Estate Wines Company were merged in 1996. He served as co-integration leader during the merger of Diageo and Seagram wine operations in 2001, which led to the formation of Diageo Chateau & Estate Wines. Chadwick holds Bachelor of Arts and Master of Arts degrees from the University of Virginia, as well as an M.B.A. from the University of Chicago. He also studied in France for several years, including a year in Bordeaux under the auspices of the Fulbright program. He currently serves on the Board of Directors of the Wine Institute.

Source: www.aboutwines.com.

ING Barings Charterhouse Securities pointed out in the same *Marketing Week* article, "There are growth and cost benefits to come—Diageo can sell the acquired brands through its own distribution network."

In an interview with *Wine Business Insider* in January 2002, Chadwick commented on Diageo's future relationships with its distributors:

Let me address this very directly. [We want] to develop a more efficient and effective way of bringing [our] total portfolio of products—including wines—to market. We want to create a new way of working with our distributors and brokers. Over the coming months we will begin a process with our distributors and brokers to develop this new kind of relationship. And we can foresee the possibility of adjustments to our distributor network in the next year or eighteen months, but that process is just beginning. In broad strokes, the new relationship will be more collaborative, more fact-based, more long-term, and more focused on delivering greater value to consumers and customers: understanding the consumer better, understanding customers and consumers better, for example, working with our distributors to really fine tune our channel strategy. I can honestly say to you that no decisions have been made yet.

Despite all the economic, social, and political turmoil that marked 2001, global retail dollars from the sale of wine, beer, and diversified spirits increased approximately 3.5 percent to $127.3 billion (from $122.8 billion in 2000), according to *Beverage Dynamics*. Spirits retail sales increased 2.9 percent, from approximately $37.3 billion to more than $38.4 billion. Wine retail sales grew about 4.4 percent, from $18.1 billion to just under $19.0 billion. Beer dollar volume sales also rose, up 3.7 percent from $67.4 billion in 2000 to almost $70 billion in 2001. Although the percentage gains over the previous year were smaller in 2001 than in 2000, consumption trends favored higher-end products.

A few months before the 2002 sale of the Glen Ellen brand to The Wine Group, Chadwick explained the segmentation of Diageo's wine brands to *Wine Business Insider*:

Super-premium wines are growing really well. The $12–$15 category continues to be a really attractive category for us. The economy and the events of September 11 have caused some business to shift from on-premise to off-premise. People are staying home but they're still drinking wine at home with friends at the table. The off-premise sector has been strong. On-premise was relatively weak for a while and has *begun to come back in many areas. There's no doubt that the low end of the business has been soft, but again, that $12–$15 category—where we've got some really good brands—continues to be very strong. BV [Beaulieu Vineyards] and Sterling are two of the great Napa Valley brands. We've got a stable of other California brands: Glen Ellen, the Monterey Vineyard, Blossom Hill, Mumm Cuvée Napa. On the European side, we have a world-renowned collection of great labels from Bordeaux and Burgundy, and we also have B&G French wines. And our other French relationships—most notably Trimbach from Alsace—we expect will continue to grow.*

Question marks still remained regarding Diageo's future in a global market where economic uncertainties increased the difficulty of forecasting and planning future growth. Much of the Chateau & Estate division's success would depend on the basic skills of marketing: well timed innovation, informed analysis of social and demographic trends, and leveraging strong distribution, particularly in the United States. Chadwick wondered how to manage the wine brands more profitably, leveraging Diageo's formidable resources and history of successfully marketing other beverages. In the January 2002 *Wine Business Insider* interview, Chadwick discussed the future of his portfolio of wine brands:

BV will remain BV and Sterling will remain Sterling. Each will operate independently and each will retain their unique character. Within our portfolio, they complement each other. BV was founded 100 years ago, it is high end in certain appellations, notably Carneros and Rutherford. Georges de Latour (the late founder) is an icon in the industry. Sterling was the first Napa Valley Winery to bottle a vintage-dated varietal—Merlot—again, it has a unique set of vineyards. Our plan is to have a focused wine division with dedicated sales and marketing teams. We're also going to have dedicated finance, human resources and operations departments within the wine division. Any overlap is minimal. As you may be aware, Guinness UDV markets wines together with spirits. And those individuals that focused on wines are being considered for opportunities within Chateau & Estates. We're still putting the company together, but we intend to have a very, very strong and large organization. We are very alert to opportunities to expand our current business, but the economics have to be right. We have to provide returns to our shareholders.

Still, Chadwick wondered, should Diageo lead or follow other conglomerates into further diversification outside of its current French and U.S. wine holdings?

BIBLIOGRAPHY

ABC News Radio (2001). "Foster's to expand its wine arm," August 29.

Adams (1999). *Adams Wine Handbook,* Adams Business Media, New York.

Anon. (2001). "2000 California wine sales up—for seventh consecutive year," http://www.thewineman.com, March 15, 2001.

Anon. (2001). "US clears $8 billion Seagram deal," http://news.bbc.co.uk, December 19.

Anon. (2000). "Diageo confirms Pillsbury sale," http://news.bbc.co.uk, July 17.

Anon. (2001). "Regional spotlight: Australia," http://www.winepros.com/, accessed 2/15/02.

Anon. (2002). "Foster's Group Limited," http://www.hoovers.com/, accessed 2/15/02.

Anon. (2002). "Allied Domecq PLC," http://www.hoovers.com/, accessed 2/15/02.

Anon. (2002). "Topsy-turvy down under," http://WineSquire.com/, accessed 2/15/02.

Anon. (2000). "All merge: Consolidation strikes the Australian wine industry," http://www.industrysearch.com/, October 5.

Anon. (2002). "The brave new world of wine," http://www.itsfood.com/, accessed 1/15/02.

Anon. (2001). "Care to see the wine list? Global drinks firms ready to buy," http://www.industrysearch.com/, May 28.

Anon. (2001). "Turning to the bottle," *Marketing Week,* November 1, 25.

Anon. (2002). "Diageo plans Napa HQ," *North Bay Business Journal,* March 17, 1.

Anon. (2000). "Globalization, who's leading the way?" *Wines & Vines,* April.

Anon. (2002). "Q&A with Diageo Chateau & Estates President Raymond Chadwick," *Wine Business Insider,* January.

Brandes, R. (2002). "Growth brands," *Beverage Dynamics,* 114(2), (March), 14–23.

De Luca, J. (2002). "The outlook for the California wine industry in 2002," Presentation to the North Bay Economic Outlook conference, Rohnert Park, CA, February 2002.

Echikson, W., *et al.* (2001). "Wine war," *Business Week,* September 3, 54–60.

Fish, T., & Gaffney, J. (2001). "Sale of Seagram's Wines & Spirits blocked by U.S. regulators," http://www.winespectator.com, October 24.

Foster's Group Inc. *Annual Reports 2000 and 2001.*

Gaffney, J. (2002). "Diageo sells Glen Ellen for $83 million," http://www.winespectator.com, March 18.

Gomberg-Fredrikson. (1999). *1999 Annual Wine Industry Review,* Gomberg, Fredrikson & Associates, 703 Market Street, Suite 1602, San Francisco, CA 94103.

Lamb, R., & Mittleberger, E. (1984). *In Celebration of Wine and Life.* New York: Drake Publishers.

Lucas, G. (2002). "Small wine merchants uncork anger," *San Francisco Chronicle,* April 16, A13.

Mansson, P-H. (2001). "Who really controls the vineyards of France," *Wine Spectator,* November 30, 89–92.

Manuel, D. (2001). "What's a premium wine?" http://www.supermarketguru.com, November 19.

Motto Kryla Fisher. (2002). "High-end California wine sales increase 10% in 2001," Unified Grape Symposium, Sacramento, CA, January 2002.

Quackenbush, J. (2002). "Diageo plans Napa HQ," *North Bay Business Journal,* January 7, 1.

Rachman, G. (1999). "The globe in a glass," *The Economist,* December 18, 91–105.

Radio National. (2001). "The business report: Fosters' wine on the march," January.

Robert Mondavi, Inc. (2001). Press release, July 25.

Simon, A. (1957). *The Noble Grapes and the Great Wines of France*, New York: McGraw-Hill.

Standard & Poor's. (2001). *Industry Surveys: Alcoholic Beverages & Tobacco*, March 1.

NOTES

1. In 1983, laws in the United States had taken effect controlling what wineries could put on their labels. A *varietal wine* meant one variety of grape—the name of a single grape could be used if not less than 75 percent of the wine was derived from grapes of that variety, the entire 75 percent of which was grown in the labeled appellation of origin.

2. *Appellation of origin* meant a general term for the label designations that indicated geographic origins of bottled wines that met specific legal requirements. Any wine, at least 75 percent of which was made of grapes grown in the area designated on its label and that conformed to the laws and regulations relevant there, was entitled to a country, state, or county appellation. *§ Title 27 Part 4 of the Code of Federal Regulations. Washington, DC: Bureau of Alcohol, Tobacco and Firearms, Regulatory Agency, United States Department of the Treasury.*

case eleven

Anne T. Lawrence
San Jose State University

On December 2, 2001, Enron Corporation filed for bankruptcy. The company's sudden collapse—the largest business failure in U.S. history to date—came as a shock to many. Just months earlier, *Fortune* magazine had named Enron the most innovative company in America for the sixth consecutive year. The Houston, Texas-based firm, ranked seventh on the Fortune 500, was widely considered to be the premier energy trading company in the world. At its peak in 2000, Enron employed 19,000 people and booked annual revenues in excess of $100 billion. At a meeting of executives in January 2001, chairman and CEO Kenneth Lay had said that the company's mission was no longer just to be the world's greatest energy company; rather, its mission was to become simply "the world's greatest company."[1]

The pain caused by Enron's abrupt failure was widely felt. The company immediately laid off 4,000 employees, with more to follow. Thousands of Enron employees and retirees saw the value of their 401(k) retirement plans, many heavily invested in the company's stock, become worthless almost overnight. "We, the rank and file, got burned," said one retiree, who lost close to $1.3 million in savings. "I thought people had to treat us honestly and deal fairly with us. In my neck of the woods, what happened is not right."[2] Shareholders and mutual fund investors lost $70 billion in market value. Two banks—J.P. Morgan Chase and Citigroup—faced major write-downs on bad loans. Not only did Enron creditors, shareholders, and bondholders lose out, confidence also fell across the market, as investors questioned the integrity of the financial statements of other companies in which they held stock.

In the aftermath, many struggled to unravel the messy story behind Enron's collapse. Congressional committees initiated investigations, prosecutors brought criminal charges against Enron executives and their accountants for obstruction of justice and securities fraud, and institutional investors sued to recoup their losses. Some blamed Arthur Andersen, Enron's accounting firm, for certifying financial statements that had arguably wrongfully concealed the company's precarious financial situation; some blamed the board of directors for insufficient oversight. Others pointed to a go-go culture in which self-dealing by corrupt executives was condoned, or even admired, while others faulted government regulators, industry analysts, and the media for failing to uncover the company's weaknesses. It will likely take years for the courts to sort through the wreckage.

ENRON CORPORATION

Enron Corporation was formed in 1985 through a merger of Houston Natural Gas and InterNorth of Omaha, Nebraska. The union created a mid-sized firm whose main asset was a large network of natural gas pipelines. The company's core business was distributing natural gas to utilities.

The central figure from the outset of Enron's history was Kenneth L. Lay. The son of a Baptist minister from rural Missouri, Lay trained as an economist at the University of Missouri and the University of Houston and briefly taught college-level economics. After a stint with Exxon, Lay accepted a post in the Nixon administration, serving in the Federal Energy Commission and, later, in the Interior Department as deputy undersecretary for energy. Following the Watergate scandal, Lay returned to the private sector in 1974, taking the first in a series of executive positions at various energy companies. Lay became CEO of Houston Natural Gas in 1984, and he assumed the top job at Enron in 1986, shortly after the merger. One observer described Lay as a man of "considerable charm, homespun roots, and economic expertise" who tended to play an "outside" role, leaving the day-to-day management of his company in the hands of others.[3]

A strong proponent of free markets, Lay felt that the deregulation of the 1980s presented an opportunity for the fledgling company. Historically, the U.S. energy industry had been highly regulated. Utilities were granted monopolies for specific regions, and regulators controlled the prices of electricity and natural gas. Pipeline operators could transport only their own natural gas, not that of other producers. In the 1980s, however, a series of legislative actions at both federal and state levels removed many of these restrictions. For the first time, energy producers were free to compete, buy and sell at market prices, and use each other's distribution networks. The promise of deregulation, touted by lawmakers at the time, was that competition would lead to greater efficiencies, lower prices, and better service for consumers.

Deregulation caused problems for both producers and users of energy, however, because prices for the first time became highly volatile. In the past, energy users (an industrial company or regional utility, for example) could buy extra natural gas or electricity from producers on the spot market on an as-needed basis. Once prices were free to fluctuate, however, this approach became riskier for both parties. The customer did not want to be forced to buy when prices were high, and the producer did not want to be forced to sell when prices were low.

Enron moved to provide an ingenious solution: the company would leverage its large network of pipelines to set up a "gas bank" that would act as the intermediary in this transaction, reducing market risk. Enron would sign contracts with producers to buy their gas on a certain date at a certain price, and other contracts with users to sell them gas on a certain date at a certain price. Presuming that both parties were willing to pay a slight premium to insure against risk, Enron could make money on the spread. Enron had clear advantages as a market maker in natural gas: it owned pipelines that could be used to transport the product from producer to user, and it had strong institutional knowledge of how markets in the industry operated.

The idea man behind this innovation was Jeffrey Skilling. A graduate of the Harvard Business School and a partner in the consulting firm McKinsey & Company, Skilling had been brought in by Lay in the late 1980s to advise Enron on the company's response to deregulation. The gas bank, in itself, was a clever idea, but Skilling went further. He developed a series of other products, called energy derivatives, for Enron's trading partners. These products included *options,* which allowed companies to buy gas in the future at a fixed price, and *swaps,* which allowed them to trade fixed prices for floating prices and vice versa. In 1990, Skilling left McKinsey to become CEO of Enron Gas Services, as the gas bank came to be known. In 1996, he was promoted to the position of president and chief operating officer of Enron and, in February 2001, to CEO.[4]

WE MAKE MARKETS

Enron's core gas services division was highly profitable, but by the mid-1990s its growth had begun to level out, as competitors entered the market and both buyers and sellers became more sophisticated and thus able to drive harder bargains. The challenge, as Skilling saw it, was to maintain Enron's growth by extending the business model that had worked so well in natural gas into a range of other commodities. As he later explained this strategy to an interviewer:

> *If you have the same general [market] characteristics, all you have to do is change the units. Enron has a huge investment in capabilities that can be deployed instantly into new markets at no cost.*[5]

In particular, Skilling sought to trade commodities in industries with characteristics similar to those of natural gas—ones that were undergoing deregulation, had fragmented markets, maintained dedicated distribution channels, and in which both buyers and sellers wanted flexibility.[6]

- *Electricity.* One of the most obvious markets for Enron to enter was electric power. Deregulation of electric utilities in many states—most notably California—presented an opportunity for Enron to use its trading capabilities to buy and sell contracts for electricity. Enron already owned some gas-fired power plants, and it moved to build and buy facilities designed to supply electricity during periods of peak demand. Enron also moved to expand this business internationally, especially in nations undergoing energy deregulation or privatization.
- *Water.* In 1998, Enron acquired Wessex Water in the United Kingdom and changed its name to Azurix, with the ambitious goal of operating water and wastewater businesses globally.
- *Broadband.* The company formed Enron Broadband Services in January 2000. Portland General Electric, which Enron acquired in 1997, provided the core fiber optic network for this service. The idea was to supply customers with access to bandwidth at future dates at guaranteed prices. Enron believed these contracts would appeal to customers who did not want to rely on the public Internet or build their own telecommunications networks.
- *Pulp, Paper, and Lumber.* Enron launched clickpaper.com, an online market for the purchase of contracts for the delivery of wood products, and bought a newsprint company to ensure a ready source of supply.

Skilling told an interviewer from *Frontline* in March 2001: "We are looking to create open, competitive, fair markets. And in open, competitive, fair markets, prices are lower and customers get better service. . . . We are the good guys. We are on the side of the angels."[7]

By 2001, Enron was buying and selling metals, pulp and paper, specialty chemicals, bandwidth, coal, aluminum, plastics, and emissions credits, among other commodities. At the height of its power, 1,500 traders housed in Enron's office tower in Houston were trading 1,800 different products. As the *New York Times* later noted in an editorial, Enron was widely viewed as "a paragon of American ingenuity, a stodgy gas pipeline company that had reinvented itself as a high-tech clearinghouse in an ever-expanding roster of markets."[8] Reflecting the general enthusiasm, Skilling replaced his automobile vanity license plate, which had read WLEC (World's Largest Energy Company) with WMM (We Make Markets).[9]

INSISTING ON RESULTS

In his 1999 letter to shareholders, Lay described the company's attitude towards its employees this way: "Individuals are empowered to do what they think is best. . . . We do, however, keep a keen eye on how prudent they are . . . We insist on results."[10]

Enron used a recruitment process designed to hire individuals who were smart, hard working, and intensely loyal. The company preferred to hire recent graduates. After an initial screening interview, candidates were brought to the Houston office for a "Super Saturday," during which they were individually interviewed for 50 minutes by eight interviewers, with only 10-minute breaks between interviews.

Even candidates who survived this strenuous hiring process, however, could not count on job security. Within the company, management used a "rank and yank" system in which new recruits were ranked every six months, and the 15 or 20 percent receiving the lowest scores were routinely terminated. Enron's highly

competitive and results-oriented culture "created an environment," in the words of one observer, "where most employees were afraid to express their opinions or to question unethical and potentially illegal business practices."[11]

On the other hand, employees were encouraged to take initiative and were handsomely rewarded when their efforts paid off. Louise Kitchen, chief of the European gas trading unit, for example, organized a team to develop an online trading system. When it was adopted as the basis for a company-wide division, Kitchen was promoted to president of Enron Online.

Executive compensation was also results-based. According to Enron's 2001 proxy statement:

> *The basic philosophy behind executive compensation at Enron is to reward executive performance that creates long-term shareholder value. This pay-for-performance tenet is embedded in each aspect of an executive's total compensation package. Additionally, the philosophy is designed to promote teamwork by tying a significant portion of compensation to business unit and Enron performance.*[12]

Executive compensation was primarily comprised of salary, bonus, and stock options, as shown in Exhibit 1. In addition, the company routinely loaned money to top executives, forgiving the loans if the terms of their contracts were fulfilled. Enron also awarded some executives equity stakes in various business units, which could be converted into stock or cash under certain conditions. For example, Skilling held a 5 percent stake in the retail energy unit, which he converted into $100 million worth of stock in 1998.[13]

During Enron's final years, many top executives sold significant blocs of company stock. Between October 1998 and November 2001, according to a lawsuit later filed by shareholders, Lay sold $184 million worth of Enron stock; Skilling, $71 million; and Andrew Fastow, Enron's CFO, $34 million. All three men sold large blocs in late 2000 or early 2001.[14]

EXHIBIT 1	Top Executive Compensation, 2000					
	Base Salary	Bonus	Other	Stock Options	Total	Stock Options as % of Total
Lay	1.3	7.0	0.4	123.4	132.1	93%
Skilling	0.9	5.6	—	62.5	69.0	91%

Note: All figures are in millions of dollars, rounded to the nearest $100,000. "Stock options" represents stock options exercised and sold in 2000, *not* granted in 2000. These figures do not include the value of perquisites, such as personal use of company aircraft.

Source: Enron, SEC Schedule 14A (proxy statement), March 27, 2001, p. 18, and Dan Ackman, "Executive Compensation: Did Enron Execs Dump Shares?" Forbes.com, March 22, 2002.

POLITICS AS USUAL

Political action was an important part of Enron's overall strategy. The company's primary policy goal was to promote deregulation and reduce government oversight in the range of markets in which it traded. It maintained an office in Washington, D.C. staffed by over 100 lobbyists and also used outside lobbyists for specialized assignments. The company spent $2.1 million on lobbying in 2000 alone.[15] Enron was also a major campaign contributor. From 1994 on, Enron was the largest contributor to congressional campaigns in the energy industry, giving over $5 million to House and Senate candidates, mostly to Republicans (see Exhibit 2). In 2000, it gave $2.4 million in political contributions.

Enron CEO Kenneth Lay also had close personal ties with the Bush family. In 1992, Lay had chaired the host committee for the Republican National Convention in Houston at which George H. Bush was nominated to run for a second term as president. Enron donated $700,000 to George W. Bush's various campaigns between 1993 and 2001. Lay and his wife personally donated $100,000 to the younger Bush's presidential inauguration.

Over the years, Enron's efforts to influence policymaking enjoyed significant success, as illustrated by the following examples:

- *Commodities Futures Regulation.* The job of the Commodities Futures Trading Commission (CFTC), a federal agency, is to regulate futures contracts traded in an exchange. From 1988 to 1993, the CFTC was chaired by Wendy Gramm, an economist and wife of then-Congressman Phil Gramm (Republican-Texas). In 1992, Enron petitioned the CFTC to exempt energy derivatives and swaps—such as those in which it was beginning to make a market—from government oversight. In January 1993, just days before President Clinton took office, Wendy Gramm approved the exemption. The following month, after she had left office, Gramm was invited to join Enron's board of directors. According to Enron's filings with the SEC, Gramm received somewhere between $.9 and $1.8 million in salary, fees, and stock option sales and dividends for her service on the board between 1993 and 2001.[16]

- *Securities and Exchange Commission (SEC).* In 1997, the SEC granted Enron an exemption for its foreign subsidiaries from the provisions of the Investment Company Act of 1940, a law designed to prevent abuses by utilities. The law barred companies it covered from shifting debt off their books, and barred executives of these companies from investing in affiliated partnerships. After it had failed to win the exemption it wanted from Congress in 1996, Enron hired the former director of the investment management division at the SEC as a lobbyist to take the company's case directly to his former colleagues. He was successful. The year 1997 was the last in which the SEC conducted a thorough examination of Enron's annual reports.[17]

- *Commodity Futures Modernization Act.* This law, passed by Congress in late 2000, included a special exemption for Enron that allowed the company to operate an unregulated energy trading subsidiary.

		Enron Contributions to Federal Candidates and Parties, 1990–2002				EXHIBIT 2
Election Cycle	Total Contributions	Soft Money Contributions	Contributions from PACs	Contributions from Individuals	% to Democrats	% to Republicans
1990	$ 163,250	N/A	$ 130,250	$ 33,000	42%	58%
1992	281,009	$ 75,109	130,550	75,350	42%	58%
1994	520,996	136,292	189,565	195,139	42%	58%
1996	1,141,016	687,445	171,671	281,900	18%	81%
1998	1,049,942	691,950	212,643	145,349	21%	79%
2000	2,441,398	1,671,555	280,043	489,800	28%	72%
2002	353,959	304,909	32,000	17,050	6%	94%
TOTAL	$5,951,570	$3,567,260	$1,146,722	$1,237,588	26%	74%

Note: Soft money contributions were not publicly disclosed until the 1991–92 election cycle. Soft money contributions were banned in 2002.

Source: Center for Responsive Politics, based on Federal Election Commission data; available online at: http://www.opensecrets.org/news/enron/enron_totals.asp.

Senator Phil Gramm, chair of the powerful banking committee, was instrumental in getting this provision included in the bill despite the opposition of the president's working group on financial markets. Over the years, Enron had been the largest single corporate contributor to Gramm's campaigns, with $260,000 in gifts since 1993.[18]

Reviewing the history of Enron's efforts to limit government oversight, one reporter concluded, "If the regulators in Washington were asleep, it was because the company had made their beds and turned off the lights."[19]

OFF THE BALANCE SHEET

As Enron forged ahead in the late 1990s as a market maker in a wide range of commodities, it began to assume increasing amounts of debt. Even though Skilling had touted the value of an "asset light" strategy, entry into markets for such varied commodities as water, steel, and broadband required that Enron buy significant hard assets. Enron's aggressive new business ventures required, by some estimates, on the order of $10 billion in up-front capital investments. Heavy indebtedness, however, posed a problem, because credit-worthiness was critical to the company's ability to make markets in a wide range of commodities. Other parties would be unwilling to enter into contracts promising future delivery if Enron were not viewed as financially rock-solid, and the company had to maintain an investment-grade credit rating to continue to borrow money on favorable terms to fund its new ventures. A complicating factor was that several of the company's major new initiatives fell far short of expectations and some—broadband in particular—were outright failures.

Beginning in 1997, Enron entered into a series of increasingly complex financial transactions with several special purpose entities, or SPEs, evidently with the intention of shifting liabilities (debt) off its books. After the bankruptcy, these transactions were investigated by a special committee of the Enron board, which released its findings in a document now known as the Powers Committee Report.

Under standard accounting rules, a company could legally exclude an SPE from its consolidated financial statements if two conditions were met: (1) an independent party had to exercise control of the SPE, and (2) this party had to own at least 3 percent of the SPE's assets. The independent party's investment had to be "at risk"; that is, not guaranteed by someone else.[20] The obvious problem was that if Enron intended to burden the SPEs with debt, no truly independent party would want to invest in them.

A key figure in many of these transactions was Andrew S. Fastow. Described as a "financial whiz kid," Fastow had joined Enron Finance in 1990. He developed a close relationship with Skilling and rose quickly, becoming chief financial officer (CFO) of Enron in 1998, at age 37. Speaking of Fastow's selection, Skilling told a reporter for *CFO Magazine*, "We needed someone to rethink the entire financing structure at Enron from soup to nuts. We didn't want someone stuck in the past. . . . Andy has the intelligence and youthful exuberance to think in new ways."[21]

The SPEs Enron set up in the five years leading up to its bankruptcy included the following:

- *Chewco.* In 1997, Enron created Chewco, an SPE named after the Star Wars character Chewbacca. Fastow invited a subordinate, Michael Kopper, to become the required "independent" investor in Chewco. Kopper and a friend invested $125,000 of their own funds and, with Enron providing collateral, got an $11 million loan from Barclays Bank. Between 1997 and 2000, Kopper received $2 million in management fees for his work on Chewco. In March 2001, Enron repurchased Chewco from its "investors"; Kopper and his friend received more than $10 million. The Powers Committee concluded that "our review failed to identify how these payments were determined or what, if anything, Kopper did to justify the payments."[22]
- *The LJM Partnerships.* In 1999, Enron created two partnerships known as LJM1 and LJM2 (the initials of Fastow's wife and children). Unlike Chewco, where he had delegated this role to a subordinate, Fastow himself served as general partner and invested $1 million of his own money. Enron proceeded to transfer various assets and liabilities to the LJMs, in a way that benefited its bottom line. For example, in the second half of 1999, the LJM transactions generated "earnings" of $229 million for Enron (the company reported total pre-tax earnings of $570 million for that period).
- *Raptor Partnerships.* In 1999 and 2000, Enron established four new even more ambitious SPEs, collectively known as the Raptor Partnerships, with such fanciful names as talon, timberwolf, bobcat, and porcupine. In a series of extremely complex financial maneuvers in the final five quarters before declaring bankruptcy, Enron conducted various transactions with and among the Raptors and between the Raptors and the LJMs that generated $1.1 billion in "earnings" for the firm. Among other actions, Enron loaned large blocs of its own stock to the Raptor partnerships in exchange for promissory notes, which were then posted to Enron's balance sheet as notes receivable.

Fastow made out handsomely on these deals. According to the Powers Committee Report, he eventually received almost $50 million for his role in the LJM partnerships and their transactions with the Raptors, in addition to his regular Enron compensation. In its review of Enron's SPE transactions, the Powers Committee Report concluded:

> These partnerships . . . were used by Enron Management to enter into transactions that it could not, or would not, do with unrelated commercial entities. Many of the most significant transactions apparently were designed to accomplish favorable financial statement results, not to achieve bonafide economic objectives or to transfer risk. . . . They allowed Enron to conceal from the market very large losses resulting from Enron's merchant investments. . . . [23]

MANIPULATING REVENUE

Moving liabilities off the books was one way to make the company's financial condition look better than it was. Another way was to manipulate revenue. In the period preceding its collapse, Enron used a number of accounting practices apparently aimed at inflating revenues or reducing their volatility.

- *Mark-to-Market Accounting.* Mark-to-market (MTM) is an accounting procedure that allows companies to book as *current earnings* their expected *future revenue* from certain assets. The Financial Accounting Standards Board (FASB), the organization that establishes generally accepted accounting principles, approved MTM in the early 1990s. Aggressively using this procedure, Enron counted projected profits from many deals in the year they were made. For example, in 2000 Enron entered into a partnership with Blockbuster to deliver movies on demand to viewers' homes over Enron's broadband network. The venture fell apart within a few months, after pilot projects in four U.S. cities failed. Nonetheless, Enron booked $110 million in profits in late 2000 and early 2001, based on the anticipated value of the partnership over 20 years.[24] In 2000, mark-to-market gains accounted for over half of Enron's reported pre-tax earnings.[25]
- *Sham Swaps.* In the wake of its collapse, Enron was investigated by the SEC for possible sham swaps. For example, on the last day of the third quarter 2001, as the company's stock price was falling, Enron entered into an agreement with the telecommunications firm Qwest to exchange assets. Qwest and Enron agreed to buy fiber optic capacity from each other, and the two companies exchanged checks for around $112 million to complete the swap. According to the *New York Times,* "the deal enabled Enron to book a sale and avoid recording a loss on . . . assets, whose value in the open market had dropped far below the price on Enron's books."
- *Prudency Accounts.* Enron traders routinely split profits from their deals into two categories—one that was added directly to the company's current financial statements, and the other that was added to a reserve fund. These so-called prudency accounts, according to Frank Partnoy, an expert in finance who testified before the U.S. Senate Committee on Governmental Affairs, functioned as "slush fund[s] that could be used to smooth out profits and losses over time." The use of prudency accounts made Enron's revenue stream appear less volatile than it actually was. As Partnoy noted, "such fraudulent practices would have thwarted the very purpose of Enron's financial statements: to give investors an accurate picture of a firm's risks."[26]

THE BEST INTERESTS OF THE COMPANY

The two groups most responsible for overseeing the legal and ethical integrity of the company's financial reporting were Enron's board of directors and its auditors, Arthur Andersen's Houston office. In January 2001, Enron's board was comprised of 17 members. Of the 15 outside members, many had long personal and business associations with Lay and were considered loyal supporters of his policies. Although the board included only two insiders (Lay and Skilling), other members of top management frequently attended, sitting around the edge of the boardroom.[27] The full board typically met five times a year. Members of Enron's board were unusually well compensated. In 2001, for example, each director received $381,000 in total compensation. (By comparison, the average director compensation for the top 200 companies that year was $152,000; and for companies in the petroleum and pipeline industries, $160,000.)[28]

The quality of the company's financial reporting was the responsibility of the audit and compliance committee. Chaired by Robert Jaedicke, emeritus professor of accounting and former dean of the Stanford Business School, the committee also included Wendy Gramm and four others.[29] The audit committee typically met for an hour or two before the regular board meetings, often for discussions with the company's professional auditors.

The board's first substantive involvement with the SPEs run by Fastow and his associates came in 1999.[30] Fastow's dual roles as both CFO and general partner of the LJM partnerships potentially violated Enron's code of ethics, which prohibited an officer from owning or participating in "any other entity which does business with . . . the company." An exception could be made if the participation was disclosed to the chairman and CEO and was judged not to "adversely affect the best interests of the company." Accordingly, in June and again in October, the board reviewed and approved the LJM partnerships and voted to suspend its code of ethics in this instance to permit Fastow to run the partnerships.

However, the board seemed sufficiently concerned that it put additional controls in place; it required both an annual board review and that the chief accounting officer and chief risk officer review all transactions with the partnerships. In October 2000, the board added additional restrictions, including provisions that Skilling personally sign off on all related approval sheets. In May 2001, an Enron attorney discovered that Skilling had not signed these documents, as the board had required, so he sent a message to the CEO that he needed to sign the papers at his convenience. Skilling never replied.[31] As for the mandated board review, the Powers Committee later concluded that although the audit committee had periodically reviewed the SPEs, "these reviews appear to have been too brief, too limited in scope, and too superficial to serve their intended function."[32]

In its oversight function, the board and its audit committee relied heavily on the professional advice of Enron's auditor, Arthur Andersen, which repeatedly told the board it was "comfortable" with the partnership transactions. Founded in 1913 and Enron's auditor since 1985, Andersen was one of the "Big Five" accounting firms. Since the early 1990s, Andersen's Houston office had acted both as the company's external and internal auditors, in an arrangement called an "integrated audit," in which Enron subcontracted much of its "inside" work to the firm.[33] Andersen also did considerable consulting and non-auditing work for its client. All told, Enron was a very important client of the Houston office. In 2000, for example, Andersen received $25 million for audit and $27 million for non-audit services from Enron. Between 1997 and 2001, Andersen received around $7 million for its accounting work on the Chewco, LJM, and Raptors transactions.

Relations between Enron and Arthur Andersen were unusually close. Many Andersen accountants had office space at Enron and easily mingled with their co-workers. "People just thought they were Enron employees," said one former Enron accountant.[34] Moreover, mobility between Andersen and its client was high; indeed, at the time of the bankruptcy, the company's chief accounting officer, Richard Causey, had formerly been in charge of Andersen's Enron audit.

Andersen's own structure gave considerable autonomy to local offices like the one in Houston. Like other big accounting firms, Andersen had a professional standards group (PSG) at its corporate headquarters whose job was to review difficult issues that arose in the field. Unlike others, however, Andersen's PSG did not have the authority to overrule its field auditors in case of disagreement. An investigation by *Business Week* showed that on four different occasions, the Enron audit team went ahead despite PSG objections to various aspects of its accounting for the Enron partnerships. Finally, Enron requested that its chief critic be removed from the PSG. Andersen headquarters complied.[35]

Later, responding to criticism of its actions as Enron auditors, Andersen simply stated that it "ignored a fundamental problem: that poor business decisions on the part of Enron executives and its board ultimately brought the company down."[36]

A WAVE OF ACCOUNTING SCANDALS

On March 5, 2001, *Fortune* magazine published a cover story, written by reporter Bethany McLean, under the title "Is Enron Overpriced?" In the article, McLean challenged the conventional wisdom that Enron stock—which had returned 89 percent to investors the previous year and was selling at 55 times earnings—was an attractive buy. Calling Enron's financial statements "nearly impenetrable," she interviewed a number of stock analysts who, although bullish on Enron stock, were unable to explain exactly how the company made money. One called the company's financial statements "a big black box."[37]

What *Fortune* did not know at the time was that the fragile structure of partnerships Enron had constructed rested on the high price of the company's stock. Much of the partnerships' assets consisted of Enron stock or loans guaranteed by Enron stock. If the share price declined too far, this would trigger a need for more financing from the company. Prior to Enron's announcement of first quarter 2001 results, and then again prior to the second quarter results, Andersen worked furiously to restructure the partnerships to prevent the necessity of consolidating them with Enron's books. The Powers Committee later commented that these efforts were "perceived by many within Enron as a triumph of accounting ingenuity by a group of innovative accountants. We believe that perception was mistaken. . . . [The] Raptors were little more than a highly complex accounting construct that was destined to collapse."[38]

In late July, Enron's stock slid below $47 a share—the first "trigger" price for the partnerships. On August 14, Skilling abruptly resigned as president and CEO, citing undisclosed personal reasons. Lay, who had been serving as chairman, resumed the role of CEO. In a memo to Enron employees that day, Lay assured them:

I have never felt better about the prospects for the company. All of you know that our stock price has suffered substantially over the last few months. One of my top priorities will be to restore a significant amount of the stock value we have lost as soon as possible. Our performance has never been stronger; our business model has never been more robust; our growth has never been more certain; and most importantly, we have never had a better nor deeper pool of talent throughout the company. We have the finest organization in business today. Together, we will make Enron the world's leading company.[39]

The following day, Sherron S. Watkins, an accountant and Enron vice president who worked under Fastow, wrote a memo to Lay to express her concerns about the company's accounting practices. She stated frankly:

I am incredibly nervous that we will implode in a wave of accounting scandals. My 8 years of Enron work history will be worth nothing on my resume, the business world will consider the past successes as nothing but an elaborate accounting hoax. Skilling is resigning now for "personal reasons" but I think he wasn't having fun, looked down the road and knew this stuff was unfixable and would rather abandon ship now than resign in shame in 2 years.

She added:

I have heard one manager . . . say, "I know it would be devastating to all of us, but I wish we would get caught. We're such a crooked company."

After a detailed review of the "questionable" accounting practices of the SPEs, Watkins recommended that Lay bring in independent legal and accounting experts to review the propriety of the partnerships and to prepare a "clean up plan."[40]

Lay followed Watkins' advice—to a point. He brought in attorneys from Vinson & Elkins, the Houston law firm that had long been Enron's outside counsel and that had helped prepare the legal documents for the partnerships. In his instructions, Lay indicated that he saw no need to look too closely into the accounting. The lawyers interviewed Fastow, Enron's auditors, and several others, and then reported back to Lay on September 21 that although the accounting was "creative" and "aggressive," it was not "inappropriate from a technical standpoint."

Yet, despite these assurances, the partnerships were unraveling as Enron's stock price dropped (see Exhibit 3) and could no longer be supported by even the most aggressive accounting. On October 16, under pressure from its auditors, Enron announced a charge against earnings of $544 million and a reduction in shareholders' equity of $1.2 billion related to transactions with the LJM partnerships. On October 22, the SEC initiated a probe of the SPEs; Fastow was fired the following day. Then, on November 8, Enron further shocked investors by restating *all* of its financial statements back to 1997 because "three unconsolidated entities [i.e., the partnerships] should have been consolidated in the financial statements pursuant to generally accepted accounting principles." These restatements had the

Enron Stock Price and Trading Volume, 1998–2002   **EXHIBIT 3**

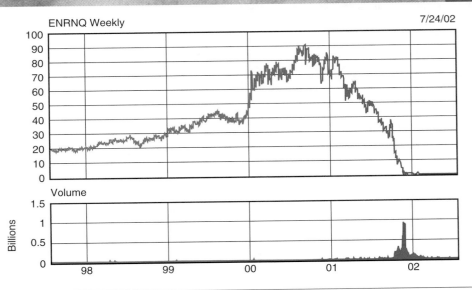

Source: bigcharts.com

effect of reducing income for 1997 to 2000 by $480 million, reducing shareholders' equity by $2.1 billion, and increasing debt by $2.6 billion.[41]

Company executives frantically went searching for a white knight to purchase the company. Dynegy, another Houston-based energy trader and longtime rival, initially agreed to buy Enron for $8.9 billion on November 9. After Dynegy's CEO and board had taken a careful look at Enron's books, however, they changed their minds and withdrew the offer. The rating agencies immediately downgraded Enron to junk status, and the stock dropped below $1 a share and was delisted from the New York Stock Exchange. (See Exhibit 3.)

As the company imploded, Enron tried to call in its political chits in one last Hail Mary move. Lay and other top executives placed urgent calls to commerce secretary Donald Evans, treasury secretary Paul O'Neill, and other administration officials, reportedly asking them to lean on banks to extend credit to the company. They declined to do so. Later asked why he had not helped Enron, Evans said that it would have been an "egregious abuse" to have intervened. O'Neill simply stated, "Companies come and go. . . . Part of the genius of capitalism is, people get to make good decisions or bad decisions, and they get to pay the consequence or enjoy the fruits of their decisions."[42]

NOTES

Sources for this case include articles appearing in the *Wall Street Journal, New York Times, Business Week, Fortune, Houston Chronicle, Newsweek, Time,* and *U.S. News & World Report.* Primary documents consulted include various Enron annual reports; "Report of the Investigation by the Special Investigative Committee of the Board of Directors of Enron Corp.," February 1, 2002 (the Powers Committee Report); William S. Lerach and Milberg Weiss Bershad Hynes & Lerach LLP, "In Re: Enron Corporation Securities Litigation" (consolidated complaint for violation of the securities laws), 2002; and transcripts of hearings before the U.S. House of Representatives Committee on Financial Services and Committee on Energy and Commerce and the U.S. Senate Committee on Governmental Affairs and Committee on Commerce, Science, and Transportation. Secondary sources consulted include Peter C. Fusaro and Ross M. Miller, *What Went Wrong at Enron* (Hoboken, NJ: John Wiley & Sons, 2002); Robert Byrd, *Pipe Dreams: Greed, Ego, and the Death of Enron* (New York: PublicAffairs/Perseus Books, 2002); Malcolm S. Salter, Lynne C. Levesque, and Maria Ciampa, "The Rise and Fall of Enron," unpublished paper, Harvard Business School, April 10, 2002; and Mark Jickling, "The Enron Collapse: An Overview of Financial Issues," Congressional Research Service, February 4, 2002.

1. "Enron's Last Year: Web of Details Did Enron In as Warnings Went Unheeded," *New York Times,* February 10, 2002. Revenue data are from Enron's 2000 Annual Report.
2. "Enron's Collapse: Audacious Climb to Success Ended in Dizzying Plunge," *New York Times,* January 13, 2002.
3. Fusaro, P.C. and Miller, R.M. *What went wrong at Enron.* Hoboken, NJ: John Wiley & Sons, 2002, p. 9.
4. Enron's early history is described in two cases, "Enron: Entrepreneurial Energy," Harvard Business School case 700-079, and "Enron's Transformation: From Gas Pipelines to New Economy Powerhouse," Harvard Business School case 9-301-064.
5. Darden School of Business videotape, May 25, 2001, cited in Joseph Bower and David Garvin, "Enron's Business and Strategy," unpublished paper, Harvard Business School, April 10, 2002.
6. Salter, M.S., Levesque, L.C., and Ciampa, M. The rise and fall of Enron. Unpublished paper, Harvard Business School, April 10, 2002, pp. 12–13.
7. "Enron's Many Strains: The Company Unravels; Enron Buffed Image Even as It Rotted from Within," *New York Times,* February 10, 2002.
8. "The Rise and Fall of Enron" [Editorial], *New York Times,* November 2, 2001.
9. Fusaro and Miller, p. 70.
10. 1999 Enron Annual Report.
11. Fusaro and Miller, *What went wrong at Enron,* p. 52. Enron's "rank and yank" system is described in Malcolm Gladwell, "The Talent Myth," *The New Yorker,* September 16, 2002.
12. Enron, SEC Schedule 14A (proxy statement), March 27, 2001, p. 15.
13. "Enron Compensation Raised Questions," *Dow Jones Newswires,* March 26, 2002.
14. Insider trading data computed by Milberg Weiss Bershad Hynes & Lerach LLP; available online at www.enronfraud.com.
15. "The Fall of the Giant: Enron's Campaign Contributions and Lobbying," Center for Responsive Politics; available online at www.opensecrets.org.
16. "Blind Faith: How Deregulation and Enron's Influence Over Government Looted Billions from Americans," Washington, D.C.: Public Citizen, December 2001.
17. "Exemption Won in 1997 Set Stage for Enron Woes," *New York Times,* January 23, 2002.
18. "Blind Faith: How Deregulation and Enron's Influence Over Government Looted Billions from Americans," December 2001.
19. "Enron's Collapse: Audacious Climb to Success Ended in Dizzying Plunge," *New York Times,* January 13, 2002.
20. A. Christine David, "When to Consolidate a Special Purpose Entity," *California CPA,* June 2002.
21. "Andrew S. Fastow: Enron Corp.," *CFO Magazine,* October 1, 1999.
22. Report of the Investigation by the Special Investigation Committee of Enron Corporation (Powers Committee Report), February 1, 2002, p. 8.
23. Powers Committee Report, p. 4.
24. "Show Business: A Blockbuster Deal Shows How Enron Overplayed Its Hand—Company Booked Big Profit From Pilot Video Project That Soon Fizzled Out," *Wall Street Journal,* January 17, 2002, and Bryce, *Pipe Dreams,* pp. 281–283.
25. "Question Mark to Market: Energy Accounting Scrutinized," CFO.com, December 4, 2001.
26. Testimony of Professor Frank Partnoy, Senate Committee on Governmental Affairs, January 24, 2002, online at: http://www.senate.gov/.
27. Jay W. Lorsch, "The Board at Enron," unpublished paper, Harvard Business School, April 10, 2002, p. 1.
28. Pearl Meyer and Partners, *2001 Director Compensation: Boards in the Spotlight: Study of the Top 200 Corporations,* 2002. Data are rounded to the nearest thousand dollars.
29. Other members of the audit committee were: John Mendelsohn, president of the M.D. Anderson Cancer Clinic; Paolo V. Ferraz Pereira, former president of the State Bank of Rio de Janeiro; John Wakeham, former British Secretary of State for Energy; and Ronnie Chan, chairman of a large property development group in Hong Kong.
30. Earlier, the board had provided a cursory review of Chewco, but had apparently been unaware of Kopper's role.
31. "Enron's Many Strands: The Company Unravels," *New York Times,* February 10, 2002.
32. Powers Committee Report, p. 24.
33. "Court Documents Show Andersen's Ties with Enron Were Growing in Early '90s," *Wall Street Journal,* February 26, 2002.
34. "Were Enron, Andersen Too Close to Allow Auditor to Do Its Job?" *Wall Street Journal,* January 21, 2002.
35. "Out of Control at Andersen," *Business Week,* April 8, 2002.
36. "Enron's Doomed 'Triumph of Accounting,'" *New York Times,* February 4, 2002.
37. "Is Enron Overpriced?" *Fortune,* March 5, 2001.
38. Powers Committee Report, pp. 131–132.
39. The full text of Lay's memo appears in Fusaro and Miller, p. 201.
40. The full text of Watkins' memo appears in Fusaro and Miller, pp. 185–191.
41. Based on data reported in the Powers Committee Report, p. 6.
42. "Enron Lessons: Big Political Giving Wins Firms a Hearing, Doesn't Assure Aid," *Wall Street Journal,* January 15, 2002.

ERG "Smart Cards": *Crafting Strategy for a New Horizon*

case twelve

F. R. Chaddad
Accenture plc

Gary J. Stockport
University of Western Australia

Based on the coastline of remote Western Australia is ERG Group, a world leader in the emerging smart cards industry. In less than 15 years, ERG grew from nothing to a market cap of around A$2bn—the equivalent of US$900m—in early 2000. According to CEO Peter Fogarty: "In 1987 we had absolutely no business whatsoever and only three people."[1] Fogarty was part of a team brought in by shareholders in 1985 to rescue an incipient automated fare collection business that was seriously haemorrhaging cash.

Upon his arrival at ERG, Peter Fogarty immediately reached out for worldwide markets. Australia was simply too small: "You won a contract. Then it was a drought for five years."[2] So ERG initiated the build-up of a broad international network of smart cards relationships from the late 1980's onwards, winning contracts first in Sweden and Canada. Through heavy but smart R&D expenditure—which according to CEO Fogarty was rigorously applied rather than "dreamy or esoteric"[3]—ERG built on its electronic display system to develop the company's first smart card project in 1989. By the late 1990's, ERG was a leader in cutting edge smart cards such as contactless, multi-function applications. ERG then operated over four continents and had recorded a compound annual growth rate of over 40% in the 1990's.

ERG was the best-performing stock in the Australian Stock Exchange Top 100 list in 2000, up an astonishing 1200% in just under 12 months. See Exhibit 1 for ERG financials. But as technology stocks around the world entered a rough bear market period and a series of events with negative connotations to ERG hit the business press in 2001, the ERG stock tumbled over 80% from its 2000 peak (see Exhibit 2). CEO Fogarty fought the bad press publicly, but he also thought about the road ahead for ERG in the 2000's. It seemed to him that the key for a bright future revolved around what technologies to pursue; how to manage knowledge and pursue these technologies; and toward what business applications. He also thought about ERG's in-house capabilities and how they should relate in the 2000's to ERG's extensive network of alliances, JV's and equity investments. Critically important to the future of ERG was the commitment to its proprietary MASS—Multi-Application Smart card Solution—technology as part of a bold effort to create an industry standard for smart cards.

THE SMART CARD TECHNOLOGY

The roots of the smart card technology date back to France in 1977, when Michel Ugon invented the first microprocessor card in the laboratories of the French technology company Bull. This card contained both memory and a microprocessor. In 1978, Ugon registered his SPOM (self-programmable one-chip microcomputer) patent that defined the enabling architecture for a self-programmable chip. This capability allowed a microprocessor to modify its behaviour in the event of an alert input, and thereby counter unwanted threats. In a worst-case scenario, the chip could self-destruct. In 1979, the first card rolled out of Bull labs. According to Ugon, who in the early 2000's was still developing smart card technologies at Bull: "I was convinced that the card should contain a self-programmable microprocessor, and not just memory, to enable an external device to modify the information stored in the card."[4]

As of the early 2000's, a smart card was a device similar in size and appearance to a credit card. It was made of plastic and contained an embedded integrated

EXHIBIT 1   Selected ERG Financials

Selected P&L Item	Fiscal year ending 30 June				
	2001	2000	1999	1998	1997
Operating Revenues [A$m]	$299	$416	$269	$243	$201
R&D [% of Revenues]	15%	14%	5%	11%	18%
EBITDA [A$m]	$ 6	$ 55	$ 38	$ 29	$ 22
Return on Shareholders' Equity [%]	2.2%	12.9%	8.8%	6.1%	7.8%
Selected Balance Sheet Item					
Cash Equivalents [A$m]	$ 32	$145	$ 28	$ 30	$ 21
Total Assets [A$m]	$711	$702	$453	$381	$298
Shareholders' Equity [A$m]	$273	$273	$232	$215	$244

Source: ERG 2001 Annual Report

EXHIBIT 2   ERG Stock Chart

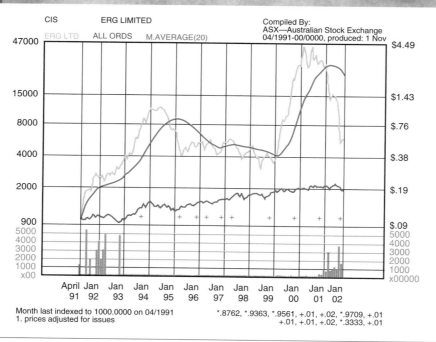

Source: www.asx.com.au, November 2001

circuit (IC) chip that enabled the storage and processing of both information and transactions. A smart card could be a memory card or a microprocessor card; disposable or reusable; contact or contactless; single or multi-functional. A smart card could be used for applications such as: access control and identification; automatic fare collection for buses, trains and airline travel; industrial automation applications in asset tracking, warehouse and inventory control; facilities and equipment management; manufacturing automation; financial transactions in banking; electronic purse applications in retail stores; loyalty programmes such as frequent flier and frequent buyer bonus plans; parking; petroleum retail; health care; as well as telecommunications application such as payphones and mobile phones network access.

Smart cards could be defined by the capabilities of the chip they contained:

- **Memory cards**: These merely stored data and had no data processing capabilities;
- **Hardwired logic** (intelligent memory cards): These contained a simple Application Specific Integrated Circuit—ASIC, usually used to control the access to the memory of the card;
- **Microprocessor cards**: These contained a microprocessor to execute a program stored inside the same silicon chip and could make decisions based on external inputs. Microprocessor cards were the "true smart cards" that were used in banking and other applications where security was essential. Very often the data processing power was used to encrypt and decrypt data, which made this type of card most appropriate for application requiring the highest security features.[5]

As of the early 2000's, several factors accounted for the increased interest in smart card technology applications. Firstly, the steady decline of smart cards costs as the technology quickly evolved made applications more feasible. Next, the increasing concern about fraud associated with magnetic strip card systems made smart cards a desirable alternative as they provided an excellent level of data security and offered very strong protection against falsification and misuse. The card and the system could mutually verify authenticity, and the identity of the cardholder could also be verified by the use of a personal identification number—PIN. Data stored on the card was secure against espionage and manipulation even during the data transmission process over a network. Further, the incorporation of a microprocessor enabled one smart card to independently manage multiple applications, such as identification functions and electronic purse functions in the same card. Smart cards also offered a much larger data storage capacity than magnetic strip cards—about 100 times larger. Therefore, they could gather demographic information for business to better understand and service their customers, and offer co-branding opportunities, leading to new marketing possibilities. In public transportation applications, for instance, bus or rail operators could use the information stored in the system to better understand customer habits and tailor their services accordingly. Another factor associated with the growing popularity of smart cards was the growing interest in remote transactions utilising telephones, personal computers, and the Internet, which required greater security than had been available in the past. Unlike magnetic strips, smart cards offered compatibility with portable devices such as mobile phones and personal digital assistants—PDA's. Finally, the transaction speeds of smart cards such as contactless ones were very high.

THE FUTURE OF THE SMART CARD

In the near future, it was expected that the major use for smart cards would continue to be for mobile telephone, access control, fare collection and banking applications. Future trends were also toward the development of multi-functional smart cards that carried more than one application—such as a parking card that is automatically reloaded from a bank account—and thus offer convenience to users who did not have to carry many cards. Along with the development of multi-functional smart cards went a growing demand for chips with higher processing capability and memory space.[6]

In the not-too-distant future, industry visionaries believed that smart cards would ultimately influence the way that humans shopped, saw the doctor, used the telephone and enjoyed leisure. Modern society already needed an enormous amount of information in the early 2000's: whereas computers processed the information, smart cards individualised the handling and control of this information. Further, advances in science would soon mean that a person could be reliably identified by his or her hand, fingerprints, eye retina or voice sound. Furthermore, it would be possible to authorise the use of electronic information in smart cards using a spoken word or the touch of a hand. The use of smart card technology would benefit individuals and increase their quality of life.[7]

SMART CARDS: GLOBAL MARKET AND SEGMENTS

The smart card industry was still in its infancy but certainly booming in the late 1990's. In 1994, 420 million smart cards were in use around the world; in 2000, this number had jumped to 1.79 billion.[8] The industry thus experienced a compound annual growth rate of 27%. And according to consultancy Frost & Sullivan, the number of smart cards in use worldwide was expected to increase to 3.6 billion by 2004[9] despite a global technology slowdown in 2001. In 2000, the fastest growing segment in the smart cards market had been SIM cards for mobile telephones. Europe was the biggest market and accounted for 53% of the world's share while Asia accounted for 24%; America was a newcomer as a smart card market with a small 2%-share.[10] See Exhibit 3 for an evolution of smart card applications from 1994 to 2000. In the late 1990's, smart card applications were classified mainly around four industries:

EXHIBIT 3   Evolving Smart Card Applications

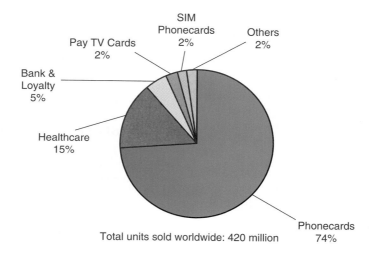

Smart Card Worldwide Applications in 1994

Total units sold worldwide: 420 million

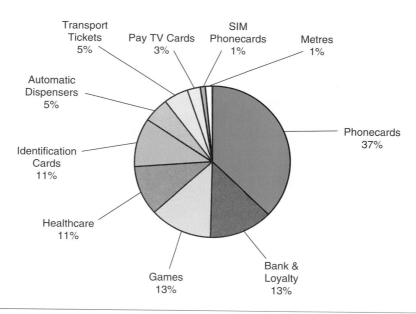

Smart Card Worldwide Applications in 2000 (est.)

Source: Hong Kong: Smart Card Technology Market, Industry Sector Analysis, December 12, 1997

- Within **public transportation**, the smart card technology meant an elegant way of automating fare collection systems in bus, ferry and rail networks. This meant lower operational costs for public transportation operators—usually municipalities, which no longer had to dedicate personnel for the physical ticketing and manual handling of payment monies from passengers. Smart cards also meant speed and convenience for passengers, who no longer had to carry small change for daily commutes;

- Within **telecommunications**, smart card applications could be materialised in a variety of ways. The simplest application was the prepaid phone card that was already ubiquitous in many countries around the world in the early to mid-1990's. A fast-growing application in the late 1990's emerged from mobile telephony: the development of digital mobile telecommunications led to the use of smart cards in mobile phones as subscriber identification modules—SIM. Such modules identified and "signed on" callers on the network every time a call was made. Further, in addition to SIM applications, telecommunications companies and banks could also team up to provide multi-functional smart cards, turning mobile phones essentially into portable automatic teller machines. Other sophisticated functions, such as the reloading of debit cards via mobile phones, were already available in pioneer markets in the late 1990's;

- Within **financial services**, growth opportunities for smart card applications around the world were immense in the early 2000's as most financial transactions were still settled by cash, even in the most sophisticated of markets. In the late 1990's, "electronic purses" that used contact reloadable smart cards embedded with a microprocessor were common. Another kind of financial smart card was the on-line stored-value system, which operated like a debit card to access a traditional deposit account. This type of system involved on-line access to a database for transaction authorisation and data capture purposes;

- **Other applications** such as parking systems or loyalty programmes: traditional coin-operated mechanical parking meters were expensive to operate, as collection could be a complex logistical exercise. Smart card-operated electronic parking devices, on the other hand, could be combined with both smart card-operated electronic payment terminals and pay-and-display machines in car parks. This type of application typically used a disposable contact hardwired logic card on a prepaid credit basis. Another emerging application for smart cards in the late 1990's was the loyalty programme. Cardholders were able to accumulate and redeem bonus points at participating retail stores. Another example was the residential membership smart card system, which aimed to incorporate different functions into a residential card, including parking, electronic purse, Internet booking of club facilities, credit card, shuttle bus and residence identification.

THE VALUE CHAIN SYSTEM FOR SMART CARDS

The value chain in the smart card technology involved several types of suppliers of different functions or capabilities. See Exhibit 4 for an illustration of the industry's value chain. The main functions or capabilities were:[11]

- **Smart card suppliers**: These were the companies that manufactured the smart card. As of the late 1990's the leading smart card manufacturer was France-based Gemplus with an estimated world share of 25%. See Exhibit 5 for a world market share break-up;

- **Smart card IC chip suppliers**: Smart card manufacturers sourced IC chips from semiconductor companies. The leading IC chip manufacturer in the late 1990's was US-based Motorola with an estimated

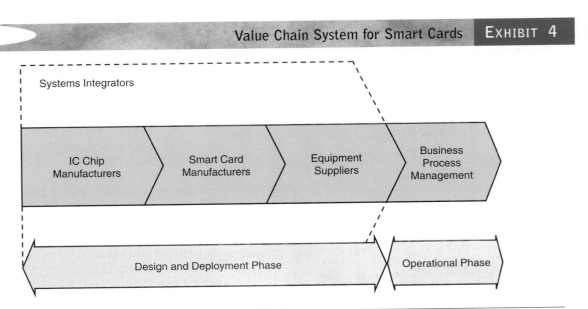

Value Chain System for Smart Cards   EXHIBIT 4

Systems Integrators

IC Chip Manufacturers → Smart Card Manufacturers → Equipment Suppliers → Business Process Management

Design and Deployment Phase | Operational Phase

Derived from Hong Kong: Smart Card Technology Market, Industry Sector Analysis, December 12, 1997

EXHIBIT 5 — Global Smart Card Suppliers (2000 est.)

Company	Origin	World Market Share
Gemplus	France	25%
Schlumberger	USA	21%
Giesecke & Devrient	Germany	12%
Solaic (Schlumberger-owned)	Germany	8%
CP8 (Bull-owned)	France	6%
Orga	USA	5%
Others	—	23%

Source: Hong Kong: Smart Card Technology Market, Industry Sector Analysis, December 12, 1997

EXHIBIT 7 — Global Smart Card Suppliers of Systems and Terminals (2000 est.)

Company	Origin	World Market Share
VeriFone	USA	27%
Schlumberger	USA	15%
Hypercom	USA	13%
Fortronic	United Kingdom	9%
Dassault	France	8%
Others	—	28%

Source: Hong Kong: Smart Card Technology Market, Industry Sector Analysis, December 12, 1997

world share of 18%. See Exhibit 6 for a world market share comparison;

- **Equipment suppliers:** The hardware needed to run smart card systems were typically developed and manufactured by a third group of companies. The leading systems company in the late 1990's was US-based VeriFone with an estimated world share of 27%. See Exhibit 7 for a world market share breakdown. In the software arena, 20% of all microprocessor cards in use worldwide operated with software developed by Bull, the company that had pioneered smart cards in the 1970's. ERG was active in this part of the value chain in its earlier days, albeit the company progressively moved away from manufacturing and into systems integration in the mid-1990's;

- **Smart card systems integrators:** These were the companies that invested heavily in R&D, actively sought out and won bids from clients throughout the world typically by partnering with chip suppliers, smart card suppliers and terminals suppliers. In the late 1990's, ERG was well known as a smart card systems integrator. Other players included (see Exhibit 8): US-based CTS—Cubic Transportation Systems; US-based Catuity; Belgium-based Intellect; France-based Welcome Real-time; and Australian arch-rival Keycorp. In the early 2000's, ERG initiated a bold effort to re-define the industry by developing its MASS—Multi-Application Smart card Solution. With this initiative, ERG aimed for no less than a new industry standard for multi-application smart cards;

- **Business process management:** Once the smart card solution was agreed upon and developed; the hardware and software were installed; and the smart cards were in circulation, there was a need to run the daily operations as well as upkeep and eventually upgrades of the system. Daily operations included the physical collection of fares, hardware maintenance, security and administrative tasks such as accounting and human resource functions. As an example of business process management, the company that operated Hong Kong's successful smart card system—Octopus—upon its commissioning was Creative Star, the joint venture led by ERG. Due to the complexity of certain systems, some customers expressed the desire to award long-

EXHIBIT 6 — Global Smart Card IC Chip Suppliers (2000 est.)

Company	Origin	World Market Share
Motorola	USA	18%
Texas Instruments	USA	15%
SGS Thomson	France	12%
Siemens	Germany	10%
Atmel	USA	6%
Hitachi	Japan	4%
Others	—	35%

Source: Hong Kong: Smart Card Technology Market, Industry Sector Analysis, December 12, 1997

Company	Financials (2000)	Business description
Catuity—USA	Revenues: US$0.7m Net income: (US$3.8m)	Catuity is a loyalty software specialist. Major relationships with Visa, IBM, Schlumberger, and Gemplus.
Cubic Corporation—USA: • CTS • Defence Division • Industrial Division	Revenues: US$531.1m Net income: US$0.6m (Cubic Corporation)	CTS is an automated fare company. Major projects included London, New York City, Washington DC, Chicago, Shanghai, Bangkok and Singapore.
Intellect—Belgium (also traded in the Australian Stock Exchange)	Revenues: A$71.4m Net income: A$9.4m	Intellect offers a range of highly secure electronic commerce solutions, including smart card technology, secure data transmission and electronic funds transfer.
Keycorp—Australia	Revenues: A$105.7m Net income: (A$14.7m)	Keycorp are providers of secure electronic transaction terminals, cards, and payments engines.
Welcome Real-time—France	Financials not available. Headcount in 2000: +/−60	Welcome Real-time are providers of smart card customer loyalty and electronic coupon software.

Source: Company websites

term operational contracts to systems suppliers themselves. Thus, ERG operated by the early 2000's their systems in Melbourne, Rome, San Francisco and Manchester.[12]

In the early 2000's, most smart card solutions required a certain degree of custom development given specific client needs. A technical solution for a specific client problem did make use of technology applied elsewhere, still this young industry had yet to experience the potential of industry standards—such as the industry standard already long in use in personal computer software, for instance. It was widely believed that the impact of industry standards in the smart cards industry could be phenomenal, dramatically bringing down the costs of smart cards applications and add-ons. The smart cards industry was also characterised by the fact that most smart card clients were either governmental agencies—such as the local authorities that operated or granted operation of public transportation networks—or companies in industries with some degree of government regulation in most markets around the world—such as mobile telephony or financial services.

Within the smart card industry, it was not unusual for companies to compete in more than one function of the value chain. Smart card player Schlumberger, for instance, was a manufacturer of both smart cards and systems or terminals. Thus, it could be both a competitor and a supplier to ERG. The need for client customisation—usually within regulated markets—combined with a complex value chain in the industry meant that smart card players typically formed consortia of companies prior to tackling specific bids as put forth by prospective clients. And in this global industry, it was not unusual for such smart card consortia to incorporate new companies geographically close to the prospective client. These "bid-focused" companies were typically structured with stock ownership from smart card players in different functions of the industry value chain.

Due to the need for custom solutions and given a certain degree of regulation, smart cards tender processes were typically complex and time consuming, with several months or even quarters elapsing before the announcement of the finalists and then winners of the tender. For smart cards players such as ERG, this required upfront investments—sometimes millions of dollars—in the tender process, for which there was no guarantee of success. In case of a successful tender, ERG could foresee a steady stream of revenues, but it still could take ERG two years to break even in the specific project. Typically from the second year onwards, the smart cards player could reap the benefits of all its hard work. A smart cards player in early business stages—with plenty of outstanding bids but few completed projects in its portfolio—had to be careful about managing cash. This was important because tender costs were expensed immediately when incurred, whereas the related revenue stream might not be achieved for a few years. Thus, a critical mass of ongoing projects was necessary for funding purposes of future opportunities.

EARLY DAYS AT ERG: A ROUGH START

The city of Perth is one of the most isolated enclaves on Earth. Sydney and the east coast are a four-hour flight away whereas northbound Singapore cannot be reached before a five-hour jet haul. Perth is the capital of hot, dry Western Australia, a state better known for mineral resources than for high tech. The Perth-based company Energy Research Group Australia Limited—later to be known as the ERG Group—was publicly listed in 1984. ERG was then struggling in the automated fare collection business with an annual turnover of only A$1m and losses of twice that amount.[13] In 1986, a shareholder revolt led to the hiring of a new management team. Peter Fogarty, who had joined the ERG board as a non-executive director in 1984, was appointed Executive Chairman in 1985 and CEO in 1991. He led ERG into the early 2000's. See Exhibit 9 for a brief bio on CEO Fogarty and other ERG board members.

In 1987, ERG started to expand in the automated fare collection business by acquiring a controlling interest in Associated Electronic Services—AES, a small company that then focused on fare collection but had tentative plans to pursue smart card opportunities. In 1989, ERG went beyond its core smart card application—then in public transportation—to pursue related applications for potential telecom clients by acquiring Radiolab, a then small telecom equipment contractor.[14]

It was also in 1989 that ERG executed its first smart card project. The move into telecom applications subsequently led to an important coup for ERG in 1990: the negotiated strategic alliance with Nokia, the world leader in mobile telephony from Finland. ERG and Nokia subsequently launched a joint venture to supply mobile phone equipment to Australia, a market that was growing rapidly in the wake of privatisation. ERG became responsible for the manufacturing of Nokia phones in a Perth-based facility. In 1992, ERG and Nokia won critical contracts with Optus Communications, Bell South NZ and Telstra.[15] These provided ERG with a stream of regular cash flow and helped compensate dips between discrete fare collection contracts.[16]

Following its first smart card project in 1989, ERG expanded its beachhead in public transportation by acquiring Belgium-based Prodata in 1993 and combining it with previously acquired AES.[17] AES Prodata then became ERG Transit Systems, the division that was later responsible for two major breakthroughs for the company in the early 1990's: the Hong Kong project and the Melbourne project.

THE HONG KONG PROJECT: A SHOWCASE FOR ERG

In June 1994, Hong Kong's five major privately-owned public transportation operators—including rail, bus and ferry operations—formed a joint venture company, Creative Star, to develop an automated fare collection system based on contactless smart cards. The fare collection contract, then valued at US$55m, was awarded to ERG and its subsidiary AES Prodata, which subsequently awarded the contactless card portion of the

---

contract to Sony and Mitsubishi. These contactless reloadable smart cards, known as Octopus cards, were fully operational in September 1997. An estimated 10 million passenger journeys were then made each day on Hong Kong's multi-modal public transport services.[18]

The Octopus project was highly successful and became a showcase for potential ERG clients. Unlike most ticketing systems, which required the ticket to pass through a mechanical device, the secret to the smart card ERG introduced in Hong Kong was that it did not come into contact with anything. A microprocessor embedded in plastic—which possessed the computing power of IBM's first personal computer—was activated when passed over a target device. This device powered the card and enabled it to communicate with the target. Once a form of radio contact was established, there was a two-way exchange of information between the card and the target. The card was identified and reported its remaining value; the target assessed if there was enough value in the card to enter the station. If so, it transmitted date, time and station of entry. If not, the passenger would not be able to enter the boarding premises. A similar process occurred at the end of a journey, with the cost of the fare being deducted on exit. A user did not have to take the plastic out of his or her purse: it sufficed to pass it over the target to gain access to the station or bus.[19] When the Octopus system was commissioned in 1997, there were 3 million cards in use. By 2000, this number had more than doubled to 7 million. Passengers could travel on ferry, bus, light rail, heavy rail and underground services provided by 30 service operators using their Octopus card.[20]

In 2000, the Octopus system was the largest integrated contactless smart card fare collection system in the world. The Hong Kong project became a global reference for smart card applications within public transportation: by 2001, about 60 cities around the world were actively reviewing the Octopus system to determine their own requirements.[21] And following Hong Kong, ERG won contracts to install and run smart-card transit systems in Singapore, Melbourne, San Francisco, Berlin and Rome.

THE MELBOURNE PROJECT: A FINANCIAL BURDEN

At the same time that ERG was awarded the hugely important Hong Kong project, the company became heavily involved with a bid for a second project of equally large scale in Melbourne, Australia. Like Hong Kong, ERG subsequently won the bid, this time with partner Fujitsu. Unlike Hong Kong, Melbourne became a frustrating experience that eventually led to a serious financial impact on the ERG balance sheet.

When commissioned in 1999, the Melbourne Automated Fare Collection Project was the world's first fully outsourced fare collection system in operation.[22] However, a series of technical difficulties led to delays that caused the project to be commissioned and signed-off later than expected. This led to tie-ups of ERG capital to the project until it was refinanced in 1999, negatively impacting ERG's fiscal year 1998 as CEO Fogarty reported an "increase to A$6.7m in interest expense caused largely by capital committed to the Melbourne project."[23] Even though the Melbourne project had a Government-guaranteed revenue stream of approximately A$370m over the remaining term of the contract, the bad press that it generated depressed ERG shares. ERG voluntarily suspended trading of its shares on September 29, 1997 after a plunge of around 40% in its share price following adverse press coverage of its fare-collection contract with the Victorian Government.[24]

Most of the blame for contract variation cost claims and broken ticket machines—as well as consumer complaints—was later geared towards Victoria's Public Transport Authority for not foreseeing these contract-related problems. Meanwhile, Sydney awarded in 2001 its smart card system—due to be commissioned in 2003—to ERG and Motorola. Sydney would use completely different technology to Melbourne's, but the operator of both contracts would be the same: ERG. CEO Fogarty did not expect problems similar to Melbourne's to occur in Sydney: "The fundamental difference is that Sydney already has a modern ticketing system, unlike Melbourne which went straight from an old to a new system. ERG has learnt out of bitter experience and we are doing everything we can to eliminate risk in the [Sydney] structure. The [Sydney] department has conducted a very detailed request for tender process." This project would encompass more than 5,000 buses, the train and ferry network, monorail and Sydney airport link. Between 1.5 million and 3 million smart cards, both anonymous and personalised, would eventually be distributed.[25]

THE MOTOROLA PARTNERSHIP

Partly as a result of Melbourne-related financial commitments, ERG and Motorola—the American technology giant—formed a worldwide alliance in 1997 to pursue transportation-related smart card projects. ERG thus issued unsecured subordinated convertible notes to raise A$30m. The notes would convert into 18 million ERG shares at a conversion price of A$1.65 per share. The rest of the deal involved the issue of 27 million shares in ERG at the same issue price of A$1.65 to Motorola to raise an additional A$45m. At conversion, Motorola came out with a 20%-stake in ERG.[26] ERG then entered the development of smart card travel systems in a venture with Motorola. This venture would later win many contracts around the world.[27]

EXPANDING IN ASIA: THE SINGAPORE PROJECT

The alliance with Motorola started to pay off almost immediately. In 1999, ERG and Motorola's Worldwide Smartcard Solutions Division (WSSD) were awarded a US$75m contract to supply an integrated smart card fare collection system for the public transport network of Singapore. The Land Transport Authority of Singapore awarded the contract for the Enhanced Integrated Fare System to the ERG-Motorola alliance following an extensive international tendering process over several months. Five public transport operators were expected to use the system, which included approximately 3,750 buses as well as mass rapid transit (MRT) and light rapid transit (LRT) operations.

The system was expected to involve a total of 22,000 readers and an initial 5 million smart cards, making the Singapore System one of the largest integrated smart card based transit systems in the world. Additionally, the contract provided for the ERG-Motorola alliance to deliver the infrastructure for smart card and central clearinghouse operations. The central clearinghouse system was based on ERG's automated clearinghouse and data processing network. Motorola provided customised support services, including systems integration and maintenance. The system was expected to be commissioned in 2002, and was designed so that further smart card applications could be added to the initial transit application. In the future, the system could also integrate electronic cash payments and other non-financial applications. The ERG-Motorola alliance bid for the project as a consortium that also involved key local Singaporean companies—including Singaporean Technologies Computer Systems, Keppel Engineering and Knowledge Engineering—to help carry out the work.[28]

ALLIANCES AS A CATALYST FOR GROWTH

ERG's alliance with Motorola continued to yield results as Dutch authorities awarded in July 1999 a contract to Motorola and ERG for approximately A$3.8bn to enhance bus services in the city of Groningen. The city implemented a field trial of an integrated smart card automated fare collection system called Tripperpas. Passengers simply waved their cards in front of a reader to board the bus—reducing long queues at bus stops and eliminating the need to search for change, making their commute more convenient and efficient. Additionally, passengers could take advantage of the technology to receive the best price for the distance they travel on buses. According to Kees Arends, Managing Director of bus operator Arriva: "The flexibility of Tripperpas will allow integration with other forms of public transport, like train, taxi and disabled transport and the innovative back office solution captures operational data that can be used to determine how to operate the transport system more efficiently. We are very pleased that the co-operation with Motorola will lead to an open market of public transport."[29]

ERG expanded its network once more in June 1999 by announcing an alliance with Westpac Banking. According to then ERG Card Systems Managing Director Richard Fleming: "We are currently looking at developing customised smart cards solutions for [other parties] in transit, and we'll see some announcements about that in the next two to three weeks. We, on purpose, didn't take an exclusive arrangement with them, but clearly there are other banks in the marketplace who we wish to keep open the option to discuss with."[30] Under the alliance, Westpac became the principal EFT-POS (electronic financial transaction at point-of-sale) transaction processor for ERG's e-purse reload and ticketing products.[31]

Another important relationship started in September 1999 as UK-based Stagecoach Holdings and ERG launched a joint venture—Prepayment Cards—to provide smart card technology for transport services across the UK. The company believed the system would set industry standards within UK transport groups and operators. The joint venture was owned by Stagecoach, Sema Group—a smart card manufacturer—and ERG. This ERG-developed system acted as a clearinghouse by issuing cards, holding funds and acting as a settlement facility between transport operators. It also provided real time passenger journey information.[32]

This joint venture then signed a deal with the UK Post Office in June 2000 to introduce smart cards for the British travel and ticket markets. Under the agreement, the UK Post Office provided a card issuing and recharging service across the UK to the 28 million customers that visited their outlets per week.[33] In September 1999, this joint venture also announced Prepayment Cards had been awarded a contract by the Greater Manchester Passenger Transport Executive to manage a smart card scheme for the city's bus services.[34]

The role of strategic alliances and JV's was central to the ERG growth strategy. See Exhibit 10 for a reference of key ERG alliances as of 2001. The strong presence of financial services partners on this list indicated that ERG expected plenty of smart card activity in this area.

ERG Alliances as of 2001 — EXHIBIT 10

ERG retains a policy of developing strategic alliances in areas, which can lead to technology transfer and commercial advantage. ERG has formed alliances with a number of companies to provide a broader depth of expertise and professional service to its customers. ERG's alliance partners include:

- The Bank of Western Australia
- card.etc AG
- Downer Group Limited
- ECard Pty Limited
- Prepayment Cards Limited
- Proton World International SA
- Sun Microsystems
- The Post Office (UK)
- Triumphant Launch Sdn Bhd
- Unisys Corporation
- Westpac Banking Corporation

Source: www.erggroup.com, November 2001

REDEFINING FOCUS FOR THE 2000'S

To ERG, the early 1990's had been very successful. The company not only entered the smart card business, but it also established itself in this global industry by winning important contracts in Belgium, Hong Kong, Australia and Argentina.[35] See Exhibit 11 for a list of key ERG contracts for transportation clients. By the mid-1990's, ERG's internal structure followed clients and their main smart card applications. ERG had then three main divisions: transit systems, which focused on public transportation; card systems, which focused on financial and loyalty applications; and telecommunications, which focused on telecom applications.

But in the late 1990's, telecom clients were becoming less important as ERG's growth focus shifted to the expansion of the smart card business through software systems that also allowed cards to be used for other purposes. Already in pioneer markets such as Hong Kong, ERG's cards could be used in pay telephones and photo booths. This was leading to the establishment of new kinds of alliances with banking and telecommunications groups.[36]

Thus, ERG made a major strategic move in 2000 as US-based SCI Systems and ERG announced a global telecom manufacturing services alliance. To initiate the alliance, SCI acquired ERG's telecom manufacturing businesses in Perth—Western Australia—and Belgium. This transaction represented another major global alliance for ERG and provided a significant opportunity for SCI to benefit from continued growth of telecom and wireless outsourcing. ERG gained access to SCI's global distributed manufacturing capacity and engineering expertise, which operated in 39 locations across 17 countries. SCI assumed ERG's contract to manufacture Nokia base stations at the Perth facility, as well as assuming the manufacturing contract between ERG's telecommunications and transit businesses. According to ERG CEO Fogarty, "ERG's clear strategy has been to maximise its capability of exploiting its

ERG Transit Systems Update as of Late 2001 — EXHIBIT 11

Project	Status
Manchester	Equipment largely installed, commissioning Q1-02, A$11m invested
San Francisco	Commissioning scheduled Q4-01, A$26m invested
Singapore	Implementation commenced, commissioning Q4-01, A$80m invested
Rome	Implementation finalised, commissioning Q4-01, over A$70m invested
Bordeaux	Commenced Sep 2001
Gothenburg	Commenced Oct 2001
Rhein-Ruhr region	Scheduled to begin Dec 2001
Oslo	Scheduled to begin Dec 2001
Sydney	Scheduled to begin Dec 2001
Hong Kong LRT	Scheduled to begin Jan 2002
Seattle	Scheduled to begin Mar 2002

Source: ERG presentation to shareholders, October 2001

EXHIBIT 12 ERG Main Divisions as of 2001

ERG Transit Systems is a world leader in automated fare collection products and systems for all modes of transport utilising all types of ticket technology including paper, magnetic stripe and contactless and dual interface (contact/contactless) smart cards. The company specialises in providing fully integrated systems for transit operators, from backend processing to depot computer software, to on-vehicle or on-station equipment.

ERG Card Systems provides smart card systems and solutions which can incorporate membership programmes, loyalty schemes, security access, biometric data and social security information; as well as electronic purse functions including retail, public transport ticketing, telephone, road tolling, vending and parking. The Company provides smart cards system design, integration expertise and project management services for all types of smart card projects.

Source: ERG 2000 Annual Report at www.erggroup.com, November 2001

leading edge technology in the rapidly expanding smart card industry. The sale of the telecommunications manufacturing business positions ERG to continue its rapid growth." SCI, on the other hand, continued to focus on its commitment to manufacturing and related services for its clients.[37]

Thus in 2001, ERG's number of main divisions was focused down to two—Transit Systems and Card Systems—with revenues almost equally split between the two. See Exhibit 12 for divisional descriptions and see Exhibit 13 for ERG's presence worldwide. ERG was by then a company that generated revenues from five different sources:[38] the licensing of its technology; revenue shares of its equity and JV's; sale of equity investments; systems build and supply; and systems operations.

A VISION OF MULTIPLE APPLICATIONS: MASS

ERG had a vision for the future of the smart cards industry. It went beyond the belief that the general public clearly saw the benefits of using smart cards for shopping, taking the train, making a phone call or proving identification. ERG was convinced that the general public would be interested in all of those functions with the use of just one card—the multi-application card. And central to the development of multi-application smart cards were financial applications, without which any multiple-application smart card was hard to conceive. ERG believed that its Card Systems division would be in the best position to reap the benefits of widespread multiple-application smart cards.

According to a rights issue prospectus to ERG shareholders dated November 2001: "ERG has had a long-held view that smart cards will ultimately have widespread usage for a variety of applications such as

transit, tolls, telephones, security, healthcare, identity and memberships. [One] of the inhibiting factors in developing smart card usage to date [has] been the lack of compatibility between major vendors' operating systems. [. . .] ERG's strategy has been targeted at reducing some of these barriers in order to attempt to position itself at the forefront of the development of the smart card industry. ERG's smart card strategy is to add more functionality to the cards it and its customers use and to create a unified smart card platform."[39]

Hence the importance of the ERG effort labelled as MASS—Multi-Application Smart card Solution.

EXHIBIT 13 ERG Offices as of 2001

ERG has offices in the following countries:

Continent	Offices
Americas	• Brazil • Canada • USA
Australasia	• Australia—Perth, Brisbane, Melbourne, Sydney • Hong Kong • Malaysia • Singapore
Europe	• Belgium • Germany • France • Italy • United Kingdom • Sweden

Source: www.erggroup.com, November 2001

MASS was a central computer processing system that was capable of managing a smart card database including financial reconciliation and management data gathering for multiple applications. The development of MASS started in 1997 and consumed over four years of internally funded investments—which totalled A$100m by 2001.[40] For a company of 2001 sales of A$299m, this was a large investment in the dream of ubiquitous multi-application smart cards around the world. ERG management reasoned that, in the near future, their installed systems—in addition to the transit systems being installed—would handle 29 million transactions per day in 200 cities around the world; this project base was expected to demonstrate the benefits of the funds devoted to the development of MASS.[41]

Moving forward towards its multi-application dream, ERG joined in 1998 other smart card players to create Proton World, giving a boost to common smart card and electronic purse standards. The partnership included: American Express (the US financial services giant), Banksys (a Belgian company of automatic teller machine networks), Interpay (a JV between ERG and all major Dutch banks such as ING, Amro and Rabobank) and Visa (the largest credit card company in the world). Proton World was a high-tech company focused on the delivery of smart card solutions worldwide. It developed and licensed Proton smart card applications, which had already been chosen by over 20 countries. The first application had been launched in Belgium in 1995. The Proton technology was the most broadly implemented in national roll-outs and was also the most actively used worldwide: by mid-2000, Proton-based smart card schemes had together performed more than 166 million e-purse transactions since its introduction. It also had the largest acceptance base, with more than 280,000 terminals installed worldwide. In June 2000, the Computerworld Smithsonian Award (CWSA) in the Finance, Insurance & Real Estate category was awarded to Proton World at a gala dinner at the National Building Museum in Washington, DC.[42]

By 2001, over 500 banks had deployed Proton technology around the world. And in October 2001, ERG announced the full acquisition of Proton in a stock-and-cash deal. Upon the sale of their shares, former shareholders American Express, Banksys and Interpay announced they remained committed to the use of the Proton platform for their own applications.[43] See Exhibit 14 for a snapshot of the merged ERG-Proton organisation and Exhibit 15 for a systems architecture. ERG described its Proton investment as "critical to gaining a central position in the development of the smart cards industry by supporting an open security platform as an industry standard."[44]

ERG Acquisition of Proton — EXHIBIT 14

ERG:
- World leader in fare collection equipment and software systems for the transit industry with globally diverse customer base: 13 countries over 4 continents
- Recurring revenue from ongoing operations of transit systems and maintenance revenue from ticketing

Proton:
- Global leader in the development of high-security smart card applications, and offers end-to-end solutions from card through to hosting
- Alliance with high margin bank and finance services

Merged entity:
- The acquisition is consistent with ERG's strategy of penetrating the higher value end of the smart card value chain, providing ERG with an entry point into banking and finance services
- ERG's smart card systems and services business represents an area of significant growth, especially in light of Proton
- Merged group will have strong alliances with a number of key strategic partners, including AmEx, Banksys, Interpay, Visa

Source: ERG presentation to shareholders, October 2001

During ERG's annual shareholders' meeting in 2001, Chairman Sandy Murdoch referred to the Proton acquisition as follows: "The new ERG balance sheet will have an amount of goodwill attributed to the acquiring company. Current Australian accounting standards require this amount to be amortised through the P&L statement. On a global stage, this treatment prejudices companies like us. Under US accounting standards, no such amortisation charge is required. Our auditors [. . .] have made submissions to the standard setters on this point in an effort to align Australian standards with the US."[45]

Strengthening its technology base further for a multi-application future, ERG announced in November 2001 the acquisition of a licence to Motorola's Venus Platform smart card technology. The Venus technology was the only smart card technology in the world today capable of supporting high-speed contactless smart card transactions that also had Proton World certification.

EXHIBIT 15   ERG-Proton Systems Architecture

Smart Cards Systems Architecture

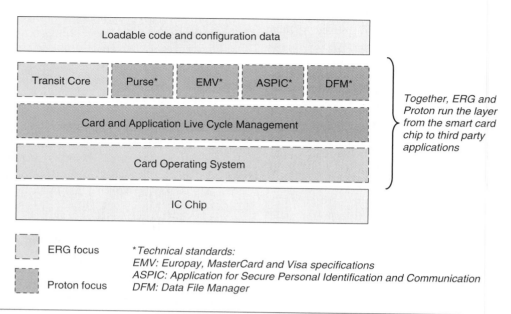

Source: ERG presentation to shareholders, October 2001

The Venus technology provided an operating system embedded on the chip of a smart card. Its presence facilitated the use of applications such as those developed by Proton World. ERG already used the technology in transit projects such as San Francisco, Rome and Manchester.

ERG's Chief Technology Officer, Viv Miners, said the Venus technology was important to ERG's expansion beyond transit applications of smart cards: "The ERG portfolio now includes Venus—a platform that ideally complements our Proton acquisition. The two transactions are significant steps in ERG's strategy to penetrate markets beyond the transit sector. The Venus platform's compliance with international standards ensures ERG can offer smart cards for any application. ERG is a true 'one-stop-shop' for the multiple applications of smart cards demanded by our customers."[46]

The concept of "one-stop-shop" that ERG was pursuing meant another advantage vis-à-vis potential competitors: the use of a shared back-office infrastructure for multiple applications given a common geography. In City A, for instance, ERG had to build a back-office infrastructure to handle its first-time installation of a transit system. For nearby City B, on the other hand, any tendered application could be run on the back-office initially built for City A. This cascading

effect could give ERG considerable cost advantages versus competitors in the near future (see Exhibit 16).

LOOKING INSIDE ERG

Over a 10-year period, ERG experienced a significant transformation as it moved away from a manufacturing company to a systems integrator and smart card leader. According to CEO Fogarty, "not all of our [1,000] employees or management have been able to make the adjustment. This has necessitated constant restructuring and reinventing of the company as a whole and of our people. Many employees who are valuable to the organisation have changed their role and become better contributors. Our staff turnover has been relatively low and all employees feel they have contributed to and shared in the group's success."[47]

As the company went global in the early 1990's, ERG top management came to the conclusion that they lacked some of the skills—particularly languages—necessary to succeed as a global business. Thus, ERG embarked on a plan to acquire multilingual staff through acquisition and/or alliances so that ERG could expand globally with the right personnel and skills. For Perth-based executives in search of business around the world, ERG plans meant a very demanding travel

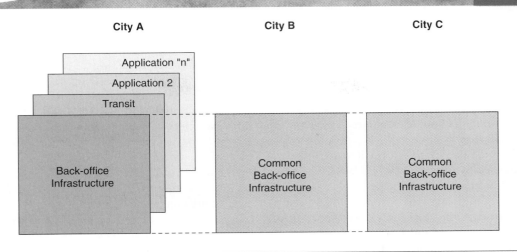

City A   City B   City C

Application "n"

Application 2

Transit

Back-office Infrastructure

Common Back-office Infrastructure

Common Back-office Infrastructure

Source: 2001 annual meeting of shareholders, November 2001

schedule. During ERG's 2001 shareholders' meeting, CEO Fogarty thanked his top management for the hard work as he mentioned that "some of our executives tendering overseas found themselves working 21 to 23 hours a day in critical phases of the process."[48] In late 2001, ERG restructured to reflect its global nature.

In late 2001, CEO Fogarty appointed three Managing Directors for key ERG markets: Asia Pacific, Europe and the Americas. Rob Noble, former CEO of Creative Star in Hong Kong, was appointed Managing Director for Asia Pacific. Armand Linkens was appointed Managing Director for Europe reporting to Franky Carbonez, Executive Chairman of European Operations. A Managing Director for the Americas was yet to be announced.[49]

According to CEO Fogarty, "the selection of Board members was also an important part of the ERG global expansion plan: the company saw its business as marketing-driven and a more conservative Board may have restricted ERG's ability to expand."[50] Finally, believing that employees should be stakeholders and not just workers, ERG management introduced a broad employee stock-ownership plan. According to CEO Fogarty, "the shares have restrictions that tie the employee to the company and [. . .] extend their commitment period. I believe that the employee shareholder plan has been fundamental to our success."[51]

ERG STOCK TAKES OFF IN 2000

Fiscal year 2000 was good for ERG. Global equity markets—especially technology issues—entered in Q2-2000 a bear market of epic proportions that dragged deep

into 2001. But in faraway Perth, the stream of good news from ERG was too strong to remain ignored.

Positive announcements included:[52] a technology concessionary scheme agreement for Greater Manchester; a new contract from LaTrobe University in Victoria to provide smart cards; together with Telstra and ANZ, the formation of a joint company to provide a common standard infrastructure for smart cards in Australia; and a new contract to design and install equipment to extend the use of the Octopus system in Hong Kong. In addition, ERG won three awards in 2000: the Business Asia Award for best use of Australian technology in Asia; the Australian Technology Award for excellence in commercialisation of technology; and the Australian Technology Award for excellence in the development of electronic commerce and Internet technology.

As a result, the ERG stock jumped in 2000 from a split-adjusted A$0.35 to A$4.50 per share and the company announced a 3-for-1 stock split. It was the best performing Top 100 stock in the Australian Stock Exchange that year as ERG announced substantial increases in both revenues (up 54%) and earnings (up 44%) for fiscal year 2000.

ERG STOCK DID POORLY IN 2001

As ERG confidently entered fiscal year 2001, the company landed a series of new contracts in addition to ongoing projects. New contracts included:[53] a joint venture with the New South Wales Road Motoring Association to issue smart cards to all of its 2 million members; a joint venture with the operator of the Victorian Road Tolling network, to integrate smart card with existing tolling technology; the creation of a joint venture in the Netherlands with ABN Amro, Rabobank and ING via a bank-owned entity—Interpay—to take a licence of ERG's multi-application technology (MASS); selection as preferred proponent for the major Sydney integrated transit project in a joint venture with Motorola; new contracts in Gothenburg and Oslo for smart cards; and a new contract to supply an integrated transit solution to the region of Bordeaux in France with Schlumberger—in addition to winning 11 out of 14 contracts tendered in France in the 18 months prior.

But unlike the previous year, fiscal year 2001 was also characterised by negative news on ERG. The flow was constant throughout the fiscal year:

- On 26 February 2001, ERG announced the restructuring of one of its most successful alliances—Motorola. Financial markets interpreted the announcement as a negative development, since ERG and Motorola had together won several smart cards contracts worldwide since their 1997 agreement. ERG shares fell 24% to A$1.87, after the company revealed it would pay A$46m to dissolve a ticketing system alliance formed with Motorola. The shares then fell further on news that Motorola's remaining 13% stake in ERG was up for sale. This drop occurred despite ERG's announcement of a 7%-rise in net profit to A$16m for the six months to December 2000 on revenue of A$184m, up 4% on an annual basis.[54] CEO Fogarty disagreed with the market's interpretation of the ERG-Motorola relationship restructuring, particularly given the fact that it had been ERG that had approached Motorola: "ERG will be free to pursue a broader range of projects such as the important win in Bordeaux in association with a different partner—Schlumberger. Further, the restructuring did not mean severance: ERG-Motorola will continue a relationship, but without the restrictions of the former structure."[55]

- In August 2001, more bad news on ERG hit the Australian business press as ERG announced profits for fiscal 2001 of only A$6m on revenues of A$299m.[56] These results were unexpectedly low, and followed an agreement by ERG management to change the accounting treatment of licence fees. ERG auditors Pricewaterhouse Coopers had refused to sign off a A$31m of contribution to earnings from the sale of its multi-application software system—MASS—in return for equity in the German smart card joint venture card.etc.[57] The auditors' final opinion was that the considered receivable was not sufficiently measurable and that

there was no sufficient probability that the economic benefit would follow. Had this receivable been recognised as revenue, ERG profits would have been A$37m rather than the reported A$6m. Financial analysts mentioned lack of financial transparency. ERG suspended trading on its shares, and when trading resumed, the stock plunged to A$0.58 from around A$1 in heavy trading.[58] The newly appointed ERG CFO, Michael Slater, later mentioned: "We will continue discussions with our auditors in order to assess whether this transaction will be booked in the current financial year. As we have stated on previous occasions, the revenue has not been lost or disallowed, but deferred until future events allow its recognition."[59]

- In the same month of August, the Motorola relationship restructuring was once more the source of bad news as one broker report mentioned: "Also questioned is the impact the overhang of the Motorola convertible notes have on the Company now that the stock is trading near the conversion rate of A$0.55 per share. Motorola converting these notes would potentially extract the full remaining cash balance of [ERG] of A$35m thus leaving the balance sheet weak for taking advantage of future opportunities."[60] In the meantime, ERG continued to slide in heavy trading volume. CEO Fogarty vigorously fought this claim on the Motorola notes, pointing out that the convertible notes issued to Motorola did not mature and would thus not be redeemable until October 2002. But the markets did not react symmetrically to good and bad news.

The overall effect on the ERG stock was devastating. The share price that had started 2000 at a split-adjusted price of A$0.35 and skyrocketed to A$4.50 by year-end 2000, was soon back to A$0.60 by late 2001 (see Exhibit 2). CEO Fogarty summarised the fortunes of the ERG stock as follows: "There is no rhyme or reason to what institutions are doing in the market. They sell stock when it suits them best, not caring what they get for it, not caring what damage they do to companies by doing it. On the other side of the ledger, you've got retail day traders playing games in the market. We see things in analysts' reports like ERG being on the verge of global success but it is only missing one thing: it needs to tie up a relationship with more banks. We then announce a deal with every major bank in Holland, and the same analyst says 'not bad, but they must win Sydney.' We win Sydney and they say we must question whether Sydney will ever get signed."[61]

In reply to CEO Fogarty's statements, analysts mentioned that ERG remained a high-risk stock: the company had a solid chance of capitalising on MASS and breaking into new markets given the strength of its banking and telecom JV's around the world. But MASS had yet to run live in any site by 2001, let alone become the industry standard. According to Deutsche Bank analyst Noel Webster: "ERG is banking everything on the possibility of owning or being a part-shareholder in processing enormous amounts of card transactions as well as owning the software. Shareholders are therefore buying an option on the potential for ERG to be extremely successful with MASS. It's an all-or-nothing strategy."[62]

During the November 2001 annual general meeting of shareholders held in Perth, ERG Chairman Sandy Murdoch commented: "Despite [our continuous operational success], you will no doubt be aware that our share price has not performed well this year. We are conscious of the concerns of the shareholders and are working hard to ensure the value of the company is fully reflected in the share price. We acknowledge that we will have to clearly demonstrate sound cash flows and profitability for the market to re-rate our stock."[63]

WHAT LIES AHEAD: ERG BEYOND 2002

CEO Fogarty completed 10 years of service at the rudder of ERG in 2001. He was proud of what ERG had accomplished since the mid-1980's. Even though he was convinced that the wild ERG stock price fluctuations were caused by inaccurate media reports, CEO Fogarty knew he would prove rumours wrong by returning ERG to the fast-growth track and keeping it there in the immediate future.

He believed that, once the entire ERG project pipeline was executed, the company would be capable of "bringing in A$300m of recurring revenues"[64] per year. He was also optimistic about new contracts. For instance, Visa and MasterCard had just announced that they would require every affiliated bank in Europe to swap their magnetic stripe cards for smart cards by 2005, or else bear any fraud-related liability.[65] This development was great news for ERG. CEO Fogarty believed the following questions were of highest importance:

1. **How should ERG define itself**: ERG evolved from an incipient electronics display company in the late 1980's to a smart card leader in the early 2000's. CEO Fogarty knew what ERG's competencies were but still he wondered how should ERG define itself for the 2000's. Regarding industry focus, CEO Fogarty had already started to pursue a strategy of multi-function applications by betting heavily on MASS. Should ERG focus solely on MASS or should it also look elsewhere for growth?

2. **How to enable growth**: In this young industry, central to ERG's strategy was the network of relationships it developed around the world. These took form as strategic alliances, JV's, equity investments and M&A activity. But the question as of how to enable growth was intrinsically linked with the question centred on how ERG should define itself. Looking at the industry value chain, CEO Fogarty knew that he had to have critical skills in-house and that less critical skills could be dealt with differently. For the critical skills, R&D was essential. See Exhibit 17 for an R&D expenditure comparison with major companies in high-tech industries. Which skills would be key for ERG's success in the 2000's? What would be the role of ERG's extensive network in the future?

3. **How to measure success**: CEO Fogarty was proud of the fact that, in the 1990's, ERG had been able to clock a compound average growth rate of over 40%—despite a disappointing fiscal year 2001. But he also knew that the industry itself as well as some key players were growing at not too dissimilar rates. How should he measure success? Should CEO Fogarty consider players such as CTS and Keycorp his competitors and thus worry about market share? If positive, should he think broadly or about specific segments of the value chain? Additionally, should he measure success based on revenue growth rates, EBITDA, or both? Should he report recurring cash flow streams to the financial community more frequently? Following the wild swings in ERG stock prices in 2000 and 2001, CEO Fogarty learned that expectations management was an integral part of his job.

4. **How to deal with stock market speculation**: To CEO Fogarty, this hardly seemed a strategic issue on the surface but he knew that the implications of ignoring it could run deep. Regarding share ownership by broad segments of the general population, Australians already ranked number one in the world by the early 2000's, surpassing the Americans (see Exhibit 18). In the short term, this meant increased volatility for stocks in general vis-à-vis less liquid markets. With this in mind, CEO Fogarty announced in late 2001 that the new senior position of Investor Relations officer had been created, and that Shaun Duffy would be responsible for this function. It was clear to CEO Fogarty that the recent battering on ERG stock affected his company's capacity to expand its network of strategic relationships, not to mention the negative impact

| EXHIBIT 17 | R&D Expenditure Comparison (R&D as % of Sales) |

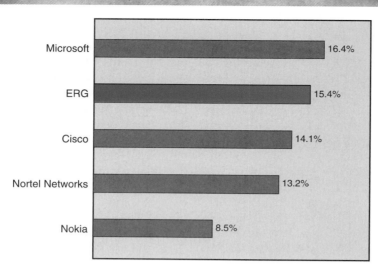

Source: Annual reports. All figures for fiscal year 2000, except ERG (FY2001)

| EXHIBIT 18 | Direct Stock Ownership by Country |

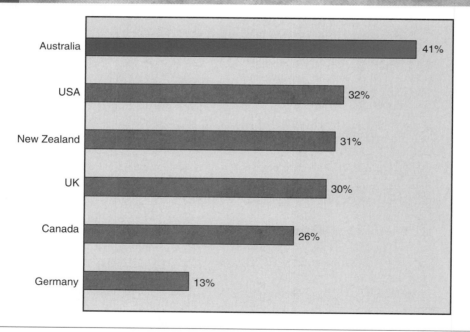

Source: Share Ownership Survey 2000 at www.asx.com.au

on employee morale as ERG stock was also widely held within the company's ranks. After the 80%-slide of its stock price, was ERG a likely takeover target? See Exhibit 19 for a sample of ERG typical trading volumes. In the area of investor relations, what else could CEO Fogarty do to avoid wild fluctuations in ERG stock?

5. **How to structure internally for the future:** ERG announced in 2001 a new structure of three regional Managing Directors. Was this structure the most appropriate one for a global industry? Should ERG maintain its focus on large-ticket projects and not proactively chase smaller tenders? Closely linked to this issue was the fact that ERG top management

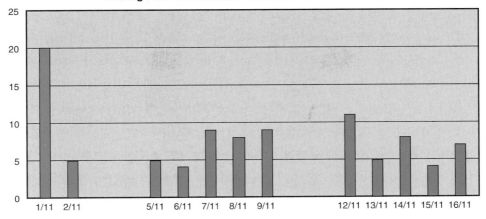

Trading Volume in Millions of Shares—Nov 1 to Nov 16, 2001

Note: Number of ERG outstanding shares in 2001 was 673 million.

Source: www.asx.com.au

seemed stretched as the company grew over the years. Should the management team be strengthened? How dependent was ERG on CEO Fogarty and how would the company perform if he were no longer around in the short to midterm?

The early 2000's were exciting days at ERG. As another week of hard work went by in beautiful Perth and heavy international travel, CEO Fogarty woke up early on a Saturday morning to think about the questions outlined above. Was he thinking about the right questions or was he missing something? CEO Fogarty brushed aside thoughts about golfing or sailing for the day as he tried to vision ERG in year 2010 instead. He watched the warm Western Australian sun rise and reasoned that the smart card industry too was still at the dawn of its technological and business possibilities. CEO Fogarty was committed to guaranteeing a front seat for ERG in the smart card industry of the future and crafting strategy for a new horizon.

NOTES

1. "Smart growth is on the cards for ticket pioneers [. . .]," *Financial Times*, July 4, 2000.
2. "Smart growth is on the cards for ticket pioneers [. . .]," *Financial Times*, July 4, 2000.
3. www.erggroup.com, November 2001.
4. www.cp8.bull.net, November 2001.
5. "Hong Kong: Smart Card Technology Market," Industry Sector Analysis, Asia Intelligence Wire, December 12, 1997.
6. "Hong Kong: Smart Card Technology Market," Industry Sector Analysis, Asia Intelligence Wire, December 12, 1997.
7. www.gemplus.com, November 2001.
8. "Frost & Sullivan release new report for the smart card market," Telecomworldwire, September 10, 2001.
9. "Frost & Sullivan release new report for the smart card market," Telecomworldwire, September 10, 2001.
10. "Frost & Sullivan release new report for the smart card market," Telecomworldwire, September 10, 2001.
11. "Hong Kong: Smart Card Technology Market," Industry Sector Analysis, Asia Intelligence Wire, December 12, 1997.
12. "ERG Limited ABN 23 009 112 725," Prospectus to shareholders regarding PWI Rights Offer, November 2001.
13. "Smart growth is on the cards for ticket pioneers [. . .]," *Financial Times*, July 4, 2000.
14. www.erggroup.com, November 2001.
15. www.erggroup.com, November 2001.
16. "Smart growth is on the cards for ticket pioneers [. . .]," *Financial Times*, July 4, 2000.
17. www.erggroup.com, November 2001.
18. "Hong Kong: Smart Card Technology Market," Industry Sector Analysis, Asia Intelligence Wire, December 12, 1997.
19. "Technology: Smart cards take to the streets—Hong Kong's public transport system is about to be revolutionised," *Financial Times*, 14 July 1994.
20. "ERG wins again in Hong Kong," news release by Melissa Frost, March 1, 2001 at www.erggroup.com.
21. "ERG technologies scoops two coveted awards," news release by Melissa Frost, June 2, 2000 at www.erggroup.com.
22. "ERG announces record revenue and profit for 1998," news release by Wendy Watson-Ekstein, August 31, 1998 at www.erggroup.com.
23. "ERG announces record revenue and profit for 1998," news release by Wendy Watson-Ekstein, August 31, 1998 at www.erggroup.com.
24. "ERG, Motorola in global smart card venture," Newsbytes, October 16, 1997.
25. "Chaos ahead for smart cards," T. Denton and K. Dearne, August 14, 2001 at www.australianit.news.com.au.
26. "ERG, Motorola in global smart card venture," Newsbytes, October 16, 1997.
27. "Digital money is the way to go," Sydney *Morning Herald*—ABIX—Australasia, August 18, 1999.
28. "ERG/Motorola alliance wins contract to supply smart card system for Singapore Public Transit Network," news release by Leonie Mawkes, June 4, 1999 at www.erggroup.com.
29. "ERG Motorola alliance brings advanced smart card solution to the Netherlands." M2 Communications, July 12, 1999.
30. "ERG says more smart card alliances to be unveiled," AFX (AP)—Asia, June 24, 1999.
31. "Westpac, ERG form smart card alliance," AFX (AP)—Asia, June 24, 1999.

32. "Stagecoach, Sema, ERG in smart card venture; Wins GTR Manchester contract," AFX Europe, September 23, 1999.

33. "UK post office in smart card deal with prepayment cards," AFX (UK), June 21, 2000.

34. "Stagecoach, Sema, ERG in smart card venture; Wins GTR Manchester contract," AFX Europe, September 23, 1999.

35. www.erggroup.com, November 2001.

36. "Smart growth is on the cards for ticket pioneers [. . .]," Financial Times, July 4, 2000.

37. "SCI systems and the ERG group announce telecommunications manufacturing alliance," PR Newswire USA, September 13, 2000.

38. "Addresses by the Chairman, CEO and CFO" at the 2001 AGM, November 26, 2001.

39. "ERG Limited ABN 23 009 112 725," Prospectus to shareholders regarding PWI Rights Offer, November 2001.

40. "ERG Limited ABN 23 009 112 725," Prospectus to shareholders regarding PWI Rights Offer, November 2001.

41. "ERG Limited ABN 23 009 112 725," Prospectus to shareholders regarding PWI Rights Offer, November 2001.

42. "Proton World wins 2000 Computerworld Smithsonian Award [. . .]," PR Newswire USA, June 13, 2000.

43. "ERG announces acquisition of Proton World," news release by Shaun Duffy, October 31, 2001 at www.erggroup.com.

44. "ERG Limited ABN 23 009 112 725," Prospectus to shareholders regarding PWI Rights Offer, November 2001.

45. "Addresses by the Chairman, CEO and CFO" at the 2001 AGM, November 26, 2001.

46. "ERG announces acquisition of Venus Card Platform," news release by Shaun Duffy, November 15, 2001 at www.erggroup.com.

47. www.erggroup.com, Peter Fogarty's address to shareholders, Full Year Results 2001, November 2001.

48. "Addresses by the Chairman, CEO and CFO" at the 2001 AGM, November 26, 2001.

49. "Addresses by the Chairman, CEO and CFO" at the 2001 AGM, November 26, 2001.

50. www.erggroup.com, Peter Fogarty's address to shareholders, Full Year Results 2001, November 2001.

51. www.erggroup.com, Peter Fogarty's address to shareholders, Full Year Results 2001, November 2001.

52. www.erggroup.com, November 2001.

53. "ERG Limited," Australian Stock Exchange company news release, August 31, 2001.

54. "ERG sinks as Motorola alliance is disconnected," Sydney Morning Herald—ABIX, February 27, 2001.

55. "Restructure of the ERG Motorola Alliance and Company Update," news release by Melissa Frost, March 30, 2001 at www.erggroup.com.

56. "ERG result affected by revenue recognition deferral," Australian Stock Exchange news release, August 22, 2001.

57. "ERG plays its smart cards in all-or-nothing strategy," Australian Financial Review, September 6, 2001.

58. "ERG plays its smart cards in all-or-nothing strategy," Australian Financial Review, September 6, 2001.

59. "Addresses by the Chairman, CEO and CFO" at the 2001 AGM, November 26, 2001.

60. "ERG Limited," Australian Stock Exchange news release, August 31, 2001.

61. "Fogarty flogs ERG's foggy analysts," www.brw.com.au, November 19, 2001.

62. "ERG plays its smart cards in all-or-nothing strategy," Australian Financial Review, September 6, 2001.

63. "Addresses by the Chairman, CEO and CFO" at the 2001 AGM, November 26, 2001.

64. "Addresses by the Chairman, CEO and CFO" at the 2001 AGM, November 26, 2001.

65. "Addresses by the Chairman, CEO and CFO" at the 2001 AGM, November 26, 2001.

case thirteen

Michael Moffett
Kannan Ramaswamy
Thunderbird

"The brewing battle for Gucci is emblematic of the New Europe that is taking shape with the launch of the common currency and the globalization of industry: two Frenchmen squaring off for control of a Dutch-based Italian company run by a U.S.-educated lawyer and an American designer, and advised by London-based American investment bankers."

"Gucci Watch," Wall Street Journal,
March 22, 1999.

The Gucci Group N.V. 2000 Annual Report really said it all. Tom Ford, Creative Director, and Domenico De Sole, President and CEO, stood side-by-side facing the camera with eyes of steel. Ford, unshaven and shirt provocatively opened, was the American designer who had single-handedly revitalized the Gucci name. Domenico De Sole, dressed in a dark suit, white shirt, with finely trimmed beard, was the Italian lawyer-turned-businessman who had returned Gucci to profitability and promise. The photograph, of course, by the famous fashion photographer, Annie Leibovitz. These two men represented the defiant spirit of Gucci, a molten mix of high-powered fashion and high-powered finance.

These two men had, in the first six months of 1999, been the centerpiece of one of the most highly contested hostile takeover battles ever seen on the European continent. Under attack by LVMH Moët Hennessy Louis Vuitton, the French luxury-goods conglomerate, Gucci had implemented the age-old strategy of "the enemy of an enemy is a friend." Gucci successfully enticed Pinault-Printemps-Redoute of France, a retailer, to act as a white knight, grabbing Gucci from LVMH's clutches. Now, in September of 2001, it appeared this particular chapter of the fashion wars was finally over.

But in the end, when all was said and done, had Gucci's shareholders been winners or losers?

GUCCI GROUP N.V.

Guccio Gucci founded Gucci in 1923 after being inspired by extravagant and elegant baggage while working in a London hotel. Gucci's expensive leather goods (shoes, handbags, and ready-to-wear)—and the Gucci red and green logo—became internationally recognized for the next half-century. The Gucci family, however, sold its remaining interest in the company in 1993 after a decade of turmoil and scandal.

Although always considered chic by international standards, the Gucci business lines had grown old in the 1970s and 1980s. Gucci's rebirth in the 1990s was credited, strangely enough, to two Americans, Domenico De Sole and Tom Ford. De Sole was Italian by birth, but had attended Harvard Law School, married an American (gaining U.S. citizenship), and began his climb up the corporate ladder in a Washington D.C. law firm. De Sole first worked for the Gucci family, then eventually headed Gucci America. When control of Gucci passed from Maurizio Gucci and the Gucci family in 1993 to a Bahraini investment bank, Investcorp, De Sole moved to the corporate headquarters in Florence, Italy, to head Gucci International.

Gucci's owner, Investcorp, spun out 49% ownership in October 1995 in an initial public offering in Amsterdam. The original issuance price averaged $22 per share. Investcorp sold its remaining stake six months later for $48 per share. Gucci was now owned by everyone and no one in particular. The company was De Sole's to run.

Upon his arrival in Florence, De Sole found a design team with one real remaining talent, Tom Ford, a transplanted Texan. De Sole allowed Ford a free hand in the revitalization of Gucci's product line and operations, naming him Creative Director in 1994 at the age of 36. In the next five years, Ford successfully transformed what many considered a tired and sad Gucci image into a sexy of-the-moment revolution.

The new Gucci was, by 1999, considered a potential takeover target. Analysts believed the firm was undervalued, well-managed, and possessed significant growth potential. Gucci was also extremely widely held. The Italian fashion house Prada had acquired a 9.5% interest in Gucci in June of 1998, making it the single largest shareholder. Prada's move led to much speculation that it might attempt a takeover. Although silent as to its intentions, Prada's move was later seen as the first move to put Gucci into play.

CREEPING ACQUISITION

On January 6, 1999, LVMH Moët Hennessy Louis Vuitton, the French luxury-goods conglomerate, announced that it had passed the 5% shareholding level in Gucci Group N.V. Because both Gucci and LVMH were traded in the United States in addition to their home markets (Gucci's shares are traded in Amsterdam, LVMH in Paris), US Securities and Exchange Commission regulations applied, requiring public notification of a firm taking a 5% or more stake in another publicly traded company. Gucci's share price in New York moved from $50 to $70 per share (see Appendix 1).

LVMH was inseparable from its President and CEO, Bernard Arnault. Arnault was widely known for his aggressive and persistent drive to continually build the French luxury-goods conglomerate through acquisition. Arnault had pursued a steady strategy of buying up hundreds of small fashion brands and business lines with established brands but lagging results. The acquisitions were then folded into the LVMH conglomerate, building mass and exerting its size in marketing and positioning negotiations globally. Arnault had considered buying Gucci back in 1994, but the asking price, $350 million, had been too much.

LVMH's surprising move on Gucci led quickly to widespread speculation that this was only the first step in a hostile takeover of Gucci. LVMH was ten times the size (by sales) of Gucci. Six days later, LVMH announced that it had acquired an additional 9.5%—the shares previously held by Prada—for $398 million.[1] Two days later, on January 14, LVMH stated, "in the present circumstances it has no intention of making a tender offer" for Gucci.

But Bernard Arnault and LVMH were not through yet. On January 26, LVMH confirmed that it had now increased its stake in Gucci to 34.4%. As illustrated in Exhibit 1, Arnault was buying Gucci shares rapidly and globally. Arnault's 34.4% totaled 20.15 million shares

and represented an investment estimated at $1.44 billion. This last step was significant, in that under French law, LVMH's home, a company was required to launch a general tender—an offer for all of the shares held publicly—of any company once a 33% share ownership position was attained. US law had no such requirement. Bernard Arnault described his intentions towards Gucci as "not unfriendly."[2]

On Wednesday, February 11, LVMH informed Gucci by letter that it was requesting a shareholder meeting to vote on its proposal to add its own nominee to Gucci's board, expanding it from eight to nine members. Bernard Arnault again assured both Gucci's management and shareholders that his interests were only those of a passive investor—Gucci's largest investor.

"I reiterate my complete faith in the creative talent of Tom Ford and in the development strategy implemented by Gucci's management team. Our proposal today is provided for within the statutes of Gucci, allowing LVMH to exercise its rights as a shareholder without altering in any way the independence of the company."

Gucci's corporate bylaws, as incorporated under Netherlands law, stipulated that a shareholder with a stake of 10% or more was entitled to call a special shareholder meeting to implement board changes. The meeting must then be held within six weeks of the request. Gucci's CEO, Domenico De Sole, publicly

EXHIBIT 1	LVMH's Creeping Acquisition of Gucci Group
Gucci, total shares outstanding (January 31, 1999)	58,510,700
LVMH's accumulation of shares:	
Purchased on the open market before Jan 19	10,068,185
Purchased from Prada of Italy on Jan 14	5,560,000
Purchased on the NYSE, Jan 19–22	919,800
Purchased on the Amsterdam stock exchange, Jan 19–22	47,000
Purchased from private transactions with Capital Research	3,550,000
Total holdings in Gucci	20,144,985
LVMH's proportional ownership of Gucci	34.4%

admonished Bernard Arnault's moves and characterized the strategy as a "creeping takeover" in which LVMH gradually acquired more and more shares of Gucci until it gained effective control without ever paying existing shareholders any premium for the change in ownership.

THE POISON PILL

Gucci reacted quickly and radically. Less than one week later, on February 18, Gucci announced the creation of a new employee stock ownership plan (ESOP) and structure, the Employee Trust. Gucci granted the Trust the right to purchase up to 37 million newly issued shares. The Trust instantly purchased 20,154,985 shares.

The Trust's ownership in Gucci was now 25.6% (if it exercised its right to purchase all 37 million, its stake in Gucci would rise to 38.7%). This matched LVMH's ownership, and diluted LVMH's position from 34.4% to 26% by the issuance. Gucci had extended an interest-free loan to the Employee Trust to purchase the shares (a Note), with the stipulation that the shares could not be transferred to a third party.[3] Exhibit 2 details the new share structure. A subtle yet significant feature of the ESOP plan was that it did not dilute earnings. Because the ESOP shares were issued to a Trust, the shares carried no dividend rights. The new shares would not be included in Gucci's earnings per share (EPS) calculations.

Gucci CEO De Sole defended the action as necessary. It was not a poison pill in Gucci's opinion. It was instituted in order to prevent a creeping acquisition in which the controlling ownership of Gucci would change hands without all shareholders receiving a payment—a *premium*—for that control. Gucci continued to oppose LVMH's advances on the basis that having a competitor as a part owner and director was not consistent with Gucci's best interests. De Sole went on to invite LVMH to make a public tender:

"We are telling them they can make a takeover bid for 100% of the company's shares any time they want.... We've had a lot of contacts with LVMH in the past month. We made it very clear that a minority position held by a major competitor is an impossible situation. It's like Coke having a seat on Pepsi's board."

LVMH's response was equally as quick and as defiant.

"Far from raising new cash, this amounts to creating virtual shares, without putting a cent into the company. They're not issuing shares; they're issuing voting rights to control . . . to management."

One week later, on February 25, LVMH filed suit in the Enterprise Chamber of the Amsterdam Court of Appeals seeking an injunction that would strip the newly issued Employee Trust share voting rights and bar Gucci's management from issuing new shares. LVMH's argument was that Gucci's management was not acting in the interests of shareholders (of which LVMH was arguably the largest), but rather acting in the best interests of management. LVMH went on to point out that the new share issuance had not raised any capital, and that the shares issues were restricted (could not be sold to a third party, for example, LVMH), preventing employees from redeeming their newly acquired shares for capital.

One week later, the Amsterdam court postponed any decision on the legitimacy of Gucci's defense until May, but did invoke a voting rights injunction on both the newly issued employee shares and LVMH's shares. The court stated that the suspension of LVMH's voting rights was based on the company not acting as a responsible shareholder in that it had failed to fully disclose its intentions. Both sides claimed victory, and the battle moved into a two-week period in which calm was quickly replaced with a new harsher and more personal battle. (See Exhibit 3.)

	Gucci's Share Ownership after the ESOP		EXHIBIT 2	
	Prior to ESOP		Post ESOP	
	Shares	Percent	Shares	Percent
LVMH's	20,144,985	34.4%	20,144,985	25.6%
Employee Trust*	—	—	20,154,985	25.6%
Free floating shares	38,365,715	65.6%	38,365,715	48.8%
Total shares in Gucci	58,510,700	100.0%	78,665,685	100.0%

*The employee stock ownership plan was authorized to issue up to 37 million shares; 20 million were actually exercised upon initiation of the program.

THE WHITE KNIGHT

Gucci had retained Morgan Stanley Dean Witter's London office in February to aid in its defense strategy. Joseph Perella of Morgan Stanley had immediately contacted Mr. Francois Pinault, the President and CEO of Pinault-Printemps-Redoute (PPR), a French retail conglomerate. Pinault controlled 42.6% of PPR via his personal investment vehicle, Artemis. Pinault had been on an acquisition binge recently, including the famed London auction house Christie's in 1998. Pinault told Morgan Stanley he would think about it.

Pinault flew to New York where he visited Gucci's Fifth Avenue showplace. After returning from New York, he met in London with De Sole of Gucci. In the meeting, De Sole explained Gucci's emerging strategy of becoming a multi-brand luxury-goods company. This goal fit neatly with Pinault's own goal of expanding PPR's business breadth to include luxury goods. Negotiations began immediately, with the two parties discussing the size of PPR's potential investment, managerial implications, and, of course, price.

Francois Pinault, known for his rapid moves, simultaneously undertook the acquisition of Sanofi Beauté, the beauty-products division of the French firm Sanofi. Beauté owned the Yves Saint Laurent brand. Pinault intended to buy the division and resell the business to Gucci.[4] Pinault followed the words of his favorite French poet Rene Char, "Think strategically, act primitively."

On March 19, Gucci announced the entry of Francois Pinault's PPR in the role of white knight.[5] Gucci would issue 39 million new shares to PPR for $75 per share ($2.9 billion), giving it a 40% stake in Gucci. PPR would hold four of the nine seats on the Gucci board, and three of the five seats on the newly created strategic and financial committee. LVMH's share in Gucci was once again diluted (as were the shares of all shareholders), falling to 21%, as illustrated in Exhibit 4. Gucci's share price jumped on Friday, March 19, from $70 to $81 per share, a 15.7% increase in one day.[6] See Appendix 2 for share price movements around this date. (See Exhibit 4.)

Francois Pinault was considered the richest man in France; Bernard Arnault was considered to be the second richest. The entry of Pinault made the issue as much personal as it was business. Pinault made no secret that he saw LVMH as his new competitor:

> *"We want to make Gucci our beachhead for development in the luxury sector and create a rival to LVMH. LVMH was practically a monopoly. There's room for two in this business."*

Arnault and Pinault were very rich, very French, but ultimately very different. The 50-year old Arnault was born into a family real estate business, and a graduate of the elite Ecole Polytechnique. The 62-year old Pinault was a high school dropout, starting from the ground up in a small family partnership running a sawmill. Both had obviously built personal financial empires over many years of hard work. And in a truly French touch, both owned wineries; Pinault owned Chateau Latour and Arnault, in a partnership, Chateau Cheval Blanc.

Morgan Stanley's London offices provided most of the financing behind PPR's entry. Morgan Stanley extended a $3 billion bridge loan to PPR in order for it to purchase the agreed-upon stake in Gucci. $2 billion of the loan was based on a refinancing of existing credit lines held by PPR, and the additional $1 billion was funded through the issuance of a convertible bond (issuance led by Morgan Stanley). The bonds were convertible into PPR's ordinary shares.

Within hours, LVMH was once again in the Amsterdam courts asking for injunctions to stop the capital infusion by PPR into Gucci and block Gucci's acquisition of Sanofi's beauty-products division. LVMH now stated that if the PPR transaction was nullified, it could "envision" an offer at $85 per share for those shares needed for control. It did not define *control*. Four days later, the Dutch courts ordered Gucci to consider

	Without ESOP Shares		With ESOP Shares	
	Shares	Percent	Shares	Percent
LVMH's	20,144,985	20.7%	20,144,985	17.1%
Employee Trust*	—	—	20,154,985	17.1%
PPR's strategic investment	39,007,133	40.0%	39,007,133	33.1%
Free floating shares	38,365,715	39.3%	38,365,715	32.6%
Total shares in Gucci	97,517,833	100.0%	117,672,818	100.0%

*The ESOP shares were typically not included in most discussions of Gucci's new share ownership ("without ESOP shares") structure after the investment by PPR.

LVMH's offer(s). Over the following weeks, LVMH sold investments it held in other companies in order to put sufficient funds in place to make additional offers. Over the first two weeks of April 1999, LVMH continued to come forward with alternative offers of a variety of kinds, at one point having four different offers on the table (see Appendix 4).[7] The fight was increasingly public as both sides continued to make accusations regarding the practices of the other.

On April 20, Gucci's board, hoping to quell the feud, told LVMH that it would be willing to recommend to stockholders an unconditional offer for the company at $88 per share. LVMH responded that the position was untenable because of PPR's continuing stake in the firm.[8]

On April 22, the Amsterdam court heard arguments over the legality of Gucci's defensive maneuvers. The court postponed any ruling until June, putting the debate on ice for a month.[9] During the interim, all parties were busy. LVMH and Gucci continued to wage a public fight in which both urged Gucci shareholders to support their disparate initiatives (see Appendix 5).

> *"More than anyone else, De Sole is looked to as the man who can save the heart of Gucci, keep it from becoming just another profitable listing in a voluminous corporate annual report. He is the man who can salvage the swagger of Gucci as a fashion house founded on Italian craftsmanship and signifying classic Italian chic. And he is the American who can defend Gucci against the French, making sure that the company remains Italian. This is a matter of national pride, supported by folks such as Santo Versace, president of Italy's fashion industry association and the financial brains behind the Versace empire."*
>
> *"Gucci's Strong Suit: CEO Domenico Is Defending the Firm Against Takeover Designs,"*
> The Washington Post, *May 6, 1999,*
> *by Robin Givhan.*

The Amsterdam court released its findings on May 27, upholding PPR's investment in Gucci, but rejecting the poison-pill defense used by Gucci in the issuance of employee shares to the Employee Trust. By most principles, the court's decision signaled a clear defeat for LVMH. Arnault then threatened further legal actions, and also pointed out that LVMH owned 20% of the Gucci Group and expected "to see superior results from Gucci's management."

Gucci and PPR moved quickly. Gucci used the capital injections from PPR to purchase—from Francois Pinault—the Sanofi Beauté division and the Yves Saint Laurent's couture and fragrance business. At PPR's annual shareholder meeting, it was announced that Tom Ford had agreed to stay on at Gucci for at least another four years. The PPR investment was formally approved by 80% of Gucci's shareholders at the regularly scheduled stockholder meeting in July 1999.

THE DENOUEMENT

The problem Gucci now had was an awkward one. PPR now controlled Gucci in cooperation with Gucci's management. But LVMH still held a 20.7% interest. The question was how to get LVMH out, while simultaneously making good on the long-term promise that stockholders were entitled to a premium when ownership had changed. LVMH, given the intensifying consolidation of luxury-goods brands in the European marketplace, wanted to free its $1.4 billion invested in Gucci. Negotiations continued.

- In September 1999, Gucci/PPR and LVMH (with Prada of Italy) once more entered into a bidding war, this time for a third party, the Fendi Italian fashion house. Both parties had offered the same $850 million in the end, but Fendi chose LVMH/Prada over Gucci because Fendi designer Karl Lagerfeld preferred LVMH/Prada's management teams. Prada eventually sold its interest in Fendi to LVMH.

- In May and June 2000, representatives of Francois Pinault and Bernard Arnault tried once again to find a resolution to the ownership impasse. "Impossibility of common ground" was given in late June for breaking off talks.
- All parties were back in court in November 2000 when LVMH charged that Tom Ford and Domenico De Sole were secretly granted Gucci stock options in the spring of 1999 as part of the PPR strategic investment. Gucci denied the charges. The charge was part of a new filing by LVMH in Amsterdam's Enterprise Court claiming that PPR's purchase of the Gucci shares short-changed minority shareholders and constituted mismanagement. This would be grounds for rescinding the PPR investment. (The Dutch court was rehearing many of the previous arguments as part of a Dutch Supreme Court ruling that the Amsterdam lower court had failed to conduct a thorough investigation of the mismanagement charge prior to its ruling in May of 1999.)
- In March 2001, the Amsterdam Enterprise Court agreed to a new demand for an investigation into Gucci's management practices. The probe was expected to take between three and six months. PPR shares fell 3% on the announcement of the ruling as speculation increased that PPR might eventually have to sell its 40% share in Gucci. The court, however, urged the parties to reach a settlement on their own.

More than two-and-a-half years after it started, it ended. On September 10, 2001, PPR, Gucci, and LVMH reached a termination agreement. LVMH would be able to cash out of Gucci at a profit, and the minority shareholders of Gucci would indeed—finally—reap a premium from the change in ownership (see Appendix 3).

LVMH's Exit

PPR would pay $812 million to raise its stake in Gucci to 53.2% by acquiring 8.6 million Gucci shares from LVMH for $94 per share. This was a $2 premium over the closing price on the Amsterdam close on the previous Friday. This left LVMH with 12% interest in the Gucci Group.

PPR would then offer to buy out all of Gucci's remaining minority shareholders, including LVMH's 12%, in March 2004 at a price set at $101.50 per share.[10] (The assumption was that LVMH would take PPR up on its offer in March 2004, but many minority share-

holders may not.)[11] A member of Gucci's management team termed the exit agreement for LVMH *greenmail*. LVMH in return agreed to forego all legal claims against PPR and Gucci.

SHAREHOLDER BUYOUT PREMIUM

Gucci agreed to distribute a special dividend of $7 per share to all shareholders except those held by PPR (see Appendix 6). A number of investment analysts were publicly annoyed, noting that the premium should be at least 15%, or a dividend of about $15 per share, not $7.

Gucci Group continues to refer to LVMH's large investment as an "uninvited acquisition of a 34.4% stock interest in the Company." Gucci consider's PPR's current dominant ownership position as a *strategic investment.*

> *"In 2000, our strategy of unparalleled product design and quality, global distribution, and outstanding communication had its natural progression to other brands. For our development in this direction, we are fortunate to have had the partnership of Pinault-Printemps-Redoute (PPR), which in the Spring of 1999, not only brought us the capital to move in this direction, but the cultural breadth to enable us to acquire on proper terms and conditions the pre-eminent French brand, Yves Saint Laurent, and which more recently assisted us in the acquisition of Boucheron."*

> *President and CEO's Letter to Shareholders, Gucci Group N.V. Annual Report 2000, pp. 14–15.*

NOTES

1. Prada's investment return was impressive. Prada's original investment of $258 million netted a profit of $140 million, a 54% return in approximately six months.
2. Details of Tom Ford's contract with Gucci as filed with the US Securities and Exchange Commission included a provision that in the event of any one shareholder gaining a 35% stake in Gucci, Ford could sever his relationship with Gucci and a variety of specified salary, bonus, and stock options could be exercised.
3. There is some disagreement on the roots of the ESOP plan. The creation of an ESOP was provided for in Gucci's prospectus in its 1995 initial public offering. But Gucci CEO Domenico De Sole reportedly had an American law firm design the specific employee share issuance structure used the previous fall (1998) after Prada of Italy had purchased its 9.5% interest in Gucci. The plan could be triggered on the first sign of a hostile takeover.
4. Ironically, both Gucci and LVMH had previously considered buying Sanofi's beauty-products line. LVMH had come very close, deciding against the purchase only minutes before signing papers making the acquisition. Both Gucci and LVMH had backed away from Sanofi on the basis of price.
5. The move was particularly galling to LVMH as the two parties were scheduled to meet that very day in Amsterdam to search for an amicable solution to LVMH's request for managerial influence at Gucci.

6. The strategic investment agreement contained a five-year *standstill clause* which restricted PPR's holdings to 42% in Gucci. The standstill agreement could only be terminated by either a vote of Gucci's board or by a full public tender offer by a third party. In the event of a third-party bid, PPR could purchase additional shares only if it were to make a full and open tender offer for all shares outstanding.

7. Most of the offers had a clause specifically stating that the offers were only applicable if the PPR transaction was nullified and Gucci Creative Director Tom Ford agreed to stay on at Gucci for at least two years following the closure of LVMH's new controlling position.

8. If PPR's investment was canceled, a full bid for Gucci would require LVMH to purchase all shares outstanding which it did not already own, 38,365,715 shares. This assumed the ESOP shares were also canceled. If, however, the PPR investment was not canceled, the share total would rise to 77,372,848 shares, which would double the price.

9. The two principals filled the interval with legal suits and countersuits. Pinault first filed suit in Paris accusing Arnault of libel in a published interview in *Paris Match*. In the interview, Arnault described Pinault's actions as "defrauding minority shareholders." Arnault responded in-kind with a countersuit against Pinault.

10. PPR, in order to fund the completion of its takeover of Gucci, announced an additional issuance of 700 million of new shares and 700 million in convertible bonds. Francois Pinault's private investment company Artemis committed to subscribing to both to maintain Pinault's 45% control of PPR.

11. LVMH arranged a bank securitization of its remaining 12% share holdings against the March 2004 sale, allowing it to receive the money up front and declare a capital gain immediately.

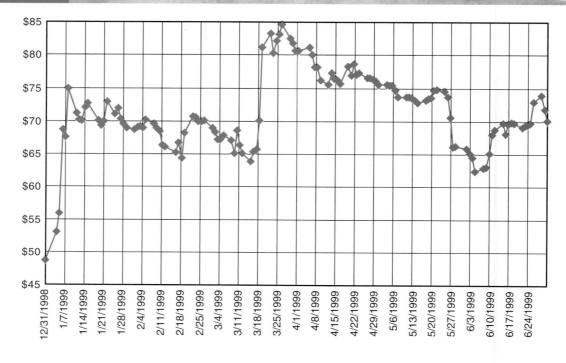

Event	Date (1999)	Closing Day	Share Price	Percent Change in Share Price
LVMH Takes Position in Gucci				
First trading day of year	Jan 4	Mon	$53.00	9.0%
	Jan 5	Tue	55.81	5.3%
	Jan 6	Wed	68.63	23.0%
	Jan 7	Thu	67.44	−1.7%
(Peak price until March)	Jan 8	Fri	74.88	11.0%
	Jan 11	Mon	$71.06	−5.1%
LVMH purchases Prada's 9.5%	Jan 12	Tue	70.06	−1.4%
	Jan 13	Wed	70.00	−0.1%
LVMH: "no intention of tender offer"	Jan 14	Thu	72.00	2.9%
	Jan 15	Fri	72.63	0.9%
PPR Enters as White Knight				
	March 15	Mon	$63.81	−1.8%
	March 16	Tue	65.25	2.3%
	March 17	Wed	65.63	0.6%
	March 18	Thu	70.00	6.7%
Gucci announces PPR investment	March 19	Fri	81.00	15.7%
	March 22	Mon	83.13	2.6%
	March 23	Tue	80.13	−3.6%
	March 24	Wed	82.00	2.3%
	March 25	Thu	83.00	1.2%
(Peak price until August)	March 26	Fri	84.56	1.9%
Amsterdam Court Makes Final Rulings				
	May 24	Mon	$74.50	−0.3%
	May 25	Tue	73.56	−1.3%
	May 26	Wed	70.50	−4.2%
Court confirms PPR, rejects LVMH	May 27	Thu	65.94	−6.5%
	May 28	Fri	66.13	0.3%

Date	Event
Jan 6, 1999	Gucci is informed that LVMH has increased its holdings in Gucci above 5%.
Jan 12, 1999	Gucci announces that it has not been consulted by LVMH regarding LVMH's stake in Gucci. LVMH increases its stake in Gucci by purchasing Prada's (Italy) 9.5% stake in Gucci.
Jan 13, 1999	Arnault praises Gucci management, CEO De Sole and Creative Director Ford.
Jan 25, 1999	LVMH increases its stake (over previous weeks) to 34.4%. LVMH does not "rule out" additional share purchases.
Feb 10, 1999	Gucci Group receives request from LVMH for special shareholder meeting to approve a request for gaining a seat on Gucci's board.
Feb 18, 1999	Gucci launches a poison pill, an employee stock option plan, which dilutes LVMH's share in Gucci to 26%.
Feb 25, 1999	LVMH files suit in the Enterprise Chamber of the Amsterdam Court of Appeals seeking a stop to the Gucci ESOP defense.
March 1, 1999	Gucci announces a special shareholder meeting, to be held on March 25, in accordance with the Gucci Group's bylaws and a request presented by LVMH for a special shareholder meeting.
March 3, 1999	Amsterdam court postpones any decision on the LVMH suit until a subsequent hearing to be held on April 22, but imposes an injunction on the voting rights held by both the ESOP and LVMH.
March 4, 1999	LVMH withdraws its request for a special shareholder meeting and its nominee to the Supervisory Board of Gucci.
March 19, 1999	Gucci announces that the Pinault-Printemps-Redoute Group has made a strategic investment of $2.9 billion in Gucci. This is to represent 40% of Gucci's capital. PPR signs a five-year standstill agreement in which PPR agrees not to increase its ownership position in Gucci past 42%. Stock issued to PPR totals 39 million shares at $75 per share, a 13% premium over the average share price of the preceding ten days. Domenico De Sole and Tom Ford are said to be "fully committed to new alliance."
March 22, 1999	LVMH's request that Gucci's management be removed is denied by the Amsterdam court. Gucci's Supervisory Board is given approval to consider LVMH's proposed $81 per share offered.
April 15, 1999	LVMH publicizes a five-page "Letter to Gucci Shareholders" and other correspondence with Gucci management. LVMH charges Gucci's board with "total lack of good faith and sincerity in negotiations." LVMH again accuses Gucci's management of violating the rights of minority shareholders. LVMH repeats its offer to make a full bid if PPR's investment is canceled.
April 19, 1999	Gucci's board tells LVMH it will recommend to stockholders an unconditional offer for the company at $88 per share. LVMH responds that this position is untenable with PPR's presence.
May 27, 1999	Amsterdam court releases its findings that the PPR investment is legal, but rejects the poison-pill ESOP issuance.
October 1999	Gucci officially acquires Sanofi Beauté from PPR for $1 billion.
Sept 10, 2001	Gucci, LVMH, and PPR reach a termination agreement whereby PPR will buy out LVMH's investment in Gucci and PPR will make a tender offer to all remaining minority shareholders.

1. If PPR's investment was rescinded, $91/share.

2. $85/share for all outstanding shares, but under which Gucci would help LVMH pass the 50% threshold in share ownership through a reserved capital increase if LVMH obtained a majority of shares held by independent shareholders, but not those of PPR.

3. $85/share under which LVMH would have the same rights and board representation as PPR if it ended up with less than 50%.

4. $85/share including PPR's stake, but only if Gucci helped deliver PPR's stake and guaranteed that most of Gucci's top management stayed on for at least two years.

Source: "Gucci Board Invites Unconditional Bid from LVMH of $88 a Share to End Battle," *Wall Street Journal*, April 20, 1999.

A Brief Overview of Takeover Laws in Selected European Countries   APPENDIX 5

Great Britain
- Decisions are made by a takeover panel and not appealable to courts
- A final offer is generally final
- Threshold of 30% where an acquirer has to make a full offer

France
- Threshold of 33% beyond which an acquirer has to launch a full offer
- Some defensive measures allowed during a bid
- Regulatory decisions appealable to courts

Germany
- A voluntary takeover code lets companies opt in or out

Netherlands
- Allows companies to adopt a broad array of defenses during a bid
- No rules requiring a company to launch a full offer at a certain threshold

Italy
- Limits the defenses a company can employ during a takeover

Switzerland
- Allows a broad array of defensive steps to a hostile takeover
- An acquirer can force a cash buyout of minority shareholders only after it achieves 98% control

Spain
- Panoply of defenses that can be put in place before a takeover is launched
- Limited defenses after takeover offer is made
- No compulsory buyout of minority shareholders

Source: "Pressure Grows to Unify Europe's Takeover Laws—Mazes of Rules Baffle Investors, Hurt Shareholders," *Wall Street Journal*, December 13, 1999.

GUCCI
GUCCI GROUP

GUCCI ANNOUNCES SPECIAL DIVIDEND OF $7 PER SHARE

Amsterdam, The Netherlands, November 2, 2001: Gucci Group N.V. (NYSE: GUC; Euronext Amsterdam: GCCLAS) announces today that the Special Dividend of $7.00 per Common Share to all shareholders, except Pinault-Printemps-Redoute S.A. ("PPR") will be paid on the following schedule:

December 12, 2001	New York registered shares commerce trading ex-dividend.
	Dutch ordinary shares commence trading ex-dividend.
December 14, 2001	Record date for New York registered shares.
	Gucci Group pays to payment agent (Kas Associate N.V.) the amount of Distribution due to all shareholders.
	Kas Associate and Bank of New York make payment to shareholders as soon as practicable thereafter.

In order to prevent any possibility of arbitrage between the two types of Gucci shares, the Bank of New York will close its books between December 12 and December 14.

The Special Dividend is part of the settlement among Gucci Group, PPR and LVMH Moët Hennessy Louis Vuitton S.A. announced on September 10, 2001, which closed on October 22, 2001.

Gucci Group N.V. is one of the world's leading multi-brand luxury goods companies. Through the Gucci, Yves Saint Laurent, Sergio Rossi, Boucheron, Roger & Gallet, Bottega Veneta, Alexander McQueen, Stella McCartney, Balenciaga and BEDAT & C* brands, the Group designs, produces and distributes high-quality personal luxury goods, including ready-to-wear, handbags, luggage, small leather goods, shoes, timepieces, jewelry, ties and scarves, eyewear, perfume, cosmetics and skincare products. The Group directly operates stores in major markets throughout the world and wholesales products through franchise stores, duty free boutiques and leading department and specialty stores. The shares of Gucci Group N.V. are listed on the New York Stock Exchange and on the Euronext Amsterdam Stock Exchange.

For media inquiries:

Tomaso Galli
Director of Corporate Communications
Gucci Group N.V.
+39 02 7712 7373
+39 335 737 8435 (mobile)

For investors/analysts inquiries:

Cedric Magnella / Enza Dominlianni
Directors of Investor Relations
Gucci Group N.V.
+39 055 759 2456
+44 20 7898 3053

Source: www.guccigroup.com/press.

The Gillette Company

case fourteen

Bulat Abishev
Kate Butler
Bruce Fraley
Andy Sherrer

There is no other article for individual use so universally known or widely distributed [as the safety razor]. In my travels, I have found it in the most northern town in Norway and in the heart of the Sahara Desert.[1]

—*King C. Gillette*

The Gillette Company (Gillette), best known for its dominant position in the shaving industry, celebrated its 100th anniversary in 2001. As a result of brands such as Mach3, Venus, Duracell, Oral-B, and Braun, Gillette is the world leader in eight product categories, including blades and razors for men and women, manual and power toothbrushes, and alkaline batteries. In its mission statement, Gillette emphasizes the goal of achieving or enhancing worldwide leadership in the consumer product categories in which it chooses to compete. This goal is achieved by producing superior products that define excellence and value in their respective categories.

Gillette diversified into the oral care and portable power markets in 1984 and 1996, respectively, and in recent years, Gillette has expanded the range of its shaving product line. By 1991, Gillette ranked twentieth among *Fortune* 500 companies, and two years later, Gillette entered the *Fortune* 100 for the first time. In 2001, Gillette served 1.2 billion consumers each day, with sales and distribution in 200 countries.[2] However, several of Gillette's strong brand names have been poorly managed. In 1994, *Financial World* ranked the Gillette brand as the ninth most valuable brand in the world,

but by 2000, Gillette had slipped to seventeenth place.[3] (See Exhibit 1.)

Therefore, in 2000, Gillette initiated several actions that sought to remedy its competitive situation. These actions included firing the company's newly appointed CEO.[4] Gillette also initiated the sale of its non-core businesses and focused its efforts on core grooming and hygiene products, the products that it knows best. In 2001, Gillette should start realizing some efficiencies from these cost-cutting measures, and if the new CEO is as effective as hoped, Gillette's turn-around may soon follow.[5]

BACKGROUND

COMPANY HISTORY[6]

Gillette's $9.2 billion global business began on September 28, 1901 when King C. Gillette launched a company to manufacture his revolutionary invention, the safety razor, invented in 1895, and patented in 1904. The company's operations began in Boston, Massachusetts and slowly expanded from a one-room workshop with a single employee to the world's largest facility designed exclusively for razor blade manufacture. The company recorded its first sales of 51 razors and 168 blades in 1903. The following year, sales reached 90,884 razors and 123,648 blades as a result of the increased shaving performance and comfort offered by a Gillette Safety Razor. One year later, razor sales had tripled, and blade sales were 10 times the 1904 results.

In 1905, Gillette began expanding internationally by opening an office in London and a manufacturing plant in Paris. By 1920, Gillette had international branch offices operating on four continents. Today, Gillette, which officially changed its name to The Gillette Company in 1952, operates 51 factories in 38 countries (see Exhibit 2).

EXHIBIT 1   Gillette's Awards and Social Responsibility

1977	The Super Cricket lighter and the Braun mini coffee mill made Fortune Magazine's list of the 25 best-designed factory-made products sold in the U.S.
1981	Three Braun products (the Micron Plus electric shaver, the Multiquick food processor, and the International hair dryer) were cited for design excellence at the 1981 Hanover Fair in Germany.
1982	The Governor of Massachusetts recognizes Gillette's leadership role in implementing water conservation programs.
	Gillette is the world's largest marketer of a broad range of writing instruments with a unit volume of one billion units for pens and refills.
1985	Gillette ranks #23 in Fortune Magazine's "most admired companies" surveys and #1 in the Metal Products Group category.
1986	Gillette contributes over $100,000 in earthquake relief aid to Mexico.
1988	The Braun solar-operated pocket calculator is the 39th Braun product to be included in the Museum of Modern Art collection.
1989	Gillette Puerto Rico contributes $60,000 in product donations following Hurricane Hugo.
	Gillette contributes more than $1.1 million in product donations to the California Earthquake Fund.
1990	Gillette receives the "Governor's Environmental Achievement Award" in Massachusetts.
1991	Gillette ranks #20 among Fortune 500 companies.
1992	Gillette receives a Special Merit recognition Award from Renew America for its worldwide conservation program.
1993	Gillette vaults into the Fortune 100 for the first time.
1994	Financial World ranks the Gillette brand as the ninth most valuable in the world.

Source: 2001, "Historical Timeline," The Gillette Company, http://www.gillette.com/100Celebration/flash/index.asp, October 22.

As a result of World War I, Gillette closed its European factories in 1917. However, other facilities substantially increased production when, in 1918, Gillette contracted with the U.S. government to supply the entire U.S. Armed Forces with 3.5 million razors and 36 million blades, thereby creating tens of thousands of new lifetime customers. This agreement was reinstated in 1942 when the War Production Board limited the production of razors and blades to quantities authorized for sale to the Armed Forces.

Gillette continued to innovate and expand its business. (See Exhibit 3.) The introduction of the Lady Gillette razor occurred in 1963, and Gillette moved into the electric razor market with the acquisition of Braun AG in 1967. Having entered the market for writing instruments when it acquired Paper Mate in 1955, Gillette expanded its presence with the later purchase of Waterman and Parker Pen Holdings. Diversification continued when Gillette acquired The Liquid Paper Corporation in 1979 and Oral-B Laboratories, Inc., an oral hygiene company, in 1984. Gillette bought Dura-

cell International, a battery company, in 1996. (See Exhibit 4.)

Although Gillette owns many well-known brand names, they have been poorly managed, and Gillette is retrenching. Gillette's original strategy was continuous growth through diversification and expanding product lines. However, such actions resulted in a decrease in net sales. Gillette is attempting to cut costs by reducing manufacturing costs and increasing efficiency. In addition, the company is concentrating on its core products and divesting unrelated product lines. Under new CEO James Kilts, the pen division was sold and Gillette's current divisions are: the Safety Razor Division, the Toiletries Division, Gillette International, and Braun AG/Braun North America.[7]

GILLETTE TODAY

Today, Gillette focuses on three core businesses: grooming, portable power, and oral care. Gillette's core businesses account for nearly 80 percent of sales and 90

1905	Gillette opens an office in London and a manufacturing plant in Paris.
1906	Gillette establishes a plant in Montreal, Canada.
1908	Gillette establishes a sales company in Germany.
1919	Gillette Belgium, Gillette Denmark, and Gillette Italy are incorporated.
1920	Gillette has international branch offices operating on four continents.
1921	Gillette establishes a plant in Slough, England.
1922	Gillette is appointed as the Purveyor to the Prince of Wales.
1924	Gillette Holland is incorporated. Gillette is appointed as the Purveyor to King Gustav of Sweden.
1926	Gillette acquires a controlling interest in Roth-Buchner Berlin Company.
1929	Gillette Sweden is incorporated.
1930	Gillette Safety Razor Company and AutoStrop Safety Razor Company merge; Gillette South Africa is incorporated.
1932	Gillette Australia is incorporated.
1937	Gillette opens a plant in England.
1953	Gillette France opens a factory in Annecy.
1959	Gillette Puerto Rico and Gillette Colombia are incorporated.
1965	Gillette Finland, Gillette Brazil, and Gillette Spain are incorporated.
1966	Gillette Austria, Gillette Chile, and Gillette Portugal are incorporated.
1967	Gillette acquires Braun AG of West Germany and moves into the electric shaving and small electrical appliance business.
1971	Gillette acquires a 48 percent interest in S.T. Dupont Company, a French manufacturer of luxury writing instruments and disposable lighters.
1972	Gillette International introduces more than 60 new products in 50 markets.
1973	Gillette increases its ownership in S.T. Dupont to 80 percent.
1974	Braun opens a manufacturing facility in Argentina and completes an addition to its plant in Spain. Gillette expands its GII manufacturing facilities into West Berlin and Rio de Janeiro.
1978	Gillette opens a facility in Brazil to manufacture blades, razors, writing instruments, and disposable lighters.
1983	Gillette's first joint venture with China begins production of double-edge blades and razors.
1987	Gillette purchases Waterman, a leading French marketer and manufacturer of premium writing instruments.

Source: http://www.gillette.com/100Celebration/flash/index.asp.

percent of profits.[8] The brand names in each of these segments possess loyal customers and are perceived as the best. As a result of their technology, they command premium prices and have a high profit margin.[9]

THE SHAVING INDUSTRY (GILLETTE'S DOMINANT MARKET)

In 1981, Gillette blades and razors outsold all competitive brands combined in most competitive markets. Four years later, Gillette ranked twenty-third in *Fortune* magazine's "most admired companies" survey and first in the Metal Products Group category. Gillette's global share in the men's blade and razor business was 20 percent and growing steadily in 1999.[10] In 2000, sales and profits grew 8 percent and 11 percent, respectively.[11] (See Exhibit 5 for current market share.)

Gillette is currently the market leader in the blade and razor segment of its business and in the women's wet shaving market. In 1990, Gillette introduced the Sensor shaving system with its automatically adjusting

1895   King C. Gillette invents the safety razor.
1903   The publication of Gillette's first advertisement occurs.
1908   Gillette adopts the diamond trademark.
1921   Gillette introduces the New Improved razor.
1923   Gillette introduces a $1 gold-plated razor.
1932   Gillette introduces The Gillette Blue Blade in June.
1934   Gillette introduces Probak Junior Blades and the Aristocrat one-piece razor.
1936   Gillette introduces Gillette Brushless shave cream.
1937   National distribution of Gillette Brushless shave cream begins.
1938   Gillette introduces the Gillette dry shaver, the Company's first electric shaver, on a limited basis in the U.S. and Canada.
       Gillette introduces the Gillette Thin Blade.
1939   Gillette introduces the Tech three-piece razor.
1940   Gillette lather shaving cream is marketed for the first time.
1942   Gillette begins a series of advertisements describing how to make blades last longer due to the serious shortage of Gillette products among civilians.
1946   The Gillette Blue Blade dispenser is invented, eliminating the need for unwrapping blades.
1947   The Gillette Super-Speed Razor is introduced.
1951   Gillette patents a double-ended blade dispenser.
1953   Gillette introduces Foamy aerosol shave cream.
1956   Paper Mate introduces the $1.95 Capri ballpoint pen with Piggy-Back refill.
1957   Gillette introduces the Gillette Adjustable safety razor.
1958   Paper Mate introduces the Capri Mark III pen that has a skip-free refill.
1959   Gillette creates the Super Blue Blade by applying a plastic coating to the carbon blade edge.
1960   Gillette introduces Right Guard aerosol deodorant.
1963   The coated stainless steel blade is introduced nationally.
       Gillette introduces the Lady Gillette razor.
1964   Paper Mate introduces the $1.95 Profile Trio ballpoint pens in Slim, Regular, and Husky grips.
1965   Gillette introduces Super Stainless Steel Blades and the Techmatic Razor.
       Dippity-Do setting gel and Casual hair color are marketed in the U.S.
1966   Gillette distributes its Techmatic razor nationally.
1968   Gillette introduces the Super Stainless Steel Injector, the first injector blade.
       Braun North America is formed to market Braun AG products in the U.S. and Canada.
1969   Gillette launches Soft & Dri, a nonsting antiperspirant for women.
1970   The Toiletries Division introduces the Dry Look men's hair groom.
1971   The Safety Razor Division introduces the Trac II twin blade shaving system.
1972   Gillette International introduces more than 60 new products in 50 markets.
1973   The Safety Razor Division introduces the Gillette Twinjector razor.
1974   The Cricket disposable lighter is introduced in 27 new markets for a total of 91 markets.
1975   The Safety Razor Division introduces Daisy, a disposable shaver designed for women.
       The Toiletries Division introduces Right Guard Double Protection aerosol antiperspirant, Right Guard roll-on antiperspirant, Soft & Dri Super Dry aerosol antiperspirant, and Soft & Dri roll-on antiperspirant.
1976   The Safety Razor Division introduces the Good News disposable twin blade razor in the U.S.
       The Toiletries Division launches the Right Guard deodorant stick.
       The Super Cricket lighter and Fashion Cricket lighter are distributed throughout the U.S.
1977   Braun AG introduces the battery-operated Sprint shaver.
       Gillette introduces the Atra shaving system.
1978   Gillette launches Dry Idea antiperspirant.
       Distribution of the Atra automatic-adjusting twin blade system expands to the European and Australasian markets.

1979 Paper Mate launches Eraser Mate, the first ballpoint pen with erasable ink.

   Braun introduces the Multiquick food processor system and electric toothbrushes and water jets to enter the dental hygiene appliance field.

1980 Gillette introduces the Swivel disposable razor with a pivoting head.

1981 The Personal Care Division introduces Right Guard solid antiperspirant.

   The Paper Mate Division introduces the Eraser Mate 2 and the Refillable Ultra Fine Flair.

1982 Braun broadens electric shavers, its most important product category, by introducing three lower-priced cord shavers for men.

   Gillette is the world's largest marketer of a broad range of writing instruments with a unit volume of one billion units for pens and refills.

1983 Gillette introduces Foamy gel shave cream.

1984 Gillette launches the Good News Pivot disposable twin blade razor.

1985 Improved versions of the Braun Lady Elegance women's electric shaver are distributed in major markets.

1986 The Paper Mate Division introduces the Metal Roller rolling ball pen.

1987 Gillette relaunches Right Guard, Soft & Dri, and Dry Idea deodorants/antiperspirants with new packaging, formulas, and fragrances.

   Oral-B launches Muppets toothpaste in a pump dispenser.

1988 The North American Shaving Division introduces four new products: Atra for Women, Daisy Plus, Good News Pivot Plus, and Trac II Plus.

1989 Gillette launches "The Best a Man Can Get" advertising theme for Atra Plus/Contour Plus.

1990 Gillette introduces the Sensor shaving system in 16 countries, its first pan-Atlantic launch.

   Gillette revitalizes Dry Idea with new packaging and graphics.

   The Liquid Paper pen applicator is launched in Japan under the brand name "Guppy."

1991 Braun introduces the Oral-B plaque remover.

1992 Gillette launches the Sensor for Women shaving system.

   Braun introduces the Flex Control electric shaver in the U.S., and it performs strongly.

1993 Gillette introduces the Sensor Excel shaving system across Continental Europe and Canada.

   Gillette unveils a new corporate Omnimark.

1994 Oral-B introduces two new toothbrushes: Advantage Control Grip and Contura.

   Oral-B Ultra floss is introduced nationally.

1995 Gillette introduces Satin Care for Women, a non-soap-based shaving gel, in the U.S.

   Oral-B launches two innovative products for children: the Squish Grip and the Gripper toothbrushes.

1996 Gillette launches Duracell PowerCheck AA batteries.

1997 Gillette introduces the new Agility women's disposable razor in North America.

   Braun expands the Flex Integral family of pivoting head shavers with two new rechargeable models.

1998 The Duracell Ultra alkaline battery is launched.

   The revolutionary Mach3 shaving system is launched in North America and Europe achieving unprecedented sales and market share results.

   Braun introduces the Oral-B 3D plaque remover in North America and Western Europe.

   Gillette launches the new CrossAction premium toothbrush in the United States.

1999 Gillette Comfort Blades are introduced.

   Gillette for Women Sensor Dazzlers is launched to target teens with colors that sparkle and shine.

2000 Gillette introduces The Gillette for Women Fashion Collection of Sensor Excel razors in high-fashion colors and Satin Care shave gels in two new scents.

   Braun launches Syncro, the first self-cleaning men's electric shaving system.

2001 Gillette introduces The Gillette for Women Venus (a triple blade shaving system designed exclusively for women), the Mach3 Cool Blue Razor, and Soft & Dri Anti-Perspirant and Deodorant in Flirty Flowers and Zensational Spring.

   Duracell relaunches Duracell CopperTop batteries.

Source: 2001, "Historical Timeline," The Gillette Company, http://www.gillette.com/100Celebration/flash/index.asp, October 22.

EXHIBIT 4   Gillette's Acquisitions and Mergers

1926	Gillette Safety Razor Company acquires a controlling interest in Roth-Buchner Berlin Company.
1930	Gillette Safety Razor Company and AutoStrop Safety Razor Company merge.
1948	Gillette purchases Toni Company, a U.S. manufacturer of home permanents for women.
1955	Gillette acquires the Paper Mate Company, a manufacturer of ballpoint pens for $15 million.
1967	Gillette acquires Braun AG of West Germany and moves into the electric shaving and small electrical appliance business.
1971	Gillette acquires a 48 percent interest in S.T. Dupont Company, a French manufacturer of luxury writing instruments and disposable lighters.
1973	Gillette acquires Jafra Cosmetics, and Gillette increases its ownership in S.T. Dupont to 80 percent.
1979	Gillette acquires The Liquid Paper Corporation.
1983	Gillette's first joint venture with China begins production of double edge blades and razors.
1984	Gillette acquires Oral-B Laboratories, Inc.
1987	Gillette purchases Waterman, a leading French marketer and manufacturer of premium writing instruments.
1993	Gillette acquires Parker Pen Holdings Limited.
1996	Gillette acquires Duracell International.

Gillette's Divestments

1986	Gillette sells the Cricket lighter business to Swedish Match.
1987	Gillette sells the S.T. Dupont business to Dickson Concepts Limited.
2000	Gillette sells the Stationery Products business to Newell Rubbermaid.

Source: 2001, "Historical Timeline," The Gillette Company, http://www.gillette.com/100Celebration/flash/index.asp, October 22.

EXHIBIT 5   Competition in the Shaving Industry

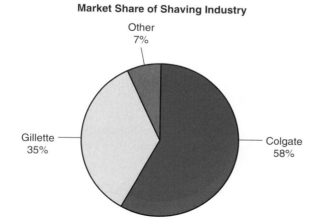

Market Share of Shaving Industry

Other 7%

Gillette 35%

Colgate 58%

Source: http://www.businessweek.com.

twin blades, followed two years later by the introduction of the Sensor for Women shaving system. The Sensor Excel shaving system was launched across Continental Europe and Canada over the next year.

The revolutionary Mach3 system was launched in North America and Europe in 1998, and it achieved unprecedented sales and market share results. Since its launch in 1998, the Mach3 triple blade shaving system, touted as the biggest shaving innovation in decades, has captured more than 20 percent of the global blade and razor market, generating over $2.5 billion in worldwide sales and delivering record profits. As a result of a successful advertising campaign, the Mach3 had generated more than $1 billion in cumulative sales by 1999, and in 2001, the Mach3 system posted strong worldwide results through a 25 percent increase in retail sales.[12] Gillette further developed the Mach3 into the Cool Blue Mach3 razor in 2001, and the Mach3 Turbo in 2002. In 2001, Gillette also introduced The Gillette for Women Venus, a triple blade shaving system that was immediately popular.

Since the introduction of the Sensor for Women shaving system in 1992, female shaving products have become the fastest growing part of Gillette's grooming portfolio, attaining a cumulative annual growth of 27 percent. Gillette offers women razors in many colors and patterns in an attempt to capitalize on this. Another women's product, the Braun Silk-epil electric hair epilator is number one worldwide with more than half of the market. Moreover, in 2001, Venus remained the country's top-selling razor, and became the number two brand in the U.S. shaving category after only six months on the market.[13]

In addition to razors, Gillette has a product line of personal toiletries. It markets four deodorant brands: Right Guard, Soft & Dri, Dry Idea, and Gillette. It also offers shaving accessory products such as shaving cream and aftershave, including a shaving gel for women called Satin Care.

THE ORAL CARE INDUSTRY

In 1984, Gillette entered the oral care industry by acquiring Oral-B Laboratories. Braun, another Gillette company, introduced the Oral-B plaque remover power toothbrush in 1991. As a result of its oscillating brush head, the Oral-B provided superior cleaning and quickly became the best-selling power toothbrush brand. Leadership in the power toothbrush market is partially based on two factors: competitors in this segment are usually smaller than in other areas of the oral care industry, and competitors do not have a background in the oral care industry.

Oral-B continued to invent and innovate and today offers a full lineup of toothbrushes of all types and sizes as well as dental floss, toothpaste, and other oral care products. Although Gillette's $5 billion market share of the oral product market is smaller than its market share for the grooming or portable power products, oral care has been Gillette's fastest growing business in recent years. The power-assisted Oral-B plaque remover reached a market share of 70 percent in 1999, and Oral-B sales increased by 10 percent the following year. However, in 2000, profits declined 3 percent.[14] (See Exhibit 6 for product introduction comparison.)

THE PORTABLE POWER INDUSTRY

In 1996, Gillette acquired Duracell International and in 1998 introduced the Duracell Ultra alkaline battery as the first battery especially designed for today's high-drain devices. Two years later, the Duracell brand expanded its market share in the rapidly growing alkaline battery market to greater than 40 percent. However, in 2000, sales and profits of the core battery brand fell 5 percent and 28 percent, respectively, from the previous year, despite the fact that sales of Duracell products account for about 27 percent of Gillette's total sales.[15] On the bright side, Duracell CopperTop batteries were relaunched in 2001 and increased market share in the United States, reversing 21 months of market share decline. (See Exhibit 7 for market share.)

COMPETITORS

PFIZER'S SCHICK PRODUCT LINE

Pfizer Inc., primarily a pharmaceutical company, also manufactures and sells razors and blades under the Schick brand name, offering razors for both men and

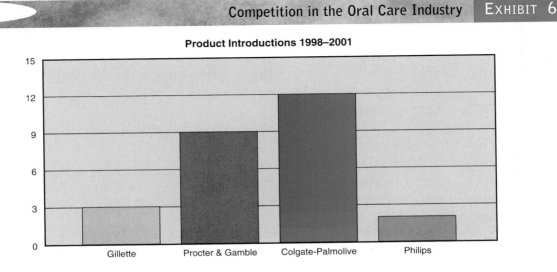

Competition in the Oral Care Industry EXHIBIT 6

Product Introductions 1998–2001

EXHIBIT 7 Competition in the Portable Power Industry

Market Share for Portable Power

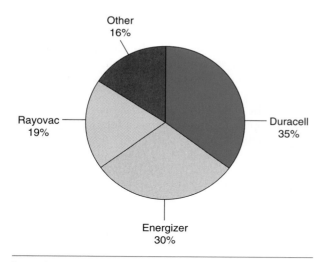

Source: http://www.quicken.com.

women called Fx Diamond, Silk Effects, and the Xtreme 3. Schick holds the number two market-share position, after Gillette, in shaving products worldwide. In 1998, it increased its sales of shaving products by 14 percent in the United States. Unlike Gillette, Pfizer Inc. has grown tremendously over the past few years. The five-year growth rate of net sales for the company was 15.04 percent, and the three-year growth rate was 21.37 percent. During the last year, when Gillette had a negative change in net sales, Pfizer Inc. increased its net sales by 20.34 percent.[16] (See Exhibit 8 for Pfizer financials.)

AMERICAN SAFETY RAZOR COMPANY

American Safety Razor Company manufactures shaving razors, blades, bladed hand tools, specialty industrial and medical blades, and custom bar soap. The company has the smallest market share of the three mentioned competitors in the shaving products market segment. American Safety Razor Company experienced a growth of 13.47 percent of net sales over the last five years and 8.88 percent of net sales in the last three years. Like Gillette, American Safety Razor Company faced a slowdown in sales over the last year, and the company barely increased sales, by 0.3 percent.[17]

EXHIBIT 8 Pfizer Financial Highlights

| (millions, except per share data) | Year ended December 31 | | | % Change | |
	2001	2000	1999	01/00	01/99
Revenues	$32,259	$29,355	$27,166	10	8
Income from continuing operations before provision for taxes on income and minority interests	10,329	5,781	6,945	79	(17)
Provision for taxes on income	2,561	2,049	1,968	25	4
Discontinued operations—net of tax	36	8	(20)	337	*
Net income	7,788	3,726	4,952	109	(25)
Research and development expenses	4,847	4,435	4,036	9	10
Property, plant, and equipment additions	2,203	2,191	2,493	1	(12)
Cash dividends paid	2,715	2,197	1,820	24	21
Diluted earnings per common share	1.22	.59	.78	107	(24)
Cash dividends paid per common share	.44	.36	.30 2/3	22	17
Shareholders' equity per common share	2.95	2.58	2.28	14	13
Weighted average shares—diluted	6,361	6,368	6,317	—	1
Number of common shares outstanding	6,277	6,314	6,218	(1)	2

Source: 2001 Pfizer Annual Report, http://www.pfizer.com/are/investors_reports/annual_2001/p2001ar00.html.

COLGATE-PALMOLIVE

Colgate-Palmolive is a $9.4 billion global corporation that competes with Gillette in marketing toiletries and, more particularly, in marketing oral care products. Colgate-Palmolive toiletry brands include Softsoap, Speed Stick, Teen Spirit, Irish Spring, and Colgate. While Gillette is an industry leader in the toothbrush market, Colgate-Palmolive has traditionally been the industry leader in toothpaste sales.[18] By inventing new products such as the Colgate Actibrush and by increasing advertising, geographic expansion, and efficiency, Colgate-Palmolive is challenging Gillette for market share in the oral care industry. In 1999, 38 percent of sales resulted from products that had been introduced to the market within the last five years, and 19 new products were introduced into the United States market alone.[19]

Colgate-Palmolive also sells household cleaning chemicals like cleanser (Ajax), dish detergent (Palmolive), and laundry detergent (Fab). The company is a formidable competitor because of its global reach. Colgate-Palmolive's operations occur in over 200 markets, and 70 percent of its sales come from international operations. In 1999, Colgate-Palmolive's personal and household products accounted for 24 percent and 16 percent of worldwide sales, respectively.[20] (See Exhibit 9 for Colgate-Palmolive financials.)

PROCTER & GAMBLE

Procter & Gamble (P&G), an enormous consumer product company, provides 250 brand names to five billion consumers in 130 countries around the world. Last year it chalked up $40.2 billion in sales.[21] Procter & Gamble markets many different consumer products, including dish detergent, disposable diapers, shampoos and hair dyes, and paper towels. It competes with Gillette mainly in its oral care segment under the brand name Crest. P&G is currently focusing on developing its oral care product line because this industry is fast-growing and asset-efficient. This strategy led to the introduction of Crest Whitening Strips and the Crest Spinbrush, which recently became the number one selling electric toothbrush in the United States.

In 2000, Procter & Gamble produced five of the top new U.S. consumer products. Over the last four years, Procter & Gamble has only launched 13 new

	Colgate-Palmolive Financial Highlights		EXHIBIT 9
Dollars in millions, except per share amounts	2001	2000	Change
Unit volume			
Worldwide Sales	$9,427.8	$9,357.9	+.7%
Gross Profit Margin	55.1%	54.4%	+70 basis points
Earnings Before Interest and Taxes	$1,834.8	$1,740.5	+5%
Percent of Sales	19.5%	18.6%	+90 basis points
Net Income	$1,146.6	$1,063.8	+8%
Percent of Sales	12.2%	11.4%	+80 basis points
Earnings per Share, diluted	$1.89	$1.70	+11%
Dividends paid per share	$.675	$.63	+7%
Operating Cash Flow	$1,599.6	$1,536.2	+4%
Percent of Sales	17.0%	16.4%	+60 basis points
Return on Capital	29.7%	26.4%	+330 basis points
Number of Registered Shareholders	40,900	42,300	−3%
Number of Common Shares Outstanding (in millions)	550.7	566.7	−3%
Year-end Stock Price	$57.75	$64.55	−11%

Source: 2001 Colgate-Palmolive Annual Report, http://investor.colgatepalmolive.com/annual_highlights_01.cfm.

products in the U.S. market,[22] but net sales have risen over five years, although the company stumbled in 2001.[23] (See Exhibit 10 for P&G financials.)

PHILIPS ELECTRONICS

While Philips Electronics is known in the electronics industry, it does not have a background in the oral care industry. Recently, however, Philips Electronics entered the oral care industry by producing the Sonicare plaque remover. The success of Philips Electronics in the oral care industry is currently uncertain.[24]

ENERGIZER HOLDING, INC.

Energizer Holding, Inc., which manufactures dry cell batteries and flashlights, is Gillette's major competitor in the area of portable power products.[25] Its subsidiaries offer a full line of products in five major categories: alkaline batteries, carbon zinc batteries, miniature batteries, rechargeable batteries, and lighting products, but Energizer Holding, Inc. concentrates on the production of alkaline batteries. Over the last year, Energizer Holding, Inc. has experienced a decrease in net sales of 2.58 percent.[26] (See Exhibit 11 for Energizer financials.)

RAYOVAC

Rayovac sits as the third most powerful portable power producer in the world. It currently controls 19 percent of the market within the industry. However, since 1998, Rayovac has gained market share, primarily from Energizer. Rayovac attributes much of its success to a focus in Latin America and the use of proven spokesmen like Michael Jordan. With a focus on international growth and brand recognition, Rayovac pins its future on cre-ating a niche that differs from Energizer and Gillette's Duracell. (See Exhibit 12 for Rayovac financials.)

FINANCIAL RESULTS

Gillette has been growing at the rate of 4.52 percent of net sales over the last five years and 0.68 percent of net sales during the last three years. However, last year, Gillette's sales decreased by 1.58 percent as a result of weakened foreign markets combined with foreign exchange rate fluctuations.[27] (See Exhibit 13 for Gillette financials.)

Compared to its competitors, Gillette has a low quick ratio of .4 and a low current ratio of .8, indicating that the company may have difficulty meeting its current financial obligations. Gillette's receivable turnover of 4.8, inventory turnover of 1.9, and asset turnover of 0.83 lag behind its competitors, signifying that Gillette is inefficient in its operations, explaining the recent decline in sales. In addition, Gillette has a gross margin of 63.11 percent. Unlike its competitors, Gillette has a high net profit margin of 13.09, a positive return on assets of 3.8 percent, and a return on equity of 20.4 percent.[28] Thus, despite low liquidity ratios and poor efficiency, Gillette manages to stay very profitable.

CHALLENGES AND PLANS

Gillette as a company has many important strengths, including a broad product portfolio of highly recognizable global brands, a worldwide presence and a broad network for distributing products, and manufacturing capabilities that produce billions of reliable products

EXHIBIT 10 Procter & Gamble Financial Highlights

Amounts in millions except per share amounts	2001	Year ending June 30 2000	% change
Net sales	$39,244	$29,951	−2%
Operating Income	4,736	5,954	−20%
Core Operating Income	6,586	6,768	−3%
Net Earnings	2,922	3,542	−18%
Core Net Earnings	4,397	4,230	4%
Per Common Share			
Diluted Net Earnings	2.07	2.47	−16%
Core Diluted Net Earnings	3.12	2.95	6%
Dividends	1.40	1.28	9%

Source: 2001 Procter & Gamble Annual Report, http://www.pg.com/annualreports/2001/pdf/highlights.pdf.

Selected Historical Financial Information
(Dollars in millions except per share data)

| | For the Year Ended September 30 | | |
	2001	2000	1999
Statement of Earnings Data			
Net sales (a)	$1,694.2	$1,927.7	$1,878.5
Depreciation and amortization	79.8	82.0	94.9
Earnings from continuing operations before income taxes (b)	31.5	279.2	248.2
Income taxes	70.5	99.0	88.4
Earnings/(loss) from continuing operations (c)	(39.0)	180.2	159.8
Net earnings/(loss)	(39.0)	181.4	80.0
Earnings/(loss) per share from continuing operations:			
Basic	$(0.42)	$1.88	$1.56
Diluted	$(0.42)	$1.87	$1.56
Average shares outstanding: (d)			
Basic	92.6	96.1	102.6
Diluted	94.1	96.3	102.6

Source: 2001, Energizer Annual Report, http://media.corporate-ir.net/media_files/NYS/ENR/reports/enr_120601.pdf.

In millions, except per share amounts	2001	2000
Total Revenue	$675.5	$693.3
Adjusted Gross Profits	$329.5	$335.1
Adjusted Operating Income	76.7	89.3
Adjusted EBITDA	96.8	108.6
Net Income	11.5	38.4
Adjusted Net Income	31.1	38.4
Diluted Net Income per common share	$0.39	$1.32
Adjusted Diluted Net Income per common share	$1.05	$1.32

Source: 2001 Rayovac Annual Report, http://ir.thomsonfn.com/investorrelations/IRfiles/169/2001AR/04_FRMSET.htm.

each year in a cost-effective, efficient manner. As a result of selling these innovative products at a fair price, Gillette developed another strength, its worldwide customer loyalty. Innovations in technology, products, and marketing are key to Gillette's success. Fifty patents apply to the Gillette for Women Venus alone.

While Gillette is perceived as an excellent example of a successful company, the leader in its respective industry, the company currently faces several challenges. Despite Gillette's leadership in its core product categories and its stock price growth rate of 30.4 percent from 1990 to 1997, the recent lack of a clear and

EXHIBIT 13 Gillette's Financial Results

Consolidated Statement of Income
The Gillette Company and Subsidiary Companies

Years Ended December 31, 2000, 1999 and 1998 (Millions, except per share amounts)	2000	1999	1998
Net Sales	$9,295	$9,154	$9,200
Cost of Sales	3,384	3,392	3,499
Gross Profit	5,911	5,762	5,701
Selling, General and Administrative Expenses	3,827	3,675	3,485
Restructuring and Asset Impairment Charges	572	—	400
Profit from Operations	1,512	2,087	1,776
Nonoperating Charges (Income)			
Interest income	(5)	(7)	(8)
Interest expense	223	136	94
Other charges—net	6	46	34
	224	175	120
Income from Continuing Operations before Income Taxes	1,288	1,912	1,656
Income Taxes	467	664	583
Income from Continuing Operations	821	1,248	1,073
Loss on Disposal of Discontinued Operations, net of tax	(428)	—	—
Income (Loss) from Discontinued Operations, net of tax	(1)	12	8
Net Income	$ 392	$ 1,260	$1,081
Net Income (Loss) per Common Share, basic			
Continuing Operations	$ .78	$ 1.14	$ .95
Disposal of Discontinued Operations	(.41)	—	—
Discontinued Operations	—	.01	.01
Net Income	$ .37	$ 1.15	$ .96
Net Income (Loss) per Common Share, assuming full dilution			
Continuing Operations	$ .77	$ 1.13	$ .94
Disposal of Discontinued Operations	(.40)	—	—
Discontinued Operations	—	.01	.01
Net Income	$ .37	$ 1.14	$ .95
Weighted average number of common shares outstanding			
Basic	1,054	1,089	1,117
Assuming full dilution	1,063	1,111	1,144

See accompanying Notes to Consolidated Financial Statements.

Consolidated Balance Sheet
The Gillette Company and Subsidiary Companies

December 31, 2000 and 1999 (Millions, except per share amounts)	2000	1999
Assets		
Current Assets		
Cash and cash equivalents	$ 62	$ 80
Trade receivables, less allowance: 2000—$81; 1999—$74	2,128	2,208
Other receivables	378	319
Inventories	1,162	1,392
Deferred income taxes	566	309
Other current assets	197	315
Net assets of discontinued operations	189	1,174
Total Current Assets	4,682	5,797
Property, Plant and Equipment, at cost less accumulated depreciation	3,550	3,467
Intangible Assets, less accumulated amortization	1,574	1,897
Other Assets	596	625
	$10,402	$11,786
Liabilities and Stockholders' Equity		
Current Liabilities		
Loans payable	$ 2,195	$ 1,440
Current portion of long-term debt	631	358
Accounts payable and accrued liabilities	2,346	2,149
Income taxes	299	233
Total Current Liabilities	5,471	4,180
Long-Term Debt	1,650	2,931
Deferred Income Taxes	450	423
Other Long-Term Liabilities	767	795
Minority Interest	41	38
Contingent Redemption Value of Common Stock Put Options	99	359
Stockholders Equity		
8.0% Cumulative Series C ESOP Convertible Preferred, without par value, Issued: 1999—.1 shares	—	85
Unearned ESOP compensation	—	(4)
Common stock, par value $1 per share Authorized: 2,320 shares Issued: 2000—1,365 shares; 1999—1,364 shares	1,365	1,364
Additional paid-in capital	973	748
Earnings reinvested in the business	5,853	6,147
Accumulated other comprehensive income		
Foreign currency translation	(1,280)	(1,031)
Pension adjustment	(34)	(30)
Treasury stock, at cost: 2000—312 shares; 1999—299 shares	(4,953)	(4,219)
Total Stockholders' Equity	1,924	3,060
	$10,402	$11,786

See accompanying Notes to Consolidated Financial Statements.

EXHIBIT 13 Gillette's Financial Results *(continued)*

Consolidated Statement of Cash Flows
The Gillette Company and Subsidiary Companies

Years Ended December 31, 2000, 1999 and 1998 (Millions)	2000	1999	1998
Operating Activities			
Income from continuing operations	$ 821	$1,248	$1,073
Adjustments to reconcile income to net cash provided by operating activities:			
Provision for restructuring and asset impairment	572	—	440
Depreciation and amortization	535	464	421
Other	5	(7)	(46)
Changes in assets and liabilities, excluding effects of acquisition and divestitures:			
Accounts receivable	(100)	(48)	(442)
Inventories	149	(140)	(62)
Accounts payable and accrued liabilities	(45)	65	72
Other working capital items	(136)	97	(104)
Other noncurrent assets and liabilities	(197)	(252)	(142)
Funding German pension plans	—	—	(252)
Net cash provided by operating activities	1,604	1,427	958
Investing Activities			
Additions to property, plant and equipment	(793)	(889)	(952)
Disposals of property, plant and equipment	41	124	65
Acquisition of businesses, less cash acquired	—	—	(91)
Sale of businesses	539	—	200
Other	(1)	2	5
Net cash used in investing activities	(214)	(763)	(773)
Financing Activities			
Purchase of treasury stock	(944)	(2,021)	(1,066)
Proceeds from sale of put options	23	72	56
Proceeds from exercise of stock option and purchase plans	36	149	126
Proceeds from long-term debt	494	1,105	500
Repayment of long-term debt	(365)	—	(12)
Increase (decrease) in loans payable	(385)	484	708
Dividends paid	(671)	(626)	(552)
Settlements of debt-related derivative contracts	279	42	9
Net cash used financing activities	(1,533)	(795)	(231)
Effect of Exchange Rate Changes on Cash	(5)	(2)	(2)
Net Cash Provided by Discontinued Operations	130	111	45
Decrease in Cash and Cash Equivalents	(18)	(22)	(3)
Cash and Cash Equivalents at Beginning of Year	80	102	105
Cash and Cash Equivalents at End of Year	$ 62	$ 80	$ 102
Supplemental disclosure of cash paid for:			
Interest	$ 243	$ 126	$ 120
Income taxes	$ 480	$ 457	$ 473
Noncash investing and financing activities:			
Acquisition of businesses			
Fair value of assets acquired	$ —	$ —	$ 100
Cash paid	—	—	91
Liabilities assumed	$ —	$ —	$ 9

See accompanying Notes to Consolidated Financial Statements.

Source: http://www.gillette.com.

coherent vision for the future and a growth strategy that included several unrelated diversifications and acquisitions have resulted in a decline in the effectiveness of operations and in sales.[29] A stock repurchase plan and a failure to effectively utilize Gillette's asset base further aggravated these problems.

In October 2000, Gillette's board of directors (see Exhibit 14) ousted Michael Hawley 18 months after appointing him CEO. James Kilts was named Gillette's new CEO and chairman of the board as of February 12, 2001 (see Exhibit 15). As the CEO at Nabisco, James Kilts was a driving force behind the company's revitalization. Gillette's board of directors is hopeful that his 30 years of experience in consumer goods, which requires the development of strong brands for long-term market differentiation and success, will revive profit and sales growth for Gillette.

James Kilts is also concentrating on returning Gillette to its historical focus on growth and increasing shareholder value.[30] His biggest challenge will be to transform a corporate culture "that has become far too insular, provincial, and inbred."[31] In addition, Mr. Kilts will have to address Gillette's poor relations with retailers, as Gillette is not as involved with Wal-Mart and other globally dominant chains as are its competitors.[32]

Gillette's 2000 Annual Report lists areas targeted for improvement. To improve annual results that were less than expected for the past two years, the CEO suggests increasing understanding of Gillette's businesses and marketplaces. He hopes to establish consistency in performance by exceeding current growth rates in order to outperform Gillette's competitors over time. Gillette's innovativeness will continue to be encouraged. To make it an asset to the company, the cost of research and development and the cost of bringing products to market must have positive returns, and Gillette must increase its return on invested capital. Last, Gillette must increase its marketing efforts to generate awareness and customer value for its new products as its advertising-to-sales ratio was only 6.5 percent last year. Currently, Gillette's advertising spending lags behind most of its competitors. Gillette has never had the reputation of a first-rate sales and marketing company.[33] To remedy this situation, James Kilts has already announced plans to increase spending on advertising and promotion and to cut costs in order to improve asset and inventory management, free cash flow, operating efficiency, and market share.

However, in order to increase advertising, Gillette must have funds available. Therefore, Gillette must improve its operating and cash cycles by becoming more effective and efficient regarding the handling of inventory and accounts receivable and by controlling its general and administrative spending. Increasing the available funds may also lead to acquisitions and alliances, increased global penetration, and expansion into high-growth product categories.[34] Thus, the main issue facing Gillette's management is whether the company should return to its historical focus in the shaving industry or whether it should continue to diversify in order to restore growth and to gain beneficial synergies in areas such as product distribution.

Board of Directors EXHIBIT 14

Warren E. Buffett, Chairman and Chief Executive Officer, Berkshire Hathaway Inc.
Edward F. DeGraan, President and Chief Operating Officer, The Gillette Company
Wilbur H. Gantz, Chairman and Chief Executive Officer, PathoGenesis Corporation
Michael B. Gifford, Former Chief Executive, The Rank Organisation Plc
Carol R. Goldberg, President, The Avcar Group, Ltd.
Dennis F. Hightower, Former Chief Executive Officer, Europe Online Networks, S.A.
Herbert H. Jacobi, Chairman of the Supervisory Board, HSBC Trinkaus & Burkhardt KgaA
James M. Kilts, Chairman of the Board and Chief Executive Officer, The Gillette Company
Henry R. Kravis, General Partner, Kohlberg Kravis Roberts & Co., L.P.
Jorge Paulo Lemann, General Partner, GP Investimentos
Richard R. Pivirotto, President, Richard R. Pivirotto Co., Inc.
Marjorie M. Yang, Chairman, Esquel Group of Companies

Source: 2001, "Board of Directors," The Gillette Company, http://www.gillette.com/company/boardofdirectors.asp, October 22.

EXHIBIT 15 Officers

Chairman of the Board and Chief Executive Officer

James M. Kilts

President and Chief Operating Officer

Edward F. DeGraan

Senior Vice Presidents

Charles W. Cramb — *Finance*

Edward E. Guillet — *Human Resources*

Peter Klein — *Strategy and Business Development*

John F. Manfredi — *Corporate Affairs*

Richard K. Willard — *Legal and General Counsel*

Vice Presidents

Duncan J. Adamson — *Internal Audit*

Gian U. Camuzzi — *Treasurer*

A. Bruce Cleverly — *Global Business Management*

James P. Connolly — *Legal*

Michael T. Cowhig — *Global Supply Chain and Business Development*

Joseph F. Dooley — *Commercial Operations North America*

A. Wallace Hayes — *Corporate Product Integrity*

Peter K. Hoffman — *Global Business Management*

Eric A. Kraus — *Corporate Communications*

Mark M. Leckie — *Global Business Management*

John M. McGowan — *Taxation*

Claudio E. Ruben — *Controller and Principal Accounting Officer*

Edward D. Shirley — *Commercial Operations Europe*

John C. Terry — *Corporate Research and Development*

Dieter Timmermann — *Corporate Information Technology*

Michelle E. Viotty — *Finance, Global Technical and Manufacturing*

Patent and Trademark Counsel

Donal B. Tobin

Secretary

William J. Mostyn III, Esq.

Associate General Counsels

Carol S. Fischman

Kevin Loftus

Timothy N. MacCaw

Assistant General Counsels

John Gatlin

Deborah Marson

Peter G. V. Mee

Assistant Treasurer

Gail Sullivan

Source: 2001, "Board of Directors," The Gillette Company, http://www.gillette.com/company/executives.asp, October 22.

NOTES

1. King C. Gillette, 2001, "Gillette at a glance," The Gillette Company, http://www.gillette.com/, October 22.

2. Ibid.

3. 2001, "Historical Timeline," The Gillette Company, http://www.gillette.com/, October 22; 2001, "The world's most valuable brands 2000," Finfacts — The Irish Finance Portal, http://www.finfacts.com/brands.htm, October 22.

4. William C. Symonds and Julie Forster, 2001, Can James Kilts put a new edge on Gillette, *BusinessWeek Online*, http://www.businessweek.com/, January 26.

5. LouAnn Lofton, 2001, Gillette's Q4 and more, *The Motley Fool*, http://www.fool.com/, January 26.

6. 2001, "Historical Timeline," The Gillette Company, October 22.

7. 2001, "Fundamental Strengths," 2000 Annual Report, The Gillette Company, http://www.gillette.com/, October 22.

8. 2001, Gillette reports results for the fourth-quarter and full-year 2000, *Business Wire*, http://www.corporateir.net/, January 26.

9. 2001, "Investor Relations Overview," The Gillette Company, http://www.gillette.com/, October 22.

10. 2001, 1999 Annual Report, The Gillette Company, http://www.gillette.com/, October 22.

11. 2001, Gillette reports results for the fourth-quarter and full-year 2000, January 26.

12. 2001, "Fundamental Strengths," The Gillette Company, October 22.

13. 2001, Gillette reports third-quarter and nine-month results," *Business Wire*, http://www.corporate-ir.net/, October 19.

14. 2001, Gillette reports results for the fourth-quarter and full-year 2000, January 26.

15. Ibid.

16. 2001, Pfizer 2000 Annual Report, Pfizer, http://www.pfizer.com/pfizerinc/investing/annual/2000/pfizer2000ar29.html, October 22.

17. 2001, "Company Overview," The American Safety Razor Company, http://www.asrco.com/, October 22.

18. Gillette reports results for the fourth-quarter and full-year 2000.

19. 2001, 2000 Annual Report, Colgate-Palmolive, http://www.colgate.com/cp/corp.class/investor_relations/annualReportContents00.jsp, October 22.

20. Colgate-Palmolive 2000 Annual Report.

21. 2002, 2002 Annual Report, Procter & Gamble, http://www.pg.com/annualreports/2002/financial/highlights.html, January 8.

22. 2001, "Latest from Our Brands—Crest Spinbrush," 2001 Annual Report, Procter & Gamble, http://www.pg.com/annualreports/2001/editorial/crest.jhtml, October 22.

23. 2002 Annual Report, Procter & Gamble.

24. 2001, "Our Body," Home & Body, Philips Electronics, http://www.philips.com, October 22.

25. 2001, Gillette reports results for the fourth-quarter and full-year 2000, *Business Wire*, http://www.corporateir.net/ireye/ir_site.zhtml?ticker=g&script=411&layout=7&item_id=14772, January 26.

26. 2001, "Fundamentals," Quicken, http://www.quicken.com/investments/stats/?symbol=ENR,+g, October 22.

27. 2001, 2000 Annual Report, The Gillette Company, http://www.gillette.com/investors/annual_report/2000/, October 22.

28. 2001, "Fundamentals," Quicken, http://www.quicken.com/investments/stats/?symbol=ENR,+g, October 22.

29. 2000 Annual Report, The Gillette Company, October 22, 2001.

30. Lofton, LouAnn. January 26, 2001.

31. Symonds and Forster, January 26, 2001.

32. 2001, "Gillette reports third-quarter and nine-month results," October 19.

33. Symonds and Forster, Can James Kilts put a new edge on Gillette."

34. 2000 Annual Report, The Gillette Company.

case fifteen

Lisa-Marie Mulkern
Alan N. Hoffman
Bentley College

My focus today, 100 percent, is making Handspring successful, making handheld computing successful. I still view the handheld computing industry as very embryonic; it's very early on. It's like 1982 of the PC world. And the big things haven't happened yet. As much success as Palm has had, and as much success as Handspring is currently having, it's just the beginning, and it takes a lot of concentrated effort to build a big business. And we think Handspring's going to be a very big business.[1]

—*Jeff Hawkins, Handspring's Chairman and Chief Product Officer*

JEFFREY HAWKINS: THE JOURNEY FROM GRID SYSTEMS TO TREO

Handspring was founded in 1998 by three key executives from Palm Computing—Jeff Hawkins, currently Handspring's chairman and chief product officer; Donna Dubinsky, president and CEO; and Ed Colligan, the chief operating officer. At Palm Computing, Hawkins had been the chief inventor, Dubinsky the president and CEO, and Colligan the vice president of marketing. The three veterans of handheld computing were credited with reviving the industry through their successful launch of the PalmPilot in 1996.

The widespread success and ongoing technological improvements found in today's handheld computing devices are a direct result of Handspring chairman Jeff Hawkins' design work at GriD Systems back in the early 1980s. After graduating from Cornell University in 1979 with a Bachelor of Science degree in electrical engineering, and after a short tenure at Intel, Hawkins began working at GriD Systems in 1982. While at GriD Systems, Hawkins developed a high-level programming language called GriDTask that would later fuel further technological advancements in handheld computing, particularly in the area of text entry. Hawkins' work on GriDTask also increased his interest in the area of brain research.

In response to this interest, Hawkins left his position at GriD in 1986 to pursue his Ph.D. at Berkeley. As Hawkins explained, he was in search of answers to such questions as, "What does it mean for a brain, or for a system like a brain, to understand its environment? What is a reductionist approach to understanding language, vision, and hearing? And what are the concepts underlying that?"[2] Although his Ph.D. thesis proposal was rejected because no professors at Berkeley were pursuing similar research, a pattern classifier program that Hawkins had written was patented and used as a hand-printed-character recognizer. With his thesis proposal rejected and experiencing difficulties with being a graduate student after having had a successful career, Hawkins decided that he would return to the computer industry in lieu of pursuing his academic interests. Hawkins returned to GriD Systems as the vice president of research and began working on the first handheld computing device, the GriDPAD, which was released in 1989. Hawkins' personal goal at the time he rejoined GriD Systems was "to become famous enough and wealthy enough to really promote and sponsor significant research in neurobiology and theoretical neurobiology."[3]

The GriDPAD measured $9 \times 12 \times 1.4$ inches and ran on a 10MHz 80C86 processor with a DOS platform. The handheld used GriD's own software solu-

This case was prepared by Professor Lisa-Marie Mulkern, MBA student, and Professor Alan N. Hoffman of Bentley College for the purpose of classroom discussion only and not to indicate either effective or ineffective management. Reprinted by permission of Dr. Alan N. Hoffman, *ahoffman@bentley.edu*, 781.891.2287, AAC320, Bentley College, 175 Forest Street, Waltham, MA, 02452-4705.

The authors would like to thank Scott Barry, Wendy Dalwin, Lindsey Fuller, Bob Mammarella, and Diane Shaffer for their research and contributions to this case.

tions that were written in GriDTask. With a Color Graphics Adapter (640 × 400) display, the GriDTask cost $2,370 exclusive of software and used 256 or 512KB battery-backed RAM cards. Using the character recognition engine that Hawkins developed, users were able to enter text using either a pen or a keyboard. The GriDPAD was marketed primarily to data collection users in such areas as transportation and warehousing as well as to police, nurses, and census takers.

In Hawkins' mind, the GriDPAD was only a first step toward his revolutionary vision for handheld computing. Hawkins believed that the success of handheld computers depended upon developing a product that was both small and lightweight enough for people to carry around with them all the time. Hawkins developed the specifications for a handheld computing device that was aptly named "Zoomer"—short for consumer, the device's intended market. However, the executives at GriD were opposed to plans for entering the consumer market. Unable to find support from within, Hawkins left GriD in 1992 with a software license for the GriD-PAD and founded Palm Computing.

CORPORATE GOVERNANCE

Exhibit 1 shows the seven members of the board of directors of Handspring, Inc. Five members are external directors. The exhibit also shows the ten members of Handspring's executive team.

THE PALMPILOT ERA

On the heels of the GriDPAD's success, several high-tech companies, including IBM, NCR, NEC, and Samsung, joined in the rush to develop the next small computing device. Apple had been in the development phase of a handheld computing device since 1987. In 1992, John Sculley, then CEO of Apple, coined the term "personal digital assistant," or PDA.[4]

Following an initial commercial failure with the launch of the Zoomer, Palm went back to the drawing board and re-emerged in 1996 with its second product, the PalmPilot. U.S. Robotics funded the development of the PalmPilot through its acquisition of Palm Computing in 1995 for $44 million in stock. It was at this time that Palm transformed itself from a strictly software company to one that would develop an entire product—both hardware and software. Hawkins created what he calls "a virtual company" by partnering with several hardware design and contract-manufacturing companies to bring the product to market. The PalmPilot was a success, and as a result, Jeff Hawkins and his colleagues Donna Dubinsky and Ed Colligan were cred-

ited with reviving the handheld computing industry. The PalmPilot was the most successful product launch in computing history, selling faster than VCRs, color TVs, cell phones, and personal computers.

THE EXODUS AT PALM

By 1998, however, Hawkins, Dubinsky, and Colligan were already setting the stage for their departure from Palm and the formation of their own handheld computing company. Collectively, the three executives did not believe that Palm was a strategic match for 3Com and requested that Palm be spun off as a separate company. Eric Benhamou, 3Com's CEO, insisted that Palm would never be spun off because it was simply too important to the business. In addition to wanting a Palm spin-off, the trio felt pressured to deliver products too quickly. As an example, Hawkins pointed to the fact that he felt pressured to deliver a wireless handheld in the form of the Palm VII. As Hawkins describes, "We were still at U.S. Robotics at the time, and the CEO, Casey Coswell, kept saying, 'I want you to do a wireless Palm.'" Hawkins objected on the basis that he would not have a great solution to deliver, but he ultimately yielded to the pressure by "doing the best that he could" with the development and subsequent release of the Palm VII wireless handheld in 1999.[5]

In response to these frustrations and armed with a license for the Palm operating system as well as the confidence that they could develop improved handheld computing devices, the three executives left Palm in July 1998 to form Handspring. On September 14, 1999, one day after 3Com announced its plans to spin off Palm, Handspring unveiled its first handheld computing device, the Visor.

HANDSPRING VISOR

The Visor featured the Springboard expansion slot consisting of a series of modules for adding the capabilities of a digital camera, a wireless Web device, a cellular phone, or an MP3 music player. Many Palm enthusiasts followed Hawkins and his colleagues over to Handspring. The new company was overwhelmed with orders, and it took nearly four months before the supply was satisfying consumer demand for the new product. By the summer of 2000, Handspring's market share for Palm-based PDAs had reached 40 percent. Handspring went public in June 2000 with an IPO price of $20.00 per share. By October 2000, Handspring's stock price skyrocketed to $95.00 per share. These successes attracted the attention of Palm and, throughout most of 2001, Palm and Handspring engaged in a price war

EXHIBIT 1   Board of Directors and Executive Team: Handspring, Inc.

A. Board of Directors

Donna L. Dubinsky
*President, Chief Executive Officer
and Acting Chief Financial Officer
of Handspring, Inc.*

Jeffrey C. Hawkins
*Chairman and Chief Product
Officer of Handspring, Inc.*

Kim B. Clark
*Dean of Harvard
Business School*

L. John Doerr
*General Partner of Kleiner
Perkins Caufield & Byers*

Bruce W. Dunlevie
*Managing Member of
Benchmark Capital*

William E. Kennard
*Managing Director of
The Carlyle Group*

Mitchell E. Kertzman
*Chief Executive Officer and
Chairman of Liberate
Technologies*

B. Executive Team

Jeffrey Hawkins
Founder, Chairman, and Chief Product Officer

Jeff Hawkins cofounded Handspring with Donna Dubinsky in July 1998 after five years together at Palm Computing. In 1994, Hawkins invented the original PalmPilot products and founded Palm Computing. He is often credited as the designer who reinvented the handheld market.

   An industry veteran with nearly 20 years of technical expertise, Hawkins currently holds nine patents for various handheld devices and features. His vision for handheld computing dates back to the 1980s, when, as vice president of research at GriD Systems Corporation, he served as principal architect and designer for the GriDPAD and GriD Convertible. Prior to that, he held key technical positions with Intel Corporation. Hawkins earned his B.S. in electrical engineering from Cornell University.

   He is also the founder and executive director of the nonprofit Redwood Neuroscience Institute, a scientific research institute working on theories and mathematical models of brain function (http://www.rni.org).

Donna Dubinsky
Founder and CEO

Donna Dubinsky cofounded Handspring with Jeff Hawkins in July 1998 to create a new breed of handheld computers for consumers. As president and CEO of Palm Computing, Dubinsky helped make the PalmPilot the best-selling handheld computer and the most rapidly adopted new computing product ever produced. When Dubinsky first joined Hawkins at Palm Computing in 1992, shortly after the company was founded, she brought with her more than ten years of marketing and logistics experience from Apple and Claris. Dubinsky and Hawkins introduced the original PalmPilot in February 1996, a move that revitalized the handheld computing industry.

   In addition to her position as CEO of Handspring, Dubinsky currently serves as a director of Intuit Corporation and is a trustee of the Computer History Museum. She earned her B.A. from Yale University and her M.B.A. from the Harvard Graduate School of Business Administration.

Ed Colligan

Founder, President, and COO

Ed Colligan joined Handspring to lead the development and marketing efforts for a new generation of handheld computers. As the vice president of marketing for Palm Computing, Ed Colligan worked with Jeff Hawkins and Donna Dubinsky to lead the product marketing and marketing communications efforts for Palm, including the successful positioning, launch, and marketing of the popular Palm product family.

Prior to Palm, Colligan was vice president of strategic and product marketing at Radius Corporation. During his eight years there, Colligan helped make Radius the brand leader in Macintosh graphics, graphic imaging, and hardware development.

Colligan's multiple successes have earned him several marketing industry accolades. *Marketing Computers* magazine named him the 1997 Marketer of the Year, and *Advertising Age* named him one of the Top 100 Marketers of 1997, an award that spanned all product categories. He holds a B.A. from the University of Oregon.

Bill Slakey

Chief Financial Officer

Before joining Handspring in September 2002, Bill Slakey was chief financial officer at WJ Communications, a leading RF semiconductor company. Prior to that, he was CFO at SnapTrack, a Qualcomm company that pioneered the industry's most advanced GPS-based wireless tracking system for pinpointing wireless phones, PDAs, pagers, and other wireless devices.

Slakey has over 16 years of experience in financial management, including a senior controller position at 3COM's Palm Computing Division and various financial roles spanning ten years at Apple Computer. Slakey holds a B.A. from the University of California and an M.B.A. from the Harvard Graduate School of Business Administration.

John Hartnett

Vice President, Worldwide Operations

John Hartnett joined Handspring from MetaCreations, where he served most recently as senior vice president of marketing, support and operations for the United States. At MetaCreations, he was responsible for developing the marketing, branding, and advertising strategies, including online marketing and website redesign.

Prior to his tenure at MetaCreations, Hartnett served as director of international operations at Claris, where he developed and managed the operations business plan and was part of the lead team in the merger of the Applesoft and Claris businesses. Hartnett also spent time at AT&T, GIS, Digital Equipment, and Wang. Hartnett earned a marketing degree through the Marketing Institute of Ireland and a postgraduate diploma in finance through the ACCA.

Patricia Tomlinson

Vice President, Human Resources

With over 20 years of experience in the human resources field, Patricia Tomlinson came to Handspring from Edify Corporation where she was responsible for the worldwide human resources department. She also designed and implemented all HR-related programs and led the worldwide integration of all HR functions for the merger of Edify with Security First Technologies.

Prior to Edify Corporation, Tomlinson grew her experience at Xerox Corporation; Synopsys, Inc.; and Apple Computer, Inc. She holds a B.A. in sociology from Pomona College in Claremont, California, and completed the Program for Management Development from Harvard Business School.

Celeste Baranski
Vice President, Engineering

Celeste Baranski joined Handspring with over 18 years of engineering, design, and management experience in the mobile computing industry. Most recently, Baranski worked at Hewlett-Packard Company as research and development manager of its Mobile Computing Division, where she led R&D, manufacturing introduction, and quality assurance for the company's laptop computer product line.

Before Hewlett-Packard, Baranski worked as a consultant and director of R&D for Norand Corporation, where she was in charge of product design and engineering management for various companies, including Plantronics, Kalidor, IDEO, and Divicom. Prior to that she cofounded and served as vice president of hardware engineering for EO Incorporated, and was also among the first employees at GO Corporation where she designed the first GO pen-based computer.

Baranski has also held technical staff positions at GriD Systems and Rolm Corporation. She holds both a B.S. and an M.S. in electrical engineering from Stanford University.

David Pine
Vice President and General Counsel

David joined Handspring in May 2000 as vice president and general counsel. Prior to Handspring, he served as senior vice president and general counsel for Excite@Home, a broadband online service provider. Before that he was vice president, general counsel of Radius Inc., a manufacturer of Macintosh computer peripherals. He started his career in private practice with Fenwick & West, LLP, a Silicon Valley law firm representing start up and high-growth technology companies. He also has been involved in government and politics, and has served as a state representative in the New Hampshire legislature.

He holds a B.A. degree in government from Dartmouth College, where he was awarded a Harry S. Truman Scholarship, and a J.D. degree from the University of Michigan Law School.

Joe Sipher
Vice President, Worldwide Marketing

Joe Sipher joined Handspring in May 2000. Sipher is a long-time veteran of the handheld industry, having joined Palm, Inc. in 1993. His most recent role there was serving as Palm's first and only Palm Fellow. Before his fellowship, Joe ran Palm's wireless business, including the definition, development, and introduction of the Palm VII wireless Internet handheld. Joe was responsible for the hardware and software development of the breakthrough Palm VII product, and spearheaded the creation of Palm's wireless Internet service, Palm.Net. Before the Palm VII, Joe managed the PalmPilot product line and was a product manager on the original Pilot project.

Prior to Palm, Inc., Joe's work experience included positions at Microsoft and Apple. He holds five patents pertaining to handheld and wireless technology. He earned a B.A. and an M.B.A. with high distinction from the University of Michigan.

Gregory Woock
Vice President, Worldwide Sales

Gregory Woock joined Handspring in 1999 with over ten years of experience in sales and marketing within the high-tech industry. Prior to Handspring, Woock served as vice president of sales at Creative Labs, Inc. As one of the original members of the pre-IPO team, Mr. Woock helped build Creative from a small start-up into a dominant brand. Mr. Woock was responsible for sales, channel marketing, sales training, and sales operations in the United States, Canada, and Latin America.

Woock earned his B.A. from Columbia College in Chicago.

with their competing handheld computing devices. Meanwhile, Microsoft was pressing ahead with its own version of a handheld computer, the Pocket PC, which had been introduced in early 1998.

In response to the increasing competition and pricing pressure in the handheld computing market, Handspring refocused its strategy with the introduction of the Treo line of communicators in fall 2001. Handspring's executives had decided that the market for strictly PDAs had become too crowded. The resulting price wars had eroded Handspring's margins and prevented the start-up from achieving its much-anticipated profitability.

The Treo Communicator

Handspring had learned some valuable lessons through the development of its Visor product line. In particular, the two-year development process of the VisorPhone module taught the company several valuable lessons about phone and radio technology. In turn, Handspring's designers were able to utilize this experience in the development of the Treo product line, which began in summer 2000 and was completed within 14 months.

Operating under the code name Manhattan, the Treo product development team consisted of both hardware and software developers. Each of the communicator's component parts also had New York–inspired names, such as Shea Stadium for the Graffiti handwriting system, Central Park for the screen, and Metro for the circuit board. In stark contrast to their rival Palm Computing, which had recently split its hardware and software subsidiaries into two separate companies, Handspring's hardware and software developers worked together to design a communicator that addressed how and where people actually used their wireless devices. Additionally, rather than employing traditional focus groups, Handspring employed an ethnographer who observed how people used both their cell phones and PDAs in everyday situations such as while driving or riding the subway.[6] Such observations indicated that people preferred to use their cell phone with one hand to avoid the distractions of juggling. The Treo combines a thumb touch QWERTY keyboard with the capability to look up addresses and telephone numbers by typing initials, and Handspring's executives are confident that it will set the company back on course toward near-term profitability.

In December 2001, Dubinsky announced that the Visor line would be phased out of production and that the company planned to achieve profitability by its fiscal year end on June 30, 2002. Handspring would eventually focus exclusively on the Treo platform of communicators, which, in contrast to the hardware-based Visor products, allow users to increase functionality through additional software as opposed to bulky hardware expansions (see Exhibit 2).

Handspring's Competitors

Since Handspring continues to serve the traditional PDA market while refocusing its strategy on becoming a leading provider of communicators, the company faces competition from a variety of providers. The competition between PDAs and smart phones continues to fuel the convergence of these two traditionally separate markets. PDA sales after 2004 will be strongly affected by smart phones.[7] A recent Strand Consult report stated that Palm and Handspring would have difficulty surviving in the smart phone market because they lack experience in the mobile phone market and are faced with strong competition. Some analysts believe that Microsoft's 2.5G Smart Phone platform will succeed because of the company's strong customer base.[8] Nokia, Sony Ericsson, Siemens, and Motorola have more financial strength to compete in the market for smart phones and smart handheld devices.[9] Traditional PDA providers such as Palm, Sharp, and Sony compete most directly with Handspring's Visor product line, while software and cell phone giants such as Microsoft and Nokia are concentrating their resources on combining the capabilities of wireless and handheld computing into their own versions of communicators that will compete for market share alongside Handspring's Treo products.

Palm i705

Palm is still the undisputed market share leader in the PDA market. However, the company has been under fire by competitors for several years and is clearly in the crosshairs of Microsoft and its Pocket PC operating system. Palm's current competitive advantage is its operating system, which is licensed to many PDA makers. The Palm i705 is the upgrade from the Palm VIIx. The i705 provides wireless e-mail and Internet access, but lacks a long battery life and a color screen, and has only 8MB of memory. Although the Palm i705 does not have cellular capability, it has "always-on" access to e-mail. This feature notifies the user by a blink, beep, or vibration when there is a new e-mail and has a very comprehensive support system that is second to none.

Sharp Zaurus SL-500

Sharp is not a major player in the PDA market, but it is making some changes to its product in order to gain

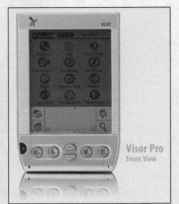

Visor™ expandable handheld computers.

The Visor model line features both B&W and color screens, uses rechargeable or alkaline batteries, and ranges in list price from $169 to $229. This is Handspring's original product offering.

Springboard™ modules transform the Visor into a digital camera, wireless web device, MP3 player, and more.

Handspring offers more than 70 different modules. Some modules are included free with the purchase of a Visor handheld while other modules have a list price in excess of $400.

Treo™ 90—handheld computer organizer.

The Treo 90 features a color screen, rechargeable battery, QWERTY keyboard, and SD/MMC expansion capabilities. It currently lists for $299.

Treo™ communicators are combination phone, messaging device, data organizer, and Web access devices.

The original Treo 180 lists for $399, while the improved Treo 270, offering global telephone coverage, released in 2002, lists for $499. The Sprint PCS Treo 300, the result of a highly collaborative partnership, scheduled for release in late 2002, will run on Sprint PCS' nationwide 3G data network. The Treo 300 will list for $449 after mail-in rebate.

Software and accessories (cases, cables, cradles, keyboards, etc.) for Visor and Treo products.

A variety of accessories and additional software are available from Handspring and other third-party providers. Accessories for Handspring's family of products range in price from $10.00 to $50.00 and are model specific. The Treo e-mail annual subscription ranges in price from $49.99 to $99.99.

recognition and market share. The Zaurus SL-500 offers a hidden thumb keyboard as well as built-in handwriting-recognition software. Perhaps most noteworthy, the Sharp PDA is operating on a Linux operating system, which is getting some attention from software developers. The Zaurus also has a wide range of accessories, 64MB of RAM, and an Intel processor. Although Sharp has taken a big step forward, there are still some bugs that must be worked out to simplify software installation and Outlook access before it becomes a force in the current market.

SONY CLIE PEG-N760C

Sony has one of the best products in the PDA market. Its long-term commitment to R&D and innovation makes it a market leader in almost every industry in which it competes. Although it is more expensive than other Palm OS devices, the CLIE offers a 65,334 color display screen along with MP3 audio capability, easy-to-use controls, remote control headphones, and picture/video viewing software. With some changes in its price and improvements in memory, Sony has the potential to utilize its deep pockets and strong product development capabilities to either enter the cellular PDA market or work with a phone producer to enter the market.

COMPAQ IPAQ 3835

The iPaq is one of the newer products in the PDA market. With a color screen, 64MB of RAM, the Pocket PC 2002 operating system, and improvements to its memory card and speakers, Compaq is positioned to increase its market share. Compaq's only setback at this time is the price of its PDA. At $699, it is more expensive than its competitors. With the merger of HP and Compaq, the market for the iPaq has the potential to increase through the combined efforts of these two leaders in personal computing.

RIM/BLACKBERRY 957

With a more solid financial backing, Blackberry would be a force in the market. Blackberry 957 has PDA and phone capabilities with a battery that lasts upwards of

80 hours. Blackberry was the first to develop the thumb keyboard and is widely preferred by its users. Compatible to applications such as Outlook and corporate networks, Blackberry has over 13,000 companies using its product. Although you cannot receive attachments via e-mail, the system is always ready to receive mail. Even with a price tag of $499, Blackberry is struggling to improve its financial performance.

SAMSUNG SPH-M330

The Samsung PDA is positioned to compete directly with the Handspring Treo, Blackberry, and Kyocera models. The SPH-M330 has a color screen, support for an external camera, and cellular capability, and runs on the Palm OS. The device also uses gpsOne, a service that can display a map of the user's location and the immediate vicinity on the LCD screen. The company will launch the product through Sprint PCS, but still lacks the brand recognition of Handspring and the other market share leaders.

KYOCERA SMARTPHONE QCP 6035

Kyocera is Japan's version of the smart phone. The PDA portion of the device runs on a Palm OS and is compatible with most third-party applications. Kyocera is new to the U.S. market but will likely thrive in the Japanese market, which is usually protected by strict tariffs and import regulations.

NOKIA 9290 COMMUNICATOR

The Nokia 9290 Communicator was released into the U.S. market in 2002. It runs on the Symbian operating system and offers a full color screen. The 9290 is capable of sending and receiving images, sound, and video clips. The handheld combines phone, fax, e-mail, calendar, and Internet access as well as support for PC applications such as Microsoft Word, Excel, and PowerPoint. It is currently being marketed as "the one device that does it all" and lists for $599.

MICROSOFT POCKET PC PHONE EDITION

Microsoft is focused on the enterprise/corporate users who will use products compatible with the operating systems and software that are also likely controlled by Microsoft. It is more profitable to sell and support 5,000 Pocket PCs to one business than to 5,000 consumers. It is Microsoft's deep pockets and R&D capability that pose the largest threat to reposition the PDA/phone market share. Although the product does not possess the capabilities of the Treo, Microsoft has just entered this market. The current device provides access to Outlook, e-mail functions, and browsing and eventually will be tied into Microsoft's new Mobile Information Server software, acting as a liaison between phones and Exchange. The Microsoft Pocket PC 2002 Phone Edition combines a phone and an organizer into a device that contains versions of Microsoft Word and Excel with an Internet browser. The device currently lists for $549.

HANDSPRING'S STRATEGY FOR THE TREO COMMUNICATORS

Treo = phone + organizer + e-mail + Web

In the seemingly overcrowded market for traditional PDAs (see Figure 1), Handspring is committed to setting itself apart from the competition with the introduction of the Treo line of communicators. In pursuit of this objective, Handspring is seeking to reach beyond the consumer market and become a force in the corporate wireless market. Corporate customers using the Treo will be able to access e-mail and more-sophisticated corporate data through the Wireless Business Engine, or opt for the try-then-buy desktop software. Handspring is marketing this new product as "several digital products all in one tiny package."

The company has recently formed an Enterprise Alliance Partnership (EAP) Program to assist in its objective of bringing communications solutions and wireless handheld devices to corporations. Handspring plans to maximize its existing relationships with retailers, enterprise-focused resellers, corporate systems integrators, and wireless service providers to branch out toward a broader set of corporate clients. A primary example of the company's commitment to the EAP Program is its highly collaborative experience in developing the Sprint PCS Treo 300. The Treo 300, scheduled for release in fall 2002, was designed exclusively for Sprint's nationwide 3G data network. According to Handspring chief operating officer Ed Colligan, "By working with the best integrators and back-end software providers in the industry, we can leverage each other's experience to give corporate customers exactly what they want."[10]

Handspring is also committed to increasing its marketing and distribution channels through similar partnership arrangements. On December 17, 2001, Handspring announced a strategic marketing and sales partnership with Neomar, a leading developer of wireless enterprise software solutions. The companies will work together on product evaluation, testing, and training. They will also combine sales and marketing efforts for Handspring's Visor and Treo product lines with Neomar's mobile infrastructure software for corporate customers.[11] Other strategic partnerships include Wireless Knowledge, Inc. (a subsidiary of Qualcomm Incor-

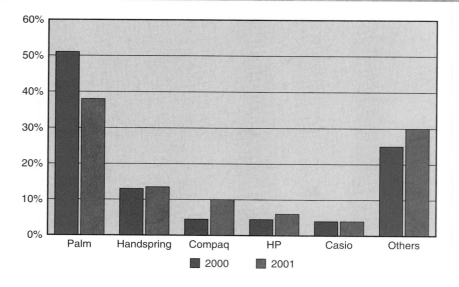

FIGURE 1   PDA Worldwide Market Share

porated), Visto Corporation, Aether Systems, AvantGo, Extended Systems, and Synchrologic.

HOW IMPORTANT IS THE MICROSOFT OS?

According to Neil Ward-Dutton of Ovum, most consumers of PDAs are business users who are reimbursed by their companies. There is not yet a general consumer market. This gives Microsoft and companies using the Microsoft operating system an advantage over Handspring's use of the Palm operating system. Company IT departments will prefer products that use the same operating system as the company computer systems.[12] The Microsoft Pocket PC will run versions of Word and Excel. Others contend that compatibility with the desktop is more important than compatibility with back-end applications.[13] In a 2001 interview with *Business 2.0*, Jeff Hawkins claimed that he does not believe the OS is nearly as important to handhelds as it was to PCs. When asked if he has made a decision to use another operating system in lieu of continuing to license Palm's technology, Hawkins responded, "Long term, if Handspring grows as large as I think it will be . . . it is almost certain that we will have products that do not run on Palm. But that is not a product announcement."[14]

ENSURING PROFITABILITY PROJECTIONS ON THE BASIS OF TREO'S INITIAL SUCCESS

In the midst of Handspring's attempts to refocus its strategy on the communicator market, the young company is still struggling to achieve profitability. It has had a net loss every year since its inception.[15] While its sales are increasing, net profit is decreasing. Worldwide, the market for PDAs is increasing. According to Gartner Dataquest, the number of PDAs shipped increased 18 percent from 2000 to 2001[16] (see Figure 2). Handspring's net profit, however, decreased as a result of downward pricing pressures from an increasing number of competitors. Gross margins fell from 31 percent to 9 percent during FY2001. Although Handspring received an additional $57 million in funding in January 2002, Donna Dubinsky knows that the shareholders are expecting profitability in the near future.

Dubinsky was reviewing her comments from the company's quarterly and fiscal year-end conference call for June 30, 2002. During the conference call, Handspring announced that Jeff Hawkins has recently formed the nonprofit Redwood Neuroscience Institute to pursue his lifelong passion for brain research. He would split his time between the Institute and serving as Handspring's chief product officer and chairman of the board of directors. With Hawkins no longer 100 percent focused on Handspring, Dubinsky wants to assure shareholders that the company will continue to successfully execute its plans for the Treo communicators in both the near and long term.

When Handspring unveiled its plans to transition to a communicator-based company, Dubinsky also predicted profitability by mid-2002. However, consumers were still taking a "wait and see" approach and looking for a compelling technological breakthrough to convince them that an upgrade to a

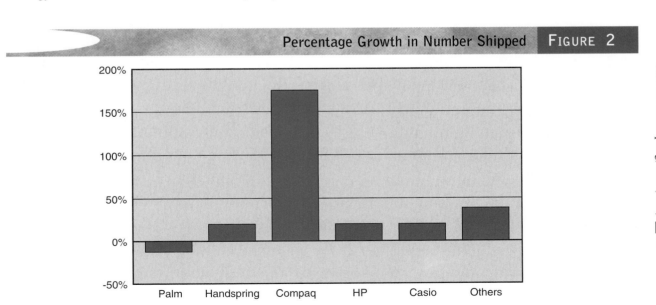

Percentage Growth in Number Shipped | FIGURE 2

Data Source: Gartner Dataquest, February 2002.

communicator was warranted. Consumer reluctance combined with an economic slowdown prevented the company from achieving its fiscal year-end profitability as predicted.

Although profitability objectives were still unmet, Dubinsky reported that the Treo is being well received in the marketplace with over 93,000 units shipped to date. Additionally, the Treo product line has significantly improved margins from 9.2 percent to 24.5 percent over the prior fiscal year-end. Unlike the Visor product line, the Treo products are not experiencing any pricing pressure from competing products. Telecommunications service providers are reportedly very happy with the Treo line, and studies indicate that Treo users represent a 20 percent to 90 percent increase in average revenue per user over traditional cell phone users. (For an overview of financial and operating performance, see Exhibits 3 and 4.)

Handspring remained confident that its new line of Treo communicators would succeed in the marketplace and revised its outlook by stating that the company intended to achieve profitability by the second quarter ending December 30, 2002. Dubinsky needed to decide how Handspring could best realize this goal and considered the following approaches to ensure the company's profitability objectives were met:

1. Accelerate the company's plans to phase out the Visor product line and concentrate all of Handspring's resources on the development and marketing of the Treo communicators through increased alliances with telecommunications service providers.

EXHIBIT 3

Consolidated Statement of Operations: Handspring, Inc.
(dollar amounts in thousands, except per share amounts)

	Year Ended June 29, 2002	Year Ended June 30, 2001	Year Ended July 1, 2000
Revenue	$240,651	$ 370,943	$101,937
Costs and operating expenses:			
Cost of revenue	205,917	292,311	69,921
Research and development	24,739	23,603	10,281
Selling, general and administrative	85,612	145,132	42,424
In-process research and development	—	12,225	—
Amortization of deferred stock compensation and intangibles(*)	20,181	32,830	40,077
Total costs and operating expenses	336,449	506,101	162,703
Loss from operations	(95,798)	(135,158)	(60,766)
Interest and other income, net	5,259	12,195	675
Loss before taxes	(90,539)	(122,963)	(60,091)
Income tax provision	1,050	3,000	200
Net loss	$ (91,589)	$(125,963)	$ (60,291)
Basic and diluted net loss per share	$ (0.71)	$ (1.21)	$ (1.77)
Shares used in calculating basic and diluted net loss per share	128,221	103,896	34,015
(*) Amortization of deferred stock compensation and intangibles:			
Cost of revenue	$ 2,586	$ 4,521	$ 5,904
Research and development	4,672	6,926	8,059
Selling, general and administrative	12,923	21,383	26,114
	$ 20,181	$ 32,830	$ 40,077

2. Dedicate resources to a costly marketing and advertising campaign to increase awareness of communicators rather than relying on the early adopters of the new Treo products to educate other consumers.

3. Focus resources on developing an operating system to compete with products offered by Palm, Microsoft, and Symbian.

By following these objectives, Dubinsky believes that Handspring will achieve success in the PDA industry.

EXHIBIT 4

Consolidated Balance Sheet: Handspring, Inc.
(dollar amounts in thousands, except share and per share amounts)

	June 29, 2002	June 30, 2001
Assets		
Current assets:		
Cash and cash equivalents	$ 85,554	$ 87,580
Short-term investments	15,235	33,943
Accounts receivable, net of allowance for doubtful accounts of $3,711 and $2,239 as of June 29, 2002 and June 30, 2001, respectively	20,491	12,850
Prepaid expenses and other current assets	3,667	19,473
Inventories	20,084	2,857
Total current assets	145,031	156,703
Long-term investments	50,644	80,237
Property and equipment, net	19,092	15,041
Other assets	1,408	1,254
Total assets	$216,175	$253,235
Liabilities and Stockholders' Equity		
Current liabilities:		
Accounts payable	$ 44,490	$ 37,881
Accrued liabilities	48,779	70,152
Total current liabilities	93,269	108,033
Commitments and contingencies		
Stockholders' equity:		
Preferred stock, $0.001 par value per share, 10,000,000 shares authorized; nil shares issued and outstanding at June 29, 2002 and June 30, 2001	—	—
Common stock, $0.001 par value per share, 1,000,000,000 shares authorized; 143,126,516 and 129,949,768 shares issued and outstanding at June 29, 2002 and June 30, 2001, respectively	143	130
Additional paid-in capital	419,256	368,166
Deferred stock compensation	(9,468)	(29,445)
Accumulated other comprehensive income (loss)	(793)	994
Accumulated deficit	(286,232)	(194,643)
Total stockholders' equity	122,906	145,202
Total liabilities and stockholders' equity	$216,175	$253,235

NOTES

1. Shawn Barnett, 2001, Jeff Hawkins, *Pen Computing*, http://www. pencomputing.com/palm/Pen33/hawkins1.html, April.

2. Ibid.

3. Ibid.

4. Pat Dillon, 1998, The next small thing, *Fast Company* 15, http://www. fastcompany.com/online/15/smallthing.html, June.

5. James Lardner, 2001, Hawkins talks, *Business 2.0*, http://www.business2. com/articles/mag/0,1640,146233,FF.html, March.

6. Vanessa Hua, 2002, Three in one: Meet the innovative force behind the new Treo, which combines PDA, wireless Internet access and a mobile phone, *San Francisco Chronicle*, http://www.sfgate.com/, January 6.

7. 2002, Future trends for mobile technologies outlined by Gartner, *EDP Weekly's IT Monitor*, April 8, 5.

8. 2002, Palm, Handspring fighting a losing battle against Microsoft? *CommWeb*, April 2.

9. 2002, Palm and Handspring may be victims of mobile convergence, *Europemedia*, March 25.

10. Jay Wrolstad, 2001, Handspring vaults toward corporate market, *CRM-Daily*, http://www.crmdaily.com, November 13.

11. http://www.handspring.com/.

12. 2002, Ovum comments PDA market stumbles as yuppie buyers dry up, http://www.ovum.com/go/ovumcommens/005354.htm, April 4.

13. Carl Zeite, 2002, PDA wars: Round two, *InformationWeek*, http://www. informationweek.com/story/IWK20020328S0007, April 1.

14. Lardner, Hawkins talks.

15. 2002, Handspring SEC filing 10-Q, February 12.

16. 2002, Worldwide PDA shipments scoot up, http://www.pdacortex.com/ worldwide_PDA_shipments_up.htm, February 19, April 9.

case sixteen

Randel S. Carlock
Elizabeth Florent-Treacy
INSEAD

Dear Shareowners,

"Forty-five years ago, a remarkable meeting took place in Sonoma, California, among Bill Hewlett, Dave Packard, and a handful of HP executives.

The people who gathered at the aptly named Mission Inn came together to define a set of values and principles that would help shape a new kind of company, one that would be known for its character as well as its creativity, for its people as well as its products. They crafted six primary objectives, later expanded to seven.

Unique to their time, those principles came to be the underpinning of what is now known as the HP Way. As Bill and Dave understood, the real genius of the HP Way is that it's a legacy built on innovation, bold enough to embrace change and flexible enough to absorb it. The spirit of those original seven principles continues to guide us to this day.

They have helped guide the Hewlett-Packard Company through war and recession, through mergers and acquisitions, through corporate reinvention and industry revolution. But rarely have they been called upon to guide us through all of these things in a single year. . . ."

(letter from Carleton Fiorina, CEO and Chairman of HP, in HP's Annual Report)

2001 was the year of war, recession, acquisition and reinvention to which Carly Fiorina referred in her letter. It was the year of the HP-Compaq merger—and it was either the best of times for HP, or it was the worst of times, depending on whom you asked. In any case, quite aside from the debate surrounding the merits of the merger, it was also one of the first major skirmishes in a revolution in corporate governance. It certainly was a year for the history books . . .

THE NEW HP

On September 4, 2001, Carly Fiorina of HP and Michael Capellas, CEO of Compaq, announced that they were negotiating a merger between HP and Compaq. The new company would be called HP, and Fiorina would be the CEO and chairman. They promised that the $25 billion deal was strategically rational and would result in a new organization large and diversified enough to rival both IBM and Dell.

HP was a Silicon Valley original, founded by William Hewlett and David Packard in 1939. It had a long and impressive history of innovation, but was hit in the late 1990s by intense competition among PC manufacturers and by a general economic downturn. Fiorina, who joined HP in 1999 as its first outside CEO, had a mandate from HP's board of directors to shake the company up and transform it into an Internet powerhouse.

The Texas-based Compaq had started as notes on a paper placemat in a Houston pie shop in 1982. The company was enormously successful in the 1980s as a maker of IBM-compatible PCs and laptops. By the late 1990s, however, Compaq was struggling in a mature market with stronger competitors. In addition, its acquisition of DEC in 1998—designed to transform Compaq into a one-stop shop for clients looking for computer hardware and software backed by a global service organization—had proved to be more difficult than expected, and Compaq had not yet reaped much benefit from it. Michael Capellas's predecessor, Eckhard Pfeiffer, was pushed out by Compaq's board in 1999, partly because board members were convinced that he had bungled the integration of DEC. Capellas was a relative unknown, a Compaq insider who was one of the few willing to consider the job. One of his first moves as the new CEO was to cut thousands of jobs and announce restructuring charges of $700 to $900 million. He did manage to pull Compaq back from the brink in 2000, but the increasingly difficult economic climate in 2001 left Capellas open to considering the idea of a merger.

When Fiorina came calling in mid-2001, Capellas let himself be convinced. The two CEOs saw a merger as the best strategy for both companies. Together, they would have a more balanced business portfolio with improved profitability in services and enterprise and access businesses, and a better position in servers and storage. They would have a large market share in enterprise computing and PCs and would double HP's service and support capacity. They believed that combining the two companies would increase operating margins and save $2.5 billion by 2004, adding from $5 to $9 to HP's share price. The new HP would have projected annual revenues of around $87 billion and profits of around $3.9 billion. It would employ 145,000 (before anticipated layoffs of 15,000 people—layoffs some critics claimed would account for 75% of the $2.5 billion cost savings). And although high-tech marriages (including Compaq's semi-digested acquisition of DEC) had had some recent bad press, the boards of Compaq and HP were confident that the two companies were complementary.

A SHOTGUN WEDDING

When Wall Street opened on the day after the merger was announced, HP shareholders began to dump their stock. By the end of the day, HP's share price had dropped 25%, reducing the value of the deal by $6 billion. Compaq's stock tumbled as well, dropping 16% in two days. Over the next few weeks, the reactions from a wide range of observers continued to be mostly negative. Some critics expressed concerns about the difficulty of combining employees from three very different corporate cultures—HP's Silicon Valley old-timers, Compaq's aggressive Texas upstarts, and DEC's Ivy League eggheads. Others, seeing the proposed merger as

a risky gamble to save two companies with too much invested in commodity-like PCs, expressed their reservations in terms such as ". . . a shotgun wedding," "two drunks holding each other up," ". . . a sudden embrace that smacks of deathbed desperation." The merger was described in one analysis as "two new CEOs ignoring history while simultaneously seeking to out-Dell Dell and out-IBM IBM."[1] One large investor compared the merger to tying two stones together, then throwing them in a river to see if they would float. Many HP and Compaq business clients were at best lukewarm fearing, as one CIO (chief information officer) said "disruption of customer focus during merger machinations."[2] One admittedly biased observer, Michael Dell, gleefully approved of the uproar:

"I don't know what happens if they don't merge, but it certainly creates even more confusion and uncertainty. Gotta love that!"[3]

FAMILY STILL MATTERS

It was not long after the September 4th announcement that the Hewlett and Packard families in their role as successors to the original founders William Hewlett and David Packard, neither of whom was still living) began to make public their concerns about the merger. David Woodley Packard (whom detractors described as an "emotional philanthropist"), the son of founder David Packard, said he was very concerned about the vast number of layoffs that the merger would cause. The other second-generation heir to speak out publicly against the merger was 57-year-old Walter Hewlett, one of the founder William Hewlett's five children (and his oldest son). Walter was a reserved intellectual, soft-spoken and private, who had never tried to outshine his famous father.

Walter had always been very close to his father, who took the young Walter to the office regularly. Both William Hewlett and David Packard were known as generous men who had lived modestly in spite of their wealth. They had instilled their values in their children, and had pushed each youngster to excel. After graduating from Harvard with a degree in physics, Walter went on to earn advanced degrees in music, operations research and engineering. He was also an outdoorsman, running the Boston Marathon as a young man and participating in grueling mountain-bike races in his 50s. Much of Walter's time as an adult was devoted to carrying on his parents' commitment to philanthropy and education. Like his father, Walter had fairly simple tastes. For example, he drove a Ford minivan—although he never sold the 1965 Volvo that his father had given him for his 21st birthday.

Walter Hewlett had led a life out of the public eye before the merger was announced. He was the chairman of the Hewlett family charitable foundation and was elected to the Board of Overseers of Harvard University in 1997. He participated in the formation of Vermont Telephone Company and was currently its chairman. He founded the Center for Computer Assisted Research in the Humanities in 1984 and still served as its director. He had also been a member of the board of Hewlett-Packard since 1987.

Throughout the summer of 2001, when the HP board was debating whether or not to go ahead with the merger, Walter Hewlett had apparently respected his obligation as a board member not to discuss the merger with outsiders, including family members. Therefore, the Hewlett and Packard families read the first official announcement of the deal in the newspaper on September 4th, along with the rest of the world. The president of the Packard Foundation said that the foundation had not received specific details about the merger until ten days after it was announced, when Fiorina first presented it to their board. An HP spokeswoman said that the board was disturbed by the families' complaint that they had not been consulted or kept informed: "We didn't want to single the families out. We have treated both families the way we treat other shareholders." (Indeed, in the past the Packard Foundation had specifically asked HP to treat them this way.)

Then, on November 7th, came a bombshell. Walter Hewlett filed a proxy statement with the American Securities and Exchange Commission (SEC), outlining his opposition to HP's plans. The move laid the groundwork for a proxy fight. Hewlett's filing said that he would be joined by his sisters, Eleanor Hewlett Gimon and Mary Hewlett Jaffe, the William R. Hewlett Revocable Trust and one of its trustees, Edwin van Bronkhorst, who had previously been chief financial officer of Hewlett-Packard. The board of the David and Lucile Packard Foundation did not immediately say whether they would support Walter Hewlett, but this was the first official sign of dissent from the families, and it took HP by surprise.

In his SEC filing and statements to the press, Walter Hewlett said that, although he had finally voted with the rest of the board to approve the transaction in September, he (as an HP board member) had informed the board of his doubts about the rationale behind the

merger as they deliberated the merits of the move over the summer. Now, in November, he announced publicly that he believed Fiorina was mistaken about the economies of scale to be gained. As he saw it, HP would be handing over one-third of the equity in its high-profit printing and imaging business in exchange for a share in Compaq's low-margin PC business—not such a great deal in a shrinking PC market. He also saw the merger as a dangerous distraction for HP managers. In short, he said,

> "We profoundly disagree with management's assertion that HP needs to make this large and very risky acquisition. To undertake the proposed merger is to make a big, long-term, bet-the-company move."[4]

It soon became obvious that, in spite of his board vote, Walter would be the family spokesman and leader for the heirs' anti-merger campaign. (Months later, he would remark, "This is not what I normally do. . . . [I]t's been hard work and I've had to recalibrate myself. It's been a bit like stepping into an alternative universe."[5])

Carly Fiorina had been aware that Hewlett had been personally opposed to the deal, but she had not expected him to launch a full-scale attempt to win others over to his side. After Walter Hewlett filed his proxy statement with the SEC, she commented that family shareholders have a powerful incentive to "preserve wealth rather than to create it." She also criticized Hewlett, saying,

> "There is a big difference between an individual managing his own personal assets and the assets of the foundation, and a board member going out and actively soliciting against a board's decision. And I don't know how to explain Walter's behavior."[6]

Some heavyweight CEOs shared her view: Jack Welch, then CEO of General Electric, said that it was "unpardonable" for a member of a board of directors to approve a merger and then head the opposition.

In any case, HP appeared to be in too deep to back out of the negotiations. There was a mutual $675 million breakup fee included in the terms of the agreement, to be paid by either HP or Compaq if one of them broke off the deal—unless, of course, the merger was not approved by shareholders of either company. In addition, if the merger did not take place, the two companies would become rivals again after having shared a great deal of proprietary information. Critics also pointed out that the two CEOs personally would lose huge bonuses if the deal broke down. (Fiorina's compensation package was estimated to be in the region of $70 million over the next two years.) Finally, if the merger failed to gain approval, Fiorina would almost certainly be forced to resign.

A BATTLE BY PROXY

By December 2001, a full proxy battle raged. The Hewlett and Packard families and their foundations announced that they would vote their shares with Walter Hewlett, against the merger, thereby solidifying the family front (and their block of 18% of HP shares). With this news, HP's share price rose 17%. In mid-December, Richard Hackborn, a top HP executive and board member who was also a member of the Hewlett Foundation board of directors, announced that he was resigning from the Hewlett Foundation board. Hackborn was a 33-year HP veteran who had created HP's printing and imaging products—ironically, the highly profitable business that Hewlett thought should be the cornerstone of HP. Not only did Hackborn think that the merger was a good idea; he felt that the families were opposing it without adequate groundwork: "I have seen no plan from the heirs. Their opposition does not address any of the issues. . . . Standing still does not serve share owners or employees." Touché.

Hewlett riposted: on December 27th he filed another proxy statement with the Securities and Exchange Commission, urging shareholders to vote against the merger. He made his side of the story public, saying that he had first learned about the proposed deal in May 2001 (although others say that Fiorina and Capellas first met in June). He said that as talks continued over the summer months, he had expressed strong reservations but had been told three days before the board's final vote that the merger would go ahead even if he voted no, although the price might have to be renegotiated. (HP's lawyer asserts that he was told no such thing.) Hewlett bowed to pressure, believing that he could later vote his own shares against the deal: he reported that on the day of the board vote, September 3rd, he voted in favor of the merger but warned the board that he would later most likely cast his own and his foundation's shares against it.

The HP board immediately and strongly denied Hewlett's version of events, saying that not only was he *not* coerced into approving the board vote, but he had missed several critical board discussions about the merger in July—one because he was bike-racing and another because he was playing his cello in a concert at the Bohemian Grove, a "gentlemen's retreat" north of San Francisco.

February 2002 was equally eventful. In the first week, the European Commission approved the merger. While Fiorina saw this barely contested approval as the removal of an important obstacle, Hewlett argued that it only proved *his* point, saying,

> "We understand that HP's rivals raised almost no objections to the proposed merger, helping it to gain Commission approval. We are not surprised. We believe Dell, Sun and IBM must be delighted at the prospect of a merger that would so greatly distract and damage two of their rivals."[7]

On February 11th, Hewlett finally addressed Richard Hackborn's criticism that the Hewlett and Packard heirs had no alternate plan, by putting forth a three-point proposal. Hewlett recommended, first, that HP invest in and expand its printer and imaging (digital cameras) unit. This strategy had merit: by getting into the exploding market for digital cameras early, HP would set itself up to reap profits through its printers down the line. He also hinted that an eventual spin-off of the printing and imaging business might be worth considering. Second, he recommended that HP optimize its software and consulting businesses by acquiring smaller companies (a strategy that the HP founders had used to grow HP in the past). Finally, he argued that the company should restructure and rationalize its PC business, possibly by closing some plants. He said,

> "Strapping together boxes [PCs] and selling them is not an area where HP is doing well. Why get further into that business?"[8]

An HP spokeswoman quickly shot the plan down:

> "Once again, Hewlett offers platitudes, not a plan. He offers no specifics. All he offers is targeted acquisitions of unidentified companies in who-knows-what businesses."[9]

Clearly, Fiorina and the HP board had underestimated the importance of winning the Hewletts and the Packards over early in the negotiations, instead concentrating their efforts on their large institutional and retail shareholders. The fight carried on, bare-knuckled, with front-page headlines, advertisements from both sides with pro- or anti-merger messages, letters to the 900,000 shareholders, and even his-and-hers dueling websites:

"vote*no*hpcompaq.com" and "votethe*hpway*.com." Each side sent out seven to ten separate shareholder mailings over the final four weeks of the campaign. Deal-related costs, including advertising and marketing directed toward influencing shareholders' votes, reached an estimated $232 million for HP, Compaq and Hewlett combined. *Business Week* satirized,

> *"Really Carly . . . Miss Nuptials always urges families to respect a bride's choices, but announcing that you were 'not surprised' when the founding families of HP came out against this hookup was a blast of snippishness unbecoming a well-compensated CEO. After all, we have come to that part of the ceremony when people with a few billion dollars on the line don't have to hold their peace."*[10]

In mid-February, HP announced better-than-expected revenues for the previous quarter. Although Walter Hewlett said his news proved that HP could do well on its own, the favorable report seemed to finally turn the tide of public opinion toward approval of the merger. On March 5th, the proxy advisory firm Institutional Shareholder Services (ISS) announced that they supported the HP board's strategy and plans for implementation, and they recommended that the merger take place. ISS, who normally advises clients on corporate governance issues, did not control any shares, but their clients held 23% of HP shares, making their recommendation a weighty one in the proxy battle. This appeared to be a final blow to Walter Hewlett.

Then, in a nearly last-minute surprise development, several heavyweight HP shareholders announced that they would vote *against* the merger—and some of them were ISS clients. Banc of America, one of HP's top five shareholders (with 2.8% of the total), said that they would vote no. The New York State Common Retirement System Fund and Wells Fargo, a US banking group, also disapproved. CalPERS, a huge California state pension fund, and the Canadian Ontario Teachers' Pension Plan—both ISS clients—also joined the "no" group. CalPERS emphasized that their decision was based simply on what would be best for their portfolio.

It became fairly clear that these shareholders, the majority of whom were holders of retirement and pension funds, had investment goals similar to those of the Hewletts and Packards and their foundations. People began to wonder: Had Fiorina and the HP board analyzed shareholders' investment strategies early in the planning stage? If the HP board had made the deal more palatable to Walter Hewlett, would the outcome have been different?

HP Shareholders—January 2001[11]

Institutional investors	57%
Retail or individual investors	25%
The David and Lucile Packard Foundation	10%
Families of William Hewlett and David Packard	8%
Management and company insiders	<1%

THE DIE IS CAST

The date and place for the ultimate confrontation were finally set: all 900,000 shareholders (controlling approximately 1.9 billion shares) were called upon to vote March 19, 2002, in person in Cupertino, California, or by proxy. There was a great deal at stake. The *Financial Times* reported: "It appears to be a battle for control of the company, pitting management against descendants of HP's co-founders."[12] Thomas Perkins, a Compaq board member, observed that Walter Hewlett and Fiorina were proxies in a battle for the heart and soul of HP.

As the proxy battle waged on, many people had the same fundamental question: Why did HP let this battle happen in the first place? In an interview Fiorina said,

> *"Walter's behavior publicly has been a complete surprise. I think it is an insult to this board."*[13]

Many people didn't buy that argument. One academic said, "You have to question her business judgment. Either [the board] failed to persuade him, or they ignored him. Either way, it's bad."[14] Another business school professor said, "Win or lose, she loses . . . unless there's a god of perfect women."[15]

People also wondered how Fiorina could have underestimated the influence of the Hewlett and Packard families, both within HP and in the community. Fiorina probably drove past Stanford University every day, seeing there a tangible reminder not only of HP's early history—as the place where William Hewlett and David Packard met and formed their lifelong partnership—but also of the families' philanthropy. Likewise, the Monterey Bay Aquarium—a prime tourist destination and a world-renowned center for marine research—had been built with funds from the Packard Foundation and was directed by Julie Packard, one of

David Packard's daughters. James Hewlett, Walter's younger brother, was an active volunteer worker in the Silicon Valley. Susan Packard Orr was the founder of a software development firm that worked with nonprofit organizations and was the head of the huge David and Lucile Packard Foundation. Why hadn't Fiorina—with her much-touted people skills—done more to win this powerful and extremely well respected family and their foundations to her cause?

The March 19th shareholders' vote turned out to be so close that the official result would not be known until weeks later, although it was clear who the sentimental favorite was: Walter Hewlett got a standing ovation from a crowd waving green fluorescent glow sticks; Fiorina was booed. (Compaq shareholders, on the other hand, decisively voted "yes" at their meeting the following day.) Even before the final HP count was announced, some people were threatening lawsuits, claiming that dirty politics had swayed the vote. For example, many of the 6,000 HP executives eligible for the combined $337 millions retention bonus package for successful completion of the merger undoubtedly chose to take the easy money. (One HP executive said that he voted for the merger even though he wasn't convinced it was a good idea: "I know it's pathetic, but the old HP is gone. I'm giving up on the stock and taking the cash. The bribe worked."[16])

After what must have been a heart-stopping delay for Fiorina, a last-minute change of heart to a "yes" vote by Deutsche Bank for 17 million of the more than 25 million HP shares it held came through during the shareholders' meeting. HP's corporate lawyer had been waiting backstage for Deutsche Bank's vote. As soon as he heard it, he radioed HP's general counsel, Ann Baskins, who was seated onstage near Fiorina. Ann Baskins handed Fiorina a note with the good news—but they both knew the game was not over yet.

Indeed it was not. Within days of the shareholder vote, rumors surfaced that Deutsche Bank's vote switch had come only four days after the bank had arranged a $4 billion line of credit for HP. There was even a smoking gun: in a voicemail to chief financial officer Bob Wayman about Deutsche Bank and another big American bank, Fiorina said that HP would have to do something "extraordinary for those two to bring them over the line." Although HP denied any impropriety, Walter Hewlett immediately filed a lawsuit, which would delay the official results even further. As a result, Walter Hewlett was not re-nominated to the HP board of directors, meaning that for the first time in HP history, the families were not represented on the board. (Hewlett's lawsuit was dismissed in April 2002, exonerating HP.)

Decidedly, from beginning to end—from mudslinging to back-office deals—the financial world had never seen a merger battle like this one before. Whatever the outcome of the vote, the proxy battle was a watershed. It had brought issues of corporate governance to the fore—issues that would likely have repercussions on similar decisions in other companies. For HP it was the decisive battle in a cold war that had been waged within the organization, albeit less visibly, during the previous year between the old HP hands on one side and Fiorina on the other. As people reflected on the proxy battle, many realized that to fully understand what had happened, it would be necessary to look back to the egalitarian, decentralized culture created and nurtured at HP for 40 years by the founders, William Hewlett and David Packard. As the world tuned into the HP soap opera, people were asking themselves: *What would Bill and Dave say about this?*

WILLIAM HEWLETT AND DAVID PACKARD

William Hewlett and David Packard can be described without exaggeration as American icons. The company they created has long been a symbol worldwide of organizational best practices, both technological and human. The meeting of two engineering students at Stanford, and the birth of their company under the guidance of their professor and mentor Fred Terman, has become a legend. The California ethos of the company's early days—based on respect and responsibility for individuals, love of nature, and the belief that there are practically no limits to what one can invent—is credited as being the foundation of the famous HP Way (see Exhibit 1). The story really begins much earlier, however, with the values and experiences that not only shaped the young Bill Hewlett and Dave Packard but also continued to influence their heirs as HP moved into the 21st century. HP was founded on family values and run according to those same values for 60 years.

DAVE AND BILL

David Packard was born in 1913 in Pueblo, Colorado, a tough mountain mining town. His home town had the frontier mentality of the miners and cowboys who had shaped the western United States.

As a boy, young Packard had many interests beyond the outdoors: chemistry, electronics, team sports and music. While his father had a strong influence on him, the youngster also enjoyed other signifi-

1. Recognize that profit is the best measure of a company's contribution to society and the ultimate source of corporate strength;

2. Continually improve the value of the products and services offered to customers;

3. Seek new opportunities for growth but focus efforts on fields in which the company can make a contribution;

4. Provide employment opportunities that include the chance to share in the company's success;

5. Maintain an organizational environment that fosters individual motivation, initiative and creativity;

6. Demonstrate good citizenship by making contributions to the community;

7. Emphasize growth as a requirement for survival.

cant mentoring relationships. Packard learned to fish with one friend's family, played music with another friend, and was coached by a track and field champion who worked in his father's law office. Packard's management style, with its commitment to teamwork and mentoring, was influenced by these relationships.

As a student at Stanford University, he met a young radio engineering professor, Fred Terman, who would become a lifelong mentor to both Packard and Hewlett and is credited with being the "father" of Silicon Valley. It was through Packard's interest in electronics that the young student developed a friendship with classmate Bill Hewlett.

William Hewlett, who was also born in 1913, was a fourth-generation Californian. Hewlett's early interests, like Packard's, were in science and electronics. During their junior year at Stanford, Hewlett and Packard, on a field trip to visit a hydroelectric plant, took time out to go fishing. Their mutual love of the outdoors and respect for each other became the foundation of their friendship.

After graduation from Stanford, Packard took a job with General Electric on the East Coast as a manager in a research laboratory that made mercury-vapor control tubes. The process used in the lab was very uncertain, and the failure rate was high. Packard soon realized that although his employees *wanted* to do the job right, they weren't getting enough guidance to do so. There were written instructions for procedures, but employees were expected to simply follow these on their own. Packard became involved in the work in a much more hands-on way, and results improved. His insight about the importance of the human factor in manufacturing quality would later become part of his practice of "management by walking around."

Professor Terman continued to play a helpful role in the lives of Hewlett and Packard: in the summer of 1938 he secured funding for a Stanford Fellowship for Packard so that he could return to the Bay Area. After moving back to Palo Alto, the newly married Packard and his wife rented a small house on Addison Avenue. Bill Hewlett and his new wife moved into a small cottage on the property. Behind the house was a one-car garage that soon became the friends' workshop.

In 1939 they formed their own engineering firm. Hewlett won the coin toss, so his name came first: their new company would be called Hewlett-Packard. Hewlett focused on R&D, and Packard worked on manufacturing and management. The partners began looking for ways to develop their concepts into products. Their headquarters were in the little garage at the rental house. Terman (who continued to send ideas and contacts their way) would later say that if the car was parked in the garage, he knew business was slow; if it was parked in the driveway, there was a healthy backlog of work. The first invention to come out of the garage was an audio oscillator (designated *model 200A* so that it would appear to be from an established product line), an instrument for generating the audio frequencies required in communications, physics, medicine and military equipment. (In 1989, the garage on Addison Avenue was designated a California Historical Landmark, "the birthplace of the Silicon Valley.")

THE HP WAY

In the 1940s the company grew from two employees and sales of slightly over $5,000 to 166 employees and sales of $2.2 million. It had moved out of the garage and was earning an enviable reputation among young engineers and scientists. As the organization grew, Bill and Dave began to formalize a unique management style based on their personal philosophy and values. Practices included "management by walking around" and management by objectives (the latter giving employees flexibility to achieve the broader objectives that Bill and Dave had set for the company). Hewlett-Packard also became one of the first companies to have an open-door policy and an open-plan office space to encourage information-sharing and networking. The founders emphasized the importance of creating an egalitarian organization in which everyone was on a first-name basis. William Hewlett set the example by sitting at the middle of the table rather than at the head during business meetings.

Early in 1957 the company held its first off-site senior management meeting. Hewlett and Packard realized that with 1,200 employees, they had to delegate responsibility for running the business. The goal of the off-site meeting was to get their senior management team fully involved in developing the values and corporate objectives that came to be known as "the HP Way." When the company held an IPO later that year, all employees who had been with the company six months or more received automatic stock grants and became eligible for the company's stock option program. This financial move reflected the founders' strong belief in the importance of employee support and participation. When Hewlett-Packard moved its headquarters to the Stanford Industrial Park in 1960, it was into a building designed to enhance employee satisfaction and performance—in other words, to support the HP Way. The site, over-looking San Francisco Bay, included outdoor patios, horseshoe pits, volleyball and badminton equipment, and a large cafeteria for all employees. At the annual company barbeque, Bill and Dave flipped the burgers.

The HP Way was also about strategy. Although Bill was considered "the engineer" and Dave "the business-man," they had always agreed on one thing: HP would focus on innovation and organic growth, not economies of scale. HP's ability to morph its core technologies to stay ahead of the wave of technological development in the coming decades was seen as a result of Dave Packard and Bill Hewlett's far-sighted philosophy that their company was "built to last," not to break up and spin off as a market peaked.

THE GLORY DAYS

HP was not left on the beach as new waves of technological development washed through Silicon Valley in the 1960s. In 1966 the company entered the computer market with the HP 2116A, which by virtue of its relatively small size eliminated the need for special computer rooms and changed the nature of the computing industry. HP also introduced the world's first desktop scientific calculator and was the first to use the term "personal computer" in an advertising campaign. The company ended the 1960s with sales over $300 million and nearly 16,000 employees.

In the 1970s the innovative, entrepreneurial spirit of the early days was nurtured: HP became an *intra*preneurial organization, with product groups being split off into autonomous units as soon as they became large enough. Bill made sure that people had the tools and the time they needed to be creative. Once when he encountered a storeroom door that was chained and padlocked, he got a bolt cutter and cut the lock off, then left a note that said, "Please don't chain this again—Bill." Bill and Dave also encouraged engineers to work on personal projects (such as building speakers for stereo amplifiers) with company equipment and parts. Bill told his engineers to spend every Friday thinking about new ideas rather than pursuing ongoing projects. Bill and Dave thought that these (and similar) learning experiences could pay off for the company, and they often did.

In 1971 sales took a dramatic downturn and drastic cutbacks were required. Instead of laying off 1,000 people as he had been advised to do, Bill decreed that virtually all employees, including himself, would take Fridays off without pay for the next six months. Many grateful employees worked a full week anyway. Sales picked up as HP introduced more path-breaking products, including the HP 35, the first handheld scientific calculator. The company continued its expansion globally, and by the mid-1970s sales had passed the $1 billion mark. Three years later sales had doubled again.

THE FOUNDERS BOW OUT

By 1978, Bill and Dave had retired from operational management after overseeing the first top-management transition in the company's history. John Young, a long-time HP executive, became CEO, while Hewlett stayed on as chairman. Bill and Dave's old offices became near-shrines: they were left open and untouched, complete with the original linoleum floors and a one dollar bill that Hewlett had left on his desk. (He put it there as proof of the integrity of HP employees, saying, "I could leave it there and it would be there forever." It's *still* there, along with a pile of change that other employees have added over the years.)

Young had taken control of a major computer corporation, and he kept it focused for many years, something that top executives at AT&T, Honeywell, RCA and other competitors were not able to do during that period. The company glided through the early 1980s— with the notable introduction of several new PC models and a desktop printer with a Canon inkjet technology— but by the end of the decade, the HP Way philosophy and structure had gotten out of hand. For example, Young discovered that two HP divisions had independently invented microprocessors! Young attempted to establish order, but his efforts apparently added bureaucracy without solving the underlying problems. In addition, after several years of double-digit sales growth, Hewlett-Packard found itself competing directly against IBM and Digital Equipment in the minicomputer market, Sun Microsystems in engineering workstations and Dell, Apple and Compaq in the PC market.

In 1990 HP faced a serious financial challenge due to these factors. After watching earnings drop 10%, Bill and Dave, who were both nearing 80, roared back and took control of HP once again. (They still owned 25% of the company.) In a summary that, with hindsight, is extremely ironic, one observer said,

> *"Hewlett-Packard might well have gone the way of IBM and DEC, but in HP's case powerful shareholders cracked down at the first sign of trouble rather than waiting for it to get out of hand."*[17]

Bill and Dave decentralized, moving people away from headquarters to other locations and shifting power back to the operating units. For the first time, they laid off employees—a total of 3,000, but mostly by attrition. They also orchestrated the retirement of John Young, who was 60. Young helped them to handpick Lewis Platt, a 30-year HP veteran and head of the computers systems group, to become the next CEO.

Lewis Platt, HP's CEO from 1992 to 1999, attempted to reinstate the innovative culture for which the early HP had been known. As a result, there was a pattern of steady growth and profitability for several years, particularly for printer products and high-margin ink cartridges (also based on Canon technology). Unfortunately, there were flaws in the rest of the company's product and marketing strategies, and the decade ended much as it had begun.

Despite a lack of important new products to introduce to the market, Platt had continued through the late 1990s to focus on "stretch goals" such as promoting diversity and a more humane balance of work and personal life for employees. One former HP worker said,

> *"[IBM CEO] Gerstner wasn't running around talking about work and life balance. It was like our own*

> *chairman [Platt] didn't realize how tough it was out there."*[18]

Decentralization had gone to the other extreme; the company now had 130 independent product groups whose main goal was to meet their own financial targets. The Laser-Jet and ink-jet printer divisions were competing with each other.

This inward focus became a dangerous myopia as HP concentrated on hardware while competitors such as Sun and IBM were reinventing themselves as Internet dot.coms. A consultant who worked with HP at the time said: "They had this 'ready, aim-aim-aim, fire' culture. These days it has to be 'aim, fire, re-aim, re-fire.'"[19] Although the company had developed Internet-compatible technology years ahead of the curve, risk-aversion kept top HP leadership from factoring the growth of the Internet into its technology and marketing decisions. The local wisdom was that if HP ever went into the sushi business, it would advertise the products as "cold, dead fish."

HP was once again in trouble. The computer industry was consolidating, with Microsoft, IBM and Dell becoming the dominant players and HP consigned to the also-rans. But David Packard had died in 1996, and William Hewlett was frail; the company couldn't look to them for help this time. Second-generation family members Walter Hewlett, David Woodley Packard, and Susan Packard Orr were members of the HP board of directors, but they all had other professional interests and obligations. Revenue growth had slowed to below 5%. In December 1997 a survey of 300 top employees showed that people saw a need for new thinking and increased customer focus. Platt took drastic action, exploring radical restructuring options. In March 1999, he announced the spinoff of HP's venerable test and measurement units, which became Agilent. (David Packard then resigned from the HP board of directors, since he did not approve of splitting the company.) Platt also asked the HP board of directors to consider hiring a new, Internet-savvy CEO. They took his advice.

CARLY FIORINA AND THE NEW HP

Enter Carly Fiorina, former president of Lucent's $19 billion global service-provider group. She had earned a reputation as one of the most powerful women in corporate America. In 1996, Fiorina had managed AT&T's successful spinoff of Lucent (at $3 billion, the largest IPO up to that time), and then had launched a $90 million brand-building and product development campaign that transformed Lucent from a manufacturer of phone equipment to an icon of the New Economy.

Fiorina was the daughter of an abstract painter and a California judge. She earned a degree in medieval history and philosophy at Stanford (working as an intern at HP!), then attended law school before changing direction and joining AT&T. She later earned business degrees from the University of Maryland and MIT. She flew up through the ranks at AT&T, earning a reputation for having aggressive marketing skills, a deft human touch, a silver tongue, and most of all an iron will.

After considering 300 potential candidates, on July 19, 1999, the HP board of directors announced that 44-year-old Carly Fiorina would become the company's new CEO. Her appointment was in itself a signal that change was in the wind: she was the first outsider, the first non-engineer, the first woman, and the youngest person to become CEO in HP's history. HP was quite a catch for Carly as well—she was now head of the 14th largest industrial company in the world. Given her record at Lucent, the HP board was convinced that she was their messiah.[20] Board member Jay Keyworth recalled that they asked her to "totally recreate and reinvent HP according to the original HP Way."[21]

HP employees were equally excited. Fiorina was greeted by standing ovations from HP employees around the world. One manager commented,

"We were looking for a CEO who would shake up a company that had grown slow and stale. The moral of the story: watch out what you wish for, because you may get it!"[22]

Fiorina's take? HP had become "a gentle bureaucracy of entitlement and consensus." The company was suffering from turf battles and complacency, and the famous HP Way had become a smokescreen for sluggishness and risk aversion. Management needed to clear out "layers of sediment that clogged up the company." Fresh from her experience with Lucent, she made it clear that successful companies have to accelerate change and embrace risk. Her modus operandi: "Preserve the best, reinvent the rest."[23]

As a self-described "brand evangelist," her first move was to come up with a new list of "rules of the garage," invoking the legacy of the HP culture of the early days, with the original garage as an unmistakable metaphor. She also championed a brand-building strat-

egy, starting in November 1999 with the announcement of a $200 million "global brand initiative." She stylized the company's logo—eliminating the name Hewlett-Packard and replacing it with a simpler HP. The purpose of the new logo was to reposition HP as a strong brand uniting diverse product groups. Fiorina went on the road, visiting clients and branch offices, promising that the new HP would offer not only innovative technology, but also better solutions for customer's problems and service requirements. To show that she meant business, in a nationwide ad campaign Fiorina posed next to the iconic one-car garage in Palo Alto, proclaiming that HP was reinventing itself: "HP is a one-car garage in need of paint," she said.

Fiorina's goal was to position HP for the Internet's second wave: e-services. Toward that end, she reduced the number of product groups from 83 to 12, and she divided the organization into six divisions—two front-end for sales (consumer and business) and four back-end for products (computer systems, personal systems [clients], printing and imaging, and services.) The new HP, she promised, would create new e-services and the hardware and software to deliver them. At the end of fiscal 2000, HP had met its revenue growth goal of 15% for the year. Carly—now president, CEO and chairman of HP—was hot, and analysts were bullish on the company again.

Fiorina's next big move came in September 2000, with the announcement that HP was negotiating an acquisition of PricewaterhouseCoopers' (PwC) global management and information technology consulting business. HP simply didn't have the ability in-house to cash in on the lucrative consulting work that implementation of its high-end enterprise applications required. Grafting PwC onto the company would provide a quick fix. Fiorina said, "We believe that the days of talking to one company about business strategy and another company about technology are, frankly, over."[24] Some observers were skeptical, expressing concern that HP might have trouble integrating the 31,000 PricewaterhouseCoopers employees who would come with the deal.

This was a valid concern. Fiorina's rapid and radical restructuring thus far had created disenchantment rather than excitement for many workers, particularly HP department heads and employees who were accustomed to running their outfits as they saw fit. Worse—from their point of view—the restructuring and the concurrent economic downturn now led to inevitable layoffs. More and more employees began to complain that Fiorina had turned her back on the HP Way. One said that she seemed to have come in with the attitude that it was time to "shake up the country club." (Paradoxically, some outside observers said that HP's problems were exacerbated by long-term employees who were lulled by the HP's safe, paternalistic ways.) There was concern, given her lack of engineering and technical experience, that Fiorina had not appointed top lieutenants with this type of background to advise her in these areas. Some clients and customers described a climate of confusion and gridlock within the company. One computer reseller said,

> *"It's beyond my ability to communicate our frustration. It's painful to watch them screw up million dollar deals."*[25]

Given Fiorina's problems with her own employees, it was not at all clear that the integration of the PwC consultants would work. By December 2000, it was clear that the pessimists had been at least half right: Fiorina announced that HP was dropping the PwC acquisition; negotiations would not continue. She blamed the "current market environment" and missed fourth-quarter earnings targets for the breakdown in the acquisition process, and stated,

> *"I am unwilling to subject the HP organization to the continuing distraction of pursuing this acquisition any further."*[26]

She also acknowledged concerns that HP might have difficulty retaining PwC employees. In addition to this public statement, it was rumored that PwC partners had been "unnerved" by the 26% decline in HP's share price in the months since the deal was announced.

Despite her disappointment, Fiorina quickly bounced back, promising revenue growth of 15 to 17% for HP in 2001. However, the end of the PwC negotiations also seemed to signal the end of Fiorina's honeymoon period at HP. In January 2001, HP missed profit expectations, and Fiorina cut the revenue growth projection to 5% for the year. HP stock was trading down 19% since Fiorina's arrival as CEO.

To be fair, Fiorina had done many things right. HP tripled patent applications in 2000 and the services division—Fiorina's top priority—was growing rapidly in both turnover and revenues. The restructuring of the divisions into front-end and back-end operations had streamlined customer service and was generally seen as a good move—although many managers were still confused about whether sales reps or back-end R&D managers should make production and development decisions. As one employee said,

> *"The idea was to move the pain away from the customer and deal with it inside the company, but for whatever reasons the managers under Carly have not been able to execute it well."*[27]

Unfortunately for Fiorina, many internal and external stakeholders expected more and better things from HP. Many of the 8,000 HP employees surveyed in February 2001 said they were angry about poor internal communication and a visible disconnect between top executives' stated intent and their actions. A former HP employee who left the company to become a venture capitalist said,

> *"HP is the anchor to the moral system of the [Silicon] Valley. There is a concern that they may be adrift."*[28]

Employees' grumbling grew to a roar in July 2001, when HP announced that "deteriorating global economic conditions" would force a reduction of 6,000 jobs—and this just after 80,000 employees had taken voluntary pay-cuts in the month before. Many employees expressed dismay; one posted an open letter to Fiorina on an Internet site:

> *"Dear Carly,*
>
> *I was at HP for 15 years until you showed me the door. And you still haven't told me why. It was only last March that you paid me a retention bonus to stay with the company as a key contributor. And in May you sent me a generous stash of stock options and said, "This award represents a significant vote of confidence by your managers that you have and will continue to play a critical role in achieving HP's ambitious goals to reinvent the company." And then you told the press that I and 6000 others were dismissed because of job performance. Well shucks, Carly, you lied. . . ."*

Meanwhile, during the summer months of 2001, Fiorina, the HP board of directors, and Michael Capellas of Compaq were working behind the scenes on a restructuring of a much larger scale—a merger of their companies.

HP board members and Fiorina publicly said that they had spent at least two years considering all possible alternatives for HP's future. In May 2001 Fiorina hired McKinsey consultants to look for strategic options. As a result of their findings, the board considered three choices: a) continue as a stand-alone company; b) split HP up; or c) consider high-tech acquisitions. According to official reports, in June 2001 Fiorina met with Capellas to discuss Compaq's licensing of HP software, but the talks turned instead to the possibility of a merger. McKinsey consultants analyzed the potential deal for Fiorina and gave board members a report on a Thursday in July—the day that Walter Hewlett was playing his cello at the Bohemian Grove.

McKinsey concluded that there was enough synergy between the two companies that the benefits would outweigh the risks. By August, the HP board was negotiating with Compaq and formulating an integration plan. Two of the HP board members had prior experience with big acquisitions: Boeing CEO Philip Condit (who led Boeing's 1997 acquisition of McDonnell-Douglas) and Sam Ginn (who was CEO at AirTouch Communications when it was sold to Vodafone in 1999).

Three days before the deal was announced in September, Fiorina asked 32-year veteran executive Webb McKinney, along with Compaq's chief financial officer, Jeff Clarke, to co-chair the team that would plan how to fit the two companies together. She asked McKinney to define the ways in which the merged company would achieve the cost savings and revenues she would be presenting to Wall Street when the deal was announced. McKinney later said that it was a complete surprise and a short conversation; he walked out of Fiorina's office thinking, "Oh, my Lord." He considered the job and what it entailed for two days, then called Fiorina and told her he was willing to do it.

The merger was announced on September 4, 2001, and the rest is history—although history itself is never objective. In February 2002, Walter Hewlett categorically stated in a press release:

"The claim that Hewlett-Packard developed the plan to acquire Compaq as the result of two and a half years of careful consideration and evaluation of alternatives is pure fantasy. In fact, nothing could be further from the truth.

The plan to acquire Compaq came as a result of a phone call from Michael Capellas to Fiorina just a few months prior to the announcement of the transaction, according to HP's own proxy statement. We believe that it was only after this that HP created its purported strategy to justify spending $25 billion to acquire Compaq.

The notion that HP's full board has considered, debated and rejected every alternative we now suggest completely defies the record and common sense."

Although there were several sides to the story, by the end of March 2002, even before the result of the vote was announced, people were beginning to draw conclusions. Walter Hewlett was one of the first to come forward with an analysis of the governance issues involved. Speaking at the Council of Institutional Investors' conference, he said that he had learned a lot about the way corporate governance should change in the United States (see Exhibit 2). In merger negotiations, he said, the board and management should have separate counsel to ensure unbiased advice and fair representation of shareholders' views. Boards are often too insulated, he noted, with few ties to company employees or shareholders. As a result, they usually share management's perspective. Hewlett said that he hoped his independent stand in the Compaq-HP merger would inspire other corporate boards to exert more independence.

Other observers saw the proxy battle as another example of the pitfalls of combining the CEO and chairman positions, a practice which is common in the US but less so in Europe. It also seemed as though HP was lacking a strong second-in-command. Fiorina was functioning as CEO, chairman, de-facto COO (chief operating officer) and visionary; in addition, she was the lightning rod for everyone's discontent. She was the chief strategist as CEO, *and* the chief decision maker as chairman. It could be argued that Fiorina had too much responsibility, although she dismissed the idea that she needed a COO, saying, "I'm running the business the way I see fit."[29] Certainly that's true: it appears that she arrived at HP with a deliberate strategy that she had devised *before* her meetings with HP executives and managers around the world.[30]

Some HP employees severely criticized the HP board members for appearing to put their own financial gain ahead of the long-term health of the company. Their point was that a CEO and directors are the virtual

Thank you. I am delighted to be here today.

I wish to thank you for your support over these past several months. I thank those of you who spoke out publicly on behalf of HP stockholders and, in doing so, spoke out for all shareholders everywhere. . . .

We took on quite a powerful machine. It had many levers of influence at its disposal and a firm determination to employ them. I believe, however, that what we lacked in relative resources, we made up for in passion and conviction. Regardless of how one voted, I think everyone understood that we are taking an important stand in this effort—one with potentially far-reaching repercussions. . . .

Indeed, it is my hope that the experiences of the past several months will come to be viewed as a turning point in the evolution of accountability and transparency in the governance of corporations. Issues of corporate governance—from fiduciary responsibility to boardroom ethics—can be highly complex, difficult for even sophisticated shareholders to grasp. These issues arise in a sometimes turbulent environment of strategic risk, corporate politics, personal ambition and high finance. Even in stable, successful companies, such waters can be treacherous. In companies grasping for new strategic direction of reinventing businesses in a changing marketplace, they can at times be downright destructive.

Despite the fact that billions of dollars and the future of great companies are at stake, standards of corporate governance are neither robustly developed nor rigorously examined or enforced. To be blunt: the stakes are high; the standards are not. I have been a director of Hewlett-Packard for 15 years. I believe my recent experiences as a director might provide a useful case study—for this group, for my peers on other boards, and for others engaged in managing and monitoring corporate behavior. If nothing else, I believe my experience makes a clear and compelling case for aligning a director's fiduciary duties as squarely as possible with the interests of stockholders.

Of that I have no doubt.

But we still have a long way to go toward achieving that end. Boards are too easily insulated from the stockholders whose interests we [board members] are obligated to protect. Board members talk to one another and to management. And most often it is management's perspective that they share. Rarely do they have substantive, ongoing relationships with employees, stockholders, clients and other key stakeholders. Rarely do they acknowledge these other, highly valuable perspectives. . . .

At the very least, boards must be pried loose from the grip of management and their hired hands. I firmly believe that, in considering grand strategic designs such as mergers and acquisitions, boards must have access to legal and financial counsel that is separate and distinct from management's team. Boards need independent sources of information in order to evaluate plans and ask the tough questions of management. They need to probe executive decisions to be certain the right choices are made. And they need to do so in an environment that rewards honest inquiry, not conformity. Executive committees should meet periodically outside the presence of company managers to assist the free flow of ideas and information.

Despite more than 200 years of political practice in the United States, democracy remains an ideology strangely alien to many corporate boardrooms. And too many corporate executives still fail to distinguish dissent from disloyalty. Above all, too many corporate managers too readily forget who owns the company: the shareholders. . . .

Is this the beginning of a new wave of advocacy for corporate democracy and accountability? Or is this simply further proof that if you take on a corporate giant, you'll have a heck of a time getting out from under the heel of his boot? The answer is up to all of us. . . .

Thank you.

owners of an organization, but because they are non-permanent members, their priority is often to cash out as quickly as possible. Walter Hewlett put it bluntly: "Boards must be pried loose from the grip of management and their hired hands."

What is notable in this case is that the key people on both sides of the merger battle appeared to feel genuinely that HP was a great company, and to be acting according to their vision for a viable future. There really were no villains in this melodrama. However, people were beginning to realize that corporate governance was of interest to a wide—and influential—constituency, and was therefore too important to be left to a select group behind closed doors. This realization would undoubtedly affect corporate governance in the future—and not only at HP.

THE BATTLE FOR THE HEART AND SOUL OF HP

If Fiorina had made the merger proposal a year earlier at the height of her popularity (and in the stronger economic climate of 2000), it might have sailed through with little objection from shareholders or the founders' heirs. But by 2002, Fiorina's reputation had dimmed somewhat, partly because of missteps and bad timing, but also, in some people's minds, because of her hubris. (As one observer said, "She brought to her stewardship a star quality at a company where no one was a star"[31]—and within a corporate culture where, it could be added, no one was *supposed* to be a star.) As a result, Fiorina came under far closer scrutiny not only from Wall Street, but also from the Hewlett and Packard heirs, than she otherwise might have.

The heirs had rational reasons for opposing the merger, and they offered some valid alternative strategies. But the reasons articulated weren't the only possible explanations for the Hewlett and Packard families' rejection of the Compaq-HP merger. Another far more significant event had occurred only a few months before Fiorina proposed her "bet-the-company" move to the board of HP—the death of William Hewlett on January 13, 2001. Steve Jobs remarked that when David Packard died in 1996, it was the beginning of the end of an era; with William Hewlett's death, the era ended.

Years ago, Walter Hewlett was asked what his life's motivation was. He answered, "The privilege of my life is to be my father's son."[32] Therein lies a clue, perhaps, to some of the irrational forces that sparked the battle for the heart and soul of HP.

Perhaps the connection that he felt with his father also helps to explain why, in a letter from Walter Hewlett sent to shareholders the week before the vote, Hewlett wrote:

> *HP Is Not Just Another Company*
> *March 19th Is Not Just Another*
> *Stockholder Meeting*
>
> *Behind all of the . . . heated rhetoric from HP lies this simple truth: you as a stockholder have the opportunity to decide what kind of company HP will be. HP management has consistently tried to present this decision as a choice bewtween HP's past and HP's future. **Rather, it is a choice between different futures. For many decades, HP has represented unique vision of the best an American corporation could be. This merger threatens everything that has made HP great** [bold appeared in original text].*

On May 9th, two days after the final approval of the merger (by a margin of 2.8%) was announced, David Packard posted an open letter on the door of the Stanford Theatre in Palo Alto, which had been restored by the family's foundation. He wrote,

> *"The HP Way touched many people's lives. Most of us expected that it would last forever—that it would prove as timeless as a Frank Capra movie. . . . It's hard to imagine that [the leaders of the new HP] can invent something better than what they left behind. . . . The old HP is gone, R.I.P. (rest in peace)."*

THE HP WAY IS DEAD—LONG LIVE THE HP WAY!

R.I.P.—or the beginning of a new lease on life? By late spring, the value of HP stock was rising (see Exhibit 3). When Carly Fiorina and Michael Capellas appeared on stage to launch the new HP, they were greeted by a standing ovation from employees. Although everyone realized that there was a tremendous amount of integration work to be done, many observers, HP clients and other stakeholders were optimistic. There seemed to be a feeling of: "The die has been cast; now let's get on with it."

Walter Hewlett, on the other hand, was no longer on center stage, but he was still active nonetheless. He seemed determined to carry on his advocacy of more effective—and responsive—corporate governance. The

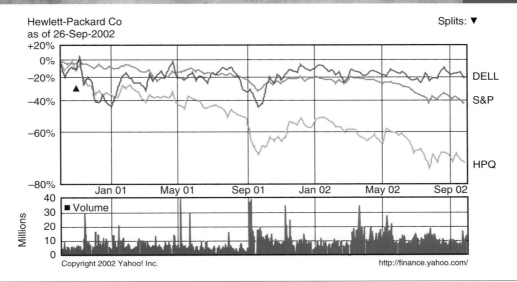

Hewlett-Packard Co
as of 26-Sep-2002

Splits: ▼

Copyright 2002 Yahoo! Inc.

http://finance.yahoo.com/

Used by permission: Data Source: Commodity Systems, Inc. (CSI) Web Site: http://www.csidata.com

collapse of Enron and the deflation of WorldCom (the latter a victim of what one observer called "takeover-itis run amok") had sensitized people to governance issues. Would Walter Hewlett now become the leader of a grassroots revolution?

In retrospect, the proxy battle and merger were only the first act. After a short pause to regroup, HP and Walter Hewlett would undoubtedly continue to make history—in one Way or another.

NOTES

1. D. Yoffie and M. Kwak, (2001). "Manager's Journal: HP and Compaq Should Return to Their Roots." *Wall Street Journal,* New York, December 17, A18.

2. B. Evans, (2001). "HP + Compaq = ?" *Information Week,* 866 December 3, 78.

3. A. Park, (2001). "A Stunning Reversal for HP's Marriage Plans," *Business Week,* 3758, November 19, 42.

4. Quotes from Walter Hewlett in this paper for which no citation is given appeared in several sources: his website, press releases, and letters to shareholders.

5. P.-W. Tam, (2002). "Walter Hewlett's Counterplan." *Wall Street Journal,* New York, February 11, B1.

6. P. Burrows and K. Rebello, "Q&A: Fiorina: The Deal Is the Right Thing for Shareholders," *Business Week,* 3763, December 24, 68.

7. Hewlett's press releases, website, and letters to shareholders.

8. C. Taylor, (2002). "HP's Fierce Face-Off." *Time,* March 4, 46–48.

9. Quoted in several sources.

10. J. Hamilton, (2001). "Happily Ever After?" *Business Week,* 3760, December 3, 32.

11. Adapted from Copeland, L. 2(2001). *Computerworld,* 35, 51, December 17, p. 1.

12. S. Morrison, (2001). *The Financial Times,* Section: Companies and Finance International, November 13, 37.

13. M. Blake, (2001). "Q&A Fiorina: The Deal Is 'the Right Thing for Shareholders.'" *Business Week,* 3763, December 24, 68.

14. P. Burrows and A. Park, (2001). "Carly's Last Stand." *Business Week,* 3763, December 24, 62–70.

15. In a private interview.

16. P. Burrows, (2002). "Doubts about HP-Compaq's Financial Goals." *BusinessWeek Online,* March 18.

17. J. Pitta, (1993). "It Had to Be Done and We Did It." *Forbes,* April 26, 148–153.

18. P. Burrows and P. Elstrom, (1999). "The Boss." *Business Week,* August 2, 76–83.

19. Burrows and Elstrom, "The Boss."

20. This kind of "consecration" is a classic example of what has been called the *myth of the messiah:* "[People in the organization have] the notion that redemption and salvation will come from an omnipotent source. The person anointed as the messiah walks into an environment overburdened with expectations. He or she is supposed to make right everything that is wrong in the organization. Usually, messiahs are outsiders coming into the family firm to set things right. The messiah can be . . . a highly praised, recently arrived (non-family) president, for exmaple." M. F. R. Kets de Vries, (1996). *Family Business: Human Dilemmas in the Family Firm.* London: Intl. Thompson Business Press. p. 64.

21. *Economist,* (2001). "In the Family's Way." *The Economist,* December 15, 64.

22. From private interview.

23. Fiorina's comments appeared in company documents and in press releases.

24. N. Mayes, (2001). "Compaq Won't Fix HP's Services Problems," *Global Computing Services*, September 6.
25. P. Burrows and W. Echikson, (2001). "HP's Woes Are Deeper than the Downturn." *Business Week*, 3731, May 7, 48.
26. Fiorina's comments appeared in several sources.
27. Anonymous website comment.
28. Q. Hardy, (2001). "Backstabbing Carly." *Forbes*, June 11, 55.
29. P. Burrows, (2001). "The Radical." *Business Week*, February 19, 70–80.
30. Dr. Henry Mintzberg, McGill University, in private discussion.
31. M. Simon, (2002). "Whatever the Vote, HP Way Is Long Gone." *San Francisco Chronicle*, San Francisco, March 20. A18.
32. P. Burrows, (2002). "What's the Truth about Walter Hewlett?" *Business Week*, 3769, February 11, 2002, 74–77.

case seventeen

James J. Kennelly
Skidmore College

"What future have they on the land?" asked a leading IFA (Irish Farming Association) officer. "Will they be able to follow their fathers and grandfathers into farming?" Nobody in the attendance of well over 800 in the ballroom of Ballygarry House Hotel said "yea" or "nay" but, by their stony silence, they answered the question in their own way.[1]

"These (the small farmers of Kerry) are our people. We feel for them. They started Kerry Group and they'll be there to see the success of the Kerry Group as it goes through and we'll make sure of that".

—Mr. Dick O'Sullivan, head of Kerry Group's Agriculture Division[2]

Gazing out his window, Kerry Group Managing Director Denis Brosnan could see, past the busy streets of the provincial town of Tralee, the expanse of the Dingle Peninsula creeping out into the Atlantic Ocean. With the sun shining intermittently amidst billowing clouds blowing in from the ocean, the mottled colors of the changing landscape made for a powerful and beautiful sight. But Brosnan hadn't time to be long distracted by the view, as he turned again to reviewing his notes for the first of two special general meetings of the Kerry Co-op scheduled for that afternoon. As the prime architect of the crucial proposal to be voted on that day, Brosnan wanted to be certain that his case was clear and convincing.

The most controversial item on the agenda was a vote on a rule change that would allow the Co-op, an association of local County Kerry farmers then functioning as essentially a holding company, to reduce its ownership stake in Kerry Group to below 51%. To achieve this, a vote of 75% in favor of the rule change, at two

consecutive meetings scheduled two weeks apart, was required. This afternoon's meeting promised to be the biggest meeting in the Co-op's history, with over 2,000 members expected to pack the conference center at the Brandon Hotel. Although the proposal was expected to pass, the "no" forces had mounted an intensive, and emotional, door-to-door and telephone lobbying effort in an attempt to gain the necessary 25% "no" vote necessary to derail the proposal. As he prepared his opening remarks, Brosnan wondered if their efforts would have any effect. Despite his confidence, he knew that when it came to Irish farming politics, there was never any such thing as a "sure thing".

INTRODUCTION

From its beginnings as a collection of small dairy cooperative societies in rural County Kerry, Ireland in 1974, Kerry Group plc had, by 1996, grown to the status of a full-fledged multinational corporation with manufacturing operations and markets throughout the world. As a major player in the international specialty food ingredients business (particularly in North America), and with a growing presence in consumer foods in European markets, it was well on its way to becoming a substantial global business.

Over the course of twenty-five years, sales revenue had grown to £1.2 billion (all financial amounts are stated in Irish Punts [£]; in 1996, the Irish £ was valued at approximately $1.60) and after tax profit to £49 million (Exhibit 1 provides an eleven year summary of financial results). Over 60% of sales revenue and 69% of operating profit were now sourced outside of Ireland (Exhibit 2 provides geographical segment data). Most of this growth was a result of a continuous program of strategic acquisitions in North America and Europe. The Kerry Group was led by an experienced management team, most of whom had been with Kerry since its inception (as a cooperative society) in 1974. Indeed, one

10 Year Summary of P&L Statements (IR£1,000)   EXHIBIT 1

	1986	1987	1988	1989	1990	1991	1992	1993	1994	1995	1996
Turnover	265,242	291,289	396,721	559,551	584,099	754,931	826,737	879,975	882,697	1,199,093	1,233,253
Operating Profit	11,157	11,397	17,906	31,397	31,963	42,084	46,403	50,196	55,549	85,739	90,594
Loss (Profit) on Disposal of Assets	(14)	65	(97)		(112)	(30)	243	10	(359)	1,685	
Interest Payable and Similar Charges	4,842	3,223	4,987	12,229	10,854	14,753	13,889	10,991	11,578	29,726	27,876
Profit before Taxation	6,329	8,109	13,016	19,168	21,221	27,361	32,271	39,195	44,330	54,328	62,718
Taxation	37	216	322	467	666	1,645	3,901	5,959	7,480	5,055	7,103
Profit after Taxation	6,292	7,893	12,694	18,701	20,555	25,716	28,370	33,236	36,850	49,273	55,615
Minority Interest	451	480	548	428	(305)	205	156	185			
Profit to Ordinary Shareholders	5,841	7,413	12,146	18,273	20,860	25,511	28,214	33,051	36,850	49,273	55,615
Dividend	819	1,152	1,497	2,281	2,746	3,355	3,527	4,057	4,608	5,456	6,268
Retained Profit	5,022	6,261	10,649	15,992	18,114	22,156	24,687	28,994	32,242	43,817	49,347
Earnings Per Share (After Goodwill)	6.01p	6.63p	9.40p	11.38p	12.60p	14.50p	15.80p	18.50p	20.50p	23.30p	26.90p
End of Year Exchange Rate (to US Dollars)	1.3995	1.6755	1.5075	1.5563	1.7794	1.7513	1.6234	1.4085	1.5456	1.6000	1.6584

Notes:
1. 1986 was the first year of the firm's results as a public limited company.

Source: Kerry Group Annual Report, 1997. All results are restated for current goodwill policies.

Geographical Market of Origin	1994 Turnover IR£1,000	1994 Operating Profit IR£1,000	1995 Turnover IR£1,000	1995 Operating Profit IR£1,000
Ireland	428,153	24,447	447,212	26,353
Rest of Eurpoe	178,474	5,186	313,522	20,554
North America	190,423	25,649	363,361	38,347
	797,050	55,282	1,124,095	85,254
Discontinued Operations	85,647	267	74,998	485
Total	882,697	55,549	1,199,093	85,739

Geographical Market by Destination	1994 Turnover IR£1,000	1995 Turnover IR£1,000
Ireland	247,959	255,918
Rest of Eurpoe	275,385	437,441
North America	262,834	424,566
Rest of World	10,872	6,170
	797,050	1,124,095
Discontinued Operations	85,647	74,998
Total	882,697	1,199,093

Source: 1995 Kerry Grup Annual Report

element often cited by the local Kerry community for the success of the group was the leadership and vision of its Managing Director, Denis Brosnan. In the public houses of Kerry Brosnan was widely reputed, only partly in jest, to have the "Midas Touch".[3] Certainly, in Kerry's first twenty-two years, serious blunders appeared to have been few. Meanwhile, its shareholders, primarily "land rich but cash poor" small farmers based in rural County Kerry, had profited over the years as the group's share price rose from £.35 in 1986 to over £6.00.

BACKGROUND AND HISTORY

THE FORMATION OF THE KERRY CO-OP

The Kerry Group began business as the Kerry Co-operative Creameries (or, more affectionately, the Kerry Co-op). It was formed in January 1974 by the amalgamation of a number of small independent cooperative societies and milk suppliers in County Kerry, Ireland and the purchase of the assets of the state run Dairy Disposal Board.[4] The dairy farmer/milk suppliers of North Kerry, who now took an ownership stake in the new, larger cooperative, had owned these small cooperatives. Similarly, independent farmers from South Kerry who had supplied milk to the Dairy Disposal Board also "bought into" the new co-op. It had taken a small

group of managers, all aged in their late 20's, about 18 months (since mid-1972) to get the enterprise off the ground. During that time the small group, led by Denis Brosnan and his "twelve apostles", thirteen in all, worked together in cramped quarters in the parking lot of a milk processing plant owned by North Kerry Milk Products, Ltd.[5]

> We started from a caravan (similar to a construction trailer, or a camper) outside Listowel in 1972. We rented that for twenty pounds a week. Hugh Friel, myself and others, thirteen in all, we lived in that cramped space for about eighteen months.[6]

Central to the formation of the Kerry Co-op was its acquisition of an 83% stake in North Kerry Milk Products Limited and its aforementioned milk processing plant, located in the twenty acre "Canon's Field" just outside of Listowel. The cost of this purchase was £1.5 million, an amount raised by the farmers of Kerry who reached into their own pockets to fund the purchase. This was accomplished through the farmer-suppliers contributing a set amount per gallon of milk supplied to the Co-op over a six year period, in return for which they received shares in the Co-op (up to a maximum of 1,000 shares). Membership was open to all milk suppliers. Democratic control of the Co-op was ensured by entitling all shareholders to vote (on the basis of one member, one vote) for various governing committees and, ultimately, for the Board of Directors. Fully nine thousand dairy farmers in Kerry answered the call and became co-owners of the Kerry Co-op by the time it opened its doors in January 1974.[7] The management of the Co-op quickly set about consolidating and rationalizing the various operations involved with the collection, processing and distribution of milk, butter and other dairy products, as well as the production of casein (a protein powder extracted from milk) for the export market. (A brief primer on the cooperative form of organization in Ireland is included as Exhibit 3.)

Despite its modest beginnings, the creation of the Kerry Co-op was greeted with great anticipation in County Kerry, for the times demanded larger, more efficient, dairy organizations. Ireland's entry into the EEC in 1973 provided not only large and rich markets for Irish dairy products, but also put pressure on the national government to privatize its state-owned holdings (e.g. the quasi-government Dairy Disposal Board). Similarly, the farmers in the county, who for generations were wed to their own small, independent, but relatively inefficient cooperatives and creameries, had by now become sufficiently frustrated to see the wisdom of banding together into large and more scale efficient cooperative ventures that could better compete with the large milk producers in the rest of the EEC. With milk prices in the EEC high, and demand rising, farmers hoped that at long last their historically depressed farm incomes would rise.

THE EARLY YEARS OF THE KERRY CO-OP

A cooperative can be defined as "an enterprise that is collectively owned and operated for mutual benefit".[8] As such, the Kerry Co-op was owned by, and for the benefit of, the small farmer/milk suppliers of Kerry. This, however, did not prevent Kerry Co-op's management group from engaging in a vigorous program of expansion from almost the very beginning. This growth reflected both continuous internal expansion and a series of strategic acquisitions.

Between 1974 and 1982, the Kerry Co-op acquired various milk businesses throughout the west of Ireland, building in the process an extensive distribution system in that area.[9] Indeed, these were halcyon days for the dairy business. Milk yields were increasing, prices were high, and EEC milk quota schemes were still in the future. With the exception of a 33% stake in a joint venture to manufacture packaging material with Union Camp in 1980 (an ill-fitting venture from which they soon exited), Kerry "stuck to its knitting" and remained largely anchored in its traditional dairy businesses of

consumer milk, butter and cheese, and in the export market for casein. This was entirely consistent with the activities of other milk producers throughout Ireland, and Europe, at the time, except that Kerry Co-op was consistently (but not spectacularly) profitable. (See Exhibit 4 for Kerry Co-op P&L Statements.) In 1980, however, an event occurred that clearly exposed Kerry's reliance upon the vagaries of the dairy business.

THE BRUCELLOSIS "WAKE-UP CALL" AND DIVERSIFICATION

In 1980, the Irish government decided to introduce a program for the eradication of brucellosis, a disease carried in cows. Given County Kerry's remote location at the extreme southwest of the country, it was decided that Kerry would serve as the pilot area in which to begin implementation of the scheme. Unfortunately, enforcement of the eradication scheme led to a substantial decline in the number of cows in the county (as herds were thinned to eliminate animals exposed to the virus). By most accounts, the productive capacity of the farmer-suppliers of the Kerry Co-op was reduced by some 20%. Additionally, the weather was particularly bad, even by Irish standards, further reducing milk production. Finally, major construction projects around Shannon (by the international airport) provided construction jobs to quite a number of smaller, more marginal dairy farmers who decided that this was an ideal time to leave the farm. As Brosnan describes it, this "war on three fronts" occurred at a particularly bad time, since the Co-op's £15 million investment in new processing capacity was just coming on line. But, rather than having 50% more milk to process, the Co-op had 20% less! As the firm suffered under the weight of this substantial idle capacity, profits for 1980 and 1981 declined from prior years.

It was clear to the management and, importantly, to the directors of the cooperative, that if the cooperative were to survive and thrive, it would need to reduce its reliance on dairy products by diversifying into more "value-added" activities, and away from milk processing. In the eyes of some observers, this was a "radical move" that "redirected the group beyond the geography and tradition of County Kerry".[10] Says Brosnan, "I clearly remember stating categorically in a meeting of the Board of Directors that we will never again be dependent on manufacturing milk!"[11] In 1982, the Co-op made a major foray outside of the milk sector with the purchase of a pig meat processing plant in Tralee (Denny's) and a meat processing plant (Duffys) in County Carlow. It followed this up with the purchase of two additional beef processing plants in March 1986. These plants were in serious financial trouble; one, in

Case 17 / The Evolution of an Irish Multinational: Kerry Group plc

Cooperation means people working together for their mutual benefit. By combining their efforts, people gain from one another's ideas, talents, skills and energies. In this way, they are able to achieve things they could not do as well (or at all) on their own. . . . Modern cooperatives developed in the context of the Industrial Revolution, the expansion of the cash economy and the growing concentration of power in the hands of those with capital. These cooperatives were set up initially as a means of safeguarding and promoting the interests of some of the less powerful members of society—whether workers, consumers, farmers or other producers. *

In the simplest terms, cooperatives are organizations that are formed solely for the benefit of their members. Cooperatives can be formed by supplier-members who sell their produce to the organization, consumer-members who buy products or services from the cooperative organization, or other types of members who somehow use the services (that is, are "patrons") of the organization. In the purest sense, these cooperative organizations are owned by the members and serve to provide a vehicle for the members to produce efficiently, have their products marketed effectively, combine their resources to realize some reasonable level of economic (and perhaps even political) power, and maintain some control over their productive resources and their economic destiny. The equity capital for these enterprises is provided solely by the member-patrons.

Cooperatives in Ireland date to the time of Sir Horace Plunkett (1854–1932) who, with the able assistance of one of the giants of the Irish Literary Renaissance, the writer, mystic, and surprisingly practical A.E. (George Russell) and the organizing genius of R.A. Anderson, spurred the development of Irish cooperative organizations around the turn of the century. They realized their greatest successes with the dairy industry in Ireland. By the mid-1970's, nearly all the island's milk supply was being produced by cooperative dairy organizations, which numbered perhaps 200 in all. These cooperatives were owned by the dairy farmers who sold their milk to the cooperative society. The co-op, in turn, was charged with finding markets for the milk . . . either through the supply of consumer liquid milk markets, the production of cheese products, or the processing of milk into any number of related products such as milk powder, evaporated milk, casein, fat-filled animal feed supplements, etc.

The Irish Co-operative Organisation Society (ICOS), which is the umbrella organization of Irish cooperatives, notes the reason for the existence of cooperatives in Ireland as follows:

[cooperatives] were set up in the first instance to help farmers build strong, self-help businesses which the country needed and which have succeeded in contributing substantially to the Irish economy. These businesses have now grown to a high degree of sophistication and will contribute even more to the economy and to agriculture in the future. **

The heart of cooperative philosophy and principles are reflected in these guidelines for the structure of cooperative organizations: ***

- **Open Membership**—Membership is voluntary, but confined to persons who wish to, and are able to, use the services of the cooperative (including the workers). Membership *is based on use and not on financial ownership*. Once members have ceased to use the services of the cooperative, their initial capital contributions in the cooperative are returned (typically at a level of £1/share . . . which is usually their initial contribution per share). There is no "market valued" return.
- **Members Are Owners**—Ownership is confined to the members . . . they retain control over the enterprise. External investors cannot have any influence over the cooperative. Also, ALL members should be owners (that is, they make a capital contribution to the enterprise). This disburses the ownership over the widest possible area.
- **Members Control Equally**—Cooperatives should be governed democratically, with equal opportunities for participation in the governance of the enterprise and EQUAL VOTING RIGHTS. That is, ONE MEMBER, ONE VOTE . . . regardless of the financial contribution of any particular member, or the amount of patronage, etc.
- **Benefit in Proportion to Use**—Financial returns to owners are not based on contributed capital, but rather based on the member's use of the cooperative. A "return on investment" (ROI) is anathema to cooperative thinking.
- **Limited Return on Capital**—At best, the return on any member's contributed capital should be no more than the market rate.

Additionally, it should be noted that cooperative organizations in Ireland, as in the United States and most of the world, are generally tax exempt. This permits cooperatives to pass along patronage dividends (that is, dividends based upon the member's transactions with the cooperative) to members free of income tax. This also permits the cooperative to retain its earnings (for capital investment) without taxation. Such benefits are not available to publicly-owned corporations.

---

*Briscoe, B., Grey, S., Hunt, P., Linehan, M., McBride, H., Tucker, V. and Ward, M. 1982. *The Co-operative Idea*. Cork: The Centre for Co-operative Studies.
**Henry, M. (ed) 1994. *Fruits of a Century*. Dublin: The Irish Co-operative Organisation Society, p. 117.
***Ibid.

	1981	1982	1983	1984	1985
Turnover					
Dairy Products	58,516	72,263	80,646	92,462	115,641
Foods	13,985	30,179	43,848	51,540	61,311
Agricultural Trading	23,157	26,817	33,585	36,468	34,287
Total	95,658	129,259	158,079	180,470	211,239
Trading Profit before Interest and Depreciation	6,417	9,940	9,948	11,421	12,330
Interest (Net)	1,409	2,479	1,953	2,778	3,016
Depreciation (Net)	2,776	3,248	3,688	3,887	4,201
Profit before Taxation	2,232	4,213	4,307	4,756	5,113
Taxation	0	0	0	0	0
Profit after Taxation	2,232	4,213	4,307	4,756	5,113
Minority Interest (Erie Cassein)	376	591	533	457	586
Profit Attributable to Kerry Co-op	1,856	3,622	3,774	4,299	4,527
Share Interest (Dividends)	363	365	360	358	710
Retained Profit	1,493	3,257	3,414	3,941	3,817

Notes:
1. 1985 was the last full year of the firm's results as a cooperative organization.

Source: Prospectus for the Private Placing of "A" Ordinary Shares in Kerry Group plc—July 1986.

fact, had already been closed. Kerry Co-op reopened it only after extensive renovations.

These actions reflected the execution of Kerry's plan for diversifying its business, a strategy called by company official Frank Hayes its "equation for growth".

The Board of Kerry Group Co-operative and its management realised that the future lay with strong diversified businesses capable of competing in a world market. In terms of the food sector Kerry viewed this as a momentum towards the development of large international companies, financially strong, with a significant share of any market in which they choose to compete. A five year corporate plan was defined and agreed by the Board, research and development became a priority, overseas offices were opened and the quiet search for suitable acquisitions began. Kerry was determined to become a large scale food business and an appropriate management structure was put in place to cater for this strategy. Kerry's strategy was based on an equation for growth which read: Strategy × Capability × Capital = Sustained Profitable Growth. The organisation was and indeed remains convinced that where one of the

elements in this equation is missing, the result at best is zero profitable growth.[12]

By 1986, this strategy appeared to be working, and Kerry Co-op had become one of Ireland's more successful food processing businesses. Yet, it was clear that to attain (or even to maintain) such a position, yet more extensive growth would be required. The problem was, however, that the Co-op had only two of the three required components to accelerate its growth. Certainly, it had the people, and it had the technology, but it was severely constrained by its organizational structure in its access to capital. Up to that point, the funding for acquisitions had come from both internally generated funds and debt, as well as from the farmer-shareholders of the cooperative who had answered the call to provide (a modest amount of) additional funds on several occasions. Yet, banks were still cautious in their loans to agricultural cooperatives (where tradition had it that "farmers always paid themselves first"), and the farmer-shareholders of the cooperative were nervous about having so much of their funds invested in an illiquid investment (shares in the Co-op did not trade and there was no easy way to ascertain the value of a share; additionally, when members decided to "cash out" their Co-op shares, they were typically paid out on the basis of £1 per share, with no capital appreciation). To continue on their path of strategic acquisitions, therefore, Kerry Co-op would have to tap other sources of equity capital. This would require the involvement of "outside" shareholders in the ownership and affairs of the Kerry Co-op.

A Defining Moment—The Formation of the Kerry Group

In February 1986 the Kerry Co-op took a novel and innovative step, one never before done by a cooperative organization in Ireland. It began the process of converting its enterprise into a public limited company (a plc, the equivalent of a publicly-owned corporation). This conversion was accomplished in three distinct steps. First, Kerry Group (which was formed as a subsidiary of the Kerry Co-op) acquired all of the assets and property of the former Kerry Co-op in return for consideration of "B" ordinary shares in Kerry Group plc. The Kerry Co-op thus became the equivalent of an investment holding company, with no direct operational connection to the Kerry Group. It also, at this point, owned 100% of the share capital of Kerry Group plc. A second placing of "A" ordinary shares was accomplished by offering additional shares (totaling 10,350,000 shares) to existing shareholders in the Kerry Co-op, as well as milk suppliers and employees of the Kerry Co-op, at £.35 per share. Finally, the Kerry Group choreographed an additional offering of 8,000,000 "A" ordinary shares to institutions and the general public (at £.52 per share). At the end of this recapitalization scheme in July 1986, the ownership structure of the Kerry Group was 83% owned by the Kerry Co-op (which still existed as essentially a "holding company"), and 17% owned by individuals and institutions (although predominantly farmer-shareholders, suppliers, and employees of the Kerry Co-op). The stock was also listed for trading on the Dublin and London Stock Exchanges. Exhibit 5 provides details of the ownership structure of Kerry Group plc.

Although this step was overwhelmingly supported by the majority of the Co-op's farmer-shareholders, it was not completely without opposition. Some farmers felt that "going public" was essentially selling out on fundamental cooperative principles (see Exhibit 3). These objections, however, were overridden by 1) the necessity of the firm to have access to additional capital to maintain its growth program, 2) the fact that the shares of the firm would now have a market value and some liquidity so that farmers could begin to realize some of the appreciation in their investment and importantly, 3) the creation of a complex governance structure that provided the cooperative and its shareholders with a means to continue to exercise control over the activities of the enterprise. The articles of association for the creation of the publicly-traded Kerry Group stipulated that no less than 52% of the shares of the enterprise were to be held by the Kerry Co-op, and that this required percentage of ownership could not be changed without a vote of at least 75% of the shareholders of the Co-op. With this "fail-safe" provision, the farmers of Kerry could maintain control over the activities and future strategies of the Kerry Group, and be protected from the rule of Dublin-based institutional investors.

The Creation of a Multinational Corporation—1986–1996

From a sales turnover of £265 million in 1986, the Kerry Group grew at an annual rate of approximately 20% over the next decade, to a turnover of £1.2 billion in 1996. This growth was the result of the Group's strategy of external expansion in a number of targeted business segments in the food ingredients and consumer foods businesses. The acquisition program is detailed in the following explanations, by major business line.

Kerry Ingredients

The largest and most important business group in the Kerry Group's portfolio, accounting for £707 million, or 57% of group sales in 1996, was Kerry Ingredients, which developed and produced a wide array of food coatings, flavorings, seasonings and other ingredients. These products are quite specialized, and include such products as cheese powder coatings for convenience foods, processed fruit preparations, clear batter coatings for french fries, and dry marinates and glazes for dessert foods.

This industry segment was among the fastest growing segments of the food industry, driven by the growth of convenience foods and the global snack markets, as well as the continued growth of food service enterprises. As described in one Kerry publication:

Key drivers in specialist ingredients markets are the accelerating trends towards snacking and convenience, together with the internationalisation of food markets through the global expansion of food manufacturing and foodservice companies and their mission to provide consistent high quality prepared food products. The growth in demand for convenient foods to match modern lifestyles and for fresh natural food products which yield higher flavour impact, ranging from savoury to traditional to ethnic tastes, has led to a proliferation of new product development thereby providing significant growth opportunities for competent ingredient suppliers capable of deliv-

Ownership Structure of Kerry Group plc   EXHIBIT 5

	1986	1987	1988	1989	1990	1991	1992	1993	1994	1995	1996*
Kerry Co-operative Creameries	83.10%	78.70%	66.00%	66.00%	60.00%	57.70%	57.70%	57.70%	52.20%	52.20%	38.00%
Irish Life Assurance plc						13.51	6.40	6.06	6.20	6.00	5.80
IBI Nominees Limited							5.32	4.90	5.90	5.40	4.30
Norwich Union Life Insurance Soc.						7.13	4.27	3.78	3.70	3.70	3.60
Standard Life Assurance Co.						5.79	2.45				
New Ireland Assurance Co. plc							2.26				
Trustees of Electricity Supply Bd.						5.76	1.53				
Trimark Investment Mgmt. Ltd.										3.10	
Bank of Ireland Nominees											3.10
Other Direct Shareholdings	16.90	21.30	34.00	34.00	40.00	10.11	20.08	27.56	32.00	29.60	45.20
	100.00%	100.00%	100.00%	100.00%	100.00%	100.00%	100.00%	100.00%	100.00%	100.00%	100.00%

Notes: Until 1991, only shareholders with 5% or more of the outstanding stock in a company needed to be reported. In 1991, this was changed to a 3% reporting requirement. 1996* percentages reflect the ownership structure after the proposed restructuring plan is put into effect. "Direct shareholdings" of Co-op shareholders were projected to be approximately 23% of the total outstanding stock in the company, after the proposed restructuring plan is put into effect.

*ering the requisite technologies and range of ingredi-
ent systems to service the global marketplace.*[13]

It was also extremely competitive, both in terms of firms and products. The major competitors on a global basis included McCormicks, International Flavors and Fragrance, Unilever and Monsanto, although the industry was extremely fragmented. It was a segment that saw the introduction of literally thousands of new products each year, making R&D and process technologies key factors for success in the industry. Such core technologies also represented a distinctive competence of Kerry Group.

Kerry's initial foray into the food ingredients business can actually be traced back to the very beginnings of the processing facility in Listowel in 1973, where it built a processing center for the production of casein from skim milk. (A timeline of Kerry Group's investments and acquisitions can be found in Exhibit 6.) This casein was initially exported to North America through Erie Casein, an American firm with a minority interest in the facility. Casein is a feedstock for many food ingredients, including infant formula and other supplements. In 1984, Kerry opened its first sales office in North America, intending to build the relationships necessary to market its casein and other products directly to the food industry (rather than through Erie Casein as a middleman).

This was followed by the acquisition of a pharmaceutical plant in the United States in 1987, Kerry's first investment in manufacturing in North America. This plant, located in Jackson, Wisconsin in the heartland of American dairy country, specialized in the coating and drying operations associated with the manufacture of various food ingredients. Nevertheless, until 1988, Kerry's North American operations were insignificant.

This abruptly changed with the Group's acquisition of Beatreme Foods in 1988. Beatreme was the premier specialty food ingredients supplier in the U.S. and, at the time, was larger than the entire Kerry Group. Beatreme had been an acquisition target for some time; indeed, there is a story, perhaps apocryphal, that back in 1984, when Kerry made its first appearance at the International Food Fair in Los Angeles, Denis Brosnan had looked across at the extensive and impressive display fielded by Beatreme and remarked that "someday we'll own that company". Kerry's chance came when Beatreme, sold off by parent company Beatrice Foods, fell into the hands of a succession of investors during the M&A craze of the 80's, with owners who were more interested in short term profit considerations than in the long run management of the business. Although other investors (from New Zealand) were interested in purchasing Beatreme, the Kerry Group succeeded in moving

Ingredients Business Segment

1972	Commissioning of Dairy & Specialty Ingredients Facility in Listowel (Ireland)
1974	Purchase of assets of Dairy Disposal Board (Ireland)
1987	Commissioning of Jackson, WI Facility (USA)
1988	Beatreme Food Ingredients (USA)
1990	Milac, GMBH (Germany)
1991	Eastleigh Flavours (UK)
	Dairyland Products (USA)
1992	Northlands (USA)
1993	Malcolm Foods (Canada)
	Research Foods (Canada)
	Tingles Ltd (UK)
1994	Commissioning of Kerry de Mexico Facility in Irapuato (Mexico)
	Acquisition of DCA (USA, Canada, UK)
	Margetts (UK, Poland)
1996	Ciprial S.A. (France, Italy)
	DCA-Solutech (Australia)

Consumer Foods Business Segment

1972	Commissioning of Dairy & Specialty Ingredients Facility in Listowel (Ireland)
1974	Purchase of assets of Dairy Disposal Board (Ireland)
1974–82	Purchase of Independent Dairies of Killarney, Limerick, Cork & Galway (Ireland)
1982	Denny, Duffy Meats (Ireland)
1986	Convenience Foods (Ireland)
	Snowcream Daires, Moate (Ireland)
1987	Denny Meats (Northern Ireland)
1988	Grove & Ballyfree Turkeys (Ireland)
	S.W.M. Chard (UK)
1990	A.E.Button (UK)
	Miller-Robirch (UK)
1992	Buxted Duckling (UK)
	Kanthoher Food Products (Ireland)
1993	Kerry Spring Water (Ireland)
1994	Commissioning of Porkmeat Products Facility in Shillelagh (Ireland)
	Mattessons Wall's (UK)

quickly to line up financing and effect the purchase. It was also not without risk, as the Kerry Group financed the acquisition primarily through debt financing, pushing its debt to equity ratio inordinately high. Still, the purchase of Beatreme was a critical breakthrough for the Group; they were now a major player in the largest specialty food ingredients market in the world.

Kerry's strategic focus on the expansion of its global food ingredients business continued with a number of smaller acquisitions in the U.S. and U.K. between 1990–1993, culminating in the largest acquisition ever undertaken by the group, a £250 million takeover of DCA Food Industries, Inc. and its subsidiaries in 1994. DCA, headquartered in the United States, and its Margetts Foods subsidiary based in the U.K., were global competitors in food ingredients, with operations in five countries. These, and several smaller strategic acquisitions, placed Kerry Ingredients in the front rank of the specialty food ingredients segment, particularly in the European and North American markets. Acquisitions were primarily funded through debt, since the requirement to maintain at least 52% Co-op ownership in the Group effectively constrained additional equity issues.

The global food ingredients business remained the cornerstone of the Group's growth strategy in 1996. The sector was expected to continue experiencing strong growth in the future, particularly in the emerging markets of the Pacific Rim, where the Kerry Group had little presence. The ingredients segment also represented the foundation of the Group's profitability, returning approximately 72% of the Group's total operating profit in 1995 (see Exhibit 7 for product segment data).

KERRY FOODS

The Kerry Group's second major business segment is the consumer foods business, which constituted 39% of

the Group's sales and 27% of its operating profit in 1996. From its beginnings as a supplier of milk and dairy products to a few regional markets in Ireland in the early 1970's, the consumer foods business had grown to encompass a wide array of prepared and chilled meat products (beef, pork, lamb and poultry), snack foods, pastries, microwavable prepared food products and flavored spring water and other juice drinks, as well as its more traditional milk and dairy products. The growth of this business segment, like that of the ingredients sector, came about through a continuing strategy of external expansion. It also represented the production and marketing of a mixture of both branded and unbranded (private or own label) products.

Although the business began, understandably, with a focus upon the domestic Irish market, it had expanded by 1996 to a major presence in the U.K. and selected markets of the European Community. It should be noted that the Group's mission statement articulates its goal to be "a leading consumer foods processing and marketing organization in selected EU markets". The statement pointedly excludes reference to the consumer markets of North America and Asia.

KERRY AGRIBUSINESS

The Agribusiness segment of the Kerry Group is the business most directly linked to the Group's farmer-shareholders in County Kerry, and to the group's heritage as an agricultural cooperative. Ironically, this business segment had, by 1996, dwindled to the least important component of the Group's operations, at least in terms of direct sales and profits. In 1996, the Agribusiness segment returned 4% of group sales revenue and 1% of operating profit.

The contribution of the business to the Kerry Group, however, may be overlooked by a focus upon sales and profit contributions exclusively, since the

Case 17 / The Evolution of an Irish Multinational: Kerry Group plc

EXHIBIT 7	Business Group Segment Data			
Business Group	1994 Turnover IR£1,000	1994 Operating Profit IR£1,000	1995 Turnover IR£1,000	1995 Operating Profit IR£1,000
Kerry Ingredients	369,687	35,091	620,987	60,517
Kerry Foods	383,864	17,509	445,460	22,517
Kerry Agribusiness	43,499	2,682	57,648	2,220
	797,050	55,282	1,124,095	85,254
Discontinued Operations	85,647	267	74,998	485
	882,697	55,549	1,199,093	85,739

intended function of the agribusiness segment is more that of an internal service center than a profit center. Kerry Agribusiness is charged with all aspects of the Group's milk supply and assembly business. It is charged with providing various technical and advisory services to the Group's milk suppliers in the southwest of Ireland (primarily County Kerry), operating a bulk milk collection system consisting of a sizable fleet of computerized tankers, providing feeds, fertilizers and other farm inputs to the Group's suppliers, and operating an animal breeding research center and providing breeding technology and services to its suppliers. It is this division that services a host of needs of the group's Irish farmer-suppliers, and represents in great measure the "old" Kerry Co-op to the rural community of Kerry.

Despite the reduced importance of this sector, however, Denis Brosnan has continued to assure farmers that they remain important to the group. Says Brosnan, "Agribusiness will still be with us for a very long time because we still look after the farmers in the Southwest of Ireland".[14]

COMPETITIVE ENVIRONMENT
The global food sector in which Kerry competes is fragmented and far-reaching, encompassing a wide range of industries and product segments. The Kerry Group itself is unique, defying easy categorization into a specific industry segment. For example, there is no one particular firm which competes "head to head" with Kerry across its entire product line. Rather, Kerry competes with particular rivals in very specific product segments, market niches, and in the case of consumer foods, in a limited geographical area. Most typically, Kerry is classified under "Other Diversified Food Manufacturers", reflecting its mix of consumer goods (marketed in limited geographic markets) and food ingredients (industrial sales targeted at very specific product niches and marketed globally). Table 1 details those "diversified food manufacturers" who compete with Kerry businesses either in the consumer food sector in Ireland and the U.K., or in various global food ingredients markets. It should be noted that many of the firms who compete with Kerry in consumer foods may, in fact, be customers of Kerry on the food ingredients side of the business.

THE KERRY GROUP—1996

THE MANAGEMENT "TROIKA"
The management at Kerry Group had been unusually stable over the years. Indeed, of the "twelve apostles"

	Competitive Environment ($ Millions)		TABLE 1
Firm	1995 Sales	1995 Net Income	Avg. 5-Yr. Sales Growth
Unilever NV (Netherlands)	$49,566	$2,317	2.02%
Nestle (Switzerland)	48,946	2,529	4.03%
Unilever PLC (UK)	48,938	2,287	6.24%
Eridania Beghin-Say (France)	10,358	311	6.17%
Monsanto (USA)	8,962	739	−.07%
Bestfoods (USA)	8,432	501	7.84%
Ajinomoto (Japan)	8,382	135	4.80%
Orkla (Norway)	3,345	226	121.07%
Nisshin Flour Milling (Japan)	3,236	59	−.78%
Unigate PLC (UK)	3,198	406	−5.05%
Northern Foods PLC (UK)	2,973	132	10.41%
Danisco (Denmark)	2,606	186	3.41%
Kerry Group PLC (Ireland)	1,799	61	13.99%
McCormick & Co. (USA)	1,733	42	—
Express Dairies (UK)	1,607	−12	−6.90%
International Flavors & Fragrance (USA)	1,439	249	8.38%
Cultor Oyj (Finland)	1,316	76	2.86%
Cerebos (Singapore)	655	68	11.07%

who, along with Denis Brosnan labored in the caravan in the parking lot in 1972, ten were still with the firm nearly 25 years later. The trio of managers, Managing Director (MD) Denis Brosnan, and Deputy Managing Directors (DMD's) Denis Cregan and Hugh Friel who, in the early 1970's, organized the farmers of North Kerry into a sizable and profitable cooperative organization, still led the firm in 1996 (and in identical capacities). By all accounts, these were managers with skills that complemented each other well. Brosnan was credited with a sense of strategic vision and an absolute, utter, and relentless focus upon the achievement of that vision. Hugh Friel, as DMD for Finance and Administration, handled the financial elements of the many acquisitions, the relations with investors, and impor-

tantly, orchestrated the strategic planning process that had become so intrinsic to the firm's operations. Finally, Denis Cregan, as DMD for Operations, was the man who "made things happen", particularly in the integration of newly acquired firms into the "Kerry way" of doing things.

Similarly, the Board of Directors had had only two chairmen over the course of twenty-two years. Michael Hanrahan, a local farmer from the seaside resort of Ballybunion, had been the chairman since 1980. Exhibit 8 provides a listing and brief biography of the top management team and Board of Directors.

Still, if there is one name associated with the Kerry Group in the public eye, it is Denis Brosnan. He is the prototypical "local boy who made good". His ID card

---

EXHIBIT 8   Officers and Directors of Kerry Group plc—1996

Chairman

Michael Hanrahan, aged 68, is a non-executive director. He is a small farmer in Ballybunion, County Kerry, a director of ACC Bank plc, An Bord Bia (Irish Food Board), and Kerry Co-operative Creameries Limited.

Executive Directors

Dr. Denis Brosnan, aged 52, is Managing Director and has been with the Kerry Group since its inception. He is Chief Executive of Kerry Co-operative Creameries Limited, Chairman of the Irish Horseracing Authority and is a Director of a number of other public and private companies.

Hugh Friel, aged 52, is joint Deputy Managing Director and has been with Kerry Group since its formation.

Denis Cregan, aged 50, is joint Deputy Managing Director and has been with Kerry Group since its formation. He is Chairman of Kerry Airport plc.

Jerry Houlihan, aged 47, is Executive Director of the Company and is Chief Executive Officer of Kerry Ingredients (Ireland) Limited.

Michael Griffin, aged 49, is an Executive Director of the Company and is Chief Executive of the Group's Consumer Foods Division, Kerry Foods.

Non-Executive Directors

Denis Buckley is a Director of Irish Agricultural Wholesale Society Limited and is Chairman of Kerry Co-operative Creameries Limited.

Philip Healy is a Director of Irish Co-operative Society Limited.

Michael Fitzgerald, Michael Harty, Stephen Kelliher, Michael Leslie, Eugene McSweeney, John Joseph O'Brien, Diarmuid O'Connell and **Patrick O'Connor** are Directors of Kerry Co-operative Creameries Limited.

Dan Barry, Patrick O'Connell, Richard Fitzgerald and **Alexander O'Donnell** are former Directors of Kerry Co-operative Creameries Limited.

Note: Additionally, all of the non-executive directors are, or have been, engaged in agriculture, principally dairy farming.

Source: 1996 Kerry Group Annual Report.

number with Kerry Group reads "employee #1", which he is, quite literally. He is also the first, and only, Managing Director of the organization. His roots in Kerry, and in farming, run deep:

> *I am a native of Kilflynn, about five miles from Tralee. My parents, Dan and Mary, are both dead. My brother James is farming at home . . . the farm is at Fahavane on the main Tralee-Listowel road. I went to the national school in Kilflynn. We milked about 25 cows then on 130 acres and nowadays with modern farming it could carry 100 cows. We used, when we were very young, get a lift in the horse and cart to school when it was on its way to the creamery with milk.[15] It was said when I was growing up that I loved farming so much that I would surely end up farming, but that was not to be.[16]*

Brosnan did B.S. and M.S. degrees in Dairy Science at University College Cork, and spent several years working for Golden Vale, the largest dairy co-op in Ireland at the time. Although his tenure at Golden Vale was short, his rapid rotation into increasingly important positions clearly earmarked him as a rising young executive there. He was, in fact, even considered for the top position of General Manager of the cooperative, but was apparently considered too young. Coincidentally, the movement to amalgamate the cooperatives in Kerry was in full swing at the time, and they were in need of a General Manager. When the call came to return to Kerry and create a county-wide cooperative organization, he took advantage of the opportunity, although he was leaving the largest cooperative organization in Ireland (in the most productive farm region) to attempt to form what would be among the smaller ones (in one of the more hardscrabble farm regions). This decision itself may be characteristic of Brosnan, for he has acquired a reputation for taking risks. From the start, Brosnan pursued the development of Kerry's international businesses with a nearly missionary zeal, spending enormous amounts of time on the road. Yet, his philosophy of business was deceptively simple:

> *I always try to keep things simple. Look, there are usually only about six simple things to be done. Do those and it will work. You need money, patience and commitment . . . if I say we are going to get to that goal, when all the advice has been given, when all the pitfalls have been pointed out, we still get there. It is the goal that has to be right.*

This business philosophy has become a core element of the Kerry way of doing things. Numerous senior managers at Kerry have explained that, when being assigned a new challenge such as an acquisition or a poorly performing business, they'd come to expect a "flying visit" from Denis Brosnan which would result in a list with five or six things to be done. This simple list would serve as the "brief" for that executive until the list was fully executed. This straightforward, "can do" ethos has been indelibly imprinted upon the organization by the personality and philosophy of Denis Brosnan. He has clearly set the tone in the organization he has so dominated since its creation.

Patience is not Brosnan's strong suit. Although he is a good listener, he does not suffer fools gladly. He listens intently, and actively, but has little tolerance for those he feels are "just blowing smoke". If he has a bias, it is a bias towards action. As a leader, he has developed a knack for remaining "grounded" and connected to his roots in Kerry even while he travels the world in search of further acquisitions or to visit existing operations. Each year, in advance of the annual meeting, he visits each of the farmers' advisory council meetings (there are eight) to talk with them informally about the performance of the business and to hear from them directly of their own particular, local concerns (most typically the price of milk). He still knows most of the farmer-suppliers (about 5,000 in 1996) by name.

Brosnan, however, does *not* have a reputation for telling people what they want to hear. He can be very direct.

> *If I was to be remembered as an individual, I think I would like to be remembered because I was never afraid to speak the truth, regardless of the consequences. Whether I go into a hostile or a friendly audience, I never have any difficulty laying the bare facts before them. And I think I usually come away with a higher reputation than I went in with.[17]*

STRATEGIC FOCUS

There is little that is confusing about the Group's strategy. First, it is clearly to be a major player in the global food ingredients business. Second, it is to have a major position in selected consumer food markets in the U.K. and Europe. Ask any employee of any level, in any location, or any farmer-supplier, or any shareholder, and they will be able to quickly and clearly articulate this straightforward strategic agenda. Both of these foci imply continued growth through external, as opposed to primarily internal organic, expansion. As stated in the Annual Report:

> *Kerry is committed to being a leader in its selected markets through technological creativity, total quality*

and superior customer service. The Group is focused on continuing to expand its presence in global food ingredients markets and on the further development of its consumer foods businesses in Europe.

ORGANIZATIONAL CULTURE

Denis Brosnan described the Kerry culture, or ethos, in this way:

> *We feel we have the edge being from Kerry. Maybe we are biased, but that is what we harnessed back in the early 1970's. We harnessed Kerry farmers and people to come together. And right through to 1986, when Kerry plc, Kerry farmers and workers took shares and they are all as interested in what is taking place in Mexico as perhaps the institutional share holders. So that pride, that togetherness is still there. And long may it remain.*[18]

The Kerry Group is the largest employer of new business graduates in the County, providing opportunities for young managers to work all over the world. It is known to be a demanding place to work, with rigorous standards and a very strong work ethic. Less sympathetic wags say managers have to "sell their souls" to succeed there. But, Denis Brosnan puts it differently:

> *The unforgivable sin is half-doing a job and we have a very strong ethic in Kerry, apart from how we are seen—tough or otherwise—and that is whatever we say we do, we'll do it, even if we have to do it to our own cost. If we are betrayed, we never forget or forgive.*[19]

Kerry employees were also expected to show singular commitment. Says Conor Keane, a local journalist who has covered the Group for many years:

> *There is a Kerry way of thinking, a Kerry way of doing things. One of them is "Second Best" is not an option. If you are in a business, you are the best, or you are out, in the manure business. That's where they strive to be, the main player. It stems from part of the football code of the County. We've got to be the best!*

This ethos is not limited to the firm's Irish employees. More and more, nationals from the Group's increasingly far flung locations are being brought into the headquarters at Tralee. Says Keane:

> *They have Spanish speakers who have been "Kerry-ized" in Tralee. They bring them over, and if they don't learn to think Kerry, they're out. And they get into the ethos. Color or creed it doesn't matter.*

THE KERRY GROUP AND LOCAL COMMUNITY

IN THE "KINGDOM" OF KERRY

It is said that Ireland is composed of 31 counties and one kingdom; it is only the county of Kerry, in the relatively remote southwest corner of the island, that presumes to call itself a kingdom. From the Ring of Kerry with its Lakes of Killarney, to the windswept beauty of the Dingle Peninsula, to the smooth expanse of the Shannon Estuary, Kerry, the "Kingdom County" has been blessed with spectacular natural beauty. For the 120,000 souls residing in this little corner of the world, however, agriculture remains a primary economic activity, one that has shaped the culture and traditions of Kerry indelibly.

However, for all of its bountiful scenery, Kerry has historically been an economically depressed area, relying on the dairy industry, tourism, and emigration. Indeed, emigration has been, until quite recently, often the only way for improving one's economic condition. For generations Kerry's youth have fled to England, the States, or even further abroad in search of employment. Jobs in Kerry were simply nonexistent, industry was nil, agriculture was in the doldrums. Such jobs as were available tended to be in the service sector, catering to the needs of the growing tourist trade. These were often unattractive, both in terms of job satisfaction and compensation, for the young, well educated, and highly skilled workforce. The sadness of this experience is summed up in the "American Wake", the Kerry equivalent of a farewell party, given as a sendoff to the emigrant on the night before the journey to the States, or England, or Australia, or Canada. Emigration from Kerry has been among the highest of any part of Ireland, leading to a large and vocal diaspora of Kerry people around the world. The pain of emigration is seared in the soul of the people.

Yet, the economy of Kerry has revived along with the fortunes of Ireland itself during the 1990's. Ireland, with an annual growth in GDP of nearly 7.2% annually during the period of 1992–1996, had achieved the status of the fastest growing economy in Europe, the "Celtic Tiger".

> *Ireland's economic buoyancy reinforces a new self-confidence. In marketing terms, Ireland is changing its homely, bucolic image into an international brand increasingly recognised in business and the arts. The changes have been tumultuous. Dublin's skyline is being transformed by new hotels and apartment blocks. Car sales are at record levels. The new affluence is evident in shops selling foreign-made luxury goods. . . . Ireland has rarely had such a benign economic climate.*[20]

As Ireland emerged from the economic doldrums, the positive spillover in County Kerry was quite pronounced. Although unemployment remained a serious issue, foreign investment in Kerry was up, housing starts and construction were booming, and there was a new air of optimism quite at odds with the dismal economic past.

COMMUNITY RELATIONS

Since every moment of the clock

Accumulates to form a final name,

Since I am come of Kerry clay and rock

—*From the poem "My Dark Fathers" by Brendan Kennelly, Ballylongford, County Kerry*

The connections between the Kerry Group and the people of County Kerry are strong and myriad and not susceptible to easy untangling. Even as the Group has grown from a simple regional milk processor to a diversified international food products company, its ties to the local community have in many ways grown deeper and more varied. Worldwide, in 1996, the firm had approximately 7,000 employees, roughly half of them in Ireland. Approximately 6,000 local farmers both supply milk to them and are shareholders in their own right through both the Co-op and the publicly-traded company. These "men of the soil" have made up the preponderance of Kerry Group investors and occupy all of the non-executive director positions on the Board of Directors. Their involvement with the Kerry Group had been continuous, direct and influential. Said Denis Brosnan:

The farmers are very involved there and as management we enjoy that and the farmers do as well. We listen to the farmers at area advisory meetings and have a pint in the pub afterwards and that keeps one's feet on the ground. We work tightly to five-year plans. So we have plans from now to the end of the decade and that plan will take Kerry Plc around the world spread out more internationally.[21]

The Kerry Group played a large role in the development of the Kerry Airport, and has been influential in many other areas of the county's life, particularly in its many contributions to the arts and culture, as in its support of both the Kerry Museum and the National Folk Theater of Ireland which are located across from the Group's corporate offices in Tralee. As a local politician from Listowel remarked as he dedicated a new grandstand at the racetrack:

As the largest and most successful company in the area it is inundated with requests for sponsorship. All are considered, and very few of merit go unaided. The fine new stand we saw on the (Listowel) race course today would not have got off the ground without their assistance. The Kerry Cultural and Literary Centre, another major project for Listowel, is indebted also to Kerry Group.[22]

As a provider of jobs, a buyer of milk products (often at above market prices) from Kerry farmers, and the creator of substantial financial gains for its many Kerry investors, the Kerry Group has become a leader in the economic revival of Kerry. Indeed, more than a few of its farmer-shareholders have, by virtue of the conversion of their shares in the Co-op to the more liquid shares in the plc, become "seriously rich", with the value of their shareholdings gleefully reported in the local newspapers.

It should be noted that, in matters affecting County Kerry, Managing Director Denis Brosnan has never been accused of keeping a low profile. Indeed, Brosnan has been a leading figure not just in his leadership of the Group, but as a prominent booster for economic development throughout Kerry. But, his perspective on the economic future of the region differs markedly from past notions, and has added to the discomfort of some of the small farmers in the area. He has been clear, and articulate, in his belief that the future of Kerry lies in tourism rather than in farming.

I think it would be wishful thinking to imagine into the future local industries centering around the local creamery making butter or whatever. That has all gone and will never come back. . . . If we are to keep Kerry alive as a county and keep our young people there, it will come from tourism related activity. Not out of farming.[23]

Nor can it be said that such a perspective is Brosnan's alone. In conversations with farmers throughout the County, the predominant sense is that farming as a way of life is destined to disappear, as the seemingly inevitable machinations of the global economy demand farm enterprises of such efficiency that small farmers can never hope to meet.

THE PROPOSAL TO REDUCE THE COOPERATIVE'S SHAREHOLDING IN KERRY GROUP

In 1986, when the Kerry Co-op agreed to float their company on the stock market and create Kerry Group plc, it also created a complicated rule structure that stipulated that the Co-op would continue to own at least 51% of the new public company. This, they hoped would ensure continuing farmer control of the enterprise. In the ensuing decade, however, a number of factors had surfaced which led to Kerry Group's proposal that the Co-op further reduce their share:

- First, the Kerry Group's continuing rapid growth had required a high level of borrowing, since the 51% rule effectively limited its ability to finance further growth by issuing additional equity stakes. This, in turn, left the firm highly leveraged (or "geared"). For example, the firm's debt to equity ratios for the years 1993–95 were 71%, 130%, and 101% respectively.
- Second, market analysts had speculated that Kerry Group had bypassed some acquisition opportunities due to its reluctance to further increase its debt load and its inability to raise funds in the equity markets. Although the firm denied such assertions strenuously, such speculation continued.
- Finally, the farmer-owners of the cooperative, with their 51% stake in the Group, owned an asset of some considerable value, but had no liquidity since cooperative shares did not trade on the market. Given the position of many farmers as "land rich and cash poor", there did exist pressure to provide farmer-shareholders a means to *realize* at least some portion of the gains in the value of their Kerry Co-op (and thus Kerry Group) holdings.

The proposal on the table called for the transfer of 21.4 million shares in the Group, now held by the cooperative, to be turned over directly to the Co-op's shareholders. This would have the effect of 1) handing over roughly £130 million in Kerry Group shares to some 6,000 Kerry Co-op shareholders (these were all farmer-suppliers of the Group, over one hundred of whom would become millionaires overnight), 2) reducing the Co-op's current share in the Group to 39% (from 51%), 3) creating a new minimum share holding level in Kerry Group (the level below which Co-op holdings cannot be allowed to drop without a "rule change") of just under 20%, enabling the group to issue up to 20,000,000 new shares in the future, and finally 4) reducing the number of farmer representatives on the Kerry Group Board of Directors from fifteen to nine, with the six vacancies filled "by 6 people whose expertise is of major value to the plc".[24] The Group also provided the Kerry Co-op an option to purchase the Agribusiness segment (exercisable between 2001 and 2010), so that the farmers could maintain control of those assets most directly related to them in the event of a further decline in Co-op ownership of the Group. Table 2 details the potential gains for Kerry Co-op shareholders.

Earlier, at the annual meeting of Kerry Group, a shareholder had asked whether the reduction in shares owned by the Co-op would lead to the Co-op losing control of the Group. Denis Brosnan had replied, "the question of control has been raised, but it's not an issue. Control is too emotional a term. I have always said that having an organization functioning well is much more important than who has 50, 40 or 30 percent".[25]

TABLE 2	Potential Gain from Conversion of Kerry Co-op Shares			
	# Shares 12/31/95 (000's)	Mkt. Value 12/31/95 (£4.90/Sh) (000's)	# Shares 7/30/96 (000's)	Mkt. Value 7/30/96 (£6.07/Sh) (000's)
Kerry Co-op Holdings	85,535	£419,122	64,135	£389,300
Other Outstanding Shares (Note 1)	78,325	383,792	78,325	475,400
Share Distribution to Co-op Members (Note 2)			21,400	129,900
Total	163,860	£802,914	163,860	£994,600

Note 1:
Exhibit 5 provides further details on these shareholdings. Approximately 10% of these shares are directly held by Kerry Co-op shareholders (farmers and milk suppliers).

Note 2:
The Kerry Co-op had approximately 6,000 shareholders; the average value of the stock transferred to these shareholders was £21,650. With an average paid-in-capital per share of .62 pence, and a market price of £6.07 per share, the gain per share approximated £5.45. This represents a nearly ten-fold increase in the stock value since the firm went public in 1986. It should also be noted that Ireland, at the time, had a capital gains tax of approximately 40%, providing a significant disincentive to those contemplating an immediate sell-off of their shares.

Case 17 / The Evolution of an Irish Multinational: Kerry Group plc

DISSENTING VOICES

Although Kerry Group management had done their homework thoroughly, believed in the proposal fully, and had communicated the proposal personally to farmers at the local Area Advisory Meetings (with little apparent objection), there *were* some who objected to the proposal. The opposition centered on philosophical rather than practical grounds, and focused upon the issue of continuing farmer control of the enterprise and adherence to fundamental cooperative principles.

The general concern centered upon the evolution of the Group from a co-op to a plc, and the continued dilution of "farmer control" of the Group (see Exhibit 5). More and more, shares in the Kerry Group were controlled by "outside" shareholders, particularly large financial institutions. As one farmer who campaigned against the proposal said, "what do these institutions know, or care, of the concerns of small farmers?" Some farmers, as they watched the number of people involved with agriculture in Kerry dwindle (from 17,000 fifteen years ago to 12,000 in 1995), worried that as the emphasis at Kerry Group changed to being a global player in food ingredients, its commitment to local farmers and, indeed, to farming as a way of life in Kerry would weaken. As Donal Hickey reported in *The Cork Examiner*:

> *When co-ops changed to plc's this was a worry that bothered many farmers: would they lose control of their own enterprises to financiers who hence-forth be calling the shots? . . . Not so long ago, the Kerry Group (still referred to by farming folk as the more intimate Kerry Co-op) was regarded as the savior of dairy farmers in the widely-scattered county, but many men of the land now have grave reservations . . .*[26]

Opponents, with more than a little hyperbole, suggested that farmers who voted for the proposal would be "selling out" the cooperative for "thirty pieces of silver". "It's just not right", said one prominent dissenter, "they are appealing to no more than people's greed". "After the deed is done, what will the farmers of Kerry have left but a few bob in the bank?" Yet the more reasoned core of such emotional objections can be found in basic cooperative principles which hold that (and see Exhibit 3):

- Owners are members of the cooperative, and they retain control of the enterprise. With the conversion, the cooperative members were taking their shares from the cooperative holding, and becoming direct owners of the public limited company, Kerry Group. They were moving, said opponents, from "cooperators to capitalists".

- Cooperative members control equally, that is, one member–one vote. This "one member–one vote" applied to decisions involving the Co-op's 51% stake in the plc. With the conversion, control of the plc will increasingly be based on "one share–one vote".

- Limited returns on capital. To pay a large return on invested capital is anathema to cooperative thinking . . . yet in this case, cooperative shareholders would be receiving a substantial return on their original investment in the cooperative.

Many of the objections, explicitly or not, also focused upon fears concerning the future of farming in Kerry. Would Kerry Group continue to help the farmers of Kerry, even when those farmers no longer held substantial control of the enterprise?

> *Many rural communities are gravely threatened by current farming trends. Townlands in remote parishes, once densely populated by growing families, are now practically deserted, with derelict home-steads and overgrown farm buildings bearing mute testimony to policies devoid of any social feelings.*[27]

Mr. Phil Healy, former president of the Kerry branch of the Irish Farmers Association, summed it up succinctly:

> *The lack of confidence among many farmers is frightening and there's a terrible fear among the smaller men that they're on the way out (Phil Healy, Kerry Irish Farming Association chairman).*[28]

There were concerns that as the Kerry Group matured into an increasingly large and diversified multinational firm, with large blocks of shares held outside of County Kerry, the embeddedness of the group in Kerry, and the strength and extent of its roots in this rural Irish county would be likely to weaken.

In the run-up to the vote, however, it seemed that such sentiments were very much in the minority. However, opponents suggested that few farmers in Kerry were anxious to openly cross the management of Kerry Group. They hoped that given that the proposal would be voted upon by secret ballot, enough farmers would side with them to protect their ownership of this enterprise that they had brought to life. After all, they needed only 25% of the vote!

THE FIRST SPECIAL GENERAL MEETING

It was most uncharacteristic of Irish, and particularly Kerry, weather. Monday, July 15th, was sweltering, and the Brandon Conference Center was not air conditioned! Even more, it seemed that attendance might be even higher than anticipated, for there were already traffic tie-ups outside the conference center an hour before the start of the meeting. Interestingly, their wives apparently accompanied many of the farmers. This fact alone demonstrated the serious nature of the meeting, for, as one wag at the hotel bar suggested, "the wives are there to make sure they vote the right way".

Although Brosnan remained confident that the proposal would pass, a considerable lobbying effort had taken place by those who objected to the change. Could the vote be as unpredictable as this weather? The first of the shareholders were already beginning to trickle into the conference center as Denis Brosnan, no longer lost in reverie as he gazed on Mount Brandon, reviewed his notes.

NOTES

1. Hickey, Donal. 1990. Kerry Group AGM likely to be a stormy get-together. *The Cork Examiner.* May 28. This article reports on an emotionally charged meeting of some Kerry farmers in 1990 in a dispute with Kerry Group over certain policies, but particularly in reaction to a drop in milk prices.
2. Ibid.
3. Garavan, T.N., O Cinneaide, B., Garavan, M., Cunningham, A., Downey, A., O'Regan, T. & Hynes, B. 1996. *Cases in Irish business strategy and policy.* Dublin: Oak Tree Press, p. 493.
4. The formation of the Kerry Co-op was actually the culmination of a multi-stage process, one element of which was the purchase of the assets of the Dairy Disposal Board, a quasi-government body charged with the collection of milk from farmer-suppliers in the area, the setting of milk prices, and the processing of it into usable consumer products such as cheese and butter.
5. North Kerry Milk Products, Ltd. was owned by the Dairy Disposal Board (47.5%), the Kerrykreem Cooperative Creameries, an association of five cooperatives in North Kerry (47.5%) and finally a minority stake (15%) owned by Erie Casein, an American firm that had provided financing for the construction of the milk processing plant and was a major purchaser of casein, a protein product extracted from milk. Erie Casein's interest was ultimately bought out by the Co-op in 1983.
6. Woulfe, Jimmy. 1994. *Voices of Kerry.* Dublin: Blackwater Press, p. 229. This book consists of a series of interviews with prominent people from County Kerry.
7. Brosnan, Denis. Farmer's desire to expand a key factor for future progress. *The Kerryman*, February 1, 1974, page 2 of a special supplement entitled "Kerry's giant new dairy co-operative".
8. The American heritage dictionary of the English language. 1975. Boston: Houghton Mifflin Company. Cooperative societies were introduced to Ireland in the late nineteenth century by Horace Plunkett and others who saw them as offering farmers a way to attain and maintain some control over their economic destiny. Co-op's typically provided support to farmers by way of farm inputs, provision of financing, advice on better agricultural methods and technology, as well as providing a marketing organization for the farmers' produce.
9. The Co-operative acquired creameries in Killarney, Limerick, Ballinahana Dairies in Cork, Galway and Moate.
10. Garavan, T.N., et al., 1996, p. 491.
11. Interview with Denis Brosnan, May 28, 1999, at Croom House, Croom, County Limerick, Ireland.
12. Hayes, Frank. Kerry Group: Building an Irish multinational. In *Food for Thought*, a limited edition publication of the 1996 Listowel Quality Food Fair.
13. *Kerry: Building a Global Business*, p. 4. An in-house publication of the Kerry Group plc.
14. Keane, Conor. 1995. *The Kerryman.*
15. Woulfe, J. 1994, p. 235.
16. Kenny, I. 1987. *In Good Company: Conversations with Irish Leaders.* Dublin: Gill and Macmillan, p. 59.
17. Kenny, I. 1987, p. 75.
18. Woulfe, J. 1994, p. 230.
19. Kenny, I. 1987, p. 74.
20. *The Financial Times*, July 30, 1997.
21. Woulfe, J. 1994, p. 231.
22. Carroll, B. 1997. Listowel honours Kerry Group for 25 years of excellence. *The Kerryman*, September 26, 1997.
23. Woulfe, J. 1994, p. 232–233.
24. McGrath, B. 1996. Co-op to cut stake in Kerry Group to 39%. *Irish Times*, May 16.
25. McGrath, B. 1996. Reduced Co-op holding dominates Kerry AGM. *Irish Times*, May 28.
26. Hickey, Donal. 1990. Kerry Goup AGM likely to be a stormy get-together. *The Cork Examiner*, May 28.
27. Ibid.
28. Ibid.

The McDonald's 'Beef Fries' Controversy

case eighteen

A. Mukund
Icfaian Centre for Management
Research

"Hindus and vegetarians all over the world feel shocked and betrayed by McDonald's deception and ultimate greed."

—*Attorney Harish Bharti, on filing the lawsuit against McDonald's, in May 2001.*

"These are the ways the fries are made in the US, and we don't have any plans to change."

—*Walt Riker, McDonald's spokesperson, in May 2001.*

A CONTROVERSY ERUPTS

In May 2001, a class action lawsuit[1] was filed against the world's largest fast-food chain McDonald's, in Seattle, US. The lawsuit alleged that the company had, for over a decade, duped vegetarian customers into eating French fries[2] that contained beef extracts. The lawsuit followed a spate of media reports detailing how the French fries served at McDonald's were falsely promoted as being '100% vegetarian.'

Although McDonald's initially declined to comment on the issue, the company issued a 'conditional apology,' admitting to using beef flavoring in the fries. The furor over the matter seemed to be settling down, when to McDonald's horror, some of its restaurants in India were vandalized. Activists of Hindu fundamentalist groups—the Shiv Sena, the Vishwa Hindu Parishad (VHP) and the Bajrang Dal—staged a demonstration in front of the McDonald's head office in Delhi protesting the alleged use of beef flavoring. They submitted a memorandum to the Prime Minister, demanding the closure of all McDonald's outlets in the country.

Activists also staged protests in front of McDonald's restaurants in south Mumbai and Thane. Mobs ransacked the outlet at Thane, broke the glass panes and smeared the McDonald's mascot Ronald with cow dung. About 30 people were arrested and later let off on bail. Company officials estimated the loss to the outlet at Rs 2 million.

Officials at McDonald's India quickly announced that the vegetarian products served in India did not have any non-vegetarian content (Refer to Exhibit 1 for details). However, despite this reassurance, the anti-McDonald's wave refused to die down.

Meanwhile, more cases were being filed against McDonald's—this time in California, US and Canada. It seemed certain that the company would have to shell out millions of dollars to settle the class action lawsuit representing the 1 million US based Hindus and 15 million other vegetarians.

BACKGROUND NOTE

McDonald's was started as a drive-in restaurant by two brothers, Richard and Maurice McDonald in California, US in the year 1937. The business, which was generating $200,000 per annum in the 1940s, got a further boost with the emergence of a revolutionary new concept called 'self-service.' The brothers designed their kitchen for mass production with assembly line procedures.

Prices were kept low. Speed, service and cleanliness became the critical success factors of the business. By the mid-1950s, the restaurant's revenues reached $350,000. As word of their success spread, franchisees started showing interest. However, the franchising system failed because the McDonald brothers observed very transparent business practices. As a consequence, they encouraged imitators who copied their business

This case was written A. Mukund, ICFAI Center for Management Research (ICMR). It is intended to be used as a basis for class discussion rather than to illustrate either effective or ineffective handling of a management situation.

The case was compiled from published sources.

EXHIBIT 1   What Happened in India

In May 2001, Managing Directors of McDonald's India—Vikram Bakshi (Bakshi) of Delhi's Connaught Plaza Restaurants and Amit Jatia (Jatia) of Mumbai's Hardcastle Restaurants—said at a press conference, "We are open to any kind of investigation by the authorities, from the state or central governments. We categorically state that the French fries and other vegetarian products that we serve in India do not contain any beef or animal extracts and flavoring of whatsoever kind."

Bakshi said that the company had developed a special menu for Indian customers taking into consideration Indian culture and religious sentiments. McDonald's officials circulated official statements by McCain Foods India Pvt. Ltd. and Lamb Weston, suppliers of French fries to McDonald's India, stating that the fries were par-fried in pure vegetable oil without any beef tallow or any fat ingredient of animal origin.

People were however skeptical of the company's assurance because it had made similar false promises in the US as well. Their fears came true when it was revealed that Lamb Weston's supplies had been rejected after they failed to meet standards set by McDonald's. McCain Foods was still in the process of growing the appropriate potatoes and needed another two years to begin supply. The French fries were being sourced from the US.

However, tests conducted on the French fries and the cooking medium by Brihanmumbai Municipal Corporation (BMC) and the Food and Drug Administration (FDA) confirmed the fries contained no animal fat.

Source: ICMR.

practices and emerged as competitors. The franchisees also did not maintain the same standards for cleanliness, customer service and product uniformity.

At this point, Ray Kroc (Kroc), a distributor for milkshake machines, expressed interest in the McDonald brothers' business. Kroc finalized a deal with the McDonald brothers in 1954. He established a franchising company, the McDonald System Inc., and appointed franchisees. In 1961, he bought out the McDonald brothers' share for $2.7 million, and changed the name of the company to McDonald's Corporation. In 1965, McDonald's went public.

By the end of the 1960s, Kroc had established over 400 franchising outlets. McDonald's began leasing/buying potential store sites and then subleased them to franchisees initially at a 20% markup and later at a 40% markup. To execute this, Kroc set up the Franchise Realty Corporation. The real estate operations improved McDonald's profitability. By the end of the 1970s, McDonald's had over 5000 restaurants with sales exceeding $3 billion.

However, in the early 1990s, McDonald's was facing problems due to changing customer preferences and increasing competition. Customers were becoming increasingly health conscious and they wanted to avoid red meat and fried food. They also preferred to eat at other fast-food joints that offered discounts. During this time, McDonald's also faced increased competition from supermarkets, convenience stores, local delicatessens, gas stations and other outlets selling reheatable packaged food. McDonald's added only 195 restaurants during 1991–92.

In 1993, McDonald's finalized an arrangement for setting up restaurants inside Wal-Mart retail stores. The company also opened restaurants in gas stations owned by Amoco and Chevron. In 1996, McDonald's entered into a $1 billion 10-year agreement with Disney. McDonald's agreed to promote Disney through its restaurants and opened restaurants in Disney's theme parks. In 1998, McDonald's took a minority stake in Chipotle Mexican Grill—an 18-restaurant chain in the US. In October 1996, McDonald's opened its first restaurant in India.

By 1998, McDonald's was operating 25,000 restaurants in 116 countries, serving more than 15 billion customers annually. During the same year, the company recorded sales of $36 billion, and net income of $1.5 billion. McDonald's overseas restaurants accounted for nearly 60% of its total sales. Franchisees owned and operated 80% of McDonald's restaurants across the globe. However, much to the company's chagrin, in 1998, a survey in the US revealed that customers rated McDonald's menu as one of the worst-tasting ever.

Undeterred by these developments, the company continued with its expansion plans and by 2001, it had 30,093 restaurants all over the world with sales of $24 billion (refer to Exhibit 2 for key statistics of McDonald's). By mid-2001, the company had 28 outlets in

McDonald's—Financial Performance Summary — EXHIBIT 2

Dollars in millions, except per share data	2001	2000	1999	1998	1997	1996	1995	1994	1993	1992	1991
Franchised sales	$24,838	24,463	23,830	22,330	20,863	19,969	19,123	17,146	15,758	14,474	12,959
Company-operated sales	11,040	10,467	9,512	8,895	8,136	7,571	8,883	5,793	5,157	5,103	4,908
Affiliated sales	4,752	5,251	5,149	4,754	4,639	4,272	3,928	3,048	2,674	2,308	2,061
Total Systemwide sales	$40,630	40,181	38,491	35,979	33,638	31,812	29,914	25,987	23,587	21,885	19,928
Total revenues	$14,870	14,243	13,259	12,421	11,409	10,687	9,795	8,321	7,408	7,133	6,695
Operating income	$ 2,697•	3,330	3,320	2,762•	2,808	2,633	2,001	2,241	1,984	1,862	1,679
Income before taxes	$ 2,330•	2,882	2,884	2,307•	2,407	2,251	2,169	1,887	1,676	1,448	1,299
Net income	$ 1,637•	1,977	1,948	1,550•	1,642	1,573	1,427	1,224	1,083	959	860
Cash provided by operations	$ 2,688	2,751	3,009	2,766	2,442	2,461	2,296	1,928	1,680	1,426	1,423
Capital expenditures	$ 1,906	1,945	1,868	1,879	2,111	2,375	2,064	1,539	1,317	1,087	1,129
Free cash flow	$ 782	808	1,141	887	331	86	232	387	363	339	294
Treasury stock purchases	$ 1,090	2,002	933	1,162	765	605	321	500	628	92	117
Financial position at year end											
Total assets	$22,535	21,684	20,983	19,784	18,242	17,386	15,415	13,592	12,035	11,681	11,349
Total debt	$ 8,918	8,474	7,252	7,043	6,463	5,523	4,836	4,351	3,713	3,857	4,615
Total shareholders' equity	$ 9,488	9,204	9,639	9,465	8,852	8,718	7,861	6,885	6,274	5,892	4,835
Shares outstanding (in millions)	1,280.7	1,304.9	1,350.8	1,356.2	1,371.4	1,389.2	1,399.5	1,387.4	1,414.7	1,454.1	1,434.5
Per common share											
Net income	$ 1.27•	1.49	1.44	1.14•	1.17	1.11	.99	.84	.73	.65	.59
Net income-diluted	$ 1.25•	1.46	1.39	1.10•	1.15	1.08	.97	.82	.71	.63	.57
Dividends declared	$ .23	.22	.20	.18	.16	.15	.13	.12	.11	.10	.09
Market price at year end	$26.47	34.00	40.31	38.41	23.88	22.69	22.56	14.63	14.25	12.19	9.50
Franchised restaurants	17,395	16,795	15,949	15,086	14,197	13,374	12,186	10,944	9,918	9,237	8,735
Company-operated restaurants	8,378	7,652	6,059	5,433	4,887	4,294	3,783	3,216	2,733	2,551	2,547
Affiliated restaurants	4,320	4,260	4,301	3,994	3,844	3,216	2,330	1,739	1,476	1,305	1,136
Total Systemwide restaurants	30,093	28,707	26,309	24,513	22,928	20,884	18,299	15,899	14,127	13,093	12,418

• Includes $378 million of pretax special operating charges primarily related to business reorganization in the US and other global change initiatives, and the closing of 163 underperforming restaurants in international markets.

• Includes the $378 million of pretax special operating charges noted above and $125 million of net pretax special nonoperating income items primarily related to a gain on the initial public offering of McDonald's Japan, for a net pretax expense of $253 million ($143 million after tax or $0.11 per share). Net income also reflects an effective tax rate of 29.8 percent, primarily due to the one-time benefit of tax law changes in certain international markets ($147 million).

• Includes $162 million of Made For You costs and the $160 million special charge related to the home office productivity initiative for a pretax total of $322 million ($219 million after tax or $0.16 per share).

Source: www.mcdonalds.com.

India, spread across New Delhi, Bombay, Pune, Jaipur and on the Delhi-Agra highway.

THE TROUBLED HISTORY

McDonald's claims to be a good corporate citizen (see Exhibit 3). However, McDonald's has had a long history of lawsuits being filed against it. It had been frequently accused of resorting to unfair and unethical business practices—October 16th is even observed as the 'World Anti-McDonald's day.' In the late 1990s, the company had to settle over 700 incidents of scalding coffee burns. Reportedly, McDonald's kept the coffee at 185°—approximately 20° hotter than the standard tem-

---

| EXHIBIT 3 | McDonald's—Social Responsibility Statement |

The McDonald's brand lives and grows where it counts the most—in the hearts of customers worldwide. We, in turn, hold our customers close to our heart, striving to do the right thing and giving back to the communities where we do business. At McDonald's, social responsibility is a part of our heritage and we are committed to building on it worldwide; some of our efforts to do so are described here.

Ronald McDonald House Charities—McDonald's supports one of the world's premier philanthropic organizations, Ronald McDonald House Charities (RMHC). RMHC provides comfort and care to children and their families by awarding grants to organizations through chapters in 31 countries and supporting more than 200 Ronald McDonald Houses in 19 countries.

Environmental Leadership—We take action around the world to develop innovative solutions to local environmental challenges. Ten years ago, we began a groundbreaking alliance with the Environmental Defense Fund (EDF) to reduce, reuse and recycle. Since then we eliminated 150,000 tons of packaging, purchased more than $3 billion of recycled products and recycled more than one million tons of corrugated cardboard in the US. We continue to set new waste reduction goals and are focusing on reducing energy usage in our restaurants. In Switzerland, we annually avoid 420,000 kilometers of trucking and, in turn, the use of 132,000 liters of diesel fuel by shipping restaurant supplies via rail. In Latin America, we have partnered with Conservation International to create and implement a sustainable agriculture program to protect the rainforests in Costa Rica and Panama. In Australia, we have committed to meet that country's Greenhouse Challenge to reduce greenhouse emissions.

Diversity—We believe a global team of talented, diverse employees, franchisees and suppliers is key to the company's ongoing success. We work to create and maintain an inclusive environment and expand the range of opportunities, thereby enabling all our people to reach their highest potential and generate the most value for McDonald's and the best experience for customers. McDonald's also provides opportunities for women and minorities to become franchisees and suppliers and offers a wide range of support to help them build their businesses. These efforts have paid off: Today, more than 30 percent of McDonald's franchisees are women and minorities, and in 1999, we purchased about $3 billion worth of goods and services from women and minority suppliers.

Employment—Being a good corporate citizen begins with the way we treat our people. We are focused on developing people at every level, starting in our restaurants. We invest in training and development programs that encourage personal growth and higher levels of performance. These efforts help us attract and retain quality people and motivate superior performance.

Education—As one of the largest employers of youth, education is a key priority. So the company, our franchisees and RMHC proudly provide about $5 million in educational assistance through a variety of scholarship programs. We also honor teachers' dedication and commitment to education with the McDonald's Education Award.

Safety/quality—We are committed to ensuring safety and quality in every country where we do business. Accordingly, we set strict quality specifications for our products and work with suppliers worldwide to see that they are met. This includes ongoing testing in labs and on-site inspection of supplier facilities. Restaurant managers worldwide are extensively trained in safe handling and preparation of our food. Also, we continually review, modify and upgrade the equipment at PlayPlaces and Playlands to provide a safe play environment. Our quality control efforts also encompass animal welfare. Notably, we are working with a leading animal welfare expert in the US to implement an auditing process with our meat suppliers to ensure the safe and humane treatment of animals.

Source: www.mcdonalds.com.

perature at other restaurants—which could cause third degree burns in just 2–7 seconds. An 81-year old woman reportedly suffered third degree burns on her lower body that required skin grafts and hospitalization for a week. After McDonald's dismissed her request for compensation for medical bills, she filed a lawsuit against the company.

A McDonald's quality assurance manager testified in the case that the company was aware of the risk of serving dangerously hot coffee, but it had no plans to lower the temperature or to post a warning on the coffee cups about the possibility of severe burns. In 1994, the court declared McDonald's guilty of serving 'unreasonably dangerous' hot coffee. The court awarded punitive damages of $ 2.7 million, which was later lowered to $480,000.

The company also had to settle multi-million dollar lawsuits in many other cases such as the one filed by a woman who was permanently scarred by an extremely hot pickle slice in a hamburger and a customer who reportedly found the crushed head of a rat inside his hamburger. There were a host of other allegations

against the company (refer to Exhibit 4 for some notable allegations).

Most of these allegations were made way back in the early 1980s in a movement spearheaded by two London Greenpeace[3] activists Helen Steel (Steel) and Dave Morris (Morris). They started their protests by distributing leaflets containing allegations against the company. Soon, the issue snowballed into a bitter £10 million courtroom battle against the activists.

The company was severely criticized for hiring detective agencies to break into the activist group. According to an analyst, "The company had employed at least seven undercover agents to spy on Greenpeace. During some London Greenpeace meetings, about half the people in attendance were corporate spies. One spy broke into the London Greenpeace office, took photographs, and stole documents. Another had a six-month affair with a member of London Greenpeace while informing on his activities."

Steel and Morris were later found to have libeled McDonald's by a British court. However, the company was also found guilty of endangering the health of its

---

Allegations against McDonald's | EXHIBIT 4

Nutrition—McDonald's high fat, low fiber food can cause diseases such as cancer, heart problems, obesity and diabetes, which are responsible for about 75% of premature deaths in the West. McDonald's refuted the allegation saying scientific evidence has never been conclusive and that its food can be a valuable part of a balanced diet. The company also argued that it had the right to sell junk food just like chocolate or ice-cream manufacturers did. However, critics claimed that the company should at least refrain from advertising the products as nutritious, sponsoring sports events and opening outlets in hospitals.

Environment—McDonald's has been accused of destroying tropical forests to facilitate cattle ranching. Although the company claimed that the one million tons of packaging it used was recyclable, it still was accused of causing environmental pollution due to the litter generated.

Advertising—McDonald's annual ad spend of over two billion dollars was criticized for exerting a negative influence on children and exploiting them. Through its collectable toys, Ronald the clown, TV advertisements and promotional schemes in schools, it has an extremely strong hold on children.

Employment—Though McDonald's has generated millions of jobs worldwide, it is accused of offering low wages and forcing local food outlets out of business. Charges of discrimination, curtailing workers' rights, understaffing, few breaks, illegal hours, poor safety conditions, crushing unionization attempts and kitchens flooded with sewage, and selling contaminated food were also leveled against the company.

Animals—As the world's largest user of meat, McDonald's slaughters hundreds of thousands of cows, chickens, lambs and other animals per year.

Expansion—By opening restaurants in developing countries, McDonald's is creating a globalized system in which wealth is drained out of local economies into the hands of a very few rich elite. This results in self-sufficient and sustainable farming being replaced by cash crops and agribusiness under control of multinationals.

Free Speech—McDonald's uses its clout to influence the media, and legal powers to intimidate people into not speaking out against it. Many media organizations that voiced strong opinions on the above issues have been sued by the company.

Source: ICMR.

customers and paying workers unreasonably low wages. The case, chronicled completely at www.mcspotlight. org, has become a classic example of a corporate giant's struggle to uphold its image amidst allegations of unethical practices.

In the light of the company's chequered history of legal problems, the French fries controversy seemed 'run-of-the-mill.' However, when McDonald's issued a conditional apology, the matter acquired serious undertones. This was because it was one of the very few instances where the company seemed to have publicly acknowledged any kind of wrong-doing.

THE BEEF FRIES CONTROVERSY

With an overwhelming majority of the people in the West being non-vegetarian, products often contain hidden animal-based ingredients. Incidents of vegetarians finding non-vegetarian food items in their food abound throughout the world. Whether a person has chosen to be a vegetarian for religious, health, ethical or philosophical reasons, it is not easy to get vegetarian food in public restaurants. According to the manager of a Thai food cafe in the US, "We have a lot of customers already. We don't need to have any vegetarian food." Commenting on this dilemma, a US based Hindu vegetarian said, "We can't blame anybody. You have to find out for yourself. If you have any doubts, try to avoid it. Otherwise, you just have to close your eyes and try to eat."

The French fries controversy began in 2000, when a Hindu Jain software engineer Hitesh Shah (Shah) working in the US happened to read a news article, which mentioned that the French fries at McDonald's contained beef. Shah sent an e-mail to McDonald's customer service department, asking whether the French fries contained beef or not and if they did, why this was not mentioned in the ingredient list. Shah soon got a reply from Megan Magee, the company's Home Office Customer Satisfaction Department.

The reply stated, "Thank you for taking time to contact McDonald's with your questions regarding the ingredients in our French fries. For flavor enhancement, McDonald's French fry suppliers use a minuscule amount of beef flavoring as an ingredient in the raw product. The reason beef is not listed as an ingredient is because McDonald's voluntarily (restaurants are not required to list ingredients) follow the 'Code of Federal Regulations' (required for packaged goods) for labeling its products. As such, like food labels you would read on packaged goods, the ingredients in 'natural flavors' are

not broken down. Again, we are sorry if this has caused any confusion."

A popular Indian-American newspaper 'West India' carried Shah's story. The news created widespread outrage among Hindus and vegetarians in the US. In May 2001, Harish Bharti (Bharti), a US based Indian attorney, filed the class action lawsuit against McDonald's.

McDonald's immediately released a statement saying it never claimed the fries sold in the US were vegetarian. A spokesperson said that though the fries were cooked in pure vegetable oil, the company never explicitly stated that the fries were appropriate for vegetarians and customers were always told that the flavor came partly from beef. He added that it was up to the customer to ask about the flavor and its source. This enraged the vegetarian customers further. Bharti said, "Not only did they deceive millions of people who may not want to have any beef extraction in their food for religious, ethical and health reasons, now McDonald's is suggesting that these people are at fault, that they are stupid. This adds insult to injury."

Interestingly enough, McDonald's statement that it never claimed its French fries were vegetarian was proved completely wrong after Bharti found a 1993 letter sent by the company's corporate headquarters to a consumer in response to an inquiry about vegetarian menu items. The letter clearly bundled the fries along with garden salads, whole grain cereals and English muffins as a completely vegetarian item.

The letter stated, "At McDonald's, we are always reviewing our menu, developing new products and looking for ways to satisfy the diverse tastes of our customers. We feel it is important to offer a variety of menu items that can be enjoyed and fit into any well-balanced diet. With that in mind, we presently serve several items that vegetarians can enjoy at McDonald's—garden salads, French fries and hash browns (cooked in 100% vegetable oil), hotcakes, scrambled eggs, whole grain cereals and English muffins to name a few." Further, it was reported that many McDonald's employees repeatedly told customers that there was absolutely no meat product in the fries.

The whole controversy rested on a decision McDonald's had taken in 1990 regarding the way French fries were prepared. Prior to 1990, the company made the fries using tallow.[4] However, to address the increasing customer concern about cholesterol control,[5] McDonald's declared that it would use only pure vegetable oil to make the fries in the future. However, after the decision to change from tallow to pure vegetable oil, the company realized that it could have difficulty in retaining customers who were accustomed to beef flavored fries.

According to Eric Scholsser, author of the best-selling book 'Fast Food Nation: The Dark Side of the All-American Meal,'[6] "For decades, McDonald's cooked its French fries in a mixture of about 7% cottonseed oil and 93% beef tallow. The mix gave the fries their unique flavor." This unique flavor was lost when tallow was replaced by vegetable oil. To address this issue, McDonald's decided to add the 'natural flavor,' that is the beef extract, which was added to the water while the potatoes were being partially cooked.

The 'beef fries' controversy attained greater dimensions in India as 85% of the country's population was vegetarian. Non-vegetarians also usually did not consume beef because Hindus consider cows to be holy and sacred. Thus, eating beef is considered a sacrilege. A US based Hindu plaintiff in one of the lawsuits said, "I feel sick in the morning every day, like I want to vomit. Now it is always there in my mind that I have done this sin."

Experts commented that the issue was not of adding beef extract to a supposedly vegetarian food item—it was more to do with the moral and ethical responsibility of a company to be honest about the products and services it offered. According to James Pizzirusso, founder of the Vegetarian Legal Action Network at George Washington University, "Corporates need to pay attention to consumers who avoid certain food products for religious or health reasons, or because they have allergies. They say they are complying with the law in terms of disclosing their ingredients, but they should go beyond the law."

While it was true that McDonald's complied with the Federal Food and Drug Administration[7] (FDA) guidelines by classifying beef extract as 'natural flavor,' critics claimed that the company was trying to 'play with words' to brush off the allegations. This prompted analysts to remark that a large part of the blame was with the weak guidelines stipulated by the FDA. The guidelines did not require the flavor companies or the

---

McDonald's Response to the Allegations | EXHIBIT 5

It has always been McDonald's practice to share nutrition and ingredient information with our customers, including facts about our French fries. In the US, we consistently communicate this information through in-store posters, wallet-sized cards and various brochures, which offer a wide variety of dietary details.

McDonald's USA is always sensitive to customer concerns. Because it is our policy to communicate to customers, we regret if customers felt that the information we provided was not complete enough to meet their needs. If there was confusion, we apologize.

Meanwhile, here are the details of our French fry production in the U.S. A small amount of beef flavoring is added during potato processing—at the plant. After the potatoes are washed and steam-peeled, they are cut, blanched, dried, par-fried, and frozen. It is during the par-frying process at the plant that the natural flavoring is used. These fries are then shipped to our US restaurants. Our French fries are cooked in vegetable oil at our restaurants.

McDonald's 1990 switch to vegetable oil in the US as our standard cooking oil was made for nutritional reasons, to offer customers a cholesterol-free menu item. This nutrition announcement received national media coverage, widely broadcasting the facts about our switch and why we made it.

As a local business in 121 countries, our French fry process varies country-by-country to account for cultural or religious dietary considerations. For example, in predominantly Muslim countries—as in Southeast Asia, the Middle East and Africa—McDonald's strictly conforms to halal standards. This means no use of beef or pork flavorings or ingredients in our French fries. In India, where vegetarian concerns are paramount, no beef or pork flavorings are used in our vegetarian menu items.

Our 'McDonald's Nutrition Facts' brochure uses the term 'natural flavor' in the ingredient list for French fries. This description is in full compliance with and permitted by the US Food and Drug Administration (FDA).

Source: www.mcdonalds.com.

restaurants buying these flavors to disclose the ingredients in their additives as long as they were generally regarded as safe (GRAS[8]). Analysts added that as long as the FDA did not make the guidelines more specific, companies could legally get away with serving dishes containing animal-based products.

Meanwhile in June 2001, another class action lawsuit was filed in the District Court in Travis County, Austin, Texas on behalf of all Hindus in Texas, alleging that Hindu moral and religious principles had been violated by their unintentional consumption of French fries that were flavored with beef. As public outrage intensified, McDonald's released its conditional apology on its website, admitting that the recipe for the fries used 'a minuscule trace of beef flavoring, not tallow' (refer to Exhibit 5 for McDonald's response to the allegations).

McDonald's said that it issued an apology only to provide more details about its products to customers. A company spokesperson said, "Customers responded to the news about the lawsuit. In the end, we are responding to those customers. We took a fresh look at how we could help customers get more information about natural flavors."

Unsatisfied by the apology, Bharti said, "Apology is good for the soul if it comes from the heart. It is not an unconditional apology. Why do they go around using words like 'if there was any confusion' in their apology?" Further, news reports quoting company sources said that the apology did not mean McDonald's was admitting to claims that it misled millions of customers by adding beef extract to its fries. Bharti said that the legal battle would continue and that McDonald's would have to issue an unconditional apology and pay a substantial amount of money. By this time, two more lawsuits were filed in Illinois and New Jersey, taking the total number of cases to five.

THE AFTERMATH

The courtroom battle had entered the 11th month when McDonald's announced that it would issue a new apology and pay $10 million to vegetarians and religious groups in a proposed settlement of all the lawsuits in March 2002. Around 60% of this payment went to vegetarian organizations and the rest to various groups devoted to Hindus and Sikhs, children's nutrition and assistance and kosher dietary practices.[9]

The company also decided to pay $4,000 each to the 12 plaintiffs in the five lawsuits and post a new and more detailed apology on the company website and in various other publications. McDonald's also decided to convene an advisory board to advise on vegetarian matters.

In April 2002, McDonald's planned to insert advertisements in newspapers apologizing for its mistakes: "We acknowledge that, upon our switch to vegetable oil in the early 1990s for the purpose of reducing cholesterol, mistakes were made in communicating to the public and customers about the ingredients in our French fries and hash browns. Those mistakes included instances in which French fries and hash browns sold at US restaurants were improperly identified as vegetarian. We regret we did not provide these customers with complete information, and we sincerely apologize for any hardship that these miscommunications have caused among Hindus, vegetarians and others."

Unhappy with the monetary compensation the company was offering, Bharti said, "Wish I could do better in terms of money. But our focus was to change the fast food industry, and this is a big victory for consumers in this country because we have brought this giant to this."

Though $10 million was definitely a pittance for the $24 billion McDonald's, what remained to be seen was whether the case would set a precedent and make corporates throughout the world more aware and responsible towards their customers or not.

QUESTIONS FOR DISCUSSION

1. Analyze the various allegations leveled against McDonald's before the French fries controversy. Why do you think the company attracted so much hostility and criticism despite being the number one fast-food chain in the world?
2. Discuss the French fries controversy and critically comment on the company's stand that it had never claimed the fries were vegetarian. Do you think the company handled the controversy effectively? Give reasons to support your answer.
3. Discuss the steps taken by McDonald's to deal with the French fries controversy and critically comment whether the company will be able to come out of this unscathed.

NOTES

1. A class action suit is a suit filed to protect the interests of a group of individuals who are affected or may be affected by a perceived fraud or misconduct of a similar nature. The number of people could be as few as under 10 to millions. Typically, class action suits in the US drag on for years and very often parties settle out of court within the first year of filing.
2. Thinly sliced, finger-sized pieces of potato, deep fried and served with a sprinkling of salt.
3. A social activist group based in UK that has been campaigning for a variety of environmental and social justice issues since the early 1970s. The

group predates the more well known Greenpeace International and the two organizations are unconnected.

4. Tallow refers to shortening made from beef fat.

5. Cholesterol is a soft, waxy substance found in the lipids (fats) in the bloodstream and in all body cells. It forms cell membranes, hormones and other needed tissues in the body. However, a very high level of cholesterol in the blood causes cardiovascular diseases and leads to heart attacks and strokes. Foods rich in saturated fats cause the cholesterol level to rise thereby increasing the chances of cardiovascular diseases.

6. The book provides a detailed account of the negative aspects associated with the products and operations of fast-food giants such as Burger King and McDonald's.

7. A US governmental consumer protection body, the FDA promotes and protects public health by helping safe and effective products reach the market in a timely way and monitoring products for continued safety after they are in use.

8. GRAS status is awarded after the FDA conducts scientific tests on a product and the product meets the criterion set for approval. Products which are GRAS are explicitly excluded from requirement for FDA pre-market approval.

9. The term 'kosher' is used to describe foods/animal products that are fit for consumption according to the religious rules of the Jewish community. By ensuring that the food is kosher, the Jews believe that they recognize the value of the life taken, while at the same time integrating religion into their dietary practices.

case nineteen

Jamie Anderson
London Business School

"More than 500 million PCs are already in use around the world, and another 130 million or more will be purchased in calendar 2001—more than the number of TVs that will likely be purchased this year. The majority of these machines are installed with one or more Microsoft products. Increasingly, the PC is moving to the center of an ever-expanding network of smart, connected devices—from mobile phones to televisions and handheld devices, even household appliances. There has never been a more exciting time in the history of our industry. The coming digital decade will be a time of enormous opportunity: for consumers, for the technology industry, and for Microsoft as we realize the vision of empowering people through great software—any time, any place and on any device."

—Bill Gates, Chairman and Chief Software Architect, Microsoft Corporation

I. INTRODUCTION

Microsoft Corporation was founded as a partnership in 1975 and incorporated in 1981. As of June 30, 2001, the Company employed approximately 47,600 people on a full-time basis, 33,000 in the United States and 14,600 internationally. Today the company is the largest producer of software for personal computers in the world, with 2001 revenues of almost $25.3 billion and net income of $7.35 billion (see Tables 1–4). It has also diversified into other business sectors such as e-commerce, multimedia and broadband communications. Details of Microsoft's corporate structure and organization are provided at Appendix A.

Microsoft develops, manufactures, licenses, and supports a wide range of software products for a multitude of computing devices. Microsoft software products include scalable operating systems for servers, personal computers (PCs), and intelligent devices; server applications for client/server environments; knowledge worker productivity applications; and software development tools. The Company's online efforts include the MSN network of Internet products and services and alliances with companies involved with broadband access and various forms of digital interactivity. Microsoft also licenses consumer software programs; sells hardware devices; provides consulting services; trains and certifies system integrators and developers; and researches and develops advanced technologies for future software products.

The Company's customers include consumers, small- and medium-sized organizations, enterprises, educational institutions, ISPs, application developers, and OEMs. Most consumers of Microsoft products are individuals in businesses, government agencies, educational institutions, and at home. The consumers and

The Founding Members of Microsoft, 1975

Financial Highlights (In millions, except earnings per share) TABLE 1

Year Ended June 30	1997	1998	1999	2000	2001(1)
Revenue	$11,936	$15,262	$19,747	$22,956	$25,296
Income before accounting change	3,454	4,490	7,785	9,421	7,721
Net income	3,454	4,490	7,785	9,421	7,346
Diluted earnings per share before accounting change	0.66	0.84	1.42	1.70	1.38
Diluted earnings per share	0.66	0.84	1.42	1.70	1.32
Cash and short-term investments	8,966	13,927	17,236	23,798	31,600
Total assets	14,387	22,357	38,625	52,150	59,257
Stockholders' equity	10,777	16,627	28,438	41,368	47,289

(1) Fiscal year 2001 includes an unfavorable cumulative effect of accounting change of $375 million or $0.06 per diluted share and $3.92 billion (pre-tax) in impairments of certain investments, primarily cable and telecommunication investments.

Income Statements (In millions, except earnings per share) TABLE 2

Year Ended June 30	1999	2000	2001
Revenue	$19,747	$22,956	$25,296
Operating expenses:			
Cost of revenue	2,814	3,002	3,455
Research and development	2,970	3,772	4,379
Sales and marketing	3,238	4,126	4,885
General and administrative	715	1,050	857
Total operating expenses	9,737	11,950	13,576
Operating income	10,010	11,006	11,720
Losses on equity investees and other	(70)	(57)	(159)
Investment income/(loss)	1,951	3,326	(36)
Income before income taxes	11,891	14,275	11,525
Provision for income taxes	4,106	4,854	3,804
Income before accounting change	7,785	9,421	7,721
Cumulative effect of accounting change (net of income taxes of $185)	—	—	(375)
Net income	$ 7,785	$ 9,421	$ 7,346
Basic earnings per share:			
Before accounting change	$1.54	$1.81	$1.45
Cumulative effect of accounting change	—	—	(0.07)
	$1.54	$1.81	$1.38
Diluted earnings per share:			
Before accounting change	$1.42	$1.70	$1.38
Cumulative effect of accounting change	—	—	(0.06)
	$1.42	$1.70	$1.32
Weighted average shares outstanding:			
Basic	5,028	5,189	5,341
Diluted	5,482	5,536	5,574

TABLE 3 Balance Sheets (In millions)

June 30	2000	2001
Assets		
Current assets:		
Cash and equivalents	$ 4,846	$ 3,922
Short-term investments	18,952	27,678
Total cash and short-term investments	23,798	31,600
Accounts receivable, net	3,250	3,671
Deferred income taxes	1,708	1,949
Other	1,552	2,417
Total current assets	30,308	39,637
Property and equipment, net	1,903	2,309
Equity and other investments	17,726	14,141
Other long-term assets	2,213	3,170
Total assets	$52,150	$59,257
Liabilities and stockholders' equity		
Current liabilities:		
Accounts payable	$ 1,083	$ 1,188
Accrued compensation	557	742
Income taxes	585	1,468
Unearned revenue	4,816	5,614
Other	2,714	2,120
Total current liabilities	9,755	11,132
Deferred income taxes	1,027	836
Commitments and contingencies		
Stockholders' equity:		
Common stock and paid-in capital—shares authorized 12,000; Shares issued and outstanding 5,383 and 5,359	23,195	28,390
Retained earnings, including accumulated other comprehensive income of $587 and $583	18,173	18,899
Total stockholders' equity	41,368	47,289
Total liabilities and stockholders' equity	$52,150	$59,257

organizations obtain Microsoft products primarily through resellers and OEMs, which include certain Microsoft products with their computing hardware.

Microsoft distributes its products primarily through OEM licenses, organizational licenses, online services and products, and retail packaged products. OEM channel revenue represents license fees from original equipment manufacturers who preinstall Microsoft products, primarily on PCs. Microsoft has three major geographic sales and marketing regions: the South Pacific and Americas Region; the Europe, Middle East, and Africa Region; and the Asia Region. Sales of organizational licenses and packaged products via these channels are primarily to and through distributors and resellers. For further information on sales and marketing see Appendix B.

Microsoft has been involved in an anti-trust trial in the United States for a number of years. The European Union has also taken action against the company, due to alleged anti-competitive behavior. A summary of the status of these actions as of November 2001 is provided at Appendix C.

Year Ended June 30	1999	2000	2001
Operations			
Net income	$ 7,785	$ 9,421	$ 7,346
Cumulative effect of accounting change, net of tax	—	—	375
Depreciation, amortization, and other noncash items	926	1,250	1,536
Net recognized gains/(losses) on investments	(803)	(1,732)	2,221
Stock option income tax benefits	3,107	5,535	2,066
Deferred income taxes	(650)	(425)	(420)
Unearned revenue	5,877	6,177	6,970
Recognition of unearned revenue	(4,526)	(5,600)	(6,369)
Accounts receivable	(687)	(944)	(418)
Other current assets	(235)	(775)	(482)
Other long-term assets	(117)	(864)	(330)
Other current liabilities	1,469	(617)	927
Net cash from operations	12,146	11,426	13,422
Financing			
Common stock issued	1,350	2,245	1,620
Common stock repurchased	(2,950)	(4,896)	(6,074)
Sales/(repurchases) of put warrants	766	472	(1,367)
Preferred stock dividends	(28)	(13)	—
Other, net	—	—	235
Net cash used for financing	(862)	(2,192)	(5,586)
Investing			
Additions to property and equipment	(583)	(879)	(1,103)
Purchases of investments	(34,686)	(42,290)	(66,346)
Maturities of investments	4,063	4,025	5,867
Sales of investments	21,006	29,752	52,848
Net cash used for investing	(10,200)	(9,392)	(8,734)
Net change in cash and equivalents	1,084	(158)	(898)
Effect of exchange rates on cash and equivalents	52	29	(26)
Cash and equivalents, beginning of year	3,839	4,975	4,846
Cash and equivalents, end of year	$ 4,975	$ 4,846	$ 3,922

II. STRATEGIC CHALLENGES FOR THE NEW MILLENNIUM

Since 1975 Microsoft's business strategy has developed to emphasize the development of a broad line of software products for information technology (IT) professionals, knowledge workers, developers, and consumers, marketed through multiple channels of distribution. While Microsoft management is optimistic about the Company's long-term prospects at the start of the new millennium, the following issues and uncertainties have impacted recent strategy making.

Rapid change, uncertainty due to new and emerging technologies, and fierce competition characterize the software industry, which means that Microsoft's market position is always at risk. Microsoft's ability to maintain its current market share may depend upon the Company's ability to satisfy customer requirements, enhance existing products, develop and introduce new products, and achieve market acceptance of such products. This process grows more challenging as the pace of change continues to accelerate. Open source software, new computing devices, new microprocessor architectures, the Internet, and Web-based computing models are among the competitive challenges the Company must meet. If Microsoft does not successfully identify new product opportunities and develop and bring new products to market in a timely and cost-efficient manner, the Company's business growth will suffer and demand for its products will decrease.

The nature of the PC marketplace is changing in ways that may reduce Microsoft's software sales and revenue growth. Overall market demand for PCs can significantly impact Microsoft's revenue growth. Recently, manufacturers have sought to reach more consumers by developing and producing lower cost PCs—PCs that come without preinstalled software or contain software with reduced functionality. In addition to the influx of low-cost PCs, a market for handheld computing and communication devices has developed. While these devices are not as powerful or versatile as PCs, they threaten to erode sales growth in the market for PCs with preinstalled software. This may affect Microsoft's revenue growth because manufacturers may choose not to install Microsoft software in these low-cost PCs or consumers may purchase alternative intelligent devices that do not use Microsoft software. These lower-priced devices require Microsoft to provide lower-priced software with a subset of the original functionality. As a result, the Company may generate less revenue from the sale of software produced for these devices than from the sale of software for PCs.

The Company continues to face movements from PC-based applications to server-based applications or Web-based application hosting services, from proprietary software to open source software, and from PCs to Internet-based devices. A number of Microsoft's most significant competitors, including IBM, Sun Microsystems, Oracle, and AOL-Time Warner, are collaborating with one another on various initiatives directed at competing with Microsoft. These initiatives relate in part to efforts to move software from individual PCs to centrally managed servers, which would present significant challenges to the Company's historical business model.

Other competitive collaborative efforts include the development of new platform technologies that are intended to replicate much of the value of Microsoft Windows operating systems. New computing form factors, including non-PC information devices, are gaining popularity and competing with PCs running Microsoft's software products.

The Company's competitors include many software application vendors, such as IBM (Lotus), Oracle, Apple (Filemaker, Inc.), Sun Microsystems, Corel, Qualcomm, and local application developers in Europe and Asia. IBM and Corel have large installed bases with their spreadsheet and word processor products, respectively, and both have aggressive pricing strategies. Also, IBM and Apple preinstall certain of their application software products on various models of their PCs, competing directly with Microsoft's desktop application software. Sun Microsystems' Star Office is also very aggressive with its pricing, offering a free download from the Web or nominal charge for a CD. Additionally, Web-based application hosting services provide an alternative to PC-based applications such as Microsoft Office.

III. RESPONDING TO CHANGE: EMERGING STRATEGY AT MICROSOFT

"We believe that the PC is one of the most flexible, valuable tools ever invented. And we're taking everything we know about the PC and applying it to smart, mobile devices, to the Internet, and to gaming. So that what the PC has done for your working life can be brought to every other aspect of your life. From your PC to your TV and everything in between, Microsoft is delivering a new level of technology that will keep you in touch, informed, entertained, and connected, all on your own terms. It's a watershed year for new ideas: the latest version of MSN, and the upcoming releases of Xbox, Pocket PC, and Smart Phone will expand your idea of what's possible."

Bill Gates

In response to a rapidly evolving competitive marketplace, Microsoft has diversified its core software business. Microsoft's major strategic initiatives of the past five years are summarized below.

MICROSOFT .NET

Microsoft is laying its framework for the future with a projected investment of approximately $5 billion in research and development in fiscal 2002. At the center of the company's R&D efforts is Microsoft .NET, a project that Microsoft believes is as significant in the development of computing as the graphical user interface and the introduction of the Internet.

.NET is Microsoft's platform for a new computing model built around XML Web Services. Just as the Web revolutionized how users interact with content, XML is revolutionizing how applications communicate with data and how computers and devices communicate—by providing a universal data format that lets information be easily shared, adapted, or transformed. .NET will create new opportunities for Microsoft and for thousands of developers and industry partners by enabling constellations of PCs, servers, smart devices, and Internet-based services to collaborate seamlessly. As part of Microsoft's vision, businesses will be able to integrate their processes, share data, and join forces to offer customers much more dynamic, personalized, and productive experiences—across the PC and an expanding universe of devices—than are available today.

> *"We launched, about nine months ago, a software platform to help people take advantage of the XML revolution. We called it .NET. And .NET is a set of software that we will put in Windows, we will put in Windows servers, we will run out in the Internet as a service for end users and carriers alike, and as software that we will embed in non-PC devices like the television, the cell phone and other handheld mobile devices. This set of technologies makes it easy to build XML-based applications. It provides a user interface that's been tailored to work with XML applications, and it lets the user have control of their information, whether it's stored in the Internet or on their cell phone or in their PC. There's one view of my state, my calendar, my time, my preferences, my health records. And we give you an infrastructure, an XML-based infrastructure to seamlessly manage that information."*

> *Steve Ballmer, CEO Microsoft, March 2001*

.NET services are oriented around people, instead of around a specific device, application, service, or network. They also protect personal information by allowing the user to control who can have access to their information and providing a new level of ease of use and personalization. For example, a company offering an online or mobile electronic payment service can expose its service to its partners, so that they can offer it as their own offering—regardless of what platform they are using. An airline can link its online reservations system to that of a car rental partner, so travelers can book a car at the same time that they book a flight—even from their mobile telephone or other handheld digital device.

Clients are PCs, laptops, workstations, phones, handheld computers, Tablet PCs, game consoles, and other smart devices. These smart clients and devices use software that supports XML Web services, which enable users to access their data regardless of the location, type, and number of clients used. Smart clients and devices leverage XML Web services to create .NET experiences that allow users to access information across the Internet and from stand-alone applications in an integrated way. Some of the products that Microsoft is transitioning into .NET experiences are Hotmail, Passport, Office, Outlook, and MSN.

> *"The Internet is the Internet. It will be accessed via PC, via TV and via a variety of wireless devices. The XML revolution will change the way people interact with the Internet. The XML revolution requires software to live in these devices and out in the Internet cloud. We look forward to partnering with device manufacturers and carriers alike in the enterprise space and the consumer space to help you unlock the XML version of the Internet for your customers. From our perspective, the key to the XML revolution and the key to mobility intersect. The issue is how do you build great mobile applications. Is there a platform that allows for the development of great applications? Can you integrate easily with existing consumer and line of business applications? And we've really put our energy into designing the tools, the development tools and the services to support these devices."*

> *Steve Ballmer, CEO Microsoft*

With .NET, Microsoft is betting that it will be able to have a leading role in delivering the advanced platform and software services that will make different digital devices work together and connect seamlessly. Some say that Microsoft's concept for .NET is like a funnel: easy to get into, but hard to get out. Most .NET applications will allow programmers to write software in different languages. But the code the .NET code writing tool generates runs only on .NET. Similarly .NET services can be accessed on any device, but it will be hard for users to switch to competing XML offerings and still take their data with them. Microsoft executives justify such lock-ins by arguing that the company has to make money somehow given the otherwise open nature of the .NET platform. Microsoft intends to charge users a monthly fee for a .NET My Services account. It also plans to charge developers for .NET My Services tools and also charge every Web site that uses Passport (see below) or other My Services data.

MICROSOFT SERVICES NETWORK (MSN)

MSN is a Web-based online portal and content division of Microsoft that provides services on the Internet, encompassing MSN properties such as Homepage, Hotmail, Messenger, and Search, as well as other services such as music, news, sports, weather, communities, an online calendar, and e-commerce. MSN Internet access includes MSN Explorer, an Internet search engine. MSN Internet access subscribers can access their account from multiple sources, including a computer, television, Internet appliances, and Personal Digital Assistants. In total, the MSN network of Internet services hosted over 270 million unique users per month by October 2001. MSN has the broadest deployment of any portal, available with localized content in 34 global markets and 18 languages around the world—a broader global presence than any other network.

MSN HOTMAIL

Hotmail, which was acquired by Microsoft in 1997, is the world's leading free Web-based e-mail service. It has more than 118 million registered account holders, with more than 80 million users checking their Hotmail accounts at least once a month by late 2001. There are 20 million Hotmail users in Europe. MSN Hotmail has grown tenfold since Microsoft acquired the service. In August 2001 Microsoft announced the creation of MIGway, a joint venture of TDC Mobile International, a Denmark-based European mobile operator, and CMG Wireless Data Solutions, a global provider of messaging solutions for the wireless industry, and the MSN network of Internet services, to allow MSN to extend its interactive mobile offering to the MSN Hotmail Web-based e-mail service via two-way short message service (SMS) to certain operators across Europe (see MIGway Joint Venture below). The first companies to begin trials of the new service are Sunrise, the second-largest operator in Switzerland, and TDC Mobile, the leading provider of mobile communications solutions on the Danish market and the Danish branch of TDC Mobile International.

"Hotmail is the number one free Web-based email service in the world. We have over 100 million Hotmail customers worldwide, 100 million people who are regular users of email. If you don't use your Hotmail account within I think 60 days we kick you off the service. So these are people who use their email, who want access to it in all ways. They want it on their PC. They want it on their TV. They want it when they're offline. They want it when they're on their phone."

Steve Ballmer

MSN MESSENGER SERVICE

Messenger is a free Internet messaging service that enables users to see when others are online and exchange instant messages with them. The more than 42 million users of MSN Messenger can exchange online messages with users of the MSN Hotmail Web-based e-mail service. MSN Messenger has grown more than 100 percent worldwide between November 2000 and November 2001. MSN Messenger Service is available in 26 languages and used in nearly every country in the world.

MSN MOBILE

MSN Mobile offers MSN content and services delivered directly to digital cell phones, Personal Digital Assistants, or alphanumeric pagers. Services include news, sports, weather, stock quotes, horoscopes, instant messaging from the MSN messenger services, and alerts for MSN Hotmail messages. If users have a Web-enabled phone or a Microsoft Windows CE-based Pocket PC or Palm OS mobile computing device they can sign up for free Mobile Web service to access the following content: Expedia.com Travel, MSNBC News, MSNBC Weather, MSNBC Sports, MSN MoneyCentral Stocks, Yellow Pages, Calendar, Horoscope, and MSN Hotmail alerts. MSN was the first of the major Internet portal sites to provide wireless information services, starting in June 1999. Since then, MSN has registered over 3.9 million unique users and, through its relationships with industry-leading carriers, is available on more Web-enabled phones in the U.S. and Canada than any other major portal.

MSN TV

Microsoft's TV service provides Web access from the television. WebTV receivers and the MSN TV Service subscription are designed to enhance the TV viewing experience. While it provides access to the Internet and e-mail, the current service is not designed to offer spreadsheet, word processing, or other capabilities often associated with PCs. These possibilities will become available, however, with the introduction of .NET services for MSN TV subscribers.

MICROSOFT PASSPORT

Passport is a core component of the Microsoft .NET initiative and allows consumers to use the same user name and password at any participating Web site. Single sign-in also helps Web sites eliminate the need to create, protect, and manage user names and passwords for their users. A Passport account also allows consumers to create an electronic wallet that stores all their billing and shipping information as well as a single sign-in name for use at participating Passport sites. Once users sign in, they can avoid the redundant data entry often required to make a purchase. They open their "wallet" and select a credit card and shipping address, then Passport encrypts and transfers the information to the merchant for processing the transaction. The service is available on more than 100 e-commerce sites, including Hilton International, eBay, Barnes and Noble, Starbucks, and OfficeMax, among others. With more than 165 million accounts as of November 2001, Passport is the leading authentication service providing single sign-in across multiple Web sites. Microsoft is inviting the entire industry, including Web sites, enterprises, and competing service operators, to participate in the creation of the broader Passport network, which would work in a manner similar to that of the ATM network created by the banking industry.

BCENTRAL

The Microsoft bCentral™ portal provides online subscription services to help small businesses get online for B2C and B2B opportunities without making an investment in their own large-scale IT infrastructure. bCentral aims to improve marketing effectiveness, increase sales, and provide better customer service. With more than 1.6 million registered users, bCentral is a key part of Microsoft's overall .NET strategy to deliver software as a service to consumers and businesses of all sizes.

XBOX

Microsoft Xbox™, scheduled for North America release in November 2001, is Microsoft's future-generation video game console system that delivers high quality graphics and audio gameplay experiences and will ultimately enable Internet connectivity and new online gaming scenarios. Aimed at the $6.9 billion console gaming market, Microsoft plans to sell the XBox for $299, well below its component cost. Before breaking even in 2005, the Xbox business is likely to lose $2 billion according to some analysts. Xbox will compete head-to-head against systems such as the Nintendo GameCube and the Sony PlayStation.

POCKET PC

Microsoft released its latest generation software platform for Personal Digital Assistants (PDAs) in April 2001. More than 60 manufacturers have adopted Pocket PC software for their PDA products. Partners include Casio, Compaq, Hewlett-Packard, and Symbol Technologies, among others.

E-HOME

A new business unit formed in mid-2001 with the mission of developing technologies that bring simplified whole-home entertainment, communications, and control experiences to everyday consumers using Microsoft's Windows XP and .NET platforms. In October 2001 Microsoft announced an alliance with Samsung Electronics of Korea to develop an entire "ecosystem" of PCs, digital devices, intelligent home appliances, and services to easily and cost-effectively transform average households into next-generation digital homes.

TABLET PC

The Tablet PC is a new evolution of the laptop that combines the power of the PC with the simplicity of pen and paper. It is a full-featured, highly mobile PC that runs Windows and supports all current Windows-based applications. When it launches in fall 2002, there will be applications that will leverage the Tablet PC's pen and speech capabilities, wireless support, long battery life, and best-of-breed portability.

MICROSOFT SMARTPHONE

Since 1998 Microsoft has been working on a smartphone solution development project, currently code-named 'Stinger' or 'Smartphone'. Smartphone combines the best of the PDA and the best of the phone to create a platform to keep people intelligently connected—whether by voice, e-mail, or other means—any time, anywhere.

> *"We're moving into a world of next-generation devices. The phones that people have today are not the phones that people are going to want to use in the world of the XML revolution. The software doesn't really do data. It doesn't do XML. It doesn't plug into the global Internet in as rich a way as other devices. There's a lot of work to do to provide a rich runtime environment that runs in the phone, and that really connects the user up, that authenticates the user, lets the user give permission, gives him full access to the things that they need."*
>
> *Steve Ballmer*

The Smartphone platform will include a Web browser that supports HTML, WAP (WML), and XML formats.

Samsung Electronics Co. Ltd., Mitsubishi Trium, Sendo Ltd. and HTC, the company that designed and builds the Compaq iPAQ Pocket PC, are the first handset manufacturers to design a range of phones using the Microsoft Smart Phone platform, with Mitsubishi launching its first Microsoft Mobile Explorer product in the U.S. in March 2001, equipped with a browser capable of supporting WAP, iMode, and HTML. Mobile operators VoiceStream Wireless Corp., Vodafone, Telefonica, Telstra Corporation Ltd., and T-Mobile have agreed to provide service for Microsoft's Smartphone solution.

In May 2002, Microsoft completed a significant deal in China which will see its mobile phone software used in the devices of one of the country's leading mobile handset manufacturers. Microsoft and TCL Mobile signed an agreement which will see TCL develop its next-generation OMIT (open multimedia information terminal) devices on Microsoft's Windows Powered Pocket PC 2002 Phone Edition and Smartphone 2002 platforms. Wan Mingjian, president of TCL Mobile, said in a statement: "Wireless data is the direction next generation communications is taking. We believe that mobile devices with only voice functionality will end up in the same category that pagers are in today. According to CCID Consulting, the number of mobile phone users in China leapt 71.3 percent in 2001 to 144.8 million, accounting for 44.13 percent of the total phone market."

"Stinger takes the same concept of .NET and the ties to the XML world and literally embeds it down into a cellular phone. It's a real smart phone. It is a phone first and foremost. It wasn't designed to be a PC. It's really quite small and nice, smaller than most of the phones people carry today. It's got Outlook access built into it. It's personalized. We broadcast your information, your .NET service information down to the device. It supports the Windows Media technologies, digital media support. And from a carrier perspective, it ties in and leverages off of the base of Exchange customers we have, of Hotmail customers, the development tools, which will let people build next generation applications that run down in the device, and it's a device, of course, that a carrier can take and brand and differentiate and make their own."

Steve Ballmer

MICROSOFT TV

Microsoft TV is a family of software products for the television industry. Microsoft TV software powers a range of current digital and next-generation TV devices—from advanced set-top boxes and digital video recorders, to integrated TVs and combination devices. Microsoft believes that broadband technologies present enormous opportunities for the television industry worldwide. The television is one of the most ubiquitous devices in the world, with approximately 1.5 billion TV sets in use. The Microsoft TV platform aims to provide the technological building blocks for bringing interactive TV functions to these devices. The TV Group is also a key part of Microsoft's .NET vision of helping to ensure that people have access to the information and services they want, and is providing the television-related components of this vision. To build market share in the TV connectivity market, Microsoft has entered a series of equity partnerships, joint ventures, and strategic alliances with cable, satellite, and technology companies (see below).

HOMESTATION

In March 2002 industry insiders revealed that Microsoft is working on a top-secret home entertainment device code-named HomeStation. It is believed the PC/Xbox hybrid would run a version of Windows to form a home entertainment hub, and that the device will finally turn the idea of digital convergence into a living room reality. Following in the footsteps of the PC-influenced Xbox, the device will likely be a non-upgradeable sealed unit, with advanced graphics capabilities and Dolby Digital sound. It is believed HomeStation will come equipped for an array of online and offline activities: a sizeable hard drive, broadband connection, and compression technology—all pointing to a video-on-demand role. It is believed that HomeStation will connect to a Microsoft .NET server providing movies, music, messaging, games, and TV programming—and with a huge hard drive, HomeStation might also double up as a digital TV recorder. In addition, it might wirelessly interface with portable devices such as digital cameras, PDAs, MP3 players, and telephones using HomeRF or Bluetooth protocols. It might even manage home automation through a link to Microsoft's e-Home initiative.

HomeStation: Artist's Impression

It is anticipated that HomeStation will play both PC and Xbox titles. Because HomeStation will function through a Microsoft gateway, the device will be poised to profile the activities of its users straight back to Microsoft.

Industry insiders believe that the device's launch will be heavily dependant on broadband becoming widely available (perhaps via the Teledesic satellite system—see Appendix D below), but expect the HomeStation marketing machine to be gearing up by early 2003.

ONGOING RESEARCH AND DEVELOPMENT

During fiscal years 1999, 2000, and 2001, Microsoft spent $2.97 billion, $3.77 billion, and $4.38 billion, respectively, on product research and development activities excluding funding of joint venture activity outlined below. Those amounts represented 15.0 percent, 16.4 percent, and 17.3 percent, respectively, of revenue in each of those years. The Company is committed to continue high expenditures for research and product development.

IV. MAJOR EQUITY INVESTMENTS AND STRATEGIC ALLIANCES

In addition to diversifying into the products and services outlined above, Microsoft has pursued an aggressive strategy of equity investments, joint ventures, and strategic alliances in recent years. Some of the company's most significant initiatives are outlined below.

QWEST EQUITY STAKE

Late in 1998 Microsoft became a shareholder in Qwest, a provider of broadband Internet-based data, voice and image communications for businesses and consumers. Committing $200 million to the deal, Microsoft also licensed a broad range of its software to allow Qwest to deliver a range of e-commerce, enterprise network, and managed software solutions. In 2001 Qwest had revenues of $19 billion and served more than 30 million customers in the U.S. The Qwest Fiber Network now spans more than 113,000 miles globally and combines the world's fastest, most powerful network with Web hosting services, managed solutions, high-speed Internet access, private networks, wireless data, and other technologies and applications that are redefining global communications around the power and potential of the Internet.

QUALCOMM ALLIANCE

Also in 1998, Qualcomm, world leader of Code Division Multiple Access (CDMA) digital wireless technology, and Microsoft formed Wireless Knowledge LLC, a joint venture, to develop wireless platforms and services to corporate customers and application providers to enable applications for the mobile Internet. Qualcomm Incorporated (Nasdaq: QCOM) and Microsoft Corp.'s relationship was strengthened in early 2000 through a strategic alliance to jointly define and develop advanced wireless, multimedia-capable devices. The companies will focus on developing hardware reference designs for mobile devices including smart phones and wireless Pocket PCs.

1997 MICROSOFT INVESTMENT IN COMCAST CORPORATION

Microsoft invested $1 billion in Comcast, one of the world's leading communication companies, focused on broadband cable, commerce, and content. Today, under President Brian L. Roberts, Comcast is the third-largest U.S. cable operator and a Fortune 500 corporation, with 2000 revenues of $8.2 billion and 8.4 million customers. Comcast has transformed itself from a single-product cable provider into a leader in the delivery of broadband, serving 1.56 million digital cable subscribers and 542,000 high-speed Internet subscribers at the end of the first quarter of 2001.

$5 BILLION AT&T BROADBAND INVESTMENT

In May 1999 Microsoft announced a $5 billion investment in U.S. telecommunications and cable television company AT&T. The deal between Microsoft and AT&T Broadband guaranteed that 5 million of the set-top digital TV boxes used by AT&T would carry Microsoft's Windows CE operating system, with the potential to add another 5 million boxes. Analysts suggested that Microsoft's investment acknowledged the possibility that set-top boxes might one day drive the future of the Internet. And access to its MSN Internet services. Microsoft officials have often described a vision in which the cable television replaces the PC as the consumer's gateway to the Internet. AT&T had access to more than 60 million U.S. homes through its cable operations.

NEXTEL INVESTMENT AND OTHER MOBILE DEALS

Just days after the AT&T deal, Microsoft bought 16.67 million shares of Nextel Communications, a mobile telecommunications provider, for $600 million. The deal was intended to promote MSN Mobile, and Nextel chose Microsoft over Netscape Communications, a unit of AOL. Analysts believed that MSN's main attraction to Nextel was its cache of e-mail customers who would likely want to access their accounts through Web-enabled phones. At the time of the agreement, there were 70 million users of Hotmail.com, Microsoft's e-mail service. MSN Mobile deals were also concluded in 2000 and 2001 with network providers such as Sprint, AirTouch Cellular, and British Telecom.

TELIGENT EQUITY STAKE

In November 1999 Microsoft invested $200 million in Teligent, a company offering bundled wireless services—including high-speed Internet access and local and long-distance phone service—to small businesses. Instead of using cables or copper wiring, Teligent delivered its 'last-mile' broadband access services from base station antennas to antennas mounted on its customers' buildings. Other investors in Teligent include NTT Corp of Japan, IDT, and Nortel, among others. Due to continuing financial losses and a downturn in the U.S. market, in May 2001, Teligent announced that it had voluntarily filed a petition under Chapter 11 of the U.S. Bankruptcy Code in order to reorganize its operations and financial structure. The future of the company remained uncertain in mid-2001.

INVESTMENT TO CREATE StarBand SATELLITE BROADBAND COMPANY

In addition to its investments in telecommunications and wireless services, Microsoft also invested $50 million in an Israeli-based satellite network in February 2000 for a 26 percent stake. The investment resulted in the creation of a new company, StarBand, America's first consumer two-way, always-on, high-speed satellite Internet service provider which began operations in April 2000. StarBand is one of a number of new ventures hoping to provide satellite broadband Internet access to consumers and businesses underserved by digital subscriber line (DSL) and cable companies. The company offers tiered services at different prices. At market-entry price, the service has download speeds up to 400 Kbps, though its upload speeds will reach only 56 Kbps.

JOINT VENTURES WITH NBC

Microsoft also owns 50 percent of MSNBC Cable L.L.C., a 24-hour cable news and information channel, and 50 percent of MSNBC Interactive News L.L.C., an interactive online news service. National Broadcasting Company (NBC) owns the remaining 50 percent of these two joint ventures. MSNBC distribution includes delivery of broadband content on highspeed.msnbc. com and for Qwest, Road Runner (broadband service provider owned by Time Warner Cable), and Excite@ Home. MSNBC.com wireless content distribution is delivered through agreements with MSN Mobile, i3 Mobile, Digital Paths, and Omnisky. In addition, MSNBC.com programs interactive content for MSNBC TV and NBC News on WebTV Plus.

BILL GATES AND TELEDESIC

Bill Gates also has a substantial investment in satellite broadband company Teledesic, but the investment is a personal one not associated with Microsoft. For details of Gates' involvement with Teledesic see Appendix D.

GEDAS AND MICROSOFT LAUNCH MOBILE E-SERVICES

In June 2001 Microsoft and Gedas, one of the leading international system integrators in the field of information technology, announced a new cooperation in the field of mobile e-services based on Microsoft's .NET technologies. The partnership aims to guarantee far-reaching mobile services for the wireless transmission of comprehensive information contents and services to both consumers and enterprise clients. In the field of mobile e-services, gedas has developed various products such as nicepace, a mobile Internet portal for e-business. With nicepace, news, entertainment, personal information, and a wide range of other services can be accessed not only from stationary, networked computers, but also from mobile PDAs (Personal Digital Assistants), which use the cellular network to log in from on the road. A long-term relationship is planned between gedas and Microsoft, which will cover all of the latest technologies and products. Both companies strongly believe in the future of "pervasive computing" with portable high-tech devices. Gedas is based in Berlin and is a wholly-owned subsidiary of Volkswagen AG.

MICROSOFT $10M INVESTMENT IN MOBILE HANDSET MANUFACTURER SENDO HOLDINGS

In July 2001 Microsoft invested more than $10m in the Birmingham-based mobile handset manufacturer Sendo Holdings. The investment was aimed to increase Microsoft's foothold in the developing wireless data market and marked the first equity stake in a mobile handset manufacturer. Microsoft's shareholding in Sendo will be under 10 percent. Microsoft believed that allying itself with a handset manufacturer will help it to build closer relationships with mobile phone operators such as Vodafone and Orange. Hugh Brogan, chief executive of Sendo, said that Microsoft had also purchased options to increase its stake. Sendo's other major shareholders include the Hong Kong-based cordless phone maker CCT and the California investment fund Bowman Capital. Sendo ships to 10 countries and has supply deals with Vodafone Telecel in Portugal, BT Telfort in the Netherlands, and Virgin Mobile in the UK. By late 2001 Sendo had a 0.5 percent share of the world mobile handset market.

MIGWAY JOINT VENTURE

In August 2001 Microsoft announced the creation of MIGway, a new joint venture of TDC Mobile International, a Denmark-based European mobile operator, and CMG Wireless Data Solutions, a global provider of messaging solutions for the wireless industry, and the MSN network of Internet services. The new service to be created by the venture will allow users of MSN Hotmail the option to receive e-mail sent to their MSN Hotmail accounts by SMS on their mobile phones. They also will be able to reply to those e-mail messages directly to the sender's inbox via SMS as well as perform other common tasks directly from their phone. Under the terms of the alliance, MIGway will be the first company to distribute MSN interactive mobile services via two-way SMS. According to Microsoft, the alliance with MIGway "is the first SMS deal MSN has announced and is part of the MSN global strategy to provide mobile consumers with its best-of-breed services, such as MSN Hotmail and relevant integrated MSN features, through a link to the wireless Web." The announced alliance shortly followed the release of MSN Mobile 4.0, the latest version of MSN Mobile's platform that delivers customisable communications services to interactive pagers, mobile phones, and handheld devices.

GERMAN ISP T-ONLINE

It was rumored in May 2002 to be considering selling a 25 percent stake in the company to Microsoft. The move could help T-Online's major shareholder, Deutsche Telekom, reduce its huge level of debt. Microsoft and T-Online already had a partnership in place to develop 3G applications. A stake in T-Online would give the software company a larger foothold in Europe.

V. THE FUTURE

Speaking on the future of Microsoft in May 2001, CEO Steve Ballmer declared:

"Number one, we're a company that believes in having a clear vision, or at least a vision and a clear set of priorities, at least as clear as we can make them, and we make big bets. And in a certain sense, that sounds obvious, and yet I think it is very difficult for companies to maintain clarity of vision and clarity of priority. It's easy to lose your way and it's easy to confuse your people about what the priorities are. Frankly, not all companies should, or do, make big bets. Their economics don't allow it. They're not paid to make big bets. They're paid to be flexible. They're paid to adapt. They're paid to have vision. But some companies can't go spend $2 billion and then hope the thing is popular. We're a company that makes big bets. And if they pay out, that's great, and if they don't pay out, frankly it's reasonably cataclysmic. That's the nature of the kind of work that we do, whether it's on .NET—the original work we did on Windows was that kind of big bet. The work we did on our Windows NT technology to try to be in the server business; these are bets where you build a piece of technology, you ship it, people don't like it, you improve it, they don't like it, you improve it again; five years later, a billion dollars into it, they like it and then you get huge businesses that spring from that. That's the one thing we've learned about big bet vision and priority is you have to be willing to be flexible about the vision. In a way it's a very kind of scary and risky proposition but it's the nature of big bets and it will be a fundamental part of our future success."

Microsoft is structured around the following core groups: the Business Groups; the Worldwide Sales, Marketing, and Services Group; Microsoft Research; and the Operations Group. The Company's product segments, which are based on the Business Groups, are Desktop and Enterprise Software and Services, Consumer Software, Services, and Devices, Consumer Commerce Investments, and Other. The Desktop and Enterprise Software and Services segment includes the Platforms Group and the Productivity and Business Services Group. The Platforms Group has responsibility for continuing to evolve the Windows platform. In addition, the division includes the .NET Enterprise Server Group, the Developer Tools Division, and the Windows Digital Media Division. The Productivity and Business Services Group drives Microsoft's broad vision for productivity and business process applications and services. This group includes the Office Division, the Emerging Technologies Group, the Business Tools Division, and the Business Applications Group, which includes bCentral™ and Microsoft Great Plains.

The Consumer Software, Services, and Devices segment contains the MSN Business Group; the Personal Services Business Group; and the Home and Retail Division. MSN Business Group runs the network programming, business development, and worldwide sales and marketing for MSN and Microsoft's other services efforts, including MSN eShop, the MSNBC venture, Slate, and MSNTV. The Personal Services Group (PSG) focuses on making it easier for consumers and businesses to connect online and to deliver software as a service on a variety of devices. PSG encompasses Microsoft's Personal .NET initiative, the Services Platform Division, the Mobility Group, the MSN Internet Access, Consumer Devices Group, and the User Interface Platform Division. The Home and Retail Division develops and markets learning and entertainment software and the future Xbox game console.

The Consumer Commerce Investment segment includes Expedia, Inc., the HomeAdvisor™ online real estate service, and the MSN CarPoint online automotive service.

For financial reporting, revenue from Microsoft Press and Hardware is included in the Other segment.

The Worldwide Sales, Marketing, and Services Group integrates the activities of Microsoft's sales and service partners with the needs of Microsoft customers around the world. In addition, the group includes Microsoft Product Support Services, the Network Solutions Group, the Enterprise Partner Group, the Central Marketing Organization, and all three of Microsoft's major business-sales regions worldwide.

Microsoft Research works on devising innovative solutions to computer science problems, such as making computers easier to use, designing software for the next generation of hardware, improving the software design process, and investigating the mathematical underpinnings of computer science.

The Operations Group is responsible for managing business operations and overall business planning. This includes corporate functions such as finance, administration, human resources, and information technology.

Distributors and Resellers. The Company licenses and sells its products in the finished goods channels primarily to and through independent non-exclusive distributors and resellers. Distributors and resellers include Ingram Micro, Tech Data, Software Spectrum, Corporate Software & Technology, SOFTBANK, Software House International, ASAP Software Express, and Tech Pacific Group. Microsoft has a network of field sales representatives and field support personnel who solicit orders from distributors and resellers and provide product training and sales support.

Enterprise Accounts. The Microsoft Select program offers flexible software acquisition, licensing, and maintenance options specially customized to meet the needs of large multinational organizations. Targeted audiences include technology specialists and influential end users in large enterprises. Marketing efforts and fulfillment are generally coordinated with large account resellers. The Microsoft Open program is a licensing program that is targeted for small- and medium-sized organizations. It is available through the reseller channel and offers discounts based on initial purchase volumes. The Microsoft Enterprise Agreement program is a licensing program designed to provide a flexible licensing and service solution tailored to customers making a long-term licensing commitment. The agreements are designed to increase customer satisfaction by simplifying license administration, payment terms, and the contract process.

Certified Partners. Microsoft Certified Partners are independent companies that offer their clients leading-edge technology through consulting, deployment, remote and on-site maintenance, helpdesk support, packaged software applications, hosting services, training, and more. Microsoft Certified Partners encompass a broad range of expertise and vendor affiliations and have experience ranging from networking, e-commerce, collaboration, business intelligence, and other leading edge disciplines.

International Sales Sites. The Company has established marketing and/or support subsidiaries in more than 80 countries. Product is generally delivered by the Company's owned or outsourced manufacturing operations, which are located in the geographical region in which the product was sold. By organizing geographically, the Company is able to provide service to international channel customers and access to Microsoft professionals located in the same region to serve their specific needs. Subsidiaries have the responsibility for selling products to customers, managing licensing programs, and providing support to all types of customers based in international countries.

The Company's international operations, both OEM and finished goods, are subject to certain risks common to foreign operations in general, such as governmental regulations, import restrictions, and foreign exchange rate fluctuations. Microsoft hedges a portion of its foreign exchange risk.

OEM Channel. Microsoft operating systems are licensed primarily to OEMs under agreements that grant the OEMs the right to distribute copies of the Company's products with their computing devices, principally PCs. The Company also markets and licenses certain server operating systems, desktop applications, hardware devices, and consumer software programs to OEMs under similar arrangements. In almost all cases, the products are distributed under Microsoft trademarks. The Company has OEM agreements covering one or more of its products with virtually all of the major PC OEMs, including Acer, Actebis, Compaq, Dell, eMachines, Fujitsu, Fujitsu Siemens Computers, Gateway, Hewlett-Packard, IBM, Micron, NEC, Samsung, Sony, and Toshiba. A substantial amount of OEM business is also conducted with system builders, which are low-volume customized PC vendors.

"Microsoft is committed to continuing to deliver innovations to customers and new opportunities for partners and the technology industry as a whole. The U.S. Court of Appeals ruling in the antitrust lawsuit significantly narrowed a lower court ruling that threatened to stifle industry innovation. We are continuing to work vigorously to resolve the remaining issues in the case in a manner that will provide clarity to Microsoft and the marketplace while enabling Microsoft to meet the needs of consumers and the industry."

Microsoft Annual Report, 2001

At the time of writing Microsoft is a defendant in *U.S. v. Microsoft*, a lawsuit filed by the Antitrust Division of the U.S. Department of Justice (DOJ) and a group of 18 state Attorneys General alleging that Microsoft has pursued monopolistic and anti-competitive practices that stifle innovation. An initial judgment was handed down on 2 November 2002 with three major implications: It limits Microsoft's ability to restrict competition through agreements with original equipment manufacturers (OEMs) that make products using Microsoft's software and want to include competing software and its desktop icons; it forbids Miscrosoft from retaliation against the OEMs whether by discriminatory agreements or refusal to deal with them; and it requires the company to release software code under certain circumstances to encourage competition.

In addition to the U.S. action, the European Commission has instituted proceedings in which it alleges that Microsoft has failed to disclose information that Microsoft competitors claim they need to interoperate fully with Windows 2000 clients and servers and has engaged in discriminatory licensing of such technology. The remedies sought, though not fully defined, include mandatory disclosure of Microsoft Windows operating system technology and imposition of fines. Microsoft denies the European Commission's allegations and intends to contest the proceedings vigorously.

Investor Craig McCaw and Microsoft founder Bill Gates are the two primary founding investors of ICO Teledesic Global, a broadband Internet-satellite network (Mr. Gates' investment is a personal one not associated with Microsoft). Teledesic aims to be the first licensed satellite communications network that will enable affordable, worldwide access to advanced telecommunications services such as computer networking, broadband Internet access, interactive multimedia, and high-quality voice. Other strategic investors include Motorola, Saudi Prince Alwaleed Bin Talal, The Boeing Company, and The Abu Dhabi Investment Company.

The Teledesic Network will consist of 288 operational satellites, divided into 12 planes, each with 24 satellites. To make efficient use of the radio spectrum, frequencies are allocated dynamically and reused many times within each satellite footprint. Within any circular area of 100 km radius, the Teledesic Network can support more than 500 megabits per second (Mbps) of data to and from user terminals. The Teledesic Network supports Bandwidth-on-Demand, allowing a user to request and release capacity as needed. This enables users to pay only for the capacity they actually use, and for the network to support a much higher number of users. The service is planned for launch in 2005.

The Teledesic Network's low orbit eliminates the long signal delay experienced in communications through traditional geostationary satellites and enables the use of small, low-power terminals and antennas. The compact terminals will mount on a rooftop and connect inside to a computer network or PC.

The Teledesic Network is designed to support millions of simultaneous users. Most users will have two-way connections that provide up to 64 Mbps on the downlink and up to 2 Mbps on the uplink. Broadband terminals will offer 64 Mbps of two-way capacity. This represents access speeds up to 2,000 times faster than today's standard analog modems. For example, transmitting a set of X-rays may take four hours over one of today's standard modems. The same images can be sent over the Teledesic Network in seven seconds. Narrowband services, such as mobile and voice paging, will not be available from Teledesic.

End-user rates will be set by service providers, but Teledesic expects rates to be comparable to those of future urban wireline rates for broadband connectivity.

MTV vs. Channel V

case twenty

Paul Ellis
Hong Kong Polytechnic University

ABSTRACT

The American music channel MTV was the first to broadcast music television in Asia when it entered the market via Star TV's satellite feed in 1991. However, when Rupert Murdoch's News Corporation acquired Star TV two years later, MTV left the scene over a disagreement regarding the amount of local programming and a new player emerged in the form of Star TV's own Channel V. In contrast to the global approach of MTV, Channel V placed more emphasis on local artists and VJs and for a while enjoyed a monopoly position in the market. Later, in 1995, MTV returned to Asia with a new strategy of adapting the content while projecting a common brand image. MTV has since enjoyed rapid growth in the region resulting in fierce competition between the two channels. In 1999 the rivalry manifested itself in an escalating war of words between Steve Smith of Channel V and Frank Brown of MTV with each alleging that the other was misrepresenting distribution figures. The case documents this feud and its effect on advertisers in the context of the emerging Asian market for televised music.

> *Channel V was first in the market with a localized approach, and MTV copycatted that.*
>
> —*Steve Smith, managing director, Channel V*

> *We've tried to stay clear of the mud-slinging. But Channel V is throwing out more smoke than the ice machine at a rock concert.*
>
> —*Frank Brown, president, MTV Networks Asia*

This case was prepared from secondary sources for the purposes of classroom discussion. All dollar amounts in this case are U.S. dollars unless stated otherwise. An earlier version of this case was awarded a High Commendation in the Fourth Regional Case-Writing Competition, Management Development Council (Hong Kong). Reprinted by permission of Paul Ellis, PhD., Associate Professor, Department of Business Studies, Hong Kong Polytechnic University, Hong Kong and World Scientific Publishing Co Pte Ltd.

INTRODUCTION

If the global music industry has a wild frontier, it is Asia. Here record labels, media giants, and entertainment conglomerates are engaged in a battle to win the affections—and spending dollars—of the so-called MTV Generation, a group of 10–24-year-olds representing an estimated one billion consumers. This struggle is perhaps most aggressive on the airwaves where two foreign-owned music channels, lured by the promise of attracting mega-advertising dollars, are competing for viewers. Since the mid-1990s, Singapore-based MTV Networks Asia and its Hong Kong–domiciled counterpart Channel V have been investing heavily in their distribution networks around the region. In 1999 the competition degenerated into a personal war of words between the two energetic heads of each channel, with each alleging the other has misrepresented viewer figures. These allegations exasperated advertisers and led some analysts to wonder whether there is room for two large music channels in the Asian market. In the interim, MTV appears to have the upper hand in terms of attracting advertisers, although Channel V, with its lower operating costs, is set to recover its investment in the region sooner.

THE HISTORY OF MUSIC TELEVISION IN ASIA

It could be argued that no other company has been as much a catalyst for globalization of youth culture as the music channel MTV. MTV Networks, a division of entertainment giant Viacom, debuted in the United States in 1981, and later expanded into Europe (in 1987), followed by Central America (MTV Latino) and South America (MTV Brazil). In the vast markets of Asia, MTV pioneered music television when it first began broadcasting via satellite on the Star network in 1991. With its ever-expanding reach, MTV was able to attract advertising from global brands such as Levi-Strauss, Apple Computers, and Coca-Cola.

However, MTV's position in Asia changed when Star TV was acquired by Rupert Murdoch's News

Corporation in 1993.[1] Shortly after News Corp.'s acquisition of Star TV, MTV left the Asian scene and a new channel was launched in its place. The new arrival was called Channel X, later renamed Channel V, and quickly grew to encompass five 24-hour satellite feeds to audiences in China, Taiwan, India, Thailand, and Australia. Currently the music channel is owned by a consortium of companies led by majority shareholder Star TV (57 percent), and four of the world's six largest record labels, including Japanese media giant Sony, British record label EMI (both holding 12.5 percent), along with the German entertainment conglomerate BMG and Turner Broadcasting of the United States (each holding 9 percent). Headquartered in Hong Kong, Channel V is run by the American Steve Smith.

What had caused MTV to be dropped from Star TV in 1994? According to Gary Davey, the chief executive officer of Star TV, there had been a disagreement over the amount of local content in MTV's programming. In Star's assessment, MTV wasn't adapting its product sufficiently to the Asian market. Star TV requested MTV to split the music channel in two, broadcasting in Chinese on Star's northern satellite beam and English and Hindi on the southern beam.

But MTV, with its proven global formula that had brought success in markets around the world, was reluctant to comply. When MTV disappeared from Asian screens on May 2, 1994, Channel V was created to fill the vacuum. In contrast with MTV's standardized approach, Channel V introduced different channels for each of its main markets, emphasized local over international music, and used home-grown Video Jockeys (VJs). The new approach proved successful—see Exhibit 1 for a list of advertisers—and for a time Channel V was, in the words of Gary Davey, "competing with air." But one year later a new and improved MTV was relaunched with a redesigned product to cater to local tastes.

MTV Networks Asia, a joint venture of MTV Networks, the American parent firm, and Polygram NV of the Netherlands, went to air in May 1995. Customizing its product to each major target market, MTV enjoyed a rapid rise in the region expanding its reach from 50 million homes in 1997 to 100 million in 1999. As Richard Cunningham, MTV Asia's vice president for Network Development, explained: "What took MTV ten years to achieve in the United States and five in Europe only took two years in Asia." Following the pat-

---

EXHIBIT 1 Selected Firms Advertising on Channel V

Acer computer	Jashanmal National	Ponds
Adidas	Killer Jeans	Ray Ban
Australian Tourism Corp.	Kinetic Engineering	Reebok
BMG Records	Kodak Film	Rock Records
Cadbury Foods	Korea Racing Association	Rotary International
Canon	Lancome	Rotomac Pens
Carlsberg	L'Oréal	Royal Enfield Motors
Citizen Watches	Maybelline	Samsung
Coca-Cola	McDonald's Restaurants	Shiseido
Colgate Palmolive	Motorola	Smirnoff
Columbia Tristar	Nestlé	Sony Music
Decca Records	Nike	Strepsils
EMI Records	Nin Jiom Medicine	Times of India
Femcare India	Old Spice	Uncle Chips
Gillette	Pacific Telecom	Vidal Sassoon
Goodyear	Panasonic	Watson's
Himalaya Drug Co.	Pepsi	Wrigleys
HMV	Philips	Yamaha
Indian Oil Co.	Polygram	Za

Source: Channel V.

tern set by Channel V, a concerted effort was made to increase the amount of local programming. Often this took the form of introducing country-specific shows intended to strengthen MTV's position in particular markets. For example, in 1997 the channel introduced the one-hour *MTV WOW Thailand,* which mixes Thai hits with international videos and is produced and packaged entirely in Thailand. But while the music played around the region is different, all MTV channels follow the same basic formula and project the same image. This is in contrast with Channel V, which follows a different positioning strategy in India, for example, than the one adopted in China.

MTV Networks Asia is structured into three divisions: (1) MTV Asia, covering Indonesia, the Philippines, and Singapore; (2) MTV India; and (3) MTV Mandarin, which broadcasts to Hong Kong, mainland China, and Taiwan (set up in 1996). Each division relies on a mix of 24-hour satellite transmission and partnerships with local stations to distribute the product. By selling programs to terrestrial broadcasters and cable companies, MTV is able to increase its exposure and gain access to homes that don't have satellite dishes. Headquartered in Singapore, the company is run by the Scottish-born Frank Brown.

The "Twilight Zone" of the Asian Market

With 1.9 billion consumers under the age of 30, it is not difficult to appreciate the appeal of the Asian market to firms seeking the young, hip, and uber-cool. The main difficulty for foreign firms seeking to access this market is the delivery of promotional campaigns that span cultural barriers yet do not offend local tastes. This is where the music channels come in. In an environment characterized by the overlap of linguistic barriers, cultural differences, and distinctive broadcasting regulations, there is an economic incentive to generate a product mix that appeals to large numbers of people, thus attracting advertisers, while using an assortment of media to circumvent the technological and regulatory entry barriers. The aim of the game, in other words, is to find the right mix of hardware (satellite, cable, and terrestrial broadcasting) and software (the programs themselves) that maximizes channel viewership while minimizing the investment outlay. The problem is, not only are the rules of the game in a continual state of flux, reflecting the differing rates of development of the various Asian economies, but it is almost impossible to keep score of who is attracting the most "eyeballs on screen."

In "the twilight zone of Asian satellite television," as one Hong Kong journalist aptly put it, the only claim that can be made with any certainty is that both music channels are spending money hand-over-fist without showing any profits. In the five years since it was founded, Channel V admitted losing $100 million. By most optimistic estimates, Channel V won't break even until 2002. Although MTV is coy about its own expenditure in the region, *The Economist* has predicted that the channel won't recoup its estimated $150 million investment until 2005. These fortunes have been spent in the hope of cashing in on an anticipated bonanza in advertising revenue, particularly as cable and satellite subscriptions increase. At the end of the year 2000, there were 149 million multichannel (i.e., cable and satellite) households in Asia, representing a 32 percent penetration of 470 million television homes. Within a decade analysts estimate that there will be 294 million multichannel households representing a 49 percent penetration of 610 million television households (see Exhibit 2). In the run-up to profitability, both companies are now positioning and repositioning themselves to maximize their visibility and reach. Nowhere is this more evident than in the key market of India.

Competing in India: Road Shows and Dance Parties

MTV launched an Indian channel in 1996 and is now available in 10 million homes via 24-hour satellite distribution. Previously MTV had been distributed on syndication on the Indian state broadcaster *Doordarshan* and before that on Star TV's satellite feed. Channel V arrived on the scene in the mid-1990s, but as recently as 1998 was still ranked number two in the market after MTV. In response to losing the ratings war, and in light of MTV's perceived mass market appeal, Channel V's management decided that it needed to reposition the channel's image and differentiate the service from the competition. Consequently, in 1999 Channel V changed its image from a music channel to that of a youth channel targeted at 12- to 29-year-olds. The aim of the repositioning was, in the words of Jules Fuller, general manager of Channel V India, to develop the music industry from an "Indian kid's point of view."

India is seen as a key growth area for Channel V. As Steve Smith has said, "We are quite bullish on India." Recently the Indian division was given "full operational independence" in order to improve the company's responsiveness to needs of the local market. This means that the responsibility for scheduling and promotion activity, formerly done in Hong Kong, has now shifted to India. Divisional autonomy has also been extended into production with four new fully equipped studios being set up in Delhi, Bangalore, Chennai, and Calcutta. In addition to producing more local programs,

EXHIBIT 2　Asian Cable and Satellite Subscription Growth (2000–2010)

Cable Subscribers (000)	2000	2010	DTH Satellite Subscribers (000)	2000	2010
China	90,000	150,000	Japan	14,100	23,650
India	29,000	62,000	Malaysia	435	1,315
Taiwan	4,780	5,260	Thailand	214	650
Japan	4,000	16,000	Taiwan	90	520
Korea	2,500	7,800	Indonesia	85	725
Philippines	1,100	4,210	China	0	5,500
Hong Kong	510	923	Hong Kong	0	700
Thailand	350	692	India	0	5,200
Singapore	250	755	Philippines	0	500
Malaysia	135	580	Singapore	0	240
Indonesia	50	465	Korea	0	2,300

Source: *Asia Cable & Satellite World* (November 2000), p. 47.

the division is remixing the content of the show's broadcast. Formerly, about 90 percent of the local music aired was Hindi film music. Now the number of Hindi film clips has been reduced to allow more programming in Tamil and Bengali. By the same token, the channel is increasing the amount of Western music delivered, dedicating a full day every weekend to international music. The aim of this scheduling decision is to attract the wealthy decision makers of the higher social classes. In Fuller's words: "We want the decision makers to stay by us, which is what is happening. Let MTV have the mass audiences, we want the classes."

In spite of these recent strategy changes, Channel V has yet to make a profit in the market. Figures made available in early 1999 showed that Channel V was earning $9 million annually from its Indian operations on expenditures of $15 million. Part of this investment outlay is directed toward market development activities, an area in which both music channels are highly active.

As India has only recently been opened up to foreign broadcasters, both Channel V and MTV are engaged in events marketing in the form of hosting spectacular roadshows and dance parties. While the shows themselves are not directly profitable, the aim is to develop the local music scene, ultimately generating benefits for all players in the market. These heavily promoted events are held around the country in many of the smaller cities such as Goa and Bangalore and are very popular with local music lovers. Tickets are given away in advance and fans get a chance to see the rising stars of the local music scene. For example, those who

attended Channel V's *Coke V Live* concert in Calcutta in January 1999 were entertained by singers such as Shankar Mahadevan and local band Krosswindz. For larger events, such as the *Channel V Music Awards* held in Jawahar Lal Nehru Stadium, New Delhi, in November 1998, local artists Kamaal Khan and Daler Mehndi shared the stage with international bands Aqua and Def Leppard.

Channel V conducted six roadshows in 1997 and four in 1998. However, the number of shows is likely to increase significantly after Channel V recently secured a three-year sponsorship arrangement with Coca-Cola. For a fee of $2.5 million, Coca-Cola will be the major sponsor of no less than 18 Channel V roadshows across several Indian venues. In those cities where shows will be held, Coke will distribute specially manufactured cobranded cans of drink promoting the event and fans will be able to exchange a certain number of cans for free tickets and merchandise such as badges and T-shirts.[2]

Although popular across the country, not all the roadshows have been successful. A show held in Bangalore in April 1998 was characterized in the local press as an occasion where "everything that could go wrong did." After a fortnight of intense promotional buildup, an unprecedented crowd of 15,000 showed up for the event creating chaos in the surrounding streets. Some in the crowd were drunk. Others were there apparently intending to create trouble. During the concert, security personnel were unable to contain a surging crowd of spectators who broke through barriers and entered the VIP enclosure. To cap it all off, the venue was hit by a freak rainstorm with thunder and lightning that damaged equipment and caused the crowd to wrench out the barriers for use as umbrellas. In the end the decision was made to finish the show early. Unfortunately the promoters were unable to announce the early closure because of the danger of switching on the public address system.

COMPETING IN CHINA: MUSIC AWARDS

While markets such as India and Taiwan are the major sources of revenue for the music channels, China, with its 330 million television sets, is considered a major growth market. In 1999 China was Asia's largest advertising market with gross expenditures of US$2.7 billion (see Exhibit 3). Because of the sheer size and growth potential of the Chinese market, both channels are actively courting local partners in anticipation of reaping future benefits. According to Harry Hui, senior vice president of MTV Mandarin, "in the long term, China will be the most promising market." Presently access to the market is strictly regulated by the central government. Satellite broadcasts are officially banned, so foreign satellite TV must be filtered through registered cable operators approved by the State Administration for Film, Radio and Television. Both Star TV and MTV are lobbying for freer access to the market and both are distributing programming via syndication. In addition, Star TV has estimated that more than 20 million Chinese households receive Channel V via illegal satellite dishes.

Asian Advertising Expenditures (1999)	EXHIBIT 3	
	Gross Expenditures (US$m)	Year-on-year growth (%)
China	2,746	3
Korea	1,976	21
Hong Kong	1,378	7.5
Taiwan	916	3
Philippines	558	11
Thailand	516	22
Indonesia	496	32
Singapore	320	−7
Malaysia	279	5
Vietnam	34	3

Source: *Asia Cable & Satellite World* (December 1999), p. 24.

Unlike India with its roadshows and dance parties, the jockeying for position in the potentially lucrative Chinese market has largely been in the form of hosting televised music award ceremonies. Award ceremonies have been held in the region for years, but prior to 1999 no such ceremony had been conducted in China. In December 1998 MTV announced in a press release the inaugural *MTV Music Honors* in China to be held on February 4 in Beijing. Although Frank Brown has flatly denied that MTV was motivated by one-upmanship, industry observers couldn't help but notice that the event was scheduled to precede Channel V's own awards show by mere days. For their event MTV had chosen the country's capital over Shanghai, where Channel V's ceremony was to be held. Clearly the prestige of being first was at stake and both channels worked feverishly with local partners to get the shows off the ground.

To get permission for their awards ceremony, Channel V's Smith and mainland-born Star TV chairman Gareth Chang had met with senior Communist party officials who endorsed the show and suggested avenues for further cooperation in the future. In MTV's case, assistance had been sought from the state broadcaster China Central TV (CCTV), which signed a cost and revenue sharing agreement in January. This proved to be a late start for, as it turned out, MTV had not left itself or their partners sufficient time to get all the requisite permits and, at the last minute, their show was indefinitely postponed due to "procedural delays." In contrast, the Channel V ceremony went to air as planned four days later.[3]

According to Channel V's glossy press kit, mainland China's first music awards ceremony was beamed out to "a staggering potential 500 million viewers in China and across Asia." The show had received three million votes for 20 categories through ballot boxes distributed in record stores, campuses, and karaoke lounges in Hong Kong, China, and Taiwan as well as on Channel V's website. Not unexpectedly, Taiwan's Mandarin-singing artists fared better than Hong Kong's Canto-pop superstars, while Beijing-based Faye Wong and Taiwan's Ritchie Jen were named best female and male artist, respectively. After the ceremony, Steve Smith optimistically concluded: "I think we've opened a lot of doors in this market with this event."

MTV was finally able to stage its own awards ceremony three months later. This was the first time CCTV had co-staged an event with a foreign broadcaster like MTV, but any doubts regarding the state broadcaster's degree of professionalism proved unfounded as the show turned out to be a success. At the end of the evening Frank Brown, who was in Beijing for the ceremony, expressed his hope that "tonight is the beginning of a long and successful friendship between MTV and CCTV."

The winners at the 1999 MTV Music Honors Awards Show included a number of international celebrities such as Ricky Martin and Celine Dion who accepted awards via prerecorded videos. To the delight of local fans, Danish group Michael Learns to Rock accepted the award for Asia's biggest international band in person and followed it up with a performance of the song "Strange Foreign Beauty." Locally Liu Huan and Na Ying were named China's best pop male and female, respectively, while film star and sometime singer Jackie Chan received the title of "Asia's biggest superstar" in a prerecorded message from Elton John.

To comply with state regulations, MTV's award ceremony had been recorded on May 7 for a delayed broadcast scheduled for the weekend immediately following. Unfortunately for MTV, the date of the awards ceremony coincided with an infamous incident half a world away that was to have a direct impact on the show. The incident in question was NATO's accidental bombing of the Chinese embassy in Belgrade. The widespread protests which followed over the weekend led CCTV officials to express their wish to MTV that the tape of the ceremony not be aired. This "advice" came just hours before the scheduled broadcast on MTV Mandarin. In Hong Kong, MTV issued the following statement on May 11:

> In light of the recent incident at the Chinese embassy in Belgrade, CCTV has advised that the broadcast of the 1999 CCTV-MTV Music Honors should be postponed until the situation stabilizes. MTV Asia will comply with the recommendation to postpone the broadcast of the show inside and outside China.

IMPACT OF THE ASIAN ECONOMIC CRISIS

While accidental bombings may have created short-term operational difficulties for MTV, a larger concern for both competitors was presented by the Asian economic crisis. In the late 1990s Asia was hit by successive currency devaluations, rising unemployment across the region, and a general loss of both consumer confidence and purchasing power. How did this crisis affect the music channels? While it could be expected that advertising expenditures would fall in tandem with declining consumer spending, this was not the experience of MTV. In the year following the start of the crisis, MTV reported record growth in distribution (60 percent), advertising (40 percent), and viewership (an eightfold increase). In explaining this surprising result, Frank Brown reasoned that in an indirect way the crisis had helped the industry:

> In the cloud of economic crisis there is a silver lining. People have less disposable income to spend on external entertainment outside the home, so inevitably they spend more time on home entertainment. And in many cases it pushes them over the edge to finally subscribe to cable, because it's a great, inexpensive way of getting 24 hours a day of entertainment.

Other important factors behind MTV's growth during the recession were the attitudes and spending power of Asia's young adults. On this point Brown observed that "young people see this crisis as a very short-term blip in their life" and although the impact has been felt, "they don't actually believe it's going to change their destiny." In terms of spending power he added:

> The impact of the crisis is less on young people than it is on the older generations because the older generations have a lot of financial commitments, whether it's a mortgage or rent or feeding the kids. . . . For young people, they may have a little less income, but it's still all disposable. They don't have the same financial commitments, and so all the money they have, they're still going to spend on the same interests as before.

PROBLEMS IN MEASURING VIEWERSHIP

At base, music channels are advertising vehicles; music is the platform by which companies like MTV and Channel V attract advertisers. In the music broadcasting business the competition for the advertising dollar is measured in terms of viewership, which is a computation of distribution, ratings, and the amount of time spent viewing the channel. (This broadly defined measure of viewership is preferred over straightforward ratings for the simple reason that cable and satellite-rating information is not available in Asia except in Taiwan and India.) The main problem stems from the fact that viewership is inordinately tricky to measure across Asia's diverse markets. China, in particular, is troublesome because it is hard, if not impossible, to count the number of illicit users with access to satellite television. This makes it difficult for Channel V to sell the Chinese audience to advertisers.

The latitude for interpretation presented by poor quality data and measurement imprecision combines with fierce competition for the advertising dollar to create a powerful incentive for both channels to interpret the available market data to their best possible advantage. Consider MTV's recent claim that at the end of 1998 more than 100 million households in Asia had access to MTV by satellite, cable, or terrestrial TV, representing a 60 percent increase in viewership from 1997. In the eyes of Channel V, MTV was fudging its numbers by mixing 24-hour distribution, where the channel is aired around the clock either via satellite or cable, with syndication, where the channel is available only part-time, for example, when a program is sold to a terrestrial broadcaster. According to Steve Smith, 24 hour distribution is better than syndication because that's where most of the revenue is generated. The problem with combining distribution figures in this way is that no distinction is made between a Singaporean or Taiwanese customer who receives a music channel 24 hours a day and a Hong Kong resident who has ATV, a terrestrial broadcaster, but doesn't even know that MTV is on.[4]

In response to MTV's claim of 100 million households, Channel V published its own distribution, figures in early 1999. In 24-hour distribution, Channel V claims it reaches 40.4 million homes compared to 19.6 million for MTV (see Exhibit 4). In syndication, Channel V reaches 126 million homes versus 85 million for MTV. In the aggregate, Channel V is received by 147 million homes, leading Smith to conclude "that Channel V is Asia's leading and most-watched music channel."

In response to Channel V's counterclaims, Frank Brown sent a lengthy letter to a group of trade journalists questioning the objectivity of Channel V's figures (Appendix A). Brown argued that while MTV relies heavily on syndication, much of that distribution, unlike the situation for Channel V, includes six-hour blocks of programming. "Channel V plays down the impact of our daily programming blocks on terrestrial TV by lumping those numbers in with syndication." MTV's programming blocks—on which the broadcaster retains full rights to sell advertising—reach 77 million homes daily, "almost twice Channel V's advertising opportunity."

While Channel V was originally concerned with the way in which MTV was combining different types of distribution to arrive at the impressive figure of 100 million households, Frank Brown's complaint was that Channel V was making claims based on "vague estimates and extrapolations." For example, in China, Channel V claims 24-hour distribution to 21 million homes versus none for MTV, and syndication to 100 million households, compared with 37.7 million for MTV. Frank Brown disputes these figures, which he argues were arrived at by analyzing "nine different pieces of research," whereas MTV claims it can break down its figure of 37.7 million (see Exhibit 5) by individual cable operators (all legal operators). Brown later added:

They were muddying the waters and making outrageous claims. They know they have to catch up and

Channel V's Distribution Figures

EXHIBIT 4

	Channel V	MTV
North		
Mainland China	21,000,000	0
Hong Kong	362,000	20,000
South Korea	3,500,000	—
Taiwan	4,300,000	4,400,000
Others	270,000	6,000
Total	29,432,000	4,426,000
South		
India	10,000,000	10,000,000
Pakistan	10,000	10,000
Others	—	1,350,000
Total	10,010,000	11,360,000
International		
Japan	50,000	0
Philippines	450,000	450,000
Malaysia	185,000	185,000
Middle East	—	250,000
Thailand	320,000	250,000
Singapore	—	145,000
Indonesia	—	2,500,000
Others	80,000	50,000
Total	1,085,000	3,830,000
Grand Total	40,527,000	19,616,000

Source: *AdWeek Asia*, March 26, 1999.

they're creating total confusion, so therefore everyone becomes equal. If you look at their research, it's all very woolly and foggy. Yes, there's a need for more research and data in the industry, but I think Steve's exaggerating when he talks about the poor quality of surveys overall.

In reply to Brown's letter, Channel V sponsored two "wraparound" covers folded around the front of trade journals *Adweek Asia* (March 26) and *Media* (April 2). The cost of these covers was approximately HK$24,000 (or just over US$3,000). On the front page of each wraparound under the heading "EXPOSED!" ran the statement "The Truth About Music Channels." Inside the cover was a short personal letter to Frank Brown written by Steve Smith and a chart showing distribution figures. (A longer letter, not published but circulated in the

EXHIBIT 5 — MTV's Distribution Figures

Country	Households
MTV Southeast Asia	
Brunei	36,431
Hong Kong	19,223
Indonesia	16,000,000
Malaysia	184,204
Papua New Guinea	2,600
Philippines	5,081,919
Thailand	248,667
Vietnam	1,200
Singapore	145,339
South Korea	2,179,649
Hotel Rooms	28,372
Sub-Total	23,927,604
MTV Mandarin	
Brunei	1,000
China	37,715,000
Taiwan	4,394,000
Singapore	145,339
Hotel Rooms	5,575
Sub-Total	42,260,914
MTV India	
Bangladesh	175,000
India	10,000,000
Middle East	250,000
Nepal	125,000
Pakistan	10,000
Sri Lanka	1,000,000
Hotel Rooms	29,117
Sub-Total	11,589,117
Sub-Total (Southeast Asia/ Mandarin/India)	77,777,635
Syndication	
Hong Kong (ATV)	1,700,000
Malaysia (RTM)	3,300,000
Maldives (TV Maldives)	15,000
Thailand (Ch3)	12,000,000
Vietnam (VTV 1 & 3)	7,000,000
Sub-Total	24,015,000
Grand-Total	101,792,635

Source: MTV table circulated to advertisers in March 1999.

industry, was also written and is included in Appendix B.) On the back page was a list of advertisers already signed with Channel V. A few weeks later even Rupert Murdoch got in on the act. On a copy of *Adweek Asia* addressed to its editor Rhonda Palmer, Murdoch scribbled an enigmatic message right above the "EXPOSED!" headline: "Dear Rhonda, This is what it's all about! Rupert Murdoch." When told of the message, Brown responded by distancing himself from the fracas:

After initial amusement I felt it was a silly and wasteful way to spend valuable trade dollars. We don't want to be associated with mud-slinging in the industry. We choose to promote progress rather than taking directly negative potshots and dragging other channels into the mud. Why Channel V chose to spend so much money on this, rather than promoting their success stories is a mystery. Steve's a nice guy. I'm kind of surprised he'd approve this.

Smith was similarly polite in his assessment of his rival:

I've no problem with Frank. Before this little thing came up I'd say we were—well, friends is a bit much, but we were quite cordial. But what's gone on in the past has been ugly; in the last five years we've been more focused on trashing each other than building up music television.

THE RESPONSE OF THE ADVERTISING INDUSTRY

Although the purpose of calculating viewership is to attract advertisers, potential clients were anything but impressed by the fuss over figures. Their collective disapproval was voiced by Paul McNeill, a media specialist who complained that neither channel was talking to their consumers: "They're talking to advertisers, the media, people like us. And if they spent as much money on actual research as they do slagging each other off, we, the media planners, would have more information at our disposal." He added: "Until Channel V and MTV start taking planners more seriously by funding some real research into the viewing habits of Asian youth, then print, with a fraction of the possible reach and opportunity to see, will receive the lion's share of the pan regional budget."

Some potential advertisers seem to have been confused by MTV's attempt to combine different types of distribution, and at least one advertiser has said that it is easier to plan a campaign with a 24-hour network such as Channel V. But while Channel V's reliance on satellite technology may make it easier to plan promotional campaigns, MTV makes no apologies for using any means possible to reach the Asian consumer.

According to Richard Cunningham, "in Asia you have to be open to different distribution or you won't have a business."

Nevertheless, MTV and Channel V's recent feud has given rise to the feeling that both channels are more concerned with promoting themselves to advertisers than they are with developing the customer appeal of their products. After looking at the distribution chart on Channel V's wraparound, Paul McNeill opined:

> According to this, 362,000 people in Hong Kong watch Channel V. That's the maximum reach if they all switch on . . . The numbers mean absolutely nothing. We're making assumptions based on nothing. Anyway, I've always believed people watch programs, not channels; if you hear a song you like, you stay with it, but that doesn't mean you're MTV-loyal.

Rhonda Palmer, the editor who received the message from Rupert Murdoch, perhaps expressed the advertisers' view best when she said, "It should be a battle about better programming, not about whose figures are believable." Others have gone so far to suggest that rather than fight, the two rivals would do well to join forces. Janine Stein, editor of *Cable and Satellite Asia*, has been quoted as saying:

> There's so much more at stake now because they've both lost so much money and they've got to start showing profits. And these days the trend is to merge: in business television there was a merger between two rivals, CNBC and ABN, in sports television there was a merger between two rivals, ESPN and Star Sports—so they're really fighting for their lives.

Another voice in support of a merger came from Simon Davies, editor for the media publisher Baskerville Communications:

> Of course they should merge. There isn't a viable business for two music operators in the region. You've got to remember—nobody is watching these channels, *the real numbers are tiny, but the pressure on these guys from advertisers to demonstrate audience reach is immense. And the financial realities are so horrific neither side can face telling the truth. Both are losing in the region of $15–20m, each, per year. That's a hell of a lot by anybody's standards.*

In developing a regional network, there are valuable returns to generating cost-saving economies of scale in both distribution and production. The present situation is characterized by some duplication of activities. For example, both MTV and Channel V have independent production units in India creating programs for the local market. A merger between the two channels would thus offer a number of benefits and there is some evidence to indicate that the idea has been considered in both camps. Steve Smith noted that for a merger to take place, "what has to happen is that Rupert (Murdoch) and (Viacom CEO) Sumner Redstone have to get MTV Asia and Channel V on their radar screen for the same 10 minutes or so." But according to Brown, this is not going to happen: "There has been no conversation about a merger for many months, and from our point of view it's a dead issue."

LICENSING AND MERCHANDISING

While advertising revenue is the main source of income for the music channels, revenue is also generated by other means, including sales of programming to cable systems, terrestrial broadcasters, and airlines. For example, in June 1998 Channel V executives signed a deal with ALMA TV to beam their International channel to 50,000 homes in Kazakhstan. Another source of income includes royalty fees earned from brand extensions into related product lines. With its globally recognized logo, MTV has a clear advantage in this area (see Exhibit 6). MTV Networks, the American parent company, has a proven track record of successful brand extensions in the form of record compilations such as the "Unplugged" series and the CD "MTV Alternative Nation" released by Seagram's Universal Music Group in 1997. In Asia, MTV has sought to capitalize on the appeal of its brand name by placing its logo onto clothing, notebooks, backpacks, or basically any product that young people use for their lifestyle. In Singapore, teenagers can even sport an MTV-branded personal pager, reflecting a deal made in conjunction with Singapore Telecommunications. Although licensing fees only account for around 5 percent of MTV's business in the region, MTV projects that licensing revenue will grow at around 20 percent annually as the channel finds new products and new retailers keen to carry the brand.

According to Richard Cunningham, MTV's move into licensing and merchandising represents a natural extension of MTV's activities in Asia. "We felt the brand and channel awareness were strong enough." Dan Levy, MTV Asia's vice president for licensing and merchandising, concurred: "In the past three years MTV has become quite a strong brand in Asia, so it's quite natural to move into consumer products." But while the brand name may be global, the extensions are adapted to suit local tastes. For example, the MTV logo is featured prominently on merchandise in the Philippines but is smaller in Singapore where, according to Dan Levy, "branding is important, but in a much more

EXHIBIT 6   Positioning Strategies Compared

	MTV Networks Asia	Channel V
Target age group	15–34-year-olds	12–29-year-olds
Positioning strategy (pre-1995)	more international	pan-Asian
Positioning strategy (post-1995)	Asia, India, Mandarin	3 feeds: Greater China, India, other Asia
Flavour	more global/foreign	more local
Image	"cool & hip"	"trend-setting modern youth"
Format	similar	similar
Sex appeal	lower	higher
Advertising appeal	higher	lower
Brand equity	higher	lower
Potential for brand extensions	high	minimal
Variety of music played	higher	lower
Greater China image	international flavour	heavy Taiwanese (mando-pop) flavour
Indian image	as above, mass market appeal	youth channel with lifestyle programming
Other Asia	mix of country-specific shows + Western music	100% Western music
Distribution	satellite, cable, broadcasting, webcasting	satellite, cable
Operating costs	higher	lower
Investment cost	$150 million	$100 million
Headquarters	Singapore	Hong Kong

subtle way." The different retail prices for branded products also reflect local purchasing power. For example, an MTV shirt in Singapore costs around $15 but only $6.25 in the Philippines.

An alternative view of licensing emerges from Channel V. Although Channel V's brand extensions include albums and T-shirts sold in India, the scale of licensing activities is considerably less than at MTV. Channel V merchandise is generally limited to promotional giveaways at concerts or apparel sold for a limited time in conjunction with a particular program (such as the clothing range promoted on the David Wu show). One possible reason for Channel V's comparatively subdued attempts to promote brand extensions is a lack of managerial enthusiasm for splashing the corporate logo on to disparate products. This explanation is suggested by a recent comment made by Jasper Donat, Channel V's vice president of advertising sales: "I'm not sure that a T-shirt with the channel name on it is that exciting." However, a more likely reason behind the low level of licensing, as some outsiders explain it,

is that the Channel V logo is not sufficiently distinguishable from MTV in the minds of Asian consumers. According to Rhonda Palmer, the original choice of logo back in 1994 "did little to differentiate itself from MTV and a lot of people didn't even know that MTV was out of the market for that time." Perhaps at the time Star TV executives had been hoping to manufacture some level of familiarity among viewers. Whatever their motives, Palmer notes that by making their logo similar to MTV's, Channel V's creators "shot themselves in the foot."

Did the management team at Star TV choose a poor logo for the new music channel back in 1994? Or was Channel V handicapped from the beginning by virtue of the fact that since the early 1980s their competitor's acronym "MTV" has become widely adopted as a generic term for all music television?[5] Whatever the reason, it is undeniable that Channel V does not enjoy the same level of brand equity as its rival and opportunities for profitable brand extension are correspondingly lesser. This has compelled Channel V to pursue more creative options in the pursuit of licensing agreements. For example, in Taiwan and Hong Kong, consumers can make purchases on their Channel V MasterCard featuring a color photograph of their favorite artist.

RESTRUCTURING FOR THE NEXT PHASE OF INDUSTRY DEVELOPMENT

With rapid growth and zero profitability, the late 1990s can be characterized as the investment stage of the Asian televised music channel business. Having laid the groundwork on which future growth will be based, both MTV and Channel V are now gearing up for the next stage of development. For Channel V this has meant a complete restructuring of its operations, reducing its original five feeds to three—one each to Greater China and India and an international feed with 100 percent Western music content to cater to audiences from Israel to Japan. The company is now structured into four operating divisions with one division running each feed and a central support unit based in Hong Kong. In addition, the channel has recently been converted to digital encryption. While this has meant that some households in the region are no longer able to receive the channel, the switch should save the company $1.8 million annually in operating costs.

WEBCASTING—THE WAY OF THE FUTURE?

In preparing for an increasingly wired Asia, both channels are also increasing their online presence (see *www.channelv.com* and *mtvasia.com*). In May 1999, MTV Asia relaunched its website as part of a joint venture with Tricast Ltd., a Singapore-based Internet publishing firm. Previously the site had been simply a promotional vehicle, albeit one which attracted one million hits per month or four times the number of impressions received at Channel V's site. The revamped site now contains a mix of local material and repackaged content taken from the very popular U.S. site of the parent firm.[6] Surfers can now get access to news, audio and video clips, chat rooms, contests, and cool downloads. MTV upgraded its website for several reasons. First, having an online presence provides an additional means with which to disseminate MTV's brand name in the region. As Brown has said: "The Internet is yet another medium to reach out and connect with young people in Asia." Most of Asia's rapid Internet growth is driven by Chinese-language usage. Accordingly, a Chinese-language version of the site was launched in late 1999. Second, the channel hopes to generate revenue from the site by attracting advertisers and selling merchandise. Third, MTV intends to use its site as a proprietary research tool to glean data from its target market. In the fickle music business, the audience's perception of what is cool can change very quickly. The instantaneous nature of the Internet, whereby a site can require visitors to fill out a simple survey, is ideally suited to keeping abreast of consumers' changing tastes. Finally, in the not too distant future, it is likely that the Internet will evolve to fulfill a fourth function—delivering programming. In May 1999, MTV Asia Online hosted its first webcast live from the closing party of the MTV-Billboard Asian Music Conference.

DISCUSSION QUESTIONS

1. Is there room for two music channels in Asia? Do you think Channel V and MTV should merge? Is a merger a realistic scenario?

2. In this age of globalized markets, is it really necessary to adapt the music channels? With the introduction in 1999 of Channel V's all-Western international feed, hasn't the situation returned to where MTV was at the beginning of the 1990s?

3. Has Channel V done enough to differentiate its logo from that of MTV (see Appendices A and B)? Should Channel V adopt a re-branding strategy? If so, what new brand would you suggest that would convey the image Channel V is currently trying to promote while simultaneously distinguishing itself from its major rival?

4. Assuming the Channel V brand remains unchanged, what options exist for extending the brand into other product categories, if any? How can Channel V distinguish its brand extensions from those of MTV?

5. China has been earmarked as the market of tomorrow. How can the foreign music channels develop the China market? Do you think that the means used to develop the Indian market (e.g., spectacular roadshows, dance parties) would work in China?

SOURCES USED IN THIS CASE

"Murdoch Star deal transforms Asia," *Broadcasting & Cable*, 2 August 1993, pp. 34–35.

"Murdoch's Star targets Asian cable networks," *Hongkong Standard*, 30 May 1994.

"Sleeping with the enemy," *Far Eastern Economic Review*, 22 June.

"MTV cranks up the volume in Asia," *Business Week (International)*, 23 June 1997, p. 29.

"MTV Asia sets local programs," *Hollywood Reporter*, 5 August 1997, p. 15.

"The rise of Asia's 'MTV generation,'" *The Atlanta Journal*, 9 September 1997, p. E:02.

"Star woes," *The Economist*, 11 April 1998, p. 61.

"Rains, unruly crowds hit Channel V show," *Business Line (The Hindu)*, 1 May 1998.

"Coke unplugs $2.5m for Channel V," *Financial Express (India)*, 9 May 1998.

"MTV Networks Asia makes a licensing bet on popularity of logo," *Asian Wall Street Journal*, 20 November 1998, p. 16.

"At Channel V it's that time of year again," *Financial Express (India)*, 19 November 1998.

"Channel V uses awards platform to advantage," *Business Line (The Hindu)*, 24 November 1998.

"MTV decides what's 'in' for music—and clothes," *Inter Press Service*, 1 December 1998.

"MTV rocking on in Asia despite crisis," *Deutsche Presse-Agentur*, 9 December 1998.

"Channel V projects '99 revenue to grow 30%," *Asian Wall Street Journal*, 22 January 1999, p. 5.

"MTV thrives in Asia despite financial crisis," *Agence France-Presse*, 24 January 1999.

"MTV Asia breaks 100 mil.," *Hollywood Reporter*, 2 February 1999, p. 65(1).

"Channel V aims at 'decision makers,'" *Business Standard (India)*, 3 February 1999.

"Channel V hikes budget outlay by 20%," *Financial Express (India)*, 9 February 1999.

"MTV Networks Asia aims to boost web site's allure," *Asian Wall Street Journal*, 9 February 1999, p. 12.

"V Awards help Star prospects," *Adweek Asia*, 12 February 1999, p. 1.

"Channel V holds awards show in mainland China," *Billboard*, 27 February 1999.

"Cool customers," *Far Eastern Economic Review*, 4 March 1999, p. 50.

"MTV Asia revamps companion web site," *Billboard*, 6 March 1999.

"Star claiming twice reach of Asia MTV," *Daily Variety*, 16 March 1999, p. 10.

"Music channels hit sour notes," *Adweek Asia*, 26 March 1999, p. 1.

"MTV Asia and Channel V feud," *Billboard*, 27 March 1999.

"Tuned in to China," *Far Eastern Economic Review*, 1 April 1999, p. 50.

"When two tribes go to war . . .," *Postmagazine (Hong Kong)*, 9 May 1999, pp. 8–11.

"First ever MTV Asia webcast," *Newsbytes News Network*, 20 May 1999.

"Channel V, MTV Asia hit disharmonious note in war against red ink," *Asian Wall Street Journal*, 21 May 1999, p. 7.

"MTV Asia awards delayed," *Billboard*, 22 May 1999.

"Asia's Channel V restructured," *Billboard*, 19 June 1999.

"Channel V to raise budget, production in recast bid," *The Economic Times of India*, 19 June 1999.

"MTV Network Asia ad revenue shows 70pc rise," *South China Morning Post*, 30 June 1999, p. 2.

"Sumner's Gemstone," *Forbes*, 21 February 2000, pp. 107–111.

"Frank Brown—the elder statesman of Asia media?" *Asia Cable and Satellite World*, February 2001, pp. 24–25.

NOTES

1. Murdoch's company purchased 63.6 percent of Star TV's shares for $525 million from Hutchvision, an equal joint venture owned by Richard Li of Hong Kong and Hutchison Whampoa, the company owned by Richard's father Li Ka-shing. Although the deal was considered a lucrative windfall for the Li family, returning them a profit of three times their original investment, the acquisition gave Murdoch a chance to leverage expertise from years of experience in setting up the U.K. satellite venture BskyB. Murdoch acquired the balance of Star TV for $299 million in 1994.

2. While the roadshows help Channel V to build brand recognition in different Indian cities, the recent Coke deal itself probably had more to do with the ongoing Cola Wars than with the competition in the music industry. Prior to Coca-Cola's arrangement, MTV had formed a joint-sponsorship with Pepsi whereby the two companies share the cost of promoting *Pepsi Dance Parties* in 22 cities.

3. Although Channel V's ceremony was broadcast on schedule, there were some last-minute hiccups brought on, no doubt, by the novelty of the experience for the mainland partner, Shanghai Oriental TV. For example, Channel V was informed the day before the event that it could only use two VJs instead of the five it had been rehearsing for a week. In addition, OTV's overzealous security staff cut the guest list repeatedly and made stringent checks on clothing and hairstyles. Even sunglasses were forbidden.

4. The problem with combining distribution figures is clearly seen in Hong Kong where MTV can claim distribution to 1.7 million households at some point during the week. Of this figure only 19,000 homes in the SAR receive the channel around the clock. The remainder receive only a few hours of MTV programming per week via terrestrial broadcasts, which is usually shown at odd hours (for example, on Saturday morning).

5. Indeed, one of the problems of measuring viewership is that uninformed members of the public may interpret the terms "MTV" and "music video" interchangeably. (Executives groaned when Andy Lau casually announced at a Channel V event that he had just made an "mtv," by which he meant a music video.) Such people are quite likely to answer "yes" if asked whether they've watched MTV in the last week when in fact they have been watching Channel V.

6. MTV's U.S. website has been ranked as the number one news/information/entertainment site among 12–24-year-olds by Media Metrix, a N.Y.-based web-traffic research firm.

From: Frank Brown

Date: 15 March, 1999

Dear

I have been asked by some journalists to respond to the recent presentation pack and press release distributed by Ch V on the issue of music channel distribution. I have a few general points and a few specific points to make:

General Points

I think what's important about data that we in the cable & satellite industry issue or present to journalists/client/advertising agencies is:

1) The data on distribution should be (a) the most recent possible and (b) objective, from a third party, not commissioned by the channel in question, and/or provable by means of relatively easy verification by any interested party.
2) The focus should be on real, actual TV channel reception and more importantly, real VIEWERSHIP, rather than vague estimates and extrapolations about how many homes might possibly be receiving a signal.
3) There are many issues of nuance/detail that I could take issue with in the 'Information' provided by Ch V which when taken collectively would give a very different picture than the one they are painting, but below are just some of the examples (not to be exhaustive).

   The general issues to be raised are:
   a) Ch V's distribution ESTIMATES seem much too over-aggressive compared with perspectives from other objective outside sources.
   b) Although they try to 'belittle' the importance of MTV's terrestrial distribution, grouping it with simply syndication, the bottom line is that these MTV programming blocks get great viewership and we have advertising rights. As a result, we can offer advertisers 77 MILLION HOMES ON A DAILY BASIS (almost twice Ch V's advertising opportunity, even according to their own claims!).
   c) Ch V's focus seems still to be on their broad brush distribution claims, rather than real, measured viewership ratings. There seems to be no reference to either the pan regional surveys that have been conducted, nor much of the on-line data available at national level (such as MARG, in addition to IMRB/Nieisen, in India or SRT in Taiwan?). ALMOST ALL OF THAT OBJECTIVE DATA shows significant leadership for MTV in terms of actual viewership.

Specific Detail

4) Ch V's distribution claims seem clearly to be based (still) on subjective estimates of their own (or research commissioned by them). Additionally, they seem to be making very few comparisons about real actual levels of viewership ratings, but rather selective information on 'viewership profiles' or 'reach'. Neither of these say anything about absolute aggregate levels of total viewership.
   By contrast, the data MTV uses is from uncommissioned industry sources for both distribution and viewership, giving a better, more accurate picture of the reality.
5) The data we are given to understand that Ch V presented seems very selective:
   a) why did they use data for India from November/December 1998 when January/February 1999 is available?
   b) some of the data they use seems to date back to 1996 (Korea)
   c) it also contradicts their own data on their current website (eg. for Korea their presentation claims 3.5 million homes for Ch V but their current website claims total Star distribution of 1.7 million as at November 1998. Surely they are not suggesting a growth of almost 2 million homes in the last few months? Is it more likely an inconsistency in their subjective claims?
   d) More than half of Ch V's estimate of 40 million comes from China. This estimate of 21 million, I understand, is based on an estimate, which itself is based on yet another estimate of the distribution of the Phoenix channel (and both estimates are highly debatable, not supported by the industry at large). They also don't seem to give a breakdown of the number of households by city, just a list of cities they claim to reach?
      Meanwhile, MTV's distribution numbers in China can be supported in detail not only city by city, but also even by cable system.

e) In India, the advertising industry generally believes that Ch V's distribution is much less than 10 million, especially following their conversion to an encrypted signal recently. General opinion in the market seems to be that, given the number of decoder boxes that Ch V has provided to cable operators in India, it seems obvious that 10 million is clearly an over-aggressive claim.

   Again, even in India, MTV's distribution claims can be supported in detail, by cable system, easy to check either comprehensively or by random sample.

f) The same vagueness by Ch V applies also to Korea.

6) Although Ch V tries to play down the impact of our daily programming blocks on terrestrial TV by lumping those numbers in with simple 'syndication,' the reality is that we do have full rights to sell advertising on our daily programming blocks. No advertiser needs to have his commercial shown every hour of the day on any TV station, especially when the viewership is as high as it is for these terrestrial programming blocks of MTV.

   So we can offer our advertisers 77 million homes on a daily basis. And we have the distribution data AND the viewership data to show clearly to advertisers the impact they receive for their advertising spend on MTV. Ch V are unable to do this, I believe, in most markets, since their distribution is based on estimates and they have very little continuous viewership data.

7) MOST NOTABLY, all of the available, objective viewership data on a regional basis in the last 12 months, which I'm sure you are familiar with, clearly supports significant leadership in favour of MTV, as does the current national research data on-line, where it is available, which can be checked at any time:

   a) all pieces of regional research (PAX, CabSat, etc) demonstrate large percentage leadership by MTV over Ch V (see attachments).

   b) where it is available (in the 4 major markets of India, Taiwan, Indonesia, Philippines) the available national data also supports the same significant leadership.

   When you filter out all of the subjectivity, those sources of data are the most reliable and consistently demonstrate that same fact.

8) Many other issues are too detailed to cover in this written response (eg. MTV's higher penetration of cable homes in Taiwan—according to SRT, 98% for MTV, 87% for Ch V, as well as higher ratings in Taiwan for MTV; or that much of the programming transmitted by Ch V is not locally relevant to the market targeted by them—Korea and Philippines receiving predominately their mandarin programming, etc.).

9) Further, due to our different feeds to different markets, including our terrestrial blocks, we can offer advertisers great FLEXIBILITY to choose which individual markets they want to advertise with us in, much more so than Ch V.

Finally, the lack of detail in the Ch V document and the specific information selected is obviously designed to create the best possible interpretation, especially on a competitive basis with MTV. However, the true reality is much more to be seen in the objective data. For many weeks recently even Ch V management themselves have been reported as confessing that MTV had at least 'caught up' (according to them) in recent times, so it seems strange and self-contradictory to me that they are now suddenly coming up with a claim of their own leadership? Perhaps it is merely an attempt to counteract to recent press about MTV's own significant distribution and viewership progress?

   If you have any other questions, or points that you would like further clarification on, I would be happy to talk to you further about this issue.

Best regards,
Frank A. Brown
President
MTV Networks Asia

Frank Brown
President
MTV Networks Asia
March 26th, 1999

Dear Frank,

Here's the long one.

We absolutely agree that distribution data should be the most recent possible. The figures we have quoted **are indeed based on the most recent, independently commissioned research available.** The fact that there are too few 'establishment' surveys covering multichannel TV is a fault of our industry at large. Some TV channels are refusing to fund the surveys, and research companies, like all of us, have to turn in a profit.

- Where there is no data available we are forced, on behalf of our clients, to commission proprietary studies. If this can be done on a syndicated basis, so much the better. It gives credibility to the figures and eases the pressure on funding. A national distribution survey in China can cost over a quarter of a million dollars to be done properly.

Sometimes even the research companies admit that the independent third party data they publish can be difficult to interpret. In China the interviewer cannot gain access to many of the state owned enterprise systems. This clustering is unique to China and can also cause enormous variation in projected distribution figures. Let's not forget that all these surveys are based on relatively small samples are subject to fluctuation.

Let's go back to China and use Chengdu as an example. Channel [V] subscribes to 6 different sources of data from Chengdu. The estimates of Channel [V] distribution in homes accessible to survey varies from 1% to 6.4%. Which one would you use? They are all "recent" and "objective" and by a "third party" and or "provable" and easily verified. Free-to-air Phoenix penetration in Chengdu is 23%. If Phoenix is available, Channel [V] is available. Should we use 23%? That's where common sense comes in.

I digress—In your letter you raise some other general issues.

Channel [V] distribution figures differ from **other objective outside sources.** That's news to us. What other sources? We subscribe to all of them. Do you?

Actually it's rather amazing that according to you Channel [V] distribution in India is 'much less than 10 million.' If that is so where are all these viewers coming from sitting at home pressing their buttons on their peoplemeters? In February (is that recent enough for you?) over 8 million people tuned into Channel [V]. That number comes from just nine cities, no projection. 10 million is probably underestimating the audience out there but until the next new national survey is done none of us can claim to have 100% accurate figures. We could commission that survey from one of the internationally acclaimed research companies but that wouldn't be a **third party recent objective provable verified survey** would it? We know where the boxes are and we know where the cable operators are. We assume that these are the same 5000 cable operators that make up your figure of 10 million homes—or are there another 5000 cable operators that we may have missed?

That's just distribution. What about 'Real Viewership' (your term not ours). We love **real** viewership. Let's look at television viewership measured by peoplemeters. I have attached a chart which looks at your bottom line—'great viewership'—ACTUAL REAL AVERAGE RATINGS FROM PEOPLEMETERS. Is that 'real' enough for you?

Let's take India as another example. The Joint Industry Body, representing agencies, advertiser and broadcasters commissioned AC Nielsen to operate the only industry approved national peoplemeter panel. We understand that you haven't subscribed to that one.

Anyway, that OBJECTIVE data shows that Channel [V] reaches more people than MTV. Not only more people, but more people aged between 15 and 34 and more young people in the upmarket segment. That data is so recent you may not have seen it. Give us a call and we'd be happy to show it to you.

Thank goodness for peoplemeters. That's why we have commissioned AC Neilsen to set up a peoplemeter panel across 6 cities in China to measure viewing to satellite TV.

No-one their right mind in a multichannel market considers **recall** surveys to be either accurate or objective.

Actual MTV programme blocks do not get great viewership—they get some viewership in a few places at different times. Would you like us to send you some more data from the AC Nielsen peoplemeters in Beijing or the Taylor Nelson Sofres CSM diary data from Guangzhou for your reference?

You may not be aware of the new survey in Korea published by KRC Research International. (reliability: 95% +/-2.8). Nearly 50% of Korean homes receive foreign satellite channels (7 million TV homes). Channel [V] is the third most popular channel. Channel [V] is free-to-air in Korea and is the only STAR TV Channel to produce Korean specific shows. 'Mirror in Seoul' and the 'Korean Top 20' provide 7 hours a week of Korean programming. Oddly enough there is a demand for international as well as Korean shows, which is why Channel [V] is voted the preferred music channel (see above for evidence from a **third party recent objective provable verified survey**).

Onto 'Pan Regional' research. Which region are we talking about? Asia, South East Asia, South Asia, North Asia, China, India or Greater China? Total countries or just a handful of cities? There are several issues here. Neither of the recent 'regional' surveys included total China or any part of India. The seven cities covered by PAX do not represent the whole STAR TV market. I will admit that Indonesia is tough one for us—but we don't claim 24 hour distribution there.

Let's just spend a few minutes putting the rest of your figures straight. We feel it is always better to use the most up-to-date information.

Most notably, SRT is now called AC Nielsen in Taiwan, and has been for over a year. Channel [V] has 90% distribution on their peoplemeter panel.

Effective April 3rd Channel [V] will add a further 3.2 million homes to our Malaysian number so forgive us if our figures are moving too fast to keep up with.

Thank you for pointing out that the Indian figures were rather old. The latest figures from AC Nielsen for Jan/Feb are indeed much better. We can see an improvement for the upmarket AB segment for 15 to 24 year olds, up to 44% reach. Yours is 40%.

A minor point regarding the Philippines which in fact receives Channel [V] International as well as Channel [V] China. In this market it is more appropriate to offer an international service with localised programming blocks.

Finally, by publishing our syndicated distribution totals we are attempting to level the playing field. Until now we felt that claiming distribution figures of over 100 million was a little misleading if most of that figure was redistribution via cable. But if you think its acceptable, then we can do it too right?

The numbers that Channel [V] chose to make public recently simply reaffirm our leadership position in Asia (that includes India *and* China). We initiated multichannel research in Asia over six years ago and we know how difficult it has been to establish accurate figures in this market.

We are not contesting MTV's figures but simply giving the most accurate reflection of our own.

Yours sincerely,

Steve Smith
Managing Director
Channel [V] Music Networks

c.c. Owen Hughes; Rhonda Palmer; Janine Stein; James Kelly; Suzanne Miao; Simon Twiston-Davies; Normandy Madden; Maureen Sullivan; Karen Chan; Hamish Champ; Henry Parwani; Adam White; Jeff Clark-Meads, Dominic Pride

case twenty-one

Brian Rogers
IMD

"Nestlé needs entrepreneurs, not just functionally minded people," remarked Peter Brabeck, chief executive officer of Nestlé. He added, "Functional thinking keeps people from seeing business solutions." Since taking over the top post in June 1997, Brabeck encouraged managers to think differently about the company's business in order to better achieve real internal growth targets.

In contrast to external growth, which focused on expanding into new markets and broadening existing product lines via acquisitions, Brabeck emphasized real internal growth rates, because he believed that they were a better measure of Nestlé's competitiveness in the global marketplace. Internal growth involved achieving higher volumes by focusing on internally developed new products and/or renovating existing ones. Because the food industry had become fiercely competitive and margins had declined, many of Nestlé's traditional products were becoming commodities; therefore, achieving internal growth targets through innovation and renovation had become increasingly important for sustaining long-term profitability.

LC[1], a "yogurt" that Nestlé launched in 1994, symbolized what could be accomplished if managers pursued an internal growth strategy. Two of the product's internal champions, James Gallagher and Andrea Pfeifer, joined forces in an effort to grow the chilled dairy business, which led to the rollout of LC[1]. Nestlé experienced many challenges in bringing LC[1] to market, both internally and externally, and in the process, gained further insight into how the company could better coordinate its research and business-related activities.

Top management, aware of the opportunities for Nestlé if more LC[1]-type innovations occurred, pondered how to create an environment in which managers not only focused more on developing innovative ideas, but also learned how to transform their ideas into successful products.

Nestlé was the world's largest food company in 1998, with 552 factories in 81 countries. The company, which had over 8,000 brands, employed over 230,000 people worldwide and posted 1998 sales of 71.7 billion Swiss francs. (*Refer to Exhibit 1 for more detailed financial information.*) Nestlé's principal lines of business included: (1) beverages; (2) milk products, nutrition, and ice cream; (3) prepared dishes and cooking aids; (4) chocolate and confectionery; and (5) pharmaceutical products. Beverages represented 27.7% of sales; milk products, nutrition, and ice cream contributed 26.7%; the remaining lines of businesses represented 26.2%, 14.6%, and 4.8% of sales, respectively.

Yogurt products, including LC[1], were part of Nestlé's fresh dairy business, a subset of the milk products and nutrition businesses. The fresh dairy business accounted for 5% of the company's overall sales revenue in 1998.

INTERNAL GROWTH

Nestlé had real internal sales volume growth of 3.3% for all of 1998, which was below the company's target of 4%. Nestlé defined real internal growth as the growth in volume; changes in price were not reflected in the calculation or measurement of real internal growth.

During a conference in late 1998, Peter Brabeck proclaimed, "Internal growth can be structured by redefining our markets for each brand, setting up extended and ambitious targets, identifying obstacles to growth, selecting growth levers, and launching a series of growth initiatives." Brabeck also identified four pillars that he believed would drive Nestlé's internal growth worldwide:

EXHIBIT 1   Consolidated Income Statement, December 31, 1998

Consolidated Income Statement in millions of Swiss francs: CHF 1.5 = US$1	1998	1997
Sales to Customers	71,747	69,998
Cost of Goods Sold	(35,963)	(35,816)
Distribution Expenses	(4,887)	(4,713)
Marketing and Administration Expenses	(22,465)	(21,142)
Research and Development Costs	(807)	(770)
Restructuring Costs	(224)	(360)
Amortization of Intangible Assets	(301)	(140)
Trading Profit	7,100	7,057
Net Financing Costs	(1,168)	(1,056)
Net Non-Trading Items	189	(63)
Profit before Taxation	6,121	5,938
Taxation	(2,002)	(1,842)
Net Profit of Consolidated Companies	4,119	4,096
Share of Profit (Minority Interests)	(128)	(170)
Share of Results (Associated Companies)	300	256
Net Profit for the Year	4,291	4,182
As Percentage of Sales		
Trading Profit	9.9%	10.1%
Net Profit for the Year	6.0%	6.0%
Earnings per Share (in Swiss francs)		
Basic Earnings per Share	109.2	106.3
Fully Diluted Earnings per Share	108.1	104.4

By Major Product Group	Sales 1998	Sales 1997	Results 1998	Results 1997
Beverages	19,879	19,142	3,253	3,243
Milk Products, Nutrition, and Ice Cream	19,175	19,334	1,837	1,932
Prepared Dishes and Cooking Aids	18,765	17,660	1,617	1,525
Chocolate and Confectionery	10,485	10,663	976	1,054
Pharmaceutical Products	3,443	3,199	915	825
	71,747	69,998	8,598	8,579
Unallocated Items[a]			(1,498)	(1,522)
Trading Profit			7,100	7,057

[a]Mainly corporate expenses, research and development costs, amoritzation of intangible assets and restructuring costs.

Source: Nestlé Managemement Report, 1998.

1. **Operating excellence:** "We want to go from being a low cost producer to a low cost operator. We want to look for operational excellence on a regional and global level, not just on a country level."

2. **Innovation and renovation:** "The goal is to create innovative products and renovate existing lines. I want to see more proprietary technology applied when we design products. We need to overcome the 'not invented here' syndrome and use good ideas no matter where they come from."

3. **Product availability:** "Products should be available whenever, wherever, however."

4. **Communication:** "Communication with our employees, consumers and customers is vital to our success."

Innovation was particularly important because Brabeck believed that Nestlé could overcome problems of mature markets and intense competition by constantly coming up with innovative ideas and concepts like LC[1].

Brabeck also continued to emphasize performance. In the past, operational plans and budgets had been revised quarterly to reflect changes in the market, but Brabeck and other top managers decided to end such revision. This approach to business was markedly different from the past; Nestlé's top management wanted to convey the message that managers should be aggressive in their pursuit of growth opportunities.

YOGURT: AN OVERVIEW

HISTORY

The term yogurt, derived from the Turkish word "yogurut", was used in several ancient Middle Eastern languages. For some cultures, the word yogurt was even synonymous with life. Although researchers speculated that people began making and eating yogurt in various parts of the world 4,000 years ago, one of yogurt's earliest appearances in the West was in the early 16th century at the court of French Renaissance king, François I. The king, who suffered from persistent intestinal problems, was believed to have eaten yogurt to cure the ailment.

In the early 1900s, the Nobel prize-winning scientist, Ilya Metchnikoff researched how the lactic acid-producing bacteria in yogurt increased human longevity. As a result, interest in yogurt gradually began to spread throughout Europe and America.

Isaac Carasso of Spain, one of the first manufacturers of yogurt, began production in 1919. His son, Daniel, or "Danone," as his father affectionately called him, expanded his father's business, first across Europe and eventually around the entire world. After World War II, yogurt consumption increased considerably and its reputation as an exceptional source of health and nutrition spread. Yogurt also became known as a food that was pleasurable to eat. Researchers indicated that yogurt helped restore and maintain a healthy environment in the intestinal tract, aided digestion, and reduced the incidence and duration of some types of diarrhea.

Manufacturers responded by adding new varieties of yogurt, which included different flavors, low-fat offerings, super creamy yogurts, and even products targeted toward children. By the late 1990s, more than 30% of the world's population ate yogurt regularly. Worldwide per capita consumption was estimated at 4.3 pounds per year, and was expected to rise in the 21st century. (*Refer to Exhibit 2 for volume sales of yogurt around the world from 1993–1997.*)

Yogurt was primarily made from cow's milk, although milk from sheep, goats, and buffaloes could also be used. (*Refer to Exhibit 3 to see how yogurt is produced.*) In order to be considered yogurt, the final product had to contain live, active cultures. By far the most common cultures were *Lactobacillus bulgaricus* and *Streptococcus thermophilus*, but some yogurts contained additional cultures.

THE STORY OF LC[1]

In the early 1990s, the Nestlé Research Centre in Lausanne, Switzerland investigated a group of cultures called *Lactobacillus acidophilus*. Referred to internally as La-1, one of these cultures was selected for development because it had the characteristics of a probiotic agent. Probiotics were live microbial feed supplements that improved the function of the lower intestines and promoted good health.

Once in the lower intestines, La-1 helped balance the mix of aerobic and anaerobic bacteria in the intestinal flora, the area of the intestines that was important for digestion and the absorption of nutrients. However, Nestlé researchers also found the La-1 enhanced the functioning of the small intestines. They believed that by placing the La-1 strain in the small intestines, they improved the body's immune system, which was critical to disease prevention.

When Nestlé first developed La-1, there was no decision taken as to which of Nestlé's products would be the carrier for the bacteria. Although researchers knew they had come across an interesting idea, there was no immediate plan to introduce it into yogurt.

Traditional yogurt products were fermented with *Lactobacillus bulgaricus* and *Streptococcus thermophilus*, but Nestlé found that when it replaced *Lactobacillus bulgaricus* with La-1, the sensory properties of yogurt were retained. La-1 also had a high chance of surviving through the acidic part of the gastrointestinal tract, while most other yogurt cultures had no chance of survival.

A MEETING OF THE MINDS: JAMES GALLAGHER & ANDREA PFEIFER

In 1993, James Gallagher, who was the European coordinator for chilled products at the time, attended a presentation at the Nestlé Research Centre. During his visit, he had a discussion with Andrea Pfeifer, who was then a leading scientist at the Research Centre. Pfeifer mentioned to him that the research team had been working

EXHIBIT 2   Yogurt Volume Sales, Selected Countries, 1993–1997

Yogurt Volume Sales '000 tonnes	1993	1994	1995	1996	1997
Argentina	210	224	251	275	310
Australia	61	63	67	72	75
Brazil	179	209	252	314	370
Canada	87	89	87	92	93
Chile	43	71	77	83	88
China	331	392	444	532	615
Colombia	64	68	72	77	83
France	1050	1140	1200	1250	1300
Germany	690	740	720	708	705
Hong Kong, China	3	3	3	3	4
India	199	204	205	213	217
Indonesia	61	68	74	81	88
Japan	342	390	405	419	449
Malaysia	16	17	18	19	21
Mexico	176	215	139	151	153
New Zealand	12	13	13	14	15
Philippines	80	92	107	124	143
Singapore	12	13	13	14	15
South Africa	59	60	63	67	69
South Korea	118	121	125	131	135
Taiwan	17	19	20	21	21
Thailand	36	38	40	44	47
Turkey	96	99	104	106	109
USA	606	660	719	777	836
Venezuela	72	70	68	66	63
Vietnam	2	2	2	4	5

Source: Consumer International, 1998.

on cultures that could improve the immunity of the body. Gallagher, who was anxious to grow his stagnating yogurt business, was initially excited about the idea. He later recalled, "The scientific results were encouraging, and I thought we had hit upon a good idea."

Soon after his visit, the Nestlé Research Centre worked on preparing the cultures to be used in yogurt. Researchers tested the cultures repeatedly in clinical trials. Gallagher, who had also been the managing director of Chambourcy France, Nestlé's largest yogurt business, prompted his team to get the product on the French market quickly.

Nestlé organized a task force and researched prod-

uct concepts in a very short period of time, although there was some internal resistance at first. Researchers were not accustomed to working under business constraints, and initially wanted to continue researching. Gallagher felt that researchers were looking for a level of perfection that might not be necessary for a food product.

Gallagher later came up with the idea that the new product could be sold as a functional food, in part because Danone was already on the market with a health yogurt named Bio. Functional foods were foods that, by virtue of physiologically active food components, provided health benefits beyond basic nutrition.

Step 1: The pasteurized[1] milk is fortified with powdered skim milk.

Step 2: The fortified milk is homogenized.[2]

Step 3: The cultures are added (*Lactobacillus bulgaricus & Streptococcus thermophilus*)

Step 4: The culture is allowed to incubate in warm tanks.

Step 5: The mixture is cooled.

Step 6: The yogurt is placed in containers and refrigerated for immediate resale.

[1] Pasteurization: the partial sterilization of a substance at a temperature and for a period of exposure that destroys objectionable organisms without major chemical alteration of the substance.

[2] Homogenization: In milk, it is the process of breaking up fat globules into very fine particles by forcing them through minute openings.

Source: International French Daily; Webster's Ninth New Collegiate Dictionary.

Positioning the product as a functional food was a way of differentiating it from competitors. Furthermore, Nestlé had scientific results to back their claims.

When the yogurt was finally ready to be manufactured, Gallagher thought of many product names, but none were satisfactory. The names either sounded too generic, or were insufficiently different from yogurts that were already on the market. In a flash of inspiration, he decided to call his new product La-1, much to the surprise of Pfeifer and the rest of the scientific team. However, due to some unanticipated registration issues, Gallagher settled for the name LC[1]. After much deliberation, the decision was made to sell the product to consumers with the claim, "LC[1] helps your body to protect itself." (*Refer to Exhibit 4 to view an advertisement for LC[1].*)

THE LAUNCH OF LC[1] IN FRANCE

On September 10, 1994, LC[1] was launched in France. Although LC[1] initially performed well, it was not the success that Nestlé had hoped, and managers at Nestlé believed that the outcome was due to several reasons.

First, Nestlé arrived late to the marketplace with LC[1]; by the late 1980s, Nestlé's biggest competitor, Danone, had already entered the market with yogurts that suggested health-based properties. Second, consumer research revealed that while consumers like the taste of LC[1], they did not believe that it tasted better than other yogurts. Research also revealed that although some customers initially purchased the product based on its claims, their decision not to repurchase was primarily based on taste. Third, the product might have been positioned as too scientific. Nestlé suspected that the consumer did not clearly understand its beneficial properties; or worse, consumers might have embraced the idea that LC[1] was a drug instead of a palatable food product.

THE LAUNCH OF LC[1] IN GERMANY

Approximately one year after LC[1] was initially launched in France, the product was ready for launch in Germany. More testing was done and the yogurt was introduced into the market as a stirred yogurt rather than a set style yogurt.

EXHIBIT 4 LC¹ Advertisement

Source: Nestlé S.A.

Believing that scientific support and adequate communication were critical for success, Andrea Pfeifer personally made more than 180 presentations over a one-year period to promote LC¹. She added, "The biggest challenge of LC¹ was communication. I wanted to make sure that people understood the product. Furthermore, it is very important for the media to see the scientists behind the research."

LC¹ became hugely successful in Germany, and within two years of its launch, it had captured 60% of the health segment of the yogurt business. When asked why LC¹ was more successful in Germany than in France, top managers at Nestlé speculated that it was primarily due to the level of the development of the German market. There was no clear market leader in Germany, whereas in France, Danone had established a leadership position in the yogurt market. A second reason for Nestlé's success was that yogurts that made health-based claims were newer to the German market; therefore, Nestlé was able to clearly differentiate itself in the marketplace and communicate the benefit of LC¹ to consumers. In particular, Nestlé had been careful not

to pitch the product as medicinal. Third, managers believed that many German consumers simply preferred the taste of LC¹.

Shortly after the success of LC¹ in Germany, it was successfully introduced in several other European markets, Brazil, and Australia. In the meantime, James Gallagher was promoted to chief executive officer of Friskies Europe, the only European-wide product position at Nestlé. He applied the LC¹ concept of enhancing the body's natural defenses to Friskies' pet food products, and subsequently developed products that improved digestion in pets. Andrea Pfeifer was promoted to the top post at the Nestlé Research Centre.

REFLECTING ON THE SUCCESS OF LC¹

In January 2000, Evan Kaloussis, head of the Nutrition division, reflected on what he believed were key reasons for the success of LC¹:

Back in 1994, there was already an increased emphasis on nutrition. People began to view nutrition as more than dietetics; they began to consider nutrition as the key to health and well-being . . . The increase in life expectancy around the world, the changing views of the consumer, and the fact that Nestlé happened to launch a value-added product at the moment the customer was changing, contributed to our success.

Gallagher added, "A product like LC[1] is the function of seeing a good idea because you've got people around who have this risk-taking mentality and who *want* to see the ideas in research. Everything is about the follow-through. You've got to have sheer determination to make it work. You need people who can understand technical ideas and how these can be transformed into marketing ideas. These people need to be talking regularly to people in the research environment."

A challenge for Nestlé had been the tendency of local markets to develop their own objectives. The ability of local markets to resist ideas from outside had come to be known inside the company as the *Not Invented Here Syndrome.* Local markets often had their own priorities and their own projects, and it was sometimes difficult to persuade them to set aside their ideas and adopt different ideas. Gallagher believed that a possible strategy to deal with this problem was for the heads of the Strategic Business Units (SBUs) to get buy-in from zone managers, who could then in turn persuade country managers. He commented, "If you find a good idea, you've got to get it through Europe fast and worldwide fast. It's extremely difficult because everybody locally has the power to say, 'Yes, it's a good idea, but it doesn't apply here.'"

On a similar note, Andrea Pfeifer added, "In the past, R&D thought of a project, set up an experimental design, tested for results, and then conducted a second test. After all of these steps, researchers would then think about a product. Today, this is no longer possible. R&D people must talk with business people early on in the process, and people must think in terms of product concepts. They should ask, 'Where could this scientific finding be possibly used'?" In an organization that was not accustomed to working in this fashion, Pfeifer, as well as many others, saw the challenges in attempting to adapt the current system.

EXECUTING A STRATEGY FOR THE FUTURE

The success of LC[1] subsequently contributed to the decision to create the Nutrition division at Nestlé in 1997. For the most part, Nestlé organized its products into SBUs; however, the Nutrition division was considered a Strategic Business Division (SBD). Evan Kaloussis was chosen to head the Nutrition division, which reported directly to Peter Brabeck. (*Refer to Exhibit 5 to view an organizational chart.*)

Brabeck considered the Nutrition division to be of high strategic importance at Nestlé because it signified the future direction of the company. Nestlé was very committed to the vision of moving from a more agri-food business to developing foods with higher R&D content that promote good health and well-being. In line with this new focus, Nestlé began to actively explore other uses for the LC[1] bacteria or other "functional" ingredients in other food products. As a result, the concept of "performance nutrition" began to take shape.

In parallel, other changes had started to be implemented at Nestlé. For example, Brabeck began placing greater emphasis on developing a stronger sense of shared values throughout the organization. Upon taking over as CEO, he communicated the importance of real internal growth and the need to develop value-added products. He also, accordingly, prepared a document, "Blueprint for the Future," in which he detailed how the company should evolve.

Another important change at Nestlé was the increased emphasis on the business performance of managers. Managers were specifically encouraged to take more risks and develop entrepreneurial ideas. To drive home the message, Nestlé even restructured its compensation package to reward those who took initiatives to aggressively grow the respective businesses. Kaloussis added, "If you have initiative, you can define your job. Nobody will block you at Nestlé if you have an idea and you dare to move ahead."

Moreover, Nestlé attempted to further increase the proximity between R&D, the SBUs, and the markets. Kaloussis and others believed that the increased communication and coordination between these three functions were keys to what ultimately led to the meeting between James Gallagher and Andrea Pfeifer. He recalled, "Gallagher was under pressure to grow his business, and was preoccupied with how to get value-added products. It was then that he ran into Andrea, who had the key."

Understanding the need to continue developing innovative ideas, Nestlé actively considered ways to replicate the success of LC[1]. The company worked diligently to change the attitudes of its managers and to inspire them to be more business-oriented, proactive, and faster to market with innovative products. Brabeck concluded:

EXHIBIT 5 Organizational Chart, Nestlé

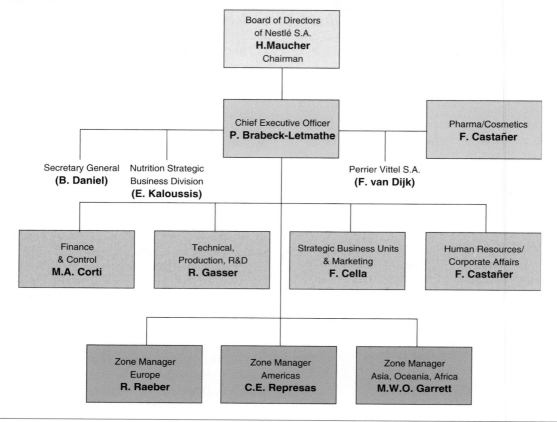

Source: Nestlé S.A.

To just keep pace in this industry, you need to change at least as fast as consumer expectations. That's renovation. *To maintain a leadership position, you also need to leapfrog, to move faster and go beyond what consumers will tell you. That's* innovation.[1]

NOTES

1. From "*Innovation and Renovation: The Nespresso Story*," an IMD case study (M 543) written by Professor Kamran Kashani and Research Associate Joyce Miller.

Nextel: Looking to the Future

C-22

case twenty-two

Bryan Brooks
Olivier Jonart
Adam Marshall
Heather Mayes
Kristen Rogstad

INTRODUCTION

On October 24, 2002, the headline to Nextel Communications, Inc.'s quarterly earnings release boasted: "Nextel Reports Record-Setting Third Quarter 2002 Results." In the release, the company highlighted a 26 percent increase in revenues and a 67 percent increase in domestic operating cash flow. Nextel also reported significant reduction of its debt burden over the period.[1] This news represented significant results considering the current economic and industry troubles.

Although the company's CFO, Paul Saleh, was quoted as saying "today's financial results show that Nextel continues to deliver on [its] business plan,"[2] investor reaction to third quarter results was not wholeheartedly optimistic. Nextel's stock on that day jumped over a dollar on the open, indicating the announcement was a positive surprise to investors. Over the course of the trading day, however, the stock faced downward pressure, ending below its preannouncement level. Obviously not everyone had the same faith in Nextel's business plan as did Paul Saleh.

The puzzle of Nextel's performance was partially wrapped up in the general uncertainty the entire wireless telecommunications industry was experiencing. The industry was maturing and appeared to be at a turning point. There were questions about how much competition the current players could withstand and about when, and if, the next generation of technology would

deliver on future growth. Nextel and the industry were taking a good look at this complex environment. To fully appreciate Nextel's present opportunities, its unique niche, and the issues facing the company, the history of the entire industry and its current problems need to be understood.

THE TELECOMMUNICATIONS INDUSTRY

In 1946, AT&T and Southwestern Bell introduced the first American commercial mobile radio–telephone service to private customers. This radio-based telephone service (MTS or Mobile Telephone Service) had neither direct dialing capabilities nor the ability for both parties to talk simultaneously (see Glossary for definitions of technical terms). This service essentially allowed a caller to use two-way radio dispatch technology (like a CB radio) to contact an operator who would connect the radio signal to a landline. MTS evolved into IMTS (Improved Mobile Telephone Service), which allowed a caller to directly dial from his or her phone and talk back and forth as if on a landline, without the need to press a button to talk as on the MTS. IMTS remained in operation in North America until the mid-1990s.[3]

Although the cellular concept and technology were known in the 1960s, development was stagnant until the late 1980s because of the high financial investment, unproven technology, and delays by the Federal Communications Commission (FCC) in making certain spectrum bandwidths available. In 1974, the FCC decided to open an additional 115-megahertz spectrum for future cellular telephone use and, in 1975, permitted Bell Systems to begin a trial cellular system. This opened the door to the first analog cellular networks that gained consumer acceptance throughout the 1980s and early 1990s.[4]

This case is intended to be used as the basis for class discussion rather than to illustrate either effective or ineffective handling of an administrative or strategic situation. We appreciate the direction of Professor Robert E. Hoskisson in the development of this case. Reprinted by permission.

Wireless telecommunications technology evolved rapidly from the first-generation analog cellular systems that were primarily used for voice service. Development of second-generation (2G) wireless technology began in the late 1980s. 2G digital infrastructure was introduced during the 1990s, and network expansion continued through the early 2000s. The 2G business focused on voice communication, with the introduction of additional value-added services such as voice mail, call waiting, and text messaging.[5]

Technological developments have improved the quality of service while decreasing costs of network deployment. Additionally, competition among service providers and device manufacturers has lowered prices and fueled a global demand for wireless services that has surpassed many analysts' expectations. As a result, the last decade saw demand for wireless telecommunication spread rapidly around the globe as services became more accessible to consumers. Subscriber growth in the United States averaged 25.3 percent over the period 1997 to 2000, reaching a customer base of approximately 110 million people (see Exhibit 1).[6]

A MATURING INDUSTRY

A trend toward industry maturity is evident in a number of ways. For example, wireless service is taking on the air of a commodity now that at least six carriers offer national flat-rate pricing plans. With wireless phone penetration currently at approximately 50 percent, usage is approaching the saturation level. At saturation level, estimated to be between 60 and 70 percent, companies will have to battle over existing market share. Also, the industry is restructuring through consolidation and alliances to expand service territory, increase brand awareness, and share the cost of technology upgrades.[7]

GOVERNMENT REGULATION

Federal Communications Commission (FCC). Established by the Communications Act of 1934, the FCC regulates interstate communications by radio, television, wire, satellite, and cable. Since passage of the Telecommunications Act of 1996, the role of the FCC has been to promote the forces of competition in determining the form of the telecommunications industry. In this pursuit, the FCC auctions radio spectrum and monitors the industry to uncover any anticompetitive behavior by carriers.[8]

A primary duty of the FCC is to regulate sharing of the airways by law enforcement, emergency agencies, radio and TV stations, cellular operators, the military, and other broadcasters. The radio spectrum has been divided among these interests to facilitate orderly transmission and to prevent interference. As cellular services took off in the 1980s, the FCC allocated spectrum for cellular carriers in each geographical region as follows: the local Bell monopoly received a share and the other share was offered to a competing carrier by lottery.[9] Since 1994, available spectrum has been allocated through competitive auctions at a high cost to wireless carriers, increasing their debt burden.

Not everyone sees the limited spectrum size as a problem, however. A movement known as Open Spectrum argues that current technology is capable of constructing transmitters that send signals over the same band of spectrum yet don't interfere with each other. If

EXHIBIT 1	United States Wireless Industry Statistics						
	1994	1995	1996	1997	1998	1999	2000
Total service revenues (in billions)	14.2	19.1	23.6	27.5	33.1	40.0	52.5
Ending subscribers (in millions)	24.1	33.8	44.0	55.3	69.2	86.0	109.5
Subscriber growth (%)	50.8	40.0	30.4	25.6	25.1	24.3	27.2
Subscriber penetration (%)	9.4	13.0	16.3	20.2	25.1	30.9	38.9
Average monthly service revenue per subscriber, including roaming revenue ($)*	59.08	54.91	50.61	46.11	44.35	42.96	44.72
Average monthly service revenue per subscriber, excluding roaming revenue ($)*	51.48	47.59	44.66	41.12	39.66	38.57	41.41

*Calculated by Standard & Poor's.

Source: Cellular Telecommunications & Internet Association.

there were no interference problem, there would be no need to auction parcels of spectrum. Implementation of such technology is expected to occur within ten years.[10]

In November 2001, the FCC announced a plan to lessen the hypercompetitive environment for wireless operators. Historically, carriers had faced an FCC-imposed spectrum cap in each market area: no organization was allowed to hold more than 45 MHz or 55 MHz in metropolitan or rural areas, respectively. The plan included the elimination of the spectrum cap in January 2003, an increase in the spectrum cap to 55 MHz in the interim, and the immediate lifting of a restriction which prevented carriers from holding different blocks of cellular licenses in overlapping Metropolitan Statistical Areas (MSAs).[11]

TECHNOLOGY: FROM 2G TO 3G

Throughout the 1990s, U.S. carriers invested heavily in deploying wireless networks to deliver 2G mobile services. The 2G wireless services included digital cellular and PCS. PCS dominates the wireless communications industry in the United States because PCS services are transmitted at lower power and higher frequencies than digital cellular voice services. U.S. wireless carriers developed 2G PCS networks based on four incompatible technology platforms: GSM, CDMA, TDMA, and iDEN. In the United States, GSM networks host 15 million subscribers; CDMA hosts 39 million; TDMA, 37.5 million; and Nextel's iDEN network hosts 7.2 million subscribers. A carrier's adoption of one of these standards depends on cost to implement, available frequencies, and the types of services the carrier wishes to provide to customers. Each of these 2G standards allows for a host of wireless services, such as call-waiting, caller ID, text messaging, data transfer, and limited mobile Internet access. The desire to improve these existing services and to offer additional, enhanced wireless services is driving competitors to move to third-generation (3G) infrastructure. These technology platforms will enable multimedia capabilities, interactive gaming, and streaming video.

As with 2G technology, the industry remains fragmented over 3G, as carriers do not agree on a single globally accepted standard. Two 3G technologies are vying to become the global standard—WCDMA and cdma2000. Most TDMA and GSM carriers will likely transition to WCDMA, but others have already announced a plan to implement cdma2000 in their networks. 3G implementation will come at a steep price for all carriers. Initially the advantage will fall to cdma2000 carriers because WCDMA will take longer to implement due to increased spectrum requirements and FCC requirements. WCDMA will also come with a higher price tag than cdma2000. However, the much larger global adoption rates for WCDMA will likely result in a greater variety of hardware at lower prices.[12]

Since the migration to 3G infrastructure will be a lengthy process, carriers are adopting intermediate technologies dubbed 2.5G. These intermediate solutions offer faster data transfer and increased voice capacity because they allow carriers to segregate data from voice transmissions. Each 2.5G solution varies from carrier to carrier, depending on the carrier's current technology and which 3G technology it is moving toward.

SUPPLIERS

Carriers rely on technology suppliers for both network infrastructure and consumer electronics, such as mobile phones, connected personal digital assistants (PDAs), and pagers. Qualcomm, a Japan-based technology firm, was the inventor of CDMA technology and holds many key patents on both CDMA and cdma2000. Ericsson pioneered TDMA technology and helped AT&T build its vast network in the United States. However, as TDMA becomes obsolete, Ericsson's importance as a supplier has diminished. For GSM and other technologies, major companies like Nokia, Motorola, Siemens, and Alcatel are among the largest firms competing to supply the world's wireless networks.

Consumer device suppliers include an even broader range of players vying to supply mobile devices that meet the various wireless network specifications. This is often done through a co-branding effort because a device without a mobile service is useless to consumers. Sony-Ericsson, Samsung, Nokia, LG Electronics, Sanyo, Kyocera, and Motorola are among the notable suppliers of mobile devices. Most carriers choose to partner with two or three suppliers for their mobile devices.

TRENDS

Subscribers. Subscriber growth took off during the 1990s and is still increasing, albeit at a slower rate. Jefferies & Co. analyst Ben Abramovitz estimated the penetration level in the United States at 48 percent as of the end of the second quarter of 2002.[13] However, penetration levels in the United States are behind those of Europe and Japan.

Average Revenue Per User. An important measure in the wireless telecommunications industry is Average Revenue Per User (ARPU). Analysts monitor this figure as a tool to evaluate trends in profitability for carriers. Industry-wide, ARPU saw steady declines throughout the 1990s as competition drove down prices. The average ARPU in the industry bottomed out at $39.43

in December 1998 and has since been increasing. Nextel has repeatedly produced the highest ARPU in the industry.

Financial markets. The burst of the telecommunications bubble did not leave wireless carriers untouched. In 2000, wireless companies began to see continuing downward pressure on their stock price (see Exhibits 2 and 3). The summer of 2002 was especially hard as concerns over lowered credit rating outlooks on the industry as a whole and high debt burdens scared investors away. Most wireless carriers will continue to face problems as they have high debt on their balance sheet and have yet to produce positive free cash flow.

Consolidation. In the face of continuing, debilitating competitive pressures, the industry is looking to consolidation to provide needed relief. Reducing the number of national players would help to lessen price pressure and bring economies of scale to the networks of those who consolidate. Various rumors of consolidation have circulated, and many of them mention as candidates these three national carriers: Cingular Wireless, AT&T Wireless, and T-Mobile. All three operate on the same GSM/GPRS technology and would be in a position to achieve cost savings and economies of scale in the event of a merger.

3G and data. As incremental penetration is slowing, carriers and equipment manufacturers are seeking future growth in new technology that will facilitate high-speed data transmission. Since network upgrades are costly, handset manufacturers are still working out "bugs," and compelling software applications have yet to surface, most carriers are only cautiously migrating to the new 3G technology. What 3G will ultimately look like and whether it will deliver promised growth fast enough for investors is yet to be seen.

COMPETITIVE LANDSCAPE

VERIZON WIRELESS

In July 1998, Bell Atlantic and GTE Corporation agreed to a merger, which was completed in June 2000. Shortly after that, Vodafone and AirTouch agreed to join forces to build a national wireless business. In April 2000, Bell Atlantic, GTE, and Alltel Corp. agreed to exchange wireless interests, which eliminated service areas that overlap each other. Soon the Federal Trade Commission (FTC) approved this merger, and in April 2000, Verizon Wireless was born. As of 2002, the newly formed company had over 31.5 million customers, revenues of more than $17.4 billion, EBITDA of $6.0 billion, and net income of $2.3 billion.[14]

The services that Verizon provides to customers include wireless service, text messaging, and wireless

---

EXHIBIT 2   Nextel Five-Year History Compared to Industry

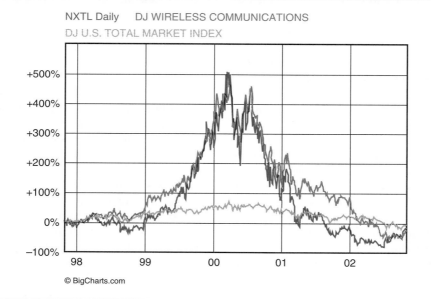

NXTL Daily   DJ WIRELESS COMMUNICATIONS
DJ U.S. TOTAL MARKET INDEX

© BigCharts.com

Source: 2002, www.bigcharts.com, October 31.

Performance during Past:	Nextel Communications Inc.	DJ Wireless Communications	DJ U.S. Total Market Index
3 Months	112.43%	40.07%	1.99%
6 Months	104.72%	−27.84%	−18.54%
Year-to-Date	2.92%	−59.31%	−23.94%
12 Months	41.89%	−55.59%	−16.06%
2 Years	−70.65%	−78.75%	−38.69%
5 Years	−14.06%	−24.17%	−5.38%

Source: 2002, Company Research, www.wsj.com, October 17.

Internet. The firm also offers business solutions to large and small clients. With the backing of parent company Verizon Communications, it is able to provide comprehensive services that cover wireless usage, home or office usage, or Internet usage. The company utilizes CDMA technology.[15] Additionally, Verizon is committed to spending over $3 billion in capital improvements to maintain and expand service.

A recent service that Verizon has unveiled is called Get It Now. This next-generation service allows customers to download games, use e-mail programs, send and receive pictures, and play music on their phones. Another service that Verizon offers with its phones is the ability to "pay as you go."[16] This service, called FreeUp®, allows users to pay for minutes and text messaging as they are used.

CINGULAR WIRELESS

Cingular Wireless is the result of a joint venture between the wireless divisions of SBC and BellSouth. This joint venture produced the second largest wireless company in the United States. In 2002, the company reaches over 22 million customers domestically, and provides service to 43 of the top 50 markets nationwide. In all, Cingular's service region covers 93 percent of the population. Revenues totaled over $14.3 billion in the most recent fiscal year, with EBITDA at $4.5 billion and net income at $1.65 billion.[17]

Services that customers can receive through Cingular include traditional wireless service, interactive messaging, and wireless Internet service (including an e-mail service). The company uses either GSM or TDMA technology to provide service to customers, depending on which part of the country the service is in. TDMA has been in existence since 1996 when it was unveiled in

Atlanta to handle the high volumes of wireless resulting from the Olympic Games that year.[18] Cingular has already launched trials of 3G technology.

Among the service plans that Cingular offers, the newest lets the customer roll over any unused minutes from the current month into the next month. Currently Cingular is the only provider to offer this option. Cingular also offers nationwide long distance and nationwide roaming with all of its wireless plans.

AT&T WIRELESS

AT&T Bell Laboratories invented cellular phone service in 1947. The firm's first commercially available cellular systems, however, did not appear until 1984, in Chicago and Washington, D.C. In the early 1990s, a company called McCaw Cellular Communications created a technology that made it possible for wireless customers to have automatic roaming. In 1994, AT&T purchased McCaw Cellular, eventually transforming it into the AT&T Wireless that exists today. Other innovations that came from AT&T include Digital One Rate, the first plan to offer no roaming or long-distance fees and two-way text messaging.[19]

AT&T Wireless is the third largest wireless company in the United States, serving almost 20 million customers. AT&T Wireless offers many wireless solutions, including voice, data, Internet, and text services. It holds licenses to provide service to over 99 percent of the country, and service is enabled in almost 8,000 cities in North America. Additionally, AT&T Wireless provides service in over 100 countries across the globe. Revenues in 2001 were in excess of $13.6 billion; EBITDA was approximately $3.1 billion; net income totaled $598 million.[20]

AT&T Wireless is able to offer more than just wireless service to its customers through its relationship with parent company AT&T Corporation. Using this relationship, like other wireless providers, it can bundle other telecommunications services to the customer, which increases convenience and lowers cost to the customer. The additional services that can be provided include long-distance service and Internet service.

The newest service from AT&T Wireless, called mLife, offers a phone that will give customers more flexibility and opportunities to access information more easily. This service offers traditional wireless service, two-way text messaging, and access to the wireless Internet. The technology used to offer these wireless solutions is a GSM/GPRS (General Packet Radio Service) network.[21]

SPRINT PCS

Sprint PCS is the fourth largest wireless carrier, with 16.7 million customers. Sprint PCS boasts the largest all-digital network, covering over 87 percent of the country. Sprint PCS has chosen this all-digital network because of the "clarity and quality of calls on its system."[22] One benefit of this all-digital network is the ability to give all customers nationwide long-distance phone service at no extra charge. Revenues in the most recently completed fiscal year were in excess of $9.7 billion, with EBITDA of $1.5 billion and a net loss of $637 million.[23]

Sprint PCS has an additional advantage in providing service to customers through bundling its wireless products with those of parent company Sprint. Included are home or office long-distance telephone service, home or office Internet service, and wireless Internet options. A consumer choosing to purchase more than one of these services from Sprint PCS will receive a discount on his or her total bill.

Sprint PCS uses CDMA technology for its phones, which is billed as "the most advanced digital wireless communications technology available."[24] CDMA offers high security, high voice quality, and increased call and data capacity. The newest service that Sprint PCS offers customers is the PCS Vision$_{SM}$ plan, which provides wireless service that acts as more than just a phone or pager. The new phones (using 3G technology) are enabled to make phone calls, receive pages and text messages, browse the World Wide Web, take pictures, and send and receive pictures. This service was launched nationwide in August 2002.

T-MOBILE USA

The history of T-Mobile USA began in 1994, when two companies, General Cellular and Pacific Northwest Cellular, merged to form Western Wireless. Over the next two years, Western Wireless launched wireless ser-

vice in a number of cities. The service was called Voice-Stream Wireless. In 1999, VoiceStream Wireless was spun off from Western Wireless and extended its coverage by merging with Omnipoint and Aerial Communications. Over the next few years, VoiceStream merged several more times (with PowerTel and MobileStar Network Corp.), and in 2001, German firm Deutsche Telekom AG acquired VoiceStream. In September 2002, VoiceStream was converted to the T-Mobile brand name, aligning it with Deutsche Telekom's European brand.[25]

T-Mobile USA has over 8 million customers domestically. Its service is available in 90 percent of the top 50 markets in the United States, with a reach of over 95 percent of the population. Together with parent T-Mobile International, the company includes over 72 million customers worldwide. T-Mobile International was the first company to offer service on both sides of the Atlantic under the same brand name. Domestic revenues for the most recent fiscal year were $1.9 billion; domestic EBITDA loss was $388 million; net loss was $3.0 billion.[26]

T-Mobile USA provides some of the most advanced communication services currently available. Services offered include two-way text messaging, AOL Instant Messenger, and high-speed wireless data transfer. The firm is also the exclusive provider of a PDA that will be enabled for voice calls as well as full-color Internet service.

T-Mobile USA uses GSM technology, a standard currently used by 70 percent of the world. This means that when T-Mobile customers are traveling globally, they can use their regular phone. For its high-speed data service, the company uses 2.5G GPRS, which allows customers to access the Internet and send/receive faxes through their wireless phones. Another new technology that T-Mobile is attempting to develop is Wi-Fi broadband Internet service. This service will provide broadband Internet access at such locations as coffee shops and airports.[27]

The service plan that T-Mobile USA offers is called Get More From Life® and is intended to provide "more minutes, more features, and more service" than competitors' plans. Through this plan, T-Mobile USA offers such services as free text messaging, unlimited weekend calling, and no roaming charges.

COMPANY HISTORY

Nextel's roots were formed in the 1930s when mobile radio systems were created to connect emergency personnel and taxi drivers to a centralized dispatch (see Exhibit 4 for a chronology of company history). This

Case 22 / Nextel: Looking to the Future

1987	Morgan O'Brien and Brian D. McAuley found Fleet Call to develop mobile telephone service on specialized mobile radio (SMR) network frequencies. Because SMR networks can be converted to digital signaling, which requires much less bandwidth than analog signaling, limited radio bands can be used to handle thousands of calls.
1987	Recognizing that SMR will eventually be able to compete with cellular phone systems, O'Brien and McAuley begin purchasing SMR properties.
1988	By now, Fleet Call has acquired ten mobile radio companies, and the company continues to focus on acquiring SMR licenses. O'Brien and McAuley approach Motorola, the leading SMR company, with their plans to build a new communications network based on SMR frequencies.
1988	Motorola agrees to partner with Fleet Call in the venture, providing the expertise to build portions of the new system in exchange for an equity stake in Fleet Call. By now, 74 mobile radio companies in major metropolitan areas have been acquired.
February 1991	The Federal Communications Commission (FCC) grants Fleet Call permission to build its new SMR system.
1991	Northern Telecom, a Canadian telecommunications network equipment manufacturer, agrees to join Fleet Call and Motorola in the construction of the new network. Japan's Matsushita agrees to supply handsets, or subscriber units, for the venture.
January 1992	Fleet Call lists publicly, floating 7.5 million shares. The $112.5 million raised is used to construct Fleet Call's first network cell site in Los Angeles, California.
December 1992	By merging with mobile radio company Dispatch Communications, Fleet Call secures coverage in nine of the ten largest U.S. markets.
1992	Comcast, a leading U.S. cable television operator, invests $230 million in Fleet Call for a 30 percent stake in the SMR venture.
March 1993	Fleet Call changes its name to Nextel Communications.
August 1993	Service in California is officially online.
February 1994	MCI Communications Corp. agrees to purchase a 17 percent stake in Nextel in exchange for certain marketing rights.
July 1994	The company exchanges several of its Midwestern and Western SMR properties for a 37 percent share of CenCall Communications, Inc.
August 1994	Nextel merges with Questar Telecom, Inc., as well as with a unit of Advanced MobilCom, Inc. that holds operating rights in Utah, Nevada, and other mountain states. Motorola grants Nextel its SMR licenses for a larger stake in the company.
April 1995	Craig O. McCaw, considered a trailblazer in the wireless telecommunications industry, agrees to invest up to $1.1 billion in Nextel.
January 1996	Nextel acquires Dial Page, Inc., the largest SMR provider in the southeastern United States Timothy Donahue, a former AT&T Wireless executive, is hired as president.
March 1996	Former MCI president Daniel F. Akerson is hired as chairman and CEO.
September 1996	Nextel introduces the Nextel phone, based on Motorola's new iDEN technology, which incorporates digital cellular, two-way radio, and alphanumeric paging technology in a single unit. The iDEN service is officially offered in Chicago, Illinois.
1996	Sales total $332.9 million.
March 1997	A new pricing program that rounds calls to the nearest second is launched, along with Nextel's first national advertising campaign.

September 1997	McCaw International Ltd., a wholly owned subsidiary of Nextel, changes its name to Nextel International, Inc. It oversees operations in Canada, Mexico, the Philippines, Indonesia, Argentina, Brazil, Japan, Shanghai, and Peru.
1997	Sales jump 122 percent to $738.8 million. During the year, Nextel adds 970,400 digital customers in the United States. Although it is one of the fastest growing wireless companies in the United States, Nextel has not yet reached profitability.
1998	By now, iDEN digital wireless service is offered in Minnesota, Kansas, Oklahoma, Texas, Florida, Utah, Ohio, Arizona, Washington, New Hampshire, South Carolina, North Carolina, and Michigan. Nextel Business Networks is launched, as is the Nextel i600 phone, a smaller and lighter model of its original unit.
1999	Nextel announces Nextel wireless data services, which integrates wireless voice, data, and messaging. To further its pursuit of providing nationwide service, Nextel acquires the 2,000 towers of SpectraSite Communications, Inc. Nextel enters into an agreement with Microsoft to deliver wireless access on an MSN portal. Akerson resigns and is replaced as president and CEO by Tim Donahue.
January 2000	Nextel introduces the i700plus Internet-ready phone nationwide.
April 2000	Nextel Online, a wireless Internet solution for business, is launched. The firm announces Nextel Worldwide, the largest all-digital wireless coverage in the United States, with operations in more than 65 countries. Nextel signs its five millionth subscriber.

Source: Gale Group, 2002, Nextel Communications, Inc. chronology, Business and Company Resource Center.

mobile radio system used transceivers dispersed throughout a market that would allow transmission to switch from antenna to antenna as a radio or phone moved throughout the area. As technology advanced, the system became practical for the larger consumer market, and the FCC stepped in to limit competition in each market to only two companies in hopes of protecting the fledgling industry. By the early 1980s, this FCC protection had created a strong duopoly system dominated by large, established telephone companies such as the "Baby Bells" and GTE. In 1984, the FCC chose to eliminate the duopoly system in favor of more open competition. To protect the limited cellular frequencies from overcrowding, the FCC supported the development of specialized mobile radio (SMR) frequencies, which effectively broke existing national frequencies into local or regionalized frequencies. The rights to these SMR frequencies were then offered for sale.[28]

One of the people most interested in buying SMR frequencies was Morgan O'Brien. O'Brien entered the wireless telecommunications industry in 1987 and established a sizable reputation as a telecommunications lawyer representing SMR operators in their drive to obtain SMR frequencies. O'Brien joined forces with accounting executive Brian D. McAuley and together they established Fleet Call, Inc. Initially, Fleet Call

focused only on purchasing mobile radio companies in order to develop a network of SMR licenses in large regional markets. O'Brien and McAuley were just beginning to develop a plan that would change the wireless communications landscape.[29]

ENTER MOTOROLA

Motorola was both the dominant radio system producer in the SMR industry and a major player in the SMR frequency network. Fearing Motorola's power, O'Brien and McAuley decided to present their plans to use existing SMR frequencies to develop a new communications network to Motorola chairman George Fisher. SMR operations had long been one of Motorola's strengths, and the changes proposed by Fleet Call would likely radically change the SMR business, which might lead Motorola to use its considerable clout to put a stop to O'Brien and McAuley's plans. Not surprisingly, O'Brien and McAuley went into their meeting with Mr. Fisher with considerable trepidation.[30]

Upon hearing their plans, not only did Mr. Fisher not object, he saw considerable promise in their vision of the future of the SMR industry. Fisher wanted Motorola to be a part of this future and proposed a partnership with Fleet Call wherein Motorola, as an equity partner, would act as the primary supplier of

Case 22 / Nextel: Looking to the Future

parts for the new network. This unforeseen partnership was key to the success of Fleet Call.[31]

GOING DIGITAL

By the end of the 1980s, Fleet Call, Inc. owned 74 mobile radio businesses in six of the largest markets in the country. Its primary business remained the operation of radio dispatch networks to some 120,000 subscribers. Fleet Call's network primarily served state and local agencies and businesses using existing radio bands. As the company entered the 1990s, however, it was prepared to introduce a new technology that would change both its primary business operations and the face of wireless communications.[32]

Prior to the 1990s, SMR frequency use was dominated by antiquated analog technology. These systems significantly limited the amount of traffic a network could carry. In April 1990, Fleet Call presented the FCC with a proposal to introduce a digital communications system used on SMR radio bands, and by February 1991, the FCC had unanimously approved the proposal. The digital technology Fleet Call adopted was TDMA, which allowed more capacity to be carried over the existing networks by filling the statistically predictable breaks in conversations to share capacity with multiple calls.[33]

With a green light to develop its new digital communications network, Fleet Call expanded its alliance network. Motorola would provide parts needed to build the network, as would Northern Telecom, a Canadian company; Matsushita, a Japanese electronics firm, would develop handsets for the new network. Fleet Call used the capital and equipment it received from its alliance partners, roughly $345 million, along with $230 million invested by cable giant Comcast (itself a cellular provider), and $112.5 million it raised in a 7.5-million-share IPO to fund the development of the network. By May 1992, a local network was complete in the Los Angeles area and was prepared for launch.[34]

The new system could provide services ranging from mobile telephone to two-way radio to alphanumeric paging and messaging. This allowed customers to get in one bill what they used to get in three. The geographic size of California, coupled with heavy car travel in the market, prompted the realization that providing seamless service throughout California was necessary to satisfy these demanding customers. This drive for coverage was taken to the national level in December 1992, when Fleet Call merged with Dispatch Communications, giving the company coverage in nine of the nation's ten largest markets and a potential customer base of 95.5 million. Despite all of its potential, though, Fleet Call had yet to offer wireless services to the general public and wouldn't for nearly another year.[35]

THE NAME CHANGE

Fleet Call, Inc. stood on the verge of revolutionizing the nation's wireless communications industry. However, as the company began to test its new system throughout California, using only a limited number of customers, it became apparent that a new brand name must be established. "Fleet Call" seemed an inappropriate throwback to the days of radio dispatch. As the company moved in a new direction, guided by new technology, a new name seemed appropriate; thus, Nextel was born.[36]

In August 1993, after honing billing services and trafficking patterns during test runs in California, Nextel officially went live. Once Nextel had its digital network up and running, it turned its focus to expanding its coverage. Four mergers in 1994 significantly expanded the company's reach. First, a merger with Questar Telecom expanded Nextel further in California and into Utah and Nevada. Next, a merger with Rocky Mountain and Midwestern SMR gave Nextel a 37 percent share in what would become OneComm, opening up much of the mountain states and the Midwest. A subsequent merger with PowerFone Holdings gave Nextel access to SMR frequencies throughout much of the Midwest. Most important, however, was an exchange with Motorola that further linked the two companies. In exchange for a larger equity stake in the company, Motorola agreed to provide Nextel with its SMR licenses in 21 states, encompassing 180 million potential users. Nextel was now poised to provide seamless nationwide coverage.[37]

At this point, Nextel stood alone atop the digital communications market. Its competitors in the cellular market were now driving to develop national presence through mergers and shared marketing. Atop the cellular heap stood AT&T, which, through a merger with McCaw Communications, had created a national network of cellular customers and could provide access to long-distance services. To compete, Nextel entered into an alliance with MCI in February 1994. Nextel now had the power of the nationally prominent MCI brand name, an extensive national network, and a superior platform in Motorola's Integrated Radio System, MIRS. Moving forward, these two alliances continued to be central to the success of all three parties, giving Motorola an outlet for its new technology, MCI access to millions of wireless customers, and Nextel the ability to provide leading wireless network services.[38]

NEXTEL NATIONAL NETWORK

As Nextel entered the second half of the 1990s, the company was poised for significant growth. The company's management team was now led by president

Timothy Donahue, formerly of AT&T Wireless Communications, and chairman and CEO Daniel F. Akerson, formerly of MCI. Craig McCaw and the McCaw family shocked the wireless world by investing $1 billion in Nextel. McCaw and his company were early leaders in wireless communications and had been acquired by Nextel competitor AT&T in 1994. Building on these three events, Nextel led the wireless industry by introducing the Nextel National Network, seamlessly linking Nextel services across the country and eliminating roaming fees.[39]

The Nextel National Network signaled the company's dedication to its customers and gave Nextel a market leader position with much sought-after business travelers. Nextel furthered this advantage by changing its pricing structure to charge calls to the nearest second, rather than the next-highest minute. Nextel was also able to introduce Motorola's new iDEN technology, which provided digital wireless services, alphanumeric paging, and two-way radio service, called Nextel Direct Connect®, bundled into a single handset. These events helped Nextel reach its millionth subscriber in October 1997.[40]

The Direct Connect® feature, in particular, provided Nextel with a new competitive advantage. Nextel phones could be used as long-distance walkie-talkies, something other wireless companies were not offering. This feature offers multiple advantages:

- Instant access: Pressing a simple button opens the local area Nextel customers network
- Value: Using Direct Connect® does not use up cellular minutes
- Control: No one but the user has access to his or her Direct Number
- Privacy: For regular cell phone calls, Direct Connect® can be set on vibration mode

However, there are some limitations to this feature. First, both parties must own a Nextel phone and must subscribe to a Nextel calling plan. Also, only the more advanced, more expensive phones have the ability to support Direct Connect®. Finally, all parties must be located in the same local calling area. While Nextel's Direct Connect® feature considerably enhanced the National Network offerings, its success is still to be seen.

In January 1998, Nextel expanded its product offerings with the lighter, more compact i600 phone from Motorola. The phone provided vibration alert, an optional second line, nation-wide caller ID, and three-way calling. By March of that year, the Nextel National Network covered 80 percent of the nation, and by June the subscriber list reached two million.[41]

Beginning in mid-1998, the wireless telecom industry began to garner considerable attention throughout the investment community as the size of the wireless market continued to grow and the technology supporting it improved. Nextel benefited from this new interest and saw its stock price increase approximately 450 percent from its low of $18.06 in the third quarter of 1998 to its peak of $159.63 in March 2000. This dramatic increase was followed by an equally dramatic fall as the wireless telecom sector experienced the now famous "bubble." Nextel's stock reached its all-time low of $4.34 in April 2002. During this time Nextel also saw a decline in its new customer growth and increasingly fierce competition. As competition increased so did the need for ever-evolving technology and more efficient ways to serve wireless customers. Nextel entered the new millennium under extreme pressure and with considerable uncertainty. (For additional information on Nextel's historical performance, see Exhibits 5–8.)

NEXTEL TODAY

Although Nextel is one of the smaller national players in the wireless telecommunications industry, the company is well positioned to face its future. Nextel's technology is both very effective and state-of-the-art. Nextel has the largest potential customer base in the United States, with a network covering over 230 million people (of whom 9.64 million are subscribers) and 197 of the 200 largest American markets. The company and its affiliates offer consumers a four-in-one package as a standard product: Digital Cellular, Direct Connect®, Mobile Messaging (Internet-based two-way messaging), and Wireless Web (provides access to office or personal e-mail, wireless-enabled Internet sites, and company databases).[42]

TECHNOLOGY

Nextel's partnership with Motorola remains central to the company's success. Motorola's all-digital iDEN technology is highly compatible with Nextel's four services. Furthermore, in 2001, Nextel partnered with Motorola to launch the first JavaScript technology usable through a wireless phone. This technology allows business professionals to customize their phones with the latest office tools and network applications.

Also in 2001, iBoard was launched for Nextel customers. iBoard allows its users to write e-mails and manage address books and calendars from their cell phone with the help of a foldaway keyboard. By the end of 2002, Nextel plans to collapse all these services into one product, the handheld Blackberry™ device. It will be fully wireless and will include all-digital cellular, Direct Connect® digital walkie-talkie service, text and numeric messaging, e-mail, Java technology, and Nextel Wireless Web.[43]

Case 22 / Nextel: Looking to the Future

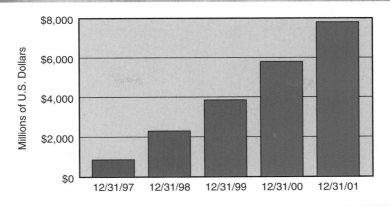

Source: 2002, www.wsj.com, October 17.

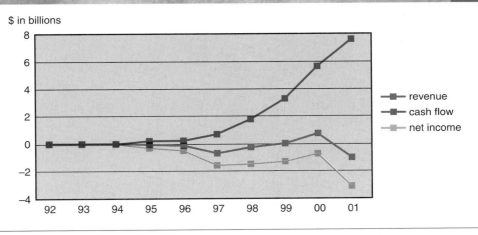

Source: 2002, Nextel Communications, Inc. Stock Evaluator, www.quicken.com, November 1.

$ in millions	1992	1993	1994	1995	1996	1997	1998	1999	2000	2001
Revenue	53	67.9	83.7	225.2	332.9	738.9	1846.8	3326	5714	7689
Net Income	−9.6	−56.9	−125.8	−331.2	−556.0	−1568	−1519	−1270	−711.0	−3094
Cash Flow	16.3	1.5	−29.2	−91.3	−149.4	−724.5	−322.4	−49	734	−1077

Source: 2002, Nextel Communications, Inc. Stock Evaluator, www.quicken.com, November 1.

EXHIBIT 8   Nextel Financial Data (Previous Five Years)

	12/31/97	12/31/98	12/31/99	12/31/00	12/31/01
Operating Revenues	739	2,295	3,786	5,714	7,689
Radio Service	—	—	—	—	—
Equipment	—	—	—	—	—
Total Revenue	739	2,295	3,786	5,714	7,689
Cost of Revenues	289	1,218	1,579	2,172	2,869
Sell./Gen./Admin.	862	1,297	1,672	2,278	3,020
Restr./Impairment	—	—	—	—	1,769
Depreciation	526	832	1,004	1,265	1,746
Cost Eqpt. Sales	—	—	—	—	—
Cost Radio Service	—	—	—	—	—
Corporate/SARs	—	—	—	—	—
Total Expenses	1,677	3,347	4,255	5,715	9,404
Operating Income	(938)	(1,052)	(469)	(1)	(1,715)
Interest Expense	(408)	(656)	(878)	(1,245)	(1,403)
Other, Net	36	(3)	49	502	(111)
Income before Taxes	(1,309)	(1,711)	(1,298)	(744)	(3,229)
Income Taxes	259	(192)	(28)	(33)	(135)
Income after Taxes	(1,568)	(1,519)	(1,270)	(711)	(3,094)
Preferred Dividends	(29)	(149)	(192)	(209)	(233)
Net Available to Common, before Extraordinary Items	(1,597)	(1,668)	(1,462)	(920)	(3,327)
Extraordinary Item	(46)	(133)	(68)	(104)	469
Net Available to Common, Including Extraordinary Items	(1,643)	(1,801)	(1,530)	(1,024)	(2,858)
Average Shares (basic)	498.64	557.00	639.00	756.00	778.00
Earnings per Share (basic), before Extraordinary Items	(3.203)	(2.995)	(2.288)	(1.217)	(4.276)
Earnings per Share (basic), Including Extraordinary Items	(3.295)	(3.233)	(2.394)	(1.355)	(3.674)
Average Shares (diluted)	498.64	557.00	639.00	756.00	778.00
Earnings per Share (diluted), before Extraordinary Items	(3.203)	(2.995)	(2.288)	(1.217)	(4.276)
Earnings per Share (diluted), Including Extraordinary Items	(3.295)	(3.233)	(2.394)	(1.355)	(3.674)

Source: 2002, Company Research, www.wsj.com, October 17.

So far Nextel has postponed implementation of 2.5G or 3G communication technology. In 2001, Nextel considered upgrading to 3G technology, following the industry pattern. The estimated cost of adopting Qual-comm, Inc.'s cdma2000 3G technology in 2003/2004 would have been about $5 billion. However, Nextel already has a heavy debt load. Currently, managers believe the firm can continue upgrading its robust iDEN platform. This strategy will allow Nextel to postpone these very costly investments until 2004/2005 and to keep its costs to upgrade to 3G to an estimated $3 billion, a savings of 40 percent.[44]

By building on iDEN with Motorola, Nextel seems to have achieved a level of technical performance on par with its major competitors, all of which have begun their move toward 3G. However, some experts are wondering if Nextel will be able to keep up as 3G technology becomes more effective. Currently, the company is biding its time and waiting for standardization in the 3G technology. Reinforcing that strategy, Nextel and Motorola have an agreement with Qualcomm, Inc. to eventually develop Direct Connect® compatibility with cdma2000.

One significant change related to Nextel's migration to 3G will be a decreased reliance on Motorola. Currently, Nextel is dependent on Motorola for the entirety of its technology from network equipment to handsets. The move toward 3G will allow the company to work with more infrastructure partners, providing the company with better leverage with suppliers. Looking further into the future, Nextel has approached manufacturers like Flarion about a 4G technology. Depending on the evolution of the industry, Nextel might even choose to leapfrog 3G and move directly to 4G technology.[45]

TARGETED CUSTOMERS

Nextel's primary focus is on attracting professional users. The company prides itself on serving over 80 percent of America's *Fortune* 500 companies, as well as several government organizations. Indeed, 90 percent of Nextel customers are business users, and Nextel focuses its communication on demonstrating that its products and services provide a high return on investment to its users. It also advertises its partnerships with other technology leaders like Microsoft and IBM, promoting itself as a state-of-the-art solution provider for communications issues.[46]

More precisely, Nextel is targeting the following customer segments, with services and price packaging tailored for each:

- Transportation and logistics
- Government and education
- Financial services
- Manufacturing
- Professional services
- Field sales and service[47]

Nextel also serves small businesses and personal accounts. These markets, however, do not enjoy the same level of performance. They can obtain the same basic products and services, but with low customization and at a set price. Customer service is also not emphasized as much as with the larger accounts.

DISTRIBUTION

In late 1998, Nextel turned its attention to developing a distribution channel that could expand its access to the customer. To stay competitive, Nextel sought lower cost alternatives and options that would allow the company to maintain a focus on its core competencies of developing and managing a wireless network. To provide retail sales, a distribution agreement with national retailer Let's Talk Cellular & Wireless and a retail agreement with Office Depot were secured.[48] Nextel continued to expand its retail partnerships, and, by 2001, the company had expanded its retail presence to include some 1,600 authorized dealers and 5,000 authorized Nextel storefronts. The year 2001 also saw the acquisition of Let's Talk Cellular & Wireless, and, for the first time, Nextel directly entered the retail market with 200 newly named Nextel stores.[49]

To reach the general consumer, the company created a direct marketing strategy built around targeted telephone sales and Internet sales. In 2001, Nextel decided to outsource the TeleSales function, allowing the company to leverage the abilities of telemarketing specialists and lower overhead costs. This decision resulted in a 209 percent increase in year over year phone sales through the TeleSales channel. Nextel's web operations not only provide the latest Nextel offerings, but also give customers access to support services. Web sales grew by 240 percent in 2001, making web sales the most efficient of Nextel's distribution channels.[50] As mentioned earlier, two specialized sales teams serve vital large account customers, providing personal service to key business and enterprise customers. The company's vital enterprise customers were served by a well-trained Direct Sales Staff, who effectively captured 80 percent of *Fortune* 500 companies. The primary object of the Direct Sales Staff by 2001 had become growing existing accounts. To further segment and better serve large industry customers, a Data Sales team was developed in 2001 to directly serve the needs of valued industries. The team's goal was to target customer needs and provide specialized solutions to customers in the transportation, government, and education sectors.[51]

THE FUTURE FOR NEXTEL?

While Nextel has long held a competitive advantage over other carriers with its proprietary Direct Connect® service, competitors are quickly evolving to address the Direct Connect® advantage. A direct threat is a service called "push-to-talk," which is comparable to instant messaging on a computer. The difference is that the user, instead of typing the message, speaks.[52] With Nextel facing this impending technology migration, will it still be able to compete without this advantage?

Nextel Communications is at a crossroads. The company cannot simply watch as larger carriers copy its direct service features and push down prices in this profitable segment. To survive in this cutthroat industry, managers must make big decisions regarding what to do in the "push-to-talk" market as well as meeting other challenges by competitors.

GLOSSARY

1XRTT A transitional 2.5G technology for CDMA networks which will enable CDMA providers to offer value-added services such as voice recognition, two-way messaging, data services (weather, sports, stock quotes), location-based m-commerce (distributing ads to handsets), and interactive gaming.

2G The second generation of wireless technology characterized by the first networks deploying digital technology. 2G networks have the capacity to provide advanced voice services such as voice mail, caller ID, call forwarding, and short messaging. GSM, TDMA, CDMA, and iDEN are the four major 2G technologies deployed in the United States.

2.5G The intermediate, transitional technology platforms that enable "always on" connections and the transmission of limited data services via wireless. The main 2.5G standards are GPRS and 1XRTT.

3G The third generation of wireless technology, beyond cellular and PCS. It combines mobile technology with high data transmission capacity, enabling multimedia applications. Under the aegis of the International Telecommunications Union, the universal mobile telecommunications system (UMTS) was adopted that enables transition to 3G from all major existing platforms through transitional (2.5G) technology.

4G Descriptions of fourth generation wireless networks vary, however, analysts predict that 4G will be 50 times faster than 3G technology and enable a seamless combination of existing 2G wireless networks with LAN (local area networks) or Bluetooth (short-range radio technology). 4G networks are not expected until between 2005 and 2011.

Bandwidth A measure of two characteristics of an electronic transmission: range and capacity. Bandwidth describes the range of electrical frequencies, from short to long waves, that a device can handle without distortion: the higher the bandwidth, the better the quality of the voice or data transmission. It also describes the capacity of a channel, which determines what kinds of communications can be carried on it. A voice-grade bandwidth is four kilohertz.

CDMA (Code Division Multiple Access) A digital cellular system technology invented by Qualcomm, Inc. that features up to ten times the capacity of traditional analog wireless technologies.

cdma2000 A 3G wireless standard that most carriers offering CDMA service plan to adopt.

Digital Electronic equipment that uses discrete digital signals (a series of 0s and 1s), as opposed to an analog signal (a variable electronic signal).

GPRS (General Packet Radio Service) A transitional 2.5G technology for GSM and TDMA networks expected to transition to WCDMA for their 3G platform. GPRS service allows continuous connections to the Internet and can handle e-mails and streaming video.

GSM (Global System for Mobile Communications) The most widely used digital cellular standard, this was adopted by the European Union. It is similar to TDMA.

Handset The part of the telephone terminal through which the user speaks and listens. In the case of a portable phone, the handset is the entire unit.

iDEN (integrated Dispatch Enhanced Network) An enhanced TDMA standard developed by Motorola that provides users with the additional capability of two-way radio service over an iDEN network. Rather than adopting a completely different technology standard, iDEN enables the integration of traditional dispatch radio technology and digital cellular communication. Nextel is the sole carrier utilizing iDEN.

PCS (Personal Communications Services) A term encompassing a wide range of digital wireless mobile technologies, chiefly two-way paging and cellular-like phone services. These services are transmitted at lower power and higher frequencies than cellular digital voice service.

Roaming Traveling outside a carrier's local network.

TDMA (Time Division Multiple Access) A digital cellular technology that offers a threefold increase in capacity over analog technology.

WCDMA A 3G wireless technology standard to which current TDMA and GSM carriers will ultimately transition.

Notes

1. 2002, Nextel Communications, Inc., Press release: Nextel reports record-setting third quarter 2002 results, October 24.
2. Ibid.
3. T. Farley, 2002, Mobile telephone history, digital wireless basics, http://www.telecomwriting.com.
4. Ibid.
5. C. Shere and K. D. Abreu, 2001, Telecommunications: Wireless, *Standard & Poor's Industry Surveys*, November 1, 24.
6. Ibid., 1.
7. Ibid.
8. Cara Cunningham, 2000, Wireless crossroad, *Red Herring*, 83.
9. Ibid.
10. Lee Gomes, 2002, Visionaries see a day when radio spectrum isn't a scarce commodity, *Wall Street Journal*, September 30, B1.
11. Federal Communications Commission, 2001, FCC announces wireless spectrum cap to sunset effective January 1, 2003, November 1.
12. Shere and Abreu, Telecommunications: Wireless, 6.
13. Ben Abramovitz, 2002, Wireless Telecom Services Quarterly Preview, July.
14. 2002, Financial Performance—Verizon Wireless.
15. 2002, Welcome to Verizon Wireless.
16. Ibid.
17. 2002, Cingular Wireless.
18. Ibid.
19. 2002, AT&T Wireless—About Us.
20. 2002, AT&T Wireless 2001 Annual Wireless.
21. 2002, AT&T Wireless—About Us.
22. 2002, About Sprint PCS.
23. 2002, Sprint 2001 Annual Report—Financial Highlights.
24. 2002, About Sprint PCS.
25. 2002, T-Mobile—About Our Company.
26. 2002, VoiceStream Investor Relations.
27. 2002, T-Mobile—About Our Company.
28. Gale Group, 2002, Nextel Communications, Inc. history, Business and Company Resource Center.
29. Ibid.
30. Ibid.
31. Ibid.
32. Ibid.
33. Ibid.
34. Ibid.
35. Ibid.
36. Ibid.
37. Ibid.
38. Ibid.
39. Ibid.
40. Ibid.
41. Ibid.
42. 2002, http://www.nextel.com/about/corporateinfo/profile.shtml, October 28.
43. Ibid.
44. Dan Meyer, 2002, Nextel's technology waiting game, *RCR Wireless News*, June 10.
45. Ibid.
46. 2002, http://www.nextel.com/about/enterprise/corporate/index.shtml, October 28.
47. Ibid.
48. 2002, http://www.nextel.com/about/enterprise/corporate/index.shtml, October 28.
49. 2001, Nextel Communications, Inc. Annual Report, Targeted sales and distribution.
50. Ibid.
51. Ibid.
52. 2002, http://www.wirelessdevnet.com/symbian/rb_30.html, November 21.

Pacific Cataract and Laser Institute: Competing in the LASIK Eye Surgery Market*

case twenty-three

John J. Lawrence
Linda J. Morris
University of Idaho

Dr. Mark Everett, clinic coordinator and Optometric Physician (OP) of the Pacific Cataract and Laser Institute (PCLI) office in Spokane, Washington, looked at the ad that Vancouver, Canada based Lexington Laser Vision (LLV) had been running in the Spokane papers and shook his head. This was not the first ad nor the only clinic advertising low-priced LASIK eye surgeries. Dr. Everett just could not believe that doctors would advertise and sell laser eye surgery based on low price as if it were a stereo or a used car. The fact that they were advertising based on price was bad enough, but the price they were promoting—$900 for both eyes—was ridiculous. PCLI and its cooperating optometric physicians would not even cover their variable cost if they performed the surgery at that price. A typical PCLI customer paid between $1750 and $2000 per eye for corrective laser surgery. While Dr. Everett knew that firms in Canada had several inherent cost advantages, including a favorable exchange rate and regulatory environment, he could not understand how they could undercut PCLI's price so much without compromising service quality.

PCLI was a privately held company that operated a total of eleven clinics throughout the northwestern United States and provided a range of medical and surgical eye treatments including laser vision correction. Responding to the challenge of the Canadian competitors was one of the points that would be discussed when Dr. Everett and the other clinic coordinators and surgeons who ran PCLI met next month to discuss policies and strategy. Dr. Everett strongly believed that the organization's suc-cess was based on surgical excellence and compassioned concern for its patients and the doctors who referred them. PCLI strived to provide the ultimate in patient care and consideration. Dr. Everett had joined PCLI in 1993 in large part because of how impressed he had been at how PCLI treated its patients, and he remained com-mitted to this patient-focused value.

He was concerned, however, about his organiza-tion's ability to attract laser vision correction patients. He knew that many prospective PCLI customers would be swayed by the low prices and would travel to Canada to have the procedure performed, especially since most medical insurance programs covered only a small por-tion of the cost of this procedure. Dr. Everett believed strongly that PCLI achieved better results and provided a higher quality service experience than the clinics in Canada offering low-priced LASIK procedures. He also felt PCLI did a much better job of helping poten-tial customers determine which of several procedures, if any, best met the customers' long-term vision needs. Dr. Everett wondered what PCLI should do to win over these potential customers—both for the good of the customers and for the good of PCLI.

PACIFIC CATARACT AND LASER INSTITUTE

Pacific Cataract and Laser Institute (PCLI) was founded in 1985 by Dr. Robert Ford and specialized in medical and surgical eye treatment. The company was headquartered in Chehalis, Washington and operated clinics in Washington, Oregon, Idaho and Alaska (see Exhibit 1 for a map of PCLI locations). In addition to laser vision correction, PCLI provided cataract surgery, glaucoma consultation and surgery, corneal trans-plants, retinal care and surgery, and eyelid surgery. Dr. Ford founded PCLI on the principle that doctors must go beyond science and technology to practice the art of healing through the Christian principles of love, kind-

*This case was prepared by the authors for the sole purpose of providing mate-rial for class discussion. It is not intended to illustrate either effective or inef-fective handling of a managerial situation. The authors thank Dr. Mark Everett for his cooperation and assistance with this project. The authors also thank the anonymous *Case Research Journal* reviewers and the anonymous North American Case Research Association 2000 annual meeting reviewers for their valuable input and suggestions. An earlier version of this case received the Cooper Award as the best case in Healthcare presented at the NACRA 2000 Annual Meeting.

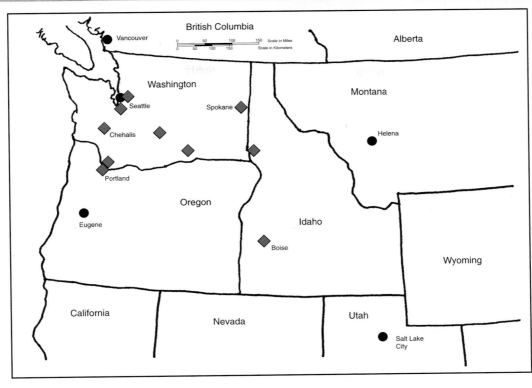

[Clinics designated by a ◆ ; Anchorage, AK clinic not shown]

Case 23 / Pacific Cataract and Laser Institute: Competing in the LASIK Eye Surgery Market

ness and compassion. The organization had defined eight core values that were based on these principles. These core values, shown in Exhibit 2, guided PCLI's decision-making as it attempted to fulfill its stated mission of providing the best possible "co-managed" services to the profession of optometry.

Co-management involved PCLI working closely with a patient's optometrist, or OD (for Doctor of Optometry). In co-managed eye care, family ODs were the primary care eye doctors who diagnosed, treated and managed certain diseases of the eye that did not require surgery. When surgery was needed, the family OD referred patients to ophthalmologists (e.g., PCLI's eye surgeons) for specialized treatment and surgery. Successful co-management, according to PCLI, depended upon a relationship of mutual trust and respect built through shared learning, constant communication and commitment to providing quality patient care. PCLI's co-management arrangements did not restrict ODs to working with just PCLI, although PCLI sought out ODs who would use PCLI as their primary surgery partner and who shared PCLI's values. Many ODs did work exclusively with PCLI unless a specific patient requested otherwise. PCLI-Spokane had developed a network of 150 family ODs in its region.

PCLI operated its eleven clinics in a very coordinated manner. It had seven surgeons that specialized in the various forms of eye surgery. These surgeons, each accompanied by several surgical assistants, traveled from center to center to perform specific surgeries. The company owned two aircraft that were used to fly the surgical teams between the centers. Each clinic had a resident optometric physician who served as that clinic's coordinator and essentially managed the day-to-day operations of the clinic. Each clinic also employed its own office support staff. PCLI's main office in Chehalis, Washington also employed patient counselors who worked with the referring family ODs for scheduling the patient's surgery and a finance team to help patients with medical insurance claims and any financing arrangements (which were made through third party sources). Dr. Everett was the Spokane clinic's resident optometric physician and managed the day-to-day activities to that clinic. Actual surgeries were performed in the Spokane clinic only one or two days a week, depending upon demand and the surgeons' availability.

Pacific Cataract and Laser Institute's Core Values — EXHIBIT 2

- We believe patients' families and friends provide important support and we encourage them to be as involved as possible in our care of their loved ones.
- We believe patients and their families have a right to honest and forthright medical information presented in a manner they can understand.
- We believe that a calm, caring and cheerful environment minimizes patient stress and the need for artificial sedation.
- We believe that all our actions should be guided by integrity, honesty and courage.
- We believe that true success comes from doing the right things for the right reasons.
- We believe that efficient, quality eye care is provided best by professionals practicing at the highest level of their expertise.
- We believe that communicating openly and sharing knowledge with our optometric colleagues is crucial to providing outstanding patient care.
- We believe that the ultimate measure of our success is the complete satisfaction of the doctors who entrust us with the care of their patients.

LASER EYE SURGERY AND LASIK

Laser eye surgery was performed on the eye to create better focus and lessen the patient's dependence on glasses and contact lenses. Excimer lasers were the main means of performing this type of surgery. Although research on the excimer laser began in 1973, it was not until 1985 that excimer lasers were introduced to the ophthalmology community in the U.S. The FDA approved the use of excimer lasers for photorefractive keratectomy (PRK) in October, 1995, for the purpose of correcting nearsightedness. PRK entailed using computer controlled beams of laser light to permanently resculpt the curvature of the eye by selectively removing a small portion on the outer top surface of the cornea (called epithelium). The epithelium naturally regenerated itself, although eye medication was required for three to four months after the procedure.

In the late 1990s, laser in-situ keratomileusis, or LASIK, replaced PRK as the preferred method to correct or reduce moderate to high levels of nearsightedness (i.e., myopia). The procedure required the surgeon to create a flap in the cornea using a surgical instrument called a microkeratome. This instrument used vacuum suction to hold and position the cornea and a motorized cutting blade to make the necessary incision. The surgeon then used an excimer laser to remove a microthin layer of tissue from the exposed, interior corneal surface (as opposed to removing a thin layer of tissue on the outer surface of the cornea as was the case with PRK). The excimer laser released a precisely focused beam of low temperature, invisible light. Each laser pulse removed less than one hundred-thousandth of an inch. After the cornea had been reshaped, the flap was replaced. The actual surgical procedure took only about five minutes per eye. LASIK surgery allowed a patient to eliminate the regular use of glasses or contact lenses although many patients still required reading glasses.

While LASIK used the same excimer laser that had been approved for other eye surgeries in the U.S. by the Ophthalmic Devices Panel of the FDA, it was not an approved procedure in the U.S., but was under study. LASIK was offered by clinics in the U.S., but was considered an "off label" use of the laser. "Off label" was a phrase given to medical services and supplies which had not been thoroughly tested by the FDA, but which the FDA permitted to be performed and provided by a licensed medical professional. Prescribing aspirin as a blood thinner to reduce the risk of stroke was another example of an off label use of a medical product—the prescribing of aspirin for this purpose did not have formal FDA approval but was permitted by the FDA.

The LASIK procedure was not without some risks. Complications arose in about 5% of all cases, although experienced surgeons had complication rates of less than 2%. According to the American Academy of Ophthalmology, complications and side effects included: irregular astigmatism, resulting in a decrease in best corrected vision; glare; corneal haze; over-correction; under-correction; inability to wear contact lenses; loss of the corneal cap, requiring a corneal graft; corneal scarring and infection; and in an extremely rare number of cases, loss of vision. If lasering were not perfect, a patient might develop haze in the cornea. This could make it impossible to achieve 20/20 vision, even with glasses. The flap could also heal improperly, causing fuzzy vision. Infections were also occasionally an issue.

While PRK and LASIK were the main types of eye surgery currently performed to reduce a patient's dependence on glasses or contact lenses, there were new surgical procedures and technologies that were in the test stage that could receive approval in the U.S. within the next three to ten years. These included intraocular lenses that were implanted behind a patient's cornea, laser thermokeratoplasty (LTK) and conductive kerato-plasty (CK) that used heat to reshape the cornea, and "custom" LASIK technologies that could better measure and correct the total optics of the eye. These newer methods had the potential to improve vision even more than LASIK and some of these new processes also might allow additional corrections to be made to the eye as the patient aged. Intraocular lenses were already widely available in Europe.

LASIK MARKET POTENTIAL

The market potential for LASIK procedures was very significant and the market was just beginning to take off. According to officials of the American Academy of Ophthalmology, over 150 million people wore glasses or contact lenses in the U.S. About 12 million of these people were candidates for current forms of refractive surgery. As procedures were refined to cover a wider range of vision conditions, and as the FDA approved new procedures, the number of people who could have their vision improved surgically was expected to grow to over 60 million. As many as 1.7 million people in the U.S. were expected to have some form of laser eye surgery during 2000, compared to 500,000 in 1999 and 250,000 in 1998. Laser eye repair was the most frequently performed surgery in all of medicine.

Referrals were increasingly playing a key role in the industry's growth. Surgeons estimated that the typical patient referred five friends, and that as many as 75% of new patients had been referred by a friend. A few employers were also beginning to offer laser eye surgery benefits through managed care vision plans. These plans offered discounts from list prices of participating surgeons and clinics to employees. Vision Service Plan's (VSP) partners, for example, gave such discounts and guaranteed a maximum price of $1800 per eye for VSP members. The number of people eligible for such benefits was expected to grow significantly in the coming years. PCLI did not participate in these plans and did not offer such discounts.

LASIK AT PCLI

The process of providing LASIK surgery to patients at PCLI began with the partnering OD. The OD provided the patient with information about LASIK and PCLI, reviewed the treatment options available, and answered any questions the patient might have concerning LASIK or PCLI. If a patient was interested in having the surgery performed, the OD performed a pre-exam to make sure the patient was a suitable candidate for the surgery. Assuming the patient was able to have the sur-

gery, the OD made an appointment for the patient with PCLI and forwarded the results of the pre-exam to Dr. Everett. PCLI had a standard surgical fee of $1400 per eye for LASIK. Each family OD added on additional fees for pre- and post-operative exams depending on the number of visits per patient and the OD's costs. Most of the ODs charged $700 to $1200, making the total price of laser surgery to the patient between $3500–4000. This total price was presented to the patient rather than two separate service fees.

Once a patient arrived at PCLI, an ophthalmic assistant measured the patient's range of vision and took a topographical reading of the eyes. Dr. Everett would then explain the entire process to the patient and discuss the possible risks and have the patient read and sign an informed consent form. The patient would then meet the surgeon and have any final questions answered. The meeting with the surgeon was also intended to reduce any anxiety that the patient might have regarding the procedure. The surgical procedure itself took less than 15 minutes to perform. After the surgery was completed, the patient was told to rest his/her eyes for a few hours and was given dark glasses and eye drops. The patient was required to either return to PCLI or to his or her family OD 24 hours after their surgery for a follow-up exam. Additional follow-up exams were required at one-week, one-month, three-months, six-months and one-year to make sure the eyes healed properly and to insure that any problems were caught quickly. The patient's family OD performed all of these follow-up exams.

Three of PCLI's seven surgeons specialized in LASIK and related procedures. The company's founder, Dr. Robert Ford, had performed over 16,000 LASIK procedures during his career, more than any other surgeon in the Northwest. His early training was as a physicist, and he was very interested in and knowledgeable about the laser technology used to perform LASIK procedures. Because of this interest and understanding, Dr. Ford was an industry innovator and had developed a number of procedural enhancements that were unique to PCLI. Dr. Ford had developed an enhanced software calibration system for PCLI's lasers that was better than the system provided by the laser manufacturers.

More significantly, Dr. Ford had also developed a system to track eye movements. Using superimposed live and saved computer images of the eye, PCLI surgeons could achieve improved eye alignment to provide more accurate laser resculpting of the eye. Dr. Ford was working with Laser Sight, a laser equipment manufacturer developing what PCLI and many others viewed as the next big technological step in corrective eye surgery—custom LASIK. Custom LASIK involved developing more detailed corneal maps and then using special software to convert these maps into a program that would run a spot laser to achieve theoretically perfect corrections of the cornea. This technology was currently in clinical trials in an effort to gain FDA approval of the technology, and Dr. Ford and PCLI were participating in these trials. Although Dr. Ford was on the leading edge of technology and had vast LASIK surgical experience, very few of PCLI's patients were aware of his achievements.

COMPETITION

PCLI in Spokane faced stiff competition from clinics in both the U.S. and Canada. There were basically three types of competitors. There were general ophthalmology practices that also provided LASIK surgeries, surgery centers like PCLI that provided a range of eye surgeries, and specialized LASIK clinics that focused solely on LASIK surgeries.

General ophthalmology practices provided a range of services covering a patient's basic eye care needs.

They performed general eye exams, monitored the health of patients' eyes, and wrote prescriptions for glasses and contact lenses. Most general ophthalmology practices did not perform LASIK surgeries (or any other types of surgeries) because of the high cost of the equipment and the special training needed to perform the surgery, but a few did. These clinics were able to offer patients a continuity of care that surgery centers and centers specializing solely in LASIK surgeries could not. Customers could have all pre- and post-operative exams performed at the same location by the same doctor. In the Spokane market, a clinic called Eye Consultants was the most aggressive competitor of this type. This organization advertised heavily in the local newspaper, promoting an $1195 per eye price (see Exhibit 3). The current newspaper promotion invited potential customers to a free LASIK seminar put on by the clinic's staff, and seminar attendees who chose to have the procedure qualified for the $1195 per eye price, which was a $300 per eye discount from the clinic's regular price.

Surgery centers did not provide for patient's basic eye care needs, but rather specialized in performing eye

EXHIBIT 3 Eye Consultants' Advertisement

Special Offer

LASIK
$1195 PER EYE*

INCLUDING pre- and post operative

WHEN: Thursday
June 1
6:00 p.m.

WHERE: Clear Vision Laser Center
Quail Run Office Park
2200 E. 29th Avenue
Suite 110

CALL TODAY
Seating is Limited

See LASIK Live!

Come to this free LIVE LASIK seminar
to receive this special offer.

*ONLY for seminar attendees who
schedule a procedure within 90 days!

Compare our Quality ~ Compare our Price
Save $600 on Both Eyes!

The Doctors You Trust
For Excellence
In Local Eye Care

EYE CONSULTANTS
David Cohen, M.D.
Chris Sturbaum, M.D.

CALL XXX-XXXX

surgeries. These centers provided a variety of eye surgeries, including such procedures as cataract surgeries and LASIK surgeries in addition to other specialty eye surgeries. PCLI was this type of a clinic. The other surgery center of this type in the Spokane area was Empire Eye. PCLI viewed Empire Eye as its most formidable competitor in the immediate geographic area. Empire Eye operated in a similar way as PCLI. It relied heavily on referrals from independent optometric physicians, did not advertise aggressively, and did not attempt to win customers with low prices. It did employ a locally-based surgeon who performed its LASIK procedures, although this surgeon was not nearly as experienced as Dr. Ford at PCLI.

LASIK clinics provided only LASIK or LASIK and PRK procedures. They did not provide for general eye care needs nor did they provide a range of eye surgeries like surgery centers. These clinics generally had much higher volumes of LASIK patients than general ophthalmology or surgery centers, allowing them to achieve much higher utilization of the expensive capital equipment required to perform the surgeries. The capital cost of the equipment to perform the LASIK procedure was about U.S.$500,000.

The largest of these firms specializing in LASIK surgeries was TLC Laser Eye Centers, Inc. TLC was based in Mississauga, Ontario, and had 56 clinics in the U.S. and 7 in Canada. During the 1st quarter of 2000, TLC generated revenues of U.S.$49.3 million by performing 33,000 surgeries. This compared with 1st quarter of 1999 when the company had revenues of U.S.$41.4 million on 25,600 procedures. TLC was the largest LASIK eye surgery company in North America and performed more LASIK surgeries in the U.S. than any other company. The closest TLC centers to Spokane were in Seattle, Washington and Vancouver, British Columbia. The second largest provider of LASIK surgeries in the U.S. was Laser Vision Centers (LVC), based in St. Louis, Missouri. Its closest center to Spokane was also in Seattle.

Almost all of the Canadian competitors that had been successful at attracting U.S. customers were clinics that specialized solely in LASIK surgeries. The largest Canadian competitor was Lasik Vision Corporation (LVC), based in Vancouver, British Columbia. LVC operated 15 clinics in Canada and 14 in the United States, and was growing rapidly. LVC had plans to add another 21 clinics by the end of 2000. During the 1st quarter of 2000, LVC generated revenues of U.S.$20.1 million by performing 26,673 procedures. This compared to 1st quarter of 1999, when the company had revenues of only U.S.$4.3 million on 6300 procedures.

In total, there were 13 companies specializing in providing LASIK surgeries in British Columbia, mostly in the Vancouver area. One of the British Columbia firms that advertised most aggressively in the Spokane area was Lexington Laser Vision (LLV). LLV operated a single clinic staffed by nine surgeons and equipped with four lasers. The clinic scheduled surgeries six days a week and typically had a two-month wait for an appointment.

The service design process at LLV was designed to accommodate many patients and differed significantly from PCLI's service process. To begin the process, a patient simply called a toll-free number for LLV to schedule a time to have the surgery performed. Once the patient arrived at the LLV clinic he/she received a preoperative examination to assess the patient's current vision and to scan the topography of the patient's eyes. The next day the patient returned to the clinic for the scheduled surgery. The typical sequence was to first meet with a patient counselor who reviewed with the patient all pages of a LASIK information booklet that was sent to the patient following the scheduled surgery date. The patient counselor answered any questions the patient had regarding the information in the booklet, and ensured that the patient signed all necessary surgical consent forms. Following this step, a medical assistant surgically prepped the patient and explained the post-care treatment of the eyes. After this preparation, the surgeon greeted the patient, reviewed the topographical eye charts with the patient, explained the recommended eye adjustments for the patient, and reiterated the surgical procedure once again. The patient would then be transferred to the surgery room where two surgical assistants were available to help the doctor with the five- to ten-minute operation. Once the surgery was completed, a surgical assistant led the patient to a dark, unlit room so that the patient's eyes could adjust. After a 15-minute waiting period, the surgical assistant checked the patient for any discomfort and repeated the instructions for post-care treatment. Barring no problems or discomfort, the surgical assistant would hand the patient a pair of dark, wrap-around sunglasses with instructions to avoid bright lights for the next 24 hours. At the scheduled post-operative exam the next day, a medical technician measured the patient's corrected vision and scheduled any additional post-operative exams. If desired, the patient could return to the clinic for the one-week, one-, and three-month post-operative exams at either the LLV clinic or one of the U.S.-based partner clinics of LLV. In some cases, the patient opted to have these post-operative exams performed by his/her family OD.

U.S. patients traveling to LLV or the other clinics in British Columbia to have the surgery performed needed to allow for three days and two nights for the surgery. A pre-exam to insure the patient was a suitable candidate for the surgery was performed the first day, the surgery itself was performed the second day, and the 24-hour post-exam was performed on the third day. Two nights in a hotel near LLV cost approximately $100US and airfare to Vancouver, B.C., Canada cost approximately $150US from Spokane, WA. Lexington Laser Vision had a sister clinic in the Seattle area where patients could go for post-operative exams. LLV requested patients undergo follow-up exams at one week, one month and three months. These exams were included in the price as long as the patient came to either the Seattle or Vancouver clinics. Some patients outside of the Seattle/Vancouver area arranged with their family ODs to perform these follow-ups at their own expense to avoid the time and cost of traveling to Seattle or Vancouver, B.C.

A breakdown of the estimated cost structure for each of these different competitors is shown in Exhibit

4. Dr. Everett believed that both Eye Consultants and LLV were probably incurring losses. Both were believed to be offering below cost pricing in response to the significant price competition going on in the industry. Eye Consultants was also believed to be offering below cost pricing in order to build volume and gain surgeon experience. PCLI's own cost structure was fairly similar to Empire Eye's cost structure, as both operated in a similar fashion.

THE CANADIAN ADVANTAGE

LASIK clinics operating in Canada had a number of advantages that allowed them to charge significantly less than competitors in the U.S. First, the Canadian dollar had been relatively weak compared to the U.S. dollar for some time, fluctuating between C$1.45 per U.S. dollar and C$1.50 per U.S. dollar. This exchange

EXHIBIT 4[1]	LASIK-related Revenue and Cost Estimates for PCLI's Competitors (all figures are in U.S.$)			
Competitor	Eye Consultants	Empire Eye	TLC Clinic	Lexington Laser Vision[2]
Type of Operation	General Ophthalmology Practice	Eye Surgery Center	Specialized LASIK Clinic	Specialized LASIK Clinic
Location of Operation	Spokane, WA	Spokane, WA	Seattle, WA	Vancouver, B.C.
Number of Procedures/Year	600	1000	4000	10,000
Price to Customer, per Eye	$ 1,195	$ 1,900	$ 1,600	$ 500
Estimated Revenues	$717,000	$1,900,000	$6,400,000	$5,000,000
Estimated Expenses				
Payments for Pre- and Post-Operative Care[3]	120,000	450,000	1,400,000	1,500,000
Royalties	150,000	250,000	1,000,000	0
Surgeon's Fees/Salary	120,000	300,000	1,200,000	1,500,000
Medical Supplies	30,000	50,000	200,000	500,000
Laser Service	100,000	100,000	200,000	400,000
Depreciation	125,000	125,000	250,000	500,000
Marketing	75,000	75,000	400,000	500,000
Overhead	200,000	350,000	500,000	600,000
Total Annual Expenses	$920,000	$1,700,000	$5,150,000	$5,500,000

[1]This table was developed based on a variety of public sources on both the LASIK industry in general and on individual competitors. In a number of cases, the figures represent aggregated 'estimates' of data from several sources. Estimated expenses are based largely, but not entirely, on discussion of the LASIK industry cost structure provided in "Eyeing the bottom line: Just who profits from your laser eye surgery may surprise you" by James Pethokoukis, U.S. News and World Report, March 30, 1998, pp. 80–82.

[2]This cost structure was thought to be typical of all of the specialized LASIK clinics located in British Columbia, Canada that competed with PCLI.

[3]In some cases, these costs are paid directly by the patient to the post-operative care provider; they have been included here because they represent a part of the total price paid by the customer.

rate compared to rates in the early 1990s that fluctuated between C$1.15 per U.S. dollar and C$1.20 per U.S. dollar. On top of this, the inflation rate in Canada averaged only 1.5% during the 1990s compared to 2.5% in the U.S. This dual effect of a weakened Canadian dollar combined with somewhat higher inflation in the U.S. meant that Canadian providers had, over time, acquired a significant exchange rate cost advantage.

Second, laser surgery equipment manufacturers charged a $250 patent royalty fee for each surgery (i.e., each eye) performed in the U.S. The legal system in Canada prevented equipment manufacturers from charging such a royalty every time a surgery was performed, amounting to a $500 cost savings per patient for Canadian clinics. Competitive pressure among surgery equipment manufacturers had caused this fee to drop in recent months to as low as $100 for certain procedures performed on some older equipment in the U.S., giving U.S. clinics some hope that this cost disadvantage might decrease over time.

Third, clinics in the U.S. generally paid higher salaries and/or fees to surgeons and support staff than did their Canadian rivals. The nationalized health system in Canada tended to limit what doctors in Canada could earn compared to their peers in the U.S. LASIK clinics themselves were not part of the Canadian national health system because they represented elective surgeries. However, Canadian LASIK clinics could pay their surgeons a large premium over what they could make in the nationalized system, but this was still significantly less than a comparable surgeon's earnings in the U.S. This cost differential extended to the referring optometrists who provided pre- and post-operative exams and whose fees were typically included in the price quoted to customers. Many Canadian clinics relied more heavily on advertising and word-of-mouth customer referral rather than referrals from optometrists and de-emphasized pre- and post-operative exams.

Fourth, there was some speculation among U.S. clinics that some low-priced Canadian clinics were making a variety of care-compromising quality trade-offs, such as not performing equipment calibration and maintenance as frequently as recommended by the equipment manufacturers and reusing the microkeratome blades used to make the initial incision in the cornea. Canadian clinics denied that the choices that they made compromised the quality of care received by the patient. Finally, it seemed clear to Dr. Everett that Canadian providers were in the midst of a price war and that at least some of the clinics were not generating any profit at the prices they were charging.

Canadian providers also had significant non-cost advantages. Because of differences in the approval process of medical equipment and procedures, laser eye surgery technologies were often available in Canada before they became readily available in the U.S. Approval of new medical technologies in Canada was often based on evidence from other countries that the technology was safe, whereas approval of new medical technologies in the U.S. required equipment manufacturers to start from scratch with a series of studies. As a result of this, and combined with the volume that the Canadian clinics' low prices generated, many Canadian clinics had more experience with laser eye surgery than comparable clinics in the U.S. Experience was a critical factor in a clinic or specific surgeon having low rates of complications. Further, the differences in the approval processes between the countries allowed Canadian providers the ability to offer advanced equipment not yet available in the U.S. For example, the FDA approved the first generation of excimer laser for use in the U.S. in October of 1995. No centers in Canada, however, had purchased this particular laser since 1995 because more advanced versions of the technology had become available for use in Canada. While some of these equipment advances have had minimal impact on the results for the average patient, they have, at the very least, provided Canadian clinics a marketing advantage.

U.S. COMPETITORS' RESPONSES TO THE CANADIAN CHALLENGE

The surgeons and staff at PCLI knew from reading a variety of sources and from following changes in the industry that most U.S. based clinics were experiencing some loss of customers to Canadian competitors. These companies were responding in a variety of ways in an attempt to keep more patients in the U.S. One company in the industry, LCA, had created a low-priced subsidiary, LasikPlus, as a way to compete with lower priced competitors in Canada. LasikPlus had facilities in Maryland and California and charged $2995 compared to the $5000 price charged by the parent company's LCA Vision Centers. One way that the LasikPlus subsidiary had cut cost was by employing its own surgeons. Regular LCA Vision Centers provided only the facilities and equipment, and contracted out with independent surgeons to perform the procedures.

Another strategy that U.S. firms were using to compete was to partner with managed care vision benefits firms, HMOs, and large businesses. TLC Laser Eye Centers had been the most aggressive at using this strategy. It had partnered with Vision Service Plan (VSP) to provide the surgery to VSP members at a $600 discount, and had partnered with HMO Kaiser Permanente to provide Kaiser members a $200 discount. TLC was also attempting to get employers to cover part of the cost for their employees, and was letting participating companies offer a $200 discount on the procedure to their employees. Over 40 businesses had signed up by late 1999, including Southern California Edison, Ernst and Young, and Office Depot. TLC was not the only provider pursuing this strategy. LCA Vision Centers had partnered with Cole Managed Vision to provide the surgery to Cole members at a 15% discount.

One of the significant advantages that U.S. providers had over their Canadian competitors was convenience, since patients did not have to travel to Canada to have the procedure performed. Most facilities providing the surgery in the U.S., however, were located in major metropolitan areas, which may not be seen as being all that much more convenient for potential patients living in smaller communities and rural areas. One competitor had taken this convenience a step further. Laser Vision Centers was using mobile lasers to bring greater convenience to patients living in these smaller communities. It used a patented cart to transport the laser to ophthalmologists' offices, where it could be used for a day or two by local surgeons. LVC could also provide a surgery team in locations where no surgeons were qualified to perform the procedure. The company was serving patients in over 100 locations in this manner and was expanding its efforts.

Technological or procedural advances offered clinics another basis upon which to compete. For example, during the summer of 1999, Dr. Barrie Soloway's clinic was the first in the U.S. to get an Autonomous laser. This laser was designed to overcome a major problem in eye surgery, the tendency for the eye to move while the procedure was being performed. In an interview with *Fortune* magazine, Autonomous's founder, Randy Frey, described the advantages of this new technology.

At present, doctors stabilize the eye merely by asking the patient to stare at a blinking red light. But, says Frey, aiming a laser at the eye is "a very precise thing. I couldn't imagine that you could make optics for the human eye while the eye was moving." The eye, he explains, makes barely perceptible, involuntary movements about five times a second. This "saccadic" motion can make it difficult to get a perfectly smooth correction. "The doctor can compensate for the big, noticeable movements," Frey says, "but not the little ones."...

Frey's machine uses radar to check the position of the eye 4,000 times a second. He's coupled this with an excimer laser whose beam is less than one mil- *limeter in diameter, vs. six millimeters for the standard beam. Guided by the tracker, this laser ablates the cornea in a pattern of small overlapping dots. (Murray, 1999)*[1]

There were a number of technological advances under development like the Autonomous laser system that could have a significant impact on this industry. With approvals for new procedures generally coming quicker in Canada than the U.S., however, it was unclear whether technological advances could help U.S. providers differentiate themselves from their Canadian competitors.

THE UPCOMING STRATEGY AND POLICY MEETING

Every time Dr. Everett saw an exuberant patient after surgery, or read a letter of gratitude from a patient, he knew in his heart that they were doing something special. He was energized by the fact that the laser vision corrections they were performing were changing people's lives. He was also proud of the fact that they continued to treat all of their customers as special guests. But he knew that for every LASIK patient they saw at PCLI, there was another potential PCLI patient who went to Canada to have the surgery performed. PCLI had the capacity to do more laser vision correction surgeries in Spokane than they were presently doing, and he wanted to make use of that capacity. He felt both PCLI and prospective patients from Spokane and the surrounding communities would be better off if more of these patients chose PCLI for laser vision correction surgeries.

But Dr. Everett was not sure what, if anything, should change at PCLI to attract these potential customers. PCLI had already begun to advertise. Advertising, in general, was not a commonly used practice in the U.S. medical community, and some in the medical profession considered much of the existing advertising in the industry to be ethically questionable. While Dr. Everett was comfortable with the advertisements they had started running three months ago (see Exhibit 5), he was still unsure whether PCLI should be advertising at all. More importantly, he felt that advertising represented only a partial solution, at best. What was needed was a clear strategic focus for the organization that would help it respond to the Canadian challenge.

One obvious answer was to also compete on price. But he simply could not conceive of PCLI treating eye surgery like a commodity and competing solely on price. Such a strategy seemed inconsistent with PCLI's

Thinking About LASIK?

Ask your optometrist first.

The question I asked my eye doctor was "Who would you trust to treat your eyes?"

The reason is simple. Excellent visual results are highly dependent on the skill of the surgeon you select.

Optometrists – also known as optometric physicians – do not perform surgery. However, these doctors provide most of the after-surgery care. This gives them the unique opportunity to see first hand the good and not-so-good outcomes of numerous surgeons.

Your optometrist can guide you to a surgeon who consistently obtains excellent results and is appropriate for your type of correction.

The results of surgery last a lifetime. See your optometric physician!

LASER VISION CORRECTION
PACIFIC CATARACT and LASER INSTITUTE

www.pcli.com
(509) XXX-XXXX
(800) XXX-XXXX

SPOKANE YAKIMA KENNEWICK TACOMA BELLEVUE CHEHALIS VANCOUVER, WA BOISE LEWISTON PORTLAND ANCHORAGE

core values, unwise from a business standpoint since PCLI's operating costs were much higher than its Canadian competitors, and simply wrong from an ethical standpoint. The problem was, he was not sure what strategic focus PCLI should pursue in order to retain its strong position in the Pacific Northwest LASIK market. What he did know was that whatever this strategy was to be, it needed to emerge from next month's meeting, and he wanted to be prepared to help make that happen. He wanted to have a clear plan to bring to the table at this meeting to share with his colleagues, even if it was simply a reaffirmation to continue doing what they were presently doing.

Notes

1. Murray M. 1999. Should you have your eyes lasered? *Fortune*, Sept. 27, 194+.

Paper Storms: Turbulence Arrives in Germany's Newspaper Publishing

case twenty-four

Heather A. Hazard
Copenhagen Business School

Claudia Loebbecke
Markus Kamrad
University of Cologne

"Competition jolts Germany's press: New foreign entrants and tough competition in domestic markets are forcing German newspaper publishers to reinvigorate their editorial and design in this now turbulent sector."

—Headline Marketing Week,
4 November 1999

"Everyone wants 'brand' and 'content' which both [the Wall Street Journal and the Financial Times] have in spades [yet both] face new competition—from on-line services and from each other with the FT launching a US edition in September 1997, the WSJE "hitting back" with a relaunch in early February 1997, followed by the FT's "second strike" of launching the FT Deutschland."

—*Paper Wars,* The Economist
19 February 2000

German newspaper publishers long enjoyed what pundits described as a stable and staid oligopolistic coexistence. Germany (Figure 1) was not only one of the five largest newspaper markets in the world, it had consistently been Europe's largest market for the circulation of dailies (Figure 2) and for advertising revenue (Figure 3). Of the dailies considered to be important business reading by Europe's decision-makers, *Handelsblatt Wirtschafts und Finanzzeitung's* strength in Germany had translated into leadership in the entire EU based on the weight of the German market (Figure 4). A warning of unprecedented turbulence came, however, when the *Financial Times* (*FT*) began to recruit journalists late in 1998 for what its owners (the Pearson Group) hoped would be a high profile launch of a German language edition. The idea that David Bell of the *FT* and Gerd Schulte-Hillen of the German publishing house, Gruner and Jahr, had kindled at a dinner meeting at a publishers' conference in Greece had flowered into a concrete agreement. *Handelsblatt* had the brand, the portfolio (Figure 5), the reputation, and the readership but even a privately owned newspaper insulated from financial market pressures could not afford to take this threatened market entry lightly. On the first of June 1999, The Street.Com reported what was "being billed as a strategic—although the cynical might term it defensive—alliance" between Dow Jones and the Verlagsgruppe Georg von Holtzbrinck to swap minority stakes in their flagship newspapers: *The Wall Street Journal Europe* (49% to Holtzbrinck) and *Handelsblatt* (22% to Dow Jones). These deals marked Germany as the latest battleground between the Pearson Group and the Dow Jones Group and *Handelsblatt* as an important strategic player in that battle.

TRENDS IN THE WORLD NEWSPAPER INDUSTRY

All over the western world, newspapers had faced declining circulation for two decades, migration of advertising investments, and increased competition for the consumers from many new and non-traditional sources. For an industry that was characterized by a broker model and the joint production of readers for

This case was prepared under the auspices of SIMI, the Scandinavian International Management Institute. It was written by Professor Heather A. Hazard, Copenhagen Business School and Professor Claudia Loebbecke, with the support of Doctoral Candidate Markus Kamrad, Department of Media Management, University of Cologne. It is intended to be used as the basis for class discussion rather than to illustrate either effective or ineffective handling of a management situation.

The case was made possible by the co-operation of Von Holzbrink Group.

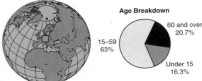

Germany

In the early 19th century German nationalists displayed black, gold, and red on their uniforms and tricolor flags. The current flag was used officially from 1848 to 1852 and readopted by West Germany on May 9, 1949. East Germany flew a similar flag but only the flag of West Germany was maintained upon reunification in 1990.

Age Breakdown

- 60 and over 20.7%
- 15–59 63%
- Under 15 16.3%

Official name: Bundesrepublik Deutschland (Federal Republic of Germany).

Form of goverment: federal multiparty republic with two legislative houses (Federal Council [69]: Federal Diet [672]).

Chief of state: President.

Head of government: Chancellor.

Population: (1998): 82,148,000.

Population projection: (2000) 82,510,000; (2010) 84,346,000.

Natural increase rate per 1,000 population (1995): −1.4 (world avg. 15.7).

Gross national product (at current market prices; 1996): U.S. $2,364,632,000,000 (U.S. $28,870 per capita).

Land use (1994): forest 30.6%; pasture 15.1%; agriculture 19.9%; other 34.4%.

309

---

advertisers and content for readers, these were serious threats. At their World Congress in 1999, the International Newspaper Marketing Association claimed that five consumer issues were driving these trends:

- Consumer time poverty,
- Consumer lack of concern for community,
- Rising standards of corporate service,
- Saturation of marketing messages in society, and
- The technological revolution.

In an explicit acknowledgement of these threats, Dow Jones went so far as to enumerate the risks and uncertainties facing them at their mid-year media review in June of 1999. These included:

- the impact of global business, economic, and stock market conditions on advertising sales and sales of products and services,
- increased competition in the markets for financial news and information and advertising from the rise of the popularity of the Internet, financial television programming and other new media,

- their ability to diversify their print publications' advertising base,
- their ability to expand their production and service capacity for electronic publishing products on a timely basis, and
- the cost of newsprint and labor.

As multi-dimensional as they were, however, the threats were not universally viewed as negative for the industry. According to the WAN Director General, Timothy Balding:

"The new and intensifying competition, with the increasingly fragmented nature of media markets, is proving to be a remarkable stimulus to newspaper companies both to play better on their traditional strengths and to exploit to the full the new media opportunities, using all the assets they have gained as dominant players in many new markets." [Presenting at the 53rd World Newspaper Congress in August 2000].

Indeed, the 2000 World Press Trends Survey revealed that in 1999, newspaper sales were actually up in 25 of

FIGURE 2 — Circulation of Dailies in Europe 1995–99 (000s of copies)

	1995	1996	1997	1998	1999
Austria	2,088	2,382	2,500	2,669	2,896
Belgium	1,628	1,621	1,602	1,588	1,585
Denmark	1,613	1,631	1,617	1,583	1,528
Finland	2,368	2,335	2,324	2,343	2,331
France*	8,770	8,656	8,952	8,799	
Germany**	25,557	25,456	25,260	25,016	24,565
Greece*	728	758	719	672	
Ireland	546	544	552	557	567
Italy	5,977	5,890	5,894	5,969	5,937
Luxembourg	135	135	121	124	124
Netherlands	4,752	4,753	4,753	4,522	4,482
Norway	2,582	2,578	2,603	2,600	2,591
Portugal	610	697	634	673	686
Spain	4,237	4,180	4,265	4,300	4,300
Sweden	4,041	3,874	3,871	3,807	3,721
Switzerland	2,721	2,715	2,711	2,676	2,679
United Kingdom	19,742	19,226	18,994	18,666	18,939

*1999 figures not yet reported.

**In 1999, Germany was the fifth largest market in the world. It trailed only Japan (72,218,000); the US (55,979,000); China (50,000,000); and India (25,587,000).

Source: World Association of Newspapers, World Press Trends 2000

FIGURE 3 — Advertising Revenues in Europe 1999 (USD millions)

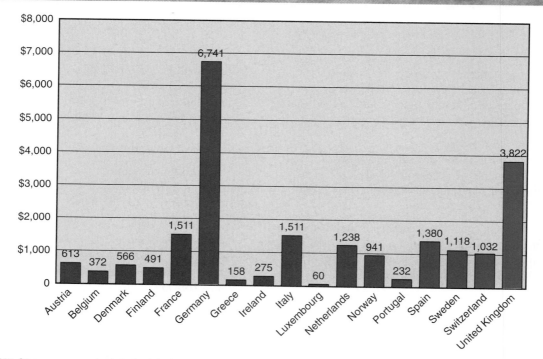

Note: In 1999, Germany was second only to the United States at $46,925,000,000.

Source: World Association of Newspapers, World Press Trends, 2000.

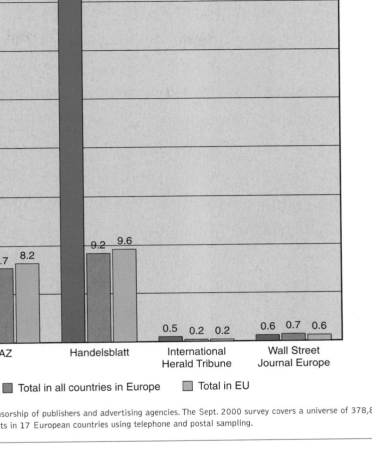

Note: The EBRS was started in 1993 with the joint sponsorship of publishers and advertising agencies. The Sept. 2000 survey covers a universe of 378,822 senior decision makers in 54,287 leading business establishments in 17 European countries using telephone and postal sampling.

Source: European Business Readership Survey, 2000.

the 46 countries for which comparable data was available. Even in the European Union where circulation had been sliding for many years, the rate of decline had slowed to −0.1% (from five times that rate in 1998 and ten times in 1997) as gains in seven countries almost offset declines in six others (see Exhibit 1).

But even the declines in circulation were discounted by Mr. Balding who proposed that:

"Reading habits do change. But more and more, the newspaper is establishing itself as a platform, or you might even say as a portal, for news and information, that you access in various formats. In countries where we continue to report decline in readership, the figures are in some ways misleading. Where internet penetration is high, newspapers might have lost

slightly in the paper format—but they have in many cases more than compensated for this through readership on their web sites... As a matter of fact, many newspapers can report a huge increase in reading but it comes in two ways: the traditional newspaper and the internet site. The combination is proving very strong and has strengthened the image and reach of many newspapers."

When Joseph McGrath, head of Unisys Global Industries, was asked to address the challenges of the newspaper industry in a presentation to the World Newspaper Congress and the World Editors Forum he optimistically stated his belief that the newspaper industry had "one of the most significant opportunities to take advantage of the new economy". Not only

FIGURE 5 — Market Spectrum Spanned by Handelblatt's Brand Portfolio

Brand Handelsblatt

Fields	Wirtschafts und Finanzzeitung	Junge Karriere	Digitally distributed	Specialized Literature	Conferences	Television	Research
Products	Handelsblatt (Daily newspaper)	Handelsblatt Junge Karriere (Newspaper published six times a year) Handelsblatt Junge Karriere.com	Handelsblatt.com Handelsblatt News am Abend (News in the evening) Handelsblatt Global Edition	Handelsblatt Books Handelsblatt Brochures	Handelsblatt Forums Handelsblatt Financial Trainings Handelsblatt Investors' Seminars	Handelsblatt Ticker Handelsblatt TV	Handelsblatt Annual Report Service

EXHIBIT 1

Austria	+8.5%
Portugal	+2.0%
Ireland	+1.8%
United Kingdom	+1.5%
Italy	+1.1%
Luxembourg	+0.3%
France	+0.2%
Greece	−5.5%
Denmark	−3.5%
Sweden	−2.3%
Germany	−1.8%
Netherlands	−0.9%
Finland	−0.5%

because of strong brand identification and a reputation for credibility but because the dot.coms shouldn't be able to compete effectively against the newspapers because of the skills and talents newspapers already had. He advised the papers against going it alone however for "This world has gotten far too complex to be able to do all the things on our own, so we really need to partner aggressively in this world."

ECONOMIC FUNDAMENTALS OF NEWSPAPER PUBLISHING

As Hal Varian and Carl Shapiro point out in *Information Rules* (Harvard Business School Press, 1999) today's business environment may be frenetic, but there are durable principles of economics. These can serve as a guide for the production and sale of information goods and that anything that can be digitized is information. What makes the nature of competition so special in information markets is its unusual cost structure: information can be extremely costly to produce and cheap (or even essentially costless) to reproduce. Thus, volume is widely considered to be the cornerstone of newspaper economics (See Patrick Hendricks, *Newspapers: A Lost Cause, Strategic Management of Newspaper Firms in the United States and The Netherlands,* Kluwer Academic Press, Dordrecht, 1999 for empirical evidence and an extended analysis of the following model). The sharp decline of unit costs with volume implies that the newspaper industry is subject to sharp economies of scale. Long run average costs are minimized when the firm has reached a so-called minimum efficient scale. Given the size of a market, there will only be room for a select number of firms at the mini-

mum efficient scale, i.e., we expect to see the concentration of market share. If there are barriers to entry then the incumbent firms may exercise their market power and behave as oligopolies (if there are few) or as monopolists (if there is only one) to charge higher prices. Assuming that achieving economies of scale has allowed the firms to achieve a favorable cost structure, then the higher prices and lower costs are expected to combine to produce solid firm profitability (see Exhibit 2). In considering *The Future of the European Media Industry,* Helen Bunting and Paul Chapman observed a general trend towards consolidation in the industry as companies moved to take advantage of opportunities to generate economies of scale and reuse content, and to offer more attractive packages to larger advertising customers. [FT Telecoms and Media Publishing 1996]

Historically, the physical production process drove economies of scale. Printing presses were expensive, high-capacity, physical assets that traditionally demanded long print runs to achieve adequate utilization. Once printed newspaper companies utilized elaborate distribution networks to get their product to the customer. According to Treucura Branchenvergleich, production and distribution accounted for 38% and 22% of the costs for German newspapers in 1997 with the remainder going to editorial (22%), administration (8%) and advertisements (13%). A perpetual problem for newspaper publishers is the cyclicality of newsprint prices.

As other distribution channels emerged, however, the logic that bound the value chain of the traditional newspaper together could no longer be taken for granted according to Philip Evans and Thomas Wurster (see their case study of the newspaper industry in *Blown to Bits: How the Economics of Information Transforms Strategy,* Harvard Business School Press, 1999). They proposed that the informational value chain and the physical value chain would be unraveled and that each had to be allowed to evolve in accordance with its own economics or value would be suppressed.

A key aspect of the newspaper industry is that it enjoys the potential for achieving significant economies of scope by producing two products simultaneously. It is possible for the newspaper to act as a broker delivering content and advertising messages to customers in return for their subscription fees and attention while delivering that attention to advertisers in return for revenues for carrying the advertising messages (see Exhibit 3). (See Peter J.S. Dunnett, *The World Newspaper Industry,* Croom Helm, London, 1988 for an elaboration of this model). While all variants on this basic model are possible (e.g. free newspapers funded only by advertising revenues, paid newspapers carrying free advertising, paid newspapers carrying no advertising, etc.) the industry

EXHIBIT 2

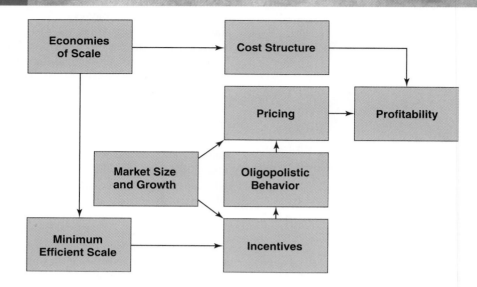

EXHIBIT 3

norm is joint production with the ratio of advertising revenues to subscription revenues varying by country, market niche, and degree of competitive rivalry.

Certain types of new goods must be experienced to be valued (so-called "experience goods") but as Varian and Shapiro note information must be experienced every time it is consumed. This is a potential problem for publishers since consumers may be reluctant to pay for a product whose value is uncertain. The main keys for overcoming the consumers' skepticism over purchasing information are branding and reputation. As such, these are critical issues for newspaper publishers.

NEWSPAPERS AND THE NEW MEDIA

The digitalization of the newspaper production process was well established before direct distribution to the consumer became possible. While the role of the World Wide Web as a distribution channel for news, entertainment, product information, and advertising was indisputable, the 2000 merger between AOL and Time Warner had underscored the ability of new and old

media to act as complements. On the one hand, multi-channel distribution made the central product of news-papers, high quality information of relevance to a wide audience, more valuable. Moreover, interactivity enriched the possibilities for exchange, personalization, and search. The challenge, however, was competition on the digital platform from other media that formerly were in separate channels and from independent producers who had been able to enter because of the ease of access to production and distribution tools. While the investment and infrastructure needed to start up a new newspaper remained high (creating a significant barrier to entry) the threat of substitutes had increased dramatically. Thus, paper sales revenues were under threat as readers turned elsewhere and advertising revenues were at risk as advertisers discover alternative channels. Newspaper publishers had two basic options: to either develop their own site or to become a content provider to an independent host. According to the World Association of Newspapers, as of 1999, there were 1,321 newspapers published in Europe and 632 of these had an online edition. The ratio for Germany was similar with 387 papers or which 179 had websites.

The Development of the German Newspaper Market

Following World War II the Allies decided only to allow publishing in Germany under license and that licenses would be restricted to publishers who had not had any connections with the Nazi regime. Control of the press was seen not only as a way of preempting resurgence of the defeated regime but of ensuring that the Allies' goals of "reeducation" were fulfilled. 176 licenses were issued starting promptly in June 1945 with terms lasting until September 1949. Although this controlled access period lasted only four years the licensed papers had enough time to establish themselves in a market where competition was limited. In fact, many of the existing, dominant German papers were founded during this period, including the *Süddesche Zeitung* and *Die Welt.*

After the end of controlled access period, new entrants flooded into the market. In the first half-year alone, 400 new titles were issued. Many of them published by so-called "Alt-Verlegern" that is publishers who were active before 1945 but who had not been allowed to publish their old titles after the war because of their connections to the Nazis. The following period was one of intense competition that many did not survive.

The German newspaper "market" was more generally divided between the markets for papers that are regional in character, German language "supraregional" papers, and internationally oriented papers (see Exhibit 4). Germany's history as a collection of states meant that no single population concentration equivalent to London or Paris developed in the nineteenth century thus fostering the growth of regional papers. By 1999, 52% of German cities had only one regional paper serving them and another 42% had two. Thus within these some 400 geographic markets the competition was extremely limited. The market for national newspapers was oligopolistic as it was shared between just a few newspapers (including *Börsen Zeitung, Frankfurter Allegemeine Zeitung (FAZ), Handelsblatt, Süddeutsche Zeitung,* and *Die Welt*). After reunification the majors increased their dominance by taking over former East German newspapers but there was no immediate action against these publishers by the competition authorities. A last significant segment of the market was the so-called yellow press, that is the papers that are sold on the street (such as Bild and Express), for which no subscriptions were available. While important in general market share numbers, (Figure 6) these papers did not serve the business market.

While only 8% of German households participated in the stock market by 1999 (as compared to 40% in the US) this was expected to increase. Already, "a growing interest in business matters and finance has led to a demand for a fresher editorial, particularly in the business pages." (Haig Simonian, the FT's correspondent in Berlin in *Marketing Week*)

Industry analysts believed that the German newspaper industry's challenges as it entered the 21st century were not dissimilar to those faced by the US industry:

"Germany enjoys a fully developed newspaper market, which makes it more vulnerable to emerging competition from new media. The long delay in developing commercial broadcasting, cable TV and more liberal broadcasting regulations have created pent-up demand among advertisers for radio and airtime. Unlike the US market, where broadcasting and cable are mature industries and are unlikely to make dramatic inroads into newspaper revenues in the future, in Germany the competition from broadcasting is just beginning for the newspaper industry. Finally, the German newspaper industry suffers from the same high cost structures, economic downturn,

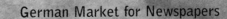

German Market for Newspapers   **EXHIBIT 4**

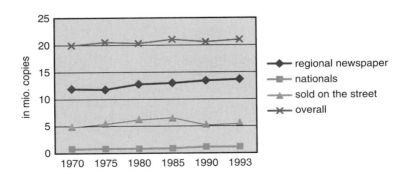

Source: BDZV

FIGURE 6 — Market Share Percentage of Top 10 Newspaper Sales in Germany (only for high-income households)

In percent	1998	1997
Bild-Zeitung	12.7	14.0
Frankfurter Allegemeine Zeitung	7.9	8.4
Die Welt	4.7	3.7
Handelsblatt	4.4	4.3
Süddeutsche Zeitung	4.4	4.4
Neue Zuercher Zeitung	0.4	0.2
Financial Times	0.4	0.7
International Herald Tribune	0.4	0.4
Wall Street Journal Europe	0.3	0.4
USA Today	0.2	0.2

Source: European Media & Marketing Survey

and fallout from reunification that have troubled German industry during the 1990s."

—Alan Abarran and Sylvia Chan-Olmsted in
Global Media Economics, *Iowa State Press, 1998.*
pp. 127–128

THE GERMAN MEDIA MARKET IN 1999

There was no question that the battle for market share between the *Wall Street Journal,* the *Financial Times* and the *International Herald* was intense across many markets (see Exhibit 5).

The sheer size and wealth of the German market (recall Figures 1 and 2) made it stand out as a publisher's prize, however. As such it was here that observers such as *Advertising Age* were "anticipating the rush on international newspaper publishers muscling into the host German media market." (1 November 1999). It would be a task for strong incumbents, such as *Handelsblatt,* to defend themselves.

HANDELSBLATT AND THE VON HOLTZBRINCK GROUP

Verlagsgruppe Georg von Holtzbrinck GmbH & Co KG is a German-oriented, media holding and administration company with a complex portfolio and structure. It is privately help by the von Holtzbrinck family. Verlagsgruppe Handelsblatt is a cornerstone within that structure with interests in publishing (newspapers, magazines, and trade publications), electronic media, and services. (Figure 7). While the group in under no obligation to publish accounts publicly although it is known to have an excellent company capital ratio (45%) and to have had a turnover of 1.86 billion Euros in 1998. With over 11,000 employees it has an extensive web of holdings. As a German media company its direct competitors are Bertelsmann (the number three media group in the world behind Time Warner/AOL and Disney), the Kirch-Gruppe (mainly in TV, music, Video and movies), Axel Springer (mainly in print), and WAZ (mainly regional newspapers).

Handelsblatt began publication on 10 May 1946 with a print run of 10,000 under a British license for the

EXHIBIT 5 — Sold Copies January to June 1999

	Wall Street Journal Europe*	International Herald Tribune	Financial Times
United Kingdom	16,347	15,387	176,218
Germany	7,855	25,331	22,088
Netherlands	6,717	10,609	9,594
Switzerland	6,172	16,313	9,018
Italy	6,031	12,795	6,747
France	5,246	36,891	9,777
Rest of Europe	29,160	47,973	55,725
Europe	77,528	165,299	289,167

*In addition to the *Wall Street Journal Europe*, the *Wall Street Journal* produces its main edition for the US market (which was then translated into ten languages for sale into 14 other markets) and also the English language *Asian Wall Street Journal* with intensive regional reporting.

Source: Horizont 06/2000 page 61

Newspapers	Magazines	Trade Publications	Electronic Media	Services

Newspapers

Handelsblatt
Wirtschafts- und Finanzzeitung

HandelsblattgruppeZeitung GmbH   78.0%

Handelsblatt
News am Abend

Handelsblatt
Junge Karriere

Shares:

The Wall Street Journal Europe	49.0%
Handelsblatt/ Dow Jones, Brüssel	58.4%
Economia, Prag	56.5%
VDI-Verlag	40.0%

Magazines

Wirtschafts Woche

DM

DIE TELE BÖRSE

Trade Publications

fachverlag
· absatzwirtschaft
· handelsjournal
· DER BETRIEB

LEBENSMITTEL PRAXIS

Spotlight

SCHÄFFER POESCHEL

Verlag Wirtschaft und Finanzen

Shares:

| Kurs | 75.0% |
| Verlag form | 49.0% |

Electronic Media

Handelsblatt.com

Wirtschafts Woche heute

ONLINE DM

GENIOS

Shares:

n-tv	28.49%
TV Media	51.0%
Dt. Börsenfernsehen	29.8%
vwd	33.33%
Market Maker	30.0%

Services

GWP media-marketing

prognos

Shares:

| corps | 50.0% |
| EuroRatings | 19.0% |

March 2000

distribution and sale of a business and financial newspaper. It is published in Düsseldorf where it was founded and also in Frankfurt. Holtzbrinck acquired *Handelsblatt* in the late sixties. At that time the daily circulation was 30,000 but after merging with the "Industrieanzeiger" in 1970, *Handelsblatt* became the leading business and financial newspaper in Germany. To respond to the demands for international news reported with sensitivity to its relevance for German readers *Handelsblatt* built the largest international network of German speaking correspondents.

The paper is divided into four main sections plus supplements. The first section examines the interaction and interdependence of economic and political events with the intention of covering "what is economically essential and politically relevant" in Germany and abroad. The next section reports on and analyzes the activities of businesses from all sectors. The third section covers equities, bonds, warrants, currencies and financial markets worldwide. The final core section provides in-depth reporting on special topics such as communication and computers. The core of the paper is then periodically supplemented with coverage of job markets, leisure activities, investing, and e-commerce.

Handelsblatt is the only German national daily focused on business and financial news and considers itself to be "an essential source of information for entrepreneurs and senior executives. The mother group, Verlagsgruppe Handelsblatt generated a consolidated turnover of 679 million DM in 1999 (up from 404 in 1995, 410 in 1996, 476 in 1997, and 526 in 1998). By 2000, it employed some 1,800 people of whom 600 were on the editorial staff (360 at the newspaper itself) and *Handelsblatt* had reached a daily circulation of approximately 234,000 (see Figure 8). As a German national daily *Handelsblatt* has traditionally competed for readership with *Börsen Zeitung, FAZ, Süddeutsche Zeitung,* and *Die Welt*. As such, Handelsblatt was careful to monitor its paper's influence among executives and high-income readers (Figures 9 and 10). With its focus on business news, a number of *Handelsblatt* readers supplemented their intake with another national daily. While 58% read no other national daily, 13% of *Handelsblatt* readers also read *SZ*, 13% also read *Die Welt,* and 29% also read *FAZ*. (Source: LAE 2000/Decisionmakers)

The market spectrum covered by the Handelsblatt brand extends well beyond the flagship newspaper to

Quarter/ Year	Printed- Circulation	Subscription	Newstand Sales	Other Circulation	Board (Airline) issues	Paid Circulation	Free + Advert.	Covered Circu- lation
I/1990	153,145	96,557	19,278	11,953	6,008	127,788	4,951	132,739
II/1990	159,047	98,041	18,362	12,046	6,238	128,449	3,927	132,376
III/1990	161,228	98,128	15,754	11,819	6,102	125,701	4,542	130,243
IV/1990	179,551	99,836	14,829	29,396	7,042	144,061	4,127	148,188
Jahres-DS	163,243	98,141	17,056	16,304	6,348	131,500	4,387	135,887
I/1991	158,196	103,721	15,311	11,992	6,863	131,024	5,647	136,671
II/1991	156,473	103,694	16,505	12,011	7,573	132,210	5,113	137,323
III/1991	155,618	101,961	15,713	13,874	8,279	131,548	5,537	137,085
IV/1991	171,178	101,991	14,250	31,415	8,282	147,656	4,942	152,598
Jahres-DS	160,366	102,842	15,445	17,323	7,749	135,610	5,310	140,919
I/1992	151,717	101,733	15,200	12,718	8,188	129,651	5,266	134,917
II/1992	150,357	101,265	13,435	12,023	7,674	126,723	5,627	132,350
III/1992	148,609	99,873	14,596	12,131	7,706	126,600	5,996	132,596
IV/1992	163,613	100,390	14,444	25,435	7,934	140,269	5,073	145,342
Jahres-DS	153,574	100,815	14,419	15,577	7,876	130,811	5,491	136,301
I/1993	155,965	100,978	16,140	11,216	8,143	128,334	5,341	133,675
II/1993	153,742	100,669	14,938	11,431	8,370	127,038	5,684	132,722
III/1993	152,914	99,939	15,983	11,781	8,446	127,703	6,559	134,262
IV/1993	170,432	101,554	17,089	28,074	8,866	146,717	6,574	153,291
Jahres-DS	158,263	100,785	16,038	15,626	8,456	132,448	6,040	138,488
I/1994	166,881	102,293	17,892	11,719	8,982	131,904	17,114	149,018
II/1994	173,266	103,294	18,731	11,949	9,553	133,974	16,564	150,538
III/1994	167,262	103,255	16,903	12,534	9,280	132,692	7,838	140,530
IV/1994	179,351	104,094	14,436	29,835	8,720	148,365	6,940	155,305
Jahres-DS	171,690	103,234	16,991	16,509	9,134	136,734	12,114	148,848
I/1995	156,625	103,115	14,967	11,603	9,516	129,685	7,049	136,734
II/1995	157,553	102,469	14,259	12,834	10,808	129,562	7,402	136,964
III/1995	155,617	100,705	13,921	14,523	10,844	129,149	7,286	136,435
IV/1995	177,737	101,085	14,066	31,977	10,941	147,128	7,841	154,969
Jahres-DS	161,883	101,844	14,303	17,734	10,527	133,881	7,395	141,276
I/1996	155,971	100,869	15,711	12,729	10,805	129,309	7,152	136,461
II/1996	156,929	101,039	14,688	12,531	10,591	128,258	6,854	135,112
III/1996	155,085	100,161	13,636	13,172	9,941	126,969	6,870	133,839
IV/1996	176,977	100,557	14,660	30,337	9,190	145,554	9,551	155,105
Jahres-DS	161,241	100,657	14,674	17,192	10,132	132,523	7,607	140,129

Quarter/ Year	Printed-Circulation	Subscription	Newstand Sales	Other Circulation	Board (Airline) issues	Paid Circulation	Free + Advert.	Covered Circulation
I/1997	160,974	100,706	15,816	11,108	9,226	127,630	10,510	138,140
II/1997	169,648	103,540	18,628	11,567	9,576	133,735	7,500	141,235
III/1997	173,419	104,370	20,163	12,691	9,947	137,224	7,307	144,531
IV/1997	195,615	106,370	17,874	33,029	10,539	157,273	7,748	165,021
Jahres-DS	174,914	103,747	18,120	17,099	9,822	138,966	8,266	147,232
I/1998	178,685	107,967	20,724	12,743	10,647	141,434	7,574	149,008
II/1998	191,213	110,277	21,986	17,695	11,708	149,958	7,798	157,756
III/1998	188,300	110,132	22,637	14,586	11,734	147,355	8,103	155,458
IV/1998	206,211	111,287	17,763	32,297	11,812	161,347	8,330	169,677
Jahres-DS	191,102	109,916	20,778	19,330	11,475	150,024	7,951	157,975
I/1999	187,409	113,072	21,870	13,514	11,412	148,456	8,285	156,741
II/1999	195,707	113,547	21,185	16,831	11,823	151,563	8,423	159,986
III/1999	198,307	112,442	21,192	15,602	12,396	149,236	8,356	157,592
IV/1999	230,182	114,558	25,363	31,035	12,139	170,956	11,318	182,274
Jahres-DS	202,901	113,405	22,403	19,246	11,943	155,053	9,096	164,148
I/2000	224,359	119,553	33,192	14,665	12,148	167,410	9,330	176,740
II/2000	233,839	120,994	28,203	17,009	12,490	166,206	9,465	175,671

Source: ivw

include other printed publications, electronic media, conferences, television, and research services. Six times a year, *Handelsblatt* publishes *Junge Karriere* on matters relating to career, personal finances, and lifestyle. With a print circulation of around 250,000 it is targeted towards success-oriented 20 to 35 year olds including students and young professionals. An online edition supplements the print version. *Handelsblatt* also publishes two to three brochures a year on specialist topics. *Handelsblatt* journalists who receive additional payment to write these and the brochures are sold through *Handelsblatt's* shop. In addition, *Handelsblatt* publishes some 25 books a year under its own brand. *Handelsblatt* has also experimented with tailored micro-editions that can be digitally distributed for remote printing. Passengers flying Lufthansa receive a preview of the next day's news in *News am Abend* that is produced by a separate editorial staff. International, Global and other editions have been added to reach other groups.

In 1998, *Handelsblatt* launched an online interactive service, *Handelsblatt Interaktiv,* with an independent editorial staff. *Handelsblatt Interaktiv* was packaged as a premium package for economic and financial information. Free four week trials were made available to users before they committed themselves to a subscription. The site offered news, company profiles, a personal portfolio manager and an English language summary. Once again, the company was careful to monitor the attractive demographics of its online users. (Figure 11). W3B data contrasts Handelsblatt.com user with the average internet user in Germany. In general, Handelsblatt.com users are more likely to be older, better off males with higher education than the average. They are also more likely to frequently go online for business related use (78% vs. 60%) and to be interested in business information (54% vs. 37%).

While *Handelsblatt's* senior managers viewed the brand as the most established and best in its niche they also recognized in August 2000 that "the arguments of the FTD are not bad—an own idea of economy, modern themes. So *Handelsblatt* has to continue the change process" and that they needed to "use all chances to

FIGURE 9   Executive Positions Held by Decision-makers

Dailies	TOTAL	Chairman, President, CEO, or Managing Director	Director, Vice President, or Human Resources	Other Senior Management or Executives
Financial Times	17.7	22.3	19.9	11.7
FAZ	13.1	13.9	15.0	9.6
Handelsblatt	14.1	14.1	16.6	9.6
International Herald Tribune	3.3	5.0	3.2	2.5
USA Today	1.6	2.1	1.9	1.0
Wall Street Journal Europe	3.0	4.3	3.3	1.5

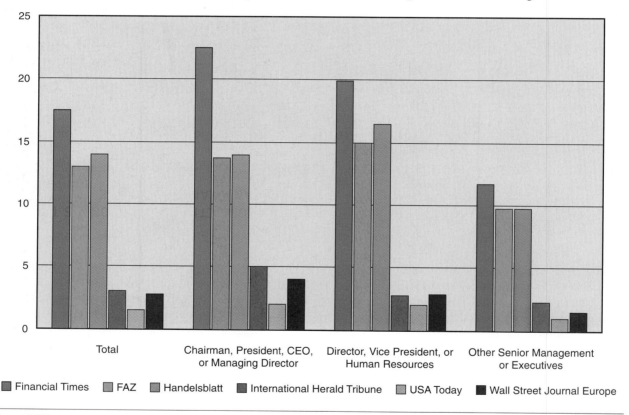

Executive Positions Held by Decision-makers Reading Dailies (Percentage)

■ Financial Times   ■ FAZ   ■ Handelsblatt   ■ International Herald Tribune   ■ USA Today   ■ Wall Street Journal Europe

Source: EBRS 2000

remain the best". Indeed one of the opportunities they focused on was to extend the strong brand of the newspaper to the other products in the portfolio and one important factor driving their performance was their "good competitors". A challenge they saw, however, was to live up to their full potential in a creative sector such as media and to exploit unused possibilities (such as Handelsblatt TV) and potential cross-media synergies. It was their perception that all products in the brand portfolio were under constant development and would always remain so since the market would continue to grow and change.

THE FINANCIAL TIMES DEUTSCHLAND AND THE PEARSON GROUP

The Financial Times Group is one of five major publishing groups that has been acquired by the Pearson

Dailies	TOTAL in %	Medium	High
Financial Times	17.7	13.6	33.6
FAZ	13.1	12.5	12.8
Handelsblatt	14.1	13.6	12.9
International Herald Tribune	3.3	2.7	6.0
USA Today	1.6	1.5	2.5
Wall Street Journal Europe	3.0	2.0	6.6

Income Groups of Decision-makers Reading Dailies (Percentage)

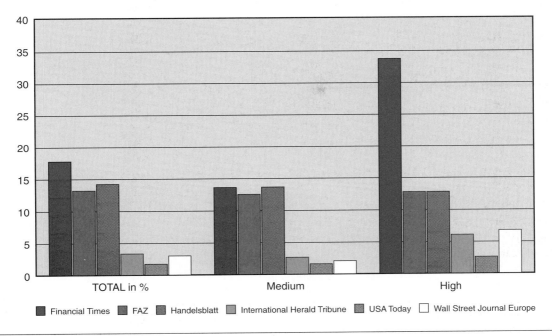

Source: EBRS 2000

Group with all five groups focused on "rich content, powerful brands, and true international reach". The Financial Times Group stated aim is "to be the leading source of strategic information, intelligence and context for senior managers and institutional and individual investors around the world." The FT branded businesses constitutes a group of operations that Pearson intends to have build on the strength of the Financial Times brand. The FT has been aggressive about boosting sales outside of the United Kingdom (its home market). In September 1997, it successfully launched a US edition bringing it into the home territory of its archrival, the *Wall Street Journal.* In 1999 the *Financial Times* newspaper posted a year of record growth with profits up 33% to £56m. In December 1999, average daily circulation topped 435,000 (up 14% from 1998). In the US, the FT reached a circulation milestone of 100,000 daily sales, some two years earlier than they had forecast and continued with plans to open new print sites in Boston and San Francisco. In continental Europe, the FT reached average daily sales of 120,000 (a 20% increase from 1998) while the UK sales grew at 7%, their fastest rate for a decade. Such strong worldwide circulation and a buoyant global economy enabled the *Financial Times* newspaper to increase advertising revenues by 19% in 1999. (See Exhibit 6.)

In 1995, the FT quietly launched an online edition, free of charge, with only five articles a day that was

FIGURE 11 The Handelsblatt.com Reader Compared to the Average Internet User in Germany

	HB.com in %	Overall in %	HB Index
Sex			
Female	17.5	26.1	67
Male	82.5	73.9	112
Age			
to 20	1.4	4.8	29
20–29	26.2	30.4	86
30–39	35.1	33.9	104
40–49	22.1	18.6	119
older than 50	15.1	12.4	122
Net-income			
below 2000 DM	14.3	21.9	65
2.000–4.000 DM	28.3	35.4	80
4.000–6.000 DM	21.5	16.8	128
6.000–8.000 DM	9.1	5.5	165
more than 8.000 DM	10.6	4.8	221
Graduation			
A-level	76.4	62.3	123
Degree-training			
University / Fachhochschule (typical German similar to University)	51.2	38.1	134
PhD			
Field of studies			
Computer science	7.0	8.8	80
Law	6.3	4.7	134
Technology/Engineering	15.7	19.1	82
Business Administration/Economics	38.9	22.8	171
Form of employment			
Self-employed/freelance	18.9	14.1	134
Staff/worker	47.0	36.5	129
Official	3.9	5.3	74
Partial sample staff/worker/official in the industry/craft/government			
Executive/executive board	2.4	1.3	185
Executive staff	30.8	22.5	137
Normal (middle) staff	43.2	42.6	101
Usage of the net for business related procurement			
Responsible for the budget. Involved in decisions concerning procurement	19.3	15.5	125
Deciding what to buy in the group/department	20.6	18.3	113
Advising position concerning procurement	23.5	21.5	109

	HB.com in %	Overall in %	HB Index
Participating in the procurement of new computers/EDP			
Deciding about budget/how to finance	16.4	11.3	145
Participation in purchase decision	30.9	28.0	110
Exclusive responsibility	15.4	14.4	107
Interest in information about finance, markets, stocks			
Business related	3.3	2.5	132
Business related and private	53.8	36.8	146
Planned capital investment in the next 6 months			
Fixed-interest security	13.3	12.3	108
Stocks (blue chips)	77.0	64.4	120
Stocks (IPO)	77.9	66.7	117
Options, futures	21.3	11.8	181
Funds	55.8	53.2	105
Capital-life-insurance	5.9	4.9	120
Private pension-insurance	6.1	6.4	95
WWW—Use since			
5 years or more	26.4	19.5	135
WWW-Use in days/week			
7 days	37.8	32.0	118
Themes about one would like to get informed online			
International news	83.5	67.7	123
National news	78.8	62.9	125
Politics	56.1	44.2	127
Economy	89.9	56.5	159
Facts about companies	71.1	41.5	171
Finance	73.5	41.1	179
Stock markets	80.8	48.2	168
Capital investments	54.8	35.3	155
Real estate	21.1	15.0	141
Insurances	23.7	17.1	139
Job, career	48.7	45.7	107
Science, technology	43.9	41.6	106
Computer science, IT, Internet	62.2	61.9	100
Telecommunications	50.1	43.3	116
Travel, holiday, tourism	46.9	43.2	109
Why using the www.			
(Further) training	58.7	57.0	103
Get up to date news	92.9	82.2	113
Information about products	70.3	64.2	110
Business related research	78.4	65.5	120

	HB.com in %	Overall in %	HB Index
Frequency of business related use			
Very often/often	77.9	60.1	130
Business related use of the www.			
Procurement	34.9	32.1	109
Sales	21.7	17.4	125
Liable for costs databases	20.2	11.0	184
Free databases	56.3	47.2	119
Online job markets	32.1	31.2	103
Subscription of newsletters	44.7	37.6	119
Use of telecommunication categories: "often"			
Mobile (without www.)	65.8	53.0	124
Mobile (with www.)	8.7	4.8	181
Laptop/notebook	45.3	25.9	175
Personal organizer (PDA, Palmtop)	21.9	13.6	161
Use of the www. for shopping			
Answer: very good	31.6	25.5	124
Online buying desire			
Books	80.6	75.3	107
Studies, reports	31.5	19.4	162
Software	57.5	53.5	107
Hardware	47.8	42.8	112
Entertainment—electronics/photo/film	30.6	26.8	114
Telecommunication (e.g. mobile)	34.0	27.8	122
Financial services (overall)	39.2	24.7	159
Securites/stocks	67.7	40.6	167
Options/stocks	30.2	15.0	201
Tickets (plane, train)	68.2	60.3	113
Travel (journeys)	51.3	45.5	113
Cars (new or used)	17.3	13.9	124
Max. amount per online purchase			
500–1000 DM	12.9	12.2	106
1000 and up	43.7	30.1	145
Online buying in the next 6 months			
Answer: Yes, for sure	65.9	55.3	119
Already bought via web			
Up to 20 times	10.8	7.5	144
More than 20 times	18.2	12.2	149

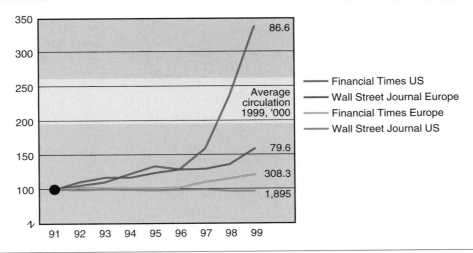

Legend:
- Financial Times US
- Wall Street Journal Europe
- Financial Times Europe
- Wall Street Journal US

Average circulation 1999, '000

- 86.6
- 79.6
- 308.3
- 1,895

Source: The Economist, February 2000

primarily intended to promote its Los Angeles office. In 1996, the site was relaunched as an editorially led site. The stated mission of Financial Times Electronic Publishing (FTEP) is to help business people be more effective and efficient in their careers and personal lives and for FT.com to serve as a "partner in business." *Financial Times* editorial coverage on industries, financial markets and companies is the featured core. This is complemented by extensive content on a full range of business topics, and by tools that are designed to be relevant to the consumer's job and ambitions. FT Business is intended as a spearhead for the Group's efforts to add more specialist in-depth information to professionals throughout the world, specializing in finance and energy. On a free access with registration model, FT.com had grown to being one of the ten top ranked news sites in the world by October 2000. (See Figure 12.)

THE WALL STREET JOURNAL AND THE DOW JONES GROUP

Dow Jones and Company was founded in 1882 and by 1999 it employed 8,200 people and revenues had grown to $2.06 billion with a net income of $272 million. Dow Jones Newswires was founded the same year and began distributing news electronically over a hundred year ago (in 1897). Dow Jones embraces *Barron's* (the Dow Jones Business and Financial weekly), *Smart Money* ("The Wall Street Magazine of Personal Business"), a number of electronic services (including Factiva, a joint venture with Reuters formed in 1999 combining Dow Jones

Interactive with Reuters Business Briefing). Dow Jones is involved in extensive syndication of its content to television and radio and has an alliance with NBC. It owns 50% of CNBC Europe and CNBC Asia. In 1999 Dow Jones co-founded, *Vedmosti,* an independent business newspaper for the "new Russia" with its rival Pearson plc.

The *Wall Street Journal (WSJ)* is the flagship print product of the Dow Jones Group. Founded in 1889, it reached an average paid circulation of 1,840,000 by 1999 (the largest paid circulation in the US). A Sunday edition was added in 1999 and had reached a circulation of 5.8 million. With potential saturation in its home market the *WSJ* also looked for growth abroad and the *Wall Street Journal Europe (WSJE)* was founded in 1983. The *WSJE* is headquartered in Brussels and printed in Bologna, Brussels, London, Frankfurt and Zurich. By 1999, it had reached a circulation of 83,000. Wall Street Journal Special Editions were added in 1994 and, by 1999, a circulation of 2.8 million had been reached through 13 newspapers in ten languages. For its print publishing, Dow Jones reported 1999 revenues of $1.32 billion and an operating income of $372 million.

WSJ.com was founded in 1995–96. While most other newspapers chose to launch their online sites with free subscriptions to generate traffic and attract advertisers, the Dow Jones Group launched WSJ.com with an annual subscription rate of $59 (or $29 for subscribers to the print edition). By January 2000, the Newspaper had 375,000 subscribers paying the full fee with 15% living outside the US and revenues of $30.9 million. Despite skepticism that it could maintain its payment

FIGURE 12 — Top Ranked Internet News and Information Sites, October 2000

This Week	Last Week	
1.	1.	cnet.com
2.	2.	cnn.com
3.	3.	msnbc.com
4.	4.	weather.com
5.	5.	nytimes.com
6.	6.	usatoday.com
7.	7.	go.com
8.	8.	ft.com
9.	9.	washingtonpost.com
10.	10.	newsworks.com
▲ 11.	12.	rediff.com
▼ 12.	11.	theonion.com
13.	13.	foxnews.com
▲ 14.	15.	tminterzines.com
▼ 15.	14.	timesofindia.com
▲ 16.	19.	unitedmedia.com
17.	17.	discovery.com
▲ 18.	20.	yahoo.com
▼ 19.	16.	headbone.com
▼ 20.	18.	freep.com
▲ 21.	22.	sjmercury.com
▲ 22.	23.	salon.com
▲ 23.	25.	herald.com
24.	24.	wsj.com
▲ 25.	26.	detnews.com

scheme (both the *New York Times* and *Slate* had been forced to abandon theirs, for example) by October 2000, WSJ.com was still one of the top 25 news sites in the world. According to the head of the group, Peter Kann, "We have lost maybe a few thousand readers who have cancelled their print subscriptions—but that's all. Two thirds of our online readers are new readers. If cannibalization is going to happen, it may as well be us that benefit from it." [*Connectis,* July 2000]

COMPETITIVE MANEUVERING IN THE GERMAN NEWSPAPER INDUSTRY

McGrath's words of advice about pursuing partnerships aggressively certainly were consistent with the observed competitive maneuvers in Germany, Europe's biggest

press sector and Europe's largest economy. On 15 January 1999 Dr. Heinz-Werner Neinstedt, CEO of Handelsblatt, was informed about a Pearson/Gruner & Jahr "project" to launch a German language paper with a strong international focus. The CEO of the Pearson Group announced "our new product will be totally different . . . The reader will discover something completely new". Within days, *Handelsblatt* built a team to collect information about the project, to reflect on the strengths and weaknesses of *Handelsblatt,* and to prepare strategies for confronting the "invader". The team was readily able to assess the players: Pearson was an expert in the British newspaper market; Gruner & Jahr was an expert in the German magazine market; and both had virtually unlimited resources but neither were considered to be experts in the German newspaper market. The team also knew that time and patience were required for success in the newspaper market (in contrast to the magazine market). They knew far less, however, about the proposed product. They did not know:

- what the title would be
- what format and paper color it would have
- whether it would have a four color layout
- what the copy price would be
- how often it would be published
- how it would be positioned
- who its intended audience was
- what its lock-up time would be, and
- what its launch date was.

The team did know a lot about *Handelsblatt* though. They knew that the paper was second in circulation among the national dailies only to *FAZ* and that it had the highest circulation among business newspapers in Germany. They felt that their relaunches had proven that they were "aggressive, innovative, and fast" and, of potential strategic importance, that the invaders did not know about the strengths of *Handelsblatt*. On the other hand, they believed that the invaders did know about *Handelsblatt's* weaknesses: that it was perceived as "German", that the writing was sometimes in a boring style, and that they had only one printing plant.

In 1999, Philipp J. Fleischmann had been promoted from being product manager for *Handelsblatt* to being joint CEO with Dr. Neinstedt. Assessing the alternative responses to the invaders they knew they could either "wait and see" or they could be faster than their enemy. They chose the latter and the *Handelsblatt* team evaluated four strategic issues:

- partners
- people
- public, and
- product.

On the first day of June 1999: Pete Kann of Dow Jones and Dieter von Holtzbrinck announced that they had agreed to swap shares between *Handelsblatt* and *The Wall Street Journal Europe* in a strategic alliance at the German stock exchange in Frankfurt. In a world hungry for content, the *WSJE* editors would be gaining access to material from *Handelsblatt* translated by Journal translators into German on a "real-time" basis for same day publication. Reciprocally, the *Handelsblatt* would be translating *WSJE* material into German on the same basis. While they would exchange editors to intensify editorial cooperation, both papers, however, would maintain full editorial control over their own products. Together they would have the largest network of journalists worldwide and the largest German network of business correspondents. Moreover, they would have the opportunity to produce joint supplements.

The management of Verlagsgruppe Handelsblatt felt the need to keep pushing, however—the strategic alliance was to be just the start. On 19 July 1999, 50 executive officers of Verlagsgruppe Handelsblatt were called together to engage in two days of war-gaming and brainstorming over the FTD launch in a secluded setting. The session ended with the executives highly

motivated by what they viewed as a challenge rather than a threat to overcome *Handelsblatt's* weaknesses as expediently as possible. Agreeing that the worst-case scenario was that the invaders might launch as early as the 15th of November they made a decision to relaunch at the beginning of the fourth quarter. Their 1994 relaunch had taken a year and they had managed to relaunch in less than half that time in 1997, but now they were going to press themselves to more than halve their time again—this relaunch was going to be allowed only two months. A week later a new approach was worked out with nine teams from the international ad agency, BBDO. It was decided that the campaign would have two base lines: a brand campaign to support *Handelsblatt* subscriptions and a sales campaign to support *Handelsblatt* newsstand sales. Since *Handelsblatt* expected the invaders to mount a massive launch campaign, a choice was made to occupy all communication channels of the target group of decision-makers in 1999 and 2000. This meant that they would double the marketing budget in 1999 and 2000 (see Figure 13), take early placement on n-TV and major radio stations, and use outdoor advertising space strategically. On 18 October 1999: *Handelsblatt* was relaunched for the third

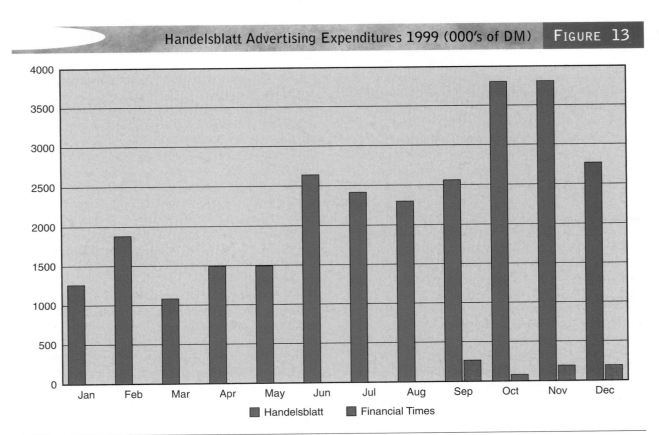

Handelsblatt Advertising Expenditures 1999 (000's of DM)   FIGURE 13

Legend: ■ Handelsblatt   ■ Financial Times

Source: Firmen und Ihre Werbekampagnen

time with the intention of being "fresher, younger, more international". Four new sections were added: Report, Inside, Technology and Media, and Investor. The effort was supported with approximately 50 additional editors and correspondents. A new, clean layout by Mario Garcia was used and orange became the signature color of the brand.

More action was to come, however. In October 1999 the *Frankfurter Allgemeine Zeitung* (*FAZ*, a leading German language daily that included strong financial coverage) and the *International Herald Tribune* (*IHT*, an English language daily owned 50% by the *Washington Post* and 50% by the *New York Times*) announced a planned Spring 2000 launch of an English language version of *FAZ*. This version was to be sold as an eight-page insert in the *IHT* in its Belgium, German, and Austrian markets. The move was backed by the largest promotional campaign that the *IHT* had ever run in Germany (its second largest market) with direct mail, outdoor and press advertising. Within two months the total circulation in Germany of the *IHT* jumped from 25,445 to 30,836 copies. Michael Getler, the executive editor of the *IHT* heralded the business and editorial alliance:

"We believe the combined coverage of Germany and the world will be second to none. The FAZ is the most authoritative and prestigious paper in Germany. It is fitting that it should be the one to open this door to greater understanding of Germany—the economic powerhouse of Europe—for the English speaking world."

The *IHT's* enthusiasm for partnering was not confined to Germany, however: they had also recently teamed up with the *Rizzoli Corriere della Sera* in Italy, *Ha'artez* in Israel and *Katherimerini* in Greece. Moreover, they were reporting dramatic circulation increases of 30%, 1,300% and 130% respectively.

Meanwhile, Dow Jones looked to the partnership with *Handelsblatt* as the foundation for the largest and most ambitious growth program they had ever undertaken for the *WSJE*. They also planned to:

- double the newspaper's circulation within five years to more than 140,000,
- expand the European reporters and editors by more than ten from a base of more than 70,
- up the page capacity from 32 to 40 pages a day and from 8 to 12 color pages,
- add two new print sites (in Italy and Scandinavia) to their existing four, and
- support their initiatives with a multi-million dollar advertising and marketing campaign.

On 7 February 2000: Dow Jones relaunched the *WSJE* "with more staff, more technology coverage, and a less archaic front page" (*Economist* 19 February 2000). The most notable feature of the new *Wall Street Journal Europe* was a daily third section called "Networking". Focusing on the "New Economy", "Networking" was positioned as the leading source for news and analysis of new media, technology and management. It was intended to be an invaluable guide to readers trying to understand, or "get", the volatile and dynamic forces shaping the technology-driven global economy. According to Peter Kann, chairman and CEO of Dow Jones:

"This investment is testament to our belief that the concept of a pan-European newspaper has come of age, that European business-people 'get it'. The Wall Street Journal Europe is Europe's international business daily. From the New Economy to the New Equity Culture, our unrivalled global resources allow us to provide the best summary anywhere of business news everywhere. This is as essential to our readers in the New Europe as it is in Asia, Latin America and the U.S."

On 21 February 2000, the *Financial Times Deutschland* was launched with a starting circulation of 50,000 and 130 journalists. Newsstand sales reached an estimated 33,000 copies. One question was how much this would cannibalize the circulation of 22,000 that the English language version had enjoyed before the launch. Two weeks after the public reaction appeared mixed (see Exhibit 7).

In April, the *FAZ/IHT* product came online as scheduled. *Handelsblatt* continued to move and relaunched *Handelsblatt Interaktiv* as Handelsblatt.com in May adding a 28 day archive (Handelsblatt Topix) to their offering that was free to print subscribers (and available on a pay per month scheme to non-subscribers). The WSJ.com link was now prominently featured on the Handelsblatt.com site. The site now shared the distinctive orange signature look of the print version. In July, *Handelsblatt* announced a joint venture with the Reuters Group to launch a personal finance website (50%/50% ownership).

By October Hr. Fleischmann could look with satisfaction at the battle to date. Every circulation figure was above where it had been the year before (refer back to Figure 8). The newsstand sales of the FTD were deteriorating sharply (see Figure 14) and *Handelsblatt* had also captured the pole position from *FAZ* for the first time. Still, overall circulation of the *FTD* was rising (Figure 15). Moreover, Hr. Fleischmann knew that his competitors were seriously committed, that they had deep pockets, and that they were unlikely to accept defeat. So the question became: what next?

EXHIBIT 7

	Global	Compared to Handelsblatt*
"FTD" is able to compete	45	29
"FTD" is an alternative	39	25
"FTD" is a good complement	16	8
Provides interesting services	4	1
Has a higher quality	1	1
Reaches a broader target-group	1	—
I do not like it as much	15	8
Is less clear (übersichtlich)	4	3
Cannot judge it that early	28	21

*includes only persons who saw a competition between the FTD and the Handelsblatt (84% of the people asked)

Source: "Kohorten Meinungsforschung" after Horizont 12/2000

CHRONOLOGY OF SIGNIFICANT ACTIONS AFFECTING THE GERMAN BUSINESS NEWSPAPER MARKET (1994–2000)

1994: *Handelsblatt* is relaunched for the first time. The relaunch takes one year from inception to execution.

May 1995: FT.com slides quietly onto the web with five stories a day. It is intended primarily as a promotion of the newspaper's printing in Los Angeles.

April 1996: WSJ.com launched.

April 1996: FT.com relaunched as an editorially led site.

1997: *Handelsblatt* is relaunched for the second time. The relaunch takes five months from inception to execution.

February 1997: *The Wall Street Journal Europe* is relaunched.

1998: *Handelsblatt Interaktiv,* an online edition of *Handelsblatt* is launched.

1998: Wallstreet Online founded as a free service providing stock quotes. By 2000, it has the most page impressions and visits for any provider of financial information in Germany. Revenues grew from 300,000 DM the first year to 2 million in 1999.

329

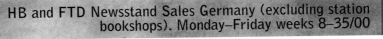

HB and FTD Newsstand Sales Germany (excluding station bookshops). Monday–Friday weeks 8–35/00 — FIGURE 14

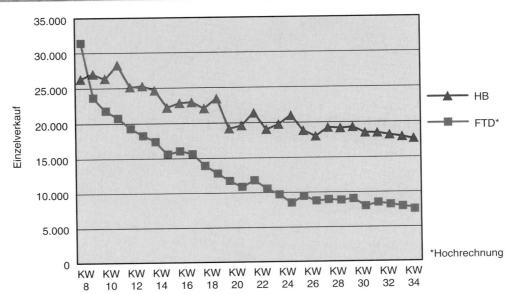

Source: Verlagsgruppe Handelsblatt

FIGURE 15 Circulation of the Financial Times Deutschland

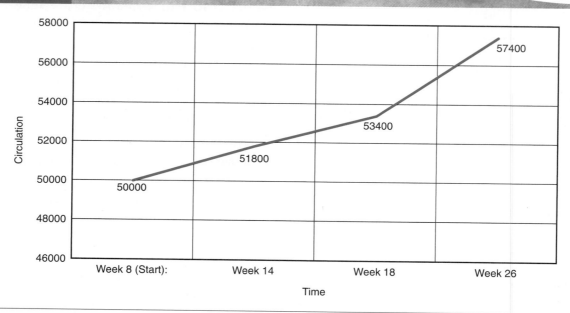

Source: Horizont 30/2000

1998: The Pearson Group starts talks with Gruner & Jahr to launch a product in Germany. Gruner & Jahr is a majority owned print subsidiary of Bertelsmann with magazine, printing, trade, and central services divisions. It is one of the 50 largest media groups in Europe in its own right.

March 1998: Holtzbrinck signs an agreement with Infoseek to launch a co-branded search engine service. Infoseek simultaneously signs deal with Axel Springer and Deutsche Telekom Online Service (a major Internet access provider).

Late 1998: The Pearson Group's planned entry into German market with a German language daily is rumored as Pearson starts to poach journalists from other newspapers.

15 January 1999: Dr. Heinz-Werner Neinstedt, CEO of *Handelsblatt,* is informed about the Pearson/Gruner & Jahr "project".

1 March 1999: Pearson and Gruner & Jahr publicize their concrete plans for launching a German language newspaper on pink paper with *Financial Times* as part of the title. The editor-in-chief will be drawn from the *FT* and the publishing manager will be drawn from Gruner & Jahr.

1 June 1999: Pete Kann of Dow Jones and Dieter von Holtzbrinck announce that they have agreed to swap shares between *Handelsblatt* and *The Wall Street Journal Europe* in a strategic alliance at the German stock exchange in Frankfurt.

19 July 1999: 50 executive officers of Verlagsgruppe assemble for two days in a secluded setting to engage in two days of war-gaming and brainstorming over the *FTD* launch.

26 July 1999: A new brand and sales campaign is worked out with BBDO. (BBDO is an international ad agency with 291 operating companies across 73 countries. The group's most international clients are Bayer and Pepsi, handled in over 60 countries each. Excluding specialized marketing subsidiaries, BBDO was ranked by *Advertising Age* as the number three agency network worldwide in 1999 with gross income of $1.4bn and billings of $12.2bn.)

Fall 1999: *Handelsblatt* extends market that will support a relaunch.

October 1999: The *International Herald Tribune* and the *Frankfurter Allgemeine Zeitung* announce that they are launching an English edition of *FAZ* in the Spring of 2000 both in print and online.

8 October 1999: Reuters signs an agreement to supply 26 news media services to ft.com including online reports (covering breaking news in business, technology, and international sports) and specialist reports (about individual financial markets).

18 October 1999: *Handelsblatt* is relaunched for the third time with the intention of being "fresher, younger, more international". New sections are added: "Report, Inside, Technology and Media, and Investor." The effort is supported with approximately 50 additional editors and correspondents. The relaunch takes two months from inception to execution.

7 February 2000: Dow Jones relaunches the *WSJE* "with more staff, more technology coverage, and a less archaic front page" (Economist 19/2/00). The most notable feature of the new *Wall Street Journal Europe* is a new daily third section called "Networking".

14 February 2000: *FT* relauches FT.com with the aim of making it the world's leading global business portal. The service is free to use and is intended to generate revenue from advertising, sponsorship and e-commerce. Certain premium services such as the share monitoring service and access to the searchable archive require registration. The *FTD* also issues a press release promoting its cross-media opportunities under a "One Brand, all media" campaign to attract advertisers.

21 February 2000: Pearson Group announces joint venture with Gruner & Jahr to launch *Financial Times Deutschland* (both print and online).

May 2000: *Handelsblatt Interaktiv* relaunched as Handelsblatt.com.

13 July 2000: *Handelsblatt* announces joint venture with Reuters to offer a personal finance website.

Handelsblatt Product History

(Launch years for products in the Handelsblatt brand portfolio)

1946	*Handelsblatt:* First printing of **Handelsblatt**
1987	*Junge Karriere:* Launch **Junge Karriere**
1993	*Conferences, etc.:* Handelsblatt **Veranstaltungen**
1994	*Specialized literature:* Handelsblatt **Books** (approx. 180,000 units)
1995	*Conferences etc.:* Handelsblatt **Financial Trainings**
	Television: **Handelsblatt Ticker** auf n-tv
	Online: **Handelsblatt News am Abend,** (News in the evening) Lufthansa Edition
1996	*Online:* Handelsblatt Internet Edition
1997	*Junge Karriere:* **Junge Karriere Online**
	Conferences etc.: Handelsblatt **Investor Seminars**
1998	*Research:* Handelsblatt **Annual Report Service**
	Online: Handelsblatt Interaktiv
1999	*Digital:* Handelsblatt **Global Edition**
	Digital: News am Abend Metropolitan and International Editions
2000	*Digital:* News am Abend Business Travel Edition
	Television: **Investor Sport Börse** DSF, Handelsblatt TV
	Online: **Handelsblatt.com** and **Handelsblatt Topix**
	Online: Founding of **Handelsblatt Online AG**

Source: Verlagsgruppe Handelsblatt

case twenty-five

Stephen Bowden
University of Waikato

"This really is a fantastic company to be part of.

Every day presents new opportunities to build on the great legacy we have"

Nick Nightingale, General Manager,
Resene Paints

As Nick Nightingale, General Manager of Resene Paints, walked along a corridor between his office and the manufacturing plant, he looked at the can of Stipplecote cement-based paint that sat in a display case. Stipplecote was the original product that his grandfather, Ted Nightingale, had developed and based the company on in 1946. While that paint-can represented the humble beginnings of Resene, the position of the company in September 2001 was far removed. In 55 years, Resene had grown into an integrated manufacturer and retailer of a wide array of high quality paints and surface coatings. Resene operated four manufacturing plants in New Zealand, one in Australia and one in Fiji. In addition, a chain of 54 company-owned ColorShops and 19 franchised outlets provided the retail arm of Resene in New Zealand. A total of 600 employees worked for Resene generating over $100M in group annual revenue and healthy profits (all figures are in New Zealand dollars unless otherwise stated). Resene had cultivated a stellar reputation for innovation throughout its history—especially from water-based paints, colour development and environmental awareness.

Still, despite the enormous pride that Nick felt in the company's achievements over the last 55 years, he knew that Resene faced many challenges in the future. Resene competed against large multinationals in an industry facing rising research costs. Could Resene continue to be such an innovator or did they need to change in some way? While dominant in the commercial market, Resene trailed the paint sales of Dulux overall. Resene was not as strong in retail sales—particularly in Auckland. But could they gain market share without sacrificing profits? Currently Resene's sales in Australia were about the same as those in Hawkes Bay. Obviously there was massive potential for growth, but how should Resene approach Australia? Were there better opportunities than Australia elsewhere in the world? Essentially, what should the focus of Resene be in the future—what range of products and markets should they be in and how should they structure the company to best take advantage of that identity?

A HISTORY OF INNOVATION AND GROWTH

Ted Nightingale, a builder with no chemical or technical training, developed Stipplecote, a paint for concrete, simply because no such paint existed (*www.resene.co.nz/ pdf/nostalgia.pdf* offers a more complete history). In 1951, Ted also developed New Zealand's first water-based paint under the brand name Resene and formed the Stipplecote Product Company in 1952. Ted developed water-based paint after he heard that the resin he was familiar with through Stipplecote, PVA, could be used to make other paints. In an experimental way, with very limited resources, Ted was able to solve the problem and develop the water-based paint. In many ways, it was a process that would be repeated again and again over the history of Resene as the company continued to innovate in terms of both paint types and colours. Being a pioneer, Ted actually had to convince people that the paint would not just wash off. After considerable effort, demand for the company's water-based paints grew strongly. Indeed, for some time it appeared as though

Resene would become the generic name for water-based paints. The growth necessitated expansion and resulted in moves from the original Kaiwharawhara factory to Seaview in 1967 and then to the current site in Naenae in 1992. In 1977 the company changed its name from Stipplecote Products to the present Resene Paints Ltd.

Paint and protective coatings have long been produced for a wide range of purposes. Resene really conceives of five different markets that they sell to. First, there is a commercial market consisting of tradespeople, architects and specifiers. It is an important aspect of paint sales that the person who applies the paint is not necessarily the decision-maker about which paint is used. Often an architect, an interior decorator or even a project manager will specify the paint to be used. While on small jobs a painter may dictate the paint to be used, this is rarely the case on larger projects. The second market is the retail market, consisting of do-it-yourself (DIY) consumers who paint their own houses and are infrequent purchasers of paint. Though the retail and commercial market will use similar paints, there can be differences. For example, a thicker paint may be used on the exterior of a high-rise building than on a home. The combined commercial and retail markets are often referred to as the architectural and decorative coatings market. Third, often treated separately, is the specialty finishes market, which mainly involves textured coatings. These textured coatings are considered almost a construction product. Fourth, there is a protective coatings market that includes marine products as well as industrial coatings and some architectural products like anti-graffiti systems. Coatings like those supplied to steel manufacturers to create different finishes are also included in the protective coatings market. Finally, there is an automotive market for paints that is distinct.

While Resene began as a manufacturer of basic paints for buildings and houses, focused mainly on water-based paints, the company has widened its range of paints and coatings considerably since to now offer an extensive range of products for each market. Resene moved into solvent-based paints and has a specialised plant in Upper Hutt. Resene also operates two acquired subsidiaries based in New Zealand—broadening their range considerably. Altex Coatings, with manufacturing facilities both in Tauranga and Australia, is a manufacturer of protective coatings for industrial and marine surfaces. Resene Automotive & Performance Coatings, located in Auckland, manufactures its own brand of automotive, furniture and industrial paints and a range of car care products for the New Zealand market. Resene Automotive is also the distributor in New Zealand for the world's leading brand in automotive refinish paint—DuPont car paints. In addition, Resene operates two international subsidiaries. Resene Ltd (Australia) focuses on manufacturing marine coatings as well as a full range of industrial and architectural coatings from its factory on the Gold Coast. Resene Paints Fiji Limited in Suva manufactures a full range of architectural, industrial and marine paints as well as furniture lacquers for the commercial and retail customer. Outside of the paint industry, Resene owns the Cellier Le Brun Ltd wine-maker in Blenheim.

At the same time that Resene has been going from strength to strength, however, other paint companies have been disappearing. The New Zealand market has consolidated considerably over the last 30 years. Where previously a large number of small independent paint manufacturers existed—probably 30 or 40—now the industry is dominated by the largest three firms: Orica, Resene and Wattyl. Both Orica and Wattyl are large Australian companies for whom the New Zealand paint market represents a small aspect of their operations. Orica, formerly ICI Australia, operates in New Zealand through brands including Dulux, British Paints and Levenes. Wattyl distributes both Wattyl and Taubmans branded paints in New Zealand. Even among the smaller paint companies in New Zealand, these tend to have links to major international paint companies such as Benjamin Moore. Resene is the only paint company still doing research and development in New Zealand and as a group currently manufactures the most paint in New Zealand.

By comparison to the corporate size of their major competitors, Resene is a very small company. Indeed, Resene has always worked from the premise that they are vulnerable to the deep pockets of competitors. Consequently, the need to be different from the competition has always been strong, but the resources to achieve that difference have been limited relative to the competition. The history of innovations that Resene has achieved is all the more remarkable because of those resource constraints. However, the resource constraints do not infer low profitability—Resene has enjoyed considerable success over the years. In fact, financial performance has been strong enough that auditors have advised Resene that they keep too much money on term deposit. More the issue is that major investments are difficult to justify given the potential returns from their current markets.

THE NIGHTINGALE FAMILY

The contrast between Resene and its competitors could not be stronger in terms of ownership. Resene is a privately-owned, family business that is still headed by the Nightingale family that founded the business. While there are still family paint manufacturers around the world, their numbers have diminished globally and most of those remaining are niche players. One consequence of being a private firm is that Resene does not report its results publicly, while its competitors, as publicly-owned companies are required to make public a great deal of financial and strategic information. As a consequence, competitors can only guess at Resene's sales and profits. A significant difference from competitors that stems from the ownership by the Nightingale family has been the tenure of the boss. Resene has always been headed by a member of the Nightingale family and the orientation to the long-term has been strong as a result.

Initially, the founder Ted Nightingale ran the company until his retirement. Ted's retirement was a major event in the history of Resene. In the early period of the company, Ted was the innovator as well as the marketer and manager and everything else. In the succession plan that was implemented with Ted's retirement, the company was structured to be less reliant on a single individual and more specialised in the management structure. Ted's son Tony became Managing Director, while the recently hired Technical Director, Colin Gooch, was given considerable autonomy for the technical issues. Tony focused more on the marketing and managerial issues, although he has always debated other issues with Colin. Given the importance of technical issues within the company, the legacy of the succession was probably that Tony and Colin were forced to work together and agree on how to proceed. Their relationship, and the mutual respect they have for each other's complementary skills, has been critical to the development of Resene to the present. While the company was no longer completely reliant on one individual, the loss of both Colin and Tony would have been disastrous and as a result they tried not to travel together.

Currently, Resene is gradually moving through the next stage in the succession of the company. Tony is still the Managing Director, although illness has limited his involvement over the last few years. Two and a half years ago, Nick became General Manager, directly under his father, with all other senior managers reporting to Nick. In the near future Tony will probably become Chairman of the Board and Nick will assume the Managing Director's position. Potentially compounding that succession issue, Colin Gooch is set to retire in five years time and no obvious successor to Colin is yet apparent. Nevertheless, the average tenure of managing directors at Resene has been close to 30 years, while its competitors often view New Zealand as a training ground and turn over senior management on approximately a two-year cycle.

TOP MANAGEMENT

Nick Nightingale, like his father Tony, has grown up around the business. Nick has been involved in jobs around the company since his youth. He was even the first person to staff one of their stores on a Saturday. After completing a commerce degree at Victoria University, Nick spent a few years overseas before returning to New Zealand and the family business. He has worked on the sales side since his return, being a Regional Sales Manager prior to General Manager. Since early in his tenure, Nick has taken on most of the operational running of the company. Reporting to Nick are all the functional managers (see Figure 1 for the organisational chart). In addition, the heads of each of the subsidiary companies throughout New Zealand, Australia and Fiji—except Altex who report directly to Tony—are responsible to Nick. The degree of centralisation of the activities of the subsidiary companies varies, but is generally very low. A small amount of R&D work is done in Naenae for the Australian and Fijian subsidiaries, but this is limited because of product differences. Recently, Resene has switched suppliers for a major resin raw material to its Australian subsidiary to the same supplier that the Naenae operation uses. This has generated cost savings, quality improvement, and means that the knowledge that Resene has accumulated in Naenae about that resin can be utilised in Australia. Resene Automotive and Altex, serving different markets with different products, are treated as stand-alone business units.

One common bond among top management is their orientation to quality and the pride they take in having that quality show through. One reason that the current marketing manager, Karen Warman, has been so successful within the company is that she also shares those common values and infuses the quality orientation throughout the company's marketing efforts. In fact, managers who do not share that orientation have not lasted at Resene. Often, the orientation to quality comes at a cost to the company in terms of materials used. For example, Resene has recently increased the weight of card used as the backing on a colour chart for metallic paints. This has increased the cost of producing those colour charts by 20 cents per card or 9%, but means that the card holds up better, looks more attractive and better supports the quality proposition.

Nevertheless, within a company with such a strong orientation toward quality and innovation the potential for conflict across functional areas can be strong. While the tradition of largely separating technical aspects from marketing aspects has been continued through to the present day, clearly the two areas are interdepend-

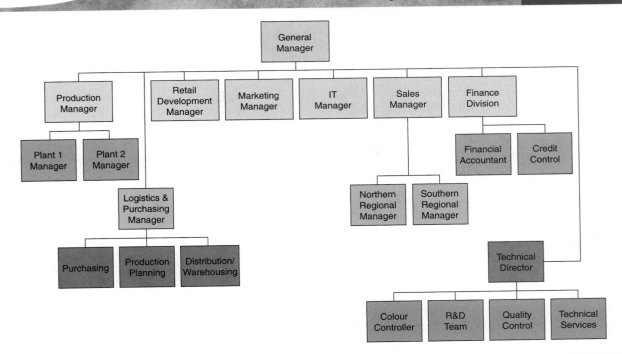

*Subsidiaries not included

ent. Of primary importance, if marketing is unable to convey to consumers why Resene paint is technically superior in ways that can be understood, the capacity to charge a premium is diminished. In reality, this is a real issue within Resene. Due to both the myriad of ways that Resene makes its paint better, and to the technical complexity of the ways in which Resene's paint is superior, even professional painters probably do not truly understand how good Resene paint is. Colin Gooch, the Technical Director, will only use the best quality ingredients in the paint and he will seek standards for the paint that go far beyond either industry norms or even customer expectations. This has been a major aspect of Resene's success, but it is not a short-term process that lends itself easily to product-specific marketing. However, the quality has at least been recognised by the New Zealand Consumer Institute, identifying Resene as standing out above all other brands of interior acrylic paints.[1]

Despite the fact that Resene has introduced many new products to the market, the idea of product launch has been regarded as "a bit of a foreign concept." Instead, people would come up with a name and "then sort of sneak the product onto the market." This can work as an approach if people recognise that Resene paints are the best quality paint. While, as noted, this is

difficult to convey, over time painters will notice that they have less come-backs (repairs) on Resene paints. Fundamentally, there was a belief that quality would sell—eventually. The cost structure certainly led to arguments—Tony would try to get Colin to look at the cost of producing the paint to see if they could get that down. Eventually, Colin would agree to look at how they might reduce the cost structure, but it never actually happened. Colin noted that he could honestly say, "there had never been a decision to reduce quality over the last 30 years—only to increase it."

The board of directors for Resene presently consists of Tony Nightingale; Lindsay Lewer, the Finance Director; Colin Gooch; and Wellington lawyer, Adrian Ellingham. At present, particularly since the board is heavily weighted towards active employees, meetings of the board are not highly formalised, nor are they regular. Important decisions involve consultation between Nick and Tony. Specific expertise is sought as necessary either within the company or, occasionally, through consultants. Nick sees the board as likely evolving into a more formalised role with additional members added such as the manager of Altex Coatings, Nick himself and perhaps Nick's brother.

One task that management at Resene has recently pursued has been the development of a vision for the company—for internal purposes only at this stage. Two alternatives have been under discussion among the management team: *"Resene will be an innovative supplier of paint solutions to the retail and commercial marketplace"* or *"Resene will be a world leader in the provision of paint products, colour and their technologies. We will be driven by our successful, world class New Zealand team which will celebrate our success."* In mid-September, the management team chose to go with, **"To be acknowledged as the leading provider of innovative paint solutions and technologies."**

HUMAN RESOURCES

The orientation towards quality is infused into every aspect of the company—even the manuals that cover the technical specifications for its paints have won awards. That means that there has to be attention to detail throughout the organisation from people who are committed to the success of Resene. While that is very difficult to achieve over an entire organisation, the company is small enough that employees can feel a very strong sense of identity with Resene. Indeed, a significant proportion of employees have worked for Resene for many years. When Resene does recruit new staff there is a general preference for avoiding employees who have worked for other paint companies. For example, the sales force has, in recent times, recruited only four employees from competitors. This is because the philosophy of competitors tends to be more towards making sales, even at the expense of profits. Resene prefers to recruit from other industries—people who have an understanding of selling a quality product for a profit. Hiring technical staff, in particular, is very difficult. Resene has recently had to hire two scientists from India to obtain suitably qualified and trained staff. In general, technical recruits from competitors are typically more used to a sterile environment with well-resourced labs, but less orientation toward creativity.

Resene does place significant emphasis on continued training after recruitment, but probably no more than competitors. However, in retail, because it operates its own chain of ColorShops, Resene is at least more in control of the way its products are presented and sold. Moreover, training can be more product specific.

PRODUCT RANGE

At its most basic level there are two types of paint—water-based and solvent-based. The difference refers to the type of solvent used in the paint for thinning—water or a petroleum derivative. While Resene pioneered water-based paints in New Zealand, as noted,

Resene later began producing solvent-based paints as well. Currently these are produced in its Upper Hutt plant—separately from the main plant in Lower Hutt. Solvent-based paints can have certain properties that make them desirable over water-based paints—particularly for high-gloss products. However, in general water-based paints have many advantages over oil-based paints. Water-based paints are not considered dangerous goods because there is not the fire danger of a petroleum-based product. Water-based paints also clean up easier, have less dangerous fumes and are generally more environmentally friendly. Because of these advantages, water-based paints now dominate production in Australasia. As such, paint companies are always looking to develop water-based versions of paints that have previously only been available as oil-based. One recent example is where Resene has pioneered the first truly water-based enamel in the world.

Within these two types of paint, Resene produces literally hundreds of product types, and thousands of specific SKUs (just think of test pots) for use on the huge variety of surfaces that paint can be applied to. The product range of Resene includes all-manner of primers, sealers, undercoats and topcoats for wood, steel, concrete, plaster or any other building material. There is literally no type of paint that a painter could want for any surface that Resene does not supply. Indeed, an important part of the service they offer to retail customers, professional painters, and architects and specifiers is the advice available on the appropriate product for particular surfaces. Resene produces specification manuals to aid this, but also works at a personal level with clients on specific problems. Both the decorative and protective functions of paint can be compromised—no matter how good the paint is—if the paint is not able to bond with the surface it is applied to.

MANUFACTURING

The actual manufacturing of paint is relatively simple and involves the mixing together of the basic ingredients of pigment, binder, solvents and additives. At Resene, like the vast majority of paint manufacturers in Australasia, paint is produced in batches. Industry-wide these batches vary from 200 litres to 20,000 litres at a time. Resene produces in batches ranging from 200 litres to 10,000 litres. The technology for batch manufacturing is not capital intensive—particularly for the production of less complex paint. The technology for continuous production of particular lines of paint does exist, but is only economic for the most popular lines of the largest manufacturers. Currently, no continuous manufacturing is done in New Zealand. Those compa-

There are four basic components in paint: pigments, binder, solvent and additives. **Pigments** are naturally occurring or synthetically produced fine powders that are dispersed or ground into a binding medium and provide the colour and covering power as their major function in paints. The **binder** is the portion of the dry paint film that binds the pigment particles together and to the painted surface. The binder gives the film many necessary properties such as gloss, adhesion, hardness, toughness, flexibility, durability and speed of drying. The **solvent** or dilutant is the material with which the binder and pigment are mixed in order that the paint may be of the correct consistency to be applied to the surface by brush, roller, spray, dipping and other methods. **Additives** are materials which are added to the paint, usually in small quantities, to help it dry more quickly or flow out evenly to remove brush marks and to stop skinning in the can. One example is silicone; this makes the surface of the paint film more resistant to marking and scratching.

Source: Australian Paint Manufacturer's Federation

nies that do use continuous manufacturing claim quality and efficiency advantages over batch processing. Continuous manufacturing is not suitable, however, for producing multiple different product lines. The majority of paint manufacturers emphasize product range, making continuous manufacturing less practical. As well as demand constraints, the type of product may limit the size of batch production. Resene has a product called Zylone Sheen which, if produced in too large a batch, turns into a jelly-like substance. While each new product is tested prior to full production through small batch production, it is not always the case that the move from small batch to large batch production is seamless.

The manufacturing facility at Naenae has recently been expanded. An additional 8% capacity has been built, aiding the manufacture of industrial tinters and generally streamlining the manufacturing process. One outcome of the expansion is that less stock needs to be carried as the plant has greater capacity to produce paint as needed. Currently Resene typically has approximately 1000 pellets of paint on hand and hopes to reduce that by 30–40%. Resene has the space on its present site to be able to double capacity. Dulux has recently invested $4M on upgrading its plant in Grace-

field, Lower Hutt. The introduction of robot technology has enabled increased production, in addition to improvements in waste treatment, for the two factories on site. Dulux claims to currently produce 12 million litres of paint per year at the site and wants to grow—taking market share from competitors. Wattyl, on the other hand, has been rationalising its manufacturing sites, reducing from three sites to one in New Zealand.

RAW MATERIALS

As noted the manufacture of paints involves the mixing together of numerous pigments, binders, solvents and additives. Resene uses approximately 1000 raw materials in the manufacture of its paints and coatings. For each raw material there are many suppliers globally. While there is variation in the exact type of product and the quality of products, there is usually a choice of quality suppliers for each important chemical. Resene estimates that for the vast majority of raw materials they purchase there are at least ten suppliers. As an example, titanium dioxide is an extremely important and very widely used component in most paint—it is generally considered the best available white pigment. There are many suppliers of titanium dioxide around the world, including DuPont, the company who developed the chemical, but also many others who produce just as high quality titanium dioxide. Quite often, those suppliers who did not develop particular raw materials will charge lower prices—because they did not have the development costs of the innovator. This has created somewhat of a dilemma within Resene from time to time. Employees involved in purchasing, whose job it is to obtain required supplies at the best cost they can, would often prefer to purchase from these lower priced imitators. However, Resene has always placed a premium on maintaining relationships with innovating suppliers like DuPont. The primary reason is so that technical staff at Resene can be kept abreast of the latest innovations. In part this is to keep Resene ahead of its competitors—who often have purchasing decisions made separately from technical decisions—but partly because Resene always wants to produce the best paint possible. One outcome of Resene's orientation is that they likely face a cost disadvantage relative to competitors on raw materials—although their paint is better because "it has more goodies in it."

Suppliers also know that Resene is enthusiastic about innovations—so Colin Gooch feels that he sees more samples of new products than potentially any competing paint company. Suppliers know that if they have something 'magic', as Gooch refers to it, then Resene will be interested. Suppliers have expressed to Resene the view that there has been an increasing trend amongst other paint companies toward a cost orientation—certainly among US companies but also the Australians—where price has become the dominant concern. Innovative supply companies get extremely frustrated by this attitude—often not even getting to meet technical people which stymies the opportunity to work together to develop new products. The strong relationships of Resene have enabled it to be the first company in the world to adopt a number of new technologies. In return, Resene does provide good information back to the supply companies. This is aided by the fact that New Zealand is a good test market with sophisticated customers and harsh conditions. But the relationships are the key—principally the willingness to share. As an example, Resene was able to obtain new pigment dispersion technology from DuPont that was the best available—which DuPont had up until that point refused to release to anyone. However, when Colin Gooch met with the key people at DuPont he told them about a technology that Resene was involved in developing as well as an idea for how the DuPont technology might be developed that were sufficiently valuable to DuPont that they agreed to allow Resene access. Resene gains time from this—not a lock on the innovation. For one technology, Resene had commercially available paint incorporating a new technology for two months in New Zealand before paint manufacturers in the US were even aware of the technology.

PRODUCT DEVELOPMENT

Ideas for new products at Resene have principally come from three sources: marketing, usually where Tony Nightingale has come up with some 'wild' idea; technical staff, developing a new product; or suppliers, coming up with a new material that allows new paints to be developed. In reality, any new development may involve all three elements: a basic product concept in part based on either consumer demand or predicted demand, technological advances from a supplier, and adaptation to the particular characteristics desired. Colin Gooch has always enjoyed the problem-solving aspect of R&D more than anything else, so even Tony's 'wild' ideas have been treated as challenges by the technical staff. As Colin notes, "If they said to us make paint jump out of the can and onto the walls itself, then it was our job to try and get to the guts of the idea behind that to see what could be done."

While typically Resene prefers not to be imitated, sometimes Resene does want competitors to copy its ideas. A case in point is the development of a new lid for plastic paint tins that dramatically reduces the amount of paint skinning (this is when a skin is formed on the paint). When this happens the skin can fall off the lid into the paint and leave 'blobs' of skin in the paint—which can be a real problem. Resene has developed a lid that dramatically reduces this effect and licensed the technology to the ICI Group. Resene will gain income from every paint can of this type used by its competitors. The reason that the technical staff at Resene developed the new lid, rather than leaving it to a manufacturer of containers, was simply because it was a problem that adversely affected the quality of the paint.

An extremely promising recent innovation has been the joint development with a Norwegian life-sciences company, Polymer Systems Ltd, of 'spheromers'. This is a paint-flatting agent used currently in Resene's Zylone Spacecote, a low sheen water-based enamel. Spheromers are perfectly spherical particles that control gloss, side-sheen and meld perfectly with the paint binder, blurring the distinction between pigment and binder. That translates into an extremely tough, cleanable, burnish resistant surface. The dramatic performance improvements for low sheen paints are attracting significant international interest. The problems with prior low sheen paints were the stimulus for Resene to try to find a technology to improve performance. That search led to contact with Polymer Systems, who were developing the technology, but blissfully unaware of the potential in paints. Resene has developed the base technology, not without problems, for the paint industry. The benefit to Resene has not just been in being first to market with the paint, but a share of the future sales of the spheromers to other paint companies.

There is no such thing as a technician—who would run experiments and report back results to more senior colleagues who decide what experiments to run—at Resene. All the scientists run experiments so that they can see what is happening for themselves. Part of the reason for this is because the process of writing up results is imperfect—just by its very nature. There will be subtle observations that are very difficult to record. If technicians alone observed these, then key researchers would not hold valuable information. Instead, there is a strong emphasis on technical expertise at the micro-level—to the point where one acquaintance once observed to Gooch that Resene "builds paint from the molecules up." Resene really takes pride in doing just that—of having an absolutely thorough understanding of all the constituent parts involved in developing a great paint. Importantly, one of the constituent parts is the surface that is to be painted. Therefore, Resene goes to considerable lengths—far more than its competitors—to understand potential surfaces. However, the fact that so much of the knowledge that

Resene possesses is tacit makes the cost of losing staff considerable—particularly experienced staff since knowledge develops cumulatively.

COLOUR

One area that Resene has long had a strong reputation is in the quality of its colours. Any serious paint manufacturer has available for purchase a very large number of colours. However, the production of paint in every colour they offer would be impractical. Resene, for instance, has the capacity to produce 10,000 colours. Instead what is typically done is to produce in the factory a base paint, typically white, and then add tinting pastes in-store, according to preset formulas, to create the final paint colour. This whole process of creating the final colours that consumers buy, however, varies considerably across paint companies. The variation is in part because tinting pastes vary—not just in their colour, but also in their concentration. The concentration is important because all tinting pastes contain 'gunge', so the more concentrated the tinting pastes, the less 'gunge' is in the final paint. The quality of the final product will, therefore, be lowered as more tinting paste is used. Resene was the first company in the world to produce multiple base paints from the factory to allow less tinting paste to be used to create final colours. Resene produces 14 different coloured bases from the Naenae factory. While much tinting paste may be necessary to create a shade of green from a white base paint, if a green base paint is produced then much less tinting paste is needed to adjust the shade of green.

While Resene has employed its basic colour system for many years—only this year has Dulux adopted something similar. The cost of changing a colour system is enormous—Colin Gooch compares it to changing the side of the road that we drive on. As an example, in the most simple change one could make—changing the concentration of one tinting paste without altering the shade—Gooch estimates that 30,000 pieces of paper would have to be produced to effect the change. Resene's blue tinting paste, for example, is used in approximately 2500 colour formulas of the 10,000 total formulas that Resene has. Each of those 2500 formulas would have to be changed because of the change in concentration. Any change to base paint or tinting paste will have a major effect on the colour system because of the scope of colours that need to be able to be produced and the interdependence of each aspect of the final paint colour. Hence, for Resene to change from a system of one base colour to 14 base colours of paint was a monumental undertaking. It was less difficult for Resene than for its competitors because of Resene's

smaller size—particularly at the time of the change. Resene felt vulnerable to its competitors, but also recognised it had an opportunity to steal a march on them.

Resene also used the opportunity created by changing its whole colour system to completely remove lead-based pigments from its paints. Whilst its competitors continued to manufacture lead-based paints for many years, Resene saw the writing on the wall for lead-based paints. Technically, lead-based pigments have superb properties and finding suitable non-lead replacements was difficult and required the modification of some raw materials. However, lead was clearly environmentally hazardous and delaying its removal would mean further modifications to the colour system at a later date.

The vast majority of paint manufacturers in New Zealand, Australia, the United States and Scandinavia use tinting systems. Colin Gooch estimates that the penetration rate in these countries is approximately 85%; whereas elsewhere in Europe penetration rates would be more like 40%, and even lower throughout Asia. The only alternative is to either produce a very limited range of colours or produce a full range of colours from the factory. In reality, the sophistication of the market and the demand for colours by customers is what drives the penetration of tinting systems. Firms find it very difficult to compete with a limited range of colours in more colour-sophisticated markets like New Zealand.

Customers pick paint based on colour to a significant extent. Therefore, customers need to be able to see colour and preferably visualise the final look of any colour on the surface they want to paint. Two critical aspects of colour visualisation that paint companies use are colour charts and test pots. Resene has been a leader in many areas of colour charts. Resene introduced a new system of colour that included strong colours for the first time in New Zealand in 1969. This was based around the British Standards Register system of colours. That system was never intended as a colour chart—rather the focus was on safety colours. But Resene developed the system into a series of colour charts that were the largest available internationally. Key to that process was the strong relationships that Resene had with a number of Wellington architects who pushed hard for Resene to develop those ranges. In 1976 the 'Total Colour Chart' was launched, having been completely developed in-house, and replacing previous charts as the largest available. Colour charts clearly have to reflect colours available, so need to be developed in concert with the technical capabilities of a firm. Resene has continued to develop its colour ranges and has even produced an innovative fan deck colour chart that better enables the isolation of particular colours on a chart.

Resene was also the first company in New Zealand to introduce a full range of test pots in 1975. Test pots enable customers to try a small amount of paint on a particular surface before making their full purchase of paint. Even though colour charts and newer computer programs (such as Resene's recently introduced 'Ezypaint') can aid colour choice enormously, there is no perfect system as yet for taking into account the specifics, such as lighting, in any given space without actually applying paint to the surface. Hence, test pots continue to play a critical part in colour selection and are complementary to the other colour selection tools. Test pots were introduced as a promotional device for Architects and Interior Designers, although retail customers have always been charged. However, Resene does now charge Architects and Designers for the test pots, which account for more than a million dollars in sales per year.

MARKETING

Resene has always placed great emphasis on the commercial segment of the market. Indeed, the primary phrase that is used in marketing is, "Resene: the paint the professionals use." Partly, this focus dates back to the origins of the company and the difficulties in selling to the retail market. But professionals, particularly architects and specifiers, are also more discerning about the type of paint to be used—fitting better with Resene's quality orientation. As noted, architects were very receptive to, and even encouraged the development of, the strong colours that helped Resene to distinguish itself from competitors. Architects, therefore, have not

just been a central target of the company's promotions, but have also been a critical source of market research. The strong relationships with architects have allowed Resene to more fully understand the needs of that market, helping Resene dominate the commercial segment.

Appealing to the commercial market involves direct marketing more than mass advertising. Even now, with a concerted effort under way to increase its retail profile, Resene spends approximately the same amount on direct marketing as wider advertising. Since Nick Nightingale has been General Manager the database that Resene uses to target its marketing has grown from 2500 to 12,000. This has not resulted from pulling random names out of the phonebook, but from thorough research including actively tracking down the owners of buildings throughout New Zealand. That database is itself segmented and each person targeted specifically. A quarterly colourful newsletter is one way that Resene promotes itself to the trade. The newsletter features new products and services as well as case studies of recent projects involving Resene paints. Resene also sends out calendars, coasters and many other promotional items throughout the year. Perhaps the highest profile way that Resene promotes itself to the trade though is through the sponsorship of the Architecture Awards of the New Zealand Institute of Architects.

Consistent with its emphasis on the commercial segment, Resene has traditionally advertised less than the other major paint companies in New Zealand. However, this situation is changing as shown in Table 1. The trend of increasing advertising is continuing this year with expenditures expected to be up 20% with the introduction of a new series of three television com-

TABLE 1	Advertising Expenditures 2000					
	TV $000s	Press $000s	Mags $000s	TOTAL $000s	% Chg 99-00	%Chg 98-99
Paint Companies						
Benjamin Moore	1304	251	68	1623	33.9	12.3
Dulux	1295	17	87	1399	−41.8	20.0
Resene	1098	123	143	1364	31.2	12.4
Retailers						
Mitre 10	4234	2381	138	6753	9.7	38.0
PlaceMakers	2074	1981		4055	4.5	−19.3
Benchmark	2544	640		3184	56.1	19.6
Guthrie Bowron	2739	193		2932	−18.6	62.1

Source: Marketing Magazine, April 2001, p23 (based on ratecard only, not actual expenditures)

mercials. In addition, Resene also managed to get some free advertising through Air New Zealand when Nick Nightingale was included as one of a series of executives on a high profile commercial about Air New Zealand's business customers. An aspect of the advertising that is quite different from competitors is that Resene advertises the brand generally—emphasizing the ColorShops in particular. The competition, especially Orica, focus on particular products to a far greater degree in their advertising. For example, $696,000 of Orica's total advertising expenditure was on Dulux Exterior and Wash & Wear paints alone. In advertising to the retail segment of the market, the key for Resene is to get customers inside a ColorShop where those customers can then be directed to the appropriate Resene product. For Orica and Wattyl, who operate through independent retailers, they try to influence a particular purchase decision prior to entering a store. The advertising of Orica and Wattyl is also aimed at fighting for extra shelf-space from retailers. However, countering this, Orica and Wattyl do benefit from the advertising of the retailers themselves.

SALES

A major difference between Resene and its two main competitors is that Resene owns its own retail outlets. Resene currently operates 54 company-owned Color-Shops as well as 19 franchised outlets (see Exhibit 1). The franchised outlets tend to operate in smaller towns, where demand may not justify a dedicated ColorShop. However, a few of the franchises are products of the history of the company where those franchises came into existence as the company was experimenting with its retail strategy. Historically, Resene opened its own stores because it could not get its product distributed through independent retailers because the larger paint companies had control of those channels (Dulux formerly owned Guthrie Bowron). During the 1970s Resene had an agent who was not particularly fervent in his attempts to move Resene products. Eventually Resene decided to branch out on its own and sell through its own stores—it had always sold direct from the factory, however, this was obviously limited. Through the purchase of a hand-made wallpaper manufacturing operation it acquired a store on Mason St. in Wellington and started selling paint through that. The store turned out to be a very effective tool and Resene was genuinely surprised at how much it could sell like that. From that original store has grown the whole chain. As such the control of retail distribution has become a central component of Resene's overall approach. That approach has been very successful with

New Zealand Retail Locations		EXHIBIT 1
Region	**ColorShops (54)**	**Franchises (19)**
Northland	Whangarei	Kaitaia Kerikeri Dargaville Kaikohe Wellsford
Auckland	Wairau Park Takapuna Birkenhead Orewa Warkworth Mt Eden Newmarket Onehunga Parnell Henderson New Lynn Manukau City Howick Pukekohe Albany Papakura	Ponsonby Devonport Browns Bay
Waikato	Hamilton Cambridge Te Awamutu Tauranga Mt Maunganui Whakatane Matamata Rotorua Taupo	Thames Gisborne
Lower Central	Napier Hastings New Plymouth Palmerston North Wanganui	Dannevirke Hawera Stratford
Wellington	Levin Masterton Paraparaumu Lower Hutt Upper Hutt Naenae Wellington City Wellington City Wellington City Kilbirnie Johnsonville	Porirua
Nelson/ Marlborough	Nelson Blenheim	Stoke
Canterbury	Christchurch Central Hagley Park Papanui Shirley Timaru Riccarton	New Brighton Sydenham
Otago/ Southland	Oamaru Dunedin Invercargill Queenstown	Winton Alexandra

double-digit growth in retail sales throughout its history. Since Nick became General Manager in 1999, nine new stores have been added.

Even more important than the expansion in the number of ColorShops has been the upgrading of the stores generally. A number of stores have been relocated to better locations, and more broadly, significant renovation has occurred. The new style stores are larger, brighter and more sophisticated than their predecessors. The latest ColorShops in Christchurch, Dunedin and Palmerston North are viewed as the biggest, brightest and best yet, with quiet study spaces, colour libraries, areas for children and plenty of parking. The upgrading was the result of a conscious decision by Resene that in order to go after the retail market more aggressively it had to have a format that was consistent with the high-quality image of Resene. The increased advertising has been complementary to the better stores and improved training—Nick was determined to only promise what they could deliver. In the ColorShops themselves, Resene offers a full complement of paint, wallpaper, and accessories as well as a paint tinting service. Most of the merchandise in the ColorShops is sold under the Resene brand name, but there is also a limited amount of 'ColorShop' brand paint that is lower in price and quality, but also manufactured by Resene. Independent suppliers manufacture the wallpaper and accessories, such as brushes, for Resene.

Both trade and DIY customers are served in the ColorShops. In the stores the importance of relationships with customers, particularly trade customers, can hardly be overstated. In one town, Resene had a manager who was rather ornery and had such a poor relationship with one major trade client that the client ceased business with Resene. Even though the manager has long since been replaced, the customer has never returned. Particularly in smaller towns, where there is no other possible ColorShop to go to, Resene is very exposed to poor staff service. This is generally not a problem, however.

Dulux and Wattyl do operate trade stores throughout New Zealand, numbering 20 and 12 respectively, and these are open to the public. However, given the importance of their other distribution channels through independent retailers such as PlaceMakers, Mitre 10 and Guthrie Bowron, DIY sales are not targeted by either trade store chain. Benjamin Moore, a smaller operator, however, does distribute through a chain of 38 owner-operated retail outlets for its paint under the Benjamin Moore Colourworks banner. In addition to selling under their own brands all the major paint companies manufacture house brands for specific stores. Resene sells a very small amount of paint through The Warehouse, using the "NZ Paints" brand.

Dulux manufactures house brands for Mitre 10 and Guthrie Bowron, while Wattyl manufactures for Place-Makers and Carters.

Distribution of paint and other supplies to the ColorShops is done on a daily basis. However, information systems to track the movement of paint through to sale are limited. At present there is no way of knowing exactly how much inventory is on hand at any particular store until a manual stock take is undertaken. Relatedly, the profitability of each store is not known with precision. In general, a key measure that is tracked is the average price per litre that paint is sold for. This gives a very strong indication of the degree of discounting occurring and is indicative of profitability as well. Resene also purchases market share data from Neilson, which is broken down by region. From that research Resene is able to track its performance relative to competitors on a monthly basis. In general, Resene's weakest market has been Auckland.

Resene's successful introduction of the ColorShops has been complementary to the long-standing success that Resene has enjoyed among commercial customers. A key factor in the commercial success has been the emphasis that Resene places on sales reps. Resene currently employs almost twice as many reps as its nearest competitor with 65 reps to Dulux's 35. While Resene is competitively priced in the retail segment, relative to other premium paints (see Exhibit 2), these factors have led to Resene being able to charge a 10–15% premium over competitors in the trade segment.

DISCOUNTING

Paint companies charge different prices to different customers and also offer a wide variety of discounts. For example, Resene has a loyalty card—called a 'Color-Shop card'—that entitles the user to a 20% discount off purchases. Currently, Resene has in excess of 100,000 cards on issue. In general, trade prices are 25% below general retail prices—although this may be for trade products that are not exactly the same product as that sold to non-trade customers. Moreover, although Resene sells paint in 1-litre, 4-litre and 10-litre pails, the trade market is dominated by 10-litre pails so exact comparison is made even more difficult.

The tradition of discounting in the industry and the complexity of the pricing systems create challenges for paint companies. Often the emphasis of sales staff is on sales rather than profits and the result can be excessive discounting. Profitability at Resene has been improving in part because the level of discounts is being more closely monitored. Previously there had been very little monitoring and sales staff had become somewhat habitual about giving discounts without assessing cus-

WHITE		Price ($)
Benjamin Moore	Benjamin Moore Moorglo 119	93
Orica	British Paints 40 Seasons Gloss	65
	British Paints Solarscreen Gloss	80
	Dulux Weathershield	80
	Levene Goldline 100% Acrylic Gloss	80
Resene	Resene Enamycryl	87
	Resene Hi Glo	87
Wattyl	Taubmans All Weather Gloss	56
	Wattyl Solargard	80
Others	Damar House and Roof Gloss	55
	Protec Master Stroke 300	55
	Protective Paints Duralon Acrylic	61
House Brands	Guthrie Bowron Dimensions UVB	60
	Hammer Hardware Acrylic High Gloss	40
	ITM Supreme Acrylic Gloss	43
	Kmart The Performer Acrylic Gloss	60
	Mitre 10 Acrylic Gloss	45
	The Warehouse NZ Paints 100% Acrylic Gloss	35

BROWN		Price ($)
Benjamin Moore	Benjamin Moore Moorglo 119	93
Orica	Dulux Weathershield	100
	Levene Goldline 100% Acrylic Gloss	130
Resene	Resene Enamacryl	103
	Resene Hi Glo	103
Wattyl	Wattyl Solargard	85
Others	Damar House and Roof Gloss	71
	Protective Paints Duralon Acrylic High Gloss	95
House Brands	Guthrie Bowron Dimensions UVB	80

Resene price includes standard 20% ColorShop card discount.

Although the table is accurate for the paint shown, house paint is largely purchased in 10-litre pales and tends to range in price from $100 to $150 approximately.

Source: Consumer Institute of New Zealand, House Paint Test, 6/8/01

tomer needs. One example was that retail staff, when asked for a discount by customers, were often giving a trade level discount—far more than was necessary to obtain the sale—simply because they were familiar with that level of discount. Training has improved this area. Additionally, Nick Nightingale has instituted a system whereby he monitors every discount offered to trade customers and pricing guidelines are more closely adhered to. While that process has involved Nick reject-ing some discount offers, it has gradually led to a sales force who understand the general pricing approach bet-ter. Although it is more complex than this, basically there are two reasons why a trade customer may be offered a discount—volume and visibility. Clearly, larger volumes of product can be produced more effi-ciently and, therefore, tend to attract discounts. Also certain paint projects—like the Museum of New Zealand, Te Papa—are prestigious and gain publicity for the paint chosen. In those cases, paint companies will have added incentive to supply the paint, leading to further discounts.

The highest discounts are given to Plunket and the IHC—where Resene sees the discount as a means of helping out a worthy cause. Resene essentially forgoes profit on these sales. In general, major contractors receive the second highest level of discount, smaller contractors a lower discount, and occasional trade customers a lower discount still. Even most retail customers typically receive up to 20% off the retail price through the use of the ColorShop card and other means of discount. However, in addition to general discounts, particular projects may attract further discounts and Resene also has the capacity to reduce the price on a particular item for a customer. For example, a trade customer may generally not buy from Resene, but may want to purchase an ongoing supply of one particular sealer. Resene has the capacity through 'contract pricing' to lower the price on that sealer, without having to give a larger general discount. Throughout the industry paint companies are notoriously reluctant to make public the exact level of discounts. One major painter described the paint companies' attitude as, "a bit cloak and dagger."

ENVIRONMENTAL CHOICE

The paint manufacturing industry has traditionally faced a number of environmental challenges. Paints are chemicals and many components have potential environmental consequences in manufacture, storage, use and removal. The two most prominent issues have probably surrounded paints containing lead or solvents. Although lead-based paints are no longer manufactured, Resene aided its reputation for environmental awareness by removing lead from its paints long before its competitors. Solvent-based paints, being thinned with petroleum-derived products, are flammable and considered a hazardous good. Resene, as noted earlier, was also the first company in New Zealand to introduce water-based paint and has continued to maintain an edge over competitors to this day. Resene moved aggressively on pursuing water-based paints prior to many of its competitors because it could see that was where the industry was heading. However, challenges remain from waste products produced during manufacture and from solvent-based paints. In general, regulations governing the manufacture and distribution of potentially hazardous goods have also become more stringent in New Zealand and elsewhere as environmental awareness has increased.

More recently Resene has begun to explicitly promote the environmental friendliness of its paint through its Environmental Choice range. Environmental Choice New Zealand is a programme endorsed by the Minister for the Environment and administered by International Accreditation New Zealand (IANZ). It is aimed at improving the quality of the environment by minimising the adverse environmental impacts generated by the production, distribution, use and disposal of products. Resene promotes the following pledge to customers regarding its environmentally friendly products, *"With no increase in price, Resene customers will enjoy safer, less hazardous paints, which are either of the same quality as before or higher."*

Resene paints carrying 'the big tick' meet the criteria of the Environmental Choice programme. The Environmental Choice product range covers a comprehensive range of paints—about 70% of Resene's paint products are Environmental Choice—far ahead of any other manufacturer. Hence, there are Environmental Choice paints for almost all painting situations. The aim is to improve the painting environment, leading to improved concentration levels and a greater feeling of well-being for users, as well as placing less stress on the body's natural defences. Whilst Resene Paints odour levels are not high, the new low odour paints—Zylone Sheen, Zylone 20 and Ceiling Paint—provide more pleasant living conditions during painting, and little waiting for unpleasant smells to disappear.

E-COMMERCE

Resene has been proactive in developing a website (*www.resene.co.nz/*) that offers a number of features for consumers. The website was developed in collaboration between senior management, in-house IT staff and a privately commissioned web page design company. Resene's Marketing Manager Karen Warman manages the site. Contained on the site are company information, product advice and tips as well as purchasing options. In using the website as a sales channel, Resene has outsourced the purchasing service to a complementary website located at *www.diy-online.co.nz*. This service provides a complete set of payment options that encompassed mail and fax to a secure online credit card option. Additionally, small test pots of paint are able to be ordered and couriered to the customers' street address directly from the Resene website. Resene also has recently added web partners onto the website who provide complementary products: Feltex (carpets); Diamond (roofing); Melteca (laminates); and Firth (masonry).

Resene also offers for download at its website the colour scheming tool 'Ezypaint'. Imaging company Itech International developed the complex software required for Ezypaint. Ezypaint, which is also available from the ColorShops for purchase on CD-Rom, allows customers to experiment with paint schemes using the full range of available colours on photos of interior or exterior surfaces to be painted. Users can select a wall or other surface, select a colour, and see how that colour looks—particularly in combination with other colours. In the original version of Ezypaint, only a limited range of photos of sample rooms and houses were available. However, in late June 2001, Ezypaint 2 was launched which allows for scanned photos of a customer's actual room or house to be used for scheming. Available online is also a paint specification system, EzySpec, which identifies the correct Resene product to use based on the answers to a series of questions about the surface to be painted.

Dulux also has a website (*www.dulux.co.nz*), although it does not allow for the purchase of paints by retail customers. Trade customers, on a separate website (*www.duluxtradeonline.co.nz*), do have the capacity to make purchases online, however. Dulux does offer its own paint scheming tool, 'Mycolour', and paint specifying tool, 'Which Product Where' through its main retail site. Wattyl at present only has an Australian corporate website with very limited consumer functionality (*www.wattyl.com.au*). Benjamin Moore has been the only other paint company in New Zealand to offer significant purchasing options online, though this option has only sporadically been available during 2001. Benjamin Moore does, like Dulux, offer a scheming tool with limited preset images.

New Zealand Subsidiaries

Altex Coatings is a paint and coatings manufacturer for the heavy industrial and marine markets, having been purchased as a going concern by Resene in 1989. Started over 45 years ago, Altex now supplies a wide range of coatings to almost every major industry sector. Structures as diverse as petro-chemical plants, commercial ships, electricity pylons, rail cars, wind turbines and even the Auckland Harbour Bridge have been supplied by Altex. Complementing its own range of coatings, Altex has also been a long-standing licensee for Devoe Coatings. More recently Altex has obtained the license from the US Paint Corporation to produce their renowned 'Awlgrip' and 'Awlcraft' range of high performance marine coatings. Altex has quickly established a strong market position in the high performance pleasure marine market. The vision of Altex is: *"To be recognised as Australasia's leading supplier of specialised liquid coatings and custom services for the protection and enhancement of structures in damaging environments."* When Altex was acquired, Resene already held licenses for some competing technologies from Ameron Coat-

ings. This necessitated the Altex business being kept more separate from Resene than might otherwise have occurred. As such, the stand-alone nature of Altex is partly a reflection of that history. However, Resene also believes that Altex operates better under a separate identity.

Resene has been in the automotive paint market since 1990, both manufacturing and distributing for DuPont outside of Auckland. In Auckland, a company called Santano was the DuPont distributor, but in 1995, after encouragement from DuPont, Resene acquired Santano. Originally called Resene Santano, the subsidiary has recently changed its name to Resene Automotive & Protective Coatings. The company's business is approximately evenly divided between manufacturing its own paint range, and acting as a local distributor for other paint companies like DuPont. The market for automotive paint has been a very difficult one. The painting of an entire car normally takes a half to one litre of paint. As such, the business involves very low volumes of paint. Moreover, since there is no car manufacturing industry in New Zealand, the market is completely reliant on repainting vehicles being repaired after accidents. However, in recent years, there has been a trend among car insurers toward writing off damaged cars rather than repairing them. Consequently, demand for automotive paint has been in decline. Nevertheless, recent changes have meant the business does now contribute profits to the group.

One other feature of Resene that distinguishes it from its competitors is that Resene has a wine subsidiary, Cellier Le Brun. Tony Nightingale decided in 1996 to purchase Cellier Le Brun principally because he has had a long-standing interest in wine. Resene does use some of the wine produced for promotional purposes and in turn the vineyard is painted with Resene paints. Other than these, however, the degree of synergy created by the acquisition has been limited. Nevertheless, Cellier Le Brun does share Resene's orientation toward quality, producing some excellent wines. The name Cellier Le Brun has become synonymous with high quality methode traditionelle wines. In recent years, the Terrace Road label has also been developed for more moderately priced table wines with some success.

International Operations

While Resene has had international links throughout its history, those links have traditionally been limited to either the purchase of raw materials or overseas technology. More recently, however, Resene has become involved in supplying paint and paint technologies to international markets. Through a combination of exporting, international alliances, licensing its own technologies, and even manufacturing and distributing in overseas markets, Resene has begun to establish a true international presence. While the revenue from outside New Zealand is still very small, Nick sees much potential, as well as some real difficulties, in pursuing markets in the Asia-Pacific region particularly.

The most obvious market for New Zealand companies looking to expand internationally is Australia. Unfortunately, there is a long history of successful New Zealand companies failing in Australia. Resene is keen to avoid becoming the next Air New Zealand. Nevertheless, Resene does currently have a small presence in Australia, and there is clearly a large growth potential with the Australian market being approximately five times the size of New Zealand's paint market. Resene has very recently consolidated the previously separate manufacturing operations of Resene and Altex Coatings down to one plant on the Gold Coast in Queensland. Nick Nightingale has also explored the possibility of supplementing Australian manufacture by exporting paint from Naenae at cost, but the Inland Revenue Department will only allow them to charge the lowest price they offer to a customer (to avoid transferring profits offshore). The Australian manufacturing plant has been complemented by a small retail distribution network consisting of four Resene ColorShops and 14 independent stockists (see Exhibit 3). No push for trade sales has been attempted in Australia because intense competition has driven prices down to virtually profitless levels.

There are a relatively large number of independent paint stockists in Australia, who compete with the massive hardware chains like Mitre 10 and BBC Hardware. The major brands in Australia—Dulux, Wattyl and Taubmans—all distribute through those large hardware chains. The independent paint retailers try to differentiate themselves from the big chains by greater customer service. However, ultimately the customer is still buying the same paint they could get from a hardware store—probably cheaper. At present the only alternative paints available are low-cost, 'me-too' type paints. Resene believes that this has created a gap for a top-of-the-line paint such as theirs. The approach to date has included offering greater margins to retailers, while still keeping prices within range of Dulux. In general, Australian paint shops are not as upscale as either ColorShops or Guthrie Bowron in New Zealand. Therefore, there may also be a potential gap in the retail paint market. Consequently, Resene has taken the ColorShop concept into Australia, although in a very limited way. While Nick Nightingale is not enthusiastic about waiting 55 years to develop a full chain of ColorShops throughout Australia in the same manner as New Zealand, the financial implications of a much faster rollout are a serious concern.

In Fiji, Resene operates one small plant, as do some Australian competitors. The Fijian operation produces a very wide variety of paints and coatings in small volumes. Making matters more difficult, the Fijian market shrank about 10% after the recent political turmoil—maybe more. Resene, though, has had a big advantage over their Australian competitors who haven't been able to get raw materials into Fiji because of Australian sanctions. By contrast, Resene had large

EXHIBIT 3	Australian Retail Locations	
State	**ColorShops (4)**	**Stockists (14)**
Queensland	Woolloongabba, Brisbane Geebung, Brisbane Brisbane	Butcher's Paint Barn, Townsville. Cairns Hardware, Atherton. Cairns Hardware, Edmonton. Cairns Hardware, Cairns. Classic Paint Supplies, Cleveland, Brisbane. Goodfellows Handy Hardware, Kallangur, Brisbane. Innisfail Plumbing and Paint, Innisfail. Paint City Coolum, Coolum Beach. Paint City Currimundi, Currimundi. Paint City Maroochydore, Maroochydore. Paint City Noosa, Noosaville. Goodfellows Handy Hardware, Kallangur, Brisbane.
New South Wales	North Rocks, Sydney	Taree Builders Bargain Centre, Taree South.
Victoria		Morgans Paint Spot, Moorabbin, Melbourne.

inventories of key raw materials and also New Zealand wharfies continued loading goods to Fiji. There is a market in Fiji for up-market paints, but that market is under threat if more affluent sections of the community leave Fiji over the current problems. Interestingly, however, there is little difference in the types of paint that work in Fiji and Australia.

Resene has been involved in a limited amount of paint exporting to date. It is currently investigating opportunities in Thailand and Japan. In Japan, where prices are quite high, Resene could cover the cost of transportation and still be profitable. Currently, paint companies in Japan are very unsophisticated with respect to colour. Traditionally the emphasis has been on white, some off-whites and perhaps beige. More recently, European colour influences have been coming through in magazines potentially signalling future growth in the demand for stronger colours.

The principal element of Resene's technology licensing to date has been of a tinting technology system. Resene has supplied this technology to South Africa, Zimbabwe, the Dominican Republic, Malaysia, Indonesia and China. Most international markets tend to have an 'ICI-type' player, a major multinational paint company who drip-feeds technology into those markets after a lag-time from their primary markets. The general approach of Resene has been to supply a local competitor, facing competition from a multinational competitor, with technology that allows it to compete better. In China, it is providing technology to a major Chinese player who has been losing market share to multinationals ICI and Nippon. In Bangladesh, Resene has taken this a step further, and holds a 20% stake in Resene Bangladesh. The products manufactured are very basic, but it has the potential to provide an avenue into the massive Indian market. The development of 'spheromers' with its Norwegian partner, as well as any other innovations, offers the opportunity to expand the technology transfer aspect of Resene's business. To cater better for this, Paint Technologies Ltd, a holding company, was recently formed.

THE PAINT INDUSTRY

On a world scale the Australasian market is small and the New Zealand market is a drop in the bucket, as it were. After the divestment of Orica by ICI, none of the major competitors in Australasia are among the top ten decorative paint sellers in the world. The three largest decorative paint companies in the world are American firm Sherwin Williams (US$4.3B), British firm ICI (US$2.5B) and Dutch company Akzo Nobel (US$1.3B). Sherwin Williams alone operates 2488 paint stores as well as selling through independent retailers and spends US$84M on technology expenditures and US$276M on advertising per year. These companies all have multinational operations with ICI in particular reporting strong growth in Asian markets (14%), particularly China and Thailand. ICI, which controls the Dulux brand outside Australasia, attributes part of their success in China to advertising and partly to China being "a market that is acutely conscious of quality." Resene hasn't seen the same quality consciousness in China, however. North America and Europe have been static markets, as one might expect with such a mature product as paint. In Latin America currency issues have been acute, particularly in Brazil, making trading difficult. Worldwide there has been pressure on margins from rising raw materials costs, particularly those associated with petroleum.

At present total sales in the Australasian architectural and decorative paint market slightly exceed A$1B, with New Zealand representing approximately NZ$190 million per year. Both Australian and New Zealand markets have shown the same limited growth as other mature markets for a number of years at about 1–2% per year (Resene has been growing at around 6% recently). As shown in Figure 2 and Figure 3, based on Dulux's own estimates, Dulux is the market leader in both Australia and New Zealand. Only 6% of paint sold in Australasia is imported. Generally paint markets are quite strongly affected by the wider economy

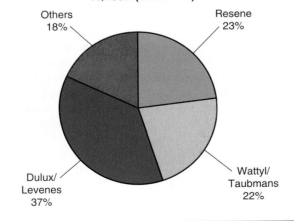

New Zealand Architectural & Decorative Coatings Market
A$150M (25M Litres)

Others 18%
Resene 23%
Dulux/ Levenes 37%
Wattyl/ Taubmans 22%

Source: Orica

FIGURE 3   Australian Market
            Shares

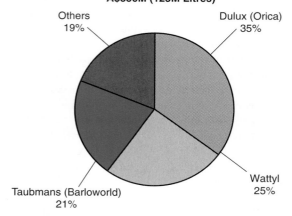

**Australian Architectural & Decorative Coatings Market
A$850M (125M Litres)**

Others
19%

Dulux (Orica)
35%

Taubmans (Barloworld)
21%

Wattyl
25%

Source: Orica

and, in particular, by the level of construction being undertaken. Apart from the obvious, that new construction needs to be painted once built, owners of pre-existing buildings also tend to renovate more when new buildings are being built and competing for tenants. In residential property, major renovations are less likely in the current market because it is frequently cheaper to move to a house that you like, rather than to fix up the house that you have. As such, the limited amount of residential and commercial property construction recently has made for a rather stagnant paint market. Another macroeconomic influence on the industry has come from the relatively weak New Zealand and Australian dollars, particularly relative to the American dollar. As a result, the costs of many supplies have risen substantially in recent times while the capacity to pass on those rising costs has been limited. Unfortunately though, most paint companies in Australasia are only marginally profitable, leaving little capacity to just absorb cost increases. Dulux (NZ) did raise both trade and retail prices approximately 7% during August 2001.

The primary brands in Australia are identical to New Zealand with the exception of Resene itself—Dulux, Wattyl and Taubmans. A significant difference exists in terms of ownership, however, with Taubmans in Australia being owned by South African company, Barloworld, rather than Wattyl. Wattyl did attempt to acquire Taubmans in Australia and New Zealand in 1995, but was only successful in New Zealand due to concerns from the Australian Competition and Con-

sumer Commission that a duopoly would be formed. Barloworld also acquired Bristol Paints who has their own chain of 120 stores. In addition to the Dulux brand, Orica also offers the Berger range and a number of smaller brands. Generally, the market is very much concentrated in the hands of the three largest players.

Throughout Australasia 55% of sales are to the trade and 45% to the retail DIY market. Although Resene does not sell to any independent hardware or decorating stores in New Zealand, a majority of retail paint sales in New Zealand, and Australia, occur through such outlets. The dominant trend in retail globally has been away from small single-store outlets toward chains of stores. Hardware and decorating stores have been no exception to this trend, with both New Zealand and Australia dominated by chains of stores. Some of those chains are owned by single companies, such as Benchmark, while others are essentially co-operatives of independently-owned stores, such as Mitre 10. The reasoning for the dominance of chains has been two-fold. First, the larger number of stores has made the development of a brand more cost effective, particularly in advertising. Second, the collective bargaining power of chains has enabled them to negotiate better prices from suppliers. Inevitably, this has squeezed the margins of those suppliers to retailers. In Australia, paint is the highest margin hardware product sold, generating gross margins of 35.5% on average for retailers. Paint is also the single biggest category of sales for hardware stores—representing approximately 15% of their retail sales in Australia. No comparable information is available for New Zealand, but the margin and sales proportion are likely to be very similar.

The biggest of the hardware chains in both New Zealand and Australia is Mitre 10. In Australia three chains operate within the group: Mitre 10 (377 stores); Mitre 10 Home & Trade (48 stores); and True Value Hardware (228 stores). In New Zealand the group operates 135 Mitre 10 stores and 70 True Value Hardware stores. As an example of how important these chains are to paint companies generally, when Mitre 10 in Australia switched from Taubmans to Dulux for the supply of their house brand of paint, Taubmans lost 7% of their total sales—with the account representing a full percent of the total market. In general, price-cutting on paint is endemic, particularly in Australia. Typically, the price-cutting is led by retailers, especially the newer hardware superstore chains and supported by manufacturers. "Discounting, plus the cluttered appearance of most sales outlets, has encouraged consumers to view paint as a commodity."[2] One result is that tinting is not paid for by customers in Australia if done off a white base, where it is in New Zealand.

COMPETITORS

Dulux is the leading paint brand of the Orica group. Orica is an Australian headquartered company formerly known as ICI Australia before the parent company ICI (UK) sold its 64% stake in 1998. A condition of the sale was that the ICI name be replaced, and so the name Orica was introduced. Orica is involved in mining services (explosives), chemicals, agricultural chemicals and consumer products such as paint in numerous countries. The paint business operates only in Australia and New Zealand, primarily under the brand name Dulux. Orica has had poor financial performance in its recent history and in June 2001 a new CEO was hired with the express aim of turning around the business. Partly as a result of its poor performance, Orica has been reducing the number of product areas it competes in to focus more on the areas that are perceived as strengths. In New Zealand, the Dulux name itself has been around since 1939, when British Australian Lead Manufacturers Pty Ltd entered the market. Eventually the company's name was changed to Dulux in 1971 with manufacturing facilities in Auckland and Lower Hutt. In 1986, the company was acquired by ICI, who later changed the name of the company to ICI Paints. Subsequently, ICI Paints made two significant acquisitions—BJN Holdings in 1988, who manufactured the British Paints range, and the Levenes brand in 1996.

The principal paint business for Orica is in Australia, predominantly through the Dulux brand there. As such, Australia is the focus of operations and New Zealand is treated to some extent as a State of Australia. This is partly signalled by the centralised location of R&D in Clayton, Victoria at the new A$12M technology centre for the Consumer Products division opened in November 2000. About the facility Consumer Products General Manager Jerry Adams said, "We have a track record of outstanding technical innovation in our business. Despite having had less than ideal facilities in the past, our team has come up with the world's best new products like Dulux Wash and Wear 101, Dulux Weathershield X10 and the Dulux Tuscan and Dulux Suede Effects Systems. The sky is the limit with what they now have to work with in this marvellous new facility."[3] Overall within Orica, the Consumer Products division generated A$638M (17%) of corporate sales and 21% of the A$235M corporate profits in 2000. The Consumer Products division is divided into further business units—Decorative (Dulux), Woodcare, Selleys, Powder Coatings and Asia Pacific. Within the Decorative area, further distinctions are made according to markets: retail; trade; texture coatings; and protective coatings.

For the Consumer Products division 74% of sales come from renovating/decorating/maintaining, while 19% is generated by new commercial projects and only 7% from new domestic construction. The approach of the division is to emphasize leading brands, established technology, overlapping customers and overlapping channels surrounding a customer focus. Dulux Trade operates 69 Dulux Trade Centres throughout Australasia, has 175 aligned depots and distributorships and boasts a customer base of 40,000. Overall, as market leader, Dulux sells 35% of the paint purchased in Australasia by volume and 38% by value of what they estimate to be a A$1.1B total market. Dulux believes its strategy for success is based around brands, technology, innovation, colour leadership, distribution and customer satisfaction. No wonder a senior executive at Dulux (NZ) told Resene recently that he believed Dulux should be charging a premium over Resene. Without question however, Dulux is a very powerful brand name. In unaided awareness tests in Australia, Dulux trailed only Telstra and McDonald's for awareness, beating out Coca-Cola and far outstripping any other paint brand.

Dulux operates four manufacturing facilities, in Queensland, West Australia, South Australia and Wellington. The Rocklea plant in Queensland completed a A$17M upgrade in 2000 that incorporated two fully automated and six semi automated robotic filling lines and the implementation of flexible manufacturing technology. The Rocklea plant is the largest paint manufacturer in Australia, the upgrade increasing the capacity from 40 million litres per year to over 60 million. While Orica does not divulge specific profitability for paint, Dulux is believed to be profitable.

Wattyl is also a multinational competitor headquartered in Australia. Wattyl is solely a paint company with manufacturing operations in Australia, New Zealand, the United States, Thailand, Malaysia and Indonesia. Founded in Sydney during 1915, Wattyl became a public company in 1959. Since then Wattyl's development has been heavily influenced by acquisitions, having purchased at least nine other Australian paint companies, including National Paints and Gransonite. Wattyl has had a presence in New Zealand since 1970, when it acquired Solway Products. In 1989 that presence was expanded greatly through the acquisition of Samson Gold-X. A further small company, Norfolk Paints in Auckland, was purchased in 1995. However, the most important acquisition was of Taubmans in 1995, which really established Wattyl as a major player in the New Zealand market. Outside Australasia, expansion has been driven by the acquisition of companies such as the Dimet Group (Asia) and Coronado Paint (USA).

Performance has been poor in recent times. During its most recent financial year to June 30th 2001, Wattyl had corporate revenues of A$528M, but experienced losses of A$22M. In March 2001, Wattyl's Managing Director resigned. Subsequently, the management and board of Wattyl have instigated a major strategic review of operations. The company did actually make a very small operating profit of A$1.5M for the year, but faced a number of one-off items. In particular, the company wrote-off large US bad debts, incurred a two-week strike in Australia, felt the effects of the newly imposed GST and the Olympics in Australia, and incurred the costs of changing its Managing Director and US leadership team. But Wattyl also believes that it had not re-invested sufficiently in plant in recent times leading to major current expenditure in this area that will not quickly be recouped. Geographically, the difference in Wattyl's results by region has been very stark. Wattyl is profitable in both Australia and New Zealand, while unprofitable in Asia and the USA as shown in Table 2. As a result, Wattyl has written down its investments in both Asia and the USA and is looking to exit Asia completely.

As can be seen in Table 2, even profits in Australia nearly halved in the last year. Indeed, both Wattyl and Orica are viewed as potential takeover targets. In seeking to remedy the situation in Australia, Wattyl has reduced the number of plants from eight to three, established more efficient warehousing, sold surplus proper-

ties, and introduced a major new premium interior wall paint. The move to premium paint could be interesting as both Resene and Dulux view Wattyl as something of a 'rogue' operator—aggressive on price, but otherwise directionless.

Barloworld is a large South African conglomerate with interests including cement, lime, laboratory equipment, lasers, and steel tubes. Barloworld has paint manufacturing operations in three countries: South Africa, under the Placson brand; the United Kingdom, under the International brand; and in Australia under the Taubmans and Bristol brands. Barloworld Australia also operates a number of car dealerships. The Taubmans brand has been in Australia for over 100 years, however, prior to its sale to Barloworld in 1996 it had begun to flounder, benefiting Wattyl and Dulux. In 1992 Taubmans had market share of 22%, but that fell to 15% by the time of the sale. The new ownership has turned that around and the combined market share of Taubmans and Bristol Paints in decorative coatings has risen from 23% to 29% since 1998, taking over the number two spot in the industry according to Barloworld.[4] Nevertheless profits have been more difficult to come by and the Taubmans/Bristol group had losses in 2000 (Table 3) that appear to be continuing. Speculation exists that Barloworld may look to exit Taubmans.

The 120-store retail arm of Bristol Paints has been moving towards increased franchising of late, with

TABLE 2	Wattyl's Regional Results							
(A$000s)	Australia		New Zealand		USA		Asia	
	2000	2001	2000	2001	2000	2001	2000	2001
SALES	332,523	321,097	38,226	39,478	147,077	140,540	18,957	19,503
EBIT (LOSS)	31,472	18,655	3,191	3,201	8,327	(22,158)	(159)	(12,039)
ASSETS	256,194	251,865	32,729	34,075	163,046	164,788	25,166	16,421

Source: Wattyl Limited, Preliminary Final Report, 12/9/01

TABLE 3	Barloworld's Regional Paint Results							
(A$M)	Australia		South Africa		Other Africa		Europe	
	1999	2000	1999	2000	1999	2000	1999	2000
SALES	192	218	216	220	9	17	19	21
OP PROFIT	0.8	(2.3)	12	12	0.2	1.2	1.8	2
ASSETS	104	109	102	101	5	7	9	9

Source: Barloworld Limited, Annual Report 2000.

company-owned stores being converted into franchises. The stores employ 500 staff throughout Australia and represent the largest chain of retail and trade stores for paint and wallpaper. In addition, six franchised Bristol decorator centres opened in China in 1999 and a further four in 2000. The entire range sold in China is produced in Australia. As part of Barloworld both Bristol and Taubmans have access to the Nova Paint Club. The Nova Paint Club is a worldwide association of 15 paint companies that provides a framework for the exchange of technical information, technology and expertise across all their areas of operation.

Smaller paint companies exist in both Australia and New Zealand. Benjamin Moore Pacific in New Zealand, for example, began as a joint venture between Benjamin Moore, the large US paint company, and local owners. However, the local owners have subsequently taken full ownership and operate under a licensing agreement from Benjamin Moore (US). As noted, Benjamin Moore does have a retail presence through franchised retail outlets around New Zealand. However, the number of Benjamin Moore Colourworks stores has been diminishing in recent times as stores have switched to competing retail chain Colour Plus. Colour Plus is associated with Wattyl products, so the switching allegiance is cutting off the primary outlets that Benjamin Moore has. Retailers are believed to be switching in order to gain better brand support. The potential exists for those problems to snowball since reducing stores will put the advertising spent under more pressure.

Most small paint companies do not have chains of stores associated with them, however. Often they are specialised firms who have a reputation in a particular product allowing them to sell direct to the trade. In New Zealand, Rotorua-based Damar has an alliance with Amway that has resulted in the website PaintDirect. This may reflect the difficulty in gaining access to distribution that smaller companies face. Damar concentrates more on the low margin road-marking business. Other small competitors try to sell direct or through any independent retailers who will stock them. In general, their volumes are very small and face limited opportunities to grow.

THE FUTURE

Throughout its first 55 years in existence Resene Paints had shown that it had the capabilities to compete effectively in New Zealand against its larger multinational competitors. Having traditionally been strong in the commercial market, Resene had, in more recent years, made a concerted and successful push at the retail market through its own chain of ColorShops. Without question, that success had been built around the innovativeness, quality and presentation of its products. But within New Zealand the prospects for growth in its current markets were not limitless. Although there was still room for growth in the New Zealand market, longer-term growth prospects appeared to be outside New Zealand. The world economy appeared headed for recession, however, and at the very least economic uncertainty was high. Internationally, Resene had very small operations in Australia and Fiji. Clearly Australia was a large opportunity, but was it the right opportunity for Resene given the differences from New Zealand? Were Asia or elsewhere more desirable regions? If Resene made a concerted push on any markets outside New Zealand, how much would the competitive approach have to change? Should Resene itself even look to operate in other countries, or should it focus on developing technologies in New Zealand to be licensed overseas, such as the newly developed spheromer paint flatting agent? Or should Resene focus its resources on continuing to grow the New Zealand market for the time being? Were there other markets in New Zealand that were better to pursue? As Nick Nightingale stepped off the 18th green at Paraparaumu Beach Golf Club, having shot 91 in a losing effort, he knew he couldn't afford to be as wayward in his choice of markets.

NOTES

1. Consumer Institute of New Zealand (1998) 'Interior Acrylic Paints', April.
2. Shoebridge, N. (1997) 'Taubmans, 'with imagination', tries to paint its way out of a corner', Business Review weekly, 10/11/97, p78.
3. Orica Limited (2001) 'New Technology Centre for Orica Consumer Products', Press Release, 20/11/00.
4. Barloworld Limited (2000) Annual Report, p32.

Andrew Inkpen
Thunderbird

In August 2001, Martha Van Gelder, the group vice president of products and international television at Sesame Workshop, was faced with various issues. Sesame Workshop was the producer of *Sesame Street*, the highly acclaimed children's educational show. Since its American debut more than 30 years ago, *Sesame Street* had achieved great success in many other countries. In virtually every country where it was introduced, *Sesame Street*, or a locally produced version of the show, had become an immediate success. By 2001, the show was broadcast in almost 150 countries, making Sesame Workshop the largest single teacher of young children in the world. The show was co-produced in the local language in 20 countries with local actors, writers, musicians, animation, and sets. In the other countries, the show was either the English-language American version or the American version with some segments dubbed in the local language. International revenue represented about 20% of total revenue.

Within Sesame Workshop, there was a consensus that many interesting international growth opportunities existed. For example, *Sesame Street* was not broadcast in Brazil, France, or India. There were also opportunities for co-productions in many of the countries where the English-language version of the show was broadcast. However, capitalizing on the opportunities had to be balanced with various factors. Sesame Workshop's mission was to educate children and their families globally. But, even though Sesame Workshop was a not-for-profit organization, creating a financially viable and growing organization was a necessity. Van Gelder described it this way:

> How do we take all the wonderful ideas and convert them into a real business? We often have broadcasters asking us to do special programs for outreach or to develop a special video. But, when we look at the time and resources, we have to come back to the main charge of developing the business and the brand. The most important thing is to deliver on the promise of what the brand and mission are; that means doing things well and may mean doing less.
>
> We face the dilemma every day: why is the pre-schooler in India more important than the one in France? They are not different. Our mission does not say that we should focus more on developing markets. We want to help all children. It really comes down to the opportunity and the feasibility; whether we have the staff and resources to do it; and how near or long-term it is.

BACKGROUND

In 1966, Joan Ganz Cooney was commissioned by the Carnegie Corporation, an American foundation, to do a study on the feasibility of using television for the education of preschool children. At the time, Cooney was a successful producer in educational television. Based on the study's findings, Cooney urged that an experimental television series devoted to preschool children be established. The Carnegie Foundation agreed, and with the support of the Ford Foundation and the U.S. Office of Education, a grant of $8 million was raised from government and private sources. The grant was to be used for pre-broadcast research and production, a seven-month broadcast period, and national evaluation of the broadcast seasons.

The Children's Television Workshop was founded in 1968 to conduct the study. A set of curriculum goals was developed in various categories: social, moral, and affective development; language and reading; mathematical and numerical skills; and reasoning, problem-solving, and perception. Research was conducted to determine how to best develop an operational model. Five test shows were developed and evaluated in August 1969. Based on the results of the tests, the first show, called *Sesame Street,* aired in November 1969 on stations of the Public Broadcasting Service, a commercial-free television network supported by government and private funding. The show was an immediate success and in the first season, the estimated audience was about seven million of the 12 million target audience. Over the next several decades, the show became a fixture on American television and in 1999, *Sesame Street* was in its 31st season in the United States. In 2000, Children's Television Workshop changed its name to Sesame Workshop.

THE MISSION OF SESAME WORKSHOP

According to Sesame Workshop, "Our mission is to create innovative, engaging content that maximizes the educational power of media to help all children reach their highest potential."[1] Sesame Workshop core values were described as:

Innovation: *We seek new ways to make the world of media more valuable for children, with a keen appreciation of children's imagination and inquisitive spirit.*

Optimism: *We champion the educational potential of media in the lives of children.*

Knowledge: *We ground our work in research to expand our understanding of what appeals to children and what helps them learn, develop, and grow.*

Diversity: *We create places where all children can see themselves and appreciate others.*[2]

Sesame Workshop was a not-for-profit company chartered by the Board of Regents of the University of the State of New York under the Education Law of New York. Income generated by educational activities was exempt from taxation. Income generated by activities unrelated to Sesame Workshop's educational mission was taxable. Sesame Workshop's board of trustees had 16 members and included Joan Ganz Cooney.

Sesame Workshop had three financial goals. The first was to assemble public and private funding partnerships to support educational initiatives. For example, the development and production of the Israeli/Palestinian co-production of *Sesame Street* had a diverse group of funders, including the Netherlands Ministry of Foreign Affairs, the Ford Foundation, and the Israeli Ministry of Education. The second goal was to support educational activities with self-generated revenues. Various revenue-generating activities were undertaken: foreign and domestic product licensing, foreign licensing and distribution of local language adaptations and co-productions of Sesame Workshop programs, syndication of *Sesame Street* and other series, magazine and book publishing, and interactive software. These activities supported more than 80% of the cost of *Sesame Street.* The third financial goal was to establish underlying financial stability by maintaining an investment portfolio to cover operating deficiencies when necessary and to ensure the long-term financial viability of *Sesame Street.*

SESAME STREET

In the United States, a six-month broadcast season for *Sesame Street* consisted of 130 hour-long programs. Each program was made up of 30–40 segments. The segments were in four categories: street scenes produced in a studio, animation, live action from outside the studio, and puppet scenes. Street scenes contained both the series' live cast of characters and such popular puppet characters as Big Bird, Elmo, and Oscar the Grouch. Each show closed with a 15-minute segment called *Elmo's World.* The puppets were Muppet characters that were originally created by the late Jim Henson. Muppet characters were integral to *Sesame Street,* and according to Joan Ganz Cooney, "The most fortunate thing that happened to us was when Jim Henson walked through the door. His puppets made us viable in the marketplace."[3] In 2000, Sesame Workshop acquired complete control over the rights of all *Sesame Street* characters; previously, they were shared with the Jim Henson Company, which was acquired by the German company EM.TV & Merchandising AG in 2000.

Each segment of the show addressed at least one highly specific educational goal. Extensive testing (*Sesame Street* has been the subject of more than 1,000 studies) found that viewers of *Sesame Street* made significantly greater gains than non-viewers in most tested areas of the series' curriculum. Three of the more recent studies demonstrated that the show made a significant and lasting contribution to preschoolers' cognitive and social development. Studies also showed that children who watched more learned more and that gains were made by children from both middle- and low-income backgrounds. Following its debut, *Sesame Street* won numerous awards in the United States and other countries. In the United States, *Sesame Street*'s 76 Emmy Awards were the most ever awarded to a single program.

THE GLOBALIZATION OF SESAME STREET

Soon after *Sesame Street* premiered in 1969, Children's Television Workshop began receiving inquiries from producers in Canada, Australia, New Zealand, and other English-speaking countries about the rebroadcast rights to the series (Exhibit 1 shows international milestones).

EXHIBIT 1 Sesame Workshop International Milestones

1968: Children's Television Workshop formed.

1969: *Sesame Street* premieres on U.S. public (commercial-free) television.

1969: Sesame Workshop launches licensed product program.

1971: U.S. version of *Sesame Street* debuts in Australia and in Japan.

1972: First international co-production of *Sesame Street* in Germany.

1975: *Barrio Sésamo* launched in Spain; *Plaza Sésamo* launched in Mexico.

1983: U.S. version of *Sesame Street* debuts in U.K.

1996: *Sesame Street* wins Japan Prize for best program in preschool education category; *Ulitsa Sezam* begins in Russia; *Ulica Sezamkowa* begins in Poland; *Sesame Park* begins in Canada.

1997: *Sacatruc*, a French-language co-production of *Big Bag*, premieres in France.

1998: *Zhima Jie* launched in China; *Rechov Sumsum/Shara's a Simsim* premieres on Israeli and Palestinian television.

1999: *Open Sesame* premieres in Pakistan and Italy.

2000: Children's Television Workshop changes its name to Sesame Workshop; *Takalani Sesame* launched in South Africa; *Alam Simsim* launched in Egypt.

2001: Mediatrade, Italy's largest commercial broadcaster, licenses *Tiny Planets*.

In addition, producers from other countries where English was widely spoken approached Children's Television Workshop with requests to rebroadcast the series with slight modifications. In Israel, for example, the series first aired in English with occasional commentary in Hebrew. In Japan, the American version of *Sesame Street* was broadcast until 1998 unedited and unaltered, with the purpose of teaching English as a second language to children, teenagers, and adults. In 1998, NHK, the Japanese broadcaster, began offering a dubbed version of the show. Similarly, countries in the Caribbean used the series as a means of teaching English. As was the case for any television show, international distribution was quite profitable. For Children's Television Workshop, the only real incremental costs for rebroadcasting were for duplicating tapes and residuals for actors and musicians.

In addition to requests to rebroadcast the series in English, requests to alter the linguistic content for foreign audiences increased rapidly after the show's U.S. introduction. As a result, Children's Television Workshop needed policies and procedures for proposed international adaptations of *Sesame Street*. In late 1969, Children's Television Workshop created an international division charged with the responsibility of overseeing *Sesame Street*'s licensing abroad. Four main licensing policies were developed:

- All non-U.S. versions of *Sesame Street* must be commercial-free.
- Changes to the series must meet the highest production standards.
- All non-U.S. versions of *Sesame Street* must reflect the values and traditions of the host country's culture.
- Any proposed changes to the series must be approved, initiated, and supervised by a local committee of educators working with Children's Television Workshop.

In 1970, a German network, NDR, began broadcasting *Sesame Street* dubbed in German. In 1971, NDR began producing and inserting a few segments that incorporated elements of the German national educational curriculum. In Canada and New Zealand, local segments also were produced and inserted into the show. In Canada, the segments focused on bilingualism, and in New Zealand, the focus was the heritage of the local Maori population.

In 1973, the international evolution continued with the introduction of a new series of 130 half-hour episodes entirely in Spanish for the Mexican market. Half the material came from the U.S. series and the other half was produced in Mexico. To avoid duplicating the look of the American series, a distinctive Latin American-looking set was designed around a neighborhood square. New music was recorded, and writers and producers were hired from Mexico and other Latin American countries. Two new puppet characters were created exclusively for the series. Financial support came from several Latin American sources and a grant from Xerox Corporation. Xerox received an institutional credit before and after each show but had no influence over content or distribution. *Plaza Sésamo*'s debut in 1973 achieved the highest audience share of any television program ever broadcast in Mexico.

Based on the model pioneered in Mexico, 18 other *Sesame Street* co-production agreements were developed over the subsequent two decades. In Norway, for example, *Sesam Stasjon* immediately became the country's most popular children's show. In Portugal, *Rua Sesamo* became the most widely viewed children's program in the history of Portuguese television. In the Arab states, *Iftah Ta Simsim,* co-produced in Kuwait, was the top-rated preschool program for 15 years.

In 2000, *Talakani* (which means "be happy") *Sesame* debuted on South African television and, for the first time in *Sesame Street's* history, on radio. *Talakani Sesame* was initiated by Sesame Workshop, United States Agency for International Development (USAID), and the South African Department of Education. The street in *Talakani Sesame* combined aspects of both rural and urban South Africa and was designed as a street where all South African children could feel welcome and safe. Given the diversity of languages in South Africa, it was decided that the characters would be multilingual. Also in 2000, *Alam Simsim* debuted on Egyptian television as a daily series. *Alam Simsim* was co-produced with Karma Productions, a new firm formed solely to produce *Alam Simsim* and other programs. USAID was involved in the initiation of *Alam Simsim* and the official sponsor was Americana, a leading Middle East food company.

THE CO-PRODUCTION MODEL

Co-productions were set up as follows (Exhibit 2 shows the different countries in which *Sesame Street* co-productions have been aired). First, Sesame Workshop worked with local co-producers, usually a local broadcaster, to establish a board of advisors to set local

	International Co-Productions of *Sesame Street*				EXHIBIT 2
Country	**Series Title**	**Language**	**Year First Broadcast**	**Number of Seasons Produced**	**Currently in Production and/or Broadcast**
Brazil	Vila Sésamo	Portuguese	1972	2	No
Canada*	Sesame Park	English (with some French segments)	1973	27	Yes
China	Zhima Jie	Mandarin	1998	1	Yes
Egypt	Alam Simsim	Arabic	2000	2	Yes
France	1, rue Sésame	French	1978	2	No
Germany	Sesamstrasse	German	1973	29	Yes
Israel	Rechov Sumsum	Hebrew	1983	4	Yes
Israel/Palestinian Territories	Rechov Sumsum/ Shara's Simsim	Hebrew and Arabic	1998	1	Yes
Kuwait**	Iftah Ya Simsim	Arabic	1979	3	No
Mexico***	Plaza Sésamo	Spanish	1972	7	Yes
Netherlands	Sesamstraar	Dutch	1976	24	Yes
Norway	Sesam Stasjon	Norwegian	1991	4	Yes
Philippines	Sesame!	Tagalog and English	1983	1	No
Poland	Ulica Sezamkowa	Polish	1996	2	No
Portugal****	Rua Sesamo	Portuguese	1989	3	No
Russia	Ulitsa Sezam	Russian	1996	2	Yes
South Africa TV	Takalani Sesame	Multi-lingual	2000	1	Yes
South Africa Radio	Takalani Sesame	Zulu, Xhosa, Sepedi with English segments	2000	1	Yes
Spain	Barrio Sésamo	Castilian, Catalan	1979	7	Yes
Sweden	Svenska Sesam	Swedish	1981	1	No
Turkey	Susam Sokagi	Turkish	1989	2	No

*The U.S. version of *Sesame Street* with some Canadian segments began broadcasting in 1973. The Canadian co-production, Sesame Park, began in 1996.
**Also broadcast to 16 Arab-world countries.
***Also broadcast in Spanish-speaking Latin America and Puerto Rico.
****Also broadcast in Angola, Mozambique, Guinea, Cape Verde, and São Tomé.

curriculum standards. Based on the establishment of local goals and standards, Sesame Workshop collaborated extensively with co-producers on all production issues: writers, musicians, animation, sets, etc. Because Sesame Workshop believed that good writing was the key to success, about 25–30 people would be brought to New York for training on writing educational and entertaining segments for the show. Sesame Workshop also constructed puppets for local productions that reflected local cultures and customs. For example, in Israel, the main body puppet was a porcupine representing the Israeli culture: prickly on the outside and soft on the inside. In Germany, the puppet was a bear, and in Mexico, a parrot. In South Africa, puppets included a Zulu-speaking meerkat called Moshe, chosen in part because male and female meerkats share the task of looking after their young.

Sesame Workshop owned the characters and licensed them to the foreign productions. About half the shows' content came from Sesame Workshop and was dubbed into the local language. Typically, street scenes were 100% local production. Live action and animation were 50% Sesame Workshop and 50% local. Muppet segments, such as Bert & Ernie and Cookie Monster, were drawn from Sesame Workshop material and dubbed. The co-producer could also use material from Sesame Workshop's library of culturally neutral international segments.

Contractual arrangements with broadcasters had many variations. In Portugal, the broadcaster had the right to broadcast in Angola and Mozambique. The Netherlands partner had the right to broadcast in places like Aruba, in the Caribbean, where Dutch was spoken. With *Plaza Sésamo,* the Mexican show, Sesame Workshop retained the right to distribute the show in Latin America. With all international agreements, when the broadcast term expired, all rights reverted to Sesame Workshop.

Open Sesame was another international television product broadcast in international markets (Exhibit 3 shows the countries where *Open Sesame* was broadcast). *Open Sesame* was much cheaper to produce because it relied on dubbing the local language. *Sesame Street* could not be dubbed in its entirety because of the segments using live actors. For example, if the actors were talking about the letter *b,* and *b* was for *book,* it could not be easily dubbed. However, other segments were easy to dub. Live action, such as showing a farm where milk came from, could easily be dubbed. Animations and puppet scenes could be dubbed, although Sesame Workshop insisted on final approval for the voices chosen. *Sesame English,* created in association with Berlitz International, was introduced in 2000 in

EXHIBIT 3 *Open Sesame* International Productions

Country	Date First Broadcast	Currently in Production and/ or Broadcast
Arab World	2001	Yes
Armenia	1997	No
Australia	2000	Yes
Canada	1998	No
Czech Republic	1997	Yes
Denmark	1997	No
Finland	1996	Yes
France	1974	No
Greece	1999	Yes
Hong Kong	1999	Yes
Hungary	1998	No
Iceland	1993	No
Indonesia	1997	No
Italy	1999	Yes
Korea	1999	No
Malaysia	1999	Yes
Morocco	1996	No
New Zealand	1999	No
Pakistan	1999	Yes
Philippines	2000	Yes
Singapore	1997	Yes
South Africa	1998	No
Spain	1979	Yes
Sweden	1996	Yes
Thailand	1997	Yes
Turkey	1989	No

China and Taiwan as a daily series focused on conversational English. The series was supplemented by print, audio, video, and CD-ROM products.

SESAME STREET IN CHINA

Entry into China began when Sesame Workshop contacted four Chinese universities with the message that Sesame Workshop was interested in China and would like to visit to discuss education and children's programming. Several people from Sesame Workshop went to China and conducted three-day seminars about Sesame Workshop, writing for children's programming, and possible partnerships. The seminars were sponsored by universities and their departments of education. The result of the trip was that almost every broadcaster contacted was interested in partnering with Sesame Workshop. Eventually, the firm signed a contract with Shanghai Television, which broadcast to about 100 million people. The contract, negotiated over a year, included a provision for syndication throughout China, which at the time was a difficult process. The contract also required that Sesame Workshop find $5 million for the co-production. Eventually, Sesame Workshop secured General Electric as the primary sponsor for the Chinese co-production.

Even though Sesame Workshop preferred to use locally created puppet characters in its co-productions, the Chinese partner insisted on Big Bird, a mainstay of the U.S. show. A compromise was made with the creation of Da Niao as the Chinese cousin to Big Bird. The Chinese show, *Zhima Jie,* became the only non-U.S. production to use a puppet similar to Big Bird. A 21-year-old former auto mechanic was selected to play the character. The other two main puppet characters were Hu Hu Zhu (Snoring Pig), an ageless, furry, blue pig who loved to sing, was very punctual, and had recently moved from the country to the city, and Xiao Mei Zi (Little Plum), a bright red, three-year-old monster.

In February 1998, the first show aired in China and was an immediate success. Later in the year, a syndication deal was signed (China had more than 2,000 broadcasters). For the first season, 130 half-hour shows were developed with plans to develop new shows. With China Educational Television in Beijing, Sesame Workshop also produced 200 15-minute educational shows called "I Love Science." The first *Sesame Street* season was syndicated in 39 markets, including Beijing and several other large cities. In 2001, a second series of *Sesame Street* shows was being planned with a new sponsor.

SESAME STREET IN RUSSIA

Sesame Street in Russia was initiated as part of a USAID program to the former Soviet Union. The program had three objectives: democratization, business principles, and education. *Ulitsa Sezam,* Sesame Workshop's Russian co-production, was launched in 1996 after six years in the making. Many issues, such as transportation, communications, office accommodations, and electricity proved to be major hurdles. A grant from George Soros and sponsorship by Nestlé S.A. made the production possible.

The initial production included 52 half-hour shows, which created the first educational television series produced in Russia. About 70% of the show was written, filmed, and produced in Russia. The *Ulitsa Sezam* set was a Russian courtyard—part city, part village, and more rural than the American *Sesame Street*

set. Aunt Dasha was a central figure in the courtyard. She lived in a traditional Russian cottage and loved folklore and dispensing homespun wisdom. The main puppet character, named Zeliboda, was a seven-foot tall creature covered in blue feathers, with a large orange nose. Other Muppet characters, conceived in Russia and produced in New York, were pink Busya and orange Kubik. Bert and Ernie were also regular characters in their dubbed versions of Vlas and Yenik. In 2001, Sesame Workshop was in negotiations for a third series of shows, with Nestlé playing a key role in the negotiations with the broadcasters.

SESAME WORKSHOP IN 2001

Sesame Workshop was involved in multiple activities. Television, film, and video included television programming, feature films, home video, and various products on cassette and CD. Noggin, a joint venture between Sesame Workshop and the cable channel Nickelodeon, was launched in 1998 as the first commercial-free 24-hour cable television channel and online service dedicated to educating and entertaining children. In 1999, Sesame Workshop launched *Dragon Tales,* a half-hour animated fantasy-adventure program designed to encourage children to approach new experiences with confidence. *Dragon Tales* quickly became a huge success in the United States and markets such as Australia, U.K., and Hong Kong. *Dragon Tales* was being dubbed for markets such as Brazil and Mexico. A new series called *Sagwa, The Chinese Siamese Cat* would premiere in 2001. *Sagwa,* an animated series inspired by a book by Amy Tan, was targeted to children ages 5 to 8 years old. *Tiny Planets,* a multimedia learning system targeted to children 3 to 5 years old was to be launched online and on television in 2002.

The publishing and media division produced a variety of magazines with a readership of more than 12 million children and adults. Sesame Workshop's publishing library included more than 150 *Sesame Street*-based books. Sesame Workshop also produced curriculum-related materials for elementary school children. Sesame Workshop was actively expanding its Internet presence through *SesameStreet.com* and developing new Web-based content, much of it tied to television shows. Sesame Workshop's Interactive Technology Group developed CD-ROMs, video games, and DVD content. *Sesame Street* CD-ROMs were among the best-selling educational titles.

Including co-productions and the U.S. version of programs, Sesame Workshop's television programs were shown in almost 150 countries. International product licensing tended to follow the introduction of the television show. As a country became more familiar with *Sesame Street,* it then became possible to introduce products based on *Sesame Street* characters. Sesame Workshop's licensing agreements stipulated that products could not be advertised on television if the audience was more than 10% preschoolers. The products were required to meet strict quality and safety standards. *Sesame Street* characters themselves could not be used in advertising to sell products.

With more than 400 licenses, Sesame Workshop licensed its brands throughout the world, with the revenue generated used to support Sesame Workshop's educational projects. Tens of thousands of Sesame Workshop products were available globally, produced in partnership with firms like Mattel, Sony, Kmart, Keebler, and Procter & Gamble. Mattel was the primary toy company partner with about 50% of Sesame Workshop's business. Target markets spanned all age groups. In 1996 and 1997, Sesame Workshop had the leading toys in the United States: Tickle Me Elmo and Sing & Snore Ernie. In 2000, *Sesame Street* brand cookies were rolled out successfully in the United States.

There were also *Sesame Street* theme parks in four locations: Pennsylvania; Monterrey, Mexico; São Paulo, Brazil; and Tokyo, Japan. Finally, Sesame Workshop's Outreach and Strategic Partnership division extended the use of *Sesame Street* as an educational resource. Outreach products were created through national and community partnerships and were designed to reach children in need and low income and minority families. Outreach programs included *Sesame Street Fire Safety Program; Sesame Street A is for Asthma Awareness Project* and *Sesame Street Beginnings: Language to Literacy.*

2000 OPERATIONS

Financial results for 2000 are shown in Exhibits 4 and 5. After an operating surplus in 1998, Sesame Workshop's first since 1992, Sesame Workshop returned to deficit positions in 1999 and 2000, although the 2000 deficit was significantly less than in 1999. The 1999 deficit, the largest in the firm's history, resulted in various new product initiative and fundraising efforts.

In 2000, the *Sesame Street* show and related products accounted for the majority of revenue generated by Sesame Workshop. Revenue in 2000 grew by 19%, mainly as a result of the introduction of *Dragon Tales.* Publishing and product licensing revenues increased 1% and 2%, respectively. Reductions in corporate staff resulted in a decrease in general and administrative costs. The total number of employees was about 300, down from more than 400 in 1999.

EXHIBIT 4	Consolidated Statement of Activities		
For the years ended June 30 (000s omitted)		**2000**	**1999**
Revenues			
Grants and contracts in support program production		$ 14,276	$ 5,923
Publishing, program and product licensing and royalties		132,766	117,925
Total operating revenues		$147,042	$123,848
Expenses			
Program production		$ 36,552	$ 26,563
Publishing, product licensing, development and distribution		91,816	84,275
Educational research, marketing and communications		14,429	13,631
General and administrative		10,901	11,796
Other expenses		4,008	2,813
Total operating expenses		$157,706	$139,078
Excess (deficiency) of operating revenues over operating expenses		$(10,664)	$(15,230)
Net investment income and change in unrealized appreciation		$ 15,958	$ 9,553
Other income, net		(5,411)	(3,323)
(Provision) benefit for income taxes		(1)	(17)
Increase in net assets		$ (118)	$(9,017)

Source: Sesame Workshop Annual Report.

For the years ended June 30 (000s omitted)	2000	1999
Assets		
Current assets:		
Cash and short-term investments	$ 13,338	$ 6,930
Receivables—		
Subscriptions, program and product licenses, less allowance for doubtful accounts, of $6,411 in 2000 and $5,279 in 1999	34,286	33,230
Grants and contracts in support of programs	2,296	1,132
Other	551	729
	37,133	35,181
Programs in process	16,028	10,547
Prepaid publishing costs	1,520	2,485
Other current assets	1,145	967
Total current assets	69,164	56,110
Deferred tax asset, less valuation allowance of $3,977 in 2000 and $4,212 in 1997	1,196	1,196
Marketable securities	174,928	180,914
Investment in Sesame Workshop Publishing Company LLC	88	3/4
Furniture, equipment, capitalized information systems, and leasehold improvements, at cost, net of accumulated depreciation and amortization of $16,257 in 2000 and $13,115 in 1999	11,983	9,753
Total assets	$260,447	$248,468
Liabilities and net assets		
Current liabilities:		
Accounts payable	11,387	5,686
Accrued expenses	31,547	32,562
Deferred subscription, program and product license revenues	35,710	29,895
Total current liabilities	78,644	68,143
Deferred rent payable	4,572	2,979
Total Liabilities	83,216	71,119
Net assets:		
Unrestricted	175,124	174,818
Temporarily restricted	2,107	2,531
Total net assets	177,231	177,349
Total liabilities and net assets	$260,447	$248,468

Source: Sesame Workshop Annual Report.

THE INTERNATIONAL ORGANIZATION FOR TELEVISION

Until 1992, Sesame Workshop had separate international sales forces for the English-language show, co-productions, and product licensing. In 1992, the international television sales group was created to eliminate the problem of having different sales forces targeting the same broadcasters. Also in 1992, markets and customers were categorized as follows:

1. Current customers.
2. Broadcasters that had shown a real interest in televising *Sesame Street*. For these potential customers, funding issues were a major element in continuing discussions. About $5–8 million was necessary for

a co-production of 130 half-hours of programming that could be used for 2–3 years. This category included countries like Poland.

3. Countries that had been in co-production and had stopped producing, such as Brazil and France.

4. Countries that Sesame Workshop would like to enter but where few, if any, established relationships existed.

ENTRY STRATEGIES

Market-entry decisions through co-production typically were initiated by a broadcaster that had seen the English version of *Sesame Street* and wanted the show for its country. Various issues would then be considered by Sesame Workshop: 1) What is the level of television penetration? 2) Does Sesame Workshop have a relationship at the government level and, if not, can a relationship be established? 3) Does the market have financial viability, i.e., is it at least a breakeven proposition? 4) Does Sesame Workshop have people available to develop the show? 5) Are Sesame Workshop's license and publisher partners, Mattel and Random House, established in that market?

Initially, co-productions were funded entirely by local broadcasters. Assuming a decision was made to move forward and a contract was signed with a broadcaster, a co-production could take from a year to four or more years to produce. During this phase, Sesame Workshop would work with the product partners to develop a product strategy, which would follow the launch of the television show once the brand was established.

1996 REORGANIZATION

A reorganization of international operations in 1996 resulted in a new structure headed by a group president for products and international television. A group vice president for international and two regional vice president positions were created: one for Latin America and Asia and one for Europe, Africa, and the Middle East. There was also a vice president for co-production. Each regional vice president had profit and return-on-investment responsibility for all Sesame Workshop business. For each region, there were regional directors responsible for television and licensing. Given the size and complexity of the China activities, there was also a senior director responsible for the television activities in China. The reorganization resulted in a revised classification of markets and countries. Non-U.S. markets in which Sesame Workshop either broadcast or planned to broadcast could be broken down as follows:

1. Large growth potential markets in which Sesame Workshop had strong recognition, e.g., U.K., Germany, Japan.

2. High potential markets that could generate more revenue, e.g., China, Mexico.

3. Maintenance markets, smaller markets that were currently generating revenue but had limited growth potential, e.g., Australia, Canada, Netherlands.

4. Social impact markets, e.g., Israel/Palestine, South Africa.

The reorganization of international activities resulted in a decision to reduce the managerial time spent on smaller markets and focus on the larger markets with high potential. However, selling the English version of *Sesame Street* or doing a co-production required roughly the same amount of effort regardless of the market size. As well, many of the smaller markets were some of Sesame Workshop's oldest customers, which raised the issue whether relationships with smaller customers should be scaled back. Within Sesame Workshop, the obvious answer was no, but there was a consensus that priority markets had to be established. As well, some market-entry decisions did not fit neatly into this model. For example, after the successful launch in Russia, USAID asked Sesame Workshop to consider Egypt, which was not initially considered a high potential market.

1999 CHANGES

In 1999, the group president for products and international television resigned. As of mid-2001, the position remained unfilled. A new division was created to manage projects that involved governments and NGOs, such as in South Africa, Egypt, and Israel. This division, called project management, consisted of four directors and focused on issues such as educational outreach, fundraising, and government contacts. These projects had limited product licensing opportunities. With the creation of this new division, the products and international television group headed by Martha Van Gelder, which consisted of 16 people, concentrated on developing markets in which both a product license and television businesses could be supported. However, there were close linkages between the groups, as Van Gelder explained:

Every market we are in is mission—there is no market where Sesame Street is not reaching and teaching kids. When we go to meetings, we don't say, "How will we make the most money?" We say, "How will we reach the most kids?" This is a concept that is very comfortable to everybody.

In 2001, Sesame Workshop had no offices outside the United States. Agents were used to manage day-to-day business relationships in international markets. The firm began shifting away from having different agents in each country. Sesame Street now had one agent for all of Europe, which helped streamline decision-making. The same approach was being implemented in Latin America. Sesame Workshop was considering how to more effectively use alliances to support marketing and advertising while still maintaining control over the brand and program content.

NEW MARKETS

A Sesame Workshop manager described the challenge of identifying new markets:

> *We need to be a profitable enterprise because if we are not profitable, we won't be around for very long. Even if we are not-for-profit, we compete against for-profit companies. We need good people, great shows, and good business systems and planning. We look at Sesame Workshop like a normal business: I have a certain overhead, I have production costs and marketing expenses and profit. We have to hit those numbers and we have to operate in a way that is as smart and professional as Warner Bros. or Disney. The difference between us and Disney is that we don't have to look for a certain profitability target in order to make a decision.*
>
> *Social responsibility is critical for us. We have pure mission countries, such as South Africa, that the company has decided are strategically important. We can and do vary costs and pricing for poorer countries. In these countries, there is not a self-sustaining model around licensing. That means we have to come up with a different model that may have government or corporate sponsorship. In contrast, in a territory like Germany, the combination of the broadcaster and licensing makes this a great market.*
>
> *Sesame Workshop celebrates diversity because it is at the heart of what we do. We believe the Sesame Street co-productions in China and Israel/Palestine help bring the world together. In Israel and Palestine, we saw that there was such a need for people to learn how to get along. For the Israel and Palestine show, there are two streets, one Arab and one Israeli. The same for Egypt—there was such a need for education on the role of women in society. By producing in Cairo, we end up with a series that can be broadcast throughout the whole Arab-speaking region. In South Africa—a total need for education for the masses.*

India was a country that was considered a potentially interesting market, as another Sesame Workshop manager explained:

> *We have some English being shown on cable and maybe 5–6 million viewers. But from a licensing perspective, India is not very interesting because there are limited distribution channels. With television there is tremendous potential for reaching people and even getting some reasonable licensing fees. But given the language and cultural differences, how can one show play to the whole country? We have had discussions with Indian organizations. But it comes down to the problem that we only have a certain amount of people who can do co-production development. When South Africa comes along and we have millions of dollars of funding and only so many hours and bodies, India and other markets have to wait.*

Brazil, France, and Italy were also obvious target markets:

> *The big holes in Europe have been France and Italy. We had versions of the series on the air back in the 1970s that did not work very well and did not leave us with a strong relationship. Both countries are known as difficult markets for American programming. Clearly, those are two markets that are very important for us with great potential. We recently signed a deal in Italy to broadcast Sesame English and Elmo's World on Rai and RaiSat. In Latin America, Brazil has great potential. We are always trying to find ways to enter new markets appropriately. But, it is a time-consuming process and every market is different. We cannot just take the same people and throw them against multiple projects that require an intense amount of work. That is why our head of global distribution focuses more on understanding markets than on actual selling.*

Another manager summed up her views on Sesame Workshop's international strategy:

> *We make decisions differently from other companies developing children's programming. That's what makes it so interesting to be here and sometimes frustrating. There are some huge markets for co-production opportunities, such as Brazil and India. It's a little hard for me to fit together how we make the decision about allocating resources to these different markets. What drives our willingness to make commitments to these markets? We are still in the process of trying to figure out what we want financially and what we want the business to look like.*
>
> *It is not feasible to do co-productions in every market. But because we are a not-for-profit, we have the freedom to go into new markets and break even. For example, I could have a great project for a small market and it would be as well received as a project*

for a huge market like China or Brazil. We want to do unique small projects. For example, we are doing a conflict resolution series for Cyprus using live action with an organization called Search for Common Ground. The producers could not even meet in Cyprus so they went to London. There is no profit in the project, but it is consistent with the mission.

INVESTMENT CRITERIA

The usefulness of specific investment criteria as the basis for guiding new international investments had been debated, as an executive explained:

Several years ago, I felt we were not making decisions in a consistent manner. We need consistent breakeven on ongoing operations. I tried to establish criteria such as mission, cash flow, financial return, and management time involved. What I wanted was a consistent list so that we understood the implications of doing a project. The problem was how to weight the criteria. Which ones are the most important?

We need to look at the overall property and what can be generated from the property. We have not done this so well, or at all, in the past. A show that production-wise is at the highest level but that nobody can afford—how valuable is that? Is Elmo's World *so successful because of the high-quality production or because of Elmo and the simple story lines? There is probably a bit of both and it is very hard to test.*

We are being pushed to find new revenue sources while staying true to our brand and mission. Now, when we look at new properties as we develop them, we are looking at all its tentacles. It is not just revenue—there are outreach components and online ways to extend the experience. Trying to capture all the revenue and all the expense around the property is something we have to get better at.

BROADCAST COMPETITION

When Sesame Workshop internationalized in the 1970s and 1980s, television in most countries was dominated by public broadcasters. Many of these broadcasters were prepared to pay Sesame Workshop fees to cover production and other costs. In the 1990s, especially with the growth of commercial broadcasting via satellite and cable, the television industry worldwide became much more competitive. With new competition, audiences dropped for individual broadcasters and especially for the former monopoly public broadcasters. As well, the

children's programming area was not a primary area for most commercial broadcasters.

In some markets, such as Taiwan, cable reached 80% of the households. In other markets, only a small percentage of households had cable. To deal with situations where cable and terrestrial (traditional broadcasters) coverage both existed, Sesame Workshop was beginning to structure deals whereby one company was given terrestrial rights and another company cable rights, with both rights exclusive and separate. However, co-productions were only done with terrestrial broadcasters.

A Sesame Workshop manager explained the new competitive challenges:

In the old days we were it. We invented education through entertainment and we always took for granted that people knew who we were. We had a quality property that we were putting on the screen. People kept watching the show and the broadcaster said, "This is great." As competition has increased and the windows for the show are shrinking, the audience we are going after is also shrinking. So, with the number of programs that are available to the shrinking audience continuing to increase, if your program loses popularity, it is hard to come back.

There are two different kinds of competition we face. We can no longer assume that Sesame Street *will be the broadcaster's first choice. There are now dozens of preschool programs, not just on* PBS. *To be successful, a show has to be good, the product has to be on the cutting edge, and there must be a fabulous product offering in every category. There is increased competition from preschool shows across the board. Shows like* Teletubbies *and* Rugrats *are financed and designed for global exploitation from the beginning. We have taught the world how to do that. At one of the major conferences, broadcasters were saying to us, "We know you make* Sesame Street, *but I have tons of preschool shows. What do you have in live action for 7–12-year-olds?"*

Although there are now more channels and options for programming, license fees [paid by broadcasters] around the world have been going down and down. We have broadcasters who are willing to pay zero but still want us to deliver a fully produced show, promote it, and guarantee a percentage of ancillary revenue. If Sesame Street *is too expensive, broadcasters will take something else. When U.S. broadcasters can fill their educational requirement by airing* GI Joe *because it shows good over evil, how much more would you pay for* Sesame Street *if your goal is just to sat-*

isfy a mandated educational requirement and you cannot use advertising on Sesame Street? *Unfortunately, the marketplace does not always put the same value on our product as it costs us to produce it.*

The other competitive situation is that many broadcasters in the United States and globally own the shows and own the airtime. That means broadcasters like Nickelodeon, Disney, and Time Warner can decide they want to back a show like Rugrats. *They own the rights and can keep it on the air, let it incubate, and slowly develop an audience. It is a lot more difficult if you don't own a channel, which is one of the strategic reasons why we launched* Noggin *on the Nickelodeon channel. We have to have strategic alliances with the broadcasters and we have to become a more flexible and creative partner. We also have to become more innovative in developing funding sources for co-productions. And we can no longer view 130 shows per season as essential. We can do 65 shows and perhaps get better quality shows.*

Historically, most government-owned channels were not allowed to interrupt programming for young children with commercials. However, the increase in cable and satellite broadcasting was putting pressure on Sesame Workshop's commercial-free philosophy.

If you are PBS or another public broadcaster, commercial-free television is accepted. But increasingly we are talking to commercial channels that want a commercial break. It is becoming difficult to ask somebody to show an entire hour commercial-free. In Mexico, we started a commercial break in the show as an experiment because they have been asking for it for so long. We were worried the kids wouldn't be able to make the distinction between the show and the commercial. The research that has come back from Mexico shows that kids clearly understand where the commercial is. I think in many markets the company will have to rethink its stance on commercial breaks.

OPPORTUNITIES AND CHALLENGES

Looking towards the future, the managers of the international group saw many opportunities and plenty of challenges. For example, Japan provided an interesting situation. Unique for Sesame Workshop, a large market in Japan was teenage girls and young women. Because the show until recently had been broadcast in English (in 1998 a dubbed version was introduced which was very successful), Sesame Street was watched primarily as a vehicle for learning English, which was never Sesame

Workshop's intention for Japan. As well, Japanese girls were very fond of characters on products like clothing, purses, T-shirts, key chains, earrings, etc. The Sesame Street characters were very popular, and many offers for product licenses had to be turned down because they were deemed inconsistent for the brand. More recently in Japan, opportunities for wireless Internet were emerging, especially for English-language training.

Production deals were also changing, which meant an increasingly complex network of partners, customers, sponsors, and other relationships.

To make the co-production model work, we need first-run revenues, syndication if possible, international sales, and international product sales. The old model was that broadcasters paid for everything, including a management fee and some profit for us. A few years ago we started going into markets where there was government money available and where we had to raise sponsorship money. The broadcaster was not paying for the whole thing. Ultimately, Sesame Workshop *was taking the risk if sufficient money could not be raised. Now, we have some broadcasters, who used to pay for the whole co-production, telling us they can no longer pay and asking us to help raise sponsorships for them.*

Another manager expressed concerns about the heavy reliance on Sesame Street:

We need new programs. We are a one-hit wonder that's been wonderful worldwide. But we need a follow-up success. We have had some other shows that have done pretty well but nothing near the global scale of Sesame Street. *We have put a lot of energy into* Dragon Tales, *which is beautifully animated.*

Product licensing was also an area that offered interesting challenges. Products could go from hot to cold very quickly, as a manager explained:

We saw that happen with Tickle Me Elmo. Sesame Workshop was considered "fashion" for awhile through Tickle Me Elmo. Moms and dads were buying Elmo ties, Elmo boxer shorts, and Elmo this and that. It was the hot brand. Then all of a sudden the fashion side of it went away and we lost 60% of the business in less than six months time. Where did it go? It went to other licensee and new properties like Teletubbies.

We have to work very hard to make sure the brand does not erode to the point where moms and dads say, "I don't want junior to watch the show anymore." If that ever happens, you are out of business.

The show is what drives everything we do at Sesame Workshop. People can tell you all day long that our products sell on their own because they are cute and fun. But eight out of every ten people buy our products because their children have seen this property on the TV show.

In some markets, we are severely limited by being with a public broadcaster in terms of television commercials and exploiting the brands the way other companies do. We can sell toys but we cannot promote them on television.

Our goal is to find ways to sustain our licensing activities but do it in a way that sets us apart from most other licensee/licensors. Our television competitors often pay for their television programming just to feed the licensing program. When Sesame Workshop enters international markets we don't say, "Here's Mickey Mouse, take him; here's Teletubbies—*you can't do anything to change it." We can make our products local because our show is local.*

CONCLUSION

Final comments from two Sesame Workshop executives:

In international, we have grown so quickly over the last few years that we worry about overextending ourselves. Sesame Street *is a very powerful series and a lot of people want to work with us. But, we cannot respond to everybody. That's why we came up with things like* Open Sesame. *Our challenge is to remain true to our roots and develop programming that's enticing and educational. We need to address where we are as a brand today because that should underpin everything that we do.*

We are a small firm with limited resources and unlimited dreams. Our mission of educating children is so important to us. But how many mission projects can we take on? I think what will drive it is what makes sense for our own survival and what it does to the overall health of the organization, both mission and financial health.

NOTES

1. Sesame Workshop 2000 Annual Report.
2. 2000 Annual Report.
3. Cynthia Crossen, "Class Act: *Sesame Street,* at 23, Still Teaches Children While Amusing Them," *Wall Street Journal,* Feb. 21, 1992, A1.

Sonic: America's Drive-In

case twenty-seven

James Beth
Charles Dunaway
Aimee Ellis
Eric Johnson
Ken Rowe

INTRODUCTION

Despite a tumultuous history, Sonic has emerged as the largest drive-in chain in the United States. Although smaller than leading "quick service" restaurant chains McDonald's, Burger King, and Wendy's, Sonic is a significant competitor in its core markets, and it beats the national chains on service measures such as customer satisfaction and loyalty. With continued expansion planned, Sonic must prepare to compete head-to-head with the burger behemoths. In fact, on a hundred-point scale, operators in the "quick service" restaurant business on average rated competition intensity at 83, up from a rating of 76 in 2000. The domestic market for fast food is so crowded that many fast-food players have been forced to expand overseas. In addition to intense rivalry among competitors, new entrants appear in the market with regularity. Not only do these companies face intense competition among themselves, but they must also contend with rivalry from convenience stores and prepackaged meals.[1] Another issue for industry members is employee turnover. Recent figures show average annual turnover at fast-food restaurants at 85 percent.[2] In spite of the drawbacks to the industry, however, there is money to be made for the ably managed company, especially in America. United States per capita spending on fast food in 1998 was $376.23, six times the amount spent in the United Kingdom and eight times the amount spent in Germany and France.[3]

Since the mid-1990s, Sonic's CEO, Cliff Hudson, has led several initiatives to bring the chain to this point. Sonic has improved its relationships with franchisees and employees, offered unique menu innovations, invested in information technology, and initiated new and creative marketing campaigns. As these measures come to fruition, Hudson knows that he must push himself and his staff toward increasingly inventive methods to achieve growing profits, to compete more effectively in the quick-service restaurant industry, and to provide strong financial returns.

HISTORY[4]

HUMBLE BEGINNINGS

In 1953, Troy Smith founded the prototype of the first Sonic Drive-In in Shawnee, Oklahoma. Smith's dream was to own his own business. Before 1953, he had already tried opening two other restaurants. Smith eventually bought a steak house that had a root beer stand on the lot. He intended to tear the stand down to add more parking for the steak house, but the root beer stand, called Top Hat Drive-In, proved to be more profitable and even outlasted the steak house. While traveling in Louisiana, Smith saw homemade intercom speakers at a hamburger stand that let customers order right from their cars. He liked the idea so much that he contacted the innovator and asked him to make an intercom for Top Hat. The speaker system was installed, a canopy was added for cars to park under, and "carhops" delivered food directly to customers' cars. The Top Hat Drive-In was now the prototype of the future Sonic.

BIRTH OF A FRANCHISE

Charlie Pappe was managing the local Safeway supermarket in Woodward, Oklahoma, but he was looking to get out of the grocery business and into the restaurant business. Pappe had dined at a Top Hat while visiting friends in Shawnee and was so impressed with the whole concept that he introduced himself to Smith. In 1956, Pappe successfully opened the second Top Hat Drive-In. Four Top Hats had been opened by 1958, when Smith and Pappe discovered that the Top Hat name was copyrighted and began searching for a new name. Top Hat's slogan had been "Service With the Speed of Sound," so they agreed on Sonic, which means moving at the "speed of sound." The first Sonic Drive-In was in Stillwater, Oklahoma, and still serves hot dogs, root beer, and frozen favorites on the same site today.

The change in name sparked requests from many aspiring Sonic operators. The first formal Sonic franchise agreement was a one-and-a-half-page double-spaced document. Smith and Pappe helped the new partners with the layout, site selection, and operation of their new Sonic Drive-In. They charged a royalty fee of one penny per sandwich bag used by the franchisee. Pappe died in 1967, and Smith was left alone to run the company along with two franchisees who had been invited to run the supply and distribution division of Sonic.

In the early days, there was no national advertising and there were no territorial rights. In 1973, a group of ten principal franchise owners, who became the officers and board of directors, restructured the company into Sonic Industries. This group of directors purchased the Sonic name, slogan, trademark, logos, and supply company and offered shares of stock to each store operator. Sonic was now owned by its franchisees and was a publicly traded company. At this point, there were 165 Sonics in the chain. From 1973 to 1978, Sonic experienced a period of tremendous growth. During this time, 800 new stores were opened. Sonic Advertising Trust was introduced during this period, which established a Sonic School to formally train new managers and launched Sonic's first television advertising campaign.

THE TURNAROUND

When Cliff Hudson joined the Sonic legal department in 1984, the franchise was a loose collection of 1,000 independent restaurants operating in 19 states. Sonic still had no national advertising program or purchasing cooperative. Accounting was done manually. Packaging and store design across the chain were inconsistent. Menus varied from store to store—"Slaw Dogs served up in the Carolinas; ice cream sundaes peddled by a renegade franchisee in Texas; deep-fried 'Pickle-Os' furtively sold in Sonic's own backyard [Oklahoma City]. Even within the same city, it was easy to find radical taste variations in Tater Tots because franchisees bought ingredients from different vendors."[5] Hudson realized that significant changes were necessary to turn

around Sonic's poor financial performance. He led the management team in a successful leveraged buyout of Sonic from its franchisees in 1986 for $10 million. Hudson was instrumental in restructuring the company, and in 1991, he facilitated an initial public stock offering for Sonic. In 1995, a second stock offering raised enough money to repay all of Sonic's debt. The same year, Hudson became CEO of Sonic Corporation. He recruited personnel from competitors and sought to reduce costs and increase efficiencies in the organization.[6] For example, Sonic started using 24-pound boxes instead of 10-pound boxes to ship burgers. At a price reduction of fifty cents per box, the simple change equated to thousands of dollars saved in the long term.[7] Meanwhile, franchisees in 17 markets began purchasing together, and increased advertising to 1 percent of sales.

In 1995, Sonic introduced "Sonic 2000," an aggressive "multi-layered strategy to further unify the company in terms of a consistent menu, brand identity, products, packaging and service."[8] A key element of Sonic 2000 was a "new, retrofitted exterior that features futuristic red pylons with fiber-optic lights, oval roofs and a new logo."[9] *Architecture* magazine noted the design "revives the streamlined look of the golden age of automobility."[10] After Sonic showed franchisees that the new design helped increase growth by 8 percent in company-owned same-store sales, they began remodeling their restaurants despite the $55,000 to $75,000 price tag. Sonic 2000 also promoted Sonic as a brand and added a new, expanded menu, standardized throughout the chain. Because of the standardized menu, the company went from five to two sizes of hamburger patties, and franchisees enjoyed reduced operating costs.[11] The company began opening more restaurants, and franchising boomed. Between 1996 and 1997, the percentage of customers who recognized the Sonic brand increased from 43 to 66.[12] In 2001, Hudson took Sonic international by opening a store in Monterrey, Mexico, with more restaurants planned in Mexico City. By 2002, 2,432 Sonic Drive-Ins operated in more than 30 states and two countries. Sonic had grown to be a strong regional competitor, but as Sonic executives pondered additional growth, understanding the nature of the competitive environment became increasingly important.

RESTAURANT INDUSTRY

The restaurant industry has long been considered mature, yet numerous outlets open and close each day. Although competition is fierce (there are about 8 million restaurants in the world and some 300,000 restaurant companies[13]) and profit margins are small, start-up costs are relatively low to enter the market. Unlike the ingenious chef who opens a small local eatery, companies primarily use acquisition strategies, rather than construction of new units, to grow, giving them a larger revenue base over which to spread costs and more leverage with suppliers to keep costs down.[14]

The restaurant industry can be divided into full-service and quick service, or fast food. Sonic competes directly with other quick-service restaurants such as McDonald's, Wendy's, and Burger King. During economic downturns, patrons tend to dine at less-expensive quick-serve facilities; consequently, as the economy stays weak, quick-service restaurants can expect better sales than their full-service counterparts. A weak economy also offsets a shrinking labor force by keeping wages (often minimum) stable, thus posing less threat to profits.[15] The restaurant industry tends to rely on hiring retirees and on automation. However, restaurants are trying to make their companies more attractive to younger generations. Many chains try to entice potential employees by designating themselves as fun places to work.

Estimates indicate that the overall economic impact of the restaurant industry should reach $1 trillion in 2002.[16] This impact includes the complete supply chain from agriculture to transportation to wholesale trade to food manufacturing. The restaurant industry has experienced approximately 5 percent annual growth, and, on a typical day in 2002, posts average sales of more than $1.1 billion.[17] The restaurant industry is the nation's largest employer, behind the government, employing approximately 11.6 million people.[18]

A National Restaurant Association survey shows that three out of ten consumers agree that meals prepared at a restaurant or fast-food place are essential to the way they live. The survey also states that "three out of five consumers reported that they plan to eat on the premises of quick-service restaurants and seven out of ten said they plan to eat takeout or delivery food in 2002 as often as they did in 2001." Because Americans have less time and energy to prepare their own meals,[19] the restaurant industry appears to be on solid ground for the time being and demand should remain steady. However, the majority of fast-food diners are young, since older diners tend to prefer slightly more upscale restaurants.[20] Consequently, as the population ages, quick-service restaurants are left to battle for share in a slow-growth market.[21]

COMPETITION

As noted above, within the quick-service restaurant industry, Sonic identifies McDonald's, Burger King, and Wendy's as its major competitors[22] (see Exhibit 1). Although Sonic is smaller and more regional than the three bigger players, the feeling of competition is mutual. McDonald's opened its first drive-through facility in Oklahoma City, Oklahoma, in 1975 to compete with the local Sonic drive-ins.[23]

MCDONALD'S[24]

The leading operator in the quick-service restaurant industry, McDonald's was founded in 1955 in San Bernardino, California. Since then, the company has grown to over 30,093 locations in 121 countries around the world, with 13,099 restaurants in the United States.[25] In 2001, McDonald's had total worldwide sales of $40.6 billion and net income of $1.64 billion, and served approximately 46 million customers per day.[26] The menu includes such favorites as the Big Mac, Quarter Pounder with Cheese, Filet-O-Fish, and Chicken McNuggets, as well as limited-time promotions such as the McRib sandwich and McDLT. In the United States, the company also serves breakfast items, including the Egg McMuffin, the Sausage McMuffin, and pancakes. Other brands owned by McDonald's include Boston Market, Chipotle, and Donato's Pizzeria. Although these operations do not represent a significant portion

	Total Number of Restaurants	U.S. Locations	International Locations	Corporate Stores	Franchise Stores
McDonald's	30,093	13,099	16,994	12,698*	17,395
Burger King	11,455	8,146	3,309	1,014	10,441
Wendy's International	6,043	5,315	728	1,228	4,815
Sonic	2,432	2,431	2	511	1,921

EXHIBIT 1

*McDonald's Corporation operates 4,320 stores in cooperation with local partners (joint ventures).

of McDonald's operations, they allow it to capture other meal occasions.

Corporate-owned restaurants account for approximately 27 percent of McDonald's total revenues, while franchisees account for 61 percent, and joint ventures the remaining 12 percent.[27] To assure that each restaurant meets McDonald's high consistency and quality standards, the company is very selective about the choice of franchisees and typically requires that all franchisees be active participants in the management of their restaurants. Generally investor groups or passive investors are not awarded franchises.

To encourage active participation by franchise owners, the McDonald's franchise contract requires that the operator provide capital for the store's equipment, signs, seating, and décor and reinvest in the business over time. McDonald's retains ownership of the land, and the franchise operator has the option of purchasing or leasing the building from the company. Franchises generate income for the company through the payment of rent and service fees based upon a percentage of sales.

Although McDonald's currently accounts for 12 percent of total commercial meals, it accounts for less than 1 percent of total meals consumed.[28] Therefore, it continues to have a growth strategy that focuses on opening profitable restaurants and expanding operations in locales where the potential for returns is strong, and it plans to open from 1,300 to 1,400 new restaurants in 2002.[29] In addition to its consistent growth strategy, McDonald's is refocusing on several other key areas. Because it believes it has suffered from a perception of poor service in the last few years, it aims to deliver an outstanding experience each time a customer visits one of its locations. Through improving its quality, service, cleanliness, and value, the chain expects to increase the number of customer visits. The company is revamping its corporate structure to allow managers to better focus on the core business. It has also elevated the importance of corporate strategy and business development to better identify opportunities for growth in its current businesses and in new businesses that offer growth potential. In November 2002, McDonald's announced plans to restructure operations in four countries, liquidate operations in three countries, and close approximately 175 underperforming restaurants in ten other countries, eliminating 400 to 600 positions to control costs and reallocate resources.[30] In addition, McDonald's continues to appeal to children with Disney tie-ins, a new "Mighty Happy Meal" for kids ages eight to ten, and enhanced play areas, some with electronic game centers.[31]

BURGER KING[32]

In 2001, Burger King Restaurants, the second largest quick-service hamburger restaurant chain, and its franchisees operated 11,455 restaurants worldwide with systemwide sales of $11.3 billion.[33] There are 8,146 locations in the United States with at least one location in each of the 50 states and with total 2001 domestic sales exceeding $8.6 billion.[34] The restaurant serves approximately 15.8 million customers per day worldwide.[35] Primary products include the Whopper, chicken sandwiches, onion rings, fries, BK Veggie Burger, and Chicken Tenders.

Burger King operates 1,014 locations worldwide, and franchisees operate the remaining 93 percent, or 10,441.[36] Franchise owners are required to provide capital to either lease a location for approximately $400,000 or purchase a location for approximately $1.2 million.[37] In addition, the franchisee pays a $50,000 franchise fee as well as an ongoing royalty fee of 4.5 percent and advertising fee of 4.0 percent based on total sales revenue.[38] The franchise owner is also required to attend a minimum of 700 hours of classroom and restaurant training before being given a franchise contract.[39]

In September 2002, Burger King introduced a 99-cent value menu with 11 items, including burgers, fries, tacos, salads, shakes, and baked potatoes.[40] The same month, it signed comedian Steve Harvey as the new company spokesperson. During October 2002, the chain will promote a Halloween tie-in with *The Simpsons* TV show, offering Simpsons toys in Kids Meals and selling a limited "chilling" Halloween Freaky Float™.[41]

The chain encourages diversity and supports volunteerism and civic involvement among employees.[42]

WENDY'S[43]

Wendy's Old Fashioned Hamburgers, the third largest quick-service hamburger restaurant, operates 6,043 restaurants worldwide with over $8.3 billion in systemwide sales and net income of $194 million.[44] There are 5,315 locations in the United States with 334 locations opening in 2001.[45] Wendy's total sales are 13.1 percent of the quick-service restaurant market.[46] Its primary products include hamburgers, chicken sandwiches, Frostys, and fries. The company also owns Tim Horton's, the largest coffee and fresh baked goods chain in Canada, and Baja Fresh Mexican Grill, a leader in the fast-casual Mexican food market.

Approximately 80 percent of Wendy's store locations are franchise operations, with the remaining 20 percent corporate owned.[47] Corporate management makes periodic visits to franchises to ensure that they meet specifications and to make recommendations to improve the location. The company also provides franchisees with detailed manuals that specify the standards for food preparation, service, and presentation. Although Wendy's does not supply food products to franchisees directly, it does have cooperative arrangements with independent distributors to allow franchisees to purchase their supplies at a discount. These arrangements provide a more efficient distribution system that ensures products meet Wendy's standards for quality and guarantees product availability. In 2001, the company also vertically integrated by opening a bun baking factory to supply both corporate and franchise locations.

Wendy's plans to pursue a "smart" growth strategy in 2002 through expansion into profitable areas.[48] It has committed to expanding only into areas where market research determines the restaurant will be profitable and where economic conditions are relatively strong. Wendy's will also consider product expansions: It has acquired other fast-food chains such as Tim Horton's and Cafe Express, and it has directly invested in other chains such as Pommodoro, an Italian eatery. The company also anticipates that technology will make the organization more efficient, improve restaurant service, enhance its competitive position, and produce superior results. It is upgrading its network to more fully integrate its information systems with its business units. Technology will also play an important role in supply chain management techniques that link suppliers, distributors, restaurants, and corporate supply managers with real-time information and that deliver significant cost reductions for the supply channel. These cost reductions will allow Wendy's to deliver competitively priced products and remain profitable.

SONIC TODAY

Despite Sonic's smaller size, Fitzburg Taylor, a Banc of America securities analyst, favorably compares Sonic Corporation to its competition, citing the company's flexibility and quick response.[49] He explains, "It's always a bit of David and Goliath, and you have to win by being smarter. I think this management team has been able to accomplish that over quite a period of time. They deliver impressive and predictable results."[50]

During its 50-year history, Sonic, the nation's largest drive-in chain, has experienced phenomenal success, despite a downturn in the 1970s. Located primarily in the Sun Belt states, Sonic is known for its personal carhop service and unique made-to-order menu items, including Toaster sandwiches, Extra-Long Cheese

Coneys, and Frozen and Fountain Favorites™. Sonic's specialty menu has allowed the chain to differentiate itself from other fast-food outlets and to avoid price wars with its major competitors.[51] Sonic also distinguishes itself on small but important points of quality. Hamburgers are made to order and served in aluminum foil, preserving the heat. Drinks are served in Styrofoam rather than paper cups, preserving the cold.[52] While these features are more expensive than the standard paper goods commonly used in the quick-service restaurant industry, Sonic Corporation feels the improved quality and customer satisfaction are worth the cost.[53]

FINANCIAL AND OPERATING RESULTS

Although Sonic is not the largest chain, it leads the fast-food industry in real sales growth, with higher same-store sales each year since 1987 (see Exhibit 2).[54] Accolades include a spot on *Business Week*'s Hot Growth Companies 2002 list, recognition from *Restaurants & Institutions* Annual Choice in Chains Award as an overall Gold Winner in March 2002 for the fourth consecutive year, placement on *Entrepreneur*'s Franchise 500 list, inclusion on *Forbes'* list of the 200 Best Small Companies in America for the eighth consecutive year, and placement on *QSR Magazine*'s America's Hottest Chains list. In 2002, Sonic reported record earnings, which had risen 22 percent. Sonic also posted record quarterly earnings, which met analysts' consensus expectations and represented an increase of 19 percent.[55] Revenues have grown from $54 million in 1991 to over $400 million in 2002. (See Exhibit 3.) Net income has increased during this period from $4 million to over $48 million, and return on equity has gone from a respectable 12.8 percent to over 21 percent. Much of the growth has been fueled by the expansion of both company-owned and franchised restaurants. However, Sonic has also continued to steadily increase same-store sales. The company experiences high levels of customer satisfaction and has achieved the highest level of customer loyalty in the quick-service segment.[56] More than one million customers eat at Sonic each day,[57] and the average Sonic customer eats at the chain seven times each month.[58]

Sonic attributes its successful operations to five essential components: a multilayered growth strategy, a highly differentiated concept, an accelerated expansion program, strong sales trends, and a solid financial performance.[59] Designed to diversify growth potential and strengthen profitability, Sonic's multilayered growth strategy calls for increased numbers of restaurants, higher media expenditures, and unification of chain

EXHIBIT 2 Sonic Sales by Year (in millions)

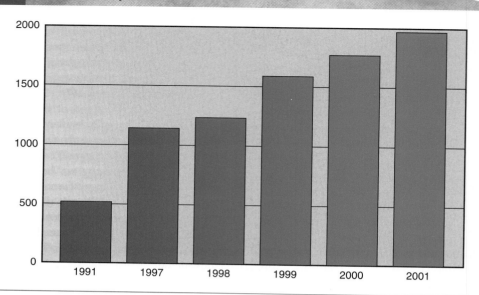

Source: Sonic Corporation, Annual Report, 2001

EXHIBIT 3 Sonic Annual Financial Data

Balance Sheet
Annual Assets (000s)

Fiscal Year Ending	8/31/ 2001	8/31/ 2000	8/31/ 1999	8/31/ 1998	8/31/ 1997	8/31/ 1996	8/31/ 1995	8/31/ 1994	8/31/ 1993	8/31/ 1992
Cash	6,971	3,477	1,612	2,602	7,334	7,706	3,778	6,013	5,397	4,251
Marktable Securities	683	625	645	1,092	856	783	NA	NA	NA	4,753
Receivables	12,142	9,685	7,652	7,587	5,890	5,229	6,089	5,502	4,968	2,662
Inventories	2,030	1,677	1,460	1,363	1,239	1,868	2,252	2,060	2,140	1,455
Raw Materials	NA	NA	NA	NA	NA	NA	NA	NA	NA	NA
Work In Progress	NA	NA	NA	NA	NA	NA	NA	NA	NA	NA
Finished Goods	NA	NA	NA	NA	NA	NA	NA	NA	NA	NA
Notes Receivable	NA	NA	NA	NA	NA	NA	NA	NA	NA	NA
Other Current Assets	1,703	1,413	1,207	3,895	3,380	591	595	534	1,076	1,073
Total Current Assets	23,529	16,877	12,576	16,539	18,699	16,177	12,714	14,109	13,582	14,194
Prop, Plant And Equip	273,198	222,318	207,890	188,065	136,522	100,505	70,171	40,980	31,695	20,050
Accumulated Dep	NA	NA	NA	NA	NA	NA	NA	NA	NA	NA
Net Prop And Equip	273,198	222,318	207,890	188,065	136,522	100,505	70,171	40,980	31,695	20,050
Invest And Adv To Subs	7,148	7,220	5,795	3,494	3,361	3,421	3,048	NA	NA	2,969
Other Non-cur Assets	7,375	7,679	5,871	3,579	3,314	3,063	2,731	5,487	4,274	1,535
Deferred Charges	NA	NA	NA	NA	NA	2,184	257	548	NA	NA
Intangibles	46,750	24,277	24,545	21,503	22,945	22,094	16,410	15,858	13,967	11,555
Deposits And Oth Asset	NA	NA	NA	NA	NA	NA	NA	NA	NA	NA
Total Assets	358,000	278,371	256,677	233,180	184,841	147,444	105,331	76,982	63,517	50,303

Annual Liabilities (000$)

Fiscal Year Ending	8/31/ 2001	8/31/ 2000	8/31/ 1999	8/31/ 1998	8/31/ 1997	8/31/ 1996	8/31/ 1995	8/31/ 1994	8/31/ 1993	8/31/ 1992
Notes Payable	NA	NA	NA	NA	NA	NA	NA	NA	NA	NA
Accounts Payable	8,052	7,455	5,104	10,740	4,635	2,904	1,691	2,433	1,907	867
Cur Long Term Debt	1,083	652	838	118	116	517	107	85	61	143
Cur Port Cap Leases	NA	NA	NA	950	1,030	823	481	472	436	462
Accrued Expenses	16,709	14,363	13,564	11,140	8,629	7,841	5,353	3,186	3,450	2,838
Income Taxes	NA	NA	NA	NA	NA	NA	NA	NA	NA	NA
Other Current Liab	1,020	778	813	883	780	601	833	620	346	398
Total Current Liab	26,864	23,248	20,319	23,831	15,190	12,686	8,465	6,795	6,199	4,709
Mortgages	NA	NA	NA	NA	NA	NA	NA	NA	NA	NA
Deferred Charges/Inc	1,735	3,110	2,504	3,805	756	NA	NA	NA	854	908
Convertible Debt	NA	NA	NA	NA	NA	NA	NA	NA	NA	NA
Long Term Debt	108,972	83,860	72,331	61,400	37,517	11,884	24,795	6,334	1,182	1,099
Non-Cur Cap Leases	12,801	6,668	7,279	7,429	8,153	8,985	5,793	6,351	5,400	4,866
Other Long Term Liab	6,909	6,222	4,489	4,704	5,051	4,206	2,921	3,125	3,132	2,756
Total Liabilities	157,281	123,108	106,922	101,169	66,667	37,761	41,974	22,605	16,767	14,339
Minority Int (liab)	NA	NA	NA	NA	NA	NA	NA	NA	NA	NA
Preferred Stock	NA	NA	NA	NA	NA	NA	NA	NA	NA	NA
Common Stock Net	319	313	207	206	135	135	121	79	79	78
Capital Surplus	78,427	69,786	67,212	63,866	59,891	59,107	30,355	28,152	27,948	25,395
Retained Earnings	188,434	149,478	116,851	89,455	69,666	50,584	39,340	26,857	19,214	10,571
Treasury Stock	66,461	64,314	34,515	21,516	11,518	143	6,459	711	492	80
Other Equities	NA	NA	NA	NA	NA	NA	NA	NA	NA	NA
Shareholder Equity	200,719	155,263	149,755	132,011	118,174	109,683	63,357	54,378	46,750	35,964
Tot Liab & Net Worth	358,000	278,371	256,677	233,180	184,841	147,444	105,331	76,982	63,517	50,303

Annual Income (000s)

Fiscal Year Ending	8/31/ 2001	8/31/ 2000	8/31/ 1999	8/31/ 1998	8/31/ 1997	8/31/ 1996	8/31/ 1995	8/31/ 1994	8/31/ 1993	8/31/ 1992
Net Sales	326,091	276,192	254,746	216,966	181,205	149,211	122,315	98,078	82,409	65,141
Cost Of Goods	195,338	163,570	155,521	135,806	112,588	75,119	64,692	52,996	54,043	41,605
Gross Profit	130,753	112,622	99,225	81,160	68,617	74,092	57,623	45,082	28,366	23,536
R & D Expenditures	NA	NA	NA	NA	NA	NA	NA	NA	NA	NA
Sell Gen and Admin Exp	30,602	27,894	25,543	22,250	19,318	43,770	28,268	26,817	9,572	8,625
Inc Bef Dep and Amort	100,151	84,728	73,682	58,910	49,299	30,322	29,355	18,265	18,794	14,911
Depreciation and Amort	23,855	20,287	18,464	14,790	12,320	8,896	5,910	4,165	2,918	2,130
Non-operating Inc	−7,586	−6,212	−6,512	−8,052	−4,415	−2,179	−1,405	−788	−1,422	−866
Interest Expense	6,628	6,234	5,047	3,446	2,154	1,184	1,823	1,084	800	666
Income Before Tax	62,082	51,995	43,659	32,622	30,410	18,063	20,217	12,228	13,655	11,250
Prov for Inc Taxes	23,126	19,368	16,263	12,152	11,328	6,819	7,733	4,585	5,012	4,436
Minority Int (inc)	NA	NA	NA	NA	NA	NA	NA	NA	NA	NA
Invest Gains/Losses	NA	NA	NA	NA	NA	NA	NA	NA	NA	NA
Other Income	NA	NA	NA	NA	NA	NA	NA	NA	NA	NA
Net Inc Bef Ex Items	38,956	32,627	27,396	20,470	19,082	11,244	12,484	7,643	8,644	6,814
Ex Items and Disc Ops	NA	NA	NA	−681	NA	NA	NA	NA	NA	NA
Net Income	38,956	32,627	27,396	19,789	19,082	11,244	12,484	7,643	8,644	6,814
Outstanding Shares	26,885	26,372	18,582	18,862	13,532	13,467	11,652	7,926	7,913	7,783

Source: Global Access, http://www.primark.com/ga/dga.asp

Case 27 / Sonic: America's Drive-In

371

operations. Sonic's differentiated concept consists of personalized, fast, and convenient carhop service as well as unique menu items. Relying on franchise expansion and same-store sales increases, the accelerated expansion program promotes a low-risk, high-return development strategy. Investments in information technology and increased marketing expenditures support ongoing efforts to build the chain.

EXPANSION

Sonic relies heavily on the opening of new franchisee-owned restaurants to maintain its continued expansion. Between 190 and 200 new drive-ins are expected to open in fiscal year 2003. Past trends indicate that almost 80 percent of the new restaurants will be opened by franchisees. This approach to development limits Sonic's risks, reduces the capital that the chain requires to fund its expansion, and plants future franchising income growth.[60] Despite the increase in restaurants, Sonic shows reluctance to enter new geographic regions. "We want to be the preferred brand of consumers in every market we go into," CEO Hudson says. "The fact that we're not national doesn't bother us one minute."[61] Consequently, Sonic plans to support ongoing expansion in core markets. In addition, the chain plans to build developing markets. Through limiting new restaurants to these areas, Sonic anticipates that it can enhance its operating efficiencies. However, some

reports indicate that Sonic plans to open restaurants in Wyoming and Ohio.[62] Entering these northern states represents a departure for the chain. Sonic has tended to cluster restaurants in warm climates because the drive-in format is not ideal in cold climates.[63] (See Exhibit 4.)

To facilitate expansion in nontraditional areas, Sonic, in its first national contract, partnered with Sodexho, the leading food and facilities management services company in North America.[64] As a result of the licensing agreement, Sodexho will open walk-in Sonics through its Corporate and Campus Services divisions. Although these locations will serve Sonic favorites, the menu will be scaled down. "Sonic is always looking for innovative ways to introduce the brand to new customers," said Dave Vernon, vice president of franchise sales for Sonic Corp. "We also want to align ourselves with partners who are committed to outstanding customer service. Sodexho is the leading service company in its industry and this agreement will allow existing and new customers to enjoy the Sonic experience in a variety of new locations and environments."[65] Franchisees have the option of opening nontraditional Sonics in mall food courts, co-branded travel plazas, hospital food courts, campus dining facilities, airports, arenas, and military facilities. While these generally don't have drive-in or carhop service, they offer Sonic's standard menu. Financial commitments

EXHIBIT 4   Sonic Map

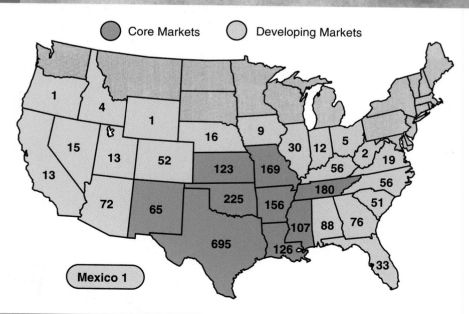

Source: http://www.sonicdrivein.com

for franchisees are similar for both traditional and non-traditional outlets.[66]

FRANCHISEES AS OWNER-OPERATORS

Sonic requires all franchisees to possess successful restaurant experience and strong entrepreneurial skills. The franchise fee is $30,000, initial investment ranges from $650,000 to $1.2 million, royalty fees are 1 to 5 percent, and advertising fees are 4 to 5 percent of total sales revenue.[67] The company offers a 12-week training program that includes one week of classroom instruction on leadership development, management skills, food safety, and business development, three weeks at new store openings, and eight weeks of on-site restaurant training.[68] Franchisees are actively involved in the company's operations through advisory councils and a national franchisee association.

Long-time franchisee Chuck Harrison lauds the company's relationships with owners: "The franchisor [sic] has been a real help to all franchisees in every area of the business—purchasing, marketing, advertising, operation. . . . [Sonic Corporation] wants input from the franchise community, they listen to what we want, and they give us help and feedback to make sure everybody's on the same page."[69] The chain's financial success, combined with its positive interactions with franchisees, gives Sonic one of the lowest franchisee turnover rates in the quick-service restaurant industry.[70] Sonic provides promotional materials and marketing advice, and keeps franchisees updated on company issues and developments through refresher training courses, seminars, and newsletters.[71]

However, the current level of cooperation between the parent company and the franchisees took years to develop. As recently as 1994, Sonic Corporation and its franchisees were embroiled in a bitter contract dispute over royalties and how many miles of protection radius a franchisee would enjoy.[72] Isolation between Sonic's various departments contributed to the tension between the corporation and the franchisees. Since then, Sonic has worked to create a more open environment that encourages communication. CEO Cliff Hudson explains, "We've moved the level of collaboration with our franchisees to a new level. There is no aspect of our business—marketing, product development, building, design—that we do not filter through our franchise advisory council. These guys are putting up millions of bucks and taking a lot of risk and helping craft our brand. We need to be partners with them."[73]

EMPLOYEE RELATIONS

As Sonic has worked to improve its relationship with franchisees, it has also tried to create a positive environment for employees. Like other restaurants in the industry, Sonic battles high turnover, low employee morale, and difficulty attracting applicants. The Oklahoma City, Oklahoma, corporate headquarters tries to lure employees with the promise of a positive work culture and comprehensive benefits: "Besides awesome food and tons of fun, Sonic offers a comprehensive benefits package including medical, dental, vision, long-term disability and life insurance, 401K, stock options, eight paid holidays, paid parking, a tuition assistance program, a stock purchase plan, paid vacation and paid personal leave."[74] Drive-in positions are advertised to appeal to the teenage applicant pool. Sonic tries to lure employees from this age group by describing drive-in jobs as "having fun while you work and learning life skills along the way. Not only do you make or work with great friends, you'll get great pay, flexible hours and a uniform that looks cool with roller blades."[75]

Additionally, the annual Dr Pepper Sonic Games were created to motivate employees, enhance performance, develop customer service skills, and promote employee retention. During the Olympic-style competition, crew members compete over a four-month period in six basic categories—Fountain, Carhop, Dresser, Grill, Swamp, and Switchboard—through written tests and actual trials.[76] At each participating drive-in, the employee with the highest rating is named station champion. The entire drive-in crew also competes against other restaurants, and the ten restaurants with the highest ratings advance to the national championship. Jerry Ruiz, manager of the Duncanville, Texas, Sonic Drive-In, winner of the 2000 Dr Pepper Sonic Games, commented on the impact of the games on his staff: "Following the 2000 Dr Pepper Sonic Games, turnover at our drive-in was dramatically reduced. In fact, we're getting a much higher number of job applicants because of all the positive publicity surrounding our participation."[77] Pattye Moore, Sonic's president, explains, "The Dr Pepper Sonic Games is a competitive and fun way to recognize crew members who are dedicated to enhancing their own skills as well as the customers' experience with better service and quality."[78] The games also impact the bottom line: Participants report an average 7.5 percent sales increase over the previous year, five points higher than nonparticipating restaurants.[79]

MENU INNOVATIONS

Although Sonic prides itself on its unique menu items, the chain continues to support menu innovations. To build business during evening hours and diversify sales among a wider array of products, in 2000, Sonic developed the "Sonic Summer Nights" campaign to promote the sale of Frozen Favorites™ on warm summer evenings. Subsequently, the high-margin drinks and ice cream desserts comprised 30 to 35 percent of system-wide sales.[80] To further distribute sales throughout the day, Sonic introduced a new breakfast menu to 400 drive-ins in 2001. Departing from the standard fast-food breakfast fare, menu items include breakfast burritos, fruit taquitos, Breakfast Toaster™ Sandwiches, French Toast Sticks, and other unique items. Moreover, the breakfast selection is available from open to close. After Sonic introduced breakfast items to the menu, same-store sales surged.[81] In addition, opening during breakfast hours "makes the drive-in more efficient by leveraging its fixed costs over extended hours." Some restaurants offering the breakfast menu have already had a 7 percent sales increase.[82] The success of the breakfast menu spurred Sonic to initiate a progressive rollout that will include ten new markets and double the number of participating drive-ins to 800 during 2002. With these initiatives, Sonic sees more consistent sales throughout the entire day than do its competitors. (See Exhibit 5.)

INFORMATION TECHNOLOGY

Until this year, Sonic did not have a systemwide information system to track sales data or share resources. Unveiled at Sonic's 2002 national convention, the Sonic PartnerNet portal provides Sonic operators with centralized access to a broad range of communications tools, sales data reporting features, and franchise group communications and support resources. SEI Information Technology, which began working with Sonic in 1998, will provide software and hardware technical support for the new portal as well as training for Sonic employees and franchisees.[83] Mirapoint, a provider of Internet messaging systems, worked with Sonic Drive-Ins to develop a Sonic-branded, web-based e-mail and

calendaring solution for the portal. Sonic operators enrolled in the PartnerNet system will be able to access special e-mail distribution lists featuring other PartnerNet members. They will also be able to keep track of their events using personal and business calendar options.[84]

Sonic's PartnerNet will also provide training on operational procedures and customer service best practices using Vuepoint's technology. The program will initially include training for Sonic's assistant managers through courses that cover opening- and closing-shift management, training techniques, receiving and storing products, sanitation, staff training, and SoniCARE Guest Service, a program that helps individuals realize and exceed guest expectations to provide great customer service.[85] "At Sonic, we're committed to providing not only the freshest, unique flavors and food for our customers, but also consistent, superior service. Vuepoint helped us realize the potential for using PartnerNet as a training channel to further enhance our ability to provide the best experience possible to customers in every Sonic Drive-In," said Diane Prem, Sonic's vice president of operations.[86]

MARKETING

To draw customers to the restaurants, Sonic has invested significant time and personnel resources to improve the chain's marketing efforts.

Sonic 2000

As Sonic 2000 was conceived and implemented in the mid-1990s, Sonic Corporation increased marketing expenditures (see Exhibit 6). Consumers often identified Sonic with a former spokesman instead of with unique food and carhop service. Thus, brand building became an important component of the Sonic 2000 plan. After identifying points of differentiation (menu and service), Sonic began an aggressive marketing push. Sonic diligently solicited feedback and was rewarded in finding customers slowly beginning to identify "made-to-order food" and "carhop service" with the drive-ins.[87]

Promotions

Since the successful Sonic 2000 marketing campaign to improve brand awareness and foster brand identity, Sonic has implemented more focused promotions. According to Sonic, target markets in 2002 include families and men age 18 to 34.[88] For families, the Wacky Pack program, geared toward children, provides a choice of entrée, Tater Tots or French fries, and a slushie or soft drink. With the Wacky Pack, children receive a learning activity and a free toy. Unlike its competitors, Sonic provides season-based or generic toys

EXHIBIT 5	Day Part Mix Comparison	
Time of Day	Sonic	Quick-Service Restaurant Industry
Morning	3%	11%
Lunch	33%	48%
Afternoon	21%	3%
Dinner	26%	36%
After Dinner	17%	2%

Source: Sonic Corporation, Annual Report 2001

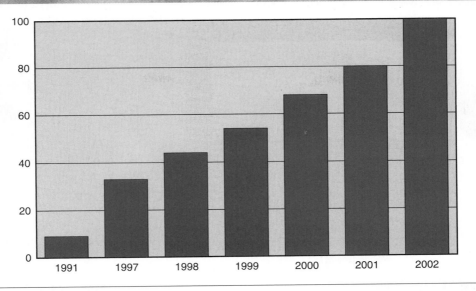

Source: Sonic Industries, Annual Report, 2001

rather than toys with movie or television tie-ins. For example, the October 2002 toy selection includes "Wacky Lollipop Lockers™," glow-in-the-dark lollipop holders in the shape of a bat, a ghost, an eyeball, or a jack-o'-lantern, that come with a Jolly Rancher® Fruit Chew Lollipop. However, few, if any, national advertising spots promote the Wacky Pack.

Advertising

To increase its exposure to the male demographic segment, Sonic sponsors NASCAR drivers Kevin Harvick and Richard Childress who participate in the Winston Cup and Busch Series, respectively (see Exhibit 7). Sonic's sponsorship gives the company exposure at the national races and helps enhance brand identity. Recent television spots have also been targeted to men in the 18–34 age bracket. A summer 2002 advertisement featured an early-thirties man who was delighted that his wife brought home Sonic for dinner—until she informed him that the dinner consisted of Sonic's new wraps, which he perceived as health fare. He imagined himself doing yoga and drinking wheat grass juice. Fortunately, the dinner was redeemed when the wife revealed hidden Frozen Treats™. A fall 2002 television spot showed the dilemma of a man in his late twenties who was asked by a buddy which Sonic sandwich he'd like. The man turned to his girlfriend and asked, "Now what was your question?" She replied, "Let's get mar-

ried." The man turned away from his girlfriend, back to his buddy, and responded, "Back to your question."

STRATEGIC LEADERSHIP: MEETING THE FUTURE

In 2000, Pattye L. Moore was one of only three restaurant executives included on the prestigious "Marketing 100" list of "the best minds in marketing today" published by the magazine *Advertising Age*. After joining Sonic in 1992 as vice president of marketing, Moore became executive vice president and then, in January 2000, president of Sonic, second only to chairman and CEO Clifford Hudson (see Exhibit 8). Lynne Collier, an analyst in Dallas, said Sonic excels at advertising with Moore in charge. "Their television commercials are more well-known in some places than McDonald's," she says.[89] "Our vision is to become America's most-loved restaurant brand," Moore said. "That's a pretty bold vision. That's not necessarily being the biggest or being everywhere. That means being the best."[90]

Sonic has enjoyed increasing success over the last decade despite the current economic downturn. Certainly, the leadership of CEO Hudson and President Moore, as well as the dedication and effort of Sonic's franchisees, has propelled Sonic's record-breaking growth through improved operations, creative marketing,

EXHIBIT 7   Sonic's NASCAR Promotion

Source: http://www.sonicdrivein.com/sports/drivers.jsp

EXHIBIT 8   Sonic Organizational Chart

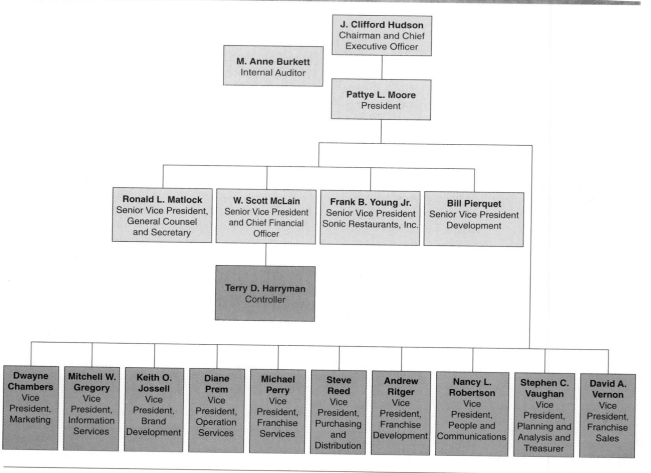

Source: Sonic Corporation, Annual Report 2001

Case 27 / Sonic: America's Drive-In

and unsurpassed customer service and will continue to be a great strength for the company.

CEO Cliff Hudson believes Sonic remains positioned to deliver 18 to 20 percent growth in earnings per share in 2003[91] based partially upon expected same-store sales growth of 1 percent to 3 percent.[92] (See Exhibit 9.) While marketing and menu management have been the primary tools used to increase same-store sales growth, incremental increases may become more difficult to attain given the slow growth in the industry and the financial might of Sonic's competitors. Earnings per share growth also depends on opening 190 to 200 new drive-in restaurants during the year.[93] To do this, due to limited capital available to the company, Sonic will continue to rely primarily upon new franchises to meet expectations for expansion.

Sonic has exhibited a preference for financing growth through debt rather than equity as well as for very aggressive cash management practices. Consequently, its financial position is not designed to fund robust growth during a possible downturn in revenues. The current debt to equity ratio is over 50 percent and the current ratio is at 69 percent.[94] Diminished sales could quickly create a cash shortage. With the high debt to equity ratio, securing additional debt to transition through the downturn could be difficult, and there are no significant liquid assets. Therefore, a major issue for Sonic is how to continue to finance the planned growth and manage the balance sheet while allowing successful navigation of an unforeseen downturn.

Sonic also operates in an industry dominated by larger competitors. Continued success requires Sonic to maintain its ability to differentiate its products in a way that appeals to customers and to increase brand recognition in developing markets. Another overlying challenge will be cost containment, since competitors continue to improve the use of technology in innovative ways and develop distribution models to gain a cost advantage.

NOTES

1. Standard and Poor's Industry Survey, Restaurants.
2. Ibid.
3. National Restaurant Association, 2001, Restaurant Industry Forecast.
4. This section partially adapted from "The Sonic story," http://www.sonicdrivein.com/about/sonicstory.shtml.
5. Lea Goldman, 2002, Greased lightning, *Forbes*, October 28, 246.
6. Anita Lienert, 1996, Setting off a Sonic boom, *Management Review*, December, 9.
7. Ibid.
8. http://www.sonicdrivein.com/about/sonicstory3.shtml.
9. Kate Arellano, 1999, The Sonic boom, *Denver Business Journal*, http://denver.bizjournals.com/denver/stories/1999/07/05/story6.html, July 2.
10. Mary Boltz Chapman, 1999, Drive in force, *Chain Leader*, http://www.chainleader.com/archive/0699/0699cov.html, July 2.
11. Lienert, Setting off a Sonic boom.
12. Arellano, The Sonic boom.
13. Rob Reynolds, Restaurants, http://www.hoovers.com/industry/snapshot/profile/0,3519,36,00.html, 1.
14. Ibid.
15. Ibid.
16. 2002, Quickservice Restaurant Trends—2002, http://www.restaurant.org/research/qsr.cfm, June 17.
17. Ibid.
18. Ibid.
19. Ibid.

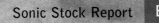

Sonic Stock Report EXHIBIT 9

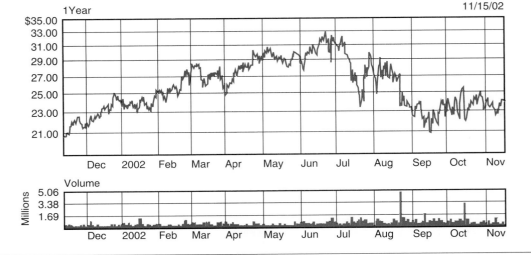

Source: http://www.nasdaq.com

20. Amy Reeves, 2002, Oklahoma City, Oklahoma business is hopping for restaurant chain, *Investor's Business Daily*, June 17.
21. Ibid.
22. Celina Abernathy, 2002, personal email.
23. Lienert, Setting off a Sonic boom.
24. Details from this section adapted from http://www.mcdonalds.com.
25. McDonald's Corporation, 2001, Annual Report 2001, http://www.mcdonalds.com.
26. Ibid.
27. Ibid.
28. Ibid.
29. Ibid.
30. McDonald's Corporation, 2002, Press Release, McDonald's announces additional plans to optimize its existing business; reports October sales, November 8.
31. McDonald's Corporation, 2001, Annual Report 2001.
32. Details from this section adapted from http://www.burgerking.com.
33. http://www.burgerking.com/CompanyInfo/onlinepressroom/corp_facts.asp.
34. Ibid.
35. Ibid.
36. http://www.burgerking.com/CompanyInfo/onlinepressroom/corp_bkgrd.asp.
37. http://www.burgerking.com/CompanyInfo/FranchiseOpps/FastFacts/index.html.
38. Ibid.
39. Ibid.
40. http://www.burgerking.com.
41. Ibid.
42. http://www.bkcareers.com/cultDiv.html.
43. Details from this section adapted from http://www.wendys.com.
44. Wendy's International, Inc., 2001, Annual Report 2001.
45. Ibid.
46. Ibid.
47. Ibid.
48. Ibid.
49. Reeves, Oklahoma City, Oklahoma business is hopping for restaurant chain.
50. Ibid.
51. Megan Rowe, 2002, Sonic: America's drive-in, *Restaurant Hospitality*, May, 72.
52. Reeves, Oklahoma City, Oklahoma business is hopping for restaurant chain.
53. Ibid.
54. http://www.sonicdrivein.com/about/sonicstory3.shtml.
55. Don Mecoy, 2002, Sonic sees record earnings; chain cites new stores, rising sales, *The Daily Oklahoman*, October 15.
56. Sonic Corporation, 2001, Annual Report 2001, http://www.sonicdrivein.com/invest/annreports.shtml.
57. Rowe, Sonic: America's drive-in.
58. Jennifer Brown, 2002, Sonic Drive-In sees room for expansion, *Salt Lake Tribune*, May 30.
59. http://www.sonicdrivein.com/invest/whysonic.shtml
60. Ibid.
61. Boltz Chapman, Drive in force.
62. Reeves, Oklahoma City, Oklahoma business is hopping for restaurant chain.
63. Ibid.
64. 2002, Sodexho, Sonic strike deal for contract sites, *Restaurants and Institutions*, August 1, 24.
65. Sodexho Press Release, 2002, Sodexho signs agreement with Sonic, June 27.
66. http://www.sonicdrivein.com/franchise/faqs.shtml.
67. http://www.sonicdrivein.com/franchise/ownfranchise.shtml.
68. Ibid.
69. Devil Smith, 2001, Sonic Drive-In booms, http://www.entrepreneur.com/article/0,4621,285407,00.html, January 15.
70. Michael Swanger, 2002, Carhop, nostalgia fuel business at Sonic Drive-In, *Business Record (Des Moines)*, July 9, 10.
71. http://www.worldfranchising.com/Top50/Food/SonicDrive1.html.
72. 1994, Sonic franchisees settle contract, *Nation's Restaurant News*, October 17, 2.
73. Christina Wise, 2002, Flexibility took him to the top, *Investor's Business Daily.*
74. http://www.sonicdrivein.com/careers/corppos.shtml.
75. http://www.sonicdrivein.com/careers/driveinpositions.shtml.
76. Sonic Corp. Press Release, 2002, Sonic Drive-In recognizes customer service excellence, February 14.
77. Sonic Corp. Press Release, 2002, Sonic Drive-In's employee recruitment, retention program hitting the mark, November 3.
78. Sonic Corp. Press Release, 2002, Oswego, Kan. is named top Sonic Drive-In in the nation, September 13.
79. Lienert, Setting off a Sonic boom.
80. Rowe, Sonic: America's drive-in.
81. Sonic Corporation, Annual Report 2001.
82. Goldman, Greased lightning.
83. SEI Information Technology Press Release, 2002, Sonic Corp. expands partnership with SEI Information Technology to support Sonic Partner-Net portal, September 19.
84. Mirapoint Press Release, 2002, Sonic Drive-In orders up email and calendar services from Mirapoint, October 15.
85. Vuepoint Press Release, 2002, Sonic selects Vuepoint to roll out operational & customer service training across 2,500 drive-in restaurants to insure consistent quality service at the speed of sound, October 21.
86. Ibid.
87. Ibid.
88. Abernathy, personal email.
89. Ibid.
90. Ibid.
91. Sonic Corporation, 2002, Annual Report 2002.
92. Ibid.
93. Ibid.
94. Ibid.

Southwest Airlines 2002

case twenty-eight

Andrew C. Inkpen
Valerie DeGroot
Arturo Wagner
Chee Wee Tan
Thunderbird

September 11 thrust the airline industry into economic chaos, resulting in layoffs, bankruptcies, and the prospect of a tenuous future. On September 22, 2001, President Bush signed into law the Air Transportation Safety and System Stabilization Act. The Stabilization Act provided up to $5 billion in cash grants and $10 billion in loan guarantees to qualifying US airlines to compensate for direct and incremental losses. Immediately after the terrorist acts, most major carriers announced significant service reductions, grounded aircraft, and furloughed employees. At Southwest Airlines (Southwest), there was no loss of pay for employees from layoffs, furloughs, or unpaid leaves. By September 18, 2001, Southwest was operating its pre-September 11 flight schedule with 100% job security. Because Southwest had the strongest balance sheet and the highest credit rating in the US airline industry, the company was able to avoid the severe cash flow problems experienced by its competitors. According to the Southwest 2001 annual report:

> Southwest was well poised, financially, to withstand the potentially devastating hammer blow of September 11. Why? Because for several decades our leadership philosophy has been: we manage in good times so that our Company and our People can be job secure and prosper through bad times. . . . Once again, after September 11, our philosophy of managing in good times so as to do well in bad times proved a marvelous prophylactic for our Employees and our Shareholders.

THE US AIRLINE INDUSTRY

The nature of the US commercial airline industry was permanently altered in October 1978 when President Jimmy Carter signed the Airline Deregulation Act. Before deregulation, the Civil Aeronautics Board regulated airline route entry and exit, passenger fares, mergers and acquisitions, and airline rates of return. Typically, two or three carriers provided service in a given market, although there were routes covered by only one carrier. Cost increases were passed along to customers and price competition was almost non-existent. The airlines operated as if there were only two market segments: those who could afford to fly, and those who couldn't.

Deregulation sent airline fares tumbling and allowed many new firms to enter the market. The financial impact on both established and new airlines was enormous. The fuel crisis of 1979 and the air traffic controllers' strike in 1981 contributed to the industry's difficulties, as did the severe recession that hit the US during the early 1980s. During the first decade of deregulation, more than 150 carriers, many of them start-up airlines, collapsed into bankruptcy. Eight of the 11 major airlines dominating the industry in 1978 ended up filing for bankruptcy, merging with other carriers, or simply disappearing from the radar screen. Collectively, the industry made enough money during this period to buy two Boeing 747s[1] (Exhibit 1). The three major carriers that survived intact—Delta, United, and American—ended up with 80% of all domestic US air traffic and 67% of trans-Atlantic business.[2]

Competition and lower fares led to greatly expanded demand for airline travel. By the mid-1990s, the airlines were having trouble meeting this demand. Travel increased from 200 million travelers in 1974 to 500 million in 1995, yet only five new runways were

Airline Operating Data 1986–2001

Exhibit 1

Seat-Miles Flown

	American	America-West	Continental	Delta	Eastern	Northwest	Pan-American	Southwest	TransWorld	United	USAir	Total All Majors
2001	152,920	26,500	81,270	141,280		98,330		65,400	31,400	164,770	66,680	828,550
2000	160,910	27,080	84,850	147,060		103,320		59,940	37,630	175,400	66,490	862,680
1999	158,220	25,870	80,950	144,650		99,410		52,900	35,590	176,540	59,120	833,250
1998	155,170	24,260	76,120	141,960		91,270		47,550	34,450	173,890	56,720	801,390
1997	153,750	23,460	68,310	138,700		96,920		44,490	36,480	169,000	58,290	789,400
1996	152,620	21,470	61,530	133,610		93,900		40,710	40,590	162,650	56,880	763,960
1995	155,300	19,400	61,006	130,500		87,500		36,180	38,186	158,569	58,163	744,804
1994	110,658	17,852	49,762	98,104		52,110		29,624	27,938	95,965	58,311	540,324
1993	117,719	16,980	49,690	99,852		52,623		34,759	25,044	98,652	55,918	551,237
1992	114,418	18,603	49,143	100,904		52,430		21,371	30,483	89,605	56,027	532,984
1991	104,616	19,460	48,742	94,350	25,299	48,847	9,042	18,440	29,684	88,092	56,470	517,743
1990	102,864	18,139	48,385	87,748	15,489	47,210	12,157	16,456	33,942	86,085	58,014	536,299
1989	98,638	13,523	47,107	82,440	41,126	44,372	11,670	14,788	35,246	82,758	40,652	486,683
1988	88,620	11,994	53,343	79,719	50,156	39,349	10,331	13,370	35,024	84,240	28,234	485,350
1987	77,274	10,318	54,626	71,504	50,156	41,499	8,217	11,457	33,566	86,246	20,014	465,327
1986	66,901	4,296	27,778	50,448	52,556	27,561	8,901	9,712	29,534	78,568	18,254	374,509
Total	1,971,048	299,205	942,612	1,742,829	184,626	1,076,651	60,318	517,147	534,787	1,971,030	814,237	10,114,490

Revenue per passenger-miles (RPMs) (in cents)

	American	America-West	Continental	Delta	Eastern	Northwest	Pan-American	Southwest	TransWorld	United	USAir
2001	13.27	10.14	12.44	11.75		11.24		11.89	11.33	11.55	14.32
2000	14.05	11.39	13.11	12.92		12.04		12.78	11.92	13.09	16.14
1999	13.12	11.44	12.10	12.61		11.58		12.33	11.39	12.32	16.91
1998	14.97	12.12	13.20	14.17		13.05		13.25	13.35	14.07	20.74
1997	14.83	11.67	14.61	14.26		13.54		13.46	13.26	14.07	20.45
1996	14.47	11.47	14.95	14.17		14.21		12.58	13.11	14.00	19.78
1995	15.06	12.03	14.55	14.11		14.53		12.31	13.24	13.36	19.87
1994	13.11	10.81	11.50	13.93		13.93		11.65	12.67	11.81	15.92
1993	13.65	11.13	11.97	14.66		13.06		11.92	12.78	12.49	17.94
1992	12.03	10.36	11.01	14.02		12.21		11.78	11.13	11.88	16.97
1991	13.11	10.00	11.79	14.30		12.79	10.02	11.25	11.31	12.21	16.93
1990	12.86	11.14	12.48	14.21		13.24	11.65	11.48	12.34	12.71	16.37

EXHIBIT 1

Airline Operating Data 1986–2001 (continued)

Revenue per passenger-miles (RPMs) (in cents)

	American	America-West	Continental	Delta	Eastern	Northwest	Pan-American	Southwest	TransWorld	United	USAir
1989	12.27	11.84	12.04	13.91	11.71	13.02	11.98	10.49	12.10	12.18	15.83
1988	11.92	10.52	10.61	13.52	12.00	12.54	10.94	10.74	11.47	10.86	15.33
1987	11.06	9.66	9.34	131.10	11.02	11.73	9.97	10.02	11.02	10.10	14.91
1986	10.23	9.90	8.56	13.54	11.26	10.48	10.12	10.59	10.07	9.87	14.93

Passenger Load Factor (percent)

	American	America-West	Continental	Delta	Eastern	Northwest	Pan-American	Southwest	TransWorld	United	USAir
2001	69.40	71.90	72.80	69.10		74.30		68.00	66.10	70.80	68.90
2000	72.40	70.50	74.90	73.30		76.60		70.50	72.30	72.30	70.40
1999	69.60	68.40	73.50	72.40		74.60		69.00	73.10	71.00	70.10
1998	70.20	67.40	72.10	72.70		73.10		66.10	70.90	71.60	72.70
1997	69.60	68.90	71.00	71.80		74.30		63.70	68.80	71.80	71.30
1996	68.50	71.20	68.10	70.30		73.10		66.50	66.80	71.70	68.50
1995	66.26	68.56	65.51	66.21		71.43		64.48	65.65	70.51	64.68
1994	63.25	67.99	62.48	64.68		64.88		66.80	62.73	69.80	62.02
1993	59.21	65.56	62.20	61.52		63.51		68.09	62.38	63.80	58.59
1992	63.12	61.62	63.14	60.59		62.24		64.52	62.94	66.15	58.60
1991	60.86	64.94	61.80	59.95		62.90	60.53	61.14	60.94	64.23	58.22
1990	61.48	60.99	58.42	57.98	60.80	62.53	60.00	60.60	58.90	63.85	59.54
1989	63.60	57.70	60.30	63.60	61.90	60.90	61.20	62.70	59.40	65.40	61.20
1988	63.10	57.90	58.80	57.60	61.80	61.80	63.40	57.70	59.90	67.10	61.30
1987	63.70	56.10	60.70	55.50	65.30	61.80	64.10	58.90	62.00	65.00	65.30
1986	65.60	61.00	62.70	57.40	60.60	54.90	51.40	58.30	59.50	65.60	61.10

Operating Revenues in millions of dollars

	American	America-West	Continental	Delta	Eastern	Northwest	Pan-American	Southwest	TransWorld	United	USAir	Total All Majors
2001	15,639	2,036	8,200	12,800		10,302		5,555	2,633	16,087	8,253	81,505
2000	18,117	2,309	9,449	15,321		10,957		5,650	3,585	19,331	9,181	93,900
1999	16,086	2,164	8,382	14,901		9,868		4,736	3,309	17,967	8,460	85,873
1998	16,299	1,983	7,908	14,630		8,707		4,164	3,259	17,518	8,556	83,024
1997	15,856	1,887	7,090	14,204		9,984		3,817	3,328	17,335	8,502	82,003

Airline Operating Data 1986–2001 (continued)

Exhibit 1

Operating Revenues in millions of dollars

	American	America-West	Continental	Delta	Eastern	Northwest	Pan-American	Southwest	TransWorld	United	USAir	Total All Majors
1996	15,126	1,752	6,264	13,318		9,751		3,407	3,554	16,317	7,704	77,193
1995	15,501	1,600	5,825	12,194		9,080		2,873	3,320	14,943	7,474	72,810
1994	10,631	1,414	4,091	9,514		5,325		2,417	2,555	8,966	6,394	51,307
1993	10,828	1,332	4,128	9,653		4,928		2,067	2,325	8,794	6,364	50,419
1992	9,902	1,281	3,840	9,164		4,464		1,685	2,510	7,861	5,974	46,681
1991	9,429	1,359	4,014	8,593		4,356	596	1,314	2,464	7,790	5,895	45,810
1990	9,203	1,322	4,036	7,697		4,298	946	1,187	2,878	7,946	6,085	45,598
1989	8,670	998	3,896	7,780	1,295	3,944	957	1,015	2,918	7,463	4,160	43,096
1988	7,548	781	3,682	6,684	3,423	3,395	804	860	2,777	7,006	2,803	39,763
1987	6,369	577	3,404	5,638	4,054	3,328	625	699	2,668	6,500	2,070	35,932
1986	5,321	330	1,676	4,245	4,093	1,815	553	620	2,064	5,727	1,787	28,231
Total	190,525	23,125	85,885	166,336	12,865	104,502	4,481	42,066	46,147	187,551	99,662	963,145

Net Operating Income (Loss) in millions of dollars

	American	America-West	Continental	Delta	Eastern	Northwest	Pan-American	Southwest	TransWorld	United	USAir	Total All Majors
2001	(2,558)	(320)	(323)	(1,383)		(395)		631	(503)	(3,743)	(1,181)	(9,775)
2000	1,243	(13)	589	1,459		664		1,021	(233)	741	(44)	5,427
1999	1,003	197	449	1,261		769		782	(343)	1,358	202	5,678
1998	1,748	198	621	1,793		(129)		684	(65)	1,435	990	7,275
1997	1,447	163	646	1,621		1,203		524	(29)	1,226	586	7,387
1996	1,316	69	472	571		1,108		350	(199)	1,130	369	5,186
1995	989	114	120	340		1,134		393	(139)	735	(75)	3,611
1994	432	146	(145)	123		725		290	(81)	262	(466)	1,286
1993	357	121	56	335		268		281	(63)	184	(143)	1,396
1992	(251)	(64)	(183)	(225)		(203)	(186)	182	(191)	(354)	(397)	(1,686)
1991	40	(79)	(218)	(115)		17	(280)	62	(233)	(412)	(233)	(1,357)
1990	103	(32)	(191)	(176)		(132)	(118)	82	(134)	(34)	(437)	(1,231)
1989	709	48	124	677	(666)	57	(181)	98	10	302	(239)	1,002
1988	794	18	(87)	441	(187)	19	(260)	86	113	461	144	1,621
1987	483	(35)	(56)	383	66	72	(283)	41	79	97	263	1,133
1986	378	4	91	212	61	(25)		81	(77)	51	164	657
Total	8,233	535	1,965	7,317	(726)	5,152	(1,308)	5,588	(2,088)	3,439	(497)	27,610

Source: Department of Transportation.

built during this time period. During the 1980s, many airlines acquired significant new debt in efforts to service the increased travel demand. Long-term debt-to-capitalization ratios rose dramatically: Eastern's went from 62% to 473%, TWA's went from 62% to 115%, and Continental's went from 62% to 96%. In contrast, United and Delta maintained their debt ratios at less than 60%, and American Airlines' ratio dropped to 34%.

Despite the financial problems experienced by many airlines started after deregulation, new firms continued to enter the market. Between 1992 and 1995, 69 new airlines were certified by the FAA. Most of these airlines competed with limited route structures and lower fares than the major airlines. The new low-fare airlines created a second tier of service providers that saved consumers billions of dollars annually and provided service in markets abandoned or ignored by major carriers. One such start-up was Kiwi Airlines, founded by former employees of the defunct Eastern and Pan Am airlines. Kiwi was funded largely by employees. Pilots paid $50,000 apiece to get jobs, and other employees paid $5,000. In 1999, Kiwi went bankrupt and liquidated its assets. At its peak in the mid-1990s, Kiwi had 1,200 employees, leased 15 jets, and flew 65 flights daily.

Although deregulation fostered competition and the growth of new airlines, it also created a regional disparity in ticket prices and adversely affected service to small and remote communities. Airline workers generally suffered, with inflation-adjusted average employee wages falling from $42,928 in 1978 to $37,985 in 1988. About 20,000 airline industry employees were laid off in the early 1980s, while productivity of the remaining employees rose 43% during the same period. In a variety of cases, bankruptcy filings were used to diminish the role of unions and reduce unionized wages.

INDUSTRY ECONOMICS

About 80% of airline operating costs were fixed or semi-variable. The only true variable costs were travel agency commissions, food costs, and ticketing fees. The operating costs of an airline flight depended primarily on the distance traveled, not the number of passengers on board. For example, the crew and ground staff sizes were determined by the type of aircraft, not the passenger load. Therefore, once an airline established its route structure, most of its operating costs were fixed.

Because of this high fixed-cost structure, the airlines developed sophisticated software tools to maximize capacity utilization, known as load factor. Load factor was calculated by dividing RPM (revenue passenger miles—the number of passengers carried multiplied by the distance flown) by ASM (available seat miles—the number of seats available for sale multiplied by the distance flown).

On each flight by one of the major airlines (excluding Southwest and the low-fare carriers), there were typically a dozen categories of fares. The airlines analyzed historical travel patterns on individual routes to determine how many seats to sell at each fare level. All of the major airlines used this type of analysis and flexible pricing practice, known as a "yield management" system. These systems enabled the airlines to manage their seat inventories and the prices paid for those seats. The objective was to sell more seats on each flight at higher yields (total passenger yield was passenger revenue from scheduled operations divided by scheduled RPMs). The higher the ticket price, the better the yield.

Although reducing operating costs was a high priority for the airlines, the nature of the cost structure limited cost reduction opportunities. Fuel costs (15.6% of total operating costs at Southwest in 2001) were largely beyond the control of the airlines, and many of the larger airlines' restrictive union agreements limited labor flexibility. The airline industry's extremely high fixed costs made it one of the worst net profit margin performers when measured against other industries. Airlines were far outpaced in profitability by industries such as banks, health care, automobile manufacturing, consumer products, and publishing.

In the early 1990s, most airlines sharply lowered their new aircraft orders to avoid taking on more debt. At the end of June 1990, US airlines had outstanding orders to buy 2,748 aircraft. At the end of June 1996, orders had fallen to 1,111.[3] (A new Boeing 737 cost about $28 million.) By 1999, the global airline industry had improved substantially, and orders rose to about 2,700. After September 11, 2001, both Boeing and Airbus reported substantially reduced orders, although the industry showed signs of a revival in early 2002.

To manage their route structures, all of the major airlines (except Southwest) maintained their operations around a "hub-and-spoke" network. The spokes fed passengers from outlying points into a central airport—the hub—where passengers could travel to additional hubs or their final destination. For example, to fly from Phoenix to Boston on Northwest Airlines, a typical route would involve a flight from Phoenix to Northwest's Detroit hub. The passenger would then take a second flight from Detroit to Boston.

Establishing a major hub in a city like Chicago or Atlanta required an investment of as much as $150 million for gate acquisition and terminal construction. Although hubs created inconveniences for travelers, hub systems were an efficient means of distributing services across a wide network. The major airlines were very protective of their so-called "fortress" hubs and used the hubs to control various local markets. For example, Northwest handled about 80% of Detroit's passengers and occupied nearly the entire new Detroit terminal that opened in February 2002. And, Northwest's deal with the local government assured that it would be the only airline that could have a hub in Detroit. When Southwest entered the Detroit market, the only available gates were already leased by Northwest. Northwest subleased gates to Southwest at rates 18 times higher than Northwest's costs. Southwest eventually withdrew from Detroit, and then re-entered, one of only four markets Southwest had abandoned in its history (San Francisco, Denver, and Beaumont, Texas, were the other three).

RECENT AIRLINE INDUSTRY PERFORMANCE

US airlines suffered a combined loss of $13 billion from 1990 to 1994 (Exhibit 1).[4] High debt levels plagued the industry during this period. In 1994, the earnings picture began to change with the industry as a whole reducing its losses to $278 million.[5] Overall expansion and health returned to the industry by 1995, and in 1997 and 1998, virtually all US carriers hit record profit levels. Together, the US major airlines made $4.9 billion in net profit in 1998, down from 1997's record of $5.2 billion. After profitable years in 1999 and 2000, the eight major US airlines had a combined loss for the first quarter 2001, the first since 1993. After September 11, 2001, the US domestic and global industries were devastated, leading to the bankruptcies of many airlines, such as SwissAir, Sabena (Belgium), Canada 3000, and Ansett (Australia). America West Airlines was forced to seek a government-backed loan through the federal Stabilization Act. Exhibits 2, 3, and 4 provide comparative data for the major airlines.

FUTURE PRESSURES ON THE INDUSTRY

In addition to the difficult revenue environment for airlines in 2002, the industry was faced with several other issues:

1. **Security.** The airlines needed increased war risk insurance, and passenger security costs were expected to rise.
2. **Customer dissatisfaction with airline service.** Service problems were leading some to call for re-regulation of airline competitive practices.
3. **Labor costs.** Although the average salary per airline employee from 1987 to 1996 rose at a rate faster than the increase in the CPI index (4.4% increase in labor costs compared with a 3.7% CPI increase over the same period), in recent years labor costs were up less than a percentage point. However, pressure from labor was expected to increase.
4. **Aircraft maintenance.** The aging of the general aircraft population meant higher maintenance costs and eventual aircraft replacement. The introduction of stricter government regulations for older planes placed new burdens on operators of older aircraft.
5. **Debt servicing.** The airline industry's debt load greatly exceeded US industry averages.
6. **Fuel costs.** Long-term jet fuel cost was uncertain. In 1997, the average price per gallon of fuel was $.62. In 1999, the average price was $.53, and in 2001, $.71.
7. **Air-traffic delays.** Increased air-traffic control delays caused by higher travel demand and related airport congestion were expected to negatively influence airlines' profitability.

EXHIBIT 2	Airline Performance 2001		
Airline	**Load Factor (%)**	**Break Even**	**Above/Below BE**
American	69.4	83.6	70.9
America West	71.9	87.2	83.4
Continental	72.8	76.4	73.0
Delta	69.1	76.0	72.5
Northwest Airlines	74.3	85.0	81.5
Southwest Airlines	*68.0*	*58.9*	*57.3*
TWA	66.1	82.8	84.0
United	70.8	94.7	89.4
US Airways	68.9	85.3	7.2

Source: Airline Quarterly Financial Review, Fourth Quarter 2001, Department of Transportation Office of Aviation Analysis, Economic and Financial Analysis Division.

flyer program based on the number of flights taken by a passenger, not miles flown.

Over the years, Southwest's choice of markets resulted in significant growth in air travel at those locations. In Texas, traffic between the Rio Grande Valley (Harlingen) and the Golden Triangle grew from 123,000 to 325,000 within 11 months of Southwest entering the market.[10] Within a year of Southwest's arrival, the Oakland-Burbank route became the 25th largest passenger market, up from 179th. The Chicago-Louisville market tripled in size 30 days after Southwest began flying that route. Southwest was the dominant carrier in a number of cities, ranking first in market share in more than 50% of the largest US city-pair markets. Exhibit 5 shows a comparison of Southwest in 1971 and 2002.

SOUTHWEST'S PERFORMANCE

Southwest bucked the airline industry trend by earning a profit in 29 consecutive years (see Exhibit 6 for Southwest financial performance). Southwest was the only major US airline in 1990, 1991, and 1992 to make both net and operating profits. Even taking into account the losses in its first two years of operations, the company averaged more than 12% annual return on investment. As of February 2002, Southwest's 10-year average return to shareholders was 23.6%. Southwest has ranked number one in fewest customer complaints for the last 11 consecutive years as published in the Department of Transportation's Air Travel Consumer Report.

Southwest ranked second among companies across all industry groups, and first in the airline industry, in *Fortune* magazine's 2002 America's Most Admired Companies list.

Southwest accomplished its enviable record by challenging accepted norms and setting competitive thresholds for the other airlines to emulate. The company had established numerous new industry standards. Southwest flew more passengers per employee than any other major airline, while at the same time having the fewest number of employees per aircraft. Southwest maintained a debt-to-equity ratio much lower than the industry average and was one of the few airlines in the world with an investment grade credit rating.

Southwest had a fleet of 355 737s in 2002, up from 106 in 1990 and 75 in 1987. Of the total fleet, 256 aircraft were owned and the remainder leased. At the end of 2001, Southwest was committed to 132 orders for the 737-700 aircraft.

HERB KELLEHER

Herb Kelleher was CEO of Southwest from 1981 to 2001. In 2001, at age 71, Kelleher stepped down as CEO but remained Chairman. Kelleher's leadership style combined flamboyance, fun, and a fresh, unique perspective. Kelleher played Big Daddy-O in one of the company videos, appeared as Elvis Presley in in-flight magazine advertisements, and earned the nickname the

	Southwest 28-Year Comparison		EXHIBIT 5
	1971	1999	April, 2002
Size of fleet	4	306	355
Number of employees	195	29,005	34,000
Number of passengers carried	108,554	52.6 million	64.6 million
Number of cities served	3	55	58
Number of trips flown	6,051	602,578*	940,426**
Total operating revenues	2,133,000	4,164,000,000*	5,555,174,000**
Net income (losses)	(3,753,000)	433,400,000*	511,147,000**
Stockholders' equity	3,318,000	2,397,900,000*	4,014,053,000**
Total assets	22,083,000	4,716,000,000*	8,997,141,000**

*1998 Figures
**2001 Figures

Sources: *Nuts: Southwest Airlines' Crazy Recipe for Business and Personal Success*, K. Freiberg and J. Freiberg, 1996, Austin, TX, Bard Press, p. 326; *Hoovers* Online; Bureau of Transportation statistics at www.bts.gov/programs/oai; Southwest Airlines Fact Sheet at www.southwest.com/about_swa/press/factsheet.html.; 2001 Annual Report.

Southwest Airlines Ten-Year Financial Summary EXHIBIT 6

Selected Consolidated Financial Data[1] (In thousands except per share amounts)	2001	2000	1999	1998	1997	1996	1995	1994	1993	1992
Operating revenues:										
Passenger[9]	$5,378,702	$5,467,965	$4,562,616	$3,963,781	$3,639,193	$3,269,238	$2,760,756	$2,497,765	$2,216,342	$1,623,828
Freight[9]	91,270	110,742	102,990	98,500	94,758	80,005	65,825	54,419	42,897	33,088
Other[9]	85,202	70,853	69,981	101,699	82,870	56,927	46,170	39,749	37,434	146,063
Total operating revenues	5,555,174	5,649,560	4,735,587	4,163,980	3,816,821	3,406,170	2,872,751	2,591,933	2,296,673	1,802,979
Operating expenses	4,924,052	4,628,415	3,954,011	3,480,369	3,292,585	3,055,335	2,559,220	2,275,224	2,004,700	1,609,175
Operating income	631,122	1,021,145	781,576	683,611	524,236	350,835	313,531	316,709	291,973	193,804
Other expenses (income), net	(196,537)	3,781	7,965	(21,501)	7,280	9,473	8,391	17,186	32,336	36,361
Income before income taxes	827,659	1,017,364	773,611	705,112	516,956	341,362	305,140	299,523	259,637	157,443
Provision for income taxes[3]	316,512	392,140	299,233	271,681	199,184	134,025	122,514	120,192	105,353	60,058
Net income[3]	$511,147	$625,224[10]	$474,378	$433,431	$317,772	$207,337	$182,626	$179,331	$154,284[4]	$97,385[5]
Net income per share, basic[3]	$.67	$.84[10]	$.63	$.58	$.43	$.28	$.25	$.25[4]	$.21[4]	$.14[5]
Net income per share, diluted[3]	$.63	$.79[10]	$.59	$.55	$.41	$.27	$.24	$.24[4]	$.21[4]	$.13[5]
Cash dividends per common share	$.0180	$.0147	$.0143	$.0126	$.0098	$.0087	$.0079	$.0079	$.0076	$.0070
Total assets	$8,997,141	$6,669,572	$5,652,113	$4,715,996	$4,246,160	$3,723,479	$3,256,122	$2,823,071	$2,576,037	$2,368,856
Long-term debt	$1,327,158	$760,992	$871,717	$623,309	$628,106	$650,226	$661,010	$583,071	$639,136	$735,754
Stockholders' equity	$4,014,053	$3,451,320	$2,835,788	$2,397,918	$2,009,018	$1,648,312	$1,427,318	$1,238,706	$1,054,019	$879,536
Consolidated Financial Ratios[1]										
Return on average total assets	6.5%	10.1%[10]	9.2%	9.7%	8.0%	5.9%	6.0%	6.6%	6.2%[4]	4.6%[5]
Return on average stockholders' equity	13.7%	19.9%[10]	18.1%	19.7%	17.4%	13.5%	13.7%	15.6%	16.0%[4]	12.9%[5]
Consolidated Operating Statistics[2]										
Revenue passengers carried	64,446,773	63,678,261	57,500,213	52,586,400	50,399,960	49,621,504	44,785,573	42,742,602[6]	36,955,221[6]	27,839,284
RPMs (000s)	44,493,916	42,215,162	36,479,322	31,419,110	28,355,169	27,083,483	23,327,804	21,611,266	18,827,288	13,787,005
ASMs (000s)	65,295,290	59,909,965	52,855,467	47,543,515	44,487,496	40,727,495	36,180,001	32,123,974	27,511,000	21,366,642
Passenger load factor	68.1%	70.5%	69.0%	66.1%	63.7%	66.5%	64.5%	67.3%	68.4%	64.5%
Average length of passenger haul	690	663	634	597	563	546	521	506	509	495
Trips flown	940,426	903,754	846,823	806,822	786,288	748,634	685,524	624,476	546,297	438,184
Average passenger fare[9]	$83.46	$85.87	$79.35	$76.26	$72.81	$66.20	$61.80	$58.44	$59.97	$58.33
Passenger revenue yield per RPM[9]	12.09¢	12.95¢	12.51¢	12.76¢	12.94¢	12.13¢	11.86¢	11.56¢	11.77¢	11.78¢
Operating revenue yield per ASM	8.51¢	9.43¢	8.96¢	8.76¢	8.58¢	8.36¢	7.94¢	8.07¢	8.35¢	7.89¢
Operating expenses per ASM	7.54¢	7.73¢	7.48¢	7.32¢	7.40¢	7.50¢	7.07¢	7.08¢	7.25¢[7]	7.03¢
Fuel cost per gallon (average)	70.86¢	78.69¢	52.71¢	45.67¢	62.46¢	65.47¢	55.22¢	53.92¢	59.15¢	60.82¢
Number of Employees at yearend	31,580	29,274	27,274	25,844	23,974	22,944	19,933	16,818	15,175	11,397
Size of fleet at yearend[8]	355	344	312	280	261	243	224	199	178	141

(1) The Selected Consolidated Financial Data and Consolidated Financial Ratios for 1992 have been restated to include the financial results of Morris Air Corporation (Morris)
(2) Prior to 1993, Morris operated as a charter carrier; therefore, no Morris statistics are included for 1992
(3) Pro forma for 1992 assuming Morris, an S-Corporation prior to 1993, was taxed at statutory rates
(4) Excludes cumulative effect of accounting charges of $15.3 million ($.02 per share)
(5) Excludes cumulative effect of accounting changes of $12.5 million ($.02 per share)
(6) Includes certain estimates for Morris
(7) Excludes merger expenses of $10.8 million
(8) Includes leased aircraft
(9) Includes effect of reclassification of revenue reported in 1999 through 1995 related to the sale of flight segment credits from Other to Passenger due to the accounting change implementation in 2000
(10) Excludes cumulative effect of accounting change of $22.1 million ($.03 per share)

"High Priest of Ha-Ha" from *Fortune* magazine.[11] Although Kelleher was unconventional and a maverick in his field, he led his company to consistently new standards for itself and for the industry. Sincerely committed to his employees, Kelleher generated intense loyalty to himself and the company. His ability to remember employees' names and to ask after their families was just one way he earned respect and trust. At one point, Kelleher froze his salary for five years in response to the pilots agreeing to do the same. Often when he flew, Kelleher would help the ground crew unload bags or help the flight crew serve drinks. His humor was legendary and served as an example for his employees to join in the fun of working for Southwest. He was called "a visionary who leads by example—you have to work harder than anybody else to show them you are devoted to the business."[12]

Although Kelleher tried to downplay his personal significance to the company, especially when he gave up the CEO position in 2001, many analysts following Southwest credited the airline's success to Kelleher's unorthodox personality and engaging management style. As one analyst wrote, "the old-fashioned bond of loyalty between employees and company may have vanished elsewhere in corporate America, but it is stronger than ever at Southwest."[13] Kelleher had a three-year employment contract signed in January 2001. From October 1 to December 2001, Kelleher, CEO James Parker, and COO Colleen Barrett voluntarily relinquished their salaries.

THE SOUTHWEST SPIRIT

Customer service far beyond the norm in the airline industry was not unexpected at Southwest and had its own name—Positively Outrageous Service. Some examples of this service included: a gate agent volunteering to watch a dog (a Chihuahua) for two weeks, when an Acapulco-bound passenger showed up at the last minute without the required dog crate; an Austin passenger who missed a connection to Houston, where he was to have a kidney transplant operation, was flown there by a Southwest pilot in his private plane. Another passenger, an elderly woman flying to Phoenix for cancer treatment, began crying because she had no family or friends at her destination. The ticket agent invited her into her home and escorted her around Phoenix for two weeks.[14]

Southwest Airlines customers were often surprised by "Southwest Spirit." On some flights, magazine pictures of gourmet meals were offered for dinner on an evening flight. Flight attendants were encouraged to have fun; songs, jokes, and humorous flight announce-

ments were common. One flight attendant had a habit of popping out of overhead luggage compartments as passengers attempted to stow their belongings, until the day she frightened an elderly passenger who called for oxygen.[15] Herb Kelleher once served in-flight snacks dressed as the Easter Bunny.

Intense company communication and camaraderie was highly valued and essential to maintaining the *esprit-de-corps* found throughout the firm. The Southwest Spirit, as exhibited by enthusiasm and extroverted personalities, were important elements in employee screening conducted by Southwest's People Department. Employment at Southwest was highly desired. In 2001, 6,406 employees were hired and 194,821 applications received. Once landed, a job was fairly secure. The airline had not laid off an employee since 1971. Employee turnover hovered around 7%, the lowest rate in the industry.[16] The number of employees has increased from 6,000 in 1987 to 34,000 in 2002.

During initial training periods, efforts were made to share and instill Southwest's unique culture. New-employee orientation, known as the new-hire celebration, included Southwest's version of the Wheel of Fortune game show, scavenger hunts, and company videos including the "Southwest Airlines Shuffle" in which each department introduced itself, rap style, and in which Kelleher appeared as Big Daddy-O. To join the People Department (i.e., Human Resources), employees had to have front-line customer experience.

Advanced employee training regularly occurred at the University of People at Love Field in Dallas. Various classes were offered, including team building, leadership, and cultural diversity. Newly promoted supervisors and managers attended a three-day class called "Leading with Integrity." Each department also had its own training department focusing on technical aspects of the work. "Walk-a-Mile Day" encouraged employees from different departments to experience firsthand the day-to-day activities of their co-workers. The goal of this program was to promote respect for fellow workers while increasing awareness of the company.[17]

Employee initiative was supported by management and encouraged at all levels. For example, pilots looked for ways to conserve fuel during flights, employees proposed designs for ice storage equipment that reduced time and costs, and baggage handlers learned to place luggage with the handles facing outward to reduce unloading time.

Red hearts and "Luv" were central parts of the internal corporate culture, appearing throughout company literature. A mentoring program for new hires was called CoHearts. "Heroes of the Heart Awards" were given annually to one behind-the-scenes group of workers, whose department name was painted on a specially designed plane for a year. Other awards honored an employee's big mistake through the "Boner of the Year Award." When employees had a story about exceptional service to share, they were encouraged to fill out a "LUV Report."

Southwest placed great emphasis on maintaining cooperative labor relations. Within the firm, 81% of all employees were unionized. Southwest pilots belonged to an independent union and not the Air Line Pilots Association, the union that represented more than 60,000 pilots. The company encouraged the unions and their negotiators to conduct employee surveys and to research their most important issues prior to each contract negotiation. Southwest had never had a serious labor dispute that grounded the airline. At its 1994 contract discussion, the pilots proposed a 10-year contract with stock options in lieu of guaranteed pay increases over the first five years of the contract. In 1974, Southwest was the first airline to introduce employee profit sharing. Through the plan, employees owned about 10% of the company's stock.

Herb Kelleher summed up the Southwest culture and commitment to employees:

> We don't use things like TQM. It's just a lot of people taking pride in what they're doing. . . You have to recognize that people are still the most important. How you treat them determines how they treat people on the outside. . . I give people the license to be themselves and motivate others in that way. We give people the opportunity to be a maverick. You don't have to fit in a constraining mold at work—you can have a good time. People respond to that.[18]

SOUTHWEST IMITATORS

Southwest's low-fare, short-haul strategy spawned numerous imitators. By the second half of 1994, low fares were available on more than one-third of the industry's total capacity.[19] Many of the imitators were start-up airlines. The Allied Pilots Association (APA) claimed that approximately 97% of start-ups resulted in failures. According to the APA, only two of 34 start-up airlines formed between 1978 and 1992 were successful, with success defined as surviving 10 years or longer without bankruptcy. Two of the most successful start-up firms, Midwest Express and America West, both went through Chapter 11 bankruptcy proceedings. Three of the 19 start-ups folded by 1996 and ValuJet was grounded after its May 1996 crash in the Florida Everglades, re-emerging a year later as AirTran.

The major airlines tried to compete directly with Southwest. The Shuttle by United, a so-called "airline within an airline," was started in October 1994. United's objective was to create a new airline owned by United with many of the same operational elements as Southwest: a fleet of 737s, low fares, short-haul flights, and less restrictive union rules. Although offering basically a no-frills service, the Shuttle provided assigned seating and offered access to airline computer reservation systems. United predicted that the Shuttle could eventually account for as much as 20% of total United US operations.

United saturated the West Coast corridor with short-haul flights on routes such as Oakland-Seattle, San Francisco-San Diego, and Sacramento-San Diego. Almost immediately, Southwest lost 10% of its California traffic. Southwest responded by adding six aircraft and 62 daily flights in California. In April 1995, United eliminated its Oakland-Ontario route and proposed a $10 fare increase on other flights. By January 1996, United had pulled the Shuttle off routes that did not feed passengers to its San Francisco and Los Angeles hubs. In early 1995, United and Southwest competed directly on 13% of Southwest's routes. By 1996, that number was down to 7% and down to 5% by 1998.

Cost was the major problem for United in competing with Southwest. For four main reasons, the Shuttle's cost per seat mile remained higher than Southwest's. First, many passengers booked their tickets through travel agents, which resulted in commission fees. Second, many of the Shuttle's flights were in the San Francisco and Los Angeles markets, both of which were heavily congested and subject to costly delays. Third, the Shuttle offered reserved seating. Fourth, the Shuttle was unable to achieve the same level of productivity as Southwest. After September 11, United discontinued the Shuttle service and folded the remaining flights into its regular service. US Airways did the same with its Metrojet discount service.

Some of the attempts to imitate Southwest were almost comical. Continental Lite (CALite) was an effort by Continental Airlines to develop a low-cost service and revive the company's fortunes after coming out of bankruptcy in April 1993. CALite began service in October 1993 on 50 routes, primarily in the southeast. Frequency of flights was a key part of the new strategy. Greenville/Spartanburg got 17 flights a day, and in Orlando daily departures more than doubled. CALite fares were modeled after those of Southwest, and meals were eliminated on flights less than 2.5 hours.

In March 1994, Continental increased CALite service to 875 daily flights. Continental soon encountered major operational problems with its new strategy.[20] With its fleet of 16 different planes, mechanical delays disrupted turnaround times. Various pricing strategies were unsuccessful. The company was ranked last among the major carriers for on-time service, and complaints soared by 40%. In January 1995, Continental announced that it would reduce its capacity by 10% and eliminate 4,000 jobs. By mid-1995, Continental's CALite service had been largely discontinued. In October 1995, Continental's CEO was ousted.

Morris Air, patterned after Southwest, was the only airline Southwest had acquired. Prior to the acquisition, Morris Air flew Boeing 737s on point-to-point routes, operated in a different part of the US than Southwest, and was profitable. When Morris Air was acquired by Southwest in December 1993, seven new markets were added to Southwest's system. In 1999, Morris Air's former president announced plans for a new airline to be based at New York's JFK Airport. The new airline was called JetBlue Airways. JetBlue had a successful IPO in April 2002, with the stock rising 70% on the first day of trading. JetBlue had a geographically diversified flight schedule that included both short-haul and long-haul routes. Although JetBlue was viewed as a low-fare carrier, the airline emphasized various service attributes, such as leather seats, free LiveTV (a 24-channel satellite TV service with programming provided by DirecTV) and pre-assigned seating. JetBlue had 24 Airbus A320 aircraft and orders for 60 more.

WESTERN PACIFIC AIRLINES

Western Pacific (WestPac) was founded by Ed Beauvais in 1995. Beauvais was also the founder and former CEO of America West Airlines. Originally, the plan was for three planes and five well-chosen cities by the end of the first year. By the end of the third year, the plan was to increase to 12 planes and 13 cities. This original plan was soon abandoned for a more aggressive start-up. WestPac began flying out of a new airport in Colorado Springs in April 1995 with a fleet of 12 leased Boeing 737s. The airline started with 15 domestic destinations on the west coast, east coast, southwest, and midwest, and all medium-length routes. Offering an alternative to the expensive Denver International Airport, business grew quickly. The company made a profit in two of its first four months of operation. Load factors averaged more than 60% in the first five months of operation. Operating cost per available seat mile averaged 7.37 cents during the early months and dropped to 6.46 within five months, the lowest in the industry. The Colorado Springs airport became one of the country's fastest growing as a result of WestPac's market entry. WestPac had one-third of the market share and had flown almost 600,000 passengers during its first seven months.

One of WestPac's most successful marketing efforts was the Mystery Fare program. As a way to fill empty seats, $59 round-trip tickets were sold to one of the air-

line's destinations, but which one remained a mystery. Response greatly exceeded the airline's expectations; thousands of the mystery seats were sold. Logo jets, also known as flying billboards, were another inventive approach by the start-up company. Jets painted on the outside with client advertising raised more than $1 million in fees over a one-year period. The airline also benefited from advances in ticketless operations. A healthy commission program to travel agents, and a diverse, non-union workforce were other features of WestPac operations.[21]

By 1996, WestPac was flying to 23 cities and had 18 planes. Not surprisingly, the major carriers reacted aggressively. WestPac was unable to match the large firms in service and did not have the financial resources to withstand a protracted price war. WestPac's fixed costs escalated and load factors dropped, leading to more aggressive pricing in late 1996. Soon, WestPac was losing money on most of its routes, forcing the airline to withdraw from several markets. In January 1997, Beauvais was replaced as CEO by a former TWA executive. Various changes were made, including a new focus on business travelers, the addition of inflight meals and new uniforms for flight attendants similar to those of other airlines, the introduction of a frequent-flier program, and a decision to join a national computer reservation system. In June 1997, WestPac announced that it would move most of its flights from Colorado Springs to Denver. The result was that WestPac's cost advantage largely disappeared because boarding charges at Denver International Airport were about $15 per passenger higher than at Colorado Springs.[22]

In October 1997, with losses mounting and rising debt, WestPac filed for Chapter 11 bankruptcy protection and abandoned all flights to Colorado Springs. Unable to find new financial backers, the company ceased operations in February 1998.

SOUTHWEST EXPANSION

Southwest grew steadily over the 30 years prior to 2002, but the growth was highly controlled. New airports were carefully selected, and only a few new cities were added each year. As Kelleher wrote to his employees in 1993, "Southwest has had more opportunities for growth than it has airplanes. Yet, unlike other airlines, it has avoided the trap of growing beyond its means. Whether you are talking with an officer or a ramp agent, employees just don't seem to be enamored of the idea that bigger is better."[23]

In January 1996, Southwest began new flights from Tampa International to Fort Lauderdale, Nashville, New Orleans, St. Louis/Lambert International Airport,

Birmingham, Houston/Hobby Airport, and Baltimore/Washington International Airport. Saturation and low initial fares were part of Southwest's expansion strategy. Some of the routes had as many as six daily flights. In April, service began from Orlando International Airport, with 10 flights headed to five different airports. Southwest's goal was to operate 78 daily flights to Tampa, Ft. Lauderdale, and Orlando.

In October 1996, with the initiation of flights to Providence, Rhode Island, Southwest entered the northeast market. The entry into the northeast region of the US was, in many respects, a logical move for Southwest. The northeast was the most densely populated area of the country and the only major region where Southwest did not compete. New England could provide a valuable source of passengers to Florida's warmer winter climates. Southwest's entry into Florida was exceeding initial estimates. Using a low-fare strategy, ValuJet had, until its crash, built a strong competitive base in important northeast markets.

Despite the large potential market, the northeast offered a new set of challenges for Southwest. Airport congestion and air-traffic control delays could prevent efficient operations, lengthening turnaround time at airport gates, and wreaking havoc on frequent flight scheduling. Inclement weather posed additional challenges for both air service and car travel to airports. Nevertheless, Southwest continued to add new northeast cities. A few years later, Southwest was flying to various northeast airports, including Long Island, New Hampshire, and Hartford. In 2001, Southwest began flying to Norfolk, Virginia.

FUTURE CHALLENGES

With the airline industry in turmoil in 2002, Southwest was in an interesting and unique position. Southwest was the only major US airline to earn an operating profit in 2001 and in the first quarter of 2002. With its strong financial position, perhaps this was the time to expand more aggressively to take advantage of competitor weaknesses. Southwest's market share in the northeast

was still quite small, and US Airways was in dire financial condition. Could Southwest quickly expand share in the northeast and still ensure that customer service and company performance were satisfactory? Or, maybe Southwest should look at internationalization options. One new initiative announced in May 2002 was that Southwest would begin nonstop flights from Los Angeles to Baltimore for an introductory one-way fare of $99. Clearly, 2002 and the years following would result in dramatic changes to airline industry structure. In all likelihood, Southwest would continue to prosper through these challenging times.

NOTES

1. P.S. Dempsey, "Transportation Deregulation: On a Collision Course," *Transportation Law Journal*, 13, 1984, p. 329.
2. W. Goralski, "Deregulation Deja Vu," *Telephony*, June 17, 1996, pp. 32–36.
3. "U.S. Airlines Finally Reach Cruising Speed," *New York Times*, October 20, 1996, Section 3, p. 1.
4. *Business Week*, August 7, 1995, p. 25.
5. C.A. Shifrin, "Record U.S. Airline Earnings Top $2 Billion," *Aviation Week & Space Technology*, January 29, 1996, p. 46.
6. K. Freiberg & J. Freiberg, *Nuts: Southwest Airlines' Crazy Recipe for Business and Personal Success* (Austin, TX: Bard Press, 1996) pp. 14–21.
7. Ibid., p. 31.
8. Ibid., p. 55.
9. Herb Kelleher, @ www.iflyswa.com/cgi-bin/imagemap/swagate 530.85.
10. Freiberg & Freiberg, p. 29.
11. K. Labich, "Is Herb Kelleher America's Best CEO?," *Fortune*, May 2, 1994, p. 45.
12. "24th Annual CEO Survey: Herb Kelleher, Flying His Own Course," *IW*, November 20, 1995, p. 23.
13. Labich, p. 46.
14. *IW*, p. 23.
15. B. O'Brian, "Flying on the Cheap," *Wall Street Journal*, October 26, 1992, p. A1.
16. *Training & Development*, p. 39.
17. A. Malloy, "Counting the Intangibles," *Computerworld*, June 1996, pp. 32–33.
18. H. Lancaster, "Herb Kelleher Has One Main Strategy: Treat Employees Well," *Wall Street Journal*, August 31, 1999, p. B1.
19. "Industry Surveys," *Aerospace & Air Transport*, February 1, 1996, p. A36.
20. B. O'Brian, "Heavy Going: Continental's CALite Hits Some Turbulence in Battling Southwest," *Wall Street Journal*, January 10, 1995, pp. A1, A16.
21. "Rapid Route Growth Tests WestPac's Low-Fare Formula," *Aviation Week & Space Technology*, December 4, 1995, pp. 37–38.
22. E. M. Olson & J. M. Ferguson, "Crash Landing," *Marketing Management*, Summer, 1998, pp. 54–58.
23. Freiberg & Freiberg, p. 61.

Sun Life Financial Services

case twenty-nine

K. Subhadra
A. Mukund
ICFAI Center for Management Research

"Extremely strong consolidated capital, very strong business profile, and very strong operating perform-ance. Partially offsetting these strengths are strong competitive pressures in most insurance markets in which Sun Life competes, and operating challenges associated with the insurer's UK operations."

—*Standard & Poor, explaining its AA+ (Very strong) rating for Sun Life, in 2001.*

INTRODUCTION

By 2001, with revenues of C$ 16.7 billion,[1] Sun Life Financial Services (Sun Life) had emerged as the largest insurer and lead-ing financial services provider in Canada. Sun Life served institu-tional and individual customers through an extensive distribution sales force network, independent agents, investment dealers and financial planners. The company operated in the wealth manage-ment and protection businesses in more than 16 countries with over 11,800 employees. It had over seven million customers in Canada alone. Sun Life's common stock was listed on the stock exchanges of Toronto, New York, London and Manila (Philippines).

Sun Life offered integrated financial services, in the areas of wealth management and protection. Wealth management included asset management, mutual funds, and pension plans, while protection included life insurance, general and health insur-ance. The company had formed strategic alliances with leading companies in countries across the globe, in addition to the many

This case was written by K Subhadra, under direction of A. Mukund, ICFAI Center for Management Research (ICMR). It is intended to be used as the basis for class discussion rather than to illustrate either effective or ineffective handling of a management situation.

The case was compiled from published sources.

mergers and acquisitions it had undertaken. In 1999, the com-pany announced its decision to exit the reinsurance[2] business due to continuous losses incurred in the business. In the same year, the company's policyholders approved the company's move towards demutualisation.[3]

In 2001, with a market capitalization of $ 9.6 billion, Sun Life was strongly established in all markets it was operating in. With the takeover of Clarica Life Insurance Company,[4] Sun Life emerged as the sixth largest life insurer in North America in terms of market capitalization.

On March 31, 2002, the group had C$ 359.9 billion of assets under management of which the wealth management busi-ness accounted for C$ 320.3 billion—90% of Sun Life's total assets. It was ranked 241 on the Forbes International 500 list in the Forbes 2002 survey.

New insurance laws were promulgated in Canada, allowing acquisitions in the insurance industry. This resulted in consolida-tion in the insurance industry with only a few strong players remaining in the market. Many Canadian companies had adopted the acquisitions route as the strategy for rapid expansion. Indus-try watchers commented that Sun Life might become an easy prey to its rival Manulife,[5] as the latter's stock market perform-ance had been much better than that of Sun Life. They felt that to avoid a takeover bid from Manulife, Sun Life needed to inte-grate the operations of its acquired companies and look for fresh takeover targets in the US.

HISTORY

The history of Sun Life dates back to 1865, when a group of businessmen in Montreal met to discuss the possibility of starting a life insurance company. In 1871, the company was incorporated, and soon its agents were working in seven regions, from Halifax, Nova Scotia to Woodstock, Ontario.

Sun Life expanded its operations to overseas markets, very early on. In 1892, it entered Hong Kong, and in 1893 it started its operations in the United Kingdom (UK). In 1895, it entered the United States (US) through Sun Life Assurance Company. The company operated in 49 states (all except for the state of New York), the District of Columbia and Puerto Rico. In the same year, it entered the Philippines and West Indies. The company also moved into other areas of insurance. In 1919, Sun Life became the first Canadian company to issue group insurance, and by 1942, assets under its management touched the C$1 billion mark. Sun Life entered the health insurance business in 1956 and in the same year it was converted from a shareholders' ownership into a mutual company, owned by its policyholders.

In 1982, it acquired Massachusetts Financial Services Company (MFS) and entered the mutual funds business in the US. The following year, it entered into the unit trust business in the UK and expanded its operations. The growth of Sun Life as a financial conglomerate was attributed to its acquisitions, which gave it significant market shares. In 1986, Sun Life entered the mutual fund business in Canada through Spectrum Mutual Fund Services. By the early 1990s, the company reached the C$ 300 billion mark in life insurance, and assets under its management were around C$ 107 billion. In 1995, it opened a representative office in Beijing to explore the business opportunities in the world's most populous country.

The company had a diversified product range including financial services such as mutual funds, pension plans, annuities, and investment management services. It offered its services through different affiliates such as Sun Life Assurance Company of Canada, Sun Life Securities Inc. and Spectrum Investment Management Limited (Refer to Table I for the subsidiaries of Sun Life).

In 1998, it signed an MoU with a Hong Kong-based financial services firm, China Everbright Group, and got a license to operate in China in 1999. In the same year, Sun Life entered the mutual fund business in India through a joint venture with the Aditya Birla group, one of India's largest business conglomerates.

TABLE I	Group Subsidiaries and Holdings
Canadian Operations	Nova Scotia Company
	McLean Budden Company
	Spectrum Investment Management Limited
	Sun Life Capital Trust
	Sun Life Financial Trust
	Sun Life Financial (India) Insurance Investments Inc.
	Sun Life (India) AMC Investments Inc.
United States	Independent Financial Marketing Group, Inc.
	Keyport Life Insurance Company
	Sun Capital Advisors, Inc.
	Clarica Life Insurance Company—US
	Sun Life Assurance Company of Canada (US)
	Sun Canada Financial Co.
	Sun Life of Canada (US) Distributors, Inc.
	Sun Life Insurance and Annuity Company of New York
	Massachusetts Financial Services Company
United Kingdom	Sun Life of Canada Nominees Limited
	SLC Financial Services (UK) Limited
	Sun Life Assurance Company of Canada (UK) Limited
	Sun Life of Canada (UK) Group Services Limited
	Sun Life Financial of Canada Trustee Limited

Source: Company Annual Report, 2001.

Sun Life stated its vision as 'To be a world-class provider of financial security to individuals over their lifetimes.' In order to realize this vision, the company identified the core values to which it was committed (Refer to Table II).

By 1999, assets under the company's management reached C$ 300 billion. In 2000, Sun Life's demutualisation process was completed and its shares started trading on stock exchanges in Toronto, New York, London and Manila (Philippines).

MERGERS AND ACQUISITIONS

Sun Life adopted mergers and acquisitions to expand in new markets and also to consolidate its position in markets where it already had a presence. (See Figure I.) In

---

Core Values | **TABLE II**

- **Integrity:** We will operate to the very highest standards of business conduct. We will strive to treat people fairly and to communicate promptly, completely and accurately with our employees, policyholders, customers, regulators, shareholders and others with whom we do business. We will not mislead these stakeholders or make promises to them that we cannot keep.

- **Customer Focus:** We appreciate the trust our policyholders and customers have in us. We will seek to reward that trust by creating and offering innovative financial solutions that address their needs.

- **Excellence:** We recognize that the contributions made by our employees and representatives are vital to our success. We will try to recruit the very best people, provide them with a challenging and rewarding work environment, and give them opportunities to enable them to enhance their capabilities and realize their full potential.

- **Building Value:** Investors demonstrate their confidence in us when they purchase Sun Life Financial securities. Other stakeholders, including our employees, demonstrate their confidence in us when they purchase our products, provide services to us or otherwise work with us to achieve common goals. We are committed to rewarding their trust and exceeding their expectations by consistently working to build value.

Source: www.sunlife.ca

1982, it acquired an 85% stake in the US-based Massachusetts Financial Services (MFS), which was an established player in the management and distribution of mutual funds and institutional funds. It was also a leading player in the variable annuity products[6] management for other companies, including financial services companies. In 2001, MFS was ranked fourth in the mutual funds industry, on the basis of new flows generated in retail mutual funds. By the end of 2001, MFS was managing US$ 120 billion in assets for more than five million individual and institutional mutual fund and annuity investors worldwide. In the same year, MFS contributed $231 million, representing 14% of Sun Life's total earnings for the year.

In 1994, Sun Life UK acquired the London-based Sun Bank, a mortgage and savings bank. (Sun Bank was sold in 2001 to Portman Building Society based in London for £95 million.) In 1997, Sun Life acquired McLean Budden Limited (McLean Budden), one of the oldest Canadian investment-counselling firms operating from Toronto, Montreal, and Vancouver. It (McLean Budden) offered investment management services, and by the end of 2001, had $24.8 billion in assets under its management.

In 1998, Sun Life's management set its sights on becoming a top ten player in North America and in the emerging markets of Asia. It planned to deliver strong internal growth across all its operations, and to acquire companies, which fitted into its larger plans for growth. The company also decided to exit the markets where it was unable to achieve its targets. The focus of its acquisitions was on achieving a leadership position in Canada and pursuing high growth segments in the US. The acquisition strategy was worked out on the basis of the following parameters:

- Discipline—Exiting or scaling back operations where the company had failed to achieve a critical mass or profitability.
- Strategic Fit—Fitting the overall strategy of becoming a top ten player in North America and the emerging Asian markets.
- Value accretion—The end result of the exercise would be enhanced value for the company.

In accordance with the above criteria, Sun Life entered into an agreement with the Boston-based group of asset management companies, Liberty Financial Companies (Liberty) in May 2001. The agreement involved Sun Life's acquisition of two of Liberty's companies, Keyport Life Insurance Company (Keyport) and Independent Financial Marketing Group (IFMG), for US$ 1.7 billion (C$ 2.6 billion). Keyport's product profile included fixed and variable annuities, which complemented Sun Life's

FIGURE I   Acquisitions & Disposals of Sun Life in 2001

	Acquisitions		Disposals				
	Keyport/ IFMG	Birla	SLCAM	SB	NLT	MCIC	SLT
Invested assets acquired / disposed of	$22,504	$ 4	$ 67	$2,604	$419	$365	$1,929
Other assets acquired / disposed of	1,328	17	41	37	6	17	52
	23,832	21	108	2,641	425	382	1,981
Actuarial liabilities and other policy liabilities acquired / disposed of	22,554	–	–	–	–	316	–
Amounts on deposit acquired / disposed of	–	–	–	2,417	394	1	1,739
Other liabilities acquired / disposed of	482	13	41	100	24	5	77
	23,036	13	41	2,517	418	322	1,816
Net balance sheet assets acquired / disposed of	796	8	67	124	7	60	165
Cash cost of acquisition / net proceeds of disposal	2,744	43	242	144	41	51	160
Goodwill on acquisition / pre tax gain (loss) on sale	$ 1,948	$35	$175	$ 20	$ 34	$ (9)	$ (5)
Goodwill amortization period in years[1]		15					
Cash acquired (disposed of)	$ 919	$ –	$(23)	$ –	$ (32)	$ –	$ –

[1]Goodwill arising from the acquisition of Keyport and IFMG is not amortized.

Source: www.sedar.com

product profile and distribution capabilities. Keyport had around US$ 19.0 billion (C$ 29.5 billion) in assets under management and generated total annuity sales of US$ 2.7 billion (C$ 4.2 billion) in 2000. With the acquisition of Keyport, the combined business emerged as the tenth-largest company in the US variable annuity business. Sun Life also acquired New York-based IFMG, a marketing group for annuities and mutual funds distributing wealth management products to small and mid-size banks. (IFMG was ranked first in fixed and variable annuities sales through banks in 1998 and 1999.)

According to Sun Life's management, the acquisitions of Keyport and IFMG would help the company achieve the goal of entering the 'Top 10' in targeted product markets in North America. It was added that Sun Life's strong presence in variable annuity franchise and Keyport's impressive fixed annuity business would result in a wealth-management powerhouse, which would cater to the full array of client needs. IFMG's extensive distribution network and positioning were expected to complement Sun Life's distribution system, whose strengths were its brokers and financial planners.

Sun Life financed the purchase through a combination of existing cash resources and money raised from the capital market. The merger was expected to raise the earnings per share (EPS) by 15–20 cents (CDN) in 2002. According to Sun Life, the acquisitions were in line with its business strategy and there existed a strong complementary fit between their operations. The company felt that the purchase of Keyport and IFMG would:

- Add scale to its operations in the US
- Provide a diversified product portfolio
- Strengthen Sun Life's product portfolio
- Enhance the distribution network

In December 2001, Sun Life and Clarica Life Insurance Company (Clarica) announced a decision to combine their operations. As per the agreement, Clarica was to become a wholly owned subsidiary of Sun Life but retain its name. With this acquisition, Sun Life:

- Moved from the fifth position in the Canadian insurance industry, to become number one, with total revenues of $21.7 billion, assets under administration of $344 billion and total assets of $140.2 billion
- The leader in Canada's group life and health insurance markets
- The number one player in Canadian group retirement services
- The market leader in terms of retail insurance premiums in force in Canada
- Number one in terms of market capitalization of Canadian insurance companies
- The insurance company with the largest customer base of approximately seven million Canadians
- One of the top five publicly traded North American life insurance companies, measured by market capitalization.

According to Sun Life sources, the cultural and business similarities between Clarica and Sun Life helped lower cost structures, increase revenue and expand distribution capabilities. The company also decided to amalgamate its two subsidiaries, Clarica Life Insurance Company and Sun Life Assurance Company of Canada, by December 2002. It was reported that the amalgamated company would operate under the 'Sun Life Assurance Company of Canada' name but would market products under both the Sun Life Financial and Clarica brands. It was expected that the deal would simplify business processes and operations, and operating costs would also be reduced.

The Sun Life Financial brand was to be used in selected retail products and distribution channels, and in group retirement services and group insurance, as it had a strong presence in these areas. The Clarica brand would be used to serve individual retail customers through more than 4,000 direct sales personnel. Clarica and Sun Life Financial drew up plans to ensure smooth integration, and to maintain their shared focus on customer service excellence. In May 2002, the government of Canada granted approval to Sun Life's acquisition of Clarica. Sun Life claimed that pre-tax synergies would be around $97 million in 2002, $236 million in 2003 and in 2004 savings would reach around $270 million. Analysts pointed out that these savings would arise, as the integrated company would have a single management team, only one set of associated expenses, economies in operating units and in information technology. Though Sun Life expected to gain substantial amounts as sav-

ings, its equity base increased by more than 40% because of the stock issued to Clarica shareholders. Analysts pointed out that Sun Life's investment performance would depend on uncertain gains from size and synergy and on the management team.

For the reasons stated above, stock markets reacted cautiously to the merger, and Sun Life's stock traded below the $33.60 price it commanded when the deal was announced. However, some analysts argued that the success of the Sun Life-Clarica deal was not dependent on stock price movements, and that the stock prices did not reflect adequately the excitement and positive views about the merger in the market. From the point of view of customers, some analysts felt that the ongoing trend of consolidation in the Canadian insurance industry would leave customers with very little choice, and their bargaining power would be reduced considerably.

BUSINESS SEGMENTS

Sun Life's business, spread across four geographic segments, Canada, the US, the UK and Asia, was divided into two principal business segments—'Wealth Management' and 'Protection.' (See Table III.)

WEALTH MANAGEMENT

The wealth management business consisted of asset management, mutual fund, pension, and annuity & brokerage operations. Considered to be the 'growth segment' of Sun Life, the wealth management segment managed assets worth C$ 315.2 billion in 2001—90% of the company's total assets under management. In the same year, wealth management represented around 55% of the total revenues earned by the company. During 1997–2001, it grew at a CAGR of 22% in assets under

Sun Life—Segmentwise Revenue Break Up (in CDN$ billion)		TABLE III
Year	Wealth Management (Fee Income)	Protection (Premium Income)
1996	1.0	3.8
1997	1.3	4.0
1998	1.9	4.5
1999	2.5	4.6
2000	3.2	4.7

Source: Company Annual Report, 2000.

management and 24% in fee income. The revenues for the wealth management business came from:

- Investment advisory fees
- Distribution and servicing fees
- Mortality and expense fees: (Denotes the first fee imposed by an annuity for insurance guarantee, commissions, selling and administrative expenses of the contract.)
- Annuity premiums
- Net investment income on general fund assets, which were held in pension and fixed annuity business.

PROTECTION

Sun Life's protection business consisted of individual life, and group life and health insurance operations, contributing 45% of its total revenues in 2001. During 1997–2001, the segment grew at a CAGR of 7%. The revenues for the protection business came from:

- Premiums earned on individual life, group life and group health insurance contracts
- Net investment income on assets supporting actuarial liabilities[7] in the protection business.

PRODUCTS AND SERVICES

The products and services offered by the company under its wealth and protection businesses were divided into the following categories—Insurance Products, Investments, Savings & Loans, and Services (Refer to Table IV for the insurance products).

INSURANCE PRODUCTS

In its life insurance plans, Sun Life offered various products, which targeted different segments of customers. The insurance products were broadly classified into the categories of Individual Insurance and Group Insurance (Refer to Table IV for the product profile).

TABLE IV	Insurance Products

Life Insurance
Permanent Life Insurance:
– Sun Life Universal
– Whole Life Participating:
  • Sun Classic Life
  • Sun Premier Life
– Non Participating Whole Life:
  • Sun Term 100
  • Sun 50 Plus

Term Life Insurance

Critical Illness Insurance

Group Insurance
Group Life Insurance:
• Basic Life and Accidental Death & Dismemberment
• Optional Life and Accidental Death & Dismemberment
• Dependent Life
• Voluntary Accidental Death & Dismemberment (AD&D)

Group Disability:
Short Term Disability
Long Term Disability
Disability Services for Self-funded Plans

Medical Stop-loss:
Specific Stop-loss
Aggregate Stop-loss
Aggregating Stop-loss
Small Business Solutions:
Group Life and AD&D
Short Term Disability
Long Term Disability

Source: www.sunlife.com

Sun Life's individual life insurance business was divided into the following three categories:

- Permanent Life Insurance—life insurance
- Term Life Insurance—health insurance
- Critical Illness Insurance—disability insurance

Permanent Life Insurance

Permanent Life Insurance products of the company offered safety for the whole life. Under this category, Sun Life offered a range of flexible permanent life insurance solutions, which provided tax-deferred savings and protection to customers. In this category, the company offered the following policies:

- Sun Universal Life: Sun Universal Life policy combined two features, savings and customized life protection, into one policy.
- Participating Whole Life: A policy for the whole life, which enabled customers to meet their long-term financial goals. In addition to ensured life protection, it allowed customers the alternatives of using policy dividends declared by the company to buy additional life insurance coverage, receiving the dividends in the form of a cash payment, or investing them with the company. Under participating whole life insurance policies, Sun Life offered two types of policies, Sun Classic Life and Sun Premier Life.
- Non-Participating Whole Life: This was a permanent life policy, in which non-participating policyholders did not receive any policy dividends but were provided guaranteed cash returns. Both permanent and temporary covers were made available under this policy. Sun Life offered two types of policies under this scheme, namely, Sun Term 100 and Sun 50 Plus.

Term Life Insurance

Under Term Life Insurance, customers were offered policies for a fixed period of time with lower premiums. SunTerm offered a simple six-class system—three for non-smokers, one for cigar smokers, and two for smokers. Policy premiums were determined on the basis of the prospective customer's current health, medical history and lifestyle. Under SunTerm, the company offered 5-, 10- and 20-year term plans and customers were given the option of renewing the policy for another term or converting it into a permanent life insurance policy.

Under term life insurance, Sun Life offered temporary policies as well. The term life insurance portfolio consisted of three non-participating plans covering short-term needs, such as mortgage or debt protection. Financial protection was offered in 5-, 10- and 20-year renewable terms. Another unique feature of the policies

was that customers were allowed to change their term life policies into permanent life insurance policies without medical evidence, within a specified time limit. The term life policies also offered supplementary benefits such as accidental death benefit, total disability benefit and guaranteed insurability benefit.

Critical Illness Insurance

Sun Life's Sun LifeAssist policy was designed to provide protection to individuals, families or businesses in the event of a critical illness. Under this scheme, payment of benefit was not dependent on the inability to work or the severity of customer's condition—payment was made even if the customer recovered fully.

The company's group insurance business was also divided into various categories:

Group Life Insurance Products

- Basic Life and Accidental Death & Dismemberment: This policy allowed employers to provide employees with accidental death benefits, equal to the employee's basic life insurance amount.
- Optional Life and Accidental Death & Dismemberment: This policy provided employees with an accidental death benefit, equal to their optional life insurance amount.
- Voluntary AD&D: This policy provided employees with a high level of financial protection in the event of death or qualifying injury.

Group Disability

- Short Term Disability: This policy protected the insured person against financial loss resulting due to injury or illness over a limited period of time (usually 26 weeks or one year). During that period, the insurer (not the employer) paid the injured person's monthly income.
- Long Term Disability: This policy protected the insured against financial loss resulting from injury or illness, through monthly payments as long as the insured person remained disabled.
- Disability Services for Self-funded Plans: Sun Life provided disability management services to professionally manage the sick leave plans of employers with SunAdvisor disability management services. Through SunAdvisor, employers were allowed to select the type of help needed without paying for unwanted services. Sun Life offered four SunAdvisor modules with different suites of services. The services ranged from enabling employers to manage sick leave plans to complete claim management, including claim reviews, benefit checks, and monthly data reporting.

Medical Stop Loss

Medical Stop Loss was defined as insurance purchased by employers who self-insured their medical plans in order to protect themselves against unexpected losses. Under Medical Stop Loss, Sun Life provided the following policies:

- Specific Stop Loss: This policy provided coverage to employers on large medical claims from a single employee. Coverage was based on the employer's medical coverage plan.
- Aggregate Stop Loss: This policy protected employers from higher-than-expected medical insurance coverage plan utilization.
- Aggregating Specific Stop Loss: This policy provided employers a chance to reduce their insurance premiums if they assumed more risk.

Small Business Solutions

Under this category, Sun Life provided special packages within the financial constraints of small businesses, through its Group and AD&D, Short-term disability and Long-term disability policies.

By 2001, Sun Life's group insurance business unit emerged as one of the largest group insurers in Canada. Its earnings from group insurance increased by 19%, largely due to the strong sales of group insurance products and improved operating efficiency. Revenues from group insurance for the year increased by 5% to C$ 1.5 billion and premium income and administrative services increased by 15% to C$ 2.3 billion. In the life insurance business, the company promoted universal life products, which offered opportunities for growth in the individual life market, more strongly. In 2001, the universal life products represented more than 75% of the company's Canadian individual life insurance sales.

INVESTMENTS

Along with its insurance products, Sun Life also offered investment services to its customers. The products and services under investment services were:

- Mutual funds—The Company offered various kinds of accounts through which customers could invest in mutual funds.
- Segregated funds—These funds ensured that an individual's investment was secure, no matter how the market performed. The investor was guaranteed to receive 75% of the initial investment.
- Annuities—These provided a guaranteed interest rate while protecting the savings. Sun Life offered various kinds of annuity plans such as Superflex, Non-redeemable Guaranteed Investment Account, and Income master.

SAVINGS AND LOANS

Sun Life also offered savings and loan products at competitive rates. It offered the following savings and loan products to customers:

- Premium Savings Account
- Premium Line Personal Line of Credit
- Residential Mortgage Service Program.

SERVICES

Sun Life offered its customers Brokerage and Advisory services as well, wherein a company-appointed advisor helped customers choose from its products and services by providing information and helping select the right kind of instruments.

MARKETING

Sun Life believed in 'always working with the customers' perspective in the mind.' From the time it was set up, the company catered to the needs of customers by creating innovative products and services. It was one of the first insurance companies to issue unconditional policies. Over the decades, Sun Life devised many innovative policies, which helped it gain a competitive advantage in the insurance market the world over. Many insurance companies charged extra premium from military personnel, as the risk involved for their lives was higher. Sun Life eliminated this extra charge for military personnel. Similarly, many companies charged extra premium from people traveling to Europe—on account of the sea travel involved. Sun Life eliminated this extra charge as well. As a result of such initiatives, the company was able to gain a substantial amount of business. Over the years, Sun Life continued to focus on marketing to expand the reach of its business.

In 1995, the company undertook a major restructuring exercise. It redefined the roles and responsibilities of the management and support staff in its customer service division, and assigned functional managers the role of 'coaches.' The role of these coaches was to help the teams develop superior customer service skills. In the new set-up, the customer service division was divided into five groups. Each of these groups had its own set of roles and responsibilities:

- Process owners set overall performance targets and objectives, and were ultimately responsible for performance.
- Process teams managed day-to-day work and were accountable to the process owners.
- Coaches guided teams to high performance—they were accountable to the teams and were responsible for ensuring the quality of team projects.

- Product managers contributed technical expertise on product standards to the teams; their responsibilities were similar to those of coaches.
- Central support ensured maintenance and development of functional expertise, and supported systems development and implementation.

These measures helped Sun Life reduce the cycle time taken for key services by over 75% and on-time process performance increased by 25%. To reach out to a larger number of customers, Sun Life started selling policies through private banks and trust companies.

To boost the sales of its fixed and variable annuity products, Sun Life offered broker incentive programs by creating a 'Laureate Circle' on its website that gave recognition to the top salesperson. When a representative or broker reached a certain sales level, he was given access to a dedicated group of customer service staff, a toll-free number to contact them and quarterly conference calls with fund managers and attorneys. The company targeted two groups: affluent clients were offered insurance products that covered the taxes charged when an estate passed to a beneficiary; and businesses were offered succession insurance, providing money to hire a replacement for an executive who had died, and continuation insurance, which allowed surviving partners to buy out the deceased partner's share of the company.

In 1998, the company conducted a market research exercise to find out how to market its various new products in the best possible manner. According to the findings of this research, there was a need to educate customers on the different types of products available. The company then started providing customers educational materials in the form of 'client-friendly' literature and prospectuses. It also expanded its sales force to sell new products throughout the year.

In 2001, Sun Life entered into a distribution alliance with the Canada-based financial services company, IPC Financial Network Inc. (IPC). The arrangement allowed IPC's clients to gain access to selected co-branded financial products and services such as chequing/savings accounts and personal lines of credit, supported by call center and debit card services. In the same year, Sun Life entered into an agreement with the Canada-based Berkshire Investment Group Inc.,[8] and launched the Berkshire Premium Program. According to the agreement, financial advisors in the Berkshire Investment Group solicited applications for various Sun Life products.

In order to extend its reach, the company entered into a strategic marketing and distribution alliance with Hub Financial Inc.,[9] in June 2002. According to the agreement, Hub Financial provided IQON advisors[10] with sales and support services. They were also given access to multiple carriers for third-party life, health and disability insurance and segregated fund products. Hub Financial was also made a preferred distributor of Sun Life's insurance products. According to the agreement, the advisors were given integrated compensation systems which included wealth and insurance products offered by Sun Life. This agreement also allowed the advisors to access Hub Financial's top-of-the-industry web-based technology and tools, allowing them to track industry developments in financial, taxation and estate planning. According to analysts, this marketing agreement was expected to help ensure that Sun Life's customers received outstanding service.

GLOBALIZATION

Sun Life's international growth began in the early 1890s, with the company expanding into the Asia-Pacific region, the United States, the United Kingdom and Latin America. By the 1930s, Sun Life was operating in nearly 60 countries—however, due to political instability, currency devaluation and war, the company was forced to withdraw its operations from most of these countries. In 2001, Sun Life had operations in over 17 countries and derived around 77% of its total revenues from its global operations. The United States was the largest source of revenues, contributing around 47% of total revenues.

UNITED KINGDOM

In 1893, Sun Life started operating in the United Kingdom, offering insurance products. Initially, it offered individual life insurance policies to consumers. For several years, it catered to the individual life insurance market only, expanding its operations to group insurance as well, in 1978. Its wealth management business in the UK consisted of unit trusts, unit-linked pension products, pension fund management services and banking operations. The company operated through various subsidiaries, which included Sun Life of Canada Unit Managers Limited which managed unit trusts, and SLC Asset Management which managed the company's UK assets, excluding those of Sun Bank and assets of third parties. Its protection business offered individual insurance (participating and non-participating whole life and term insurance), unit-linked life insurance products in which contract-holders could actively engage in the investment funds, as well as group life and health insurance.

In 1994, Sun Life acquired Confederation Life Insurance Company Ltd. (UK), which had a strong presence in the pensions business. But the business reported losses due to costs associated with the minimum annuity rates on its pensions which were higher than preliminary estimates. In order to minimize losses, Sun Life initiated a cost-reduction exercise.

In 1998, Sun Life's wealth management business (UK) reported a net operating loss of $521 million, which was attributed to the cost of annuity rate provisions. In 1999, Sun Life (UK) reported a net operating loss of $332 million attributed to pension sales provisions.

In 2001, Sun Life (UK) reported total revenues of $2,067 million, of which the wealth management business contributed $789 million as against $855 million in 2000. The decrease was attributed to Sun Life's decision to scale down its operations in the country. Individual life business contributed $850 million in 2001 as compared to $987 million in 2000 (Refer to Table V for the revenues of UK operations). Sun Life abandoned distribution through direct sales personnel, and also stopped selling its individual life insurance and pension products to new customers in the UK, in 2001.

Other income included investment income, asset provisions and expenses that were not directly associated with UK operations. As on December 31, 2001, these operations reported $95 million in losses compared to $50 million in 2000. Increase in losses was attributed to restructuring expenses due to the rationalization initiative.

By December 31, 2001, Sun Life's UK operations contributed revenues of $180 million—a rise of $61 million or 51% over that in 2000. In February 2001, Sun Life initiated measures to rationalize its business profile as it felt that its existing business model had failed to meet its long-term strategic business goals.

UNITED STATES

Sun Life started its operations in the United States in 1895. Its insurance operations concentrated on individ-

ual annuity products and high-end individual insurance markets. The business was organized into two areas: 1) individual life (fixed and variable universal life), term life, non-participating and participating whole life insurance; and 2) group life and health insurance (short and long-term disability benefits and medical stop-loss plans). Sun Life's group insurance business was focused on small and medium-sized companies.

For the year ended December 31, 2001, US operations reported revenues of C$ 7.8 billion as compared to revenues of C$ 7.1 billion in 2000. Though Sun Life saw decreased sales in the annuity business (due to the economic slowdown and the poor performance of the equity markets in the US), increased revenues from the protection business and Keyport were cited as reasons for the increase in overall revenues. ROE decreased to 11.8% from 20.1% in 2000, which reflected the increased equity base due to the acquisition of Keyport and IFMG. By 2001, US operations represented 25% of Sun Life's earnings and 47% of total revenues. In a survey of 34 mid-size variable annuity providers in the US, Sun Life was ranked 'number one' for overall marketing support in 2001 (Refer to Table VI for the revenues of US operations).

ASIAN OPERATIONS

Sun Life's Asian operations included individual insurance businesses in the Philippines, Hong Kong, Indonesia, and India, and group insurance businesses in the Philippines and India. Wealth management was included in the Indian and Philippine operations. Revenues from Sun Life's Asian operations increased by C$ 51 million in 2000 to C$ 464 million in 2001 (a 12% rise) due to increased sales in Hong Kong and improved investment performance. However, ROE for 2001 decreased to 4.2% from 6.7% in 2000 due to reduced earnings and increased investments in the region. In

TABLE V	Revenues of UK Operations (in C$ millions)		
	2001	2000	1999
Wealth Management	789	855	1,082
Protection:			
Group Life and Health	420	418	411
Individual	850	987	1,127
Other	8	–	33
Total UK Operations	2,067	2,260	2,653

Source: Company Annual Report, 2001.

TABLE VI	Revenues of US Operations (in C$ millions)		
	2001	2000	1999
Wealth Management	4,672	4,406	3,270
Protection:			
Group Life and Health	871	699	622
Individual	2,206	1,981	1,863
Other	62	73	80
Total Revenues	7,811	7,159	5,835

Source: Company Annual Report, 2001.

2001, the company expanded its presence in selected Asian markets.

In the Philippines, the company was the number two player in the individual life insurance business. It strengthened its market position continually by expanding its product range and providing enhanced customer service. Sun Life's Philippine operations contributed around 55% of its total insurance premiums revenues in Asia, and in 2001, it posted a growth of 14% in total premium, measured in local currency.

In Hong Kong, Sun Life adopted aggressive marketing strategies, focusing on investment-linked life insurance products through a multi-channel distribution network. In 2001, the company launched its variable life insurance business line, and entered into a bancassurance[11] partnership with Hong Kong-based CITIC Ka Wah Bank to sell its products. It targeted high-end customers with strong customer services. The bancassurance channel accounted for 18% of its total sales in Hong Kong in 2001. In 2001, Sun Life's sales in Hong Kong increased by 38% and it also focused on strengthening its distribution network. In the same year, the company's agents increased in number to 346, from 271 in 2000.

Sun Life entered India in 1999, through a joint venture called Birla Sun Life, with one of the largest business conglomerates of India—the Aditya Birla group. Initially the joint venture operated in the mutual fund business in India through its asset management joint venture, Birla Sun Life Asset Management Company Limited (BSLAMC). BSLAMC was ranked as India's second largest private mutual fund. In December 2001, it had $1.3 billion in assets under management and approximately 350,000 investor accounts. After the Indian insurance sector was opened to private players, Sun Life started insurance operations through its joint venture with the Aditya Birla group—Birla Sun Life Insurance Company Limited (BSLIC)—in March 2001. It started operating in both individual life and group insurance. By December 2001, the company had built a distribution network of 11 branches in 10 cities and had sold more than 8,000 policies. It entered into two bancassurance alliances as well to strengthen its distribution network.

Sun Life's joint venture in China, Sun Life Everbright Life Insurance Company Limited (SLEB) was granted a license to commence operations in Tianjin, a major city in China. SLEB was the first foreign life insurance joint venture in China to start operations in Tianjin.

Sun Life sources revealed that the company's decision to concentrate on the Indian and Chinese markets was prompted by the relaxing of the regulatory framework in both countries, where, for the first time, foreign investment was being allowed in the insurance sector. According to Sun Life, both the countries offered tremendous potential, being the world's most populous countries with very low insurance penetration rates by global standards (Refer to Table VII for the revenues of Asian operations).

HUMAN RESOURCES

Sun Life focused on employee development and offered a comprehensive package of benefits to ensure that its employees were happy to work for the organization. The culture of the organization was people-focused. The company had developed a set of shared values, which served as a guide for all employees. Sun Life encouraged employees to *'deliver excellence, make a difference, anticipate the future, be open-minded and act with integrity',* as was stated in its business code for its employees. To fulfill its role as a socially responsible corporate entity, Sun Life encouraged its employees to support a variety of non-profit organizations and to participate in charitable activities.

Sun Life tried to provide a work environment, which allowed its employees to grow and develop in various ways. Every year, senior managers interacted directly with the staff, so as to gain an insight into the actual work environment. At Sun Life, communication was given vital importance as the management believed that good internal communication practices helped initiate ideas and enabled the company to seize new opportunities. The company believed in encouraging its employees to be proactive.

Sun Life considered communication skills an important element in the wider competence of individual employees. The set of competencies required and

Asian Operations—Financial Performance (in C$ millions)	TABLE VII		
	2001	**2000**	**1999**
Revenues	464	413	401
Shareholders Net Income	20	27	31
Shareholders Equity	514	401	405
Return on Equity	4.2%	6.7%	8.2%

Source: Company Annual Report, 2001.

the communications profile for each job were laid down. These were used for the appraisal of personnel for particular jobs, and were also used to determine their salaries. If an employee was in a customer-service job, then the pay was directly linked with the individual's communication skills, and a certain level of competence in communication was a definite prerequisite for moving up in the salary scale. In support areas, the link was not direct, but the communication skills of the employee had a bearing on pay hikes.

The company followed an open policy regarding annual appraisals and used the 360° appraisal tool for its employees. In this appraisal technique, views were sought from the individual's peers, bosses, customers, people reporting to them and the individual being assessed. In addition to the annual appraisal, there were general quarterly appraisals.

In order to enhance employee productivity and development, the company initiated many programs. Some of the programs undertaken by the company were:

- **The Galaxy Program:** The company organized six seminars every year, in which well-known external speakers participated. The aim of the program was to expand the knowledge of the employees attending the seminar. Initially, the sessions were targeted solely at managers; later on they were opened to any employee who was interested in attending. To improve the communication skills of employees, the speakers had question-and-answer sessions with senior managers on the issue addressed at the seminar.
- **Inter-lunch Meetings:** Sun Life organized Inter-lunch meetings during which the top management team met employees from all levels and areas of business over lunch. About 15–30 employees attended each meeting with one or two managers. Each manager aimed to conduct six such meetings a year. This gave the senior management a chance to talk directly to employees and to learn their views on various policies of the company. These meetings usually started with a short presentation from the manager on a specific topic, followed by a general discussion, which gave employees a chance to ask questions or express views on the subject.
- **Branch Visits:** Senior managers visited branches to converse directly with employees and also to oversee the functioning of the branches.
- **Managers' Conferences:** Held every 18 months, these conferences were attended by top-rung managers to review broad business strategies. At these meetings, the company focused on issues such as the company's vision and the role of managers in driving the company forward. They also discussed and tried to envisage different scenarios for the future.

In order to increase the productivity of employees, Sun Life provided many benefits, covering the personal, professional and health concerns of its employees (Refer to Exhibit I for some of these benefits). In addition, Sun Life provided employees the following benefits:

- **Incentive Compensation:** Sun Life gave cash bonuses in addition to the regular salary if an employee met team and individual objectives that were set at the beginning of the year.
- **Vacation:** New employees of Sun Life earned 15 days of vacation per year, and if an employee accumulated monthly leave, he/she could take vacation time after the first three months of employment. Employees were also given 11 paid statutory holidays per year.
- **Flexible Business Attire:** In order to make the work environment at Sun Life comfortable, the management gave employees the option of wearing casual business clothes from Monday to Friday. But for employees working in departments where client interaction was high, traditional business attire was mandatory.
- **Alternative Work Arrangements:** Sun Life allowed its employees flexible work arrangements of four types: Regular Part Time, Compressed Workweek, Telecommuting, and Job Sharing.
- **University of Sun Life Financial:** Sun Life provided employees an opportunity to develop their career through Sun Life Financial's Corporate University. Under this program, 10 schools and colleges offered resources and courses to help employees align their skills and knowledge with the company's future business needs.
- **On-site Fitness:** Sun Life provided fitness classes and individual weight-training programs for a nominal fee. It also employed registered nurses who were available for health care assistance, information and counselling on health-related issues.
- **Employee Assistance Program:** Sun Life provided professional counselling and referral services—24 hours a day, seven days a week—to the employees and their families. An external organization was employed to provide these services, and personal information was not disclosed to the company.

CORPORATE GOVERNANCE

Sun Life followed a strong 'code of business conduct' right from its inception that formed the basis of its principles of corporate governance in later years. The objectives of Sun Life's 'code of business conduct' were:

- To demonstrate to the public and stakeholders that Sun Life's ethics were sound;

Insurance Plans:

- Health Insurance: Sun Life provided comprehensive coverage by subsidizing the cost of several health insurance programs for employees and their families.
- Life Insurance: Sun Life provided every employee group life insurance coverage worth of one and a half times their salary without charging them. It also provided full-time and part-time employees working for more than 30 hrs per week insurance coverage worth C$ 5,000 for their spouse and C$ 1,500 for each dependent child.
- Disability Coverage: Sun Life provided 15 days of paid sick leave each year, a short-term salary continuance plan for employees taking leave for more than five consecutive days and long-term disability insurance for employees taking leave for more than six months.
- Flexible-Spending Accounts: Flexible-spending accounts provided tax advantages for employees when paying for health expenses not covered under their benefit plans, and for dependent care expenditures.

401(K)* and Pension Plans:

Sun Life employees could save for their retirement through contributions of 1–16% of their salary to any of nine investment options. Sun Life matched employee contribution by 50 cents for every dollar up to a certain percentage of employee compensation. Sun Life contributed at a rate of 20% for each year of work at Sun Life.

Pension Plan: Employees were automatically enrolled in the company's pension plan when they were hired and participated fully in the plan after five years of service.

Professional Development:

- Tuition Reimbursement: The company reimbursed about 75% of tuition cost of approved courses after six months of service.
- Insurance Industry Courses: Sun Life offered to pay exam fees for insurance industry courses such as Life Office Management Association and Health Insurance Association of America courses for employees who completed the course successfully, and also awarded a cash bonus.
- Company Seminars: Sun Life's Human Resource Development Department regularly conducted seminars on management development, communication skills, stress management and other workshops for the benefit of employees.
- Toastmasters: Sun Life opened its own chapter of Toastmasters International, an organization that develops public speaking skills and self-confidence.
- Library: The company managed a library for its employees providing access to a wide variety of magazines, reference materials, books, audiocassettes and videotapes.
- Electronic Job Posting: The company provided information on within-company jobs through Sun Life's electronic mail system or through the HR on-line kiosks.
- Performance-based compensation increases: Sun Life rewarded excellent performances through annual performance-based compensation increases and bonus programs. It also had a 360-degree performance appraisal.
- Referral Bonus Program: Sun Life gave a bonus to employees if a candidate referred by them was selected.

*401(K) plans refer to employee retirement plans as specified by Section 401(K) of the US Internal Revenue Code. These plans allow employees to make pre-tax contributions that are automatically deducted from their paycheque. The contributions are invested at the employees' direction into one or more funds provided in the plan. While the investments grow in the 401(K) account, they do not pay taxes on them.

Source: www.sunlife.ca

- To describe Sun Life Financial's values and standards of business conduct;
- To guide employees on how to resolve potentially difficult situations and conflicts of interest;
- To promote principles of respect and fairness in the workplace and in dealings with the public and stakeholders.

Sun Life's corporate governance principles conformed to the Toronto Stock Exchange Guidelines for Effective Corporate Governance. The structure and practices of corporate governance were designed to assist the company board and strengthen its ability to monitor the organization's management, and also to create shareholder value. The mission of the board was stated as follows: 'To be a strategic asset of the organization which was measured by the contribution the directors make—individually and collectively—to the long-term success of Sun Life Financial.'

Sun Life's board approved a charter that outlined its overall responsibilities, including norms for the selection, evaluation and compensation of the CEO and other senior executives. In addition the charter also specified the guidelines for: succession planning for senior positions; approving strategic plans and monitoring performance against the plans; approving the risk management framework for the enterprise; approving material transactions; and, reviewing the performance of the company. Sun Life had a Lead Director, whose responsibilities included ensuring independent management of the board. Sun Life's board had six committees, to assist in carrying out its responsibilities—members of board committees were non-management directors (Refer to Table VIII).

The board had six scheduled meetings every year with additional special meetings held whenever necessary. Most of the board committees met quarterly to discuss the company's affairs, and a yearly Directors' seminar was held to provide non-management directors with the background to and perspective on the ongoing activities. A comprehensive orientation program was also given to new directors. To promote greater alignment of interests between the non-management directors and shareholders, the board adopted a share ownership policy which required every non-management director to acquire 2,000 common shares or the number of shares equivalent to three times the value of the annual board retainer (C$ 26,000 per year), whichever was less.

In 2001, Sun Life's management adopted a charter and mission statement, revised the charters for each of the board committees and also updated the description of the post of the Lead Director. It also introduced a

---

TABLE VIII Board Committees of Sun Life Financial

Board Committee	Function
Audit Committee	It oversees the integrity of financial statements and information provided to shareholders. Checks the adequacy and effectiveness of the internal control and performance of the external auditors who are accountable to the Audit committee, the Board of Directors and the shareholders.
Conduct Review Committee	It reviews the procedures and practices of the organization in accordance with statutory requirements.
Executive Committee	It oversees matters of general policy and administration and also reviews the investment portfolios.
Governance Committee	It oversees the effectiveness of the corporate governance process and recommends nominees for election as directors. It also gives its recommendations to the Board about processes relating to Board meetings.
Management Resources Committee	It oversees the succession planning for the position of CEO and other senior management positions. It also reviews the performance of the CEO and senior management, approves their remuneration, assesses compensation policies and also oversees employee pension plans.
Risk Review Committee	It oversees the major areas of risk faced by the organization. It also approves and reviews compliance with investment, risk management and regulatory compliance policies.

Source: www.sunlife.ca

formal peer review process for directors and undertook a 'board effectiveness review' exercise.

Better Business Bureau, Inc., a public serving organization based in Eastern Massachusetts, awarded Sun Life (USA) the 2002 Torch Award for Excellence, for its corporate governance and ethical business practices. The Torch Award was intended to honor outstanding businesses that were committed to promoting ethical business practices. Sun Life was given the award for its integrity and for consistently meeting very high standards in its relationship with customers, employees, vendors/suppliers and industry peers. Sun Life won the award in the large business category (1,000–1,500 employees). It was judged on the following criteria:

- High ethical standards of behavior toward customers, suppliers, shareholders, employees, and communities in which the company does business.
- Demonstrated ethical practices surrounding its buyer/seller relationships.
- Longstanding history/reputation of ethical practices in the marketplace.
- Marketing, advertising, communications, and sales practices, which reflect a true representation of what is being offered in the marketplace.
- Acknowledgment of ethical marketplace practices by industry peers and in the communities where the company does business.
- Management practices and policies that give long-term value to shareholders, customers, employees, vendors, and surrounding communities.
- Training programs that assist employees in carrying out established ethics policies.

SOCIAL RESPONSIBILITY

Sun Life believed that corporate responsibility for a company extended beyond day-to-day business practices. It provided support for many social causes in countries where it operated. The company supported various non-profit organizations offering services in the areas of health, culture, education and environment. It also encouraged its employees to contribute generously for the victims of the September 11, 2001 terrorist attacks in the US, and offered financial help for the victims of the January 2002 earthquake in Gujarat, India.

Sun Life offered support to the 'Heroes of Hope' campaign for raising money to construct and equip the Durham region's[12] first cancer centre. The centre was staffed by professional oncologists, and was equipped with state-of-the-art technology. In 2002, Sun Life agreed to sponsor the Canadian Foundation for AIDS Research (CANFAIR)'s national campaign—'Have a Heart'. The campaign was a bilingual project, which encouraged Canada's youth to work together towards the goals of increasing awareness and prevention of AIDS, and of raising funds to support research into a cure for HIV infection.

FINANCIAL PERFORMANCE

Sun Life's revenues increased to C\$ 16.7 billion in 2001 from C\$ 16.2 billion in 2000, an increase of C\$ 483 million or 3% (Refer to Table IX for Sun Life's financial performance summary). The company's strong performance in insurance premiums and higher investment income was offset by decreases in annuity premiums and fee income. (See Exhibit II.) In 2001, ROE declined to 12.8% from 13.1% in 2000—this decrease was attributed to the increased equity base in 2001. Another reason for the decrease was that Sun Life had invested some excess funds, which had been raised for the acquisition of Keyport Financial, in low-yield short-term securities. This adversely affected the company's overall performance in 2001. Sun Life was not severely affected by the September 11 attacks, as it was not directly involved in the property and casualty insurance business, and was not involved in underwriting individual life insurance policies in the state of New York.

In 2001, the operating expenses of the company increased to C\$ 2.5 billion from C\$ 78 million in 2000. The increase was attributed to the restructuring and

Financial Performance of Sun Life (1995 to 2001)			TABLE IX		
	1997	1998	1999	2000	2001
Assets Under Management (C\$ billion)	186.2	250.6	301.3	328.5	351.7
Shareholders' Net Income (C\$ in million)	–	719.0	649.0	792.0	882.0
ROE	12.5	12.0	11.7	13.1	12.8
Total Capitalization (C\$ billion)	7.3	7.8	7.2	8.1	10.4

Source: Company Annual Report, 2001.

EXHIBIT II   Consolidated Statement of Operations

(in millions of Canadian dollars, except for per share amount) Years ended December 31	2001	2000	1999
Revenue:			
Premium income:			
Annuities	$ 4,196	$ 4,371	$ 3,494
Life Insurance	3,749	3,455	3,332
Health Insurance	1,409	1,287	1,196
	9,354	9,113	8,022
Net investment income	4,120	3,776	4,113
Fee income	3,215	3,317	2,606
	16,689	16,206	14,741
Policy Benefits and Expenses			
Payments to policyholders, beneficiaries and depositors			
Maturities and surrenders	2,604	2,267	2,864
Annuity payments	952	1,076	923
Death and disability benefits	1,197	1,048	1,005
Health benefits	1,091	1,041	980
Policyholder dividends and interest on claims and deposits	960	1,040	1,206
	6,804	6,472	6,978
Net transfers to segregated funds	2,606	2,562	2,327
Increase in actuarial liabilities	1,660	1,604	874
Commissions	1,577	1,612	1,276
Operating expenses	2,511	2,433	2,240
Premium taxes	113	116	87
Interest expense	168	159	161
	15,439	14,958	13,943
Operating Income before Income Taxes and Non-Controlling Interests	1,250	1,248	798
Income taxes	301	379	418
Non-controlling interests in net income of subsidiaries	68	67	46
Net Income from Continuing Operations	881	802	334
Loss from discontinued operations, net of income taxes	—	—	170
Total Net Income	881	802	164
Less:			
Net income from mutual operations (prior to demutualization)	—	179	164
Participating policyholders' net income (loss) after demutualization	(1)	(6)	—
Shareholders' Net Income (after Demutualization)	$882	$629	$ —
Basic earnings per share	$2.08	$629[T]	$ —
Diluted earnings per share	$2.07	$1.48[T]	

[T] Basic and diluted earnings per share cover period from March 22 to December 31, 2000.

Source: Company Annual Report, 2001.

outsourcing activities of the UK operations, the acquisition of Keyport Financial and the unfavorable impact of currency translation. The money for the acquisition was raised through an IPO of C$ 500 million. In 2001, the company also adopted new accounting standards and policies, but these did not have any significant impact on the company's financial results. Investor Relations[13] magazine selected Sun Life for the Best Investor Relations Award for an IPO. The magazine surveyed around 250 fund managers, analysts, retail brokers and investors in order to select the winner. (See Exhibit III.)

Sun Life had good ratings from various independent-rating agencies for its financial strength. It was placed among the top companies in the financial services sector in North America. The ratings indicated the group's extremely strong consolidated capital, strong business profile, and strong operating performance. It was ranked 'very strong' by S&P, Moody's ranked it as a company with 'excellent financial security', while A. M. Best rated it 'very strong' (Refer to Table X).

Sun Life was converted into a shareholder company from a mutually held company,[14] in 2000, after policy owners voted for its demutualisation. After this, it was listed on the New York, Toronto, London and Philippines stock exchanges. By 2001, Sun Life's total capitalization increased to C$ 10,405 billion from C$ 8,166 billion in 2000. (See Exhibit IV.)

FUTURE OUTLOOK

With the acquisition of Keyport, IFMG and Clarica, Sun Life emerged as one of the largest players in the North American insurance markets in 2002. The company's management stated that it would strive to consolidate its business operations and achieve its objective of being among the top ten players in the North American market. Analysts pointed out that with the enactment of new financial services legislation in Canada in late 2001, consolidation in the industry would increase, and by 2004, the Canadian insurance market would be dominated by only three or four players.

Analysts felt that the acquisition of Clarica would help Sun Life in consolidating its position in the Canadian market. However, they pointed out that integration of the operations would be very critical. Agreeing with this observation, Sun Life stated that it would try to consolidate its position through operational efficiencies and financial strength.

Analysts also felt that in order to consolidate its position in the Canadian and international markets, the company would have to focus on building stronger customer relations through its innovative and value-added products and services. It was also pointed out that the company would have to focus on operational efficiencies and capital optimization in order to enhance its financial performance. In line with its decision to exit from non-profitable markets, Sun Life had exited from the UK individual insurance business, and had initiated cost savings measures on a large scale.

In its Asian operations, Sun Life identified India and China as growing markets, and planned to increase its exposure in those markets with more investments. According to insurance industry observers, Sun Life projected a positive outlook for the year 2002 and beyond. This was largely because the North American insurance industry was expected to turn around soon with the changing business cycle.

THE GLOBAL LIFE INSURANCE INDUSTRY

Insurance is essentially a social device to reduce or eliminate risk of loss to life and property. A large number of people form an association that shares risks attached to individuals. The risks, which can be insured against, include fire, the perils of sea, death, accidents and burglary. Any risk contingent upon these may be insured against at a premium commensurate with the risk involved.

The insurance business is divided into 1) life insurance and 2) non-life (general) insurance, which includes fire, marine, social, and various other forms of insurance. The life insurance industry across the world has evolved over many decades based on the principle of insurance being a collective bearing of risk, which offers individuals an opportunity to protect themselves.

Ratings of Sun Life	TABLE X
Rating Agency	**Rating**
Standard & Poor's	AA+* (second of 21 rating levels)
Moody's	Aa2** (third of 21 rating levels)
A. M. Best	A+ (first of 16 rating levels)
Fitch	AAA*** (first of 24 rating levels)

*With negative outlook
**With positive outlook
***Credit watch negative

Source: Company Annual Report, 2001.

Exhibit III   Consolidated Statements of Cash Flows

(in millions of Canadian dollars) Years ended December 31	2001	2000	1999
Cash Flows Provided by (Used in) Operating Activities			
Net income from continuing operations	$ 881	$ 802	$ 334
Items not affecting cash:			
Increase in actuarial and other policy related liabilities	1,389	1,494	1,226
Amortization of:			
Net deferred realized and unrealized gains on investments	(445)	(543)	(620)
Goodwill and deferred acquisition costs	324	283	252
(Gain) or loss on sale of subsidiaries	(195)	5	(25)
Future income taxes	42	82	79
Provisions for losses on investments	4	104	30
Other changes in other assets and liabilities	259	836	797
New mutual fund business acquisition costs capitalized	(296)	(506)	(504)
Redemption fees of mutual funds	105	101	95
Net cash provided by operating activities	2,068	2,658	1,664
Cash Flows Provided by (Used in) Financing Activities			
Borrowed funds	(104)	(294)	432
Payments to certain participating policyholders and underwriters	(29)	(658)	–
Issuance of common shares	330	844	–
Issuance of Sun Life Exchangeable Capital Securities— Series A	950	–	–
Purchase and cancellation of common shares	(35)	–	–
Dividends paid on common shares	(204)	(51)	–
Net cash provided by (used in) financing activities	908	(159)	432
Cash Flows Provided by (Used in) Investing Activities			
Sales, maturities and repayment of:			
Bonds	13,379	9,604	10,188
Mortgages	1,424	1,566	2,506
Stocks	3,241	3,807	2,721
Real estate	240	378	221
Purchases of:			
Bonds	(13,833)	(11,848)	(10,695)
Mortgages	(2,001)	(1,771)	(2,877)
Stocks	(3,278)	(3,190)	(2,458)
Real estate	(118)	(282)	(230)
Policy loans	(88)	(46)	(75)
Short-term securities	(255)	(461)	(475)
Other investments	(319)	30	(321)
Acquisitions, net of cash acquired	(1,825)	–	(43)

(in millions of Canadian dollars)
Years ended December 31

	2001	2000	1999
Disposals, net of cash disposed of	$ 363	$ 160	$ 60
Net cash used in investing activities	(3,070)	(2,053)	(1,478)
Net cash provided by discontinued operations	6	23	47
Changes due to fluctuations in exchange rates	168	36	(132)
Increase in cash and cash equivalents	80	505	533
Cash and cash equivalents, beginning of year	2,503	1,998	1,465
Cash and cash equivalents, end of year	2,583	2,503	1,998
Short-term securities, end of year	2,226	1,459	1,445
Cash, cash equivalents and short–term securities, end of year	$ 4,809	$ 3,962	$ 3,443
Supplementary Information			
Cash and Cash equivalents:			
Cash	$ 396	$ 476	$ 698
Cash equivalents	2,187	2,027	1,300
	$ 2,583	$ 2,508	$ 1,998
Cash disbursement made for:			
Interest on borrowed funds, subordinated debt and cumulative capital securities	$167	$159	$161
Income taxes, net of refunds	$269	$357	$76

Source: Company Annual Report 2001.

Stock Price Chart (1999–2002) Exhibit IV

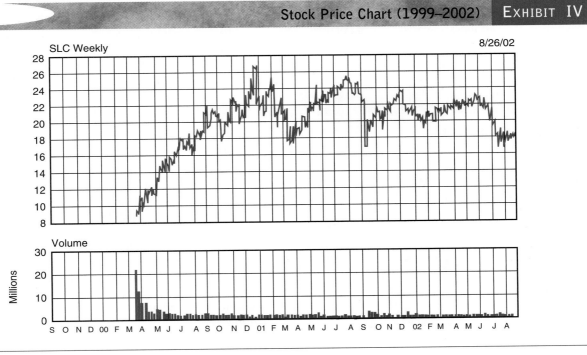

SLC Weekly 8/26/02

Source: www.bigcharts.com

According to a survey conducted by Swiss Re,[15] during 1990–2000, total world insurance premiums increased by 72.8%, and in the same period, the life insurance business grew by 104.6%. In 2000, life insurance accounted for 62% of the total worldwide premiums while non-life accounted for the remaining 38%. The total premiums worldwide in 2000 were $2,244.3 billion and North America constituted the largest market for the insurance industry. It contributed around 37.32% of the total premiums in 2000.

US emerged as the largest market for insurance in 2000 with total premiums of $865.3 billion, followed by Japan with $504 billion. According to analysts, with reforms having been initiated in the insurance sector in China and India, they had emerged as the largest and most attractive markets for many global players (Refer to Tables XI and XII).

In the late-1990s, the global insurance industry underwent great upheavals. The changes in the industry included—new channels for distribution of insurance products; consolidation in insurance markets across the world; globalization; new technology; and, changes in regulations for the industry. During this period there was a spate of acquisitions, takeovers and mergers, in many parts of the world. According to industry watchers, only companies with a huge capital base would be able to achieve global dominance and establish presence in all the lines of the highly competitive industry. However, it was also being felt that with the falling stock markets in many countries, it would be very difficult for companies to raise money for acquisition/merger/takeover deals to establish themselves as big players.

Companies that focused on their areas of core competency were likely to emerge as the most successful. Analysts expected that outsourcing of non-core activities would increase and there would also be an increasing number of strategic alliances with financial services and non-financial services companies in the future.

The Internet was expected to become a strong channel for the distribution of simple products in the insurance industry. But some analysts pointed out that distribution in the insurance industry was 'self selected' by consumers and in the Internet age it would be difficult to retain customers. On the other hand, it was expected that the Internet would support complex business models by integrating all methods of distribution, besides reducing costs for companies and simplifying the claims-management process.

Advancements in health care were helping extend the lifespan of people across the globe. At the same time, in several countries, governments were withdrawing from providing extensive health care facilities to citizens. These factors fuelled the growth of the products relating to savings for retirement and health care. Although conventional life insurance products continued to dominate the market, analysts expected that there would be rapid growth in wealth management products, which gave the consumer a wide investment choice. In the US, it was expected that life insurance would be linked with investment choice and fund management. Also, many life insurance agents were expected to become personal financial planners.

Most importantly, insurance markets were being deregulated worldwide, leading to the emergence of universal financial services rather than the conventional stand-alone banks, insurers and brokerage firms. This seemed to affect the Asian industries the most, particularly those in Malaysia and Singapore. Simultaneously, there were more regulations regarding the way products could be sold. An analyst at Price Waterhouse Coopers said, "There is a shift from regulation of what is sold by a particular institution to regulation of how it is sold." Many countries were forming regulatory bodies for this purpose, such as the Financial Services Authority in the UK, APRA in Australia and IRDA in India.

Many analysts felt that national borders were no longer important in the industry—labor-intensive tasks were being shifted to low-wage countries, using the Internet. Many US companies shifted service centers to Canada in order to reduce processing costs. Claims management, policy administration, accounting and underwriting were the processes most suited to this kind of relocation. Many European companies were establishing back-office operations in countries like India.

TABLE XI	Top 10 Markets	
(Total premiums, in $ billion)		
Country	1999	2000
United States	688.5	865.3
Japan	490.6	504.0
United Kingdom	158.0	237.0
Germany	136.7	123.7
France	128.9	121.9
South Korea	56.7	58.3
Italy	47.7	63.1
Canada	46.3	46.6
Netherlands	34.2	36.5

Source: www.bimaonline.com

Rank	Company	Revenues[2] (in $ millions)	Country
1	AXA	92,782	France
2	ING Group	71,196	Netherlands
3	Nippon Life Insurance	68,055	Japan
4	CGNU	61,499	UK
5	Assicurazioni Generali	53,333	Italy
6	Dai-ichi Mutual Life Insurance	46,436	Japan
7	Prudential	43,126	UK
8	TIAA-CREF	38,064	U.S.
9	Sumitomo Life Insurance	37,536	Japan
10	MetLife	31,947	U.S.

[1]Includes stock and mutual companies.

[2]Revenue includes premium and annuity income, investment income and capital gains or losses, but excludes deposits; includes consolidated subsidiaries; excludes excise taxes

Source: Fortune.

The importance of branding came to be strongly established. Brands for financial services, including insurance products, came to be promoted as strongly as brands for consumer product brands such as Coca-Cola or Levi's. Many global companies, such as Allianz, AXA and ING, were establishing their own brand names across the world. Companies like Sun Life (in Canada), HSBC (in Hong Kong) and Tokio Marine and Fire in Japan, which had very strong domestic brands, were now concentrating on building up a global brand.

THE CANADIAN LIFE INSURANCE INDUSTRY

Canada, like the US, is a high-tech industrialized country. Its market-oriented economic system, pattern of production, and high living standards are points of similarity with the US. Canada had an annual growth rate of 3% on average since 1993. In the same period, unemployment was falling and government budget surpluses were being diverted to the reduction of public sector debt. There was a dramatic increase in trade and economic integration with the US due to the 1989 US-Canada Free Trade Agreement and the 1994 North American Free Trade Agreement (which included Mexico).

The Canadian insurance market consisted of about 230 private property and casualty insurers, and 27 providers of insurance for life and accident and sickness. In the general insurance category, automobile insurance constituted the largest single class of general insurance in Canada followed by property insurance and liability insurance. Federal and provisional governments governed general insurance operations in the country. The life insurance and health insurance market was divided into: life insurance, retirement and investment products, and health insurance products.

The Canadian life and health insurance industry comprised 117 firms—107 publicly traded companies and 10 mutual companies. As in the insurance industry in other countries, the Canadian life insurance industry was also undergoing consolidation mainly through the sale of firms by foreign insurers to Canadian insurance companies. The top five companies held approximately 57% of the Canadian life and health insurance market. It was reported that Canadian-controlled firms were gaining market share while the share of foreign insurers was declining.

Insurance in Canada was distributed through full-time career agents, who represented a single company, and also through independent agents, who sold the products of several insurers. Both career and independent agents were paid commissions on sales. Career agents usually received additional payments such as pension benefits and access to employer-paid training. In Canada, though most individual insurance products were sold through agents, other distribution channels, such as telephone and mail solicitation, and sales through the Internet, were gaining acceptance fast. Total premium income in 1999 was $39.4 billion, of which the life insurance business contributed around

27%. (See Exhibit V.) Total premium income increased by 9.7% in 1999, above the annual average rate of 6.4% over the 1990s. Besides Sun Life, the other strong players in the Canadian life insurance market were Manulife, Great-West, Canada Life and Industrial Alliance. In 1997, the Canadian government formed a task force on the financial services industry for restructuring the regulatory environment of the financial services industry to make it more competitive. In line with the recommendations of the task force, the government allowed mutual companies to go in for demutualization. This was considered an important turning point in the country's insurance industry. According to analysts, this decision allowed the insurance industry to move towards consolidation. Companies could now expand their international operations through money raised in the capital markets.

By the end of 2000, there were around 120 life and health insurance companies in Canada. Canadian companies held $267.1 billion in assets on behalf of Canadian life and health insurance policyholders. Most of the funds with Canadian life insurers were invested in government bonds, corporate bonds, stocks and mutual funds. In 2000, it was reported that Canadian health and life insurers generated $49.1 billion in revenues from foreign clients for life insurance, health insurance and annuities and according to reports, 12.6 million people in more than 120 countries outside Canada owned life policies with Canadian companies.

In 2001, Bill C-8 was passed by the Canadian parliament. This bill would increase the competitive flexibility of life and health insurers through various enhancements including the ability to set up holding companies, and access to the national payments system.

NOTES

1. In August 2002, 1 C$ equaled 0.64 US $.
2. Reinsurance is defined as the process through which an insurance company shares the risk involved in a policy by reinsuring with multiple insurers in order to reduce the risk.
3. Through demutualisation, a company held by its policyholders is converted into a company with common shares. The company's net worth is distributed to policyholders in exchange for their membership rights.
4. Clarica is one of the leading financial services companies in Canada with more than 4 million customers offering a diversified range of financial services. It has the largest sales and service force in Canada.
5. Manulife is a leading Canada based financial services company offering a diversified range of financial protection products and wealth management services. It is the second largest player in the individual life insurance market based on annualized premiums.
6. An annuity is a tax-deferred contract with an insurance company in which contributions are invested to provide a stream of income at a later date. The investment may be variable or fixed, and payouts can be deferred or immediate. Variable annuities invest the accumulated contribution of investors in high-yield assets with a relatively higher level of risk. It is a kind of a personal retirement account in which money grows tax-deferred until it is withdrawn.
7. Actuarial liabilities include estimated future premiums and net investment income for covering the outstanding claims, future benefits, policyholders' dividends, taxes and expenses on in-force policies.
8. Berkshire was established 1986 and provided a full range of investment and insurance products and services to the clients of independent financial advisors.
9. Hub Financial Inc. is one of the leading Canadian insurance brokerage companies providing life and health insurance for independent financial advisors.
10. IQON is one of Canada's leading financial services organizations that runs a network of independent financial advisors. IQON advisors are independent financial advisors who do not sell proprietary insurance products but offer unbiased advice to the consumer regarding the insurance products.
11. A bancassurance agreement can be defined as an agreement between an insurance company and a bank for selling insurance products through banking channels.
12. Durham is a highly developed and populated economic centre of Ontario stretching from Ottawa to Niagara Falls. Durham lies to the east of Toronto.
13. A London-based magazine reporting on the investor relations of various companies.
14. A company held by the participating policyholders.
15. Swiss Reinsurance Company (Swiss Re) based in Zurich was founded in 1863 and provides services of risk transfer, risk financing and asset management to its clients.

(in millions of Canadian Dollars)	2001	2000	1999	1998	1997	1996	1995	1994
Assets (as on December 31)								
General Fund Assets [1]	80,327	55,010	54,241	54,319	49,700	45,709	42,382	40,297
Segregated Fund Assets [1]	48,544	49,533	46,524	39,213	30,519	26,250	23,709	20,313
Other Assets Under Management	222,875	223,990	200,538	157,074	106,035	69,820	57,196	46,465
Total Assets Under Management	351,747	328,533	301,303	250,606	186,254	141,779	123,287	107,075
TOTAL EQUITY [1]	7,725	6,517	5,690	6,081	5,175	5,152	4,868	4,576
Operating Results (for the Year Ended December 31)								
Revenue								
Premiums								
Annuities	4,196	4,371	3,494	2,409	2,488	1,916	2,241	2,409
Life Insurance	3,749	3,455	3,332	3,313	2,955	2,822	2,658	2,418
Health Insurance	1,409	1,287	1,196	1,110	1,602	994	941	789
Total Premiums	9,354	9,113	8,022	6,832	6,505	5,732	5,840	5,616
Net Investment Income	4,120	3,776	4,113	4,035	3,788	3,482	3,408	2,759
Fee Income	3,215	3,317	2,606	2,014	1,427	1,107	830	679
Total Revenue	16,689	16,206	14,741	12,881	11,720	10,321	10,078	9,054
Payments to Policyholders, Beneficiaries and Depositors[2]	9,410	9,034	9,305	8,492	7,620	6,459	6,242	4,676
Increase in Actuarial Liabilities	1,660	1,604	874	480	697	928	1,238	2,141
Commissions and Expenses	4,201	4,161	3,603	3,027	2,528	2,132	1,947	1,798
Interest Expenses	168	159	161	182	145	95	68	29
Income Taxes	301	379	418	274	201	221	177	120
Non-controlling interests in Net Income of Subsidiaries	68	67	46	24	8	–	–	–
Net Operating Income	881	802	334	142	521	486	406	290
Confederation Life Goodwill Write-off	–	–	–	260	–	–	–	–
Net income from Continuing Operations	881	802	334	142	521	486	406	290
Loss/(Net Income) for Discontinued Operations, net of income taxes	–	–	170	88	10	(4)	(1)	(14)
Total Net Income	881	802	164	54	511	490	407	304
Business Statistics								
Life Insurance in Force [3]	607,801	561,389	673,322	670,094	588,773	514,337	476,657	421,082
Mutual Fund Sales	39,466	45,614	38,123	33,849	18,791	13,150	7,453	6,628
Managed Fund Sales [4]	31,953	25,869	13,939	12,255	10,304	3,860	3,448	3,324
Segregated Fund Deposits	5,851	8,318	4,137	4,345	3,430	3,719	3,619	2,174
Employees	11,787	11,328	11,406	10,717	10,200	9,750	9,150	9,150

[1] The 1999 and 2000 amounts were restated in 2001 as a result of the adoption, in October 2001, of the new Canadian standards of practice issued by the Canadian Institute of Actuaries for the valuation of policy liabilities of life insurers.
[2] Includes net transfers to segregated funds.
[3] Includes reinsurance assumed.
[4] Includes inter-company sales.

Source: Company Annual Report, 2001.

Sylvan Learning Systems, Inc.

case thirty

Kemi Ashaye
Diane Cotts
Doug Gray
Belinda Perry

Sylvan Learning Systems, an organization that provides educational and instructional services to students of all ages and skill levels, faced challenges as it moved into the 21st century. Despite a dominant brand presence, recent cost increases from acquisitions contributed to declining earnings performance. In 1999 net losses totaled $15 million, and sales of profitable business divisions prevented the company from reporting net losses in 2000. In addition to earnings challenges, Sylvan's acquisition strategies from 1998 to 2000 did not appear to coincide with the capabilities and competencies that built the Sylvan brand. Sylvan's franchise business model allowed the company to operate with low overhead and capitalize on expertise of local owners. Additionally, Sylvan capitalized on a niche segment of a fragmented education market. Recent acquisitions and franchise purchases, however, appeared to be contrary to Sylvan's successful structure and niche strategy. As a result of its financial performance and strategic decisions, Sylvan's share price declined by over 50 percent during 1999 and 2000.

Douglas Becker, Sylvan Learning Systems chairman and CEO, responded to these challenges by presenting a new vision for the company that focused on "the transformation of Sylvan into a consumer-oriented company focused on the high-growth areas of the global education marketplace in postsecondary and K–12 education."[1] During 2000, management worked to restructure the organization to build on Sylvan's dominant brand in K–12 supplementary education. Additionally, aggressive acquisition strategies were implemented to expand Sylvan's position in the postsecondary market segment. Both supported management's additional objectives of "developing an international business that matches the company's U.S. presence."[2] Becker's hope was that acquiring complementary business lines in international markets and pioneering innovative education-related technology initiatives would result in improved future financial performance.

In the wake of Becker's announcement to shareholders about Sylvan's restructuring efforts, Sylvan faced a crossroads leading to difficult questions. Would the strategic reorganization of Sylvan in 2000 prepare the company for changing market dynamics in domestic and international markets? Would the acquisition of international universities be consistent with core competencies and lead to stronger financial performance? Would overseas expansion alone allow for increased profitability? These and other issues faced Sylvan's top management team. To address these questions, the following sections of this case have been compiled. First, the history of Sylvan is discussed to provide background. Second, Sylvan's organizational development, acquisitions and divestitures, and financial performance are reviewed. Next, the role of the education industry as a whole is summarized. Finally, Sylvan's organization and key businesses are explained, along with an overview of its competitors.

HISTORY AND CORPORATE LEADERSHIP

As in any organization, personal experiences of Sylvan's leaders played a significant role in the historical development of Sylvan's successful business lines and corporate activities. By capitalizing on the strengths of each leader, Sylvan itself became a leader in the education services industry.

1979–1985: W. BERRY FOWLER

With an investment of $14,500, W. Berry Fowler opened the first Sylvan Learning Center in 1979.[3] Fowler, a

This case is intended to be used as the basis for class discussion rather than to illustrate either effective or ineffective handling of an administrative or strategic situation. We appreciate the direction of Professor Robert E. Hoskisson in the development of this case. Reprinted by permission.

mediocre student, was able to complete college only after receiving tutoring help to improve his subpar reading abilities. After a couple of other entrepreneurial ventures, Fowler acted on the need to augment educational services offered by the public school systems. As a former teacher, Fowler hoped to prevent other students from falling short academically. His supplemental education business was designed to fill learning gaps experienced by students. During his six-year tenure, Fowler developed the franchise business model, training programs, educational programs, and teaching methodology that provided Sylvan with a competitive advantage in the education industry. As one writer noted, Sylvan was "poised to carve out a hefty slice of what business people refer to as the $300 billion education industry."[4] In 1985, after molding the process and direction of Sylvan Learning Centers, Fowler sold the business to KinderCare for a $5 million profit.

1985–1991: KINDERCARE

Under KinderCare ownership, Sylvan grew from 100 tutoring centers to over 300. In 1988, 50 percent of Sylvan was acquired by KEE, a software company owned by Doug Becker and Chris Hoehn-Saric. By 1991, the two took over management of Sylvan and moved the headquarters to Columbia, Maryland. Very little change in Sylvan's business model, materials, or methodology took place during the KinderCare years.

1991–PRESENT: BECKER AND HOEHN-SARIC

Douglas Becker and Christopher Hoehn-Saric were entrepreneurs and best friends who met while they were employees at the same Baltimore-area ComputerLand store.[5] In 1983, the pair (ages 17 and 21, respectively), along with three other friends, developed LifeCard, a credit-card-sized device used to store a person's medical history. Two years later, the group became millionaires following the sale of LifeCard to Blue Cross and Blue Shield of Maryland.[6] After this sale, Becker and Hoehn-Saric purchased some software development companies. One of these companies, KEE, was used to acquire Sylvan. Initially, Becker and Hoehn-Saric bought 50 percent of Sylvan Learning Corp. from KinderCare, Inc. On the advice of a friend, they decided to see if they could "do something" with it.[7] Seeing many similarities between the health-care industry and the education industry regarding the potential role of the private sector, Becker and Hoehn-Saric decided to commit to the development of Sylvan.

While Becker served officially as president and Hoehn-Saric as CEO, both used the same word to describe their roles: "interchangeable."[8] Both individuals had received quality secondary education at Gilman, a renowned boys' prep academy in Baltimore. In 1984, Becker chose to continue with entrepreneurial opportunities rather than attend Harvard Business School. Hoehn-Saric dropped out of Johns Hopkins for the same reason. Both men provided vision and entrepreneurial creativity to the development of Sylvan. While Becker received most of the credit for Sylvan's success during the 1990s, both contributed to its expansion and success.

In 1993 many key developments took place at Sylvan. First, Sylvan purchased its single largest supplementary educational services competitor, Britannica Learning Centers. Second, it partnered with the Baltimore City Public Schools to provide education to disadvantaged students. This strategy placed Sylvan in six public elementary schools. Sylvan's success at this level soon led to additional partnering in schools across the nation. In 1993, when Sylvan Learning Systems, Inc. (NASDAQ: SLVN) became a publicly traded company, its corporate staff had grown to about 500.

ORGANIZATIONAL DEVELOPMENT

Sylvan's organization changed as the company grew. The founder, Mr. Fowler, developed a set of competencies that fostered success for Sylvan. The foundational principle for Sylvan was the use of positive reinforcement to reward students for mastery of material. As students completed assignments during a tutoring session, they would receive tokens or other similar rewards. After accumulating a sufficient number of tokens, the students could redeem them for merchandise at the Sylvan store, which contained various toys, books, or other fun objects.[9] Fowler believed that the use of positive reinforcement would make learning fun for children and in the process students would learn at a faster rate. Speed was critical to parents who wanted their children to perform well in school.

In addition to using positive reinforcement, Fowler developed materials designed to fill in "learning gaps" in a student's educational background. When a student arrived at Sylvan for the first time, directors of education (DEs) administered diagnostic tests for reading and math that would indicate skills in which the student lacked proficiency. DEs then tailored a program to that student with the goal of closing those skill gaps. Fowler was so certain of the program that he began implementing guarantees of success. If a student testing below grade level failed to improve by one grade level after 36 hours of instruction, then the student would receive an additional 12 hours of instruction at no charge. This approach to bringing students back in line with peers placed Sylvan in a complementary position with public school systems. Fowler was quick to point out, "We're [Sylvan] not here to compete, we're here to complement." He recognized that public school referrals were a significant source of Sylvan's business.[10]

An additional strength created under Fowler's leadership was the development of the franchise business model. Fowler lacked the capital to expand by opening new centers. Instead, he decided to sell franchises to other individuals who had the funds available. By 1985, 100 franchised centers were opened with about 140 franchises sold. The typical franchise fee was approximately $27,500. In addition, franchise owners would pay approximately $37,500 to $57,500 for advertising, materials, supplies, and furniture.[11] This business model allowed Fowler to develop the materials and brand recognition of Sylvan without focusing on the logistics of expansion. This type of franchising has remained the dominant model for Sylvan Learning Centers.

Becker and Hoehn-Saric brought new capabilities to Sylvan, the most critical of which was an entrepreneurial spirit. In the corporate office, Sylvan was no longer exclusively committed to the franchise approach to growing learning centers. Rather, Sylvan's strategic focus expanded beyond K–12 education and U.S. markets. This was evident in the adult education, corporate training, and English language businesses acquired during the early 1990s. Tapping earlier experiences with LifeCard and software businesses, the pair displayed proficiency in identifying strategically important companies and developing partnerships or acquiring the companies. Their acquisition strategy allowed Sylvan to meet its international growth objectives. The market recognized the duo's abilities and, as such, share prices increased sharply during this period.

Becker and Hoehn-Saric also had connections that provided access to both debt and equity markets. During the early years of Sylvan, capital was not sufficient to expand corporate activities, so Becker and Hoehn-Saric used their understanding of the financial markets both in function and in practice to obtain funding for a variety of activities. Sylvan's initial public offering in 1993 provided the needed equity to develop the company's diversified business lines. Becker and Hoehn-Saric's resourcefulness gave Sylvan a first-mover advantage in the education industry.[12]

In 1998, Becker changed Sylvan's vision. He stated, "Every couple of years I can see us spinning off a company. I want Sylvan to be a generator for the education industry."[13] With this new vision, Sylvan's corporate strategy shifted to focus on expanding globally within the education industry through acquisitions. Sylvan acquired businesses in complementary areas when opportunities arose and spun businesses off when they matured. The Sylvan vision maintained two key guiding principles: to provide high-quality education and to look to the future in order to prevent missed opportunities.

SYLVAN ACQUISITIONS AND DIVESTITURES

As the company developed and corporate strategy changed, Sylvan's method of growth changed. During the first 14 years of business, Sylvan expanded from within, but now its expansion strategy shifted to procuring related acquisitions. Beginning in 1993, the company made significant acquisitions as part of its competitive strategy in the education industry. In 1995, Sylvan's acquisition of Drake Prometric combined with a 1991 deal to make Sylvan the exclusive commercial testing partner for Educational Testing Services (ETS) and helped make testing services Sylvan's key moneymaker.[14] The company expanded its adult education activities in 1996 by buying the Wall Street Institute (WSI), an English language instruction company, and forming a joint venture (Caliber) with MCI Communications to provide professional education.[15] Caliber went public in 1998, and Sylvan retained a 9 percent stake. In 1997, the company purchased Block Testing Services L.P., Block State Testing Services, and the outstanding shares of National Assessment Institute, Inc. ("NAI block").[16] These companies were involved in designing, marketing, and administering paper tests for licensing of individuals. Sylvan paid for the acquisition by issuing common stock worth $24.6 million.[17]

Sylvan extended its reach with a string of acquisitions in 1998, including Aspect International Language Schools and Canter Group (training and staff development for educators).[18] Its acquisition of Schulerhilfe brought 900 international learning centers in Austria, Germany, and Italy under the company's umbrella.[19] Sylvan International Universities (SIU) was launched in 1999, with an acquisition of 54 percent in the Universidad Europea de Madrid, a private, for-profit university in Spain.[20] In November 2000, the company added three global universities to its network: Universidad del Valle de Mexico, Universidad de las Americas (60 percent, Chile), and Gesthotel SA Hotel Management School (Switzerland), also known as "Les Roches" (100 percent).

In 2000, Sylvan announced it would launch an Internet investment company with several partners. It also joined a consortium and created a new company that provided elementary and high schools with mobile computing infrastructures. Sylvan contributed about $30 million to own approximately 42 percent of the organization, MindSurf.[21] During 2000, Sylvan Learning Centers completed its acquisition of Ivy West, a provider of instructor-led college admission test preparation.[22] In February 2001, Sylvan Ventures made an investment of 41 percent in Walden University, a pioneer in distance-learning education.[23] The purpose of the acquisition was to develop Sylvan's position in the emerging distance-learning market.

To reduce overhead and debt associated with its various acquisitions, management elected to divest business segments that were unrelated to core business lines or that were not considered opportunities for future expansion. During 1999, the company sold PACE group, a corporate consulting, training, and development firm.[24] In March 2000, the company opted to sell 100 percent of Prometric, the testing company, to The Thomson Corporation (Canada) for about $775 million.[25] This divestiture marked a significant change in strategy for Sylvan. Testing would no longer compose a primary revenue source for the company.

Sylvan announced the sale of Aspect in September 2000 following an earlier Chapter 11 bankruptcy. Aspect, a subsidiary of SEL, offered English language immersion programs to college students. The sale was completed in October 2000 for $22 million in cash. In addition, Virtual University Enterprises, Inc. (Bloomington, MN) acquired the Smarts education center management system from Sylvan for an undisclosed amount. Finally, the Internet-based Zapme! was sold in 2000 at a loss of $11.4 million.[26] Zapme! was one of the venture capital investments under the newly created Sylvan Ventures subsidiary. The company was designed to provide private, secure networks to schools, but it drew harsh criticism for exploiting teachers and students through unwanted online advertising.[27]

FINANCIAL PERFORMANCE

While management aggressively pursued an acquisition strategy expanding into related customer and business segments, low earnings performance created challenges. Sylvan's revenues grew significantly following its IPO in 1993. In the same year, revenues totaled $18.1 million and net losses $300,000. The following year, revenues doubled to $39.6 million and earnings improved as net income totaled $2.8 million. Sylvan Prometric was a significant contributor to improved earnings performance between 1993 and 1997 due to increased utilization of GRE, GMAT, and TOEFL testing services. In 1997, this segment contributed $64 million of the $81 million revenue increase. Corporate net income before extraordinary items grew to a high of $27.9 million in 1997. (See Exhibit 1 for Financials before restatement.)

Between 1997 and 2000, revenues increased sharply, but operating income began to dwindle (see Exhibit 1).[28] The declining profitability was the result of Sylvan's shift in corporate strategy. Prior to 1998, Sylvan grew primarily through increases in both domestic and international franchising. Under the franchise business model, Sylvan's costs were low due to low levels of fixed assets and related costs. Beginning in 1998, Sylvan's strategy shifted to rapid growth via multiple acquisitions. These acquisitions created significant depreciation and operating expenses. In Learning Centers and SEL centers, costs increased due to corporate acquisition of former franchise centers, which operated at lower margins.[29] Losses from Sylvan Ventures also contributed to deteriorating earnings performance. By 2000, Sylvan's earnings performance resulted in net losses (before extraordinary items). Management acquired substantial debt (up by $134 million in 1999) to finance acquisitions. Consequently, interest expense increased to $18.8 million in 2000, resulting in a net loss before tax of $5.9 million. Profitability was salvaged only through multiple divestitures of profitable businesses, as the company funded its new acquisitions through old business line divestitures.

At the beginning of December 1993, Sylvan's stock traded at $4.89 per share. The stock performed extremely well from 1994 through 1998, reaching a high of $33.50 per share in February 1999. Following poor earnings performance and divestiture of profitable business lines, Sylvan's stock fell to $11.93 per share in December 1999. By the end of 2000, the stock price remained low at $13.92 per share (see Exhibit 2 for a chart of trended stock performance).

TRENDS IN THE EDUCATION INDUSTRY

Sylvan's former profitability testifies to the fact that there is indeed profit to be made in the education industry. It is not surprising that, with frustration growing toward the nation's public education systems and with new technology and investment opportunities, a number of alternatives to the public school system have surfaced over the last decade. Education entrepreneurs, companies, and investors have seized opportunities during the past decade to develop this industry. In January 2000, Michael Sandler of Eduventures.com noted, "Right now, the education industry is a collection of private companies. As companies enter the public market in increasing numbers, we are witnessing the formation of an industry."[30] The efforts of education entrepreneurs sparked the evolution of an increasingly competitive collection of education companies during the 1990s.[31]

EXHIBIT 1

Annual Income Statement

In Millions of U.S. Dollars (except for per share items)	12/31/2000	12/31/1999 Restated 12/31/2000	12/31/1998 Restated 12/31/2000	12/31/1997 Restated 12/31/1999	12/31/1996 Restated 12/31/1998
Revenue	316.7	277.0	178.8	170.6	220.0
Other Revenue	–	–	–	–	–
Total Revenue	316.7	277.0	178.8	170.6	220.0
Cost of Revenue	270.6	220.6	134.1	148.9	187.8
Gross Profit	46.0	56.4	44.7	21.6	32.2
Selling/General/Administrative Expenses	20.3	26.9	15.5	19.7	8.0
Research and Development	–	–	–	–	–
Depreciation/Amortization	–	–	–	–	–
Interest Expense (Income), Net Operating	–	–	–	–	–
Unusual Expense (Income)	–	3.6	3.2	–	–
Other Operating Expenses	18.2	–	–	–	–
Total Operating Expense	309.1	251.0	152.9	168.6	195.9
Operating Income	7.5	26.0	25.9	1.9	24.1
Interest Expense, Net Non-Operating	(7.3)	(4.0)	(0.3)	(0.5)	(1.3)
Interest/Investment Income, Non-Operating	(11.4)	–	–	–	–
Interest Income (Expense), Net Non-Operating	(18.8)	(4.0)	(0.3)	(0.5)	(1.3)
Gain (Loss) on Sale of Assets	–	(13.4)	–	–	–
Other, Net	5.3	(1.6)	0.5	31.2	2.1
Income before Tax	(5.9)	7.1	26.1	32.7	24.9
Income Tax	(4.3)	(1.3)	6.6	10.2	9.1
Income after Tax	(1.6)	8.3	19.4	22.5	15.8
Minority Interest	–	–	–	–	–
Equity In Affiliates	–	–	–	–	–
Net Income before Extra. Items	(1.6)	8.3	19.4	22.5	15.8
Accounting Change	–	(1.3)	–	–	–
Discontinued Operations	306.8	(22.0)	16.3	5.4	–
Extraordinary Item	–	–	–	–	–
Net Income	305.2	(15.0)	35.7	27.9	15.8
Basic/Primary Weighted Average Shares	43.50	51.55	48.96	42.41	36.63
Basic/Primary EPS Excl. Extra. Items	(0.037)	0.162	0.397	0.530	0.430
Basic/Primary EPS Incl. Extra. Items	7.016	(0.291)	0.729	0.658	0.430

Annual Balance Sheet

In Millions of U.S. Dollars (except for per share items)	12/31/2000	12/31/1999 Restated 12/31/2000	12/31/1998 Restated 12/31/2000	12/31/1997 Restated 12/31/1999	12/31/1996 Restated 12/31/1998
Cash and Short Term Investments	318.6	29.9	39.3	112.8	27.6
Total Receivables, Net	99.3	66.1	48.7	69.9	38.1
Total Inventory	5.8	6.1	8.6	5.0	4.5
Prepaid Expenses	21.0	9.1	7.9	6.3	3.1
Other Current Assets	6.5	290.3	13.8	7.9	4.2
Total Receivables, Net	451.2	401.5	118.3	201.9	77.5
Property/Plant/Equipment—Gross	210.8	143.9	69.2	72.9	43.5
Accumulated Depreciation	(39.0)	(28.1)	(22.9)	(21.5)	(15.6)
Property/Plant/Equipment, Net	171.8	115.8	46.3	51.4	27.9
Goodwill, Net	278.0	191.0	114.1	168.9	—
Intangibles, Net	—	—	0.6	14.3	110.3
Long Term Investments	83.9	39.2	60.8	40.5	28.1
Note Receivablele—Long Term	10.7	7.2	10.1	6.2	0.6
Other Long Term Assets	21.4	9.9	276.0	13.6	15.3
Total Assets	1,017.0	764.6	626.1	496.8	259.6
Accounts Payable	20.1	23.5	—	—	—
Payable/Accrued	—	—	31.0	40.8	28.6
Accrued Expenses	40.5	21.2	—	—	—
Notes Payable/Short Term Debt	—	—	—	—	0.0
Current Port. LT Debt/Capital Leases	20.3	14.3	0.6	1.3	3.2
Other Current Liabilities	212.9	58.1	71.6	47.0	16.1
Total Current Liabilities	293.7	117.2	103.2	89.0	47.9
Long Term Debt	128.6	146.1	12.5	2.4	2.2
Memo: Total Debt	148.9	160.4	13.1	3.7	5.4
Deferred Income Tax	4.8	12.2	8.3	7.6	2.3
Minority Interest	32.9	12.1	—	—	—
Other Liabilities	3.7	3.0	13.3	57.3	26.9
Total Liabilities	463.7	290.5	137.3	156.3	79.3
Preferred Stock	—	—	—	—	—
Common Stock	0.4	0.5	0.5	0.5	0.2
Additional Paid-In Capital	205.3	414.6	410.7	302.0	168.5
Retained Earnings (Accum. Deficit)	360.2	60.8	75.9	39.1	11.6
Treasury Stock—Common	—	—	—	—	—
Unrealized Gain (Loss)	—	—	1.8	(1.2)	0.0
Other Equity	(12.7)	(1.7)	—	—	0.0
Total Equity	553.3	474.1	488.8	340.5	180.3
Total Liability and Shareholders' Equity	1,017.0	764.6	626.1	496.8	259.6
Total Common Shares Outstanding	37.28	50.90	50.95	45.45	35.97
Employees (actual figures)	5,300	4,252	3,800	2,000	—
Number of Common Shareholders (actual figures)	383	462	435	—	—

Source: 2001, Annual Report; Fundamental Data provided by Market Guide, http://yahoo.marketguide.com.

EXHIBIT 2   Sylvan Stock Performance

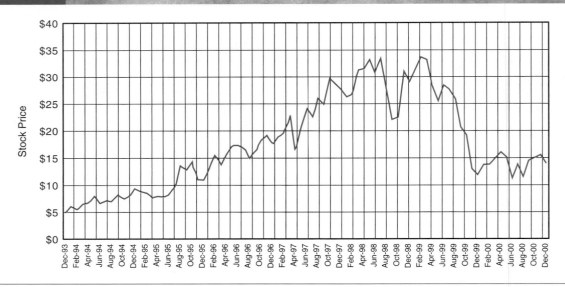

Source: Fundamental Data provided by Market Guide, http://yahoo.marketguide.com.

A few alternatives, representing some of the most popular trends in the education industry today, are discussed below. Sylvan has approached these trends by choosing to align some of its divisions as complements to the school system (Sylvan Learning Centers, Sylvan English Language Instruction) and others as competitors of the school system (Sylvan Education Solutions, Sylvan International Universities).

ALTERNATIVE SCHOOLS

Alternative schools have been developed primarily for "hard-to-educate" and misbehaving youngsters. Districts, rather than parents, typically have chosen these schools for children who have been problems in "regular" classrooms. Characteristically, these schools are secondary schools with low student–teacher ratios, modified curricula, and flexible schedules. Eight states now require alternative education, and many other districts appear to be moving in this direction. Political and legal pressures from the community to not just "suspend" or "expel" youngsters onto the streets fuel the growth of alternative schools as well.[32]

CHARTER SCHOOLS

Charter schools span a wide range, including "back-to-basics" schools, Montessori methods, schools for disabled children, and a number of other models in between. Charter schools are a hybrid of public and private schools. As public institutions, they're open to all who wish to attend, are paid for with tax dollars, are accountable to public authorities for their performance (especially student achievement), and are nondiscriminatory. They also enjoy such features as self-governance, freedom from most regulations, freedom to hire whom they like (usually without a union contract), and control of their own (secular) curricula. Because they are private schools, attendance is allowed only for students whose parents choose to send them. Besides accountability to state or local authorities, charter schools must satisfy parents and students in order to maintain enrollment. The charter movement now has about 700 schools enrolling some 170,000 youngsters.[33]

HOME SCHOOLING

Data indicate that parents teach between 1 and 4 percent of U.S. children at home. All states allow home schooling, and 16 states have no regulations for curricula, testing, or parent qualifications. Historically, home schoolers have come from religious families dissatisfied with public schools and uncomfortable with or unable to afford private schools. Growing numbers of parents cite mediocrity in the public school system as a reason for home schooling their children. An intriguing twist in home schooling practices involves part-time home schooling with part-time school attendance. Idaho, for example, requires public schools to allow home-schooled children to participate in any school activity, including academic and extracurricular activities. Several charter schools also offer this kind of arrangement, providing the best of both worlds.[34]

AFTER-SCHOOL SCHOOLS

Partly because of changing family patterns and work schedules, and partly because of dissatisfaction with regular schools, more and more families (and churches, community organizations, etc.) are augmenting children's schooling with a wide array of programs and offerings. Many are nonprofit, but some of the fastest growing are owned by commercial firms. For its after-school program, Sylvan Learning Centers joined with the National Geographic Society to provide "hands-on experiments and exploration activities" in school facilities. In addition, Voyager Expanded Learning offers after-school programs on school grounds, utilizing teachers from the school to work after-hours to teach its thematic curriculum.[35]

VIRTUAL SCHOOLS

Using the Internet and e-mail, students in virtual schools can interact with teachers, obtain lesson plans, and turn in homework assignments without leaving home. Video streaming technology makes possible 24-hour classrooms with online access to instructors. California's Choice 2000 program enrolled approximately 130 middle- and high-school students. Combining a computerized bulletin board and downloaded curriculum software, students can work at their own speed. For those who need help, chat rooms and online communication allow teachers to interact with their students.[36]

PRIVATELY MANAGED PUBLIC SCHOOLS

Based on charters or management contracts, approximately a dozen firms provide "school-management" services in the United States. The best known among these firms are Educational Alternatives, Inc., which embarked on large but ill-fated ventures in Baltimore and Hartford, and the Edison Project. Although public education is apparently becoming amenable to "outsourcing," profitability remains an issue.[37]

CORPORATE REORGANIZATION

The education industry is truly fragmented, and as Sylvan strove to become a bigger player in such a disparate industry, a reorganization became necessary. Between 1998 and 2000, management's efforts centered on reorganizing Sylvan to build on a dominant brand in K–12 supplementary education and on developing new postsecondary opportunities. By the end of 2000, restructuring resulted in five primary business segments organized to meet the needs of two primary customer segments.

CUSTOMER SEGMENTS

During the past 20 years, Sylvan has established a dominant brand in the K–12 supplementary education cus-

tomer segment. Market dominance has been established through Sylvan's substantial franchise network, commitment to quality, and record of success. In the 2000 annual report, management pointed to additional opportunities for the K–12 segment. According to Becker's observation in the annual report, "Parents, students, school administrators, and political leaders alike are focused on raising academic performance and improving schools."[38] Becker believes existing businesses are well positioned to capture deeper market penetration in the K–12 segment. Additionally, the export of Sylvan's K–12 strategy through the Schulerhilfe acquisition in Europe has expanded Sylvan's global domination of the K–12 segment.

In recent years, Sylvan has attempted to translate its K–12 educational service expertise to international postsecondary customer segments. Target customers in this segment include both undergraduate and graduate students outside the United States. Sylvan also hoped to attract adult students to its English language courses in other countries. In domestic markets, Sylvan hoped to focus on teacher training to attract postsecondary customers. Becker believes that teacher training is closely related to K–12 business activities. Management believes that after eliminating training programs for private corporations, Sylvan will be better suited to focus exclusively on teacher training in the domestic postsecondary market.

BUSINESS SEGMENTS

To meet the K–12 customer segment needs, Sylvan is split into two primary business segments, Sylvan Learning Centers and Sylvan Education Solutions. (See Exhibit 3 for segment financial information.) Sylvan Learning Centers (SLC) offers supplementary education services in the United States and Europe. Sylvan Education Solutions (SES) partners with public and nonpublic schools to provide in-school educational support services. Sylvan markets its teacher training business, Canter, through SES with the purpose of improving teacher quality nationwide.

To meet the postsecondary customer segment's needs, Sylvan is split into two primary business segments, Sylvan International Universities and Sylvan English Language Instruction. Recent acquisitions of both international universities and online instructional companies are part of the new Sylvan International University division. Franchised English language instructional facilities make up the Sylvan English Language Instruction division. A description of each business segment is included below.

Sylvan Learning Centers

Sylvan Learning Centers has become the most significant brand name in the "consumer education services marketplace."[39] Sylvan's traditional product offerings

EXHIBIT 3   Segment Financials (000's)

	Sylvan Learning Centers	Sylvan Education Solutions	Sylvan International Universities	Sylvan Ventures	Company Totals
2000					
Revenues	$98,943	$105,177	$62,582	$0	$266,702
Segment profit (loss)	$22,015	$16,132	$4,977	($50,846)	($7,722)
Segment assets	$84,895	$120,756	$239,166	$82,006	$526,823
Long-lived assets	$5,820	$9,890	$127,098	$3,728	$146,536
Segment ROA	26%	13%	2%	−62%	−1%
1999					
Revenues	$90,664	$101,263	$32,275	$0	$224,202
Restructuring charges	$170	$2,537	$447	$0	$3,154
Segment profit (loss)	$21,768	$17,371	$2,408	$0	$41,547
Segment assets	$71,097	$105,273	$69,042	$0	$245,412
Long-lived assets	$5,041	$10,582	$80,862	$0	$96,485
Segment ROA	31%	17%	3%		17%
1998					
Revenues	$64,755	$86,293	$0	$0	$151,048
Segment profit	$19,339	$14,339	$0	$0	$33,678
Segment assets	$56,841	$96,438	$0	$0	$153,279
Long-lived assets	$3,823	$14,656	$0	$0	$18,479
Segment ROA	34%	15%			22%

Sylvan Learning Systems Segment Data

	2000	1999	1998	1997
Revenues:				
Sylvan Learning Centers	31%	33%	36%	27%
Sylvan Education Solutions	33%	37%	48%	30%
Sylvan English Language Instruction	16%	19%	16%	43%
Sylvan International Universities	20%	12%	0%	0%
Total Revenues	100%	100%	100%	100%
Direct				
Sylvan Learning Centers	24%	25%	25%	23%
Sylvan Education Solutions	28%	29%	40%	26%
Sylvan English Language Instruction	15%	15%	9%	38%
Sylvan International Universities	18%	11%	0%	0%
Total Direct Costs	85%	80%	75%	87%
General and Administrative Expenses	6%	10%	9%	12%
Sylvan Ventures Operating Costs	6%	0%	0%	0%
Costs Related to Pooling of Interests and Restructuring Costs	0%	1%	2%	0%

	2000	1999	1998	1997
Operating Income (Loss)	2%	9%	14%	1%
Other Non-Operating Income(Loss)	6%	−4%	2%	18%
Interest Expense	−2%	−1%	0%	0%
Sylvan Ventures Investment Losses	−4%	0%	0%	0%
Equity in Loss of Affiliates	−7%	−1%	−2%	
Minority Interest	2%	0%	0%	
Income from Discontinued Operations Net of Tax				3%
Income (Loss) from Continuing Operations before Taxes	−2%	3%	15%	19%
Tax Benefit (Expense)	1%	0%	−4%	−6%
Income (Loss) from Continuing Operations	−1%	3%	11%	13%

Source: Fundamental Data provided by Market Guide, http://yahoo.marketguide.com.

are tutoring services in reading and math. Sylvan has developed its study skills and advanced reading programs, which are aimed at enhancing the performance of students with adequate performance. It has proliferated its new ACT/SAT prep program through the Ivy West acquisition. Sylvan continues to develop eSylvan, an online delivery mechanism for traditional learning center services. These new services help Sylvan accomplish its new goal of helping children "catch up, keep up, and get ahead in school."[40]

Sylvan Education Solutions

Sylvan Education Solutions (SES) provides tutoring services in public schools, nonpublic schools, and welfare agencies. Contractual agreements are concentrated in large metropolitan areas such as Atlanta, Chicago, Cleveland, Los Angeles, New York, and six other cities. SES partners with inner-city school districts to help improve students' standardized test scores. SES' ability to provide measurable improvement in reading and mathematics skills has positioned SES to expand successfully in other major markets. Additionally, Becker believes that in combination with Sylvan Teachers Institute, SES could provide an alternative route for teacher certification in many states.[41]

Sylvan International Universities

Becker has stated that the mission of Sylvan International Universities (SIU) is "to meet the tremendous demand for university education by operating profitable, high-quality universities that prepare students for the career opportunities of today and tomorrow."[42] The strategy for SIU is to grow newly acquired institutions, acquire new universities in key markets, and cautiously develop universities where acquisitions are not available in key markets.[43] This strategy marks a significant change from the franchise approach used in the Sylvan Learning Centers business model. Becker and Hoehn-Saric are accustomed to buying and selling businesses, but operating private universities in international markets represents a new challenge. Becker, however, sees growth in university acquisitions as the key to improving Sylvan's position in both the postsecondary customer segment and in international markets. Strategic plans also include coupling international universities with online education holdings to gain a first-mover advantage in international distance learning.

Sylvan English Language Instruction

Franchised English language instructional facilities make up the Sylvan English Language Instruction division. Through its Wall Street Institute (WSI), Sylvan hopes to meet "growing demand by offering adult students in their home countries practical, results-oriented English language instruction in a comfortable, relaxed atmosphere."[44] WSI has recently entered seven new countries, with the most remarkable growth in China. As stated in the 2000 annual report, "in just one month, WSI's charter locations in Beijing each generated as much revenue as an average WSI center in Europe or Latin America produces in a full year."[45] Plans for 2001 include further expansion into China, Europe, and Latin America, as well as other promising Asian markets (i.e., Taiwan, Korea, and Japan).[46]

Sylvan Ventures

A fifth business segment has recently been created as a complement to both customer segments. This business segment, Sylvan Ventures, is a venture capital entity established to partner with technology-oriented companies offering educational services. The primary purpose of Sylvan Ventures is to establish a foothold in emerging technologies as they relate to education. Sylvan Ventures will provide strategic direction to portfolio companies pointing them in a successful direction. This is an effort by Sylvan's leadership to capitalize on its entrepreneurial talent without requiring full ownership. Sylvan has invested significant sums in this venture, but has left one-third of its capital uncommitted in order to provide flexibility for future investment strategies.[47]

Sylvan Ventures did not generate revenues for the company in 2000. Costs related to developing eSylvan (an online version of the learning centers), start-up of Sylvan Ventures, and recently incurred investment losses from the sale of Zapme! brought Sylvan Ventures' losses to $51 million during the same year.

COMPETITORS

Sylvan Learning Systems faces competition in each of its business segments introduced above. That competition focuses on price, educational quality, and location in the franchise businesses. In the Education Solutions and International Universities businesses, the competition is primarily based on price and educational quality.[48]

The company is aware of only three direct national corporate competitors to its Sylvan Learning Centers segment: Huntington Learning Centers, Inc.; Kumon Institute of Education; and Kaplan Educational Centers. The company believes these competitors operate fewer centers than Sylvan and that these firms concentrate their services within a smaller geographic area. In most areas served by Sylvan Learning Centers, competition also exists from individual tutors and local learning centers. State and local education agencies also fund tutoring by individuals, which compete with the company's Sylvan Learning Centers segment.[49]

The company's Education Solutions segment's most significant competitor today is the public school system. On the surface, this contradicts management's assessment of the partnership between Sylvan and public school systems. However, improvement in public school system performance would result in higher standardized test scores and reduce the need to hire Sylvan. Sylvan also competes with school reform efforts sponsored by private organizations and universities and with consultants hired by school districts to provide assis-

tance in the identification of problems and implementation of solutions.[50]

The English Language Instruction market is highly fragmented with numerous public and private sector operators. These included Berlitz/ELS, E.F. (a Swedish company) and Opening (a Spanish company). Berlitz is the largest of these companies in this market segment, with annual revenues of approximately $330 million.[51] Below is a brief description of Sylvan's most significant competitors.

HUNTINGTON LEARNING CENTERS

Huntington Learning Centers, founded in 1977, are located throughout the United States. These centers enroll over 10,000 students a year focusing on tutoring services for children in kindergarten through 12th grade. Huntington helps students improve math, reading, writing, and study skills, as well as prepare for the SAT and ACT exams. The programs provide regularly scheduled parent conferences. Based on diagnostic test results that identify a student's exact academic needs, Huntington prescribes a comprehensive, individualized program of instruction to produce skill mastery. Children spend an average of three to four hours a week with certified teachers in programs focused on personalized, noncompetitive, and structured environments to build academic independence and self-esteem. A major goal of Huntington is teaching children how to replace frustration and failure with confidence, motivation, and a desire to learn.[52]

Huntington was a $52 million company by the end of 1998. It operated over 200 centers in 48 states, and had plans to open 50 more centers during 1999. During the same time period, Sylvan was operating over 700 learning centers throughout the United States and Canada. The U.S. tutoring industry was estimated to be a $2 billion business at that time.[53]

KUMON INSTITUTE OF EDUCATION

Kumon Institute is located locally in Japan, Australia, Canada, and the United Kingdom, but its educational programs reach 3.5 million students in more than 22 countries. Kumon offers classes in both math and English. The math and English programs provide skills training ranging from kindergarten through college preparation. Kumon has created a program that focuses on the individual student and progression of knowledge set by the student's rate of learning. The program includes repetition, so that knowledge already learned is reinforced. Students at Kumon are given diagnostic tests to determine their existing skills level. The results are then used to establish a program for a student that is just under the student's current abilities. By starting the student at a level just less than his or her current ability to perform, the program creates 100 percent success rates. Kumon's managers believe that 100 percent success rates provide the confidence needed by students to encourage them to think for themselves.[54]

KAPLAN, INC.

Kaplan, a subsidiary of the Washington Post Company, is perhaps Sylvan's most direct competitor. It provides educational and career growth services. Its Test Preparation and Admissions division publishes course materials, books, software, and Web content to prime students for standardized and licensing examinations, such as the SAT, GRE, and medical board exams. Kaplan, in addition to providing training and continuing education services for a variety of industries, operates Score! Learning after-school learning centers. Kaplan also offers Internet-based distance learning through Kaplan Colleges. Recent Kaplan acquisitions include Quest Education, an operator of postsecondary schools, and Speer Software Training.[55]

Kaplan Colleges offer nearly 500 professional development, continuing education, certification, and degree courses and programs in nursing, education, criminal justice, real estate, legal professions, law, management, general business and computing/information technology (see Exhibit 4 for a detailed listing of programs). Many courses are available online in either instructor-led or self-study formats. The remaining courses are offered through Kaplan's existing distance learning programs: Concord School of Law and the National Institute of Paralegal Arts and Sciences. Kaplan is one of the largest distance education providers in the United States.[56]

Kaplan Professional is a corporate partnership program that allows organizations to offer Kaplan Colleges' education programs directly to employees and members. These training programs specialize in courses designed to increase critical business skills, increase employee productivity, and improve overall performance. The partnership's staff tailors programs to meet individual organizational needs. The professional program also provides licensing, certification, and compliance tracking educational tools.[57]

Kaplan's Test Preparation and Admissions Program offers testing preparation services for school admission and professional licensing exams. Exams include GMAT, LSAT, GRE, MCAT, SAT, etc. and cover areas such as high school, college, graduate, business, law, pre-med, medical licensing, dental, nursing, allied health, and English/TOEFL.[58] Kaptest.com, the online division of Kaplan Test Prep and Admissions, is a provider of online test preparation, reaching 2 million users worldwide. Kaptest.com added a variety of new

---

| The Kaplan Colleges Program Listing | EXHIBIT 4 |

School of Business
- Certificate in Financial Planning
- Bachelor of Science in Management/Applied Management
- Associate of Science/Interdisciplinary Studies
- Associate of Science/Applied Management
- Bachelor of Science in Management/ Information Technology Management

School of Information Technology
- Associate of Applied Science in Computer Information Systems
- Bachelor of Science in Management/ Information Technology Management
- Microsoft® Solution Developer Certificate
- MNE (MCSE 2000) Microsoft® Network Engineer Certificate Program
- MNE (MCSE + Site Builder 2000) Microsoft® Network Engineer Certificate Program

School of Paralegal Studies
- Paralegal Diploma Program
- Paralegal Specialized Associate's Degree Program
- Bachelor of Science Degree in Paralegal Studies

School of Legal Nursing Consulting
- Legal Nurse Consultant Certificate Program
- Legal Nurse Consultant Paralegal Diploma Program

School of Criminal Justice
- Criminal Justice Diploma Program
- Criminal Justice Specialized Associate's Degree Program
- Bachelor of Science Degree in Criminal Justice

Source: http://www.kaplancollege.com

---

online courses, workshops, and live online events related to test preparation and admissions during 2000. The site also provides informative articles and guidance about the admissions process for colleges and graduate and professional schools..

Kaplan recently developed a subsidiary, Kaplan Ventures, to invest in high-growth, Internet education sector companies. With this subsidiary, Kaplan is attempting to leverage its resources, relationships, and expertise to help accelerate the growth of its portfolio companies. One of the most noteworthy ventures, Apollo International, plans to open accredited University of Phoenix campuses around the world, beginning in Europe.[59]

Kaplan, Inc., through its efforts to expand its reach and position as a broad-based provider of education and career services in 2000, increased revenues by 37 percent, reaching a total of $353.8 million. The breakdown of revenue by division, as well as how many students each division reached, can be found in Exhibit 5.[60]

INTERNATIONAL UNIVERSITIES

The university market in Spain is dominated by public universities, which own a 95 percent market share. In the Madrid area, where UEM operates, the main competitors are C.E.U, Alfonso X el Sabio, and Universidad Pontificia de Comillas. C.E.U. is believed to be the largest, with several campuses in the Madrid area and approximately 10,000 students.[61] UVM, another competitor, is considered a leader within the growing segment of private universities in Mexico. It accounts for 29 percent of the total university enrollments. UVM's market share among private universities is 7 percent at a national level and 14.5 percent in the Mexico City metropolitan area. The Chilean higher education system is composed of a group of traditional, publicly funded universities (25) and a growing number of private universities (48). The private universities account for 31 percent of the total higher education enrollments. UDLA, which is considered another international competitor, has a market share within the private university sector in Chile of 5.7 percent.[62]

SYLVAN'S FUTURE

Sylvan enjoyed tremendous success in the early 1990s due to brand strength and appropriate business models. Earnings performance, however, lagged in the late 1990s due to ongoing acquisitions of businesses with high operating and fixed-asset costs. Trends in the education industry indicate further fragmentation as parents seek alternatives to the public school system. With the recent restructuring, management hopes to position Sylvan to capture many of the customers disenchanted with public education. Teacher training and Internet ventures aim to complement Sylvan's efforts to garner larger customer bases in each segment. However, recent financial performance raises questions regarding management's ability to translate its vision and strategy into corporate profits. Sales of profitable business segments raise further doubts about the ongoing profit potential of the organization. Additionally, Sylvan's entry into technology ventures comes at a time when the equity market for technology firms is not favorable. As the company wanders away from the activities and business models that were critical to historic brand success, management must determine how significant a role Sylvan Ventures will play for future development. Additionally, management must determine the appropriate scope of its many business segments and multiple international markets, while at the same time keeping a close watch on other competitors and their actions in the fragmented education market.

NOTES

1. Sylvan Learning Centers, 2000, Annual Report to Investors.
2. William Glanz, 1998, Business person of the year, *Baltimore Business Journal*, December 25, 4 (reprinted at request of Sylvan Learning Systems, Inc.).
3. LenNell Hancock, 1994, A Sylvan invasion, *Newsweek*, December 19, 52.
4. Ibid.
5. Allison Rogers, 1994, With a little help from their friends, *Fortune*, September 19, 238.
6. Glanz, Business person of the year, 2.
7. Rogers, With a little help from their friends.
8. Ibid.
9. Dennis A. Williams, Sylvester Monroe, Tracey L. Robinson, and Rebecca Boren, 1985, The McDonald's of teaching, *Newsweek*, January 7, 61.
10. Ibid.
11. Ibid.
12. Glanz, Business person of the year, 2.

EXHIBIT 5	Kaplan's Revenue in 2000 by Division		
Division	Revenue	Students Reached	Program Reach
Quest Education Corporation	$56.9 million	13,000	34 school relationships
Kaplan Colleges	$11.1 million	8,000	
Score! Learning	$41.2 million	50,000	140 centers
Kaplan Professional	$79.7 million	115,000	200 online courses
Kaplan Test Prep	$165.2 million		650 school relationships

Source: http://www.corporate-ir.net/media_files/nys/wpo/reports/ar00/wp2000ar24.html

13. Ibid., 4.
14. http://www.hoovers.com/premium/profile/7/0,2147,17087,00.html
15. Ibid.
16. 2000, Sylvan Learning Systems Annual Report to Shareholders.
17. Ibid.
18. http://www.hoovers.com/premium/profile/7/0,2147,17087,00.html
19. Ibid.
20. 2000, Sylvan Learning Systems Annual Report to Shareholders.
21. http://www.hoovers.com/premium/profile/7/0,2147,17087,00.html
22. 2000, Sylvan Learning Systems Annual Report to Shareholders.
23. http://www.hoovers.com/premium/profile/7/0,2147,17087,00.html
24. 1999, Sylvan Learning Systems Annual Report to Shareholders, Highlights, 4.
25. http://www.hoover.com
26. 2000, Sylvan Learning Systems Annual Report to Shareholders, 20.
27. http://www.commercialalert.org/zapme/
28. 1999, Sylvan Learning Systems Annual Report to Shareholders.
29. 2000, Sylvan Learning Systems Annual Report to Shareholders.
30. http://www.eduventures.com/pdf/whatiseduindstry.pdf
31. Ibid.
32. http://www.eduventures.com/news/education_industry_report/eirs_mainpage.cfm.
33. Ibid.
34. Ibid.
35. Ibid.
36. Ibid.
37. Ibid.
38. 2000, Sylvan Learning Systems Annual Report to Shareholders, 5.
39. Ibid., 14.
40. Ibid.
41. Ibid., 10.
42. Ibid.
43. Ibid.
44. Ibid., 11.
45. Ibid.
46. Ibid.
47. Ibid., 16.
48. http://news.moneycentral.msn.com/sec/business.asp?Symbol=SLVN
49. Ibid.
50. Ibid.
51. Ibid.
52. http://www.zip2.com/columbian/huntingtonlearning
53. http://baltimore.bcentral.com/Baltimore/stories/1998/12/07/story5.html
54. http://members.ozemail.com.au/~samsuen/kumon.htm
55. http://www.kaplancollege.com/info/press
56. Ibid.
57. http://www.kaplan.com/professional/index.html
58. http://www.kaptest.com
59. http://www.kaplan.com/ventures/index.html
60. http://www.corporate-ir.net/media_files/nys/wpo/reports/ar00/wp2000ar24.html
61. http://news.moneycentral.msn.com/sec/business.asp?Symbol=SLVN
62. Ibid.; http://www.hoovers.com/co/capsule/7/0,2163,17087,00.html, and http://www.planetpress.org/fin.htm

The Long Road to Value Creation: Restructuring and Spin-Offs at Tredegar Industries (1990-2003)

case thirty-one

D. Robley Wood, Jr.
Virginia Commonwealth University

Gerard George
University of Wisconsin–Madison

John Daniels
University of Miami

COMPANY BACKGROUND

Tredegar Industries became an independent company on July 10, 1989, when Richmond, Virginia–based Ethyl Corporation spun off its plastics, aluminum, and energy businesses. General Motors and Exxon (Standard Oil of New Jersey) had formed the Ethyl Corporation as a joint venture in 1924 to produce tetraethyl lead that was added to gasoline to reduce engine "knock." The Albemarle Paper Manufacturing Company of Richmond, Virginia, purchased Ethyl Corporation in 1962 and adopted the Ethyl name for all of its operations. Ethyl Corporation faced the eventual ban of tetraethyl lead being used as a gasoline additive and therefore decided to use its strong cash flow to diversify into plastics, aluminum extrusions, energy, life insurance, pharmaceuticals, and petroleum additives. In the late 1980s, Ethyl's management did a tax-free spin-off to its shareholders of its aluminum, plastics, and energy units. The new company was named Tredegar Industries. Tredegar's name was adopted from an iron foundry business started in 1836 in Richmond, Virginia. Throughout its history, Tredegar Iron Works had a reputation for producing high-quality products and Tredegar Industries was built on that commitment to quality. Subsequently, Ethyl completed two more spin-offs, and today its primary focus is on the fuel and lubricant additives businesses.

MANAGEMENT TEAM

A team of veteran managers was assembled to lead Tredegar. The president and CEO was John D. Gottwald, who had previously been the corporate vice president of Aluminum, Plastics and Energy of Ethyl. He was supported by two executive vice presidents: Richard W. Goodrum who previously held the position of divisional vice president of Aluminum, Plastics, and Energy for Ethyl; and Norman A. Scher, who had been a partner in the law firm of Hunton & Williams where he had worked in the areas of corporate financing, mergers, and acquisitions. In 1995, Mr. Goodrum retired after 39 years of service to Ethyl and Tredegar. Mr. Gottwald was elected chairman of the board of directors in 2001, and Mr. Scher was elected president and chief executive officer in 2001. Tredegar is headquartered in Richmond, Virginia, and employs about 3,500 people in operations spread around the world.

RESTRUCTURING THE BUSINESS UNITS

PLASTICS SEGMENT

Tredegar Industries was initially comprised of three business segments that operated in the plastics, aluminum, and energy sectors of the U.S. economy. The plastics segment was composed of the film and molded products divisions. The film products division supplied plastic films for products such as diapers, greenhouses, food packaging, and masking. Permeable films were supplied to Procter & Gamble for use in infant and adult diapers and feminine hygiene products. Procter & Gamble and Tredegar jointly held patents applicable to the production of these films. The molded products division competed in the following four markets: packaging, beverage closures, industrial products, and injection-mold tools. The molded products division was the leading

Reprinted by permission of the authors.

producer of lip balm sticks in the United States, and it held patents on plastic carbonated beverage closures that are used in such countries as Japan, Canada, and Australia.

ALUMINUM AND VINYL SEGMENT

The aluminum segment produced soft alloy aluminum extrusions for the construction, automotive accessories, and marine industries. This segment was also a leading producer of vinyl extrusions for new and replacement windows and doors.

ENERGY SEGMENT

The energy segment owned mineral rights on 133,000 acres of land through its 97percent ownership of The Elk Horn Coal Corporation. These mineral rights were primarily for substantial low-sulfur coal reserves in eastern Kentucky. In addition, the energy segment owned interest in oil- and gas-producing properties in western Canada and the U.S. Gulf Coast.

THE EVOLUTION OF TREDEGAR FROM 1990–2003

In 1990, Tredegar was comprised primarily of under-performing businesses, was $100 million in debt, and had 5,000 employees in 35 different locations. The three business units, plastics, aluminum, and energy, were analyzed and Tredegar's management concluded that the best strategy was to invest in businesses in which it had a sustainable source of competitive advantage and to exit all others. Management devoted its attention to restructuring its three business units and making investments for future growth.

The firm sold U.S. oil and gas assets for $16.5 million resulting in a pretax loss of $7.6 million and announced its exit as a supplier of molded products for the automotive market. The process of reducing non-strategic assets continued in 1991. The molded products business segment (plastics) announced that plants in California and Kentucky would be closed within one year. The molded products tooling plant in Massachusetts was put up for sale, and the beverage closure business was sold for a gain of $894,000. In 1991, Tredegar invested $2.4 million in Emisphere Technologies, Inc., a pharmaceutical research and development organization that was developing an oral delivery system for drugs currently administered by injection.

In 1992 and 1993, Tredegar sold parts of its investment in Emisphere Technologies, Inc., for a gain of $3.3 million. Also in 1993, it was announced that Tredegar had invested in a research effort called Molecumetics located in Bellevue, Washington. Molecumetics was

working to improve the drug discovery process through proprietary chemistry. In 1994, Tredegar sold its 97 percent ownership in the Elk Horn Coal Corporation for approximately $71 million and its oil and gas properties for $8 million and completed its exit from the energy business. In 1995 and 1996, Tredegar sold the molded products division for $57.5 million. During 1996, Tredegar Investments was created as a separate business segment to identify and invest in early-stage, technology-based companies with substantial growth potential.

During 1997, Tredegar added to its aluminum extrusions business by purchasing an aluminum extrusion and fabrication plant located in Texas from the Reynolds Metal Company. The Texas plant had sales of $25.7 million and most of the sales were to the transportation, electrical, and consumer durables market. Acquisitions worth more than $70 million took place during 1998. In early 1998, Tredegar acquired two Canada-based aluminum extrusions and fabrication plants from Reynolds Metals Company whose 1997 collective sales were approximately $53 million. Both facilities manufacture products for the construction, transportation, electrical, machinery, and consumer durables markets. Also in early 1998, Tredegar sold APPX software which had been part of its technology division. Tredegar completed more than $200 million in acquisitions in 1999. Tredegar acquired Exxon Films in May 1999, and this expanded its technology and customer base. The acquisition included 350 employees and two plants. The plants are in Lake Zurich, Illinois, and Pottsville, Pennsylvania, and manufactured films used primarily in packing, personal hygiene, and medical markets. Acquisitions of aluminum extrusion operations in Aurora, Ontario, and Pickering, Ontario, were completed in 1999. Also, the Film Products division finished construction of its new plant in Budapest, Hungary, in 1999. In 2000, Tredegar divested its Fiberlux division, which produced rigid vinyl extrusions for windows and patio doors for a pretax gain of $525,000 and shut down its films manufacturing facility in Manchester, Iowa. In 2001, Tredegar closed an aluminum extrusion plant in El Campo, Texas. In 2002, Tredegar shut down films manufacturing facilities in Carbondale, Pennsylvania, and Tacoma, Washington.

CURRENT BUSINESS SEGMENTS

By 2003, Tredegar was a diversified firm with three main business segments: plastic and film products, aluminum extrusions, and technology. The three businesses have diverse operations and are located in different parts of the world (Exhibit 1). Each of the three businesses is discussed below:

FILM PRODUCTS

The Film Products division manufactures plastic films for disposable personal products (primarily feminine hygiene and diaper products) and packaging, medical, industrial, and agricultural products. Tredegar makes these products at various U.S. locations and sells them both directly and through distributors. Tredegar also has films plants located in the Netherlands, Japan, China, Hungary, Brazil, and Argentina, where it produces films primarily for the Asian, European, and Latin American markets. During 2000, Film Products acquired ADMA and Promea of Italy and started construction of a plant in Shanghai, China. ADMA manufactures and sells plastic films to small and private label converters that serve the hygiene markets in Europe, China, and the Middle East. Promea designs and manufactures equipment for producing specialty films.

The plastic film extrusion process begins with small plastic resin pellets that are fed into a high-pressure extruder. The pellets are heated to form a homogenous liquid melt stream that is then pushed through a forming die, where it begins to take the shape of the finished material. Once through the die, the film can be (a) perforated through a vacuum-forming process, (b) laminated to another fabric, or (c) embossed to impart a three-dimensional structure. The film can be treated to modify its surface chemistry so that inks or adhesives will adhere to its surface. The production line may

---

EXHIBIT 1   Plant Locations and Principal Operations

Film Products Locations
Cincinnati, Ohio
LaGrange, Georgia
Lake Zurich, Illinois
New Bern, North Carolina
Pottsville, Pennsylvania
Terre Haute, Indiana (technical center and production facility)
Retsag, Hungary
Chieti, Italy
Guangzhou, China
Kerkrade, the Netherlands
San Juan, Argentina
Sao Paulo, Brazil
Shanghai, China

Principal Operations
Production of plastic films

Aluminum Extrusions Locations
Carthage, Tennessee
Kentland, Indiana
Newnan, Georgia
Aurora, Ontario
Richmond Hill, Ontario
Pickering, Ontario
Ste. Therese, Quebec

Production of aluminum extrusions, fabrication, and finishing

Tredegar Investments
Richmond, Virginia

Investments

Therics
Princeton, New Jersey

Microfabrication for bone replacements and drug delivery

include heating or cooling sections to enhance the product's clarity, strength or rigidity.

The primary raw materials for films are low-density and linear low-density polyethylene resins, which are obtained from domestic and foreign suppliers at competitive prices. Management believes there will be an adequate supply of polyethylene resins in the immediate future. Film Products has a technical center in Terre Haute, Indiana, and holds 35 U.S. patents and 14 U.S. trademarks. The introduction of new products on a regular basis is critical for success in the films business. Film Products produces films for two major market categories: disposables (65 to 70 percent of production volume) and industrial (30 to 35 percent of production volume).

Disposables

Film Products is one of the largest U.S. suppliers of embossed and permeable films for disposable personal products. Film Products supplies permeable films for use as liners in feminine hygiene products, adult incontinent products, and hospital underpads. Film Products also supplies embossed films and nonwoven film laminates for use as backsheets in such disposable products as baby diapers, adult incontinent products, feminine hygiene products, and hospital underpads. Film Products' primary customer for permeable films, embossed films, and nonwoven film laminates is the Procter & Gamble Company (P&G), the leading global disposable diaper manufacturer. P&G and Tredegar have had a successful long-term relationship based on cooperation, product innovation, and continuous process improvement.

Industrial

Film Products produces coextruded and monolayer permeable films under the VisPore® name. These films are used to regulate fluid and vapor transmission in many industrial, medical, agricultural, and packaging markets. Specific examples include filter plies for surgical masks and other medical applications, permeable ground cover, natural cheese mold release cloths, and rubber bale wrap. Film Products also produces differentially embossed monolayer and coextruded films. Some of these films are extruded in a Class 10,000 clean room and act as a disposable, protective coversheet for photopolymers used in the manufacture of circuit boards. Other films sold under the ULTRAMASK® name are used as masking films to protect polycarbonate, acrylics, and glass from damage during fabrication, shipping, and handling. Film Products produces a line of oriented films for food packaging, in-mold labels, and other applications under the name Monax® Plus. These are high-strength, high-moisture-barrier films that provide cost and source reduction benefits over competing packaging materials.

ALUMINUM EXTRUSIONS

The Aluminum Extrusions segment is composed of the William L. Bonnell Company, Inc., Capitol Products Corporation, Bon L Campo Limited Partnership, and Bon L Canada Inc., which together produce soft alloy aluminum extrusions primarily for the building and construction, transportation, electrical, and consumer durables markets. Aluminum Extrusions manufactures plain, anodized, and painted aluminum extrusions for sale directly to fabricators and distributors that use aluminum extrusions in the production of curtain walls, moldings, architectural shapes, running boards, tub and shower doors, boat windshields, window components, tractor-trailer shapes, ladders, and furniture, among other products.

The aluminum extrusion process begins with aluminum ingot and scrap that are melted in a furnace exceeding 1200 F. The molten aluminum is then poured into logs that are then placed in a homogenizing oven, where the heat is evenly distributed in the metal. They are then cut into smaller sizes, called billets. The billets enter the extrusion process, where they are pushed through dies to form shapes. Finally, the extrusions are stretched and cut into required lengths and hardened in an aging oven at approximately 360°F for four hours. The final finishing stage may include wet paint, powder coat paint, buffing, and drilling.

Sales are made primarily in the United States, principally east of the Rocky Mountains. Revenues are primarily generated in the building and commercial construction (61 percent), distribution (15 percent), transportation (10 percent), and other miscellaneous industries. The Aluminum Extrusions division depends on the growth and strength in these industries. Aluminum Extrusions competes primarily on the basis of product quality, price, and service. Competitors include Alcoa, Hydro Aluminum, and Kaiser. Customers include GE, Wilson Trailer, and Polario Industries. Recent acquisitions have been in Canada, and Tredegar is open to more acquisitions if the current economic environment presents opportunities at attractive prices.

TECHNOLOGY

Tredegar's technology interests in 2002 included Molecumetics Ltd., Therics, and Tredegar Investments Inc.

Molecumetics, a subsidiary of Tredegar, operated a drug design research laboratory in Seattle, Washington, where it used its patented chemistry to develop novel small molecule drug candidates for licensing to pharmaceutical and biotech companies in exchange for upfront fees, research and development support payments, milestone-driven success payments, and future royalties. Tredegar has been funding Molecumetics since 1992. Molecumetics had collaboration agreements with pharmaceutical companies such as Bristol-Myers Squibb, Pharmacia, and Asahi Kasei. Molecumetics never made a profit and on March 22, 2002, Tredegar announced its intention to divest this subsidiary. Tredegar was not able to sell Molecumetics and on July 2, 2002, all operations were ceased. Tredegar reported a $7.5 million loss in 2002 on the disposal of Molecumetics.

Therics went from partially owned (19 percent) in 1996 to fully owned by Tredegar in 1999. Therics is developing a microfabrication technology that can be used to manufacture very complex internal architectures. By using the "comb polymer" technology developed at MIT, Therics is developing the microfabrication technology under the brand Theri Form™ and sees applications in reconstructive tissue engineering. Currently, Therics is developing the capability to manufacture bone replacement products that encourage cell and tissue growth, with its initial target market being reconstructive products for above-the-neck surgeries. Tredegar believes that a substantial market exists as more than two million orthopedic and plastic reconstructive surgeries are performed each year in the United States. Therics incurred an operating loss of $13.1 million in 2002 and Tredegar is planning a divestiture in the near future.

Tredegar Investments division identifies and invests in early-stage, technology-based companies that have substantial growth potential. "The primary reason why we invest in new technologies is that we are constantly learning and seeking new ways to maximize shareholder value," says chairman Gottwald. As of December 31, 2002, Tredegar Investments portfolio had an estimated fair value of $99.4 million. On October 15, 2002, Tredegar announced that it was exploring the sale of its entire investment portfolio in secondary market transactions. The investments were primarily in the life sciences, communications, and information technology industries. A complete list of the Tredegar Investments portfolio is published quarterly on Tredegar's website (www.tredegar.com) in conjunction with its earnings release.

PERFORMANCE

Tredegar has come a long way since 1990. The firm has evolved by shedding unproductive units and turning non-performing units around within a short time frame. The company's earnings have grown from a loss of $24.7 million in 1990 to a remarkable profit of $111.4 million in 2000 (see Exhibits 2 and 3 for a five-year summary of financial statements). The earnings of $111.4 million in 2000 were the best in Tredegar's ten-year history but dropped drastically to $9.8 million in 2001 and to a loss of $2.5 million in 2002. Long-term debt totaled $204.3 million in 2002 and was down slightly from 2001 but up considerably from the 1998 total of $25.0 million. At the close of 2002, Tredegar had more than $100 million in cash and short-term investments, so financial liquidity was not a problem. Shareholders' equity was $462.9 mil-

EXHIBIT 2	Selected Income Statement Data (5-Year Summary)				
Income Statement In Millions of U.S. Dollars	12 Months Ending 12/31/02	12 Months Ending 12/31/01	12 Months Ending 12/31/00	12 Months Ending 12/31/99	12 Months Ending 12/31/98
Total Revenue – Net	677.3	745.2	1,007.5	816.0	703.8
Cost of Goods Sold	582.7	618.3	706.8	648.3	553.2
Gross Profit	94.6	126.9	162.4	172.2	146.6
Selling/General/Admin./R&D Expenses	78.2	74.6	80.5	69.7	54.0
Depreciation/Amortization	0.1	4.9	5.0	3.4	0.2
Interest Expense, Net Operating	9.4	12.7	17.3	9.1	1.3
Unusual Expense (Income)	(2.3)	16.0	23.2	4.1	(0.1)
Total Operating Expense	668.0	726.5	832.9	734.5	608.6
Operating Income	9.2	18.7	174.5	81.5	95.2
Income Tax	3.0	4.6	63.2	28.9	31.1
Discontinued Operations	(8.7)	(4.3)	–	–	4.7
Net Income	(2.5)	9.8	111.4	52.6	68.9

Balance Sheet In Millions of U.S. Dollars	As of 12/31/2002	As of 12/31/2001	As of 12/31/2000	As of 12/31/1999	As of 12/31/1998
Cash and Short Term Investments	109.9	96.8	44.5	25.8	25.4
Trade Accounts Receivable, Net	92.9	79.3	96.7	121.8	94.3
Other Receivables	12.9	5.4	0.3	0.0	0.0
Total Inventory	44.0	45.3	46.8	53.1	34.3
Prepaid Expenses	4.0	2.9	2.8	2.7	3.5
Other Current Assets	21.0	16.0	17.6	11.2	8.8
Total Current Assets	284.6	245.7	208.8	214.6	166.3
Property/Plant/Equipment, Net	250.6	267.3	273.5	243.4	156.0
Goodwill, Net	132.3	136.5	139.6	152.5	32.9
Long Term Investments	93.8	155.1	232.3	140.7	60.0
Other Long Term Assets	76.7	60.4	49.7	41.2	41.9
Total Assets	838.0	865.0	903.8	792.5	457.2
Accounts Payable	35.9	46.5	51.8	61.5	47.6
Accrued Expenses	42.4	47.6	36.6	45.0	41.1
Other Current Liabilities	55.0	5.0	0.0	1.7	0.2
Total Current Liabilities	133.3	99.1	88.4	108.2	88.9
Total Long Term Debt	204.3	259.5	268.1	270.0	25.0
Deferred Income Tax	27.4	19.0	40.6	33.2	24.9
Other Liabilities	10.0	9.5	8.9	8.8	8.1
Total Equity	462.9	477.9	497.8	372.2	310.3
Total Liability and Shareholders' Equity	838.0	865.0	903.8	792.5	457.2

lion and total assets were $838 million, of which $132 million was goodwill. Tredegar's stock was trading near its three-year low but still outperformed the S&P 500 and the Dow market indices. The closing market price per share for Tredegar's common stock in 2002 was a high of $24.72, a low of $12.25, and an end of year price of $15.00 (Exhibit 4).

THE LONG ROAD TO VALUE CREATION: AN INTERVIEW WITH THE CEO

Corporate restructuring and spin-offs are commonplace. Many firms are successful with their spin-offs while others are not as successful. A spin-off has an existing culture, customer base, and staff with a corporate strategy that must be redirected quickly. An interview with Tredegar CEO John Gottwald highlights some fundamental operating philosophies that are critical for a successful turnaround. Below are excerpts of that interview:

- *Understand who you really are.* The company's key strengths were in specialty product niches, where it held patent protection and broad distribution. We quickly began channeling our resources into product categories that we felt were the strongest. By doing so, we extend the lines that yield results and detract from unproductive units.

- *Identify committed managers, guide them in setting their goals, and then let go.* We lost many good people in the early years. We did not make any real

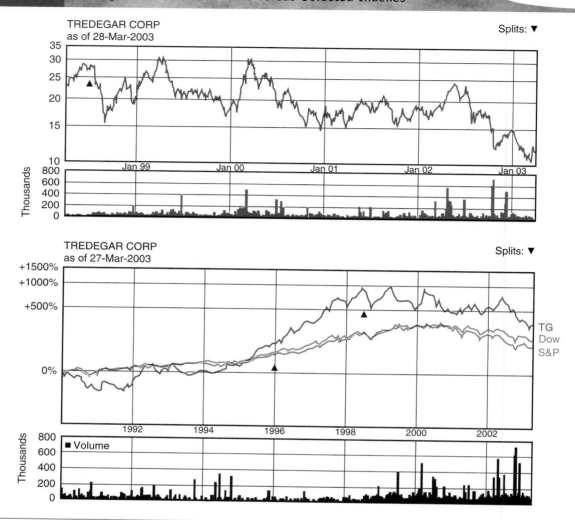

TREDEGAR CORP
as of 28-Mar-2003

Splits: ▼

TREDEGAR CORP
as of 27-Mar-2003

Splits: ▼

TG
Dow
S&P

Copyright 2002 Yahoo! Inc.

effort to entice them to stay, deciding instead to see who would stay and be committed to a turnaround strategy. For example, the original corporate staff consisted of over 100 employees many of whom considered themselves to be in an oversight and control capacity. We decided that we needed to change the culture to one of value creation where the corporate staff viewed the line divisions as their customers. To accomplish this, we divided the line managers into three groups and instructed them to think like owners of the business. They were charged with identifying the staff services that they would like to purchase out of their operating budgets and the people that they would like to work on their team. This exercise produced dramatic results.

By 1998, the corporate staff had less than 40 employees, the reporting structure was flatter, costs were down, and teamwork was greater.

- *Spend like a start-up.* Cash is king for any small company that cannot go back to dip into its parent's deep pockets. In the first few years, we ruthlessly cut back on costs, including saving on recurring costs associated with non-profitable businesses. Disposing of units that did not contribute to the bottom line not only helped improve cash positions but also stopped the drain caused by maintaining unproductive units.

- *Increase efficiency and quality.* We saw the creation of Tredegar as a rare opportunity to introduce a new management philosophy and culture to a group of under-performing businesses and product lines. We decided to stress quality as the most important driver of performance because we saw quality as a way to differentiate us from the competition. We defined quality as exceeding the customer's expectations for the life of the product by constantly reducing variation in all processes. We had a company-wide training effort to teach employees to use statistical process control and improve job skills. The goal was to increase material efficiency (i.e., good pounds versus total pounds produced), sales pounds per employee, reduced rework, more on-time deliveries, and fewer customer returns. The end result of this effort was products of consistent high quality, shorter lead times, more on-time deliveries, and ultimately, more satisfied customers.

- *Reward to the lowest possible level.* Directors, officers, and employees own almost half of Tredegar shares so that management, employee, and shareholder interests are directly linked. Most of our workforce receives performance-based compensation and many own stock options. We think that this strengthens the link between employees, customers, and shareholders. We reward highly competent self-starters who enjoy winning. Building this performance-driven culture has taken a lot of time and effort but is our most important competitive advantage.

FORGING NEW BRIDGES TO VALUE CREATION

As Tredegar looks for ways to continue growth in sales and earnings, it has many alternatives. One such alternative is to place more emphasis on foreign operations. These may be sales-oriented, such as to spread fixed developmental or production costs over a larger output, a key factor in capital-intensive industries such as aluminums. Another possibility is in resource-acquisition to secure differentiated or lower-cost capabilities from foreign locations or serve as a defensive ploy by preventing competitors from gaining a foothold in other strategic foreign markets. But any foreign alternative must be weighed against the use of resources domestically, such as to move into new potential growth industries. Each of Tredegar's product divisions has taken different strategies for international operations.

Film Products is the most international of Tredegar's divisions. In its 1996 annual report, this division listed "continued expansion into Asian, Latin American, and European markets" as one of its primary strategies. In 2000, Tredegar's Film Products division

added capacity in Brazil, Hungary, and China and purchased ADMA and Promea that sell specialty films and equipment in Europe, China, and the Middle East. Tredegar's expansion strategy mirrors that of Procter & Gamble, Tredegar's largest customer. If Tredegar does not supply P&G for, say, the Chinese market, Procter & Gamble might switch to a competitive supplier, such as Clopay or CT, for that market. A satisfactory relationship between P&G and Clopay or CT in China might erode Tredegar's position vis-à-vis P&G in the United States.

Between 1990 and 2002, the Film Products division's dependence on non-North American sales grew from 21 percent to 38 percent. The major growth was in Latin America, where 11 percent of sales were located in 2000—up from zero in 1990. By 2001, the Far East and Europe accounted for 8 percent and 19 percent of sales, respectively. In spite of a sales decrease and challenging economic conditions, profits from ongoing operations in the Film Products division increased by 17 percent to $72,307 million in 2002. Profits from ongoing operations had previously increased by 31 percent in 2001 in the Film Products division. Commenting on the future prospects of Film Products, President Scher stated, "We're optimistic that continual growth from new products and cost reductions will have an increasingly positive impact as the year progresses. By year-end, we should be well positioned to resume growth in both sales and profits during 2004." Tredegar's Film Products division continues to develop relationships with more firms in the personal hygiene business and sell more components per product.

Film Products' current strategy is to carve out a unique niche as the only company that offers a full range of components for diapers and feminine hygiene products for all regions of the world. In support of this strategy, Tredegar reported in early 2003 that it has established sales and product development relationships with all the major global producers of diapers and sanitary napkins as well as most regional and private label manufacturers. Tredegar continues to work closely with P&G on several new personal care products and has announced a new apertured topsheet for P&G's sanitary napkin business which will be introduced in Europe in 2003.

The Aluminum Extrusions division includes only Canada in its international strategy. In 1998, Tredegar acquired two Canada-based aluminum extrusions and fabrications plants from Reynolds Metals. In 1999, Tredegar acquired two more Canada-based aluminum extrusions and fabrications plants. These purchases were motivated primarily by the growth in the construction and building industries that fueled growth in aluminum demand. To meet that demand quickly, Tredegar needed to acquire additional capacity. In aluminum extrusions, Tredegar sees itself as a consolidator in an industry undergoing rapid consolidation. Unfortunately, the distribution, transportation, and construction markets slowed significantly and orders were expected to be weak in the near future, reflecting the general malaise in the United States and global economy. Through improved execution and cost control, profits in the Aluminum Extrusions division were up 7 percent to $3.6 million in 2002. Sales decreased by 5 percent to $360.3 million and significant sales growth was not expected in 2003. According to President Scher, "Our aluminum business continues to be affected by poor economic conditions. Until the economy strengthens, we do not expect to see meaningful improvement in this business."

There are some deeper questions raised about strategy of spin-offs from Tredegar's technology businesses. Can a diversified firm with a primarily manufacturing orientation successfully segue its operations into a high-technology start-up world? Apparently, Tredegar has not had the relative success for which it aspired in this segment, but as students of strategy we must question ourselves to see if there are true benefits that underlie

shifts from low to high tech; probably the most pressing questions include the issues of complementarity of resources and transferability of organizational capabilities. Perhaps this can be done; it could just be a question of "under what conditions?"

In the near future, Tredegar's management will face many challenges of which the following are examples. First, how can Tredegar deal with the growing presence of Chinese imports in a number of the aluminum extrusions markets? Second, P&G continues to comprise approximately 30 percent of Tredegar's net sales. Third, will they be able to sell Therics, a company with high potential and substantial risks? Fourth, in spite of expected growth, the market price for Tredegar stock remains low. Is the low market valuation truly representative of Tredegar's potential? Tredegar has grown from a spin-off with a combination of successful and unsuccessful units in 1989. It has managed to divest its unproductive units while improving productive units. After a lot of hard work and a success story under his belt, Mr. Gottwald notes, "When I think about how much Tredegar has changed since its creation in 1989, I can't help but wonder if external perceptions have kept pace. It is clear that we are facing several challenges, but I want to send a clear message—now is a time to look forward, not back."

case thirty-two

Richard C. Scamehorn
Ohio University

It was cold, early on the morning of December 4, 2002, as Glen F. Tilton, Chairman and CEO of UAL, the parent of United Airlines drove along Chicago's Dan Ryan Expressway. Tilton was on his way to Chicago's O'Hare International Airport. UAL, the world's second largest airline had just filed for bankruptcy the previous day and Tilton wanted to get a message to several groups of people.

A MESSAGE OF ASSURANCE

Glen Tilton wanted to meet with customers of United Airlines to assure them that United would be flying its usual routes, notwithstanding the previous day's filing. Moreso, he wanted to tell them that United Airlines would continue to fly these routes during the busy holiday season. The holiday season was the country's second busiest for the airline industry (Thanksgiving being the busiest) and Tilton wanted to minimize any cancellations resulting from customers' fear of flight cancellations.

Secondly, but almost equally important, was to meet one-on-one with many of United's employees to assure them that United would continue to fly and that their jobs were secure (at least, for the time being). If Tilton could not retain the loyalty of employees, he would be unable to meet the commitment he was making to the customers.

Finally, he knew that if he was seen talking to customers and employees, the media would want to capture these scenes and broadcast them over the networks. In this regard, he hoped to reach (at no cost to United) at least five important groups: 1) the flying public, at large; 2) stockholders; 3) suppliers to United; 4) Wall Street and United's creditors; and 5) United's partners in the Star Alliance of global cooperative code-sharing airlines.

In fact, the media would probably broadcast his statement about the airline providing it was short and to the point. To further this event he welcomed the cameras as he talked to both customers and employees. Before long he was standing before a battery of microphones, issuing his pledge that United Airlines could be depended upon to keep flying throughout the holidays.

UNITED'S BANKRUPTCY

United Airlines financial problems were frequently viewed as a result of the terrorist attacks of 9/11. However, a review of United's statement of operations presents a different picture. In the first six months of 2001, well before the terrorist attacks, United experienced a pre-tax loss of $1,051,000,000 and a net loss (after a credit for income tax) of $678,000,000 (see tables 1 and 2).

This paints a clear picture that United's operating problems, although exacerbated by the events of 9/11, were inherent within the company's revenue–cost structure. Over a longer time, prior to filing, United experienced a net loss of more than $10 billion during the period between 2001 and mid-2002 (see charts 1 and 2).

Bankruptcy, although related to losses, is more directly focused on cash availability and flow. On the surface United's cash balance seemed impressive: $2,700,000,000 in the bank at mid-year, 2002. Unfortunately the company's losses were creating a cash-burn rate in the range of $2–5 million per day, reducing the cash balance to less than $800,000,000 by early December, 2002. This was insufficient to repay the $850,000,000 portion of a loan which was due December 3, 2002.

AIR TRANSPORTATION STABILIZATION BOARD

As a result of the terrorist attacks of 9/11, Congress established the ATSB in late 2001 as a method for the United States government to guarantee up to $10,000,000,000 to commercial banks for loans made to troubled airlines. Although fifteen airlines had applied for this guarantee only four had been approved and

	2001	2000	1999
Operating revenues			
Passenger	$13,788	$16,932	$15,784
Cargo	704	931	906
Other operating revenues	1,646	1,489	1,337
	16,138	19,352	18,027
Operating expenses			
Salaries and related costs	7,080	6,877	6,426
Aircraft fuel	2,476	2,511	1,139
Commissions	710	1,025	1,139
Purchased services	1,650	1,711	1,575
Aircraft rent	827	888	876
Landing fees and other rent	1,009	959	949
Depreciation and amortization	1,026	988	650
Aircraft maintenance	701	698	689
Cost of sales	1,280	1,061	602
Other operating expenses	1,722	1,841	1,737
Special charges	1,428	139	17
	19,909	18,698	16,636
Earnings (loss) from operations	(3,771)	654	1,391
Other income			
Interest expense	(525)	(402)	(362)
Interest capitalized	79	77	75
Interest income	105	101	68
Earnings (loss) of affiliates	(23)	(12)	37
Gain on sale of investments	261	109	731
Non-operating special charge	(49)	(61)	–
Airline stabilization grant	652	–	–
Miscellaneous	(86)	(35)	2
	414	(223)	551
Earnings (loss) before tax, etc.	(3,357)	431	1,942
Provisions for income taxes	(1,226)	160	699
Earnings before distributions	(2,131)	271	1,243
Distributions and other	(14)	(221)	(8)
Net earnings (loss)	$(2,145)	$50	$1,235
Net earnings per share (diluted)	$(40.04)	$0.04	$9.94

seven had been turned down. The reason for such limited action was that approval required a highly credible business plan for successful loan repayment. The Federal government did not want to end up owning a lot of used airplanes in return for paying-off the banks who had made the loans.

United Airlines determined they would require $1,800,000,000 in an ATSB loan guarantee and made such application during the Summer, 2002. The business plan they submitted to justify such an amount was based upon achieving $5,800,000,000 in operating cost reductions.

	2001	2000
Assets		
Current assets		
Cash and cash equivalents	$ 1,688	$ 1,679
Short-term investments	940	665
Receivables, less doubtful accounts	1,047	1,216
Aircraft fuel and spare parts	329	424
Income tax receivables	174	110
Deferred income taxes	272	225
Prepaid expenses and other	636	460
	5,086	4,779
Operating property and equipment owned		
Flight equipment	14,745	14,888
Advances on flight equipment	566	810
Other property and equipment	3,919	3,714
	14,514	13,829
Less accumulated depreciation and amortization	4,716	5,583
	14,514	13,829
Capital leases		
Flight equipment	2,667	3,154
Other property and equipment	99	99
	2,766	3,154
Less accumulated amortization	472	640
	2,294	2,514
	16,806	16,343
Other assets:		
Investments	278	435
Intangibles, less accumulated depreciation	984	671
Aircraft lease deposits	667	710
Prepaid rent	374	567
Deferred income taxes	97	—
Other	903	850
	3,303	3,233
	$25,197	$24,355
Liabilities and Stockholders' Equity		
Current liabilities		
Notes payable	133	—
Long-term debt maturing within one year	1,217	170
Current obligations under capital lease	237	269
Advance ticket sales	1,183	1,454
Accounts payable	1,268	1,188
Accrued salaries, wages and benefits	1,227	1,236

| TABLE 2 | Statements of Consolidated Financial Position *(continued)* |

	2001	2000
Accrued aircraft rent	$ 903	$ 840
Other accrued liabilities	1,898	1,352
	8,066	6,509
Long-term debt		
Long-term obligations under capital leases	1,943	2,261
Other liabilities and deferred credits		
Deferred pension liability	1,241	136
Postretirement benefit liability	1,690	1,557
Deferred gains	827	912
Accrued aircraft rent	551	408
Deferred income taxes	–	1,241
Other	1,049	783
	5,358	5,037
Commitments and contingent liabilities		
Company-obligated mandatorily redeemable liabilities	98	99
Preferred stock committed to Supplemental ESOP	77	304
Stockholders' equity		
Common stock at par	1	1
Additional capital invested	4,995	4,797
Retained earnings (deficit)	(199)	1,998
Stock held in treasury, at cost		
Preferred	(305)	(305)
Common	(1,180)	(1,179)
Accumulated other income	(275)	152
Other	(4)	(7)
	3,033	5,457
	$25,197	$24,355

Almost the day after the application was filed, United's competitors launched a lobby attacking the business plan. They argued that United, in some cases, would actually be paying employees more than at the start of the year. One competitor attempted to show that United would be paying an additional 16% increase to pilots during the course of their business plan. The competitors, notably American, Continental and Delta airlines argued that United was poorly managed and as such should not be subsidized by taxpayer guaranteed loans.

The fight drew an immediate reaction from United management as well as employees. Paul Whiteford, chairman of United pilot's union said, "We have been stunned at how far other carriers [competitors] are willing to go to sabotage United's application. We invite anyone who doubts the extraordinary employee sacrifices at United to spend an afternoon with a group of our pilots."

A response to a claim that ramp agents and machinists would be paid retroactive pay, costing $65,000,000 per quarter for the next two years was refuted by Joe Tiberi, spokesman for the International Association of Machinists (IAM). Tiberi noted that these workers had been working since 1994 without a pay raise and the (above) claims were, "ridiculous" and that "the concessions are real."

JUST SAY NO

On November 27, 2002, the day before the IAM was to vote on a revised company contract proposal, the ATSB

CHART 1

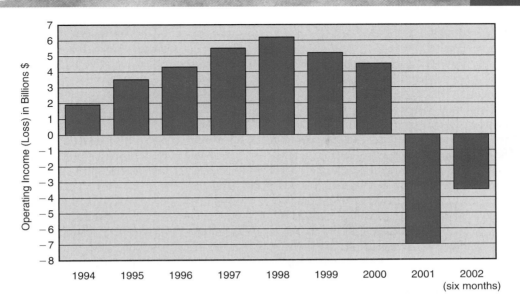

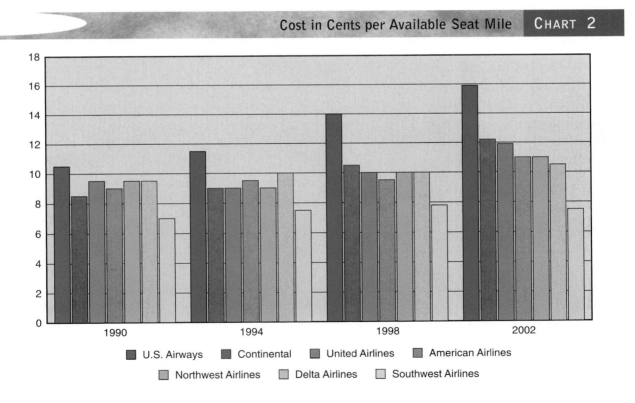

■ U.S. Airways   ■ Continental   ■ United Airlines   ■ American Airlines

■ Northwest Airlines   ■ Delta Airlines   ■ Southwest Airlines

rejected United's application. The Board's explanation was that United's recovery, as outlined in their business plan, was "not financially sound." Further, "United would face a high probability of another liquidity crisis [cash flow] within the next few years."

Later it was leaked that United's business plan had puffed-up their revenue projections. This was done by assuming that the airline industry market growth would escalate far more rapidly than all the rest of the industry was forecasting. The ATSB concluded that if industry growth followed the consensus forecast, United would be unable to repay the loans. United joined six other airlines who had their application rejected (see table 3).

The die was now cast.

THE AIRLINE INDUSTRY'S TURBULENT HISTORY

The United States Post Office decided to experiment with the concept of delivery of mail by airplanes, and in 1917 it received a Federal grant of $100,000 for that purpose. The experiment proved worthwhile and in 1918 the U.S. Air Mail Service was started using a JN-4 "Jenny" biplane for service between Washington, D.C. and New York City. In what might be called an omen of the industry, the pilot of the inaugural flight started flying the wrong direction from Washington. By the time he realized his mistake and corrected his course, there was insufficient fuel to reach New York City. So, he landed in Maryland and the nation's first air mail was actually delivered to its destination by train.

Private firms were awarded air mail routes across the country giving conception to an embryo of an airline industry. With the development of higher performance aircraft, which could fly faster and carry heavier loads than the "Jenny," the cost of an air mail letter was established at 34 cents, or about $4.00 in current value.

Government control over the infant industry was made certain by the Watres Act of 1930. This gave U.S. Postmaster General Walter Brown control over which airlines received the lucrative air mail contracts. Believing that a few larger airlines were more stable than many small ones, Brown forced the mergers of these small airlines into fewer, but larger ones: a trend which continues today.

Unfortunately, a scandal in 1932 concerning the corruption in the awarding of air mail routes resulted in President Roosevelt re-militarizing the air mail service under the U.S. Army. This quickly proved to be a mistake and the Air Mail Act of 1934 re-privatized air mail service. Other benefits of the act resulted in a broadening of the airlines which received contracts, the opposite of Brown's practice. The act also eliminated holding companies such as Boeing, who manufactured aircraft and also owned two airlines which delivered air mail.

Passenger travel had become common, although it remained a luxury. However, the industry was without direction so Congress passed the Civil Aeronautics Act of 1938. This created the Civil Aeronautics Authority (CAA, later called Civil Aeronautics Board, CAB) with

TABLE 3	Air Transportation Stabilization Board Activity through 12-05-02 $ millions			
Airline	Annual Revenue	Requested Loan	Date of Request	Board Action
United Airlines	16,138	1,800	5-24-02	Reject
U.S. Airways	8,288	900	6-07-02	Approve
America West	2,066	380	11-13-01	Approve
Frontier Air	455	63	5-28-02	Approve
Spirit Airlines	450	54	3-28-02	Reject
National Airlines	276	50.5	5-03-02	Reject
Aloha Airlines	N/A	40.5	6-28-02	Approve
World Airlines	318	27	6-28-02	Pending
MEDJet Int'l	N/A	7.7	6-28-02	Reject
Vanguard Airlines	119	72	12-06-01	Reject
Frontier Flying	16	72	1-29-02	Reject
Corporate	N/A	7	6-28-02	Reject
Evergreen Int'l	N/A	N/A	2-25-02	Pending
Gemini Air Cargo	N/A	N/A	6-28-02	Pending
Great Plains Air	N/A	N/A	6-28-02	Pending

authority to regulate the airlines' routes, fares, air mail rates and most every other aspect of the airline industry. Further development of the industry proceeded slowly as the nation sequentially prepared for World War II, fought it and then returned to a peacetime economy.

In 1956, two passenger planes collided over the Grand Canyon, killing 128 people, causing Congress to pass the Federal Aviation Act of 1958. This act created what is now called the Federal Aviation Administration (FAA) with a primary mission to oversee airline safety and traffic control. The CAB, however, continued as oversight of the economic aspects of the airline industry, maintaining an industry similar to that of a public utility with nearly guaranteed rates of return.

Following the 1973 oil embargo and its resultant fuel price spike, the CAB authorized major airline fare increases which drew heavy public criticism. By 1975, the CAB staff had concluded the airline industry was no longer an "infant industry" and was "naturally competitive." As a result, under the Jimmy Carter administration and led by CAB Chair Alfred Kahn, Congress passed the Airline Deregulation Act of 1978 eliminating restrictions and control of routes by 1981 and fares by 1983. The act also eliminated the CAB.

ENTER A NEW TYPE OF AIRLINE

However, it did much more. It increased competition among the existing airlines and stimulated the entry of a series of new airlines in the 1980s and 1990s: People Express, ValuJet, JetBlue, AirTran, America West, Southwest Airlines and others. All of these had one characteristic in common, but different from the old airlines. They were all based upon low operating cost and offered highly discounted fares.

The new entrants, along with competition of the older major airlines, resulted in price discounting which saved the flying public an estimated $20,000,000,000 per year. As flying became less expensive more people flew more often and the industry grew at a pace nearly twice that of the economy.

It should be noted that the newly intensified competition resulted in the demise of several major "old line" airlines: Braniff, Eastern, Pan American and Trans World.

UNITED AIRLINES' HISTORY

Following the merger of a half-dozen small airlines, the new owner appropriately chose the name of United Airlines. In the 1930s, United pioneered a new route from San Francisco to New York. United's busiest route developed between Chicago and New York. As a result, Chicago's O'Hare Airport became United's home base with administrative headquarters located in nearby Elk Grove Village. United's growth took a leap forward with the acquisition of Pan American's Pacific Ocean routes and aircraft, placing United for the first time as a major carrier to the Far East.

United elected to utilize the "hub-and-spoke" strategy, created by Delta Airlines. This plan attempted to capture flyers on their entire journey from city "A" to city "C," which was previously not possible with the traditional "point-to-point" strategy.

With point-to-point routes, airlines not flying directly to city "C" could not offer any customer service. However, utilizing hubs (which we will now call city "B,") an airline could pick up a passenger at city "A", fly a shortened spoke to city "B", where the passenger would transfer aircraft and fly another shortened spoke to city "C." This hub-and-spoke system was more costly since more landings and takeoffs were involved along with more ground crews, but revenues as well as market shares would be increased.

United, the world's second largest airline had amassed the most elaborate and complex hub-and-spoke network in the United States with hubs in Chicago, San Francisco, Los Angeles, Denver and Dallas (see table 4).

Some individual routes were more important to United than others (see table 5).

THE INFRASTRUCTURE OF AN AIRLINE

Airlines are inherently capital intensive. Aircraft, costing up to $250,000,000 must be acquired by equity or debt, capitalized and depreciated over a number of years. New aircraft technology, such as wide body, fly-by-wire controls, quieter engines, improved fuel economy or upgraded passenger features (in-seat video, phones, high-tech seats, et al.) required all airlines to purchase the new technology aircraft to avoid falling behind competitors.

Airlines must also acquire flight simulators for pilot training, airport hangars for maintenance, ground equipment and computer systems.

The industry is also labor intensive, the most costly category being their pilots. Other labor costs include flight attendants, mechanics, baggage handlers, and company agents at gates, ticket and reservation desks. One third of all airline revenue is consumed by employees who are among the highest paid of any industry. Many of these employees are unionized, which reduces the amount of management flexibility and job control. Industry average costs are:

TABLE 4 United Airlines' Hub Activity First Six Months—2002

City	Total Passengers Boarding	UAL % Share
San Francisco	5,373,064	53.1
Los Angeles	9,513,554	23.1
Denver	7,860,886	64.1
Chicago	12,488,553	49.0
Dallas	2,254,265	53.3

TABLE 5

Route	Daily Average Passengers (6 Mo.)	United Share % 2002
Chicago–New York	2,333	33.7
New York–San Francisco	1,727	42.0
Chicago–Washington	1,561	72.9
Los Angeles–New York	1,403	21.7
Chicago–Los Angeles	1,360	35.3
Chicago–San Francisco	1,345	54.7
Chicago–Denver	1,207	51.4
Denver–New York	1,175	47.1
Denver–San Francisco	1,009	70.0

27%	Flying—pilots and fuel
13%	Maintenance
16%	Ground services
13%	Promotions and travel agent commissions
9%	In-flight service: cabin crew, food, etc.
6%	Depreciation
6%	Administration
10%	Other

Revenue is derived primarily from passengers:

80%	Passengers
10%	Cargo (freight and air mail)
10%	Other

A SOCIAL EXPERIMENT IN EMPLOYEE OWNERSHIP?

United Airlines is unique among the major domestic airlines: 55 percent is employee owned. That is a story in itself.

In 1995, Gerald Greenwald, a former Chrysler Corporation executive was named United's chief executive, replacing Stephen M. Wolf. United was experiencing profit and cash flow problems at that point and in order to achieve an operating cost (salary) reduction of $4,800,000,000, the pilots, machinists and non-union salaried employees agreed to accept the wage cuts provided they were given 55% ownership of the airline and each group was awarded one seat on the board of directors.

The flight attendants union refused to participate in this plan which irked the other three employee groups.

Patrick Palazzolo, a pilot of 24 years with United called this agreement "a new dawn." He also said,

"There were extremely high hopes that Gerald Greenwald could change the culture, the culture that had been calcified here over the years, the 'us versus them' mentality. He said all the right things. But, he made a fatal mistake, which is he didn't clean house. The middle management structure, and most senior managers around him, never changed."

Palazzolo also blamed the old-time managers for not following through on what was called "seamless contracts." This concept brought negotiators from both sides to work out new contracts before the old ones expired, thereby eliminating the need for a union "strike vote" at the eleventh hour. The lead negotiation with the seamless concept was the pilot's union where negotiations were started in December, 1988, way ahead of the contract expiration of April, 2000.

Greenwald retired (early) and James E. Goodwin became CEO and was most interested in United's acquisition of U.S. Airways. When the pilots discovered Goodwin's plans, they were afraid that many of the pilots' jobs at United would be given to more senior U.S. Airways pilots. The pilots' contract negotiations fell apart.

Airline pilots have a career concern which exceeds the other airline employee groups. Ticket and gate agents are able to find employment in other industries which require meeting and directing the public. The same is true for cabin attendants. Machinists are in demand by many industries much of the time. The skills of a professional airline pilot are essentially of no value in any other industry. Once a pilot establishes a career in the airline industry, particularly a mid-life pilot, they become entrapped in that industry, for better or worse, for their working life. Accordingly, in order to achieve job security, a pilot might sacrifice wages but not seniority.

Senior United Airlines pilots make more than $300,000 per year. Forfeiting a 10 percent salary cut is much less threatening than job loss. So, when the April contract expired, the pilots continued to work without a contract with what is called "work to rule."

No pilot would accept any overtime, which meant if the 80 hour per month time was used-up, and the plane was on the ground in Paris, France, the company would need to fly another pilot to Paris for the return flight. In addition, all work rules were now strictly adhered to: no "sneaking in line" for a faster takeoff or landing or willing to take off if storms were present, etc. The result was that many flights were hours late, causing missed connections at the hub transfer point. It was a job slowdown. Customers became irate.

United management said it lost $700,000,000 as a result of the slowdown. As the pressure on management became unbearable, Goodwin gave in to the most liberal contract of any airline: pay raises of between 22 percent and 28 percent. The pilots had won a bonanza. After it was all over, the pilots were in a state of disbelief. T. Scott Cooper, a first officer (co-pilot) on one of United's AirBus A320s said, "Had there been a good faith contract proposal, we would have settled for less."

BAD BLOOD

Goodwin made an offer to acquire U.S. Airways which was tentatively accepted, subject to approval by the U.S. Department of Justice relative to anti-trust. In July, 2001 the Justice Department blocked the acquisition and United had to eat $116,000,000 of costs related to the attempt. United employees were further embittered stating that United had just squandered money the unions had sacrificed. That same summer, United's management wrote off $102,000,000 in a failed attempt to use non-union flight attendants in a new business-jet division.

Expecting to see profits improve, the losses shown in United's release of the first half, 2001 statement of operations made employees wonder what happened to all the salary cuts made by the pilots, machinists and non-union clerical. To make matters worse, the unions started to blame each other.

In October, 2001 Goodwin made a public statement that United Airlines would go bankrupt in 2002 unless it was able to straighten out its financial mess. Just about everybody had lost confidence in the company management. This caused Wall Street to substantially lower the valuation of United's stock.

The unions then demanded Goodwin's resignation. Goodwin was replaced by John W. Creighton, Jr. who issued a warning in the summer of 2002 that United was about to go bankrupt. As United's stock slid further, along with the employees' 401K retirement accounts, the unions demanded his resignation. He was replaced in the summer of 2002 by Glen F. Tilton.

The pilots criticized the machinists for not contributing more to the cost reduction program. One pilot said, "It's hard for us pilots to understand why the machinists' union leadership would rather let the company slide into bankruptcy than try to save it." In addition, the pilots were still smarting from the machinists' vote in 2001 to approve the merger with U.S. Airways.

The flight attendants have been most adamant about not giving wage concessions for two reasons: first, they never achieved industry-leading wages (like the pilots and machinists did) and second, their wages are much less—$23,000 to a maximum of $50,000, including overtime.

Patrick Palazzolo owned 4,627 shares of United stock, which were worth nearly $390,000 in early 1999. The day before United filed for bankruptcy they were worth $4,627. (See chart 3.)

A CAN OF WORMS

Glen Tilton left O'Hare Airport late that day, exhausted and drained of adrenaline. He had met with the flying customers, the national media, pilots, machinists, cabin attendants, baggage handlers, ground support crews, gate and ticket agents. Although he felt he had made contact and attempted to ensure everyone that United Airlines would continue to fly, he also knew that there were so many unresolved issues that neither he, nor anyone else, could answer at this time.

He also recognized the strife which was present among the company employees. Nearly every group mistrusted one or more of the others. He also recognized that each group's position would defend its own enlightened self-interest before any of the others.

Every employee knew that cost reduction was the only answer for survival of the airline. Tilton knew, as did the unions, that as soon as United Airlines had filed under Section 1113 of the United States Bankruptcy Code that the company has a right to ask a judge to cancel labor contracts.

However, treatment of the three unions would certainly be different, because the three union groups were so widely diverse in two categories.

The first category was political power. Pilots were the "captains of the ship." Although they certainly were not imbued with the power of a ship's captain at sea, their word was law regarding most decisions once the aircraft was airborne. As a result, their direction of leadership swayed other employees' thinking more than anyone else (including that of management).

The second category was wage scale. Senior United Airlines pilots' annual earnings were more than $300,000, while junior cabin attendants earned barely $25,000. Machinists' annual earnings were around $50,000, counting overtime. What sort of wage concession must the pilots sacrifice in order to motivate the other union groups to add to the inevitable forthcoming cost reductions?

While driving back to Elk Grove Village, Glen Tilton was thinking about this can of worms knowing that if he didn't arrive at a workable solution, United Airlines would become a candidate to fly the same final route flown by Braniff, Eastern, Pan American and Trans World.

CHART 3

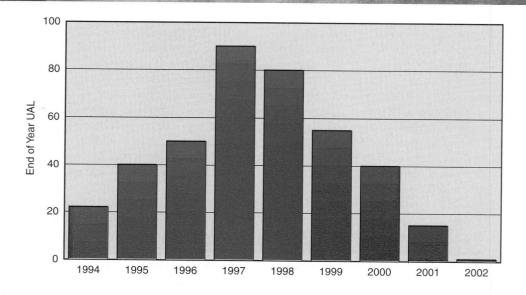

case thirty-three

Isaac Cohen
San Jose State University

In 1997, Federal Express (FedEx) was flying high. Its share price had increased by nearly 70 percent in one year, its international earnings (fiscal 1997) accounted for 20 percent of its total income, and its foreign income was expected to exceed its domestic income in five years. FedEx's commanding lead in the domestic air express industry was also growing: between 1994 and 1997, Federal Express's market share climbed from 35 percent to 43 percent while United Parcel Service's (UPS) share stagnated at a level of 26–27 percent of the U.S. air express market.[1]

The "father" of the air express industry, FedEx's founder and CEO Frederick Smith had just concluded a merger agreement with Caliber System, a $1.3 billion trucking company which owned a fleet of 13,500 trucks—second in size to UPS's only. The new fleet was expected to help Federal Express compete successfully with United Parcel Service in non-express ground operations.[2] Additionally, FedEx benefited from UPS's recent labor troubles. During a Teamster strike in the Summer of 1997—a nation-wide UPS work-stoppage that lasted 15 days—the average daily delivery volume of FedEx jumped 15 percent, as many UPS customers switched to FedEx.[3] Another critical advantage of Federal Express over UPS was its early lead in technology. FedEx had pioneered the automated package tracking system in 1983, and by the mid 1990s, the company was operating an end-to-end client-server Unix information system that traced every package at each stage of its delivery from origins to destination. UPS, by contrast, had not begun investing heavily in information technology until the late 1980s, and trailed FedEx through the mid 1990s. In 1993 [according to one industry expert], FedEx was two years ahead of UPS in developing logistical services that helped companies coordinate storage, distribution, and assembly operations.[4] In 1994–95, a Harvard Business School study singled out Federal Express as the industry's technological leader. An industry analyst speaking in Winter 1997 estimated that FedEx's use of technology was still so far ahead of its competitors that it would have taken UPS at least one year to catch up.[5] And in 2001, FedEx formed an alliance with the United States Postal Service (USPS) which posed a serious competitive challenge to UPS.

Looking back at the 1990s, this case focuses on the growing competition between UPS and FedEx. Would FedEx manage to retain its lead in the 21st century? Would the advent of the Internet, the increasing globalization of the air freight industry, and the exploding demand for worldwide logistical services enhance FedEx's competitive advantage relative to UPS? Or would it rather allow UPS to catch up and leapfrog FedEx?

To assess the competitive advantage of FedEx versus UPS, this case pays particular attention to the strengths and weaknesses of the strategies undertaken by each of the two rival companies.

THE INDUSTRY

In the late 1990s, the parcel service industry in the United States was dominated by four large carriers: UPS, FedEx, Airborne Express, and the U.S. Postal Service. In 1998, the four carriers generated together close to 95 percent of the industry's domestic revenues. Ranked by market share, UPS (47 percent) led the way and was followed by FedEx (25 percent), USPS (16 percent), and Airborne (6 percent). One measure of the industry's increasing importance was its growth rate over time: domestic parcel revenues jumped from $2 billion annually in 1970 to $7 billion in 1980, $22 billion in 1990, and over $50 billion in 2000. Another was the industry's expanding role in the economy: the value of goods shipped by parcel carriers in the United States climbed from 2 percent of the GDP in 1977 to 11 percent of the GDP in 1997.[6]

This case was presented at the October 2002 Meeting of the North American Case Research Association (NACRA) at Banff, Canada. I am grateful to the San Jose State University College of Business for its Support. Copyright by Isaac Cohen and NACRA. Reprinted by permission. All rights reserved.

Why the parcel service industry expanded so rapidly may be explained by four interrelated changes in the ways U.S. manufacturing companies operated: the growing reliance of companies on just-in-time inventory control methods, mass customization and the increasing demand for logistical services, the growing dependency of customers (both businesses and individuals) on information technology, and the increasing use of advanced technology in all sectors of the economy.

During the last quarter of the 20th Century, manufacturing firms in nearly every industry had adopted just-in-time inventory control methods to cut storage and distribution costs. As companies sought to reduce inventories, they relied more and more heavily on parcel carriers. UPS, FedEx, USPS, and Airborne provided a faster, more reliable, and more frequent service than rail, motor, and water carriers. Because parcel service was highly reliable, manufacturers no longer needed to keep large "safety" stocks to protect against late deliveries. And because parcel service was exceedingly rapid, manufacturers no longer needed to stock sizable "in transit" inventory to ensure against long delivery journeys. One consequence of the growth in parcel shipments of all types of goods was the steep decline in inventory. Between 1980 and 1997, the total value of inventory held in the United States fell from 9.4 percent to 5.5 percent of the GDP.[7]

Closely related to the just-in-time inventory control system was a build-to-order manufacturing technique known as mass customization. Dell Computer epitomized mass customization. "When you order a customized computer-package [a UPS manager explained], the components probably come from at least four different locations, are pulled together by a small-package carrier like UPS, and are delivered at once to your doorstep."[8] While mass customization required the logistical services of parcel carriers, the supply of such services added value to their transportation capabilities, and made them more diversified. In 2001–2002, Internet-based logistics was one of FedEx and UPS's fastest growing businesses.

In addition to providing delivery and logistical services, parcel carriers supplied customers with information. "The information about the package is almost as important as the package itself," Frederick Smith had famously said, and indeed, shippers had sought to track such information for decades. Ordinarily, reliable tracking ("in transit visibility") enabled shippers to both plan ahead and minimize disruption in cases of delayed deliveries. Occasionally, reliable tracking was absolutely critical, as for example, in the case of a hospital waiting for shipments of medical supplies. Reliable tracking did not develop overnight, however. In their efforts to improve tracking, parcel carriers gained from several

technological innovations, including the development of sophisticated bar codes, laser scanners, state-of-the-art software, satellite and cell phone communication equipment, electronic information interchanges, and the Internet.[9]

Parcel carriers also benefited from the increasing demand for their services by the fastest growing industries in the 1990s. Relying heavily on parcel service, manufacturers of computer and related equipment, electronics and office equipment, precision instruments, medical equipment, medical supplies, and pharmaceutical products were among UPS and FedEx's largest clients.[10] Shipping electronic and medical products in small cardboard boxes instead of large cargo pallets was rather expensive, to be sure, but prompt delivery added value to these products, and improved customer satisfaction.

Finally, two major trends were likely to shape the future of the parcel service industry in the 21st century, the growing globalization of world trade, and the expanding role of the Internet in retailing and e-commerce.

During the early 2000s global manufacturers adopted just-in-time inventory control practices, on the one hand, and mass customization, on the other. As a result, the worldwide demand for logistical services increased markedly. An integral part of the global supply chain, parcel service supplied much of the growing demand. Between 1993 and 1998, the market for international air express service more than doubled. During the ten year period 1998–2007, global express revenues were expected to grow from $15 billion to $150 billion. In 2001, the global leader was DHL International Ltd. with a 20–25 percent share in the overnight express market. FedEx was tied in second place with the TNT-Post Group, each accounting for a 10–15 percent share. UPS was a close third with an 8–12 percent share in the international overnight market.[11]

Similarly, the explosion in e-commerce was revolutionizing retailing. The Internet enabled customers to link directly with manufacturers and retailers, place an order online, and pay electronically. In 2001, the online market was served almost exclusively by parcel carriers, and this trend was likely to continue in the foreseeable future. The value of goods ordered over the Internet and shipped to homes doubled from $20 billion in 1999 to $40 billion in 2000. Online retail sales were expected to reach $100 billion in 2003 and $180 billion in 2004.[12]

THE ASCENT OF A GIANT: UPS AND THE PARCEL SERVICE INDUSTRY

In 1907, Jim Casey founded UPS in Seattle as a six-bicycle messenger service. Casey was 19 years old at the time, and he ran the company for the next 55 years. From the start, UPS was organized as a private company "owned by its managers and managed by its owners." UPS remained privately owned for more than 90 years.[13]

During the first two decades of its operation, the company functioned as a contract carrier, delivering small packages from department stores to homes on bicycles, motorcycles, and small trucks. UPS extended service from Seattle to Oakland, California in 1919, Los Angeles in 1922, and New York City (its headquarters between 1930 and 1975), Newark, New Jersey and Greenwich, Connecticut by 1930. Following the end of World War II, UPS evolved from a contract carrier into a common carrier, serving commercial and industrial firms as well as individual customers. Operating as a "common carrier," UPS was obligated to serve any shipper located within its service territory.[14]

Postwar expansion was rapid. In 1969, UPS delivered 500 million packages to 165,000 regular customers, generating $548 million in revenues and $32 million in profits. Its 3,700 stockholders were its own executives and managers, their families, heirs, and estates.[15]

Despite regulatory restrictions on motor carriers' operations, UPS obtained federal approval to operate fully or partly in 31 states in 1970, and all 50 states in 1980. With the passage of the trucking deregulation act of 1980, UPS was free to offer services to any point throughout the continental United States without restrictions. Beginning in 1976, UPS embarked on a massive global expansion. The company bought and leased aircraft, offered air express deliveries, and extended services to Canada, Germany, Japan, and many other countries.[16] Relaxing Casey's long-standing policy of limiting stock ownership to managers only, UPS went public in 1999. In 2000, UPS was a $30 billion company with a fleet of 340 planes and 153,000 trucks, and a workforce totaling 359,000 employees. It delivered 13 million packages a day and generated $2.9 billion in net income.[17]

STRATEGY

UPS's growth strategy was based on two elements, both of which helped the company cut its operating costs: building route density and standardizing the jobs of drivers and sorters. To achieve a high route density and deliver a large number of packages per route mile, UPS drew a circle around certain cities, 150 miles in radius, and offered to ship any package meeting its size and weight limitations to any place within the circle. Increased route density enhanced labor productivity, and in turn, lowered delivery costs. To standardize the driver and sorter's jobs, UPS put strict limits on the size and weight of packages. In 1970, UPS delivered packages weighing no more than 50 pounds with a combined length, width, and height of up to 120 inches. The average package weighed ten pounds, was about the size of a briefcase, and was therefore easy to sort on conveyor belts, and convenient to carry by hand. In the 1980s, UPS increased its parcel weight limitations to 70 pounds, and redesigned its sorting facilities and transport vehicles to handle parcels not exceeding 108 inches in combined length, width, and height. Again in 1994, UPS increased its parcel maximum weight limitations to 150 pounds.[18]

UPS's drive at efficiency dates back to the 1920s. Casey was heavily influenced by Frederick Winslow Taylor's Scientific Management theories, particularly Taylor's time-and-motion studies. Utilizing the stopwatch to measure employee productivity, Casey applied Taylor's principles to the package delivery industry with an obsessive rigor.

Casey's legacy lived on for decades. Industrial engineers employed by UPS kept on improving package handling efficiency, measuring the speed of loading and unloading packages, and timing every driver's route to the traffic light. In 1988 sorters were expected to load 650 parcels per hour and unload 1,300 per hour.[19] UPS drivers were expected to comply with a rule-book called "The 340 Methods." "The 340 Methods" had originally been published in the 1920s, was revised periodically, and was still in use in 2001. It instructed drivers to walk at a pace of three feet per second, carry the parcel under the left arm and the [electronic] clipboard under the right arm, step into the truck with the right foot, and hold the keys with the middle finger of the right hand (serrated edge downward, facing out). Starting the truck, drivers were advised: "Engage the starter with one hand while fastening the seat-belt with the other." Drivers were supposed to complete the [computerized] paperwork on the way back to the truck, and fold the money they collected face up, sequentially ordered. "It is just like the military," one UPS driver said. "If you don't meet their time standards, they ride with you and tell you every little thing you do wrong." Management called drivers who fell behind "least best" drivers, a language reflecting the spirit of competition and the culture of winning which UPS inculcated among all its employees.[20]

CORPORATE CULTURE AND MANAGEMENT STYLE

Employee competition was an important element in UPS's system of internal promotion. Significantly, the vast majority of UPS managers rose through the ranks. In 1995, all 13 members of UPS's management committee were promoted from below; seven started as drivers and six as either hourly employees or first line supervisors.[21] "I don't hire anybody I don't think will retire with us," a UPS vice president told *Business Week* in 1990.[22]

UPS's practice of recruiting managers internally helps to account for the company's egalitarian culture. No one—not a manager nor an hourly wage employee— was allowed to drink coffee or sodas at his/her desk. UPS management explained the company-wide ban on drinks on egalitarian grounds: all company employees needed to defer to the drivers who were prohibited from having drinks in their vehicles. Similarly, UPS's dress code prohibited all male employees from growing beards, growing mustaches that extended beyond the corner of the mouth, and growing long hair that covered the top of the collar or the lobes of the ear. Again, UPS management insisted that the company's strict dress code was modeled on that of the drivers: UPS drivers were in direct contact with customers and therefore were required to maintain a neat, clean-cut appearance.[23]

Another aspect of UPS's egalitarian culture pertained to executive privileges. UPS did not grant its corporate officers special privileges. At UPS's Atlanta Headquarters, as at UPS's former headquarters in Greenwich, Connecticut, executives and hourly employees ate lunch in the same cafeteria, competed over the same parking spaces in the company lot, and addressed each other using first names only. James Kelley, UPS CEO between 1997 and 2001, had no private secretary, did his own photocopying, answered his own phone, and flew economy class. His predecessors had done the same.[24]

UPS's management style reflected its corporate culture. On the one side, work at UPS was governed by a long-standing tradition of Marine Corps-type rules and regulations. On the other, decisions at the top were reached through consensus, the climate of decision making resembled that of a town meeting, and executives were encouraged to act as a team, not as individuals. "It is the exact opposite of the star system," an industry analyst observed, adding: UPS managers were groomed as generalists, rotated jobs, were trained on a broad skill base, and were therefore less likely to engage in power struggles.[25] They also delegated authority to subordinates, pushing decision making down the chain-of-command to the lowest possible levels.[26] A related aspect of UPS's culture pertained to corporate spending. Management at UPS had always been fiscally conservative, eager to cut costs and reluctant to borrow. "We talk about making one tenth of a cent improvement," a UPS marketing manager said in 1990, referring to the way in which UPS pilots helped the company save money by taxiing their planes at precise intervals at the company's sorting hubs at Louisville so that they could enter the runway and take off without hitting

their brakes.[27] Cost cutting and corporate savings went hand in hand. Having a large amount of cash on its balance sheet as an insurance against possible losses, UPS rejected heavy borrowing even during years of high inflation when many other companies found it expedient to take loans. In 2000, UPS kept $2 billion in cash, and was awarded a triple A credit rating.[28]

LABOR RELATIONS

In 1916, Jim Casey invited the International Brotherhood of Teamsters (IBT) to organize UPS drivers and other employees. Motivated by the desire to avoid costly unionization battles, Casey negotiated early agreements with the Teamsters which granted the company flexible work rules, the right to utilize employees across job categories, and the right to impose mandatory overtime as needed. Over the years, labor relations at UPS were mostly peaceful but occasionally stormy. An issue over which frequent disputes occurred, and over which UPS management refused to bargain, was the company's work-load standards. Union leaders complained about the constant pressure UPS employees were subject to, claiming [in the words of one Teamster official] that the continual efforts of UPS to increase employee productivity resulted in a "never ending battle" between labor and management.[29] Disputes occasionally led to strikes. A lengthy strike involving 17,000 UPS employees from Maine to South Carolina erupted in 1976 over UPS's attempt to replace its full-time package sorters with part-time employees. Pay and working conditions of UPS part-timers were again principal issues in the 1997 company-wide strike. Still, UPS drivers were among the highest paid truckers within the Brotherhood. "If UPS announced it had 1,000 openings for drivers there would be 100,000 applicants," Ronald Carey, president of the Long Island Local and future president of the Teamsters Union conceded in 1983.[30]

THE RISE OF THE CHALLENGER: FEDEX AND THE AIR EXPRESS INDUSTRY

Frederick Smith outlined the original idea of establishing an air express company in a term paper he wrote for a Yale University economics class sometime in the 1960s. At the time, express packages were routinely shipped on commercial passenger flights, and Smith wrote the paper to disagree with the prevailing theory that placed the future of air freight transportation in the hands of the commercial passenger airlines. He argued that passenger and freight route structures were not identical, that smaller cities were not as well served by the airlines as large ones, and that the cost of shipping freight on passenger aircraft was not likely to drop with increased volume. Instead, Smith proposed to establish a whole new air express system designed specifically for the speedy delivery of packages. He received an infamous C on his term paper.[31]

Investors awarded Smith a better grade. Risking $8 million of his own family money, Smith managed to raise more than $80 million from venture capitalists between 1969 and 1971. In 1971, at the age of 28, he launched Federal Express at Memphis, Tennessee, and two years later the company began operating, flying its own aircraft, and serving 22 U.S. cities with overnight and second-day deliveries. In its first three years of operation, Federal Express had lost an average of $10 million a year, but beginning in 1976, the company experienced a spectacular success with sales jumping from $75 to $260 million and profits from $4 to $21 million in just three years (1976–1979). Federal's largest customers in the 1970s included the U.S. Air Force and the IBM Corporation, the first shipped spare airplane parts, the second, mainframe computer parts.[32] At the time, neither the air passenger industry nor the air freight business were deregulated.

Prior to the passage of the air cargo deregulation act, the passenger airlines had one key advantage over Federal Express. All major passenger airlines were certified by the Civil Aeronautics Board (CAB)—the federal agency regulating the airline industry—to fly interstate routes and operate aircraft of any size. Federal Express, by contrast, had no CAB certificate to operate, and therefore was forced to utilize small airplanes with payload weights of under 7,500 pounds, the limit under which no commercial aircraft was subject to CAB regulation. The result was an inefficient mode of operation: Federal shipped its entire air cargo on tiny French-built Falcon Jets, flying "wingtip to wingtip" five or six Falcons (instead of a single Boeing 727) on its busiest routes, and spending $9 million a year in additional operating costs. Smith, therefore, sponsored a bill in Congress ("Federal Express Relief Bill") which was intended to free the company from any restrictions on the use of large aircraft. Congress, in turn, went one step further and deregulated the entire air cargo industry in 1977, a year before it deregulated the air passenger industry. Following deregulation, Federal Express immediately bought larger planes (first Boeing 727s, and then McDonnell Douglas DC-10s), extended its service network to 300 cities, and transformed itself from a privately-owned firm to a publicly-traded company.[33]

Other companies followed Federal Express's path. First, the older "air freight forwarders" (companies responsible for picking up and delivering packages shipped on commercial flights), most notably Airborne Express and Emery Air Freight, leased and/or bought their own aircraft fleets and offered fully integrated air freight services. Then, in 1981, UPS acquired its own fleet of 727s and DC8 freighters and offered second-day delivery services. As competition intensified, Federal Express solidified its position as the uncontested leader of the air express industry. In 1980, *Business Week* described the rise of Federal Express as "one of the most astonishing business success stories of the past five years."[34] In 1983, Federal Express became the first American company to generate $1 billion of sales within the first ten years of its beginning without mergers or acquisitions.[35] By 1986, Federal Express held a 37 percent market share in the air express industry, well ahead of UPS's 15 percent share, Emery's 14 percent, and Airborne's 8 percent share.[36] And in 2000, FedEx continued to lead the worldwide overnight package delivery service, shipping three million such packages daily (against UPS's 2.2 million), and accounting for 39 percent of the market (against UPS's 29 percent).[37] So dominant was the relative position of FedEx in the industry that the company's name had become now a verb commonly used with any air express service provider: "I'll FedEx it to you."

Still, FedEx experienced setbacks as well. In 1984, the company introduced Zapmail, an early version of a fax document service. The triumph of the home and office fax machine two years later resulted in substantial losses on the service—about $350 million—and in FedEx's decision to discontinue Zapmail altogether. In its global business too FedEx incurred losses. Expanding its global delivery system at a remarkable speed, Federal Express bought the Flying Tiger cargo lines in 1989, and paid close to $900 million for the acquisition. FedEx's initial attempt to use Tiger's European routes and landing rights to improve its own European results was unsuccessful: Federal was losing $1 million a day in Europe in the early 1990s. Smith, therefore, suspended FedEx's intra-European service in 1992, and refocused the company's global business on intercontinental express service.[38]

Three years later, FedEx resumed its intra-European service, established Latin American and Caribbean divisions, and became the pioneering U.S. express carrier to operate direct flights to China. At long last, FedEx's global business had become profitable in 1995. In 2000, FedEx was an $18 billion corporation with a fleet of 44,000 delivery trucks and 650 planes serving some 210 countries and territories. Its 215,000 employees shipped five million packages worldwide each day.[39]

STRATEGY

Three distinct strategies facilitated FedEx's growth and expansion: the buildup of hub-and-spoke route systems, the supply of logistical services, and the introduction of advanced technology.

In drafting his business plan, Smith observed that airports were highly congested during the day and underutilized during the night, and therefore the key to a successful air express business was night operation. He selected Memphis as a central point, or a hub, and built a route system that connected the cities serviced by FedEx to Memphis like spokes on a bicycle wheel. In 1986, the hub-and-spoke system worked in the following way: FedEx vehicles picked up from customers across the U.S. some 600,000 packages a day, trucked them to the nearest airports, unloaded them onto 60 company-operated aircraft, and flew them to Memphis. At the Memphis hub, about 3,000 FedEx employees unloaded the planes between midnight and 3 o'clock in the morning, sorted, coded, reloaded, and shipped the packages on to their final destinations on other planes. Only after the last plane had landed would the first plane take off and fly to its home base. "The choreography has to be remarkably precise [a *Fortune* reporter remarked]: A one minute delay in Memphis can make as many as 20,000 packages miss Federal's 10:30 A.M. guaranteed delivery."[40] FedEx's unique hub-and-spoke system was quickly adopted by United Parcel Service and all other Federal competitors save the U.S. Postal Service. As Federal Express expanded its domestic air express service, the company built two additional hubs, an East Coast hub in Newark, New Jersey, and a West Coast hub in Oakland, California. The growth in FedEx's global operation, similarly, prompted the company to open continental hubs in Paris (Europe, Middle East, Africa), the Subic Bay in the Philippines (Asia), and Miami (Latin America).[41] From the outset, FedEx focused its box delivery business on high-tech, high-price products which were quite expensive to store. Grasping the significance of the just-in-time inventory control revolution early on, Smith sought to help companies compete in the global marketplace by offering them a range of end-to-end after-manufacturing product services that included warehousing, inventory accounting, shipping, billing and invoice reporting. "Our customers are very rapidly learning that inventories in the field are wasted assets," Smith said in 1980, adding: "What Federal can do is permit our customers to use their capital profitably, to roll over their assets more rapidly."[42] In order to manage the inventories of a growing number of large and small companies, FedEx converted some of its large sorting facilities in Memphis, Newark, and Oakland to warehouses, and in addition, designed and built new warehouses both at home and abroad.

In the late 1980s, Federal's logistical business ranged from the global warehousing of computer parts for IBM workstations to the shipment of auto parts to all Volvo car and truck dealers in Britain.[43] To concentrate its logistical services in one semi-autonomous unit, FedEx established in 1988 a new division called Business Logistics Services (BLS). By 1993, BLS accounted for 8 percent of FedEx's revenues and employed 3 percent of FedEx's workforce. Two examples of contracts signed by BLS in 1992 illustrate the kind of services FedEx offered in the 1990s. First, FedEx was responsible for the worldwide distribution and delivery of the finished products manufactured by the National Semiconductor Corporation (NSC) in its Southeast Asia plants. FedEx's guaranteed two-day delivery cycle improved considerably on NSC's own experience of 5- to 18-day delivery journeys. FedEx used its Singapore warehouse to store NSC's goods, pull them from inventory "as needed," pack them, clear them through customs, and ship them to their final destinations. In the same year, FedEx took over Laura Ashley's home furnishing and women's clothing global distribution network. Building warehouses, hiring former Ashley's warehouse employees, designing computerized tracking systems, and setting up a global mail-order business for Ashley, FedEx managed to deliver Ashley's products worldwide in 24 to 48 hours.[44]

FedEx's supply of logistical services required the development of an information technology (IT) infrastructure, and here too Frederick Smith led the way. In 1986, FedEx was the only air express company to offer customers a highly reliable tracking system that could locate any package within half an hour of a customer's inquiry. While FedEx's competitors planned to introduce similar IT systems, UPS did not manage to build a fully functional package tracing system until 1994, and in 1992 its customers still waited up to 24 hours to track a package. Similarly, FedEx's computerized pickup service was fully operational in the early 1980s, nearly a decade before UPS's. In 1986, FedEx's van drivers carried hand-held computers and responded within an hour or two to pickup calls that showed up on their computer screens. Using no computers at the time, UPS drivers visited each of the company's many thousands of business customers every day to check whether a pickup service was needed.[45]

Although FedEx pioneered the introduction of advanced IT in the parcel service industry in the early 1980s, its antiquated information network could no longer serve the company adequately. In 1993, consequently, FedEx launched a three-year effort to upgrade and modernize its information technology. Connecting some 38 different information systems that were mostly mainframe based and could not communicate with each other, Federal Express replaced many of its aging computers with a Unix-based integrated network of workstations.[46]

COMPENSATION, TRAINING, AND LEADERSHIP

FedEx's image of a high-tech company went hand in hand with a merit-based employee compensation system. Whereas most UPS employees were members of the Teamster's union and were paid by the hour, Federal Express's employees were paid in proportion to productivity, and the vast majority did not belong to a union. FedEx [Ground] drivers, for example, were independent contractors who owned and maintained their delivery vehicles, worked as many hours a day as they wished, and received a complex weekly pay that fluctuated according to productivity, reliability, and "job knowledge."[47]

FedEx's "pay-for-performance/pay-for-knowledge" compensation system was linked to its training program. Spending nearly three times as much as UPS on employee training—$0.90 versus $2.50 per employee annually[48]—FedEx trained and tested all its customer contact employees every six months. Because job knowledge and performance were highly correlated, FedEx encouraged its employees to undertake frequent training, offering them four hours of paid test-preparation time before each six-months test. "We place a lot of value on training," a FedEx HR vice president said in 1991. "If you can't pass the knowledge test every six months you can't stay in a customer contact position." Approximately 98 percent of the employees taking the test passed it the first time around. Transmitting its training materials on a closed TV network, FedEx was in a position to update the curriculum as frequently as eight times a year.[49]

FedEx trained and tested managers as well. In the early 1990s, every FedEx manager, whether a first line supervisor or a top corporate officer, was required to take 40 hours of leadership training per year. The company broadcasted its monthly leadership courses on FedEx's global TV network, and tested managers interactively on its electronic network anywhere they were stationed in the world. To recruit managers internally, FedEx developed an evaluation process that measured leadership potential on nine dimensions: charisma, courage, dependability, integrity, flexibility, judgment, intellectual stimulation, individual consideration, and respect of others. The evaluation process helped FedEx screen prospective candidates and thereby control the high rates of failure among newly promoted managers.[50]

LABOR RELATIONS AND CORPORATE CULTURE

FedEx's leadership philosophy was an integral part of the company's non-union culture. Smith's opposition to unions was both ideological and practical, and he sought to forestall unions by offering FedEx employees some of the benefits of unionism. To substitute for a union-based grievance-and-arbitration system, for example, FedEx introduced its own internal appeal system. Called the Guaranteed Fair Treatment Procedure, FedEx's appeal system provided employees with the opportunity to challenge a managerial decision all the way up the corporate ladder to the top. Any FedEx employee had the right to file a complaint against any manager—including his/her own immediate supervisor—and Smith acted as the final arbitrator. In the 1990s, as in the 1980s, Smith devoted four hours a week to resolving employees' complaints.[51]

FedEx's entrepreneurial culture also helped the company avoid unionization. FedEx's "pay-for-performance" compensation package, its "no lay-off policy," and its flexible system of employee cross-training, all acted rather powerfully against the prospects of unionization. Both the Teamsters and the United Auto Workers (UAW) unions made repeated efforts to organize FedEx employees, and both failed.

Yet Smith was unable to stop union organizing among the FedEx pilots. Just as UPS management signed a union contract with its pilots, so did Federal Express. FedEx pilots had remained unorganized until the company merged with Flying Tiger, and following the merger, integrated 970 unionized Tiger pilots with 1,000 non-union Federal pilots. FedEx former Tiger pilots launched a massive union drive, Smith fought long and hard to defeat the drive, and in 1993, the union finally won recognition. Five years later, in 1998, the FedEx Pilots Association signed a five-year union contract with Smith.[52]

THE COMEBACK OF UPS

"UPS used to be a trucking company with technology," wrote *Forbes* magazine in 2000. "Now it is a technology company with trucks." *Forbes* selected UPS as its "Company of the Year"[53] in 2000. Citing UPS as the leading company in integrating online and core business practices, the MIT Sloan School of Management handed UPS its "Clicks and Mortar" award for 2000. *Fortune* magazine, likewise, named UPS as the "World's Most Admired Package Delivery Company" in its 1998, 1999, and 2000 surveys.[54]

The comeback of UPS was facilitated by improvements in every important segment of the package delivery business, including online, logistics, ground, overnight, and global services. Across all business segments, UPS enhanced customer satisfaction, on the one hand, and reduced costs while increasing employee productivity, on the other. Across the parcel service industry, UPS had become now highly profitable with an annual rate of return on sales averaging 6.7 percent for the three-year period 1998–2000, or nearly double the FedEx's rate (see Exhibit 4).

CUSTOMER SERVICE

Nowhere was UPS's improvement in customer service more striking than in the area of information technology. For years, spending money on package-tracing information was considered "heresy" at UPS ("If the package is delivered why spend the money on information about it?"),[55] but as it became apparent in the early 1980s that more and more customers sought such information, UPS changed its long-standing policy. Investing billions of dollars in IT over a period of nearly two decades, UPS had first challenged its competitors, and then leapfrogged them. By 2000, UPS used the most advanced tracking information system in the industry, fast, reliable, simple, and easy to access. (See Exhibit 1). To enable customers to track a package on the Web without visiting the UPS site, UPS linked its tracking system functionality to tens of thousands of outside web sites. Federal Express's customers, by contrast, needed to use the company's own web site to track a package.

To enhance customer satisfaction further, UPS improved its on-time shipping performance as well. In 1999, 90 percent of the packages shipped in UPS's three-day ground-service arrived earlier, and the company offered customers a money-back guarantee for delayed deliveries.[56] A 2000 study conducted by a California freight consulting firm showed that between 3 percent and 9 percent of all UPS packages arrived late

| EXHIBIT 1 | Online Package-Tracking Milestones at UPS (all in December) |

1995: First Month with 100,000 Online Tracking Requests

1996: First Month with 1 Million Online Tracking Requests

1997: First Week with 1 Million Online Tracking Requests

1998: First Day with 1 Million Online Tracking Requests

1999: First Day with 2.5 Million Online Tracking Requests

2000: First Day with 5 Million Online Tracking Requests

Source: Rick Brooks, "Overnight Delivery: Outside the Box," *Wall Street Journal*, February 12, 2001.

compared to 11–15 percent of the packages shipped by FedEx [Ground]. Independent contractors (hired by FedEx Ground) were "inherently less reliable" than hourly workers (hired by UPS), the author of the study concluded, and explained: At UPS, "they go overboard on accountability. Drivers know they're going to have to answer for every service failure, and it's not going to be pleasant." At FedEx, on the other hand, "(i)f a contractor has five packages in the van at the end of the day, and he's got to drive all the way across town to deliver them, it will be in his financial best interest to wait a day."[57]

To compete successfully against Federal Express, UPS also offered customers price flexibility as well as service flexibility. "We'd always prided ourselves on saying your grandmother paid the same price General Motor did,"[58] Kent Nelson, UPS CEO in 1993, recalled. But as the company shifted its focus from home deliveries to corporate shipments in the early 1990s, it abandoned its single-price policy. Implemented in 1991, the new pricing flexibility helped UPS attract new business among large corporate clients. At first, UPS offered large clients a standard 10 percent discount, but as its price war with FedEx intensified in the late 1990s, UPS's sale representatives sought to take away business from FedEx by offering clients bigger discounts. "(I)f you tell UPS that your client has been using FedEx for the last three years," an industry consultant told *Fortune* magazine in 2000, "their pencils come out in a hurry."[59]

During the 1990s, finally, UPS expanded its service options to include one-day (morning and afternoon) delivery, two-day delivery, three-day delivery, and time-definite service. The company also expanded its marketing workforce. Until 1992, UPS had no marketing department and no sizable sales force. By 1997, UPS employed a sales force of 3,000 representatives and support staffers.[60]

ONLINE BUSINESS

As the package delivery industry entered the 21st century, United Parcel Service benefited from two advantages over its competitors: first, it had become the preferred home delivery carrier on the Web, and second, it adopted an "open system" of online services.

In 1998, 1999, and 2000, UPS delivered 55 percent of the packages ordered over the Internet and shipped to American homes. FedEx delivered 10 percent of the items ordered online, and the U.S. Postal Service 30 percent. One reason why FedEx lagged far behind UPS and the Postal Service was Federal's underdeveloped system of ground transportation. Although residential service accounted for just 20 percent of all UPS's deliveries in 2000 (business to business accounted for 80 percent), home deliveries were projected to increase rapidly over the next five years, as the online market expands. Home deliveries, to be sure, were less profitable than business deliveries (UPS charged extra for home deliveries), yet combining business and residential service, UPS was expected to build a high route density, and in turn, cut delivery costs.[61]

UPS's decision to adopt an open system of online services had become a key element in the company's competitive advantage. Federal Express forced its customers to use the company's proprietary software to ship and track packages, and to redesign their computers to do so. UPS, by contrast, developed software that was compatible with any corporate software and could be linked to—and operate from—outside web sites. In 1999, UPS's tracking system functionality was built into 10,000 business web sites, and in 2001, 60,000 web sites were linked to the UPS system. UPS's outside web sites generated 30 percent of the four million package tracking requests the company received each day in 2001.[62]

UPS, additionally, formed alliances with IT companies while Federal Express avoided such alliances for years. To provide customers with improved information services, UPS formed partnerships with IBM, Oracle, PeopleSoft, and many other large and small companies. At the close of the 1990s, UPS partnered with more than 2,000 information technology firms.[63]

LOGISTICS

It took FedEx five years (1988–1993) to generate $500 million in logistics services. In 1993, Federal Express employed 3,000 workers in its Business Logistics Services (BLS) division, and BLS's logistics revenues were growing at a yearly rate of 10–15 percent. UPS launched its Worldwide Logistics division (WWL) in 1993. Hiring just 60 managers and support staffers in 1993, WWL's logistics revenues reached $1 billion in five years (1993–1998), and were growing at a rate of 40 percent a year.[64]

The key to UPS's success in supplying logistical services was the company's IT system. UPS's WWL created the logistical software necessary to provide customers with supply chain services such as inventory management, material management, warehousing, packing, shipping, production planning, engineering, marketing, and electronic billing. In 1998, WWL provided the health care industry with supply chain management technology tailored to the needs of large hospitals. In 1998, likewise, UPS offered the wireless industry a package of supply chain management software targeted to the needs of cell phone manufacturers and wireless network providers.[65]

UPS's principal logistics center was located near the company's airport hub at Louisville, Kentucky, a 500-acre facility where each night 90 planes landed every two minutes in a three-hour period. Goods were transported by UPS planes to the Louisville hub, trucked a few miles away to the logistics center, and later shipped back to the hub. The logistics center was highly automated. To minimize delay in deliveries, the center employed dozens of computer repair technicians. On a typical night shift in 2000, some 60 technicians wearing white lab gowns and armed with analyzers and screwdrivers were busy fixing 800 pieces of jammed equipment.[66]

Many of UPS's clients were low-tech "old economy" firms. For Nike, UPS managed Nike.Com, taking orders for Nike shoes at UPS's call center at San Antonio, stocking Nike shoes at UPS's Louisville warehouse, filling orders hourly, and shipping the shoes to their destination via the Louisville air hub. UPS also managed the return of warranty parts for the General Motors Corporation, collecting the warranty parts from GM dealers, shipping them to a warehouse in Detroit, and monitoring their entire return cycle. For the Ford Motor Company, UPS coordinated the shipments of cars from factory floors to dealership showrooms, cutting delivery times from nine to five hours, and thereby saving the auto maker $240 million in 2000 alone. Similarly, WWL managed the North America supply chain of GNB Technologies, a manufacturer of batteries, coordinating the shipments of GNB batteries between factories, warehouses, recycling centers, and retailers. UPS's WWL, lastly, ran the distribution center of Hamilton Standard, an aircraft-part manufacturer owned by United Technologies, in Singapore in 1997. Responsible for shipping thousands of aircraft parts to more than 20 airline customers in the Asia/Pacific region, WWL helped Hamilton cut order-to-delivery times from 10–12 days to 1–2 days.[67]

UPS, like FedEx, sought to provide logistics services to high-tech companies too. FedEx ran the supply chain of Philips Semiconductor in the United States, and coordinated Cisco's worldwide shipping. UPS managed the spare parts network of Compaq Computer in North America, and the supply chain of Lucent Technologies in Asia.[68] But while UPS's WWL was growing, FedEx's BLS was retrenching. In 2000, UPS's logistics services generated $1.4 billion from some 50,000 companies worldwide, and one transportation analyst told *Business Week*: "I expect UPS to double its logistics business within the next four or five years."[69] FedEx, by contrast, experienced a setback which was reflected in a new strategic initiative announced by Frederick Smith in 2000: FedEx would no longer provide logistics services to customers; only logistics solutions, i.e., new ways to ship, track, and store packages. To implement the new strategy, FedEx's BLS was reexamining all of its logistics accounts.[70]

The examples of two clients who moved their accounts from FedEx to UPS shed some light on the problems FedEx faced in competing over the supply of logistics services. The first was the National Semiconductor Corporation. In 1999 NSC terminated its contract with FedEx and handed it to UPS. According to NSC's director of logistics, FedEx had failed to reduce NSC's inventory and transportation costs for two reasons: first, FedEx lacked the logistical resources necessary to manage NSC's central warehouse in Singapore efficiently; and second, FedEx had routinely used the fastest and most expensive shipping choice—overnight delivery—to transport NSC's products, even in cases where speedy deliveries were unnecessary. UPS, by contrast, managed to cut NSC's costs by 15 percent in two years, 1999–2001.[71]

The second client was SmartHome.Com, an online retailer of home-building products. Initially, FedEx had supplied SmartHome.Com with logistical services, but as UPS extended an offer to cut costs and speed up deliveries, the e-tailer transferred its account from Federal to United Parcel. UPS redesigned SmartHome's web site, built its package tracking software into SmartHome's site so that visitors could link directly to UPS, and provided customers with the choice of selecting shippers other than UPS. "FedEx just didn't have the software to do something like this," SmartHome's purchasing director told *Business Week* in 2000, adding: "SmartHome no longer receives any phone calls from customers, down from 60 daily calls in the past."[72]

OVERNIGHT AND GLOBAL SERVICES

UPS's worldwide logistics business contributed to the company's international operations. For years, United Parcel was unable to match FedEx's reputation for speed and reliability, but by the late 1990s and early 2000s, UPS was gaining over FedEx. Federal, to be sure, had remained the uncontested leader of the air express industry generating in 1999 $11.2 billion in U.S. overnight and international revenues compared to UPS's $8.8 (Exhibit 2). Yet United Parcel was closing the gap quickly: UPS's overnight global delivery business was growing at more than double the FedEx's rate: 8 percent against 3.6 percent in 2000.[73]

UPS had first launched a global air express service in Europe in 1976, but the company did not turn profits from its international operations until 1998. In 2000, UPS ran 300 international daily flights to Europe, and in 2001, UPS operated a larger number of direct flights to China than any of its competitors. One reason why UPS managed to improve its international results was the company's decision to hire local executives abroad. In the five-year period 1995–2000, UPS reduced the number of American managers working abroad from 400 to 40 and replaced many of them with local managers steeped in the host country's culture.[74]

COST STRUCTURE

While FedEx was the industry's air express leader, United Parcel was the industry's cost leader. UPS's cost advantage was rooted in efficient management. On the one hand, increased productivity of UPS's employees helped the company reduce its overall labor cost (salary and wage expenses) from 60 percent to 57 percent of total revenues between 1996 and 1999. On the other,

	FedEx		UPS	
EXHIBIT 2 — UPS versus FedEx: 1999 Revenue	Revenue (billions)	% of Revenue	Revenue (billions)	% of Revenue
International Operation	$3.8	22%	$3.6	13%
U.S. Overnight	$7.4	42%	$5.2	19%
U.S. Two-Day Air	$2.3	13%	$2.7	10%
U.S. Ground	$3.0	17%	$14.4	53%
Other	$1.0	6%	$1.3	5%
	$17.5	100%	$27.2	100%

Source: *Fortune* estimate, Brian O'Reilly, "They've Got Mail," *Fortune*, February 7, 2000, pp. 102–103.

UPS's 1999 decision to integrate its overnight and ground services enabled the company to shift packages from costly airplanes to inexpensive trucks, and thereby save customers the high cost of air transportation. Ordinarily, UPS used trucks on short-haul overnight routes of up to 500 miles. Federal Express, in contrast, continued operating its ground and overnight services as two separate, independent businesses, and as such, failed to take advantage of the cost-saving opportunities available to UPS. Shipping five out of every six packages by air, FedEx's cost per package was the highest in the industry. In 2001, FedEx's cost per package was $11.89 or five dollars-plus above UPS's $6.65.[75]

FedEx's cost was higher than UPS's also because Federal's air express service—compared to competing air express services—was more expensive to operate.

Industry statistics show that in 2000 (fourth quarter), UPS's cost per available ton-mile (ATM) of air transport was lower than FedEx's in five out of six major cost categories, as shown in Exhibit 3.

PROFITS AND RATES OF RETURN

UPS's cost leadership played a key role in the company's financial results. During the great economic boom of the 1990s, UPS's rate of return on sales exceeded that of FedEx for every year except 1999.[76] Partly because FedEx invested heavily in capital equipment such as expensive aircraft, and also because of various management inefficiencies, Federal's return on equity for the ten-year period ending 1999 was less than half the UPS's rate: 8 percent versus 20 percent.[77] During the subsequent recession of 2000–2001, FedEx continued to

---

EXHIBIT 3

Unit Labor, Maintenance, Rental, Interest, Advertising, and Landing Fees Costs of UPS's Air Service and FedEx's Air Service in Cents per Available Ton-Mile, 2000 (Fourth Quarter)

	UPS	FedEx
Labor	7.88 cents	13.97 cents
Maintenance	7.08	8.80
Rentals	1.07	7.80
Interest	0.40	0.53
Advertising	0.00	0.33
Landing Fees	1.10	0.92
Totals	17.53 cents	32.35 cents

Labor. UPS's labor cost advantage was not based on lower pay (union contracts covering 1998 show that the average hourly pay of UPS pilots was comparable to that of FedEx's) but, instead, on higher labor productivity.

Maintenance. UPS operated an all cargo fleet of 340 Boeing (including McDonnell Douglas) and Airbus jets whereas FedEx's fleet included 360 Boeing (including McDonnell Douglas) and Airbus jets, and in addition, 290 Cessna and Fokker light airplanes. UPS's dependency on an all jet fleet of a limited number of aircraft makes provided the company with ample opportunities to streamline maintenance costs.

Rentals. By contrast to FedEx, UPS paid cash for many of its aircraft, and owned a large proportion of its aircraft outright.

Interest. UPS's debt to total capitalization rate was relatively low, resulting in unit interest cost lower than that of FedEx whose fleet purchases required the expensive use of debt.

Advertising. UPS's fiscal conservatism and strict cost control help to explain why the company was reluctant to invest in advertising, just as FedEx's constant drive at expansion helps to account for Federal's generous spending on promotions.

Landing Fees. Because FedEx pioneered the air express industry, it had gained access to a large number of major airports early on, and therefore achieved a landing fee cost advantage over UPS.

Source: ECLAT Consulting, reprinted in Aviation Daily, June 1, 2001, pp. 7–8, June 5, 2001, p. 7, June 6, 2001, p. 7, and June 7, 2001, pp.7–8.

underperform and to remain narrowly profitable while UPS generated an annual *average* rate of return on sales of nearly 8.8 percent (Exhibit 4). Contrasting the two rival companies, one securities analyst, speaking in Winter 2000, observed:

> *At some point you begin to question if [FedEx is] such a great company. It's got great morale, great service, and all that. But how great a company can it be when its returns are so poor? FedEx has a tendency to over-engineer. In the basic operations where FedEx does something that UPS doesn't, its not clear that FedEx makes money.*[78]

For other financial comparisons, see Appendixes 1 and 2.

FUTURE CONCERNS

Despite its respectable results, UPS's comeback strategy did not adequately address two major concerns that could have affected the company's future success. One concern pertained to the state of labor relations; the other, to the prospects of increased competition with "outsiders," that is, DHL International, and the U.S. Post Office.

LABOR RELATIONS

In August 1997, United Parcel experienced a costly work-stoppage when 185,000 IBT-affiliated employees struck UPS for 15 days, crippling the supply chains of thousands of business customers, disrupting the nation's parcel delivery system, and costing the company about $750 millions in lost revenues. During the strike, FedEx's average daily delivery volume rose by 800,000 packages, as many UPS customers defected, searching for alternative shippers. The strike ended in a clear cut union victory. Signed reluctantly by UPS management, the 1997 collective bargaining agreement granted full-time employees an average hourly wage of $23 (the highest in the industry), and part-time employees an average pay of $11 an hour. The contract also authorized UPS to convert 10,000 part-time jobs to full-time positions.[79]

Following the expiration of the five-year contract in the Summer of 2002, UPS negotiated a new IBT contract with 220,000 teamsters. Notwithstanding the sluggish economy, and the slack labor market of 2002, Teamster President James Hoffa demanded "substantial" increases in wages and pensions for UPS's 220,000 IBT members, and the creation of 12,000 new full-time jobs for part-time employees. Given the strike experience of 1997, many of UPS's business clients diverted shipments to other carriers earlier than they had done in 1997, and in some cases, as early as six months before the expiration of the contract.[80]

But in July 2002, just days before the old agreement was expected to expire, UPS and the IBT signed a six-year contract. Seeking to avoid a costly strike, United Parcel Chairman Michael Askew agreed to sign a contract the terms of which were quite generous to the union; they included a $5 pay raise for full-time workers, a $6 pay raise for part-time workers, and the creation of 10,000 full-time jobs for part-time workers over the life of the contract. Competing head to head with non-union carriers like FedEx, the new contract placed UPS at a distinct disadvantage insofar as labor cost was concerned.[81]

INCREASED COMPETITION

As the parcel service industry entered the 21st century, foreign delivery companies were seeking access to the U.S. market. In 1999, Deutsche Post—the German Post Office—had begun operating in the United States, and two years later, it acquired the Brussels-based DHL International. The world's leading air express company outside the United States, DHL's share in the American market stood at less than 1 percent in 2001, as shown in Exhibit 5. To protect their market share, UPS and

EXHIBIT 4	Sales, Net Income, and Income as % of Sales, UPS versus FedEx, 1997–2001									
	1997		1998		1999		2000		2001	
	UPS	FedEx	UPS	FedEx	UPS	FedEx	UPS	FedEx	UPS	FedEx
Sales ($bil.)	22.5	14.2	24.8	15.9	27.1	16.8	30.0	18.3	30.6	19.6
Net Income ($bil.)	0.9	0.2	1.7	0.5	0.9	0.6	2.9	0.7	2.4	0.6
Income as % of Sales	4.0%	1.4%	7.0%	3.2%	3.3%	3.8%	9.7%	3.8%	7.8%	3.0%

Source: *Hoover's Handbook of American Business*, 2001, pp. 587, 1433; *UPS 2001 Annual Report*, p. 65; *FedEx 2001 Annual Report*, p. 34.

Market Shares in the Domestic U.S. Parcel Service Industry, 2001	EXHIBIT 5
United Parcel Service	52.8%
Federal Express	26.4%
U.S. Postal Service	13.9%
Airborne Express	6.3%
DHL International	0.6%

Source: Rick Brooks, "FedEx, UPS Join Forces to Stave Off Foreign Push," *Wall Street Journal*, February 1, 2001.

FedEx joined forces together and sought to revoke DHL's right to operate in the United States, arguing that Deutsche Post (which had recently been privatized with the German government retaining a majority ownership) could use profits from its monopoly on German mail to compete unfairly against American delivery companies. But UPS and FedEx failed. In June 2001, the U.S. Department of Transportation (DOT) ruled in favor of DHL and Deutsche Post, stating that there was no evidence that DHL competed unfairly with U.S. companies, and that foreign air express companies had not gained a substantial share in the U.S. market.[82] DHL's victory had far-reaching implications on the prospects of competition in the domestic package delivery industry. One possible result of the DOT ruling was a future merger between DHL and Airborne, as a Bears Stern logistics analyst suggested:

> *DHL Airways is in need of domestic express product to complement its export/import U.S. business, and ABF [Airborne Express] needs to improve its international operations. . . . We believe there is real potential for DHL either through its U.S. entity DHL Airways or its Brussels entity DHL International to take equity stake in ABF.*[83]

Increased competition in the parcel service industry was also the outcome of improvements in delivery services launched by the U.S. Postal Service. In 2001, USPS offered customers unprecedented discounts on two-day and three-day delivery services between the U.S. and 200 foreign countries (the post office was prohibited by law from offering discounts on most domestic services, notably, first class mail). To deliver packages to foreign cities, the post office linked with DHL International, taking advantage of DHL's fast, reliable, and cost-effective global service network.[84] Similarly, to develop a state-of-the-art information-technology tracking system, the post office signed a contract with the Lockheed Martin Corporation. Once fully functional in 2003, USPS's tracking system was expected to rival UPS's for efficiency. One industry analyst predicted that USPS's share in online business-to-customer package delivery service would climb from 30 percent (2001) to 50 percent in just a few years.[85]

Finally, a recent alliance between FedEx and USPS was likely to enhance the competitive advantage of both carriers relative to UPS. In January 2001, the post office agreed to pay FedEx $7 billion over a seven-year period to ship mail across the country. The USPS agreed to place FedEx Drop Boxes outside the nation's post offices. For the post office, the new arrangement was expected to save $1 billion a year while speeding up deliveries. For FedEx, the transport of U.S. mail by air was projected to cut costs significantly because FedEx planes were flying partially empty. And for UPS, the alliance between USPS and FedEx constituted perhaps the single most serious potential threat, as the industry was consolidating at the dawn of the 21st century.[86]

NOTES

1. Linda Grant, "Why FedEx Is Flying High," *Fortune*, November 10, 1997, pp. 155, 158, 160; Douglas Nelms, "World Class Speed," *Air Transport World*, April 1998, p. 56; Standard & Poor's, "Aerospace & Air Transport," *Industry Survey*, February 1, 1996, p. A49.
2. *Fortune*, November 10, 1997, pp. 155–156.
3. Nicole Harris, "UPS Puts Its Back into It," *Business Week*, October 27, 1997, Start p. 50. Online. ABI data base.
4. Joan Feldman, "Now More Than Ever Time Is Money: Logistics, Managing Movement and Storage, Is the Newest Concept in the Package-Delivery Industry," *Air Transport World*, March 1993, pp. 48, 50.
5. Joan Feldman, "The Price of Success: FedEx Is Solidly No. 1 in Express Shipping," *Air Transport World*, September 1994, p. 47; *Fortune*, November 10, 1997, p. 158.
6. Edward Morlok and Bradley Nitzberg, "The Parcel Service Industry in the United States: Its Size and Role in Commerce." A study prepared for the Dept. of Transportation, the Commonwealth of Pennsylvania (University of Pennsylvania, Philadelphia, 2000), pp. iii, 12, 14.
7. Morlok and Nitzberg, "The Parcel Service Industry," p. 34.
8. Quoted in John Quinn, "Strange Bedfellows," *Logistics Management and Distribution Report*, November 2000, Start p. 47. Online. ABI data base.
9. Brian O'Reilly, "They Got Mail: The Growth of Internet Commerce Has Raised the Stakes in the Boxing Match between UPS and FedEx," *Fortune*, February 7, 2000, p. 106; Morlok and Nitzberg, "The Parcel Service Industry," p. 11.
10. The "old economy" manufacturers of apparel, printed, and plastic goods were also among UPS and FedEx's largest clients. See Morlok and Nitzberg, "The Parcel Service Industry," pp. 30–31.
11. Nelms, "World Class Speed," p. 56; *Fortune*, November 10, 1997, p. 160; Charles Haddad, "Ground Wars," *Business Week*, Industrial/Technology Edition, May 21, 2001, Start p. 64. Online. ABI data base.
12. *Fortune*, February 7, 2000, p. 110; Charles Haddad, "Big Browns Big Coup," *Business Week*, Industrial/Technology Edition, September 18, 2000, Start p. EB76. Online. ABI data base; Jim Kelly, "You'll Do It My Way," *Executive Speeches*, June/July 1999, Start p. 1. Online. ABI data base.
13. "The Quiet Giant of Shipping," *Forbes*, January 15, 1970, p. 38.
14. "Why United Parcel Admits Its Size," *Business Week*, July 18, 1970, p. 96; "United Parcel Service, Inc.," *Hoover's Handbook of American Business 2001*, p. 1432.
15. *Business Week*, July 18, 1970, pp. 94, 96.

16. *Forbes*, January 15, 1970, p. 38; Jeffery Sonnenfeld, "United Parcel Service," Harvard Business School, Case No. 9-488-016, March 23, 1992, pp. 3–4.

17. *Business Week*, May 21, 2001, Start p. 64; "Aircraft Fleet Fact Sheet." Online. UPS.Com.

18. *Business Week*, July 18, 1970, pp. 94, 96; *Forbes*, January 15, 1970, p. 38; James Heskett, *Managing in the Service Economy* (Boston: Harvard Business School Press, 1986), p. 71; Kenneth M. Jennings, "The UPS Strike: Lessons for Just in Timers," *Production and Inventory Management Journal*, Fourth Quarter, 1998, Start p. 63. Online. ABI data base.

19. Kenneth Labich, "Big Change at Big Brown," *Fortune*, January 18, 1988, p. 58.

20. The quotations, in order, are from Lea Soupata, "Managing Culture for Competitive Advantage at United Parcel Service," *Journal of Organizational Excellence*, Summer 2001, p. 25; and Richard Tomkins, "Where a Bad Hair Day Breaks the Rules: The Business Culture of UPS," *Financial Times*, August 16, 1997. Online. Lexis Nexis. Academic Universe. But see also "Behind the UPS Mystique," *Business Week*, June 6, 1983, p. 68, and Todd Vogel, "Can UPS Deliver the Goods in a New World?" *Business Week*, June 4, 1990, p. 80.

21. Charles Day, "Shape Up and Ship Out," *Industry Week*, February 6, 1998, p. 20.

22. *Business Week*, June 4, 1990, p. 82.

23. Soupata, "Managing Culture," p. 24; *Financial Times*, August 16, 1997.

24. *Fortune*, January 18, 1988, p. 58; *Financial Times*, August 16, 1997.

25. *Business Week*, June 4, 1990, p. 81.

26. Soupata, "Managing Culture," p. 23, but see also *Business Week*, June 6, 1983, p. 66.

27. *Business Week*, June 4, 1990, p. 81.

28. *Business Week*, June 6, 1983, p. 73; Sarah Rose, "UPS vs. FedEx," *Money*, February 2000, Start p. 34. Online. ABI data base.

29. Quoted in *Fortune*, January 18, 1988, p. 64, but see also *Business Week*, June 6, 1983, pp. 68–69, and Sonnenfeld, "United Parcel Service," p. 3.

30. Quoted in *Business Week*, June 6, 1983, p. 68, but see also "Unions: The 'Casual' Issue at UPS," *Business Week*, November 1, 1976, pp. 28–29.

31. Robert Flaherty, "Breathing Under Water," *Forbes*, March 1, 1977, pp. 36–37; Dean Foust, "Mr. Smith Goes Global," *Business Week*, February 13, 1989, p. 68.

32. "FedEx Corporation," *Hoover's Handbook of American Business 2001* (Austin: Hoover Business Press, 2001), p. 586; *Forbes*, March 1, 1977, pp. 37–38; "Federal Express Rides the Small Package Boom," *Business Week*, March 31, 1980, p. 111; *Business Week*, February 13, 1989, p. 68.

33. James C. Wetherbe, *The World on Time: The 11 Management Principles That Made FedEx an Overnight Sensation* (Santa Monica, Ca.: Knowledge Exchange, 1996), Chapter 6; *Forbes*, March 1, 1977, pp. 37–38; *Business Week*, March 31, 1980, p. 108; "Federal Express," *International Directory of Company Histories* (Detroit: St. James, 1992), p. 451.

34. *Business Week*, March 31, 1980, p. 108.

35. "Federal Express," *International Directory*, p. 452.

36. Brian Dumaine, "Turbulence Hits the Air Couriers," *Fortune*, July 21, 1986, p. 101.

37. *Business Week*, May 21, 2001, Start p. 64.

38. *Business Week*, February 13, 1989, pp. 66–67; "Federal Express," *International Directory*, p. 452; Feldman, "The Price of Success," p. 49.

39. "FedEx Corporation," *Hoover's Handbook of American Business 2001*, p. 586; Nelms, "World Class Speed," p. 56; *Business Week*, May 21, 2001, Start p. 64; "FedEx Aircraft . . . FY1995-FY2004." Online. FedEx.Com.

40. *Fortune*, July 21, 1988, p. 40, but see also *Forbes*, March 1, 1977, p. 37.

41. Nelms, "World Class Speed," p. 55; Dean Foust, "Why Federal Express Has Overnight Anxiety," *Business Week*, November 9, 1987, p. 66.

42. Cited in *Business Week*, March 31, 1980, p. 108.

43. *Business Week*, November 9, 1987, p. 66, and February 13, 1989, p. 72; Wetherbe, *The World on Time*, p. 18.

44. Feldman, "Now More Than Ever Time Is Money," pp. 47–50.

45. *Fortune*, July 21, 1986, p. 104; Mary Thyfault, "Tracking Technology—The First Nationwide Cellular Data Network Puts UPS Back on the Leading Edge," *Information Week*, May 18, 1992, p. 12.

46. Danna Henderson, "FedEx Upgrades Tracking System," *Air Transport World*, March 1993, p. 48.

47. Dave Hirschman, "A Tale of Two Drivers: UPS, FedEx Treaded Different Paths," *Atlanta Constitution*, December 5, 2000. Online. Lexis Nexis. Academic Universe.

48. The figure for UPS pertains to 2000; for FedEx, to the early 1990s. See Soupata, "Managing Culture," p. 20, and Patricia Galagan, "Training Delivers Results to Federal Express," *Training and Development*, December 1991, p. 29.

49. Galagan, "Training Delivers Results," pp. 29–31. The quotation is on page 30.

50. Galagan, "Training Delivers Results," pp. 31–33.

51. Wetherbe, *The World on Time*, pp. 29–32; *Business Week*, November 9, 1987, p. 66.

52. Feldman, "The Price of Success," p. 50; "Status of Airline Labor Contracts," *Aviation Daily*, January 26, 2001, p. 7; *Hoover Handbook of American Business 2001*, p. 586.

53. Kelly Barron, "Cover Story: UPS Company of the Year," *Forbes*, January 10, 2000, p. 79.

54. See *UPS Annual Report, 2000*, p. 71.

55. Cited in Day, "Shape Up and Ship Out," p. 19.

56. *Fortune*, February 7, 2000, p. 106.

57. *Atlanta Constitution*, December 5, 2000.

58. Cited in Chuck Hawkins, "After a U-Turn: UPS Really Delivers," *Business Week*, May 31, 1993, p. 93.

59. *Fortune*, February 7, 2000, p. 108.

60. Day, "Shape Up and Ship Out," p. 19; *Forbes*, January 10, 2000, p. 81; Melanie Berger, "The Missing Link," *Sales and Marketing Management*, December 1996, Start p. 18. Online. ABI data base.

61. *Fortune*, February 7, 2000, pp. 108, 110; *Business Week*, May 21, 2001, Start p. 64.

62. Jim Kelly, "You'll Do It My Way," Start p. 1; Rick Brooks, "Overnight Delivery: Outside the Box," *Wall Street Journal*, February 12, 2001; *Business Week*, September 18, 2000, Start p. EB76.

63. J. P. Donlon, "Big Brown Books Up," *Chief Executive*, March 1999, Start p. 30; *Business Week*, May 21, 2001, Start p. 64.

64. Feldman, "Now More Than Ever Time Is Money," p. 50; Doug Bartholomew, "IT Delivers for UPS," *Industry Week*, December 21, 1998, p. 58.

65. Bartholomew, "IT Delivers for UPS," p. 62.

66. *Forbes*, January 10, 2000, p. 82.

67. *Forbes*, January 10, 2000, p. 82; Bartholomew, "IT Delivers for UPS," p. 64; *Business Week*, September 18, 2000, Start p. EB76, May 21, 2001, Start p. 64.

68. *Wall Street Journal*, February 12, 2001; Rose, "UPS vs. FedEx," Start p. 34.

69. *Business Week*, September 18, 2000, Start p. EB76, May 21, 2001, Start p. 64.

70. *Business Week*, May 21, 2001, Start p. 64.

71. *Business Week*, May 21, 2001, Start p. 64.

72. *Business Week*, September 18, 2000, Start p. EB76, May 21, 2001, Start p. 64.

73. *Business Week*, May 21, 2001, Start p. 64.

74. *Forbes*, January 10, 2000, pp. 82–83; Donlon, "Big Brown Books Up," March 1999, Start p. 30.

75. *Forbes*, January 10, 2000, p. 81; *Fortune*, February 7, 2000, p. 106; *Business Week*, May 2, 2001, Start p. 64.

76. *Hoover's Handbook of American Business, 2001*, pp. 587, 1433.

77. *Fortune*, February 7, 2000, p. 106.

78. Cited in *Fortune*, February 7, 2000, p. 112.

79. *Business Week*, October 27, 1997, Start p. 50; "Highlights of the Proposed UPS Contract Agreement," and Shari Caudron, "Part-timers Make Headline News," both in *Workforce*, November 1997, pp. 2–3 and pp. 50–60. Online. ABI data base.

80. Rick Brooks, "UPS and Teamsters Ready Themselves for Contract Brawl," *Wall Street Journal*, January 28, 2002.

81. Rick Brooks and Christine Whelan, "Hoffa Wins with UPS Pact," *Wall Street Journal*, July 17, 2002; Steven Greenhouse, "UPS and Teamsters Reach Deal for a 25 percent Raise," *New York Times*, July 17, 2002.

82. Rick Brooks, "FedEx, UPS Join Forces to Stave Off Foreign Push," *Wall Street Journal*, February 1, 2001; "DOT Rules in Favor of DHL," *Logistics*

Management and Distribution Report, June 2001, Start p. 18. Online. ABI data base.

83. Cited in "DOT Rules in Favor of DHL."
84. Rick Brooks, "U.S. Postal Service Offers Price Breaks on Global Service," *Wall Street Journal*, August 17, 2001.

85. *Fortune*, February 7, 2000, p. 110.
86. *Wall Street Journal*, February 12, 2001; *Business Week*, May 21, 2001, Start p. 64; *FedEx 2001 Annual Report*, p. 4.

UPS: Five Year Financial Summary (Years Ended December 31) — APPENDIX 1

(Dollars in millions except per share data)	2001	2000	1999	1998	1997
Revenues	$30,646	$29,771	$27,052	$24,788	$22,458
Operating Expenses	26,684	25,259	23,147	21,785	20,815
Operating Profit	3,962	4,512	3,905	3,003	1,643
Income before Income Taxes	3,937	4,834	2,088	2,902	1,553
Net Income	2,399	2,934	883	1,741	909
Per Share Earnings					
Basic	$2.13	$2.54	$0.79	$1.59	$0.82
Diluted	2.10	2.50	0.77	1.57	0.81

Source: *UPS 2001 Annual Report*, p. 65.

FedEx: Five Years Financial Summary (Years Ended May 31) — APPENDIX 2

(Dollars in millions except per share data)	2001	2000	1999	1998	1997
Revenues	$19,629	$18,257	$16,773	$15,873	$14,238
Operating Income	1,071	1,221	1,163	1,011	507
Income before Income Taxes	928	1,138	1,061	900	426
Net Income	584	688	631	503	196
Per Share Earnings					
Basic	$2.02	$2.36	$2.13	$1.72	$0.67
Diluted	1.99	2.32	2.10	1.69	0.67

Source: *FedEx 2001 Annual Report*, p. 34.

case thirty-four

David Bardolet
Jordi Canals
IESE

On January 12, 2000, Chris Gent, CEO of Vodafone AirTouch, the world's largest mobile phone group, and his board were facing a difficult decision: whether or not to raise the hostile takeover offer of €120 billion ($122.5 billion) that Vodafone AirTouch had announced on November 19, 1999 to acquire Mannesmann, the largest mobile phone operator in Germany. Vodafone posted its final offer on December 23, 1999 and offered 53.7 of its own shares for each Mannesmann share, which meant valuing each Mannesmann share at €266.4. On that day, Mannesmann share price was €239 and Vodafone share price was 305.75 pence, up from €193.1 and 283.5 pence, respectively, on November 19, 1999.

Mannesmann's board, which in October 1999 had rejected a negotiated agreement, was once again adamant. On November 19, 1999, Klaus Esser, CEO of Mannesmann, declared: "The Vodafone AirTouch offer is too low and does not reflect the true value of the company's shares. €350 is a reasonable price in order to start having discussions with Vodafone." A fierce battle for control of Mannesmann began. In the weeks that followed it saw all kinds of defensive manoeuvres and considerable tension between the two companies. According to the rules of the German regulatory body for mergers and acquisitions, the Mannesmann board had to make a decision to accept or reject the offer before February 7, 2000.

David Bardolet, MBA 2000, and Professor Jordi Canals prepared this case as the basis for class discussion rather than to illustrate either effective or ineffective handling of an administrative situation, January 2001.

Mannesmann's board considered that the price offered by Vodafone AirTouch was too low. Also, the Mannesmann board had insisted that it wanted 58.5 percent of the new company for its shareholders. Under the initial offer, Mannesmann shareholders would have only 47.2 percent of the new company.

Vodafone AirTouch's board knew that their offer would be more likely to be accepted if it could be improved. There were huge doubts concerning the risks of the operation. Should Vodafone AirTouch raise its bid? Should Vodafone throw in some cash to entice shareholders? Was Mannesmann worth that much money? Would the acquisition put Vodafone AirTouch in a better competitive position?

THE TELECOMMUNICATIONS INDUSTRY IN EUROPE

At the beginning of the year 2000, the telecommunications industry in Europe was in the throes of a major transformation at all levels. This upheaval was driven mainly by three factors: the privatization of the large European monopolies, the gradual liberalization of national markets, and the appearance of new technologies for voice and data transmission. These factors put the industry's traditional incumbents in what for them was a very new position. Large, national carriers had been used to operating in conditions that favoured their interests, with rapid growth (up to 50 percent per year in some segments such as mobile telephony), a regulatory regime that enabled them to maintain their dominant position, and minimal pressure from competitors. On average, they continued to be highly profitable.

However, the transformation process was under way and traditional companies such as BT, Deutsche Telekom and Telefónica had to do battle with new competitors who had either already entered the sector or were planning to do so. These new companies had a very different way of operating, with much lower costs, and were changing the structure of the industry.

Some analysts predicted certain basic trends in the strategies of the incumbents. The first of these was rationalization. The situation they had enjoyed up until then had allowed them to survive with low efficiency and inadequate cost. This would not be permitted in the new environment, so those companies were putting a lot of effort into their cost reduction programmes.

Secondly, all the companies in the industry were trying to expand internationally. This trend was driven by a variety of factors, two of which are worth mentioning. On the one hand, companies were afraid they would lose market share in their home markets to new entrants. International expansion was seen as a good way to maintain revenues. On the other hand, the consolidation of the euro-zone seemed to require companies to have a solid presence in the main markets of the area.

Finally, a concentration process seemed to have begun in the industry. As reasons for the mergers, companies cited the need to reach economies of scale and reduce-costs, though some observers saw these mergers more as an attempt to extend geographical presence as fast as possible.

Companies tried to find factors that would differentiate them from their rivals. One such factor might be the control of a solid international network that could connect customers from any part of the world. This type of service (roaming) was very profitable for mobile phone companies if they had an equity interest in the operator that received the call. This gave them a strong incentive to extend their network of alliances and equity interests. In any case, it seemed vital to deploy a good marketing strategy to get new customers. Distribution networks, advertising campaigns or aggressive pricing and promotions were factors that could influence customers' choice of one operator over another. Accordingly, the mobile phone companies were spending a lot of money on marketing and brand building. Those with the most proactive marketing approach, such as Telefónica Móviles in Spain or Orange in Great Britain, enjoyed faster and steadier growth.

THE MOBILE PHONE INDUSTRY

At the beginning of 2000, the mobile phone market was one of the fastest-moving segments in the telecommunications industry. Its growth in recent years had beaten all forecasts. From 1997 to 1999 the world mobile phone market had gone from 203 million to 475 million clients. Dollar sales, however, had grown by only 66 percent due to the general drop in prices. Another indicator of worldwide growth in the sector was investment in infrastructure (equipment and transmission networks), which in 1997–1999 had increased by 50 percent.

The figures for Europe were particularly impressive (Exhibit 1), All this raised the question of whether there was any limit to growth, and if there was, where exactly it was. Some experts were confident that the rapid growth would continue for a few more years, though the European market would inevitably approach saturation.

The European market was far from homogeneous. One of the most attractive markets was Germany. It had the lowest penetration rate in Europe (Exhibit 2), a large number of potential users, and a potential revenue per customer well above the European average. The growing competition between the three operators existing at that time was expected to lead to sharp price reductions.

Italy was one of the countries with the highest penetration rate (39.3 percent), second only to the Scandinavian countries. Having reached a certain degree of saturation, it was expected to have slower growth than the rest of Europe. Nonetheless, the marketing strength and innovativeness of the three Italian operators suggested that this market still had considerable growth potential. Telecom Italia (TIM) was the European operator with the largest number of clients (Exhibit 3).

The United Kingdom had a penetration rate of 25 percent and excellent prospects. France and Spain had penetration rates of around 21 percent and seemed to have great potential. Several countries already had three operators competing with one another. The Scandinavian countries, in contrast, seemed to have settled down to lower rates of growth, though their companies were more profitable.

In mobile telephony there was another factor to be taken into account: the growing tendency for fixed-line telephony and wireless telephony to converge. This convergence was due, firstly, to the appearance of technologies such as WAP (Wireless Application Protocol), which allowed mobile telephony to offer virtually the same voice and data services as fixed telephony. Secondly, regulation in Europe favoured this tendency, allowing direct competition between fixed and mobile operators. Thus there arose a debate over whether mobile phones were a real substitute for conventional fixed-line phones or a complementary product.

A particularly interesting prospect was the imminent introduction of the third generation (3G) of mobile phones, UMTS (Universal Mobile Telecommunications System), which would be a step forward with respect to the existing GSM (Global System for Mobile Communications) standard. The basic difference between the two lay in the quantity and quality of information that could be carried. GSM was very effective for carrying voice but

EXHIBIT 1   The Mobile Phone Industry in Europe

Mobile Phone Customers (In thousands)

	1997	1998	1999	2000E	2001E
France	5,760	10,245	13,995	16,895	19,395
Germany	8,393	14,547	21,213	27,728	33,591
Italy	11,712	18,738	22,646	26,568	30,422
Spain	4,290	6,873	9,651	11,981	14,022
Sweden	3,300	4,526	5,265	5,913	6,409
United Kingdom	7,083	9,027	14,619	19,711	24,162

Revenue per Customer (In dollars)

	1997	1998	1999	2000E	2001E
France	85.5	76.1	68.1	61.9	57.0
Germany	92.6	75.6	61.6	55.9	52.6
Italy	67.1	50.5	45.8	44.0	42.8
Spain	54.4	48.6	44.0	41.1	38.9
Sweden	68.6	68.1	60.1	56.4	55.1
United Kingdom	64.9	62.8	56.6	47.4	43.3

Customer Turnover (In percentage)

	1998	1999	2000E
Cellnet	28.8	25.9	24.5
D2 Mobilfunk	19.0	20.0	20.0
Europolitan	19.7	19.4	18.8
NetCom GSM	26.8	22.6	20.3
Orange	15.8	15.5	15.0
SFR	23.7	23.2	22.9
Europe (average)	22.6	22.1	21.6

Source: Morgan Stanley Dean Witter.

very limited for other types of data. UMTS was set to become the new standard of the future, allowing the transmission of voice and data at high speed to any part of the world. This opened the door to broadband communications, unrestricted Internet access by mobile phone and the probable convergence of multimedia services (TV, music, etc.) with mobile telecommunications. UMTS was expected to be introduced into many European countries by the end of 2001.

However, mobile phone companies were aware that the existence of two digital standards (W-CDMA in Europe and Japan, and CDMA in the United States) and the absence of mobile applications that would make use of the greater bandwidth of third-generation systems could become a major obstacle to the rapid deployment of UMTS. This could give GPRS (General Packet Radio Service) technology, which had been created as a temporary solution between the second and the third generation, a longer lease of life than originally expected.

With UMTS, the biggest battle would take place on the small screen of the cell phone. This precious real estate—the mobile portal—is what Internet surfers would see when they turned on their phones. From Vodafone to AOL, everybody seemed to be eager to control it. Multimedia content would become more important for mobile phone operators. Some experts thought that the factor that could differentiate mobile phone operators in the future would be the ability to offer a wide variety of contents (information, entertain-

The Mobile Phone Industry in Europe: Customer Growth and Penetration (1999) EXHIBIT 2

	Net Growth (thousands)	Share of Total Growth	Penetration (%)
Austria	101	2.3	30.8
Belgium	178	4.0	22.1
Denmark	54	1.2	35.8
Finland	−50	−1.1	58.6
France	394	8.9	21.2
Germany	550	12.4	18.8
Greece	155	3.5	22.3
Holland	353	8.0	26.3
Ireland	29	0.7	27.7
Italy	953	21.5	39.5
Norway	118	2.7	51.6
Portugal	62	1.4	34.4
Spain	568	12.8	21.5
Sweden	113	2.6	53.8
Switzerland	83	1.9	24.7
United Kingdom	764	17.3	25.3
Total Europe	4,425	100	26.8

Source: Morgan Stanley Dean Witter.

ment and electronic commerce). Consequently, some operators were already considering acquiring stakes in content providers.

Phone companies seemed to enjoy an advantage in this new game, since they already had a billing relationship with the final customer. This positioning could offer those firms the ability to track customers' movements and phone companies could be in the middle of e-commerce transactions. The development of new software to do it involved very high costs.

At the beginning of 2000, tenders for UMTS licenses were under preparation in some European countries. In each case it was expected that five or six consortia would compete for the three or four licenses on offer. It was a good opportunity for European operators to obtain a larger European presence.

High growth rates had attracted a large number of new companies, which fought for a place in the industry. In all European countries the entry of new competitors was conditional upon obtaining a license. Governments tended to auction such licenses. The conditions that would-be participants had to meet were such that only groups with considerable financial muscle could consider bidding for a license.

Mobile phone companies were expanding internationally at a fast pace. The largest among them had sought to gain a presence in the main European markets in two ways: by acquiring or forming alliances with existing operators in other countries, or by bidding (on their own or as part of a group) for new licenses. International expansion enabled them to maintain the growth rate and, so some thought, also developed economies of scale in R&D and network exploitation. These latter benefits, however, remained unclear.

It was also argued that the consolidation and expansion of the European operators were driven by the need to secure a dominant position in Europe. This would be an advantage when it came to exploiting the mobile Internet market, currently in its infancy. Expectations of a gradual increase in the use of mobile phones as a platform for Internet access were very high. Many observers thought that the mobile phone would be the principal medium of electronic commerce in the future. Furthermore, technology would make it possible to provide new, value added services (payment, localization, leisure, etc.).

Among mobile phone manufacturers, three companies (Ericsson, Nokia and Motorola) controlled 61

EXHIBIT 3   Main Competitors in Europe

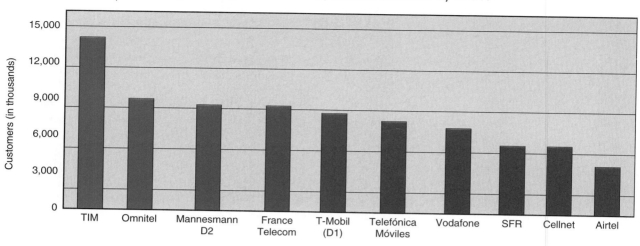

Top Ten Digital Cellular Operators (October 1, 1999)

percent of the market. They enjoyed major economies of scale in production, marketing and R&D, which gave them a clear advantage over the rest. Their domination was expected to continue for several years. For many consumers, these companies brands were more important than those of the mobile phone operators.

The future of the mobile phone industry was uncertain. Firstly, it was not clear whether the market would maintain recent years' exceptional growth. Some predicted that, although growth in the number of new customers would slow, new opportunities for data transmission by mobile phone would lead to sustained growth in revenue. It was also suggested that the increase in traffic (in minutes consumed by each customer) would be another factor driving revenue growth. Despite the uncertainty of the situation, many companies were willing to take every available opportunity to secure a privileged position in the market.

COMPETITORS

DEUTSCHE TELEKOM

In January 2000, it was the largest telecommunications operator in Europe and the third largest in the world. Deutsche Telekom exploited the full range of telecommunications businesses in an integrated fashion. In mobile telephony it had around 11 million customers distributed among its German subsidiary T-D1 and some European operators in which it held equity interests. Most important of these was One2One, the British

company with almost 2.5 million customers. Deutsche Telekom also operated a huge fixed-line business with almost 50 million lines, and its business as an Internet access provider (ISP), through T-Online, a subsidiary, had grown rapidly to reach 3.3 million customers. In the future, Deutsche Telekom intended to continue to be a large integrated operator offering a complete range of telecommunication services with a presence in all the important markets.

FRANCE TELECOM

It was very similar to Deutsche Telekom. Until recently, France Telecom had concentrated on its home market, with 34 million fixed lines and a mobile telephony business that had close to 9 million customers. France Telecom also had an Internet service provider and cable television businesses. It had ambitious plans for the future, involving aggressive international expansion.

TELEFONICA

One of the most active companies in the industry, Telefonica was exploiting its scale and constantly expanding its services to new countries and customers. In fixed telephony it served around 38 million customers in 1999. Its mobile phone company, Telefónica Móviles, had experienced very rapid growth since its launch and had about 18 million customers, half in Spain and the rest in Latin America. Telefonica was aiming to be an integrated company (including content), had interests in TV (1 million pay-TV customers) and the Internet, with the launch of Terra.

BRITISH TELECOM (BT)

It offered fixed and mobile telephony, Internet access, and other data transmission services. Its fixed telephony business covered 28 million customers in the United Kingdom. Its mobile phone subsidiary, BT Cellnet, ranked second in the UK market behind Vodafone AirTouch. BT was expanding internationally through acquisitions and alliances, such as the alliance formed recently with AT&T.

TELECOM ITALIA

It held the control of 60 percent of Telecom Italia Mobile (TIM), the operator with the largest number of customers in Europe, thanks to its strong leadership in the Italian market. TIM had close to 15 million customers in 1999. Telecom Italia had other businesses (fixed telephony and Internet), in which it was also the market leader. TIM was acquiring stakes in operators in Asia, Latin America and some European countries.

VODAFONE AIRTOUCH PLC

At the end of 1999 Vodafone AirTouch plc was the world's largest mobile phone operator. It operated in 23 countries and had around 28 million customers. Vodafone's activities were focused entirely on providing mobile telephony services. Vodafone's offer included the sale and rental of handsets and the transmission of voice and data by mobile telephony, with a wide range of products and a variety of payment systems.

Vodafone AirTouch was the result of a $62 billion merger between Vodafone, a British company, and Air-Touch, a Canadian company. The merger was announced on January 18, 1999. Vodafone was formed in 1982 to operate a mobile phone service in the United Kingdom. For almost ten years this service used analog technology. In 1991 Vodafone launched the UK's first digital GSM service. At the end of 1999 it had a total of 6.8 million customers in the UK market. AirTouch, for its part, was the largest mobile operator in North America, with a customer base of approximately 9 million users. Its presence in the European market, however, was very weak. Thus, the two companies had great complementary strengths from a geographical point of view. As Vodafone CEO Chris Gent stated, " the merger with AirTouch will be a major step forward in our strategy to expand the penetration of mobile phone services to the largest possible number of customers and to the largest possible number of markets that offer prospects of profitability in the medium and long term."

In 1999 Vodafone generated £3,360 million in revenues, with strong growth and a sound financial structure (Exhibits 4 and 5). Fifty-five per cent of its revenues came from the United Kingdom.

From the outset, Vodafone had single-mindedly focused its business on mobile telephony, avoiding other segments of the telecommunications services. It did not own any interest in any fixed-line operator or any other business that was not mobile phones. Similarly, it had not tried to diversify into other sectors. This determination to be a pure wireless operator had been manifested on many occasions. For Vodafone, owning fixed-line operations could be a distraction from the new wave of mobile data. Chris Gent thought that as

Vodafone: Profit and Loss Account (In millions of pounds)					EXHIBIT 4
	1999	1998	1997	1996	1995
Net revenues	3,360	2,470	1,749	1,402	1,152
Cost of goods sold	1,512	1,026	762	605	495
Gross margin	*1,848*	*1,444*	*987*	*797*	*657*
Selling expenses	460	380	222	154	125
General expenses	246	180	116	78	80
Other expenses	296	238	154	116	92
Operating profit	*846*	*646*	*495*	*449*	*360*
Interest expense	90	65	36	16	3
Extraordinary expenses	−81	−21	−45	−25	−21
Profit before taxation	*837*	*602*	*504*	*458*	*378*
Tax	240	196	166	164	132
Net profit	**597**	**406**	**338**	**294**	**246**

EXHIBIT 5   Vodafone: Balance Sheet (In millions of pounds)

	1999	1998	1997	1996	1995
Assets					
Fixed assets	2,525	1,775	1,780	1,334	1,039
Current assets	775	578	487	335	305
Inventories	45	30	20	10	13
Debtors	497	349	281	190	166
Other assets	227	184	144	123	110
Cash and checking accounts	6	15	42	12	16
Other assets	343	149	154	94	65
Total assets	3,643	2,502	2,421	1,763	1,409
Liabilities					
Equity shareholders' funds	924	380	828	1,024	818
Capital	252	233	213	204	195
Reserves	563	50	557	819	622
Minority interests	109	97	58	1	1
Total creditors	2,719	2,122	1,593	739	591
Short-term liabilities	1,529	1,432	1,013	583	442
Long-term liabilities	1,148	648	531	148	143
Other liabilities	42	42	49	8	6
Total liabilities	3,643	2,502	2,421	1,763	1,409

voice was moving to wireless, so would data and the Internet for the same reason, convenience. On the other hand fixed-line networks offered a lower return than mobile networks.

Vodafone was investing heavily in international expansion. Its acquisitions and alliances in the international arena were growing rapidly. In 1999 it had acquired AirTouch, established itself in New Zealand, and won a license to operate in Hungary and Egypt. On September 21, 1999 Vodafone AirTouch and Bell Atlantic had announced an agreement to create a new mobile phone company in the United States under a single brand and would use the same digital technology. This company would have 20 million customers, making it the largest in the US. Vodafone AirTouch would own 45 percent of the new company, leaving the management to Bell Atlantic.

Vodafone needed this expansion if it was to maintain the rate of acquisition of new subscribers it had had until then: in 1998 it was close to 65 percent growth. Also, the EU was starting to become a genuine single market and, despite its dominant position in the UK, Vodafone did not have high market shares in the other EU countries. Vodafone AirTouch had interests in operators in France, Germany and Spain, but none of these companies was the leader in its market (Exhibit 6). In the UK, Vodafone was suffering the effects of Orange, a very innovative new entrant that was gaining market share very quickly.

It was Vodafone AirTouch's ambition to be the technological leader in the industry. Up until then it had successfully applied GSM technology, the European standard that accounted for 50 percent of the world market, and had created new developments such as the radio connection protocol. At the end of 1999 it was developing new ways of transmitting voice and data. Vodafone had expressed an interest in bidding for UMTS licenses in the auctions to be held in various European countries.

Vodafone AirTouch's shares were expensive. On January 12, 2000, its market capitalization was €164 bn. It had risen steadily throughout the 1990s. Chris Gent said that "Vodafone AirTouch aims to become one of the largest companies in the world in the next five years." To achieve this, it would rely on the strengths that had taken it to its current position as world leader. These strengths included a clear focus on GSM mobile telephony (allowing it to concentrate its investments),

Country	Company	Holding	Partner
Germany	D2	35%	Mannesmann
Belgium	Proximus	25%	Belgacom
Spain	Airtel	21%	BT
France	SFR	20%	Cégétel
United Kingdom	Vodafone	100%	–
Greece	Panafon	55%	Government
Holland	Libertel	70%	Government
Italy	Omnitel	21%	Mannesmann
Poland	Plus GSM	19%	TDK
Portugal	Telecel	51%	Government
Romania	Connex GSM	10%	TIW
Sweden	Europolitan	71%	Government

and the excellent infrastructure network it had built. Another key factor in the company's growth was its audacity in acquiring or merging with other companies. The acquisition of AirTouch or the takeover bid for Mannesmann were deals that could double Vodafone revenues.

MANNESMANN

Mannesmann AG was created in 1885 by the brothers Max and Reinhard Mannesmann, who had invented a new process for manufacturing steel tubes. Together with ore extraction, this business fuelled the company's activities for almost half a century. At the end of 1990 Mannesmann embarked on a process of diversification and formed a telecommunications division to operate a mobile phone license in Germany. During the 1990s this division expanded its activities to include fixed telephony and data services. Exhibits 7, 8 and 9 show main financial figures.

In 1999 Mannesmann had three basic lines of business: telecommunications (39 percent of total sales), engineering and automotive (53 percent of total sales), and tubes (8 percent of total sales). While in 1990 telecommunciations was not a major part of Mannesmann's business, in 1999 it contributed 39 percent of the group revenues and around 70 percent of its earnings. With 36 million customers in Europe, Mannesmann had become one of the top firms in European telecommunications. Its total market capitalization tripled during the year 1999 from €38, billion in 1998, to about €110 billion at the end of 1999.

Its telecommunications division encompassed three basic businesses. First, mobile telephone services in several countries (Exhibit 10). Mannesmann had started to offer these services in 1990 through its subsidiary Mobilfunk, of which it owned 65 percent. Mobilfunk operated under the D2 brand and in 1999 had around 8.1 million customers, making it the leader in the German market. In 1999 it had sales in excess of €4 billion. Mannesmann had a significant presence in other markets outside Germany. It owned 55 percent of Omnitel, one of the main mobile phone operators in Italy, with close to 9 million customers. In France, Mannesmann had a 15 percent stake in Cégétel, a fixed and mobile operator belonging to the Vivendi group. Mannesmann's presence in mobile telephony had been considerably strengthened in October 1999 by the acquisition of Orange, one of the main mobile phone operators in the United Kingdom.

Mannesmann's second activity in the telecommunications industry was fixed-line telephony. In Germany it operated through Arcor. Arcor offered a full range of voice and data services and had a 5.3 percent market share. Its sales amounted to €1.1 billion. In Italy, Mannesmann had acquired 100 percent of Infostrada, a fixed-line operator previously belonging to the Olivetti group, with 2.3 million customers. Mannesmann's international presence in fixed-line telephony further included stakes in Tele.ring, an Austrian operator, and France's Cégétel.

Thirdly, Mannesmann had a growing activity as an Internet service provider. In Germany it had acquired the provider germany.net. In Italy and France it offered

EXHIBIT 7 Mannesmann: Profit and Loss Account (In € millions)

	1999	1998	1997	1996	1995
Net revenues	23,265	17,375	18,218	16,162	14,955
Cost of goods sold	15,804	11,026	14,224	12,818	12,033
Gross margin	*7,461*	*6,349*	*3,994*	*3,343*	*2,922*
R&D expenses	701	284	n.a.	n.a.	n.a.
Selling expenses	3,041	1,014	n.a.	n.a.	n.a.
General expenses	1,482	541	n.a.	n.a.	n.a.
Other expenses	169	312	438	2,273	2,039
Operating profit	*2,068*	*1,019*	*423*	*123*	*38*
Interest expense	520	142	69	70	85
Extraordinary expenses	−210	132	143	271	349
Profit before taxation	*1,338*	*1,293*	*635*	*465*	*472*
Tax	841	719	350	184	145
Net profit	497	574	284	281	327

EXHIBIT 8 Mannesmann: Balance Sheet (In € millions)

	1999	1998	1997	1996	1995
Assets					
Fixed assets	22,455	12,841	11,602	9,499	8,461
Current assets	36,418	17,532	21,133	18,956	17,068
Inventories	1,993	6,374	12,192	10,154	8,959
Debtors	4,615	6,229	6,025	5,358	5,163
Other assets	1,277	1,650	711	778	1,667
Cash and checking accounts	946	3,279	2,205	2,666	1,279
Other assets	1,371	5,579	4,176	2,062	2,269
Total assets	60,244	35,952	36,911	30,517	27,798
Liabilities					
Equity shareholders' funds	23,720	12,440	8,798	7,710	7,294
Capital	1,633	8,221	4,821	4,774	4,730
Reserves	19,999	2,745	2,103	1,815	1,777
Minority interests	2,088	1,474	1,874	1,121	787
Total creditors	36,524	23,512	28,113	22,807	20,504
Short-term liabilities	34,712	14,947	16,689	13,575	13,098
Long-term liabilities	1,791	8,474	11,307	9,109	7,274
Other liabilities	21	91	117	123	132
Total liabilities	60,244	35,952	36,911	30,517	27,798

	Gross Operating Assets (in €m)	Result from Ordinary Activities (in €m)	Goodwill Amortization (in €m)	Net Interest and Miscellaneous (in €m)	Gross Operating Result (in €m)	Return on Gross Operating Assets 1999 (in %)	Return on Gross Operating Assets 1998 (in %)
Mobilfunk	2,147	1,684	47	−11	1,720	80.1	67.3
Arcor	2,826	−318	63	23	−232	−8.2	−9.1
Omnitel	4,618	474	191	13	678	14.7	–
Infostrada	1,415	−157	55	18	−84	−5.9	–
Eurokom	2,332	−59	61	6	8	0.3	−2.6
Telecommunications	13,338	1,624	417	49	2,090	15.7	21.4
Rexroth	1,274	145	6	45	196	15.4	18.0
Dematic	1,111	103	25	20	148	13.3	14.1
Demag Krauss-Maffei	1,160	64	16	7	87	7.5	1.9
VDO	1,760	11	55	26	92	5.2	8.3
Sachs	1,205	105	32	34	171	14.2	16.0
Engineering & Automotive	6,510	428	134	132	694	10.7	11.4
Tubes/Other companies	2,029	−504	1	340	−163	−8.0	2.9
	21,877	1,548	552	521	2,621	12.0	14.1

Company	Country	Percentage Stake
D2 Mannesmann	Germany	65.2
Arcor	Germany	70.0
o.tel.o (100% owned by Arcor)	Germany	70.0
germany.net (100% owned by Arcor)	Germany	70.0
Cégétel—SFR	France	15.0
Omnitel	Italy	55.2
Infostrada	Italy	100.0
Italia Online (100% owned by Infostrada)	Italy	100.0
Tele.ring	Austria	53.8

this service through Infostrada and Cégétel, respectively. It was also developing a whole series of Internet-related businesses. Specifically, it was preparing the launch of various products using WAP technology and was planning to expand into electronic commerce and hosting.

The Engineering & Automotive division (Atecs Mannesmann) had five units that were growing at 3.5 percent annual rate. Mannesmann was trying to focus the portfolio of investments on more profitable segments. For instance, in 1999, the company sold ten units. The Tubes & Other division had a serious problem, due

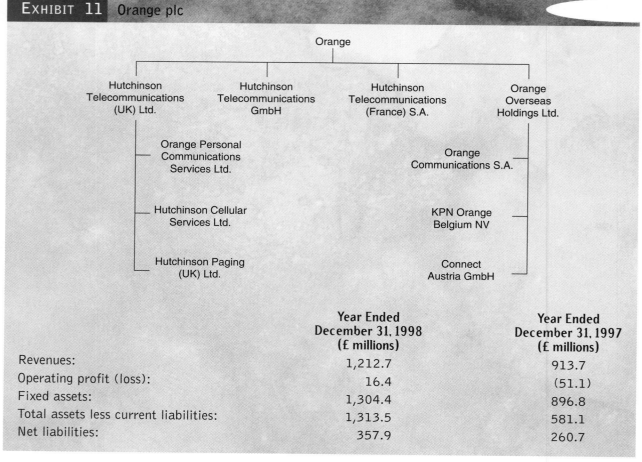

EXHIBIT 11 Orange plc

	Year Ended December 31, 1998 (£ millions)	Year Ended December 31, 1997 (£ millions)
Revenues:	1,212.7	913.7
Operating profit (loss):	16.4	(51.1)
Fixed assets:	1,304.4	896.8
Total assets less current liabilities:	1,313.5	581.1
Net liabilities:	357.9	260.7

to market conditions; their growth rate in 1999 fell by 22 percent, and the division reported a loss of €504 million.

Mannesmann's strategic objectives were clear. It aimed to become the European leader in integrated telecommunications, offering a full range of services. In September 1999 Klaus Esser had announced his intention to split Mannesmann into two separate entities. One would group together all the telecommunications businesses, and the other would include the engineering and automotive businesses. The company was considering selling off the Tubes division on account of its poor performance.

THE ACQUISITION OF ORANGE

On October 20, 1999 Mannesmann announced a bid for Orange. The Mannesmann offer was 0.0965 of its own shares plus £6.4 in cash for each share of Orange, which represented approximately £19.8 bn (€28 bn). The offer

was quickly accepted by Orange. That day France Telecom also nabbed control of E-Plus, Germany's third-largest mobile phone operator, in a deal worth €7.4 bn. Mannesmann offered Orange around €9,000 per customer, while France Telecom offered E-Plus €4,200 per customer.

Orange was the third-largest mobile phone operator in Great Britain in terms of number of clients. It had been created in 1997 and specialized exclusively in cellular telephony. In 1998 it had sales revenues of £1,212 million (Exhibit 11). At the end of 1999 its customer base in the UK was close to 5 million.

Orange was dedicated exclusively to wireless telephony and had experienced rapid growth. It had a very dynamic marketing approach and possessed the best network in the UK. Evidence of this was the 1.4 million new subscribers it had gained in the fourth quarter of 1999. Moreover, Orange's customers seemed to be more satisfied with their company than were those of any other company in the industry. Orange's rate of customer turnover (15.8 percent) was markedly lower than the average of the other European companies (22.9 percent). In view of all this, Mannesmann's interest in acquiring such a solid customer base was understandable.

Orange based its growth on innovation. The launch of the pre-payment segment had been a success and Orange had captured most of this market. It had also pioneered the offering of Internet access by mobile phone, and one of its goals was to be the leader in data services. Recently, it had started to expand, with the launch of its mobile phone service in countries such as Belgium and Switzerland, though it seemed unwilling to enter the main markets of continental Europe.

In the United Kingdom, by contrast, Orange was a serious threat to Vodafone's leadership. In the last quarter of 1999, Orange had won up to 30 percent more customers than Vodafone. In some segments, such as pre-payment, Orange had become the leader.

With the acquisition of Orange, Mannesmann was assured of a privileged position in the British market. Klaus Esser declared that, as a result of the deal, Mannesmann would improve its annual profits by an additional 5 percent in each of the following three years. Also, the company could try to exploit the synergies with Orange and transfer them to the other markets in which it was present. Some observers, however, thought that Mannesmann's acquisition of Orange was such a serious threat to Vodafone that it could provoke a series of unexpected reactions. Others thought it was a path that Mannesmann had chosen precisely in order to block any possible takeover bid by Vodafone AirTouch. Other analysts thought that Mannesmann had overpaid for Orange and, as a result, it became vulnerable to a hostile bid.

THE TAKEOVER BID FOR MANNESMANN

During October 1999 a group of Vodafone AirTouch and Mannesmann senior executives held talks to explore the possibility of Mannesmann accepting a friendly offer from the British company. Vodafone AirTouch showed great interest in gaining control of the German company. But Mannesmann's response was categorical, closing the door to any negotiated agreement. Vodafone AirTouch made a last friendly offer of €100 billion on November 14, 1999. One day later, Klaus Esser rejected the offer and applied to a British court for an injunction to prevent Goldman Sachs from acting as an adviser to Vodafone AirTouch on the grounds of a conflict of interests, since Goldman Sachs had advised Orange in its sale to Mannesmann. A London High Court judge condemned the conduct of Man-

nesmann top management when one of its members assured that Goldman Sachs promised not to help Vodafone launch a takeover of the German group.

Vodafone AirTouch's reaction to Mannesmann's refusal was quick. On November 19, 1999 it officially announced the launch of a hostile takeover bid for the whole of Mannesmann's stock. The offer consisted of an exchange of shares with no cash payment. All-share hostile bids were very risky, because the target had every incentive to undermine the bidder's share price by attacking its credibility, its share price could slide and the bid could founder. The official offer was launched on December 23, 1999 and consisted of 53.7 Vodafone AirTouch shares for each Mannesmann share (Exhibit 12). The bid thus valued each Mannesmann share at €266.4 (a total value of €120 bn), which was based on the last closing price of Vodafone. Vodafone AirTouch told Mannesmann shareholders that its offer was giving them an important premium, taking into account the value of €157.8 that had been used in the acquisition of Orange two months earlier. On November 19, 1999 the Mannesmann share price was already €193.1 and Vodafone share price 283.5 pence (Exhibits 13 and 14). On December 23, 1999 Mannesmann share price was €209 and Vodafone share price was 305.75 pence. On January 12, 2000, Mannesmann share price was €237.9 and Vodafone share price was 302.25 pence.

Mannesmann was advised by Morgan Stanley Dean Witter, Merrill Lynch, J. P. Morgan and Deutsche Bank. Goldman Sachs and Warburg Dillon Read were advising Vodafone.

It was the largest takeover bid in history. It was also the first time a foreign company had launched a hostile bid for a German company. For Vodafone AirTouch the takeover bid served various objectives. The first was to achieve a bigger scale that would stimulate cost reduction. With more than 42 million users, Vodafone-Mannesmann would be the world leader (Exhibit 15). That would open the way to new cost advantages through economies of scale. Another consideration was the possibility of reducing costs by aggregating calls in a company-owned network without having to resort to the networks of other operators. Owning the largest network in the world could multiply revenue from other operators with less extensive networks. Lastly, being bigger could give the company greater bargaining power vis-a-vis the handset manufacturers when it came to setting prices and defining the characteristics of the new generations of mobile phones.

Vodafone AirTouch's second objective was technological leadership. The development of new hardware and software applications for Internet-based services was key.

EXHIBIT 12 Vodafone AirTouch: The Acquisition of Mannesmann

December 23, 1999

Vodafone AirTouch's offer to Mannesmann Shareholders

The Offer

Vodafone AirTouch's offer (the "Offer") for Mannesmann has now been launched and will be open for acceptance from 24 December 1999, 00.01 hrs until 24.00 hrs Central European Time ("CET") on 7 February 2000.

Offer Document

Copies of the Offer Document and an Acceptance Form can be obtained by calling any of the telephone numbers detailed below. The Offer Document is available on Vodafone AirTouch's website at **www.vodafone-update.com.**

Key terms of the Offer

Mannesmann Shareholders accepting the Offer will receive:

53.7 New Vodafone AirTouch Shares for every Mannesmann Share.

The Offer values each Vodafone AirTouch Share at €266.4 based on the Vodafone AirTouch Closing Price as at 17 December 1999. The Offer gives Mannesmann Shareholders a 68.8% premium to the Mannesmann Share Price of €157.8 at which Mannesmann Shares were issued to pay for Orange.

The full terms of the Offer are contained in the Offer Document.

Acceptance Procedure

To accept the Offer please call your financial intermediary or depositary bank or for assistance please telephone the Offer Helpline on:

In Germany: toll free - 0800 088 77 66

In the UK: freephone - 0800 169 2853

Bank custodian, broker custodian and institutional investor enquiries in relation to the acceptance and settlement procedures should be directed to Paribas Frankfurt Branch (the Global Exchange Coordinator) at telephone: +49 (0) 69 1520 5630; fax: +49 (0) 69 1520 5636 and enquiries in relation to the Offer and requests for additional copies of offer materials should be directed to D. F. King (Europe) Limited (the European Information Agent) at telephone: +44 (0) 207 920 9700; fax: +44 (0) 207 588 7300.

ALL ACCEPTANCES MUST BE RETURNED TO YOUR DEPOSITARY BANK BEFORE 24.00 HRS CET ON 7 FEBRUARY 2000.

Goldman Sachs International
Peterborough Court, 133 Fleet Street
London EC4A 2BB
United Kingdom

Warburg Dillon Read
1 Finsbury Avenue
London EC2M 2PP
United Kingdom

01 Jan 97 — 31 Dec 99

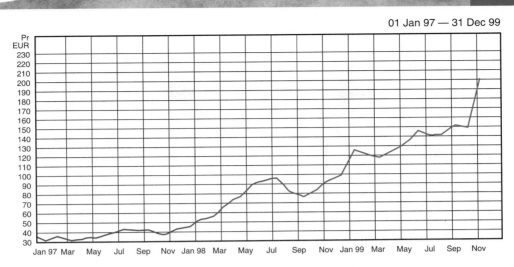

Source: Reuters.

01 Jan 97 — 31 Dec 99

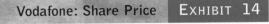
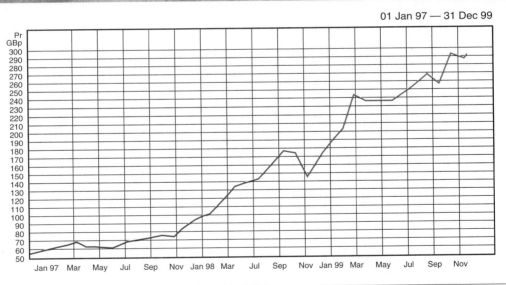

Source: Reuters.

Thirdly, Vodafone AirTouch aimed to achieve a significant presence in continental Europe, where its activity had always been fairly secondary. It was already present in markets such as Germany, Spain or France, but always with a low market share. Mannesmann, in contrast, owned leading companies in Germany, France and Italy. By acquiring Mannesmann, Vodafone could gain a dominant position in all these markets at a blow.

The valuation of Mannesmann had sowed doubts among industry analysts (Exhibits 16 and 17). There were arguments to please everyone. Supporters of the Vodafone bid thought that its success depended on three factors. First, the value of the offer, i.e., whether Vodafone really offered Mannesmann shareholders a good price. The problem lay in defining what an attractive offer was. But the offer consisted of an exchange of

EXHIBIT 15 Vodafone Air Touch and Mannesmann Combined Global Presence

Country	Operator	Rank	Customers (000)
United Kingdom	Vodafone AirTouch	1	6,865
Germany	D2	1	8,195
Italy	Omnitel	2	6,857
France	SFR	2	1,854
Netherlands	Libertel	2	1,355
Spain	Airtel	2	863
Greece	Panafon	1	818
Portugal	Telecel	2	812
Sweden	Europolitan	3	561
Belgium	Proximus	1	451
Poland	Polkomtel	2	254
Romania	Mobifon	1	53
Malta	VF Malta	–	24
Austria	Tele.ring	–	0
Hungary	Vodafone Hungary	–	0
Total Europe			28,962
Middle East/Africa			916
US	Bell & Vodafone		9,000
Asia Pacific			3,422
TOTAL			42,300

Source: Vodafone AirTouch.

shares, so its value would depend directly on the price of Vodafone AirTouch shares. For example, on the day following the announcement, Vodafone AirTouch shares slipped 3 percent, which signified an equivalent reduction in the value of the offer for Mannesmann. The same analysts pointed out that if the market was convinced that the deal would go ahead, the two shares would trade in line with the offer. At the moment that was not happening.

The second critical factor in persuading investors was the strategic logic behind the offer. Chris Gent had defined the objectives to be achieved through the acquisition of Mannesmann: scale, technological leadership, and international expansion. The takeover would create a mobile phone giant on a global scale.

The third factor that analysts identified as key to the bid's success were the cultural, legal and social barriers that Vodafone AirTouch would have to overcome. Specifically, there were various obstacles in the legal field. Firstly, Mannesmann's rules of corporate governance stated that no shareholder could control more than 5 percent of the votes. Secondly, a minority group holding 5 percent of the shares could start legal action

and delay the deal for years. A further difficulty could arise if the offer won between 50 percent and 75 percent of the votes. In that case, the current management team would not be obliged to resign.

With regard to the workforce, the takeover bid was viewed with great suspicion. In some German political and union circles, it was seen as a British invasion of German territory. Even the German Chancellor had spoken out against the Vodafone initiative. The unions at Mannesmann thought that the acquisition would lead to major job cuts and so were prepared to put up a fight. Within the EU itself Vodafone's initiative seemed to have sparked off a debate about mergers and acquisitions involving companies from different countries and thus with different cultures and ways of operating. Vodafone wanted to assure German unions and public opinion that there would not be job cutting.

In any case, the effect of all these barriers would ultimately depend on the attitude adopted by Klaus Esser and his board. If they came out in favour, the difficulties would disappear. But if they decided to resist the takeover, they could use any of these obstacles as weapons in their favour. Esser had repeatedly stated

Part	Total € (millions)	Per Share	Part	Total € (millions)	Per Share
Mobilfunk			**Omnitel Equity Value**		
Total Value	51,203		per DCF	27,873	
Mannesmann's 65.2% Share	33,384	85.6	Mannessmann's 55.1% stake (million)	15,358	39.4
Arcor			**Infostrada Valuation**		
Revenues in 2000E	2,863		Revenues in 2000E (million)	1,388	
Valued at 8x Revenues	22,906		Revenue Multiple	8	
Less: Assumed 2000E Debt	−2,045		Valued at 8x Revenues	11,100	
Equity Value in 2000E	20,861		Less: Assumed 2000E Debt	−1,033	
Discounted back at 15%	19,453		Equity Value in 2000E	10,067	
Mannesmann's 35% Share	6,808	17.5	Discounted back at 15%	9,388	
Total German Telecoms	40,193	103.1	Total Omnitel and Infostrada Stake	24,476	
Cegetel (Fixed)			Less: Stage 3 of OliMan acquisition	−320	
Revenues in 2000E	1,524		Less: OliMan Transaction	−7,600	
Valued at 8x Revenues	12,196				
Less: Assumed 2000E Debt	−762		**Total Italian Telecoms**		
Equity Value in 2000E	11,434		Valuation	16,826	43.2
90% Owned by Cegetel	10,290				
Discounted back at 15%	9,596	3.7	Total Telecoms Valuation	61,634	158.1
SFR (Mobile)			**Capital Goods and Other**		
Enterprise Value	27,075		Valuation	9,256	23.7
Less: Assumed 2000E Debt	−610				
Equity Value	28,466		Total Valuation	70,890	181.8
Cegetel's 80% Share	21,172	8.2	Less: 5% Holding	463	−1.2
Combined Fixed and Mobile	30,768		Company Discount		
			Equity Value	70,427	180.7
Total French Telecoms (15% Stake)	4,615	11.8			
			Price Target		180.0

Source: Morgan Stanley Dean Witter.

that his intention was to seek the highest possible value in the long term for Mannesmann shareholders, and that he would put up a fight only if he felt that the offer was not good enough. The board's reaction would be decisive for the final outcome. Hutchison Whampoa, the Hong Kong investment firm, owned 10.3 percent of Mannesmann stock; it was the largest shareholder of Orange when it was sold to the German firm in October 1999.

MANNESMANN'S REPLY

Mannesmann reacted swiftly to the Vodafone Air-Touch bid. Essentially, Esser's argument was that the offer did not reflect the true value of the company. Mannesmann gave three arguments to justify a higher value (Exhibit 18). First, it argued that whereas Vodafone was a company that specialized exclusively in mobile telephony, Mannesmann's telecommunications

EXHIBIT 17 What Are Mannesmann's Parts Worth?

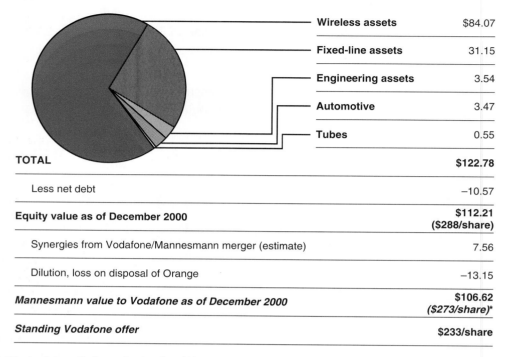

Our firm's view, based on projected 2000 results; figures are in billions of U.S. dollars converted from euros at current rate.

Wireless assets	$84.07
Fixed-line assets	31.15
Engineering assets	3.54
Automotive	3.47
Tubes	0.55
TOTAL	**$122.78**
Less net debt	−10.57
Equity value as of December 2000	**$112.21** ($288/share)
Synergies from Vodafone/Mannesmann merger (estimate)	7.56
Dilution, loss on disposal of Orange	−13.15
Mannesmann value to Vodafone as of December 2000	**$106.62** ($273/share)*
Standing Vodafone offer	**$233/share**

*Based on these estimates, Lehman Brothers estimates value of Mannesmann to Vodafone today to be $252.01 per share.

Source: Lehman Brothers, London.

business included other highly valuable segments such as Internet access or fixed-line telephony. This, it claimed, was a very valuable combination that offered better growth potential than the combination Vodafone-Mannesmann. Also, Esser argued that Mannesmann held larger equity stakes in its subsidiary companies and that this stronger influence should have a bigger value.

The second argument in Mannesmann's defensive strategy was Orange. Esser pointed out that if the acquisition went ahead, the regulatory authorities would require Mannesmann to dispose of Orange, which would involve a substantial loss of value. Esser argued that Orange had more growth potential than Vodafone AirTouch. This was part of his attempt to persuade the market that Mannesmann offered greater value as an independent company than as part of Vodafone AirTouch.

Finally, Esser insisted that "Vodafone needs a deal more than Mannesmann does." Without the deal, Vodafone would have to struggle in order to extract value from its many minority holdings in Europe.

Despite these arguments, Vodafone stuck to its initial offer. During the final weeks of 1999 Mannesmann tried other defensive tactics in an attempt to boost its value and make Vodafone AirTouch abandon its assault. Esser also announced the imminent spin-off of its engineering and automotive businesses. By this means he hoped to ensure that Mannesmann was valued as a pure telecommunications company, pushing up its share price. He also announced plans to spin off the Internet services subsidiary.

On January 3, 2000, to strengthen the company's defence against the Vodafone AirTouch bid, Esser announced that Mannesmann was working fast to present a plan to reduce costs and boost revenue by integrating Orange's business with its own. Said Esser: "We still don't know the exact figure for profit, but we're convinced it will be higher than the figure Vodafone has presented for the supposed synergies between Vodafone and Mannesmann. One of the least acceptable aspects of Vodafone's offer is that it does not value the loss Mannesmann would suffer as a result of the new Vodafone-Mannesmann group having to dispose of Orange, a great company with a great brand."

Esser also warned that if Vodafone obtained only 50 percent of Mannesmann's shares, it would have to

WHAT'S THE ONLY FLAW IN VODAFONE'S GLOBAL STRATEGY?

TICK

It doesn't include the UK's fastest growing
telecommunications brand

It doesn't add any controlled assets
in any major markets to Mannesmann

It suffers from restrictive minority agreements
in major markets that hamper growth

All of the above

Vodafone's hostile offer for Mannesmann ticks all the boxes. In the last quarter of
1999 Orange (which Vodafone has acknowledged will have to de-merge) gained
1.4m new customers, well over 30% more than Vodafone UK. Vodafone would
only bring control over markets such as Sweden and the Netherlands. In the US
and Japan Vodafone is locked into restrictive agreements that will limit its ability
to control the delivery of new products and the creation of value.

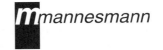

REJECT THE VODAFONE OFFER

pay the remaining shareholders around €60 billion. Such a cash offer might be necessary to gain formal control of the firm. Esser said that "this amount could only be raised by selling crown jewels in the new group, but we don't have any dogs in our portfolio that you would want to sell." He also emphasized that "it is evident that we can do better alone than with Vodafone." Esser also announced that he and his management team would take a 25 percent pay cut if the Mannesmann share price did not reach €350 by December 2001, which represented 24 percent of the Vodafone AirTouch bid.

FINAL ACT?

After more than two months of tension between the two companies the process seemed to be nearing a conclusion. Gent and his team were unsure of winning the approval of Mannesmann's shareholders and so were considering raising their initial offer and offering some cash. There was speculation that this increase would put the value of Mannesmann at €140 billion. At the same time, Vodafone AirTouch was considering modifying some of the conditions and seemed willing to allow Mannesmann to keep up to 49.9 percent of the total shares of the new firm in order to get the support of Mannesmann's board.

At Vodafone AirTouch headquarters, however, nothing was clear. Gent and his management team kept asking themselves the same questions: Was Vodafone AirTouch paying too high a price for control of Mannesmann? Would this acquisition strengthen Vodafone's leadership? Was the acquisition of Mannesmann the best way to win leadership in the European market? Were there other options?

The Battle for Wachovia Corporation

case thirty-five

Justin Webb
R. Duane Ireland
Joseph E. Coombs
University of Richmond

THE MERGER

On April 16, 2001, First Union Corporation announced its planned $12.5 billion stock purchase of Wachovia Corporation. The intended transaction would create what would become the fourth-largest bank in the United States as well as possibly the most dominant bank in the Southeast. (30, 8, 1) To be based in Charlotte, North Carolina, the new Wachovia would have $328.6 billion in assets, 19 million customers on the East Coast, and 90,000 employees. (1) If completed, the combination of First Union and Wachovia would create a bank holding either the number 1 or number 2 market share positions in New Jersey, Pennsylvania, Virginia, North Carolina, South Carolina, Georgia, and Florida. (15) The combined company's revenues would rank among the top 90 in the world, exceeding the revenues of corporations such as Cisco Systems, Coca-Cola Company, and McDonald's Corporation. (15)

However, less than a month after the announcement of the initial proposal, SunTrust Banks Inc. moved aggressively to break up the planned merger with its own stock bid of $14.7 billion, approximately 16.7 percent higher than the First Union bid. (8) "As an additional sweetener, SunTrust would increase its annual dividend to $2.22 a share from the $1.60 expected for 2001 so that Wachovia shareholders, after receiving 1.081 shares of SunTrust shares, would effectively get the same $2.40 annual dividend they already receive from Wachovia." (8) Although First Union would increase its dividend to $2.40 for the first year of acquisition, the dividend would then decrease to an equivalent of $1.92 per share for Wachovia shareholders. (8) Legal battles and expensive marketing campaigns targeted to shareholders are examples of the tactics used during the

months following SunTrust's creation of a contest for Wachovia. Both First Union and SunTrust worked tirelessly during this time period to "sell" the advantages of their individual proposals to Wachovia shareholders before they exercised their right to vote in favor of one bid over the other.

Why were First Union and SunTrust committed to acquiring Wachovia? What industry conditions caused banks to want to grow through mergers and acquisitions? As is often the case with large-scale acquisitions, the answers to these questions were complex and defied simple explanations.

THE FINANCIAL SERVICES INDUSTRY

RIEGLE-NEAL INTERSTATE BANKING AND BRANCHING EFFICIENCY ACT OF 1994 (47, P. 91; 131; 132)

Restrictions on interstate banking and branching had long been a key component of the U.S. banking system's operations. The restrictions were products of a deep-seated mistrust of financial concentration, the belief that a bank should be tied to the community it was chartered to serve, and strong notions about the rights of individual states to protect their citizens' financial interests. In combination, these restrictions created what was essentially a unit banking industry.

The late 19th century's economic expansion and the increasing distances of commerce transactions that improved transportation systems made possible created a need for financial networks with additional capabilities such as those that could be provided by further branching at the state level. However, legislation prevented Federal Reserve Bank members from branching across state lines. By the mid-1980s, however, many states did permit some form of acquisition by out-of-state bank holding companies—an action that had the net effect of allowing banks to expand their operations outside of their home state. Yet, it was not until the Riegle-Neal Interstate Banking and Branching Efficiency Act of 1994 that formal legislation was in place to address the question of geographic expansion within the banking industry. The main impetus driving this reform was the desire to buffer banks from the full effects of being linked only to the economic well-being of a specific region. Thus, in part, the reforms were intended to provide banks with some protection from the full effects of regional downturns such as happened to some financial institutions during the 1980s and the early 1990s.

The Riegle-Neal legislation allowed adequately capitalized and managed bank holding companies to acquire banks in any state beginning on September 29, 1995, and allowed the same for adequately capitalized and managed banks beginning on June 11, 1997. These interstate acquisitions were to be regulated by a number of anti-competition limits, including the restriction specifying that a newly created bank holding company could not control more than 10 percent of U.S. bank and thrift deposits nor more than 30 percent of the deposits in the home state of the bank to be acquired

(except for initial entries into a state). Moreover, the legislation's specifications indicated that individual state deposit-concentration limits would supersede the Riegle-Neal state concentration limit, or the host state could waive the limit altogether. In addition, compliance with state minimum-age laws and community reinvestment laws was required, although exceptions were allowed when transactions involved failed or failing banks. Acquisitions remained subject to other pertinent state laws as well. In Florida, for example, a person who had been convicted, pled guilty, or pled no contest to violation of the Florida Control of Money Laundering in Financial Institutions Act could not be given a certificate of approval required for the purchase or proposed change of control of a bank or trust company. (66)

COMMERCIAL BANKS

The commercial banking industry experienced record profits for ten of the fourteen years between 1987 and 2000. Net income for the industry in 2000 was approximately $72 billion—over 400 percent higher than the net income for the industry in 1990 (see Exhibit 1). This growth in profitability started in the early 1990s and was

Profit Growth for the Banking Industry **EXHIBIT 1**

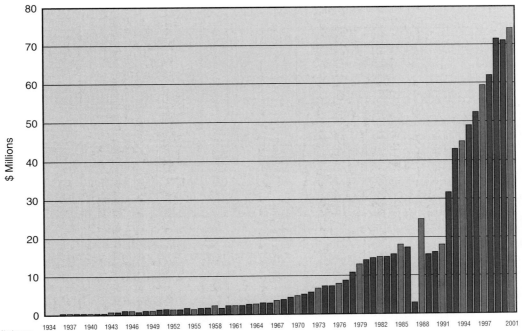

**Net Income of FDIC-Insured Commercial Banks
1934–2001 (as of Year-End)**

	1934	1937	1940	1943	1946	1949	1952	1955	1958	1961	1964	1967	1970	1973	1976	1979	1982	1985	1988	1991	1994	1997	2001
Net Income (In $ Millions)	−857	357	383	623	854	968	1,067	1,320	2,082	2,374	2,602	3,457	4,837	6,580	7,844	12,839	14,844	17,977	24,812	17,935	44,622	53,156	74,318

a product of massive consolidations and the application of new technologies such as Automated Teller Machines (ATMs) and online banking. (45) According to the FDIC, 453 mergers took place in 2000, reducing the number of banks to 8,315 from nearly 14,000 in 1987. (49) (See Exhibit 2.)

Ascendancy of the Universal Commercial Bank (45)
Beginning roughly in 1987, industry observers predicted universal commercial bank ascendancy and increased competition in the commercial banking industry. On April 13, 1997, as the Bank of America–NationsBank deal was announced, Banc One chairman John B. McCoy (who once mused that in the future the industry would have just five or six major banks) announced plans to merge his $116 billion bank with the much merged $115 billion First Chicago NBD Corp. All this came just a week after insurance and brokerage giant Travelers Group announced its intention of combining forces with Citicorp, the second-largest bank in the United States. At a value of $76 billion, this transaction was intended to bring together two large service-oriented

companies that had products and delivery channels that were to be used to create unique synergies.

WACHOVIA

Founded in 1879, Wachovia Corporation is a leading interstate financial holding company with dual headquarters in Atlanta, Georgia, and Winston-Salem, North Carolina, serving regional, national, and international markets. Through 668 branches and 1,356 ATMs, the retail bank serves 3.8 million consumers and 180,000 small businesses in Florida, Georgia, North Carolina, South Carolina, and Virginia. It is also a leading corporate bank with more than 28,000 business relationships and global activities in more than 40 countries.

Wachovia had three major strategic business units—Retail Financial Services, Corporate Financial Services, and Asset and Wealth Management—accounting for 48 percent, 32 percent, and 20 percent of 2000 net revenue, respectively. (39, p. 30) Less than 70 percent of revenue was derived from the dominant business, and the individual businesses shared product,

EXHIBIT 2   Profit Growth for the Banking Industry

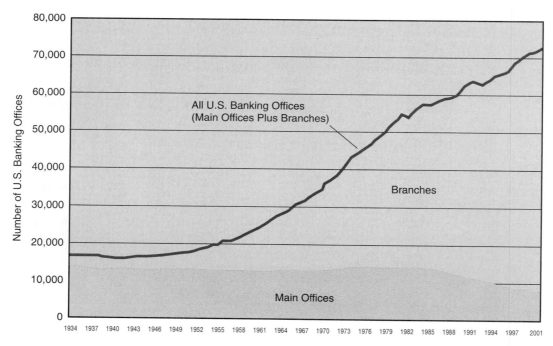

**Number of Insured Commercial Banks
1934–2001 (as of Year-End)**

technological, and distribution linkages. See Appendix A for Wachovia's financial statements.

CORPORATE-LEVEL STRATEGY (39, PP. 12–28)

Wachovia's corporate-level strategic objective was to transform the organization into a dynamic, flexible, performance-minded financial institution that was capable of performance exceeding that of competitors. Decisions to combine the best characteristics of a strong regional bank with industry leadership in selected areas were thought to be the foundation for reaching this objective.

A strong focus on relationships provided an historic competitive advantage for Wachovia in corporate and retail markets and a strong competitive platform for the rapidly growing field of wealth management. This focus has an underlying presence in each of Wachovia's strategic imperatives. Firstly, Wachovia planned to launch multiple "growth thrusts," which should create immediate results and a pipeline of future opportunities. Wachovia defined a growth thrust as a "specific new direction in a chosen business with the potential to contribute $100 million or more in profits within three or four years," achieved through heavy investment within the early years of development. (15) Wachovia's current refinement and expansion of its Private Financial Advisors approach, which provided integrated wealth management services to clients with investable assets of $500,000 to $10 million, was an example of a growth thrust.

Strengthening and pursuing business propositions in which it can create value for customers was Wachovia's second strategic imperative. The bank's decision makers believe that frequent shifts in population patterns as well as fluctuating economic conditions continuously yielded opportunities to create new types of value and to enhance existing value propositions. Information-Based Relationship Management technology made it possible for Wachovia to identify value-creating opportunities and to understand how to better serve customers' needs.

The third imperative was to accelerate entry and expansion into potential high-growth business opportunities while simultaneously exiting those business areas lacking strategic fit with the bank's intended future. Wealth management services became one of the most enviable financial services markets in the nation. Wachovia's 1999 acquisition of OFFITBANK resulted in a respectable share of this attractive market for the bank. Wachovia expanding OFFITBANK offices from New York, San Francisco, and Miami to other high-wealth markets, including Atlanta, Charlotte, Palm Beach, and Winston-Salem—all of which are locations within Wachovia's footprint of operation and area of expertise. To support its intended strategic and financial character, Wachovia exited the Master Trust business and consolidated retail branches in locations that could not significantly contribute to achievement of the primary objective associated with its corporate-level strategy.

Streamlining internal processes by reducing complexity and increasing flexibility was the fourth strategic imperative. Actions taken regarding this imperative included integrating Wachovia's mortgage company and retail division, thereby eliminating staff and system redundancies and achieving customer service efficiencies. In addition, banking regions adopted a geographically based business model that reduced management layers and costs, decentralized authority, and encouraged market-based sales strategies. The market-based sales strategy called for Wachovia to more efficiently segment its consumer market on the basis of demographic, psychographic, and behavioral consumer characteristics and consumer responses. These segmentations facilitated Wachovia's efforts to identify specific customer needs as well as products and services with the highest probability of satisfying them. (68)

The final strategic imperative revolves around implementing performance improvement methodologies that were focused on enhanced productivity, resource allocation, and cost management. This imperative found Wachovia reengineering its processes and leveraging its existing technology to increase efficiency and competitiveness without sacrificing customer service. Consolidating deposit encoding operations and developing high-speed check processing were examples of process improvements. In addition, Wachovia continually enhanced its Intranet capabilities and implemented a Web-based procurement system.

BRAND PROMISE

Financial services inherently require a foundation of trust and a belief that the provider is always acting in the customer's best interest. Wachovia conveyed and emphasized its trustworthiness through its brand promise, which was: "Financial services that work for you. Creative, innovative, on target. From a source you can trust." This brand statement was the foundation for many of Wachovia's advertising campaigns.

COMPANY CULTURE

Wachovia fostered an image of a traditional and conservative bank. Wachovia's internal, paternalistic system demonstrated and was consistent with this image. After discussions with Wachovia officials, one First

Union employee perceived them as much more trustworthy, down-to-earth, and respectful than First Union management. These characteristics contributed to what was perceived to be Wachovia's supportive, yet somewhat formal corporate environment. Few, if any, Wachovia upper-level managers were addressed by their first names. (21)

Wachovia's conservative atmosphere and strong customer service focus contributed to efforts to develop long-standing, profitable relationships. Until a number of bad loans in the years leading up to 2000, Wachovia had traditionally been one of the strongest banks in the Southeast, earning respectable profits during bull and bear cycles. Wachovia intended to provide superior service to its customers and believed that its service was one of its competitive advantages.

First Union (53)

First Union was founded in 1908 in Charlotte, North Carolina, as the Union National Bank. Over the years, it grew to become the sixth-largest nationwide banking company with over $254 billion in assets and the sixth-largest nationwide brokerage-dealer with 7,400 registered representatives. Featuring 2,200 financial centers, 375 full-service brokerage offices, 160 home equity loan originators, 3,800 ATMs, and the fastest-growing Internet channel, the bank's multi-channel distribution network was used to serve 7 million retail households, 800,000 small business customers, and 3 million brokerage accounts in 2000. First Union held the number 1 deposit share on the East Coast, with banking operations in New Jersey, New York, Connecticut, Virginia, Maryland, North Carolina, South Carolina, Georgia, Pennsylvania, Delaware, Florida, and Washington, D.C. See Appendix B for First Union's financial statements.

Corporate-Level Strategy (53)

The General Bank, Capital Management Group, and Capital Markets Group are First Union's three strategic business units—accounting for 51.4 percent, 27.1 percent, and 21.5 percent of 2000 net revenue, respectively. Supporting the business units' operations were several corporate-level competitive advantages, including a broad distribution network, a full selection of financial and investment products, and a leading share in the attractive East Coast markets.

With four primary business lines—Retail, Small Business, Commercial, and Commercial Real Estate—the General Bank was the "face" of First Union to its customers. The strategic focus of the General Bank was the growth of deposits, loans, and investment products and an increased share of the small business market by

leveraging customer information to enhance and tailor services. This concentration appeared to be a source of competitive advantage for First Union. Its multiple services customer ratio increased from 20 percent to 25 percent for the financial year 2000, and customer satisfaction scores compiled by the Gallup organization improved over seven consecutive quarters. The multiple services customer ratio is a comparison of the number of services used per individual customer. Since marketing to present customers is less expensive than acquiring new ones, and more services provided implies greater efficiency, this ratio's trend was a positive indicator of First Union's profit potential.

With the sixth-largest brokerage firm in the nation, the fifth-largest mutual fund family among banks, and the second-largest volume in annuity sales, the Capital Management Group was an asset management powerhouse. Helping to build a balanced earnings stream for First Union through fee-based businesses, the Capital Management Group business unit focused on providing to customers both maximum brokerage channels as well as financial advice for investments, trust, 401(k), and insurance services. To create intra-firm synergies, Capital Management Group tried to: (1) maximize the linkage with the General Bank, (2) capitalize on its distribution scale as well as from both existing and new, innovative product offerings, and (3) identify demographic trends suggesting commercial possibilities for the Group. A 30 percent compound annual growth rate from 1995 to 2000 and nearly quadrupled assets under management from $47 billion to $171 billion demonstrated the group's success.

The Capital Markets Group offered customers a number of diversified creative capital solutions—fixed income products, equity products, structured products, and advisory services. Capital Markets Group planned to attract and retain customers across all business units by combining industry and product expertise with an unmatched commitment to customers. Thus, customer service was an intended competitive advantage in this business unit.

Underlying the three core business units' operations as a corporate-level resource was First Union's eCommerce and Technology unit. It was the nation's third-largest and fastest-growing Internet banking channel between 1998 and 2000, with 2.4 million online enrollments, including 59,000 brokerage and 88,000 wholesale accounts. To further reduce costs and improve the customer experience, First Union intended to expand the online channel and "Web enable" internal processes and infrastructure. The hope was to effectively and efficiently extend the First Union brand name.

COMPANY CULTURE

First Union was a veteran of intense competition across a broad range of financial products and services. In one First Union employee's opinion, the General Bank has a "very aggressive sales culture that was bottom line–driven and demanding." The General Bank also had an industry-high employee turnover rate. At the same time the aggressive culture had enabled First Union to be an industry leader in extending and providing multiple services to individual customers.

First Union CEO Thompson is described as "a roll-his-sleeves-up executive who is called 'Ken' by his employees." Upper management was viewed as detached from daily operations—almost as figureheads—whose decisions rarely mattered until they affected those locally. This means that individual employees had considerable autonomy to produce and control their operations. (21, 57)

SUNTRUST (54)

Established in 1891 as Commercial Travelers' Savings and merging with Sun Banks in 1985, SunTrust owns more than 30 subsidiaries throughout the Southeast in 2000. Relying on its 1,100 branches and 1,900 ATMs, SunTrust served more than 3.7 million households in Alabama, Florida, Georgia, Maryland, Tennessee, Virginia, and Washington, D.C. SunTrust subsidiaries offer a wide range of financial services—from the traditional deposit, credit, and trust and investments services to mortgage banking, commercial and auto leasing, asset management, discount brokerage, credit-related insurance, and capital market services. SunTrust handled over $138.4 billion in assets and a mortgage-servicing portfolio in excess of $42.3 billion. As attractive as these positions were, the "crown jewel" of SunTrust was the 8 percent share of Coca-Cola it owned, having underwritten the company's initial public common stock offering in 1919. (55, 56) See Appendix C for SunTrust's financial statements.

CORPORATE-LEVEL STRATEGY

SunTrust operated with five major strategic business units—Retail Banking, Commercial Banking, Corporate and Investment Banking, Mortgage, and Personal Client Services. Appendix F compares SunTrust's business units with those of Wachovia and First Unions. SunTrust offered its customers a local orientation via a decentralized management structure. On the other hand, being one of the nation's largest banks gave it product development advantages over smaller organizations. With the acquisition of Crestar Financial Corporation on December 31, 1998, SunTrust derived the technological capabilities to standardize many of its operations, becoming more efficient and capable of serving customer needs. (65)

The Retail Banking unit served 3.7 million households as well as businesses with annual sales up to $5 million. It provided deposits, loan products, insurance, and business and private banking services through branch and other delivery channels (ATM, Internet, and phone). Commercial Banking served medium-sized businesses and entities with annual sales ranging from $5 million to $250 million. Real estate, institutional and government services, and receivables capital management were areas of expertise for this business unit. Corporate and Investment Banking handled the business of more than 1,000 of America's top corporations through traditional credit facilities, factoring, leasing, treasury management, and capital markets alternatives. In addition, this unit offered a wide array of services for raising capital and investment options as well as the technical expertise for advice in these fields. SunTrust Mortgage originated and serviced loans via 113 locations in 48 states as well as through its many retail branches in the bank's Southeast footprint, the telephone, and the Internet. Personal Client Services provided trust, brokerage, investment management, and other related services to institutions and affluent individuals. Barron's, a top mutual fund family, favorably evaluated the performance of SunTrust's STI Classic Funds. Nonetheless, some believed that this fund group lacked the focus of comparable business units in First Union and Wachovia, noting that this group has changed its name multiple times within the last few years. (65)

COMPANY CULTURE

SunTrust was considered conservative, both as an employer and as a bank. As an employer, SunTrust placed high value on ethical business practices and lending policies. In addition, the work atmosphere was termed "tight buttoned," with SunTrust having just recently started casual Fridays in *some* departments. Similarly, SunTrust's lending and investing methods were comparatively conservative, reducing the bank's susceptibility to negative conditions in different markets' economic conditions. (55) For example, SunTrust would avoid lending to companies operating in the higher risk technology and media industries, choosing to focus on serving the needs of S&P 500 companies instead.

As with Wachovia, SunTrust's conservative nature and customer orientation yielded a strong customer-based revenue stream. This combination helped build long-term trusting relationships with customers, allowing SunTrust to frequently interact with customers about the bank's comprehensive set of products and services. The breadth and depth of its relationships with customers was expected to enable SunTrust to secure loans with lower risk and higher overall returns. Observing demographic trends and becoming even more conscious of customer needs is expected to continually strengthen these relationships.

THE TRANSACTION

INTERESTS

Following the congressional action in 1994 that eliminated the ban on interstate banking, many banks sought nationwide operations through mergers and/or acquisitions. (42) Increasing competition resulting from extensive merger and acquisition activity forced banks to seek larger market share to develop scale and possibly scope economies as a foundation for profitability. The previous fragmented character of the banking industry increased the likelihood that scale and scope economies can be realized through mergers and acquisitions.

First Union was the nation's sixth-largest bank in 2001. A merger with Wachovia was intended to augment First Union's Connecticut to Florida retail chain. Both companies agreed the ability to offer and service a wide, deep set of product lines was crucial to success in the future banking industry. Neither corporation alone had the resources to create such an extensive collection of products, but a business combination would make this possible. (73) As a second stimulus to this transaction, NationsBank (now Bank of America) had previously blocked Wachovia's first attempt to enter the lucrative Florida market by winning the bidding contest for Barnett Bank. (72) This merger would allow Wachovia to capture almost 15 percent of this market, or the second-highest market share for the state. Finally, great complementarity existed between the management structures of the two banks. Most of the executives that comprised Wachovia's peak management were ready to retire, leaving no one, in CEO Baker's opinion, ready to run the company successfully. First Union would fill this looming void. (73) Despite these great advantages and even in light of the potentially attractive merger price, some analysts still questioned the transaction's necessity, favoring the higher SunTrust offer instead. SunTrust—the nation's ninth-largest bank—had retail branches from Baltimore to Florida, but was relatively weak where Wachovia was strong, namely in North and South Carolina. (6) Consequently, SunTrust argued, this would create less disruption during the integration process since fewer branches would have to be closed. Despite the apparent advantages of combining with SunTrust, Wachovia's board rejected the hostile takeover bid with a 14 to 1 vote.

TACTICS
December 2000

In late December 2000, Wachovia CEO Baker announced his bank's 11th-hour rejection of SunTrust's offer to merge with Wachovia. According to Baker, this decision was based on disagreements regarding how to operate what would be the newly formed financial institution. However, others at Wachovia suggested that the SunTrust offer appeared to be an acquisition rather than a merger. Firms acquired by others usually lose their identity and ability to control their operations. Baker and others deemed these losses to be unacceptable and not in the best interests of Wachovia shareholders.

May 2001

Following the Wachovia board's mid-May rejection of the offer, SunTrust stated that it would challenge the First Union/Wachovia merger anti-takeover provisions in court and would demand a shareholder vote. First Union/Wachovia, possibly anticipating a hostile bid after SunTrust's failed bid for Wachovia in December 2000, had developed a number of provisions to dissuade additional suitors. The legal structure of the agreement provided that if shareholders rejected the First Union proposed deal, Wachovia's board would not participate in any other transactions until January 2002. In addition, both First Union and Wachovia agreed to another deterrent that gave the banks options to purchase 19.9 percent stakes, using cash and *other assets,* in one another should a third party acquire Wachovia. Thus, if SunTrust's hostile bid was approved by shareholder vote, First Union could purchase approximately $2.5 billion in options from Wachovia using the equivalent of distressed loans and/or real estate, leaving SunTrust with a large amount of questionable assets on Wachovia's books. (7, 20)

SunTrust also highlighted the large difference between the projected premium to be received by Wachovia CEO L. M. Baker Jr. and shareholders. While Wachovia shareholders would receive a fairly small premium from the First Union deal, Mr. Baker would become chairman of the new company and would receive $2 million a year for the rest of his life as an annual retirement income and an additional $200,000 a year for life for office/secretarial/transportation uses. Should his wife survive him, she would receive no less than 60 percent of his annual retirement income. (7)

Within a few days of SunTrust's bid, a simultaneous increase in First Union's stock price and drop in the value of SunTrust's stock decreased SunTrust's premium from almost 17 percent to just 6 percent over First Union's bid. Yet, even with this lower margin, First Union's board felt the need to revise the merger agreement, enhancing shareholder return and answering SunTrust's challenges. In this context, First Union decided it would allow Wachovia shareholders to choose between the originally proposed dividend with an additional one-time 48-cent per share cash payout at the time the transaction was completed or an increase to Wachovia's normal dividend. A second revision would allow First Union to purchase a 19.9 percent stake in Wachovia, now capped at $780 million, using only cash, readily marketable securities, or preferred stock. Finally, Mr. Baker would not accept the original package, agreeing instead to one that was more comparable to that offered by SunTrust. (20)

First Union was expected to run ads highlighting the First Union/Wachovia transaction as a "friendly merger." (38) The present actions were intended to appeal to Wachovia employees and shareholders, claiming the hostile takeover would gut Wachovia—the name, culture, and management would disappear—ultimately leading to low employee morale and poor customer service. This was extremely important because one of the only other hostile takeovers in the banking industry—the Wells Fargo acquisition of First Interstate—proved to be a disaster. A convenience bank, Wells Fargo had trouble integrating its culture with that of the "relationship"-styled First Interstate. In addition, Wells Fargo terminated 75 percent of First Interstate's senior managers, resulting in massive systems problems. Customers fled, leading to a 20 percent loss of non-interest bearing deposits and a $180 million loss in a single quarter less than a year after its approval by the Federal Reserve Board. (64, 69, 70, 71)

On May 23, 2001, each side filed lawsuits accusing the other of breaking federal securities laws by making deceptive public statements. SunTrust claimed the Wachovia board misled shareholders regarding key costs involved in the merger. Later the same day, both Wachovia and First Union countered with their own lawsuits. Wachovia alleged that SunTrust used confidential information obtained during the banks' merger discussions in December 2000 to stake its claims. Both First Union and Wachovia claimed SunTrust made untrue statements of costs associated with the proposed transaction and requested federal and state courts to require SunTrust to retract its statements. (6)

The shareholder vote was set for August 3, 2001.

June 2001

SunTrust's next move was to seek an amendment to Wachovia's bylaws to permit shareholders to call a special meeting to expand Wachovia's board with new directors who would support SunTrust's takeover proposal. First Union successfully lobbied North Carolina lawmakers to change how special shareholder meetings

could be called. The net effect of this effort was to block SunTrust's move. (5, 19)

Later that month, First Union pointed to SunTrust's poor record and Community Reinvestment Act (CRA) rating in lending to low- and moderate-income borrowers. Regulators examine a bank's overall CRA rating when approving its bid to acquire another financial institution. SunTrust accused First Union of trying to distort its image by highlighting the lending rating. The overall CRA rating encompasses scores for lending, services, and investments in low- and moderate-income neighborhoods, and SunTrust's overall rating was "satisfactory." SunTrust further argued that although both First Union's and Wachovia's overall CRA ratings were "outstanding," the ratings had not been updated since 1997, when tougher CRA criteria had been established. In addition, some activists and community groups contended that First Union's rating should have been lower, because the bank did not live up to its promise to continue low- and moderate-income programs in Philadelphia after its acquisition of CoreStates Financial, and the bank had "predatory mortgage lending practices" remaining from its 1998 acquisition of Money Store. (10) In addition, Georgia state senator Vincent D. Fort stated, "For First Union to call SunTrust the bad guys is like a possum calling a skunk ugly," also noting that First Union's overall CRA rating had been questioned. (10)

July 2001

SunTrust followed First Union's allegations with its own, claiming First Union used "lease-in/lease-out" tax structures between 1994 and 1999, a practice that the U.S. Treasury Department outlawed in 1999. These structures allow banks to gain tax deferrals on the leasing of real estate and other properties. If the IRS were to order First Union to pay back taxes, the bank would possibly have to dip into reserves, an action that would decrease future earnings. In addition, SunTrust claimed that First Union carried over $5.4 billion in loans to the media, telecommunications, and technology industries, and "due to changes in market conditions and attitudes of the investment community, this sector has become extremely risky for investments." (23) Due to unpredictable market conditions, a large portion of these loans could become uncollectible in the future, leaving the potential for value creation of this merger even more uncertain. First Union stated that all tax structures were used in accordance with rules and regulations but would not comment on specifics of its loan portfolio.

SunTrust charged that Wachovia CEO Baker negotiated a merger deal with First Union without fully informing the rest of Wachovia's board about SunTrust's competing offer. (27) However, less than a week later, a North Carolina judge ended all legal actions by issuing a number of rulings. According to the judge, the provision that Wachovia could not meet with other suitors until January 2002 would be thrown out; however, the break-up fee could remain at $780 million. Finally, it was ruled that Wachovia's board was informed, intelligent, and knowledgeable in its decisions. (40, 28)

Proxy Monitor, a shareholder advisory company, recommended that Wachovia investors approve First Union's bid, citing potential for long-term growth and an increased long-term share value. In addition, Proxy Monitor stated there was no compelling reason to abandon the First Union transaction, which for most purposes is fully under way, for another "deal that is risky at best." (28, 52)

August 2001
In August of 2001, Institutional Shareholder Services (ISS) became the second shareholder advisory company to endorse the First Union/Wachovia merger. ISS stated the First Union/Wachovia merger was more of a strategic partnership seeking long-term growth, while the SunTrust deal would merely maximize immediate shareholder returns. The announcement was a great advantage for the First Union bid because it established the tone for the vote of many institutional investors. First Union had to win a majority of the 210 million shares outstanding. A shareholder's non-vote was to be tallied against First Union. (42, 52)

August 4, 2001
On this date, it was determined that Wachovia shareholders had approved the merger of First Union and Wachovia. First Union won about 55 percent of the vote, made up mostly by institutional investors. It was also confirmed that Wachovia spent approximately $550 million to purchase 18 million shares of First Union Corporation shares, beginning on April 16 and ending in late June. This purchase helped boost First Union's stock price during the battle, decreasing the difference between SunTrust's offer and First Union's to about 5 percent from 17 percent. Consequently, this made it difficult for SunTrust to highlight its bid premium. (1, 18, 30) The shareholder vote ended the expensive marketing campaigns by all parties. First Union/Wachovia and SunTrust spent $8 million apiece to advertise in newspapers and on the radio and television. The rival banks contacted thousands of individual investors to lobby for their votes. Wachovia rejected SunTrust's initial request for a list of Wachovia's 120,000 shareholders, but SunTrust successfully sued to acquire the list. SunTrust even handed out thousands of Koozies can holders at Fourth of July celebrations with

suntrustwachoviaproposal.com printed on the foam. The website hosted a number of arguments to block the merger of First Union and Wachovia. (18)

The Federal Reserve Board approved the $14.6 billion transaction between First Union and Wachovia with a 5 to 0 vote. The Justice Department also advised that this merger would not likely have any significant adverse effect on competition. (13)

FUTURE

THE NEW WACHOVIA
The Federal Reserve decision allowed First Union and Wachovia to begin the difficult task of integrating the two companies. To achieve a seamless integration, the companies began to organize a merger steering committee and organization in May 2001 (see Appendix D; 58, pp. 4–7). The main effect of the integration effort was to expand the customer base by remaining focused on the customer experience and by improving customer perception of the new Wachovia. (59) To avoid previous integration problems resulting from mergers and acquisitions, the companies planed to take the process slowly with three years being allocated for full integration to be reached. Besides no fees for Wachovia customers who use First Union ATMs, and vice versa, customers would see very few changes in the first year. The two banks would continue to market and operate as separate entities, no branches were to be closed, and new signs would not be installed until the second year of integration. (60) Although the new Wachovia wished to avoid major disruptions in its systems, which occurred with SunTrust's acquisition of Crestar and resulted in a loss of many customers, some integration consultants suggested that a failure to move quickly may prevent merging companies from creating intended value. (46, p. 88) Conversely, First Union argued that the low premium it paid to acquire Wachovia would allow the combined company to effect a slower integration while nonetheless gaining value for all shareholders.

A proposed timeline for the complete conversion can be seen in Appendix E. (58, pp. 9, 16) The new Wachovia had three major lines of business or strategic business units—General Bank, Wealth Management Group, and Capital Management Group. General Bank encompassed the retail (number 1 on the East Coast), small business, and wholesale sectors and would serve customers' needs through an extensive distribution network, a robust product line, exceptional service, and advice/knowledge. (15)

Wealth Management Group handled private banking, personal trusts, investments management, insurance services, financial and estate planning, and charitable services. With over 35 additional locations compared to its closest competitor, Wealth Management Group would have the strongest presence in the new Wachovia footprint. Taking advantage of Wachovia's heritage and geographically deployed market, Wealth Management Group would retain its position by focusing on clients, providing an extensive product solution set, and using a consistent, talented, and integrated team model. (16)

Capital Management Group included retail brokerage, insurance (annuities, mass market life, and online), asset management (Evergreen Investments), and corporate and institutional trust business lines. It would remain a leading player in this growth industry by taking advantage of its well-positioned multi-channel distribution network, a broad spectrum of investment products, and a proven track record. (17)

Identifying the business models and management for these groups were some of the earlier decisions to be made by the new Wachovia. As can be seen from the timeline under 2Q and 3Q 2001, the top three layers of management had been named by the time the Federal Reserve approved the merger. However, most of the complex decisions lay ahead, including the issue of eliminating 7,000 of the 90,000 employees of the new Wachovia. The merger integration team continually updated Wachovia employees via memos and Intranet messages. In addition, employees could apply for a certain number of new positions within the company based upon their current position. Displaced employees received a severance package amounting to half a month's pay for each year of service, with a minimum severance of 1.5 months for lower-level staff and 12 months for those in upper-level management positions. (60)

Although the new company has established various business models pre-approval, another important post-merger challenge was to integrate the widely differing cultures of First Union and Wachovia. The seamless integration of corporate cultures was extremely important to achieve organizational fit and the goals of the merger, as was demonstrated earlier by numerous failures in the industry (e.g., Wells Fargo and the two banks' own experiences). The new Wachovia decided on a "go slow" approach to culture integration, allowing the two banks to operate as separate entities until late 2002. The intent was to deliver extensive training to employees and, through that training, to articulate a new corporate culture. In addition, although the sales models of the individual companies differed greatly, the banks argued that since both were southern banks with headquarters in North Carolina, their overall culture and values were essentially the same. (73) (See Appendix E for a complete integration timeline.)

Many observers were stunned to learn that the integrated company would keep the Wachovia name and discard First Union, especially because Wachovia had virtually no name recognition in the Northeast and First Union had spent hundreds of millions of dollars in recent years to boost recognition of its own name. In fact, according to Thomson Publishing's Bank Advertising News, First Union led all banks in media spending in 1999, expending $82.6 million, with Bank of America a distant second at $64.5 million. Interestingly, Wachovia CEO Baker adamantly required that Wachovia be the name of the new company, citing the heritage and reputation of the bank, yet conceded to First Union's requirement that the company be headquartered in Charlotte. (74) First Union Chairman Ken Thompson downplayed the name change, though, jokingly stating, "I think the only problem we're going to have with Wachovia is trying to get some portion of 19 million customers to pronounce it appropriately." However, in an industry where every corporate/customer association—name, logo, slogan, typeface, and even bank décor—is vital, the new Wachovia must be extra cautious in its branding decisions. (57)

SUNTRUST AND OTHER COMPETITORS

Since First Union won the battle for Wachovia, Lehman Brothers analyst Henry Dickson noted that SunTrust *must* perform well to remain a competitive force in the East Coast banking industry. However, others were not as optimistic, claiming that SunTrust must seek a partner to remain competitive in the long term. These analysts speculated SunTrust as either the future acquirer of North Carolina–based BB&T Corp. or as a Wells Fargo target. SunTrust expressed interest in moving into the Carolinas, and BB&T's 900 branches in the Carolinas, Georgia, Kentucky, Maryland, Tennessee, Virginia, West Virginia, and the District of Columbia have been described as a good fit for achieving SunTrust's interests. On the other hand, San Francisco–based Wells Fargo, the nation's fourth-largest bank, lacks a presence in the Southeast. Feeling the challenge from the new Wachovia, Wells Fargo may be persuaded to counter with an acquisition of SunTrust. However, SunTrust spokesman Barry Koling only teased the speculators, stating, "Our eyes are always open for merger opportunities. We never needed the Wachovia acquisition. We certainly would have liked to have had it." One of SunTrust's short-term tactics was to court Wachovia customers. First Union acquisitions had generated customer complaints in the past, and with plans to close branch offices and convert bank statements and ATM cards to one system, SunTrust was adequately positioned to achieve its goal of gaining customers from the new Wachovia. (41)

By the end of 2001 SunTrust was competing against two larger banks with a strong presence in its footprint—the new Wachovia and Bank of America.

As of 2001, Bank of America was number two and three with respect to earnings and assets in the United States. These earnings were over three times as much as the new Wachovia's and the assets were almost double. Bank of America allowed its customers to bank and invest through the nation's largest financial services network, including approximately 4,400 domestic branches, 13,000 ATMs, call centers, and an Internet website. (62, 63)

The Royal Bank of Canada made aggressive moves to secure a position in the U.S. Southeast during this period as well. It completed a $2.3 billion acquisition of Rocky Mount, N.C.–based Centura Banks, Inc. This purchase gave Royal Bank a strong position in North Carolina, and a bank spokesman said it was seeking an even greater market share, having already expressed an interest in acquiring some, if not all, divested branches from the First Union/Wachovia merger. (24) Operating as Canada's leading provider of residential mortgages, personal lending, business banking services, and corporate/investment banking and wealth management services, the Royal Bank served 10 million customers through approximately 1,800 branches and would be a significant competitor for both the new Wachovia and SunTrust. (61)

THE CHALLENGE

Many mergers and acquisitions fail due to a lack of effective due diligence. (46, p. 178) Announced less than half a year after Wachovia and SunTrust called off merger talks, was the First Union/Wachovia merger a result of due diligence, in which feasible synergies were recognized, or was it spurred on by other factors, including even managerial hubris? Effective due diligence goes beyond transfer of shares, environmental issues, sale of assets, tax issues, and other financial issues to include unforeseen liabilities such as organizational and cultural barriers. (46, pp. 18, 24) Did Wachovia and First Union adequately identify costs associated with the unification of the two cultures, the extension of the new Wachovia brand and image into the Northeast, the loss of customers due to system disruptions during conversion, as well as other hidden barriers that are so crucial in deciding whether value is created during an acquisition or merger? Can the new Wachovia develop viable competitive advantages in its business units while corporate-level executions remain focused on shaping the bank's character for future success? Can synergies be realized from the integration of these two corporate cultures? Thousands of decisions will be made in the next few years to determine the fate of this new banking industry titan.

REFERENCES

1. Associated Press, "Wachovia Investors OK Merger Finances: $14.3-Billion Deal with First Union Will Create the 4th-Largest US Bank," in *Los Angeles Times*, Home Edition, The Times Mirror Company, 8/04/2001, C2.
2. Boraks, David, "Battle for Wachovia: Thompson Takes to the Stump," in *American Banker*, Trade Publications, 5/18/2001.
3. Boraks, David, "First Union Still Selling Merger Deal to Wall St," in *American Banker*, Trade Publications, 5/01/2001.
4. Boraks, David, "First Union-Wachovia: On Second Thought," in *American Banker*, Trade Publications, 4/18/2001.
5. Brannigan, Martha, "SunTrust Seeks Wachovia Bylaw Change as Part of Attempt to Achieve Takeover," in *Wall Street Journal*, Dow Jones & Company Inc., 6/05/2001, A4.
6. Day, Kathleen, "Fight over Wachovia Is Taken to Court; Merger Partners, SunTrust File Suits," in *Washington Post*, The Washington Post Co., 5/24/2001, E01.
7. Deogun, Nikhil and Carrick Mollenkamp, "Deals & Deal Makers: Wachovia Chief Faces Puzzled Shareholders—Why Did Bank Brush Off Earlier SunTrust Overture?" in *Wall Street Journal*, Dow Jones & Company Inc., 5/16/2001, C1.
8. Deogun, Nikhil and Carrick Mollenkamp, "SunTrust's Hostile Bid Ends Its Genteel Banking Position," in *Wall Street Journal Europe*, Dow Jones & Company Inc., 5/15/2001, p. 13.
9. First Union, "There Are Two Different Ways to Combine Financial Institutions," Packet of Ads provided by Wachovia Corporation.
10. Fleishman, Sandra, "SunTrust's Lending Rating an Issue in Merger Battle; First Union Points Finger in Fight for Wachovia," in *Washington Post*, The Washington Post Co., 6/27/2001, E01.
11. Gold, Jacqueline, "Ken do 1 of 2," in *Institutional Investor Magazine*, National Magazines, 6/22/2001, Cover Story.
12. Gold, Jacqueline, "Ken do 2 of 2," in *Institutional Investor Magazine*, National Magazines, 6/22/2001, Cover Story.
13. Gordon, Marcy, "Fed Board Approves Merger of Banks," in *Washington Post*, Washington Post Co., 8/14/2001, E03.
14. Jenkins, Ben, "General Bank Strategy Update Focused on Growth," at wachovia.firstunion.com, June 7, 2002.
15. Jenkins, Ben, Stan Kelly, and Don McMullen, "Wachovia Corporation: A Winning Combination," at wachovia.firstunion.com, June 7, 2002.
16. Kelly, Stan, "Wealth Management Group," New York City Media Luncheon, at wachovia.firstunion.com, June 7, 2002.
17. McMullen, Don, "Capital Management Group," New York City Media Luncheon, at wachovia.firstunion.com, June 7, 2002.
18. Mollenkamp, Carrick, "Deals & Deal Makers: Wachovia Rivals Courted Mom and Pop—Ad Battle Sought Individual Votes," in *Wall Street Journal*, Dow Jones & Company Inc., 8/13/2001, C1.
19. Mollenkamp, Carrick, "First Union Aided by North Carolina with Fast New Law," in *Wall Street Journal*, Dow Jones & Company Inc., 6/15/2001, B2.
20. Mollenkamp, Carrick, "First Union Alters Break-Up Fee Cap in Wachovia Pact," in *Wall Street Journal*, Dow Jones & Company Inc., 5/31/2001, B14.
21. Mollenkamp, Carrick, "First Union and Wachovia Shift Focus to Merging," in *Wall Street Journal*, Dow Jones & Company Inc., 8/06/2001, A3.
22. Mollenkamp, Carrick, "First Union Beats Estimates for 2nd Period, Gaining Edge in Its Bid for Wachovia," in *Wall Street Journal*, Dow Jones & Company Inc., 7/13/2001, A4.
23. Mollenkamp, Carrick, "First Union Denies Tax-Shelter Charge Made by SunTrust," in *Wall Street Journal*, Dow Jones & Company Inc., 7/05/2001, A4.
24. Mollenkamp, Carrick, "First Union Enters Talks to Divest Branches as It Prepares to Complete Wachovia Deal," in *Wall Street Journal*, Dow Jones & Company Inc., 7/27/2001, A2.
25. Mollenkamp, Carrick and Nikhil Deogun, "First Union Offers a Dividend Incentive as Wachovia Board Is Set to Weigh Offers," in *Wall Street Journal*, Dow Jones & Company Inc., 5/22/2001, A4.
26. Mollenkamp, Carrick and Nikhil Deogun, "Is Rejected SunTrust the Way for Wachovia?" in *Wall Street Journal*, Dow Jones & Company Inc., 5/23/2001, C1.

27. Mollenkamp, Carrick, "SunTrust Assails Wachovia at Hearing," in *Wall Street Journal*, Dow Jones & Company Inc., 7/18/2001, A4.

28. Mollenkamp, Carrick, "SunTrust Has Little Time Left to Divide Wachovia, First Union," in *Wall Street Journal*, Dow Jones & Company Inc., 7/23/2001, B4.

29. Mollenkamp, Carrick, "SunTrust Says Wachovia Bid Is 'Best and Final'—Investors Must Weigh Offer against First Union; Premium Stands at 4.8%," in *Wall Street Journal*, Dow Jones & Company Inc., 7/17/2001, A4.

30. Mollenkamp, Carrick, "Wachovia Bought First Union Shares in Takeover Battle," in *Wall Street Journal*, Dow Jones & Company Inc., 8/15/2001, A4.

31. Mollenkamp, Carrick and Nikhil Deogun, "Wachovia Director Confirms Vote that May Give Hope to SunTrust," in *Wall Street Journal*, Dow Jones & Company Inc., 5/24/2001, A4.

32. Nowell, Paul, "First Union: Bid for Wachovia 'Clearly Superior' to Sun-Trust," in *Associated Press Business Writer*, Wire Service, 5/15/2001.

33. Reddy, Anitha, "SunTrust Earnings Increase 9 Percent," in *Washington Post*, The Washington Post Co., 7/07/2001, E08.

34. Seccombe, Jane, "Selling the Merger—Banks' Leaders Tout Opportunities for Employees," in *Winston-Salem Journal*, Major In-Market Newspapers, 5/03/2001.

35. Serres, Chris, "Bankers Hit Road to Sell Deal," in *Raleigh News & Observer*, Major In-Market Newspapers, 5/09/2001.

36. Staff, "SunTrust Won't Boost Bid," in *Washington Post*, The Washington Post Co., 7/17/2001, E02.

37. Tannenbaum, Fred, "Bank CEOs Say Risk Was Losing Deal," in *Charlotte Business Journal*, Trade Publications, 4/30/2001.

38. Veverka, Amber, "CEOs Duel for Wachovia in North Carolina Newspaper Ads," in *The Charlotte Observer*, Major In-Market Newspapers, 5/18/2001.

39. Wachovia Corporation 2001 Annual Report.

40. Williams, Krissah, "Ruling Gives SunTrust Hope; Wachovia Can Seek New Bids Sooner if Current Deal Fails," in *Washington Post*, The Washington Post Co., 7/21/2001, E02.

41. Williams, Krissah, "SunTrust to Woo Merger Bank's Clients; Rejected Suitor Hopes Wachovia, First Union Will Alienate Customers," in *Washington Post*, The Washington Post Co., 8/08/2001, E01.

42. Williams, Krissah, "Wooed Not for Love but Money; Two Aggressive Suitors Await Wachovia Shareholders' Vote," in *Washington Post*, The Washington Post Co., 8/02/2001, E01.

43. http://www.nyse.com.

44. Sechler, Bob, "Southeast Banks' 2nd Quarter Seems As Solid Amid Positive Trends," in *Dow Jones Newswires*, provided by Wachovia Corporation.

45. Hodges, Dawn, Ernest E. Scarborough and John R. Montanari, "The Merger of US Bancorp and Piper Jaffray Companies," in *Strategic Management: Competitiveness and Globalization*, by Hitt, Michael A., R. Duane Ireland, and Robert E. Hoskisson, South-Western College Publishing, Cincinnati, 2001, pp. C612–C628.

46. Hitt, Michael A., Jeffrey S. Harrison, and R. Duane Ireland, *Mergers and Acquisitions: A Guide to Creating Value for Stakeholders*, Oxford University Press, New York, 2001, pp. 3–21.

47. FDIC, "Banking Legislation and Regulation," at http://www.fdic.gov/bank/historical/history/87_136.pdf.

48. http://www.fdic.gov/bank/statistical/stats/2002mar/industry.pdf.

49. http://www.fdic.gov/bank/statistical/stats/2002mar/fdic.pdf.

50. http://www.fdic.gov/bank/statistical/statistics/0112/nmbank.html.

51. http://www.fdic.gov/bank/statistical/statistics/0112/netinc.html.

52. http://www.wachovia.com/newsroom/news235.asp, "ISS Recommends Wachovia and First Union Shareholders Vote for Merger of Equals; Proxy Monitor Inc. Also Endorses First Union and Wachovia Combination," July 23, 2001.

53. First Union 2000 Annual Report.

54. SunTrust 2000 Annual Report.

55. http://www.iwon.com/home/careers/company_profile/0,15623,391,00.html, "SunTrust Banks Inc.: The Scoop."

56. http://www.suntrust.com/personal/wealthmgt/intlpvtbanking/history.asp, "SunTrust: Our History."

57. http://www.naca.com/new/dearticle.jsp?idt=351, "Merged Banks Use Branding Campaigns in Effort to Retain Customers' Loyalty," The Record, 5/21/2001.

58. Wachovia, "Wachovia/First Union Merger Transition Process," at http://personalfinance.firstunion.com/personal/images/integration.pdf, May 2001.

59. Wachovia, "The New Wachovia: A Compelling Combination," provided by Wachovia Corporation.

60. Van Dusen, Christine, "Battle for Wachovia: The Aftermath: Merger's Completion Brings Hard Decisions on Staff Cuts," in *The Atlanta Journal–Constitution*, Home, The Atlanta Journal and Constitution, 9/01/2001, F1.

61. http://www.marketguide.com, "Royal Bank of Canada: Business Description."

62. Stitt, Kevin and Lee McEntire, "Investor Fact Book December 2000," at http://www.bankofamerica.com/investor.

63. http://www.corporate-ir.net/ireye/ir_site.zhtml?ticker=bac&script=2100.

64. First Union, "Top Ten Reasons Why the First Union/Wachovia Combination Is Better for Wachovia Shareholders Than SunTrust's Hostile Proposal," provided by Wachovia Corporation.

65. SunTrust, "SunTrust in Brief: Second Quarter 2002," SunTrust Corporate Communications, April 2002.

66. http://www.leg.state.fl.us.

67. Hitt, Michael A., R. Duane Ireland, and Robert E. Hoskisson, *Strategic Management: Competitiveness and Globalization*, Chapter 6: "Corporate-Level Strategy," South-Western College Publishing, Cincinnati, 2001, pp. 228–271.

68. Kotler, Philip, *Marketing Management: The Millennium Edition*, Prentice Hall, Upper Saddle River, New Jersey, 2000, p. 263.

69. Anthes, Gary, "Mergers Made Easier," June 15, 1998, found at http://www.computerworld.com/news/1998/story/0,11280,31384,00.htm.

70. Carlton, Jim, "Wells Fargo Discovers Getting Together Is Hard to Do—Efforts to Merge Operations with First Interstate Result in Alienated Customers," in *The Wall Street Journal*, 7/21/1997, B4.

71. Dixon, Patrick, "Merger Fever," found at http://www.globalchange.com/mergers.htm.

72. "NationsBank, Barnett Become One Bank," October 9, 1998, found at http://www.bankofamerica.com/newsroom/press/press.cfm?PressId=press.19981009.05.htm&LOBID=9.

73. Hamrick, Spence of Wachovia Corporation.

74. Jenkins, Ben, Head of the General Bank for Wachovia Corporation.

Consolidated Statements of Condition
Wachovia Corporation and Subsidiaries

($ in thousands)	December 31 2000	December 31 1999
Assets		
Cash and due from banks	$ 3,727,441	$ 3,475,004
Interest-bearing bank balances	173,529	184,904
Federal funds sold and securities purchased under resale agreements	788,618	761,962
Trading account assets	960,838	870,304
Securities available-for-sale	7,571,696	7,095,790
Securities held-to-maturity (fair value of $1,052,535 in 2000 and $1,061,150 in 1999)	1,023,750	1,048,724
Loans, net of unearned income	55,001,721	49,621,225
Less allowance for loan losses	822,560	554,810
Net loans	54,179,161	49,066,415
Premises and equipment	911,304	953,832
Due from customers on acceptances	82,008	111,684
Goodwill and other intangible assets	1,256,227	937,225
Other assets	3,357,080	2,846,693
Total assets	$74,031,652	$67,352,537
Liabilities		
Deposits in domestic offices:		
Demand	$ 9,180,330	$ 8,730,673
Interest-bearing demand	5,116,571	4,527,711
Savings and money market savings	12,902,336	13,760,479
Savings certificates	9,534,778	8,701,074
Large denomination certificates	3,673,219	3,154,754
Total deposits in domestic offices	40,407,234	38,874,691
Interest-bearing deposits in foreign offices	4,004,948	2,911,727
Total deposits	44,412,182	41,786,418
Federal funds purchased and securities sold under repurchase agreements	6,753,164	5,372,493
Commercial paper	1,855,923	1,658,988
Other short-term borrowed lunds	1,253,058	3,071,493
Long-term debt	10,808,218	7,814,263
Acceptances outstanding	82,008	111,684
Other liabilities	2,582,560	1,878,741
Total liabilities	67,747,113	61,694,080
Off-balance sheet items, commitments and contingent liabilities		
Shareholders' Equity		
Preferred stock, par value $5 per share:		
Authorized 50,000,000 shares, none outstanding	—	—
Common stock, par value $5 per share:		
Authorized 1,000,000,000 shares; issued and outstanding 203,423,606 shares in 2000 and 201,812,295 shares in 1999	1,017,118	1,009,061
Capital surplus	731,162	598,149
Retained earnings	4,505,947	4,125,524
Accumulated other comprehensive income (loss)	30,312	(74,277)
Total shareholders' equity	6,284,539	5,658,457
Total liabilities and shareholders' equity	$74,031,652	$67,352,537

See notes to consolidated financial statements

Consolidated Statements of Income
Wachovia Corporation and Subsidiaries

($ in thousands, except per share) Year Ended December 31	2000	1999	1998
Interest Income			
Loans, including fees	$4,728,737	$4,000,541	$3,873,404
Securities available-for-sale	460,486	504,470	597,557
Securities held-to-maturity:			
State and municipal	15,124	11,673	15,044
Other investments	60,654	79,919	95,952
Interest-bearing bank balances	6,527	7,390	12,988
Federal funds sold and securities			
purchased under resale agreements	30,892	30,696	25,803
Trading account assets	42,934	32,131	44,497
Total interest income	5,345,354	4,666,820	4,665,245
Interest Expense			
Deposits:			
Domestic offices	1,417,160	1,156,113	1,224,046
Foreign offices	239,003	109,082	135,659
Total interest on deposits	1,656,163	1,265,195	1,359,705
Short-term borrowed funds	559,336	457,161	563,846
Long-term debt	614,134	474,378	390,662
Total interest expense	2,829,633	2,196,734	2,314,213
Net Interest Income	2,515,721	2,470,086	2,351,032
Provision for loan losses	588,450	298,105	299,480
Net interest income after provision for loan losses	1,927,271	2,171,981	2,051,552
Other Income			
Service charges on deposit accounts	418,611	369,646	334,980
Fees for trust services	219,476	216,392	199,949
Credit card income	297,833	255,243	171,127
Investment fees	334,795	235,350	61,556
Capital markets income	170,007	170,771	130,083
Electronic banking	102,832	88,626	74,257
Mortgage fees	25,377	33,213	44,929
Other operating income	362,758	240,882	211,238
Total other operating revenue	1,931,689	1,610,123	1,228,119
Securities (losses) gains	(417)	10,894	20,442
Total other income	1,931,272	1,621,017	1,248,561
Other Expense			
Salaries	1,086,694	1,020,384	874,750
Employee benefits	212,649	199,902	180,603
Total personnel expense	1,299,343	1,220,286	1,055,353
Net occupancy expense	160,350	151,282	138,636
Equipment expense	188,061	198,062	153,007
Merger-related charges	28,958	19,309	85,312
Litigation settlement charge	20,000	—	—
Restructuring charge	107,487	—	—
Other operating expense	778,814	661,686	564,024
Total other expense	2,583,013	2,250,625	1,996,332
Income before income tax expense	1,275,530	1,542,373	1,303,781
Income tax expense	443,222	531,152	429,611

($ in thousands, except per share)

Year Ended December 31	2000	1999	1998
Net Income	$832,308	$1,011,221	$874,170
Net income per common share:			
Basic	$4.10	$4.99	$4.26
Diluted	$4.07	$4.90	$4.18
Average shares outstanding:			
Basic	202,989	202,795	205,058
Diluted	204,450	206,192	209,153

See notes to consolidated financial statements

Consolidated Statements of Shareholder's Equity
Wachovia Corporation and Subsidiaries
($ in thousands, except per share)

Year ended December 31, 1998	Common Stock Shares	Amount	Capital Surplus	Retained Earnings	Accumulated Other Comprehensive Income (Loss)	Total
Balance at beginning of year	205,926,632	$1,029,633	$974,803	$3,098,767	$71,098	$5,174,301
Comprehensive income:						
Net income				874,170		874,170
Other comprehensive income:						
Unrealized holding gains on securities available-for-sale (net of tax expense of $16,233)					23,802	23,802
Less reclassification adjustment for gains realized in net income (net of tax expense of $7,982)					(12,460)	(12,460)
Comprehensive income				874,170	11,342	885,512
Cash dividends declared—$1.86 a share				(381,798)		(381,798)
Common stock issued pursuant to:						
Stock option and employee benefit plans	2,211,599	11,058	102,540			113,598
Dividend reinvestment plan	301,992	1,510	22,885			24,395
Acquisitions	1,127,723	5,639	77,674			83,313
Common stock acquired	(6,581,846)	(32,909)	(508,093)			(541,002)
Miscellaneous			(565)	(19,522)		(20,087)
Balance at end of year	202,986,100	$1,014,931	$669,244	$3,571,617	$82,440	$5,338,232
Year ended December 31, 1999						
Balance at beginning of year	202,986,100	$1,014,931	$669,224	$3,571,617	$82,440	$5,338,232
Comprehensive income:						
Net income				1,011,221		1,011,221
Other comprehensive loss:						
Unrealized holding losses on securities available-for-sale (net of tax benefit of $92,356)					(149,636)	(149,636)
Less reclassification adjustment for gains realized in net income (net of tax expense of $3,813)					(7,081)	(7,081)
Comprehensive income				1,011,221	(156,717)	854,504
Cash dividends declared—$2.06 a share				(418,447)		(418,447)

| | Common Stock | | | Capital | Accumulated Other | Comprehensive |
	Shares	Amount	Surplus	Earnings	Retained Income (Loss)	Total
Year ended December 31, 1999 *(continued)*						
Common stock issued pursuant to:						
Stock option and employee benefit plans	1,252,596	6,263	111,308			117,571
Dividend reinvestment plan	282,947	1,414	21,692			23,106
Acquisitions	4,801,987	24,010	399,059			423,069
Note conversions	3,065	15	235			250
Common stock acquired	(7,514,400)	(37,572)	(603,357)			(640,929)
Miscellaneous			(32)	(38,867)		(38,899)
Balance at end of year	201,812,295	$1,009,061	$598,149	$4,125,524	$(74,277)	$5,658,457
Year ended December 31, 2000						
Balance at beginning of year	201,812,295	$1,009,061	$598,149	$4,125,524	$(74,277)	$5,658,457
Comprehensive income:						
Net income				832,308		832,308
Other comprehensive income:						
Unrealized holding gains on securities available-for-sale (net of tax expense of $64,352)					104,318	104,318
Add reclassification adjustment for losses realized in net income (net of tax benefit of $146)					271	271
Comprehensive income				832,308	104,589	936,897
Cash dividends declared—$2.28 a share				(463,018)		(463,018)
Common stock issued pursuant to:						
Stock option and employee benefit plans	1,078,507	5,392	58,310			63,702
Dividend reinvestment plan	393,346	1,967	20,864			22,831
Acquisitions	2,254,947	11,275	167,673			178,948
Common stock acquired	(2,115,489)	(10,577)	(113,834)			(124,411)
Miscellaneous				11,133		11,133
Balance at end of year	203,423,606	$1,017,118	$731,162	$4,505,947	$30,312	$6,284,539

See notes to consolidated financial statements

Consolidated Statements of Cash Flows
Wachovia Corporation and Subsidiaries
($ in thousands)

Year Ended December 31 Operating Activities	2000	1999	1998
Net income	$ 832,308	$1,011,221	$ 874,170
Adjustments to reconcile net income to net cash provided by operations:			
Provision for loan losses	588,450	298,105	299,480
Depreciation and amortization	295,411	245,803	155,069
Deferred income taxes	235,174	383,302	266,451
Securities losses (gains)	417	(10,894)	(20,442)
Gain on sale of noninterest-earning assets	(6,364)	(13,485)	(7,421)
Increase in accrued income taxes	2,187	26,459	224,609
(Increase) decrease in accrued interest receivable	(94,083)	(25,158)	40,246
Increase (decrease) in accrued interest payable	134,533	11,578	(26,107)
Net change in other accrued and deferred income and expense	120,851	(163,073)	(60,053)
Net trading account activities	(90,534)	(91,125)	334,310
Net loans held for resale	(74,432)	250,632	(184,571)
Gain from branch sales	(41,618)	(7,554)	(17,155)
Net cash provided by operating activities	1,902,300	1,915,811	1,878,586
Investing Activities			
Net decrease (increase) in interest-bearing bank balances	28,185	(73,826)	23,208
Net (increase) decrease in federal funds sold and securities purchased under resale agreements	(8,339)	(40,361)	947,064
Purchases of securities available-for-sale	(1,488,647)	(2,222,574)	(3,106,977)
Purchases of securities held-to-maturity	(140,324)	(95,531)	(394,956)
Sales of securities available-for-sale	482,692	366,714	590,447
Calls, maturities and prepayments of securities available-for-sale	854,051	2,525,569	3,564,575
Calls, maturities and prepayments of securities held-to-maturity	189,461	431,963	532,922
Net increase in loans made to customers	(5,019,413)	(5,471,971)	(1,634,527)
Net credit card receivables securitized	250,000	1,395,954	—
Capital expenditures	(115,993)	(213,229)	(258,719)
Proceeds from sales of premises and equipment	16,998	27,154	38,959
Net increase in other assets	(341,355)	(279,575)	(375,080)
Business combinations	(805,754)	(11,123)	16,108
Branch sales	(378,559)	(114,761)	(111,901)
Net cash used by investing activities	(6,476,997)	(3,775,597)	(168,877)

Year Ended December 31 *(continued)*	2000	1999	1998
Financing Activities			
Net increase in demand, savings and money market accounts	377,471	757,675	1,584,124
Net increase (decrease) in certificates of deposit	2,173,930	163,578	(3,192,149)
Net increase (decrease) in federal funds purchased and securities sold under repurchase agreements	1,376,791	(151,068)	(2,870,049)
Net increase in commercial paper	196,935	299,606	325,358
Net (decrease) increase in other short-term borrowings	(1,818,435)	1,125,558	1,159,388
Proceeds from issuance of long-term debt	3,893,075	1,588,733	2,684,679
Maturities and repayments of long-term debt	(915,267)	(1,410,819)	(1,028,772)
Common stock issued	40,465	59,478	80,375
Dividend payments	(463,018)	(418,447)	(381,798)
Common stock repurchased	(116,086)	(634,623)	(531,122)
Net increase in other liabilities	81,273	154,854	38,704
Net cash provided (used) by financing activities	4,827,134	1,534,525	(2,131,262)
Increase (Decrease) in Cash and Cash Equivalents	252,437	(325,261)	(421,553)
Cash and cash equivalents at beginning of year	3,475,004	3,800,265	4,221,818
Cash and cash equivalents at end of period	$3,727,441	$3,475,004	$3,800,265
Supplemental Disclosures			
Interest paid	$2,695,100	$2,185,156	$2,340,320
Income taxes paid	204,811	119,959	159,500

See notes to consolidated financial statements

First Union Corporation and Subsidiaries Consolidated Balance Sheets

(In millions, except per share data)	December 31, 2000	December 31, 1999
Assets		
Cash and due from banks	$ 9,906	$ 10,081
Interest-bearing bank balances	3,239	1,073
Federal funds sold and securities purchased under resale agreements	11,240	11,523
Total cash and equivalents	24,385	22,677
Trading account assets	21,630	14,946
Securities available for sale (amortized cost $47,930 in 2000; $52,708 in 1999; amortized cost of collateral $25,453 in 2000)	47,603	51,277
Investment securities (market value $1,728 in 2000; $1,809 in 1999; carrying amount of collateral $827 in 2000)	1,643	1,758
Loans, net of unearned income ($6,482 in 2000; $5,513 in 1999)	123,760	133,177
Allowance for loan losses	(1,722)	(1,757)
Loans, net	122,038	131,420
Premises and equipment	5,024	5,180
Due from customers on acceptances	874	995
Goodwill and other intangible assets	3,664	5,626
Other assets	27,309	19,145
Total assets	$254,170	$253,024
Liabilities and Stockholder's Equity		
Deposits		
Noninterest-bearing deposits	30,315	31,375
Interest-bearing deposits	112,353	109,672
Total deposits	142,668	141,047
Short-term borrowings	39,446	50,107
Bank acceptances outstanding	880	995
Trading account liabilities	7,475	3,569
Other liabilities	12,545	8,622
Long-term debt	35,809	31,975
Total liabilities	238,823	236,315
Stockholder's Equity		
Preferred stock, Class A, 40 million shares, no par value; 10 million shares, no par value; none issued	–	–
Common stock, $3.3-1/3 par value; authorized 2 billion shares, outstanding 980 million shares in 2000; 988 million shares in 1999	3,267	3,294
Paid-in capital	6,272	5,980
Retained earnings	6,021	8,365
Accumulated other comprehensive income, net	(213)	(930)
Total stockholders' equity	15,347	16,709
Total liabilities and stockholders' equity	$254,170	$253,024

See accompanying Notes to Consolidated Financial Statements.

First Union Corporation and Subsidiaries Consolidated Statements of Income

(In millions, except per share data)	2000	Years Ended December 31, 1999	1998
Interest Income			
Interest and fees on loans	$11,246	$10,629	$11,109
Interest and dividends on securities available for sale	3,784	2,929	2,304
Interest and dividends on investment securities	119	129	182
Trading account interest	820	600	546
Other interest income	1,565	824	847
Total interest income	17,534	15,151	14,988
Interest Expense			
Interest on deposits	5,269	4,054	4,316
Interest on short-term borrowings	2,536	2,019	2,373
Interest on long-term debt	2,292	1,626	1,022
Total interest expense	10,097	7,699	7,711
Net interest income	7,437	7,452	7,277
Provision for loan losses	1,736	692	691
Net interest income after provision for loan losses	5,701	6,760	6,586
Fee and Other Income			
Service charges and fees	1,920	1,987	2,027
Commissions	1,591	1,014	753
Fiduciary and asset management fees	1,511	1,238	1,055
Advisory, underwriting and other Capital Markets fees	716	702	364
Principal investing	392	592	237
Other income	582	1,400	1,999
Total fee and other income	6,712	6,933	6,435
Noninterest Expense			
Salaries and employee benefits	5,659	4,716	4,250
Occupancy	622	546	561
Equipment	870	793	723
Advertising	114	234	223
Communications and supplies	503	481	480
Professional and consulting fees	348	287	311
Goodwill and other intangible amortization	361	391	348
Restructuring and merger-related charges	2,190	404	1,212
Sundry expense	1,043	1,010	948
Total noninterest expense	11,710	8,862	9,056
Income before income taxes and cumulative effect of a change in accounting principle	703	4,831	3,965
Income taxes	565	1,608	1,074
Income before cumulative effect of change in accounting principle	138	3,223	2,891
Cumulative effect of change in the accounting for beneficial interests, net of tax	(46)	–	–
Net income	$ 92	3,223	2,891
Per Share Data			
Basic			
Income before change in accounting principle	$ 0.12	3.35	2.98
Net income	0.07	3.35	2.98
Diluted			
Income before change in accounting principle	0.12	3.33	2.95
Net income	0.07	3.33	2.95
Cash dividends	$ 1.92	1.88	1.58

(In millions, except per share data) Average Shares (In thousands)	2000	Years Ended December 31, 1999	1998
Basic	970,608	959,390	969,131
Diluted	974,172	966,863	980,112

See accompanying Notes to Consolidated Financial Statements.

First Union Corporation and Subsidiaries Consolidated Statements of Changes in Stockholders' Equity

(Shares in thousands, dollars in millions)	Common Stock Shares	Amount	Paid-in-Capital	Retained Earnings	Accumulated Other Comprehensive Income Net	Total
Balance, December 31, 1997	960,984	3,203	1,456	10,198	286	15,143
Comprehensive income						
Net income	–	–	–	2,891	–	2,891
Net unrealized gain on debt and equity securities, net of reclassification adjustment	–	–	–	–	121	121
Total comprehensive income	–	–	–	2,891	121	3,012
Purchases of common stock	(49,738)	(165)	(384)	(2,507)	–	(3,056)
Common stock issued for						
Stock options and restricted stock	19,271	64	787	–	–	851
Dividend reinvestment plan	1,476	4	77	–	–	81
Acquisitions	50,230	168	2,243	129	–	2,540
Deferred compensation, net	–	–	(150)	–	–	(150)
Cash dividends paid by						
First Union Corporation $1.58 per common share	–	–	–	(1,423)	–	(1,423)
Acquired companies	–	–	–	(101)	–	(101)
Balance, December 31, 1998	982,223	3,274	4,029	9,187	407	16,897
Comprehensive income						
Net income	–	–	–	3,223	–	3,223
Net unrealized loss on debt and equity securities, net of reclassification adjustment	–	–	–	–	(1,337)	(1,337)
Total comprehensive income	–	–	–	3,223	(1,337)	1,886
Purchases of common stock	(35,508)	(118)	533	(2,228)	–	(1,813)
Common stock issued for						
Stock options and restricted stock	8,644	29	379	–	–	408
Dividend reinvestment plan	1,937	6	78	–	–	84
Acquisitions	31,019	103	1,148	–	–	1,251
Deferred compensation, net	–	–	(187)	–	–	(187)
Cash dividends paid, $1.88 per share	–	–	–	(1,817)	–	(1,817)
Balance, December 31, 1999	988,315	3,294	5,980	8,365	(930)	16,709
Comprehensive income						
Net income	–	–	–	92	–	92
Net unrealized gain on debt and equity securities, net of reclassification adjustment	–	–	–	–	717	717
Total comprehensive income	–	–	–	92	717	809
Purchases of common stock	(19,060)	(63)	(79)	(548)	–	(690)

(Shares in thousands, dollars in millions) Balance, December 31, 1999 *(continued)*	Common Stock Shares	Amount	Paid-in-Capital	Retained Earnings	Accumulated Other Comprehensive Income Net	Total
Common stock issued for						
Stock options and restricted stock	6,922	23	131	–	–	154
Dividend reinvestment plan	2,599	9	68	–	–	77
Acquisitions	1,187	4	30	–	–	34
Deferred compensation, net	–	–	142	–	–	142
Cash dividends paid, $1.92 per share	–	–	–	(1,888)	–	(1,888)
Balance, December 31, 2000	979,963	$3,267	6,272	6,021	(213)	15,347

See accompanying Notes to Consolidated Financial Statements.

First Union Corporation and Subsidiaries Consolidated Statements of Cash Flows

(In millions)	2000	Years Ended December 31, 1999	1998
Operating Activities			
Net income	$ 92	3,223	2,891
Adjustments to reconcile net income to net cash provided (used) by operating activities			
Cumulative effect of a change in accounting principle	46	–	–
Accretion and amortization of securities discounts and premiums, net	264	281	249
Provision for loan losses	1,736	692	691
Securitization gains	(265)	(417)	(529)
(Gain) loss on sale of mortgage servicing rights	2	(44)	(22)
Securities transactions	1,134	63	(357)
Depreciation, goodwill and other amortization	1,253	1,172	1,141
Goodwill impairments	1,754	–	–
Deferred income taxes	91	1,079	624
Trading account assets, net	(6,684)	(6,626)	(380)
Mortgage loans held for resale	381	1,677	(1,464)
Gain on sales of premises and equipment	(18)	(16)	(11)
Gain on sales of credit card and mortgage servicing portfolios	(1,008)	–	–
Other assets, net	1,384	79	(2,513)
Trading account liabilities, net	3,906	2,027	878
Other liabilities, net	3,838	(3,535)	2,212
Net cash provided (used) by operating activities	7,906	(345)	3,410
Investing Activities			
Increase (decrease) in cash realized from			
Sales of securities available for sale	16,356	17,391	28,698
Maturities of securities available for sale	3,089	4,104	5,201
Purchases of securities available for sale	(8,127)	(27,954)	(47,477)
Calls and underdeliveries of investment securities	23	–	387
Maturities of investment securities	324	523	1,480
Purchases of investment securities	(234)	(263)	(366)
Origination of loans, net	(9,334)	(9,986)	(872)

(In millions)	Years Ended December 31.		
	2000	1999	1998
Investing Activities *(continued)*			
Sales of premises and equipment	398	280	475
Purchases of premises and equipment	(884)	(957)	(1,139)
Goodwill and other intangible asses, net	(40)	(101)	(179)
Purchase of bank-owned separate account life insurance	(135)	(576)	(359)
Cash equivalents acquired, net of purchase acquisitions	3	168	366
Net cash provided (used) by investing activities	1,439	(17,371)	(13,785)
Financing Activities			
Increases (decrease) in cash realized from			
Purchases (sales) of deposits, net	1,621	(1,420)	5,139
Securities sold under repurchase agreements and other short-term borrowings, net	(10,661)	7,637	7,525
Issuances of long-term debt	17,491	17,612	11,493
Payments of long-term debt	(13,662)	(8,586)	(3,153)
Sales of common stock	152	143	700
Purchases of common stock	(690)	(1,813)	(3,056)
Cash dividends paid	(1,888)	(1,817)	(1,524)
Net cash provided (used) by financing activities	(7,637)	11,756	17,124
Increase (decrease) in cash and cash equivalents	1,708	(5,960)	6,749
Cash and cash equivalents, beginning of year	22,677	28,637	21,888
Cash and cash equivalents, end of year	$24,385	22,677	28,637
Cash Paid For			
Interest	$ 9,759	7,568	7,566
Income taxes	203	30	152
Noncash Items			
Transfer to securities available for sale from trading account assets	–	1,529	–
Transfer to securities available for sale from loans	9,342	8,259	–
Transfer to trading account assets from loans	–	–	2,212
Transfer to other assets from securities available for sale	1,335	–	–
Transfer to assets held for sale from loans	$ 7,901	–	133

See accompanying Notes to Consolidated Financial Statements.

(Dollars in thousands)	At December 31	
	2000	1999
Assets		
Cash and due from banks	$ 4,110,489	$ 3,909,687
Interest-bearing deposits in other banks	13,835	22,237
Funds sold	1,267,028	1,587,442
Trading account	941,854	259,547
Securities available for sale – Note 4	18,810,311	18,317,297
Loans held for sale	1,759,281	1,531,787
Loans – Notes 5, 13 and 14	72,239,820	66,002,831
Allowance for loan losses – Note 6	(874,547)	(871,323)
Net Loans	71,365,273	65,131,508
Premises and equipment – Note 7	1,629,071	1,636,484
Intangible assets	810,860	804,632
Customers' acceptance liability	184,157	192,045
Other assets – Note 12	2,604,221	1,997,302
Total assets	$103,496,380	$95,389,968
Liabilities and Shareholders' Equity – Notes 10 and 12		
Noninterest-bearing deposits	$ 15,064,017	$14,200,522
Interest-bearing deposits	54,469,320	45,900,007
Total deposits	69,533,337	60,100,529
Funds purchased	10,895,944	15,911,917
Other short-term borrowings – Note 8	1,761,985	2,259,010
Long-term debt – Note 9	7,895,430	4,967,346
Guaranteed preferred beneficial interests in debentures – Note 9	1,050,000	1,050,000
Acceptances outstanding	184,157	192,045
Other liabilities – Note 11	3,936,319	3,282,259
Total liabilities	95,257,172	87,763,106
Commitments and contingencies – Notes 7, 9, 13 and 16		
Preferred stock, no par value; 50,000,000 shares authorized; none issued	—	—
Common stock, $1.00 par value	323,163	323,163
Additional paid in capital	1,274,416	1,293,387
Retained earnings	6,312,004	5,461,351
Treasury stock and other	(1,613,189)	(1,013,861)
Realized shareholders' equity	6,296,434	6,064,040
Accumulated other comprehensive income – Notes 4 and 18	1,942,74	1,562,822
Total shareholders' equity	8,239,208	7,626,862
Total liabilities and shareholders' equity	$103,496,380	$95,389,968
Common shares outstanding	296,266,329	308,353,207
Common shares authorized	750,000,000	500,000,000
Treasury shares of common stock	26,896,428	14,809,500
Includes net unrealized gains on securities available for sale	$ 3,048,313	$ 2,527,705

See notes to consolidated financial statements.

(Dollars in thousands except per share data)	Year Ended December 31		
	2000	1999	1998
Interest Income			
Interest and fees on loans	$5,605,320	$4,744,609	$4,555,244
Interest and fees on loans held for sale	110,563	172,153	180,383
Interest and dividends on securities available for sale			
Taxable interest	916,573	859,002	759,653
Tax-exempt interest	25,794	30,682	35,733
Dividends	64,885	66,906	58,531
Interest on funds sold	92,782	73,382	71,639
Interest on deposits in other banks	865	2,665	5,72
Other interest	28,637	10,809	8,945
Total interest income	6,845,419	5,960,208	5,675,900
Interest Expense			
Interest on deposits	2,452,919	1,626,132	1,644,229
Interest on funds purchased	651,235	749,561	634,086
Interest on other short-term borrowings	97,903	79,521	127,800
Interest on long-term debt	534,924	359,538	340,664
Total interest expense	3,736,981	2,814,752	2,746,779
Net Interest Income	3,108,438	3,145,456	2,929,121
Provision for loan losses – Note 6	133,974	170,437	214,602
Net Interest income after provision for loan losses	2,974,464	2,975,019	2,714,519
Noninterest Income			
Trust income	493,929	495,613	453,328
Other charges and fees	525,920	471,486	398,760
Service charges on deposit accounts	459,653	438,107	401,095
Mortgage production related income	90,061	153,055	238,234
Mortgage servicing related income	32,832	27,056	2,828
Other noninterest income – Note 19	164,614	149,675	151,418
Securities gains (losses) – Note 4	6,616	(109,076)	8,207
Total noninterest income	1,773,625	1,625,916	1,653,870
Noninterest Expense			
Salaries and other compensation – Note 12	1,468,967	1,522,570	1,433,703
Employee benefits – Note 12	175,035	175,801	181,781
Equipment expense	193,709	198,464	178,766
Net occupancy expense	202,608	197,439	192,198
Marketing and customer development	106,215	105,429	107,092
Merger-related expenses – Note 2	42,444	45,556	119,419
Other noninterest expense – Note 20	639,555	660,019	657,124
Total noninterest expense	2,828,533	2,905,278	2,870,083
Income before provision for income taxes and extraordinary gain	1,919,556	1,695,657	1,498,306
Provision for income taxes – Note 11	625,456	571,705	527,289
Income before extraordinary gain	1,294,100	1,123,952	971,017
Extraordinary gain, net of taxes – Notes 3 and 11	—	202,648	—
Net Income	1,294,100	1,326,600	971,017
Net income per average common share – Note 10:			
Diluted			
Income before extraordinary gain	$4.30	$3.50	$3.04
Extraordinary gain	—	0.63	—
Net income	$4.30	$4.13	$3.04
Basic			
Income before extraordinary gain	$4.35	$3.54	$3.08
Extraordinary gain	—	0.64	—
Net income	$4.35	$4.18	$3.08
Dividends declared per common share	$1.48	$1.38	$1.00
Average common shares – diluted	300,956	321,174	319,711
Average common shares – basic	297,834	317,079	314,908
Includes dividends on 48,266,496 shares of common stock of The Coca-Cola Company	$ 32,821	$ 30,891	$ 28,960

See notes to consolidated financial statements.

(in thousands)	Common Stock	Additional Paid in Capital	Retained Earnings	Treasury Stock and Other[1]	Accumulated Other Comprehensive Income	Total
Balance, January 1, 1998	$318,571	$1,087,511	$3,967,359	$(109,503)	$2,048,153	$7,312,091
Net Income	–	–	971,017	–	–	971,017
Other comprehensive income:						
Change in unrealized gains (losses) on securities, net of taxes	–	–	–	–	40,054	40,054
Total comprehensive income						1,011,071
Cash dividends declared, $1.00 per share	–	–	(352,454)	–	–	(352,454)
Exercise of stock options	810	1,366	–	25,166	–	27,342
Acquisition and retirement of stock	(190)	–	(10,540)	(294,878)	–	(305,608)
Restricted stock activity	90	8,378	–	(8,468)	–	–
Amortization of compensation element of restricted stock	–	–	–	12,771	–	12,771
Stock issued for acquisitions	1,619	108,607	–	93,846	–	204,072
Issuance of stock for employee benefit plans	1,005	58,742	–	17,912	–	7,659
Stock issued in private placement	580	28,407	–	162,713	–	191,700
Balance, December 31, 1998	322,485	1,293,011	4,575,382	(100,441)	2,088,207	8,178,644
Net income	–	–	1,326,600	–	–	1,326,600
Other comprehensive income:						
Change in unrealized gains (losses) on securities, net of taxes	–	–	–	–	(525,385)	(525,385)
Total comprehensive income						801,215
Cash dividends declared, $1.38 per share	–	–	(440,631)	–	–	(440,631)
Exercise of stock options	575	(8,661)	–	23,116	–	15,030
Acquisition of stock	–	–	–	(954,642)	–	(954,642)
Restricted stock activity	11	735	–	(746)	–	–
Amortization of compensation element of restricted stock	–	–	–	15,557	–	15,557
Issuance of stock for employee benefit plans	92	8,302	–	3,295	–	11,689
Balance, December 31, 1999	323,163	1,293,387	5,461,351	(1,013,861)	1,562,822	7,626,862
Net income	–	–	1,294,100	–	–	1,294,100
Other comprehensive income:						
Change in unrealized gains (losses) on securities, net of taxes	–	–	–	–	379,952	379,952
Total comprehensive income						1,674,052
Cash dividends declared, $1.48 per share	–	–	(443,407)	–	–	(443,407)
Exercise of stock options`	–	(11,767)	–	29,672	–	17,905
Acquisition of stock	–	–	–	(668,391)	–	(668,391)
Restricted stock activity	–	(795)	–	795	–	–
Amortization of compensation element of restricted stock	–	–	–	9,408	–	9,408
Issuance of stock for employee benefit plans	–	(6,409)	–	29,188	–	22,779
Balance, December 31, 2000	$323,163	$1,274,416	$6,312,044	$(1,613,189)	$1,942,774	$8,239,208

[1]Balance at December 31, 2000 includes $1,568,792 thousand for treasury stock and $44,397 thousand for compensation element of restricted stock. See notes to consolidated financial statements.

(In thousands)	2000	Year Ended December 31 1999	1998
Cash Flow from Operating Activities			
Net income	$1,294,100	$1,326,600	$ 971,017
Adjustments to reconcile net income to net cash provided by (used in) operating activities:			
Extraordinary gain, net of taxes	—	(202,648)	—
Depreciation, amortization and accretion	299,957	284,993	282,599
Provisions for loan losses and foreclosed property	134,353	173,789	215,225
Deferred income tax provision	190,103	183,842	39,115
Amortization of compensation element of restricted stock	9,408	15,557	12,771
Securities (gains) losses	(6,616)	109,076	(8,207)
Net gain on sale of noninterest earning assets	(9,777)	(28,887)	(8,823)
Net (increase) decrease in loans held for sale	(227,494)	2,016,768	(2,259,825)
Net increase in accrued interest receivable, prepaid expenses and other assets	(1,494,731)	(108,769)	(897,527)
Net increase (decrease) in accrued interest payable, accrued expenses and other liabilities	323,302	(164,030)	706,691
Other, net	—	—	45,735
Net cash provided by (used in) operating activities	512,605	3,606,291	(901,229)
Cash Flow from Investing Activities			
Proceeds from maturities of securities available for sale	2,195,575	3,668,622	4,484,087
Proceeds from sales of securities available for sale	1,365,509	5,857,310	4,343,241
Purchase of securities available for sale	(3,545,929)	(11,249,089)	(10,572,056)
Net increase in loans	(6,355,547)	(4,454,927)	(6,328,474)
Capital expenditures	(145,821)	(257,179)	(259,032)
Proceeds from sale of assets	9,904	59,577	136,875
Net funds received in acquisitions	—	—	14,857
Loan recoveries	58,910	65,650	70,684
Other, net	—	—	(4,611)
Net Cash used in investing activities	(6,417,399)	(6,310,036)	(8,114,429)
Cash Flow from Financing Activities			
Net increase in deposits	9,432,808	1,067,246	4,452,499
Net (decrease) increase in funds purchased and other short-term borrowings	(5,512,998)	2,238,108	2,671,305
Proceeds from issuance of long-term debt	4,191,114	1,095,872	2,205,211
Repayment of long-term debt	(1,263,030)	(886,395)	(407,700)
Proceeds from the exercise of stock options	17,905	15,030	27,342
Proceeds from stock issuance	22,779	11,689	191,700
Proceeds used in acquisition and retirements of stock	(668,391)	(954,642)	(305,608)
Dividends paid	(443,407)	(440,631)	(352,454)
Net Cash provided by financing activities	5,776,780	2,146,277	8,482,295
Net decrease in cash and cash equivalents	(128,014)	(557,468)	(533,363)
Cash and cash equivalents at beginning of year	5,519,366	6,076,834	6,610,197
Cash and cash equivalents at end of year	$ 5,391,352	$ 5,519,366	$ 6,076,834
Supplemental Disclosure			
Interest paid	$ 3,618,302	$ 2,812,819	$ 2,770,872
Income taxes paid	540,212	530,786	482,621
Non-cash impact of securitizing loans	925,380	—	—

See notes of consolidated financial statements.

Merger Transition Organization

Balanced Representation of Wachovia and First Union Management

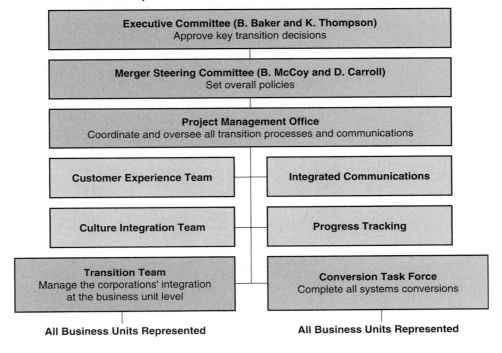

Executive Committee (B. Baker and K. Thompson)
Approve key transition decisions

Merger Steering Committee (B. McCoy and D. Carroll)
Set overall policies

Project Management Office
Coordinate and oversee all transition processes and communications

Customer Experience Team

Integrated Communications

Culture Integration Team

Progress Tracking

Transition Team
Manage the corporations' integration
at the business unit level

Conversion Task Force
Complete all systems conversions

All Business Units Represented   **All Business Units Represented**

Team Roles

Executive Committee
Merger Steering Committee
- Approve Key Merger Steering Committee decisions
- Establish strategic direction
- Provide overall leadership
- Approve recommendations
- Address issues and resolve conflicts

Project Management Committee
- Coordinate teams sequence activities and monitor progress
- Develop merger timeline and set milestones
- Identify and allocate critical resources
- Resolve issues

Customer Experience Team
- Monitor primary emphasis on customer retention through transition
- Immediately respond to any integration-related customer issue
- Provide customer perception and issue identification information associated with merger

Culture Integration Team
- Assess cultural similarities and differences
- Provide action-oriented programs to accelerate cultural integration and leverage cultural differences

Integrated Communications
- Review and approve all internal and external communications
- Ensure accuracy and consistency with merger objectives and guiding principles

Progress Tracking
- Develop and track key metrics related to merger transition information

Transition Team
- Develop combined business unit strategies, plans and organizational structures
- Integrate business units to establish merged entity
- Assess business readiness for integration
- Manage execution risk

Conversion Task Force
- Conduct technical systems review, analysis and selection
- Develop conversion schedule based on business unit strategies
- Implement project plan for systems integration

	2001			2002				2003			
	2Q	3Q	4Q	1Q	2Q	3Q	4Q	1Q	2Q	3Q	4Q
Transition Organization In Place	X										
Merger Agreement Announced	X										
Strategic Business Reviews	█	█									
Management Structure											
Executive	█										
Tier 2 Senior Management	█										
Tier 3 Management		█	█								
Shareholder Meeting		X									
Consummation		X									
Divestiture Purchase Agreements		█									
Divestitures Complete			█	█	█						
System Review and Selection	█	█									
Early Conversions (e.g. GL, HR, AP)			█	█	█						
Training Calendar Developed			█	█	█	█	█				
Core Conversions								█	█		

Draft – MOE Target Dates

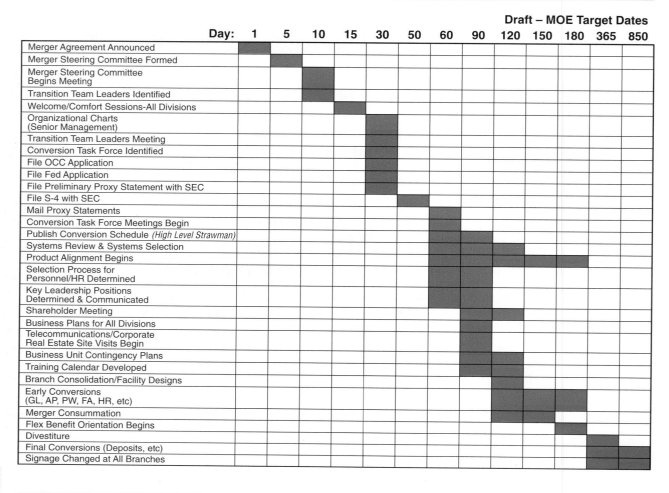

Day:	1	5	10	15	30	50	60	90	120	150	180	365	850
Merger Agreement Announced	■												
Merger Steering Committee Formed		■											
Merger Steering Committee Begins Meeting			■										
Transition Team Leaders Identified			■										
Welcome/Comfort Sessions-All Divisions				■									
Organizational Charts (Senior Management)					■								
Transition Team Leaders Meeting					■								
Conversion Task Force Identified					■								
File OCC Application					■								
File Fed Application					■								
File Preliminary Proxy Statement with SEC					■								
File S-4 with SEC						■							
Mail Proxy Statements								■					
Conversion Task Force Meetings Begin								■					
Publish Conversion Schedule *(High Level Strawman)*									■				
Systems Review & Systems Selection								■	■				
Product Alignment Begins								■	■	■			
Selection Process for Personnel/HR Determined								■	■				
Key Leadership Positions Determined & Communicated								■	■				
Shareholder Meeting								■					
Business Plans for All Divisions									■				
Telecommunications/Corporate Real Estate Site Visits Begin								■					
Business Unit Contingency Plans									■				
Training Calendar Developed									■				
Branch Consolidation/Facility Designs								■	■				
Early Conversions (GL, AP, PW, FA, HR, etc)									■	■	■		
Merger Consummation									■				
Flex Benefit Orientation Begins											■		
Divestiture													
Final Conversions (Deposits, etc)												■	■
Signage Changed at All Branches												■	■

APPENDIX F Parallelism of the Banks' Business Units

Wachovia	First Union	Sun Trust
Assets and Wealth Management	Capital Management Group	Personal Client Services
Retail Financial Services	General Bank	Retail Banking
		Mortgage
Corporate Financial Services	Capital Markets Group	Corporate and Investment Banking
		Commercial Banking

Name Index

A

Aaker, D. A., 134n
Abell, D. F., 97n
Abelson, R., 62
Abrahamson, E., 165n
Abratt, R., 299n
Ackman, D., 259
Adler, P. S., 196n, 403n, 428n
Adner, R., 33n, 68n
Aeppel, T., 68n, 263n
Afuah, A., 68n, 134n, 165n, 264n, 296n
Agami, A. M., 227n
Aggarwal, R., 67n, 165n, 195n, 198n
Aggarwal, S., 93
Agle, B. R., 34n
Aguilera, R., 333n, 336n
Ahlstrom, D., 33n, 68n, 69n, 263n, 264n, 266n, 336n
Ahuja, G., 33n, 227n, 228n, 426n, 427n
Aiello, R. J., 229n
Albanese, R., 401n
Alcacer, J., 264n
Alden, D. L., 97n
Alessio, V., 297n
Alexander, D., 76
Alexander, K. L., 19
Alexander, M., 195n
Aley, J., 166n
Allen, L., 265n
Allen, M., 298n
Almanza, A., 336n
Almeida, J. G., 97n
Almeida, P., 266n, 298n
Almstedt, K., 234
Alsop, S., 279
Alvarez, S. A., 98n, 402n, 428n
Amason, A. C., 428n
Amato-McCoy, D. M., 297n
Ambrose, M. L., 403n
Ambrosini, V., 99n
Amburgey, T., 369n
Ames, C., 99n
Amihud, Y., 198n, 333n
Amit, R., 33n, 34n, 78, 98n, 99n, 197n, 428n
An, J. M., 263n
Anand, J., 228n, 229n, 335n, 336n
Andal-Ancion, A., 68n, 97n
Anders, G., 60, 227n, 383

Anderson, P., 98n, 227n
Anderson, R. C., 198n, 333n
Andersson, U., 267n
Andrews, S. M., 259
Angwin, D., 227n
Angwin, J., 60
Anhalt, K. N., 135n
Ansberry, C., 93, 99n
Ante, S. E., 38
Anthanassiou, N., 333n
Antoine, A., 266n, 296n
Aoyama, Y., 264n
Apfelthaler, G., 33n
Appel, A. M., 133n
Ardichvilli, A., 67n, 403n
Areddy, J. T., 234, 296n
Arend, R. J., 134n
Argote, L., 98n
Argyres, N., 69n
Arikan, A. M., 402n
Arino, A., 266n, 296n, 299n
Armstrong, J. C., 166n
Armstrong, L., 165n, 166n, 297n
Armstrong, R. W., 135n
Arndorfer, J. B., 72
Arndt, M., 19, 33n, 112, 135n, 182, 267n, 297n
Arnold, D. J., 33n, 263n
Arnott, R., 336n
Arora, A., 265n
Arregle, J.-L., 266n, 298n, 428n
Artz, K. W., 69n, 97n, 299n
Asakawa, K., 34n, 264n, 267n
Ashford, S. J., 401n, 403n
Ashton, J. E., 427n
Aston, A., 135n
Atamer, T., 68n
Audia, P. G., 98n
Aukutsionek, S., 336n
Aulakh, P. S., 265n
Auster, E. R., 226n
Autio, E., 67n, 97n, 427n, 428n, 429n
Avolio, B. J., 401n
Axelrod, B., 403n

B

Baden-Fuller, C., 299n, 371n
Bae, S. C., 229n
Baek, H. Y., 267n
Baglole, J., 68n

Bagozzi, R., 33n
Bailey, J., 68n, 76
Baiman, S., 370n
Baker, W., 97n
Baldwin, T. T., 98n
Balfour, F., 196n, 228n, 257
Baljko, J., 135n
Ball, D., 164n, 265n, 266n, 335n, 351, 392
Bamford, C. E., 133n
Baptiste, R. G., 228n
Barad, Jill, 374
Barbakow, Jeffrey, 305, 322, 392, 393
Barber, B. N., 228n
Barham, J., 265n
Barkema, H., 68n, 228n, 369n, 426n, 427n
Barker, R., 196n, 265n
Barney, J. B., 32n, 34n, 80, 97n, 99n, 133n, 135n, 195n, 228n, 296n, 297n, 298n, 299n, 369n, 370n, 402n, 403n, 428n
Barnir, A., 402n
Barrett, A., 33n, 60, 134n, 178, 182, 196n, 227n
Barringer, B. R., 267n, 426n
Barsade, S., 401n
Barth, H., 369n
Bartlett, C. A., 68n, 69n, 265n, 370n, 402n, 403n
Bass, K. E., 263n
Bates, K. A., 98n, 196n
Bates, T. W., 198n, 333n
Batra, R., 97n
Bauerschmidt, A., 370n
Baum, I. R., 34n
Baum, J. A. C., 165n, 369n, 426n
Baumgartner, P., 69n
Baur, A., 134n
Baysinger, B. D., 334n
Bayus, B. L., 97n, 299n
Beamish, P. W., 68n, 227n, 265n, 266n, 267n, 427n
Beard, A., 314
Becerra, M., 401n
Becker, B. E., 404n
Becker, D. O., 134n
Becker, T., 67n
Bednarski, A., 227n
Beekman, A., 428n

Beer, M., 400n
Begley, T. M., 97n, 263n, 370n, 426n
Beinhocker, E. D., 133n
Belderbos, R., 266n, 427n
Bell, David, 185, 215
Belson, K., 170
Bendor-Samuel, P., 99n
Benedict, J., 97n
Bengtsson, L., 299n
Benner, M. J., 99n, 427n
Bennis, W. G., 198n
Berenson, A., 334n
Bergen, M., 32n, 97n, 196n
Bergh, D. D., 195n, 196n, 197n, 198n, 228n, 229n, 335n, 401n
Berle, A., 334n
Berman, S., 98n
Berman, S. L., 296n
Bernardo, A. E., 197n, 226n, 298n
Berner, R., 97n, 197n, 351
Bernstein, A., 68n, 124, 263n
Bernstein, J., 264n
Berry, L. L., 134n
Berthon, P., 98n
Best, A., 229n
Bethel, J. E., 229n
Bettis, R. A., 33n, 400n
Bhambri, A., 400n, 402n
Bhappu, A., 265n
Bianco, A., 202
Biemans, W. G., 300n
Bierly, P. E., III, 296n
Bierman, L., 32n, 34n, 97n, 98n, 228n, 402n, 427n, 429n
Bigley, G. A., 35n, 369n
Bilefsky, D., 214, 227n, 267n
Billet, M. T., 196n
Birkinshaw, J., 33n, 264n, 370n, 404n, 427n
Bizjak, J. M., 198n, 333n
Black, B. S., 334n
Black, J. S., 33n, 402n
Black, Lord, 314
Black, S. S., 133n, 296n
Blank, D., 298n
Blasberg, J., 98n
Bliss, R., 198n
Bloodgood, J. M., 97n, 98n
Bluedorn, A. C., 426n
Blumentritt, T. P., 267n

Yip, P., 67n
Yiu, D., 34n, 195n, 197n, 229n, 402n, 404n
Yli-Renko, H., 67n, 428n
Yoffie, D. B., 165n
Yoshikawa, T., 227n
Youndt, M. A., 402n
Young, G., 67n, 164n, 165n, 166n
Young, G. J., 299n
Young, M., 336n
Young, S., 334n
Young, T., 135n
Young-Ybarra, C., 296n, 298n
Yu, L., 263n, 428n
Yucel, E., 69n, 336n, 402n, 429n

Yun, Jong-Yong, 396–397
Yurtoglu, R. B., 227n

Z

Zacharakis, A., 428n
Zacharakis, A. L., 98n
Zack, M. H., 33n, 67n
Zaheer, A., 69n, 134n, 265n, 299n, 370n
Zaheer, S., 33n, 69n, 264n, 265n
Zahra, S. A., 32n, 33n, 67n, 68n, 230n, 264n, 265n, 267n, 297n, 334n, 403n, 427n
Zajac, E. J., 334n, 335n, 401n

Zalewski, D. A., 197n
Zambrano, Lorenzo, 244
Zander, I., 267n
Zaun, T., 145, 326
Zbar, J. D., 134n
Zbaracki, M. J., 32n, 97n, 196n
Zeisel, S., 165n, 226n
Zeithaml, C. P., 33n, 98n, 99n, 134n
Zeitz, G. J., 428n
Zelleke, A. S., 198n
Zellner, C., 196n
Zellner, W., 19, 227n
Zetsche, Dieter, 380
Zhang, H., 196n
Zhang, Y., 401n

Zhang, Y. B., 99n
Zhao, H. W.-C., 264n
Zhao, J., 229n
Zhao, J. H., 257, 267n
Zhou, X., 135n
Zhu, G., 427n
Zimmerman, A., 392
Zimmerman, M. A., 428n
Zingales, L., 197n, 333n
Zollo, M., 228n, 297n, 298n, 299n, 428n
Zook, C., 263n, 265n, 296n
Zott, C., 33n, 34n, 99n, 134n
Zulehner, C., 227n
Zweig, P. L., 197n

Company Index

Company Index

Subject Index